Latin America

PART II

old world and new create a rich new tapestry

151

v

CONTENTS

chapter 29

PART VI

Latin America assumes an important place in international affairs

691

chapter 30

chapter 31

epilogue

PREFACE TO
THE THIRD EDITION

From our years of teaching Latin American history, we, the authors, realize that it is difficult to write as a readable text a complete factual and interpretive account of every region of Latin America in every era of its history. An ideal text contains the story of social and cultural development as well as political and economic history. First of all, our ideal text could not be encompassed within the limits of a one-volume work, and a two-volume text is not feasible. The price would be prohibitive and the material too lengthy and detailed. Thus, we have rearranged and redesigned the previous editions of our text to meet the practical situation. In doing this, we have watched, observed, and listened to our students, and have received advice from colleagues and teachers of the survey course in Latin America.

With respect to the introductory materials, we have rewritten and shortened somewhat our general chapters and the chapters relating to the colonial period. We have engaged in some rearrangement of chapters and have added a completely new chapter on the African contributions to the New World. But try as we have, we have not been able to synthesize, as a whole, the history of the Latin American republics with regard to developments in the twentieth century. We have found from experience that topical treatment of the republican era has left our students baffled in trying to understand present-day Latin America. They are best satisfied with reading and preparing on an individual country and obtaining an understanding of that country. Our attempts to have them get an overview of Latin America as a whole have resulted in inaccurate generalizations. We have, therefore, continued our practice of giving the histories of the individual Latin American countries as stories of development since the inception of their independence. Our students have been far more satisfied to have a text giving them the background of and sufficient up-to-date material for each country, with economic conditions and social problems given as much weight as political history. Artists, musicians, and writers have been given recognition also.

Each Latin American republic has its own history and differs from its sisters in almost every detail. The Latin Americans resent our lumping them all together and subjecting them to overall conclusions, even though some modern currents of fundamental agreement on common problems do present themselves.

Because of space limitations in this third edition, we have reduced our section on "Aids to Further Study" but instead have increased the length of the bibliographies at the end of each chapter.

Our previous editions have received a very cordial reception from students, colleagues, and teachers. Many have sent in suggestions and have supplied us with constructive criticisms and corrected minor errors and inconsistencies. We have been most grateful for their cooperation and help. The list of such persons is far too lengthy to detail here, but we do want to express personal thanks for help rendered by our colleagues Professor Roger Cunniff and Professor W. D. Phillips (now at the University of Minnesota) and to the library staff of the California State University, San Diego. We are also grateful to María Celia Grijalva, Carlos Rafael Lopez, and María Josefina Calderón, former students at East Los Angeles College, as well as Margaret Blander, for their many hours of assistance in preparing this third edition.

Helen Miller Bailey
Abraham P. Nasatir

two worlds meet

PROLOGUE

Thursday, October 11, 1492, at sunset! There had been several days of murmuring and mutinous talk among the hands on all three ships, the *Niña*, the *Pinta*, and the *Santa María*. Two days before, Christopher Columbus, the Admiral, had conferred with his captains, telling them, says the chronicle written from his logs, "that it was useless to complain, since he had come to go to the Indies, and so had to continue until he found them, with the help of Our Lord." Then he agreed with the captains to continue westward for three more days. Now on this second day, the eleventh, there came "floating by the vessel a green rush." The men of the *Pinta* picked up "a reed and a stick," and "those of the caravel *Niña* saw a branch of wild roses." Throughout the day the wind had blown a gale; there was a high sea, and the fleet made a record run of seventy-eight miles.

At sunset all hands were summoned; evening prayers were said in unison. On the *Santa María*, the Admiral stood on the sterncastle and gave the men a little talk, speaking of the "fair winds and clear course" throughout the voyage, and of the "comfort of signs of better things to come." Then, because of the "great desire of all to see land," he ordered the ships to carry on at full sail at night despite the unusually high wind.

At 2:00 A.M. October 12, with the moon just past the full, the lookout on the *Pinta*, a seaman named Rodrigo de Triana, saw a "white sand cliff" gleaming in the moonlight, and a dark line of land beyond. As he shouted "Tierra!" his captain, Martín Alonzo Pinzón, set off a small cannon as a signal to the other two ships. The land was then about six miles distant. Since Columbus rightly feared reefs and breakers, he ordered the ships to lower sails and lay off shore till dawn. In the morning they came to a passage through the western reefs of a tiny island in the Bahamas and "found sheltered anchor in five fathoms of water." Here on the sandy beach, says the chronicle, "presently they saw naked people, and the Admiral went ashore in the armed ship's boat with the royal standard displayed." Thus, Old World and New had officially met.

Columbus was not the first citizen of the Old World to see the New. His was the first *effective* discovery; he advertised the New World and made its occupation permanent and continuous. Surely, in remote times, Chinese or Japanese navigators touched on the Pacific Coast. Breton fishermen had known of the Grand Banks off Newfoundland for years before

Columbus, and they may have wintered on Labrador or laid over on Nova Scotia to dry and salt their codfish. Leif Ericson the Viking sailed to North America from the Norse colony on Greenland about the year 1000; his discovery was kept alive in the Norse sagas which were still being told as true history in Iceland and Norway in the late 1400's. Sailors from Bristol, England, knew these stories, knew also of the fishing banks visited by the Bretons, and of Irish tales of missionaries who, centuries before, had visited on Saint Brendan's Island somewhere in the Atlantic to the west. Bristol sailors had contacted Portuguese sailors, perhaps the very ones who had been involved in Prince Henry the Navigator's attempts to have the African coast thoroughly explored, and had given ear to all kinds of stories of western islands. It was now the second half of the fifteenth century and discovery was in the air. By the time Bartolomeu Dias came home from the tip of Africa, Christopher Columbus, promoter, man of vision, and superbly skillful navigator, had already approached the Portuguese king with his more daring scheme to reach India by way of the western islands.

Medieval Europeans, largely preoccupied with the petty wars and the restricted commerce of feudal times, had centered their interest in the Mediterranean and forgotten the geographic knowledge of the ancient Greeks. Not until the Crusades in the 11th century did the Europeans look outward. The individual Crusader became a traveler and he heard about other lands lying beyond the Near East, lands which produced silk and spices, camphor and musk, pearls and ivory. From the Crusader, other Europeans heard about these lands and soon developed new interests and new tastes. Trade routes were mapped and trading cities grew throughout Europe, providing a stimulus that caused the outside world to move inland. Surplus wealth created leisure in the young towns and cities and permitted the cultivation of the arts and learning. The new learning produced more accurate geographic knowledge and more intelligent interest in the world beyond.

Marco Polo, a young Venetian traveler in the 1200's had made known to Europe the riches of the Far East. Other travelers, including traders and ecclesiastics, made their way to India and China during the next century. Meanwhile Castile expanded into the Atlantic by occupying the Canary Islands in 1405. Prince Henry the Navigator set up scientific head-quarters for navigation at the southwesterly tip of Portugal to gather maps and information about the west coast of Africa in the hope of reaching the mythical Christian king, Prester John. His seamen sent colonists to the Madeiras and the Azores, and by 1460, when Henry died, they had reached the coast of Guinea, and in 1487–1488, Bartolomeu Dias had found the Cape of Good Hope.

Meanwhile the medieval universities had begun to produce Renais-sance thinkers who were studying the ancient Greek scholars—mathemati-cians who had proved by figures that the world was round, mapmakers who had drawn the world as a sphere—a geographer of Alexandria who in A.D. 25

had implied that circumnavigation of the globe could have been tried "except for want of resolution and the scarcity of provision." These writers, forgotten for centuries, were being reread in the Europe of 1450. Mapmaking improved as a consequence and geography became a scientific pursuit. Most learned men accepted the idea of a spherical earth, and were ready for a voyage such as Columbus proposed, for the books of all the travelers of the previous three centuries were now being read. They had been made available by the spectacular invention of movable type.

An awakened Europe hoped to enhance the trade in Far Eastern goods. But direct connections between East and West which travelers and traders had begun to establish were almost cut off by the time of Columbus' birth. Trade via the ports of the Near East became a mere trickle when the Turks captured Constantinople in 1453. After that, all trade was in Turkish hands, and although the Turks tried to stimulate trade, their excessive taxes caused prices to rise sky-high. The only European centers in touch with the Turkish monopoly were Venice and Genoa, and they squeezed out Western European traders. A nation that could find a new route to the East could corner the entire wholesale market on its luxury wares, silks, and spices. In countries that had windows on the Atlantic, in England, Portugal, Spain, and France, strong kings had money, the need for trade, and an interest in expansion. Their peoples were restless, for the Black Death had depopulated the countryside, made villagers footloose, and had broken many still-existing feudal ties. Kings of such countries might be "sold" on the idea of sending expeditions to find new sea routes. A single ship, following an all-water route, could bring back more cargo than several caravans and at much lower cost.

The seafaring world was now building ships that could weather such a trip. Vessels of the early 1400's were "caravels" steered by a rudder. Their captains knew how to use the compass, and the astrolabe, a very primitive type of sextant which gave the position north and south of the Equator—that is, latitude. Though longitude was a matter of guesswork until the 1700's, the clever mariner of the 1400's knew the direction in which he was going and his approximate distance from home—knowledge which made sailing charts possible. These charts enhanced seamanship in the Italian cities and in Spain and Portugal. Their preparation was a career in itself; in fact Columbus and his brother made their living drawing such maps in the Lisbon of the 1470's.

Shipowners were also ready to search for the all-water route to India for they were building bigger and better ships. In 1450, vessels were built in Venice that had large holds for cargo and also a forecastle and sterncastle, high platforms at each end for boarding enemy ships in case of war. By Columbus' time, the sterncastle was a poop deck with space for the captain's cabin, and later the forecastle became a covered quarters forward for the crew. Such ships could carry stores of provisions and drinking water and could be away from land for more than a month. The lateen-sailed galley of the Italian ports was giving way to the square-rigger whose sails could be held taut in a high wind and could always catch enough breeze to be independent of the oars of galley slaves.

Columbus' voyage was thus the culmination of the many-sided intellectual, technological, and commercial revolution going on at the time. His discovery had an enormous impact on the life of the New World, which is the story of the rest of this book. It marked the inception of Latin America. The life of the aboriginal inhabitants was to be changed beyond measure by the importation of the Spanish and Portuguese languages, customs, food, religion, wheeled vehicles, and domestic animals. The New World was to be ruled politically and economically by Spanish and Portuguese governments for three centuries. An immigration of European peoples started that is still going on.

Columbus' discovery had great significance for the people of Europe as well. The news of his voyage spread rapidly among learned circles in Europe. One letter from Columbus to a friend at court in 1493 ran to nine editions. The story of naked natives living in a state of nature, seemingly generous, rather timid, lacking in religion, ignorant of important weapons of war, sounded to Europeans like something approximating the lost Garden of Eden. The description of rivers yielding gold stirred world excitement since European markets were short of gold for commercial exchange. Although Columbus himself never doubted that he had reached East India, some skeptics doubted it from the start, and the idea that these lands were entirely "new" was growing rapidly by the time Columbus died in 1506.

The economic effects of the Columbian discovery came rapidly with colonization. The center of trade and finance began to shift from the Mediterranean to the Atlantic. When gold from Mexico and Peru began to pour through Spain into Europe, a price revolution resulted which brought changes in banking and finance and helped produce a new type of businessman. With new sources of raw materials, and the plantation system producing sugar and, later, cotton, new wholesale methods developed in Europe and eventually machine production. Shipping processes changed as larger and larger vessels had to be built and provisioned to handle the flow of passengers and cargo.

In the field of politics, changes were as great. Spain's metallic wealth gave her an illusion of prosperity and forced her into a more vigorous foreign policy, which led to the enlarging of navies by both Spain and her enemies. New types of warfare, fought in both hemispheres, brought new balances of power and changes in diplomacy. And traditional concepts of government had to be modified for the government of colonies with peoples entirely different from any ever before ruled by Europeans. New institutions grew up to handle these problems.

Changes were also great in religion and culture, especially with a whole pagan world for the devout to convert and money pouring in for such conversion. Literature was vitalized by the impact of adventure. The map of the world changed, and mapmaking became more accurate. Even the diet of

Europeans changed as they began eating corn and potatoes and chocolate for the first time, and began smoking tobacco as a luxury. All in all, the New World was one of the most revolutionary things that ever happened to the Old.

Thus centuries of build-up in Europe brought about Columbus' landfall on the morning of October 12, 1492, which in turn brought about changes in every phase of life in the Old World and the New.

Latin America

the age of discovery and conquest of the new world

PART I

In 1492, the old Latin Europe and the New America had come together to make Latin America. But when Columbus came searching for a sponsor, it was the Spanish rulers who accepted his challenge. Why? For the answer to that question, the student must understand not only Europe in the early Renaissance, but the backgrounds of Spanish history. Spain was, in fact, not only ready to back Columbus, but ready to follow him. Spanish America was to become a transplanted Spain in language and religion and family tradition, just as Portugal, the nation whose Atlantic exploration antedates that of Columbus, gave her lifeblood to Brazil.

The New World was a land-mass to be known as "the Americas." It was full of natural beauty and a wide range of climates and topography. But it was a mistake to call it "new." It was new only to the self-centered Europeans, for both in Middle America and in the Andes city civilization had existed for more than a thousand years before Columbus was born. The rise and fall of these city civilizations and their influence on their descendants today is of great interest to the modern "Latin Americanists."

Other Spaniards who came after Columbus beat their way up and down the hemisphere. Thus the reader must follow their footsteps to know their reactions to the geography and to the "Indians," as Columbus mistakenly called the New World's inhabitants. The story of the clash between Europeans and Indians, and the destruction of the Indian cultures introduces Latin America. But it is a story also of beautiful scenery, fascinating archeology, and breathless adventure.

include Valencia. By the time of Columbus' birth, the combined kingdom of Castile and León dominated most of central and northern Spain, flanked by Portugal on the west and tiny Navarre and powerful Aragon on the north and east, with the Moors on the defensive in Granada alone.

Although Christian Spain was not territorially united until after 1479, the Moors had been on the defensive since the middle of the thirteenth century. During the two centuries of the "reconquest," the powerful Christian kingdoms of Castile and Aragon were developing institutions that were to dominate the Spain of Renaissance times and to provide the pattern for government and social life in Spanish America. There was great pride in noble birth. Castilian nobility was made up of *ricos hombres*, or grandees. Armed noblemen fighting against the Moors were called *caballeros*, or mounted horsemen. The "sons of somebody," *hijos de algo* (as opposed to "sons of nobody," *hijos de nadie*) came to be called *hidalgos*. *Hidalgos* and *caballeros* figured strongly in the development of Latin America throughout its conquest and settlement. In both Castile and Aragon these privileged classes were strongly individualistic and separatistic.

The nonprivileged class was composed of peasants and people of the towns. The Castilian town was not only a center of commerce but an agency for holding and consolidating lands in the reconquest of Spain from the Moors. The towns thus gained special rights, *fueros*, or charters granting privileges outside the royal authority and immunities from the law. They administered their own affairs rather democratically, through a *cabildo*, or council made up of elected members called *regidores*. They maintained their own police system separate from the king's—police groups called brotherhoods, or *hermandades*. The towns furnished revenue to the king in return for self-government, and were answerable only to royal inspectors, called *visitadores*.

During the reconquest, the kings gained increasing power over the feudal nobles. Now the subjugated nobles served in the capacity of royal officials or frontier military governors and were called *adelantados*. In the king's castle a court officialdom was developed. In some cases feudal positions were held by church dignitaries who recognized the king's nominal power over them. As the king grew in power, he formed a royal tribunal, which brought justice under royal rather than local control. Then the *audiencia*, or court, in which the king held an audience to hear complaints and administer justice, became a fixed institution. In the late Middle Ages, Roman Law was revived as a code for the king's justice. The church was also a centralizing authority; church agencies received large land grants in return for cooperation with the royal government, and became wealthy and powerful.

The king often made special fiscal grants to noble or military officials. This grant was called an *encomienda*, a term destined for a fateful history in the New World. In medieval Spain the grant consisted of the right to collect taxes in a given region in return for responsibility over the welfare of the inhabitants. Similar *encomienda* grants were to form the basis of distributing Indian laborers and their village lands in the New World. Sheep valley of Andalusia. The people prospered from wise use of the land. Trees and vines were grafted to improve the fruit. Sugar cane, rice, and cotton were introduced from the Near East as products to be grown under irrigation. A textile industry developed from the cotton as well as from silkworms grown in Cordova. It is interesting to know that the conflict among farmers who used the land to graze sheep, those who raised cattle, and those who planted crops was present in Moorish Spain. The quarrel broke out again in the history of the Spanish-speaking frontier of the United States—the sheep men, the cattle men, the "nesters."

Society under the Moors consisted of the landed aristocrats, the freemen, the peasants, the merchants, the soldiers, and the slaves. Naturally, the nobility was made up chiefly of the Moslems, while the merchants were Jews and descendants of Christians who had adopted Mohammedanism. Still the culture was Moorish, and Moors comprised the chief racial element, an element so important in shaping Andalusian character and thus indelibly stamping the character of Spanish America.

the reviving Christian nations
and their institutions on the New World

Politically the Spain that was to administer the New World colonies grew from the persistence of Christianity during the Middle Ages in the northern mountains, and from the long "reconquest" as these northerners moved southward into the Moorish regions of the center and the south. Many Christians, fleeing from the Mohammedans, had hidden in the mountains in the northwest. Groups of them remained in the north as in Visigothic times, in areas that gradually became the independent kingdoms of Asturias, Navarre, Aragon, and Catalonia. Gradually two stronger kingdoms emerged in the northwest, León and Castile, which were destined to supplant Asturias and become a single nation under the ancestors of Isabella. By the eleventh century Castilians began the long process of reconquering Moslem Spain.

The influence of the church and the monastic orders gave vigor to this movement. The small northern kingdoms had become fanatically religious. The Christians had always remembered Saint James, whose bones were supposed to be in Spain. "Miraculously" discovered in Galicia, the bones were placed in a shrine called Saint James of Compostela. Saint James—San Diego or Santiago—became the patron saint of the reconquest; soldiers went into battle crying "Santiago!" Many are the towns in the New World today called Santiago.

In 1236 Cordova fell to a Castilian king known to history as San Fernando. Asked by the king of France to join in a Crusade against the Mohammedans in the Holy Land, this King Fernando had answered, "There is no lack of Mohammedans in my own land." In 1248 he came triumphantly into Seville as a conqueror. Meanwhile kings of Aragon, uniting with Catalonia, had advanced their own kingdom southward to time history was being recorded in Egypt. Via the Pyrenean passes came Celts; via the Mediterranean and the Straits of Gibraltar came Phoenicians and Greeks and Carthaginians to mix into the Iberian bloodstream. When Carthage was embroiled with the Romans, the great General Hannibal used Spain as his base; another century saw Spain a thriving Roman colony. Out of Roman rule came governmental and cultural patterns that remained as foundations of Spanish civilization. The political administration was unified, the language standardized as a dialect of Roman Latin. The Romans super-imposed their own system of law, indelibly stamping Roman law upon the Hispanic peoples and their descendants in America. Roman roads, public buildings, schools, and libraries showed the power of Rome in Spain. Spanish town and countryside used Roman ways of commerce and agricul-ture. Almost every form of scientific, literary, and artistic accomplishment that characterized Rome in her days of greatest glory was copied in Spain. Roman town and city government was later to form the basis for town strength in imperial Spain and in the Spanish American empire.

Even more important was the introduction of Christianity. The Spaniards in the Americas were to be famous for their religious devotion and the intolerance they felt toward other religions. Christianity had started as a religion in the Roman Empire, spreading from Palestine to Greece, to Rome, to North Africa, to Southern France, to Spain. Modern Spanish Christians believe that Saint James, brother of Saint John, traveled the length of Spain preaching, and that his bones are buried in a church in Galicia on the Bay of Biscay. Midway through the third century there were Christian communities all over Spain; and in 313 the Emperor Constantine made Christianity a legal religion throughout the Roman Empire. The church in Spain proceeded to hold its own conferences, to enjoy exemption from taxation, to perform all marriage ceremonies, and to take advantage of special legal rights such as maintaining separate courts for church leaders accused of crime—rights as famous as the royal *fueros*. The Spanish clergy developed a very high culture, traditional in Spanish American life to the present time.

Following the pattern of Mediterranean history, Spain fell to bar-baric hordes at the time of the Germanic invasions. With the coming of the barbarians into Italy, Roman soldiers were called home; contacts between Rome and Spain diminished. Now Spain was open to conquest by various waves of Germanic peoples, the last of whom were the Visigoths who estab-lished a Christianized kingdom with its capital at Toledo. For three cen-turies the Visigothic kings ruled most of the Iberian peninsula, administer-ing the country under an efficient code of laws, part Roman and part Germanic. The Visigothic pride in and respect for this code of laws created the strong Spanish pride in juridical practice which would later be trans-ferred to America. The Visigoths also contributed a basic trait of the nobility—the preference for living in the country rather than in the towns, the establishment of a landed aristocracy whose serfs tilled the land, as opposed to the city-dwelling ruling class of Roman times. Thus the Visi-gothic nobles may be distant progenitors of the modern Latin American *hacendados* or *estancieros*, the owners of large estates living in splendid rural isolation with their many servants and laborers. Toledo remained a cosmopolitan center, however, welcoming cultured Jews from the Near East, hiring Byzantine mercenaries from the Eastern Empire at Constantinople, and generating an atmosphere of tolerance and prosperity that was to be found in few other cities of the moribund Roman Empire.

In 711 Moslems from North Africa crossed the Straits of Gibraltar into Spain in a wave of expansionism for that new Arabian faith which was to surge across the Pyrenees until it was stopped by Charles Martel at Tours. This brought Spain into the orbit of the Mohammedan world. The invaders, called in Spanish history the Moors, settled throughout the Iberian peninsula, save for some isolated regions in the Cantabrian and Pyrenean mountains. Gone was the Visigothic rule over the Ibero-Carthaginian-Roman-Byzantine peoples. The continuous presence of this new intrusive culture and its political rule until the final defeat at Granada in 1492 were the dominant factors in Spain during the Middle Ages. The Moorish influence was especially strong in Andalusia, the province around Seville which was to become the headquarters of New World trade and government.

The first two centuries of Moslem domination brought little stability to the peninsula, for when Moslems were not fighting Christians they were fighting each other, along tribal or regional lines. Finally by 930 Moslem rule was consolidated under the Caliphate of Cordova. The Caliphs formed the strongest navy in the Mediterranean and gained for Spain the reputation of being the greatest state and the seat of the highest culture in western Europe. This "golden age" of the Moslems lasted from about 900 to 1300.

The Moorish cities grew and prospered, and the twelfth century brought luxury in living and advances in culture to both Seville and Cordova. It is said that Arab mathematicians introduced into Europe by way of Spain the Arabic numerals, the use of the zero in arithmetic, and the study of algebra and geometry. The Moslem sages knew elementary physics and chemistry. Not only the wise men, but a great majority of the common people could read and write Arabic, and many of them the Latin of the European Christians as well. In these languages Caliphs and hermits, wise men and gay young blades wrote poetry—poetry of love, of spring, of the abstract values of life. This love of verse writing persists in Latin America, for young and old. In Toledo lived many learned Jews; astronomical tables and computations worked out by a group of Jewish astronomers in Toledo in 1065 became the foundation of the work that made latitude and longitude calculations possible, and thus helped chart the New World. From the Giralda tower in Seville—to be used as a cathedral tower when Christians retook the town—learned astronomers surveyed the stars. The city had seventy public libraries, that of the Caliph containing 600,000 volumes. Many of these volumes were history books; with their fondness for historical writing, the Arabs helped build a tradition that would live on in Spain and in Latin America.

Seville was filled with the tile-roofed houses of Moorish architecture, built square around a patio. Beyond lay the wide green acres of the overland quickly to the court being held at Barcelona, the width of Spain away. The new Admiral had purchased clothing of fine white linen and red velvet suitable to his new rank; he journeyed with his officers and servants in a long mule train. The mules in the rear bore six Bahama Island Indians; donkeys carried Caribbean parrots in wicker cages. After two weeks of cross-country travel the caravan reached Barcelona, seat of Ferdinand's power in Catalonia. "All the court and the city came out to meet the Admiral," wrote Columbus' biographer son. He was received by Ferdinand and Isabella in a hall full of nobles and courtiers. The sovereigns stood up to greet him, and Columbus sat to tell of his adventures while the nobility remained standing. The members of the court were to find out within a decade that this royal guest had given a claim to a whole new continent to Spain, the Spain of the colorful cities, the great fairs, the gala processions, the deep religious devotion. The next century was to bring exploratory and colonizing activities in which much of the life of Spain that Columbus had seen in passing was to be transferred to the New World.

Spain's history gave her a drive for land and trade. The wars against the Moslems produced a spirit of national unity and expansion and created a fervent patriotism which expressed itself in terms of a fanatical religion. There was, by 1492, a strong military caste seeking an outlet for its energies, and a militant church, seeking souls to convert and new sources of funds. Columbus' discovery was an answer to all this seeking.

*early Iberian history as the background
for Iberian America*

In the decade before 1493 Columbus had occasion to see many of the geographic features of the Iberian lands which had influenced the early Iberian peoples and which prepared them for life in the New World. With a land mass about two-thirds the size of the single modern Latin American nation of Venezuela, separated from the rest of Europe by the Pyrenees mountains, dominated by a high and dry central plateau, the Iberian nations of Spain and Portugal had been conditioned by their own difficult terrain and climate. The broken highlands, the rugged river valleys, the extremes of heat and cold, the great variations between dry and rainy seasons, between low altitudes at river mouths and high altitudes up steep escarpments away from the sea—the Iberian people knew all these handicaps of climate and geography at home and could cope with them when they encountered them in the New World.

As the Spaniards were to invade areas of the New World across many difficult geographic barriers, so their ancestors had been either conquerors or conquered through many epochs of history. Spain's people represent a blending of many races and cultures. The inhabitants of the Iberian peninsula were, by 1492, the most mixed peoples in Europe; not even the proudest Spanish knight could call himself a "pure-blood." Perhaps a race known as Iberian had developed in Spain by the

chapter 1

THE RICH HERITAGE OF SPAIN AND PORTUGAL

the Spain to which Columbus returned

Columbus, aboard the *Nina*, returned from his voyage of discovery, arriving in Palos on March 15, 1493. By the 31st, Palm Sunday, he was in Seville, jewel city of the Castilian province of Andalusia. The city of Seville in the 1490's was one of the most colorful cities in Europe. When Columbus returned from the West Indies the first time, it was Holy Week, time of a great trade fair. In the crowds jostling at the market place were tradesmen from all southern Spain. Here were the fine horses of Andalusia, the bulls for the corridas or bull fights to be held Easter Sunday afternoon, the fat tawny oxen from Spain's uplands, as well as many sheep and goats and donkeys for sale—all those domestic animals which Spaniards were to carry to America. Here also were the handmade products of Spaniards and Moors from all the regions of Spain, products which deft Indian fingers were to copy in the New World: silks, embroideries, pottery, leather work. Seville merchants could not foresee that this Holy Week Fair was to be rivaled in its turn by the two great yearly fairs Seville's traders were to set up in the New World during the next two centuries.

Columbus himself was gone from Seville before the fair was over. A summons from the Queen had arrived on that Monday, an order to come

Prentice-Hall International, Inc., *London*
Prentice-Hall of Australia, Pty. Ltd., *Sydney*
Prentice-Hall of Canada, Ltd., *Toronto*
Prentice-Hall of India Private Limited, *New Delhi*
Prentice-Hall of Japan, Inc., *Tokyo*

10 9 8 7 6 5 4 3 2 1

Printed in the United States of America

Library of Congress Cataloging in Publication Data

Bailey, Helen Miller.
    Latin America: the development of its civilization.

    Includes bibliographies.
    1. Latin America—History.   2. Latin America—
Civilization.   I. Nasatir, Abraham Phineas,
joint author.   II. Title.
F1410.B16 1973   980   72-13948
ISBN 0-13-524264-9

Helen Miller Bailey
EAST LOS ANGELES COLLEGE

Abraham P. Nasatir
CALIFORNIA STATE UNIVERSITY, SAN DIEGO

Latin America
the development of
its civilization

THIRD EDITION

PRENTICE-HALL, INC., *Englewood Cliffs, New Jersey*

and cattle raisers formed their own guilds in Christian Spain as they had in Moorish Spain, and received certain chartered privileges. Their guilds were called *mestas;* their disputes were carried over to the colonies.

Special liaison officers between king and town were called *corregidores;* as the centuries passed, these royal agents served to strengthen the royal authority at the expense of self-government in the towns. Town government, chartered rights, provincial control, and strengthened royal authority in Castile were setting a pattern for the New World. The terms *cabildo, adelantado, audiencia, fueros, corregidor, visitador* all were to appear again and again in Spanish American colonial history. The system of royal taxation included such things as a royal share on the output of the mines, ships to be contributed for royal use, such as those which the town of Palos had to give Isabella for Columbus, a tax on commercial transactions called *alcabala,* royal monopolies on certain products, and customs duties on every shipment in and out of a Spanish port. This was a system to be used to tax the towns, the mines, and the trade of the colonies. All these functionaries together with the codes of legal jurisdiction, the code of the Visigothic kings, and the laws of Castilian rulers helped create respect for written law and bureaucratic procedure. The endless copies of detailed reports on all the taxes complying with all the laws were to fill the colonial archives of Seville during the three centuries after Columbus.

The treatment of minorities was to be reflected also in the colonial epoch in the New World. Special taxes were laid on Jews and Moors; they were confined to ghettos, forced to wear badges or distinctive types of clothing, kept from practicing certain trades. In fact, no occupations save those of merchant and moneylender were open to Jews. Many Moslems were also in the commercial class, but thousands of them worked as artisans and agriculturists. The quiet discrimination against such people turned at times to bitter persecution and forcible baptism. Meanwhile royal authority, and with it religious persecution, were to receive a new impetus in the second half of the fifteenth century.

the strong unified Spain of Columbus' time

In 1469 an eighteen-year-old girl named Isabella, heiress to the throne of Castile, married a seventeen-year-old boy named Ferdinand of Aragon. Within ten years' time, each of these young people had inherited his own throne; Castile, León, Aragon, and Catalonia and all their Moorish conquests were now ruled by one family. The marriage has been hailed as a love match; though that is not completely true, it was more so than most royal marriages. Isabella, auburn-haired, clear-skinned, fair of face, had a strong religious will and was determined to stamp out heretics, infidels, and Jews in her realm; the church became rich and powerful under her. Ferdinand, on the other hand, though perhaps not so sincerely religious, was a wily and successful diplomat. He made alliances with other great powers and the new Spain became a leading nation in Europe. After 1479 the young rulers, though still technically reigning separately, set about to complete the unification of all Spain within the borders it has today.

Territorially, they had first to rid the peninsula of Moslems, a goal for Isabella's religious zeal and Ferdinand's political ambition. Isabella and Ferdinand visited the holy shrine of Santiago at Compostela for inspiration in the war against Granada, the last Moorish stronghold. Then they received the support of the nobility and the blessings of the Pope, who gave them the title of The Catholic Monarchs. With their soldiers crying "Santiago!" the monarchs laid siege to Granada, and followed the campaign into the field with their entire family. Isabella was at her camp outside the city when she received Columbus. She had little interest in explorations until Boabdil, the last Moorish sultan, evacuated the Alhambra in the spring of 1492 and fled to North Africa. Now Spain was united territorially. The entire nation was still celebrating the victory when the successful Columbus went to the court at Barcelona in 1493.

Territorial unification itself is not sufficient to make a strong nation. The marriage of Ferdinand and Isabella was meant to be a mere personal association, and Spain in the 1470's was still a collection of virtually autonomous units. Administratively, feudalism had to be made to bend to royal power. This the Catholic Monarchs proceeded to do. They gave special powers to the *Santa Hermandad*, the royal brotherhood which became the centralized police force. The chivalric military-religious organizations were taken over by Ferdinand, who became their "grand master" and thereby assured for himself a strong central army and a larger income. Chartered towns were restricted and *corregidores* and *visitadores* superseded *cabildos* or town councils in power. *Residencias*, reviews of an official's administration at the end of his term of office, were instituted to insure the honesty and efficiency of the *corregidores* and became an established institution a century later in the New World. The monarchs obtained income from many types of taxation and had no reason to summon a *cortes* or parliament to lay taxes, as the earlier Christian kings in northern Spain had done. Ferdinand and Isabella did call the *cortes* at least twice. But royal councils, as opposed to the *cortes*, grew in power and became the principal instrument of government for both Spain and the colonies. There were councils of state, of finance, of justice, of religious affairs as government became more complex and Spain's power expanded. Finally the Council of the Indies, which was to wield power in the New World for three centuries, was established.

Thus Ferdinand ruled Aragon and Isabella ruled Castile, though the Queen's idea was "all for Spain," not "all for Castile." As their power grew, they raised a son and three daughters for this new Spain. Ferdinand arranged marriages for his children into several of the courts of Europe, outlived the strait-laced Isabella by twelve years and his only son by a generation. Of his daughters, the youngest was Catherine of Aragon, ill-starred first wife of Henry VIII, whose only heir was the English queen "Bloody" Mary. His eldest daughter died as the young queen of Portugal. His mentally unbalanced second daughter, Juana, had the most brilliant match, marrying Philip, the heir to Austria, Belgium, and Holland, as well as to the title of Holy Roman Emperor, and with that title heir to the leadership of the federation of German states.

Juana became insane before she came to the throne of Castile, but her son Charles inherited all these vast possessions. He was actually the first monarch of both Castile and Aragon, and Granada as well, and he called all these Iberian possessions Spain. Through his father he had vast possessions in Europe. During his reign as Charles V of the Holy Roman Empire and Charles I of Spain, while he was yet a boy, Magellan sailed around the world, Cortés conquered the Aztecs, and Martin Luther challenged the power of the Roman Catholic Church in his German possessions with the first successful "heresy." Charles was the king of Spain when many of the major grants for exploration were made. Harried and exhausted by religious disputes in Germany and wars in other parts of his realm, he could still put Castile's institutions to the test in an all-out attempt to transfer the Spanish royal will to the New World. His son enhanced the prestige and increased the power; he was that Philip II of Spain's Golden Age who "tangled" with Queen Elizabeth and lost the Armada in 1588, the first strong colonial ruler to be defeated by the British navy.

Ferdinand and Isabella and their heirs also brought about unification and strong central power in the field of religion. Before Isabella's time the Castilian clergy had been, by modern standards, scandalously lazy, immoral, and ignorant. During Isabella's reign the church and the religious orders were reformed and infused with piety and industry. The monarchs secured control of church appointments in Spain; bishops and archbishops were chosen, not by the Pope but by the Crown, a royal privilege called the *real patronato*. As "Divine-Right" monarchs, with more control over the church than had other rulers of Europe, the Catholic Monarchs transferred their religious authority to the New World. Indeed, the Latin American republics of modern times were to inherit disputes based on the same question—was the government or the Pope to choose religious leaders? In the Americas, as in the Spain of 1492, the church became a large landowner, possessing many peasant Indian villages and thousands of square miles of land, again creating an economic problem for modern times.

Once Granada had been taken, conformity in religion became synonymous with patriotism in the mind of the pious Isabella. Unity of the nation meant unity in faith, complete acceptance of Catholicism. Moors and Jews must be converted or exiled. To make sure that newly converted Christians did not backslide or secretly practice old ways, a Royal Council of the Inquisition was established to root out heresy, to make Spain orthodox from the mountains to the sea. The institution of the Inquisition was carried into the New World and used against heretics who turned up from Spain or elsewhere. It was not abolished until the nineteenth century.

Religious unity was achieved when Jews and Moors were driven out, but economic activities were temporarily blighted in Spain as a result, and the effects were felt socially in the New World for centuries. The clever artisans, the skilled metal workers, the richest merchants, the ablest financiers were gone from Spain. Because darker-skinned "heretics" had carried on the handicrafts and commerce, "pure-blooded" Spanish *hidalgos* scorned such pursuits. In the New World the gallant young Spaniards would not undertake any such occupations; until recent times the Latin American republics were retarded because educated young men would not go into commerce, engineering, or the skilled trades.

For the future colonial empire the rule of Ferdinand and Isabella had great commercial and financial importance. Government administration was efficient; commerce and trade were rehabilitated after the years of the Moorish wars. A merchant marine was developed; the sheep raising industry was strengthened and agriculture prospered with hired labor. By 1500 the Catholic Monarchs were ruling over a people who could well afford the effort of colonizing the Caribbean islands. The centralization of political and economic power, combined with the riches brought from the further discoveries in Mexico and Peru, stamped the sixteenth century as one of Spanish dominance in Europe and the world, even though these riches soon produced an imbalance, in Spain's home economy. When Charles V served as ruler of both Spain and the Holy Roman Empire and controlled realms in Europe and the Americas of a size and strength unknown since the fall of Rome, a new imperialism developed, challenging the rest of Europe to expand in opposition. Spanish metallic wealth from the New World, Spanish unity under one crown and one religion—in contrast to northern Europe's quarrels over Protestantism—combined to give Spain unprecedented prestige. American gold helped Charles in his wars in Europe against the French. As accepted champion of Catholicism he fought Protestants in Germany and Turks in Eastern Europe. Charles' son Philip II inherited the prestige of Spain, though not all the Hapsburg possessions, and brought Spanish glory to its height just before the loss of the Armada in 1588. Even Portugal was to be ruled by Spain for sixty years after 1580. In the period from 1520 to 1588 two new civilizations were conquered, and Spain's empire was expanded the length of both American continents. It was the largest empire the world has ever known. The reign of Philip II was indeed Spain's "Day in the Sun," although shadows were already being cast at midday.

golden age of Spanish culture

The serious-minded Isabella was interested in other things besides the "purification" of religion. She believed in "Culture" with a capital "C." She surrounded herself with scientific minds, some of whom eventually listened to Columbus. She sent for one of the famous figures of the Italian Renaissance, Peter Martyr, to be tutor to her children. He stayed on at her court to write the best-known contemporary account of the days of exploration. Printing had been introduced into Spain from North Europe while Isabella was still a girl, and German and Italian workmen were imported to run the presses. New universities were founded in the now united Christianized Spain to replace the great Moorish centers of learning. At Valencia, Valladolid, Barcelona, Seville, Salamanca, and Alcalá the university centers prospered. Italian teachers were brought in to tell of the new interests in ancient classics and modern science. Isabella encouraged religious painting and architecture. Spaniards in the united Spain wrote more love poetry and history-telling ballads than ever. Intellectual life was stimulated, although by modern standards it seems severely hampered by censorship and by the stress placed on theological education. The monarchs' own officials came from an educated class of lawyers, a closed administrative group which became a bureaucracy and which brought bureaucratic methods into colonial government.

During the reigns of Charles V and Philip II, the European Renaissance flowered contemporaneously with the religious conflicts over Protestantism; Spanish literature and art reflected these trends by the early 1600s. The period from about 1550 to about 1650 has been called the Golden Age of Spanish literature. The scholars at Salamanca were concerned with eclipses and calendar reform; Luis Vives contributed to European philosophy on a level with Erasmus; Father Vitoria wrote of international law before Grotius. Lope de Vega and Calderón de la Barca wrote plays still read today; Cervantes produced *Don Quixote*, the greatest Spanish novel ever written. Velázquez, El Greco, and Murillo set patterns for portraiture and religious painting for the New World to copy. The religious revival of the Counter Reformation produced the militant order of Jesuits founded by Ignatius Loyola. Some of this Spanish Renaissance of the sixteenth century was due to the inspiration and zest brought to the peninsular peoples by the discovery and conquest of America. In its turn the influence of the Spanish Renaissance was reflected in many ways in the New World.

The language of Lope de Vega and of Cervantes was the language of old Castile, the language of Isabella's court. The history of Castilian, which became the official language of the new unified nation and survives as the present-day Spanish is the history of Spain, for it contains Iberian words as well as words from the "vulgar Latin" of the Roman soldiers and from the Arabic of the Moorish invasion. The old Latin of the soldiers, spoken differently in each province, had developed different pronunciations in Portugal, Castile, Aragon, and Catalonia. Students of Latin America should remember that the first "proud Castilians" who came to the New World were from Cádiz and Seville rather than Castile; they spoke the language of Andalusia with its "ss" sound rather than "th" for *c* and *z,* as in the language of the central plateau. Today in Latin America one says, *"grassias,"* not *"grathias,"* so as not to be taken for a visitor from Madrid.

In this language, with the Andalusian pronunciation, Spanish words, Spanish place names, Spanish family names came to America. A glance at lists of the nobility, government officials, and church leaders in the Spain of 1250 to 1500 reveals many names familiar in the Americas. The names of viceroys, poets, explorers, and large landowners of the New World were the famous noble family names of Spain. But more important were the ordinary families named Chávez and Pérez, Domínguez and González, López and Morales and Fernández, who gave their names to the New

World, for they are today the Smiths and the Joneses, the Browns and the Greens, the Millers and the Carpenters of Latin America. They brought their love of music and poetry, their almost Moorish seclusion of women, their pottery and weaving, their market squares, their styles of houses. Especially they brought their devotion to religion—the colorful pageants on holydays, the patron saints for each town, the religious place names. And those who came as farmers brought their domesticated animals, especially their patient burros and their draft oxen, their methods of caring for orchard and vineyard and their Old World grains. In fact, the Chávez and Pérez and López families brought their whole pattern of life.

Spaniards also stamped the New World with their own personal characteristics. The bigotry and intolerance born of the long crusade against the Moors, the excessive pride and arrogance of the *hidalgos* who laid siege to Granada came to New Spain in the next generation. Contempt for peasant workers and for heretic tradesmen and artisans caused the well-born young Spanish soldiers in America to prefer fighting on the frontier to manual labor. On the other hand, the knightly pride was accompanied by reckless irresponsibility and an almost Arabic individualism which was to run rampant in America.

The many regions of Spain each contributed special characteristics. To the New World came self-reliant commerce-minded Basques, hard-working Gallegos from Galicia, cultured Castilians, peasants from Estremadura, and traders from Aragon. Especially is the carefree, emotional spirit of Andalusia found in the Americas—the joy of living, the gay colorful dances, the lighthearted poetry and song and speech. All these elements combined to form the psychological make-up of the sixteenth-century Spanish immigrants to America, dominated by honor, passion, and individualism, which are the best-known reflections of Spain in the development of Spanish America.

Portugal at the time of Europe's renaissance

Little has been said of Portugal, that other Christian kingdom which remained outside the union of Castile and Aragon, which kept its own language separate from the Castilian tongue, and which was the first European nation to embark on a colonial career. The Lusitanians were a tribe of Iberians on the Atlantic coast. Their city in the valley of the Tagus River came to be called Olisipo when it was under Roman dominance, a name re-pronounced Lisboa or Lisbon when the Roman Latin was no longer spoken. The Moors were in Lisbon by 720 and stayed there 400 years. Moorish influence is evident in Portugal in place names, architecture, literature, and folklore.

Meanwhile, the Valley of the Douro, with its old Roman town of Portus Cali, or Portucale—today's Oporto—was conquered by the expanding kingdom of León. As the county of Portugal, this area was given as a dowry by the king of León to his daughter when she married a young count from Burgundy. Her son proclaimed independence from León and pushed southward, winning the Tagus Valley from the Moors in 1147. Nine successors of his direct line, called the House of Burgundy, drove the Moors out of the rest of present-day Portugal. By placing the kingdom under the protection of the papacy as a papal fief, and by fending off all attempts of León and Castile to conquer it by force, Portugal was able to develop itself into a unified new state under a strong monarch, with a national language and literature. Many of the factors involved in the early history and struggles of Spain were present in the story of Portugal. By the time of John I—King John the Great (1385–1433)—Portugal was a strong unified nation, completely separate from the expanding Castilian kingdom.

King John's rule resembled that of Isabella a half century later. He consolidated the royal power and allowed his *cortes* to put but slight restraint upon him. The towns looked to the monarch for their privileges, and the nobles were loyal to the king. Owing to the piety of the people, the church remained a powerful influence. Royal courts encroached upon ecclesiastical courts and the king acquired the right of approving Papal Bulls. Yet clergymen filled most of the positions of influence and power. The King, as Ferdinand was to do later in Spain, assumed mastership of the military orders, the command of a royal army and of the newly created royal navy. Meanwhile there developed a new middle class capable of handling an increase in commerce. This class supported the king and obtained concessions, while the military were rewarded with land grants. Peace, strength, and economic and social advances made Portugal ready to act on the inviting possibilities presented her by her geographic situation.

Portugal is located in the southwest corner of Europe facing the Atlantic Ocean, and has several good ports. The Italian states had gained prosperity from their Mediterranean ports; the Portuguese could circumvent the Italian monopoly and do the same on the Atlantic. The people, physically strong, brave, sober, accustomed to hot climates, and imbued with religious zeal and the spirit of medieval chivalry, were ready to embark on any adventure. Tales of distant lands, of Christian kingdoms like that of the mythical Prester John, egged on the Portuguese. King John began the expansion in 1415 with the capture of Ceuta, a rich port on the African side of Gilbraltar, terminal of caravan routes into the heart of Africa, and a stronghold of Moslem corsairs. In this conquest the nineteen-year-old Prince Henry, born in 1394 as the third son of John I, was in naval command and was given a governorship in the corner of North Africa. This campaign started his career of discoveries down the African Coast, discoveries so important in the story told in the Prologue.

The religious Prince Henry hoped to find the land of the Christian Prester John; for profit to Portugal he sought gold, slaves, and ivory. He himself spent most of his years at home as administrator of the voyages of exploration. At his headquarters at Sagres on the southwest tip of Europe he established an "Institute," and here he surrounded himself with a group of scholars, cosmographers, cartographers, mathematicians, astronomers, and physicians. Here he built an observatory, made maps and charts, built ships, trained pilots, and received reports from his captains who were year by year working farther down the shoulder of Africa. The Madeiras were discovered by 1420 and colonized in 1425; a little later the Azores, known to antiquity, were rediscovered and explored. From Cape Blanco, Negro captives were brought back to Portugal. By the time of Henry's death in 1460, his mariners had gone within 6 degrees of the equator and had landed at Sierra Leone. His ships had started the trade in Negro slaves, gold dust, ivory, cotton, and pepper. Before the death of Henry, papal grants had confirmed the Portuguese claims along the African coast.

Far from ceasing when Henry died, the voyages down the African coast increased after the fall of Constantinople in 1453; the desire to circumvent the Turkish monopoly of the eastern trade routes created a new incentive for discovery of an all-water route to India. The eastern bend of Africa was discovered in 1462, and a settlement made on the Guinea coast. The Congo region was reached in 1484. Finally the work was climaxed by Bartolomeu Dias, who in 1488 doubled around the Cape of Good Hope; only a mutiny of his sailors prevented his achieving the goal reached ten years later by Vasco da Gama, who arrived successfully in India and returned with products of the Far East. Following up Vasco da Gama's voyage, Pedro Alvares Cabral, with a large trading fleet, touched at Brazil and then went on around Africa to lay the foundations for the Portuguese trade empire. There followed a rapid succession of Portuguese trading stations and colonies in the Far East—in India, Java, Sumatra, the Spice Islands, China, and even in Japan. Portugal, by thus finding an all-water route to India, wrested the lion's share of the India trade from the Italian city-states and became the great entrepôt of this lucrative business. The Portuguese ships, not the *Niña* and the *Pinta*, had actually reached Cathay. Thus Portugal had laid the groundwork for both trade and colonization.

Portugal now had her own century of glory. Her university at Coimbra was famous in Europe; the missionary St. Francis Xavier, though Spanish-born, took Christianity to India at the request of the Portuguese king and became a patron saint for all missionaries; the Portuguese poet Camões sang the glories of the age of East Indian exploration. Portugal's captains founded sugar-growing settlements in Brazil which she claimed under the Line of Demarcation agreement. Her merchants founded stations along the coast of Africa and became rich as slave traders for Europe and America, starting that tragic traffic in Negroes that was to be a black shadow on the New World.

But her decline as a world power came even before the defeat of Philip II's Armada at the hands of Elizabeth. For that same Philip, through his mother's line, had made himself King of Portugal when the male line died out, and thus what all early Portugal had dreaded—union with Castile—happened unexpectedly. Sixty years later, when Spain's own kings were weak, a Portuguese patriot, the Duke of Braganza, revolted and made Portugal an independent nation once again. The House of Braganza survived to see gold and diamonds discovered in Brazil. So, in the long run, Portugal had no reason for lasting regrets that she had turned Columbus down.

Spain and Portugal, by the evidence shown in this brief review of their earlier histories, were uniquely prepared for the task of colonizing the Americas which had been set for them by the voyages of Columbus.

READINGS

Abbott, W. C., *Expansion of Europe* (2 vols., 1924).

Altamira y Grevea, R., *A History of Spain,* trans. Muna Lee (1949).

Atkinson, W. C., *History of Spain and Portugal* (1960).

Baker, J. N. L., *History of Geographical Discovery and Exploration* (1937).

Beazley, C. R., *Dawn of Modern Geography* (3 vols., 1949).

Beckingham, C. F., and G. W. B. Huntingford, *The Prester John of the Indies* (2 vols., 1968).

Bertran, L., and Charles Petrie, *History of Spain* (1934).

Boxer, C. R., *Four Centuries of Portuguese Expansion, 1415–1825* (1961; 1969).

Castro, A., *The Spaniards. An Introduction to Their History* (1971).

Chapman, C. E., *History of Spain* (1918).

Cheyney, E. P., *European Background of American History* (1904).

————, *Dawn of a New Era* (1936).

Cohen, J. M., *The Four Voyages of Christopher Columbus* (1969).

Crone, G. R., *The Discovery of America* (1969).

Davies, R. Trevor, *The Golden Century of Spain 1501–1621* (1965).

Descola, J., *A History of Spain* (1963).

Diffie, B. W., *Prelude to Empire: Portugal Overseas before Henry the Navigator* (1961).

Elliott, J. H., *Imperial Spain 1469–1716* (1966).

Foster, G. M., *Culture and Conquest: America's Spanish Heritage* (1960).

Gibson, C., *Spain in America* (1966).

————, *Spanish Tradition in America* (1968).

Gordon, C. H., *Before Columbus: Links Between the Old World and Ancient America* (1971).

Haring, C. H., *Trade and Navigation Between Spain and the Indies in the Time of the Hapsburgs* (1918).

Hart, H. H, *Sea Road to the Indies* (1950).

————, *Venetian Adventurer, the Life and Times of Marco Polo* (1943).

Hechscher, E., *Mercantilism* (2 vols., 1935).

Helps, A., *Spanish Conquest of America* (4 vols., 1900–1904).

Iglesias, R., *Columbus, Cortés and Other Essays.* Trans. and ed. by L. B. Simpson. (1969).

Johnson, H. B., ed., *From Reconquest to Empire: The Iberian Background to Latin American History* (1970).

Keen, B., trans. and ed., *Life of Admiral Columbus by His Son Ferdinand* (1959).

Kirkpatrick, F. H., *The Spanish Conquistadores* (1934; 1969).

Klein, J., *The Mesta: A Study in Spanish Economy, 1273–1836* (1920).

Lane–Poole, S., *The Moors in Spain* (1886).

Lea, H. C., *History of the Inquisition in Spain* (4 vols., 1906–1907).

Livermore, H. V., *A New History of Portugal* (1967).

Lybyer, A. H., "Influence of the Rise of the Ottoman Turks upon the Routes of Oriental Trade," in *American Historical Association, Annual Report—1914*, Vol. I, 127–33.

————, "Ottoman Turks and the Routes of Oriental Trade," in *English Historical Review*, XXX (1915), 577–88.

Lynch, J., *Spain Under the Hapsburgs 1516–1598* (1964).

Marco Polo, The Book of Sir Marco Polo the Venetian (Yule ed.) (2 vols., 1903).

Madariaga, S. de, *Englishmen, Frenchmen, Spaniards* (1928; 1969).

Mariéjol, J. H., *Spain of Ferdinand and Isabella* (1961).

Merriman, R. B., *Rise of the Spanish Empire in the Old World and in the New* (4 vols., 1918–1934).

Morison, S. E., *Admiral of the Ocean Sea* (2 vols., 1942).

————, *The Caribbean as Columbus Saw It* (1964).

————, *The European Discovery of America. The Northern Voyages* (1971).

————, *Portuguese Voyages to America in the Fifteenth Century* (1940; 1965).

Newton, A. P., ed., *Travel and Travellers in the Middle Ages* (1930).

Nowell, C. E., *The Great Discoveries and the First Colonial Empires* (1954).

————, *A History of Portugal* (1952).

Nunn, G. E., *Geographical Conceptions of Columbus* (1924).

O'Gorman, E., *Invention of America* (1961).

Olson, J. E., and E. G. Bourne, eds., *The Northmen, Columbus and Cabot* (1906).

Penrose, Boies, *Travel and Discovery in the Renaissance, 1420–1670* (1952).

Pike, R., *Enterprise and Adventure: The Genoese in Seville and the Opening of the New World* (1966).

Pohl, F. J., *Atlantic Crossings before Columbus* (1961).

Prescott, W. H., *Ferdinand and Isabella* (2 vols., 3rd ed., 1839).

Prestage, E., *The Portuguese Pioneers* (1933).

Richman, I. B., *The Spanish Conquerors* (1919).

Sanceau, E., *Henry the Navigator* (1947).

Sauer, C. O., *The Early Spanish Main* (1966).

————, *Sixteenth Century North America: Land and People as Seen by the Europeans* (1971).

Savelle, M., *The Origins of the American Diplomacy. The International History of Anglo-America 1492–1763* (1907).

Skelton, R. A., et al., *Vinland Map and the Tartar Relation* (1965).

Stanislawski, D., *The Individuality of Portugal* (1959).

Stephens, H. M., *Portugal* (1893).

Sykes, P., *The Quest for Cathay* (1937).

Thatcher, J. B., *Christopher Columbus* (3 vols., 1903–1904).

Ticknor, G., *History of Spanish Literature* (3 vols., 1965).

Vicens Vives, J., *Approach to the History of Spain* (rev. ed. 1970).

————, *An Economic History of Spain* (1969).

Watt, W. M., *History of Islamic Spain* (1965).

chapter 2

THE LAND AND
CLIMATE OF
THE NEW WORLD

the surprising new land mass

"An age will come after many years, when the Ocean will loose the chains of things, and a huge land lie revealed," the Roman-Iberian Seneca had written. Christopher Columbus had read such early prophecies and had written comments on them in the margins of his personal books. And he had also promised Queen Isabella that he "had the intention to make a new chart of navigation, upon which I shall place the whole sea and lands of the Ocean Sea in their proper position under their bearings." But Columbus never made such a chart personally; he evolved no conception of the two continents, "the huge land" revealed when the ocean "loosed the chains of things." Between him and his goal of the true Indies lay half the "space" of the world.

And what "space"! Toscanelli and Behaim, the great geographers of the 1490s, thought the coast of China would be 5,000 miles westward from Europe; by actual airline it proved to be 11,766. Nearly 7,000 miles of this distance was partly occupied by the new hemisphere—from the hump of Brazil on the east to San Francisco on the west—and Iberian peoples were to put settlements somewhere along the entire 7,000-mile stretch. Spain and

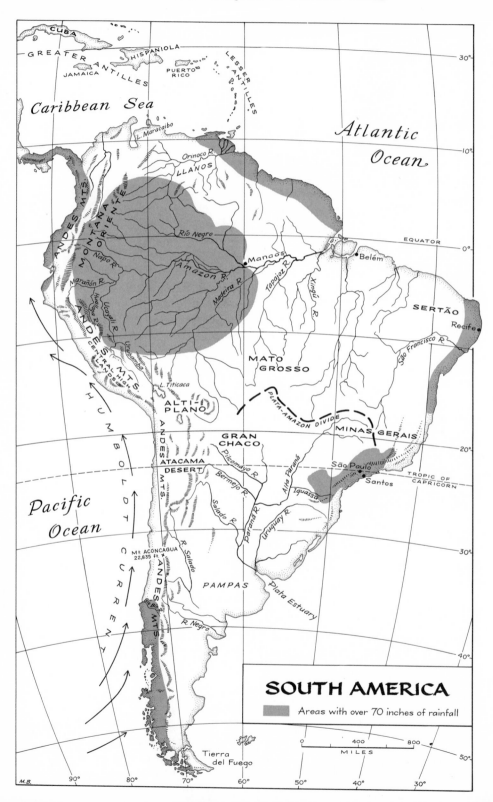

CUBA

GREATER ANTILLES

JAMAICA

HISPANIOLA

PUERTO RICO

LESSER ANTILLES

Caribbean Sea

Atlantic Ocean

L. Maracaibo

Orinoco R.

LLANOS

MONTAÑA ORIENTE

ANDES MTS.

Río Negro

Napo R.

Marañón R.

Huallaga R.

Ucayali R.

Urubamba

CENTRAL HIGHLAND

ANDES MTS.

L. Titicaca

ALTI-PLANO

GRAN CHACO

ATACAMA DESERT

ANDES MTS.

Mt. ACONCAGUA 22,835 ft.

R. Salado

PAMPAS

R. Salado

R. Negro

Pacific Ocean

HUMBOLDT CURRENT

Manaos

Amazon R.

Madeira R.

Tapajoz R.

Xingú R.

EQUATOR

Belém

SERTÃO

Recife

São Francisco R.

MATO GROSSO

PLATA-AMAZON DIVIDE

MINAS GERAIS

Pilcomayo R.

Bermejo R.

Salado R.

Paraná R.

Alto Paraná

Iguassú

Uruguay R.

São Paulo

Santos

TROPIC OF CAPRICORN

Plata Estuary

Tierra del Fuego

M.B.

SOUTH AMERICA

Areas with over 70 inches of rainfall

0   400   800

MILES

90°   80°   70°   60°   50°   40°   30°

30°   10°   0°   20°   30°   40°   50°

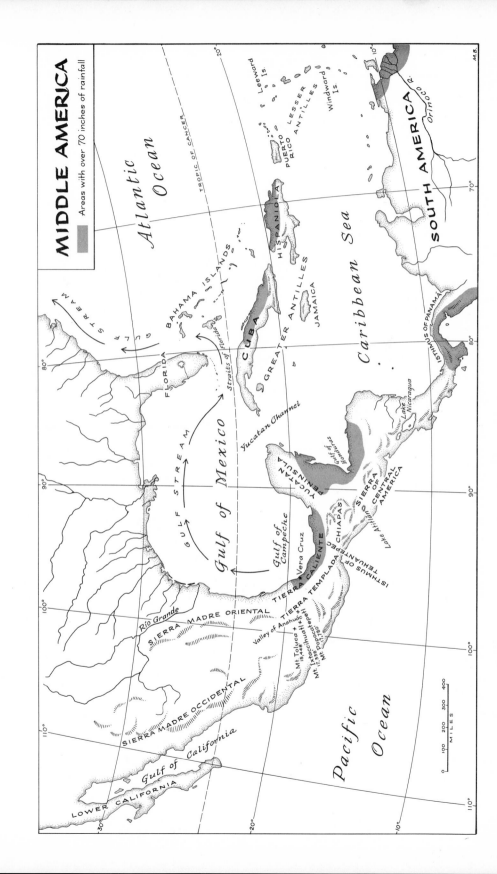

MIDDLE AMERICA

Areas with over 70 inches of rainfall

Portugal, with an area of only 225,000 square miles, were to dominate 8,600,000 square miles, an area almost forty times as great. For 200 years after the discovery, mapmakers tried to draw the contours and positions of the new continents, adding lands and islands in the wrong places, hoping to plot the strait that would show the way through to the Far East. The royal courts of Spain and Portugal regularly employed expert pilots and mapmakers to keep up with the newest information about coastlines and river mouths brought in by ship captains, but accurate knowledge was acquired only slowly, for the project was so vast. While scholars, cloistered in Europe, drew maps from secondhand information, explorers, soldiers, friars, and homebuilders tackled the lands themselves. In a thousand ways they found the new areas to be fantastically beyond previous experience. Although Spain itself was a land of severe contrasts, Spaniards entering the New World were unprepared for the great extremes of size, wealth, climate, hardships, and sheer beauty that they found in the American continents. Nothing as exciting would happen to mankind again until the exploration of space beyond the earth's atmosphere.

It is impossible to understand the history of Latin America without knowing something of its geography and the influence of that geography on the people who came to live there. For history is the story of the lives of people, and people live when and where they can earn a living, with their living depending on the geography of their living places. This is especially true of the great land mass the Spaniards had just discovered; each region of Latin America has a distinctive situation of water, weather, or mountain that has affected the lives of people there.

Latin American history is more involved with geography than is the history of most places. Latin America's geography produced her isolation from the rest of the world and her slow changes in culture; the great distances separating Latin America from Europe, and separating her various regions from each other, produced fierce local feelings for independence.

That the culture of Mexico is different from that of Brazil or of Argentina today is to some extent a matter of geography. For convenience the term Latin America is applied geographically to the twenty different regions of Spanish, Portuguese, and French colonization that make up today's twenty republics. The Latin-Europeans explored the Western Hemisphere from Nootka Sound and Chesapeake Bay to Tierra del Fuego, an area entirely surrounded by water, unconnected with any other continent. Most of South America lies east of the United States and much closer to Europe than does North America. By far the greater portion of the new continents lies within the Torrid Zone, a factor destined to make difficulties for the settlers, despite modification by some high plateaus.

Into this area, intervening between Europe and the eagerly sought–for lands of Asia, the Spaniards came—into an area unknown, uncharted, inhabited by strange red men who themselves had no concept of the extent of the land mass. The reader can follow the astounded Andalusians as they arrived in the Western Hemisphere via the Caribbean area and spread out into North and South America. In general, the Europeans were delighted at

umbus thought his new-found lands were "like
ropean invasion of the American hemisphere
nds of the Caribbean.

the Caribbean as Spaniards first saw it

; of the sea of the same name and the Antilles,
.e string of isl   sweeping arch from the coast of Venezuela near
the delta of the   the entrance to the Gulf of Mexico, as delimited
by the Yucata.   la peninsulas. The four westernmost islands—
Cuba, Jamaica, His   und Puerto Rico—are called the Greater Antilles,
due to their size in cc   to the long curve of Windward and Leeward
Islands, some volcanic in structure, some coral. All these islands together,
formed around the highest parts of submerged mountain chains contain a
total area of better than a million square miles.

Elevation and prevailing winds have always played a large part in
the economy of the Caribbean. Some islands are relatively dry, lack sufficient level places for agriculture, and have failed to develop adequate food
supplies. Others rise to a height of 5,000 feet—and in one case, the peak of
Mt. Tina, almost to 10,000 feet—receive a great deal of precipitation during
the season of the trade winds and hurricanes, and have a warm, moist
climate.

Both the Greater and Lesser Antilles loom large in the first century
of colonization. The Spaniards first introduced themselves as colonists in the
former, and then introduced their animals and plants, especially sugar. Here
they first tried out their institutions. The Greater Antilles were the strategic
steppingstones to North, Central, and South America, and the nearness to
the mainland gave the region a continuing and enduring importance. The
trade winds blew the first European ships directly to these islands; the
important commercial routes from Europe led to the Caribbean as long as
shipping depended on sails and wind directions.

Columbus came to Cuba two weeks after he first sighted land in the
Bahamas. "I sailed along its coast some distance toward the west," he wrote
of this Pearl of the Antilles, "and found it to be so large, without any
apparent end, that I believe it was not an island but a continent, a province
of Cathay." Actually, this large island stretches from east to west some 760
miles, though it averages only sixty miles in width. At all points Cuba is near
the sea, and it has many good harbors and anchorages which invited
Spanish explorers from the first. Sixty per cent of Cuban land is flat or gently
rolling. Spaniards began to clear forests along the coast and raise sugar cane
before Cortés went from there to the conquest of Mexico in 1519, and most
of Cuba's subsequent history, to the present, was to revolve around the
production of sugar. With rainfall averaging about fifty inches and temperatures averaging between seventy and eighty degrees, only an occasional
hurricane disturbs this planter's idyll.

The first Spanish homes were built on the Caribbean's second

largest island, Hispaniola, which now contains the two re
and the Dominican Republic. Much more mountainous than
much less agricultural land. Though this island was the "mother of
Spanish planters, miners, explorers, and administrators struck out fo
islands of the Antilles or for the mainland within a decade of its settlem
However, Spanish settlers and traders continued to make fortunes fro
sugar and slaves in Cuba and Santo Domingo throughout the colonial
period.

Puerto Rico, fourth of the Caribbean islands in size, is a continuation of the mountain range running from Cuba through Hispaniola. The
island of Jamaica, third largest in the Antilles, lies directly south of Cuba. It
long served Spaniards as a great producer of livestock; from here came
many of the horses and cattle utilized in the settlement of mainland Mexico,
Peru, and elsewhere. Then, for a century after it fell into the hands of the
English, Jamaica was a thorn in the flesh of the Spanish American empire,
serving as a base for naval attacks upon Spanish Caribbean cities.

The long line of the Lesser Antilles, exotic little islands with such
pretty names as Dominica, Antigua, Martinique, Guadeloupe, and Marie
Galante, was largely by-passed by the Spaniards after their first entry into
the Caribbean. This chain of islands became, during the seventeenth and
eighteenth centuries, hideouts for English and French freebooters, as well as
important bases for the English and French when they began colonial
development in the Americas.

heights and lowlands of Mexico and Central America

Across the Gulf from Cuba lies the eastern coastal plain of Mexico, an area
stretching from the Rio Grande to Yucatan and comprising sandy beaches,
swampy lagoons, mosquito-infested rivermouths. Veracruz, to be founded
from Cuba as a base for the conquest of the Aztecs, lies in the middle of the
curve. At the end of the arc, like a thumb, lies the peninsula of Yucatan, a
flat limestone tableland resembling that other dangling finger into the
Caribbean, Florida. Since its porous limestone surface absorbs the runoff,
there are no rivers in Yucatan; the tropical rains run quickly underground,
forming a below-surface water table used as a source of year-round deep
wells by the Maya Indians. It was here that the Spaniards first saw such
civilized peoples, and gained the desire to explore deeper into Mexico.

The base of Yucatan's peninsula leads into the plains of Mexico's
tropical eastern lowlands in the states of Tabasco and Chiapas. Here is
Mexico's narrowest point, but even here the traveler soon meets the main
geographic feature of the Mexican nation, the *cordillera,* or mountain range,
which forms Central America and runs on up into central Mexico where it
serves as the sheltering walls for many highland valleys. The real Mexico is
the highland plateau between its ridges. Between the two branches of the
cordillera, above the coastal plain on the east and sweeping down into the

Pacific on the west, lies an area 500 miles wide at its broadest, an area filled with valleys and basins. The altitude—4,000 feet for Oaxaca, 9,000 feet for Toluca, with many other valleys at elevations in between—produces a temperate climate conducive to European settlement.

Most important of these basins is the central valley of Anáhuac, site of the Aztec culture and home of today's Mexico City. Here is a cup 160 miles in circumference at an altitude of about 7800 feet. There are twenty-three inches of rainfall a year, distributed throughout the growing season to produce adequate crops, while temperatures stay near seventy degrees. The fertile and productive valley is rimmed by two snow-covered peaks, Popocatépetl and Ixtaccíhuatl. From the pine-covered mountains melting snows and rain pour down into the valley, and there is no outlet. In prehistoric times these streams formed a series of marshes and lakes. The Aztecs built their city on islands in the marsh known as Lake Texcoco; as it grew, they could not drain it in flood season. For the Spanish colonial city, as for the modern Mexican capital, there has been no natural drainage from the central sink of the Valley of Anáhuac, creating a problem for its rulers since 1400. Yet the valley itself has housed the population center of Mexico and is in many ways an ideal place to live.

North from the central valley lies a series of basins, some of them inhabitable areas where Indians had started agricultural settlements made possible by sufficient rainfall. On the edge of the rainfall line, just south of the Tropic of Cancer, quantities of mineral wealth lay hidden in the ranges in the silver-producing areas of Zacatecas and San Luis Potosí. One-third of the modern state of Mexico lies north of this region, outside the area of sufficient rainfall. It is an area of brush and cactus. Beyond it lie the Rio Grande, the plains of Texas, the mountains of Arizona and New Mexico, the barren peninsula of Baja California, and the Mediterranean-climate area of Alta California. All were to know the rule of Spain.

To the south of the central valley the highland country continues, beyond the mountain rim of the plateau of Anáhuac and at increasingly lower elevation. Two hundred thirty miles south from Mexico City the mountains open out to form the long, narrow, and rich valley of Oaxaca, with an average elevation of some 5,000 feet, where lived other civilized Indian tribes. Beyond this last valley the mainland of Mexico narrows down to 130 miles; here the two ridges form one in the low hills of the Isthmus of Tehuantepec, again a low hot country. Where Tehuantepec begins to widen out again, the mountains jut up steeply into the cooler valleys, deep slashing *barrancas,* or ravines, and active volcanoes standing guard over sapphire lakes of Guatemala—a land with a large Indian population that made the Spaniards fight hard for conquest. The Indian strain is still strong in Guatemala today, and the whole land is very nearly as colorful as the Spaniards found it.

Columbus himself had been the first to sail along the Central American coast, the deeps or *hondos* of Honduras, the "rich coast" of Costa Rica. The Central American area was to be colonized both from Panama northward and Mexico southward. Its 213,000 square miles of area comprise merely a narrowing and an extension of Mexico southward, running across the compass from northwest to southeast, containing many volcanic peaks and two high continuing ridges which unite at various points. The mountains tend to come closer to the Pacific Ocean side, dividing the smaller republics into tropical and unhealthy lowlands on the east and pleasanter highlands on the west. Most of the Spanish settlement in Central America took place in the valleys where an average altitude of some 3,000 feet lessens the heat of the tropics. The Negro slave population brought in by the Spaniards remained largely confined to the Caribbean coastal lowlands. Today's Central American population is white, Indian, and *mestizo,* or mixed bloods, in the thickly populated highlands on the west, and Negro in the small ports and banana plantations on the Caribbean coast.

Thus the *cordillera* of Mexico and Central America was to be a constant hindrance to conquest and settlement. But the greatest frustration this mountain chain was to offer the Europeans was at the place where it narrowed to its lowest strip in the dense jungle called the Isthmus of Panama. Only forty miles of land here separated the Caribbean from the Pacific, or South Sea—just enough land to shatter the hopes of easily reaching Marco Polo's China by water. This low mountain range of Panama is the connecting link between the Andean *cordillera* of South America and the great chain of *sierras* heading northward through Central America and Mexico. Half the voyages of exploration for a quarter century after Columbus were made in search of a way around or through this strip. The Isthmian link flattens out into swampy lands along the Caribbean coast— swamps which were to bring fever and death and to make the Isthmus famous as the pesthole of colonial trade and travel.

Pesthole the Isthmus was, but its very narrowness was to be a blessing for the Spanish empire. Its small width made it the shortest route to the riches of Peru, and it was naturally situated as the base of supply for Pizarro's Peruvian conquest. Throughout the whole colonial period Panama, with its terminal trading centers on either coast, handled the richest traffic in all the New World, the flow of silver and merchandise from Peru, Chile, and Ecuador to Mother Spain.

the South American continent

"We reached a land which we deemed a continent, which is distant westwardly from the Isles of Canary about a thousand leagues beyond the inhabited regions and within the torrid zone." Perhaps this was the first description of South America on the "hump" of Brazil, written by Amerigo Vespucci a few years after Columbus' first voyage. Here Iberians were to find and develop agricultural and mineral wealth untold, but the geography of the continent was so difficult, its whole area so much to the south of the main east-west trade routes as to make South America even today an isolated and underdeveloped region. It has been handicapped by its long, smooth coastline where good harbors lie so far apart, by the tropical climate of two-thirds of its land mass, by its rugged and lofty mountains unmatched save in the Himalayas. It was hard for Europeans to maintain contact and to interchange ideas across this difficult terrain; Spanish and Portuguese towns remained isolated, and in the mid-twentieth century whole regions are still only sparsely occupied by wild Indians.

Again, it is the contrast between mountains and lowlands that has set up the most difficult geographic barrier. In past geologic ages South America was made up of two great land masses, the Andes mass on the west, and the plateau known as the Brazilian Highlands on the east.

The Amazon and the Plata River basins make up the eastern side of the continent, and the Andes *cordillera* stands high as the backbone, dividing the continent into two unequal parts. Its ridges hug the Pacific shores, leaving only a narrow coastal strip as a shelf or stepping stone up into the highlands. The ridges and valleys that make up the Andes extend the length of the western coast from Panama to Tierra del Fuego. In southern Chile the *cordillera* is one single range forty miles wide, a region of forests, fogs, and fjords; in Bolivia the Andes area is a vast plateau of from ten to fifteen thousand feet elevation with the city of La Paz lying in a ravine. With the inhabited plateaus at lower elevations in Peru and Ecuador, the mountains continue into Colombia, where they divide into three narrow fertile valleys with rivers flowing down each. One of these chains sidetracks to form the ridges and valleys of Venezuela. Individual peaks in the Andes rival the famous mountains of the Himalayas. Illimani, at 22,000 feet, towers above Bolivia's windswept central tablelands. Osorno, a perfect cone like Fuji-yama, stands snow-covered the year round in Chile's southern range, while Mount Aconcagua is the highest peak in the Western Hemisphere at 22,863 feet. Cotopaxi and Chimborazo are near the Equator in Ecuador, but both are constantly snow-covered at the top because they reach upward of 20,000 feet.

Most prosperous of the long Andean valleys today is perhaps the Central Valley of Chile, a fertile area forty miles wide and 600 miles long, whose counterpart Spaniards were to find two centuries later in Alta California. The Inca Indians had built their capital at Cuzco in the Andean Valley to the north in Peru; Quito, capital of Ecuador, is similarly situated. The capital of the Colombian region was to be at Bogotá. The city itself is not in the river valley, but in a *savanna* or grassy plain, at 8,700 feet elevation in the Andes, 600 miles up the Magdalena River from the coast and 150 miles into the mountains beyond, extremely difficult of access until the air age. Despite their height, with few exceptions, the Andes have not formed the political boundaries of today's republics.

The geography of the Andes approaches never made transportation easy; routes to Bogotá, Quito, La Paz, and Cuzco were so precipitous as to slow down the development of those Spanish cities in the interior. The peaks of the *cordillera* raise their beautiful heads as the greatest handicap to development of five nations on the west coast, nations which are still trying to get across their mountains and develop their areas in the valleys of the Amazon's tributaries, nations whose isolated towns put sectionalism ahead of national pride. About one-sixteenth of this large area of South America has an elevation of 10,000 feet or more, a height at which Europeans have found life difficult. Along the *cordillera* from Central America to Chile runs an earthquake and volcano belt where seismic and volcanic activity persists yet with often disastrous results. The Brazilian Highlands consist of a plateau broken by mountains along the coast, making passage north and south difficult. In the far north are the Guiana Highlands which even today are little explored.

As important as the mountains in the social and economic development of South America are the vast plains, which comprise about three-fifths of the land area of the continent, making eastern South America one of the largest lowland areas of the world. Inland from the coastal plains are three great areas of low-lying fertile lands. In the north are the *savannas* or tropical grass lands of the Orinoco, the *llanos* of Venezuela. Beyond the Guiana and Brazilian Highlands lie the tropical *selvas* or hot, wet forests of Brazil, merging in the south into the rolling, grassy, treeless pampas, the meat and wheat belt for South America. The pampas start in today's modern Brazilian state of Rio Grande do Sul, and run through Uruguay, a grassland nation two-thirds the size of Spain. So devoid of mountains is this land that when a Portuguese sailor, so the story is told in Uruguay, saw a hill 700 feet high, he called, "*Monte vejo!*"—"I see a mountain!"—and Montevideo itself is there today.

Below the Plata River are the pampas of Argentina, one of the greatest pasture areas on earth. On their east lie a thousand miles of open Atlantic, on the north the Plata-Paraná River system, on the west the Andes. At the widest point the pampas are 980 miles across, enough area to make thirty Hispaniolas. Spanish-speaking peoples, coming to the area reluctantly at first as to a poor land of starvation and wild Indians, were to make of it four centuries later one of the world's richest agricultural regions, producing beef, mutton, wheat, corn, cotton, and flax for the city people of Europe. Its climate is right for this type of agriculture: warm for the crops in the heat of the Southern Hemisphere's January summer, chilly in July and August, but rarely below freezing. The flat pampas rise gradually into the Andes in the west. A mule-train-oxcart round trip from Buenos Aires to the Andes foot-hills behind Chile took four months as late as 1800. Geography south of the pampas stopped the Spaniards short, for here was windswept Patagonia. In mid-twentieth century there were still whole sections of it that had never been surveyed, although geologists found iron ore in Patagonia in the 1960's.

Equally difficult for colonization was another grassy plain of South America, the *llanos* of Venezuela, flood plain of the Orinoco, never actually settled, save by a few cattle ranchers. Lowlands on the western coastal strip, the bleak Atacama Desert of southern Peru and northern Chile, also proved uninviting for Spanish colonists. Nitrate and guano developments there, however, made the region a bloody battleground in the nineteenth century. Thus lowlands and highlands, in stark contrast with each other, both created a poor welcome to the Iberians as they wrestled with the land mass of South America.

the influence of river systems

The Iberian peoples, accustomed to the Tagus and the Guadalquivir, would want to use the rivers of America as approaches to the hinterland. Mexico's geography offered them little in this regard. Indeed, in all of Mexico there are no large rivers. Even the famous Rio Grande is important today only for irrigation. In Central America, the Chagres forms part of the Panama Canal, and the San Juan River-Lake Nicaragua waterway has historic importance in colonial commerce and in diplomatic controversy over canal routes. Harbors are good in Mexico and Central America, but they are not necessarily on river mouths. Rivers in the Antilles show as names on the map, but are not navigable, though the good harbors on the islands have been of great use since the days of discovery.

South America is as blessed with rivers as Mexico is lacking. It was at one such river that Columbus first saw South America; his third voyage touched on the mainland beyond the island of Trinidad. There he approached one of the mouths in the delta of the Orinoco, a river 1700 miles long, draining the *llanos*. Spaniards had not seen such a quantity of water issuing from so green a country. Columbus himself thought that as "neither the Ganges nor the Euphrates nor the Nile carried so much fresh water," it could not flow from a mere island, but from "a terrestrial paradise." Thus, because of the river, Columbus sensed that he had reached a continent. The Orinoco has proved of little economic use, however, though navigable for a thousand miles. There is little trade because of the floods during the rainy season. Not so the Magdalena, which, with its tributary the Cauca, served as the highway into Colombia's interior until the air age. Navigable for 600 miles, the Magdalena carried the nation's freight three-fourths of the way to Bogotá from the harbors of Barranquilla and Cartagena at its mouth until highways were completed in the late 1950s.

In southern South America the Plata estuary, a great body of fresh water a hundred miles wide at the sea, invited explorers to come in looking for a strait to the Far East. In itself, the Plata is not a hundred miles long, for it is actually a joint mouth for the Uruguay and the Paraná-Paraguay rivers. The latter, one of the great rivers of the Western Hemisphere, has its headwaters in little rivulets in Brazil's Goiás plateau, where drops of water running side by side cannot make up their minds to go either north to the Amazon or south to the Plata. One of the tributaries, near its junction with the Paraná a thousand miles upstream from the Plata estuary, rushes madly along a plateau and plunges 210 feet on a two-mile width in the second largest falls of the world, the Falls of Iguassú.

The Paraná has a sister river, the Paraguay, navigable to Spanish "brigantines" 500 miles above the two rivers' confluence. Waters reaching it from the Bolivian Andes, near Lake Titicaca down the Pilcomayo, and from the Mato Grosso plateau divide its sources from those of the Amazon. How could the Spaniard, accustomed to the short reaches of the Guadalquivir, comprehend the great river systems of South America? Pilcomayo, Paraguay, Iguassú, Bermejo, Paraná, Uruguay—draining over a million square miles of territory and providing as much navigation for his little barks as if he had crossed the Atlantic, these rivers spread out like a fan before him as he stood at the Plata estuary. Entering the estuary he was to find paths overland from it to reach his brother Spaniards in the Inca lands beyond the Andes. Today four modern republics are dependent on the Plata system for part of their life stream. The first European settlement was to be Asunción, where the Pilcomayo meets the Paraguay in the interior. To the north lay the jungles of the Mato Grosso. To the west lay the Gran Chaco, a region of swamps in the wet season, desert in the dry, through which comparatively few Spaniards passed safely in three centuries.

Largest river in the world is the Amazon, flowing majestically over 4,000 miles, draining a basin of 2,750,000 square miles, which contains 40,000 miles of navigable river. Spaniards first saw the mighty river as they worked down from the Andes at the river's sources. The first Spanish witness described the headwaters of the Amazon as a region "full of foul places, of rough forests, and rivers great and small," a region later to be called the *Montaña*, comprising the eastern sections of the modern republics of Peru, Ecuador, Colombia, and Bolivia. In fact, until very recent times the Amazon was the only means of penetrating large portions of South America, and it gives several Pacific South American republics a future hope and look toward the Atlantic. Here the rushing streams of the Andes, starting at some places less than a hundred miles from the Pacific, come leaping out of the easternmost canyons of the *cordillera*, through the humid forest belt of the foothills to form great rivers—the Napo, the Huallaga, the Urubamba, the Negro, and the Marañón. Forbidding access to the first Europeans, many Amazon tributaries are even yet unexplored; their tentacles stretch out into every South American country save three. Three thousand miles from the Atlantic the tributaries begin to meet, first one and then the other, to make the Amazon eight miles wide before it has flowed one-fourth of its journey. Many of its head streams almost touch fingers with headwaters of the Plata-Paraná system on the south, or the Orinoco system on the north.

Flood waters which start in eastern Peru in February, the rainiest season, reach the Atlantic down the Amazon four months later in June. The banks of this river that crosses a continent are so low and the tributaries are so many that the waters move sluggishly, overflowing and filling swamps as the water comes down, receding just in time for another flood. It reaches the sea in a stream fifty miles wide, goes around large islands at the mouth, and makes the ocean itself a muddy brown many miles out. The tributaries flowing from the south split the wilderness of Mato Grosso and Goiás. These rivers, the Tapajós, the Xingú, the Tocantins, are themselves half a continent long; the territory they cross is slowly being opened to colonization in the air age.

There are other bodies of water in South America. Though west coast rivers are few, the Maule and the Bío Bío have been important in Chilean history, and the Guayas in Ecuador makes a harbor at Guayaquil. Lakes in the south of Chile form a vacation area today. Lake Titicaca, home of a very early Andean civilization, is one of the highest lakes in the world, while Lake Maracaibo, actually an arm of the sea on the Venezuelan coast, is one of the world's most important sources of petroleum, black gold far more valuable than the yellow gold the Spaniards sought.

The east coast does not lack harbors, from Belém on the mouth of the Amazon, to Recife with its protecting reefs, to the beautiful Bay of Salvador known as Baía where the Portuguese first settled in Brazil, to Santos Bay, port for the São Paulo interior. Rio de Janeiro itself remains one of the most spectacular harbors of the world. That these good ports did not help develop Brazil more rapidly was due to the facts that they were too far apart down the long coast and that their backlands were not inviting. Inland from Recife lies a highland region with only twenty inches of rainfall, the *Sertão* or pastoral country; few immigrants direct from Portugal were ever to go there. Inland from Baía runs the São Francisco River, south to north and then into the sea, but so full of rapids as to be unusable for navigation, and hence little assistance to penetration beyond. Inland 300 miles to the northwest of Rio, but still only an eighth part of the distance across the continent, vast mineral treasures awaited the Portuguese in Minas Gerais. Inland from Santos harbor lay the rich uplands of São Paulo, destined to produce wealth in coffee berries undreamed of by any gold-prospecting settler. However, much of this development was to come late in Brazilian history.

The natural beauties, the breathtaking scenery of mountain, lake, and river in Latin America make today's tourists gasp as did the first explorers. The Falls of the Iguassú, part of the Plata system, are wider and higher than Niagara; the *barrancas* of Mexico are almost as amazing as the Grand Canyon; Lake Atitlán in Guatemala is bluer than Crater Lake; Angel Falls, discovered only in 1935 in the Guiana Highlands, dims the wonders of Yosemite Valley. Spanish chronicles and letters are full of descriptions of the many such wonders Europeans saw for the first time in the New World.

temperature, rainfall, and settlement

Climate has surely been an important influence on humanity and history in Latin America. It is impossible to do more than make a few generalities about climate conditions; a mere glance at the map does not tell the story. Spanish and Portuguese America stretches from 35 degrees north latitude to a few degrees from the Antarctic Circle, through temperate, torrid, and again temperate zones into the edge of the frigid zone, but there are greater variations in climate than that. The Tropic of Cancer crosses Mexico near Mazatlán a few hundred miles south of the United States border; the Tropic of Capricorn runs near Rio de Janeiro on the east, near the Bolivian-Peruvian border on the west. The areas north of Mazatlán have a cool season in December and January; south of Rio and Asunción Christmas comes in the summer, and June and July bring cold weather to Buenos Aires and Santiago. Still, the areas within these zones vary in climate because of the presence of vast mountains and many different elevations. Winds, fog, rains, and ocean currents also enter the picture.

Thus there are many exceptions to any statements that can be made about climate in Latin America. A mere glance at a relief map does not reveal the climatic differences between Quito and Guayaquil, Mexico City and Veracruz, Lima and Baía. In Mexico and in the Andes nations the temperature is based not on north and south but on elevation. Mexicans refer to the coastal lowlands of Veracruz, Tabasco, and Yucatan as *Tierra Caliente,* the hot, humid lands, the home of the mosquito as well as of the banana. The *Tierra Templada,* or temperate country, lies at 2,000 to 8,000 feet above sea level. It is a land of perpetual spring, exemplified by Mexico City at 7,800 feet, with its year-round pleasant days but chilly nights. *Tierra Fría* lies above 8,000 feet where nights are cold and one wears a coat every evening, and where there can even be severe frost to hurt the crops. Thus in crossing from east to west, from Veracruz to Acapulco, one goes from hot to temperate to cold to temperate and back to hot, all on the same parallel of latitude. The plateaus north of Mexico City are *templadas,* in varying degrees, depending on their altitude, while on the low west coast north of Acapulco, one finds the *Tierra Caliente* as far north as the Tropic of Cancer at Mazatlán and beyond. South of Mexico City the land slopes down to *Tierra Caliente* again at Tehuantepec, then up sudddenly to the cool *Tierra Templada* in the highlands of Chiapas and Guatemala. Rainfall also varies; there is heavy precipitation on the Atlantic coastal plain, especially in the south, and hardly any rain at all in the barren west and northwest Pacific coastal area.

Central America presents the same spectacle of varying climate, for it is hot and humid on the Atlantic coastal plain, but cool, healthy, and in spots delightful in the highland areas near the Pacific where most of the city population lives. There is a difference in rainfall from fifty inches a year on the west coast to more than 200 in some points on the Caribbean side. In general the rainy season is in summer, May to October, but the winter seasons are by no means dry. The Caribbean climate is that of the torrid zone, though the altitude and insular position on each island temper the heat. For example, Puerto Rico's climate, dry on one side, moist on the other, is conditioned by the trade winds, the same breezes that blew Columbus to the islands in the first place. On each island, rainfall varies greatly from coast to coast, but it is always humidly warm.

In South America great variations take place, again explained by altitude, by winds, and by ocean currents. About two-thirds of South America is in the torrid zone, and the remainder in the south temperate zone. In general the lowlands of the Amazon are damp and hot, while the places of great altitude are cool and salubrious even at the equator. In the Andean regions of the torrid zone the majority of the population lives at an altitude of from six to twelve thousand feet. On the plain of the west coast the heat is not as excessive, owing to the cooling effects of the Humboldt Current, a cold ocean current, that sweep northward from the Antarctic, as the earth turns, along the coast of Chile and Peru. It is, however, turned away from South America by the shoulder south of the Guayas and runs northwest across the Pacific to become the Japanese Black Current in Asiatic waters. Coming from the frigid zone into the tropics, the air above this current holds little moisture, and cannot release it in the form of rain as would a warm current; it brings chilliness and fog to the coast of Peru, but hardly ever rain. The high Andes reach close to the shore and have already combed out the moisture from the trade winds blowing across the Amazon Valley, and have collected it on their peaks in the form of snow. None of this moisture reaches the west coast below the Guayas, except as it flows down in the form of melted snow in swift rivers through the desert coast. Thus the Andes on the west side in Peru, Bolivia, and northern Chile get no moisture and the coast is a rainless desert. The Inca capital was in an irrigated valley 11,000 feet in altitude and 200 miles inland from the coast. These Indians developed irrigation because although the Central Highlands in Peru are well watered from the melted snow, the streams that rise there find their way eventually into tributaries of the Amazon which flow in the *Montaña* area of Peru, Ecuador, and Bolivia, where there is heavy rainfall anyway.

North of the bulge at Guayaquil the coast of Ecuador and Colombia lies in one of the rainiest areas of the world. The steaming west coast part of Colombia has 200 inches of rainfall a year. To the south of Chile's northern coastal desert the Central Valley of Chile—the California of the Southern Hemisphere—needs irrigation on both sides of Santiago. Rain falls more heavily to the south, and the wooded hills beyond the Bío Bío are one vast area of lakes, rains, and chill fogs.

Southern Argentina, where the pampas begins along the Andean Piedmont, sees little rain, but from there to the Atlantic Coast rainfall increases to keep the pastures green. In Brazil the precipitation is heaviest in the Amazon Valley and fairly heavy along the coast from March to August. Here the trade winds also blow and help take the discomfort out of the heat. They come across the Atlantic from northeast and southeast toward the equator, bearing heavy loads of moisture, most of which has been dropped in the form of rain by the time they reach the *cordillera*. Hence, the tropical interior of South America on the whole gets excessive rain, a geographic factor that has made colonization difficult.

Rain, its excess or its lack, has been one of the most significant factors in Latin American history, determining as it does the character and distribution of the lakes and rivers, and making the ultimate decision as to location of settlements and methods of agriculture. Moisture also influenced the type of game settlers would catch, fruits they would pick, and their own state of health, good or bad. Most tropical climates bring the constant menace of insect pests and diseases which we have only recently learned to combat. Dysentery, and hookworm are carried by bacteria, parasites, and fleas in the tropics. Malaria, to which natives and Negro slaves were more apt to be immune, slowed down the white European everywhere he tried to live in the tropics. So he built his most successful cities at higher altitudes— Mexico City, São Paulo, Bogotá, Puebla, Arequipa—or on drier irrigated plains such as the coast of Lima. Only the ports in the tropics flourished— ports which had to be placed there as steppingstones to something else. Mankind wants water for his civilization but not too much and not too often. Thus from this whole pattern of moisture versus dryness, a history of settlement, of successful agriculture, of the growth of cities, could be written.

the wild life of the New World

The Iberians were to see many strange animals: tapirs, iguanas, bison, jaguars, turkeys, emus, capybaras, guanacos. They noted immediately the lack of horses, cows, mules, sheep, goats, or donkeys. "So innumerable are the animals that they could not be counted," wrote an early explorer, "but all are savage, and of none of them do the natives make use for their service." When Pizarro came to Peru, he found the llama domesticated as a beast of burden, the alpaca and the vicuña raised as a source of wool; all of these animals were to be pressed into service for the Spaniards. Other New World animals were of less use to him, though deer, bison, and rabbits were often to serve him as meat, and beavers were to inspire a Spanish fur trade up into the Mississippi country in rivalry to the French. The fish of the New World—over two thousand varieties in the Amazon area alone—provided the colonist with a source of food, and led to a thriving industry into modern times, as did the pearl–bearing oysters which first brought the Spaniards to the islands off Venezuela and the Bay of La Paz in Lower California.

Tropical and subtropical fruits and many vegetables were usable for the Europeans in the New World. The Europeans were to learn to eat Indian corn, or maize, to use the beans, the squash, the tomatoes, the chiles, and the yams the Indians cultivated. The New World gave them cacao for chocolate, tobacco for smoking, quinine to cure malaria. Cortés wrote his king about a game played with a ball, which "when thrown to the ground rebounded to the player." The ball was made of rubber, one of Latin America's greatest gifts to Europe. Mexico alone produced eighty-seven kinds of fruits, fifty-two species of vegetables and cereals, 113 types of medicinal herbs and plants. South America provided the white potato, basic food of the Inca Indians, and soon to spread from Spain to Ireland and Germany to become a staple of Europe's peasantry.

Other plants produced fibers, the agave and henequén of Mexico. For building materials there were fifty-six species of lumber-producing woods, and twenty-one kinds of cabinet woods, including the mahogany of Central America and the Amazon. Quebracho trees of the upper Paraná were to produce a chemical valuable for the tanning of leather, and become one of the principal exports of Paraguay. In the soil lay mineral wealth—gold, silver, iron, tin, copper, nitrates, and finally oil. For the earliest civilized inhabitants there was stone for building materials and clay for pottery.

So the explorers and settlers were to know the islands and the Spanish Main, the Isthmus, and the *cordillera* of Mexico, with its *Tierra Caliente* at the foot and its *Tierra Templada* in the center. They were to meet and conquer the Andes, over Indian trails, or through new passes they themselves worked out. Deserts in Chile and Peru, in Sonora and Arizona and Baja California, were to be crossed by them. The Colorado and the Yaqui, the San Juan and the Chagres, the Orinoco and the Magdalena and the Bío Bío would be used for floating ships or for watering men or beasts or crops. The Amazon and the Plata drainage systems were to provide access to new regions and to become the sources of boundary disputes through centuries to come.

The settlements themselves were completely bound by geography. Where climate was temperate and soil fertile, native peoples had learned agriculture, had developed irrigation systems where they were needed, had built villages and then cities. Where mineral deposits were close to such peoples, they had begun to work them. To such areas, rich in agriculture, in mineral wealth, in labor supply, Europeans came in large numbers. Where high ranges separated these areas, even the European communities remained isolated. Where rivers helped them in and out, they kept in touch with one another. Where good harbors combined with river systems and easy passes through the mountains, they kept in touch with the world. Tropical diseases and heat drove them into the highlands; cold and barren ridges kept them in the temperate valleys. Sufficient rainfall brought them independence as to food supply and gave them products to export; excess rainfall flooded them out and made city-building impossible. Thus some areas were settled and some neglected; in some places one crop was raised and in some another; in some places natives were exploited to do the labor, in some Negro slaves were imported, and in some farmers from Spain did the work themselves—all depending on the geographic conditions. The New World offered a wide variety of such conditions.

Concerning most of this New World, later comers would agree with Amerigo Vespucci: "The land is full of immense rivers. The soil is very pleasant and fruitful; there are immense woods and forests, and it is always green, for the foliage never drops off. The fruits are so many that they are numberless."

The fruits were indeed to be many—from the pleasant soil, the immense woods, the riches under the earth, the toil of the settlers and of the natives. Truly had Columbus written to Ferdinand and Isabella that "great will be the benefit derived hence. It is certain, Lord Princes, that where there are such lands there should be profitable things without number."

READINGS

Bain, H. F., and T. T. Read, *Ores and Industry in South America* (1934).

Bates, M., *Where Winter Never Comes: A Study of Man and Nature in the Tropics* (1952).

Blakemore, H. and C. T. Smith (eds.), *Latin America: Geographical Perspectives* (1971).

Bowman, I., *The Andes of Southern Peru* (1916).

————, *Desert Trails of Atacama* (1924).

Butland, G. J., *Latin America: A Regional Geography* (1960).

Carlson, F. A., *Geography of Latin America* (3rd ed., 1952).

Cole, J. P., *Latin America; An Economic and Social Geography* (1970).

Deutschmann, P. J., *et al.*, *Communication and Social Change in Latin America* (1968).

Edel, M., *Food Supply under Inflation in Latin America* (1969).

Gruenwald, J., and P. Musgrove, *Natural Resources in Latin American Development* (1970).

Hargreaves, D. and B., *Tropical Trees in the Caribbean, South America, Central America and Mexico* (1965).

James, P. E., *Latin America* (rev. ed., 1959 and later).

Jones, C. F., *South America* (1930).

Millás, J. C., *Hurricanes of the Caribbean and Adjacent Regions 1492–1800* (1969).

Monge, C., *Acclimatization in the Andes,* trans. D. F. Brown (1948).

Phelps, D. M., *Rubber Developments in Latin America* (1957).

Platt, R. S., *Latin America: Countrysides and United Regions* (1942).

Pohl, I. and J. Zepp, *Latin America, A Geographical Commentary* (1966).

Price, A. G., *White Settlers in the Tropics* (1939).

Reid, W. A., *Ports and Harbors of South America* (1934).

Rich, J. L., *The Face of South America: An Aerial Traverse* (1942).

Russell, R. J., and F. B. Kniffin, *Cultural Worlds* (1951).

Shanahan, E. W., *South America: An Economic and Regional Geography with an Historical Chapter* (11th ed., 1963).

Smith, J. R., *North America* (1925).

Stokes, C. J., *Transportation and Economic Development in Latin America* (1968).

Suman, A. L., *Geography of Middle America* (1937).

Verrill, A. H., *Foods America Gave the World* (1938).

Whitbeck, R. H., *et al.*, *Economic Geography of South America* (3rd ed., 1940).

Wilgus, A. C., ed., *Colonial Hispanic America* (1936).

————, *Latin America in Maps* (1943).

Wollman, N., *Water Resources of Chile* (1968).

dwellers and temple builders to about A.D. 300; the Classic from about A.D. 300 to about 900; and the post-Classic from about A.D. 900 to 1500. Across the lines of these time periods went waves of migration from one region to another along with wars, famines, conquests, and rebuildings. Although towns had been built by 800 B.C. in the central valley of Mexico and in Oaxaca, Yucatán, and Guatemala, the first pyramid builders to develop a complex temple structure seem to have been the Olmecs near the Gulf of Mexico.

The Olmecs probably built earth mounds with wooden temples on top at three sites in the modern Mexican states of Veracruz and Tabasco. But at the site called La Venta, they also dragged large stone blocks for miles to carve them into heads, without bodies or even necks. They were as large as ten feet high, the faces, very realistically rendered, resembling those of young children, their heads encased in protective helmets. A clay pyramid 100-feet tall was also at the site and near it were deposits of carved jade, some representing human figures with child-like faces, some half-animal types with faces resembling jaguars, all carved carefully and smoothly in very hard material.

Carbon-14 dating, the modern scientific method of determining the approximate age of archeological sites, set the time the site was used as the period from 800 to about 300 B.C. The length of this period of occupancy indicates that the people were dominated by powerful priests and harried by few enemies. Some of the carved stones carry hieroglyphic inscriptions. From the fact that carved faces of the Olmec type are found on stones used as rubble to fill an early pyramid in the Oaxaca Valley at Monte Albán, it is deduced that these people sent out traders or missionaries. In the ruins in the Yucatán and Central America of the early Classic period that came 500 years later, the glyphic writing is extensively found in a vastly more complicated form. And the people who about A.D. 100 began the great city of Teotihuacán around the Pyramid of the Sun in Mexico's Central Valley had brought the method of building pyramids with a clay or adobe center to a high stage of development. So it appears that the Gulf Coast Olmecs, whose history was not studied until the 1930s, were perhaps the "fathers of Middle American culture."

Maya history and culture

We know more about the ancient Mayans than of any other peoples who learned from the Olmecs. Mayan languages were spoken in all parts of today's Guatemala, in sections of El Salvador and Honduras, and in the Mexican states of Chiapas, Yucatán, Campeche, Quintana Roo, and Tabasco. This area had fertile soil, no rugged mountains, and adequate rainfall for growing corn. From the Olmecs, the powerful class of Mayan priest rulers had learned to count the years on a calendar and to keep track of dates by a set form of hieroglyphics, date carvings that can now be read with fair accuracy. The date of the earliest marker found in the area is about A.D. 300 by our calendar, and the last dated stone of the Classic Maya period is about A.D. 900. After this the Classic Maya religious centers were abandoned and the dates no longer recorded.

Large cultural centers were built during this Classic period at Uaxactún and Tikal in the eastern flatlands of Guatemala, at Copán across the border in Honduras, and at Palenque in southern Mexico. Each city was independent but had satellite cities of its own. Another large center was Uxmal in western Yucatán, which had smaller centers around it such as Kabah, Edzna, and Sayah. Chichén Itzá was a smaller classical center north of Uxmal. They all were unfortified cities, which show no evidence of large numbers of human sacrifices nor of strong belief in vengeful feathered serpents. All were ceremonial centers with tall pyramids around plazas and ball courts. Their large, elaborately decorated buildings were divided into small rooms used perhaps as temporary quarters for priests during special festivities. Each center, maintained and improved upon for more than 500 years, was surrounded by the grass huts of tens of thousands of farmers, weavers, potters, and stone carvers, who, at certain fixed periods, probably came willingly to take part in great building activities.

The cultivation of corn being the most important industry, much of their ceremonial religion concerned itself with corn and with supplications to their deities for the right amount of rain at the right time. Instilled in the people was the idea that if ceremonies were not held nor carvings completed within a certain time, the rain would cease and famine would result.

At Tikal, in the Guatemala jungle, the ceremonial site had 350 temples, palaces, and carved monuments crowding an area of six and a half square miles. At the central plaza, two 100-foot pyramids face each other. On the sides are steep stairways and elaborate glyphic inscriptions that were once brightly painted, and on the top small stone temples with carved peak roofs. In the courtyard carved stone monuments or *stelae* bear the figure of a priest or a god and contain carved dates corresponding to 20-year periods from about A.D. 500 to 800. University of Pennsylvania archeologists, who started excavating at the site in 1956, found that each of the pyramids had other whole pyramids inside them with dates carved during a period beginning 400 years earlier; in other words, at the end of each 400-year period, priests ordered new pyramids built around those of the previous period. No reference is made by Spanish explorers on the Tikal site except for one report by a wandering priest in the 1700's.

At Uxmal on the Yucatán peninsula there stands on a knoll an 85-foot pyramid, the Palace of the Divination, that has at its foot three complicated courtyards, one leading into another, and on another knoll stand two large, elaborately carved buildings. Behind is a 100-foot long building with tier upon tier of carved blocks above it, called the House of Dovecotes by archaeologists. More than 20 jungle-covered mounds can be seen off in the distance from the top of the House of the Governor which are yet-uncleared buildings.

The central pyramid at Palenque in present-day Tabasco in Mexico was found in the 1950's to have a grave 72 steps down into its center containing the skeleton of a king or a high priest wearing a mask of turquoise, many necklaces of jade and pink shell, and bracelets and anklets of jade and coral. No evidence was found that the pyramid was used in any way differently from all other known pyramids of ancient America, that is, as the foundation for a temple.

A total of 25 different Maya centers have been identified, most of which are at least partially cleared.

The Mayas excelled at mathematics and astronomy and made the Olmecs' calendar system far more accurate. They knew the solar year consisted of 365 and one-quarter days and Venus had a revolution of just less than 225 days. They maintained day names and day counts on the 365-day-system and separate ones on a 260-day-cycle (probably on the basis of early miscounts of the orbit of Venus). Years were counted in terms of days, and sets of 365 days were counted in terms of twenties; thus 20 years times 20 years, or 400 years, was an extremely holy number.

In their numerical systems, a dot equaled one, a bar five, and a shell shape zero. Dates needed five sets of figures, one on top of the other, the top one signifying the number of the 400-year period, the one below the 20-year period within this larger span, the third the year within those 20-year spans, and the fourth and fifth the month and the day respectively. This counting of time in units of twenties and four hundreds shown by position in the writing of numbers indicates that the ancient Mayans had discovered the concept of the mathematical zero; and they had done it long before the introduction of the Arabic symbol of zero into Europe. They counted 20 months to the year and 18 days to the month. Mayan priests or astronomers were conscious of millions of days having passed before their time, indicated by their glyphs for periods of 365,000 days (a thousand years).

The Maya seem to have been obsessed with the measurement of time, which they based on both Venus and the sun. New stelae were raised every 20 years, whole new pyramids built every 400. None of the glyphs seem to tell a story or a legend, or to describe an incident in history or to glorify a current hero. The glyph system was used over so many centuries (five or six at least at every site) that the carvers in each city began to develop their own variations—which makes the task of the archaeologist in deciphering them all the more difficult.

The Maya also wrote their glyphs on fibre paper with watercolors and decorated them with pictographs of gods or priests. The long sheets were bound between covers. Most of the pictograph books that were still in existence in 1540 were burned by Christian zealots. Fortunately a few specimens were sent home by the conquerors and preserved in European museums. Through the generations, a literature in prose and poetry was also passed down, perhaps orally, and some of their legends, as well as descriptions of the orbit of Venus and forecasts of eclipses, were later recorded by Christianized Maya. At least two have been translated into English, the book of *Chilam Balam* of Yucatán and the *Popol Vuh* of Guatemala.

The careful observance of time and astronomical phenomena was the mainspring of their religious faith. In the Maya pantheon there were about a dozen major deities and a host of lesser gods, some to secure prosperity and happiness and some to ward off evil. At the head was a Creator, a god of the sun who was aided by lesser gods of the sky, of the north star, of Venus as a morning star and another of Venus as an evening star. There were gods of thunder, lightning, and, most important, of rain. Many carvings of a maize god depict him as a handsome young man with a headdress of corn tassels.

The Maya firmly believed in immortality and ancestor worship. For this religious devotion and careful count of time, a large clergy was needed, with orders of monks and nuns. Priests served in temples, burned incense at the corners of the fields to insure good crops, and presided over religious festivals. They also arranged and enforced a work schedule for everyone's participation in the rebuilding of pyramids, stone carving, and stone quarrying at distant sites. In the Classic period the emphasis seems to have been not on human sacrifice but on the sacrifice of time spent on the endless building and carving.

All carving of the Classic period was done with stone tools—small metal objects found in the area date from a later time. Much of Maya carving and stucco decoration was in geometric and elaborate formal designs, but in every city there were some carvings of people, birds, and animals, sometimes conventionalized, often very realistic. Jade was often used for small carvings. Turquoise was highly prized for decorative purposes and seashells from the Caribbean were evidently sent a long way north to be traded for the blue stone. Great skill had also been developed in the textile arts, judging from the decorative dress of both men and women in Maya paintings.

Their architectural planning was superb. Their principal temples, astronomical observatories, and homes for chiefs and priests were large and often as impressive as similar remains in the Old World. When constructing their massive pyramids for use as bases of temples, they heaped up earth and rubble to make a central core, then faced this with carved stones. Often these carved stones were covered with a much larger mass of rubble and faced in turn with a new set of carved outer stones, as was done at Tikal at the end of a 400-year period. But the Maya never did learn how to build a vaulted arch through the use of a keystone, and could only make a corbelled or false arch which ended in a V-shaped top. They could never build a domed roof of any size and their large rooms had to be roofed with flat timbers which have since rotted away.

In 1946, a scientist stumbled upon a previously unknown Maya site which he called Bonampak, the place of the paintings. On the inside walls under a corbelled arch roof were large mural paintings of festivals that had not been exposed to the weather and therefore were preserved in brilliant colors for more than 1100 years. Artists and photographers from the Mexican Department of Archeology went to Bonampak and made perfect copies, thus recording a unique pageant of Maya life with processions of priests and groups of warriors all dressed in magnificent costumes. Life-sized figures of women, children, lesser noblemen, and even slaves are also realistically portrayed. Nothing at any other site does as much to make Mayan life real to us as do the murals at Bonampak.

Few commoners are shown in the murals or are carved in stone at

Tikal or Copán. When common citizens were not taking part in religious ceremonies, they lived much as do people in Yucatán today. Farmers kept their land cleared of weeds, planted corn, beans, squash, and cotton, harvested crops in big cooperative festivals, tended their fruit trees and cared for their flower gardens. They lived in round huts with peaked roofs such as are seen in many villages in Yucatán today. Their women ground corn on grinding stones, wearing the long white gown with square neck and wide bands of bright embroidery around neck, sleeve, and skirt still worn today even in the larger towns.

City dwellers also owned land and went out into the country to till it. Some worked as jewelers or potters. Thousands of laborers built roads— high, wide, paved causeways, on which a heavy roller was used. But the wheel, which would have been the next step, was never developed, and so no carts traveled the roads. If the road workers were paid, they probably received cacao beans, cotton, cloth, feathers, or, later on, small bells of copper, all of which were used as money in the markets and in inter-regional trade. Men and women brought their rural produce and the results of their handwork into the markets and sold them to city dwellers. In the markets, products from other parts of Indian America were offered for barter or sale, even products from long distances such as emeralds from Colombia and turquoise from New Mexico.

Family life seems to have been serene. Marriages were arranged by the family and divorces easily attained by husbands. Personal cleanliness was practiced by the high and the low, as it still is in Yucatán. For beautifying purposes, mothers tied boards to their childrens heads to force them into a conical shape, filed their front teeth, and suspended beads in front of their eyes to make them permanently cross-eyed. A game of ball requiring great skill was one of the important Maya recreations, and it is something of a mystery how these cross-eyed babies grew up to develop this skill. The ball courts were located in the center of their religious temple complexes, indicating that the game had some religious significance.

Little is known about the Classic Maya government and society. The individual city with its outlying district was perhaps the only stable political unit. Each city was a theocratic despotism ruled by civil princes and high priests who appointed the chieftains or *caciques* of outlying villages and the local magistrates for sections of the larger cities. All officials seem to have come from a few noble families. The commoners below them were all equal, the only difference seemingly measured by the distance a family lived from the center of the city. Slaves in this society, found in temples and chieftains' houses, were persons who had been captured in war, condemned to slavery as a result of crime, or sold into slavery because of debt. Children of slaves were usually free so a permanent slave class did not develop. The serenity of Mayan life seems to indicate that no restive and rebellious masses existed at the bottom of the social scale.

Then within a single century these Classic Maya cities were abandoned. The earliest known date carved at a Classic Maya site was A.D. 320, the last 909, and at many Classic sites the last date found is about 750 or 800

A.D. There is no evidence of a long war or of a natural calamity such as an earthquake or tidal wave. A long famine or a horrendous epidemic would have resulted in all the cities being abandoned within the same decade. Perhaps land near the city became exhausted after six or seven hundred years of corn growing and, as the population grew, workers had to go farther and farther from the city to clear more land for corn. When the population outgrew its food supply, the continual building, carving, and worshipping ordered by the priests did not bring more corn per acre nor more acreage per village. And when nothing catastrophic befell the people if they refused to do the construction or obey the priests, new generations did not flock to the ceremonial centers. Later generations may have migrated to the highlands of Guatemala, where villagers speak Mayan dialects today, or maintained their village culture in Yucatán or Chiapas.

But the counting of time, the carving of glyphs, and the making of paper books were not to be entirely forgotten. Invaders called Toltecs from the highlands of Central Mexico came in the peninsula of Yucatán about A.D. 980. The history of Yucatán after that invasion is told as part of the history of the Toltecs, page 52 below.

civilizations in the Oaxaca Valley

One direction in which the Olmec ideas of glyph writing, calendar keeping, and pyramid building spread even before the beginning of the Christian era was toward the broad valley of Oaxaca, 450 miles south of Mexico City.

The influence of the Olmecs is seen in the strange, three- and four-foot high dancing figures carved on slabs used as decorative facing on the pyramids on Monte Albán at the head of the valley. About 200 B.C., villagers from the valley below, who probably spoke Zapotecan, began to build a level courtyard with a rough pyramid at each end on the flat top of the mountain; and as time went on Zapotecan farmers by the thousands willingly climbed the steep hill to serve their gods at the temple and to build finer temples. The temple base faced with the dancing figures was covered by a greater one and the dancing figures were forgotten for perhaps 2,000 years until modern Mexican archaeologists discovered them during their excavations.

The history of Monte Albán as a religious center covered more than 1300 years, from the time the dancing figures were carved until about A.D. 1000, representing probably the longest continuous use of a ceremonial center in the New World. Maya glyphs are found carved there but not in any great profusion. Below Monte Albán grew up satellite centers such as Zaachilá, which is still a little-changed Zapotecan-speaking town, and Oaxaca which today is the modern state capital. Century after century the villagers seem willingly to have climbed up the trail to the hill top (3 miles today by automobile) to carry stones for the workers, water with which to mix the mortar, and food for the builders. Life was peaceful and change was gradual. The lack of fortifications indicates the hilltop center was never used as a refuge or fort.

The Zapotecs of Oaxaca, unlike the Mayans 400 miles to the south, arranged elaborate burial places that were lined with carved rock and adorned with fresco paintings. Pottery and figurines have been found in the tombs which enable archaeologists to estimate the dates of burials.

Devotion to Monte Albán as a religious center declined when the productivity of the soil in the area began to decrease. People had to fight other language-groups north and south to gain more farming land, living farther and farther away as time went on. And when the priests in charge of the mountain became more and more rigid in their observances and demands, the common people ceased climbing the hill to worship.

Another civilized people, the Mixtecs, moved into the valley and occupied the neglected Zapotecan lands. They came from the state of Puebla, Mexico, their original center being near the present town of Tehuacán. They had built the most massive construction in the New World in the northern part of the Valley of Puebla under the south slope of Mount Popocatépetl, the pyramid of Cholula—which was still used as a center of worship for non-Aztec people when Cortés arrived. The Mixtecs knew how to use a canal system to irrigate the land. They buried their dead in old tombs in the hillsides of Monte Albán. About 1100, the Mixtecs learned to make objects of gold by modeling small earrings and pendants in beeswax, surrounding their models with clay, and pouring the molten metal through small vents in the clay to melt out the wax and solidify into shape. The only recent discovery of notable amounts of gold by archaeologists was made in 1927 when they found the Mixtec tombs with their gold necklaces, bracelets, and earrings. The skill of the goldsmith spread in a later period, to the Aztecs and to the post-Classic Mayans in Yucatán.

One of the Mixtecan centers, called Yanhutlán, kept records of its kings in careful pictographs from A.D. 1041 until the Spanish conquest. One of these "genealogical" books is preserved in a European museum. The first "real person" of whose existence we are sure, whose victories and glories are recorded, was an overlord named Eight Deer Tiger Claw. Symbols showing this name appear in the "book" and in carvings and legends of the time. He seems to have lived longer, to have had a finer character, and to have been a more respected person than Montezuma, whose story is far better known.

A center called Mitla in the Oaxaca Valley, in which lived both Mixtec and Zapotec people at the time of the Spanish conquest, is an extensive complex of palaces that are built over elaborate tombs but have no central pyramid. Long panels of geometric designs made of thousands of small stones, with no religious connotations apparently, decorate the massive palaces. Catholic missionaries after Cortés used stones from the palaces to build a church on the site. But churchgoers still speak Zapotecan and weave blankets in the designs of the stone-mosaic panels. In ancient times the Oaxaca Valley was probably as thickly populated as was Yucatán.

the culture of Teotihuacán

The Central Valley of Mexico or Anáhuac, the site of today's Mexico City and Federal District, lies at an elevation of nearly 8000 feet in a region of inadequate rainfall that has no outlet for its rain runoff and for the melting snows of the mountains that surround it. Already by 3000 B.C. villagers were growing corn around the marshy lakes that filled its lowest area. Villages expanded into towns which were influenced by Olmec traders from the Gulf Coast. A pyramid and temple of some size has been excavated at the town of Cuicuilco which with several others was covered by a lava flow about 100 B.C.

By A.D. 150, a city complex grew up across the valley, well above the marshes, where the inhabitants built the gigantic Pyramid of the Sun which remained a center of worship for 600 years. Except for the pyramid at Cholula, built perhaps a thousand years later, it is the largest building in the ancient New World, a mass of more than a million cubic yards, nearly 200-feet high. Around it grew a city in the modern sense of the word, a true urban settlement reaching ten miles in every direction from the Pyramid. Markets and ceremonials were held every day, traders came and went constantly, and a priestly bureaucracy governed the swelling population. By A.D. 650, Teotihuacán with perhaps 250,000 people was possibly the largest city in the world, for Rome had lost its grandeur, Constantinople was half that size, and no city in India or China in the 7th century contained so many inhabitants. Archaeologists working there have suggested that its culture, spreading from there, might have been more influential than the Maya area or the Oaxaca Valley. However, no Maya glyphs or other forms of carved or painted writing have been found there—although later inhabitants of the valley did use the 360-day versus 260-day calendar developed by the Maya. But no corbelled arch, no Maya zero, no stelae to mark the date, not even ball courts have been found at Teotihuacán.

The Pyramid of the Sun was never rebuilt or remodeled, but the Pyramid of the Moon, a smaller structure a half mile away, shows seven different smaller structures in the interior, each one built outside the other. Neither of these pyramids is decorated. But a large temple court, called by moderns the Citadel or the Temple of Quetzalcóatl, has very elaborate decorations in color, rain-god masks, and alternating feathered serpents and pink seashells. Palaces recently excavated prove to have walls covered with very decorative fresco paintings that show many figures in splendid costumes. One stylized heaven of the rain god shows people swimming happily and raindrops falling from the god's hands.

Teotihuacán was a trading center that thrived from the exchange of handicraft goods as well as corn sent to its markets by distant villages. Pottery remains of every 6th- and 7th-century region of Mexico have been found there. Religious pilgrims from Oaxaca, Guatemala, Yucatán, and the barbaric north must have kept coming there in a constant stream.

Eventually some group of visitors—nomadic peoples perhaps—took over the city and burned it, and its inhabitants spread south to the Mixteca country or they moved to sites across the marshes or over toward the west coast. And other cities (actually only scattered towns) dominated the Valley of Anáhuac, and became the Mexican towns eventually absorbed by the barbaric Aztecs. Generations later people remembered only that "giants" had built Teotihuacán—which is what the Aztecs told Cortés. That Spanish conqueror even sent a mastodon leg bone found in a dried lake bed to the king of Spain to illustrate the size of the builders of the Pyramid of the Sun. Archaeologists as recently as 1950 thought Teotihuacán was the legendary city of the Toltecs whose king, named after the Feathered Serpent Quetzal-cóatl, had gone off about A.D. 1000 to conquer Chichén Itzá. Actually, Teotihuacán had been burned and abandoned at least 300 years earlier.

Family life, government, agriculture, and even worship must have been very much like that of the Classic Maya. The rain god was revered even more because rain was less frequent in the Central Valley and there were more mouths to feed on less arable land. The drive to build and rebuild in time cycles to appease the rain god seems to have been less urgent, and there is no evidence of the large-scale human sacrifice which kept the decadent Aztecs hysterically offering human hearts to the rain god in the same dry valley a thousand years later. But it was lack of rain along with growth in population that eventually weakened the Teotihuacán civilization. People there became open prey to "vandals and barbarians" who raided from the north—at a time only two centuries later than other barbarians destroyed Rome. But the culture of Teotihuacán, no less than that of Rome and the Classic Maya, did not die out. Much of it remained with the people who survived in the Valley of Anáhuac.

the Toltec people in Central Mexico
and in Yucatán

Fifty miles out of Mexico City, near the present town of Cuernavaca, a complex of terraces and temple bases known as Xochicalco was recently excavated which has been identified as a "Late Classic" center to which refugees from the burned-out Teotihuacán fled in large numbers. There are carvings of Maya noblemen with flat foreheads, surrounded by curling feathered serpents. Aztec legend tells the story of a king of Xochicalco named Mixcóatl who fought to defend his city from barbarous bands and built a great fortification on a nearby cliff. Enemies killed him but a son—named for the serpent god covered with feathers, the Quetzalcóatl—was born posthumously to a beautiful woman of a tribe related to barbaric peoples called Toltecs.

In later stories about Quetzalcóatl, confusion arises as to who is being described—this hero son of Mixcóatl, the god of the same name, or later priests or rulers. At any rate the hero son revenged his father's death, conquered parts of the Central Valley around the marshy lakes, and built a

new religious complex of temples at Tula. His people, who called themselves the Toltecs, dedicated their temples about A.D. 980. Archaeologists,
knowing that this story had been told in the mid-1500's, thought this Toltec
chief named Quetzalcóatl had built Teotihuacán. But when in 1942 archaeologists began to dig in a hill in the mining town of Tula, 83 miles north of
Mexico City, they discovered a pyramid decorated almost exactly as were
Toltec buildings in Chichén Itzá. This site has now been identified as the
capital of the Toltecs, whose life style and decorations had been described by
Aztec chroniclers in the most glowing terms.

According to these chronicles, Quetzalcóatl became not only the
king but also the high priest of the feathered-serpent cult, and ruled wisely
for 20 years. But descendents of his father's murderers plotted against him
and drove him out, and about the year A.D. 1000, he and his followers went
in great numbers to the Central Valley where they occupied the lake area
near the town of Texcoco.

About ten years later Quetzalcóatl and some of his original soldiers
moved down to the Tabasco coast where they hired, perhaps as mercenaries, people speaking Maya, called Itzás. Then the group migrated to an
abandoned Classic Maya center known throughout Yucatán for its deep,
open, clear-water wells in limestone. Settling down at Chichén Itzá or "The
Wells of the Itzás," the Toltecs began to build pyramids and ball courts
exactly like those they had left behind at Tula. Chichén Itzá is thus a
combination of Classic Maya- and Toltec-inspired buildings.

Its wells became centers of human sacrifice to the rain god, carried
on as part of Quetzalcóatl's religion. On top of its Toltec-type Temple of the
Warriors and its great pyramid, human sacrifices were carried out in increasing numbers. The Toltecs also built the largest ball court found in the New
World to date, one which had goal posts 20 feet above the players' heads. If
the game was played there as it was played in Mexico City on Cortés'
arrival, it would seem to have been impossible for the players ever to
achieve a score, since only shoulders, hips, or feet and never hands touched
the ball.

The Toltecs in Chichén Itzá began to lose their individuality by
1150 as they absorbed Maya culture. Their rebuilding of the city led to a
Maya renaissance, as did the reoccupation of other city sites by city
dwellers who remembered how to write Maya glyphs and count the Maya
timetables. But the Toltec spirit of war and human sacrifice, and their
vengeful feathered-serpent god, persisted.

Three cities formed a military alliance. The people still living
around the Uxmal complex, the descendants of the Maya and Toltecs at
Chichén Itzá and the inhabitants of a more recently built center called
Mayapán, half way between, formed a League of Mayapán to fight off other
peoples, perhaps from the mainland of Mexico. But the League cities
quarreled among themselves, even over the scores of ball games. War
within the League began in earnest by 1350.

The ablest of the young men would be killed off in a decade of
fighting and the war would subside, but with the next generation brought to

manhood and trained to perpetuate the fighting, war would begin again. Through the 14th and 15th centuries, Maya men were so often at war they had little time for building. The last date-carving on any monument thus far found in the Mayapán region is the mid-1400s according to the most modern reading of the calendar. When the Spanish conquerors arrived a century later, they found the Maya living in grass-hut villages near the old city sites and priests living in the temples of the stone cities and conducting religious ceremonies, but they found grass growing through paving. Maya writings were found but few knew how to read them. Records indicate that there had been several years of epidemics and destructive hurricanes between wars. So when the Spaniards arrived, they found a people in decadence. One of the Yucatán chroniclers later wrote:

> *Eat, eat while there is bread;*
> *Drink, drink while there is water.*
> *A day comes when a blight shall wither the land*
> *When ruin shall fall upon all things*
> *When eyes shall be closed in death*
> *Father, son, and grandson hanging dead on the same tree.*
> *When ruin shall fall upon all things*
> *And the people be scattered abroad in the forest.*[1]

In 1520, when the Spaniards came, thousands of survivors of these long wars were living in a decadent center called Dzibilchaltún, which today can be called the oldest continuously occupied Maya site. Archaeologists working there have recently found more than 25,000 foundations of houses and small temples. Evidence indicates that the site was occupied when "civilization" first crept into Yucatán from the Olmecs. The Spaniards forced the majority of its residents to move to the new Spanish city of Mérida, fifty miles away. Their descendants still constitute the bulk of the population in Mérida, where both Yucatecan Maya and Spanish are used interchangeably on the streets.

Thus the Quetzalcóatl legends came to Yucatán and lingered there in the recurrent use in religious worship of the word Kukulcán or feathered serpent. The legend persisted in the Central Valley where the real King Quetzalcóatl had lived briefly among the people around the marshy lakes. He had left with the promise that he would return some day and bring the splendors of his city of Tula to the marsh towns. The Aztecs believed these prophecies and thought he would perhaps return by sea since he had gone off toward the coast. They fused into one story the many myths of priests and gods named for the feathered serpent, but the legend that he was a fair-skinned, bearded man is discounted by modern historians. Cortés undoubtedly took advantage in 1520 of all these prophecies about the folk hero when he arrived approximately 550 years after the real Quetzalcóatl had been driven out of Tula.

[1] Gregory Mason, *Columbus Came Late*. New York, Appleton-Century-Crofts, Inc., 1931. Reprinted by permission of the publishers.

Aztecs, the late comers

By 1200, the power of Tula had disintegrated in the upland central valley. Several large towns remained around the marshy lakes, 30 miles from the ghost city of Teotihuacán at the foot of the Pyramid of the Sun. Their culture was a mixture of Toltec and Teotihuacano and they kept up an interchange with Zapotecs and Mixtecs in the Oaxaca Valley. Among the most important of these towns were Texcoco, which was already keeping records of long lines of hereditary kings; Atzcapotzalco, center of handicraft and weaving; and Tlaltelolco, a market center on an island in the lake. Waves of nomads called Chichimecas invaded the Central Valley from the north and destroyed whole villages. No one people dominated the valley from 1200 to 1350.

Then in the early 1300's, nomadic tribesmen who called themselves the Aztecs and spoke a language called Náhuatl, wandered from the north into the Central Valley, looking for a sign, which their priests had described—an eagle with a snake in its mouth perched on a cactus. The symbol is today the national emblem of Mexico. According to the legend, these wanderers, led by their chief Tenoch, found their augury on the shores of a marshy Lake Texcoco, and here they decided to establish their home. Traditionally their city of Tenochtitlán was founded in A.D. 1325, but actually at the time they were building mud and reed huts on islands in shallow water. But they learned much from their more advanced neighbors in the next 200 years and finally became the dominant politico-military power of the valley and even beyond. They enlarged the original islands, filled in land to create others, and connected their dwelling places to the mainland with four giant causeways and numerous bridges.

Since the Aztecs had achieved the height of their military power when the Spanish invasion occurred, we have good descriptions of this city as the Europeans saw it. They knew nothing of the 2000 years of Mexican history before the Aztecs. To them, Tenochtitlán seemed fair and shining with its white stucco buildings and brightly colored ornamentation. Wide streets and open paved plazas served as market squares and as centers of religious pageantry. Around the inhabited islands, smaller islands had been built for flower and vegetable gardens. Some of these had originally been "rafts" on which flowers were grown in a layer of mud; as the roots grew, these "floating gardens" became anchored, and they are, today, the flower-raising group of islands and canals called Xochimilco.

The Aztecs had taken over the island market, the town of Tlaltelolco—which Cortés described in glowing terms in a letter to the King. He wrote that the market plaza was twice as large as that of the famous Spanish plaza in Salamanca. Boatloads of produce were borne by long lines of carriers from the surrounding countryside to the city markets. Special sections of the plaza were assigned exclusively for each product—vegetables, charcoal, cloth and clothing, sleeping mats and basket work, and "tools" such as copper implements, obsidian knives, stone-drilling tools, and clay or horn spinning whorls. Fresh fish from the gulf could be purchased—carried by runners in 24 hours from the coast to grace the tables of Montezuma and the nobles. Luxury goods were available such as bird feathers for the feather-embroidery of high-ranking warriors and priests, objects of jade, pink seashells, tortoise shells, and turquoise, and ornamental figurines cast from gold, copper, and silver. Medicine women sold herbs, barbers shaved men with razors of volcanic glass. A Spanish chronicler commented on the women with their luxurious raven tresses and faces not unfrequently pleasing "although of cinnamon hue." Trade was conducted by direct barter or with cacao beans as money—the bean being valuable because chocolate was a favorite drink and the cacao tree did not grow in the central plateau.

So much has been written about the Aztecs that the impression may be gained that their culture was the most important attainment of Indian America. Actually they were inheritors rather than originators and added little to what the Teotihuacaños and the Zapotecs had already achieved.

The Aztecs had kept an account of their rulers in a kind of picture record. Counting back the years, coordinating the Aztec calendar to that of the Spaniards, the date A.D. 1376 has been set down as the date of accession of the first Aztec chieftain in Tenochtitlán. By 1480, the Aztecs had begun to expand their power. They joined their neighbors in the city states of Texcoco and Tlacopán in a three-way confederacy in which each unit kept its own government but followed the Aztec emperor as military leader in wartime. The Aztec Confederacy developed an intensely military mentality, became more and more aggressive in warfare, and soon extended its conquest from Tehuantepec to Mazatlán, from the Gulf to the Pacific. The civilized and highly artistic Tarascan Indians to the west in Michoacán and the Mixtecs at Cholula were forced to pay tribute. A few independent groups such as the Tlaxcalans halfway down toward the Gulf did remain here and there, groups that were willing to help Cortés fight the hated Aztec Confederacy.

We know a great deal about Aztec society, more than about any of the earlier, more civilized people, because many Aztecs survived to learn to write about their people in Spanish and missionary teachers after Cortés studied Aztec life. We know that the Aztec Confederacy was, strictly speaking, not an empire although its vassals paid heavy taxes to the Aztec ruler. Revolts took place, which were suppressed, but some of the conquered sections were independent enough to govern themselves without having garrisons stationed among them. Officials merely supervised the collection of tribute and perhaps watched for signs of rebellion.

At the center was the city-state of Tenochtitlán, governed by a council of elders representing the 20 clans in the various wards of the city. Each clan in turn had its own council of elders. The over-all city council elected the *tlachautín,* an official who led the warriors in war and was responsible for maintaining order, and the *calpullec,* or principal civil officer who collected taxes, distributed land, and kept reports. Montezuma II, the much-touted emperor, was at first simply the war chief, this position having come to his family by election for two generations. He was also a priest, and his power held some theocratic overtones; furthermore, he served as the highest court of appeal, meting out severe punishments for serious crimes. The government was changing at the time of the arrival of the Spanish from a kinship-territorial form ruled by a council of elders to a one-man despotism.

Strict social classes developed as the nomadic Aztecs changed into rulers of a vast federation. The great feudal lords and high army officials became the nobility. The priests, who had charge of education and religion, were specially privileged and had the future in the palms of their hands. Free citizens all organized in clans and tribes, were beginning to lose their freedom and to sink into serfdom by being deprived of political privileges. Slavery existed, every village having its slave market, but no one was born into slavery. Slaves were chiefly prisoners of war or criminals or people who sold themselves or had been sold by their parents; it was not a harsh type of slavery. Merchants had status and influence, especially those who were respected tradesmen. Free peasants and artisans formed the rank and file of the nation. The warrior's position was held to be of greatest importance, of greater worth than agriculture, for wars brought spoils, tribute, and prisoners to be sold as slaves or used as sacrifices. Military education was stressed and armies were well-organized and well-disciplined, for wars were "necessary" for tribute and for prisoners to be used as slaves or sacrifices on the pyramids. All education was taken seriously; priests taught music, arithmetic, reading of hieroglyphic writing, and religion.

Family life was elaborately regulated. A few days after its birth a child was given a name and a feast was held in its honor—for which reason the people of Mexico took easily to the Catholic idea of baptism and baptismal parties. Children were generally treated well and given instruction on manners. At fifteen boys were given military or religious training in an organized "house of youth." Marriages were arranged by the parents with the young people's consent, boys marrying at twenty, girls at sixteen. Three-day marriage feasts are described during which much *pulque* and *tequila* flowed, endless speeches were made and many gifts exchanged.

Clans, not individuals, owned the land. The clans received the lands used for agriculture from the tribal council, divided the lands into lots, and distributed the lots among the heads of families. Tenancy passed to the son at the death of the landholder; or, if no son survived or if the land had not been cultivated for two seasons, it reverted to the clan for redistribution. Large land areas were reserved for the maintenance of officials and for the financing of wars, the lands evidently worked by slave labor or by the "contributed time" of nearby tenants. Much land was reclaimed in swampy areas and new lands were constantly added by conquest. So well did the irrigation systems and water rights arrangements of the Aztecs work that kings of Spain later ordered that they not be changed in rural areas.

Trade and commerce were highly respected occupations that received government protection. Away from the great market centers, each village had its special product—mats or baskets or pottery—as do Mexican villages today. Aztec travelers, with packs on their backs, covered the length and breadth of Mexico and Middle America on foot. The use of mules came later, brought by the Spaniards. Tropical parrot feathers found their way to the southwest United States, Aztec cotton cloth reached Panama. Turquoise from New Mexico and Arizona found its way to the Aztecs. No one trader covered this distance. Contacts were made from the great center of Tenochtitlán but objects passed from tribe to tribe through many hands.

The Aztecs kept track of time for purposes of trade, agriculture, and religion. Their carefully divided solar years ran in cycles of 52, but those half-century cycles were not named or numbered in any order. Every 104 years, or at the end of two cycles, a great celebration was held. The Aztecs themselves had no record of two 104-year celebrations, so their history becomes legendary a century before Cortés' arrival. The Aztec calendar stone, now in Mexico City's National Museum, has carvings to represent days and months.

Because the overcrowded Aztec city in the semi-arid Central Valley depended on regular rainfall to provide sufficient corn crops, the Aztecs had hysterical fear of drought. Toltec ideas of blood sacrifice were carried to a horrifying extreme by the Aztecs. On every public feast day, the priests led war captives and slaves up narrow steps to the top of the giant pyramid in the center of Tenochtitlán, held them over an elaborately carved altar, and tore out their hearts with a sharp obsidian knife. Wars were fought simply to capture prisoners and thousands of captives died this way every year. On special occasions members of distinguished families were chosen for sacrifice, which may have been something of an honor. The victim was pampered by the populace for weeks beforehand. The pageantry, processions, and incense-burning which accompanied the sacrifices, especially those in honor of the supreme war-god, Huitzilopochtli, made religion very dramatic to the people watching the ceremonies. It was indeed a brutal religion, in the charge of great numbers of clergy. The temple of Tenochtitlán housed over 5,000 priests, each with his specialty, whether saying prayers and chants, leading processions and dances, keeping track of the calendar, educating the young, or preparing sacrifices. As the population grew in size and foodstuffs became more scarce, any delay or lessening in the yearly rainfall brought further sacrificial orgies and more wars to obtain sacrificial prisoners. So feared and hated were the Aztecs by their neighbors that another generation might have seen the downfall of the Aztecs at the hands of some mild-mannered people, in another of the many great waves of migration and change that Mexico had seen in the previous 2000 years.

The Aztec religion retained some of the more advanced concepts of peoples to the south. Many poems and songs were sung about the puzzle of life itself. The most famous poet was a king of Texcoco, called Nezahualcoyotl, which means "hungry coyote." He sang, "The goods of this life, its glories and its riches, are but lent to us; its substance is but an illusory shadow, and the things of today shall change on the coming of the morrow. Then gather the fairest flowers from thy gardens to bind round thy brow, and seize the joys of the present ere they perish." In another song, handed down by memory through generations, he said, "The fleeting pomp of the world is like a green willow. . . . but at the end a sharp axe destroys it, a north wind fells it."[3]

The north wind that felled the Aztec culture was the Spanish army led by Cortés. Tenochtitlán was destroyed and Mexico City built on the lake site. But the imprint of the Aztecs and their predecessors remained strong. In the rural villages and among the poor of the new Spanish cities, art craft, home life, food, house construction, and marketing methods remained purely Aztec. Tortillas and beans were eaten, the agave and maguey plant were used for liquor and fibre. Náhuatl, the Aztec language, was spoken commonly in Mexico as late as 1750. The great majority of the people of Mexico are the mixed-blood descendants of the Indians.

other more primitive peoples

North of the Aztec empire, on the edges of northern Mexico's desert country, were many semi-nomadic tribes. Groups of these tribes are known by such names as the Chichimecs, tribes who put up fierce resistance to the Spaniards, the Huastecs, who lived on the Gulf Coast, and the Tarahumaras, who roamed the northern ranges of the central plateau. Withstanding Spanish domination longest were the Yaqui, who remained unconquered into the first year of the 20th century. North of the Yaqui were the Indians of Sonora who were related to the Pima, the Pápago, and the Yuma of Arizona and among whom Spanish Jesuits founded missions late in the colonial period. Farther north lived the very primitive Indians of California who lived on acorns and wore animal skins and whom Spanish Franciscans brought into missions as a last frontier effort of Spain in America. North of the Rio Grande were the uncivilized Tejas Indians, with whom the Spaniards were also in contact, and to the east of that area, across the Mississippi, were the Creeks, Cherokees, and Appalachian tribes. On the Great Plains were nomads who hunted buffalo, the Sioux, the Comanches, and the Kiowa, who were never conquered by the Spanish. But they adopted abandoned Spanish horses and in a later century became the fast, mounted terrorizers of wagon trains. In today's New Mexico were the Pueblo, an advanced, sedentary people with maize the basis of their civilization, who came under Spanish domination in the early 17th century.

In the outer islands of the Caribbean were the aborigines first encountered by Columbus, called Tainos, a group of the general Arawak culture. Columbus described them as "a gentle, peaceful people of great simplicity," who came to meet him "naked as their mothers bore them," whose spears or darts were "a kind of rod without iron" (shown Spanish swords, they grasped them by the blade and cut themselves), but who traded him cotton threads in skeins and who used tools of stone to build

---

[3] Frances Gillmor, *Flute of the Smoking Mirror, a Portrait of Nezahualcoyotl* (Albuquerque: University of New Mexico Press, 1949). P. 147.

dugout canoes fashioned all in one piece, "wonderfully made, and so big that in some came 40 or 45 men."

On Hispaniola and Cuba Columbus found more Arawak tribes, village dwellers who had driven hunting tribes away from the coasts. Their villages sometimes had three or four thousand inhabitants and consisted of a "great house," made of reeds and thatch for the chief, and many "long houses" in which the lesser families lived. They had no "nation," but each village followed its own chief and medicine man and worshiped its own crudely shaped idols. At such worship Spaniards first saw the use of tobacco for smoking and as snuff.

The Arawaks could carve wood, weave baskets, make pottery decorated in several colors, work the small amounts of gold they had into objects by hammering, and weave wild cotton into hammocks and netted bags. They planted and harvested corn, cassava, or mandioca roots for bread and yams, beans, and peanuts.

On scattered islands in the Lesser Antilles and on the Venezuelan coast were the Caribs, enemies of the Arawaks, who attacked Arawak villages and forced these weaker Indians into slavery or fattened them for cannibalistic feasts. The way of life was generally similar throughout the Caribbean area and the Carib culture seems to have been no more advanced than that of the Arawaks. The gentle Arawaks disappeared early from the cultural scene, eliminated by the diseases and the forced labor of the conquerors. They made no marked contribution to the race and culture of modern Latin America. The Caribs managed to survive in part among wild tribes in Venezuela.

READINGS

Anderson, A. J. O. and C. Dibble, eds. and trans., *Florentine Codex* (Sahagun's, *General History of Things of New Spain* (12 vols., 1950 to date).

Anton, F., *Art of the Mayas* (1970).

Astrov, M., *The Winged Serpent; An Anthology of American Indian Prose and Poetry* (1946).

Bandelier, A. F., and E. L. Hewitt, *Indians of the Rio Grande Valley* (1937).

Beckinsale, R. P., and J. M. Houston, eds., *Urbanization and Its Problems* (1968).

Bernal, I., *Mexico before Cortéz: Art, History and Legend* (1963).

———, *The Olmec World* (1969).

———, et al., *Three Thousand Years of Art and Life in Mexico* (1968).

Blom, F., *The Indian Background of the Conquest of Yucatan* (1936).

———, et al., *Studies in Middle America* (1934).

Borah, W., and S. Cook, *The Aboriginal Population of Central Mexico on the Eve of the Spanish Conquest* (1963).

———, *Indian Population of Central Mexico, 1531–1610* (1960).

Caso, A., *The Aztecs, People of the Sun* (1958).

Castedo, L., *A History of Latin American Art and Architecture from Pre-Columbian Times to the Present* (1969).

Chevalier, F., *Land and Society in Colonial Mexico* (1963).

Clark, J. C., ed., *Codex Mendoza* (3 vols., 1938).

Cook, S. and W. Borah, *Population of Central Mexico, 1548* (1960).

————, *Population History: Mexico and the Caribbean* (1971).

Cornyn, J. H., *The Song of Quetzalcóatl* (1930).

Covarrubias, M., *The Eagle, the Jaguar and the Serpent: Indian Art of the Americas* (1954).

Craine, E. R., and R. C. Reindorp, eds., *The Chronicles of Michoacán* (1969).

Díaz del Castillo, B., *True History of the Conquest of New Spain* (many editions).

Dockstader, F. J., *Indian Art in Middle America* (1964).

Driver, H. E., *The Americas on the Eve of Discovery* (1964).

————, *Indians of North America* (1961).

Durán, D., *The Aztecs: History of the Indians of New Spain* (1964).

————, (trans. F. Horcasitas and D. Hayden) *Book of the Gods and Rites of the Ancient Calendar* (1971).

Effler, L. R., *The Ruins of Chichén-Itzá* (1936).

Embree, E. R., *Indians of the Americas* (1939).

Emmerich, A., *Art Before Columbus* (1963).

Gann, T., and J. C. Thompson, *History of the Mayas* (1931).

Gann, T. W. F., *Glories of the Maya* (1939).

————, *Maya Cities* (1927).

Gates, W., *A Grammar of Maya* (1938).

Gibson, C., *Aztecs under Spanish Rule* (1964).

Gillmor, F., *The King Danced in the Market Place* (1963).

————, *Flute of the Smoking Mirror* (1949).

Goetz, D., S. G. Morley, and A. Ricinas, *Popol Vuh: The Sacred Book of the Ancient Quiché-Maya* (1950).

Griffin, C. C., ed., *Concerning Latin American Culture* (1941).

Hanke, L., *Aristotle and the American Indian* (1959).

Hardoy, J. E., and R. P. Schaedel, *The Urbanization Process in America from Its Origins to the Present Day* (1969).

Harrington, M. R., *Cuba Before Columbus* (2 vols., 1921).

Helfritz, H., *Mexican Cities of the Gods* (1970).

Hewitt, E. L., *Ancient Life in the American Southwest* (1930).

————, *Ancient Life in Mexico and Central America* (1936).

Ivanoff, P., *Mayan Enigma: The Search for a Lost Civilization* (1971).

Jenness, D., ed., *American Aborigines* (1933).

Jennings, J. D. and E. Norbeck, eds., *Prehistoric Man in the New World* (1963).

Joyce, T. A., *Central American and West Indian Archaeology* (1916).

————, *Maya and Mexican Art* (1927).

————, *Mexican Archaeology* (1914).

Kéleman, P'al, *Medieval Ancient Art* (one vol. ed., 1956).

Keen, B., *The Aztec Image in Western Thought* (1971).

Kidder, A. and C. S. Chinchilla, eds., *Art of the Ancient Mayas* (rev. ed., 1959).

Kingsborough, V., *Antiquities of Mexico* (9 vols., 1830–1848).

Koebel, W. H., *Central America* (1917).

Kubler, G., *The Art and Architecture of Ancient America* (1962).

Landa, Diego de, *Yucatan Before and After the Conquest,* ed. Gates (1937); edition by A. M. Tozzer is better (1941).

Léon-Portilla, M., *Aztec Thought and Culture* (1963).

————, *Broken Spears: Aztec Account of the Conquest of Mexico* (1961).

————, *Pre-Columbian Literature of Mexico* (1969).

Linne, S., *Archaeological Researches at Teotihuacan* (1924).

Lothrop, S. K., *Treasures of Ancient America* (1964).

Lumholtz, K. S., *Unknown Mexico* (2 vols., 1902).

MacGowan, K., *Early Man in the New World* (1950).

MacNeish, R. S., F. A. Peterson, and K. V. Flannery, *The Prehistory of the Tehuacan Valley* (3 vols., 1970–19– to be completed in 6 vols.).

Martin, P. S., G. I. Quimby, and D. Collier, *Indians Before Columbus* (1947).

Mason, G., *Columbus Came Late* (1931).

Mayas and Their Neighbors: Studies Presented to A. M. Tozzer (1940).

Mitchell, J. L., *Conquest of the Maya* (1935).

Morley, S. G., *Ancient Mayas* (3rd ed., 1956).

Motolinía, T., *History of the Indians of New Spain* (1950).

Padden, R. C., *The Hummingbird and the Hawk: Conquest and Sovereignty in the Valley of Mexico 1503–1541* (1967; paperback 1970).

Paddock, J., *Tomorrow in Ancient Mesoamerica* (1965).

Peterson, F., *Ancient Mexico: Introduction to Prehispanic Cultures* (1962).

Prescott, W. H., *History of the Conquest of Mexico* (many editions).

Proskouriakoff, T., *An Album of Maya Architecture* (1963).

Radin, P., *The Story of the American Indian* (1944).

Robertson, O., *Mexican Codices* (1959).

Rouse, I., *The Prehistory of Haiti* (1939).

Roys, R. L., *The Indian Background of Colonial Yucatan* (1972).

Sauer, C. O., *Distribution of Aboriginal Tribes and Languages in Northwestern Mexico* (1934).

————, *The Early Spanish Main* (1966).

————, and D. Brand, *Aztatlán: Prehistoric Mexican Frontier of the Pacific Coast* (1932).

Schendel, G., *Medicine in Mexico from Aztec Herbs to Betratons* (1968).

Scholes, F. V., and R. L. Roys, *The Maya Chontal Indians* (1968).

Sejourne, L., *Burning Water: Thought and Religion in Ancient Mexico* (1957).

Sellards, E. H., *Early Man in America* (1952).

Soustelle, J., *Daily Life of the Aztecs on the Eve of the Spanish Conquest* (1970).

Spence, L., *Civilization of Ancient Mexico* (1912).

————, *Gods of Mexico* (1923).

Spicer, E. H., *Cycles of Conquest: The Impact of Spain, Mexico and the United States on the Indians of the Southwest 1533–1960* (1965).

Spinden, H. J., *Ancient Civilizations of Mexico and Central America* (3rd rev. ed., 1928).

————, *Maya Art and Civilization* (1957).

Spores, R., *Mixtec Kings and Their People* (1967).

Stacy-Judd, R. B., *Ancient Mayas* (1934).

Stevenson, R., *Music in Aztec and Inca Territory* (1968).

Tax, S., ed., *Civilization of Ancient America* (1951).

Thompson, J. E., *Mexico Before Cortéz* (1933).

————, *Maya History and Religion* (1970).

————, *Maya Hieroglyphic Writing* (1971).

Tulane University, *Middle American Papers.*

Unesco, *Mexican Wall Paintings of the Maya and Aztec Period* (1963).

Vaillant, G. C., *Indian Arts in North America* (1939).

————, *The Aztecs of Mexico* (1950).

Von Hagen, V. W., *The Aztec: Man and Tribe* (1958).

————, *The World of the Maya* (1960).

Von Winning, H., *Pre-Columbian Art of Mexico and Central America* (1968).

Wauchope, R., ed., *Handbook of Middle American Indians,* Vols. I–IX (1964–1970; to be complete in 13 vols.).

————, ed., *The Indian Background of Latin American History. The Maya, Aztec, Inca, and Their Predecessors* (1970).

————, *They Found the Buried Cities* (1965).

Weatheraux, P., *Indian Corn in Old America* (1954).

White, J. M., *Cortes and the Downfall of the Aztec Empire: A Study in Conflict of Cultures* (1971).

Wicke, C. R., *Olmec, an Early Art Style of Pre-Columbian Mexico* (1971).

Willey, G. R., *An Introduction to American Archaeology,* vol. I, *North and Middle America* (1966), vol. II, *Central and South America* (1971).

Wissler, C., *The American Indian* (3rd ed., 1938).

Wolf, E. R., *Sons of the Shaking Earth* (1959).

Wormington, H. M., *Origins* (1953).

chapter 4

PRE-COLUMBIAN AMERICANS FROM THE ISTHMUS SOUTH

Oh, Pachacamac,
Thou, who hast existed from the beginning,
Thou, who shalt exist until the end,
    powerful but merciful,
Who didst create man by saying,
    "Let man be,"
Who defendest us from evil,
And preservest our life and our health,
Art Thou in the sky or upon the earth?
In the clouds or in the deeps?
Hear the voice of him who implores thee,
    and grant him his petitions.
Give us life everlasting,
    preserve us, and accept this, our sacrifice.[1]

When the Spaniards came to the coast of Peru in the 1500's they heard the
Indians who were subjects of the Incas, singing this hymn which appeals to

---

[1] Translation given in Philip Ainsworth Means, *Ancient Civilizations of the
Andes* (New York: Charles Scribner's Sons, 1931), p. 439. Reproduced by permission of
the publishers.

the universal religious sentiments of all mankind. Pachacamac, sometimes called Viracocha, was a god of the people who had lived on the coast centuries before the Incas swept down from the Andean highlands. Twenty-five miles from Lima there stands today a great ruin called Pachacamac; it was once the religious center for several different groups of ancient Peruvians whose abstract ideas of worship and songs of devotion were adapted for daily use by the later sun-worshiping Incas. Archaeological work carried out during the 1960s and early 1970s greatly expanded our knowledge of these peoples, providing evidence that their history parallels that of ancient Mexico in many ways.

pre-Inca peoples on the coasts
and in the mountains of western South America

Villagers who hunted Andean deer and wild llamas occupied the Andes at an elevation of 15,000 feet, and fishermen lived in the mouths of rivers on the coast as early as 7500 B.C. These villagers had learned to make pottery by 1500 B.C. and to farm cotton, corn and white potatoes. On the coast they domesticated the guinea pig for meat and in the highlands the llama for meat and the alpaca for wool. Between 900 to 800 B.C., perhaps before the Olmecs built the first adobe pyramid in Eastern Mexico, a large rough stone mound faced with stucco stood as a temple base in the Rímac River Valley near modern Lima.

Within the next two-hundred years, a religious cult developed in a mountain valley about 150 miles northeast of Lima called Chavin. Temples, altars and palaces there were decorated with carvings in what is known as the Chavin style. Strange, formalized figures with many mouths and eyes interwoven with snakes' bodies and jaguars' faces are carved on elaborate panels in perfect detail. The Chavin people never developed an empire, but merely converted other tribes or towns to their religion. The Chavin also knew how to work with gold and how to weave alpaca wool in intricate designs. Other peoples throughout northern and central Peru decorated altars in the Chavin style and knew these crafts.

By A.D. 300, contemporaneously with Classic Maya beginnings, two large cities of twenty to fifty thousand inhabitants had grown up south of the Chavin area. Just below Lake Titicaca, there remains an extensive ruin known as Tiahuanaco. It consists of several large plazas; the central one is paved with enormous stone slabs, and remains of buildings and gateways are carved with Chavin-type figures. This city covered an area of about four square miles and was the center of the first South American "empire" controlling more than one valley area. The small towns on the coast which had grown up from fishing villages now became Tiahuanaco-controlled governing centers. Skilled weavers and potters on the coast, called the Nazca and Paracas people, became part of the Tiahuanaco empire, which reached perhaps as far north as the famous oracle or shrine which had stood at Pachacámac since early Chavin times. But the distances were so great and the mountain barriers so high that the city of Tiahuanaco could not maintain its empire for more than two centuries. The site of Tiahuanaco was itself abandoned and never resettled. Another large, city empire arose at Huari 150 miles east of today's Lima and closer to the old Chavin center of a thousand years before. Huari was also built around a series of paved plazas and large palaces. During their period of domination the Huari people controlled Pachacámac and the fine potters and weavers who inhabited the irrigated valleys on the coast. More than 50 towns in the Huari period had pyramid-based temples of clay brick and finished stones.

By A.D. 800 the Huari control had broken, and the Huari centers in the highlands were deserted. The people on the coast fortified the towns surrounding their temples and, for the next 600 years, fought each other for water rights. In the highlands no center remained with more than a thousand people, and each one ruled itself. Only the shrine at Pachacámac was available to all. But these isolated towns in the valleys and along the river mouths maintained the Peruvian Andean culture. They improved metallurgy by using copper from northern Chile and combining it with tin from Bolivia to make hard bronze knives and plowing sticks, and by working ever more intricate patterns in gold and silver for ornamentation. The weavers produced cloth far superior to its European counterpart by making tapestry, damasks and laces, and voiles with 250 threads to the square inch; weavers in Europe produced cloth only as fine as 85 threads to the square inch. On the dry Pacific coast, the Paracas and Nazca peoples south of Pachacamac buried their dead in beautiful multicolored mantles with elegant tapestry patterns, which were perfectly preserved in the sand and can now be seen in the museums of Lima.

During this long period of "independent" towns, the idea of empire was not entirely forgotten. In the Moche Valley near modern Trujillo north of Lima, the city of Chan Chan began to expand about A.D. 1200. It was the largest city ever built in ancient Peru, having ten different *barrios*, each around a plaza and with its own reservoir of water from melted snow brought down by the swift rivers from the high Andes on their flow to the coast. When the Spaniards first saw the Chimú city of Chan Chan it was a great roofless mass of adobe buildings, square streets and ornate stucco walls in bright colors, having changed little since the conquering mountain Incas had resettled its people almost a century before. Although an unprecedented rainstorm on this rainless coast in 1925 reduced Chan Chan to piles of mud, a recent aerial survey proved that the city covered an area of twelve square miles, with a thousand square miles of irrigated cornfields and truck gardens around it. A "Great Wall" had been built from the coast to the high Andes ridge as a defense against the expanding Incas and other mountain tribes; the Chimú people depended on their river, and had to keep invaders from stealing their water rights.

Equal in skill to their irrigation projects, was the pottery of the Chimú. Jugs created as portraits (perhaps of the person in whose grave they were found) have realistic full-scale faces, moulded in the round, in the rich terra cotta color so much like an Indian's skin—faces which smile or frown or even wink at the visitor from the walls of museum shelves. Chimú plates and vases intended for daily use are decorated with scenes of home life, commerce, or religious ceremonies. Some of their colored plates suggest that they built large sailing rafts and traded extensively on the coast.

The Chimú controlled Pachacamac and sent their armies to conquer mountain villages. But it was the revival of city life in the mountains which caused their downfall. The Andes-dwelling Incas, with a far better imperial organization, came down to the coast and conquered the Chimú in 1475. The Incas were superior military men, but they never achieved a higher culture than that of the Chimú.

the empire of the Incas

When Europeans discovered America, a tribe of lama herders from north of Lake Titicaca had developed into the dominant people called the Incas or "the Children of the Sun." Their civilization and territory extended from the northern border of Ecuador a third of the way down Chile, and eastward through Bolivia into upper Argentina. Speaking the Quechua language, they were mistakenly called Incas by the Spaniards, who used the title of their ruler as a general name for all the civilized Andean peoples. These so-called Incas kept their empire together through a remarkable system of roads and communications. They emphasized the general welfare of the people as a basis for their state, and planned the development of the resources of the country so that the surplus only should be used for state and aristocracy after the needs of the workers themselves had been satisfied.

We know a mass of detailed history about the Inca kings and their subjects—more than we know about the Aztecs and infinitely more than we know about the Maya. Perhaps in Peru there was not as great a slaughter of nobility by the European conquerors as elsewhere; many upper-class Incas held their positions and married their daughters to Spaniards. The detailed memorized stories of Inca greatness were passed down in these families. Spanish priests and scholars seemed more interested in writing down facts about the Incas than they were about the Aztecs.

These memorized Inca legends say that the Sun created a man and his wife on an island in Lake Titicaca and made them "prince and princess." He then sent them to the high fertile Andes valley of Cuzco. "The prince and princess went throughout the valley calling the people together in the name of their Father, the Sun." With the "multitude thus assembled" they built the city of Cuzco. Their descendants conquered the surrounding territory and told their history to their children in turn.

By 1450 the Inca realm was as large as modern Peru. The Inca king at that time, Pachacutec, required three years to make a complete inspection of it, his empire had been so widely extended by combining guile and diplomacy with military aggression. It had become set policy of the Inca ruler to conquer peoples militarily and then reconcile them by kindness. It was Pachacútec who absorbed Nazca country, took over the shrine, and perhaps the religion of Pachacamac, and advanced to the great wall of Chan Chan. It was his son, the crown prince Tupac Yupanqui, who subdued the Chimú.

In the next generation under Huayna Cápac, the empire reached to the present Colombia-Ecuador line, and far down into the fertile valleys of central Chile as well as the sloping eastern *montaña* of Bolivia, an expanse of territory 1500 miles long and 300 miles wide, all ruled by the Child of the Sun from Cuzco. With the death of the ruler about 1527 a quarrel ensued between two of his sons for whom he had divided the empire. Was it Huáscar, born of Huayna Cápac's chief wife, a Cuzco princess, who should be the true heir, or was it Atahualpa, his favorite son, whose mother was a much-loved concubine, a princess from the recently conquered province of Quito? After several years of armed truce, these two half-brothers fought openly for three years over the Inca throne; the Spanish conquerors under Pizarro were to profit from the disorganization caused by this quarrel.

Inca statesmanship was remarkable as the empire extended itself; new conquests were made integral parts of the highly centralized kingdom. Whenever lands were conquered, subjected peoples were allowed to retain approximately a third of their territory; the Incas were given a second third for their own expansion, while the Inca ruler kept a final third for his own use. The new area would be dominated by Inca-built roads and fortresses; its people would be appeased by a policy of assimilation and Inca-acculturation. Transferred colonists from older parts of the empire came into the villages and farms to work side by side with the newly conquered inhabitants. These were always people who spoke Quechua, the language of the Incas. From them the subjects were forced to learn this official tongue. There was once more than 80 tribal groups and languages in the habitable west coast area. By the time the Spaniards came, some people in every village spoke Quechua; in fact, it was more widely spoken in the region than Spanish is today. This language helped unify the empire. No interpreters were needed, for the conquered peoples learned Quechua more quickly than the new officials could learn the speech of the conquered. The Quechuan word for the empire, *Tahuantinsuyo,* actually means *unity.* Thus were the vast Inca holdings solidified.

The actual governmental system of the whole territory was theocratic despotism. As head of the empire of eight or ten million inhabitants stood the hereditary Inca or Sapa-Inca, descendant of the Sun. Tradition and precedent required that he rule wisely and justly. As the source of all laws, administrative decrees, and religious proclamations, he was surrounded by an aura of divinity and wore special and distinctive garb. His capital was at Cuzco, city of 100,000 inhabitants at 11,000 feet elevation; a secondary capital and court were maintained at Quito by the time of the arrival of the Spaniards. Four viceroys helped him in the actual rule of the empire and served as an advisory council. He also maintained an elaborate system of messengers and itinerant officers who kept him closely in touch with every part of his vast realm.

The absolute power of the Inca, the uniform level of knowledge and culture, the generally well-fed condition of the subjects, and the lack of any strong outside enemies made the empire a paternalistic and socialistic state. Such a state called for a bureaucracy of many officials. Below the four viceroys and the provincial governors, called *camayas,* were the tribes and villages, the *hunas,* each theoretically comprising a hundred households. At the bottom of the pyramid were the headmen, the *chuncas,* in charge of ten families each. These headmen reported on the physical needs of their people, and served as justices of the peace, although their decisions could be appealed all the way up to the Inca, the supreme judge. Justice was firm and prompt; capital punishment was the penalty for theft, adultery, murder, and blasphemy against the Sun God, with justice especially severe for violations committed by public officials.

The government was supported by income from lands belonging to the Inca, from monopolies of precious stones and metals, and from tribute in the form of forced labor. Work from each household was supposed to be contributed equally; the whole governmental system emphasized equality of opportunity based solely on ability and age. But such a system called for rigid regimentation. Although no one was overworked, labor was highly specialized. Each age group was assigned a certain type of labor according to the strength required. Once an artisan of particular skill, always such an artisan. Young people under twenty-five and old people over fifty were exempted from tribute labor on the roads, on water supply systems, and on other public projects, and were assigned only light tasks. Transfers of population were sometimes undertaken for the purpose of maintaining loyalty. If a region threatened rebellion, it was soon re-colonized with many loyal families—a system of *mitimaes.* Thus there was "social security" without individual liberty. Life was safe and pleasant enough, and the government efficient and respected.

This organization of all levels of life developed a rigid class system. Royalty included legitimate descendants of the royal family who formed the highest nobility; from their number were selected principal military and civil officials and the chief priests. There was an upper class in the remote provinces also, consisting of the *curacas,* hereditary chiefs of the conquered governments whose children were educated at the court of Cuzco.

Below the official class, the only inequalities were those of physical strength, numbers of able-bodied sons and daughters in a family, or skill of craftsmanship and farming "know-how." There was also a class of slave workers. who were confined to the lands of the Inca and the temples, and kept in that position from generation to generation. In the families of the laboring class of people even marriage was arranged by the state; all the girls and boys of marriageable age in any one unit of a hundred households were married at one time in a gala public ceremony in order to provide a big fiesta, prevent private family parties, and save time for the harvesting of crops and the building of roads.

Under such a system there was no individual ownership of land. Fields belonged either to the priests for the support of the sun-worship, to the Inca for support of the royal family and the government, or to the tribes (*hunas*) and villages (*chuncas*) for distribution to the families. From the village reserves enough land was given to each family for its own maintenance according to the number of its members, their assigned occupations, and their ability to work. No land was ever bought from and sold to individuals, and adjustment of holdings was made to suit family numbers of each new generation. Food from the land went into public storehouses; craftsmen received it in return for their manufactured goods, laborers in return for their work on roads, on public works, or in mines.

The lands produced well, for the Inca people were among the best farmers in the Americas. They terraced the mountainside, fertilized the soil with *guano* or seagull dung from the coast, and used well-planned systems of reservoirs, canals, and aqueducts for irrigation of the drier valleys and the coastal shelf. In their intensively cultivated plots they raised potatoes, corn, manioc or tapioca, peppers, tomatoes, beans, and squash. They had vast herds of llamas to be used as beasts of burden and alpacas to be sheared for wool.

Roads used to maintain contact with all the empire and necessary for military purposes connected all sections; some of them were constructed on flatland paved with stones, others made of chiseled stairsteps up mountain passes. On such trails suspension bridges across deep chasms were better than many of those in use on pack trails in the Andes today. Post runners, or *chasquis*, ran regular routes on these trails with messages, and storehouses and inns were maintained for these runners, as well as for the Inca's packtrain leaders, traveling officials, and tradesmen. Signal fires helped the runners relay commands swiftly from post to post. The thousand-mile trip from Cuzco to Quito was covered by such messengers in eight days. Balsa boats on Lake Titicaca relayed the Inca's messages into what is now Bolivia.

Religion naturally ruled the people's lives in a country where the absolute ruler was also a Child of God. The Inca himself, usually son of the previous Inca by his own sister to keep the blood line pure, was also the highest archpriest. For the cult of unquestioning devotion to Sun-worship there existed an elaborate priesthood headed by the Villac Umu, a brother or close relative of the ruler under whom there were hundreds of lesser priests, keepers of the temples, and nuns or "Virgins of the Sun." Sacrifices of food and flowers, or articles of precious metals were offered. For formal ceremonies on set occasions llamas were sacrificed, and, very rarely, a human life.

Among the more sophisticated Cuzco people, there was a belief in a life after death. Those who were good went to live with the Sun. Sinners—and disobeying the emperor, or carelessness in worship was a sin equal to murder—descended to the center of the earth, where they suffered constant hunger and had no food but stones. Sins had to be confessed; bad luck, illness, and accidents came to those who failed to do so. Priests in the temples received these confessions (much as Catholic priests among the Quechua might do today) and made assignments of fasting and prayer for penitence. The temple in Cuzco was the finest building erected by the Inca;

one of its spacious rooms was 296 feet long. A curved sanctuary adjoining it made of beautifully smooth stones, still stands today in Cuzco in the foundation of a convent. Here the people prayed, "Oh, Sun! Thou art in peace and safety, shine upon us, keep us from sickness, and preserve us in health and safety." It was not difficult for these people to transfer their faith to a Christian God in the Cuzco cathedral.

Through their Sun-worship the Incas seem to have developed an abstract culture superior perhaps to that of the Maya. Although there was no system of writing, much religious poetry was recited orally and written down by the Spaniards. The Inca sages also composed love songs and philosophical verses. Pachacutec, Inca in the 1480s, is best remembered for his wise proverbs, many of which were still being widely quoted when Spaniards wrote them down a half century later:

> Envy is a worm that gnaws and consumes the entrails of the envious.
> He that kills another without authority or just cause condemns himself to death.
> Judges who secretly receive gifts from suitors ought to be looked upon as thieves and punished with death as such.[2]

Such poems and proverbs were part of the "college education" given to the sons of the upper class. In a four-year course in the temples they learned astronomy and mathematics as well as the history and legends of the Inca peoples. Classes for the noblemen's sons were taught by *amautas,* learned men of the priestly class who gave specialized training in law, priesthood, and principles of government. The youngsters of nobility were trained for a life of service to the empire as priests, tax collectors, and governors; they were also taught the elements of science, bridge building, and road construction. Recently experts in deciphering codes have reason to suspect that the intricate designs in Inca and pre-Inca weaving are a type of hieroglyphic writing. But they had no alphabet and a great deal of their learning had to be by rote in oral recitation. The sons of officials were also taught the use of the *quipu,* an elaborate and ingenious method of keeping accounts by means of knotted cords of various sizes and colors—red for accounts concerning war, white for those of peace. With these cords officials recorded population size, taxes, road-building plans, increase of herds, and every item necessarily accounted for in a vast realm. The children of commoners had no such fine training—in fact, no formal education of any kind.

With an efficient ruling class and an accurate system of accounts, the Incas developed an advanced culture in things practical as evidenced by their bridges and irrigation canals, and their terraced fields on steep mountainsides. In such activities they surpassed all other Western Hemispheric peoples. They developed even their art forms in practical ways. The Inca conquerors could not improve the pottery work of the Chimu nor the textiles of the Nazca. But they could improve their "technical excellence" in the

---

[2] Means, *Ancient Civilizations of the Andes,* p. 262. Reproduced by permission of the publishers.

Sauer, C. O., *The Early Spanish Main* (1966).

Stevenson, R., *Music in Aztec and Inca Territory* (1968).

————, *Music of Peru, Aboriginal and Viceregal Epochs* (1960).

Stewart, J. H., ed., *Handbook of South American Indians* (6 vols., 1946–1950).

————, and L. C. Faron, *Native Peoples of South America* (1959).

Tax, S., ed., *Civilization of Ancient America* (1951).

Thompson, J. E., *Archaeology of South America* (1936).

Von Hagen, V. W., *Incas, People of the Sun* (1961).

————, *Realm of the Incas* (1957).

Wissler, C., *American Indian* (3rd ed., 1938).

chapter 5

SPAIN IN THE NEW WORLD: THE FIRST QUARTER CENTURY

Columbus' first voyage

Columbus typified the new age in successfully planning his voyage and advertising his discovery. Born in 1451 at or near Genoa, he went to sea early, like other Genoese boys, aboard small cargo ships in the Mediterranean, going to Bristol and possibly to Iceland—where he himself heard tales of islands. In 1476 the young Columbus was aboard a Genoese merchantship trading with England when it was attacked by French war vessels and he had to swim ashore with other survivors to the Portuguese coast. Portugal at the time was the center for the new navigation, for exploration and geographic discovery. Columbus found help among Genoese seamen and traders who were living in Lisbon, men who knew how to handle ocean-going vessels well, to load them for long trips, to deal with primitive peoples (such as those on the West African coasts) and bring to them the kind of goods they liked.

He spent his late twenties and early thirties in Lisbon, becoming well-known in the Genoese colony, and going into the chart- and map-making business with his brother Bartholomew. He took trips with Portuguese captains to the Guinea Coast. Accepted in Portuguese society, he married the daughter of the governor of Madeira, Doña Felipa Perestrello,

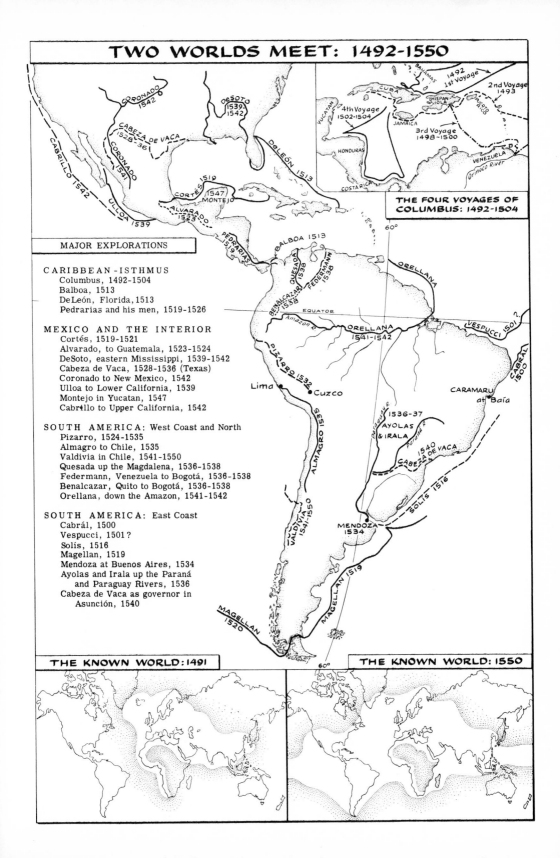

TWO WORLDS MEET: 1492-1550

THE FOUR VOYAGES OF COLUMBUS: 1492-1504

MAJOR EXPLORATIONS

CARIBBEAN-ISTHMUS
Columbus, 1492-1504
Balboa, 1513
DeLeón, Florida, 1513
Pedrarias and his men, 1519-1526

MEXICO AND THE INTERIOR
Cortés, 1519-1521
Alvarado, to Guatemala, 1523-1524
DeSoto, eastern Mississippi, 1539-1542
Cabeza de Vaca, 1528-1536 (Texas)
Coronado to New Mexico, 1542
Ulloa to Lower California, 1539
Montejo in Yucatan, 1547
Cabrillo to Upper California, 1542

SOUTH AMERICA: West Coast and North
Pizarro, 1524-1535
Almagro to Chile, 1535
Valdivia in Chile, 1541-1550
Quesada up the Magdalena, 1536-1538
Federmann, Venezuela to Bogotá, 1536-1538
Benalcazar, Quito to Bogotá, 1536-1538
Orellana, down the Amazon, 1541-1542

SOUTH AMERICA: East Coast
Cabrál, 1500
Vespucci, 1501?
Solís, 1516
Magellan, 1519
Mendoza at Buenos Aires, 1534
Ayolas and Irala up the Paraná
   and Paraguay Rivers, 1536
Cabeza de Vaca as governor in
   Asunción, 1540

THE KNOWN WORLD: 1491

THE KNOWN WORLD: 1550

and doubtless heard a lot of talk about Portuguese explorations from his wife's family. In 1479, records show, he lived in the Azores.

In 1482 he was corresponding with a famous Florentine scholar named Paolo Toscanelli who assured him of the safety of a course due west of Lisbon, which, he said, "will take you 5,000 nautical miles to the Chinese Province of Mangi." He complimented Columbus on his "great and noble ambition to pass over to where the spices grow." Thus Columbus came greatly to underestimate the distance between Lisbon and the China coast, which actually stretched 12,000 nautical miles, he had no idea of the lands that intervened between them.

In 1484 in the court of Portugal, Columbus made his first request for a group of ships to sail west to Cipangu (probably Japan). The maritime commission which considered the proposal turned it down, but the Portuguese king remained interested, and, in fact, went so far as to permit a private exploration westward in 1487 which came to naught. Disappointed in two attempts to involve the Portuguese monarch, Columbus, now a widower, went to Spain in 1485 with his young son Diego and got in contact with people close to the Queen. Isabella appointed a commission to study his plan while Columbus, cooling his heels on a royal pension busied himself gathering evidence that the voyage was possible and supported a young mistress who bore him his famous biographer son Fernando.

The commission rejected the westward voyage plan on the proper ground that the ocean was too wide and that its proponent asked for too many personal rewards for the discoveries he might make. Spain was busy expelling the Moslems and unifying the interior provinces. Columbus, who had already waited five years for Spanish action, decided to look to France or England for help. But when his brother had started for England and he himself had started for France, a royal messenger was sent after him with the news that Queen Isabella had personally decided to back the project. She had been attracted to him from the first, and gave her consent when her treasurer and some others in the court expressed willingness to invest the needed money.

He was probably a commanding figure, in the prime of life, as he stood before the Queen. He was described by his contemporaries as "tall and well built, with a ruddy and freckled complexion, hawk-nosed and long of visage, blue-eyed and with high check bones." In character he was courageous, persistent, strong-willed, and deeply devout. Undoubtedly he was also conceited and overbearing to the point that many people found him irritating or offensive.

Back in Madrid, a basic agreement was made, the first of a long series of contracts between the Spanish crown and New World explorers and conquerors. Under the contract, Columbus was to be "Admiral over all islands and mainlands he discovered not already under Christian kings," a title which was to go to his heirs in perpetuity. He was to govern all such lands, nominate officials, and receive "one tenth of all gold, silver, pearls, gems, spices, and other things produced or obtained by barter and mining within these new lands." As "Admiral of the Ocean Sea, Viceroy, and

Governor," he would have rights and titles that would have made him ruler of all the Western Hemisphere! His heirs were to carry on lawsuits about these rights for a generation after his death.

The Queen undertook to supply ships, sailors, and provisions for the voyage, the total cost of which came to be about 2,000,000 *maravedis* (about $30,000). Columbus himself invested some funds in the enterprise. The Queen, contrary to legend, did not have to pawn any of her jewels for the venture. She looked on the voyage as a lucrative enterprise, made especially attractive by the chance of expanding dominions and finding new channels for crusading zeal.

The little town of Palos was selected as the port of departure partly because this Spanish town had had experience in the African trade and in handling caravels and partly because it owed the Queen some ships as back taxes. The Pinzón brothers, Martín Alonzo and Vicente Yáñez, undertook the job of provisioning the ships and recruiting the crew, and they managed, through their influence in Palos, to persuade 90 men to undertake the questionable voyage. None of them, contrary to legend, were convicts. The Pinzón brothers captained two of the ships. In later years the family was to claim greater credit on the voyage than they had received and to bring suit against Columbus' heirs.

The ten weeks it took to get the expedition ready was a fortunate delay for it kept Columbus from the West Indies until after the hurricane season. The ships, though leaky little cockleshells to the modern sailor, were the best type known at the time, small but fast. In short, the little fleet (*Niña*, the best; *Santa María*, the biggest and the worst; and *Pinta*) was unusually well organized. And Columbus himself was not only a skilled navigator but a man of determination with faith in his plans, a Renaissance man putting *theory* to the test.

The maps of Columbus' time indicated that Cipangu was on the same parallel as the Canary Islands, so Columbus proposed to sail straight west from the Canaries to the Far East. The ships left Palos on August 3, 1492, and sailed southwest to the islands off the African coast where some repairs and adjustments were made and supplies, especially fresh food, were taken aboard.

From the standpoint of sailing, this 1492 trip was one of the easiest Columbus ever made. The weather was fine, the season the best of the year. Columbus himself worked ably and hard as navigator, using the system of "dead reckoning," laying out his course with a mariner's compass as his main instrument, estimating distances on a chart. His principal difficulty was in handling the men, a skill in which he never excelled. His seamen were experienced and not afraid of sea monsters or of dropping off the end of a flat world. Their troubles rose mainly from close confinement on small ships for such a long time and from the fear of foundering so far from home.

The crisis with the men was coming to a head by the first week of October when they were two months from home and twenty days from the Azores. They had exceeded all previously known records for ocean navigation beyond the sight of land. On October 8 and 9 conferences were held with the Pinzón brothers, captains of the *Niña* and the *Pinta,* and the agreement was made to continue three more days. Then came the glorious sunset of October 11 and Rodrigo de Triana's cry of "¡*Tierra!*" in the early hours of the 12th.

Stepping from the armed ship's-boat on the beach at San Salvador, Christopher Columbus stepped from the role of sea captain to the exalted title of Admiral of the Ocean Sea and to immortality as *the* discoverer—and stepped into a strange new world which he and his men explored excitedly. They were fascinated by the sight of naked human beings, of a color and type the Spaniards had never known. They saw the native *hamacas,* hammocks—a discovery that would soon enable the sailors to sleep more comfortably on their ships. They found a small quantity of gold—at least enough to increase the importance of their expedition to those back home. They found the natives smoking cigars through their noses, the first European view of the tobacco habit. Intent on finding the mainland of Asia beyond the Bahamas, Columbus sailed on into the Caribbean waters.

The first large island that he discovered, the home of today's Haiti and Santo Domingo, he called Hispaniola. The *Santa María* was wrecked and had to be abandoned off Hispaniola, and since the Admiral could not take all his men back to Spain on the two small remaining ships, he was forced to leave some of the men on Hispaniola in a makeshift fort he called Navidad. Thus began the first, though temporary, colony in the New World.

After much sailing among the islands and touching on Cuba (which Columbus thought might be the China coast) the *Niña* and the *Pinta* started for home. Returning to Europe, Columbus hit upon the best route east, going north far enough to pick up the prevailing westerlies which took him rapidly back to Spain. On his first voyage, he laid out the best westward as well as eastward routes across the Atlantic. The trade winds pushed him over, the westerlies took him back.

And back in Spain in April of 1493, he became a famous personage overnight. He was received in state by the whole court and declared Admiral of the Ocean Sea and Governor of the islands and mainlands he had found. He stayed for six weeks in royal lodgings provided for him. Baptismal services were held for the six Bahama Island Indians he had brought back. The Queen herself acted as godmother. Plans for a second voyage got under way immediately. A large fleet with many colonists aboard was to be sent back to Hispaniola.

Spain, however, had need for haste in 1492 if she was to prevent Portuguese encroachment on her discoveries. She appealed to the only international authority in existence, one recognized by both Spain and Portugal—the Papacy. Portuguese authorities had been quick to claim that the new Spanish discoveries were in territory already guaranteed to Portugal by papal order and by Spanish treaty of 1481 in connection with discoveries on the African coast. The Pope responded to Spain's appeal with a new papal order. Thus began the diplomatic history of the Americas.

In return for promises by both Spain and Portugal that they would evangelize the savages and colonize the new lands with Christians, the Pope drew a line between the respective areas of Spain and Portugal by two new Bulls or papal pronouncements on May 2 and 4, 1943. This Line of Demarcation was indefinitely placed at one hundred leagues west and south of any one of the islands "commonly known as Azores and Cape Verdes." Disputes over the exact location led to a meeting of Spanish and Portuguese envoys the next fall at Tordesillas which settled on a line 370 leagues west of the Cape Verdes. Spain accepted a line this far west because she erroneously assumed the other half of the line would cut through the East Indies and allow her part of the rich trade in that area. After Magellan's voyage, the line did give Spain the Philippines, but, on the other hand, the demarcation line in the Atlantic gave Portugal her legal toehold on Brazil. The exact location of the Demarcation Line remained uncertain and led to disputes over the extent of Portuguese expansion inland in South America. Modern boundary disputes in South America had their origin in the Line of Demarcation.

the continued search for a route from west to east

The court made plans to colonize Haiti, the land of "Hispaniola" on which Columbus had left the men of the shipwrecked crew, and busied itself preparing a large fleet to take settlers and their equipment to the New World. Columbus' main interest, now that the Papal Bull gave Spain a free hand to search farther west for the route to India, was in making further discoveries.

As commander of the colonizing fleet, he reached Hispaniola in November of 1493 after sighting the Virgin Islands and Puerto Rico. There he found his year-old fort destroyed and no trace of the men from the *Santa María*. The new town of Isabella then set up was the first true settlement in the New World. Columbus made further explorations in the summer of 1494 along the coasts of Cuba and Jamaica but never found the tip of Cuba that turned north and so decided he had skirted a continent.

The mistakes he made in governing the settlement at Hispaniola are part of another story. Three years after he had brought the large fleet to the Indies, he was forced by the chaos and economic failure in the colony to return to Spain to explain his difficulties. He managed to remain in good favor with Isabella and talked her into maintaining him as governor and outfitting another exploratory expedition.

On his third voyage, in 1498, he sailed south of Hispaniola, found the island of Trinidad, and saw the Venezuela coast. When he found a great body of fresh water on the south side of Trinidad, he sensed the might of the Orinoco, a river that could not rise in a small island, that must come from a continent. He made his first mention of a mainland other than Asia when he wrote to the Queen, "I believe that this is a very great continent, which until today has been unknown." He said, "Your Highnesses have here another world!"

Columbus found himself in deeper difficulties as governor when he returned from this exploration to Hispaniola with nothing but the story of a new continent and a handful of pearls from Margarita Island. In 1500 he was sent home under arrest. Isabella freed him but, tired of the chaos in his colony and his own bickering over titles and prestige, she never again allowed him to govern. She did allow herself to be persuaded to send him on one more expedition to find a strait to India through the Caribbean and Central America and to "discover lands rich in gold."

With four ships and 150 men—including his brother Bartholomew, the mapmaker, and Ferdinand, the 14-year old son who was to be his biographer—he cruised along the shore of the *hondos,* the deep waters he named Honduras, and the Rich Coast, Costa Rica. There he saw a trading raft of the civilized Maya and assumed he was close to China. Later he might have changed his mind, for a map made by his brother on this expedition calls the South American mainland *Mondo Novo,* the New World, and in his own writings in 1502, he spoke of the islands as the "West Indies Unknown to all the World."

On this last voyage, he was shipwrecked on Jamaica and marooned there a whole year. He sent a messenger by canoe to Hispaniola, 120 miles away, but the quarrelsome colony did not consider him important enough to rescue. Friends finally sent a caravel to take him home to Spain, where he died in 1506, practically forgotten. But it was the stories of his findings that led to such rapid exploration, conquest, and settlement of the Americas.

Other European nations had not been content to let Spain alone capitalize on Columbus' discoveries. A series of voyages with captains representing Portugal, France, and England as well as Spain had by 1525 examined the shoreline of the entire Western Hemisphere from Labrador to the Straits of Magellan. The English claim to the Atlantic coast of North America was established by the voyage of John Cabot in 1497, another Genoese mariner who had visited Bristol and had been hired to sail for England. His son Sebastian was unsuccessful in finding the Northwest passage or strait for England but he later did receive fame for his explorations in South America for Spain. The claim of the French kings to the northern area was established in 1524 by the search of a Florentine seaman, Verrazano, for the strait to Asia by way of Maine and Newfoundland. Portugal's mariners, the Corte Real brothers, also looked for the elusive strait along the North Atlantic coast.

By 1500, Portugal established its claim to Brazil by discovery and exploration. The Portuguese Vasco da Gama had found the round-Africa sea route to India, and in 1499 Pedro Alvares Cabral set out with a fleet of 13 ships to make permanent trading contacts in India. His fleet went west of the Cape Verde Islands, perhaps by instruction, before turning south to round Africa, and in Easter Week of 1500 found land on the shoulder of Brazil, within the Portuguese area of Demarcation. Cabral explored 25 leagues of coastline which he reported as "flat, and full of great trees, and very beautiful inland," with natives, who, he said, were naked, "painted black and red on their bodies and legs and looked very well." He sent a ship home with the news of the discovery and continued his route around Africa.

Portugal sent out another expedition immediately and by 1502 had opened the land to Portuguese commercial companies.

Spanish ships continued the desperate search for a northwest passage through or round the newly discovered lands, and despite Columbus' claim to exclusive exploring rights, sent out other captains. One of them was a young man named Alonzo de Ojeda who had gone with Columbus on the second trip to Hispaniola, and who was a personal friend of Isabella's colonial adviser, Bishop Fonseca. Ojeda was commissioned to explore the whole length of the northern coast of South America from Guiana to the Magdalena, and was the first to see "lake-dwellers' huts" on stilts in the Gulf of Maracaibo in the region he called "Little Venice" or Venezuela. He found pearls and thus made a profit out of what was actually a piratical venture. Four or five other captains and navigators who had served under Columbus undertook similar exploring and pearl-hunting expeditions within the next few years with varying success.

Thus in a little more than a decade four Columbian voyages and five trips by former companions of his had revealed the coastline from Honduras to Pernambuco and even beyond. Every larger island in the West Indies was known except Barbados. To the captains themselves, these voyages were disappointing for they had found only wild land and neither eastern cities nor a route through to them. To the future, of course, they were of vast importance.

By a quirk of fortune, the new continent was named for a man who may have been a spy for Italian commercial companies on several of these early explorations. A Florentine named Amerigo Vespucci, a commercial trader who was at one time an agent for the rich Italian house of de Medici and later a mapmaker, claimed to have made several trans-Atlantic voyages. Some of his adventures have been authenticated. A profuse and interesting letter writer, he described the coast of South America in personal and readable letters to Italian employers and friends. To him the continent he saw was a "new world," this at a time when Columbus was still claiming that Cuba and Haiti were in the Far East. Some of his letters to the de Medicis, published in Florence under the title "The New World," were widely read before any of Columbus' accounts of his later voyages were printed. Then a young geography professor in a college in Lorraine, Martin Waldseemüller, published a textbook in 1507 and enumerated in it the four parts of the world and concluded that "the fourth part of the globe, which, since Amerigo discovered it, may be called Amerigo's land." Amerigo's "The New World Letters" were added as an appendix to the book. The name was copied by other geographers and eventually applied to the whole Western Hemisphere.

By 1525, the whole eastern coastline from Nova Scotia to the Straits of Magellan had been mapped as a result of the search for the strait. Cuba was circumnavigated by Sebastian de Ocampo; Florida was discovered by the Spaniard Juan Ponce de León; the Gulf coast was mapped by three different voyages out from Cuba and Jamaica between 1517 and 1519. Slave raiders from Santo Domingo worked up and down the Carolina coast.

Europe finally became convinced that the strait to India through the New World did not lie between the nothern coast of South America and Nova Scotia and thus it lost interest in the all-water route through the Caribbean to the Indies. Isabella died in 1504; Ferdinand concentrated on Aragon; Juana the Mad inherited Castile. The colony of Hispaniola languished and only occasional voyages were made to the northern South American coast for pearls and Indian slaves.

A series of southern explorations along the coast of South America preceded the discovery of the only through passage, the Straits of Magellan. Pinzón sighted the Amazon mouth in 1500. He and Juan Díaz de Solís explored for salt-water inlets between Trinidad and the Amazon mouth in the search for the strait. Balboa discovered a great sea to the south and west of the Isthmus. When this news reached Spain in 1514, Ferdinand sent Solís out again, ordering him to explore the coast of South America. Solís passed the shores of Uruguay in 1515–1516 and entered with delight a sea of fresh water which he called the Mar Dulce. It was actually the Plata estuary, 100 miles wide at the mouth. Unfortunately when he left his caravel and went exploring in a small boat, he and his landing party were killed by Indians, and, within sight of his crew, anchored out in mid-stream, Solís was roasted and eaten. When on the homeward voyage one of Solís' vessels was shipwrecked, eighteen men survived and lived among the Brazilian Indians for eight years. There they heard stories of silver in the Inca land to the west.

Europeans were finally convinced that America was an obstacle blocking the way to the Orient and that some route must be found through or around it. A Portuguese nobleman named Ferdinand Magellan proposed to the young King of Spain that they go around it. He showed Charles V, son of Juana, a "well-painted globe in which the world (was) depicted" and indicated to him a proposed route for circumnavigation. His expedition of five ships and 270 men was provisioned for a two-year voyage and reached the Plata estuary by January of 1520. Magellan spent the Southern Hemisphere winter on the bleak coast of Patagonia exploring bays and river mouths.

He had lost two of his boats by the time he found the strait that bears his name. This was in October of his second year out. His ships had entered a harbor, driven ahead by a 36-hour hurricane. The mariners of the lead ship, "perceiving that this channel was not closed, threaded it, and found (themselves) in another." The remaining ships eventually arrived safely through the straits. So Magellan came into the open Pacific, which his ships traversed, without fresh food or water, for three months and twenty days.

Magellan stopped at Guam eventually and landed in the Philippines, claiming them for Spain. In the Philippines, he found the natives understood the Malayan speech of his East Indian slave and knew he had reached waters near Asia. He himself was killed fighting natives in the Philippines, but one of his ships, captained by Jean Sebastian del Cano, and loaded with spices enough to pay the expenses of the whole trip, "limped" into Spain around Africa. The voyage had taken three years.

The survivors aboard the ship were the first to fulfill Columbus' dream of obtaining riches from spices by sailing west. The voyage had brought a group of eastern islands into the Spanish empire, and had shown the unexpectedly great size of the Pacific and of the earth. Though the search for a better strait continued for another two centuries, Europeans now knew that the Indies were half a world away from the Caribbean and that a great land mass lay across the path. By this time, Spaniards and Portuguese had turned to the New World for conquest and settlement rather than for routes through to Asia.

Under what conditions did these men cross the Atlantic and explore the new continent? Every contemporaneous account tells of the difficult life on shipboard—the foul drinking water, the short rations of salt pork and pickled sardines, the prevalence of scurvy owing to lack of fresh supplies. Work was constant, setting the sails, hauling them in, drying and repairing them, pumping out the bilges, scrubbing the deck, and splicing rope. Seamen slept on the open deck or in crannies in the cargo among the fleas, the rats, and the cockroaches. Passengers brought their own food and cooked it themselves. Horses of the explorers and cattle for the colonists were carried on deck. In later days, the larger galleons had stalls below deck for livestock, private cabins for officers and government officials, and rooms with bunks for the passengers. Ships built in the New World by later explorers, called brigantines, had no decks or private quarters and were lucky to hold together.

The captains got them to land with what would seem today impossibly crude instruments of navigation. With the astrolabe they could measure the position of the sun at noon and know their approximate distance from the equator. But they had no maps showing longitude and latitude and no standardized ways of measuring them. The site of the Royal Naval Observatory in Greenwich, England, was not accepted as zero degree of longitude until 1675. Time was measured by hour glasses and water clocks. Captains lacked the education to apply the mathematics of the new Renaissance science to navigation. Often the preliminary crossing on the trade-winds was less dangerous than slopping about in narrow channels between islands and taking large ships into shallow river estuaries in search of straits. By risks such as these, mariners in the years from 1492 to 1522 plotted out the shores of almost a whole hemisphere.

Hispaniola: laboratory of colonial administration

The transfer of Spanish people and institutions to the New World began in November of 1493 when 1500 settlers embarked with Columbus on his second voyage, and his large fleet, loaded with equipment, seeds, and livestock, set sail for Hispaniola. When he found the fort built for the *Santa María* crew destroyed, Columbus established the newcomers at a new site, in the northeast part of the island called Isabella, where he laid out streets and a plaza and erected huts of thatch as temporary quarters. The Spaniards, however, made poor settlers. They had not come to do heavy work in the tropics. The site was unhealthy and they fell sick. When some gold was discovered in the southern part of the colony, Isabella was abandoned. The oldest permanent European city in the New World, Santo Domingo, was founded in 1496 on the southeast corner of the island.

But in Santo Domingo, the emaciated colonists—those who had not died or run off to the hills—were ready to mutiny against Columbus because of his neglectful administration. On his third visit, in October 1498, Columbus sent a ship back to Spain with a report on the "abominable knaves and villains" he had in his colony. The colonists in turn sent a message by the same ship that called Columbus and his brother "unjust, mean, cruel enemies and shedders of Spanish blood."

Shocked by the reports, Isabella appointed Francisco de Bobadilla royal commissioner over Columbus' head to investigate and adjust grievances. When the judge reached Santo Domingo in the summer of 1500, the first sight that met his eyes in the new town was seven Spaniards hanging on the gallows. Already prejudiced against Columbus, the new governor put both the Admiral and his brother in chains and sent them back to Spain. The fact that Columbus was released and allowed to make a fourth exploratory voyage does not lessen his failure as colonial administrator. Yet in the brief time he was in charge, towns had been founded, fortresses built, and a pattern for future rule had been set. Colonial policy was being established by the experimental method. Bobadillo brought peace to the colony and then embarked in his fleet to return home, only to lose the whole fleet and his own life in a West Indian hurricane.

A new royal governor, Nicolás de Ovando, was appointed and set sail from Cádiz in February of 1502 with thirty ships. With him were 2,500 new colonists, including 73 married couples with families. Also included were twelve friars with whom church policy was begun; before long two bishoprics were established. Ovando was efficient, firm, and fair, and he became the actual founder of Spain's empire in America. Under him agriculture prospered; he had brought hogs as well as cattle to the island and thus was begun a livestock industry. He interested himself in pacifying the island and putting down Indian rebellions so that the European colony could survive and prosper. He sought to keep the interests of Spain foremost—the search for wealth, the spread of religion, the development of agriculture. By 1513, gold was being mined in the interior, cotton and sugar were planted, roads had been built, and 13 chartered towns had been founded. Though interest in Spain soon transferred to Cuba and the mainland, Hispaniola remained a successful colony.

Meanwhile Diego Columbus, Christopher's elder son, had grown to manhood in the Spanish court and Ferdinand decided to make him governor, an appointment Don Diego claimed as his inherited right but one which Ferdinand considered a matter of sovereign will to be rescinded after a short term. Disagreements between the ruler and the Columbus family continued until 1536 when Don Diego's descendants finally received a dukedom and a pension and gave up all further claim to hereditary rights in America.

Don Diego's colony of Hispaniola has been called the "mother" of Spanish America because so many Spanish colonial institutions were experimented with and developed there—councils and boards to handle colonial matters in New Spain, titles and powers of administrators, the relationship between church and state. A humanitarian attitude in the abstract toward the natives existed along with a realistic "on the spot" economic exploitation of them in the "concrete." The encouragement and selection of immigrants, the granting of land and the Indians living on it to private owners, the economic policy in developing mines, the trade with the mother country via official fleets, the improvement of agriculture, the doubling and trebling of red tape and regulation as the empire grew, all these evolved from the first experimentation on Hispaniola and became set practices for more than two centuries.

Spain, after all, had no exact model, no actual precedent to follow in the world's history of colonizing nations. She had to draw on her own experiences and adapt them to the new situation. The West Indies were meant from the first to be permanent European communities that would shine as a credit to Spain and Catholicism, with only approved immigrants entering the islands and all natives converted to Christianity. Almost all-inclusive powers were given to Columbus, whose rule was canceled in less than a decade, and to Bobadilla in 1499, Ovando in 1502, and Diego Columbus in 1509. All were called "governor" (they were not called "viceroys" until later) and served as the highest court of appeal, the collectors of taxes, and the source of decisions concerning land grants. As the city of Santo Domingo grew, complaints against the arbitrary justice of Diego Columbus were made which led to the establishment of a superior court to which appeals from the governor-general could be carried. The Spanish judicial institution, the *audiencia*, was transferred to the New World to curtail the governor's power as chief justice. First formally decreed in 1524, *audiencias* followed Spanish government to the other principal colonies.

The locally elected *cabildo* or municipal council had already lost its autonomous powers in Spain under the unification policies of the Catholic monarchs. Its authority was curtailed soon after being established in the New World. In 1500, Santo Domingo had a *cabildo* which was appointed, not elected. The *cabildo* was to become a major institution of government in the New World though its membership in many places was to become hereditary.

Another representative of the crown, called the *adelantado*, was given the joint rights of founder and governor similar to the old rights given Castilian noblemen to maintain feudal holdings along the Moorish frontier. In the New World, as the conquest branched out into virgin territory, private individuals such as Ponce de León were given grants in the 1500's by which they bore the expenses of their ventures in new colonies but could keep most of the profit, including the lands they chose to hold personally.

Since the crown was directly concerned with the colonies, some special official or council had to head up colonial plans in Spain itself. When Columbus made plans for his second voyage, Isabella's chaplain, Juan de

Fonseca, was put in charge of collecting the supplies, interviewing the colonists, and chartering the ships. He acted as a sort of colonial minister for a decade and opposed Columbus' monopolies, concentrating plans in his own hands for the benefit of his sovereigns. He succeeded in transferring the port monopoly from Cádiz, where Columbus wanted it, to Seville, which became the headquarters of all colonial activity. A Board of Trade called the *Casa de Contratación* was set up to assist Fonseca in economic matters and it developed into the clearing house for all trade, navigation, and immigration to the Spanish colonies. Later, when Mexico had been added to the empire, a Council of the Indies headed up colonial affairs.

On his second voyage, Columbus had taken along brood mares, rams and ewes, donkeys, bulls and cows, as well as chickens and many types of seeds. He was able to force the new colonists to plant and harvest the first crops—wheat, barley, melons, and cucumbers—and to set out grape cuttings for vineyards and to plant sugar cane roots. He also sent prospectors to look for gold, which was found in some quantity at Cibao in the interior—where he built a fort and set miners to panning the streams.

Although rumors of gold promoted conquest, actually little gold was ever found in the Caribbean. Prosperity had to depend on agriculture. Ovando was successful, between 1502 and 1508, in increasing herds of domestic animals and promoting the planting of grapes, olives, oranges, lemons, figs, and bananas. The first two major sources of wealth in the islands were sugar cane and cattle. This energetic pursuit of agriculture not only brought prosperity for those engaged in it but also provided needed supplies for later conquests on the mainland, permitting explorers and conquerors to supply themselves over the relatively short distances from the islands. Indicative of Ovando's success is the arrival of many new settlers. By 1507 Spaniards in the islands numbered 12,000, many of them settled down in Santo Domingo or in the other 13 towns of Hispaniola.

The work of agriculture, commerce, political administration, and religious direction engaged most people. There were town councilmen, royal judges, treasury officials, friars, parish priests, artisans, merchants, planters, small farmers; there were wives from Spain and Indian wives, Spanish children born in the New World, and half-breed children called *mestizos*. Those who worked at gold mining in the interior of Hispaniola were a relatively small percentage of the population, as they were to be in the total story of Spanish conquest in America. All Spaniards were "good Catholics," kept good by the constant presence of their own religious institutions.

But what about the natives, how were they to be handled? For the "good" of the colony or for the good of the natives themselves? Queen Isabella had considered their protection and conversion one of Spain's chief duties, had wanted to bring them to a life of industry and usefulness and to teach them to till their own lands or work for pay within the Christian fold. Columbus had felt that the Arawaks were a people "who could better be freed and converted to our Holy Faith by love than by force," but he felt that the cannibalistic Caribs were fair game for slavery. On his second trip he broadened the rule and said it would include "resentful" natives. There was work to be done, precious metals to be mined, and fields to be tilled, and many Spaniards disdained work. So the Indians, although legally wards of the crown, were forced into a system hardly distinguishable from slavery. After an Indian uprising in 1495, Columbus condemned the Indians to pay tribute in gold or personal sacrifice, and later, demands for tribute to the government led to more forced work. From the beginning, economic motives clashed with the humanitarian.

How should the Indians be managed, fed, and paid, and which Spaniards should have rights to their services? Under Columbus a system of temporary allotments of labor, called a *repartimiento*, was started in which groups of Indians were assigned to a colonist for a private job or put to labor on a public project for a single set task. This policy was expanded under Bobadilla. Ovando had been instructed to consider the Indians legally free and to treat them with "kindness," but he also was faced with the necessity of finding cheap labor. The permission to enslave cannibalistic Indians and natives who "resisted Catholicism or the King," and to exact tribute and tithes from Indian villages brought deviations from the "kindness" instruction that served as an entering wedge for many abuses.

When word came to Isabella of these abuses, she ordered that Indians be congregated in villages, each under the permanent control of a "protector" or *encomendero*, a word which implied the feudal protection a lord owed his serfs. *Repartimientos* were "chain gangs" of Indians temporarily working for a colonist, separate from their land or their village. *Encomiendas* were grants of Indian workers on their own settled land, in their own villages—villages in which the Indians worked permanently for the one lord while the lord "converted, civilized and educated" them. These two systems were to figure large in Latin American history.

By 1514 there were 715 *repartimientos* in Hispaniola with perhaps 20,000 Indians bound to service. When local Indians ran away into the interior, collapsed under the unaccustomed labor, or died in the epidemics of measles and smallpox, European diseases new to them, slave raiders brought Indians from other islands, hostile Caribs at first but later peaceful Arawaks. Already during Columbus' rule, exploitation and disease started a sharp decline in the number of the island's Indians. Later on, when the mainlands were invaded, Spanish officialdom was better prepared to prevent such a decimation of the Indian population.

Church officials in the New World became concerned for the Indians. In 1511 a Dominican friar, Antonio de Montesino, who had returned from Santo Domingo persuaded Ferdinand to summon a group of theologians and learned men to suggest a remedy for the Indian problem. An effort was made in the so-called Laws of Burgos which emanated out of the ensuing discussions. Indians were declared, in the preamble of this document, to be by nature idle and given to vice. The detailed decrees went on to provide for congregating Indians into villages on or near *encomiendas;* the men who got the grants, the *encomenderos,* were to build churches, teach the rudiments of Catholicism, maintain priests, and feed the natives. The Indians in return were to work in the fields or mines. They could not engage in commerce or keep more than one wife. No one *encomendero* was to have less than 40 nor more than 150 Indians on his estate. Indians were not to be overworked or beaten, and inspectors were to be assigned to enforce good treatment. But greed and economic necessity carried out the exploitation features of the code to the exclusion of other sections. *Encomenderos* themselves were appointed inspectors for their own villages. Distance as well as lax inspection made it impossible to enforce the code's humane provisions.

Another Dominican preacher, Bartolomé de las Casas, called the "Apostle of the Indians," was better able to arouse the conscience of Spain. As a layman in Cuba he had been granted an *encomienda* and had exploited the Indians, then when he took the holy orders in 1510, he offered his services to the Dominican reformers, publicly renounced his *encomienda*, and from the pulpit preached to persuade Spanish landholders to let the Indians go in peace. After five years of effort in the Indies, he sought to lay the matter before the authorities in Spain. Granted an interview with Charles V, he made an impassioned plea in which he said that these people "with whom the New World is crowded, are quite capable of practicing the Christian faith, and likewise all the virtues and good customs." They were a people "by nature free, having their natural lords to govern them." As a result of his pleas, a commission was sent out to enforce more liberal laws and to set free "all capable Indians" under their own chiefs. Las Casas himself returned to America with the title Protector of the Indians.

He spent the rest of this life experimenting with solutions to the problem of getting the work of the Indies done without enslaving the Indians. He fought the landlords who held *encomiendas*, pleaded for the enforcement of old laws and promulgation of better ones, and he wrote a book entitled *Very Brief History of the Destruction of the Indies* in which he described in gruesome detail much of the torture and persecution he had seen. The book, widely read in England, gave rise to a somewhat exaggerated picture of Spanish cruelty which historians today call "The Black Legend." Las Casas also tried to found a Utopian colony on the mainland which failed through unfortunate circumstances. Further efforts in converting the Guatemala Indians were very successful and the state in which he worked is still called Vera Paz or "The True Peace."

If settlements were to be maintained, life in them had to be made attractive to the colonists from home. And the Indians, being weak, were exploited in mines and fields. Spain was not soulless in the matter. The moral outlook of Isabella held over into new generations. The problem vexed Spaniards sorely, bringing missionaries to the Indies, causing both crown and church to spend vast sums of money, leading Spanish scholars to study Indian languages, write grammars, prepare Indian chronicles and histories, all in the attempt to bring justice. The Spaniards, actually, were probably no more cruel to the natives than any other Europeans might have been there at the time. Church and crown meant well but accomplished little in resolving the conflict between humanitarian feelings and vested interests.

Las Casas in his pleadings for the Indians made one suggestion he was later to regret. Accustomed in Spain to the idea of the Portuguese slave trade in Negroes, he suggested that Negroes be introduced into the West Indies to do the work assigned to the unfortunate Indians. Today in the West Indies it is the descendants of African Negroes, not of Arawaks and Caribs, who make up the great mass of the population. Their story is told in Chapter 9. Thus all the problems of the Spanish empire, political, economic, and social, began on Hispaniola within the first quarter of a century.

expansion to other areas around the Caribbean

The second phase of Spanish empire development began under Don Diego's governorship with the spread of conquest and colonization using Hispaniola as a base and with each conquest followed by exploitation. Cuba, the largest island colony in the Caribbean, was to remain for the next two centuries a much greater source of wealth and a bigger center of population than Hispaniola.

Cuba was circumnavigated by Sebastian de Ocampo in 1508. In 1511, Don Diego Columbus sent Diego Velázquez, a wealthy and longtime resident of Hispaniola, to Cuba in command of settlement. Many *hidalgos* from Santo Domingo gladly followed Velázquez because Cuba provided much better land. Subjugating the island proved difficult, but a tiny settlement, called Baracoa, was established. It soon gave way to the city of Santiago, founded in 1514, as the capital of Cuba, for Santiago had a fine harbor and easy access from Santo Domingo; and it soon became the center of prosperous sugar plantations. In 1515, Velázquez also founded Havana at the Western end of the island, and within a decade settlements dotted the coast between the two cities. Inland, some mines were opened and grants of Indian workers were given out.

A few years before the settlement of Cuba, the third and fourth largest islands in the Greater Antilles, Puerto Rico and Jamaica, had been brought under Spanish sway. A protégé of Ovando's, Juan Ponce de León, who had come to Hispaniola in 1493, was given permission in 1508 to "trade with the Indians" on the nearby island of Puerto Rico. De León "pacified" the island, was made its governor, and in 1511 organized the town of San Juan—which was later to be the seat of the third bishopric in the New World. Puerto Rico continued to prosper after de León left on the voyage in which he discovered Florida.

In 1509, another *adelantado*, Juan de Esquivel, a "prudent man," conquered Jamaica, the island on which Columbus had been so long marooned. Esquivel chased the Indians into the interior and ruled quite peacefully until his death three years later. Jamaica was a thriving Spanish colony in these early years, with a yard for shipbuilding, but it was destined in a later century to be the base for English pirates and the home of English planters and traders.

From the islands, colonizing Spaniards spread to the mainland although initial endeavors came to grief. Licenses to make permanent settlements on the Isthmus and the Colombian coast were granted in 1509 to two *adelantados,* one of them the same Ojeda who had first seen Venezuela and the other to a rich Hispaniola planter named Diego de Nicuesa. Both men headed large expeditions to the pearl coast which met with starvation and disaster and with the death of the leaders. But with one had sailed an illiterate adventurer named Francisco Pizarro, and with the other a gentleman farmer escaping from his debts in Hispaniola by hiding as a stowaway in an empty provision cask, a man named Vasco Núñez de Balboa.

Balboa, then a man of thirty-five, may have been a failure in Santo Domingo but on the Isthmus he was a successful commander of men and administrator of colonies. He was elected leader by the starving survivors of the disastrous Ojeda-Nicuesa expeditions and helped find a healthy site for a town at Darién. There he made friends with the Indians who willingly brought in food. One of the chieftains told Balboa of a great body of water a few days' journey inland and passed on to him the rumors of a highly civilized people with a "silver king" far to the south along that water. Balboa decided to search for the so-called "South Sea" even though he had no legal status in the eyes of the government. He set forth across the Isthmus on foot with a small force of the men he had, including the soldier Pizarro.

On September 25, 1513, Balboa stood on a hilltop from which he could see the Pacific, and four days later he waded out into the water, and, facing south, he took possession of all lands washed by the South Sea in the name of the King of Spain.

Before Balboa returned to the now thriving colony at Darién some 60 miles back on the other side of the Isthmus, Ferdinand in Spain had appointed a legal governor for the area, a 74-year-old dynamo named Pedrarias de Ávila, who arrived in Panama with many dapper gentlemen of the court dressed in silks and brocades. He allowed Balboa to continue his plans for exploring the South Sea. New orders from Spain made Balboa *adelantade* of the "South Sea." With the help of his Indian allies, Balboa built four brigantines at new docks he constructed on the Pacific side and organized supplies to start down the coast.

Now Pedrarias and his friends from court began to fear Balboa's ambition. The jealous and wily old goveror sent for Balboa on a ruse, tried him for treason, and had him executed—some say that the executioner's sword was wielded by Pizarro, his companion in arms, who took over his private dream to find Peru. Balboa's ships were used in the exploration of the Pacific coast of Central America and his boat works were merged with Pedrarias' new town of Panama City. Balboa's name has not been remembered for his natural leadership of men, his long-range plan, his town-building, or his Indian policy but rather for the view he had from a mountain top.

Pedrarias shifted the Isthmus capital from Darién on the Caribbean to Panama City on the Pacific and a trail was begun to connect the two sides of the Isthmus. The "Men of Pedrarias," as his followers were called, explored Costa Rica and Nicaragua from these two bases and established Spanish rule. An independent adventurer, Gil González Dávila, discovered the Lake Nicaragua, so named from an Indian chief powerful in the region. Gil González had rebelled against Pedrarias, escaped to Santo Domingo, and there received a separate charter to exploit the Central American area. His men in the early 1520's were involved in open warfare with the lieutenants of Pedrarias for control of the Nicaranguan area. It was the Indians who suffered most; they were subject to every outrage and were murdered and enslaved by the thousands at Pedrarias' order. One of Pedrarias' lieutenants, the handsome young Hernando de Soto, was defeated by the adventurers in the squabble, but he was destined to play an important part in the conquest of the Incas and to die eventually on the shores of the Mississippi. But Cortés had conquered Mexico, and all these warring Spaniards in the Nicaraguan and Costa Rican area were defeated in their turn, as they advanced north into Honduras, by the agents and forces of Hernando Cortés.

The whole story of the conquest of Nicaragua, Costa Rica, and Panama is one of cruelty and jealous self-seeking. Pedrarias was removed from the governorship of Panama by royal order when news of his personal cruelty to Spaniard and Indian alike reached the young Charles V. But he proceeded to rule as governor on the new frontier of Nicaragua until he died of old age in his 91st year.

Guatemala and El Salvador were conquered by the "Men of Cortés" and the whole area was eventually ruled by Cortés' lieutenant from Guatemala City. And now, with the colonization of the Greater Antilles accomplished, a pattern for administration developed, and the Isthmus established as a part of the Spanish empire, attention turned to the invasion of the mainland of North America via Mexico.

READINGS

Anderson, C. B. G., *Life and Letters of Vasco Núñez de Balboa* (1941).

d'Anghiera, Peter Martyr, *De Orbo Novo,* trans. F. A. MacNutt (2 vols., 1912).

Bancroft, H. H., *History of Central America* (3 vols., 1883–1887).

Benson, E. F., *Ferdinand Magellan* (1930).

Bolton, H. E., and T. M. Marshall, *Colonization of North America* (1921).

Bourne, E. G., *Spain in America* (1904; new ed., 1962).

Brebner, J. B., *Explorers of North America, 1492–1806* (1933; new ed., 1955).

Chamberlain, R. S., *Conquest and Colonization of Honduras, 1502–1550* (1948).

Crone, C. R., *The Discovery of America* (1969).

Elliott, J., *Old World and the New 1492–1650* (1970).

Fernandez Guardia, R., *History of the Discovery and Conquest of Costa Rica* (1970).

Fiske, J., *Discovery of America* (2 vols., 1896).

Friede, J. and B. Keen, *Bartolomé de Las Casas—* (1971).

Gibson, C., ed., *Black Legend* (1971).

————, *Spain in America* (1966).

————, *Spanish Tradition in America* (1968).

Gonzalo, Fernández de, *Natural History of the West Indies* (1959).

Guillemand, F. H. H., *Life of Magellan* (1890).

Hanke, L., *First Social Experiments in America* (1935).

————, *Spanish Struggle for Justice in the Conquest of America* (1949).

————, *Bartolomé de Las Casas* (1952).

————, *Aristotle and the American Indian* (1959).

Haring, C. H., *Spanish Empire in America* (1952).

Helps, A., *Life of Las Casas, the Apostle of the Indies* (1896; new ed., 1970, ed. by L. Hanke).

————, *Spanish Conquest of America* (4 vols., 1900–1904).

Jane, C., *Select Documents Illustrating the Four Voyages of Columbus* (2 vols., 1930–1932).

Keen, B., ed., *Life of Admiral Christopher Columbus by His Son Ferdinand* (1959).

Kirkpatrick, F. A., *The Spanish Conquistadores* (1934).

Las Casas, B. de, *History of the Indies,* trans. A. M. Collard (1971).

Lynch, J., *Spain Under the Hapsburgs 1516–1598* (1964).

MacNutt, F. A., *Bartholomew de Las Casas* (1909).

Maltby, W. S., *The Black Legend in England 1558–1660* (1971).

Means, P. A., *The Spanish Main: Focus of Envy 1492–1700* (1935).

Merriman, R. B., *Rise of the Spanish Empire in the Old World and the New* (Vols. II–IV, 1918–1934).

Morison, S. E., *Admiral of the Ocean Sea* (1942).

————, *Journals and Other Documents on the Life and Voyages of Christopher Columbus* (1964).

————, *Caribbean as Columbus Saw It* (1964).

Moses, B., *Establishment of Spanish Rule in America* (1898).

Neasham, A., "Spain's Emigrants to the New World," *Hispanic American Historical Review,* XIX, 147–160.

Newton, A. P., *European Nations in the West Indies (1493–1688)* (1933).

Nowell, C. E., ed., *Magellan's Voyage Around the World* (1962).

————, trans. and ed., *A Letter to Ferdinand and Isabella, 1503* (1965).

O'Gorman, E., *Invention of America* (1961).

Olson, J. E., and E. G. Bourne, eds., *The Northmen, Columbus and Cabot* (1906).

Parr, C. M., *So Noble a Captain—Life and Times of Ferdinand Magellan* (1953; 2nd ed. under title of *Ferdinand Magellan,* 1964).

Pigafetta, A., *Voyage of Magellan—The Journal of Antonio Pigafetta* (1970).

Pike, R., *Enterprise and Adventure: The Genoese in Seville and the Opening of the New World* (1966).

Pohl, F. J., *Amerigo Vespucci—Pilot Major* (1944).

Richman, I. B., *The Spanish Conquerors* (1919).

Romoli, K., *Balboa of Darién, Discoverer of the Pacific* (1953).

Sauer, C. O., *The Early Spanish Main* (1966).

————, *Sixteenth Century North America. Land and People as Seen by the Europeans* (1971).

Simpson, L. B., *The Encomienda in New Spain* (1950).

————, *Laws of Burgos of 1512–1513* (1960).

Stevens, H., and F. W. Lucas, ed. and trans., *The New Laws of the Indies* (1892).

Vigneras, L. A., *Journal of Christopher Columbus* (1960).

Wagner, H. R., *The Life and Writings of Bartolomé de las Casas* (1968).

Wright, I. A., *Early History of Cuba* (1916).

Zavala, S., *New Viewpoints on the Spanish Colonization of America* (1943).

————, *Political Philosophy of the Conquest of America* (1953).

chapter *6*

THE SPANISH CONQUEST
OF NORTH AMERICA
TO 1600

the approach to Mexico

By 1519 the Isthmus had been crossed and had yielded no great riches; the coasts of North and South America were being mapped, and neither golden kingdoms nor routes through to the riches of the Far East had been found. The Caribbean itself was now an old story. The killing and dying of the natives led Spaniards on the search for slaves farther and farther away from their island bases, toward the east coast of the United States. There was a double advance during the next thirty years; one movement went directly west to the mainland of Mexico and one went northwest toward what is now the United States.

It seems ironical that in these movements away from the islands toward the mainland it took the Spaniards so long to hear of the Mayas and the Aztecs. In 1512 a ship returning from Darién to Hispaniola had been wrecked on the coast of Yucatán and eighteen survivors had reached a Mayan town. Perhaps the Mayas had heard more about the Spaniards than the whites had heard about them; at any rate, all eighteen Spaniards were immediately seized when they came in to shore, and only two of them were saved from sacrifice on the local pyramid. One of them, Gerónimo de Aguilar, a priest, spent the next eight years fretting over his fate, serving cruel taskmasters who forced him to do women's work in the houseyards, and yearning for a Spanish ship which would free him from bondage. It was to Cortés' ship, anchored off Cozumel in 1519, that he finally escaped, and his knowledge of the local languages made him of great value to Cortés' expedition. The other survivor, a seaman named Guerrero, used his skills with rope and carpentry to win the respect of the Indians; he became a petty chieftain among the decadent Mayas, and helped the towns of Yucatán fight off the Spanish conquest as late as 1540.

Other men from the colony of Darién, men whose voyages were more successful than that of the marooned priest, reported the existence of stone cities on the peninsula of Yucatán. A group of veterans of Pedrarias' first campaigns on the Isthmus had returned to Cuba and were soon hired on slave-raiding expeditions to the coasts about which they had heard rumors. Their captain was Francisco Hernández de Córdova, whose venture was partially backed by Velázquez, governor of Cuba. In 1517 Córdova's men landed at several points on the Yucatán peninsula. They were attacked by the expert bowmen of the Mayas, but not before they had traded for enough vessels and utensils of gold to whet the appetite of the Cuban governor. They were able to "limp" home to Cuba, having lost half of the men from the Darién colony. Their captain Córdova died shortly after his arrival in Cuba.

Governor Velázquez immediately dispatched another captain, his cousin Juan de Grijalba, with orders to reconnoiter for information. Grijalba's well-armed expedition made forays along the Yucatán and Tabasco coasts, entered the river now named for the commander, and proceeding cautiously according to instructions, continued to skirt the coast as far north as the Pánuco River. When Grijalba returned without making any further landing, his cousin the governor chafed at his hesitancy and planned a bigger and better-equipped expedition under a more daring and able leader. The leader he chose was Hernán Cortés.

At the time that Cortés was to begin his great adventure in Mexico, the Gulf of Mexico coast was being mapped in greater detail. Francisco de Garay, governor of Jamaica, and a rival of Velázquez, had sent Alonzo de Pineda out as his agent to explore the continental line of the Gulf in search of a strait. Pineda's work overlapped Grijalba's from the other direction; he had seen the mouth of a large river which was surely the Mississippi, and had then sailed counterclockwise to overlap Grijalba's northward exploration, thus mapping the Gulf of Mexico coast from Florida to Veracruz. Pineda's master, Garay then applied for and obtained permission to colonize Amichel, as the Texas-Tampico coast was first called; his grant and his efforts here were to run afoul of Cortés later on. In the story of the advance to Mexico, Córdova was credited as being the discoverer, Grijalba and Pineda the coastline explorers, but Hernán Cortés was the conqueror, the man who founded a really *New* Spain.

The story of Cortés and of his conquest of millions of people with a few soldiers is a romance for the ages, and has as its hero a natural leader of men. Born in Medellín, Estremadura, in 1485, Cortés had early been excited by stories of the New World. He had left his student life as a young gentleman at the University of Salamanca and had gone to Santo Domingo in 1504. Here he soon made his mark in "gallantry about town," but found no quick fortune. Unwilling to farm in Hispaniola—"I did not come to till the soil like a peasant!"—he joined an expedition for the conquest of Cuba. There his potential as an organizer attracted the attention of Velázquez. He was then thirty-three, a vigorous, resourceful man, well set up and clean-cut, by nature a born gambler ready to stake his all on a single chance, but persistent and brave, fair in his treatment of the men who served him, and capable of long-range planning.

He enthusiastically accepted the role of Grijalba's successor and was able to pay for the equipment he organized—in all, eleven vessels, 508 soldiers, and 109 seamen, as well as Cuban Indians, two Maya Indians previously captured by Córdova, sixteen horses, and several small cannon. We get to know his soldiers well, thanks to the description written afterwards by the famous chronicler and companion of Cortés, Bernal Díaz, who probably was among the original hundred men from Darién who had sailed with Córdova. Díaz, writing fifty years later, could still see the men of Cortés "before his eyes," these future *conquistadores* destined for so many individual adventures in the next two decades. Díaz particularly remembered the sixteen horses which came on the first ships—"a light bay with three white feet";—"a gray mare who was a pacer but not fast";— "a piebald horse inclining to black in the markings, with white forefeet, he turned out worthless";—"for Captain Cortés a vicious dark chestnut horse which died." How they wished there had been more horses, but they were so difficult to get in Cuba! The horses and the few small cannon were to be of great help in frightening the Indians who were unaccustomed to mounted soldiers or firearms.

Velázquez soon became suspicious and jealous of Cortés who was so successful in acquiring this retinue. When he revoked Cortés command, the dramatic Cortés lifted anchor and sailed out of Santiago in defiance while the frustrated governor bellowed with rage. This occurred on November 18, 1518. Continuing secretly to enlist men in the smaller port towns along the coast of Cuba, Cortés was able to sail from the western point of the island in February, 1519. With men and equipment organized and himself in illegal command, he left for the mainland of Mexico and his destiny.

The expedition proceeded directly to the island of Cozumel off the coast of Yucatán. Here Cortés picked up the first Spaniard enslaved by the Mayas, the priest Aguilar who was to act as interpreter among the Mayas and other coastal tribes. With Aguilar aboard, Cortés' fleet landed on the Tabasco coast, where he had a first minor skirmish with the natives, terrorizing them with his seven cannon and his sixteen horses. After their defeat by these prancing mounted "gods," the Tabascans brought Cortés presents, among them twenty girl slaves. One of these, the beautiful girl Cortés was to name Marina, then about eighteen years old, was a chieftain's daughter from the Aztec highlands who had been a slave among these Maya-speaking

Tabasco people. It was soon discovered that she spoke both the Aztec and Maya dialects; Aguilar, the marooned Spaniard, spoke Maya and Spanish. Thus Cortés, through two interpreters, spoke directly to all tribal leaders in the Aztec confederacy, and later to Montezuma. Doña Marina he took as his own mistress; he kept her with him on his way to Tenochtitlán, took her on an excursion to Honduras, and in later life granted her land, a position of respect, and legitimized her son. Through her wise counsel the expedition was saved from disaster on many occasions.

From the Tabasco coast Cortés proceeded to the harbor of San Juan de Ulúa, familiar to several men on his expedition who had accompanied Grijalba a short time before. Here Cortés founded and laid out la Villa Rica de la Vera Cruz, the first city of New Spain, on Good Friday, 1519. Immediately a *cabildo* or town council was elected; to it Cortés resigned the command bestowed upon him by Velázquez. Then the *cabildo* in turn appointed him *alcalde* and captain-general, thereby erasing the stigma of rebel (at least in Cortés' own conscience) and conferring legitimacy on the expedition in consonance with medieval Spanish practice. Thus Cortés could now consider himself independent of Velázquez and dependent directly on the crown. He persuaded his men to surrender their booty and shipped it to Spain with a long explanatory letter in support of his position. Next he secretly scuttled his ships, thus preventing desertion and giving his men the alternative of fighting to win or dying in the attempt. On the Veracruz coast Cortés heard of discontent running rampant among the many tribes subject to the Aztec Confederacy—for example, the Totonacs of Cempoalla who were anxious to free themselves from Aztec control and willing to welcome an army with which they might take common cause.

the fall of the Aztec empire

Montezuma, then "war chief" and emperor of the Aztec Federation, had heard of Córdova's and Grijalba's expeditions and he knew of Cortés' coming from afar; he feared that the Quetzalcóatl of song and story had returned in the white castles on the sea to claim his people. To placate this awe-inspiring rival, Montezuma sent messengers bearing many beautiful gifts—masks and plates of gold, silver and turquoise, cotton cloth, feather mantles—thus giving Cortés greeting and asking him to leave peaceably. The golden objects whetted the Spanish appetite; news of disloyalty and disaffection in the empire encouraged Spanish boldness. Cortés instructed the gift bearers to take back to Montezuma a picture story of the Spaniards' greeting and their determination to visit the capital at Tenochtitlán.

Cortés had now spent several months at Veracruz; fortifications were built, a church had even been constructed, and natives in the region converted. But men were dying of fever on the coast. The Cempoallans offered warriors and burden bearers by the hundreds. Leaving 150 men under Gonzalo de Sandoval to guard the Veracruz fort, in August, 1519, Cortés wound his way up through the luxuriant vegetation of the *tierra caliente* and climbed to the pine-clad slopes of the Sierra Madre, with snow-capped Orizaba gleaming on his left. Beyond Orizaba, Cortés' men fought a pitched battle with the independent nation of Tlaxcala. The natives were subdued after hard fighting and joined Cortés in an alliance against Montezuma. At Cholula, a religious capital and site of a sacred pyramid, it was learned that the natives planned to murder Cortés. Dramatically, Marina, the faithful mistress, warned Cortés in time for him to turn the tables; he massacred the nobles of Cholula, destroyed the temple on the pyramid, and founded a church in its place. Montezuma meanwhile had sent fresh envoys with more gifts and more requests to leave, but on hearing of Cortés' quick action against the Cholula conspiracy he felt that Quetzalcóatl's return was inevitable; a last brace of envoys arrived with their thousands of Indian allies and porters to guide Cortés' men to Tenochtitlán.

Now the Spaniards went in official convoy, having been proclaimed as gods. From the pass below Popocatépetl the whole valley of Anáhuac with its lakes and cities lay before them. Pine forests gave way to corn fields, to villages with orchards and gardens—then to the large lake-shore towns of Xochimilco, Ixtapalapán, and Texcoco. The four causeways led across the lakes to the fair island city of Tenochtitlán. Chieftains from all sides of the lake came to greet the Spaniards ceremoniously as they advanced down from the pass; crowds of common folk drifted about in canoes to see the white gods and their supernatural animals. At last Montezuma arrived in a sedan chair. At this dramatic meeting of the Old World and the New on November 8, 1519, Cortés and Montezuma, both handsome leaders in their middle thirties, greeted each other as equals. Their retinues joined in a single parade and went together into the city. Montezuma treated the Spaniards as his guests, and turned over a part of his own castle to them.

The Spaniards were sumptuously entertained here for a week. They felt the presence of danger all around, however, for their Indian allies were outside beyond the causeways. Cortés decided on a bold move to strengthen his position. He brought Montezuma to the Spanish quarters by forceful "persuasion" and attempted to run the government through him. Montezuma lived thus as a hostage for several months, giving all the Spanish soldiers gold and other presents, providing them with both men and women slaves, and teaching them to play the Aztec equivalent of chess. Both they and he seemed, on the surface at least, to live a gracious life of ease.

This domination of millions by a handful was rudely interrupted. Governor Velásquez back in Cuba and furious with Cortés, had sent a large expedition under Pánfilo de Narváez to arrest him. In May of 1520 Cortés was forced to make a quick journey to the coast to win this force of over 1,000 Spaniards. The wily Cortés sent men ahead with gifts of gold to tempt the men from Cuba into joining him, and easily won a brief battle against them. Most of the newcomers followed Cortés back to Tenochtitlán. When he approached the causeways, however, Cortés' luck seemed to have deserted him and his former Indian friends avoided him.

And small wonder! Inside the city, Pedro de Alvarado, the impetuous lieutenant whom Cortés had left in charge, had become alarmed at the tension he sensed at an Aztec festival and had broken up the fiesta by force. Cortés and his new followers came back to the old quarters, but the feeling in the air was one of hostility. Cortés blamed Alvarado for the difficulty, but the mischief had been done. Montezuma sulked in the Spaniards' head-quarters; Aztecs in the city brought Cortés and his band no food. Outside the palace, an Aztec prince aroused the wrath of the citizens. Montezuma himself died from wounds received from stones thrown by his own people when he appeared on the palace roof to calm them.

Then followed the sad night, *La Noche Triste,* of Mexican history, June 30, 1520. The Spaniards having decided to sneak out of the city on the shortest causeway, secretly built a portable bridge to be carried out of the palace and through the streets. Drums on the pyramid aroused the popu-lace; the Aztecs swarmed over the retreating Spaniards. The bridge helped them over the first gap in the causeway, but it stuck and could not be moved as other bridges ahead were hewn down by the Aztecs. The greedy Spanish soldiers loaded down with gold (especially the newcomers from Cuba) fell heavily into the water with their treasure. Their bodies became a bridge for others to pass over. Legend has it that Alvarado himself made a spectacular leap using his lance as a vaulting pole, and cleared the gap. For every Indian the Spaniards killed, three took his place.

In the morning Cortés sat down beyond the lake shore to weep. A cypress tree under which he is reputed to have rested that night still stands today, marked by a plaque. His most trusted lieutenants, his two inter-preters, a clever ship's carpenter, and many Tlaxcalans had been saved, as well as twenty-three cavalrymen. As for Spanish foot soldiers, of whom there had been about 1300, no accurate count was kept of losses, but a third of the force must have perished.

Fighting other Aztec armies on the way, the little Spanish band returned to Tlaxcala. However, their Indian allies now determined to reorganize and destroy the Aztecs. Here Cortés showed himself to be a master strategist. Plans for the new campaign consumed a year of his time. More Spaniards and supplies intended for Narváez' men reached him from Cuba; munitions and reinforcements also came to him direct from royal officials at Hispaniola. His rescued ship's carpenter and other craftsmen made the parts for thirteen brigantines which were carried over the pass below Popocatépetl and put together on Lake Texcoco. Meanwhile, newcomers from Cuba had brought the smallpox to Mexico, a disease to which the Indians had no immunity and which thus acted as an ally to Cortés by killing the natives by the thousands. With the brigantines, the Spaniards had command of the lake and laid siege to the city, beginning April 28, 1521. For three months the brave Aztecs in Tenochtitlán, with their fresh-water supply having been cut off, slowly starved while the young son of Montezuma's brother, Cuauhtémoc, Mexico's national Indian hero, urged them on to a spirit of resistance. The Spaniards landed from the brigantines onto the causeways and destroyed the city block by block. It is said that Cortés grieved for the destruction of the city; he had hoped to keep its beauty intact under the peaceful rule he had accomplished after seizing

Montezuma. Cuauhtémoc surrendered when the city was five-sixths destroyed. All the survivors were allowed to go to villages in the country, and
the corpse-ridden and disease-infested ruin was burned. A modern Mexican
historian, Miguel Léon Portilla, has retold the story of the Conquest from the
Aztec point of view, based on recently translated sources. His touching book
Broken Spears vividly captures the anguish caused by smallpox, the surprise
at ungrateful guests, and the woe that "regular spring dances of our youth"
were interrupted by the murderous Alvarado. It is a "must" for students of
the Spanish colonial era. So ended the Aztec Tenochtitlán. The date was
August, 1521. Martin Luther was defying papal authority for the first time
in Germany, and Magellan's ships were sailing round the world.

expansion from Tenochtitlán in all directions

The fall of Mexico-Tenochtitlán was but the prelude to an extensive and far-
flung series of conquests. The Spanish occupation spread in all directions
and was carried on by the "Men of Cortés." He sent his lieutenants out
north and south to pacify the country, while he himself devoted three years
to rebuilding the city. Indians were put to work laying out blocks after the
plan of a Spanish city, with churches, monasteries, and government buildings,
some of which are still standing today. The Spanish municipality of Mexico
City was legally organized and city officials chosen. Paganism was uprooted
as missionary fathers arrived to preach Christianity, and the Indians were
given out in *encomiendas* to individual Spaniards. Cortés was made captain-
general by order of the king in 1522.

While Cortés busied himself at constructive works, his lieutenants
Sandoval and Orozco conquered the southern part of Veracruz, set up
municipalities in the Valley of Puebla, and defeated the semicivilized
Zapotecs in the Valley of Oaxaca. North and west of Tenochtitlán, bands of
Cortés' men, chiefly under Cristóbal de Olid, conquered Michoacán and
Jalisco. Thus, much of the most thickly settled area of modern Mexico was
subdued by Spaniards while Cortés was still rebuilding the capital city. A
shipyard was even constructed at Zacatula to prepare vessels for northward
and southward expansion along the Pacific coast and to search for the
elusive strait from the west side. Cortés himself left the capital again for the
Gulf coast to crush a second group of Spanish rivals under Garay, who
claimed the mouth of the Pánuco river. Here Cortés proceeded to subdue
the Huasteca tribes and establish the town of Pánuco (modern Tampico), a
settlement which was to remain the northeast outpost of Mexico for a
number of years.

Meanwhile, Pedro de Alvarado had regained Cortés' confidence
during the long months of the siege of Tenochtitlán and had served as the
first *alcalde* or mayor in Mexico City. A handsome, swashbuckling captain
with red, curly hair, he was called "Sunlight" by the Aztecs. When the Men
of Cortés had gone out to the north and south, Cortés sent the ambitious
"Sunlight" off to distant Guatemala, from whence rumors of the highland

this expedition which discovered San Diego Bay in 1542. Cabrillo died en route but his ships, under Ferrelo, reached the present California-Oregon border. Another fleet under Ruy López de Villalobos sailed to the Philippines and made an unsuccessful attempt to oust the Portuguese from those islands legally claimed by Spain. By their very failure, these expeditions of Coronado, de Soto, Cabrillo, and Villalobos led the Spanish government to renew activity in areas closer to Mexico City and to concentrate on the economic development of agriculture and mining there.

the mines of northern Mexico

The second half of the sixteenth century (1542–1609) was to witness the occupation of parts of northern Mexico, Florida, New Mexico, and the Philippine Islands, and the further exploration of the Pacific coast. But the pace, the methods, and the reasons for this new half-century of conquest were different from those of the dashingly romantic first half. After 1550, the Spaniards, their first bloom of excitement over, were interested in developing silver mines, in raising cattle and planting crops to feed the new cities they had already founded, and in doing missionary work among primitive tribes. They also began to worry about foreign competition from other Europeans—the French and the English; they had to protect the treasure fleets and to advance their farthest outposts against encroachments. Thus the expansion of this new period was less aggressive, and a little more defensive.

Since almost every advance was begun with the idea of establishing permanent towns and settled agricultural or mineral development, the conquests were undertaken as an investment by men of means, great captains or *adelantados*. They came from settled New World communities where many docile Indians were already at work, and they used these Indians, the Tarascans or the Tlaxcalans, as settlers, farmers and miners, to countercolonize, and to guard the frontier against the wilder tribes of the north.

The first such *adelantado* was an arch enemy of Cortés, Nuño de Guzmán, "a natural gangster," who had governed in Pánuco, and who headed the first *audiencia* or "court" staff to discipline and control the Men of Cortés. He soon needed much more control himself. As governor along the Pánuco River he had amassed a fortune by shipping slaves to the Caribbean islands. *Persona non grata* in Mexico City because of these activities, he was nevertheless a friend of Velázquez and of the slave buyers in Cuba and, perhaps through them, was not punished for his Pánuco activities. Instead, he was soon carving out a private empire for himself in a region he was to call New Galicia. Cortés' lieutenants had conquered the Tarascans in Michoacán; much of the land south of the Río Santiago in the present states of Jalisco and Nayarit had already been granted as *encomiendas*. Now in 1529 came Guzmán, with a royal sanction as governor, to spend the next seven years exploring Nayarit and Sinaloa, granting *encomiendas* to himself and his friends, selling Indians into slavery, and destroying their villages. But he established the Spanish tradition of correctly founded Spanish towns, and set up Compostela and Culiacán on the two edges, north and south, of his "empire." Here were *cabildos*, the municipal councils which gave the faint color of legality to Guzmán's action. For lack of docile Indian labor and a ready market for their products, the *encomenderos* of New Galicia made no profits. Soon Guzmán was called before the reform government in Mexico City, to be imprisoned there by the new viceroy, Antonio de Mendoza. Francisco de Coronado was made governor in his place to establish firmer royal control over the frontier province, before he departed for Gran Quivira.

While Coronado was gone to the north an uprising occurred in New Galicia called the Mixton War. The natives, long abused and terrified by the Guzmán regime, took advantage of the new governor's absence in 1540 and carefully planned a full-scale war. Alvarado met his death ignominiously when a horse fell on him as he fled from an Indian ambush. Finally, the viceroy himself arrived in the midst of the Mixton carnage and crushed the revolt by force of numbers and the weapons of the fresh royal troops. By 1548 the area was organized as the province of New Galicia, with an *audiencia*, a bishop, and a cathedral at Guadalajara in 1550. It was sub-divided into districts under governors, and the Indians were organized under local *alcaldes* subject to *encomenderos*. The smallpox, which had helped Cortés devastate the area around Mexico City two decades earlier, came with the troops to New Galicia during the Mixton War; the Indians who survived it were forced into heavy work in field and mine which brought new prosperity to the region.

This was the prosperity of a "silver rush." In 1542 silver had been discovered in Michoacán, but that discovery was soon eclipsed in 1546 by the great silver strike made near today's Zacatecas by Juan de Tolosa, a captain sent out to subdue pockets of rebellious Indians left unconquered after the Mixton War. Putting the Indians to work mining for him, Tolosa had several mule loads of ore on the way to Mexico City in a few weeks. Soon he was joined by three other veteran commanders of the Mixton War, Cristóbal de Oñate, Diego de Ibarra, and Baltazar Termiño de Bañuelos, men who had money enough from previous adventures to exploit the mines, establish mining camps, contract for laborers, hire muleteers for transport-ing the ore, and support all these people until the silver profits began to flow back. The four of them became the richest men in Mexico; their fabulous fortunes were to be used in making explorations and opening mines farther to the north, in establishing packroutes back to the larger towns, and in building up the frontier provinces. Guadalajara, and the *encomiendas* in Jalisco which had failed under Guzmán, now had a new reason for exis-tence. The region lay on the silver route; Guadalajara was the new distribut-ing center for goods for the silver rush, a market for food, a center of farming and cattle raising. The cattle prospered on the fields of Jalisco, but the Indians did not. Cattle trampled the corn fields and destroyed the native agriculture. The Indians also lost their hold to the stockmen and were driven as slaves to the mines.

Under the new viceroy, Luis de Velasco, systematic exploration beyond the frontiers took place in the 1560s with the idea of establishing permanent Spanish and Indian towns for defense against the still unsubdued Chichimecas who were raiding the last line of settlement. Especially important here was the work of Francisco de Ibarra, nephew of one of the four developers of the silver boom. From New Galicia and Zacatecas he went farther north and, using his uncle's fortune to fit out mule drivers, soldiers, and Indian colonists, he worked for two decades carving out a future province called New Vizcaya, chiefly in the present states of Zacatecas, Durango, and Sinaloa. A provincial government was organized on the same plan as all Spanish government in the new territories. Francisco de Ibarra himself was named governor in 1562; the town of Durango was founded in the next year and for many years remained the military capital of all the northern country, including the settlements in southern Chihuahua.

Mines were found in this new area, but native Indians were few. Who was to be forced to work in the mines? The frontier community of Santa Bárbara, where silver deposits were found in 1563, was on the River Conchos, which drained into the Rio Grande. Down the canyons and valleys of the Conchos and across the Rio Grande went the slave raiders to capture the primitive Tejas Indians among whom de Vaca had served as a slave. Thus did the Spanish frontier reach into Texas in the time of the *adelantado* Ibarra. Interested in looking for new river valleys and harbors as well as for villages to be conquered, Ibarra explored Sinaloa, ascended the Pacific slope from Culiacán up the river valleys and across into Chihuahua. When Ibarra died in 1570 he had over twenty years of exploring, mining, colonizing, and efficient administration to his credit. Cattle were brought into his Durango region, and they remain today the chief source of wealth. San Luis Potosí, today one of the world's most productive silver mines, had been developed in 1576, and Tlaxcalan colonists were brought in to hold the frontier. By then the mines were being extended northeast of New Vizcaya and Durango by a father-and-son team, both named Francisco de Urdiñola.

On the Gulf coast, in today's state of Tamaulipas,[1] another province called New León was created in 1579, the area north and west from Pánuco and delimiting New Galicia and New Vizcaya. Its founder was Luis de Carabajal whose money-making slave raids to supply labor to the mines were stopped by the Inquisition, which condemned him as a heretic. In 1596 the lieutenant governor of New León, Montemayor, founded the city of Monterrey, which after 1600 became the center of Franciscan missionary activity. Today it is one of Mexico's chief industrial centers. Thus by the end of the century the frontier of settlement of Mexico was roughly a line drawn some hundred miles below the mouth of the Rio Grande on the Gulf of Mexico, and just north of Monterrey across Mexico to a point high up in

[1] See the map showing states of modern Mexico, p. 331.

Sinaloa on the Gulf of California. However firm that line might have been, several areas beyond it had been explored and occupied during the same half-century. Northern Mexico, with its mines, its forts, its cattle ranches, and its missions, was to be a base for Spanish expansion north of the Rio Grande.

Spanish exploration and occupation in the present United States

In the American Southwest—Texas, New Mexico, Arizona, and California, and to a lesser extent in Florida—Spanish colonial history is an important part of regional heritage. Of little importance in the development of modern Latin America, these regions deserve some attention as farthest points of the Spanish frontier, and as areas where Spain was forced on the defensive against the encroachments of other powers. Rumors that Francis Drake had found the Northwest Passage in 1579 stimulated a renewed interest in the regions to the north, which had been called "the very worst country that is warmed by the sun," in Coronado's own reports. Indians captured on slave raids north of the Rio Grande reported again on the towns of the Pueblos. Working on the idea that these people should be Christianized and a frontier set for Spain farther north nearer the "strait," explorations were made into the area in 1580–1582 and in the early 1590s. Meanwhile, rich ores had been reported on a foray into Arizona. Don Juan de Oñate, wealthy relative of two of the Big Four, was made *adelantado* for the northern region in 1595, and in 1598 went at his own expense on an extensive exploration which expanded to the area of the Arkansas River on the east and the Gulf of California on the west. Oñate, who had with him 130 soldiers and their families and 7000 cattle and horses, made a temporary settlement. He fought and subdued the pueblo of Ácoma, but could make no money from the investment, so gave up his governorship and returned to the Zacatecas mines and from there to Spain.

The Crown then assumed control of the colony, considering the risk worth the time and effort. Under direct royal authority Governor Pedro de Peralta settled the city of Santa Fe in 1609, a town which remains one of the symbols of Spanish influence in the Southwest. Its establishment a hundred years after Ojeda and Nicuesa received a grant to search for pearls on the Isthmus, marks the end of a colorful century of discovery, conquest, and occupation in North America.

There had also been a renewal of activity on the Atlantic coast. Spanish attempts to colonize Florida had not ended with de Soto. That fourth effort at Florida settlement had been followed by a fifth in 1549 under Fray Luís Cáncer, and a sixth in 1559–1561 under Tristán de Luna and Villafañe. This last failure was enough for King Philip II, who no longer considered Florida worthwhile.

The need for bases remained, however. The fleets of Spanish

treasure ships had to have refuge from hurricanes and pirates. So, when French Protestants under Jean Ribault and René de Laudonnière successfully settled 300 colonists on the northern Florida coast in 1562–1564, Philip changed his mind. He sent an able organizer, Pedro Menéndez de Avilés, to found St. Augustine within a hundred miles of the French fort; it was the first permanent settlement in today's United States. His men massacred the French settlers; a French captain in turn massacred a Spanish coastal garrison, but Menéndez de Avilés held firm in his hold on the coast for Spain. From his successful colony further exploration was carried on inland to the interior of Georgia and along the coast as far as Chesapeake Bay. Jesuits and Franciscans founded missions, and the little settlement became a buffer against both English and French in the Bahama Channel shipping lanes when Spain began to lose her monopoly on the Atlantic coast after 1600.

On the Pacific slope and in the Far West, Spain was also forced to action by the activities of other European nations. Portuguese merchants were successfully trading and exploring in the Orient via their round-Africa route, and the Spaniards had no choice at first but to leave it to them, for although they had worked out a route from Acapulco across the Pacific, they could not find a way to return with the wind. The only way home led around Africa, Portugal's own private route. Finally in 1564, Miguel López de Legazpi was sent to lay an effective claim to the Philippines, first seen by Magellan, and to work out a route back. His chief navigator, Fray Andrés de Urdañeta, found such a route via the northern Pacific. Now the Philippines were within reach going and coming by an all-Spanish route; Manila was founded and Spanish rule established in the islands. An *audiencia* was established at Manila in 1583 and attached to the viceroyalty of New Spain. A single ship, the famous Manila Galleon of the colonial trade fairs, went every year to the islands and came back loaded with the luxuries of the China and Philippine trade.

Because of the northern return route of the Manila Galleon, the California coast came into importance again in Spanish eyes. Sailors needed fresh supplies to ward off scurvy; pearl fisheries might be found; foreign intruders could be scared away if Spain developed California. Hence captains of the Galleon were instructed to search for suitable harbors as way stations along the coast. When none were found, it was decided to send explorers directly from Mexico. In 1596 a special expedition under Sebastián Vizcaíno established the colony of La Paz in lower California. Vizcaíno was also commissioned by the king to explore the upper coast, which he did in 1602, naming various points and recommending Monterey Bay as an important site for a colony. With the death of Philip II in 1598, an era had ended; the project was forgotten, and nothing was done for another century and a half about the stopping points for ships on the return trip to Mexico from the Far East.

This exploration of the California coast marked the farthest northward advance of Spanish rule in the sixteenth century. Thus passed the heroic age of Spanish colonization in North America, an age of fantastic accomplishment.

READINGS

Aiton, A. S., *Antonio de Mendoza: First Viceroy of New Spain* (1927).

Ballentine, D. K., *Ally of Cortés by Fernando de Alva Ixtilxochótl* (1969).

Bannon, J. F., *The Spanish Borderland's Frontier 1521–1821* (1970).

————, *The Spanish Conquistadores* (1960).

Barrett, W., *The Sugar Hacienda of the Marqueses' del Valle* (1970).

Bennett, C. E., *Laudonnière and Fort Caroline: History and Documents* (1964).

Bishop, M., *The Odyssey of Cabeza de Vaca* (1933).

Bolton, H. E., *Coronado on the Turquoise Trail: Knight of Pueblos and Plains* (1949).

————, *Spanish Borderlands* (1921).

————, *Spanish Explorations in the Southwest, 1542–1706* (1916).

Borah, W., *Early Colonial Trade and Navigation Between Mexico and Peru* (1954).

————, *Silk Industry* (1943).

————, *New Spain's Century of Depression* (1951).

Bourne, E. G., *Spain in America*, ed. B. Keen (1962).

Braden, C. S., *Religious Aspects of the Conquest of Mexico* (1930).

Brebner, J. B., *Explorers of North America, 1492–1806* (1933).

Cervantes de Salazar, F., *Life in the Imperial and Loyal City of Mexico in New Spain* (1970).

Cerwin, H., *Bernal Díaz: Historian of the Conquest* (1963).

Chamberlain, R. S., *Conquest and Colonization of Honduras, 1502–1550* (1953).

————, *Conquest and Colonization of Yucatan, 1517–1550* (1948).

Chávez, A., *Coronado's Friars* (1968).

Chipman, D. E., *Nuño de Guzmán and the Province of Pánuco in New Spain, 1518–1533* (1967).

Chudoba, B., *Spain and the Empire 1519–1643* (1969).

Clissold, S., *Seven Cities of Cíbola* (1962).

Collis, M., *Cortés and Montezuma* (1963; 1968).

Connor, J. T., *Pedro Menéndez de Avilés* (1923).

Craine, E. R., and R. C. Reindorp, *Chronicles of Michoacán* (1970).

Day, A. G., *Coronado's Quest* (1940).

Descola, J., *The Conquistadors* (1957).

Díaz del Castillo, B., *True History of the Conquest of New Spain* (many editions).

Fuentes, P. de, *The Conquistadors: First Person Accounts of the Conquest of Mexico* (1963).

Garcilaso de la Vega, El Inca. *The Florida of the Inca*, ed. and trans. J. G. and J. J. Varner (1951).

Gardner, C. H., *The Constant Captain: Gonzalo de Sandoval* (1961).

————, *Naval Power in the Conquest of Mexico* (1956).

Gerhard, P., *A Guide to the Historical Geography of New Spain* (1972).

Gibson, C., *Spain in America* (1966).

————, *Tlaxcala in the Sixteenth Century* (1952).

Guardia, R. F., *History of the Discovery and Conquest of Costa Rica,* trans. H. W. Van Dyke (1913).

Hallenbeck, C., *Álvar Núñez Cabeza de Vaca: The Journey and Route of the First Europeans to Cross the Continent of North America, 1534–1536* (1934).

Hammond, G. P., and A. Rey, eds., *Narratives of the Coronado Expedition, 1540–1542* (2 vols., 1940).

————, *Oñate: Colonizer of New Mexico* (2 vols., 1953).

Hanke, L., *Bartolomé de Las Casas* (1952).

Hodge, F. W., and T. H. Lewis, *Spanish Explorers in the Southern United States, 1528–1543* (1907).

Horgan, P., *Conquistadors in North American History* (1963).

Kelly, J. E., *Pedro de Alvarado, Conquistador* (1932).

Kinigan, A., trans., *Barcías Chronological History of the Continent of Florida* (1951).

León-Portilla, M., ed., *Broken Spears: The Aztec Account of the Conquest of Mexico* (1961).

Liebman, S., *The Enlightenment* (1968).

————, *Jews of New Spain* (1970).

López de Gómara, F., *Cortés; The Life of the Conqueror by His Secretary,* trans. and ed. L. B. Simpson (1964).

Lowery, W., *Spanish Settlements Within Present Limits of the United States* (2 vols., 1911).

Lynch, J., *Spain Under the Hapsburgs, 1516–1598* (1964).

MacNutt, F. A., *Fernando Cortes and the Conquest of Mexico* (1908).

————, *Letters of Cortes to Charles V* (2 vols., 1908).

Madariaga, S., *Hernan Cortés* (1941).

Maynard, T., *De Soto and the Conquistadores* (1930).

Mecham, J. L., *Francisco de Ibarra and Nueva Vizcaya* (1927).

Menucy, A., *Florida's Menéndez, Captain General of the Ocean Sea* (1965).

Merriman, R. B., *Rise of Spanish Empire,* Vols. III and IV (1934).

Padden, H. C., *The Humming Bird and the Hawk, Conquest and Sovereignty in the Valley of Mexico, 1503–1541* (1967; 1970).

Parry, J. H., *The Audiencia of New Galicia in the Sixteenth Century* (1948).

————, *The Seaborne Spanish Empire* (1966).

Powell, P. W., *Soldiers, Indians and Silver: The Northward Advance of New Spain, 1550–1600* (1952).

Prescott, W. H., *History of the Conquest of Mexico* (many editions).

Priestley, H. I., *Coming of the White Man; 1492–1848* (1929).

————, *Tristán de Luna* (2 vols., 1936).

Ribaut, J., *The Whole and True Discoverye of Terra Florida, 1563,* ed. D.L. Dowd (1964).

Ricard, R., *The Spiritual Conquest of Mexico—1532–1572* (1966).

Richman, I. B., *Spanish Conquerors* (1919).

Riley, G. M., *Fernando Cortés and the Manquesado in Morelos, 1522–1547* (1972).

Sauer, C. O., *Colima of New Spain in the Sixteenth Century* (1948).

————, *The Early Spanish Main* (1966).

————, *Road to Cíbola* (1932).

————, *Sixteenth Century North America. Land and People as Seen by the Europeans* (1971).

Simpson, L. B., *Exploitation of Land in Central Mexico in the Sixteenth Century* (1952).

Taylor, M., *Impetuous Alvarado* (1936).

Taylor, W. B., *Landlord and Peasant in Colonial Oaxaca* (1971).

Verrill, A. H., *Conquerors of South and Central America* (1943).

Wagner, H. R., ed., *Discovery of New Spain in 1518 by Juan de Grijalva* (1942).

————, *Rise of Fernando Cortés* (1944).

————, *Spanish Voyages to the Northwest Coast of America in the Sixteenth Century* (1929).

West, R. C., *Mining Community of North New Spain: The Parral Mining District* (1949).

White, J. M., *Cortés and the Downfall of the Aztec Empire: A Study in a Conflict of Cultures* (1971).

Wright, J. L., *Anglo-Spanish Rivalry in North America* (1971).

chapter 7

THE SPANISH CONQUEST
OF SOUTH AMERICA
TO 1600

the Pizarros in the land of the Incas

An Indian chieftain watching Balboa in 1511 as the Spanish captain weighed golden objects taken from his Panamanian Chibcha tribe, is supposed to have struck the scales and cried, "If this is what you prize so much that you are willing to leave your distant homes, and risk even life itself for it, I can tell you of a land where they eat and drink out of golden vessels, and gold is as cheap as iron is with you." Balboa heard other stories of Birú, or Peru, lands to the south where the fabulous Incas lived. On the Pacific coast another Indian is said to have stooped on the beach and modeled for Balboa in the wet sand a representation of a llama, as he tried to tell Balboa's men of the glamorous lands where such animals were as tame as their own horses. With Balboa at his first sight of the Pacific in 1513 was a soldier named Francisco Pizarro who was eventually to find such lands and see such animals. Stories of the riches of the Incas had already reached the Europeans from various other directions when Pascual de Andagoya sailed south along the west coast of Colombia in 1522 and reached a region called Birú. He brought back alluring stories of riches to the south, riches which he himself could not reach as a result of an incapacitating illness. Pizarro was still on the Isthmus restlessly looking for some way to travel south.

Francisco Pizarro, poor, proud, cruel, and adventurous, was actually an illiterate swineherd of Estremadura. Illegitimate son of a minor aristocrat, he spent his youth in the poorest peasant surroundings. When through the influence of his father he was able to sail to America, he had nothing save his "cloak and sword." He had come to Darién with Ojeda in 1509, a bold, resourceful, persistent man of unusual physical strength, already nearing forty. In Panama, granted an *encomienda* for his loyalty to Pedrarias, he had amassed some wealth, so life in the New World had not passed him by. But he was obsessed with Balboa's old dream of conquering the land of the Incas, and so formed a three-way partnership with two other men of Pedrarias. Diego de Almagro, second of the partnership, was, like Pizarro, a soldier of fortune of questionable birth. He had been a servant at the court of Spain, and, coming under a cloud when he stabbed a man, had left quickly for America; but he was more generous and frank than Pizarro.

The third partner was the vicar of Panama, a priest named Hernando de Luque; their business partnership was so formal and official that even Pedrarias owned a share. In 1524 each of the active partners, Pizarro and Almagro, took a ship south along the Colombian coast, returning with gold enough to interest their backers in a more elaborate expedition of 160 men. On this second trip one of their pilots made a contact with Túmbez, a prosperous port town in northern Peru, and both partners landed in rich villages of the Ecuadorean coast. Here they had such brisk opposition from the Indians—which cost Almagro an eye—that the partners decided they needed a larger force. Almagro returned to Panama for help, while Pizarro and a few loyal men stayed on tiny Gallo Island off the Ecuadorean coast till his partner should return. The next ship they saw was a vessel from Panama sent by the new legal governor there to force them to give up the whole plan. Dramatically, Pizarro appealed to his men to stay with him— "As for me, I go south!" Thirteen men stayed, half-starving on the island, till another ship came months later. This time, Pizarro and his men went as far as Túmbez, received gold vessels and vicuña wool in trade, and took a young Indian, Felipillo, to be trained as intepreter. They knew, however, that the governor was now hostile to them; any further help must come directly from Spain. Pizarro himself set out for the homeland.

It was the summer of 1529 when Pizarro appeared in the Spanish court. On July 26, Charles V gave Pizarro his written instructions for a larger expedition. In this document, both Almagro and Pizarro were given titles as legitimate gentlemen; even the thirteen who had stuck with Pizarro on Gallo Island were all made knights. Almagro was to be commander of Túmbez; their partner the vicar was to go there as bishop. Pizarro himself, being the only one on the spot at court, was granted 200 leagues of territory south of the Gulf of Guayaquil, and was made governor, captain-general, and *adelantado* for life. He had to recruit his own forces, however—a difficult task since everyone was more interested in going to Mexico. So Pizarro traveled to his old home in Estremadura, enlisted his two full brothers, Gonzalo and Juan, his father's one legitimate son, Hernando Pizarro, and Martín de Alcántara, a half-brother on his mother's side. These infamous and avaricious brothers were to bring destruction to the Incas and internecine strife to the Spaniards in Peru. Though they all survived many battles, each died by violence or imprisonment. With them also went a young nephew, Pedro Pizarro, as page; he alone was to leave a good record, and became a famous chronicler of the conquest.

Back in Panama Pizarro picked up more recruits, including Hernando de Soto who brought two ships from Nicaragua. In January, 1531, with 180 men and twenty-seven horses, Pizarro set sail from Panama—with Almagro to follow as usual—and came again to Túmbez. After destroying that town, and founding another Spanish municipality named San Miguel on the coast, he decided not to wait for Almagro and reinforcements but to march directly east over the Andes into the central valleys at Cajamarca, where the Inca ruler was holding court.

Like Cortés, Pizarro came to his new kingdom at an opportune time. The old Inca ruler Huayna Cápac had died about 1527, leaving his successors quarreling—Huáscar, the legal heir, and Atahualpa, son of a Quito-born concubine. When the Spaniards arrived, Atahualpa had just won this civil war and was consolidating his empire by setting up a capital at Cajamarca halfway between Cuzco and Quito. De Soto, now with the Pizarro brothers, had been in touch with the envoys of Atahualpa and reported this situation to Pizarro. To Cajamarca, then, came Pizarro, in November, 1532, after a difficult climb of forty-five days, with 102 infantrymen and sixty-two horses. Unlike Montezuma, Atahualpa heard with scorn of the coming of these interlopers, these destroyers of Túmbez; the llama-using Incas lacked the Aztecs' superstitious fear of horses. When Pizarro arrived in Cajamarca, Atahualpa, who had an army of 40,000 near at hand, came in from a bathing spa at the hot springs outside his city leading a large retinue, and deigned to meet the Spaniards in the square. Pizarro's chaplain, Fray Vicente de Valverde, made a long speech through Felipillo the interpreter, telling Atahualpa that Charles V was the only true king, and the Christian God the only true God. When Atahualpa asked by what authority the Christian God stood over his god, the Sun, he was shown a testament. It was a book with clasps; Atahualpa struggled to open it, looked at the strange black lines on the white paper, and scornfully cast it down. The Spaniards needed only this excuse of sacrilege to rush in, fire their cannons into the Indian crowd, and take Atahualpa captive in the midst of a general slaughter of his followers.

Atahualpa, handsome and grave of countenance with fierce flashing eyes, was in the prime of life, perhaps about thirty-five years of age. Held in captivity while the Spaniards lived in Cajamarca, he was treated much as the hostage Montezuma had been treated by Cortés. His servants and his wives waited on him; he learned to play chess with de Soto; and he was exposed to the doctrine of Christianity, expounded to him by Valverde. But Atahualpa was of a more determined character than Montezuma. He offered the treasure-hungry Spaniards gold enough to cover the floor of his quarters. When the Spaniards seemed scornful, he offered to fill the room up to a nine-foot height as a price for his release—a "king's ransom." Two smaller rooms were to be filled with silver. Pizarro hypocritically agreed, if it were to be done in two months.

Immediately runners went out with *quipu* messages to all points of the empire. Soon the treasure began to pour in; porters carried loads of vases and temple vessels, even thrones. It has been estimated that the ransom amounted to about 13,265 pounds of gold and 26,000 pounds of silver. Spaniards who went out to get more were carried on Indian litters all the way to Cuzco, where they were hospitably received as emissaries of Atahualpa's new masters. Hernando Pizarro went to the ancient city of Pachacamac and there received the same treatment; the mass of Incas were willing to accept the new rulers without a murmur. At this juncture Almagro and his men arrived from Panama.

It was not in the scheme of things to release Atahualpa, however. The Spaniards had to find some excuse to be rid of him. The half-brother Huáscar, held prisoner by Atahualpa, had offered the Spaniards even higher ransom money for his own release, but Atahualpa had secretly ordered him murdered in prison. Now the Spaniards could accuse Atahualpa of murder, ransom or not. He was condemned to be burned at the stake for this crime. When he was told that if he accepted Christianity he would only be strangled, not burned, he became "converted." He submitted stoically, was garroted in the plaza of Cajamarca, and was given a Christian burial on August 29, 1533.

The Pizarros now planned to march on Cuzco, take over the whole empire, and found a large Spanish capital on some good harbor to the south. The ransom gold was melted down and divided, one-fifth being sent to the king via that gentlemanly and only educated Pizarro brother, Hernando. The rest of the loot was given to the soldiers under the eagle eye of "fair-play" de Soto. Here commenced the greatest difficulty Pizarro was to have in Peru—not battle with the Indians, but quarrels among the Spaniards. Almagro's men received a much smaller share than Pizarro's men, because they had reached Cajamarca three months after the seizure of Atahualpa, and Pizarro's men could claim to have suffered the greater peril and hardship. As soon as the treasure was distributed, gambling began for large stakes; fortunes were won and lost, and discipline broke down. Pizarro realized that action was necessary, and set out on a long march to Cuzco. Beautiful Cuzco, city of the children of the Sun, offered no resistance and was systematically looted. Then the ever legal-minded Spaniards set up a Spanish municipality there in March, 1534; two *alcaldes* and a town council of eight members were appointed from their group. Soldiers received houses in town and large tracts of agricultural land with many Indians in *encomienda*. A younger brother of Huáscar, Manco Cápac, was set up as a puppet to maintain the pretence of Inca authority.

Two years had passed since the subjection of Túmbez. Almagro, temporarily pacified by gold looted at Cuzco, set off to Quito, a city already conquered by a lieutenant named Benalcázar and organized into a Spanish municipality. Both these Spaniards were hurrying to ward off the rumored coming of Alvarado, the conqueror of Guatemala, who was cruising with his fleet down the coast. Gonzalo and Juan Pizarro ruled Cuzco; Francisco went to seek a site for a new capital on the coast. The valley of Rimac near the harbor of Callao seemed the ideal place; there the capital was founded in 1535. The Indian word Rímac was corrupted to Lima, and Pizarro began the construction of a fine Spanish city. Here Pizarro was an efficient administrator for a time; colonists came and other cities were founded soon at Guayaquil and Trujillo. Alvarado himself, "welcomed" at Quito, was bought off for 100,000 pesos of gold, and after a pleasant visit with Pizarro, went happily back to Guatemala and died in northern Mexico, although hundreds of men who came with him stayed in Peru.

Peru—through chaos to rich colony

Although the conquest of Peru now seemed complete except for consolidation, the situation was to degenerate into civil war between factions of Spaniards. As knowledge of new riches spread like wildfire and adventurers of all descriptions came to Peru, they soon divided into two factions as a result of the Almagro-Pizarro jealousy. Hernando Pizarro had taken the king's share of Atahualpa's ransom to Spain and had returned with a royal order for the division of the new territory. Territories, "in the north for an extent of 270 leagues," were granted to Pizarro; lands 200 leagues to the south of Pizarro's grant were given to Almagro. The bishop of Panama was expected to come to Peru and set the dividing line, a trip which he never found time to make. Naturally, a dispute arose as to who should own the former Inca capital of Cuzco. The inevitable bloodshed was temporarily averted when the men of Pizarro were able to persuade Almagro that more riches lay in the unexplored south. Hernando Pizarro assumed control of Cuzco; Francisco went down to the coast to develop his new capital at Lima.

The *Almagristas*, the men of Almagro, now spent all their gold in preparing for a journey to unknown Chile. Spaniards numbering 550, thousands of Indian porters, and flocks of llamas set out over the Bolivian highlands and through the mountainous deserts of northern Chile. When Almagro finally entered the fertile valley of central Chile, he found only poverty-stricken, hostile Indians living in adobe villages. The bankrupt *Almagristas* returned to Peru more embittered at the Pizarros than ever and determined to take Cuzco for their own.

While Almagro was gone and Francisco Pizarro was busy in Lima, the Inca puppet Manco Cápac revolted and led a great army of Inca villagers in a siege of the Spaniards inside Cuzco. Other Indians harassed the new coastal cities till the return of the men of Almagro ended the many months of rebellion. Manco Cápac, hopeful that the two groups of Spaniards would destroy each other, withdrew his remaining forces and went into retirement in an Inca stronghold hidden away in the mountains; here he held court and harassed the Spaniards by forays until his death. His descendants considered themselves ruling Incas, albeit only over a few poor villages.

Manco's hope that the Spaniards would quarrel to the death among themselves almost became reality. Almagro had returned from Chile and taken over Cuzco after defeating Pizarro's troops. This meant open civil war, for Francisco Pizarro was not one to give in easily. The inevitable decisive battle took place at Las Salinas, a salt plain outside Cuzco, on April 6, 1538. Six hundred *Almagristas* fought eight hundred *Pizarristas,* while bemused Indians looked on from the hills. Two hundred Spaniards were killed and Almagro himself was taken to prison where Hernando Pizarro decided to execute him. Almagro, now a decrepit seventy-five-year-old man with no fortune to show for his years of campaigning, pleaded with Hernando, "I was the first ladder by which you and your brother mounted up." Hernando was deaf to these pleas and had him strangled in prison.

The Pizarro brothers were now in complete control. Juan had been killed in Manco Cápac's rebellion, but the other three fared well. Gonzalo went beyond Lake Titicaca to found the colony of Charcas, mother of today's Bolivia, where, at Potosí, a silver strike far richer than that of northern Mexico was to be made before the end of the century. Gonzalo granted himself a rich *encomienda* among the Aymarás, and arranged for the founding of Chuquisaca, today's Sucre, in 1539. Francisco went on to found Arequipa and to organize his own *encomienda* with 100,000 Indians northeast of Lima. Pedro de Valdivia, a faithful Pizarro supporter, was sent to Chile to make a permanent settlement. Gonzalo was appointed governor of Quito, where he had further fantastic adventures. Hernando meanwhile had gone to Spain but the king, who had already heard stories of the death of Almagro, threw him into prison. He laid in jail for twenty-two years, released eventually, to succumb to old age in his hundredth year, the only Pizarro to die a natural death.

Both Francisco and Gonzalo died by violence in the continued quarrels in Peru. A young *mestizo* son of Almagro, an eighteen-year-old called Almagro the Lad, rallied the remaining *Almagristas* and assassinated both Francisco and his half-brother Martín de Alcántara in their own house on June 25, 1541. When news of this continued feud reached the king he sent an experienced lawyer, Vaca de Castro, to restore order in Peru. His first problem was to destroy the forces of Almagro the Lad in a pitched battle in September, 1542, and to have this last of the *Almagristas* executed. This left Gonzalo, now backed by a large private army. To deal with him, Vaca de Castro, was replaced by an official viceroy, the aristocrat Blasco Núñez Vela, who with a group of judges to comprise an *audiencia* was ordered to end the rule of the Pizarro faction and to bring legal Spanish government to the chaotic new colony.

In the same year, 1542, the government in Spain had become increasingly concerned with the conditions of the Indians in all the New World colonies, and promulgated a list of regulations to end hereditary *encomiendas* and to limit many abuses of forced labor among the Indians. These were known as the New Laws, and Núñez Vela came ready to enforce them in tumultuous Peru. But the *conquistadores,* who had gambled away most of the Inca gold, now owned thousands of acres of fertile lands worked by hundreds of thousands of Indian serfs. They bitterly opposed the New Laws and rallied behind Gonzalo to defy the viceroy.

Gonzalo Pizarro, popular man of the hour to all factions except those newcomers on the viceroy's side, took Cuzco, imprisoned the viceroy, and then made himself dictator of Lima. A few loyal Spaniards came to the viceroy's aid, helping him to escape and to collect a small army near Quito, where he was met and defeated by Gonzalo. Acting with kingly power, Gonzalo had the viceroy beheaded. This last of the Pizarros was now definitely an outlaw who had committed treason although the whole colony including the settlements in Panama lived for two years under his unchallenged power. This time the king sent a scholarly priest, Pedro de la Gasca, to bring Gonzalo to heel. Under his blandishments Gonzalo's henchmen in the Isthmus "deserted" back to the king, as did the captains and sailors on the private "fleet" Gonzalo had been using to patrol the coast. By the time La Gasca landed at Túmbez with a large loyal force in June of 1547, Gonzalo realized the game was up. Retreating in a cat-and-mouse play with this new royal agent, Gonzalo was finally forced to surrender near Cuzco on April 9, 1548, while his men deserted to La Gasca by the hundreds. Gonzalo was unceremoniously beheaded. Thus came the final doom of the Pizarro brothers sixteen years after the death of Atahualpa. The "Age of the *Conquistadores*" in Peru was ended.

Pedro de la Gasca now turned his strong hand to reform in the face of seething discontent; he worked busily at balancing finances and founding new towns, including La Paz in Bolivia. He was clever in rewarding those of Gonzalo's friends who had switched to his side and was purposely lax in enforcing the New Laws against hereditary *encomiendas*. When La Gasca returned to Spain in 1550, the king replaced him with Antonio de Mendoza, who had been the successful first viceroy of Mexico for fifteen years; however, Mendoza was old and ill when he came to Peru in 1551, and died after ten months there. Subsequent viceroys, good and bad, came and went accompanied by large retinues of servants, courtiers, and relatives. Meanwhile settlers came in great numbers to Peru to take out grants of land worked by Indians, to operate mines in the Andes, and to work as shopkeepers and artisans in the new Spanish cities.

Most famous and successful viceroy of Peru in the second half of the sixteenth century was Francisco de Toledo, who in his years in Peru from 1569 to 1581, really established the Spanish colonial system on South America's west coast. Philip II had given him a long list of detailed instructions. He toured the provinces personally, increased the output of the new silver mines in Bolivia, established a mint, sent silver home to Spain in fleet after fleet, planned the founding of a university in Lima, and encouraged the recording of Inca history. Although he ended the shadowy rule of the last Incas in their mountain fastnesses by the execution of Tupac Amarú, Manco Cápac's youngest son, he improved conditions for the Indians at work in field and mine. He stiffened the morale of the clergy, introduced the Inquisition, built roads, aqueducts, and canals, and founded hospitals.

By 1600 Peru was Spain's most valuable colony, by yielding large

quantities of silver from the Bolivian Andes, supporting a cultured aristocracy in Lima, and by working its highland Indians in agriculture and
handcrafts. Two sociological processes characteristic of all Spanish colonies
were taking place—Spanish towns and cities had been founded, and
Spanish blood had been injected into the population often through legal
intermarriage, for few women came from Spain in the early years, and
Spanish law sanctioned marriage with Christianized Indian women. The
rich silver veins of Potosí had been found by 1545, and in 1563 the Spaniards had stumbled on the remarkable mercury deposit at Huancavelica;
silver refining by the mercury process became the basis of Peru's prosperity.
All was not easy for the Spanish rulers, however. A series of weak successors
to Toledo faced problems of foreign rivalry in the Pacific beginning with
Drake; earthquakes, internal disorders, and smallpox epidemics disturbed
the population. The methods of government developed in Peru and in
Mexico, the economic system, the interplay of the new social classes, the
activities of missionaries and church officials, and the development of a
scholarly culture in Lima all are topics that will be treated in Part II of this
volume.

explorations and settlement in northern South America

The story of northern South America, including the area called "the mainland," the "Spanish Main," or *Tierra Firme,* is the history of present-day
Venezuela, Colombia, and parts of Ecuador and of the Amazon Basin.
Explorations pushed into this area from all directions—from the Antilles,
from Panama, and from Peru. It began with Columbus' first sight of the
Orinoco beyond Trinidad. As it unfolded, the story was to include sagas of
pearl fishing and slave hunting among the Caribs on the coast, the attempts
of a German banking house over two decades to settle Venezuela, the
explorations of the interior by way of the Orinoco and its tributaries on the
one hand and from eastern Peru down the Amazon on the other, the advance north from Ecuador up into the southern valleys of Colombia, the
search for *El Dorado,* the Gilded Man, and the final meeting of three such
searching parties in the *savanna* or valley of Bogotá. It is a confusing story,
with many swashbuckling heroes.

Ojeda, ill-fated commander of the expedition on which Balboa
sailed, had named the Venezuela coast. Although the area had been put
under control of the *audiencia* in Hispaniola, settlement was slow; the
fierceness of the Indians and the exploitation of the coast by slave raiders
made progress difficult. Actual permanent occupation began with the founding of Coro in 1527 by Juan de Ampués. Diego de Ordaz, who had been
with Cortés in Mexico, was made *adelantado* of the Orinoco country and
was the first to go inland in search of mythical kingdoms. All subsequent
adventures in the same direction failed to bring about any permanent settlement. Caracas, today's capital of Venezuela, was not established until 1567.
The whole Venezuelan coast waited for development until Negro slaves
were imported to work in place of the untamed Caribs.

The Amazon Valley meanwhile was explored by accident from Inca-land. Before he had begun his quarrels with the viceroy, Gonzalo Pizarro, as governor of Quito, set out from that city on Christmas Day, 1539, in search of a mythical Land of Cinnamon, the land of the Omaguas and the country of *El Dorado* in the *montaña* to the east. The expedition started with 210 Spaniards driving 4,000 chained Indian bearers, 5,000 live hogs for food, and large flocks of llamas. After weeks of hardship they descended into a land where progress was difficult "without blows of the hatchet," so dense was the jungle. On an upper tributary of the Amazon, the versatile Spaniards built two boats. Many of the highland Indians they brought with them died in the low altitudes; the herd of swine had all been eaten. Captain Francisco de Orellana set out downriver in the boats with sixty men to find help and food; Gonzalo Pizarro never saw him again and always maintained that he had deserted. Gonzalo and the survivors found their tortuous way back to Quito a year later (1542), half-starved, and having eaten their 100 horses. Meanwhile, Orellana had gone rapidly on down the current until it was impossible to return. Eventually he reached the Amazon which he named after the women of the Greek myth, reporting that he had passed villages in which only women with spears emerged to view them. Halfway down the river he built a brigantine, even "forging two thousand very good nails" over a charcoal fire from the weapons and armor the Spaniards carried. When the crew of this brigantine reached the river mouth eight months after they had left Gonzalo Pizarro, they were able to sail out into the Atlantic and reach Spanish settlements in the Caribbean. A passage down the Amazon to the Orinoco was made in 1559 by a group of illegal outlaws from Peru led by the infamous Lope de Aguirre.

At this time the Venezuelan interior was in non-Spanish hands. Charles V with his German background, had borrowed money from a German banking house named Welser. He had given the Welsers a proprietary grant to the Venezuela area in 1528, from which they hoped to regain their loans to the king in slaves, pearls, and gold. Their agents made sporadic explorations along the coast from the Magdalena to the Orinoco, spurred on by stories of Meta, Omagua, and *El Dorado*, the Gilded Man, who might be found far inland. One of these agents was Nikolaus Federmann, the wisest and most daring of the German leaders, who started out with 400 men up the Orinoco-Meta system in 1536, hoping to find a back-door route to *El Dorado*. By the time they came to the upper reaches of the Meta, he and less than half his men had survived the snow of the Andes passes to emerge from the mountains emaciated, clothed in skins, with beards long and matted. They were in the high Chibcha plateau of Bogotá, but Spaniards from the Colombian coast had come there ahead of them up the Magdalena. Meanwhile, other German agents of the Welsers had ravaged the Indians on the coast and plundered the country. They lost the company's investment, and their grant was canceled by the Council of the Indies in 1546. Venezuela was neglected by the Spanish kings for many years until pirates raided the coast and forced attention to its defense.

The story of the search for *El Dorado* must now shift to the

Colombian coast. Since it faces the Caribbean and the Pacific and lies adjacent to Peru and Panama, Colombia was entered from all directions. The real beginning of permanent settlement was the founding of Santa Marta by Rodrigo de Bastidas in 1525 and of Cartagena by Pedro de Heredia in 1533. Explorers from these bases had explored the lower Magdalena, where they naturally heard many stories of the Chibcha kingdoms in the highlands. The final successful expedition which reached the highland valley was led by the chief justice of Santa Marta, Gonzalo Jiménez de Quesada; he was an earnest and honest servant of the king who took with him about 800 men. They left that colony on April 6, 1536, and, after suffering months of hardship in the lowlands of the Magdalena, 166 survivors found the upper reaches of the river and discovered an Indian trail up a steep escarpment into the Andes. Their remaining fifty-nine horses were lifted over cliffs in baskets; men and supplies were pulled up by ropes. Thus a year after leaving Santa Marta, Quesada emerged upon the savanna of Bogotá, where he found the cultivated fields of the Chibchas, who decorated their wooden huts with gold discs and their bodies with emeralds. By playing one tribe against the other, Quesada's soldiers easily conquered the Chibchas and then lived idyllically in the valley, they counted their gold and jewels and talked idly of returning to report to Spain. Quesada called this new land New Granada; Santa Fé de Bogotá was founded as his Spanish capital on August 6, 1538.

It was upon this peaceful scene that two other parties arrived in search of *El Dorado*. In February of 1539 Federmann and his emaciated men came down from the east into the valley. Since their party numbered only 160 and Quesada's well-fed, well-entrenched men was a group of 166, there was at first no challenge, only succor and sympathy. However, close on Federmann's heels came word of still a third expedition, "Spaniards well clothed and supplied with arms, riding fine horses and driving 300 head of swine for food." This second group of interlopers coming from the south through the highlands of Ecuador, was led by Sebastián de Benalcázar, who had experienced in his lifetime half the story of the Spanish conquest of the Americas. He had sailed as a boy with Columbus, settled in Santo Domingo, served in Darién under Balboa, and in Nicaragua under Pedrarias, and had then followed Pizarro to Peru, where he soon became governor of Quito. Bored after the completion of the conquest of Quito, he had struck north on his own to find *El Dorado*. He had come up through the rich valleys of the upper Cauca in 1536, founding Cali and Popayán on the way.

Thus, parties in the name of King Charles V had approached Bogotá from three directions to meet amicably in the year 1539. If the two new groups of arrivals had combined, they could have replaced the first comers but Quesada gave the Germans a gift of 4,000 gold pesos, and they supported him. After three months of guarded pleasantries, all three leaders went back down the precipitous trail to the Magdalena to Santa Marta together, and so on to Spain. Federmann asked for royal favor in vain, as the German grant was already in dispute. Quesada spent months traveling in Europe, spending the emeralds he had brought before he finally pleaded his case at court; then he was created "Marshal of Bogotá," a title of dignity but of little power. He returned to live peacefully in his new city; he lead one more unsuccessful expedition in search of *El Dorado,* and he served as town councilman until after his eightieth birthday. Benalcázar was made governor of the towns he founded in southwestern Colombia. When he returned from Spain to this royal grant, he made his rule there effective, setting up the town of Pasto and establishing successful agricultural and mining colonies.

New Granada which included the coast towns, Benalcázar's territory, and Bogotá, was made the seat of an *audiencia* in 1550; a bishopric was established there and missions started. The history of the area till 1600 is a confusion of disputes over grants of *encomienda,* the work of the Indians, and the power of the governors over the archbishops. The coast towns on the Spanish Main suffered particularly from the raids of Drake and other English privateers, ill omen of the destruction to be wreaked by pirates on that coast in the next century.

the settlement of Chile

From Peru the conquest spread moving north with Benalcázar from Ecuador to Colombia, east with Orellana down the Amazon, and south into Chile, a land only partially infiltrated by Inca civilization, and occupied by the fierce Araucanian Indians beyond the River Maule. The embittered men of Almagro had told all Spaniards in Peru that it was an inhospitable and unfruitful land. However, four years after Almagro's failure there, one of the men of Pizarro, Pedro de Valdivia, a persevering Estremaduran of gentle birth, forty years old at the time of the invasion of the land of the Incas, had asked Pizarro for the Almagrist grant in Chile. Pizarro, considering this territory unclaimed after the defeat and death of Almagro, had gladly given it to Valdivia, helping him raise an expedition of 150 Spaniards and 1,000 Inca farmers, with mares and swine for breeding and seed, grain, and tools for cultivation. Valdivia even took his mistress, a Spanish woman named Inez Suárez, known in history as "the Conqueror's Lady."

The party left Cuzco in January of 1540. When Valdivia reached the central Chilean valley, he found that the local Indians remembered Almagro's mistreatment, and resisted the Spaniards' effort to force them to work. With the help of the colonists he had brought, however, Valdivia founded the city of Santiago—today one of South America's great capitals— just a year after he had left Cuzco. He laid out Santiago as the typical rectangular Spanish city, with central plaza, church, *cabildo,* and prison. He called the settlers into an open town meeting, and had them "elect" him "captain-general and governor." The first mayor was one of his lieutenants; among his achievements, he built an aqueduct to bring water into the town, made peace with the Indians, and put the men to work planting crops and washing gold in the nearby river. Valdivia, like Cortés, was interested in expanding his colony and built ships for further exploration.

The good fortune did not last. Six months later the Indians rebelled and destroyed Santiago; the crops were burned and the Spaniards had only roots to live on while they sent to Peru for aid. They needed gold to persuade Pizarro to send reinforcements. They had found very little in Chile, but they worked up all they had into golden stirrups to cajole the Peruvians. With this show of wealth their envoy was successful in attracting more men to come to save Chile. Santiago was rebuilt, more colonists arrived, and Valparaiso was founded for sea communication with Peru in 1544. Meanwhile, the dashing Valdivia had himself been censured for mismanagement and debt and ordered either to marry or to rid himself of his mistress. Valdivia had her married to another Spaniard and returned to Peru in order to clear his name and get more help against the wild Araucanians. When he returned to Santiago in 1549 he had with him his own legal wife who had been left behind in Spain the first time; he also had clear title to the governorship granted to him by the new viceroy.

Back in Chile, Valdivia, now in his fifties, was anxious to make more of a name for himself in conquests of wilder country. The town of La Serena in the Valley of Coquimbo to the north had been founded to protect communications with Peru; now some settlements needed to be set up to the south to protect the central valley from the Araucanians. In 1550 Valdivia himself went beyond the Bío Bío River and founded the cities of Concepción, Imperial, Valdivia, and Villarica. Below these towns the Araucanians continued to inspire dissatisfaction and revolt among the Indians in the established *encomiendas* of the central valley, and to harass Valdivia's new towns to the south.

The leader of many Araucanian guerrilla raids into the valley was a young Indian named Lautaro; today he is one of the heroes of South America, a symbol of the struggle for freedom. As a fifteen-year-old boy, Lautaro had been captured by Valdivia, and had served for four years as head groom in charge of Valdivia's horses. But he burned with a zeal for the independence of all Indian peoples in Chile and secretly organized the guerrillas. Finally he ran away from Valdivia's service to lead them himself. Lautaro's insurrections gave Valdivia the excuse for a raid south of the Bío Bío with 200 men, but he was surrounded by Lautaro's men, captured, and put to death at the Indian town of Tucapel on New Year's Day in 1554.

To avenge the death of the Chilean leader another Spanish force went into Araucanian territory and fought Lautaro for an additional three years. Finally in 1557, while still in his early twenties, Lautaro was defeated and killed in battle, and the untamed Indians retreated south of the Bío Bío to remain there. The Araucanians never bowed to Spanish rule however, and presented a problem for the independent nation of Chile until the second half of the nineteenth century. The Spaniards held such respect for the independent spirit of these natives that Lautaro was made the hero of a long poem written by one of Valdivia's own men. Chile remained a "fighting frontier," and the war against the Araucanians continued at a great expense to the Crown.

After Valdivia's death his lieutenants quarreled over succession until the king intervened as he had done in Peru by sending an official governor, young Hurtado de Mendoza, son of the viceroy. Under this governor, rival claimants to Valdivia's power were expelled, founding of towns continued, and explorations toward the Straits of Magellan and Patagonia were made by sea.

From Chile's central valley and from Peru, Spaniards crossed the Andes and founded towns in today's Argentina—Santiago del Estero (1553), and Mendoza (1561) in the province of Cuyo just across the Andes from Santiago. All of these, like Chile, were colonies originally planned as agricultural ones. In spite of flood, earthquake, epidemic, and drought, the development of Chile slowly improved by 1600. Cattle, horses, sheep, and pigs brought prosperity to the settlers, although the revenue was insufficient to please the king. The irrigated lands of the valley were planted for vineyards and orchards, wheat, maize, and hemp. These products were raised by Indian laborers on large estates, the feudal holdings of a white aristocracy around Santiago. The same types of crops were also raised on smaller holdings in the outpost regions. Thus Chile remained a fighting frontier, an agricultural colony and a pleasant place to live in periods between wars. But it had to be subsidized from Peru and was never a source of pride and wealth for Spain.

the Plata river: an entry into the far south

The valley of the Plata was an area long neglected by the agencies of the mother country, although today it is Spanish South America's most cosmopolitan and prosperous area. There was no treasure there, only the wildest, most "unusable" Indians. When settlers finally came in any number—from Peru, from Chile, and from the Atlantic coast—they came for agriculture and livestock grazing, or for the purpose of keeping other nations out.

At first the Plata estuary had been the stopping place on the route around the new continents in search for the Orient. One such searcher, Juan Díaz de Solís, had been killed there and left a group of survivors, some of whom were stranded on the coast of Brazil. As the story goes, one of these survivors, Aleixo García, crossed from the Atlantic coast and ascended the Pilcomayo, one of the tributaries nearest the Andes; after reaching the land of the Incas, he returned to tell the other survivors among the Guaraní the fabulous stories of a "White King," a "Sierra de la Plata." Though García was himself later killed by the Guaraní, some of his fellow survivors were found eventually by other Spaniards, and the second-hand account they heard of Inca silver soon brought Sebastian Cabot to the region on a disappointing search for silver in 1526. Interest in the estuary died when Panama was accepted as a closer route to Inca silver.

Portuguese encroachments on the southern Brazilian coast eventually frightened the Spanish king, and although he was unwilling to spend royal money on this distant shore, he did grant the region to a very rich and famous man, Don Pedro de Mendoza, who would pay all expenses of colonization. Mendoza hoped to find an easy route overland to the rumored silver kingdom and planned for a big return on his investment. He came to South America with eleven vessels and more than 2,000 settlers, including some of the most illustrious men of Spain, together with equipment for a large colony and many cattle and horses. Mendoza himself was old and ill; his men quarreled during a stop on the Brazilian coast for fresh water, and the expedition arrived disgruntled. In early February or March, 1536, Mendoza founded the town of Nuestra Señora del Buen Aire.

At first the primitive Indians brought in guanaco meat and fish, but it took a great deal of food to feed 2,000 Spaniards, who "did not come to till the soil but to find silver kings." When the Spaniards demanded more food, they had a bloody battle on their hands. From that time on the Indians were their enemies, and the Spaniards starved inside the stockade. Too sick to continue work in the colony, Mendoza sailed for Spain but died in passage, his investment lost. An eyewitness account relates how the survivors at Buenos Aires ate the corpses of the dead.

Meanwhile, before Mendoza left he had sent a party of explorers up the Paraná to search for a better site for a colony and in addition to find a route up into the Andes to Peru. It was commanded by Juan de Ayolas, the most trustworthy and devoted of those with Mendoza. His party established a fort at Corpus Christi; they went up the Paraguay River and found friendly Guaraní Indians living in villages, cultivating fields, and raising corn and manioc. How different from the hostile guanaco-hunting pampas Indians around the stockade at Buenos Aires! Here where the Pilcomayo runs into the Paraguay, a camp was set up named in honor of the Assumption of the Virgin, or Asunción. A lieutenant named Domingo Martínez de Irala was left behind to found forts along the Paraguay while Ayolas set out across the Chaco following rumors of silver in Bolivia. Historians theorize that Ayolas reached Inca outposts but was murdered on the way back.

Meanwhile Irala built a fort at Asunción in 1537 and gathered supplies from the Guaraní Indians; he also did some exploring on his own. When he knew Ayolas was dead, he assumed leadership. The starving colonists at Buenos Aires and on the Paraná ascended to Asunción, where Irala built a large town. It was the first permanent settlement in the area, and Irala was elected its first governor. Only a third of Mendoza's colonists had survived to reach Asunción. On the pampas were left a few horses of the expedition—perhaps seven mares and two stallions—which could not be captured and put on the "brigantines" for Asunción; from them sprang the wild horses of Argentina, numbering in the thousands before the century was out. Some cattle were perhaps "marooned" there also, as later comers found great droves of wild cattle.

There was no royally appointed governor in the colony; there was only Irala, who had been chosen by the settlers and had taken things into his own hands. He put the peaceful agricultural Guaraní to work, and settled down himself, marrying all seven daughters of a Guaraní chief. He and his associates were not to be left undisturbed by the home government in their happy seclusion of the forests of Paraguay, however. Charles V determined to help Mendoza's survivors, and to send them an official governor. Cabeza de Vaca, that famous pedestrian, had become bored with the life of retirement in Spain. He asked for a governorship in the New World; was sent with 400 men to the Plata as *adelantado* and governor in 1540. Cabeza de Vaca landed four months later at Santa Catarina Island on the southern coast of Brazil. Being an experienced hiker, he sent his ships on down the coast and up to Asunción by the long river route, and walked himself, with 250 men and twenty-six horses, a thousand miles straight west to Asunción. He probably was the first white man to see the Iguassú Falls (unless it be that man of mystery, Aleixo García), and he described the lush land on his route as "a garden" compared to that which he had walked through in Texas and New Mexico.

When he arrived in March, 1542, the new governor received a very cold welcome in Irala's colony. He had been ordered to refound a city at the mouth of the Plata, but the Asunción settlers, remembering the miseries suffered there, refused to return downriver. He tried to set up a regal court in the wilds of Paraguay, and there was hostility between his men and the older settlers. Out of a sense of gratitude to the many Indians who had befriended him on his transcontinental hike in North America, Cabeza de Vaca meant to stop the abuse of Indian laborers and to check the polygamy practiced by the white men among the Indian women. While he busied himself with expeditions up the Pilcomayo, the settlers, determined to keep their many Indian wives and their easy way of life, rose up in rebellion against him. On his return from the futile trip into the Gran Chaco they put him in a dark little adobe prison in Asunción for eight months while they built a "caravel," not just a mere brigantine, in which they shipped him back to Spain. The king seems to have sided with the rebels, for Cabeza de Vaca was in disgrace at home during many years of litigation. Eventually he was given a judicial office in Seville, where he lived to a very old age.

When the "caravel" was two days downstream with Cabeza de Vaca aboard her, Irala, who had returned from a search for the headwaters of the Paraguay River on which the deported adelantado had sent him, was re-elected governor. By this time the royal court had again lost interest in the Plata, so Irala's election was confirmed. He lived on as a successful governor for twelve more years, continually sending out exploring parties. On December 7, 1548, a messenger from one of his expeditions which had crossed the Bolivian Chaco reached the viceroy at Lima, having traveled all the way on foot. Sheep and goats were introduced over this mountain trail from Peru, and cows were later brought in from Brazil. Though Agentine historians deride Irala as a bad administrator and blame him for abandoning the first Buenos Aires and for sending Cabeza de Vaca home, Paraguayan historians praise him as a true leader of men, a friend to the Guaraní, and a national hero. By proclamation of the town council of Asunción in 1602, "they weep even today in this land for Domingo Martínez de Irala"—and who wept that long afterward for Pizarro or Cortés? Before his death in 1556, 1,500 Spaniards and who knows how many half-breeds and Guaraní were living in Asunción; the city covered three square miles, had three churches, two schools, and even a weaving establishment, while three less important Paraguayan frontier towns had been founded to hold the line against the Portuguese in Brazil. But the mouth of the Plata was still a "no man's land."

During the years that followed Irala's death there was a succession of governors, some chosen by the colonists, some royal appointees. Under one of these, Ortiz de Zárate, the project of refounding Buenos Aires was taken under serious consideration. As leader for this venture he chose his own nephew, Juan de Garay, a true pioneer spirit of the New World who had come to Peru when only fourteen. As a partisan of Asunción, Garay wanted to keep the Spaniards of Peru from advancing into the Plata. He also knew that a town at the mouth of the Plata would keep out the Portuguese and establish direct communication from the sea into the interior—a port for Paraguay. In 1573, as a first step in his new project, he had taken eighty-four settlers from Asunción to found the town of Santa Fé, halfway downriver to the Plata mouth. Various other pioneer projects involved Garay until 1580. In March of that year he set out downriver with sixty-three men, only ten of them from Spain, for he wanted young men born in Asunción and used to frontier life. He also took farm implements and munitions, perhaps 1,000 horses, 500 cows, and "other equipment for founding a city" at the Plata mouth.

Having arrived at the old site, these second settlers easily fought off the pampas Indians, now all mounted bareback on those wild horses descended from Mendoza's few. Three miles from Mendoza's old fort, Garay proclaimed Buenos Aires a city on June 11, 1580, and laid out 144 square blocks. An *alcalde* or mayor was elected, and he and Garay proceeded to divide the land for farming, with a parcel for each family to work by its own labor. Then he set the new colonists to killing the wild cattle and drying the hides. When a locally built ship carried his official report of all this activity back to Spain, it took a load of hides with it, a symbol of the source of the future wealth of Argentina. Buenos Aires was now permanently established; by 1600 it had a population of 3,000. Garay spent the rest of his life maintaining authority between Asunción, Santa Fé, and Buenos Aires and traveling to and from these places. On such a journey he was ambushed by hostile Indians and killed in 1583, though he had always been a friend of the Indians and a leader of communities composed almost entirely of settlers of half-Indian blood.

But what is now the area of Argentina was not settled from Asunción alone. A thin stream of colonists crossed the Andes from Chile in 1561, to settle at Mendoza and other places in the province of Cuyo; this area was governed from Santiago until 1776. A larger trickle of colonists—Peruvians, whom the Paraguayans hated—came down from Bolivia into the northwest. They founded Tucamán in 1565, Córdoba in 1573, Salta in 1582, and Jujuy in 1591. This area was incorporated into a governmental unit under the *audiencia* of Upper Peru or Charcas. Agricultural crops were developed here which found ready markets in the mining areas of Potosí and in Lima. In spite of their Peruvian origin, Mendoza, Tucumán, and Córdoba are all cities of Argentina today, built by second-generation sons of the New World, sons who loved freedom, chose their own leaders, and often did their own work. No gold was discovered, no docile Indians served as slaves. Democratic town councils often did the governing, as Peruvian influence faded after 1600. Thus the Argentines of this area pride themselves on their democratic origins. The Plata towns, involved in constant clashes with the Portuguese on the Brazilian border, remained a frontier for two centuries. The interior towns, Córdoba, Tucumán, Santa Fe, and Salta for centuries were in large part dependent on overland trade between Buenos Aires and Peru, and were to resent the domination of Buenos Aires into modern times. By 1617, Asunción itself had been separated from Buenos Aires as a separate governmental unit.

Thus, by the end of the sixteenth century a great part of South America had been definitely colonized by Spain. The semicircle of settlement stretched from the Isthmus, down along the Andes through Bogotá, Quito, Peru, and Chile, eastward over the Andes to Mendoza, across the pampas to the Plata, and northward upriver beyond Asunción. This line enclosed an interior frontier over 7,000 miles long, everywhere bordered by savagery. Although such a frontier could not remain unchanged, yet by 1600 armed conquest had paused, and peace, if such it can be called, was to characterize the life of the colonists in the next century. Almost from the moment of the founding of all these new towns, as in Mexico, political, economic, social, and cultural institutions began to develop out of the new mixture of two races—institutions worth as serious consideration as has been given to the exciting stories of exploration and conquest.

READINGS

Arciniegas, G., *Germans in the Conquest of America* (1943).

_____, *Knight of El Dorado* (fictionalized, 1942).

Arriaga, P. J., *The Extirpation of Idolatry in Peru* (trans. L. B. Keating, 1968).

Bandelier, A. F., *The Gilded Man* (1893).

Bannon, J. F., *The Spanish Conquistadores* (1960).

Beals, C., *Nomads and Empire Builders* (1961).

Birney, H., *Brothers of Doom: The Story of the Pizarros in Peru* (1942).

Chudoba, B., *Spain and the Empire 1519–1643* (1969).

Dawson, T. C., *South American Republics* (2 vols., 1903–1904).

Eidt, R. C., *Pioneer Settlement in Northeast Argentina* (1971).

Elliott, J. H., *Old World and the New 1492–1650* (1970).

_____, *Imperial Spain 1469–1716* (1966).

Galdames, L., *History of Chile*, trans. I. J. Cox (1941).

Gibson, C., *Inca Concept of Sovereignty and the Spanish Administration in Peru* (1948).

Graham, R. B. C., *Conquest of New Granada, Being a Life of Gonzalo Jiménez de Quesada* (1922).

————, *Conquest of the River Plate* (1924).

————, *In Quest of El Dorado* (1923).

————, *Pedro de Valdivia, Conqueror of Chile* (1926).

Hart, B. T., *Conquistador, Inca Princess, and City Fathers* (1940).

Heaton, H. C., ed., *Discovery of the Amazon* (1934).

Henao, J. M., and G. Arrubla, *History of Colombia*, trans. J. F. Rippy (1938).

Kirkpatrick, F. A., *Spanish Conquistadores* (1934).

Korth, E. H., *Spanish Policy in Colonial Chile* (1968).

Kosok, P., *Life, Lord and Water in Ancient Peru* (1965).

Lee, B. T., and A. C. Heaton, *Discovery of the Amazon According to the Account of Frier Gaspar de Caravajal* (1934).

Levene, R., *History of Argentina*, trans. W. S. Robertson (1937).

Lockhart, J., *Spanish Peru 1532–1560* (1968).

————, *The Men of Cajamarca: A Social and Biographical Study of the First Conquerors of Peru* (1972).

Lowry, W., *Lope Aguirre, the Wanderer* (1952).

Lynch, J., *Spain Under the Hapsburgs 1516–1598* (1964).

Markham, C. R., *Conquest of New Granada* (1912).

————, *A History of Peru* (1892).

Martin, L., *The Intellectual Conquest of Peru* (1968).

May, S. B., *The Conqueror's Lady, Inez Suárez* (1930).

Means, P. A., *Fall of the Inca Empire and Spanish Rule in Peru, 1530–1780* (1932).

Merriman, R. B., *Rise of the Spanish Empire*, Vols. III and IV (1934).

Moses, B., *Establishment of Spanish Rule in America* (1898).

————, *Spanish Dependencies in South America* (2 vols., 1914).

Muller, R., *Orellana's Discovery of the Amazon River* (1927).

Ober, F. A., *Pizarro and the Conquest of Peru* (1906).

Penrose, B., *Travel and Discovery in the Renaissance, 1420–1620* (1952).

Pizarro, P., *Relation of the Discovery and Conquest of the Kingdom of Peru*, ed. P. A. Means (2 vols., 1921).

Polmentary, H. C., *The River of the Amazons—Its Discovery and Early Exploration, 1500–1743* (1965).

Prescott, W. H., *History of the Conquest of Peru* (many editions).

Richman, I. B., *The Spanish Conquerors* (1919).

Sancho de la Hoz, P., *An Account of the Conquest of Peru* (1917).

Service, E. R., *Spanish-Guaraní Relations in Early Colonial Paraguay* (1954).

Vernon, I. W., *Pedro de Valdivia, Conquistador of Chile* (1946).

Verrill, A. H., *Great Conquerors of South and Central America* (1943).

Warren, H. G., *Paraguay. An Informal History* (1949).

Zahm, J. A., *Quest of El Dorado* (1917).

Zárate, A. de, *A History of the Discovery and Conquest of Peru*, ed. D. B. Thomas (1933; another edition by J. M. Cohen, 1970).

Zimmerman, A. F., *Francisco de Toledo, the Fifth Viceroy of Peru, 1569–1581* (1938).

chapter 8

THE PORTUGUESE
CONQUEST OF
BRAZIL TO 1800

Portuguese interest in and settlement of Brazil to 1600

The Portuguese mariner Cabral, following the route around Africa pioneered by Vasco da Gama, had landed in 1500 far off his course on the shoulder of Brazil—either by design on orders from the king of Portugal or by chance wind. Thus the part of the New World which lay within the area granted Portugal under the Line of Demarcation and the Treaty of Tordesillas was claimed by a Portuguese explorer while Isabella was still working to make a permanent colony on Spanish Hispaniola. Therefore, from the first year of the sixteenth century this easternmost portion of South America had a separate history from that part explored by Spaniards. The great modern nation of Brazil, Portuguese in language and custom, differing from Spanish America even more than Portuguese Iberia differs from Spanish Iberia, began its individualistic course in the earliest colonial times. Portugal had spent its strength and gained its wealth in Africa and the East Indies; hence it neglected Brazil, where there were no wealthy civilized Indian tribes. The colonists who came to Brazil, in contrast to those in Spanish America, felt little centralized control and lived as a peaceful, feudal patriarchal group, controlling their own affairs.

The king of Portugal had been mildly interested in the report of Cabral's discovery, in the hope of finding a halfway station for ships on the long passage to India. He therefore granted permission to some merchants to explore and trade along the Brazilian coast. They found there the valuable red-colored dyewood which was called "brazil" and which remained the coast's only important article of commerce for a generation. Amerigo Vespucci perhaps sailed for these merchants. By 1510 French as well as Portuguese merchants were working unhindered in the dyewood trade and were bringing back Indian slaves, parrots, and monkeys. *Degredados*—a word used for escaped convicts, exiled heretics, sailors marooned for insubordination, deserters, and minor criminals—stayed in the dyewood cutting camps or roamed in the forests. One of these "squaw men," a Portuguese of noble birth named Diogo Álvares, became the patriarch of a large community of his Indian wives and his half-breed children and grandchildren. He had frightened the Indians with his musket when he was first stranded on the beach at the present site of Bahía; they called him "Man of Lightning," Caramarú. His presence on the coast when an official Portuguese governor arrived in 1531, nearly three decades later, was of great help to the new colony. He lived to be more than a century old, and many proud Bahíans were glad to claim descent from him.

Thirty years elapsed before there was formal settlement, for the coast had proved of no value on the route to India; Portugal's kings considered the Brazilian colony a "wretched business" and concentrated instead on the East Indian trade. In contrast to the opulence of the East, with its jewels, temples, and sumptuous textiles, Brazil had nothing. The real history of Brazil as a Portuguese effort begins in 1526. The ambitious John III grew alarmed at profits being made on the Brazilian coast by Frenchmen. He was also fearful of Spanish encroachments east of the Demarcation Line, now that the stories of Inca gold were being told in Spanish America, so he decided to hold the fine bay at Bahía against foreign encroachment. He knew he must establish fortified, self-sustaining posts if Portugal expected to retain the territory.

John appointed Martim Affonso de Sousa, a thirty-year-old member of the nobility and a prudent and able statesman, to head the new colony. With five vessels and 400 men he arrived on the Bahía coast in January 1531 to work out a program best adapted for colonization. Chronicler and explorer with him was his brother Pero Lope de Sousa. Caramarú, patriarch Man of Lightning, and his sons helped the expedition destroy the French logging interest and lay a permanent settlement. Ships sent out by the Sousas started another town called São Vicente near the site of modern Santos where they were helped by other *degredados*, notably one João Ramalho.

John III now instituted the second period in Brazil's early history, that of the *Donatários*. When Martim Affonso de Sousa returned to Portugal with his report, the king organized a system of grants under which Brazil was governed and settled for the next two decades. Large tracts of land, *capitania-donatários*, were granted to individuals who had economic backing. The *donatário* had rights similar to those granted to proprietors in the English colonies—jurisdiction stretching fifty leagues along the coast and inward as far as the Demarcation Line, wherever that might prove to be. He could found towns, levy taxes, hold monopolies. In return, the *donatário* had to bring settlers, organize a militia, pay a fifth of his profits to the king, and meanwhile pay all expenses. The financial outlay had to be immense, for many of the vast tracts had little economic value, the Indians were hostile, and the proceeds from such a raw country slight. Of the fifteen "middle-class noblemen" who took out the grants between 1534 and 1536, several never came to Brazil at all, and few made profits. A lasting effect was the decentralization caused by this system of private settlement, many Brazils, not one united colony, were created, and Brazil remains regionalistic to this day.

Most of the grantees or captains embarked on their Brazilian adventure in earnest, however, mortgaging their possessions in Portugal in order to set up towns, churches, and sugar plantations. The most successful was Duarte Coelho, who had already made a fortune in India and had large sums to risk on his grant of Pernambuco. A well-selected group of colonists sailed at his expense to settle at Olinda to raise sugar. Even Caramarú's help did not bring financial success to Francisco Coutinho who had been granted Bahía. Though the town itself thrived, Coutinho expended his entire fortune and was reduced to poverty. The king had to learn the hard lesson that few private fortunes were capable of standing the strain of opening up a new country, although the system did accomplish the settlement of parts of the coastline at little royal expense. By 1548 there were sixteen towns with several fortified harbors, and the colonists were raising livestock, planting European-type crops, exporting dyewood, sugar, cotton, and tobacco, and profiting from the labor of both Indian and Negro slaves.

But politically the *donatários* failed. There was no bond uniting the regions, and efforts expended were dissipated. Many of the colonists were lawless; they revolted against the captains, joined bands of Indians, or quarreled among themselves. To cope with the widespread anarchy it was imperative to establish a common code, both administrative and penal, to be organized by a superior official representing the Portuguese Crown. This decisive step was taken in 1549, when the king issued a decree limiting the power of the *donatários* and creating a governor-general for the whole of Brazil. Conformity must be brought to the region, French and Spanish dangers met with a united front, and boundary difficulties between the *donatários* settled. To produce such unity another member of the Sousa family, Tomé de Sousa, was appointed first governor-general. An able and virtuous man having political judgment and administrative experience in Africa and India, he set up his capital at Bahía and made it a direct royal colony, succeeding where the *donatários* had failed. Eventually all the *capitanias-donatários* reverted to the Crown, though in general, these subdivisions remain the modern states of Brazil.

Tomé de Sousa came to Bahía with six ships conveying 1,000 people—mechanics, civil servants, and missionaries. He had been instructed to build a fleet and to encourage sugar as a crop for export. He soon had a hundred new houses built in the colony. One of his successors as governor, Mem de Sá, an experienced judge in Portugal, prepared workable laws for all the captaincies, set the vagabonds to work, stamped out cannibalism among the coastal Indians, encouraged the Jesuit missions, founded Rio de Janeiro by driving a group of French settlers away, and remained in Brazil for the rest of his life. Pero de Magalhães, an historian, described Bahía in 1576 as being big enough to have sixty-two churches and forty-seven sugar mills, and containing both the lower town on the seashore and the upper town on the bluff, the two regions of Bahía today connected by the famous public elevator. In addition Magalhães mentioned the growing communities at São Vicente, today's Santos, and Olinda and Recife in today's Pernambuco. Olinda was so prosperous that many wealthy men "ate their meals with a fork and set their tables with silver and fine porcelain." By 1600 there were probably 25,000 Portuguese inhabitants in this New World, nearly a hundred sugar mills shipping crystallized sugar back to Portugal, and 14,000 Negro slaves to do the work. Perhaps 18,000 Christianized Indians were in the missions or working for the plantations.

expansion inland

The sixteenth century had witnessed the sprinkling of a few towns along the coast. The seventeenth century was to show long strides toward a stable society both in the towns and by the defeat of all foreign invaders. It also brought the penetration of the interior behind the settled towns, the exploration of the Amazon Basin, the extension toward Spanish lands to the south, and the conquest of the São Francisco River area. This expansion was heightened in the eighteenth century when gold and diamond mines were developed—a development which brought inflation, corruption, depopulation of the maritime areas, and increased vulnerability to foreign attack. São Paulo and Minas Gerais, modern Brazil's richest provinces, were opened in the early 1700s, and even Goiás and the Mato Grosso, still one of the world's frontier areas, were tapped. The lines of inland development for modern Brazil were set by 1750.

There would seem to be few incentives to push the settlers inland. Desert stopped them behind Pernambuco; mountains crowded the sea behind Rio de Janeiro and Santos; the unnavigable river of São Francisco kept Bahíans on the coast. However, if the government was not concerned with exploration for conquest, slave raiders, cattle ranchers, gold prospectors, and missionaries were sufficiently interested in the interior to cover thousands of square leagues, thereby opening a frontier for later comers.

Portuguese renegades had gone into the plateaus beyond the north-south axis of the São Francisco, taking cattle with them into the rich grazing grounds there. Their descendants became rich ranchers, holding hundreds of square miles in single family holdings, and sending their *vaqueros* out to drive back the Indians. To the north in the Amazon area *donatários* failed

Columbus: A portrait painted on the return from his second voyage. (Photo courtesy of the Pan American Union.)

The Alcazar at Segovia, where Queen Isabella often held court in Columbus' time. (Photo by Helen Miller Bailey.)

Primitive Caribbean Indians still offer trade goods to the ships of strangers: San Blas Indians off the coast of Panama. (Photo by Helen Miller Bailey.)

Holy Week parade in San José, Costa Rica—a direct heritage from Spain. (Photo courtesy of the United Fruit Company.)

Above, *the Falls of the Iguassú on the Argentine-Paraguay-Brazil border—one of the fantastic surprises the New World held for the Spaniards. (Photo by Helen Miller Bailey.)*

Below, *Inca field planted to corn and potatoes today under Spanish-speaking landlords. (Photo by Helen Miller Bailey.)*

The Andes Ridge between Argentina and Chile. (Photo by Helen Miller Bailey.)

The cone of Mt. Popocatepetl, Mexico, from the air. (Photo by Helen Miller Bailey.)

Mayan carving and numbered
hieroglyphs, Copán, Honduras.
(Photo by Helen Miller Bailey.)

Great stone head built by the Olmecs, La Venta. (Photo
by Helen Miller Bailey.)

Figure of a "danzante" carved by early worshippers at Monte Alban, Oaxaca, Mexico. (Photo by Helen Miller Bailey.)

Pyramid of the Toltecs at Tula, Mexico, built between 900 and 1000 A.D. (Photo by Helen Miller Bailey.)

Stairway of the Feathered Serpents, Teotihuacan, Mexico.
(Photo by Helen Miller Bailey.)

Portrait jugs made by pre-Inca peoples on the Peruvian coast. (Photo courtesy of the Pan American Union.)

Street in pre-conquest town of Pissac, Peru. Indian women here continue to dress in Inca costume. The terraced fields rising high above the town are planted with varieties of corn and potatoes derived from plants developed by the early Incas. (Photo by Helen Miller Bailey.)

Pre-Inca gateway at Tiahuanaco. (Photo by Helen Miller Bailey.)

The fortification of Sacsahuaman built by the Incas above Cuzco. (Photo by Helen Miller Bailey.)

The first Spanish towns founded in the Caribbean area were similar to this Venezuelan coastal village. Only the burros and the plaster walls changed the appearance of the Indian villages. (Photo courtesy of the Standard Oil Company of New Jersey.)

The palace built by Diego Columbus as governor of the island of Hispaniola. (Photo by Helen Miller Bailey.)

Hernando Cortés. (Photo courtesy of the Pan American Union.)

The plaza of Mexico Tenochtitlán, capital of the Aztec empire, as it might have looked when the Europeans first saw it. (Photo courtesy of the American Museum of Natural History.)

Dance of the Conquistadores in Sololá, Guatemala, reliving the conquest of that area by Alvarado. (Photo courtesy of the Pan American Union.)

Inca towns in the Peruvian Andes. The Spaniards built the buildings but changed the Indians little. (Photo by Helen Miller Bailey.)

miserably. Hostile cannibalistic Indians and French and Dutch renegades limited settlement to only a few hundred families in Maranhão and Belém at the mouth of the river by 1700. In the region behind Brazil's shoulder, the semi-desert or *sertão* of Ceará, and the treeless plains of Piauí provided slave raiders with a steady source of Indian slaves for the market farther south. The provinces of Rio Grande do Norte and Ceará were founded from slave-trading centers. To the north of the Amazon there remained a colonial no-man's land.

Just as the population filtered back from Bahía and Pernambuco to occupy the inland valleys, and moved along the northern coast and up the Amazon, so there came from Santos far to the south a similar and much more significant expansion. Martim Affonso de Sousa, the great colonizer, had ordered settlers inland from Santos to the high plateau, where they founded a village called Piratininga, which was soon combined with a Jesuit school and a mission for the nearby Indians and renamed São Paulo. Since natural features of the region made São Paulo the key to a new frontier of rolling and extensive plains, the people moved onward instead of stopping to raise sugar.

From the "crossroads" town of São Paulo, rivers led south and west into the Spanish colony of Paraguay, and northwest into the Mato Grosso, Goiás, and Minas Gerais areas. Indian slaves, gold, diamonds, and rich pasture lands waited for the pioneers in all these directions. Thus the men from São Paulo, the *Paulistas* of Brazilian history, a hardy, energetic and courageous mixture of races, spread out as frontiersmen to double the size of Portuguese Brazil. These raiders were the founders of the three modern Brazilian states of São Paulo, Minas Gerais, and Goiás, but they left few written records, since most of them could not write. Organized into raiding groups under their private banners or *bandeiras*, they were called *bandeirantes*. Not relying on the woods and Indian villages for food, these frontiersmen often drove cattle with them; many of them became frontier cowboys and later cattle farmers. Their trails into the interior were even followed by prospectors. It was they who made war on the prosperous and peaceful Spanish Jesuit missions of Paraguay, enslaving the Indians by the thousands, though most of the *bandeirantes* were themselves half-breeds, or *mamelucos*, as Portuguese mestizos were called in southern Brazil. Portuguese Jesuit missions to the north of São Paulo were not safe from their raids. When the governor of Pernambuco hired a famous São Paulo *bandeirante* to come to the coast and lead a raid against fugitive Negro slaves, the bishop there described him as "one of the worst savages I have ever encountered; except that he is a Christian, he is not different from the most barbarous Indian." The activities of slave raiders were excused on the basis of hostility against any Spanish settlement, and of the "prevention of cannibalism." Government and Jesuits combined to oppose the Indian slave trade, but the law allowed Indians to be captured if they were cannibals. The *Paulistas* said that all Indians were cannibals; the Jesuit missionaries from Portugal said that all Indians had souls to be saved; thus there was a century of dispute between frontiersmen and missionaries.

That the Brazilian boundaries were set far to the west of the Line of Demarcation was due largely to the *Paulistas*. One *bandeirante* leader reached Peru on an Indian raid; there are authenticated reports of two explorers who had gone up the Amazon tributaries into Ecuador in the 1630s. They also went to the south, inspiring the founding of Colônia do Sacramento on the Uruguayan coast and causing the fighting and negotiations concerning Misiones, the Paraguayan missions, and the north shore of the Plata. There were Portuguese governors and settlements at Santa Catarina and at Porto Alegre in Rio Grande do Sul by 1750; both of these settlements are the southernmost capitals of Brazilian provinces today.

When the *bandeirantes* discovered precious metals around 1700, they created a whole new colonial region of Brazil called Minas Gerais, the "general mines." This was to be a region as different from the plantation-sugar-slave life of Bahía as a California mining camp in 1850 was different from Charleston, South Carolina. At the news of the discovery of gold, settlers rushed into the backlands. There was no food, and malaria and starvation killed off the miners, but still they came. Negro slaves were brought into the mines; sometimes their masters sold the sugar plantations in Bahía or Olinda and brought the slaves to the mines with them. Immigrants from Portugal, runaway slaves, and half-castes from the coastal towns swelled the population. The miners chose their own leader until 1720; then Minas Gerais was made a separate province and given a government which brought a measure of order into the mining camps.

The central town grew up from straggling mining camps on two sides of a ravine. Here pure, dark gold was washed out in nuggets, called "black gold" or *ouro preto* in Portuguese. The *Paulistas* ruled by lynch law over this Ouro Preto mining camp, with its excesses in vice, its brazen women, and its smart gamblers which made it the "Potosí of Brazil." Newcomers from Europe, called by the Brazilians *emboabas*, and settlers from the plantation towns of the coast resisted the rule of the *Paulistas* in armed warfare for seven years until the newcomers won equality in the "diggings." Commerce flourished on the new trade routes to the coast. By 1780 Ouro Preto was no longer a tough mining camp, but an ornate city, a center of the Enlightenment, with churches on both hills and fine houses filling in the ravines. When the mines gave out, Ouro Preto stagnated on grazing and agricultural pursuits, changing so little that today the town has been declared a national monument of colonial architecture, to remain unaltered as a living museum, the "Williamsburg" of Brazil.

Defeated in the control of Minas Gerais, the *Paulistas* pushed almost a thousand miles inland, opening cattle trails through to Goiás, which is today as remote a frontier as any in the twentieth-century world. There were new gold mines in Goiás and the Mato Grosso by 1730, and diamonds had been discovered in northern Minas Gerais in 1728. By 1735 40,000 people were in the new town of Diamantina, working the diamond mines and living in lush style in stately houses. To serve all this new area, Rio de Janeiro, a port established by Mem de Sá on a former French site in 1567, became the most prosperous harbor on the Brazilian coast, and finally the center of government. To improve regional government, Goiás was made a captaincy in 1744, Mato Grosso in 1748, and Piauí in the north in 1750.

Thus it might be said, in summary, that the sixteenth century had been one of neglect and experimental colonization on the coast, the seventeenth century one of sugar plantations and coastal settlement in a lazy prosperity, and the eighteenth one of interior development, gold and diamond "rushes," and new frontiers. Brazil continued to carry on a "Westward Movement" similar to that of North America. The frontiers were held and expanded against the Spaniards. A mining, pastoral, democratic Brazil centering in São Paulo had developed in contrast to the sugar-planting, slave-holding north with its capital at Bahía.

foreign interventions and rivalries

All this expansion did not take place without exciting the envy of the foreigner. From the first cutting of brazil wood for dye, the French were rivals of the Portuguese in Brazil and tried to maintain trading posts in spite of Portuguese resistance and coast guards. When the struggle between Protestant Huguenots and Catholics in France led to ideas of an "Antarctic France" as a haven for the Huguenots, the Catholic French king granted "permission" to Nicolas Durand de Villegagnon for the founding of a French colony at the Bay of Rio de Janeiro. This fine harbor had been explored and then neglected by the Portuguese. When the French first came, the Portuguese settlers to the north and south had been too weak to drive them away; then the French leader himself abandoned his quarrelsome and impractical colonists in 1559, and Governor Mém de Sá determined to take the area for Portugal. After two attempts the governor's forces, in command of his nephew Eustacio de Sá, were able to drive the surviving French north for good, and to establish Portuguese Rio de Janeiro in 1567. The remaining Frenchmen, outlawed by all governments, joined other French outlaws to set up trading posts at Maranhão near the mouth of the Amazon. With the Portuguese founding of Belém, this last French outpost was destroyed, and the French menace was gone from the Brazilian coast.

English rivalry was not a serious problem for Portugal during the colonial period, for in the century of greatest colonial warfare the English and the Portuguese were fast friends. During the period from 1580 to 1640, however, when the Portuguese king had died and Philip II, claiming to be an heir to the throne, had annexed Portugal, English privateers pillaged Portuguese colonies as fair game to any enemy of Spain. Except for the Spanish king on the throne of Lisbon, there was little other change for Brazil during the years of Spanish rule. In 1640 the Duke of Braganza led a revolt in Lisbon which ousted the Spanish ruler and put the Braganza family on the throne of the Portuguese empire, where they were to remain until the twentieth century.

During the Spanish period, however, Brazil had acquired the enmity of the Dutch, whose clever ship captains went directly to India and the

East Indies by the Portuguese trade routes and won Java and other eastern possessions. After three attempts along the Brazilian coast the Dutch "Sea Beggars" were able to capture and hold the whole area of Pernambuco in 1630. Since the Spanish rulers of Portuguese possessions at that time had no spare troops to send to Pernambuco's aid, the Dutch remained in control of the northern coast of Brazil for twenty-four years, until 1654.

Actually, not Holland itself, but the Dutch West Indies Company ruled Pernambuco, although the governor from 1637 to 1644, Prince Maurice of Nassau, was a prince of the royal house of Orange (Holland). An unusually well-educated, liberal man, interested in science, literature, and efficient government, Prince Maurice gave Pernambuco its best years. Migration of other creeds and nationalities was encouraged, and the count called a legislature in which Portuguese and Dutch settlers were both represented. Unfortunately, the company was not interested in democracy, nor in the botanical specimens the count was collecting, but wished to revive the sugar industry, make more money, and expand its holdings. In a clash with the company over policy, the good count resigned, even though a European settlement at the time of the Braganza revolution recognized nearly a third of the settled coast of Brazil as a Dutch possession.

After the resignation of Prince Maurice, the Portuguese and mixed-blood settlers developed an intense nationalism against the Dutch. Mixed-bloods, freed slaves, Indians, and Portuguese citizens combined in a red, white, and black revolt to drive out the now-legal Dutch overlords. With no help from Mother Portugal they fought the Dutch for thirteen years from 1641 to 1654. Finally a fleet came from the home country to help them, and the Dutch were forced to leave, in return for which they received money indemnities and trading privileges. The Dutch withdrew all claims to Brazil in 1661. The whole episode served to show northern Brazilians an example of good government. Their revolt from the Dutch taught them local pride in their courage against a common enemy without help from home, a pride which is considered the beginning of Brazilian nationalism.

political and economic conditions

Portuguese lack of concern over the Dutch in Pernambuco was typical of the whole policy of government. Unlike the Spaniards, the Portuguese had not created special governing bodies for control of the colonies; they ruled the American territories through the existing political machinery in Portugal, which had seemingly worked well enough for the early Portuguese government in India. Administrative organization never proceeded according to any uniform plan. Until the control of Portugal by Spain in 1580 there was not even a council or minister in Portugal charged with the entire responsibility of colonial affairs. Government of the colonies, as well as that of the home country, was concentrated entirely in the hands of a Chancellor, a Royal Registrar, and a secretary of the king. An Inspector of Finance for Portugal, India, and Brazil supervised the *Casa da India,* which prepared cargoes for all colonies and enlisted soldiers for colonial affairs. Only an ecclesiastical council, *Mesa da Consciencia é Orden,* exercised some authority over officials sent to Brazil; the authorities for local government which were sent out from Portugal consisted of the viceroy at Bahía and the provincial governors.

Philip III improved on this situation, setting up a Council for the Indies in 1604 similar to that of Spain, and dividing its work into two branches, one for the East Indies and one for Brazil and Africa. Efficiency was so much enhanced that with the independence of Portugal under the Braganzas, the Spanish-founded institutions were maintained. In the seventeenth century Portugal suffered an even greater decline than Spain. Rule in Brazil became an entirely personal one, depending on the casual whim of the monarch with little organization or body of laws for Brazil. There was corruption and graft in the highest places, and venality reached its peak under John V.

After 1750 a new turn was given the Portuguese administration by the Marquis of Pombal, the great minister of "enlightened despotism" who was virtual dictator of Portugal for twenty-seven years. Government agencies in Brazil were improved, royal authority was more centralized, inefficiency and corruption were reduced, taxes and revenues for the Crown were increased, and trade and commerce more strictly controlled for the mother country. Trading companies and monopolies were established. In the line of social reform, Pombal was influenced by the French Enlightenment. He ended the political inequalities of Brazilians and Portuguese, abolished Indian slavery, and encouraged Portuguese immigration to Brazil. In his effort to reduce the importance of the Church, he expelled the Jesuits. The administration of justice, always a weak part of Portuguese colonial rule, was strengthened by the establishment of a second supreme court at Rio in 1751 to supplement the existing one at Bahía.

As for government in the colonies themselves, Bahía's governor-general had ruled with little interference from the days of Tomé de Sousa in 1549; although the area at the mouth of the Amazon—Pará and the Island of Maranhão, was not governed from Bahía, but directly from Portugal. Such a governor was called a viceroy after the Braganza revolution; under him served an attorney-general, a treasurer, and other royal officials. Various captaincies in the provincial capitals of Brazil with royal officers were created as the frontier expanded. Finally, the viceregal capital itself was moved from Bahía to the rapidly growing south and set up at Rio de Janeiro in 1763. Rio itself had grown from a thatched-roof town to a fair-sized city because of the flood of precious minerals leaving its port from Minas Gerais in the 1700s. The economic balance of the colony had shifted away from the sugar-producing north. Theoretically all the governmental posts, as well as judgeships and lesser administrative positions, could be filled by native-born Brazilians as well as by Lisbon-born Portuguese. There was no legal discrimination against creoles in Brazil, though actually, royal favorites close to the king's ear received most of the lucrative appointments.

Regionalism, still today one of Brazil's biggest administrative problems, flourished as a by-product of the laxity of central control. The Crown did not adequately support its representatives and did not provide sufficient military forces, so an independent spirit was to be expected in the provincial town councils and governors' offices. Captains-general ruled the provinces; plantation-owners were kings on their own lands; missionary fathers were the law in the mission compounds. The *câmaras* or city councils in the provincial towns were more active and democratic than the similar Spanish local councils. Though members were appointed, or were hereditary officials serving for life, they were leaders in their communities and took pride in their services. In these councils Brazilians dealt with shipping laws, customs duties, army maintenance—many such things which in the Spanish colonies were ordained from Spain. The church got its principal support from the municipalities. When, during wartime, communications with Portugal were weak, local *câmaras* took charge, even temporarily filling a vacancy in the governorship. In the interior, local militia bosses, assistants to the provincial governors, called *capitão mor,* recruited small armies and became political bosses. Since Brazilians were not in general very civic-minded, and there was no widespread culture and little self-reliance, no actual democracy developed.

The Crown made money from the colony of Brazil, though nothing to compare with the money Spain made from Spanish America. The customs duties, the royal monopolies, the *quinto* or fifth-part value on precious metals and stones brought in sufficient revenue to keep the kings interested, though taxes were farmed out to private tax collectors who kept their full share. After the discovery of gold and diamonds every attempt was made to collect taxes on these rich diggings. Entry and exit to the mining area were licensed; gold had to pass through royal smelting houses, and bullion and diamonds could be shipped only in royal craft. Smuggling, especially in the diamond fields, was rampant, and the Crown probably lost more than it gained during the eighteenth-century mining boom.

Portugal's commercial policy concerning Brazil was chiefly directed toward increasing the government's revenues, preventing competition with Asiatic goods, obtaining benefits for privileged interests in the home country, and encouraging sugar planting and mining. Commerce was free to Portuguese ships only, for free trade was inconsistent with the mercantilist theories of the time.

The homeland maintained her colonial trade by means of convoys to and from Brazil, set up by a law of 1571 when the new colony was fast being recognized as a place of some value. The Portuguese convoys had an irregular history throughout the seventeenth century until they were finally completely abolished by 1800. Meanwhile trade was carried on through monopolistic companies, the first of which had been set up to protect the Pernambuco trade and expel the Dutch. These companies received grants for twenty years at a time to trade in tobacco, slaves, or dyewoods. All the trade north of Pernambuco was carried on in this way, and the mother country never hoped to make a large income there. In the southern settlements trade thrived. Staples from Portugal were exchanged for rice, sugar, coffee, vanilla, indigo, hides, and tallow, as well as gold and diamonds, though sugar export far exceeded all other trade throughout the colonial period.

Commodities used in the colony were manufactured there in handicraft industry on the plantations and in the missions, though wealthy plantation owners imported European-made luxury goods. Simple farming and mining tools were forged in the New World, textiles were made on the plantations, and ships were built in coastal yards.

It was the plantation or *fazenda*, the great sugar-growing establishment, which was the essential feature of Brazil. "Sugar is King" was the motto. The sugar crop encouraged slavery, led to large holdings, and discouraged small tenancy. Sugar needed many unskilled hands in harvest time and required little intelligent management on the part of the owner, who could let his paunch grow fat while he lived idly in the big plantation house, keeping most of his slaves busy only a few months of the year.

Sugar had been deliberately introduced from the Madeira Islands as a quick money crop in the tropics. The sugar cane was crushed in mills and then crystallized into brown cakes or distilled into rum. A mill, called an *engenho* became a symbol of wealth; since handling the crushing entailed a large investment needing fifty slaves and twenty yoke of oxen, only the "sugar barons" could maintain one. In 1711 a report listed 146 such mills in or near Bahía. To handle this sugar the *fazendeiros*, or plantation owners, were each allowed to buy from the Africa traders 120 slaves a year. Indian laborers, still being captured in large numbers by the *Paulistas* in the 1700s were inferior to the Africans as workers, and were used on cattle ranches rather than on the "sugar coast." There were few artisans in such a colony; most labor was colored and involuntary. By the end of the colonial period slaves in Brazil outnumbered the whites by 50 per cent. The other agricultural exports from Brazil were hides, which came from the backlands in great numbers, and tobacco, of which 25,000 "twists" a year were sent to Portugal. Planting coffee, which was to mean Brazil's wealth in the twentieth century, had little importance at this time.

The population of Brazil had grown enormously in the wake of all this prosperity. In 1776 there were almost 2,000,000 "civilized" people in Brazil, in 1800 nearly 3,000,000. Of these perhaps 800,000 were whites, 300,000 were Indians, almost a million and a half were blacks, and the remainder half-castes of all types. The captaincy of Bahía had 530,000 people, Pernambuco 480,000, Rio 380,000, and Minas Gerais 600,000 in 1800. Though mining was producing $4,000,000 a year by then, agriculture, the real mainstay of Brazil, was bringing in triple that amount at the end of the colonial period.

society, religion, and culture
in Portuguese America

Social life in the sugar-producing coastal areas centered around the *fazenda*, the plantation. Life for the black African slaves there is discussed in Chapter 9, below. The *fazenda* was an isolated sugar-producing unit, with its own refinery and its own chapel.

Here on the manor the *fazendeiro* had complete authority, often kept his own militia, and lived independent of any city rule. In the manor houses the ladies would live in almost Mohammedan seclusion, marry very early, go out only to church, and then be smothered in bejewelled cloaks up to their eyes. At home they grew fat on sugar-sweets and inactivity, their very wish anticipated by a slave. The daughters were married to other *fazendeiros* in early adolescence. According to an eighteenth-century French traveler, many Brazilian girls preferred the life of a nun to such early marriage and the secluded life and heavy childbearing that followed it. Wealthy families left their land to the eldest son, sent their second to a university in Portugal so he might be a lawyer or enter the government service, and were apt to "give their third to the church" at fifteen.

In general, *fazendeiros* did not congregate in cities as did the Spanish colonial aristocracy, though they often kept town houses. The towns were more apt to be filled with middle-class Portuguese immigrants. In most towns unpaved streets ran past the Moorish-tile dwellings of the rich. Black women washed clothes in the public fountains and mule trains and oxcarts trundled by, loaded with sugar and rum or hides from the interior. At night the streets were so dark that wayfarers were preceded by a slave carrying a fish-oil lantern. But let fiesta time come, Carnival or Saint John's Day, and the streets were full and gay, while social classes mixed freely in the parades and street dances, celebrating with greater abandon than did the population of any Spanish colonial city.

The social class-lines were not so marked as in Spanish America. At the top were the *donatários*, the aristocrats or *fidalgos*. Though this was the small ruling class from Portugal, the creoles, called in Brazil the *masambos* or native-born, were not excluded from it as they were in Spanish America. Below the *fidalgos* came the *fazendeiros*, who owned the plantations, and the middle-class merchants who ran the businesses. In both these groups many mixed-bloods could be found by 1800. White peasants from Portugal, Jewish merchants and peddlers, Azores Islanders in business and on land, made a middle class. Then came the *caboclos* and *mamelucos,* the white-Indian mixtures, the mulattoes, and the *cafusos* or Indian-Black hybrids; next the free Blacks and the free Indians, and at the bottom both Indian and Black slaves. In these last groups there was much crossing over, with an ever-present opportunity to rise into a higher class in the second generation seldom found in Spanish America.

Church organization had come to Brazil with the first centralized government at Bahía and remained in a dominant position through colonial times. There was little cultural activity outside it. The Church grew with Brazil, maintaining four bishops and an archbishop by 1700. There seems to have been little effort made by the authorities to keep Brazil "pure" in the accepted faith; the Inquisition stayed in Lisbon and heard very few cases from the colonies. The Church in Brazil was never as wealthy or as powerful as it was in the Spanish colonies, and it was not an obstacle to political development after independence. The most important record of religious activity is that of the missionary workers among the Indians.

A leader among the Jesuits who came out with Tomé de Sousa was

Father Manoel de Nobrega, one of the truly great men of all the colonies, a fearless, tireless champion of the Indians against enslavement by whites. He worked in the São Paulo area where he learned Indian languages, wrote dramas and music in those dialects, and personally taught thousands of young Indians in his mission schools. He and his successors founded mission villages to protect the natives from the *bandeirantes.*

"Graduates" of these missions found their way into the economy of the colony, took half-breed or mulatto girls to wife, and helped to create a new Brazil. A co-worker with Nobrega in the mission field was José de Anchieta, a sort of "Saint Francis Xavier of the New World." As famous as a geographer and historian of the early days of Brazil as he is as a devoted missionary, he is sometimes called the "Father of Brazilian Literature." Another outstanding Jesuit writer and leader in the seventeenth century was Father Antônio Vieira, who persuaded the king to put the Indians under exclusive Jesuit control. Thus the Jesuits ran all the missions in Brazil; in this they fought openly with the other colonists and finally clashed with the kings in Europe. The Marquis of Pombal, dictator-minister of Portugal, had all members of the Jesuit order expelled from Brazil in 1759.

Jesuits in Brazil founded the secondary schools, ran the hospitals and maintained charities. But in every town there was a parish priest and a church building. Never as concerned with political life as the Spanish American Catholic Church, the Brazilian church seemed closer to the peoples' lives. Church practice was never as stiff and formal; Christianity had more of friendliness, tolerance, and affection in Lisbon and Bahía than in Seville and Lima.

Jesuits controlled education completely however. By the time of Nobrega's death there was a "school of elementary education" in every coastal town and at São Paulo. When the Jesuits were expelled two centuries later, they were maintaining nine advanced secondary schools and three seminaries. Plantation children learned to read and write from the house chaplain, were sent away to boarding schools, or grew up illiterate like their easygoing fathers. If one son of a rich family was to be sent to the university he had to go to Coimbra in Portugal; throughout the colonial period there was never a university in Brazil.

Thus Brazil approached the "Age of Enlightenment" in the eighteenth century with few educated people. There was no successful printing business in Brazil until after 1808. Brazil was behind Portugal in enlightenment, and Portugal was behind Spain. There is a spotty history of feeble little academic societies and literary clubs, especially in Ouro Preto, but few of them were able to hold more than twenty meetings or to last more than three or four years.

The Portuguese language was itself a tongue of seafarers and explorers rather than of classical scholars, and with the exception of histories and travel stories very little literature was produced in Brazil. Anchieta on the frontier was preaching in Tupi-Guaraní; priests among the freedmen in the north spoke to their flocks in Nâgo. For two centuries more town and plantation people spoke these two languages than spoke Portuguese. By

1750, when Portuguese finally dominated, it was a new language differing from "Lisbonese" as the language of Texas differs from that of London. The people who wrote for Brazil wrote of the land itself, its history and its resources—Anchieta, the missionary, Pero de Magalhães, the historian, and Father Antonil, the economist, from all of whose works much of the life and economic progress of colonial Brazil is known to modern scholars.

The 1700s at last saw formal stories of adventure and dramas written by people who set out to be writers. One such dramatist, Antônio José da Silva (1705–1739), had his satirical plays produced in Lisbon—a questionable honor, for he was burned at the stake there for heretical practices. A poet who died at the end of the seventeenth century, Gregório de Mattos Guerra (1633–1696), also wrote sarcastically about the authorities, singing with a guitar, as the gay young man-about-town, of the "fat cats" in the Portuguese colonial service. For thus lampooning society he was sentenced to several years in the prison colony in Angola, but was soon back in Brazil singing more scornful songs until his death. Two long epic poems are remembered today in modern Brazil, and both are concerned with the life of the Indians—*O Uruguay*, by José Basilio da Gama (1741–1795) and *Caramarú* by José de Santa Rita Durão (1722–1784).

The common people, with their African and Indian blood, never forgot the legends of their own people, and told the folk stories of the rivers and jungles of two tropical continents to their children and their children's children. Slave "mammies" told them to the white children; such stories of backwoods lore, of animal cunning, of moon magic were better known to most colonial Brazilians than the poems and stories in Portuguese published about Brazil in Lisbon.

Of all the colonies in the New World, only the Portuguese produced a real artist of world fame. He was Antônio Francisco Lisboa, born to a black mother of a white father and freed by his father on his baptism in Ouro Preto, in 1730. His father, an architect, apprenticed him out to craftsmen to learn woodcarving. Soon he was the best known of Minas Gerais church decorators. At the height of this local fame he was attacked by leprosy which disfigured his fingers and stunted his height. He came to be known as "Aleijadinho," the Little Cripple; under that name he is remembered as a dedicated artist. With his two devoted slaves he spent his last decades, chisel tied to his fingerless hands, carving the realistic and tragic statues of the life of Chirst which adorn churches in Ouro Preto and Bahía. The churches also reflected other art—fine colonial architecture, religious paintings, beautiful gold filigree on the altars, elaborate tile decorations— but it is all considered mediocre today compared to the work of Aleijadinho. The colony produced one famous musician, also a mulatto, José Mauricio (1767–1830), who composed more than 300 musical works during his lifetime as a leader of the musical services in the Rio cathedral.

If José Mauricio was the only well-known composer, Brazil had thousands of creators of Brazilian music in the slaves, the principal sources of Brazilian folk music. Their dances are still copied in the great Brazilian carnivals today; they were Africa with a veneer of the New World. Dances and names of song types could fill many pages; some could be analyzed as having their roots in the Tupi-Guaraní, some in the Congo.

Culturally Brazil was not the equal of the Spanish colonies. There were no universities or institutions of higher learning, few private libraries, and no printing presses. But there was no censorship over the importation of books, and there existed a much greater freedom of discussion than in Spanish America, and a toleration of races and ideas which stemmed from the absence of a powerful Church and a strongly centralized government.

Individually, Portugal's writers, missionaries, soldiers, and empire builders were on a par with the Spaniards, but Portugal lacked the lawyers and the political theorists of Spain. Therefore, the Crown never had the strength in Brazil, the Portuguese bureaucracy was never as entrenched, the viceregal pomp was never as imposing as in New Spain and Lima. Less loyal to things Portuguese, Brazil already had a separate "nationality" by 1800. But Portugal had been successful in her empire. In three centuries, her claims covered half of South America, a region eighty times the size of the mother country and twice as much as the Treaty of Tordesillas had allowed her. The great republic of Brazil today is a testimonial to the intrepid colonists who laid the solid foundation on which the modern nation rests.

READINGS

Alden, D., *Royal Government in Colonial Brazil* (1968).

———— (ed), *Colonial Roots of Modern Brazil* (1972).

Arciniegas, G., ed., *The Green Continent* (1944).

Bandiera, M., *Brief History of Brazilian Literature* (1958).

Boxer, C. R., *The Dutch in Brazil, 1624–1654* (1957).

————, *Four Centuries of Portuguese Expansion, 1415–1825: A Succinct Summary* (1961).

————, *Golden Age in Brazil, 1595–1750* (1962; 1969).

————, *A Great Luso-Brazilian Figure, Padre Antonio Vieira, S. J., 1608–1697* (1957).

————, *Portuguese Seaborne Empire: 1415–1825* (1969).

————, *Portuguese Society in the Tropics: The Municipal Councils of Goa, Macao, Bahía and Luanda, 1510–1800* (1965).

————, *Race Relations in the Portuguese Colonial Empire, 1415–1825* (1963).

————, *Salvadore de Sá and the Struggle for Brazil and Angola, 1602–1686* (1952).

Brown, R., *Land and People of Brazil* (1960).

Burns, E. B., *Documentary History of Brazil* (1966).

————, *History of Brazil* (1970).

Calmon, P., *History of Brazil* (with de Mendeiros, 1939).

Calogeras, F. P., *History of Brazil*, trans., P. A. Martin (1939).

Castedo, L., *The Baroque Prevalence in Brazilian Art, Seventeenth to Twentieth Centuries* (1964).

Correia-Afonso, *Jesuit Letters and Indian History 1542–1733* (2nd ed., 1970).

Curtis, P. D., *Atlantic Slave Trade* (1969).

Da Costa, L. E., *Rio in the Time of the Viceroys,* trans. D. H. Momsen (1936).

Davis, D. B., *The Problem of Slavery in Western Culture* (1966).

Dominian, H. G., *Apostle of Brazil: The Biography of José de Anchieta* (1958).

Foner, L., and E. D. Genovese, *Slavery in the World* (1969).

Freyre, G., *The Masters and the Slaves,* trans. Putnam (2nd ed., 1956).

————, *New World in the Tropics* (1959).

Fritz, S., *Journal of Travels and Labours of Father Samuel Fritz in the River of the Amazons between 1686 and 1723* (1922).

Furtado, C., *Economic Growth of Brazil* (1971).

Goldberg, J., *Brazilian Literature* (1922).

Goodwin, P. L., *Brazil Builds: Architecture New and Old, 1652–1942* (1943).

Greenleaf, R. E., *The Roman Catholic Church in Colonial Latin America* (1970).

Greenlee, W. B., *Voyage of Pedro Alvares Cabral to Brazil and India* (1938).

Hill, L. F., ed., *Brazil* (1947).

Jayne, K. G., *Vasco da Gama and his Successors 1460–1580* (1970).

Keith, H. H., and S. F. Edwards (eds.), *Conflict and Continuity in Brazilian Society* (1969).

Kiemen, M. C., *Indian Policy of Portugal in the Amazon Region, 1614–1693* (1954).

Labat, P., *The Memoirs of Père Labat 1693–1705* (1970).

Lathrap, D. W., *The Upper Amazon* (1970).

Lima, M. de O., *Evolution of Brazil Compared with That of Spanish and Anglo-Saxon America* (1914).

Livermore, H. O., *History of Portugal* (1947).

————, *A New History of Portugal* (1967).

Magalhães, P. de, *Histories of Brazil,* trans. J. B. Stetson (2 vols., 1922).

Marchant, A., *From Barter to Slavery: Economic Relations of Portuguese and Indians in the Settlement of Brazil, 1500–1580* (1942).

María de Jesús, C., *Child of the Dark* (1962).

Medina, J. T., *Discovery of the Amazon* (1934).

Moog, V., *Bandeirantes and Pioneers* (1964).

Morison, S. E., *Portuguese Voyages to America in the Fifteenth Century* (1940).

Morner, M., *Expulsion of Jesuits from Latin America* (1965).

————,*The Political and Economic Activities of the Jesuits in the La Plata Region* (1953).

————, *Race Mixture in the History of Latin America* (1967).

Morrill, P., *The Gold Rushes* (Chapter on Brazil, 1940).

Morse, R., *The Bandeirantes* (1965).

Nash, R., *Conquest of Brazil* (1926).

Nist, J., *Brazilian Poetry: An Anthology* (1962).

Nowell, C. E., *History of Portugal* (1952).

Parker, J., ed., *Tidings out of Brazil* (1957).

Peckham, H., and C. Gibson (eds.), *Attitudes of Colonial Powers Towards the American Indian* (1969).

Pierson, D., *Negroes in Brazil: A Study of Race Contact at Bahía* (1942).

Polmentary, H. C., *The River of the Amazons—Its Discovery and Early Exploration, 1500–1743* (1965).

Pope-Hennessy, J., *Sins of the Fathers: A Study of the Atlantic Slave Traders 1441–1807* (1968).

Prado, C., trans. by S. Macedo, *Colonial Background of Modern Brazil* (1967).

Prestage, E., *Portuguese Pioneers* (1933).

Ramos, A., *The Negro in Brazil* (1939).

Randall, L., *A Comparative Economic History of Latin America: Argentina, Brazil, Mexico, Peru, 1500–1914* (1972).

Rodrigues, J. H., *Brazil and Africa* (1966).

—————, *Brazilians: Their Character and Aspirations* (1967).

Russell-Wood, A. J. R., *Fidalgos and Philanthropists: The Santa Casa de Misercordia (1550–1755)* (1968).

Silva Rego, A. da, *Portuguese Colonization in the Sixteenth Century* (1959).

Southey, E., *History of Brazil* (3 vols., 1810–1819).

Tenenbaum, L., *Tiradentes* (1965).

Vellinho, M., *Brazil South: Its Conquest and Settlement* (1968).

Wiznitzer, A., *Jews in Colonial Brazil* (1960).

old world and new create a rich new tapestry

PART II

In the next three hundred years, Indians and Europeans, along with many forced immigrants from Africa, combined to create a new race in the New World. In this combination, the culture and the characteristics of the various bloodstreams were present.

The two highest classes were the aristocrats born in Spain and the pure whites or creoles born in the New World. These two classes quarreled among themselves for prestige in the Spanish empire. The offspring of these classes and the natives produced the *mestizo* or mixed-blood, the numbers of which multiplied during three centuries of colonial rule.

The *mestizo* worked hard, fought in the army, obeyed the Spanish administration, and suffered the domination of the upper classes. Usually he was disadvantaged economically as well as politically and socially. Only in recent times in much of Latin America is he coming into his own.

The third group adding new strands to the ethnic tapestry was the African slave, whose story is covered in the first chapter in this section. The background of this racial group, its forced transport and life in bondage brings another sad note into the story of popular confrontation in the New World.

Spain's long hold on its vast empire in Latin America attests to the fact that it was successfully administered. To understand this success along with the attendant failures, it is necessary to examine the methods used to administer both central and local government, to control trade, and to maintain church authority. The daily life of people at all social and racial levels must be understood, including the influence religious faith had on people's lives.

When riches poured from the mines and fleets sailed the oceans, other European nations became jealous of Spain—which resulted in the intercolonial wars and frontier clashes of the 17th and 18th centuries. In these, Spain managed to hold her own. But in the 18th century there also came the Enlightenment, which brought revolutionary changes to Europe. Since the culture of the colonies was always a reflection of trends in Europe, the colonists developed corresponding interests. By the end of the century, all peoples were seeking to secure more freedom from dictatorial governments, and the fact that the Spanish Americans did so indicates that the Spanish colonial empire cannot be considered a three-century failure.

chapter 9

THE AFRICANS IN THE NEW WORLD

People of Indian descent and people of European descent make up the "Latin Americans." But in addition, there are millions of people of African descent. Some black men stand out in the history of the Spanish colonies. A very tall strong black man named Estevánico was a Moorish slave of the explorer Pánfilo de Narváez who was abandoned by his ships off Florida in 1528. When the explorer and his men tried to return to Mexico in small boats built by themselves, they were wrecked off the coast of Texas. After six years of degrading captivity among the Texas Indians, only the giant slave and one ship's officer, Alvar Núñez Cabeza de Vaca, and two others survived. They wandered for years among the Indians of New Mexico, Arizona and northern Mexico serving as medicine men. Cabeza de Vaca, writing of this long journey, had nothing but praise of Estevánico as an equal. When they reported to Spanish officials in Mexico, Estevánico led another expedition up the Rio Grande to look for Pueblo Indian villages. The large black man went at the head of the expedition and arrived in the Pueblo towns alone, where the Indians, frightened at his strange appearance, shot him down with arrows. Thus a black man of African descent was one of the first Spanish-speaking people to come into the United States Southwest. Later colonizers into New Mexico took an African drum player to set the pace of the settlers' march. In South America, Sebastián Benalcázar, the founder of Quito, listed three black men as his companions and co-founders of the city, and their names are carved in stone in the original plaza there.

By a census taken in 1800, there were three million people in the settled part of Brazil, 800,000 of them white, 300,000 Christianized Indians and a million and a half or more blacks or freedmen descended from slaves brought from Africa. There was no count made of people of African descent in the Spanish colonies of the Caribbean. But perhaps ten million people of African descent, most of them slaves, lived in Cuba, the island of Hispaniola including Santo Domingo and Haiti, the sugar-producing Lesser Antilles, owned by England, France, Holland and Denmark, and on the coasts of northern South America, Panama, Central America and Mexico. They had been taken to all these areas, because large profits could be made on sugar plantations and strong, hard-working people used to the tropics were necessary to care for the cane fields and work in the sugar mills. In the ports of this "sugar belt" they worked in chain gangs as stevedores on the docks; they cut and fitted the great building stones to make the fortifications necessary against English and Dutch pirates. Their descendants are there today, often still working on the docks or in the sugar mills. Partly because they have so recently been emancipated from slavery, they remain the slum dwellers or the rural poor. But their contributions of heavy hard work in the New World, of dance, music, art, and poetry brought from Africa, make them an integral part of Latin America.

the mother land in Africa

Most Africans in the New World came from West Africa by force. North Africa and Egypt had been well known to ancient Europeans. But the Sahara desert and the forbidding coast south of Cape Verde had kept knowledge of the Niger River drainage area and the Guinea coast a secret to geographers until the beginnings of the Renaissance. If the black people were ever seen in Roman and medieval Europe, they came from the upper Nile by way of Egypt, or were traded by two's and three's up the Red Sea from Arabia. Then came the captains of Prince Henry the Navigator, who traded with Arabs who had crossed the Sahara and reached Senegal. Just before Prince Henry's death, his captains reached the Guinea Coast under the shoulder of Africa and sailed down to the Congo.

The area of today's Liberia, Ghana, Dahomey, Togoland, southern Nigeria and the Cameroons stretch east and west along 2,000 miles of Guinea coastline. Behind the harbors at the mouths of the rivers were fields planted with kaffir corn and cotton, yams and gourds, and between the fields lay many areas of dense forest. The African inhabitants of these regions were villagers who worked these lands under native kings. One of the big towns near the coast of today's Nigeria was Benin, established by 1350. Slavers came to know the coast as the "Bight of Benin." A Dutchman described it in 1602 as "built along a great, broad street eight times broader than those of Amsterdam." There were four miles of this street, with many side streets, on which "the houses stand in good order, one close and even with the other." He visited the court of the king, who maintained "many gentlemen in his army, who when they come to court ride upon horses." This king was called the Oba, and his "palace," a series of many rooms and courtyards, was decorated with bronze plaques which can be seen in European museums today. There is still a tribal chieftain called the Oba of Benin, and in the 1970's he sent his grandsons to Oxford.

Benin itself was a center for a network of trade routes long before the time of Prince Henry the Navigator. Ibadan was a similar city. Today in the large and varied market of Ibadan, native nationalists in long scarves of home weaving mingle with Moslem Nigerians in long white gowns. Many European visitors were impressed with the culture of these West Africans in the 16th century. Ibadan stayed alive through the long years of the slave trade, but Benin became a small dirty town, destroyed by the English in the 1890's. Millions of the black people later sold through Benin as slaves to the New World came from the ancient kingdoms of the West African Sudan, on the northern limits of sub-Saharan Africa. An independent nation was named Ghana, today the name of a coastal nation 700 miles to the south. In the account of an Arab traveler in A.D. 750, Ghana was described as a civilized region in which gold, cattle, horses and sheep were traded down to the coast of the Gulf of Guinea.

These Western Sudan people became Moslems after two centuries of contact with the Arabs. The Moslem horsemen of the Hausa tribes had founded the city of Kano. This became a big horse-breeding center, and Hausa-bred horses from Kano were traded far to the south at Benin. From their fine cotton, the Kano people wove scarves and dyed them with indigo dye, to trade them for other goods with the blue-veiled, camel-driving Tuaregs of the Sahara. This trade continued from the tenth century into the 1970's.

West of the Niger River lived a people called the Ife. Their ancestors, the Noks, had been working with pottery and carving shell jewelry and stone figurines as early as 500 B.C. The skills in bronze casting of the Ife people were passed on to a nation called Mali, also the name of a modern West African state. Mali people spoke the Mandingo language; some of its words are still spoken by black religious cultists in Brazil today. The Mandingo capital of Timbuktu was the largest and most famous medieval African city, known to the Moroccans on the Mediterranean. Scribes from Timbuktu could write in Arabic in the slave centers on the coast of Brazil. Caravans from towns in southern Morocco crossed the Sahara with more than a thousand horses to trade at Timbuktu for leather, iron work and cotton cloth. One Mandingo emperor of Timbuktu went to Mecca on a pilgrimage accompanied by a wealthy caravan. In 1591, the Moroccan army captured Timbuktu, which ceased to be a center of learning and luxury, but has remained a caravan market center near the Niger into modern times. Throughout the colonial period of Latin America, slave raiders from the Guinea and Senegal coasts kidnapped large numbers of people from Kano and Timbuktu.

Historians are only now beginning to study the ancient history of these West African peoples. They think that the Nigerian Sudan was the first area heavily populated, and as the land was over-used and the food supply diminished, the people moved into the forested area nearer the Gulf of Guinea, taking their agriculture and their crafts with them. But the entire area south of the waterless Sahara was filled with village people and skilled farmers and craftsmen in 1450, when the slaves were first being sold by two's and three's in Lisbon by captains trained by Henry the Navigator.

As the sugar plantations of the New World demanded more and more slaves, Portuguese slavers began to capture tribesmen from Angola and Congo. Portuguese missionaries had been sent to convert the King of Congo in 1490. The royal family became Christians as did several sub-chiefs, all governors of yam-and-millet growing villages. The crown prince was baptized in 1491 under the name of Alfonso. Other royal youths were sent from Congo to be educated and return as priests. Alfonso himself ruled as "an enlightened Christian" for more than thirty years. But slave raiders up from Angola kidnapped hundreds of Christianized people and sold them into Brazil by 1600. A Congo priest pleaded with the Pope, who in turn asked the Spanish king at that time in control of Portugal to stop "this trade in Christians." But the government in Portugal replied that "it was power-less to control its subjects in Angola."

The capital of today's Angola, Loanda, had been founded by the Portuguese as a slave-catching center. The Angola natives had no strong central kings and each village ruled itself under its own chieftain. To save their own tribesmen from capture by the Portuguese, villages began to make war on other villages for the sake of captives for sale. After two centuries of such warfare, local government in the area had collapsed and native village agriculture had been destroyed. When, late in the colonial period, the French were building up large-scale sugar production on Haiti, it was Angola and Congo natives they bought, because they were cheap and were usable only as field hands. The primitive peoples of Central Africa between the Congo and the Zambezi were seldom found in the slave trade. But it is a mistake to assume that African natives were brought to the Americas as primitive savages, "children of the forests" like the Brazilian Indians. From all the accounts of conditions of life in West Africa it is evident that the majority of the people were farmers or craftsmen. Their farming methods may have been as good as those of Spanish and Portuguese villagers in 1492. They had no wheel and no native method of writing. But they were more accustomed to the use of copper and gold than any Indians of the New World, and could also cast and forge iron. Their extensive trade routes were as long as the ancient trails from Central America to New Mexico. Unlike the American Indian village and city dwellers, they had domesticated cattle and horses.

It is true that slavery existed among the West Africans. A Scotch-man named Mungo Park, who was the first explorer from Europe to reach the curve of the Niger, traveled with an Arab-led coffle of slaves from the area of Timbuktu out to the Senegal coast. Of the line of blacks chained together at the neck with whom he made the journey, two-thirds of them had already been slaves when joined to the chain, and one-third were recent prisoners of war. But all of them had come into the status of slaves because of capture in war. While held in enemy African villages they were given land to farm as a tenant class. Many other slaves had sold themselves to pay a debt and were free when the cost was worked out. Others were sold by their kinsmen or clan as punishment or for revenge. They could be redeemed when the kinsmen decided to do so, and their children were never born into slavery. There was no slave-owning class as such, and no one clan or town lived by the product of slave labor alone.

The ancient civilizations of the Mediterranean area depended heavily on slavery. The Pyramid of Cheops, the Parthenon in Athens, the Coliseum in Rome had all been built by slaves. Such slaves, captives in war or their descendants, were themselves Mediterranean peoples or, later, Germanic ones. Such Caucasians were, by the third or fourth generation, similar in appearance to their masters, and could run away unnoticed, melt into the crowds, or be freed in some sort of general amnesty. The slave status of their ancestors did not show on their faces; they were often able to return to the home of their origin if they wished. During the long wars in the Iberian peninsula between Moslems and Christians, each side enslaved captives from the other and held them for ransom, or put them to work.

The tragedy of black African slavery in the New World was that the color of their skin, their non-Caucasian appearance, marked the imported Africans as slaves or as the descendants of slaves forever. They could not change their African looks and they had no way to get home again where all the people were Africans. It was a new and different kind of slavery in the history of the world.

The warfare to catch such people and sell them to the New World brought decadence to the native kingdoms of Africa. At the height of colonial sugar production, more than 100,000 of the strongest men and women were siphoned off yearly to start the sad journey to the New World. The best West Africans, eugenically, were lost as breeding stock for the homeland. Agriculture, horse-breeding, metal work all became subservient to the slave trade, for native kings no longer encouraged any activity save the securing of captives. European foods and European-made goods could be purchased with human flesh. War between Dutch, Portuguese, English and even Yankee slave traders destroyed the large coastal towns. The empires of the Western Sudan fell apart as village chief fought village chief to get captives and to save his own clan from slavery. Just as American Indians were demoralized by liquor and guns, so were West African communities by the slave trade. Religious feelings about the immorality of human chattel slavery were lost to both Moslems and Christians, and forgotten over three centuries of exploitation. The African kings became the puppets of the slavers and were easily bought off with firearms and glass dishes. The Portuguese traders eased their consciences by having the captives baptized and thus giving them a "chance" at Heaven. Dutch and British traders often preferred to think that the blacks had no souls to save, and trade in them was the equivalent to trade in cattle or horses.

the political history of African exploitation
for the New World

Prince Henry of Portugal had planned to send ships around Africa to the rich trading centers of the East, since he had talked to Arabs who knew that Africa was one continent. As we have seen, his captains first met black Africans when they reached Cape Verde and the Senegal River Valley in 1444. One of these captains is said to have traded for ten young Moslem blacks, perhaps the slaves of an Arab merchant. Since many Moslem slaves were at work in Portugal in the 1440's, these handsome Senegalese were easily offered for sale in Lisbon. They brought high prices as butlers and footmen. Because Prince Henry had ordered the slaves baptized so that they would not remain Moslems, he probably still thought, at the time of his death sixteen years later, that the trade he had started in black Africans was a way to save souls.

By 1471, the Portuguese traders had a permanent colony at Cape Verde, knew of the trails to reach Timbuktu, and had begun to build a fortified post on the coast near today's Accra in Ghana. It was the gold dust of that coast more than the black workers they sought. But each ship loaded with gold and tropical products also took two or three dozen slaves back for increasingly higher prices in Lisbon. The traders had only to tell themselves that the blacks were being saved from Islam or from paganism. They also could reason that the blacks fared better in Lisbon than as servants for the native kings. In 1472, the Portuguese reached Benin. Soon they had three "factories" or fortified trading posts, the last at the island of São Thomé off the Cameroons coast. All these posts were licensed to trade in gold dust, cotton cloth, ivory, and only incidentally in black human beings. Sometimes the Portuguese traders baptized a whole cargo of slaves at once, and at least the baptism gave them status as Christians. When they became family servants in Lisbon they were taken to church with the family, made confessions, received communion and were buried in holy ground. These attitudes were carried over to Brazil.

By 1492, some black slaves from Lisbon had been traded or freed to go into Spain. Perhaps two black men were with Columbus off San Salvador, for the Pinzón brothers of the *Niña* and the *Pinta* had bought slaves from the Portuguese. Some slaves were brought into Santo Domingo before 1515 as personal servants, cooks or herdsmen. By then, Father Bartolomé de las Casas had concerned himself with the pitiful conditions of the Indians in Santo Domingo, and the inefficiency of their labor in the tropics. Las Casas' pleas had one bad social effect on the New World. Accustomed in Spain to the Portuguese slave trade in Negroes, and considering Negro slavery a lesser evil than the exploitation of natives which he had seen with his own eyes, he suggested that Negroes be introduced into the West Indies to do the work assigned the unfortunate Indians, as the Africans were better adapted to plantation life in the tropics. Later las Casas repented his words and advocated abolition, but it was then too late. Ovando had brought a few Negroes to work in the mines, and they soon ran away to the hills. A consignment of 200 had been sent from Seville in 1510, but the Cardinal of Spain had stopped further trade. Now with the increased planting of sugar which called for human labor by hands accustomed to the tropics, Negroes were imported in large numbers. More than 8,000 slaves were sold in Santo Domingo from 1520 to 1530. After the middle of the sixteenth century, territorial expansion on the mainland and the official ban against the enslavement of Indians still further augmented the traffic, either directly from Africa or by way of the slave mart in Lisbon. Cuban plantations prospered on Negro slave labor from their beginning.

Later Spanish kings used the sale of a slave trade monopoly as a way to make money for the crown. The grandson of Isabella had tried a system of granting "the sale privilege or license for eight years of introducing blacks into the Indies to a maximum of 4000 to a nobleman and personal friend." But this gentleman sold the right to an Italian company for 25,000 ducats. Soon the right, or *asiento* as it was called, was resold at a large profit to two Germans at the Spanish court. Thereupon the Council of the Indies advised the king to handle the purchase of slaves from the Portuguese coast through government officials. Individual Portuguese shippers from the African "factories" often traded directly to officials or port authorities in the Spanish colonies. But when Spain held Portugal under a joint crown from 1580 to 1640, the *asiento*, or grant of right to trade in slaves, was reinstituted. The contracts specified the number, to be taken to the colonies each year, of *Piezas de Indias*, or "prime slaves sound in wind and limb between the ages of eighteen and thirty, and seven Spanish hands tall." On each such black, a duty was paid to the Council of the Indies and a bonus paid to the Spanish crown. The demand for slaves increased with the prosperity of the sugar plantations, and prices went up with demand. After the independence of the Spanish Netherlands, Dutch companies received the *asiento*, then in the early 1700's, the French Royal Guinea Company, and by 1720, the English South Sea Company. The wars of the 1700's in the Caribbean led to a great deal of smuggling and many New England ships profited from the sale of Africans into the Spanish colonies. After the 1770's, any merchant could buy slaves openly on the African coast and bring them legally into the ports of Spanish America. Dutch traders bought slaves for the islands of Curaçao and Aruba, and were the first to sell slaves into the English colony of Jamestown in 1619. Once Haiti was established as a French colony, an unusually vicious system of using unskilled Angolan slaves was introduced on the sugar plantations there.

The pirate John Hawkins was the first Englishman known to have sold slaves in Spanish America. Under the eyes of the Portuguese he had raided the Guinea Coast in 1562 and stolen 300 slaves from the slave pens there. In Santo Domingo he traded them for a cargo of sugar and hides and some quantities of pearls. His second voyage was partially financed by Queen Elizabeth I herself. With four ships, he then went to Sierra Leone, where there was no Portuguese fortification, and "spent several days there, going ashore every day to take the inhabitants with burning and spoiling their towns." He forced the governor of Caracas, Venezuela, to buy his slave goods by landing a force of armed sailors at La Guaira. When Hawkins sailed again in 1567, one of his ships, the *Judith,* was commanded by Francis Drake, Hawkins' young cousin. Local kings in Sierra Leone by this time feared Hawkins' methods and quickly rounded up 500 captives for him among their neighbors in the interior. After trading slaves into San Domingo, Hawkins took this fleet of ships right into the port of Vera Cruz, where they were caught by a hurricane and taken over by the Spanish governor. Hawkins and Drake escaped personally and Hawkins retired a wealthy man. But Drake went on to be an outright pirate rather than a slave trader.

A century later, the English king, Charles II, had an investment in the Royal African Company. The English legally owned Jamaica by this time, and this new company had "factories" of its own along the Gold Coast to supply Jamaica and Barbados with African slaves for the prosperous English sugar plantations. Two hundred and fifty ships of this company brought 30,000 Africans a year into the British held islands, and the mainland colonies, or smuggled them into the Spanish Caribbean ports. By the Treaty of Utrecht in 1713, the English had forced the Spanish to grant them the *asiento.* Now the English controlled the Grain Coast, the Gold Coast, the Ivory Coast, and the Bight of Benin. Englishmen, not Portuguese, staffed the slave-trading centers or "factories" there. Jamaica became the wealthiest English colony and the largest slave trading center in the entire New World. Spanish slave buyers could get them in Jamaica, or from "legal" English ships which entered Havana, Porto Bello in Panama, Cartagena in Colombia, or Santo Domingo. New England smugglers moved into this trade throughout the 1700's and carried it on legally after 1776.

methods of obtaining, transporting, and selling
African slaves

Slaves were being brought to the New World in a steady stream, almost an assembly-line production, by 1600. At least 300,000 had been landed by the end of the first century of colonization. In the seventeenth century another million and a half were brought, and in the eighteenth, as the sugar production boomed in Brazil and Haiti, another six million more. By 1750 African slaves were being sold from Argentina to New York, the whole length of the Atlantic Coast, some of these for transshipment across the Isthmus of Panama to Ecuador and Peru for work as stevedores. If nine and a half million Africans survived to come to the colonies, more than twenty million must have been captured in raids or purchased at the "factories." Perhaps another five million died resisting capture or perished in the coffles or chain gangs from the interior to the coast. For every slave that came to the slave markets in Havana, Bahía, or Jamaica, perhaps two had died in the process of capture and shipment.

Church authorities often worried as to whether blacks were taken from Africa "legally." In 1610, a priest in Portugal wrote to ask a missionary in Angola if many of the slaves were "carried off illegally." He was told not to "have scruples on this score." Since the kings "have obtained them among those not reached by the missions, very few of them can say they were taken illegally." Officially neither church nor Portuguese government would say that any part of the trade was "illegal." A local king had to be particularly careful in his criticism, because he, himself, and his own family stood in danger of transportation in the slave ships whenever the traders were angered.

On the Guinea coast, kings of Benin or Lagos would buy long lines or coffles of chained slaves from the interior Sudan or Niger kingdoms at low cost, paying in gold dust or salt. In fact, many of these kings hired regular Arab raiders for this purpose. The kings and the raiders divided the profits between them from the sale of the survivors at the port. At the port the Portuguese and later the English maintained "baracoons" or slave pens. The "factor," the European who managed the slave pens, would inspect all the slaves for disease and then brand them with the government, ship owner's or company brand. Food, a mush of corn, bananas and yams, would be thrown into the slave pen once a day. Here again the strongest survived for they got the lion's share of the food.

Whenever any slave ship arrived at the "factory," there were slaves ready for transport. Usually the ship stood out in the harbor and the slaves were taken out in barges. If they were from the interior, as the majority were after 1650, they were terrified by the sea and the high surf when ferried between the baracoon and the ship. Some of them flung themselves overboard, or clutched handfuls of sand in a desperate effort to stay in Africa. As a witness reported, "They had to be whipped in line by a cat-o-nine-tails," for it was evident that "they preferred to be eaten by the sharks near the sight of the beach than be taken far beyond the roaring ocean." It was as if "they thought they had already died and gone to hell." Many of them assumed they were to be taken to some nearby islands to be fattened up and eaten by the strange white men who, they assumed, were cannibals. No Africans returned to tell them of life in the New World, and few of the sailors spoke any language they understood. As late as 1800, many captured Africans thought they were to be sold as a source of meat.

For the actual voyage, slaves were crowded into the hold in narrow spaces and fed on mash made of millet grain. When slaves sickened or refused food, they were thrown overboard, but when they tried to commit suicide by jumping off the ship they were hauled back and almost flogged to death. In the hold, each slave had scarcely enough room to turn himself, they were all brought up on deck each morning only so the sailors could wash the stench of the hold with sea water. Some captains did not even bother with this cleanliness, but reasoned "crowd them in closely, throw them food, and enough will survive anyway to make a handsome profit." Captains were so afraid of mutiny that they were careful not to confine together those who spoke the same language, so that no plans could be made for mutiny. There were many such mutinies anyway during the three-hundred-year period. There is no record kept of the whole ships taken over by slaves and lost at sea, since none of the Africans had knowledge of how to return the ship to any African port out of reach of Portuguese or English cannon. Heavy losses by death due to intestinal orders, to the continually raging smallpox so deadly to the non-immune Africans, or to suffocation in the hold did not materially cut the profit. Often the voyages lasted more than three months, since the slave captains had to go north along the African coast nearly two thousand miles to reach the trade winds from the Canaries or Madeira and across to Havana or Jamaica.

Even though whole cargoes of slave ships going to Portuguese ports in Brazil were baptized, the trip to Bahía was usually just as hard. The ceremony of baptism, done in a strange language while slaves still were in chains, had no meaning. Slave ships were brought into Bahía or Recife, or later into Rio de Janeiro, and planters or their overseers came directly on board to purchase the slaves as individuals. Spanish planters could do likewise in Havana or Santo Domingo. In Panama, Vera Cruz or Cartagena, Colombia, government officials bought slaves by groups of twenty or thirty for work in quarries or on docks. In Porto Bello, the Caribbean port for Panama, slave gangs were purchased to serve as mule drivers or porters to carry goods across the Isthmus. All such government owned slaves were branded a second time as crown property and were given five to seven years to live before they were replaced by fresh workers from Africa.

Some historians consider that the very large profits on the slave trade, in spite of the losses, helped bring excess capital into Europe. Here was a commodity, the individual African, for which the enterpreneur spent only a small sum in yardage of European cloth, muskets, or barrels of rum, and which brought a profit sometimes thirty fold. Rum was distilled from molasses which was itself a by-product of the sugar refining business. Some very religious Puritans in Boston or Liverpool made fortunes this way which could be turned into more ships or into stock companies investing in the new commercial enterprises of the late eighteenth century. Portuguese traders did not always make such a large return but the slave trade made possible the survival of the sugar producing colonies in Brazil. In the earliest years of Santo Domingo and Cuba, if sugar had not been found profitable the island colonies might have been abandoned before the mainland could be explored and Mexico and Peru exploited. To this extent the survival of Latin America depended on the labor of the black Africans.

life for the black slaves in the Spanish New World

The great mass of Africans in the New World worked in the cane fields, the sugar refineries, and at any heavy work at all in the lowland tropics. The African from the agricultural villages was easier to teach than a non-agricultural Indian; also he was stronger and healthier than an Indian of similar height and age, and he was more docile, perhaps because he knew he could never return home. He was completely and forever lost from his own village culture, and thus had no alternative except to become a *cimarrón,* or runaway wild black African living free in the hinterland. So the slave assumed a resigned cheerfulness and chanted in rhythm with his fellow slaves as he staggered under the heavy burdens on the Cruces Trail across Panama, or sang as he cut cane on a Cuban plantation. He remained socially at the bottom of the scale in Spanish America. Some few who worked as freedmen in the Spanish army or in the mines had status little above the slaves and below any Indians. A *zambo,* or red-black half-breed, was spurned by all three color groups and considered a potential enemy of society. In the Spanish colonies, *mulattoes,* mixtures of white and black, remained in the slave condition of their mothers, or, if freed, had to live among the few free black men, and not as whites or *mestizos.*

From the whips of the sugar plantation overseers the blacks ran away by the thousands, establishing communities of runaway blacks, the *cimarrones* referred to above. In British Honduras, and the central mountains of the greater Antilles and northern Panama their descendants are in the majority today. English and French pirates cooperating with a band of *cimarrones* from the interior of Cuba once sacked Havana. *Cimarrones* were so numerous in Panama, that any travel away from the main trail was considered dangerous. Spanish settlers exaggerated the dangers of slave revolts and *cimarrón* attacks, and rounded up freed blacks on the slightest provocation, often considering them dangerous wild men.

In those areas where the numbers of slaves was greater than that of whites or *mestizos,* rebellions often did take place. The earliest recorded was in Santo Domingo in 1522, when forty black men murdered their masters and fled to the hills. In 1531, there was a general uprising in Panama, and in Hispaniola surviving Indians joined with slaves to wreck plantations and harass towns in a guerilla war which took ten years to suppress. But the plantations were soon rebuilt, the slaves eventually surrendered, and more slaves were purchased in Africa as sugar production and Isthmian traffic increased. This brought more Spanish soldiers to the New World to guard against more uprisings, and then more African blacks to work for the army and help build more fortifications. Thus slavery increased as the colonies expanded.

Both the Spanish crown and the Spanish church had qualms of conscience over the institution of slavery, in spite of the economic pressure to preserve it. Laws about the treatment of slaves in Spain, in those days captured Moslems, were proclaimed by King Alfonso the Wise in 1280. The laws were a direct continuation of the Roman Justinian Code guaranteeing slaves the rights of human beings. Slaves could marry, buy their freedom, even become priests. Masters and slaves were equal in the eyes of God. It was the master's duty to take the slave to church, and to enforce his conversion to Christianity. These laws, part of basic Spanish legal institutions, were carried intact to the colonies.

Queen Isabella had been deeply concerned about the treatment and the Christianity of the Indians in the New World. She died before there were more than a handful of black Africans in Santo Domingo. But her grandson Charles V tried to enforce her wishes with regards to both the Indians and blacks. He even meant to free all the slaves in the Spanish New World, it is said, but he abdicated before he had carried this out. Throughout the next century the sugar plantation system so enhanced the need for slaves in the economy that all idealistic plans to free them became impossible. But the Spanish government continued to take the position that slaves were human beings with moral identity, and the killing of a slave was considered an act of murder. Manumission, or the freeing of slaves, was considered an act of "merit." There was undoubtedly great cruelty, as in any forced system of agricultural work. But conditions on plantations were surely better than were those for slaves working in mines.

As for the Spanish Catholic Church, its position was ambiguous. When Church authorities learned that many Moslem slaves were being brought into Cartagena, they forbade the use of such slaves on public works. The Church has always had "a positive role of sympathetic conversion of virgin peoples to the true faith," and so must not let Moslems mix with slaves owned by the crown. When the Council of the Indies, the governing "cabinet" for the Spanish New World, asked a meeting of bishops about the morality of the African slave trade, the bishops replied that there could be "no doubt as to the necessity of slaves for the support of the kingdom of the Indies." As there had been "no objection on the part of any one filling the seat of His Holiness, but rather tolerance of all of them," the church in Spain could not censure the institution of slavery. Throughout 300 years of Spanish colonial rule, the Church authorities made many statements of conscience concerning kind treatment to slaves as well as to Indians, but never tried to stop any system which was bringing in profits to Spanish plantation owners or taxes to the Crown. There were, however, some abolitionists in Spanish America who spoke out and preached against slavery.

Though authorities agree that the life of African slaves in Spanish colonies was probably easier than that of slaves in Jamaica, Carolina, or Virginia, the life of a black slave was never a life of dignity or comfort. The existence of the *cimarrón communities,* the fear of slave revolts, the poverty of the descendants of the blacks in the Caribbean area today, attest to the great privations of their life throughout the three centuries of Spanish colonial rule.

life of the African in Portuguese Brazil and French Haiti

The life of the African blacks in Brazil was much more a part of the entire economy and the whole strata of social life than in the Spanish colonies. African slaves made the coastal economy possible in Bahía and Pernambuco, and they worked along with Indian slaves in the interior. Since the Portuguese had the monopoly on the slave trade for nearly two hundred years, they brought the healthiest, strongest, and most intelligent Africans to work in their own colonies. They sold the slaves directly to the planters or to agents of the miners in the interior. It is estimated that one-third of all Africans who came to the New World were brought to Brazil. The Brazilian Indians faded away into the jungles, died working for the people of São Paulo and the explorers in the interior, refused to live in the sedentary villages on plantations, or melted their bloodstream into the free class on the frontier. Very few Portuguese farmers or artisans ever came to Brazil from the mother country. Thus a large class of free men, or skilled and trusted African slaves was necessary to the Brazilian economy. And where Brazilian slave owners needed strong, docile hands to plant and harvest cane, to drive oxen in the cane crushers, and stoke the refining furnaces where the molasses boiled, more and more Africans were brought in from the Guinea coast, the Niger Valley and Angola.

Brazilian slaves were more apt to be at work with their own fellow-tribesmen; in Brazil they kept their own customs and beliefs. Some slave groups developed a common language called Nâgo, a mixture of Portuguese words and African dialects, and many of its words are in use today in Bahía.

There were instances of successful black villages in the backlands called *quilombos,* made up of escaped slaves such as the *cimarrones* in Cuba or Panama. In the 1650's for example, many slaves ran away into the wild northeast out of Pernambuco and there set up an independent "republic" called Palmares, after the palm forest in which the "capital" was situated. This capital was one of a group of well-fortified villages of corn and cotton growers in an area almost as large as Portugal. They elected their own head, set up a judicial system, and allotted agricultural land to families. Perhaps 100,000 blacks lived there by 1660. So strong was their republic that the Portuguese did not capture it until 1697. At that time, when a large force finally wiped out the settlement, more than half the adults had been born in the freedom of Palmares and had known no other life.

Those slaves who stayed docilely on the plantations received better treatment than they would have found elsewhere in the New World. Black toddlers were pets in the Big House; masters and slaves joined in festivals on religious holidays. Portuguese men, long a seafaring band who traveled without women to lands where dark-skinned beauties could be had for the asking, always mated freely in the New World with both Indian and slave. Now their mulatto children by slave women were often freed at birth, grew up as overseers or artisans, and were sometimes even sent to study in Lisbon. All Brazil in general felt no antagonism toward black people as such; anyone with a little white blood was white, in contrast to the United States plantation-life development in which anyone with a drop of Negro blood was Negro. There were many laws and customs protecting the rights of slaves, the holidays granted them, the privilege to earn private money, the rights to inherit land and shops, to complain against unjust treatment, and to form protective and religious brotherhoods with other slaves.

The slaves lived in the patriarchal villages around the Big House, the *Casa Grande,* the master's manor house of fifteen or twenty rooms and a private chapel. The establishment contained elements of a social center, a hospital, fortress, school, commissary, and army kitchen. It was an isolated, patriarchal, self-sufficient village. Beyond the scores of slave huts would be the sugar refinery, the distillery, and the stock pens.

On the mining frontier in Minas Gerais, slaves from metal working villages in Ghana brought high prices. They improved by their own knowledge the methods of smelting gold and working iron. Thousands were able to buy their own freedom and stake out their own claims. There is even a record of a group of free men who had come from Senegal and Timbuktu setting up a trading company in Bahía and trading in their own ships with Senegal in the Arabic language.

Although visitors from Europe wrote with admiration of happy conditions of slaves in Brazil, there undoubtedly was cruelty. Any sadistic master could do what he pleased with his slaves, and the only complaint that could be made was by another master, not by any black person. Little white boys were allowed to mistreat any black child or adult, and grew up knowing nothing but selfishness and arrogance. Portuguese wives could order the slave-girl mistresses of their husbands tortured to death for sheer jealousy. The death rate among blacks on the plantations always remained higher than the rate of survival of black babies, and slaves continued to be imported faster than the growth of the colony would seem to necessitate.

At the time of independence in Brazil, José Bonifâcio de Andrade, an idealistic leader, proclaimed that the new nation should abolish slavery as had the Spanish South American nations, even though slavery was more important in the Brazilian economy than in the Peruvian or the Chilean. Though the mother country, Portugal, had been responsible for the "initial sin, . . . we tyrannize over our slaves and reduce them to the state of brutish animals, and they in return initiate us in their immorality and teach us all their vices," wrote Bonifacio de Andrade. His proposals for abolute abolition fell on deaf ears, and he, himself, was exiled in the first years of independence. Brazilian slaves were not freed until 1889, though by a peaceful proclamation and without bloodshed.

The worst conditions for black Africans in the New World was in French Haiti, and it is only there that a slave revolt ever permanently succeeded. The Haitian end of the island of Hispaniola was a thriving French colony by 1700, known to the homeland as Saint Domingue. It had been organized under a French governor and its largest town, Port-au-Prince, had been made the capital. A report of 1779 showed the colony to have 40,000 whites, 25,000 mixed-bloods and freedmen, and 480,000 slaves. Great fortunes were made in the plantations and sugar mills, where the few white overseers dominated the rural slaves. Mulatto slaves were treated as confidential servants in the plantation houses, and *mulatto* mistresses were kept by most white men, with their quadroon children being freed at birth. Half the population of the town of Port-au-Prince, Cap Haitien, and Aux Cayes were freed mulattoes. In these towns the handful of ruling whites lived a life of luxury; French plays and concerts were presented, French novels read. The slaves, however—the majority of them African-born and recently purchased in Jamaica's slave market—worked on the plantations in chain gangs, died under the overseers' lashes, and were replaced by more new purchases in spite of a supposedly humanitarian French legal code.

In fact, slavery in Haiti was so vicious that slaves had to be replaced by fresh African imports, usually from the "cheaper," less-civilized regions, every four years rather than every seven or eight as in other sugar-producing islands.

The story of the successful slave revolt came out of the philosophies of the French Revolution in 1789, and its success led to a ferment of revolutionary philosophy about "Liberty, Equality and Fraternity" which influenced a group of young South Americans to work toward independence. Therefore, this story has to be part of a later chapter. But its three heroes, Toussaint L'Ouverture, Jean Jacques Dessalines and Henri Christophe are among the most famous black Africans in the history of the New World.

contributions of the black Africans
to Latin American culture

The African immigrants, though brought against their will, "saved" the economy of Brazil and the Caribbean area by their hard work under tropical conditions. But they did more than save the economy. They contributed a major part to Latin American culture, especially in music. Though blacks, and their whitened offspring the *mulattos,* or their reddened offspring, the *zambos,* were kept at the bottom of society, all classes of society were doing the "black thing." Without realizing it, they were dancing to black African rhythms, singing black African songs, wearing black African costumes at carnivals, believing in black African herb doctors. In Bahía and Recife, in Havana and in Port-au-Prince, African religious cults today carry on ceremonials direct from the mother country, using words of the African languages of centuries ago. All Haitians have some African blood; Cubans and Puerto Ricans are so mixed that color is of little importance in the 1970's. Brazilians of the northern states above the Tropic of Capricorn are more African than Caucasian or Indian, and no one in Brazil stops to ask or care. The Portuguese language as spoken in Brazil, the largest and most important Portuguese-speaking nation, is said to have softer sounds, less harsh consonants because of the African influence. The outstanding artist of colonial Brazil, Aleijandinho and the one outstanding classical composer, José Mauricio, were both of African blood. Few modern Latin Americans realize how widespread African influence has been.

READINGS

Aimes, H. H. S., *The History of Slavery in Cuba 1511–1848* (rep. 1967).

Bennett, L., *Before the Mayflower: A History of the Negro in America 1619–1966* (1966, 4th ed. 1969).

Bethell, L., *The Abolition of the Brazilian Slave Trade; Britain, Brazil and the Slave Trade Question, 1807–1869* (1970).

Boxer, C. R., *Dutch in Brazil 1624–1654* (1957).

————, *The Golden Age of Brazil 1695–1750: Growing Pains of a Colonial Society* (1964).

————, *A Great Luso-Brazilian Figure—Padre Antonio Vieira* (1957).

————, *Portuguese Seaborne Empire: 1415–1825* (1969).

————, *Race Relations in the Portguguese Colonial Empire 1415–1825* (1963).

Cohen, D. W. and J. P. Greene, eds., *Neither Slave Nor Free* (1972).

Corwin, A., *Spain and the Abolition of Slavery in Cuba 1817–1886* (1967).

Curtin, P. D., *Africa Remembered. Narratives by West Africans from the Era of Slave Trade* (1968).

————, *The Atlantic Slave Trade: A Census* (1969).

Curtis, J. C., and L. L. Gould, *The Black Experience in America: Selected Essays* (1970).

Davidson, B., *Black Mother: The Years of the African Slave Trade* (1961).

Davis, D. B., *The Problem of Slavery in Western Culture* (1966).

Degler, C. N., *Neither Black Nor White: Slavery and Race Relations in Brazil and the United States* (1971).

Diffie, B. W., *Latin American Civilization: Colonial Period* (rev. ed., 1967).

Donnan, E., *Documents Illustrative of the History of the Slave Trade to America* 4 vols. (1930).

Duffy, J., *Portuguese Africa* (1959).

Elkins, S. M., *Slavery: A Problem in American Institutional and Intellectual Life* (1959).

Fernandes, F., *Negro in Brazilian Society* (1969).

Fernández de Oviedo, G., *Natural History of the West Indies* (1959).

Fisher, L. H. and B. Quarles, *The Black American* (1970).

Foner, L., and E. D. Genovese, *Slavery in the New World* (1969).

Franklin, J. H., *From Slavery to Freedom* (1964).

Freyre, F., *The Masters and the Slaves* (2nd ed., 1956).

Furtado, G., *The Economic Growth of Brazil* (1965).

Gibson, C., ed., *The Black Legend* (1970).

————, *Spain in America* (1966).

Goode, K. G., *From Africa to the United States and Then—A Concise Afro-American History* (1969).

Greene, J. P., *The Role of the Black and Free Mulatto in Societies of the New World* (1971).

Guerra y Sánchez, R., *Sugar and Society in the Caribbean* (1964).

Hammond, R. J., *Portugal and Africa 1815–1910* (1966).

Harris, M., *Patterns of Race in the Americas* (1964).

Helps, A., *Spanish Conquest in America and Its Relation to the History of Slavery and to the Government of the Colonies* (1855).

Herskovits, F., *The New World Negro. Selected Papers in Afroamerican Studies* (1966).

Hispanic American Historical Review; issue for August, 1944, a symposium on Negro in Latin America.

Hoetink, H., *The Two Variants in Caribbean Race Relations* (1967).

Johnson, H., *Negro in the New World* (1910).

Jordan, W. D., *White over Black: American Attitudes Toward the Negro 1550–1812* (1968).

King, J. F., *Negro Slavery in New Granada* (1945).

————, "Negro in Continental Spanish America—A Select Bibliography," *Hispanic American Historical Review*, XXIV (1944) 549–559.

Klein, H., *Slavery in the Americas: Comparative Study of Virginia and Cuba* (1967).

Mannix, D. P., and M. Crowley, *Black Cargoes: A History of the Atlantic Slave Trade 1519–1865* (1962).

Mathieson, W. L., *British Slavery and Its Abolition* (1926).

————, *Great Britain and the Slave Trade* (1929).

Mörner, M., *Race and Class in Latin America* (1970).

————, *Race Mixture in the History of Latin America* (1967).

Oliver, R. A., and J. D. Fage, *A Short History of Africa* (rev. ed., 1968).

Parry, J. H., *The Spanish Seaborne Empire* (1966).

Pierson, D., *Negroes in Brazil* (1942).

Pope-Hennessy, J., *Sins of the Fathers: A Study of the Atlantic Slave Traders 1441–1807* (1968).

Prado Junior, C., *The Colonial Background of Modern Brazil* (1967).

Ramos, A., *The Negro in Brazil* (1945).

Rippy, J. F., "The Negro and the Spanish Pioneers in the New World," *Journal of Negro History*, VI, (1921) 183–189.

Sahagun, B. de, *General History of the Things of New Spain* (1960).

Sayers, R. S., *The Negro in Brazilian Literature* (1956).

Suárez, B. R., *The Color Question in the Two Americas* (1922).

Tannenbaum, F., *Slave and Citizen: The Negro in the Americas* (1947).

Wagley, C., ed., *Race and Class in Brazil* (1952).

Weinstein, P., and F. D. Gatell, eds., *American Negro Slavery: A Modern Reader* (1968).

Wesley, C. H., *The Negro in the Americas* (1940).

Williams, E., *From Columbus to Castro: The History of the Caribbean 1492–1969* (1970).

————, *The Negro in the Caribbean* (1942).

Zavala, S., *New Viewpoints on Spanish Colonizing of America* (1943).

chapter 10

POLITICAL
ADMINISTRATION
OF THE SPANISH
NEW WORLD

a long development from the first governor
at Santo Domingo

Diego Columbus, eldest son of the discoverer, took as his bride María de Toledo, a cousin of King Ferdinand—a brilliant match for the young son of a wandering foreigner. With this extra influence he received the governorship the Crown had promised his father—full power as the king's representative, supposedly governor of the entire New World. On July 11, 1509, the newlyweds landed in the midsummer heat of Santo Domingo, that first frontier town in the Americas, but dignified by the term "Capital of the Island of Hispaniola and the Spanish Empire." With Don Diego came an escort of relatives, ladies in waiting, knights, plumed horses, and a crested gilt coach. All members of the party were dressed in velvet and brocade, sweltering as they walked up the beach into the soggy little town. There was no place for this pompous array of lords and ladies to stay in the tropical huts of Santo Domingo only a decade and a half after Columbus had first seen Hispaniola. But Don Diego's bride was determined to hold court in the manner of her royal cousins. For her Don Diego built a viceregal house, with arched colonnades front and back, and a fine view of the river and harbor from the terrace. Doña María covered the walls with tapestries, paved the floor with majolica tiles, and planted lush gardens. While she tried to make raw Santo Domingo into a true royal capital, her husband quarreled with the kings of Spain over the titles and moneys due him on his father's death, and over his powers of appointment and inspection.

Don Diego's quarrelsome rule, the expansion of settlement into other islands and on the Isthmus, and the need for strong centralized agencies at home in Spain led the rulers to establish a permanent pattern for government in the New World. It grew into the full-fledged colonial political system for a vast empire which was to last three hundred years. For such an empire settlers and administrators were more important than the explorers and adventurers whose story has been told in Chapters 6 and 7.

Compared to the spectacular story of transplanting European government and culture to the Americas, the tales of the gold-hungry conquerors pale. Before Jamestown and the *Mayflower*, Spain had completed most of her full cycle of discovery, exploration, and settlement, and had transplanted her civilization, one of the richest cultures in Europe at the time. By 1574, over 160,000 Spaniards had followed Don Diego's courtiers on the route to America, Spaniards drawn from all walks of life. Santo Domingo was but the beginning; in 1600 there were over 200 chartered towns, many more mining centers and frontier garrisons. Don Diego's city of Santo Domingo declined in his lifetime, but the empire grew by leaps and bounds. So, too, the governmental institutions outgrew the pattern set up in the agreements with his father. To further the evolution of this colonial system, agencies of royal control were set up both in Spain and in the New World.

colonial administration from the mother country

The pattern for the rule in the colonies was largely established under the Hapsburg kings of the sixteenth century. In theory the colonies belonged to the Crown of Castile, and thus held as his personal property by Isabella's grandson, the young King Charles, called Charles I of Spain but Charles V in his German holdings. He and his son Philip II did their best throughout the sixteenth century, trying to solve the explosive problems of a very New World for whose rule no kings could have been prepared. The age of discovery ended in their time and in that of their immediate successors. By the 1600s the New World was an old story to the Hapsburg descendants; the colonies no longer produced glamorous adventure stories but silver and hides and sugar for Spain. As the Hapsburg line weakened, its rulers in the late 1600s being misled by favorites, with the last of them, Charles II, even feeble-minded, neither colonies nor mother country were run well by them. After 1713 French-blooded kings of the Bourbon line were to rule Spain in an era of so many changes as to deserve a separate chapter.

The Spanish monarch was absolute at home and the royal monarchs intended to maintain the same exclusive control over the people in the new possessions, natives and Europeans alike. The new institutions, though

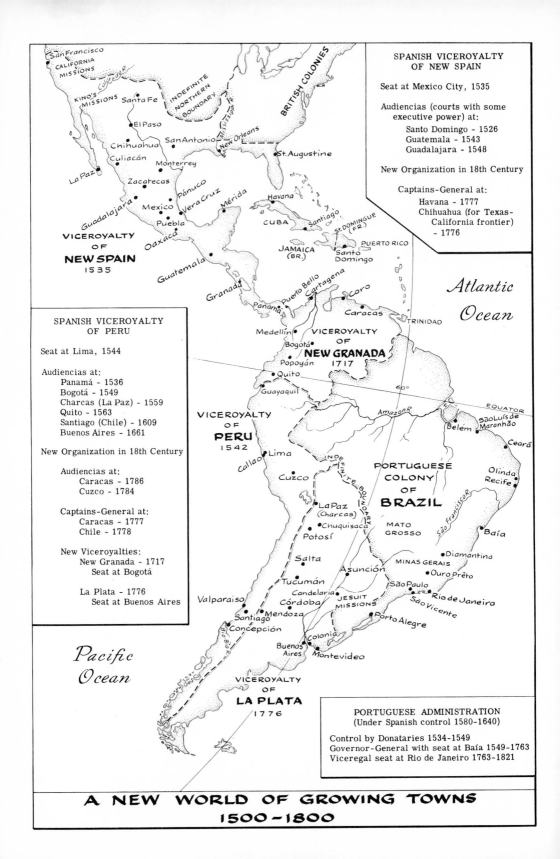

San Francisco
CALIFORNIA
MISSIONS
KINO'S
MISSIONS
Santa Fe
El Paso
Chihuahua
Culiacán
Monterrey
La Paz
Zacatecas
Guadalajara
Mexico
Puebla
Oaxaca
Pánuco
VeraCruz
Mérida
San Antonio
New Orleans
St. Augustine
INDEFINITE
NORTHERN
BOUNDARY
Colorado R.
Mississippi R.
BRITISH COLONIES

VICEROYALTY
OF
NEW SPAIN
1535

Granada
Guatemala

Havana
CUBA
Santiago
JAMAICA
(BR.)
ST.DOMINGUE
(FR.)
Santo
Domingo
PUERTO RICO

Panamá
Puerto Bello
Cartagena
Coro
Caracas
TRINIDAD

Medellín
Bogotá
Popoyán
Quito
Guayaquil

VICEROYALTY
OF
NEW GRANADA
1717

Atlantic
Ocean

EQUATOR
60°

Amazon R.
São Luís de
Maranhão
Belém
Ceará

VICEROYALTY
OF
PERU
1542

Callao
Lima
Cuzco

La Paz
(Charcas)
Chuquisacá
Potosí

Salta

Tucumán
Valparaiso
Córdoba
Candelaria
JESUIT
MISSIONS
Santiago
Mendoza
Concepción
Rio Bío R.

INDEFINITE BOUNDARY

PORTUGUESE
COLONY
OF
BRAZIL

MATO
GROSSO

São Francisco R.
Baía

Diamantina
MINAS GERAIS
Ouro Prêto
São Paulo
Rio de Janeiro
São Vicente
Porto Alegre

Asunción

Buenos
Aires
Colonia
Montevideo

Pacific
Ocean

VICEROYALTY
OF
LA PLATA
1776

Olinda
Recife

SPANISH VICEROYALTY
OF NEW SPAIN

Seat at Mexico City, 1535

Audiencias (courts with some
executive power) at:
Santo Domingo - 1526
Guatemala - 1543
Guadalajara - 1548

New Organization in 18th Century

Captains-General at:
Havana - 1777
Chihuahua (for Texas-
California frontier)
- 1776

SPANISH VICEROYALTY
OF PERU

Seat at Lima, 1544

Audiencias at:
Panamá - 1536
Bogotá - 1549
Charcas (La Paz) - 1559
Quito - 1563
Santiago (Chile) - 1609
Buenos Aires - 1661

New Organization in 18th Century

Audiencias at:
Caracas - 1786
Cuzco - 1784

Captains-General at:
Caracas - 1777
Chile - 1778

New Viceroyalties:
New Granada - 1717
Seat at Bogotá

La Plata - 1776
Seat at Buenos Aires

PORTUGUESE ADMINISTRATION
(Under Spanish control 1580-1640)

Control by Donataries 1534-1549
Governor-General with seat at Baía 1549-1763
Viceregal seat at Rio de Janeiro 1763-1821

A NEW WORLD OF GROWING TOWNS
1500–1800

modified to fit local conditions in the New World, were modeled on those of Castile. The power and control emanated from the monarch, and exercise of personal rights on the part of subjects often depended on the favor and will of whoever happened to be on the throne. When, as in the cases of Columbus, Cortés, and Pizarro, the reigning sovereigns had granted sweeping powers to the explorers and conquerors, royal jealousy and prerogative soon revoked the power and centralized the authority again in the hands of the king in Spain. This authority was from the first economic and religious as well as political.

It will be remembered from Chapter 5 that in 1493 Ferdinand and Isabella had appointed Bishop Fonseca to supervise the preparations for Columbus' second voyage. He was to serve until his death in 1524 as a counselor of the crown for American affairs. His appointment gave the position great prestige, for he was archdeacon of the cathedral of Seville and chaplain to Isabella. After a decade of control by Fonseca, the economic administration of the affairs of Hispaniola grew too large for him to handle, and the *Casa de Contratación,* or House of Trade, was created, perhaps at his suggestion. As described in Chapter 5, the *Casa* was a clearing house for commerce and immigration. As the empire expanded from the islands to the mainland, commercial regulations naturally became more complicated and the work of the *Casa* increased. Officials, secretaries, port collectors, a post-master, a chaplain, a prison staff, and scores of lawyers were added to its force. Originally housed in Seville, it had to act as arbiter for over a century in the fierce struggle between the ports of Cádiz and Seville for a monopoly of the trade of the Indies.

Fonseca's troubles in the field of politics were magnified also. He had to sign all decrees and orders from the king concerning colonies, and to act as colonial minister. On Fonseca's death in 1524, Charles set up the Council of the Indies to take over all of Fonseca's political duties and all his employees and offices. It was to become Spain's chief agency for governing the New World, and was not abolished until after the Spanish American republics were declared independent. It was the supreme legislative, administrative, judicial, and ecclesiastic body for colonial affairs, responsible only to the king.

The membership of the Council was always made up of high-born men, nobles from Spain's richest families, lawyers from the University of Salamanca, returned officials from the colonies serving emeritus. It had its own attorneys, reporters, clerks of accounts, treasurers, solicitors, a chaplain, a bailiff, a historian, a cosmographer, and a professor of mathematics. Distinguished mapmakers and historians served it. The actual membership of the board varied from nine to nineteen at different epochs of the colonial period. During the weak reigns of the last Hapsburgs, the top-heavy Council had three times as many officials and employees as it had had at its peak of success in 1600, although the salaries for all these extra dignitaries were in arrears and the state was bankrupt.

What were the duties of the Council in its heyday? Actually, it was the mouthpiece of the king in colonial affairs; it resided at court; its deliberations were secret. It proposed for the king's approval the names of appointees to fill all political positions in the New World except those few filled by the choice of the settlers themselves. The Council prepared all the laws and decrees, wording them, copying them, readying them for the king's signature, and distributing them to the officials concerned. It heard cases on appeals from the various courts in America, held powers of censorship of all books and papers going into the colonies, spied on all its own appointees as they worked in the colonies to carry out its orders, tried to preach good treatment of the Indians, and endeavored to maintain harmony among all the subjects of the king in the dependencies. It was responsible for all accounts and reports on every colonial subdivision—and there were more and more subdivisions as the colonies expanded from the Rio Grande to Tierra del Fuego.

Its members worked hard, from three to five hours every day in general council alone, as the meetings dragged on interminably. Then each member served many hours daily on small committees—committees that heard complaints from the colonies, committees that interviewed applicants for positions, committees that read books for censoring before shipment, committees that prepared the special reports for the king, committees that handled military affairs. Only of this last job were the committeemen relieved by the creation of a special committee for warfare, or *junta de guerra de Indias*, after 1600.

So many detailed records were kept of all these doings that historians know more about life in Spanish colonial times than they do about conditions fifty or a hundred years ago in many of the smaller Latin American republics. In general the records prove that the home government was trying to do a good job, and that it fell down where the frontiers were too distant, the differences in colony and homeland too great, the red tape needlessly complicated, the moneys too great a temptation to the very human administrators who handled them, or the laws themselves too involved to be successfully carried out.

The legislation for the colonies was voluminous and touched on every aspect of the duties and rights of both colonists and officials. The code of Castilian law, complicated enough of itself, had to be adjusted so that the legal spirit of the homeland was applicable to the peculiar conditions in the New World. Then there had to be elaborate new legislation with a distinct character of its own, including special laws for the Indians and even some judicial customs of Incas and Aztecs. As conditions changed, and parts of the New World became busy, settled, Europeanized places, many of these laws became obsolete but were still on the books. A codification of all the laws, decrees, ordinances, and regulations of the Council of the Indies was compiled eventually in the *Recopilación de Leyes de los Reynos de las Indias*, a notable monument of colonial legislation and a comprehensive and humane code for government. In its final form in 1681 the code contained 6,377 laws, arranged in nine books, classified by subject under 218 headings. With the law itself so confusing, small wonder that there was so much disregard of it, disregard as often stemming from ignorance as it was from corruption.

Two other institutions for the government of the colonies existed at home in Spain and controlled affairs from the home base. While the *Casa* or House of Trade existed to see that the Crown made money from the colonies, the merchants of Seville wanted their share of colonial profits also. When in 1543 the Crown made the regulation that all vessels trading with the New World sail in fleets officially sponsored and protected by the royal navy, the merchants in control of American commerce banded together in a merchant guild or *Consulado* to arrange these fleets to their own best advantage. The guild proceeded to lighten the burdens of the *Casa* with respect to the outfitting and dispatching of the fleets. It was almost official and served to settle disputes among its own members, the rival merchants, so that the Crown had little reason to interfere.

Although headquarters for the fleets were in Seville, the difficulty of the Guadalquivir entrance and the dangers of sandbars at its mouth forced many ships to load and unload at Cádiz. Thus an agency called the *Juzgado de Indias* was established at Cádiz; it handled the inspection and loading of ships, the embarkation and clearance of passengers to and from the Indies whenever tidal and river conditions made ascent to the port of Seville impossible. The fleets which left semiannually from one port or the other carried all paperwork, all officials, all cargo to the colonies; they were the link between the home government in Spain and the units of government scattered throughout the empire.

viceroys as the king's representatives

As colonial organization in the homeland evolved slowly from the time of Columbus and Don Diego to 1800, so also did the agencies of control that had their offices in America. Thus the development of colonial institutions in the Americas was a gradual process; however, in order to provide an over-all picture of colonial administration, it is best to discuss it at the height of its power.

With Columbus in the settlement of Hispaniola there had been two treasury officials to regulate finances and to guard the king's rights. Thus central authority was present from the beginning. Only in municipal organization did any vestige of ancient Castilian democracy permanently survive, and even there local self-government was overshadowed by royal authority. Though the first settlements were often made by adventurers who put up their own capital and thus had some governmental power, this period of *adelantados* did not last long. Most of the *conquistadores* only held the powers of *adelantado* for a few years. Sooner or later a governor was chosen whose appointment was revocable at the pleasure of the Crown, and the colony was administered as a royal rather than as a proprietary colony. Colonization was thus conceived primarily as a function of the state. This called for an elaborate bureaucracy, for viceroys, judges, local governments, and financial officials. The age of Charles V and of Philip II was a period of great experimentation in government; centralization, uniformity, and routine were its keynotes. Many of its experiments hardened into complex, inflexible institutions which remained unaltered until the eighteenth century.

The territorial organization, the viceroyalties, the captaincies-general and the *audiencias* all fit into this complex scheme. So large an area of settlement, from the Rio Grande to the Bío Bío river, must have many subunits of central control. As time and the Spanish pioneers advanced, the lines of control became thinner, and the vast distance between the various New World cities became of itself a problem of administration and a cause of the weakening of the empire. The administrative subdivisions—viceroyalties, captaincies-general, and seats of *audiencias*—became the independent nations of today. The feelings of independence that Quito's judges had against Peru's viceroy, that Guatemala City inhabitants felt against Mexico City, are partially responsible for the existence of Ecuador and Guatemala as separate from Peru and Mexico in the twentieth century. The subdivisions had been created for administrative and geographic convenience. They were ruled by the judges of the regional *audiencias* through the person of their chairman or president, and by a captain-general, in whose office military and civil authority were combined on the frontier. The seat or subcapital of each such factotum, although regarded as part of the viceroyalty of Mexico or Lima, was for all intents and purposes independent of viceregal intervention.

The first permanent viceroyalty erected in America was on the mainland in New Spain. Antonio de Mendoza, the experienced diplomat, popular nobleman, decisive administrator, and devoted public servant who brought peace and prosperity to Mexico after the days of Nuño de Guzmán and the Mixton War, reigned there in the king's stead for fifteen years (1535–1550) and held much greater powers over a much vaster and more populous area than ever were held by Diego Columbus. This viceroyalty included the former Aztec empire, as well as New Galicia, Central America, the Antilles, and, after Mendoza's time, even the Philippine Islands. Within this domain there were seats of *audiencias* at Mexico City, at Guadalajara for New Galicia, and at Guatemala City for Central America, which was later created a captaincy-general. As the frontier advanced in the next two centuries, New Spain's viceroyalty also included many military governments on the frontier in the silver-mining areas and as far north as California by 1769. The earliest governors, striving to bring order out of chaos in frontier Hispaniola in the first decade of the 1500s, could not have foreseen the extensive kingdom of New Spain as it existed in the 1700s.

The viceroyalty of Peru was even more far-reaching, including as it did by 1600 all of South America that was to be settled by Spain. The viceroy himself had more prestige in Lima than had his counterpart in Mexico City, and received a higher salary. Under him was the *audiencia* of Lima, 1544, the *audiencia* of Panama attached to Lima after 1567, the *audiencia* of Charcas, 1559, the *audiencia* of Bogotá, created in 1561, of

Quito in 1563, of Chile in 1565, of Buenos Aires, at least temporarily in 1661, as well as others in the eighteenth century. Many of these capitals were so far from Lima that one by one most of them were made into small captaincies-general, or *presidencias,* with little subserviency to Lima. Bogotá, seat of government for New Granada, became a captaincy-general as early as 1563. Chuquisaca, today's Sucre, Bolivia, had a governor of its own by the seventeenth century, as did Santiago, Chile. Buenos Aires and Asunción, the Plata frontier, were considered so remote and unimportant for two hundred years that they were simply ruled from Charcas, high in the Bolivian Andes, till the 1660s. Further changes were made in the eighteenth century, as will be discussed in Chapter 17.

As for viceroys themselves, those alter egos of the king, they had broad powers and heavy responsibilities. The king needed a royal representative with fullest authority who would not declare independence in his own right. Thus the king had to choose his viceroys wisely. The royal officials, living so far from home supervision in both time and distance, must have an intense devotion to the royal power. It was hard to find men with these qualifications. In many cases the noblemen of the highest Spanish blood whom the king sent for these jobs were hampered by the pride and arrogance of the higher clergy, by the jealousy of the royal judges, and by the distrust of the governing councils in Spain in everything they did. Antonio de Mendoza, fifteen years in Mexico and a term afterward in Lima, pleased the king by his lack of independent initiative. "The secret of good ruling," he told his successor, "is to do little and to do that slowly," since most matters lent themselves to that kind of treatment. After the first viceroys, the normal term for this position was fixed at three years, then later raised to five. The viceregal salary, difficult to translate into modern dollars, provided a sumptuous living from the royal treasury, and the viceroy usually had a private fortune as well.

Throughout the three centuries many decrees were passed regulating the powers and activities of the viceroy. Politically and administratively he made appointments, distributed land and titles, issued instructions to subordinates, promoted colonization, founded new towns, took the periodic census, superintended public works, maintained public health rules, protected the Indians, and enforced all royal laws. On the economic side, he collected taxes, enforced commercial restrictions, and promoted industry where it did not come into competition with that of the homeland. Ecclesiastically, the viceroy was the representative of the king in America; he founded churches, set the boundaries of bishoprics, supervised the instruction of natives in religion, acted as vice-patron to all religious endeavor, and collected tithes to support the church. Thus he was the chief agency in promoting the advancement of the faith in the New World. As an ex-officio member of the judicial body, the viceroy sat with the *audiencia* judges, although he had no vote. That body acted as the highest court of appeal this side of Spain, and decided the competency of questions of jurisdiction between civil officials and church officials. The viceroy also acted in a military capacity, serving as commander in chief of all forces within his viceroyalty, and being held responsible for the "preservation of the peace." The viceroys thus became practically kings in the New World. At first they could do here in America almost everything that the king could do in Spain, but this great power of the earliest viceroys was afterward regulated by law from Sapin, as the king became increasingly fearful of New World autonomy.

How well a viceroy did all these things depended on the character of the man himself. The viceroys of the sixteenth century were good administrators, carefully chosen by Charles V and Philip II. In the seventeenth century, military men were preferred; those of the period after 1650 were often weaklings to whom the Crown owed some favor. There were viceroys who worked for their own interests and for those of their families, viceroys who worked only for the king and for Spain, viceroys really interested in furthering the New World for its own sake. Of 103 different men who served as viceroys in the three centuries of Spanish rule in Mexico and Peru, only four were born in any part of the Americas, so determined were the kings to choose only men of noble Spanish families whose loyalty would be unquestioned. Forty-one of the viceroys served in Peru, sixty-two of them in Mexico; the portraits of all those in Mexico hang in a museum room of the Castle of Chapultepec. The subjects for these portraits were thin men and fat, old men mostly, but here and there a young one. Before 1700, they wore their own hair in curls or showed bald spots; after 1700, they wore the elaborate white wigs popularized by the kings of France. A few were church leaders in ecclesiastical robes; one or two seem to have been gallant horsemen.

We can read, in the records of their rule, the accounts of the elaborate celebrations given at the time of their arrival and departure. Two centuries after Mendoza served his term in Peru the Spaniards had established there the custom of processions of welcome stretching out over a hundred miles and lasting several weeks. The incoming viceroy, so an old account relates, was to land at a small port two hundred leagues north of Lima, so he could be entertained at every town en route. Each local governor along the coast "then provides litters, mules, and everything necessary for the viceroy and his retinue as far as the next jurisdiction," and also, at his own expense, "orders booths to be built for the entertainment of the viceroy in the halting places of the desert." In Lima the new arrival was the guest of the local town council; a parade "of all officials and all religious orders," which lasted the entire day, welcomed him as a mere civilian guest on the day of his arrival. The first evening he must attend a play "to which the ladies are admitted." Next day he went at the head of a long line of open coaches to meet the retiring viceroy, who was delayed at the port of Callao while his record was being "inspected" by the other royal officials. The militia, the college students, the judges, and all the lesser officials of the court marched in honor of the new viceroy. There were three days of such processions, with dinner parties in the homes of the elite every evening. Then followed five days of "Bull Fiestas" for the general public. For the next two weeks, the new viceroy had to spend some days at ceremonies at the university, and others at every house of a religious order. There is a final celebration in which Lima "breaks loose" because all these formalities were finished. Diego Columbus had brought the pomp and splendor of Spain with him to a thatch-and-mud town; these later viceroys to Lima and to Mexico City found the pomp waiting for them in the rich new cities. Throughout the era, the first year of a viceregal term was given over to functions chiefly social.

The use of time and money in such welcomes was matched only by the account of a funeral of a viceroy who died in Mexico City. Parades, booths on the plaza, four hundrd special readings of the mass, elaborate new mourning clothes for all well-to-do families were the order of the day. Some viceroys are famous for other things besides arriving and dying. The Count of Chinchón, a religious fanatic who would not allow ships in Lima to receive passengers who had not gone to confession the night before, and who tried to stop ladies from wearing seductive veils with one eye peeking out, is remembered because of his wife's severe case of malaria, cured by quinine bark, an Inca remedy still called *cinchona* in Peru. He introduced the malaria cure in Europe, while in Lima the defiant ladies used his anti-veil ordinance for curl papers. Another Peruvian viceroy is famous for the mistress he kept, La Pericholi, whose career as an actress and arbiter of social customs is still well known in Lima.

Few viceroys were actually corrupt, and real challenge to the royal authority was unthinkable, but furtive disobedience mixed with an outward show of respect for the king's wishes became a widespread fact. Yet for the viceroy there were many controls on his power both in theory and in actuality. He was furnished with detailed instructions when appointed, instructions which he must endeavor to carry out in every respect, and royal decrees were sent which, at least legally, had to be respected.

The kings and the Council of the Indies had a sure check on every viceroy at the end of his term of office. He was required to remain at the seat of his viceroyalty after his successor had been appointed and to submit to an inspection and auditing of his accounts which was called a *residencia,* or term of mere residence without authority. During this *residencia* a judicial review was made of the viceroy's administration. Notice was given in advance, and anyone among his subjects could bring any complaint against him, to be heard before officials appointed by the Crown. This formidable institution of royal control was probably more effectively enforced against lesser officials in the provinces than against the viceroys in Lima or Mexico City. If any official was involved in an unusually big scandal during the middle of his term, he was inspected by a special *visita* sent out by the Council of the Indies; or a general investigation could be made of a viceroyalty by a *visitador general,* and recommendations made to Spain which were reviewed by the Council of the Indies. In such investigations the *visitador general* had powers superior to the viceroy and could carry out his recommendations on the spot. His visits were usually followed by a period of marked honesty and efficiency. It was not that the Crown lacked machinery to maintain loyal, honest, efficient government, but that the long distance from Spain, the slowness of communication, the human weakness of the governors, and the lax conditions of the court life in Spain itself in the later period made real honesty in government a rarity, though flagrant dishonesty was the exception rather than the general rule. It was said of the Spanish empire the "government was never vigorously good, never intolerably bad."

In the remote capitals where a captain-general was the king's executive representative, he lived like a small-scale viceroy, kept as elaborate a court as he could afford in a frontier community, collected taxes, supervised the church, dealt with the Indians, maintained forts and garrisons, founded new towns according to royal specifications, and was a "big frog in a little puddle." He also was subject to a short inspection by a *residencia*. Captains-general reported directly to the Council of the Indies and were removable by the Council of the king, just as was a viceroy.

In all government the judicial branch is as important as the executive. Though viceroys and captains-general had some judicial function, the real center of judicial power was the *audiencia,* the court of appeal, the highest interpreter of the law. The first *audiencia* sent to Mexico had only four member judges, called *oidores,* or "hearers." By the seventeenth century the two large *audiencias* attached to the viceregal courts in Mexico City and Lima had twelve judges, some to hear criminal cases and some to hear civil cases. They listened to appeals from decisions made by various types of local governments and lower courts. *Audiencias* were required to "protect the Indians," and two days were set aside each week for the judges to hear cases involving Indians. In the two viceregal capitals, appeals of cases concerning Indians were so numerous that special branches of the *audiencias,* called *juzgado general de Indios,* had to be set up before 1600 to check abuses against the natives.

The *audiencia* judges corresponded directly with the king and acted as the king's advisors to the viceroy. They executed royal orders, administered royal property, reviewed credentials, and filled in for the viceroy. In Quito, Charcas, and other capitals where the *audiencia* was the chief agency of the Crown, the president of the court acted as governor of the province, and the area was often called a presidency. In the viceregal capital it was the president of the *audiencia* who served as viceroy during the many periods when the former viceroy had died or had served out his term and the new one was long in arriving. Since the terms of the judges were not limited, the *audiencia* was a more permanent and continuous body than any one viceroy, and thus was actually the center and core of the government of the Spanish Indies, often acting as a curb on viceregal power. Its judges were kept "Spanish" and, together with the viceroy, were not allowed to marry in the colony, to own real estate, to carry on business, or even to attend weddings or funerals in American-born families. The term *audiencia* was also often used for the territory of the *audiencia's* jurisdiction and some of these territories became modern republics in the present day.

There were many courts below the level of the *audiencia.* Some were administrative courts that acted in an executive capacity. Routine civil and criminal cases were heard by *alcaldes,* or justices of the peace. There were also special civil courts, courts of the *consulados* or merchant guilds, courts of the silver-mining interests, courts of the *mesta* or livestock ranchers' guild, a tribunal of accounts connected with the exchequer and a *proto-medicato* to regulate the medical profession. The church and the army maintained separate courts for those of their own personnel who might be in difficulties, for Spanish custom granted them *fueros,* privileges which set them apart from the jurisdiction of the civil courts.

provincial and local government

Captaincies-general were areas as large as the modern republics of Latin America; naturally, they had to be divided into smaller units to facilitate administration. These provincial divisions differed greatly in size and importance, and were governed variously by officials called *gobernadores* if in large sparsely settled areas on the frontier, or *corregidores* if in areas of many Indian villages, or *alcaldes mayores* if in areas of Europeanized settlement. All three of these types of governors had approximately equal salaries and powers, and all had political and judicial as well as military authority.

Each governor usually served only a three-year term in any one district, and was often asked to give an inventory of his personal wealth before assuming office. He could not conduct a private business or marry within the district. Occasionally landowners or merchants already resident in the New World received these appointments. Such appointees in most cases had to serve in districts apart from their residences. As with the viceroy, the multiplicity of decrees and regulations often made honesty and integrity hard to maintain, and some governors became petty tyrants. Their salaries were so low compared to those of the captains-general that they were constantly tempted by the many opportunities for graft and corruption. In general they were closely associated with the town council and could intervene, either in the public interest or in the interest of the Crown, in all affairs conducted by local council meetings.

Corregidores especially had responsibility concerning Indians, and in this connection they were often guilty of petty graft. A *corregidor,* under the guise of being their chief protector, could force the Indians to render him or his friends personal services, to sell products to him below the market price for his own resale at pleasure, and to pay excessive tributes of any kind that pleased him. So widespread were these abuses that the relationship between the *corregidor* and the Indians became the notorious weak link in the Spanish colonial administrative system.

Viceroys, *audiencias,* and *corregidores* were not the government in town and village; the governor of New York State does not tell people how to light the streets of Poughkeepsie. In every empire there must be some local government. At home in Spain, the local unit of government was called an *ayuntamiento* or a *cabildo.* This body was transferred with little change to the New World. The urban tradition was as strong in Spanish America as it was in Spain. The *cabildo* was the first institution set up everywhere the Spaniards went. Cortés established a *cabildo* to legalize his acts in Veracruz before he ever met Montezuma; Balboa strove to legalize his position on the Isthmus by founding a *cabildo* in Darién. Later municipalities might have grown out of an earlier Indian mission or a mining settlement or even a garrison or *presidio* on the frontier, but each municipality was created consciously with a predetermined plan.

The *cabildo* is usually considered a democratic institution, for it was the only area of government open to creoles, the American-born sons and grandsons of European immigrants. In the first *cabildos* the councilmen, the *regidores,* usually from five to twelve in number, were chosen by the settlers themselves. As soon as the frontier character of the town was lost the royal power moved in and *regidores* were usually no longer elected. By 1660 most *cabildo* members were chosen by the provincial governors, often from lists drawn up by retiring *regidores.* Some seats even became hereditary or were sold to the highest bidder. Thus the democracy of the *cabildo* did not last long. Municipal offices also became private property. By the beginning of the seventeenth century most local offices had become both proprietary and hereditary and municipal administration had passed into the control of a narrow circle of wealthy and influential families.

Cabildos exercised the normal routine functions of city councils today, distributing land, collecting local taxes, regulating the local militia and police force, issuing building permits, proclaiming public holidays, setting up rules for parades, supervising public markets, building bridges, controlling floods, distributing grain during famine. Because the revenues were limited, the budgets, and hence the public works and services, were small. There was nothing to create any community spirit; only in matters of grave importance—such as defense problems, floods, Indian raids, special gifts to be collected for the king to support new European wars or to honor the birth of an heir to the throne—was the main body of the citizenry called into consultation. Such a meeting was called *cabildo abierto,* or open council, even if it included only the most notable citizens, the landowners, the bishop and clergy, and the principal merchants. Though seldom held in the colonial period, open councils became of great importance during the Wars of Independence.

A number of lesser town officials were chosen by the *cabildo* members. The chief magistrate, sort of a combined mayor, city commissioner, and justice of the peace, was the *alcalde* elected by the *regidores.* He was also head of the local court system. Lesser officials, such as a constable, a public trustee of funds, an inspector of weights and measures, a collector of fines set by the court, a city attorney, a custodian of public property, all did the duties these dignitaries would perform in a modern town. There were also police magistrates for local districts, tax collectors, and officials of the exchequer. This in general is the type of town organization in the more Hispanized regions where European-type towns prospered.

Things were different on the frontier. Here the principal institutions were mission settlements in which the religious leaders formed the government, and *presidios* or garrisons in which the military officers commanded the soldiers. Such garrisons were necessary along the periphery of the empire to secure routes of travel, to protect commerce between the cities and the rich mines of northern Mexico or of Bolivia, and to check invasions of hostile Indians. Such a *presidio* consisted of a fort and a number of soldiers and their families who lived there and developed farms around the military post. Frequently, important towns grew up around the *presidio*. San Francisco, for instance, was once such a frontier garrison and mission.

A majority of the pure-blooded Indians still lived in their own *pueblos*. The Spanish government was interested in attempting to get the scattered Indians throughout the country to abandon their nomadic way of life and to settle down in concentrated villages of their own. Each such Indian village was to be provided with a church and priest of its own, in order to bring the Indians under Spanish tutelage, though the expenses of the church were to be borne by the Indians. There were to be from one to four Indian aldermen or *regidores*, and an *alcalde* or magistrate, chosen with the consent of the *corregidor*. These *alcaldes* shared jurisdiction jointly with the old time *caciques* or hereditary tribal chieftains, though Spanish policy was to substitute the Spanish form of local government and the Spanish titles of officeholder wherever the idea of tribal chieftains could be forgotten in the new *pueblos*. Even sites of Indian *pueblos* had to be carefully selected and had to be provided with a common public land for pasturing cattle. *Caciques* and *alcaldes* could punish their fellow Indians for drunkenness, for failure to attend mass, and for minor infractions of tribal rule, but more serious offenses were taken to the *corregidor* who was always of Spanish blood and seldom interested in the social well-being of the Indians. In addition to paying into the royal coffers and the *corregidor's* own expense fund, Indian villagers maintained their community funds to defray expenses for local improvements and celebrations, as would any Indian town in Latin America today.

In conclusion, it must be admitted that in spite of the abuses of the *corregidor* system, the heavy tributes on the Indians, the scandals involving occasional viceroys, the disregard of Spanish laws in the colonies and of colonial well-being in Spain, the Spanish colonial empire was as well governed as any empire in history up to that time. The paternalistic administrative system actually worked remarkably well for three centuries over a vaster territory than that ever controlled by the empires of antiquity. Eventually, red tape and restrictions led officials to think up ways to get around them, obedience to royal and viceregal orders grew lax, and corruption increased. In the course of time the complications of administrative function and the multitudinous instructions from Spain inevitably sapped the vigor of the colonial regime.

Since government jobs brought such honor and prestige and were closed to so many classes of society born in the New World, job "mania" and nepotism became the order of the day. A job with the government meant the open door to quick wealth and social standing. As the centuries advanced, there was an excessive number of officials in Spanish America and jobs were created for relatives of relatives of those in power. "Get me a relative, I have an extra government job," was supposed to be a byword. However, Spain winked at a little graft in order to save the empire from larger graft, accepted a little lawbreaking and disobedience to prevent open rebellion and to make its system work. When, by the eighteenth century, the whole empire was decaying and the system cried out for reform both at home and in America, the Bourbon kings instituted the methodical changes that are described in Chapter 17.

READINGS

Aiton, A. S., *Antonio de Mendoza, First Viceroy of New Spain* (1927).

Bannon, J. F., *Spanish Borderlands Frontier 1513–1821* (1970).

Blackmar, F. W., *Spanish Institutions of the Southwest* (1891).

Bobb, B. E., *The Viceregency of Antonio María Bucareli in New Spain, 1771–1778* (1962).

Cameron, R., *Viceroyalties of the West: The Spanish Empire in Latin America* (1968).

Castañeda, C. E., "The Corregidor in Spanish Colonial Administration," *Hispanic American Historical Review*, IX, 446–70.

Cunningham, C. H., *The Audiencia in the Spanish Colonies as Illustrated in the Audiencia of Manila, 1583–1800* (1919).

————, "The Residencia in the Spanish Colonies," *Southwestern Historical Quarterly*, XXI, 253–78.

Diffie, B. W., *Latin American Civilization: Colonial Period* (1945).

Elliot, J. H., *Imperial Spain 1469–1716* (1966).

————, *Old World and the New 1492–1650* (1971).

Fisher, L. E., *Viceregal Administration in the Spanish American Colonies* (1926).

Fisher, J. R., *Government and Society in Colonial Peru. The Intendant System 1784–1814.* (1971).

Gerald, R. E., *Spanish Presidios in the Late Eighteenth Century in Northern New Spain* (1969).

Gerhard, P., *A Guide to the Historical Geography of New Spain* (1972).

Gibson, C., *Spain in America* (1966).

————, *Spanish Tradition in America* (1968).

Haring, C. H., *Spanish Empire in America* (1952).

————, *Trade and Navigation Between Spain and the Indies in the Time of the Hapsburgs* (1918).

Henige, D. P., *Colonial Governors from the Fifteenth Century to the Present* (1970).

Hill, R. R., "Office of Adelantado," *Political Science Quarterly*, XXVIII, 646–68.

Holmes, J. D. L., *Gayoso: The Life of a Spanish Governor in the Mississippi Valley, 1789–1799* (1965).

Jones, O. G., "Local Government in the Spanish Colonies as Provided by the Recopilacion," *Southwestern Historical Quarterly*, XIX, 65–90.

Lynch, J., *Spain Under the Hapsburgs 1516–1598* (1964).

—————, *Spain Under the Hapsburgs 1598–1700* (1969).

—————, *Spanish Colonial Administration, 1782–1810: The Intendant System in the Viceroyalty of the Río de La Plata* (1958).

Madariaga, S. de, *Rise of the Spanish American Empire* (1947).

Mecham, J. L., *Francisco de Ibarra and Nueva Vizcaya* (1927).

—————, "The Real de Minas as a Political Institution," *Hispanic American Historical Review*, VII, 45–83.

Merriman, R. B., *Rise of the Spanish Empire*, Vols. II, III, IV (1918–1934).

Moore, J. P., *Cabildo in Peru Under the Hapsburgs* (1954).

—————, *Cabildo in Peru Under the Bourbons* (1966).

Moses, B., *Spanish Dependencies in South America* (2 vols., 1918).

Parry, J. H., *The Audiencia of Nueva Galicia in the Sixteenth Century* (1948).

—————, *Spanish Seaborne Empire* (1966).

—————, *Spanish Theory of Empire in the Sixteenth Century* (1940).

Pierson, W. W., "Some Reflections on the Cabildo as an Institution," *Hispanic American Historical Review*, V, 573–96.

Priestley, H. I., *Coming of the White Man, 1492–1848* (1929).

—————, *Jose de Gálvez Visitor General of New Spain* (1916).

—————, "Spanish Colonial Municipalities," *Louisiana Historical Quarterly*, V, No. 2, 125–43; see also *California Law Review*, 1919.

Roscher, W., *Spanish Colonial System*, trans. E. G. Bourne (1914).

Schurz, W. L., *Latin America* (rev. ed., 1964).

Smith, D. E., *The Viceroy of New Spain* (1913).

Te Paske, J. J., *The Governorship of Spanish Florida, 1700–1763* (1964).

Wilgus, A. C., ed., *Colonial Hispanic America* (1936).

Zavala, S., *New Viewpoints on the Spanish Colonization of America* (1943).

Zimmerman, A. F., *Francisco de Toledo, Fifth Viceroy of Peru, 1569–1581* (1938).

chapter 11

ECONOMIC TRENDS
IN THE NEW WORLD
AND THE OLD

Spain's money-making ideas for her empire

Digging for gold and silver, breeding and grazing horses and cattle, planting and harvesting the agricultural products of Europe and the Americas,
setting up small hand manufactories for weaving and ceramics, trading
directly with Spain and with Spain only—by these means were the Spanish
colonials to make profits for the mother country and, incidentally, to live
well enough themselves. European countries of the sixteenth, seventeenth
and eighteenth centuries believed in mercantilism—the colonies existed for
the benefit of the mother country. Only Spanish merchants in the towns of
Spain and Spanish-born traders in the New World should benefit from
commerce with the colonies; foreigners should be excluded positively from
the bonanza of the colonial trade, and creoles or *mestizos* born in the
Americas were to share in the wealth only when the citizens of the mother
country were abundantly prosperous. Since bullion—silver and gold in pure
metallic form—was considered by economists at the time as the only true
wealth, and the American colonies were one of the greatest sources of
bullion of all time, that wealth was intended for Spain only, to increase her
own prosperity at home and abroad. In order that all the gold and silver
should reach Spain, the colonists were to sell to Spain only, and to purchase

processed goods from Spain with the metals whenever possible, rather than to process the goods in the Americas. Prices on both sides of such trade were to be set and qualities standardized by the Spanish government or by the trade guilds Spain approved at home.

Spain was the first European nation to face the problem of colonizing the New World; but she was also a country with little experience in colonization or in overseas trade of any kind. Furthermore, more than any other trading country, Spain was busy with the spread of religion and the waging of wars against the native population. There were other handicaps: the colonies with which this heretofore nontrading nation now carried on this vast commerce were thousands of miles away; the Spanish ruling class was a landed aristocracy, not a commercial class; upper-class Spaniards considered trade as manual labor and did not wish to dirty their hands. Most of the first colonial trading centers were in the tropics, with different needs and agricultural methods from those the colonists were used to. The work force was primitive and unwilling. The semicivilized Indian centers had been accustomed to subsistence economy and usually to barter trade. Neither the Old World colonizers nor the New World subjects had traditions of seafaring or large-scale commercial enterprises.

In spite of these handicaps, Spain transplanted herself to America in matters economic. That she succeeded is due to the great wealth of the New World in field and mine. The minor failures sprang from the position of Spain in Europe's economy. The flood of bullion into Spain produced inflation. Such enormous mineral wealth and the ease of its acquisition discouraged Spanish home enterprise and Spanish trade efforts in Europe. Big money meant big power and big power meant wars and big wars meant big debt. By 1700 Spain's military might was defeated on land and sea; her people were hungry and unemployed; her agriculture and industry had deteriorated. Her monopoly failed in the Americas when her businesses were failing at home, and foreign smugglers began to edge in on the colonial trade, supplying the articles the mother country no longer provided cheaply to the colonists. When the empire ceased to be self-contained by the beginning of the eighteenth century and most of the colonial silver was passing into foreign hands, then the new Bourbon kings tried to institute reforms.

agriculture as the basis for colonial life

The Spanish American colonies reflected both New World and Old World influences in their economic life. Side by side with the subsistence and tribute-paying economy of the Indians there arose a Spanish commercial agriculture, producing foods and fibers for home use, for sale in local markets, and for transport to Europe. Geographic differences and variations in native economies determined the trend of agriculture in the various regions of Latin America. Subsistence agriculture continued to support the sedentary Indians; grazing industries were introduced on the grassy plains regions, and plantation life developed in the Caribbean and along the coasts. Over vast areas the land was fine, fertile, and unused when the Spaniards came. Farms could be laid out as big as the holdings of several Old World villages combined. Into the Indian culture producing maize, lima and kidney beans, manioc, potatoes, maguey, tobacco, cacao, pineapple, and peanuts there was transplanted the Spanish culture of wheat, barley, olives, grapes, and sugar. The pattern of land ownership varied with the type of planting, the level of Indian civilization, and the military history of each region. No matter who owned the land, its product meant wealth for Spain.

For despite the emphasis on metals, the cash value of agrarian products of the New World usually exceeded that of the metal shipped from the mines. Only in the Mexican colonies was the silver exported worth more than the various agricultural products shipped home to Spain. Even in that rich region the total value of all foodstuffs consumed on the *haciendas,* at the mines, in the cities, and in the Indian villages must have been far greater than the value of the silver ingots. The Indians had grown food to support themselves; now they and their Negro slave counterparts in the more tropical colonies produced sugar and tobacco, cacao and indigo on plantations for export, and added to their pre-Columbian products the cattle, swine, horses, and poultry introduced along with Spanish farming methods. Thus, for export and for home consumption, the geographic area of Spanish America was growing perhaps double the tonnage and the value that it had before the Spanish rule began. Indians tilled the land of their ancestors, but in most larger settlements they learned to use European animals to harvest both the old and the new crops. Nomadic Indians became herdsmen or forest gatherers for the new masters. In the Spain of 1492, the great mass of people labored in the fields; so also in the Spanish New World of 1592 or 1692, or even 1892, more Spanish-speaking and Indian peoples lived by agriculture than by any other means. Agriculture remains the basis of wealth in most of Latin America today.

At home, Spaniards lived on wheat bread and beef, on mutton cooked in olive oil, on the rich red wine of the Alicante and Malaga grapes, on the oranges of Valencia. All these things had to be grown in the New World if Spaniards were to live there happily. Though wheat was planted wherever possible for the Spanish settlers, maize remained the staple cereal crop of Latin America. In the irrigated coastal valleys of Peru the olive tree was introduced in 1560 and olive oil was exported from Lima to other colonies. Grapes did well on Mexico's plateau, in the Central Valley of Chile, and in the Argentine foothill province of Mendoza, and colonial wines competed briskly with wines imported from Spain.

The silk industry based on the mulberry-leaf-consuming worms was brought to New Spain, where many Spanish landowners encouraged the Indians to work with silk. Martín Cortés, son of Cortés and Marina, was one of those who prospered on the Indian manufacture of silk cloth; when Chinese silks began to come in cheaply on the Manila Galleon, the silk industry, and with it the mulberry trees, were allowed to die out. Hemp and flax, grown at first in abundance, also competed with the cordage and the linen of Spain, and their planting was discouraged after 1600.

Tobacco and cacao were developed as plantation crops in the New World for the European market—the demanding court ladies at Versailles had to have their cup of chocolate on retiring, and the gentlemen took up the use of snuff. Some of the fortunes of the Caribbean Islands were made on the private estates where these crops were grown. The largest single source of wealth from a planted crop, however, was the sugar grown to make rum; Negro slaves were imported to handle the crops.

The livestock industry was important from the first. Columbus brought cattle to Hispaniola and Cortés came with horses to Mexico. After a century, Indian farmers still did the work in Mexico and Peru, but their ways of farming were changed. A cow and a few pigs and a flock of chickens lived near the little farmhouses of corn and bean growers, just as they do today near the *casitas* of Mexican villagers. The Indian corn planters had oxen to pull a plow similar to that used in Spain, a step up from the primitive cornplanting stick of the Aztecs. Sheep provided wool for weaving and created a new industry. Pigs had come with the first colonists to Hispaniola, for the Spaniards wanted their pork, hams, and bacon wherever they settled. Today it is impossible for us to imagine the pampas without cattle, Uruguay without sheep, Mexico without horses and burros, any Latin American mountain community without goats. All these descended from the stock brought by the Spaniards.

The Crown had paid attention to stock raising from the early settlement of Hispaniola; in each new town there were to be "woods and grasslands for the common use of all colonists." Various decrees of the Council of the Indies attempted to regulate the size of lands to be distributed to those who were to make their living grazing cattle. An area one league in diameter was to accommodate no less than 2,000 head of cattle and to have built on it at least one permanent stone building. More than three square leagues could not be granted to one individual without a special royal license. The great cattle ranches that developed in Argentina, in northern Mexico, and on the plains of the Orinoco would indicate that it was either simple to get such a license, or else that this law to guarantee a just distribution of land was, like so many others, conveniently overlooked by the authorities in the New World. It may have been overlooked because the stockraisers' guild so powerful in medieval Spain, the *mesta*, was transferred to the colonies. Formally organized in Mexico in 1542, the *mesta* regulated branding, settled quarrels over land ownership, maintained a separate court for disputes concerning cattle, and represented the cattlemen before the authorities.

Equally important in many parts of the New World was the raising of mules and horses for transport. In the archives of Asunción there is a bill of sale, telling how Domingo Martínez de Irala, in the year 1551, bought "a black horse with the near forefoot white and some white about its face, from Alonso Parejo for 4,000 gold pesos." Fourteen years before, far down the Plata, Mendoza had abandoned seven mares and two stallions; when Irala's descendants came to refound Mendoza's colony, there were "wild horses in plenty," no need for gold pesos, nor even for bills of sale. The Crown had said that all such wild herds were royal property, but the settlers went to court in Asunción and won a case against the king in 1596. Then anyone could have the horses who cared to catch them—there were more than enough for all. In 1744, an English traveler in the Plata region reported that a young colt was not worth half a peso. He saw "great plenty of tame horses and a prodigious number of wild ones." The wild horses "wander in great troops about those vast plains."

There was more money to be made in Venezuela, Peru, or Colombia in raising mules, which were used by the hundreds on the Andes or the Isthmus crossing and which died in equal numbers from overwork, accidents on the precipitous trails, and poor fodder. On flat lands, burdens were carried by carts, the large-wheeled *carretas* pulled by oxen, but there was little profit in raising oxen for transport. Cattle produced meat for local consumption solely, as it could only be preserved by drying and salting. Profits from the grazing business lay in hides which were shipped across the pampas and up into the Andes to Lima for transport to Spain, or sent down to Veracruz from the interior. The Texas longhorn and the Indian pony of the Great Plains "grew" in the same way as did the stock of Argentina, probably from animals abandoned or lost by early expeditions. Thus, on the frontier of Spanish settlement both north and south, a cowboy-pony, bronco-busting, hide-and-jerked-beef industry developed unlike anything ever known in the Old World. So, too, developed the culture of those who worked with the cattle, the mixture of Indian and white which produced the life of the *vaqueros* near the Rio Grande, of the *gauchos* near the Plata, and the *llaneros* on the Orinoco.

If the Crown was to question private ownership of wild cattle and horses, and worry over the size of grazing acreage, how much more of a problem was the ownership of agricultural land—all those millions of acres of the new continents. Of the various factors that contributed to maintain an aristocracy in the Spanish American colonies—differences of race and religion, discriminatory economic legislation—the problem of land tenure was the most important. Land was the basis for political rights, the principal source of riches and prestige in a society which disdained trade and industrial pursuits. The value of the land was created, not by the landlord, but by the Indians and Negroes who worked it. The idea of a manor, a large area cultivated by an ignorant and depressed peasantry, was so common in Europe as to be easily transferred to the New World. Successful mine operators invested their gold and silver fortunes in land; creoles, the sons of Spanish families born in the New World but shut off from important government jobs, became wealthy through the inheritance of land.

How was land to be distributed in the first place? Most Indian communities had little conception of individual ownership; land had been owned by a tribe or village as a whole. As new lands were conquered by the Spaniards, they belonged automatically to the Crown, which granted out the tillable surface parcel by parcel and preserved the subsoil or mineral rights for royal ownership. Throughout the colonial epoch the Spanish rulers awarded deeds or charters to individual *adelantados,* town councils, or plantation developers. Of course, the lands were not surveyed, boundaries were indefinite, and many abuses were practiced. Squatters took over large areas; a decree of the late 1500s required squatters of ten years' standing to clear with the Crown. Many Indian villages theoretically kept their land, though they were often defrauded of it.

Favorites of the king or of the viceroys received great tracts of unsurveyed, new lands—estates called *haciendas* in New Spain and *latifundios* in South America. Indians on such lands were theoretically held in trust and protection by the new landowner. In actuality, of course, the Indians became the peasant workers of the feudal system. Smaller holdings—that is, free grants to a head of a family or to a common foot soldier, a *peón,* in lieu of wages—were called *peonías,* and comprised enough land for subsistence planting and pasturage for a small herd. The word *peón* came to be applied to the poor Indian who worked the lands of the rich landowner, but the *peonía* holding was the basis for an independent small-farmer class, the *rancheros,* who still farm these smaller holdings today. The church became a large owner of land, as described in Chapter 13. On the whole, land in the New World belonged to the wealthy, and was tilled by servile labor under primitive methods.

mining, industry, and handcrafts

It was the lure of gold and silver that had brought many Spaniards to the New World in the first place. Mining remained one of the great industries of Latin America. Kings were interested in mining efforts, and issued early decrees that the subsoil rights on all agricultural land belonged to the king. Mines were worked on a sort of grant or lease from the royal court, with a fifth of all metals ordinarily going to the king, but there was a large private profit in mining anyway. In fact, in the mines lay the origins of many of the private fortunes in America and the principal source of crown revenues. When the prosperity of the mines increased as the frontier advanced, there was more money in circulation, a greater demand for goods, and a sharp rise in the value of land, since mine operators invested their profits in agricultural land. Mine fortunes also brought a spur to the construction of churches and public buildings.

Gold soon gave out save in a few gold-bearing regions. The first silver mines were discovered in Michoacán, Mexico, in 1531. By 1550, Zacatecas, San Luis Potosí, Guanajuato, and later Taxco became silver-mining towns of fantastic wealth. Potosí in Bolivia became one of the most dramatic "boom" towns in all mining history; the hill of Potosí was thought to be the greatest "glory hole" on earth.

The mines produced so richly and easily that there was no need for efficiency. To bring the ore to the surface, small pits were dug with no connecting galleries; the ore was carried up ladders by Indian bearers who worked on a forced-labor basis. When the pits were flooded, they were drained by leather bags and the water handed up the same way, from Indian to Indian up the ladders. Once on the surface, the ore was crushed in an open "patio" by a revolving stone drag drawn round and round by a blindfolded mule. The ancient Indians had known how to smelt the silver out of the ore by fire. In 1554, after the ores from Zacatecas had been worked in this primitive way for six years, a German in Europe discovered a method of running mercury or quicksilver over the crushed ore and dissolving out the silver. The mercury could then be easily distilled off, leaving the pure silver. A Spanish miner, Bartolomé de Medina, heard of the method and brought it to Pachuca in 1556, and it was soon in use in both Mexico and Peru. Though at first all mercury was brought from Europe, a mercury deposit was soon found in Peru at Huancavelica, and its product was monopolized by the Crown. By the end of the seventeenth century even this method was no longer the best modern procedure, and the mining industry began to decline as a result of the lack of machinery, bad transportation, and underground flooding. Under the Bourbon kings at the close of the colonial period an attempt was made to bring technological improvements into the mines.

Silver was not the only mineral resource of the New World. Gold was still worked in some places in the late seventeenth century and was the source of boom conditions in the province of Chocó and in the Cauca Valley of Colombia and the mountains of Honduras. Diving for pearls was a major industry on Margarita Island near the Venezuelan coast and at La Paz in Lower California; a rich consignment of emeralds was sent to Spain from Colombia every three months for 150 years.

Since American treasure preserved Spain's balance of trade and financed her foreign wars, Spain endeavored to keep these valuable sources of wealth within the home country. Gold and silver were to be cast into ingots stamped with the royal stamp. At the time of stamping, the king's agents were to take his fifth. Naturally much gold and silver was never reported to the agents but was hidden away unstamped and traded to foreign smugglers for valuable French, English, or Dutch commodities. All the stamped bricks were contracted out to a half dozen private coin-making firms who minted up the pesos according to a standard set by royal decree. That is, they did so when strictly supervised; records indicate a loss to the Crown of 10,000,000 pesos in one twenty-year period because the minters made the coins "defective in weight or fineness."

This loss was small compared to all the wealth gained from Spain's New World minerals. In 1803 Alexander von Humboldt, a visiting scientist, figured the New World had sent the Old World, from 1492 to the year of his visit, a greater amount of precious metal than the entire known world had seen since the days of Solomon. In the final analysis, however, the mines proved a liability to Spain, as the great mass of metallic wealth meant inflation at home, and left Spain with an impoverished working class and a declining home industry. Only a small group of Spanish merchants actually benefited.

Naturally, manufacturing industries had no extensive development in the colonies, partly because the Spanish government discouraged or directly forbade any industry's competing with the manufacturing and trade of the mother country. The colonies existed to send raw materials to the mother country and to buy her manufactured goods. But the townspeople in the New World needed more than beef and hides, corn and wheat, or sugar and tobacco. They needed clothing in greater quantity and at lower prices than could be imported by the long slow journey from Spain. The manufacturing most widely developed in America was textile manufacturing. Factories called *obrajes,* hiring great numbers of skilled Indian hand weavers, appeared within the first decade of conquest. The Incas had always been expert textile weavers with llama wools; their descendants took easily to the use of sheep's wool. All types of fine cotton goods were produced; dyes for them were made from the cochineal insect, bright red parasite on the cactus plant, and from indigo. The weaving of velvet, taffeta, and other fine silk goods, at first from the silk produced in the new mulberry-tree industry and later from raw skeins brought over on the Manila Galleon, became a local industry, even though considered competitive to the mother country. The upper classes in the growing cities objected that "fine materials brought from Spain rotted and faded on the long sea journey."

Obrajes producing the cheap cotton and woolen goods for general consumption were found from Guadalajara to Tucumán. The exploitation of Indian labor in them was notorious, both by the Indian chieftains who abused their fellow Indians to make a profit and by the Spanish entrepreneurs. Efforts to control this exploitation were made from time to time by social-minded governors and viceroys, and by direct decree from the Council of the Indies, but to no lasting avail. Negro slaves and at one time even Chinese weavers were brought in to end the abuse of the Indians, and the number of *obrajes* was restricted by law.

Metal work, from ornamental iron bars for the windows of wealthy young ladies' bedrooms to horseshoes, had to be made by smiths in the New World. Skilled metal craftsmen could cast anything from a cannon to a church bell, even the fine needles for the ladies' embroidery work. Equally skilled were leather workers who brought their trade from Spain; they turned out shoes for the wife of the viceroy and sandals for the Indian herdsmen, saddles and suits of leather clothing for the horsemen, hand-tooled scabbards for the swords brought out from Spain. Potters continued in their ancient crafts and had an importance in the economic life of every town and market place. The wines of Chile's central valley were stored in large earthen jars made in Santiago and, which are still to be seen in some old vineyards. Refined sugar, soap, gunpowder, tanned shoe leather, basketry, glass, hardware of all sorts, carved wood cabinets, and intricate jewelry, all were made in the New World for the New World consumption. The colonists could not wait for the fleets from Spain to bring them these products, and could not pay the high prices asked when they arrived.

The new towns needed skilled builders also. The records of Asunción, Paraguay, for instance, have preserved the names of the carpenters, shipbuilders, and bricklayers, as well as of the adventurous captains who founded the town. Skilled wood-workers built ships for the Pacific coast of Mexico at San Blas and Acapulco, for the west coast of South America at Guayaquil and Valparaiso.

Many of these craftsmen, who created an in-between social class in the cities, were organized into *gremios* or guilds on the medieval pattern. The silversmiths of Mexico City were the first to organize such a guild, patterning it after the powerful one in Spain. By 1685, seventy-one silversmiths were listed in Mexico City; at the same time there were eighty organized silver workers' shops in Lima. The guild members were in evidence as leaders in public celebrations and religious processions. Only pure-blooded Spaniards could join; the years as apprentice and as journeyman were as long and arduous as in any craft guild of Europe. After two centuries of Spanish rule, Mexico had 100 other guild groups—gold beaters, harness and saddle makers, potters, weavers, hatters, candle makers. These organizations regulated apprenticeship, set standards for the quality of goods, kept up prices, and licensed journeymen, masters, and inspectors. They were also social, religious, and philanthropic organizations, the center of life and activity for their members and families.

To sample the economy of a smaller community, the people who lived in Panama City were checked by a royal "informer" as to how they made their living. "A few wealthy citizens have grain and livestock plantations for the local market; other wealthy ones own the brigantines which seek the oyster beds where the pearls are found, or are the owners of pack trains of mules which make the portage from the fleets of one sea to those of the other." There were also boat owners who "bring the wares from the fleets from Spain down the Chagres to the customs houses at Cruces and from there by mule train to Panama." There were "wealthy owners of saw mills where they make the planks used for houses and flat-bottomed boats." Some others superintended the cutting of logs in the forest, ran the slaughter houses, and owned fishing and shrimp-collecting boats. The Indians and Negro slaves, who were not even listed in the report, cut the logs and manned the boats, dived for the oysters, tilled the fields, and drove the mules.

colonial labor supply

At every step of the conquest, the conquerors expected the conquered Indians to do the heavy work. In countries in which there is a preponderance of Indian blood the Indians still today remain the toilers, the hewers of wood and the drawers of water. How to allocate Indian workers and get them to work was the problem in Hispaniola at the beginning. Groups of Indians were distributed to a private party to do an assigned task—an institution called *repartimiento*. Theoretically they were to be paid wages for this work, but as they also owed tribute to the Crown, the work was soon considered the tribute. This granting of the use of Indian laborers as separate from the land became an abuse in Peru under a system called the *mita*. Chiefs were required to send a certain percentage of the men of free villages long distances from their homes to work in the mines. They were kept there for months on a pittance of wages, as a method of collecting "tribute" from the chiefs. Thousands of them died in the mines and never saw their native villages again.

A different institution for the use of Indian labor was the *encomienda,* also first used on the Caribbean islands. This was not intended to be a grant of land, for land grants had no legal connection with the work of the Indians who happened to be living on the land. The landowner was to "protect" the Indians, and could collect from them in work the tribute they were supposed to owe the Crown. If the Indians did not work the land to the capacity the landlord decreed, they had "failed to pay the royal tribute" and were considered in debt. Thus they were soon tied to the land in the manner of feudal peasants in Europe, working as serfs on estates. In Mexico the serfs were called *peones,* in Peru *yanacones,* in Chile *inquilinos.* If the Indians could prove themselves to be out of debt, they could go to work as paid laborers. Thus there was a gradual evolution away from the forced labor of *repartimiento, mita,* and *encomienda* to the use of free labor paid in wages.

Complicating the picture of the Indians' gradual rise to free labor status were the black slaves, supplanting the Indians on the plantations. The slave trade prospered, with Cartagena and Havana as its centers. Once in the New World, the blacks, although well adapted to heavy work in the tropics, did not multiply rapidly and often ran away to the hills to become *cimarrones,* or renegade slaves living as outlaws. Though there was always a demand for more slaves freshly captured in Africa, actually black labor cost more than forced Indian labor.

White laborers entered the colonial working strata to a smaller extent. The Crown encouraged farmers, artisans, and laborers from Spain to go to the New World, and granted free transportation for chosen emigrants, giving them tools, seed, and farm animals. But the restriction on emigration counterbalanced these inducements, and, save for the craftsmen who were members of the guilds and a few technicians from foreign countries, the laboring classes were not of pure European extraction. The social problems of labor and its exploitation will be discussed again in Chapter 12.

trade and commerce as controlled by Spain

It should be apparent to the student of American history that Spain tried to control the trade of Latin America much as England did that of her colonies. Under the theory of mercantilism, the accepted theory in those days of new overseas empires, colonies existed to help the mother country, to provide the raw material for the manufacturers at home, and to buy back the manufactured articles. None of this colonial trade must be allowed to profit a rival foreign power. Spain's efforts to maintain such a policy forced her to spend large sums on army and navy to fight off foreign competitors, and on a large bureaucracy to restrict and control trade and keep foreigners from sharing it.

Control of trade in the Indies was handled through the *Casa de*

Contratación, whose founding was described in Chapter 6. It remained a gigantic agency, licensing and supervising all ships and merchants, passengers and goods, crews and equipment passing to and from the New World. It handled all gold and silver, collected all customs taxes, and even maintained a whole staff devoted to improving the science of navigation. It was assisted by the *consulado* or merchant guild in Seville and by parallel merchant guilds in the chief trading centers of the Americas. *Consulados* were local "chambers of commerce" for the American cities, performing public services, improving roads, arranging parades, handling bankruptcies and breach of contract cases. Their members were the wealthiest and most important merchants in the colonies.

The system of sending goods to the Indies narrowed the monopoly, kept up the prices, and made trade slow and difficult. Only Cádiz and Seville could be used as ports of departure, only Havana, Veracruz, Portobello and Cartagena as ports of arrival. Not only must goods be sent on Spanish ships, but the ships must all sail together. To control the trade and to protect the ships against pirates, all cargoes were sent on yearly fleets of from forty to seventy ships. All the ships which were licensed to visit the colonies in any one year met at Seville or, in the years of shallow water, at Cádiz, and traveled with six or eight armed ships. Two groups sailed, a fleet in the spring called the *flota* which went to Veracruz with cargo for Central America, Mexico, and the islands, and a fleet in August called the galleons, *los galeones,* with cargo destined for Panama and transshipment across the Isthmus. The *flota* returned laden with hides, sugar, and Mexican silver, the *galeones* with Peruvian silver, Colombian emeralds, Venezuelan pearls, drugs, spices, cacao, and dyestuffs.

The Veracruz *flota,* often delayed in Spain until late summer, might be caught in the hurricane season of the Caribbean, or, if not caught by the hurricanes, might fall as booty to English pirates. When the *flota* arrived at fever-ridden Veracruz, the produce was transshipped to mule-back and taken up into the *cordillera* to the pleasant town of Jalapa for a great yearly fair. Thousands of people came to Jalapa; profits for middlemen were enormous as goods were purchased to be transshipped to towns from Guatemala to Texas.

To the fair at Jalapa also came goods brought by the one ship which sailed alone without convoy, the Manila Galleon, the single ship a year which came from Spain's one colony in the Orient. All Spanish trade with the Philippines had to go via Mexico's west coast. If the ship survived its difficult passage, it came into Acapulco loaded with silk, both raw and woven, and all kinds of embroidery, porcelains, lacquers, carved ivories, and damascene ware. When the Oriental wares arrived in Acapulco they were transported by mule to Mexico City, and thence to other parts of the empire and to Spain via the Jalapa fair.

The fair to sell goods from the *galeones* was held at Porto Bello, the "Emporium of South America" on the Caribbean side of the Isthmus; in fact, the towns on the Isthmus existed for this fair. Here for the forty days of the fair came the wholesale merchants from Peru to exchange mule-train loads of silver and vicuña wool and Plata River hides for European-made things. To the fair through the rich Seville middlemen had come laces, tapestries, and silks from France, linens from Holland, crystalline glass from Venice, hand-tooled leather from Florence, wool hats from England, rugs and shawls from the Near East, beautiful things to find their way eventually into the colonial mansions in Lima or Quito, or even the frontier houses in Buenos Aires. In addition there were staples from Spain—cheeses, ink, shoes, hardware, Spanish pottery, wheat flour, and even beeswax.

At Portobello these things had already doubled in price. To sell them, booths were built of jungle logs around the plaza nearest the wharf and covered with sailcloth to "hold the vast stacks of merchandise." A special force of 5,000 soldiers patroled the town and the trails to Panama City across the Isthmus and protected the mule trains of silver out of Bolivia's "glory hole" from the thieves and hangers-on who followed the fairs. There was no place to sleep for the thousands who came, so they slept in the open, in the mosquito-ridden night, and died by the hundreds from yellow fever. Two thousand mules for the trans-Isthmian service were kept in near-by corrals, though they could not be carefully enough guarded, there on the edge of the jungle, from jaguars making their nightly kill. The European goods purchased by the wholesalers were taken, on the mules who survived the jaguars, to meet the "Armada of the Southern Seas" in Panama Bay, a fleet of ships mostly built in Guayaquil. At Callao and Lima smaller fairs were held; the goods were sold to other middlemen who would ship them to Valparaiso, send them by pack train up to Cuzco or to the fast-living silver towns of Bolivia, or pack them through the Andes to meet the caravans of oxcarts on the edge of the pampas at Salta to go the long trip to Buenos Aires. As far as the *Casa* and the Council of the Indies officially knew, no European goods ever reached Valparaiso or Buenos Aires except via the fair and the galleons at Portobello. Any bride in Córdoba or Santiago or Buenos Aires who wanted a wedding dress from Spain would wait two years from the time she ordered it until she got it, and then would pay ten times its original price.

And the bride, waiting for her wedding dress in Buenos Aires— could her father not get a better price for his hides and a lower price on the dress by dealing with a trader directly at the Plata harbor? This dependence of Buenos Aires on Lima and Portobello was an absurd situation creating high costs and retarding the growth of the Plata colony, but one which was perpetuated because the merchants of Lima and Panama were influential with the *Casa* and wanted to keep their cut of the Plata trade. What a temptation for smugglers, and how the settlers in these isolated ports welcomed them! English and Dutch ships often lay in Buenos Aires harbor, taking untold thousands of hides back to shoemakers in London or Amsterdam—and who in Seville was to know? Other centers of contraband were in the Antilles, especially at Jamaica and Curaçao, islands controlled by England and Holland in the eighteenth century.

African slaves were part of the contraband trade coming into the Caribbean. Spanish merchants had seldom handled slaves, since they had no access to the coast of Africa and had been forced to grant the Portuguese *asientos,* or rights to send slave ships into the island markets and to the mainland at Cartagena. As time went on these ships carried on much contraband trade as well, and England was able to cut into this profitable cargo. Spanish officials helped in the cheating, secretly opening ports as "haven for ships in distress," ships which had no greater distress than the anxiety to unload their rich cargoes.

Trade from one colony to another was less restricted by law than by poor roads, lack of bridges, difficult geography, and great distances. Every region was isolated from every other. The regions had little use for each other's products; a long trek by river boat was necessary even to start the climb to the Bogotá highland valley; the trek by oxcart across the pampas from Buenos Aires to Salta, only halfway to the hide markets at Lima, took several weeks; even the improved trail between Veracruz and Mexico City called for ten days on a good horse. On the Isthmus, that shortest route across the continent, the Cruces Trail was actually a primitive, overgrown mule path paved with irregular blocks of stone and seldom repaired, so muddy and so difficult that even though it was only sixty miles long a week's travel was necessary for a loaded mule. Meanwhile, in all parts of the New World, transportation of village food products to town markets was carried on by the same methods as in 1492, on the heads and backs of Indians. Tropical colonies needed to import cereals from temperate climate areas; tobacco, sugar, and cacao from the tropics went to Mexico City and to Lima. Commission men made fortunes supplying food and pack animals from the agricultural areas to the silver-mining regions of northern Mexico and Bolivia. From such trading a new middle class began to develop slowly by the 1700s.

money into the royal exchequer

More important than the trade and commerce of the New World—more important to the Crown and the Council of the Indies—was the wealth of funds that came from direct income on royal land, from Crown monopolies, and (mainly) from taxes. The revenues varied up and down through the decades; the total royal income from the New World had multiplied sixfold between 1550 and 1750. Though many of the smaller colonies and frontier communities never paid their own expenses, Peru and Mexico continually brought in a substantial revenue for the crown. Spain maintained a wide frontier, fought expensive wars in Europe, and championed the Catholic faith in Europe and America, so taxes could never be light. The royal exchequer hired a comptroller, a treasurer, inspectors, tax collectors, auditors, judges for special tax appeal courts, and hundreds of bookkeepers, all of whose records have been carefully preserved. The money came from more than forty different types of taxation.

A major source of income was the indirect tax on trade between Old World and New. Though such taxes brought income for the Crown, they actually hampered commerce and kept prices high. Merchants who sent goods on the fleet paid a special assessment to pay for and arm the fleet. A standard import and export duty, the *almojarifazgo,* ranging between 7 and 10 per cent, was charged on all articles coming through Seville, and another almost equal percentage was collected as a sales tax, the hated *alcabala,* on the same articles when they arrived in the colonies. At home in the colonies, individuals paid tithes to the Church, excise taxes on wines and liquors, luxury taxes on cockfights and tobacco, and many types of stamp taxes on legal documents. The Indians at the bottom paid a capitation or poll tax, as well as tribute to local authorities.

In addition to such taxes, the Spanish crown gained a personal profit from the New World. The *quinto* or fifth of all precious metal mined went to the king. He held vast tracts of agricultural land as direct proprietor and owned all cattle and crops on it. Mercury, gunpowder, playing cards, lotteries, salt, pepper, snow, and ice brought down from the mountains for cooling drinks in Mexico City and Lima—all were royal monopolies. In addition the king made private revenue from the sale of public offices, titles and honors, "forced loans," and from "kickbacks" into the treasury required of many seekers after lucrative political and ecclesiastic appointments.

To provide money to carry on all this financing, the Crown set up royal mints in Mexico City and in Lima, where the small coins called *reales* and the standard silver *peso* pieces of eight *reales* value, the "pieces of eight" of pirate days, were minted. The colonies always suffered from scarcity of small coins and had to resort to barter on the village-market level. There was never any paper currency, there were no banks, and thus there was little flexibility of credit.

Tax collecting was often farmed out to subcontractors, a system which always invites dishonesty. The heavy taxes on trade produced a chronic undersupply of manufactured goods, and all goods were sold at exorbitant prices. In return for the large tax revenue Spain gave the colonies an organized governmental system, roads, albeit poor ones, communications with the mother country, defense against Indians, the comforts of religion, and the luxury of a Spanish-born aristocracy. But there was much legitimate trade in spite of taxes, business was thriving, and wealth was being produced, no matter how badly distributed. The colonists accepted the conditions and learned to live with them, sometimes complying with the many restrictions and levies, sometimes getting around the system by bribery or smuggling.

Some historians of the Spanish colonial empire claim that the responsibility of the colonies bankrupted Spain. It is true that by 1700 colonial cities were more prosperous than Seville or Madrid, and that the power of Spain in Europe was ended. But this was partially due to the wasteful line of weak kings, to the many wars they fought against England and France, to their quarrels with their dependencies in Holland, Italy, and the German states, and to their own corrupt tax collectors. Fifty per cent of all the fabulous wealth pouring into the royal treasury must have been used to defray these expenses, for the records seem to indicate that the costs of governing the New World—maintaining the viceroys and their courts, the customs houses and their employees, the fleets and their crews, the frontier forts and their soldiers—came to only 50 per cent of the total tax revenue. The lack of adequate law enforcement, the opportunities for smuggling and tax evasion, combined with the great natural wealth and vitality of the New World itself led to the ultimate downfall of Spain's commercial system, the end of mercantilism as a colonial policy.

READINGS

Agricola, G., *De re Mettallica*, trans. H. C. and L. H. Hoover (1950).

Bakewell, P. J., *Silver Mining and Society in Colonial Mexico, Zacatecas 1546–1700* (1971).

Bannon, J. F., *Indian Labor in the Spanish Indies* (1966).

Barber, R. K., *Indian Labor in the Spanish Colonies* (1932).

Barrett, W., *The Sugar Hacienda of the Marqueses del Valle* (1971).

Borah, W., *Early Colonial Trade and Navigation Between Mexico and Peru* (1954).

———, *New Spain's Century of Depression* (1951).

———, *Silk Raising in Colonial Mexico* (1943).

Brading, D. A., *Miners and Merchants in Bourbon Mexico 1763–1810* (1971).

Chevalier, F., *Land and Society in Colonial Mexico* (1963).

Cobb, G. B., "Supply and Transportation from the Potosí Mines, 1545–1560," *Hispanic American Historical Review*, XXIX, 25–45.

Diffie, B. W., *Latin American Civilization: Colonial Period* (1945).

Dusenberry, W. M., *The Mexican Mesta: The Administration of Ranching in Colonial Mexico* (1963).

Elliott, J. H., *Old World and the New 1492–1650* (1971).

Furtado, C., *Economic Development of Latin America* (1970).

Gibson, C., *Spain in America* (1966).

———, *Spanish Tradition in America* (1968).

Hamilton, E. J., *American Treasure and the Price Revolution in Spain, 1501–1650* (1934).

———, *War and Prices in Spain, 1651–1800* (1947).

Hamnett, B. R., *Politics and Trade in Southern Mexico 1750–1821* (1971).

Hanke, L., *Bartolomé Arzans de Orsura y Vela's History of Potosí* (1965).

———, *The Imperial City of Potosí* (1956).

Haring, C. H., *Spanish Empire in America* (1952).

———, *Trade and Navigation Between Spain and the Indies in the Time of the Hapsburgs* (1918).

Harmon, E., *Trade and Privateering in Spanish Florida 1732–1763* (1969).

Howe, W., *The Mining Guild of New Spain and Its Tribunal Guild* (1949).

Klein, J., *The Mesta* (1920).

La Force, J. C., *Development of Spanish Textile Industry 1750–1800* (1965).

Loosely, A. C., "The Puerto Bello Fairs," *Hispanic American Historical Review*, XIII, 314–335.

McBride, G., *Land Systems of Chile* (1936).

———, *Land Systems of Mexico* (1923).

Merriman, R. B., *Rise of the Spanish Empire*, Vols. II, III, IV (1918–1934).

Motten, C. G., *Mexican Silver and the Enlightenment* (1950).

Muers, S. L., *The Ranch in Spanish Texas 1691–1800* (1969).

Nesmith, R. I., *The Coinage of the First Mint of the Americas at Mexico City, 1536–1572* (1955).

Parry, J. H., *Sale of Public Office in the Spanish Indies Under the Hapsburgs* (1953).

———, *Spanish Seaborne Empire* (1966).

Pike, R., *Aristocrats and Traders. Sevillian Society in the Sixteenth Century* (1972).

Powell, P. W., *Soldiers, Indians and Silver* (1952).

Priestley, H. I., *Coming of the White Man* (1929).

Purser, W. F. C., *Metal Mining in Peru, Past and Present* (1971).

Schurz, W. L., *Latin America* (rev. ed., 1964).

———, *Manila Galleon* (1939).

Service, E. R., "The Encomienda in Paraguay," *Hispanic American Historical Review*, XXXI, 230–50.

———, *Spanish-Guaraní Relations in Early Colonial Paraguay* (1954).

Simpson, L. B., *Encomienda in New Spain* (1950; rev. ed., 1966).

———, *Exploitation of Land in Central Mexico in the Sixteenth Century* (1952).

———, *Many Mexicos* (3rd ed., 1952).

———, *Repartimiento System of Forced Native Labor in New Spain and Guatemala* (1938).

Smith, R. S., *The Spanish Guild Merchant* (1940).

Stein, S. J. and B. H., *Colonial Heritage of Latin America* (1970).

Taylor, W. B., *Landlord and Peasant in Colonial Oaxaca* (1972).

West, R. C., *Colonial Placer Mining in Colombia* (1952).

———, *Mining Community in Northern New Spain: Parral Mining District* (1949).

Whitaker, A. P., *The Huancavelica Mine* (1941).

———, "Spanish Contributions to American Agriculture," *Agriculture History*, III, 1–14.

Wilgus, A. C., ed., *Colonial Hispanic America* (1936).

Woodward, Jr., R. L., *Class Privilege and Economic Development: The Consulado de Comercio of Guatemala, 1793–1871* (1966).

Zurita, Alonzo de, *Life and Labor in Ancient Mexico*, trans. B. Keen (1963).

chapter 12

RELIGION, SOCIETY AND CULTURE IN THE SPANISH COLONIES

religious organization under the crown of Spain

When Columbus returned from his first voyage in 1493, he wrote to Isabella, ". . . all Christendom should rejoice for the winning of so many peoples to our Holy Faith." When he discovered the mainland at the mouth of the Orinoco in 1498, he rejoiced that "your Highnesses have here another world where our Holy Faith may be spread." Other explorers for the next 50 years used religious terms such as "the Holy Trinity," "Saint James," "Flowery Easter," "Thanks to God" to name their new finds. Cortés, when he first met with Indians at Tabasco, set up an altar to the Virgin, and said he won his victories as he marched to Mexico because "the great mercy of God gave us strength."

Every Spaniard who went to the New World was imbued with similar missionary spirit and devotion no matter how greedy or ambitious he might personally be or how callous he was in his treatment of individual Indians. The colonies were all founded with the same provisions—a chaplain came with the conquerors, missionary brothers worked to convert the Indians, bishoprics were created and churches built as soon as towns were founded. The priests and friars, moreover, tried to protect the Indians from exploitation.

So due to the crusading spirit, courage, and persistence of church workers, Catholic Christianity came to be one of the strongest forces in colonial Spain. They must be given great credit for their part in transplanting European culture and civilization to America's rugged frontiers. True, members of the Church often failed to live up to the high standards expected of them; the church organizations became too rich and politically powerful; their institutions controlled education so rigidly they sometimes kept out new and necessary ideas; and they were always intolerant of other faiths. But in all this, they were reflecting the times in Europe. Human frailties rather than institutional evils explain the failings of the Church. It undertook many tasks in the New World, and in almost every case the only agency to attempt the work was the Church.

It is difficult for people in the modern age to understand the intensity of religious feeling in the sixteenth century. This is the century that saw the bitter wars between Catholic and Protestant and the fanatical punishment of heresies by both sides. It was a century of great missionary zeal fostered by the close connection between church and state. So zealous were Ferdinand and Isabella in championing the cause of Catholic Christianity that they were granted special powers by the Pope over the clergy in Spain. Implicit in the unity which the "Catholic Monarchs" established for all Spain was conformity to Catholicism, providing them with an absolutism that enabled them to root out all nonconformists as heretics. So wherever Spain went in the New World, the Roman Catholic Church went also, to uphold the sanctity of kings as well as to transmit the institutions and culture of Spain.

Unusual powers were given the Spanish Crown by the Church, beginning with the papal bull that set the Line of Demarcation that gave Spain her legal claim to the new lands. Other papal bulls in the next two decades gave the Spanish kings direct control over the Church in America. Under the *real patronato,* the king of Spain could make appointments to positions usually filled in other countries by the Pope alone. The Crown received control of church buildings and the right to handle taxes collected for the Church. In return, the Crown was to back all church activity financially and, above all, to "instruct and convert the natives."

Within a few years, the Church organization for the New World islands was completely separate from, though parallel to, the Church hierarchy of Seville and Madrid. Crown control over the Church was as thoroughly consolidated as was its control of the courts and of customs collection. The only exception was the *fuero,* the special privilege of church personnel to be tried only in church courts. But a royal license was required for all churchmen going to the New World. The Council of the Indies appointed bishops, created new dioceses, carried on communications between abbots and bishops in the New World and their counterparts in Seville, or between an archbishop in Mexico and the Pope in Rome, and even approved the publication of papal bulls applying to the colonies.

The Church served as a bulwark of monarchy. The clerics, beholden to the king for finances and favors, served the monarchs faithfully, instilling in the minds of their ignorant flocks an almost universal devotion to the royal person. This purpose was served by both branches of church organization, the "regulars" or members of holy orders of monks and nuns and the "seculars" or the clergy who directly served the public as parish priests and the archbishops and bishops above them.

At the head of the secular clergy for the colonies was the Patriarch of the Indies, who resided at court and served *ex officio* on the Council of the Indies. Under him were the archbishops and bishops in America. As Spain's power stretched north and south, bishoprics were created in provincial capitals; and eventually, in the 1540's, archbishops were sent to the capitals of the new viceroyalties, Mexico City and Lima, retaining only nominal subservience to the archbishop at Seville, hitherto the chief prelate for the island colonies. Growth continued until there were ten archbishops' and thirty-eight bishops' dioceses in Spanish America. These church divisions did not always coincide with political divisions, which in the early days of independence was to cause some confusion.

The new bishops and archbishops were almost always men born in Spain, of noble birth, of high ability, and the best education, ten of them becoming viceroys of Mexico during their New World sojourn. American-born Spaniards, pure whites called creoles, seldom reached eminence in the church but served as curates, priests, and missionaries. The yearly salary of the archbishop of Mexico was 130,000 pesos, of a parish priest about 125.

Every diocese had a cathedral with its many canons and prelates as dignitaries. In the town and village churches were the thousands of parish priests. The priests were responsible for the church buildings erected by law in every town, Spanish or Indian, and for such schools and hospitals as it was possible to maintain. It was the priests who were closest to the common people, and many of them were to side with the colonists during the later wars for independence while the bishops were almost always royalists.

More numerous than these "secular" clerics were the members of the "regular" orders, the missionary churchmen devoted to the Christianizing and civilizing of the natives, the most serious obligation of the Spanish Crown. Virtually every fleet bore a contingent of friars, Franciscans, Dominicans, or Augustinians, to carry on the campaign of conversion, until eventually, when Spanish power was spread to the mainland of Mexico, fifteen different organizations were engaged in the conversion of millions of Indians. After the militant Ignatius Loyola founded the Society of Jesus, the Jesuits became important in education and missionary work, the first arriving in New Spain in 1572. Each of these orders was worldwide and had its own elaborate hierarchy from its general resident in Rome and commissary-general in Madrid to its various ranking officials in America. Their members were divided into two classes, those who worked in the frontier missions, doing work for which the *padres* are best and most warmly remembered, and those who lived in monasteries or convents in or near Europeanized cities and who devoted themselves to social services and the education of children of Spanish town dwellers or who gave their lives over to meditation.

shrines, saints, and religious celebrations

Hispanized communities, with their culture imported entirely from Spain, centered their life around the Church and its parish priest as did their Spanish prototypes. The church, set on the central plaza, was the finest building in every colonial village or town. Its interior was richer, more colorful, more magnificent than anything else the children of the town would ever have a chance to see. Mexico City had a church for every three or four blocks of residences. Puebla, a hundred miles to the southeast, reportedly had the most churches per population of any city in the New World—Romanesque churches with round domes, Italian Renaissance churches, churches with roofs of brilliant blue and yellow glazed tile, façades of ornate carving or of Majolica tiles in picture patterns.

Church procedure was the center of social life, with the priest serving as the town's social arbiter and community leader. Family life was built around church traditions: a child's birth was registered in the parish register; he received a baptismal rather than a civil birth certificate; his godparents at baptism promised to help him all his life. Probably a boy's elementary education, and certainly his secondary education, was in church schools. Marriage was a religious sacrament blessed by the priest, never to be broken by divorce.

As a grown man, the town dweller belonged to a religious *hermandad* or lodge which conducted social affairs and looked after charity cases. He prayed to his own saint, promised penance and gifts if his requests were granted, often offering to bear the expense of the next fiesta as a "major domo." If life became hard, he could go into a monastery and be cared for for the rest of his life. At death he was given a church funeral and was buried in holy ground. A woman's life was bound, even more than a man's, by religious restrictions. Convent life was the only possible career other than marriage within the church fold.

Social events in towns or cities were largely religious celebrations. High points of the year were pageants and parades for Carnival, Palm Sunday, and Easter, *posadas* for Christmas, miracle plays from medieval Europe and celebrations of the birthday of the town's own patron saint. Even today towns in rural Latin America celebrate their patron saint's birthday as a week-long festival, with processions and pageantry perhaps identical to those of the 1670's and 1770's.

Latin America eventually produced saints and beatified persons of its own, commemorating religious leaders for their service to the unfortunate. Colombia has San Pedro Claver, a friar who worked for 40 years among the slaves, built the fortifications of Cartagena, and kept a mission in the slave pens where they were forced to live. Mexico has Fray Pedro Gante (Peter of Ghent) who founded schools in Mexico City among Aztec children, and Don Vasco de Quiroga who christianized the Tarascan Indians in the Lake Pátzcuaro region and helped them develop colorful handicrafts with lacquer which their descendants still sell to tourists. Paraguay has its patron saint in missionary father San Francisco Solano who died working in the inhospitable Gran Chaco. Peru has an archbishop, Toribio Alfonso de Magrobeja who learned to speak Quechua and made a tour on foot and muleback to every community he could reach in the country; Peru also has a young girl cannonized as Saint Rose of Lima, and a third one named Saint Martin de Porres, a *mulatto* born in Lima.

Pilgrimages were made to New World shrines, such as the church of Guadalupe, four miles from the center of Mexico City, which possesses a miraculous painting of a dark-haired, brown-skinned girl who is the patron saint of all Mexico's Indian people. This painting of the Virgin of Guadalupe is believed to have appeared December 9, 1531, on the *serape* or blanket of a poor Christianized Aztec Indian named Juan Diego. A vision of the Virgin had appeared to him when he was picking cactus apples on the Guadalupe Hill; she requested him to ask the bishop to build a church on the spot, and as proof she caused roses to grow among the cactus. The picture appeared on the blanket in which he carried the roses to the bishop. The bishop built the shrine, which today is visited by thousands of devout Mexicans, many of whom climb the hill on December ninth on their knees. The appearance of a brown-skinned Virgin helped the Spanish priests enormously in their efforts to convert the Indians.

The Virgin of Guadalupe had competitors during colonial days. Colonists of pure Spanish blood worshiped at the Mexican shrine of Our Lady of Los Remedios. South Americans had similar shrines. The chapel of the Virgin of Copacabana on Lake Titicaca, is still the goal of pilgrimages today. The site of the Virgin of Luján near Buenos Aires was selected when the oxen drawing the cart in which the statue was being carried inland in 1630 halted there and would go no farther. This was presumed to be evidence that the Virgin wished to stay near Buenos Aires. The Catholic Church deeply influenced colonial life at all levels and in all regions of Latin America.

the influence of the Catholic faith on the Indians

The speed with which the Indian religions were replaced by Christianity is one of the remarkable facts of the Western Hemisphere's history. The historian Motolinía tells us that over four million Indians were baptized during the first fifteen years of the conquest of Mexico. The Franciscan fathers claimed more than a million conversions between 1524 and 1531. Fray Pedro de Gante wrote to his king that 14,000 Aztecs had been baptized on a single June day in 1529 and that "many of us have baptized more than 100,000 each during our sojourn here." Isabella's fondest dream concerning the new islands of the Indies was the conversion of the Indians, and she saw the dream being realized.

On the whole the conversion was more apparent than real. Often a "requisition" giving a theological explanation of the history of Christianity was merely read aloud to the Indians in Spanish. Of course they did not understand, and after hearing the reading and watching the celebration of the Mass, they were baptized, Some of the conversion was by physical force, used to "eliminate heathen practices." Temples were torn down, idols destroyed, and severe punishments inflicted by the Spanish military on those who resisted. "Save their souls first, then teach and train them afterward" was the motto.

Teach and train the missionaries did, as more and more friars came to serve new generations of Indians more accustomed to Spanish ways. The friars who came in their coarse habits were pledged to a life of poverty and simplicity which was quite different from the life in the rich monasteries in Mexico City and Lima. They devoted themselves to the well-being of their charges in agricultural villages and frontier missions—and became famous in the annals of their orders. The papacy issued special dispensations that gave these "regulars" the right to perform the duties of ordained priests for the numbers of "secular" clergy were too few to serve the wide frontier. The jealousy between the regulars and the seculars which this caused was ended in 1757 when the secularization of well-established missions was ordered.

But in most frontier missions, the new religion was a thin veneer on the old barbarism. The natives had difficulty in comprehending the involved spiritual doctrines of the Church. They received a thin veneer of European culture along with Christian faith but they lost the old tribal ethical standards which they had understood. The ethics of the new faith they did not grasp. The clergy, in the first century of expansion, were working for numbers of converts, not the inculcation of high ideals. The *conquistadores* by their example did little to inspire the Indian to follow Christian ethics and often undid what the friars had accomplished. But, for the government, the missionaries did an excellent job in pacifying many tribes without arms, defending the frontier, and Hispanicizing entire areas.

The greatest energy and zeal was exerted on the frontier at the farthest limits of empire in both North and South America. The missionaries endured hardship, hunger, disease, and even martyrdom as they got into contact with the tribes, studied their languages and customs, "reduced" the Indians into missions and taught them the elements of a new civil and religious life. Actually the missions were schools, and the new culture, veneer or not, included agricultural and craft training as well as arts, music, and letters. The friars were trained at missionary colleges such as the Franciscan College at Querétaro and became explorers, diarists, historians, architects, geographers, and linguists as well as teachers of agriculture and agents of the Crown. They became anthropologists who made studies of tribal life of value today in analyzing primitive groups. The missions were outposts of the Empire on the most remote frontiers—Upper California, Texas, Florida, the Guiana border of Venezuela, the Araucanian territory of southern Chile, the Guaraní country of Paraguay and Iguassú—and were often fortified by *presidios* or garrisons of soldiers.

Missions in California and Paraguay became most famous. In northern Mexico the Jesuits worked for two centuries in Durango, Sinaloa, and

Sonora, moving northward as their missions became villages taken over by the seculars. Their "farthest-north worker" was Father Eusebio Kino who had spent 24 years in the Nogales-Tucson-Yuma triangle of Arizona teaching the Pima Indians. Eventually he extended his work to Lower California through his support of Father Salvatierra. His rich mission at Dolores was able to send thousands of cattle to help start farms for the mission in that inhospitable desert land.

The Franciscans extended the mission chain into Alta California, building the 21 missions in California from San Diego north through Santa Barbara and Monterey to San Francisco that are familiar landmarks today. Father Junípero Serra founded many of the missions in the chain, starting with San Diego in 1769. These missions were typical of such settlements throughout the length of Latin America. From the first reed huts, the mission buildings were transformed by Indians in the second generation into large adobe-brick chapels, many of which, restored, still stand today. At their peak of power the missions were surrounded by homes for the priest-teachers, barracks for Spanish soldiers, dormitories for unmarried Indians, huts for families, and long lines of blacksmith shops, olive and wine presses, smoke houses, leather-tooling shops, brick-making yards, pottery kilns, and tanneries.

Life in these missions has been over-romanticized for the life of the Indians was not always happy. If they tried to flee mission life with its heavy work and strict discipline, they were chased by Spanish soldiers and sometimes flogged when caught. Later generations born into mission life profited more from the experience than did their parents.

Indicative of the impact of missionaries in South America is the fact that the Argentine province on the Paraguay is called Misiones. Tourists today cruise up into the semi-tropics to view abandoned Jesuit missions. Jesuits from Peru arrived there in 1605, sent by the Crown to stop the encroachments of Portuguese slave raiders from Brazil in the area to the northeast of Asunción. They founded missions on the upper Paraná and upper Paraguay. When slave raiders destroyed the missions in Paraguay and carried off some 60,000 mission Indians into slavery in Brazil, the devoted Jesuits retreated with 12,000 neophytes and settled south of the Falls of the Iguassú, where they eventually had 30 successful mission *pueblos* with perhaps 100,000 neophytes. Provided with arms, they were able to keep the Brazilian raiders at bay and to develop an almost independent community, called "The Jesuit Republic."

Life in Candelaria, the largest of these settlements, was happy and prosperous though strictly regimented, the fathers acting as judges and using corporal punishment. They developed an agricultural empire that produced oranges, olives, grapes, wheat, and livestock. They learned the Guaraní language, wrote books in the language and had them printed on their own printing presses, with the result that the Guaraní, of all the Indian languages in the Americas, remains today a written language and is widely spoken in modern Paraguay. But when the Jesuits were expelled in 1767, the mission buildings fell into decay and the Indians relapsed into barbarism.

The mission fathers had kept their charges under constant tutelage, isolated from other Spaniards, themselves managing all funds, carrying on all trade, maintaining a theocratic quasi-communism under which the Indians never learned self-reliance.

The Indians developed their own variations of the Christian doctrine, especially in long-settled villages where missions were not founded. Sometimes it was easy for church teachers to persuade the people of such communities to adopt a patron saint to replace a local deity whose stone statue stood in the temple guarded by the medicine man. In Peru in 1620 the Spanish government faced a problem because the Inca religion persisted among the Quechuas. The Quechuas still hoped to enlist help from the mummies of their ancestors, the spirit of their "luck piece," the sacrifice of guinea pigs, and the "incantations" of sorcerers, confusing this aid with that which the saints gave in time of stress. In the Andes, where Quechua is still spoken, in the Guatemala highlands and remote parts of Mexico, the old rituals are still performed though villagers attend Mass regularly and observe the outward forms of the Catholic ritual.

activities, powers, and abuses of church officials

All the social service in the colonies—the schools, hospitals, asylums, personal relief, family charity—was done by religious orders. When fortunes were left to the Church, it was done for charity. Bequests cared for foundlings, educated the children of the poor, provided poorhouses for the destitute and hospitals for victims of the periodic epidemics of the time. Where today a socially-minded person may set up a foundation for a boys' club or cancer clinic, in the sixteenth to eighteenth centuries—when no other agencies existed to do such things—a man of wealth gave money to the Church and thus commissioned some Church group to spend the money for him. A wealthy Spaniard in Mexico City in the mid-1500's gave liberally to frontier missions, endowed a chair of theology in the new University of Mexico, and left 140,000 additional pesos to Jesuit charities.

From the primary schools for Indian children to the Jesuit universities described later in this chapter, education was in the charge of religious orders. In the true missionary spirit thousands of the clergy occupied themselves selflessly in education and charity work. Doubtless more actual social service work was done in the New World by Catholic personnel than was done during this same period in the Old World by Protestant and Catholic workers combined.

But the power of the Church was such that abuses developed. In many areas, the regular and secular branches had more members than the new colonies needed. In some parts of the New World, the Church owned more than half of the productive land, having acquired it by bequest, gift, mortgage, and tithes collected in cattle and acreage. The archbishops' salaries were comparable to those of the viceroys—while poor parish priests worked on a pittance. Bishops and archbishops lived in palaces like those of royalty and ruled vast estates like feudal lords. The Indians on these estates were just as subject to abuse, overwork, heavy tribute, and *mita* service in the mines (some of the mines were Church-owned) as were Indians working for any private person, and often they had less redress in the courts. Monasteries were exceedingly numerous, and by 1750, those in Mexico and Lima are said to have owned a fourth of all the buildings in these cities. Controlling such wealth, the monks sometimes forgot their vows, relaxed in their discipline, and lived lives of licentiousness, idleness, and intrigue—in sharp contrast to the self-sacrifice and zeal of the frontier missionaries.

Troublesome problems caused by the wealth of the Church and its influence in politics were carried over from the colonial era to that of the new republics. In some parts of Latin America this is still a cause of conflict. Many church leaders were given to misuse of funds for personal political advantage and to quarreling over jurisdiction with civil authorities or the rival branch of the Church. Special courts grew up to try cases involving priests or monks or concerning disputes over church lands or fees, a practice in line with traditions in Spain and Rome that kept such cases out of the civil courts. This privilege or *fuero* for churchmen later helped cause a revolution in Mexico, and was a sore point elsewhere. It was a sore point to other citizens that priests, friars, and nuns, who were supposed to live exemplary lives, were often no better than run-of-the-mill townspeople and sometimes worse. Powerful Spanish-born churchmen who had no knowledge of colonial conditions were sent out to head rich parishes or dioceses—which roused the jealousy of colonists born in the New World who could never hope to hold such positions themselves.

Only a small minority of the clergy were involved in such abuses, which in many ways were a reflection of conditions in Spain. (In Spain this was an age of hypocrisy and immorality under the later Hapsburgs and early Bourbons). The king was kept advised by reports sent to him on affairs of the Church in the New World. A "plainclothes" inspector in the 18th century, Antonio de Ulloa, reported a long list of church abuses and reported that in Peru "the life of the clergy was scandalous to an unbelievable degree." That the king sent such inspectors is indicative of the conflict between Church and State. Viceroys were jealous of archbishops, captains-general of bishops; the clergy threatened political administrators with excommunication, and administrators retaliated by cutting off funds to the Church. Litigations in the courts over jurisdictions and funds were interminable, with appeals to the king and court hearings dragging on for decades.

But the Church carried on its activities, in cathedrals and city and parish churches and in missions, parochial schools, hospitals, and orphanages, supporting these activities from tithes, amounting to a tenth or *diezmo* of income on all agricultural and industrial products of the New World and from the income from its own farmlands and herds. Secular churchmen also received large amounts of produce and cash for religious services such as sacraments, weddings, baptisms, and funerals, which sometimes became a cause of dispute with political authority when *audiencias* and *cabildos* tried to set standard prices and individual churchmen continued to charge "whatever the traffic would bear."

One Church activity was the exercise of "thought control." Books were censored, school curricula supervised, deviations from accepted beliefs punished. In Spain the Inquisition flourished as a board of judgment and censorship which sought to regiment religious thought and which sent heretics to the stake. As early as 1522 Inquisitorial agents were sent from Spain to protect the orthodoxy of the Church against heretical contamination. A separate Inquisition for the New World was decreed by Philip II by 1570. Three different courts were set up, at Lima in 1570, at Mexico City in 1571, and at Cartagena in 1610, for the declared purpose of punishing blasphemy and immorality among the clergy and adultery and witchcraft among laymen, and of censoring morals and maintaining "the purity of the faith."

Very few trials for heresy were held throughout the colonial period, for nonconformists were seldom able to obtain legal passage to the colonies. Penalties included fines, penance, and flogging for blasphemy and immorality, work in the galleys and exile for bigamists, and burning for "proven heresy and witchcraft." In the three centuries of colonial rule, only 30 heretics were burned in Lima and only 41 in Mexico City. Some of the victims were Protestant heretics, or *Luteranos*, as even the irreligious English pirates were called, who had been captured while raiding along the Spanish main. When, in Lima or Mexico City or Bogotá, heretics were burned or "flogged through the streets of the city" on rare occasions, the crowds felt little of the religious upheaval and intolerance wracking Europe at the time but looked on as at a carnival. The Inquisition was never as fearsome in America as it was in Spain.

To "prevent" disbelief, the Inquisition maintained the Index, prepared in Rome or Spain, of books that were not to be shipped from Europe nor sold, printed, or read in the colonies. Works by Jews, Mohammedans, and Protestants were forbidden as was any book containing the idea of popular sovereignty. Bishops and priests closely supervised the reading of parishioners. Church agents could enter homes, question crews of ships, watch out for smuggled books and papers, and check the wares of bookshops. Many hundreds of books listed by the Index got through this "thought-control screen" anyway, and some were even read by members of the clergy themselves. But the Inquisition did attempt to keep out foreign ideas and hindered intellectual progress while at the same time it kept people loyal and orthodox by its suppression of heresy and punishing of private and public scandals.

Indians, however, were never subject to the Inquisition. Because of their "ignorance and weak minds" they were excused from its regulation. It was a few misguided missionaries rather than Inquisitorial judges who destroyed Indian religious objects and punished recalcitrant pagans among the newly baptized. Only one case is on record of a converted Indian being put to death by a religious court for "backsliding to heathen practices."

Members of the Jesuit order were the most successful university teachers and most efficient missionaries. Their novices were strictly trained, their leaders highly educated, and their monasteries among the richest in the New World. They owned vast areas of fertile land and often pursued profit for their order. In Peru, for instance, they controlled the market in wheat, brandy, sugar, and hides. With such funds and power, they could defy lay authority and even challenge the viceroy himself.

Then in 1750 trouble started with the very unworldly and unselfish Jesuit missionaries on the Paraguayan frontier. By treaty with Portugal, territory on the upper Paraná, which included the populous mission settlement of Candelaria, had been ceded to Brazil. The mission fathers refused to obey the royal order and the Portuguese authorities who came from São Paulo to take over the missions. Open war against the transfer ensued with the Indians fighting in armies led by the Jesuits.

In Europe, the rich and powerful Jesuit order had roused jealousy by interfering in politics in Spain and other Catholic countries. Suddenly, by royal order, the 2,260 Jesuits in America were expelled and their property confiscated by the government. Near rebellion took place in some parts of America. In Guanajuato and San Louis Potosí in Mexico, where the Jesuits were leaders in community social projects, there was rioting in the streets. The Jesuit clerics were sent to Italy, where they remained fanatically opposed to the Spanish Crown. In fact, they were instrumental in circulating propaganda for independence thirty years later.

It cannot be denied that the most thorough work done by a religious organization in the New World was done by the Spanish Catholic Church. It must be admitted, however, that by seeking to monopolize moral and educational control, by interfering in politics, and by failing to live up to its own high standard, it created problems with which Latin American republics are still wrestling.

castes and classes: the dominant whites

After a mere half century, the people of Latin America had begun to be a new race, a mixed people combining elements and characteristics of three continents—America, Europe, and, with the introduction of the Negro culture, Africa. The amalgam in this "melting pot" did not all become a blending but a new metal formed in layers that were determined by blood and color content and dictated by nature and by official document as well. The small number of Spaniards who conquered America did not conquer an unpopulated expanse of territory but a hemisphere already full of peoples, so within the three basic colors of white, red, and black there came to be variations until the mixtures gradually came to outnumber the "pure." In areas such as Uruguay and Argentina where the Indians were barbarous, they were annihilated and the population there today is mostly white. In areas of sedentary population, of town and city civilization, the Indians remained as the work force, and since few white women came at first, intermarriage and miscegenation created modern nations of many mixed bloods. But the whites always kept the upper hand socially, politically, and economically and remained the highest caste, in which no one of color gained membership.

A social pyramid was developed by Spain, not always legally but by consistent practice, at the apex of which was not just the white man but the white man born in Spain. The colonies, according to mercantilist theory, existed for the good of the mother country, so the cream of jobs and profits in the colonies naturally went to Spaniards born in the mother country. Pure white Spaniards of noble lineage who were unfortunate enough to have been born in the colonies could easily "break into" the top social classes and gain their special advantages and privileges by exceptional means such as purchasing certificates which proclaimed the bearer to be of Spanish birth or by way of licenses available only to colonials of great wealth. But many jobs were given to parasites and relatives of the Spanish Court, especially as the royal family declined physically and mentally and increasingly distrusted anyone not born close to the Court. Only government jobs were socially acceptable since Spanish tradition disdained the commercial trades, professions and crafts. These lush jobs were received in Spain before the office-seeker left.

The American-born or creoles thus came to be separated from the Spanish-born by economic class lines as well. The colonials called the Spanish-born variously *chapetones,* tenderfeet; *gachupines,* "spurred ones"; and sometimes *peninsulares* or else *Godos* or Goths, referring to the Visigothic barbarians who had conquered Spain long before. The colonials hated them all even though they fawned on the Spanish aristocrats and aped their ways, hoping to pass as Spanish-born themselves.

Quite a few foreigners turned up in the New World despite the general Spanish restrictions on emigration. To stimulate industry Madrid at times authorized the emigration of non-Spanish Europeans who were skilled artisans, engineers, or metallurgists. Italian, Flemish, or German missionaries often were legally approved. Many men deserted from ships in New World ports, many entered clandestinely; travelers and learned men came to visit and remained. By 1700, Lima had French, Italian, German, Flemish, Greek, Irish, English, Moorish, and even East Indian and Chinese men busy at various trades. One of the five wealthiest people in Guatemala was a Genoese and two were Portuguese. The foreigners were almost entirely occupied in trade and shipping, money-making pursuits scorned by the true *gachupines.*

Already by 1600, 200,000 whites were settled in more than 200 towns in Spanish America, controlling more than 4,000,000 Indians and mixed-bloods. An increasing number of the whites came to be American-born *criollos* or creoles (a term, misused today, meaning anyone of pure European extraction native to the New World). The emigration of single women was not favored but married men coming to the colonies as settlers were required to take their families with them. Children born to them after their arrival inherited lands granted their fathers and the right to control Indian workers but their position was inferior to that of whites who had come from Spain. They had pride of blood and a sense of aristocracy, including an aristocratic scorn of manual labor. Vanity and pride kept them from working in commerce and industry, and opportunities at the top in government were closed to them. This assignment to an inferior status often worked against the young creole psychologically, and he became indolent and worthless. Spaniards wrote home that the creoles were "prone to gambling and love affairs and attendance at bullfights and cockfights" for lack of anything better to do, and expressed surprise when they found elegant manners and "gentle and discreet speech" at creole society gatherings.

The colonial aristocrats called themselves the *gente decente,* the "nice folks," wore clothes of silk, and lived better than the aristocrats born in Spain from among whom the *gachupin* officials came. Their young sons were educated in Jesuit universities in the colonies and sometimes were sent to universities in Europe for their last years of schooling. They became lawyers, doctors, professors, and priests—and they nursed their discontent. Such a wealthy creole was Simón Bolívar, the richest young man in Venezuela, who had the breeding, the polish, the education both at home and abroad, to surpass most young Spaniards, but who was embittered by the discrimination against his class and devoted his life to freeing that class from Spain forever.

The creole hated not only the *gachupín* but also the humbler classes, the *chapetones* or tenderfeet who came from Spain as farmers and artisans. The humbler Spaniards, usually Basques or Catalans from northern Spain, rated higher in importance than the creole, no matter what his education and wealth. They often gained an entrance into exclusive circles after they made a fortune in trade. They had had the prestige of Spanish birth but had not been too proud to start as peddlers. They often married wealthy creole women and created hostilities within families. Hostility carried over even into church leadership since the uneducated Spaniard had preference in promotions over the most distinguished creole.

the Indians and the mestizos

What do native populations do when militant colonizing peoples take over? Generally those natives who are leaders adopt the civilization of the colonizing power; those who have done the work for the native leaders stay and work for the new masters; and those who lived off the beaten track of the colonizers remain unchanged. To a large extent, this pattern held true in Latin America. The black picture painted by historians for centuries of the Spanish treatment of the Indians is not entirely true. Anglo-Saxons have forgotten tales just as black in the treatment of natives within their own empire.

Modern historians think cruelties were exaggerated by reformers such as las Casas, that the Black Legend of Spanish mistreatment was widely circulated by Spain's Protestant enemies in Europe, and that in the 16th century captains and adventurers from any European nation would have reacted to the peoples of the New World in much the same way. Spanish kings for a hundred years tried to enforce laws to protect the Indians, and friars served as their champions when the laws were broken.

Official Spanish policy was to reduce the Indians to village life, separated from Europeans but converted to the European religion, and to "eradicate odious practices among them" and train them in essential trades. Pure-blooded Indians remained near the bottom of the social scale, widely distributed, and differing greatly from tribe to tribe, often preserving their own language and customs. Reduced to a role of food-producer, their living standards were low; they were wretchedly housed, undernourished, and addicted to alcohol in which they found solace. Most of the Indians were serfs, held by law to be minors in a "perpetual stage of tutelage," protected by a vast legislation against exploitation by their "betters," but subject to "unlimited exactions in labor and product" by *corregidores, caciques,* and priests. Isabella's rules for good treatment were broken from the first by governors and slave raiders. New Laws passed in 1542 to stop exploitation of Indian labor were softened by viceroys in Mexico and Peru. Few Indians received a real redress of grievances even though the viceroy remained the Indians' legal protector and in Mexico they had the *Juzgado de Indios,* their own special court of appeal.

Indian labor in the form of peonage on agricultural lands and of forced drafts in mines and on public lands persisted for three centuries. The *encomienda* system was finally abolished by law but landlords worked out other ways to hold the Indians in bondage, such as keeping the Indians in debt through advance payments for seeds and equipment and for expenses of baptisms and funerals, thus preventing them from leaving the land. In Mexico this system persisted till 1910 and was partly responsible for a violent civil war which began that year.

In Peru and Bolivia, the *mita* system kept Indians laboring in the mines and on public works under slave labor conditions, as described in reports in the archives, with limited rations and high death rates among the miners. Some of the reports resulted in enforcement of royal laws protecting the Indians, and conditions for gold and silver miners in Latin America in 1700 were better than those of English coal miners in 1800. But in years of weak rule in Spain, laws such as those forbidding Indians of free villages from doing forced labor as textile weavers or as pearl divers were violated. Indian revolts took place throughout the colonial period and were all severely repressed. They were "subjects of the Crown," they had souls, but they were looked on as children.

Some of the tribal Indians who were semi-civilized peoples in 1492—the Tarascans north of Mexico City, the Zapotecans on the Isthmus of Tehuantepec, the Aymará in Bolivia, the Maya in Yucatan, the Cachiqueles of Guatemala—remained unchanged for generations. Many villages still speak their own language and follow ancient customs today. Hundreds of these communities continued to exist, unchanged except perhaps by the introduction of burros or oxen, still ruled by their own *caciques* or chieftains, often with oppressive powers over their tribesmen.

Villages remained intact where they were remote from colonial centers or where there was no gold or silver to be mined and little flat land for plantation crops. The Spaniards merely collected tribute, and did not come in as actual occupants. Indian people remain as the basis of today's population in Mexico, northern Central America, Peru, Ecuador, Bolivia, and Paraguay. On remote frontiers, Indians kept up the battle against the white man, just as did the Sioux and the Pawnee in the Mississippi Valley. In the 1680's a medicine man named Popé led the Pueblos in a revolt that caused the temporary abandonment of the colony of New Mexico. A three-century-long revolt was staged by the Araucanians in Chile, sometimes called the "Apaches of South America."

A German scientist, Alexander von Humboldt, visiting Latin America around the turn of the century, did not find Mexico's Indians living as "meanly as peasants of North Europe" lived in 1800. He found the Indians in Mexico City's markets ignorant and lazy due to the circumstances under which they had to live. The Indians "built huts of wood, clay, and uncut stone; they did not eat beef, mutton, or wheaten bread, nor drink wine. . . ." and their dress was "that of a slave, linen breeches to the calves of the legs, a cotton shirt like a sack with three openings for head and arms, and in winter a blanket with a hole in the center." The number of natives had increased for a century so that New Spain was more inhabited in 1803 than before the arrival of the Europeans.

The great mass of Latin Americans were the mixed-bloods between the "pure white" at the top and the "pure red" at the bottom. The laws of the Indies recognized differences between mulattoes, the mixture of black and white; *mestizos,* the mixture between red and white; and *zambos,* the mixture between red and black. Spanish records noted differentiations down to the nineteenth degree of blood mixture and as many as 80 different castes, with legal Spanish terms for every variation, terms often appearing in documents of the time.

It was the *mestizo* who really made Latin America. Many legal unions were made between beautiful and semi-cultured Indian women and Spaniards in the first generation after the conquest, and legally *mestizos* were *gentle de razón* or people with the ability to reason and were admitted to minor offices in church and state and to the militia. In a sense they constituted a lower middle class of farmers, stewards, shopkeepers, and artisans and formed the majority of the population in large cities and towns. Those on the upper levels often merged with the creoles, on the lower levels with the Indians. A stigma was always attached to their birth, however, and the terms illegitimate and *mestizo* came to be used synonymously by the end of the first century of colonial rule. The frontier had an appeal for such disinherited people and they became the cattle herders of the plains, the typical *llaneros* of Venezuela, the *vaqueros* of northern Mexico, the *gauchos* herding wild horses on the Argentine *pampas.* Raised by Indian mothers, often illegitimate, they were forced to stay near the bottom of the social ladder.

On the eve of the wars of independence, the *mestizos* as a class were ready to join with the creoles in winning independence. They constituted 31.5 percent (5,328,000) of Spanish America's population of 17 million, according to the estimates of von Humboldt at the time, while pure whites were 19.4 percent. Indians were 44.5 percent (7,530,000) and Negroes 4.6 percent (776,000). Of course, after 300 years, there was much more mixture than most families were willing to admit.

Class stratification paralleled the color-caste line in this hybrid population. The European whites were the ruling class; the humbler *peninsulares* were the commercial element; the wealthy creoles were the leisure class, members of professions, the lower clergy, scholars, university students; *mestizos* were in trade and industry and military service or free laborers on the frontier; Indians worked in agriculture or did heavy work in the mines; Negroes were plantation workers or domestic servants. The life of the Negro slaves has been discussed in Chapter 9. The class structure based on color still holds in those parts of Latin America where a feudal land system remains and there is only a small middle class.

social life in the colonies

The topmost class in Mexico City and Lima lived much as did the well-to-do in Madrid and even Paris, wealthy creole ladies dressing with the best of Europe, buying their silks and satins at annual fairs or the Manila galleon. Letters, diaries, and travel accounts of the time mention the silk stockings, pearl-embroidered garters, bodices laced with gold and silver, and petticoats of China silk worn by women, and the crimson velvet suits, lace cuffs, floral embroidered vests, and gold knee buckles worn by the men, and tell of fancy masked balls and endless dinner parties with a rich variety of foods and wines.

The homes of the wealthy creoles, many of them showplaces today visited by tourists, had carved balconies, tile floors, and hand-wrought grillwork. Around the first of three patios were the living rooms of the family, around the second, kitchens and rooms for domestics, and around the third, stables and carriage houses, with facilities for blacksmiths, carriage makers, and craftsmen in the greater of these establishments.

Aristocratic creole families paraded in their carriages up and down the *alameda,* the one main, paved, tree-lined street in colonial cities. Six thousand decorated mule-drawn carriages threaded the streets of Lima where they met with mule pack trains from the Bolivian mines and countless thousands of Indian burden bearers on foot. The country estates of wealthy grandees resembled those in the city (though often they had to be fortified against bandits) and entertaining in them was on the same lavish scale. Huts of the Indian workers surrounded them as slave cabins did a plantation.

The leisure class had a great deal of time for enjoyment. Gentlemen bet at cards, held lotteries, played at *pelota* or handball, wagered on gamecocks, participated in religious processions and fiestas, and watched bullfights. They gave masquerade parties, played parlor games, and conducted *tertulias* or literary society meetings. Upper class colonials were an amiable, courteous, hospitable, self-indulgent people. Their youth took classical courses in the universities. A creole with an advanced education sometimes worked as a lawyer or doctor or university teacher. The artisan classes had social contacts through their craft guilds.

Among the disinherited lower classes, with color mixtures and caste lines against them, there was much misery and ignorance. Records of Mexico City describe large numbers of homeless beggars of all kinds and colors swarming in rags around churches and plazas. There were so many criminals, gamblers, and hold-up men in the cities and bandits in the country, so many frequenters of *pulquerías* or poor-man's bars, that a police force called the *Santa Hermandad* or holy brotherhood was organized to keep order.

Family life on all levels was patriarchal, with the father, or, if living, the grandfather, the unquestioned arbiter on the comings and goings of everyone in the family, even married sons. Families could include cousins several degrees removed and the co-godfathers and co-godmothers who sponsored children at baptism. Woman's place was one of meek obedience, their influence on family affairs being only the indirect kind they could exert through force of personality. In many of the more provincial parts of Latin America, this type of family life still persists.

Ladies had more leisure than men; even the skilled craftsmen's wives had to do little housework since Indian servants were to be had for their keep. They learned little besides embroidery, music, and religious devotions. A few outstanding women in the colonial period are remembered for literature, art, or charity organization but most of them merely raised their large, well-mannered families and made the family unit with its religious observances the center of their social life. And many ladies helped the church workers in charity among foundlings and orphans and in hospitals.

The spread of disease seems to have been worse in America than in Europe, owing to the Indians' lack of immunity to European diseases. Smallpox struck in Mexico three times in the century after Cortés, bringing waves of death for hundreds of thousands. Another mysterious epidemic struck which might have been influenza, killing the friars who tried to nurse the thousands of cases suffering from this lung and throat infection. Although there were never enough doctors and hospitals, the colonial hospitals not only took care of acute cases but they also served as a refuge for the destitute old, the blind, and the orphaned. The mass of Indians followed quacks and sorcerers and believed in witchcraft, but they had some native medicinal plants such as quinine in Peru, which were ahead of current practice in Europe and which they taught the friars and nuns to use.

the towns and countryside of the Spanish-speaking new world

Mexico City, largest city in the Western Hemisphere, viceregal capital and social center, the equal of many European capitals, had 20,000 white inhabitants before there was an English town in North America. Today's narrow streets near the Zócalo or main square were laid off in the days of Cortés and Mendoza, and the great cathedral was begun on the old Aztec plaza of Tenochtitlán. The city was founded on the islands of the Aztec lake and suffered five great floods during the colonial period.

Catastrophe marked the founding and early history of many of the Latin American cities. Few cities, however, had such a tragic history as Vera Cruz, chief port of New Spain. A high sea wall built to defend the town from pirates kept the sea breezes out and sewage in, which encouraged mosquitoes that spread yellow fever. Wrecked by hurricanes, attacked by pirates, scourged by disease, the town was important during visits of fleets and viceroys but almost deserted the rest of the year.

The enemy of Guatemala City throughout history was the quaking earth. Alvarado's capital was destroyed by earthquake and flood in 1543, and the new city that grew up on a different site became, according to its own historians, "third in magnificence among Spanish colonial capitals." With a great concentration of wealth, especially in church organizations, it was a handsome city of Spanish Renaissance architecture. But the year 1773, when the city was 200 years old, saw its death. It was a year of terror, with earth tremors week after week, with people camping in the fields, nobles spending the night in coaches. Disorganization and pestilence took the town. The city was officially moved sixty miles away by the king's order to the site of the present Guatemala City while the old site with its uncleared debris was taken over by the Indians as a provincial seat known as Antigua.

Nicaragua, which had two rival cities, Granada and León, was in 1637 the "Paradise of America, so fertile, so abundant in the fruits of the earth," according to an English visitor, Thomas Gage. And Costa Rica, a settlement of middle-class farmers of European stock, was according to him a country of "good valleys, planted with corn and prosperous farms."

Panama was a hot steamy town where men sickened and died, according to Gage. Eating its fruit and drinking its water, hundreds of merchants, soldiers, and mariners died of "the flux." It was a town of 8,000 "souls who confessed," living in 750 houses along four streets, a town with an inadequate harbor, with alligators floating "like large logs in the water" behind the slaughter house. The people were forced to move when the English pirate, Sir Henry Morgan, sacked the town, the ruins of which stand in a park ten miles from the present-day Panama City.

The harbor of Porto Bello lay across the Isthmus on the Atlantic side, started on the initiative of a wise governor in 1597 who wanted to locate a better port than the first Spanish town in the general area, an unhealthy settlement on a poor harbor. Porto Bello was a fine harbor, "protected by three strong fortresses, the strongest bastion on the Spanish Main," its long sea wall lined with "cannon of the largest calibre ever cast up to the time," some of which still lie there today in a picturesque ruin.

Of the three noted Colombian towns, Cartagena had the finest fortification on the Spanish Main. Bogotá was so far inland from Cartagena that a Spanish viceroy sent to govern it stayed three years on the coast waiting for an auspicious water level on the Magdalena River to make the trip and returned to Spain without ever visiting the city at all. Bogotá prided itself on its isolation and on the purity of Spanish speech and blood and on its intellectual pursuits. In the Cauca River valley, Medellín, founded in 1675, by the end of the colonial period became a prosperous agricultural city of 9,000 inhabitants, more people than had Vera Cruz or Panama City.

To the north, Caracas, 23 miles from the Caribbean Sea, was an independent-spirited city that was destined to be the mother of the revolution. The trail leading from the port of La Guaira to the city was a precipitous approach that took two days of "stair-step climbing" among rocks on sure-footed mules.

Farther south, on the Pacific side of the continent, were two cities which the famous Spanish author, Cervantes, considered choice spots for a government post when in 1590 he sought to be a "beneficiary of one of the royal offices" in the Indies. Quito, important as the seat of an *audiencia,* was a center of art and science, though the "decent folk," according to one of the king's plainclothes investigators, were only one-sixth of the population. Quito was in mule-train touch with Bogotá by way of two fiercely loyal colonial towns founded by Benalcázar named Popayán and Pasto. But Guayaquil, not Quito, was considered the "jewel of the *audiencia's* crown," a trade and ship-building center. Mule trains came down from Quito to the city with textiles, dyestuffs, and liquor, and went back up with sugar cane, bananas, and rice.

Lima, to the south, was the literary, cultural, and social center of Spanish South America till 1800. At that time it had upwards of 70,000 inhabitants. In 1620, when Plymouth was founded, Lima "counted 4,000 houses, only 200 of which were of Indians." A viceroy in the next decade brought clear spring water by aqueduct into the city, built local fountains in "all the quarters," and made it possible to install water in the houses from the pipes running along the streets. Lima had running water before New England had houses. Arequipa, which today is the second city of Peru, was a sleepy, monotonous convent town. Cuzco was an Indian center, a provincial capital with a thin veneer of Spanish culture.

Santiago, Chile, located in the earthquake belt of the Andes, was destroyed by a quake in 1647. Over a period of years, it was gradually rebuilt until it was all new "from the cathedral to the jail." Floods of the Río Mapocho were an added calamity, coming so frequently that every year the residents of this capital were liable to see their homes destroyed. Life in Santiago moved at a much slower pace than in Lima, with even the wealthiest families boasting only mule-drawn carriages on two wheels instead of coaches.

A thin colonizing stream dribbled through the centuries into Buenos Aires from Bolivia, with its silver-mining cities and "wide-open" social life, into the valleys at Tucumán and Salta and onto the pampas below the aristocratic city of Córdova. Asunción on the Paraguay River was farther away from this current of traffic than St. Louis is from New Orleans. Travelers from Asunción going home to Spain went downriver to meet the wagon trails to Tucumán and then up the mule trails to Cuzco and over to Lima. In Guaraní-speaking Asunción there was even less society than in Santiago, the ladies there spending their time in "sewing, weaving, gardening, and taking care of babies and ducks." Buenos Aires on the Plata estuary was described in the 1650's as having "only four saloons paying the annual license tax" and "only sixteen horse-drawn coaches." "A dirty, unattractive town," a visitor called it. Montevideo, across the estuary, was not even founded until 1726.

The cattle herders, later called *gauchos*, lived on the grassy pampas beyond Buenos Aires. Descended from colonists brought by Mendoza and Irala or from Spaniards from Peru or Chile, they took Guaraní women as wives and lived in mud huts thatched with pampas grass on the treeless plain. Their front door was a steer hide, their beds piles of hides, their diet beef and *yerba maté*, their hearth an open fire of cow dung. It took weeks on horseback for these "children of the sun and wind" to get to Buenos Aires or Mendoza or Córdova.

In all these Spanish communities, life was probably as pleasant as it was in most towns in Spain, and it was certainly cleaner and more open to air and sun than was town life in 17th century England. The Spanish Indies by 1700 was a good place in which to live, full of color, excitement, and opportunity. Here in these scattered communities the culture of today's Latin America was evolving and the progress of the combined races, red, black, and white, was emerging as one of the most significant developments of New World history.

intellectual life in the colonies: schools and colleges

Education may not have been as widely spread in the New World as in the old but one should not think of the colonies as a raw, unlettered frontier. But it is true that schooling in the colonies was chiefly of the formal, classical type, made available only to pure whites and upper-level *mestizos*, maintained by the Church and guaranteed "pure" by the Inquisition. While many of the upper class young creoles went through the university, the lower classes remained in complete ignorance with illiteracy, around 1800, amounting probably to more than 90 percent. Theoretically all municipalities were supposed to support primary schools but usually they were too poor to do so; and in practice education was a church responsibility. Parish churches did try to maintain an elementary school for the children of their parishioners, often taught by the priest. Secondary schools or *colegios* maintained under church auspices may have been very good but only a small fraction of the eligible boys in town attended them. The two principal teaching orders, the Dominicans and Jesuits, worked against difficulties to keep their schools going. Sometimes they received financial aid from the Crown or from private benefactors. In general it was university rather than primary or secondary education for which these orders should be given credit, and which the Spanish colonials themselves were most interested in fostering.

In the beginning primary education had been provided for Indian children. Already in Cortés' lifetime, schools for the children of Aztec chieftains and nobility were set up to teach religion. The famous Brother Peter of Ghent directed such a school for over 40 years, his graduates becoming Europeanized and developing into artisans and skilled craftsmen who worked in the decoration and care of churches. And Father Sahagún gathered together likely young Aztecs who taught him their tongue as they learned his, while they all worked together on a monumental history of the Aztecs.

But as a new generation of children grew up under the care of *mestizo* or Indian mothers, it was without benefit of any education. The Council of the Indies had decreed that there be a school to teach Spanish in every Indian pueblo, but the decree was often ignored. Church authorities made an attempt to set up schools but there were never enough. Schools were set up for foundling boys and girls in Mexico City and Lima and other large towns. The one erected by the Franciscans in Mexico City, San Juan de Letrán, was especially famous, providing vocational education for orphan Indian children for 250 years. Eight schools for Indian girls were founded in New Spain by 1534 in which cooking, sewing, and homemaking were taught. But even today in numerous villages with a preponderance of Indian blood, only the village leaders can read and speak Spanish.

The second generation of creoles in Mexico and Lima saw the coming of full-fledged universities, the Royal and Pontifical University of Mexico predating Harvard by nearly a hundred years. It was founded by royal order in 1551 and opened in 1553 with the status and privileges of the University of Salamanca, its mother institution in Spain. Its site was that of Montezuma's old palace, its building a two-story stone structure around a flowered patio. The Crown in its first grant provided a yearly sum to pay its teachers—professors of Latin, rhetoric, philosophy, civil and canon law, and theology. Two of the first professors were judges of the *audiencia* and the rest were churchmen. Within half a century, there were twenty-four chairs, two of them in medicine and two specializing in ancient Indian languages, Nahuatl and Otomí.

The University of San Marcos in Lima was established also by royal order in 1551, but for 25 years classes were housed in a Dominican convent and taught by its monks. The Viceroy Toledo made it a separate institution in 1578 and gave it buildings of its own. The usual classical subjects were taught and also medicine and the Quechua language. By 1625, ten major colleges and fifteen lesser ones were founded in the provincial capitals, all giving aristocratic young creoles a formal and impractical schooling to brighten the luster of their family standing. On a more practical level, law schools trained men to conduct the government's business and protect the legal interests of landowners and clergy; courses in medicine were as practical as those offered in Spain, and theological schools supplied the New World with priests.

University organization was patterned after that of Salamanca; college affairs were governed by a cloister and a rector. Professors took the oath to "defend the doctrine of the Immaculate Conception, to observe modest conduct, and not to attend theaters and dances." They got their jobs after competition before an examining board, but received very low salaries; it was an honor to teach but not a means of support. Chairs endowed by wealthy patrons paid better than regular classes. The various professional schools—law, theology, medicine—were located in different parts of town, not grouped on a campus according to modern North American practice.

Students lived a strict life under the control of the rector, who had been chosen from among professors who had doctorates, and of the "masters" who corresponded to our graduate students and teaching fellows. Students were taught by rote, memorizing lectures which the professors themselves had memorized. They wore cassocks, long cloaks, and brimless hats to class much like present-day academic caps and gowns, fashions that were inherited from students in medieval times.

Teaching was based on Scholasticism and Aristotelian logic, and experimental science had no place in the schools until late in the era. Mathematics, including the geometry of Euclid, was taught to all who tried for the bachelor's degree. Classes were conducted in Latin with little or no discussion. Tuition was small but matriculation and graduation fees were high. A doctor's degree entitled one to teach, considered a great honor. San Marcos was criticized for "inbreeding," for most of its teachers through the centuries were its own graduates. Indians and freed mulattoes, supposedly eligible for university work, were granted few degrees after 1600. A "certificate of legitimacy and purity of race" and a document showing "freedom from the taint of heresy" were required for matriculation by 1700.

In spite of such restrictions, the colonial universities did produce some distinguished scholars and students. In all, the University of Mexico, in its 268 years of existence before independence, granted 37,732 bachelor's degrees, several thousand master's degrees, and 1655 law degrees and doctorates. In the later 18th century, changes came in education as in other phases of colonial life.

scholarly research and scientific pursuits

The mother country at the peak of her golden age in the 16th and 17th centuries was anxious that the colonies should be a credit to her but did not want them to outshine her. American scholars were encouraged to interest themselves in specialities in which the Spanish scholars were making no contribution; thus American researchers studied the pre-Columbian Indians, their history, customs, and language; the geography, botany, zoology, and metallurgy of the New World; and the astronomical phenomena visible along the equator and from the Southern Hemisphere. Contributions made by colonial scholars in all these fields received recognition in Europe.

Garcilaso de la Vega, an Inca *mestizo,* Bishop Landa of Yucatan, and, especially, Friar Bernardino de Sahagún wrote descriptions of Indian civilizations and of their conquest that are the best modern sources of information on the ancient cultures. Friars who had studied the Indian tongues in their own mission schools heard the Indians, in the first and second generations of the conquest, recite their stories, songs, and epic poems from their rich tribal memories, translated them into Spanish and wrote them down. The Dominican, Francisco Jiménez, living among the Maya-Quiché in Chichicastenango, Guatemala, discovered as late as 1700 the records of Mayan history and mythology known as the *Popul Vuh,* a most important source of information on the Maya to the modern student.

Gonzalo Fernández de Oviedo (1478–1557), the foremost historian of the early days of New World conquest, came to Panama with Pedrarias in 1514 (later as an authorized chronicler crossing the Atlantic at least twelve times), and wrote down in the greatest detail everything he himself saw and all the roistering history he heard from those who came and went through Panama. The Jesuit professor, Father José de Acosta, the most scientific historian of these early days, wrote down many Indian stories and then tried to write a unified history of the New World from pre-Columbian times, a work published in 1571 under the title *Natural and Moral History of the Indies,* one of the best sellers of the day. Pedro Pizarro, the nephew of the conqueror and soldiers and friars who came to Peru early in the conquest such as Pedro Cieza de León and Friar Montesinos told the story of the conquest. Bernal Díaz told the story of Cortés' adventures and Cabeza de Vaca gave an account of the long walk in the Southwest, both popular contributions to the history of the conquest. Juan Matienzo, Juan de Solórzano Pereira, and Bernabé Cobo (1582–1657) (the latter with his *History of Lima*) added detailed studies of the law and government and of civil and judicial procedures of the new *audiencias.* Today's historians find the contributions of these learned men their most important sources of information on colonial Latin America.

When the new interest in science developed in Europe from 1550 to 1700, the New World was awake to new developments. Philip II sent careful instructions to Peru that a forthcoming eclipse of the moon should be observed from the Western hemisphere and just below the equator. Scientists at the University of Mexico figured the longitude of their capital more accurately than it was done in Europe, but geographers in the Old World kept making maps with the incorrect longitude for another century because these calculations were not published outside Mexico. In 1680, writer-scientist Carlos de Siguenza y Góngora (1645–1700) studied a comet in a truly scientific spirit and quarreled with Church authorities as to its causes. He courageously wrote that "Comets, contrary to popular belief, have nothing to do with the wrath of Providence." Dr. Pedro de Peralta Barnuevo, born in Lima in 1663, became a famous mathematician, astronomer and practical engineer.

Applied science received attention. In 1608, an engineer, Enrico Martínez, worked out a fairly modern plan to drain the swamps of Mexico

City which temporarily solved Mexico's age-old drainage problem. Scientific commissions studied the possibilities of a canal through Panama and formulated no less than 20 plans which were filed away in the archives. Also studied was the Nicaragua Lake route. Royal cosmographers kept government ships posted on new explorations and on improvements in navigation, from which Spanish sea captains sometimes seemed not to benefit.

Medical science lagged behind the other sciences in America as in Europe. Practice was limited to medieval usages and Indian herb-doctoring. As early as 1535 royal orders were issued against "quackery and dishonesty" in medical practice in the New World. The first *protomédico* sent out to enforce these decrees in Mexico was appointed in 1571 by Philip II to improve standards, to license physicians and druggists, and to collect botanical specimens. When he returned to Spain in 1577, he brought back fifteen or more volumes of studies on natural history and Indian lore.

Medical science began making strides in America, as in Europe, by the 18th century, with attention being paid to clinical surgery, obstetrics, pharmacy, and scientific anatomy based on observation and dissection. But in 1723, when a debate was held in Lima on the possibility of the circulation of the blood, learned professors took the negative on a subject that had been proved by William Harvey almost a century before. Eighty years later, however, vaccination against smallpox, according to von Humboldt, was used in an epidemic in Mexico.

The Age of Enlightenment was penetrating into the colonies in the 18th century. Reforming kings introduced classes in chemistry, mineralogy, botany, astronomy, engineering, and navigation into the universities, and founded schools of mining. More and more lay teachers in the universities were of the new scientific bent. Spanish Americans traveled to Europe and to other parts of the colonies, and famous European scientists visited America. Whole new fields of thought opened up.

The new types of flora in the New World helped to make botany a new science in the latter half of the 18th century. The lush American tropics offered a rich field for plant collectors and classifiers. Botanical gardens to house specimens were set up in Bogotá and Mexico City and a Museum of Natural History was founded in Guatemala. To the Bogotá gardens came a Spaniard from Cádiz named Dr. José Celestino Mutis who was a friend of the famous botanist Linnaeus. He had come to Colombia as physician to one of the first viceroys sent there and stayed 25 years, fascinated by the wealth of plant life. With the aid of a grant from the king, he hired fifteen engravers and water colorists to make exact reproductions of each species. He had sent to Madrid more than 3,000 miniature drawings of plants. He also founded an astronomical observatory in Bogotá in 1802. His botanical work was carried on by a creole pupil of his, Francisco José de Caldas.

The distinguished natural scientist and geographer, Alexander von Humboldt, visited Mutis in Bogotá, where the city was so "science-conscious" that it declared a public holiday on his arrival. For five years von Humboldt and Aimé Bonpland, a French scientist, journeyed through Mexico and northern South America, afterwards publishing their findings in a monumental work in French called *Voyage to the Equinoctial Regions of the New Continent*. He found the new intellectual interests of 18th century Europe reflected in the cultural advances in Spanish America. He found Mexican youth gifted in science and students in the School of Mines "animated with the finest zeal" in scientific pursuits. "No city of the new continent," he concluded, "not excepting any of the United States, can show scientific institutions as big and solid as those of the capital of Mexico."

books written and books read

The book publisher in Seville who handled the sale of all the books shipped to the New World sent in 1601 a shipment of 10,000 books—80 boxes each for Puerto Rico, Santo Domingo, and Cuba, the rest for Mexico and Panama, an order that would surely delight a modern publishing house. Every year at fleet-sailing time, long mule trains carried boxes of books to the storage sheds for the fleet, where the boxes were opened by customs officials, books forbidden to good churchgoers were removed, and the boxes "resealed with the stamp of the Inquisition." More than 75 percent of the 1601 order consisted of heavy religious tomes, law books, and school books, but a surprising amount of popular fiction was included. "Romances of chivalry" were prohibited but the shipping lists show hundreds of Horatio-Alger-type light novels got by the censors. The first edition of *Don Quixote* found its way into the colonies in great quantity. In spite of strict censorship, carried on jointly by the House of Trade and the Church courts, books on history, mathematics, and medicine, and even poetry, of which Spaniards were fond, were sent to the New World. The House of Trade kept lists of every title in every box of printed materials sent to the colonies, but bills of lading often used subterfuges and many "illegal" books reached the colonies. Such lists reveal a surprising amount of reading going on in the New World.

The reading of colonials varied with the century. The 16th century, the century of expansion and mission work, saw chronicles, translations of native Indian works, *relaciones* on the conquest as well as the lives of saints, catechisms, books of sermons and missionary chronicles—and also primers and grammars in the Indian language. The 17th century saw romances, picaresque novels, the dramas and comedies of famous Spanish playwrights as well as more histories and travel books. The 18th century saw the newly popular secular philosophy, science, and even books in French and English, frowned on though they were.

Printing presses spread very slowly in the colonies. The Bishop of Mexico petitioned the king in 1533 for a craftsman who could help set up a printing press and a paper mill, and the monopolistic Seville publishing house did send an Italian who brought plates for engraving and soon was able to produce a "Brief Christian Doctrine" for use with the Indians. Before 1600 a total of 174 different works were produced. Craftsmen were sent from Mexico to Lima, and books were printed in Peru by the 1580's, but even by 1800, at the end of the colonial period, the reading public was so small and the price of books so prohibitive that only 25 presses existed in the whole of Spanish America, of which ten were in New Spain.

Newspapers were not printed until the 18th century. Spanish Americans had no learned journals or magazines and no newssheets describing the life of their own times, except the *Hojas Volantes*, which were distributed on the arrival of the fleet, and, in Mexico City and Lima, occasional copies of the special court newsletters from Spain. One such *Gazeta*, from the year 1671, tells about the peace settlement between the crowns of Spain and Great Britain in America, the repression of raids and robberies on the high seas, the fights against the Turks in the Mediterranean, and a "bull-running in Mexico" on the anniversary of Charles II. The first monthly *Gazeta de Mexico* appeared in 1722 and lasted only six issues. When later such periodicals increased rapidly as a part of the "Enlightenment," they proved very influential in the movement for independence.

Colonial Spain produced little in the way of *belles-lettres* but excelled in meaty research materials. The Spanish writer Luis de Góngora (1561–1627), who wrote in an artificial, bombastic style known in Spanish literature as "Gongorism," influenced literary efforts in Spanish America for decades with the result that little Latin American writing of the 17th century is even remembered today other than the historical chronicles. A few masterpieces came from this latter field such as the long epic poem on the conquest of Chile, *La Araucana*, by Alonzo de Ercilla y Zúñiga (1533–1594), a soldier in Valdivia's company of pioneers. Today the national epic of Chile, this history, first published in 1569, praises Lautaro and presents the Spanish as full of "swollen importance," their souls made of so much "wind and glory." But an epic written by Pedro de Oña (1570–1643) entitled *Arauco Domado* gave high praise to the Spaniards.

An Inca drama telling the love story of an Inca prince, translated into Spanish as a long metrical poem entitled *Ollantay*, has been the inspiration for a modern musical drama. The longest poem, called *Elegies of the Illustrious Men of the Indies*, was written in praise of Spain in the New World by a priest named Juan de Castellanos (1522–1606). Its 150,000 lines are a key to usages of the Spanish language in the Caribbean area in the 1580's. Garcilaso de la Vega's (1539–1643) chronicle, the *Royal Commentaries*, glorified Inca civilization and is a masterpiece of distinguished literary merit.

No important novel was produced and there were no other works of a purely literary type except occasional essays on contemporary life and short poetic works and dramas.

poetry, music, and art

Poetry was the preferred form of literary expression. Spanish colonial poetry was classical in form and stilted in spirit by the middle of the 17th century, but formal or not, everyone in the colonies who could write wrote poetry.

Scientists, drainage engineers, theology professors, judges, and even governors wrote lyrical verses. Priests encouraged their flocks to write sonnets to the Virgin and the saints; poetic contests were held in the universities. Outstanding among the gentleman poets was Bernardo de Balbuena (1568–1627) who was born in Spain, educated in Mexico, and appointed Bishop of Puerto Rico after his poetry became famous. He wrote a poem, *La Grandeza Mexicana,* in praise of Mexico City, where, in contrast to European cities, one could live a life of "plenty, peace, and happiness." The best sacred epic, *La Cristiada,* was written in a Lima monastery by Diego de Hojedo (157[?]–1615).

But the most famous poet of colonial Latin America was a woman, a beautiful little nun who lived in Mexico City a century after Balbuena. Born Juana Inés de la Cruz in 1651, she learned to read at the age of three, begged to go to the university like a man at the age of 14 but was allowed instead to live in her grandfather's city house where she had the advantage of a fine library and of meeting socially prominent people. The viceroy's wife made her a lady-in-waiting. Disillusioned in the lax society of the time, she decided at the age of 16 that she could best devote herself to writing and peaceful study if she became a nun. As Sor Juana she busied herself writing plays, sonnets, and critical essays, using several foreign languages, her phrases and ideas becoming the intellectual fashion of the day. She worked out a theory of the mathematics of harmony in music, was ahead of her time even in science. At forty she became a nun in spirit also, selling her 4,000-book library for charity, going out to nurse cases of the plague during the great epidemic of 1695, in which she herself died.

But it is as a poetess of love that she will always be remembered, and as a liberator of women. She urged her readers to burn the candle at both ends—"If my displeasure from my pleasure comes, Heaven give me pleasure even at the cost of my displeasure," she wrote, and "Happy it is to die while young and fair and not to endure the insults of old age." She blamed men for the frustrated loves of womankind—"You blame women alike whether they favor or scorn you, complaining of them if they treat you ill, making mock of them if they love you dearly." Pleading for freedom of the mind and of the soul, Sor Juana became famous in Spain as well as in the colonies and her works are read today for their sheer artistry.

The most famous dramatist was Juan Ruiz de Alarcón y Mendoza (1581[?]–1639), the author of 35 plays, who wrote sad poems about a "somewhat grey world"—with reason, for he was a short and ugly hunchback. Born in the Mexican town of Taxco, he pleaded cases as a young lawyer before the *audiencia* and wrote poetry to which no one paid attention. Receiving a legacy, he went to Madrid and began to write plays in verse for the theater. He was spurned by his contemporaries though his plays were popular, and even Lope de Vega, Spain's most famous dramatist, derided him as "the poet with a trunk on his back." In a play called *The Walls Have Ears* Alarcón had one of his leading characters address the audience and say, "Thou shalt not look for beauty and gentility in man's physique. His beauty lies in nobility of soul, his gentility in wisdom."

Mexico was to claim him gladly as a native son and to ascribe his ability to his colonial background. He retired from the theater when he received a post with the Council of the Indies. He is best remembered today for his play, *La Verdad Sospechosa*, or *The Liar*.

Mexico City before 1600, at a time when the Shakespearean theater was young in London, had a permanent public theater, to which all classes of society came, with its own buildings, its acting companies with a repertoire of plays, and a paying audience. Traveling companies from Spain played the dramas of Lope de Vega and products of local talent such as the more than 50 light comedies by the Mexican Eusebio Vela. Lima claimed an even more sophisticated theater in its *Casa de Comedias* of the 1590s and its Coliseum Theater of the early 1600s. There were private theaters, though the clergy denounced them, in convents and universities, and even one at the court of the viceroy. Indians in the villages never saw these sophisticated dramas but they had pageantry of their own in the festivals and religious plays on saints' days.

All formal art was church art, save for the occasional portrait of some dignity—sugary paintings of saints and virgins, dark pictures of martyrdom, poor copies of Spanish and Italian subjects, crude tempera drawings by mission Indians, work that still fills churches in Spanish America. Spanish artisans and Indian craftsmen produced a new art in the beautiful handiwork they learned from each other. Some noteworthy canvases were done by a school of painting in Quito but all subjects were pious. The half-breed son of Benalcázar, the adventurous *conquistador*, devoted himself to painting and gilding the churches of Quito, and many of his canvases can still be seen there.

Miguel Cabrera, a pure-blooded Zapotec, decorated several Mexican churches in the ornate Churrigueresque style and not in any Zapotec tradition. Francisco Eduardo Tresguerras (1745–1833) is remembered for the fine decoration of the church of Carmen at Celaya, Guanajuato. He lived to see the revolt against Spain and is called "the last figure of importance in Mexican art until 1920." Painting reached its apogee in the 17th century and declined in the 18th.

The true Latin American art was in crafts, which combined Indian skills with European methods. Puebla was famous for its tile-making in the Majolica style, work that can be seen there in the churches and homes today. Glass blowers working in the Venice tradition founded a "blue glass" industry in Guadalajara. Talavera-type pottery was made in polychrome, blue with yellow, red, or black, with an amazing variety of effects. Indian craftsmen learned to copy Chinese pieces that came on the Manila Galleon, to paint on ivory for the delicate fans of delicate creole ladies. Creole miniature artists copied French methods and learned to make portrait brooches on imported ivory. Indian designs in textiles were used with new dyes; the blankets of Chile and Araucanian motifs in geometric patterns, conventional plant and flower designs, stripes in harmonizing colors. The ingenious flower designs of the Araucanians decorated saddlebags of plush and velvet and rugs and tapestries for women to kneel on in the

Santiago churches. The mosaic patterns on the ruins of Mitla crept into the new sheep's-wool blankets of Oaxaca. The Indian artistry of fine gold casting was kept alive by the Spanish taste for gold jewelry and silver table service and for decorated saddles, spurs, and sword hilts.

No classical art education was offered in New Spain until the cultural renaissance brought by the late Bourbon kings in the 18th century. A School of Fine Arts was founded in Mexico City in 1773 and a famous Spanish architect and sculptor, Manuel Tolsa (1767–1825) was imported to teach there. Sculpture was religious in nature; marble and wood carvings were done as church decorations.

Architecture was essentially European in origin with a few Indian contributions. Churches reflected the periods of Spanish art—Moorish, Italian Renaissance, the declining Spanish Renaissance with its baroque styles and "gingerbread" ornamentation. Private dwellings were built in the Moorish style, with rooms and balconies around an interior patio, adobe walls on the outside and much tile decoration within.

Latin American music evolved from the melancholy strains of the Indians, the rhythmic genius of the Negro, and the technical influences of Europe. Unfortunately little record remains of music in colonial times. Every convent had its chorus, every church its singing choir boys, many big cities their own public bands. Indian villages still had their drummers, harpists, and pipers. In the Caribbean, Negro rhythms were transplanted into Spanish melodies.

Everywhere that Indian and *mestizo*, Negro and mulatto danced, for religion or pleasure, new dances and songs developed, but only in very recent times have their tunes and steps been recorded. The Gauchos in the Plata Colony produced a dance form, the *malambo*, a "nervous, jumpy, contagious form" of the old staid Spanish *fandango*, which the Bishop of Buenos Aires condemned in 1743. Only after 1780, when it was given sweep and grace and became the *tango* did it come into the drawing rooms, such as they were, in Buenos Aires. But in staid creole society, people sat in their stuffy city parlors and listened to their marriageable daughters playing European classics on the harpsichord while their suitors out in the street sang to a guitar the current popular songs of Spain.

To the dominant creoles and *gachupines*, it was European culture that mattered and few were interested in what the New World was producing that was new. The intellectual epochs in Europe were reflected in the colonies. The Golden Age of the Spanish Renaissance, the age of El Greco, Velásquez, Lope de Vega, and Cervantes, saw a paler "golden age" of culture come to Spanish America. Mexico City was the intellectual center with Lima and Bogotá as secondary centers. By the 18th century, the influence of science was turning the leisure and wealth of the creoles into new channels, but during the colonial period, the underlying culture of the Spanish New World was that of the *mestizo*, a combination of the thin European veneer of Old World interests and trends with the Indian culture as the base.

READINGS

Adams, E. B., and P. V. Scholes, "Books in New Mexico," *New Mexico Historical Review*, XVII, 226–255.

Anderson, L., *The Art of the Silversmiths in Mexico, 1519–1936* (2 vols., 1941).

Appleton, L. H., *Indian Art of the Americas* (1950).

Arriaga, P. S., *The Extirpation of Idolatry in Peru*. Tr. by L. C. Keating (1968).

Baird, J. A., Jr., *The Churches of Mexico, 1530–1810* (1962).

Bancroft, H. H., *History of Mexico* (6 vols., 1883–1887).

Bannon, J. F., *Indian Labor in the Spanish Indies* (1966).

Barth, P. J., *Franciscan Education and the Social Order in Spanish North America, 1502–1821* (1945).

Bolton, H. E., *Rim of Christendom* (1936).

————, *Wider Horizons of American History* (esp. essay on the "Mission as a Frontier Institution") (1939).

Bourne, E. G., *Spain in America* (1904).

Braden, C. S., *Religious Aspects of the Conquest of Mexico* (1930).

Bravo, Francisco, *The Opera Medicionali* (1570; reprinted, 2 vols., 1970).

Buford, N., *The University of San Marcos de Lima in the 18th Century* (1969).

Caso, A., et al., *Twenty Centuries of Mexican Art* (1940).

Cervantes de Salazar, F., *Life in the Imperial and Loyal City of Mexico in New Spain* (1970).

Charlot, J., *Mexican Art and the Academy of San Carlos, 1785–1915* (1962).

Chevalier, F., *Land and Society in Colonial Mexico* (1963).

Cleven, N. A. N., *Readings in Hispanic American History* (1927).

Coester, A., *Literary History of Spanish America* (rev.)

Conway, G. R. G., *An Englishman and the Mexican Inquisition, 1556–1560* (1927).

————, ed., *Friar Francisco Naranjo and the Old University of Mexico* (1939).

Cook, S. F. and W. Borch, *Essays in Population History*. Vol. I, *Mexico and the Caribbean* (1971).

Cooper, D. B., *Epidemic Disease in Mexico City, 1761–1813* (1965).

De La Cueva, M., et al., *Major Trends in Mexican Philosophy* (1966).

Demarest, D., and C. Taylor, *The Dark Virgin: The Book of Our Lady of Guadalupe* (1959).

Diffie, B. W., *Latin American Civilization: Colonial Period* (1945).

Disselhoff, H., *The Art of Ancient America . . .* (1966).

Dunne, P. M., *Pioneer Black Robes on the West Coast* (1940), and other works by author.

Ekdahl, Ravicz M., *Early Colonial Religious Drama in Mexico: From Tzompantli to Golgotha* (1970).

Elliot, J. H., *Old World and the New 1492–1656* (1971).

Englekirk, J. E., et al., *Outline History of Spanish American Literature* (3rd ed., 1965).

Espinosa, A. V. de, *Compendium and Description of West Indies,* trans. G. U. Clark (1942).

Espinosa, C., *Shawls, Crinolines, Filigree: The Dress and Adornment of the Women of New Mexico, 1739–1900* (1970).

Farriss, N. M., *Crown and Clergy in Colonial Mexico, 1759–1831* (1968).

Fernandez, J., *A Guide to Mexican Art from Its Beginning to the Present* (1970).

Fisher, J. R., *Government and Society in Colonial Peru: The Intendant System 1784–1814* (1971).

Friedrich, C. J., *Age of the Baroque, 1610–1660* (1952).

Gage, T., *A New Survey of the West Indies, 1648,* ed. A. P. Newton (1929); ed. J. E. Thompson (1958).

Gannon, N. V., *The Cross in the Sand: The Early Catholic Church in Florida, 1513–1820* (1966).

Garcilaso de la Vega, *Royal Commentaries of the Incas and General History of Peru* (trans. H. V. Livermore) (1969).

Geiger, M., *Franciscan Conquest of Florida 1573–1618* (1937).

Gibson, C., *Black Legend* (1970).

————, *Spain in America* (1966).

————, *Spanish Tradition in America* (1968).

González Obregón, L., *Streets of Mexico,* trans. B. C. Wagner (1937).

González-Peña, C., *History of Mexican Literature* (rev. ed., 1943).

Graham, R. B. C., *A Vanished Arcadia* (1924).

Greenleaf, R. E., *The Mexican Inquisition of the 16th Century* (1969).

————, *Roman Catholic Church in Colonial Latin Amercia* (1971).

————, *Zumárraga and the Mexican Inquisition* (1961).

Griffin, C. C., ed., *Concerning Latin American Culture* (1940).

Hague, E., *Latin American Music, Past and Present* (1934).

Hanke, L., *The First Social Experiments in America* (1935).

————, *The Imperial City of Potosí* (1956).

————, *The Spanish Struggle for Justice in the Conquest of Mexico* (1959).

Haring, C. H., *Spanish Empire in America* (1952).

Harney, M. P., *The Jesuits in History* (1941).

Henriquez-Ureña, P., *Brief History of Hispanic American Culture* (1964).

————, *Literary Currents in Hispanic America* (1945).

Houtart, F., and E. Pin, *The Church and the Latin American Revolution* (1965).

Jacobsen, J. V., *Educational Foundations of the Jesuits in Sixteenth Century New Spain* (1938).

Kélemen, P., *Baroque and Rococo in Latin America* (1951).

Kessell, J. L., *Mission of Sorrows; Jesuit Guevavi and the Pimas, 1691–1767* (1970).

Keyes, F. P., *The Rose and the Lily: The Lives and Times of Two South American Saints* (1961).

Korth, E. H., *Spanish Policy in Colonial Chile. The Struggle for Social Justice 1535–1700* (1968).

Kosok, P., *Life, Land and Water in Ancient Peru* (1965).

Kubler, G., *Indian Caste of Peru, 1795–1940* (1952).

————, *Mexican Architecture in the Sixteenth Century* (2 vols., 1948).

————, and M. Soria, *Art and Architecture in Spain and Portugal and Their American Dominions, 1500–1800* (1959).

Lanning, J. T., *Academic Culture in the Spanish Colonies* (1940).

————, *Eighteenth-Century Enlightenment in the University of San Carlos de Guatemala* (1956).

————, *University in the Kingdom of Guatemala* (1955).

Lea, H. C., *Inquisition in the Spanish Dependencies* (1908).

Leonard, I. A., "Best Sellers in the Lima Book Trade," *Hispanic American Historical Review*, XXII, 5–33.

————, *Baroque Times in Old Mexico* (1959).

————, *Books of the Brave* (1949).

————, *Colonial Travelers in Latin America* (1972).

————, *Don Carlos de Siguenza y Gongora: A Mexican Savant of the 17th Century* (1929).

————, *Romances of Chivalry in the Spanish Indies* (1933).

Liebman, S., *The Enlightened: The Writings of Luis Caravajal, El Mozo* (1967).

————, *Jewish References* (1964).

————, *Jews of New Spain; Faith, Flame, and the Inquisition* (1970).

Lockhart, J., *Spanish Peru 1532–1560: A Colonial Society* (1968).

Lucero-White, A., *Folk-Dances of the Spanish Colonials in New Mexico* (1937).

McAndrews, J., *The Open Air Churches of Sixteenth Century Mexico* (1965).

McClaskey, J. Y., *Inquisition Papers of Mexico* (1947).

Mandel, O., *The Theatre of Don Juan: A Collection of Plays and Views, 1630–1963* (1963).

Martin, L., *The Intellectual Conquest of Peru: The Jesuit College of San Pablo 1568–1767* (1968).

Marshall, C. E., "Birth of the Mestizo in New Spain," *Hispanic American Historical Review*, XIX. 161–87.

Martin, L., *The Intellectual Conquest of Peru, The Jesuit College of San Pablo 1568–1767* (1968).

Mecham, J. L., *Church and State in Latin America* (rev. ed., 1966).

Millás, J. C., *Hurricanes of the Caribbean and Adjacent Regions 1492–1800* (1969).

Moore, J. P., *The Cabildo of Peru Under the Hapsburgs, 1530–1700* (1954).

Mörner, M., *Expulsion of Jesuits from Latin America* (1965).

————, *Political and Economic Activities of the Jesuits in the La Plata Region: The Hapsburg Era* (1953).

————, ed., *Race and Class in Latin America* (1970).

————, *Race Mixture in the History of Latin America* (1967).

Moses, B., *Spain Overseas* (1929).

————, *Spanish Colonial Literature in South America* (1922).

————, *Spanish Dependencies in South America* (2 vols., 1914).

Nettl, B., *Folk and Traditional Music of the Western Continents* (1965).

Newton, N., *Thomas Gage in Spanish America* (1969).

O'Daniel, O. F., *Dominicans in Early Florida* (1930).

O'Neill, B., *Golden Years on the Paraguay: History of Jesuit Missions* (1934).

O'Gorman, F., *Invention in the Americas* (1961).

Oswald, J. C., *Printing in the Americas* (1965).

Parry, J. H., *Audiencia of New Galicia in the Sixteenth Century* (1948).

Paz, O., *The Labyrinth of Solitude. Life and Thought in Mexico* (1961).

Peckham, H., and C. Gibson, eds., *Attitudes of Colonial Powers Towards the American Indian* (1969).

Phelan, J. L., *Kingdom of Quito in Seventeenth Century* (1967).

————, *The Millennial Kingdom of the Franciscans in the New World* (1956; 1970).

Picón-Salas, N., *Cultural History of Spanish America from Conquest to Independence*, trans. I. A. Leonard (1963).

Pike, F. B., *Conflict of Church and State in Latin America* (1964).

————, ed., *Latin American History* (1969).

Priestley, H. I., *Coming of the White Man* (1929).

————,"Old University of Mexico," *University of California Chronicle*, XXI, No. 4, 369–385.

Rippy, J. F. and J. Nelson, *Crusaders of the Jungle* (1936).

Robertson, D., *Mexican Codices* (1959).

Rodrigues, J. H., *Brazil and Africa* (1965).

Royer, F., The Tenth Muse, *Sor Juana Inés de la Cruz* (1952).

Sanchez, G. I., *Development of Higher Education in Mexico* (1944).

Schendel, G., *Medicine in Mexico From Aztec Herbs to Betratons* (1968).

Scholes, F. V., *Church and State in New Mexico, 1610–1670* (2 vols., 1937–1945).

Schons, D., *Book Censorship in New Spain* (1949).

Schurz, W. L., *This New World* (1954).

Schwartz, K., *A New History of Spanish-American Fiction*, Vol. I (1972).

Shepard, M. L. B., ed., *Life in the Imperial and Royal City of Mexico— by Francisco Cervantes de Salazar* (1953).

Shiels, W. E., *King and Church: The Rise and Fall of the Patronato Real* (1961).

Simpson, L. B., *Encomienda in New Spain* (1950).

Steck, F. B., *Education in Spanish North America During the Sixteenth Century* (1943).

Stevenson, R., *The Music of Peru: Aboriginal and Viceregal Epochs* (1960).

Studies Presented at the Conference on the History of Religion in the New World During Colonial Times (1958).

Tannenbaum, F., *Slave or Citizen: The Negro in the Americas* (1947).

Taylor, W. B., *Landlord and Peasant in Colonial Oaxaca* (1972).

Thompson, L. S., *The Libraries of Colonial Spanish America* (1963).

————, *Printing in Colonial America* (1962).

Tibesar, A., *Franciscan Beginnings in Colonial Peru* (1953).

Torres-Rioseco, A., *The Epic of Latin American Literature* (rev. ed., 1946).

Vance, J. T., *The Background of Hispanic American Law* (1943).

Varner, J. G., *El Inca: The Life and Times of Garcilasso de la Vega* (1968).

von Humboldt, A., *A Political Essay on New Spain* (4 vols., 1811).

Warren, F. B., *Vasco de Quiroga and His Pueblo Hospitals of Santa Fe* (1963).

Weisman, E. W., *Mexico in Sculpture, 1521–1821* (1950).

Wethey, H. E., *Colonial Architecture and Sculpture in Peru* (1945).

Wilgus, A. C., ed., *Colonial Hispanic America* (1936).

Zavala, S., *Defense of Human Rights in Latin America Sixteenth to Eighteenth Centuries* (1964).

———, *New Viewpoints on the Spanish Colonization of America* (1943).

Zea, L., *The Latin American Mind* (1963).

chapter 13

THE SEVENTEENTH CENTURY: AN INTERNATIONAL RIVALRY AND FRONTIER EXPANSION

early challenges to Spain's power

"The sun shines for me as well as for others. I should very much like to see the clause in Adam's will that excludes me from a share of the world," said Francis I, the scornful king of France, in contemplating the papal bulls establishing the Line of Demarcation. Francis proceeded to send out a Florentine named Verrazano to lay a claim for France to the northeast coast of the new continent in 1524. Across the channel was that other king of scornful jest named Henry VIII, whose father had laid a similar claim for England through the voyage of John Cabot. Neither of these nations limited its subjects to voyages along the northern coasts, however. Corsairs and privateers went out of the ports of Bristol or Saint Malo and harried the trade of Spain in the Canaries or the ships of Portugal in the Azores. In 1527 an English three-master sailed right into Santo Domingo harbor on Hispaniola; its officers were wined and dined by the governor; then, after clearing port next day, they returned secretly and laid waste the countryside.

Such illegal goings-on hardly disturbed the Spaniards at first, for they considered the New World their exclusive property in the sixteenth century. *Mare Nostrum,* the Caribbean as Spain's own sea, was "a pontifical and regal principle" under the Demarcation Settlement. It was out of the question for Spain to make any trade or navigation concessions to her rivals, France and England, who were not yet strong enough before the 1580s to challenge the *Mare Nostrum* theory. Their alternative was to steal Spain's markets surreptitiously, to rifle her colonial treasure ships. As the sixteenth century progressed into the seventeenth there were often wars in Europe, and the battlefields were always extended to the Caribbean. Even when there was sweet peace at home between colonial rivals, there was "no peace beyond the line"; France, England, and Holland needed no excuse to attack Spanish shipping in the New World beyond the Line of Demarcation. They were determined to challenge Spain's monopoly there.

Thus the visit of the three-master in Santo Domingo was actually the beginning of a long series of intrusions by marauders, sea-borne bands who poached on the Spanish preserve. Sacking towns, plundering trade—all with the most pious reasons in the rivalry between Catholics and Protestants—English, French, and Dutch roamed the Caribbean, harried the West Coast, and sacked the Isthmus, often at the request of statesmen. After a century and a half Spain had gradually declined as a world power; her kings at home grew weaker, and by 1700 it was surprising that she had been able to hold her empire at all against her formidable enemies.

During the first half of the sixteenth century most of the attacks were carried on by French privateers, attacks which led the king of Spain to organize the convoyed fleets for New World trade. A peg-leg pirate named François le Clerc had a squadron of ten French vessels in the Caribbean in the 1550s and methodically plundered and pillaged, temporarily capturing Havana in 1555. French colonizers even attempted to found a settlement at Fort Caroline in Florida and another in Brazil. After a peace in Europe between France and Spain in 1559, the corsairs had no official French backing; they were obscure marine thieves living a hunted life, holing-in along the shores of unsettled Caribbean islands which they used as bases. Here the renegade Frenchmen gathered food by catching wild cattle escaped from unsuccessful Spanish expeditions and drying the meat. The French word for such beef is *boucan,* so free-rovers who stocked their illegal ships with such meat were called *boucaniers,* the buccaneers who became the scourge of the Spanish towns in the Caribbean.

By 1570 England, in her period of "new" commercial expansion and Protestanism, was a formidable enemy of Spain in the New World. The Englishman John Hawkins of Plymouth had formed a prosperous trading company in secret collusion with Spanish officials in the West Indies, smuggling slaves into Santo Domingo in return for hides and sugar. On his third voyage two ships of his fleet were the personal property of Queen Elizabeth, archenemy of the Spanish King Philip II. A storm in 1568 drove the whole smuggling fleet into the port of Veracruz where they were caught by the viceroy. Only Hawkins' own ship and the one captained by his young cousin Francis Drake escaped Spanish vengeance. The days of Hawkins' peaceful smuggling were over with this action. From then on, for 150 years, England and Spain, whether or not they were at war in Europe, were always at war in the Americas.

Drake became Elizabeth's "legal pirate," attacking Panama, sailing round South America and invading the West Coast ports, taking possession of California, and continuing round the world to start new rumors of a mysterious strait somewhere on the California coast. In Europe he sneaked in to burn the shipyards in the harbor of Cádiz. When Philip retaliated by building the Spanish Armada as a means of attacking England at home, Drake was instrumental in helping Elizabeth and England defeat this massive invasion fleet before a single Spaniard could land in the island. With this defeat in 1588 the sea power of Spain was weakened and her empire began to go on the defensive. Drake continued to be the nemesis of Spanish shipping until he finally died of a fever at sea in 1596; his body was cast into the bay of Portobello. Drake was not the only sea-dog; there were others, notably Cavendish, Cumberland, and Andrew Barker. Drake was followed by Sir Walter Raleigh who even dared enter the Orinoco on a long flatboat trip into the interior in search of *El Dorado* in 1595, who gave England later claim to the coast of British Guiana, and who attempted a colony in North Carolina.

French and Dutch challenges

Thus with Raleigh we close the sixteenth century, the day of Elizabethan "sea-dogs," and commence a period of official encroachment by England in the Spanish New World. Spain began an era of "aggressive defense" in the seventeenth, the so-called "forgotten century," often neglected by historians as a time of declining power, of stalemated institution, of stupid kings. But in that forgotten century Spain advanced her frontiers and kept off her enemies by land and sea to hold what she had. It is true that at home there was inefficiency and corruption. Charles I had been a fine emperor and a great man; his son, Philip II, was a prudent king and an upright man. Among their successors in the Hapsburg line in the 1600s, Philip III and Philip IV were poor kings and mediocre men; Charles II was neither king nor man but an imbecile, yet he sat on the throne for thirty-five years. His reign was characterized by cynicism on the part of political officials, hypocrisy on the part of religious leaders, and graft on the part of economic administrators. All Latin America passed through a period of vigor and prosperity up to the third decade of the seventeenth century and then went into a period of decline and corruption. Meanwhile France, England, and Holland supplemented privateering and smuggling with actual settlement in the New World in lands claimed but not occupied by Spain. There is a bright side to this picture for Spain; her "aggressive-defensive" policies held and even advanced the frontier in North America, and in the long run she lost only the island of Jamaica to her enemies.

The Lesser Antilles had been neglected by Spanish colonists as too small, too dry, or too far out of the way. By 1664 the French flag flew over fourteen of these islands, islands already serving as headquarters for buccaneers. Guadeloupe and Martinique had been made official French colonies by Cardinal Richelieu in 1635. Meanwhile the Spanish colonists on Hispaniola had allowed the western half of the island to be taken over by cattle and hogs gone wild. The buccaneers made the island of Tortuga, close to the north coast of Hispaniola, their headquarters. When a French governor, Levasseur, was sent to win them over as a part of the French island empire, he joined the pirates as their chieftain, defied the authorities at home, and founded a "pirates' union," The Brethren of the Coast. He and his successors swarmed over the Caribbean, flying the "Jolly Roger," burying their stolen treasure in hidden caves, and probably enjoying the secret complicity of the governors on the French islands.

Since many of these French renegades were originally outlawed Protestant Huguenots, and since they were joined by equally renegade Englishmen, they were all grouped by the Spaniards under the heading of heretics, or Lutherans, the *corsarios luteranos,* willing to despoil churches, rob altars, and even steal holy statutes if they were sufficiently jewel-encrusted. In the 1660s the Brethren shifted their headquarters to Jamaica; by the 1680s they found their "sweet trade," as they called it, outlawed by both the English and French governments. The year 1702 brought a young French Bourbon king to the throne of Spain, and with him began a new Franco-Spanish policy of friendship. In the last part of the seventeenth century the successful French West India Company was formed; it established sugar-planting colonists on the Antilles and in Saint Domingue, as the French-controlled Haiti was then called. Many of the buccaneers now had no choice save to settle down and raise sugar; large fortunes were amassed in the cane plantations of Haiti in the eighteenth century.

Some of the most active smugglers and pirates of the seventeenth century were Dutchmen, for in Holland there was a deep-seated hatred of Spanish rule, as well as an intense clash of religious faith. When Holland revolted from Spanish rule, the Dutch "sea beggars" attacked the Spanish Empire wherever they could. In 1621, during their war for independence, the Dutch organized the prosperous Dutch West India Company, whose ships "legally" harassed the Spanish West Indian trade. One of the greatest single hauls in the history of piracy was made by Piet Heyn, formerly one of the Brethren of the "sweet trade" who had been captured by Spain and sent for four years to the galleys. Out of chains eventually, he came back to the pirate islands and became an admiral in the Dutch fleet. He took his revenge for the four bitter years by capturing the Spanish silver fleet in 1628 and making a profit of fifteen million Dutch guilders for himself and the West India Company. Holland's gain in this exploit and Spain's loss is said to have upset the international money markets for a decade. The Dutch West Indian Company founded New York, held the coast of Pernambuco, Brazil, for forty years, and permanently colonized the formerly neglected islands of Curaçao, Aruba, and Buen Aire off the coast of Venezuela, as well as the Dutch settlement in Guiana. A parallel Danish West India Company founded a sugar-growing colony in the unclaimed Virgin Islands, which were held by Denmark until purchased by the United States in 1917.

Anglo-Spanish rivalry, 1600 to 1700

Elizabeth of England and Philip II of Spain were both dead by 1604, and Elizabeth's successor was concerned with a scheme for trade and colonization rivaling Spain's in the New World. Raleigh's successors had organized a company which founded permanent colonies on St. Kitts and Barbados, again islands Spain had never bothered to settle. The Puritans, so important in English history in the first half of the seventeenth century, were active merchants interested in colonies in Massachusetts Bay and in the Caribbean as well. The Providence Islands off the coast of Nicaragua, a nest of freebooters, were seized by an English captain under the very nose of Spain 300 miles away at Darién. A Puritan colony of "planters, artificers, and indentured servants" arrived in 1631, not on the *Mayflower* but on the *Seaflower*. They soon gave up farm work and imported slaves from Dutch smugglers while they went privateering. Though Spain eventually drove them away, they did make a success of the logwood business. Later this success gave England the idea for a toehold for dyewood cutting on the Central American coast and led to the British colony of Belize or British Honduras.

Oliver Cromwell, British dictator in the 1650s, developed the idea of a "Grand Design" to capture the Caribbean for Puritan England. The encounter between his well-organized fleet and the Spanish was a fiasco, and the Puritans were merely able to capture Jamaica, a tropical paradise with only 1,500 Spanish settlers. This was the one Caribbean possession actually settled by Spaniards that any enemy of Spain was ever to hold permanently. Jamaica was strategically placed and became the headquarters for English activity. The legal settlers established sugar plantations with a black slave basis, and the island became one of the busiest slave markets of the world. The pirates used it as the center for the Brethren, and the Jamaica freebooters became as feared in the late 1600s as Drake and the seadogs had been in the late 1500s. Even the governor, Thomas Modyford, sent expeditions against Havana and Portobello.

With Modyford's connivance, his lieutenant, Henry Morgan, made the most spectacular raid of the time on the Isthmus of Panama in 1671. Heading 2,000 armed renegades of all nationalities, he surprised Portobello with his invasion fleet, crossed to the Pacific before any word could precede him, and took Panama City from the land side. In the orgy of looting and killing which followed, some Spanish citizens escaped to sea, while Morgan burned ships in the harbor, destroyed the city, and returned by himself with his closest associates, leaving the rest of the renegades marooned amidst the destruction. For his efforts he was knighted, served as governor of Jamaica in his own turn, and died a natural death in 1688. It was after his raid that the site of Panama City was moved to a better harbor, and the forts and church towers ruined by Morgan were left standing as ghosts in the jungle.

Later English buccaneers did not fare so well at the hands of their own government. England's colonies were by now prospering overseas, as was her trade with Spain at home. The English Charles II, no imbecile, made peace with Spain in the hopes of procuring greater profits by legal means. There was to be a new alignment of European policies, and the Americas were to be brought within the realm of international diplomacy; the days of "no peace beyond the line" were to be over. In the Treaty of Madrid (1670) Spain acknowledged the existence of the British colonies in North America, and England promised to end government-sponsored piracy in the Caribbean. Morgan's raid the same year was the last of its kind. Thereafter pirates such as the famous Captain Kidd were dealt with summarily by English justice. Piracy declined because it was bad for commerce, because it menaced freedom of the seas. England proceeded to procure *asientos*—the legal rights granted by Spain to foreign ships to trade in slaves—and to make money for the Royal African Company by sending African natives to be sold to the Spaniards from the Jamaica market.

French privateering continued for another two decades after the Treaty of Madrid, but eventually the French government bought off the buccaneer leaders. However, England did not frown on smugglers and contraband traders, who continued to bite into Spanish colonial revenues for the next century. Individual English smugglers made fortunes out of Spanish commerce from Pánuco and Acapulco to Buenos Aires and Valdivia. There was even a Scottish Darién Company which established a short-lived settlement on the Isthmus in the hopes of growing rich off contraband trade and perhaps digging a canal.

What was Spain's reaction to this century of looting in *Mare Nostrum?* She had fortified her main Caribbean ports, building the fortifications that the tourist sees at Havana and Cartagena and the long sea wall at Portobello which still stands mouldering on the edge of the jungle. Santo Domingo, hard to protect because it was so open to the enemy-held islands of the Antilles, declined to a town of less than 500 Spaniards. Cartagena, on the other hand, was built up to be the best-protected city in the New World, with walls forty feet thick, a great fort commanding them, and the large end of the open channel artificially closed with sunken debris to guard the harbor. Here the Spaniards were to withstand an official English siege for many months in the 1700s.

In addition to her land forts, Spain improved her sea armaments and built better naval vessels. By these means, and by the division among her enemies, she held the Caribbean, so that the islands of the Greater Antilles, save the Haitian end of Hispaniola, remained and are still today Hispanic in language and civilization. Spain's colonies on the two continents had meanwhile advanced their frontiers north and south, and had stopped English and French encroachments on their farthest borders. It was Spanish "defensive aggression."

frontier expansion on the north

The need for "defensive aggression" was also felt on the northern frontier. By the end of the sixteenth century, as we have seen, the northernmost Spanish line had reached a point stretching from below the mouth of the Rio Grande to the Gulf of Lower California. Oñate had organized New Mexico far up the Rio Grande, and Santa Fe had been founded in 1609. Lower California, still thought to be an island, contained no permanent colonies. Alta California had been explored but not settled, while the fort at Saint Augustine gave Spain one small toehold on the Atlantic seaboard. In Spain's declining century this expansion went on. The motives were still the desire for wealth and the pursuit of missionary activity, but now a new one was added at the top of the list—defense. This new century was to see northern Sonora colonized, missionary occupation of Lower California begun, the Chihuahua and Coahuila areas settled, Pensacola permanently founded, and a border struggle carried on against the French in Texas. It was on this northern frontier that the missionary system as a civilizing institution played its function to the fullest, though the advance of the missionaries was slow and was accompanied by many Indian uprisings.

The Franciscan missionaries were working on the center of the northern frontier, in Nuevo León, Durango, and New Mexico. Western Mexico was to see even more active mission work. From the frontier of San Felipe in Sinaloa on Mexico's west coast the Jesuits entered the area in 1591 and worked along the western Sierra Madre up one dry river bed after another through Sinaloa and Sonora into the Nogales Valley in southern Arizona. Here on this long frontier the Jesuits claimed to have baptized 50,000 people, while they taught them farming and crafts. Their work was accompanied by clashes with the primitive Yaqui and Sonora tribes. An Indian grammar was written so that the fathers could teach the Yaqui in their own language, but those fiercely independent people remained un-Hispanized into the 1900s. However, the Jesuit missions in Sinaloa and Sonora had become mining and stock-raising settlements by 1700, while the pearl-diving industry had brought a small "boom" to the region of La Paz on Lower California. The pearl-fishing interests were required to colonize the region at their own expense under monopolies granted by the Crown.

With one such concessionaire in 1679 arrived that most famous Jesuit missionary in Spanish North America, Eusebio Kino. He had received permission to work the area on the mainland west coast called Pimería Alta. Over twenty towns were personally established by Father Kino between 1687 and 1711; the missions of San Xavier del Bac and Tumacácori in southern Arizona, landmarks in the Southwest today, were his special charge. From his cattle ranches, vineyards, and orchards, pack trains went weekly to the settled area of Mexico; supplies from these missions helped in the permanent settlement of Lower California. Father Kino himself, busy writing the geography and history of the region, spent more than a third of his years in the saddle on exploring trips around the frontier, proving that the mouth of the Colorado was a fresh-water estuary and that there was no body of water separating Lower California from the mainland. His map to this effect was quickly copied by the great mapmakers of Europe. Because of his work the frontiers of Spain had been extended to the Gila and the Colorado.

By 1620 New Mexico, last outpost of the sixteenth century, 600 miles north of Chihuahua, had thirty-five Spanish *encomiendas* centered around the town of Santa Fe among the civilized Pueblo Indians. From the time of Friar Marcos, who had preceded Coronado, these Indians were considered targets for missions. Father Alonzo Benavides of Santa Fe was also an historical writer, and his accounts report 250 Spaniards and 750 halfbreeds in Santa Fe in 1630. In that year he claimed twenty-five mission stations serving ninety villages comprising 90,000 Pueblo Indians as the sum total for the New Mexico frontier. His story also tells of skirmishes with the Apaches, the wild marauders who swept down on the settled towns, stealing corn and cattle and destroying the mission buildings.

Many settlers who came into New Mexico were runaways from older settlements, thieves, and cattle rustlers. They joined restless officials and military men in making new searches for Gran Quivira; they fought off the Apaches; they flogged the Indians into working for them. Because of all this misrule the thousands of alleged converts were resentful of Christian influence, tributes, and forced labor. They became sullen toward their exploiters and secretly practiced their own tribal religion under medicine men. Feelings among the Indians throughout the area became so tense that the inevitable revolt occurred there in 1680, the most successful rebellion against Spanish rule of any Indian group north of Panama.

An Indian medicine man named Popé, from the Pueblo of San Juan, formed a well-organized "terror" against the Spaniards, gaining the cooperation of the nomad Apaches who were being sent as slaves down to the mines of Zacatecas. Popé was determined to drive out the whites forever and to reestablish the ancient tribal faiths, but word of the plot, hatched over sandpaintings in the *kiva* council, leaked out to the Spaniards. Then Popé called out his conspirators in full force. Up and down the Rio Grande they threw the Spaniards out of New Mexico. Twenty-one missionaries and 400 Spaniards were killed by the enraged Indians, and the remaining settlers fled for their lives. They retreated downriver to El Paso del Norte, the present site of the Mexican city of Juárez, where a mission had been established in 1659.

El Paso now became the "last frontier" town, site of a presidio and an *alcaldía mayor*. From El Paso, missions spread down the Rio Grande in the other direction and into Texas. From the New Mexican settlements the idea of revolt spread into northern Mexico, from Nuevo León to Sonora, and mining camps, missions, and towns were destroyed in the years from 1683 to 1690. New presidio garrisons had to be set up to defend the old frontier. The Pueblos remained independent for twelve years, resiting all invasions. Then in 1692 their leaders began to disagree among themselves, and a

Spanish expedition from El Paso was able to re-invade their villages. In another four years the area was reconquered under Diego de Vargas and repopulated with Spanish and mestizo settlers; missionaries returned and, with a better administration, the Spanish occupation became permanent. Of all regions in the United States once under Spanish rule, New Mexico is today the most Spanish in culture.

Missionary groups had entered Texas on the northeastern frontier of Nuevo León. Beyond the Rio Grande there now arose a new danger, the French under the Sieur de la Salle, who had found the Mississippi River mouth in 1682 and set up an unsuccessful colony on Matagorda Bay on the Texas coast five years later, thereby creating a direct menace to Spain in the Gulf region. To answer the challenge Spaniards temporarily occupied eastern Texas, only to abandon it in 1693 when the French danger seemed to have receded.

A greater menace was the advance of the English along the Atlantic coast. The settlement of Jamestown in the face of the Spanish claim to exclusive ownership had brought a new wave of Spanish missionary activity in Florida and Georgia, with the town of St. Augustine serving as a base. Franciscan missionaries attempted to convert the hostile Indians as far north as the Carolinas. By the Treaty of Madrid in 1670 the English settlements to the north of the Savannah River were acknowledged by Spain, and further development there becomes part of the history of the United States, not of Latin America.

Thus, at the end of the seventeenth century, the extensive frontier of New Spain was held by a series of fortified points to stop either European or Indian encroachment. Farming and mining settlements followed the missions and the presidios in the continuing pattern of Spanish settlements. In similar fashion other parts of Spanish North America had been consolidated and defended in the seventeenth century. The thriving towns of Central America, ruled from Guatemala City, had only to worry about English logwood cutters and Caribbean pirates. The last native civilization in Central America, the domain of Canek, king of the Itzás in the Petén region between Yucatan and Guatemala, a dying Mayan town untouched by the Spaniards for two hundred years, had been conquered by 1697. These last of the Maya were then converted by the Franciscan friar Andrés de Avedaño y Loyola, who knew the Maya language. Guatemalan settlements in the seventeenth century lived off cattle raising, while the Costa Rican area developed around small farms owned by individual Spanish farmers.

The main centers of Mexico went through a period of depression in the seventeenth century. So many of the aborigines had died or been enslaved that agriculture and mining suffered from lack of free workers. Some farmland was abandoned and wheat cultivation fell off; livestock ranches replaced the great *haciendas*. Peons who had tilled the crops fled to the urban centers and joined the crowds of beggers in the epidemic-ridden cities. By 1650 the native population reached an equilibrium; the diet had changed from the Spanish wheat to the Indian corn for everyone, and prosperity slowly returned. With it, the physical face of Mexico changed back from cattle ranches to *latifundia* and debt peonage.

The viceroys of this century were weak and the social and political life was decadent. The last seventeenth-century viceroy (1696–1701) was the Count of Montezuma, a descendant of the line of the Aztec ruler on his mother's side. This man with Montezuma's blood in his veins saw the end of the Hapsburgs with the death of the imbecile Charles II and the ascendancy of the new Bourbon line to the throne of Spain. In New Spain, in spite of bad rule at home, foreign rivalry, and stultified trade, the colonial towns of Puebla, Guadalajara, Oaxaca, Valladolid, Guanajuato, as well as Mexico City, continued to grow and thrive.

frontier expansion in South America

Whereas in North America a frontier line had moved generally northward, in South America the frontier population tended to fan out from established nuclei. All of South America save Lima, Quito, and Bogotá was a frontier in 1600. Panama, the crossroads of the Americas and the link between Spain and Peru, was most hurt by foreign rivalries in the 1600s. Panama City itself was forced to move after Morgan's attack. Bogotá, seat of Jesuit learning, with seventeen Jesuit colleges by 1767, spent its time in quarrels between civil and ecclesiastic authorities. New Granada was a leading mineral-producing area, though methods were backward and transportation was very poor. Cartagena, its main port, was connected by a shallow sea-level canal to the Magdalena for riverboat transportation inland toward Bogotá, while Barranquilla on the sandy, treacherous mouth of the Magdalena was a frontier fishing village. Venezuela had a real frontier, the Orinoco, to protect against English and French encroachment. Here Jesuits carried Christianity to the *llanos* while Capuchins worked inland from Cumaná. Neither group was very successful, for they were dealing with untamed descendants of the cannibal Caribs in a region where there are wild Indians yet today. From the Orinoco the Jesuits carried Christianity to the *llanos of the Meta* and the Casañare, while armed forces sent out from Bogotá had to subdue the ferocious Pijaos, the "Araucanians of the Colombian highlands," before missionaries could contact them.

A more typical frontier of South America in the seventeenth century was the silver-mining region of Potosí. In 1611 this Bolivian mining town had a population of 114,000, including 65,000 Indians and 42,000 creoles. Its standard of living, its prices, its history parallel that of the gold-rush towns of California. At the beginning of the century Potosí had fourteen dancing halls, thirty-six gambling houses, and one theater, for which tickets of admission cost the equivalent of forty or fifty dollars. There were duels over mine claims and over women, while flashy streetwalkers ruled society and Indian workers died like flies in the mines.

Lima, the "shining jewel of Spain's empire," continued as the center of society; in 1680 it boasted 70,000 people of whom 10,000 were whites. The nobles lived in luxury, the church was of the richest, and the Lima branch of the Inquisition was the strongest in the Americas. University professors were honored. The élite society basked in its literary reputation, attended the theater, and considered itself as aristocratic as society in Spain. Most of the mestizos and all of the Indians and slaves were poverty-stricken. In Cuzco there were 40,000 people and a university as well, though the newer Spanish part of town had been shaken down by an earthquake in 1650. The port of Callao, a town of about 4,000 people, had to withstand numerous Dutch, French, and English raids. Peru, with its seat of the viceroyalty, its wide divergence between rich and poor, its wealth from the mines, its Indian masses, was in a state of constant "jitters" about foreign attack in the seventeenth century.

A few attempts were made in the 1600s to explore and develop the *montaña*, the region on the Amazon tributaries beyond the Andes. A few Jesuit missions among the half-savage Maynas Indians attempted to stop the work of Portuguese churchmen coming up the Amazon toward Peru. Samuel Fritz, a German Jesuit working under the Spanish flag, went among the Omaguas in the 1690s and made his way down the Amazon into Portuguese territory and back, mapping the river and studying the Indian language.

Chile was a never-resting frontier. Here the war against the Araucanians continued; in the 1590s these Indians had killed a governor of Chile and fifty of his men. Early in the seventeenth century a Jesuit missionary, Luis de Valdivia, convinced the court in Spain that peace could be won by missions and by better treatment of the Indian communities, but this policy did not work with the already bitter Araucanians. Though the Pact of Quillín was signed with the Araucanians in 1641, the peace it set up was soon broken. In the long run, missionaries were never successful among the Araucanians. The line between the settlements and the Indians became a group of forts, and permanent army was subsidized from Peru to defend the agricultural communities in Chile. A hundred thousand Christianized inhabitants were reported there at the end of the 1600s. With the southern frontier along the Bío Bío always an armed camp, the Chileans never colonized the Straits of Magellan.

The development of what is now Argentina and Paraguay, areas defined roughly in 1617, was conditioned in the 1600s, by the distance from Peru, the foreign smuggling, the pressure of the Portuguese to the north, and the neglect of the mother country. On the Plata frontier Spain faced a really aggressive enemy, the Portuguese. Here the Jesuit missionaries held the line at Candelaria in Misiones, a point to which they had retreated in 1632 from a group of successful missions in the Iguassú region which had been destroyed by the Portuguese from São Paulo. The quarrels over this frontier were to continue well into the period of independence.

Buenos Aires, with its 400 houses, its 500 men bearing arms, its 854 Spanish inhabitants, and its 1,500 slaves, ranked as the most important frontier town in the Plata area in 1650. Beginning in 1620, Spain was finally willing to allow two ships a year to come in directly from the mother country, in the face of all the open smuggling that went on in the Plata mouth, but few luxuries came in and life was still hard, simple, and cheap. Córdoba, far to the interior, had a university, founded in 1614 by Bishop Fernando Trejo, a true frontiersman, born in Asunción in 1554, and serving as bishop of Tucumán. His influence made these Argentine towns, Tucumán and Córdoba, no longer raw frontier communities.

The cattle ranches on the pampas stretched less than a hundred miles south from Buenos Aires against the wild Pampa Indians until after independence; there was so much unused pasture land that the cattle ranchers had no need to go south. Thus Buenos Aires itself was the frontier of the south on the Atlantic side, the Bío Bío at the edge of Araucanian country on the Pacific, and the Jesuit missions among the Guaraní on the Brazilian border. There was little further expansion in South America during the colonial era. Instead, the process continued to be a filling-in and a developing of the areas conquered in the sixteenth century.

Though Spain was battered from without during this "forgotten century," Latin America still had tremendous vitality. If the colonies were weakened in their position, it was because Spain at home was weakened, for she slipped during this century to a third-rate status in Europe. It was remarkable that she kept her mainland empire intact and expanded it on the North. Spanish institutions continued to grow deeper roots during the seventeenth century. There was need for reform and rejuvenation, both at home and in the New World, and that rejuvenation became the keynote of the first Bourbon century, the 1700s.

READINGS

Andrews, K. R., *English Privateering Voyages to West Indies, 1588–1595* (1959).

Bailey, J. B., *Diego de Vargas and the Reconquest of New Mexico* (1940).

Bannon, J. F., *Mission Frontier in Sonora, 1620–1687* (1955).

————, *Spanish Borderlands Frontier, 1513–1821* (1970).

Bolton, H. E., *Rim of Christendom* (1936).

————, *Spanish Borderlands* (1921).

————, *Spanish Explorations in the Southwest, 1542–1706* (1916).

Bridenbaugh, C. and R., *No Peace Beyond the Line. The English in the Caribbean 1624–1690* (1971).

Burney, J., *History of the Buccaneers of America* (1949).

Burns, Sir A., *History of the British West Indies* (1954).

Carse, J., *Age of Piracy* (1957).

Castañeda, C. E., *Our Catholic Heritage in Texas* (6 vols., 1936–1950).

Cavallero, C. J., *The Pearl Hunters in the Gulf of California* (tr. by W. Mathes, 1966).

Chatelain, V. E., *Defenses of Spanish Florida, 1565–1763* (1941).

Chudoba, B., *Spain and the Empire, 1519–1643* (1969).

Corbett, J., *Drake and the Tudor Navy* (2 vols., 1898).

————, *Successors of Drake* (1933).

Crouse, N. M., *French Pioneers in the West Indies, 1624–1664* (1940).

————, *The French Struggle for the West Indies, 1665–1713* (1943).

Davies, R. T., *Spain in Decline, 1621–1700* (1957).

Dawson, T. C., *South American Republics* (2 vols., 1903–1904).

Diffie, B. W., *Latin American Civilization: Colonial Period* (1945).

Eaden, J., ed. and trans., *The Memoirs of Pére Labat, 1693–1705* (1970).

Elliott, J. H., *Imperial Spain 1468–1716* (1966).

————, *Old World and the New 1492–1650* (1971).

Espinosa, J. M., *Crusaders of the Rio Grande* (1942).

Esquemeling, A. O., *The Buccaneers of America* (1924).

Folmer, H., *Franco-Spanish Rivalry in North America, 1524–1763* (1953).

Gerald, R. E., *Spanish Presidios of Northern New Spain* (1969).

Gerhard, P., *Pirates in Baja California* (1963).

Gibson, C., *Spain in America* (1966).

————, *Spanish Tradition in Latin America* (1968).

Galdames, L., *History of Chile,* trans. I. J. Cox (1941).

Goslinga, C. Ch., *The Dutch in the Caribbean and on the Wild Coast 1580–1680* (1971).

Hackett, C. W., ed., *Historical Documents Relating to New Mexico, Nueva Vizcaya and Approaches Thereto to 1773* (3 vols., 1923–1937).

————, ed., *Revolt of the Pueblo Indians* (2 vols., 1942).

Haring, C. H., *Buccaneers of the West Indies in the Seventeenth Century* (1910).

————, *Spanish Empire in America* (1952).

Henao, J. M., and G. Arrubla, *History of Colombia,* trans. J. F. Rippy (1938).

Holmes, M. G., *From New Spain to the Californias 1519–1668* (1963).

Kemp, P. K., and C. Lloyd, *Brethren of the Coast: Buccaneers of the South Sea* (1961).

Kino, E. F., *First from the Gulf to the Pacific* (tr. by W. Mathes, 1969).

Lanning, J. T., *Spanish Missions of Georgia* (1935).

Leonard, I. A., *Spanish Approach to Pensacola, 1689–1693* (1939).

Levene, R., *History of Argentina,* trans. W. S. Robertson (1937).

Lynch, J., *Spain Under the Hapsburgs 1598–1700* (1969).

Maltby, W. S., *The Black Legend in England 1558–1660* (1971).

Mathes, W. M., *Vizcaíno and the Spanish Expansion in the Pacific Ocean* (1968).

Means, P. A., *The Spanish Main* (1935).

Mörner, M., *Political and Economic Activities of the Jesuits in the La Plata Region: The Hapsburg Era,* trans. A. Read (1953).

Moses, B., *Spanish Dependencies in South America* (2 vols., 1914).

Newton, A. P., *European Nations in the West Indies, 1493–1688* (1933).

Parry, J. H., *Spanish Seaborne Empire* (1966).

Perez de Ribas, A., *My Life Among the Savage Indians of New Spain* (trans. T. A. Robertson) (1969).

Priestley, H. I., *Coming of the White Man* (1929).

————, *France Overseas Through the Old Regime* (1939).

————, *Mexican Nation* (1923).

Savelle, M., *Origins of American Diplomacy* (1967).

Scholes, F. V., *Church and State in New Mexico, 1610–1650* (1937).

————, *Troublesome Times in New Mexico, 1659–1670* (1942).

Thompson, J. E. S., ed., *Thomas Gage's Travels in the New World* (1958).

Tibesar, A., *Franciscan Beginnings in Colonial Peru* (1953).

Unwin, R., *Defeat of John Hawkins* (1960).

Wilgus, A. C., ed., *Colonial Hispanic America* (1936).

Williamson, J. A., *Age of Drake* (rev. ed., 1946).

Williams, E., *From Columbus to Castro: The History of the Caribbean 1492–1969* (1970).

Wright, J. L., Jr., *Anglo-Spanish Rivalry in North America* (1971).

chapter 14

CHANGES BROUGHT
BY THE
EIGHTEENTH CENTURY

a new world developing separately from the old

> *Yet, now, for those of you whom subtle genius has*
> *raised above the common herd,*
> *Put off the custom of yesterday,*
> *and clothe yourselves with the new.*[1]

So sang a poetic priest named Rafael Landívar (1731–1793) to the youth of the Valley of Tepic, north of Guadalajara, Mexico. He was writing of the beauties of Mexican rural life in a long poem called *Rusticatio Mexicana,* and had already described the "flowery countryside" of Oaxaca and the lakes at Pátzcuaro and Chapala. The last canto of this book-length literary classic brought him to Tepic, and there he exhorted this beautiful New World to throw off the yesterdays and turn to the tomorrows. Though written in Latin, as was the style at the time, the whole poem was soon translated into Spanish and is known and loved in Mexico as a Spanish classic and a vivid description of the beauties of the homeland.

[1] From the translation by Gusta B. Nance and Florence J. Dunstan in Carlos Gonzáles Peña, *History of Mexican Literature* (Dallas: Southern Methodist University Press, 1945).

But it was more than that; it was a clarion call! Throughout the eighteenth century all Latin America was changing from the old customs and "clothing itself with the new"; by 1800 many Spanish colonials were ready to think of their beautiful New World as a separate homeland. The century from 1700 to 1800 brought many changes—in the international scene, in the administration, in the economic field, and in the cultural pattern of "Enlightenment" of which the poet Landívar was himself a part.

A new line of kings, influenced by the more progressive French, came to power in Spain in 1702. Their accession was followed by a long series of wars in Europe which was reflected in the colonies. In the colonial wars of the eighteenth century Spain had to deal with an England no longer torn by Puritan strife at home, but unified, progressive, and rich in colonial possessions herself. This new England challenged France in Europe, in America, and in India, and world history of the 1700s is dominated by the Anglo-French colonial struggles. Spain often became involved as a weaker third party, but, for the most part, her loss of prestige in Europe made her concentrate on better rule in the colonies. By 1750 wiser rulers at home, less concerned with European alliances and more concerned with the New World, instituted a series of reforms in trade, in government, and even in teaching methods in order to maintain prosperity in the colonies. The result was a rapid change in economy—more industry, more commerce, more taxes paid, more wealth pouring in from mines, a trend towards city life with the increased incomes, a new well-informed middle class—till some New World cities were finer than Madrid, and individual New World fortunes often bigger.

All this change taught the colonials that they could live without Spain. French influences at the court of Madrid brought French ideologies and writings into the colonies. These French ideas challenged all the old concepts; there could no longer be unquestioned obedience to one king, one Church, one rigid set of class lines, one system of commerce.

French "Enlightenment" reached the Spanish court and brought to Spain a few shallow changes in fashions, university subjects, and industrial methods. All earlier Spanish movements had eventually had a tardy and weaker reflection in the colonies, but they had been brought to America only through Spanish contacts. French "Enlightenment," however, came through many other contacts. Rich young creoles visited Paris and attended universities there. Under the wiser, broader policies of the French-blooded Spanish kings, French books and periodicals and even Frenchmen themselves—on scientific expeditions and as professors and tutors—came to the colonies. These Frenchmen preached a doctrine that questioned the established authorities, a doctrine of the equality of classes, the rights of free trade. The creole class was most receptive to such ideas. Eagerly, the young sons of the newly enriched merchants listened to arguments that they were equal to the *gachupines*. Meanwhile the century of wars proved to the colonials that they could defend themselves, survive successfully in a competitive commerce, and live very well without any dependence on Spain.

Thus the eighteenth century made the Spanish New World philosophically, commercially, and militarily able to live as a separate entity from the Old World. The creoles were ready and willing to take the poet's advice and "clothe themselves with the new."

international conflict and the northern frontier

Dynastic and commercial wars, and the struggle for control of the seas were the international keynotes of the eighteenth century. In all of these the ruling house of Spain and its Spanish colonies were involved. With the death of Charles II, that poor bewitched moron who had been the helpless tool of intriguing politicians, the rule of the Hapsburgs had come to a sad end in 1700. The nation was bankrupt, the army demoralized. The next heir in line was the young Philip V, grandson of Louis XIV of France, to whom Charles II, under pressure from his French wife's relatives, had willed Spain. Though Philip acceded to the throne, the other powers of Europe, England and Austria, challenged this controlling influence of the powerful French kings in Spanish affairs, and fought the War of the Spanish Succession. At its end in 1713 the Bourbon prince was accepted as ruler in Madrid, independent from Bourbon rule in Paris, though still influenced by French ideas and advisers. Spain was also forced to grant England a limited legal right to slave trading in the Caribbean, an agreement called the *asiento*. Thus Spain had been dragged into the bitter Anglo-French rivalry, a titanic struggle which lasted till the end of the Napoleonic period.

For a long time there had been various causes of dispute between England and Spain, the most important of which arose from English contraband trade in the Spanish colonies. Englishmen, bent on finding a new *El Dorado* in Spanish colonial trade and dissatisfied with their limited rights, tried to increase the smuggling. But under Philip V Spain was better governed and had a more efficient coast guard. Restrictions were tightened and contrabandists treated roughly. Spanish reprisals were made against the English smugglers and a number of them were caught. One Englishman, Thomas Jenkins, was so unlucky as to have his ear cut off; he carefully preserved it and claimed the Spaniards had committed the act, all of which fitted in with English conceptions of the Spanish cruelty and furnished a pretext for the rising imperialists of England.

Claims and counterclaims led to the renewal of warfare in the War of Jenkins' Ear in 1739, which soon merged in the great European conflict called the War of the Austrian Succession. But insofar as Spain and England were concerned, it meant the Caribbean would be the princpal center of action. Fighting took place there and along the Florida-Georgia frontier. By now the energy of the Bourbon dynasty in Spain was beginning to show results, and Spain was able to fight off British attacks. Admiral Edward Vernon did take Portobello and Commodore Anson sailed a British fleet around the Horn, set fire to a Peruvian port, captured a prize ship off Panama, and held up the Manila Galleon. But the Spaniards had expended huge sums on fortifying Cartagena, which was regarded as a principal bulwark of her colonial defense, so that when Admiral Vernon laid siege to that city with a large fleet, the brave townspeople held out and he was forced to evacuate.

The peace that ended this European war in 1748 was in reality only a truce, for it led directly to the Seven Years' War in Europe. In the uneasy years between the wars Spain had, in effect, tacitly accepted the rights of free navigation of the Caribbean: England had to give up the *asiento* and Spain abandoned her fleet system in 1748, admitting the "right of effective occupation." Where other powers held island or mainland territory she no longer made claims. She had ceased to be the "mother of the Caribbean" and was now only one of the "sisters," but she had successfully defended Cuba, Panama, and the northern mainland of South America.

The Seven Years' War, concerned in Europe largely with the ambitions of Prussia, was fought in America as the famous French and Indian War of 1754 to 1763. Spain had joined the French under the Family Compact between Bourbon cousins. It was in this war that France lost all her possessions in Canada and the Mississippi Valley and Spain suffered severely in the colonies in the loss of ships and men. To regain Havana, conquered by England during the war, Spain gave up East and West Florida, but was compensated by the grant of New Orleans and its inland territory of Louisiana. However, the war was another step in the decline of Spanish prestige, for she no longer had France as an ally in the New World, and now faced England there alone.

The next international war took place mainly in the New World: the revolution of England's North American colonies. France and Spain both fought on the side of the colonies as a way to hurt England, but the independence of those colonies as a result of the war was more hurt than help to Spain, for such independence showed the Spanish American creoles that mother countries were unnecessary. Many noble words about equality and popular sovereignty were spoken in the English colonies during this period, words which were later translated into Spanish in Mexico City, Bogotá, Caracas, and Buenos Aires. Lastly, the French Revolution of 1789, itself a movement full of new ideas of equality and self-rule, quickly became an international war by 1792 and again involved Spain in further minor changes of territory in the colonies. Within a decade the French Revolution had expanded into a titanic struggle between Napoleon on the one hand and England on the other. As will be told in a later chapter, the alliance of Spain and England against Napoleon was a direct cause of the revolt of the Spanish American colonies.

As a by-product of the wars, Spain was forced into shifts on the frontier while she improved the whole colonial system. By the Treaty of Utrecht at the close of the War of the Spanish Succession in 1713, Spain had been forced to grant England an *asiento*, the right of selling 4,800 slaves a year into the Spanish colonies, as well as the privilege of bringing one 500-ton ship yearly with general cargo into Portobello, a legal entering wedge in the Spanish monopoly. Spain lost Georgia during the War of the Austrian Succession and the Floridas in the Seven Years' War, only to get the latter back in 1783. When England temporarily held Havana in the Seven Years' War, that port was opened to free trade—free trade which meant increased revenue and prosperity for the Cuban colonists and taught Spain to allow more intercolonial trade afterward.

Finally, through all this century Spain's policy of "aggressive defense" in the New World was forced to change gradually to one of "defensive defense." The empire had reached its farthest limits by 1790; in that year Spanish ships challenged English ships to rights on the remote northwest coast at Nootka Sound. Having no effective allies in the Nootka Sound Controversy, Spain was forced to abandon any exclusive claim to this unsettled coast, a humiliating moral defeat. At the same time Russian advances down the same coast from Alaska had brought a new enemy into the territory. After 1763 England and Spain had a common frontier in the Mississippi Valley, with no buffer of French colonies in between.

defensive expansion along the North American frontier

All the international complications just described—the changes and exchanges of territory as a result of wars in Europe—meant more English, French, and Portuguese advances on Spain's frontiers, and pushed Spain to a strong defensive policy—"defensive aggressive." In the eighteenth century Spain advanced its frontiers in both North and South America and tried to forge a ring of defenses around its empire, to hold the sea lanes, and to keep out further encroachments by the enemy.

At the end of the seventeenth century the frontier was north of Chihuahua and Coahuila. New Mexico, reconquered after Popé's revolt, now had two centers, Santa Fe and Albuquerque. El Paso remained a thriving town, while silver mines were booming in Chihuahua. But the upper Rio Grande towns were threatened by Navajos, Utes, and Comanches from the north and by Apaches from the east. The French were expanding in Louisiana and their traders in the Great Plains would buy any horses and cattle these marauders would steal. Expeditions were sent out to stop the raiders at their source, and Spaniards reached to the Colorado-Kansas border. In 1720 the Spanish Captain Pedro de Villasur led a well-equipped expedition from Santa Fe to oust the French, but the French traders and the Pawnees cut him to pieces on the North Platte. The first French traders from Louisiana pushed through to Santa Fe in 1739 and many other Frenchmen were arrested later for doing the same thing. Colorado itself was explored some fifty years later by Rivera and Anza, and Escalante visited the Great Basin in an effort to find a route to Monterey, California, in 1776. In spite of the roaming Indian enemies, New Mexico had 7,600 Spaniards in fourteen settlements by 1760.

More important was Texas, that vast area separating the French in Louisiana from the Spaniards in Coahuila. The temporary occupation of Eastern Texas by the Spaniards from 1690 to 1693, as a direct result of La

Salle's ill-fated colony, has already been noted. As more French traders came into the Louisiana-Texas border, Spain began to settle Texas in earnest. The presidio and the Alamo mission in San Antonio were founded, and Texas was permanently occupied by troops under the Marquis de Aguayo in 1720. This was during a period of open border conflict with the French, despite the royal family friendship at home. The entire Gulf coast from Tampico northward had been made the new colony of Nuevo Santander in 1746, and over twenty settlements were thriving along the coast. Border rivalry continued with the French there until the Seven Years' War gave Louisiana to Spain and eliminated the Franco-Spanish border.

Louisiana was small source of pride or pleasure to Spain during the forty years she ruled it. The French settlers in New Orleans threw out Antonio de Ulloa, the first Spanish governor, and his ninety soldiers; in 1769 a sterner governor, Alejandro O'Reilly, forced the Frenchmen to accept Spain. The king then established lieutenant governorships at St. Louis and Natchitoches and ordered the adoption of Spanish law. Louisiana was regarded principally as a buffer against the English; after 1790 it was attached to the captaincy-general of Havana. Trade in furs, horses, and mules took place between Spanish frontier posts in New Mexico and Texas, along the Arkansas borders, and with Frenchmen from St. Louis. Spain adopted French methods in dealing with the Osage and Comanche Indians, giving them presents and maintaining trade with them, rather than attempting conversion through established missions. Fur traders were licensed and French traders, such as the successful Athanase de Mézières, were enlisted by Spain.

During the American Revolution Spanish Louisiana, under the energetic Bernardo de Gálvez, aided the rebels. When Spain entered the war Gálvez drove the British from the Lower Mississippi Valley and conquered Pensacola and Florida. But economically Spain lost out to the English in the upper Mississippi Valley, for British traders invaded the Missouri area. To counter all this British activity and reassert Spanish claim to the entire territory west of the Mississippi, Spain chartered a private trading group, the Missouri Company, whose traders worked the Missouri, and even ascended as far as the Yellowstone, but never reached the Pacific. Thus the northeastern frontier of New Spain reached the Upper Missouri River in the interior of North America, at least temporarily. The idea of ringing the whole northeastern and northwestern frontier with a line of forts via the Missouri across to the Pacific was Spain's dream. However, by a secret deal in Europe, Spain retroceded Louisiana to France and the latter sold it to the United States in 1803.

On the west coast Sinaloa and Sonora had ceased to be the frontiers by 1750. Lower California and the Sonora coasts were held by the forts and missions of the Jesuits, started in the days of the great missionary, Father Kino, who had died in 1711. As a part of the defensive policy against both England and Russia on the Pacific, the wise Bourbon King Charles III had appointed an equally wise organizer, José de Gálvez, to make recommendations as to the strengthening of the frontier. Gálvez went to Lower California to see to it that the Jesuits left their missions intact when the expulsion of their order was decreed. From Loreto he looked to the north, felt instinctively the foreign menace, and ordered the occupation of San Diego and Monterey Bay by permanent settlements. Thus in 1769 Spain began her last great spurt of empire extension.

Gálvez felt he had reason to fear the Russians. Vitus Bering had found his strait, and by 1765 there were Russian fur traders in the Aleutians and Alaska. Against their possible southward advance by sea Gálvez ordered the occupation of Alta California. In 1769 a military expedition under Gaspar de Portolá, accompanied by a missionary leader, Father Junípero Serra (described in Chapter 13), traveled via Lower California to San Diego. Krom this base twenty-one missions were eventually founded, many of them the nuclei for modern California cities. An overland route back through Yuma to Mexico was pioneered by Juan Bautista de Anza, and settlers were brought over it to help found the presidio and mission of San Francisco in 1776. Once Alta California was occupied, exploration was undertaken up the northwest coast to counter the English and Russians, a movement that was stopped by the Nootka Sound Controversy. By treaties of 1790 and 1794 Spain was forced to admit the legality of exploration and settlement by other nations into territory which she had not yet effectively occupied above San Francisco.

Spain's North American frontier on the Atlantic side, the Florida line, shifted back and forth in the eighteenth century when Florida changed hands as a prize of war. No other nation held it permanently and it was finally sold by Spain to the United States in 1819 during the last years of the wars of Spanish American independence. Thus, in the long run, the results of the century of warfare, as they affected the border area, had little effect on the story of the modern Latin American nations and their civilization. The expansion beyond the Rio Grande was to give Texas and the southwestern third of what is now the United States to Mexico when she became an independent nation.

frontier conflict and consolidation in South America

Expansion in South America in the eighteenth century consisted chiefly of Spanish-Portuguese border warfare north of the Plata. Here again Spain's "aggressive defensive" policy was in play. The Treaty of Tordesillas had divided the world between Spain and Portugal, though no one knew just where the line was. Throughout the first two centuries of expansion neither side came near enough to building up its assigned territories to run a counter claim to the other side. By the mid-1600s, however, Brazilian slave raiders from São Paulo had entered the area of the Jesuit missions in Paraguay and Misiones and had forced the missionaries south of the Iguassú. On the Amazon the Portuguese had advanced beyond the most extreme measuring of the Line of Demarcation, had founded Manáus in 1674, and had destroyed the missions which the Spanish Jesuit Father Fritz had founded among the Omaguas. The *Banda Oriental,* or eastern strip of Uruguayan coast across the Plata from Buenos Aires, became the most important bone of contention between the two nations; contraband trade into the Plata region was a profitable business for foreigners, Portuguese as much as English.

The hub of this illicit commerce was a Portuguese station just across the estuary from Buenos Aires, a station which the Portuguese called Colônia do Sacramento, or merely Colônia. Here a permanent town with settled streets and garden plots was laid out in 1680, just in time for its smuggler-inhabitants to begin the eighteenth century with a constant harassment of Spanish port authorities at Buenos Aires. Imports from Europe came in free; cities in the interior could buy these smuggled Portuguese wares at much cheaper prices than those asked on goods that came legally overland from Lima. The citizens of Buenos Aires were torn between their desires to wipe out Colônia as a foreign intrusion against Spanish power, or to urge its growth as a source of bargains. England, France, and Holland also participated in the trade and gave the Portuguese a tacit protection. On more than one occasion the governor of Buenos Aires protested that Spanish commerce, even in cattle and charcoal, might be permanently stifled by the existence of the Portuguese base. When he received no answer to his protest, the governor finally went over and burned the town.

Thus a long controversy began. Despite the fact that Spain captured Colônia a number of times, Portugal, usually with the aid of English pressure, was able to force her to give it back. The town remained a center for illicit English and Portuguese activity. The treaty of 1750, settling other Spanish-Portuguese difficulties, set up a border commission to agree on a line. The Uruguayan coast was ceded to Spain, in return for which Portugal received the Misiones area in the interior, so coveted by São Paulo slave raiders. It was in opposition to this transfer of territory that the Jesuit missionaries there defied the king's order by forcefully opposing the exchange and eventually found themselves and all other Jesuits expelled from the New World. As for the treaty, its provisions were unenforceable in the wilderness. The Colônia coast remained a Portuguese center till it was made permanently Spanish in 1777, when Portugal's ally England was busy with the American Revolution. This permanence was sealed by the Treaty of San Ildefonso in the same year in which Spain retained the Misiones territory as well. Thus, in the long Spanish-Portuguese frontier quarrel, the Spaniards stopped the Portuguese advance south of Rio Grande do Sul, though Spain lost territory and missions in the Upper Paraguay and Paraná regions.

The Portuguese attempt to make the Plata the natural southern boundary of Brazil had induced Spain to settle the Montevideo area just outside of Colônia in order to keep both sides of the Plata Spanish. In 1726 a few families from the Canary Islands were given free transportation, free land, cattle, and sheep to induce them to come to Montevideo; there were enough colonists to set up a *cabildo* in 1728. Liberty-loving from the outset, the Montevideans quarreled constantly with the military governor, and entered the contraband trade themselves as go-betweens for Colônia and Buenos Aires. To further consolidate Spain's power and make control easier, the wise King Charles III created the viceroyalty of La Plata at Buenos Aires in 1776. This new governmental unit included Cuyo, Tucumán, Buenos Aires, Uruguay, and Paraguay, and was to be a defense against Portugal and a protection against smuggling. Buenos Aires was now to be a port with direct trade with Spain, and the days of the long hauls across the Isthmus and over the Andes were ended. The new viceroys opened the port and thus gave a new impetus to the growth of Buenos Aires after decades of stagnation. They also planned to expand the Spanish frontier into the South toward Patagonia and into the Gran Chaco on the north, but except for Río Negro their settlements in both directions failed. No longer afraid of the Portuguese, Spanish settlers encroached on Portuguese lands in Rio Grande do Sul, and more than 4,000 Spaniards were living in Southern Brazil when a final boundary was set in 1800.

There were also some small advances in the Cauca valley in Colombia. The only other frontier in South America that saw any marked change in the 1700s was along the Orinoco and beyond, where missions and cattle ranches were established in the 1730s and '40s. The Jesuits on the Meta and the Casañare were subject to Bogotá, the Capuchins in Guiana were subject to Caracas. Here Spanish missionaries came into conflict with the Dutch, for the missions of the Capuchins harbored runaway slaves who had escaped from Dutch Guiana. On the Orinoco the town of Angostura was founded in 1764; it soon had twenty *haciendas* and many herds of cattle pasturing on the grassy *llanos*. Angostura was to become immortal in the story of independence, when Bolívar set up a government there on this last "new frontier" to carry out the challenge of the eighteenth-century poet to "clothe himself with the new."

economic changes of the Bourbon century

The poet Landívar appealed for change among those "whom subtle genius has raised above the common herd." The Bourbons of the 1700s—Philip V and Ferdinand VI, his elder son—had infused a new spirit and brought some "subtle genius" into the administration of decadent Spain. Interested still in the prosperity of the mother country and the ruling class, they nevertheless felt that such prosperity depended on improvements for all, at home and in the colonies. To reorganize and rehabilitate the decadent Hapsburg monarchy, Philip V had remodeled the entire home government, bringing all administration and finance directly under the Crown. French absolutism was the model and imperial aggrandizement the ultimate end. Unfortunately, Philip V had his eyes on Spain's European interests and was willing almost to bankrupt Spain to hold them. Ferdinand VI, less involved internationally, gave Spain a breathing spell and left a treasury surplus. True to the "benevolent despotism" of the times, both these kings hoped to keep the people satisfied, but they made little attempt to bring this new spirit to the colonies.

Now came Charles III (1759–1788), a man of true genius who stands with Isabella and Philip II among the great rulers of Spain. Little concerned with the fashionable French life now at court, he devoted himself to government. He aimed to win revenge for the defeat Spain had taken from the English as an ally of the French in the Seven Years' War; he hoped to increase the military power and revive the trade of the empire. In order to strengthen the navy and fortify a new frontier he reformed the tax system, and cut graft and corruption and brought efficiency into imperial rule. In the previous reign a general survey of conditions in Spanish America had been undertaken, based on a report made by official though secret observers, Jorge Juan and Antonio de Ulloa, who had gone on a long tour of all the colonies in the 1740s. Now their recommendations and those of Charles' own agents were taken up, and a number of "visitors-general" was sent out to inspect conditions and take appropriate administrative action. The most famous of these were the "visitations" of José de Gálvez to New Spain, which led to many reforms within Mexico and the empire and to the settlement of Upper California, and the work of his opposite number, José de Areche, in Peru.

In economics as well as politics Charles III saw the need for change. Spanish economists Bernardo Ward and José del Campillo, products of the "Enlightenment," served as strong influences on the monarch. Charles saw that he must recover the trade of the colonies by enforcing the laws against contraband, while at the same time liberalizing commerce to and within the colonies and adding to the revenue of the Crown. Besides giving this encouragement to commerce, Charles hoped to expand colonial agriculture and revive mining. These economic reforms failed from Spain's point of view, owing to her own industrial weakness at home, the insecurity of shipping during the international wars, and the competition of cheap textiles and other wares from northern Europe. But from the American point of view the reforms succeeded by increasing trade, especially from one colony to another, by enhancing the prosperity of the merchants, and by giving the creoles a taste of freedom.

In the fields of commerce, therefore, Charles broke the monopoly of the Cádiz merchants, allowed all ports in Spain to trade with the colonies, opened up many ports in the New World, instituted a money-making monopoly on tobacco, and ended trade monopolies in the empire. The Crown had instituted monopolistic trading companies under the earlier Bourbons, especially in places where foreign smuggling had been heavy. A typical example was the Guipúzcoa Company of Caracas, which in 1728 had received exclusive rights to the Venezuela import trade along with special privileges and exemptions and control of the cacao market. This company of ambitious Basques had helped finance the defense of the Spanish Main against the English and had maintained the coast guard at its own expense, although the aristocratic landowners of Venezuela had staged an unsuccessful rebellion against its powers and exorbitant profits. Mail delivery had been granted as a monopoly to a single family, and other parallel companies operated in the Caribbean islands. By the 1780s Charles III had ended these private monopolies and brought the companies under the Crown. Mail was delivered on a systematic schedule by packet boats and there was an inter-colonial postal delivery.

The traditional fleet system of convoyed merchantmen had become obsolete—a hindrance to legal trade by individual merchants and an invitation to smugglers. During the century of wars fleets had seldom been able to make the trip safely, and the whole convoy system was abolished definitely with the last one to Vera Cruz in 1778.

Profiting by the lesson learned from the increased shipping in Havana during the period of English occupation in the Seven Years' War, Charles allowed a bimonthly trading ship to Buenos Aires. All West Indian ports were opened to individual private Spanish ships. No longer was it necessary to have a special license to sail with the fleet. The many taxes were consolidated into one import tax, which was then efficiently collected. The profits to the Crown increased so quickly that trade was next allowed directly between Peru and Mexico. Guatemala could trade with Caracas, Valparaiso with Buenos Aires. Between 1730 and 1740 less than 200 legal ships had come into Vera Cruz; between 1785 and 1795 more than a thousand came in. Because goods from Europe were more abundant, prices went down. Smugglers and monopolistic merchants in Spain went out of business and a new class of creole merchants began to prosper.

Trade between colonies by land was easier, for roads and trails were improved as the regular mail service from town to town was instituted. Ideas on freedom spread with the prosperity and with the mail, and thoughts of free trade with all nations began to occur to creole merchants and shipowners. Prosperity came to the individual towns in South America. Ten times as many hides were shipped from Buenos Aires in 1790 as in 1770. The population of Buenos Aires doubled; her hinterland prospered also, for there was more market for hides, tallow, and salted meat. Tucumán made a thriving business of textiles; Mendoza sold wine and brandy into Buenos Aires. Paraguay sent out *mate,* tobacco, and lumber.

Chile now had over thirty cities, with a total population of more than 150,000 creoles and mestizos; its rich lands and large herds of cattle enhanced the prosperity brought by the freer trans-Andean and intercoastal trade. Only Peru was hurt, for Lima now lost the monopoly on South American trade and merely shipped out the gold and silver from her own hills. Fewer and fewer ships came and went through Callao harbor now; gone was the lush trade, and with it much of the viceregal pomp of the old Lima, for there were viceroys now at Buenos Aires and Bogotá as well. Cartagena achieved a new prosperity as the center of an enlarged Caribbean trade; Havana and Vera Cruz thrived on the increased prosperity of Caribbean South America. Acapulco on the Pacific coast could now trade freely with Santiago or Lima or Guayaquil.

Everywhere the population increased with the exports and the subsequent buying power. It was the merchant class—creoles and even *mestizos*—who gained new wealth and felt little loyalty to the mother country because of it. Landowners felt a new prosperity because of the growing European demand for sugar, coffee, and hides, though land became more concentrated in the hands of the few. Mine owners made almost as much new profit, for, though the king's taxes were now carefully collected, mining methods had been greatly improved under royal experimentation. Young creoles could attend the new Schools of Mines in the colonies and there learn scientific mining methods. New mines were opened and with their output Mexico surpassed Peru in silver production. In general, Spain in the later eighteenth century did much to improve economic conditions in the colonies, but in the long run it was not enough.

Bourbon attempts at political reform

Reform in political administration was also badly needed in the colonies. At home in Spain the Bourbon monarchs curtailed the powers of the Council of Indies and of the *Casa de Contratación*, and most of their functions were delivered over to a minister of the Indies appointed by the king. The first Bourbon king, Philip V, had sensed the need for greater decentralization and efficiency in the colonies; in 1717 he had created the viceroyalty of New Granada, putting control of Caracas, Panama, Cartagena, Popayán, and Quito in the hands of a new viceroy at Bogotá. Though temporarily abolished in 1724, the post was recreated in 1739 because British attacks on the Spanish Main made the area of greater importance to Spain. Venezuela was made a separate captaincy-general in 1777, as was Chile in 1778. More *audiencias* were created, with those at Caracas in 1786 and at Cuzco in 1787 among the new ones. The creation of the viceroyalty of Buenos Aires put all the provinces east of the Andes under one unit.

North America, Louisiana and the Floridas were included in a new captaincy-general of Cuba; earlier Mexico lost direct control over Central America when Guatemala was made a captaincy-general in charge of that whole area. In accordance with a recommendation made by Gálvez, the *Provincias Internas* were established as a commandancy-general in 1776 to consolidate the frontier. This new unit strengthened and protected the farthest northern provinces of New Spain, centered Chihuahua and extending from Texas to California. Charles III's reforms thus continued the territorial decentralization within the empire. At the same time, this efficient monarch made plans to bring a high degree of centralism into its actual governing.

The colonial minister José de Gálvez, already mentioned as suggesting many specific economic and other reforms to Charles III as a result of his own investigation in New Spain, instituted a new type of official, the intendant, who was to be sent to the colonies to further Gálvez' suggestions. An intendant was a powerful new governor who did the work of the *corregidores, alcaldes-mayores* (which were abolished), tax collectors, and financial auditors, and even shared the powers of the viceroy. The idea of intendancies was a French institution brought into Spain earlier in the century. The new system aimed at centralizing administration, giving greater efficiency, increasing the royal revenues from the colonies, and strengthening the defense of the empire.

This new institution corrected abuses in the tax system, the treatment of the Indians, and the distribution of goods. By 1782 Gálvez himself was Colonial Minister in Spain in charge of the intendants. New Spain was divided into twelve of the new districts, Peru and the Plata into eight each, while smaller regions such as Cuba and Guatemala made one each. These units were subdivided into districts headed by subdelegates. In general intendants were superior individuals, but their subordinates, who were not, became notorious for some of their oppressive practices. Local administration improved somewhat under Charles III though *cabildos* lost power. Taxes were actually collected more scientifically.

Gálvez gave the colonials more experience by reorganizing the colonial armies and creating colonial militias, which had a brace of creole officers—a new recognition for the creoles in the army. New presidios were created on the frontiers. Militias were established with urban and provincial infantry, cavalry, lancers, artillery, and dragoons. They were recruited from all classes except Negroes and Indians. The upper class furnished the officers; the lower class filled the ranks; merchants and landowners provided the money. By 1804 there were 25,000 regulars in Spanish America and 127,000 miliamen. Some of these smartly uniformed creole lieutenants, whose fathers disliked the strict new customs control, became revolutionary colonels and generals in the next generation.

As a political reform tending toward centralization, the expulsion of the Jesuits (described in Chapter 16) should be noted. Perhaps recommended because the Jesuit missions seemed so independent of central authority, this expulsion decree had repercussions for Spain in the struggle of the colonies for independence.

The results of all the other administrative changes were very noticeable under Charles III. Revenues were increased, government strengthened and centralized, some abuses corrected, and the caliber of appointees markedly improved. With the tax collection centralized, peculation and petty graft were reduced, especially in the customs houses. The *mita* was legally abolished, the last *encomiendas* passed into history, and the empire was extended. Thus the eighteenth century produced changes in the field of government, and through them in mining, in commerce, and in agriculture.

The new viceroys who tried out these reforms, though still Spanish-born, were now required to be intelligent administrators. Don Pedro de Cevallos, the first viceroy of Buenos Aires, was a good example—a "career man" promoted up through the colonial service rather than a "political appointee" coming out to the new post direct from court. In his down-at-the-heels little capital he created a buzz of reform. He tried to break the evils of a one-crop economy—in this case hides—by forcing the cultivation of wheat, vegetables, flax, and hemp. The second viceroy, a creole born in Mexico, laid plans for a university at Buenos Aires, built a public theater in the central market, paved the two principal streets of Buenos Aires with cobbles, established secondary schools, founded a shelter for beggars, a home for orphans, and a hospital for women, set up a printing press, and even lit the main square with street lanterns containing tallow candles. Thus did Charles III's viceroys create a new Buenos Aires, just in time to lose it to a new Argentina in the next generation.

That Spain now chose executives from among those best fitted, rather than from among Spain's old families, is proved by the story of the colorful viceroy at Lima from 1796 to 1801, Ambrosio O'Higgins. Born plain Ambrose in County Sligo, Ireland, he found his way to Spain, where in an atmosphere friendly to anti-English Catholics he went into business and arrived in Peru as a "salesman" under the laxer immigration policies of the Bourbons. Later he became an engineer in the improvement of the pack trail between Chile and the pampas. Charles III spotted a good worker and made him a field marshal in charge of suppressing an Araucanian rebellion. Soon he was captain-general of Chile; then, under Charles' successor, he became Viceroy at Lima. O'Higgins' Chilean mistress bore a child named Bernardo who was destined to free Chile from the rule of viceroys forever.

All these improvements, this "clothing oneself in the new" as the poet urged, resulted in betterment for the colonies but an ultimate loss for Spain, since the reforms, despite their merits, did not cure the dissatisfaction of the colonials. Abuses by the local and provincial officials were corrected, but already creole *cabildos* had begun to correct abuses themselves without asking the crown officials. What advantages accrued to Spain under Charles III were all lost under his weak son and successor, Charles IV. In all his long-range plans as a benevolent despot, Charles III had neglected to educate his heir to responsibility.

eighteenth-century "enlightenment"
in Spanish America

Manuel Belgrano, Argentine independence leader, who was to spend his middle age fighting up and down the pampas to create a republic of Buenos Aires, wrote of his youth, "As was in Spain in 1789 and the French Revolution was then causing a change of ideas, especially in the men of letters with whom I associated, the ideals of liberty, equality, security, and property took a firm hold on me, and I only saw tyrants in those who opposed man's enjoying wherever he might, those rights with which God and Nature endowed him." To many other creole leaders besides Belgrano the ideas of "Enlightenment" stemming from France and Europe became a tremendous force. They were weary of European absolutism and of the political discrimination it brought against their own class. The concepts of natural rights, of liberty, of equality, justified their hatred of the *gachupín* "superiority" and of their own inferior position. Thus the "Enlightenment" led them to form literary and patriotic societies, to demand more liberalized university courses, and eventually to oppose the Spanish government.

The Enlightenment movement itself stemmed from the writings of

Rousseau who talked of social equality, of Locke and Montesquieu who believed in popular sovereignty, of Newton who was formulating his laws of nature, of Descartes who said that science should be based on proof through experimentation rather than on Aristotelian logic, of Adam Smith who said that economics could be scientific, and of Voltaire who challenged the authority of the Church.

Some of these ideas had reached Charles III, who read history and economics, entertained philosophers and playwrights at court, watched physics experiments conducted in the salons of the intellectuals, and is said' to have secretly read some of the new books placed on the Church Index. His economic and political reforms for the colonies were "enlightened" in that they were utilitarian and efficient and were based on "experimentation" by means of new organizations and new policies. Spain itself saw many reforms at home. Officials were appointed for their merits and their services rather than for their blood and lineage. The credo of the Enlightenment, the "Doctrine of Progress," was manifest in the new courses at the University of Salamanca, where physics, astronomy, and medicine were encouraged by Charles III, and in the many new scientific institutes, businessmen's societies, and intellectual clubs which flourished during his reign. On the other hand, progress was hampered by the "paternalistic" basis of these reforms, which were all handed down from the top and had no democratic basis, as well as by the continued censorship of books and limitations on public education.

Such restrictions and paternalism tended to retard any spread of the Enlightenment spirit to the colonies. But if Spanish policy delayed the intellectual awakening of Spanish America, the creole interest in such ideas, once they came to the colonies, tended to accelerate the Enlightenment there. While the University of Salamanca was modernizing its curriculum, so was the University of Mexico. The Universities of San Marcos and of Chuquisaca set a pace for liberalism in higher education. Many of the professors supplanted memorization by scientific experimentation. British science, French philosophy, and American political ideas were being discussed by student groups. The revolutionary attack on authoritarianism and the introduction of doubt was thoroughly achieved in the universities in Latin America during the last half of the eighteenth century. Colonial leaders corresponded with European scientists and with such Americans as Benjamin Franklin.

This new thinking, plus the examples of the American and French Revolutions, brought on a literary and scientific revival in Latin America despite the rigid Spanish censorship. There was a gradual intellectual reorientation away from Spanish leadership, a growing receptiveness to new ideas, and a willingness to question the validity of the old ones. Officials and merchants traveled to Europe, colonial students went abroad to study, scientists and travelers from Europe came to the New World. Books and newspapers from revolutionary France and the new United States were smuggled in. Botanists studied under Mutis in Bogotá in the 1770s and a medical and scientific journal, the *Mercurio Volante,* was printed in Mexico.

Influenced by all this ferment, young creoles were taking more university courses, reading more books, entering the professions in the growing colonial cities, and joining the lodges of Freemasons. They enrolled in the Schools of Mines and of Fine Arts and in the classes in engineering, astronomy, and navigation which liberal-minded professors were offering. Jesuit domination of education had been ended with the expulsion of the Jesuits in 1767—thus probably removing a major obstacle to the entry of democratic ideas into the colonies. Within twenty years the colonial universities had recovered from the shock of the expulsion of many of their classical professors; now more and more lay teachers, intellectuals not trained in the church, were leading educational developments. The scientific expeditions and projects described in Chapter 14 were a part of the Enlightenment. Scientists measured the size of the earth, identified tropical plants, and encouraged the use of vaccine to cure smallpox.

The New World produced its own philosophical and liberal writers in this period. In Mexico, José Joaquín Fernández de Lizardi, best known as "The Mexican Thinker," led other restless creole minds in discussing "radical" new ideas—popular education, abolition of Negro slavery, Indian reform, free trade, and freedom of religion and the press. In the University of Chuquisaca, in today's Bolivia, students read a study by Victoriano de Villava of the economic ineffectiveness of the *mita* system of forced labor in Peru. Solórzano Pereira's *Política Indiana* and the French Abbé Raynal's *Philosophical and Political History of the European Colonies and Commerce in the Two Indies* were also studied in the new university classes. Though written by travelers from Europe, not by colonials, they gave criticisms of the Spanish government and foretold the inevitability of revolution and self-government.

Newspapers and magazines appeared during the Enlightenment to encourage such "advanced political beliefs" on the part of all their readers. A literary *Diario de Mexico* was started, ran eight months, and was suppressed by the viceroy in 1768. In 1790, on the other hand, the viceroy in Peru was very literary minded, and was willing to support authors and poets in his court as the enlightened French despots had been doing in Europe. Under his encouragement Peru was soon issuing a very "cultural" review, half literary and scientific journal, half newspaper—the *Mercurio Peruano*. For actual dailies with news and political comment, all Latin American capitals waited till the 1800s. Paper was scarce, of course, and news from Europe was weeks old when it was printed. These early newspapers and magazines carried essays on literature and the classics, locally written poetry, notices on agriculture, trade, and current improvements.

Those who wrote for these new journals formed literary societies. In Bogotá they called themselves the *Buen Gusto* or Good Taste Club; the members wrote poetry, studied botany, and perhaps talked of independence. The Lima society, called *Amantes del País,* Lovers of the Nation, limited its membership to thirty members, as exclusive as the French Academy. In these societies everyone was a poet, but no one seems to have been an outstanding one. Of the hundreds of verse-writers in Mexico City,

Landívar, the priest and classical scholar whose verse heads this chapter, is one of the few still remembered. Books written in Spain continued to come into the New World in greater numbers than ever. French books came too; many copies of Voltaire, Rousseau, or the Encyclopedists were to be found in private libraries or even bookshops, though the violence of the French Revolution had frightened the Spanish Crown into stricter censorship.

Social life was changing also. The last decades of the eighteenth century saw notable improvements in comforts and elegance. Mexico City and Lima were both paved with cobbles and lighted with candle-lanterns. Stagecoach roads connected cities. Recreation showed new influences. Spanish bullfighting as a stylized spectacle now held the attention of Sunday crowds, and the *paseo* or evening walk around the plaza—girls in one direction, young men in the other—had been imported from Madrid as a correct pastime; it is still so today in most provincial Latin American towns. The risqué French dances were frowned on by Charles III, but *boleros, fandangos,* and *jotas* had been brought from Spain as country dances. City people attired in powdered wigs danced French minuets. Gambling had become a secret sport under Charles III and was openly enjoyed by his son Charles IV; its popular form in the colonies is said to have given rise to the national lottery, an institution which supports government charities in many Latin American countries today. The French influence in general had made society less strict and formal, less prone to accept authority, more broad-minded in its interest in the late 1700s than it had been in the late 1600s.

At the end of the eighteenth century there were between fourteen and seventeen million inhabitants in the Spanish colonies, perhaps 20 per cent of them creoles, the class which became most enlightened and most discontented. Because it caused the creoles to challenge authority and offered no solution to social and economic problems, the movement of the Enlightenment in Latin America was more destructive for Spain than constructive. It "tore away the curtain of superstition and ignorance," undermined the authority of Church and empire, and produced the "will to rebel." Thriving commercially, improving culturally, the colonies were reaching maturity. As the eighteenth century drew to a close so did the colonial period.

READINGS

Almariz, F. D., Jr., *Tragic Cavalier: Governor Manuel Salcedo of Texas 1808–1813* (1971).

Aldridge, A. O., *The Ibero-American Enlightenment* (1971).

Aschman, H., *The Central Desert of Baja California* (1959).

Bannon, J. F., *Bolton and the Borderlands* (1964).

———, *The Spanish Borderlands Frontier 1513–1821* (1970).

Bernstein, H., *Origins of Inter-American Interest, 1700–1812* (1945).

Bobb, B., *Viceregency of Anotonio María Bucareli in New Spain, 1771–1779* (1962).

Bolton, H. E., *Athanase de Mézières and the Louisiana-Texas Frontier* (2 vols., 1914).

————, *Kino's Historical Memoir of Pimería Alta* (2 vols., 1914).

————, *Outposts of Empire* (1939).

————, *Pageant in the Wilderness* (1951).

————, *Palou's New California* (4 vols., 1926).

————, *Rim of Christendom* (1936).

————, *Spain's Title to Georgia* (1925).

————, *Spanish Borderlands* (1921).

————, *Texas in the Middle Eighteenth Century* (1915).

————, and M. Ross, *The Debatable Land* (1925).

Brading, D. A., *Miners and Merchants in Bourbon Mexico 1763–1810* (1971).

Brown, V. E, "Anglo-Spanish Relations in America—the Closing Years of the Colonial Era," *Hispanic American Review*, V, 327–483.

Buford, N., *The University of San Marcos de Lima in the Eighteenth Century* (1969).

Burrus, E. J., ed., *Ducrue's Account of the Expulsion of the Jesuits from Lower California 1767–1769* (1967).

Cambridge History of the British Empire, Vol. I (1929).

Carr, R., ed., *Latin American Affairs* (1970).

Carter, H., *Doomed Road of Empire: The Spanish Trail of Conquest* (1963).

Castañeda, C. E., *Our Catholic Heritage in Texas*, Vols. II–V (6 vols., 1936–1950).

Caughey, J. W., *Bernardo de Gálvez in Louisiana, 1776–1783* (1934).

Chapman, C. E., *Founding of Spanish California* (1916).

————, *History of California: Spanish Period* (1921).

Dawson, T., *South American Republics* (2 vols., 1903–1904).

De La Cueva, M., et al., *Major Trends in Mexican Philosophy* (1966).

Diffie, B. W., *Latin American Civilization: Colonial Period* (1945).

Dunn, W. E., *Spanish and French Rivalry in the Gulf Region of the United States* (1917).

Dunne, P. M., *Black Robes in Lower California* (1952).

Espinosa, C., *Shawls, Crinolines, Filligree: The Dress and Adornment of the Women of New Mexico 1739 to 1900* (1970).

Englekirk, J. E., et al., *Outline History of Spanish American Literature* (3rd ed., 1965).

Faulk, O. B., *Last Years of Spanish Rule in Texas 1778–1821* (1964).

Fisher, J. R., *Government and Society in Peru. The Intendant System 1784–1814* (1971).

Fisher, L. E., *Background of the Revolution for Mexican Independence* (1934).

————, *Intendant System in Spanish America* (1929).

————, *The Last Inca Revolt 1780–1783* (1966).

————, *Viceregal Administration in Spanish American Colonies* (1926).

Floyd, T. S., *The Bourbon Reforms and Spanish Civilization* (1966).

Folmer, H., *Franco-Spanish Rivalry in North America, 1524–1763* (1953).

Ford, L. C., *The Triangular Struggle for Spanish Pensacola, 1698–1739* (1939).

Galdames, L., *History of Chile,* trans. I. J. Cox (1941).

Galvin, S., ed. and trans., *The Kingdom of New Spain* by P. A. O'Crouley (1972).

García Calderón, F., *Latin America: Its Rise and Progress* (1913).

Gayarré, C., *History of Louisiana* (4 vols., 1903).

Geiger, M., *Life and Times of Fray Junípero Serra* (2 vols., 1959).

Gerald, R. E., *Spanish Presidios of Northern New Spain* (1969).

Gerhard, P., *Historical Geography of New Spain* (1972).

Gibson, C., *Spain in America* (1966).

————, ed., *The Spanish Tradition in America* (1968).

Griffin, C. C., ed., *Concerning Latin American Culture* (1941).

Hackett, C. W., *Historical Documents Relating to New Mexico, Nueva Vizcaya and Approaches Thereto to 1773* (3 vols., 1923–1927).

————, ed., *Pichardo's Treatise on Limits of Louisiana and Texas* (4 vols., 1931–1946).

Hamnett, B. R., *Politics and Trade in Southern Mexico 1750–1821* (1971).

Hamilton, E. J., *War and Prices in Spain, 1651–1800* (1945).

Haring, C. H., *Spanish Empire in America* (1952).

Harman, E., *Trade and Privateering in Spanish Florida 1732–1763* (1969).

Henao, J. M., and G. Arrubla, *History of Colombia,* trans. J. F. Rippy (1938).

Henríquez Ureña, P., *Literary Currents in Hispanic America* (1945).

Herr, R., *The Eighteenth Century Revolution in Spain* (1958; 1969).

Hill, L. F., *José de Escandon and the Founding of Nuevo Santander* (1926.)

Houck, L., *History of Missouri* (3 vols., 1908).

————, *Spanish Regime in Missouri* (2 vols., 1909).

Howe, W., *Mining Guild of New Spain and Its Tribunal General, 1770–1821* (1949).

Humphrey, R. A., and J. Lynch, *Origins of the Latin American Revolution, 1808–1826* (1965).

Huck, E. R. and E. H. Mosely eds., *Militarists, Merchants, and Missionaries. United States Expansion in Middle America.* (1970).

Hussey, R. D., *The Caracas Company, 1728–1784* (1934).

Kamen, H., *The War of Succession in Spain 1700–1715* (1969).

Kinnaird, L., ed., *The Frontiers of New Spain: Nicolás de Lafora's Description, 1766–1768* (1958).

————, *Spain in the Mississippi Valley* (3 vols., 1949).

Kroeber, C. L., *Growth of Shipping Industry in the Río de La Plata* (1957).

Lanning, J. T., *Academic Culture in the Spanish Colonies* (1940).

————, *Diplomatic History of Georgia* (1936).

————, *The Eighteenth Century Enlightenment in the University of San Carlos de Guatemala* (1955).

Levene, R., *History of Argentina,* trans. W. S. Robertson (1937).

Leonard, I. A., ed., *Colonial Travelers in Latin America* (1972).

Lockey, J. B., *East Florida, 1783–1785* (1949).

Loomis, N., and A. P. Nasatir, *Pedro Vial and the Roads to Santa Fé* (1967).

Lynch, J., *Spanish Colonial Administration, 1782–1810: The Intendant System in the Viceroyalty of the Río de La Plata* (1958).

Madariaga, S. de, *Fall of the Spanish American Empire* (1948).

Manning, W. R., *Nootka Sound Controversy* (1905).

McAlister, L. N., *Fuero Militar in New Spain, 1764–1800* (1957).

McLachlan, J. O., *Trade and Peace with Old Spain, 1667–1750* (1940).

Means, P. A., *Fall of the Inca Empire and the Spanish Rule in Peru, 1530–1780* (1932).

Morfi, J. A., *History of Texas, 1673–1779*, trans. C. E. Castañeda (2 vols., 1935).

Mörner, M., *Expulsion of the Jesuits from Latin America* (1965).

Moses, B., *Intellectual Background of the Revolution in South America* (1926).

_____, *Spain's Declining Power in South America, 1730–1806* (1919).

_____, *Spanish Colonial Literature of South America* (1922).

Mottem, C. G., *Mexican Silver and the Enlightenment* (1950).

Murdock, R. K., *Georgia-Florida Frontier, 1793–1796* (1951).

Nasatir, A. P., *Before Lewis and Clark* (2 vols., 1952).

_____, *Spanish War Vessels on the Mississippi 1792–1796* (1968).

Nichols, M., *The Gaucho* (1942).

Pares, R., *War and Trade in the West Indies, 1739–1763* (1936).

Parry, J. H., *Trade and Dominion: The European Overseas Empires in the Eighteenth Century* (1971).

Petrie, Sir C., *The Spanish Royal House* (1958).

Pfefferkorn, I., *Sonora: A Description of the Province*, trans. T. Treutlein (1949).

Pierson, W. W., *Studies in Hispanic American History* (1927).

Pike, F. B., ed., *Latin American History* (1969).

Pons, F. R. J. de, *Travels in South America* (2 vols., 1807; reprint 1970).

Priestley, H. I., *Coming of the White Man* (1929).

_____, *France Overseas Through the Old Regime* (1939).

_____, *José de Gálvez, Visitor-General of New Spain* (1916).

Randall, L., *A Comparative Economic History of Latin America: Argentina, Brazil, Mexico, Peru, 1500–1914* (1972).

Roberts, A., *The French in the West Indies* (1942).

Robertson, J. A., *Louisiana Under Spain, France and the United States* (2 vols., 1911).

Savelle, M., *Origins of American Diplomacy* (1967).

Shaeffer, R. J., *Economic Societies of the Spanish World 1763–1820* (1958).

Simpson, L. B., *Many Mexicos* (3rd ed., 1952).

Spell, J. R., *Rousseau in the Spanish World Before 1833* (1938).

Steele, A. R., *Flowers for the King: Expedition of Ruiz and Pavón and the Flora of Peru* (1968).

Syrett, D., *The Siege and Capture of Havana, 1762* (1970).

Te Paske, J. J., *The Governorship of Spanish Florida, 1700–1763* (1964).

Thomas, A. B., *After Coronado* (1935).

_____, *Forgotten Frontiers* (1932).

_____, *Plains Indians and New Mexico, 1751–1778* (1940).

_____, *Teodoro de Croix and the Northern Frontier of New Spain, 1776–1783* (1941).

Thompson, J. E. S., ed., *Thomas Gage's Travels in the New World* (1958).

Thurman, M., *The Naval Department of San Blas—1767–1798* (1967).

Treutlein, T. E., ed., *Missionary in Sonora* (1965).

Ulloa, J. J. and A. de, *Noticias Secretas de America* (2 vols., 1826).

—————, *Voyage to South America* (5th ed., 2 vols., 1807; abridged ed. in English, 1964).

Vives, J. V., trans. F. M. López Morellos, *An Economic History of Spain* (1969).

von Humboldt, A., *Personal Narrative of Travels to the Equinoctial Regions of America During the Years 1799–1804* (7 vols., 1814–1829).

—————, *Political Essay on the Kingdom of New Spain* (4 vols., 1811).

Whitaker, A. P., *The Huancavelica Mercury Mine* (1941).

—————, ed., *Latin America and the Enlightenment* (1942).

—————, *Mississippi Question, 1795–1803* (1934).

—————, *Spanish American Frontier, 1783–1795* (1927).

Wilgus, A. C., ed., *Colonial Hispanic America* (1936).

Williams, E., *From Columbus to Castro: The History of the Caribbean 1492–1969* (1971).

Wright, J. L., *Anglo-Spanish Rivalry in North America* (1971).

Latin America
stirs and revolts

PART III

Basic among the causes for the wars of the revolution were the oppression of the colonial system and the growing resentment of the creole class against restrictions. Moreover this was a revolutionary age, the era of the Enlightenment, marked by the successful American and French Revolutions. In the colonies, subversive "foreign ideas" were disseminated against the Spanish system that promoted a spirit of belligerency.

The revolt began merely as a movement for the reform of a bad governmental system and a protest against Bonapartist possession of the Spanish throne. Once under way, it moved against Spanish authority, rapidly in some localities, more slowly in others. In their common fight against the Bonapartists, the colonials increasingly felt themselves the equals of the Spaniards. When local committees took over the powers of the viceroys and captains-general, the large and prosperous colonies could no longer submit to being treated as mere colonials, and the struggle became a war of independence. Local communities in revolt became independent republics.

There was no single movement, no single hero. Leaders differed among themselves over ultimate aims, the type of government desired, concepts of freedom and individual liberty, the proper position of the Church and the landed aristocracy. On the one hand were the "loyalists" the men loyal to Spain whether already New World residents or newly arrived Spanish military men. On the other were the "patriots" the enlightened, quick-witted creole leaders. Indians and *mestizos* and slaves fought now on one side, now on the other, varying in their confused loyalties from region to region, with little idea that independence might mean equality for them also.

When independence did come, it was a political change at the top only, with some economic improvements for the merchant class. The Latin American revolutions stopped short at the point where they might have evolved into social revolutions. From the beginning there was no unity—no centralized staff, no general plan of revolt, no coordination of action by various groups of revolutionaries. Venezuela and Colombia constituted one area of localized revolt, Argentina and other areas below the Tropic of Capricorn another. The Mexican and Central American war was an entirely separate movement. Peru, the seat of the loyalists and the area for the last stage of operations, was the only area of centralized planning.

Events in Spain called the tune. From 1808 to 1810, the colonies struggled for a redress of grievances and for the return of the Spanish king, Ferdinand VII, to the throne. When Ferdinand was returned to power in 1814, he disappointed his liberal supporters, and the colonists had no choice but sullen acquiescence—until a liberal party again came to the fore in Spain in 1820. The struggle resumed and the victories that then came to the colonials led on to final defeat of the Spaniards.

The independence of Brazil, though due indirectly to the invasion of Portugal by Napoleon's troops, is so different a story and so much a part of the Brazilian nation that it is told separately in Chapter 20.

chapter 15

BACKGROUNDS
OF INDEPENDENCE

disaffection within the empire

The three centuries of Spanish colonialism were rapidly coming to their inevitable end. The discussions, the agitations, the rebellions, and the military campaigns of the eighteenth century gave evidences of widespread dissatisfaction. The very colonial system itself, with its social discrimination against creoles and mestizos, was a major factor. Ten generations had grown up in America, generations which were increasingly resentful of the arrogance and exclusiveness of Spanish policy. The feeling of patriotism and loyalty among Latin races is very strong, and the devotion to the Crown, taken as seriously as personal honor, tended to prevent complaints by the masses against the *status quo*. When laws seemed foolish and administrators corrupt, the people never blamed the Crown. "Long live the King, but death to bad government!" was the battle cry of several abortive revolutionary movements. The people tended to disregard or even openly disobey laws that were laxly enforced; when force was used to bring obedience to the laws, it was to be met in turn by a new force of resistance. This resistance was largely creole, for the creoles were the intelligentsia, and they were the ones who felt the discrimination most keenly and determined on action when the time came.

Economic reasons for disaffection there were in abundance, similar to the "trade and navigation" disputes between the Thirteen Colonies and England. When trade barriers were lessened by Charles III, the colonists had a new taste of commercial freedom, which made them love Spain even less. When taxes were collected, under the fiscal reforms of Charles III, riots occurred against the tax collectors in Quito, Bogotá, and Veracruz. The high fees collected by the Church, combined with increasing resentment on the part of "enlightened" young colonials against the "thought control" of the Inquisition and against the control of upper church positions by the gachupines, made the Church seem the ally of the restrictive colonial government. The Church, therefore, was plunged, voluntarily or otherwise, into the class struggle; many of the lower clergy were later to become leaders in the wars for independence.

The administrative reforms of Charles III had come far too late to be effective, and were not given a chance because of the weakness of Charles IV and his reversion to the old system. When this change of kings came in 1788, the creoles were already conscious of their powers and their demands. Both creoles and mestizos were better off than they had been a half century before, but they were also better informed—revolutions do not take place among ignorant people unaware of their possibilities. Some "radical" young creoles stood ready to furnish leadership, mestizos swelled the army ranks and helped pay the bills, and Indians and Negroes supplied the brawn. The town councils, the cabildos, the creoles' only chance for a voice, began to demand more power, to ask that their members be locally chosen; these requests for local control in the 1790s were coming at a time when Spain was a second-rate power, when her merchant fleet and her navy had less than one-tenth the power of that of England and one-eighth that of Holland. But even all these causes for disaffection might never have broken loose in the Spanish empire, bound by the Latin chains of patriotism and loyalty, if it had not been for the temporary destruction of Spanish power by Napoleon in the first decade of the 1800s.

There had been revolts against Spanish authority in Paraguay in the 1730s, in Caracas in the 1750s, in Peru and Bogotá in the 1780s—revolts against monopolistic companies, against Jesuit control of mission Indians, against continued Indian exploitation by Peruvian authorities—against taxes on tobacco to pay for colonial wars—a wide variety of small local causes. Leaders were anxious to save themselves money, to oust a particular government official, to improve conditions for their entire class in one locality, to bring wealth and power to themselves. None of these revolts became a widespread interregional affair, and each was handled as a separate instance by Spanish authorities.

In Paraguay a judge named José de Antequera, sent to settle a local quarrel, made himself dictator for four years in the late 1720s after a dispute over Indian workers with the legal governor, who backed the Jesuit missionaries in protecting the Indians from landowners. The landowners in the cabildo supported the ambitious judge and elected him governor in defiance of the Peruvian viceroy's appointee. When Antequera was captured and taken to Lima for execution, he chose a successor who continued the rebellion for another ten years. Their followers considered themselves independent of Spain; they called themselves *comuneros* after rebellious communities that staged a famous revolt in Spain against the royal government in the 1500s. Although the rebellion in Paraguay was put down on orders of the viceroy by an army from the Plata, this outbreak of disorder was typical of later revolutions in Latin America: ambitious leaders, a parliamentarian *cabildo*, the influence of the Church, the readiness to decide issues by force rather than by compromise.

In Caracas landowners revolted for another reason—anger at the monopoly of the Basque-owned Guipúzcoa Company, which held the trade of Venezuela in a vise. An army of creoles marched in force on Caracas to appeal to the *cabildo* to expel the Basque company. Though crushed by Spanish troops, this was considered a "loyal" revolt—"Long Live the King! Death to *chapetones!* Death to bad government!"—and its leaders were granted amnesty by Spain, while the company continued to control trade until all such monopolies were broken by Charles III.

In Quito in the 1760s, in Bogotá in the 1780s, there were revolts in which the rebels called themselves *comuneros.* In Ecuador a creole-*mestizo* party protested against the government alcohol monopoly. Fifteen years later Bogotá saw a much more widespread *comunero* revolt against the strict enforcement of sales taxes by the new intendant in order to pay for the war against England. The war-tax was resisted with especial fervor in a community of tobacco growers called Socorro. Though the leader was executed and many of the Indians who had staged a simultaneous revolt were killed, some of the grievances of this armed uprising were alleviated. In it the New Granadans had learned to make protests for redress of grievances and to revolt when they got no redress.

The Indians had joined the Socorro *comunero* revolt because they heard of the great uprising among the Indians in Peru. Long abused by the *mita* system and the *corregidores,* the work in the mines and the weaving establishments, the Indians in Peru had rebelled three times in the 1740s in the hopes of ousting the Spaniards and re-creating an Inca empire. In 1780, as the *comuneros* were protesting taxes in Bogotá, an educated man from a college in Cuzco, a dignified, well-dressed young gentleman named José Gabriel Condorcanqui, who read Latin and spoke Spanish, not Quechua, was serving as the Indian agent and tax collector in an Andean valley. His forefathers had been recognized as lineal descendants of Tupac Amaru, last of the Incas, and he himself had been granted the title of marquis by the royal *audiencia* before he was twenty. As Indian agent he had tried peacefully to alleviate the conditions of the Indians. Now in protest against the conditions of the *mita*, the forced labor in the mines, he formed an Indian army, claimed to be the true ruler of Peru, and called himself Tupac Amaru II. When he went to the authorities at Cuzco to plead for reform, he received a disdainful reply; in answer, his Indians seized and killed the local Spanish governor. All the native villagers living near Cuzco rallied to his banner, and an actual war broke out from the Ecuadorean border down through Tucumán to the pampas. It took several months and 15,000 Spanish troops to quell the revolt. Tupac Amaru II was cruelly put to death when the Spanish troops captured him; his body was torn apart by horses pulling in opposite directions, but his followers kept on fighting. One of his cousins laid siege to the city of La Paz with an Indian army of 40,000. Though the army was disbanded, the wise Charles III followed the rebellion with reforms. A new viceroy made a study of the causes of the revolt, and recommended the abolition of the *mita* system. Tupac Amaru II accomplished little for the sons of the Incas; people of Indian blood live under conditions of extreme poverty in Peru today. However, the revolt taught the Indians to join with the creoles in the independence movement against Spain.

Other regions of Latin America stirred. There were disorders and uprisings against the taxation system in Mexico, Cuba, and Peru. Salta and Jujuy, in the Andean foothills of present-day Argentina, revolted against their governors in 1724 and again in 1767. The Argentine town of Corrientes rose against its local governor in 1767, imprisoned him, and replaced his power with a committee from its own *cabildo*. A baker named Jacinto Canek proclaimed himself King of the Maya in Yucatan and raised the Indians in protest against the heavy taxes and the lack of justice they received in the courts. In the same period there were separatist plots in Chile. In Caracas in 1797 José María España and Manuel Gual planned a similar conspiracy to overthrow Spanish rule, hoping for aid from British forces from Trinidad and encouraged by the governor of the island. The movement was imbued with French Revolutionary ideas and had many friends, for the creoles of Venezuela were well informed, aware of world trends, and angry at Spain; but the revolution in its turn was betrayed, and many leading creoles hanged as a result.

In Bogotá, by this time a center of intellectual activity, a young cacao exporter named Antonio Nariño, a French encyclopedist in philosophy and a typical creole in his opposition to Spain, had received a copy of the French Declaration of the Rights of Man, that stirring plea for equality. Nariño translated it into Spanish equally as stirring, had copies printed on a secret press in Bogotá, and distributed them widely. For promulgating such ideas the viceroy sentenced Nariño to ten years' imprisonment in Africa. Fortunately for the independence movement in Colombia, he escaped by jumping into a small boat when his prison ship lay in the harbor of Cádiz, and he returned to serve his native land again after 1810.

The writings of North American revolutionists had also been found among Nariño's papers. Franklin and Jefferson corresponded with leading Latin Americans; Hamilton, Knox, and others were in contact with Miranda. By 1800 the United States of North America was a going concern, economically as well as politically, and creole leaders had visited it. The revolution there influenced Spanish America in that it had proved that a rebellion against a mother country could succeed, that a republic could be a practical working entity. Members of the creole intelligentsia like Nariño had read

Montesquieu, Rousseau, and Voltaire. Secret Masonic societies were formed in Spain itself, anti-Church and anti-Crown though they were. One of the most active Masonic groups in Spain and Spanish America was named the Lautaro Lodge in honor of the Araucanian Indian youth who had revolted against the first white men in Chile. Joining in the Masons' dislike of Spanish autocracy were the exiled Jesuits, thousands of them back in Europe from their missionary and educational work in the colonies, and well organized as pamphleteers and conspirators against Spanish power in the Indies.

Forces working toward individual freedom and against Spanish control of the empire were thus very strong from the outside—the liberal philosophers, the American and French Revolutions. Propaganda concerning them came in through smugglers, through travelers and foreigners in the colonies, to add to the dissatisfaction already felt by the creoles.

the French Revolution in the Caribbean

The workability of popular sovereignty in North America, and the French Revolution, with its ideas of "Liberty, Equality, and Fraternity" and its success in overthrowing a monarch, were both watched by Spanish America's creoles. In another region of the New World the French Revolution was taken even more seriously—the French West Indies.

The "factories-in-the-field" process of producing sugar in French Haiti, or Saint Domingue, and the life of the African slaves there have been described in Chapter 9, above. A handful of luxury-loving French overseers in the capital, Port-au-Prince, many mulatto children of the overseers, and the mass of slaves at the bottom lived in a state of tension in the last part of the eighteenth century.

In 1789 the Haitians—Africans, free mulattoes, and white planters —all heard about "Liberty, Equality, Fraternity," and reacted each in his own way. White planters thought that now they would be represented in Paris; freedmen thought "equality" referred to all colors; the blacks thought that slavery was ended forever. A delegation of free mulattoes went to Paris in 1789, led by the prosperous Vincent Ogé, and brought back word from the National Assembly there that all tax-payers in the colonies could vote in new colonial legislatures. When Ogé attempted to prove himself qualified as a "voting taxpayer," he was executed in Port-au-Prince by being broken on the wheel in a gala public display. In the crowd, there were three black slaves who saw the mulatto Ogé die proclaiming liberty. They were Toussaint L'Ouverture, a coachman from a hill plantation, a slave boy named Henri Christophe, belonging to an innkeeper, and the third, an African-born member of a gang of stevedore slaves, a sullen, bitter illiterate named Jean Jacques Dessalines and called "The Tiger." The three of them were to bring death to a great number of whites and independence to mulattoes and blacks on both the French and Spanish halves of the island before any other Latin American nation was independent. But freedom was to be accompanied by fifteen years of bloodshed and massacre such as no other colony was ever to know.

A visitor to the island colony, one Abbé Raynal, had just written a book of his travels, *Philosophical and Political History of the European Establishment and Commerce in the Two Indies,* in which he wrote with horror of the treatment of slaves in the French West Indies and of the inevitability of their revolt. "All that they need is a brave leader. Who will he be? There is no doubt that he will appear; he will come and raise the sacred standard of liberty." These words were read by Toussaint L'Ouverture, son of an African-born Negro, educated by Jesuit priests to whom his father had been a slave, trained as a coachman by an indulgent and liberal-minded master who was early interested in the wiry, intelligent little boy. Other slaves in Saint Domingue—speaking only African dialects, practicing voodoo rather than Christianity since the overseers felt it dangerous to teach them too much of white ways—knew little of the French Revolutionary doctrines for which Ogé had died, but Toussaint, the educated, the well-treated, did know; he remembered Raynal's words and Ogé's death. He was determined to liberate the slaves.

On the night of August 22, 1791, five months after Ogé's death, Negro voodoo priests aroused the slaves to the first widespread rebellion in island history. Plantations were destroyed, whole families massacred; mulattoes and freedmen joined one side or the other; Dessalines and Christophe became guerrilla leaders. Toussaint bided his time for two months, his own plantation home untouched in the holocaust. Then he helped his master to safety, organized his fellow slaves, and joined the rebels, where he soon became commander in chief.

At first loyal to the French king, who, he had been told, really wanted freedom for all the slaves, Toussaint refused to deal with French commissioners who opposed the royal power. When Toussaint heard that Louis XVI had been executed, he took his well-trained guerrillas across the mountains to Santo Domingo to preserve that colony for kings against the Republican commissioners then in Cap Haitien. A new commissioner representing the Directory persuaded him that the French Republicans were his true friends. In 1798 he was called Lieutenant Governor under the French Governor, and was made commander in chief of the colonial army—in which the soldiers were all former slaves. Soon, on one legal pretext or another, he had the officials of the French Republic sent home, and ruled the island alone in their name.

As an administrator there seems to be nothing but praise for Toussaint. His problems were stupendous: to produce food in a disorganized society with all owners and all overseers gone, to encourage ex-slaves to do any work at all for their own self-preservation. Toussaint had drafted a constitution proclaiming Saint Domingue a self-governing French protectorate, with himself as governor general. He made friends with the strong mulatto leaders at Aux Cayes in the south; he took progressive white leaders into his government, enlarged agriculture, and aided commerce. Visitors described him as a true leader, far ahead of his time, intensely just and upright, inspiring respect and devotion by his character. Meanwhile he made war on Spanish Santo Domingo and controlled the whole island by 1801.

Meanwhile in Paris, a new authority with less sense of justice, Napoleon Bonaparte, was now called upon to approve Toussaint's constitution. Napoleon had grandiose schemes for controlling the Caribbean from the island colony, including in his wide empire Louisiana which he had just wrested from Spain. Hearing from his colonial advisers that the white-owned plantation system had brought great revenues to France, he sent his own brother-in-law, General Charles LeClerc, with 20,000 well-trained troops to crush Toussaint. "I will not leave an épaulette upon the shoulders of a single black," he told LeClerc. The reconquest was to be accomplished in three phases—first, Toussaint was to be lured into friendship; secondly, LeClerc's troops were to take the island; thirdly, Toussaint was to be arrested on any type of pretext and sent to France, while LeClerc made himself dictator and restored both the French owners and the sugar-cane profits for France. Phases one and two were immediately impossible, for Henri Christophe, Toussaint's general in charge of the town, would not let LeClerc land. While he delayed, Toussaint reorganized his army, inflicted heavy losses on the French as they landed, and then played hide-and-seek, waiting for the rainy season to come and bring him a stronger ally.

That ally, which killed LeClerc and 18,000 of his men, and brought victory for the blacks, was the yellow fever. In a virulent epidemic it took a hundred deaths among the susceptible Frenchmen daily, and left the immune blacks victors in three months' time. LeClerc made peace, won over Dessalines and Christophe by making them officers in his army, and showered Toussaint with compliments and favors. When, in good faith, the black leader, now fifty-eight years old, rode unarmed to a dinner meeting with the whites, he was thrown into chains—phase three of Napoleon's instructions—and taken to Europe. There Napoleon refused to see him, and sent him to a bleak prison in the Alps, where he died of tuberculosis. His last words as he left Haiti had been, "In overthrowing me they have only felled the tree of black liberty in Saint Domingue. It will shoot up again, for it is deeply rooted, and its roots are many."

Shoots grew from the roots before Toussaint was dead. By November of 1802 LeClerc himself was dead of yellow fever. Dessalines and Christophe, hearing that Napoleon had re-instituted slavery in Guadeloupe and Martinique, deserted the French army and began again raising guerrillas in the hills. Napoleon now turned his attention to renewed war with England, sold Louisiana, his other Caribbean-area possession, to the United States, and the remaining handful of French soldiers sailed home. Jean Jacques Dessalines, "The Tiger," stood on a rock before his troops when the French left, took the French tricolor in his hands, and tore the white stripe out of it to trample under his boots. Thus would he trample the whites out of the French half of the island forever. He had a declaration of complete independence written in his name on January 1, 1804, using the old aboriginal word Haiti for the nation for the first time. He, and after him Christophe, ruled Haiti as absolute dictators. The French masters never came back; Haiti, with few white men left in the entire province, was the first Latin American state to win independence. This whole drama had been watched anxiously by the Spanish colonials; events in Haiti frightened many aristocratic creole landowners, but also proved that a small force of "Americans," in hills and valleys they knew, could fight off seasoned European troops unfamiliar with the tropics.

English intervention versus Spanish authority

England was involved in the struggle for Spanish American independence. She encouraged and financed revolutionary agents and she tried to capture the port of Buenos Aires. In the confusion of the wars in revolutionary Europe, England was an enemy of Spain again for a period after 1796. Still active in the Caribbean, England enlarged her anti-Spanish activities by making an attempt to invade southern South America and by encouraging anti-colonial agents and movements in the Spanish empire. War or no war, it would be to England's commercial advantage to have the Spanish American ports completely free, ruled by weak new republics that would look to England for all their trade relations.

Through the years of Spanish neglect Buenos Aires had been served by illegal English shipping. Under the more liberal trade policies at the turn of the century there were more than a hundred English vessels coming into the Plata by 1800. English colonial planners were not satisfied—in the light of the wars against Napoleon raging in Europe, and with the position of Spain there undecided—merely to steal the trade of Buenos Aires away from the Spanish homeland. An English fleet had captured Capetown; from South Africa in 1806 its commander sent William C. Beresford with six vessels and 1650 men across the South Atlantic to take the Plate estuary. There were no regular troops in Buenos Aires, and there was a very cowardly viceroy, Rafael Sobremonte, who hastily retreated inland to Córdoba when the English landed.

> At the first gunshot and the soldiers' shout
> Sobremonte and his kin cleared out.

Thus the humiliated townspeople are supposed to have sung while watching as the British flag went up over their plaza and their public treasury moneys were shipped off to London. Word of the easy landing reached England together with the money, and plans were made there to consolidate the gains by sending more English troops inland and by making an attack on Chile. Meantime, the English held the port for two months, opened the harbor to free trade, and gave the creoles a touch of real commercial independence, while they guaranteed the rights of private property and the Catholic religion.

But the citizens of Buenos Aires were not taking the foreign occupation of their city without protest. Free commerce, yes, but foreign rule, no! Secretly they drilled and trained a local militia, some of whom under Juan Martín de Pueyrredón escaped from the city. The cowardly viceroy remained in hiding in Córdoba, to the disgust of the loyal Spanish inhabitants. After two months a reconquest, the famous *Reconquista* of Argentine history, took place dramatically under Santiago de Liniers, a Frenchman by birth but a loyal servant of Spain, who had worked with Pueyrredón in organizing the militia. An army of young creoles from Montevideo and from the pampas met outside the city on a stormy night, marched into the bull-ring at dawn, forced the English to surrender, and made Buenos Aires again a Spanish city less than sixty days after the viceroy had fled.

The viceroy soon returned, but the gallant creoles, having tasted liberty, changed his power and that of the *audiencia*. They convened a *cabildo abierto*, deposed the viceroy, and made Liniers viceroy in his place, an appointment confirmed by Spain. Meanwhile Liniers resumed charge of the militia—the idea of a locally trained, locally supported militia of townspeople and volunteers was a new one in Spanish America—and drafted 8,000 men into his raw army. They were ready to meet the British when they came again in 1807. This time the English War Office sent twenty warships, ninety transports, and 12,000 men under General John Whitelocke to make the Plata area a permanent English colony. They landed first at Montevideo, while the creoles in Buenos Aires organized every block and every house for defense. After weeks of preparation across the river, the large English forces marched into Buenos Aires, and then the citizens did their duty. They blocked every street, they poured hot water from the housetops, they dropped stones on English heads. When the English general was court-martialed in London for the defeat which followed after a few hours of such fighting, he protested that English soldiers had never been faced with "such resolution and perseverance on the part of an enemy." The British removed themselves permanently from Montevideo and Buenos Aires; the viceroy returned to quarrel with the people and with Liniers. But things were never to be the same again. The citizens of Buenos Aires had learned to scorn their viceroy and rally to their own leader; they had learned to raise and train their local militia; they had learned to carry on free trade with the world. Though they had scorned their English "guests," at first their captors and then their prisoners, the "propaganda" those guests disseminated concerning free trade under British protection did not fall on deaf ears.

The English War Office was also interested in financing the anti-Spanish agent, Francisco de Miranda. Called by South American historians "the Morning Star of Independence," he spent thirty years of his life as an "agitator" in the cause of Spanish American revolt, and served as a link between the North American and the Latin American Revolutions. Unfortunately, most of these years were spent away from his native Caracas, where he was born in 1756, and where he had grown up among the aristocratic Venezuelan families and received the standard classical education befitting his status. His family had purchased him a captaincy in the Spanish Army, and, because of his military ability, he was promoted in rank. While Spain

was fighting England during the American Revolution, Miranda participated and was raised to a full colonelcy. But he was accused of smuggling
and threatened with court-martial, so he became embittered against Spain
and ran away. By 1784 he was a fugitive in the new United States. Here he
talked to Thomas Paine and even to the aristocratic Alexander Hamilton,
and evidently formulated plans for freeing the Spanish colonies with
English or American help, though Hamilton later called him an intriguing
adventurer. He was indeed involved in intrigue. After traveling widely in
Europe for four years, he took his schemes for revenge against the Spanish
army, added to them the idealism of the revolutionary creoles, and presented a definite plan to the English Foreign Office. England was to finance
and staff an invasion led by Miranda himself; the Spanish colonials would
rise up to join it, and great would be the strategic and commercial advantages accruing to England.

The English listened to him seriously enough to put him on an
English pension and keep his ideas dangling on a string in case the British
government decided on a blow against Spain. On English money he traveled
to the continent, visited other royal courts, and became an intimate of
Catherine the Great of Russia, for he was a handsome figure of a man. After
years of adventure in revolutionary France, he was back in England in 1798,
renewing connections with the British Foreign Office, and working on his
plans for English help in an invasion. His modest rooms in London became
the headquarters for young Spanish creoles on visits to Europe. Simón Bolívar met him there, as did Chile's future liberator, the young Bernardo O'Higgins. A secret lodge of Masons, with both English and Spanish creole
members, centered around Miranda; branches of this lodge met in colonial
cities and even in royal Cádiz, where they pledged colonial independence.
The exhilaration of the London meetings and the correspondence with the
young creoles after their return home undoubtedly led the volatile Miranda
to believe that all South America was anxiously awaiting his English-
financed liberating expedition. He dubbed himself "agent for South American independence."

Miranda was again in the United States in 1805. There he hired
advertising agents to recruit help for an initial expedition to take Caracas.
He consulted with Jefferson and Madison and got help from the Collector of
the Port of New York. Only the small "spark plug" of one vessel was needed
to set off a revolution, he was sure. So he commanded the little ship *Leander*,
with 200 adventurous volunteers, toward South America. When he reached
the Venezuelan coast his young creole friends were not there to meet
him and no spontaneous force arose to help him. Venezuelan officials
had been forewarned. Miranda's name was better known in England than in
Caracas. How could South Americans who never heard of him be expected
to rally to his standard when he appeared unannounced in one small boat?
Sadly he returned to sulk in England, and to inspire creole visitors. The
creoles at home would have to feel a reasonable confidence in their ability to
beat Spain, and the right moment had to come before revolution could be
successful. Meanwhile Napoleon began to influence English policy far more

than did any hopes for trade with Spanish America. A force under Wellington which had been raised to implement Miranda's plan once Venezuela
was free, was sent to help Spain fight Napoleon at home in the Peninsula
instead. It was that very Peninsular War which was to be the "spark plug"
for independence in Spanish America, rather than any of Miranda's
schemes.

events in Europe leading directly
to the revolution

A small percentage of creoles wanted independence; some merchants
wanted freedom from the empire. A large percentage of all Spanish colonials were loyal to their king. But Napoleon changed that loyalty by his
attempt to control the Spanish throne.

It must be remembered that Napoleon and his agents did not have
to deal with a fine king and upstanding man of the Bourbon line such as
Charles III. His successor, Charles IV, was completely under the control of
the prime minister Manuel Godoy, who was the queen's paramour. The son
and heir, Ferdinand, was also a weakling and a reactionary, Their vacillating
foreign policy of Spain's government lost Trinidad to the English; the
Louisiana colony with its port at New Orleans, Spanish since 1763, went to
Napoleon in a treaty. After Nelson's victory at Trafalgar Napoleon completely distrusted the unstable government and decided to put an end to the
Bourbon rule of Spain.

To accomplish this, Napoleon resorted to trickery. Hostile to Portugal as a long-time ally of his enemy England, he sent an army through Spain
with Godoy's connivance and into Portugal from the east. This force
captured Lisbon, while the English navy helped the Portuguese royal family
escape to Rio de Janeiro, an escape on which the whole subsequent history
of Brazil hinged. Godoy had been promised a share of the Portuguese spoils,
but now Napoleonic troops were pouring into Spain, and Godoy saw he had
been duped. The terrified Charles IV abdicated, and then recanted to save
his favorite Godoy, while Godoy's mistress, the queen, made plans to flee
Spain. Then Crown Prince Ferdinand declared his father, who had abdicated and then recanted to save his favorite Godoy, a traitor and threatened
to take over the government. The wily Napoleon invited both father and son
to meet him as arbitrator in southern France. Thus both the Spanish
Bourbons became Napoleon's "house guests," which they remained, practically as prisoners, until the death of Charles IV and the return of Ferdinand
to the throne of Spain in 1814 after the defeat of Napoleon. Napoleon's
brother Joseph was made king of Spain, and kept himself in power by
means of 100,000 French troops who overran the Peninsula.

Now those Spaniards loyal to their king had no Spanish king. They
armed themselves as guerrillas and, with help from the English, kept Napoleon's soldiers busy for seven years in the Peninsular War. They tried to run
the government first through regional *juntas* or revolutionary committees

and then, by September of 1808, through a central *junta* of thirty-five members which moved from Madrid to Seville to Cádiz as the French advanced, and which tried to rule the entire disrupted empire in the name of Ferdinand VII. Napoleon was now fighting the whole nation.

And what of the colonies in all this confusion? Joseph Bonaparte had sent agents to the various Latin American cities—at least sixty different Frenchmen—who were scorned, exiled, or imprisoned. He appointed pro-Bonaparte Spaniards as viceroys in Mexico and in New Granada, but his appointees refused the honor. Meanwhile the *junta,* taking refuge at Cádiz, chose a regency to arrange for the calling of a congress, a *cortes,* which included a small group of Spanish colonials then resident in Spain. This congress, under the influence of French revolutionary ideas, wrote a very liberal, limited-monarchy type of constitution for Spain in 1812.

The Constitution of 1812 declared the colonies an integral part of Spain, but did not end the restrictive system of colonial trade. Apart from allowing a small representation, the *cortes* merely demanded money from the colonies to fight Napoleon but did nothing to win colonial loyalty. Colonials who went before the *cortes* for consideration of specific New World problems received scant attention. Most colonials had no reason to feel that the Cádiz government was an actual substitute for the king.

In fact, the colonials did not want a substitute for the king. They set up their own *juntas* in the name of Ferdinand VII, proclaiming "The old king or none." Public opinion was not yet ready for independence, but throughout 1808 and 1809 Spanish prestige in the New World began to totter. At La Paz and at Quito there were armed revolts against the Spanish troops still in the New World to protect the now "un-legal" viceroys—revolts which declared independence yet protested loyalty to Ferdinand VII. Bogotá, Caracas, and Valladolid in Mexico saw revolutionary movements under local *juntas.* Their leaders claimed that if Seville or Cádiz could set up interim ruling *juntas* so could any Spanish American city. Not knowing what the imprisoned Ferdinand thought, and having found out that the *cortes* of Cádiz still considered the colonies as colonies, the New World cities proclaimed for Ferdinand and against the Cádiz government. This was actually the moment that began the Revolution. Under the flag of Ferdinand the creoles struck for independence in 1810.

The wars that achieved that independence are the exciting story of the next chapter. However, events in Spain between the proclamation of the liberal Constitution of 1812 and the winning of independence must be here summarized for the reader, as they had so many repercussions on the progress of the Spanish American revolutions. With Wellington's ousting of French troops from the Iberian Peninsula and the defeat of Napoleon in Europe in 1814 and 1815, his brother Joseph was forced off the Spanish throne, and the wily Ferdinand VII returned. Raised as a reactionary, he immediately declared the liberal Constitution of 1812 null and void and all the actions of the Cádiz *junta* and the *cortes* illegal. Members of those bodies were arrested, even though they had acted in Ferdinand's name and in hopes of his return. Most areas in the New World that had proclaimed their independence were again reconquered.

Liberal citizens of Spain were no happier over this turn of events than their counterparts in Spanish America, and the next five years saw revolt after revolt. However, the general tenor of the times in Europe, under the reactionary policies of Prince Metternich of Austria, made liberal successes impossible. Finally in 1820, when Spanish soldiers, assembled on the docks at Cádiz to be sent to fight Bolívar and other independence leaders to "save the empire," revolted against their own officers, a revolution against Ferdinand and for the Constitution of 1812 broke out under the leadership of Rafael Riego. Ferdinand was powerless before the storm and promised to summon a *cortes* to return to the liberalism of the Napoleonic period and the Constitution of 1812. During the three years of the government by this "limited monarchy" there were many victories for the South American patriots. Spain could not attempt reconquest in the Americas because of her own internal difficulties. This "rosy" period ended with the invasion of Spain by reactionary troops from France and Austria who restored Ferdinand to absolute power.

The next decade was a period of terrorism and confusion at home in Spain. First this group and then that prevailed with the weak Ferdinand, and various possible heirs plotted to take over the throne. In 1829 he surprised the plotters by marrying again. On his death in 1833, the child of this late marriage, the infant princess Isabella II, became Queen of Spain. By 1836 the advisers of this child ruler began tardily to recognize the New World daughter nations, who had, for all practical purposes, been independent a decade. Thus the rise and fall of the fortunes of King Ferdinand from 1810 to 1833, and the acceptance or rejection by the Spanish monarchy of the principles of constitutionalism, were as much factors in the successes of the Latin American patriots as were their own fierce battles in mountain and jungle.

Note: Readings for this chapter are given at the end of Chapter 17.

chapter 16

THE WARS FOR
SPANISH AMERICAN
INDEPENDENCE

Venezuela the prototype and Bolívar its hero

With the coming of Napoleon's troops into Spain, the stage was set and the fuses were sputtering, ready to set off the series of explosions known as the Wars for Independence in Latin America. The movements toward rebellion had broken out simultaneously in many places. Events on the Plata were speeded by the English intervention there. Then in 1809 the Plata uprisings were reflected in La Paz and Chuquisaca and even in loyalist Peru, where a serious revolt was put down by the Spanish troops. Between April and September, 1810, revolutionary juntas or provisional governing committees set up in the name of Ferdinand VII were formed in Santiago, Quito, Bogotá, and Caracas, beginning with the last. None of these were hypocritical maneuvers to deceive the masses concerning a false loyalty to the king, but they were attempts to avoid obedience to the Bonapartists. Creole leaders who joined in these juntas, however, were determined never again to return to a purely colonial status. Thus in 1810 revolutions broke out almost simultaneously in all parts of Spanish America—municipal outbreaks which became regional and national by extension.

Venezuela is a prototype of the new nations that struggled under these conditions. The methods used there were in general followed elsewhere. It is on the movement there and along the Spanish Main, where Bolívar became the heroic figure, that attention must first be centered, that area in which Miranda had tried to land the *Leander*, when he was the "Morning Star."

When in July of 1808 Napoleon had sent a special captain-general to Caracas, Venezuela, the people had rioted, carrying Ferdinand's picture through the streets with the label *Fernando el Deseado*, Ferdinand the Desired One. Within a year, however, they had to bow to the strict rule of a Spanish "stooge" of Joseph Bonaparte named Vicente de Emparán. A small group of patriots, driven underground, now met secretly in the home of the young Simón Bolívar. These patriots welcomed the news that a central junta had been set up in Seville. Then when word came that Seville had fallen to the Bonapartists, they assumed that there was no government left in Spain, and they decided to force the issue when agents arrived demanding recognition of the regency as supreme in Spain. They called a *cabildo abierto* in April, 1810, deposed the false captain-general, and established for themselves in the name of Ferdinand a junta composed of Bolívar's secret society.

The junta issued a clarion call to other cities in nothern South America, but it did not even have all of Venezuela behind it. Followers of the Archbishop of Caracas were devoted to the old regime; Maracaibo and Coro to the west were jealous of the leadership of Caracas; out in the plains of the Orinoco the *llaneros* were to remain loyal to the government of Spain for years. Meanwhile, the Caracas junta debated in fine-sounding words and sent three of its members to England for recognition and aid. The rich young Simón Bolívar, aristocratic plantation owner, led the delegation. His errand in England was futile but, needless to say, he got in touch with Miranda in his same old London lodgings. The "Morning Star" had been busy writing articles which were sent out secretly to the new presses of South America; he had a blueprint for government in Caracas based on the writings of Locke and Rousseau. Bolívar was then twenty-seven, Miranda fifty-four. "Why not come home with us to Venezuela? The time has come!" said the younger man.

So Miranda arrived in Caracas on a British ship in December, 1810, and this time Caracas was ready to receive him. He soon got himself elected to a new congress called by the junta. His wide experience, soldierly bearing, and shock of white hair gave him great prestige, as did his now-popular stories of the *Leander* expedition; he was elected commander in chief of the rebel armies and put in charge of finances. Also influential in the congress was Simón Bolívar, now returned himself from London and appointed as military leader.

The junta and the congress were busy with reforms. A federation of the seven eastern provinces was set up. Indian tribute was abolished, the *alcabala* tax discontinued, the importation of slaves forbidden. Federalism won out over the strong objection of Miranda and Bolívar. Independence was voted at the insistence of the Patriots' Club, July 7, 1811, creating the First Venezuelan Republic. The flag used by Miranda on the *Leander* was adopted for the United Provinces of Venezuela. The constitution for these

United Provinces, emphasizing the regional differences and local rivalries, weakened the new nation from the beginning, and began the Federalist versus Centralist quarrels that plagued all Spanish America for a century. Not only jealous regions, but also colored elements among the poor who were hostile to the creoles, as well as church leaders and the strong Spanish army contingent were all against the new government. Nature itself turned against the revolutionists. On the day before Good Friday in 1812, March 26, a terrific earthquake hit Venezuela, all along a fault line, bringing greatest destruction to the very towns that had been most active against Spanish authority. Priests who supported the Spanish government headed by the Archbishop of Caracas shouted that it was the judgment of God on the sinful republicans. "Down with the Republic! Acknowledge our King!" they told the frightened crowds. Simón Bolívar, working to free victims from the ruins, yelled back, "If nature opposes herself to us, we will wrestle with her, and force her to obey!"

But nature had given Miranda's republic a death blow. Congress quit quarreling and accepted Miranda as dictator in the emergency, but it was too late to save the government. Royalist soldiers made rapid progress against the rebellious sections of the country; the ports had been blockaded by Spanish ships, the patriot armies were undisciplined and many deserted; the congress was quarreling over the constitution; the lower classes, frightened by the earthquake, became hostile to the revolution. The popular young Bolívar, actually jealous of Miranda, had been put in command of the key fort of Puerto Cabello, and as the republic weakened, Bolívar had to give up the fort without a fight because of heavy desertions among his men. Thus the military situation was completely lost for the patriots. Miranda knew he had lost the confidence of the people also, and believed the whole Venezuelan republic hopeless for the time being. In desperation he made a treaty with the commander of the Spanish forces, General Domingo de Monteverde, in July 1812. All patriots were to be pardoned, and Miranda and the other leaders would be allowed to leave the country.

Then the perennially optimistic old soldier took the funds of the republic, planning to go to New Granada to use the money to further the more successful revolution that had started there—at least so his friends later insisted. An English ship awaited him in the harbor, but he delayed on shore one night too long. The Spanish commander had broken the treaty and was arresting patriots, cruelly persecuting civilians, and confiscating their property right and left. The younger leaders considered Miranda to blame; they thought he had sold out for the money. Led by Bolívar, they took Miranda prisoner in his lodgings and turned him over to the Spanish commander, listing him among the rebels as a traitor to his cause. Miranda was taken to a prison in Spain where he was kept in chains until he died four years later. The last attempt of the "Morning Star" had not been in vain, however, for his Venezuelan Republic was to be permanently revived within a decade.

Bolívar, with a passport from the Spanish commander, perhaps as a price for the arrest of Miranda, was permitted to go to Curaçao in August of

1812; from there he, rather than the "Morning Star," went to join a group of revolutionists who were seemingly succeeding in Cartagena, and to accept from their new governor a commission as colonel in the New Granadan army. Thus ended the First Venezuelan Republic.

What manner of man was Simón Bolívar—idealist, patriot, or, as one of his biographers calls him, "The Passionate Warrior"? How could he thus send his revered older leader to the dungeons? His treatment of Miranda is still unexplained, and is one of the few blots on an otherwise spectacular career of service and self-sacrifice. A very wealthy young creole born in 1783 in Caracas, heir to a four-million-peso estate, he had been orphaned at an early age and was raised by uncles and tutors. As a youth of great intellectual ability he had watched with interest the French Revolution and the rise of Napoleon. After an early and very romantic marriage he had lost his young bride in an epidemic. To ease his sorrow he traveled extensively in Europe, accompanied by Simón Rodríguez, a wise old tutor and scholar of the Enlightenment. On the Aventine Hill in Rome, after he and his tutor had spent the afternoon discussing South America's problems, Bolívar suddenly fell on his knees and made a solemn oath to "never allow my hands to be idle nor my soul to rest until I have broken the shackles which chain us to Spain."

A short man with irregular features, Bolívar had such "alert and penetrating eyes" as to inspire all who met him. Though he never remarried, he was a favorite with the ladies. The girls of Caracas threw roses ahead of his horse's feet when he came triumphant into the city; ladies in Quito rivaled each other in giving him parties, and his devotion to a mistress or two did not deter other ladies from patriotic adulation. On the trail and the battlefield his skill in handling arms and horses won men's admiration also. The war was his whole life; his personal fortune was spent for the cause, his plantations were ruined by the fighting; he himself freed all his slaves.

It is difficult to follow his activities from his betrayal of Miranda in 1812 to the surrender of the last Spanish army in South America in 1826, while he wrote and made speeches, danced and made love, crossed rivers and mountains and fought in the thick of battle. We left him en route by British ship to Cartagena after the fall of Venezuela in 1812. He arrived there, an unknown young upstart, full of a dream of a great federation of Gran Colombia, a free union of all northern South America.

winning northern South America

New Granada, today's Colombia, had meanwhile followed a very complicated course, corresponding to the rough and mountainous character of the land and the confusing variations of population. Bogotá and Cartagena each had a separate revolution, while the towns on the passes into Ecuador, Popayán and Pasto, remained hotbeds of royalist feeling. Bogotá, the center of science and intellectual pursuits, with a vivid memory of the comunero revolts against excessive taxation in the 1780s and the secretly printed

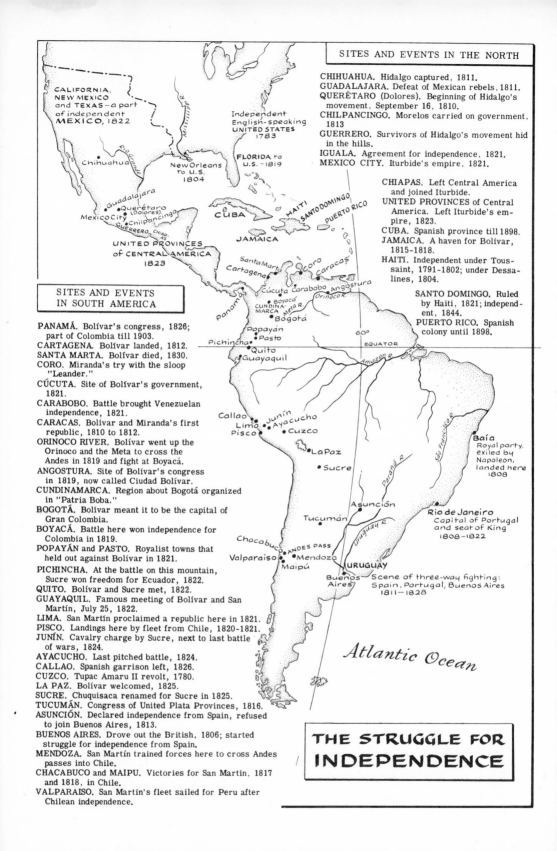

CALIFORNIA,
NEW MEXICO
and TEXAS—a part
of independent
MEXICO, 1822

Independent
English-speaking
UNITED STATES
1783

Chihuahua

New Orleans
to U.S.
1804

FLORIDA to
U.S.-1819

CHIHUAHUA. Hidalgo captured, 1811.
GUADALAJARA. Defeat of Mexican rebels, 1811.
QUERÉTARO (Dolores). Beginning of Hidalgo's
movement, September 16, 1810.
CHILPANCINGO. Morelos carried on government,
1813
GUERRERO. Survivors of Hidalgo's movement hid
in the hills.
IGUALA. Agreement for independence, 1821.
MEXICO CITY. Iturbide's empire, 1821.

CHIAPAS. Left Central America
and joined Iturbide.
UNITED PROVINCES of Central
America. Left Iturbide's empire, 1823.
CUBA. Spanish province till 1898.
JAMAICA. A haven for Bolívar,
1815-1818.
HAITI. Independent under Toussaint, 1791-1802; under Dessalines, 1804.

SANTO DOMINGO. Ruled
by Haiti, 1821; independ-
ent, 1844.
PUERTO RICO. Spanish
colony until 1898.

CUBA
HAITI
SANTO DOMINGO
PUERTO RICO
JAMAICA

Guadalajara
Querétaro
(Dolores)
Mexico City Chilpancingo
GUERRERO CHIAPAS
UNITED PROVINCES
of CENTRAL AMERICA
1823

Santa Marta
Cartagena
Coro
Caracas
Cúcuta Carabobo Angostura
Boyacá Orinoco R.
CUNDINA-
MARCA Meta R.
Bogotá
Popayán
Pasto
Pichincha Quito
Guayaquil

60°
EQUATOR
Amazon R.
Panamá

SITES AND EVENTS
IN SOUTH AMERICA

PANAMÁ. Bolívar's congress, 1826;
part of Colombia till 1903.
CARTAGENA. Bolívar landed, 1812.
SANTA MARTA. Bolívar died, 1830.
CORO. Miranda's try with the sloop
"Leander."
CÚCUTA. Site of Bolívar's government,
1821.
CARABOBO. Battle brought Venezuelan
independence, 1821.
CARACAS. Bolívar and Miranda's first
republic, 1810 to 1812.
ORINOCO RIVER. Bolívar went up the
Orinoco and the Meta to cross the
Andes in 1819 and fight at Boyacá.
ANGOSTURA. Site of Bolívar's congress
in 1819, now called Ciudad Bolívar.
CUNDINAMARCA. Region about Bogotá organized
in "Patria Boba."
BOGOTÁ. Bolívar meant it to be the capital of
Gran Colombia.
BOYACÁ. Battle here won independence for
Colombia in 1819.
POPAYÁN and PASTO. Royalist towns that
held out against Bolívar in 1821.
PICHINCHA. At the battle on this mountain,
Sucre won freedom for Ecuador, 1822.
QUITO. Bolívar and Sucre met, 1822.
GUAYAQUIL. Famous meeting of Bolívar and San
Martín, July 25, 1822.
LIMA. San Martín proclaimed a republic here in 1821.
PISCO. Landings here by fleet from Chile, 1820-1821.
JUNÍN. Cavalry charge by Sucre, next to last battle
of wars, 1824.
AYACUCHO. Last pitched battle, 1824.
CALLAO. Spanish garrison left, 1826.
CUZCO. Tupac Amaru II revolt, 1780.
LA PAZ. Bolívar welcomed, 1825.
SUCRE. Chuquisaca renamed for Sucre in 1825.
TUCUMÁN. Congress of United Plata Provinces, 1816.
ASUNCIÓN. Declared independence from Spain, refused
to join Buenos Aires, 1813.
BUENOS AIRES. Drove out the British, 1806; started
struggle for independence from Spain.
MENDOZA. San Martín trained forces here to cross Andes
passes into Chile.
CHACABUCO and MAIPU. Victories for San Martín, 1817
and 1818, in Chile.
VALPARAISO. San Martín's fleet sailed for Peru after
Chilean independence.

Callao
Lima Junín Ayacucho
Pisco Cuzco
La Paz
Sucre

Baía
Royal party,
exiled by
Napoleon,
landed here
1808

São Francisco R.

Asunción
Tucumán

Rio de Janeiro
Capital of Portugal
and seat of King
1808-1822

Chacabuco ANDES PASS
Valparaiso Mendoza
Maipú

Paraná R.
Uruguay R.

URUGUAY
Buenos
Aires

Scene of three-way fighting:
Spain, Portugal, Buenos Aires
1811-1828

Atlantic Ocean

THE STRUGGLE FOR
INDEPENDENCE

French revolutionary literature of Nariño, was quick to respond to Caracas' example. On July 20, 1810, influenced by the stirring writings of an idealistic Bogotá lawyer named Camilo Torres, the Bogotá creoles set up their own junta, "loyal to Ferdinand VII and to no other." Cartagena went further and on November 11, 1811, declared independence. But each town wanted to head a confederation of New Granadan cities. Cartagena called its organization the United Provinces of New Granada, while Bogotá proclaimed the independent republic of Cundinamarca—the name of the province around Bogotá—on July 16, 1813.

Under Camilo Torres and the fiery Nariño, now returned from prison, the idealists of Bogotá argued endlessly over a model constitution. At the critical moment when a compact union was required, petty details involved the parochial civilians to such an impractical extent that Colombians call the following five-year period of Bogotá history *La Patria Boba,* the Foolish Fatherland. Its idealistic laws were never carried out, its fine speeches never listened to, while Nariño fought the republicans of Cartagena in a civil war on one hand and the Spanish loyalists on the other. He was captured and sent to Spain in chains, while New Granada was being reconquered by the royalists.

Bolívar, exile from the First Venezuelan Republic, had been made first a colonel and then a general in the Cartagenan forces. While the two New Granadan cities fought each other, he issued a famous manifesto to the people of New Granada, appealing for their aid to liberate Venezuela. Then, after campaigning brilliantly along the lower Magdalena and ridding the area of loyalists, he proclaimed "War to the Death" and took Cartagenan troops into Venezuelan territory. After ninety days of unexpected victories he entered Caracas in triumph a second time on August 6, 1813, and had his first taste of flower-strewn streets. Given the title of "Liberator" he soon became dictator of the Second Republic of Venezuela which was set up.

This republic was as short-lived as the first. Many Venezuelans were blindly loyal to the king, including poor Indian cowboys from the Orinoco who joined an army under a savage cowboy general named José Tomás Boves. Boves then made a counter declaration of "War to the Death" against the rebels from Cartagena. It was brother against brother, without mercy to prisoners, wounded, or noncombatants on either side. Running from the half-savage army of *llaneros* and Spanish regulars, taking with him 10,000 of the terrified population in a dismal column of half-naked and starving people, Bolívar abandoned Caracas, found refuge for his people in the villages in eastern Venezuela, and escaped alone to Cartagena.

It was September, 1814, and Napoleon had already been defeated in Europe. New troops of the now-reinstated King Ferdinand were on the way to the Cartagena coast. Back in New Granada Bolívar had succeeded in an expedition to force Cundinamarca and Bogotá into confederation with Cartagena, but his short-lived success there was ended by the arrival of 10,000 new Spanish troops. In May of 1815 the "Liberator" had no choice save resignation and ignominious flight to Jamaica. Cartagena stood 106 days of bitter siege and fell to the new royalist troops. The year 1815 was a black one for the patriot cause. Ferdinand's most capable general, Pablo Morillo, occupied Venezuela, by then mainly royalist, and went on to Cartagena and up to Bogotá. All northern South America was again a "loyal" Spanish colony, while the stauncher patriots of *La Patria Boba* went underground.

In exile in Jamaica, the Liberator wrote letters, made plans for model governments and large-scale South American confederations, and seethed with ideas of reconquest of the mainland to win the liberty of the Americas. After other defeats in Venezuela his plans changed. His hopes centered on the Orinoco Valley, where the *llaneros,* such fierce fighters for the king three years before, had turned in wrath against their cruel General Boves and now craved excitement on the patriots' side. A rebel army of 1,500 of them was formed under their own illiterate and colorful leader, José Antonio Páez. In the spring of 1818 Bolívar joined Páez at Angostura, today called Ciudad Bolívar, on the Orinoco. There the Liberator called a congress and set up the Third Venezuelan Republic. He eloquently addressed the tiny group of patriots who attended his congress and announced plans to cross the Andes and liberate New Granada. At that congress which met on February 15, 1819, Bolívar was elected president and dictator of the war areas.

Bolívar's real success started from Angostura. Leaving Páez to command in Venezuela and harass Caracas from the rear, he took 1,300 infantrymen and 800 cavalrymen and set out on his daring scheme. Unbelievable as it seems, for no explorer would start such a trip on foot today, he took his little army of ragged plainsmen up to the headwaters of an Orinoco tributary, then into the Andes and up to 13,000 feet elevation across a snow-covered plateau at the top, and then down upon the surprised Spanish garrison outside Bogotá. His losses had been high, men had slipped to their death in the narrow passes or frozen in the snow, but the clash with the Spanish troops at Boyacá on August 7, 1819, was brief and overwhelmingly victorious, a turning-point in the struggle for independence in northern South America. New Granada was free. In seventy-five days he had "marched a thousand miles and emancipated a nation." Leaving his lieutenants in charge in the now exuberant Bogotá, he himself went back to Angostura via Cúcuta in the foothills, to report to his little government still existing there and to create the Union of New Granada and Venezuela.

To Angostura had come help from Britain, the long-awaited result of that first mission of Bolívar's to London. Perhaps 5,000 foreign legionnaires, veterans of Wellington's Napoleonic campaigns and now unemployed in postwar London, were glad to go to fight in South America. American privateers had joined in the struggle and helped free the Caribbean of Spanish ships. Now with Bolívar's victory at Boyacá the Angostura congress was a successful government; it proclaimed the creation of the Republic of Gran Colombia, Bolívar's idealistic federation of all northern South America. In 1821 the congress was moved to a new capital, Cúcuta, near today's Colombia-Venezuela border.

The congress of Cúcuta proceeded to make a new constitution for the larger nation. Bolívar was chosen president with command of the army,

while an ambitious Colombian civilian leader, Francisco de Paula Santander, was made the vice president in Bogotá, to do the actual governing.
Bolívar was now ready to take his combined new army—the veterans of
Boyacá, the *llaneros* of Páez, the foreign legionnaires—on to liberate the
heart of Venezuela and then to Quito or Lima. For a few months it seemed
that he would not have to; the liberals at home in Spain, under Riego, had
revolted against Ferdinand and wished to pacify the colonists. There was to
be a six-month truce while commissioners came from Spain to set up the
new arrangements. Not liking to make a truce, Morillo resigned and was
succeeded by General Miguel de la Torre. Bolívar had been suspicious of
the truce and its proponents; his followers had lost their loyalty to Ferdinand and yearned for the complete independence they had fought for.
When the visiting commissioners asked for an oath of allegiance to the
Spanish constitution and merely promised that delegates from South
America should sit in the Spanish *cortes,* Bolívar broke the truce. His troops
fought a last decisive battle against the Spanish garrisons of Venezuela at
Carabobo, June 24, 1821, and freed Venezuela from Spain forever.

Now the Spanish Main was one united state, and Bolívar turned his
attention southward. Cities in Ecuador had tried to establish juntas in 1809
and 1811, but their revolutions had been wiped out by troops from loyalist
Lima and the independence movement had remained quiescent. Between
Colombia and Quito lay the staunchly loyalist towns of Popayán and Pasto.
Bolívar planned to win over these towns with his own personal persuasion,
and set out overland through them with a small army. Fortunately, he sent a
trusted lieutenant and military genius, Antonio-José de Sucre, down to
Guayaquil by sea with another army. Sucre proceeded to win and lose and
win again in the country inland from Guayaquil, and then to move his
troops up the Andes toward Quito. While Bolívar was meeting one of his
most serious personal reverses in the narrow passes approaching Pasto,
Sucre lined up what troops he had on the side of a volcano overlooking
Quito, and won a decisive victory for the Colombian forces at Mount
Pichincha on May 24, 1822.

When Bolívar arrived three weeks later he proclaimed the annexation of Quito and Guayaquil to his Gran Colombia republic. Thus Boyacá
had won Colombia; Carabobo, Venezuela; and Pichincha, Ecuador—a firm
foundation of victories upon which lasting independence could be built.
Peru, most loyal of Spanish colonies, remained for the patriots to attack, but
this was eventually done with aid from Argentina and Chile, where similar
movements had been taking place from 1810 to 1820, and other heroes had
been crossing the Andes and liberating cities.

independence in southern South America

The creoles in Buenos Aires had already learned to fight independently of
Spain, for in 1807 they had beaten off the second English expedition against
the Plata colony. The hero of that victory, Liniers, had served as viceroy,
and had then been replaced by the unpopular Baltazar de Cisneros. The

creoles were already plotting against him when they received news that Napoleon had overrun Spain. The patriots then arranged for a *cabildo abierto*, which soon appointed a creole junta and ousted the viceroy, this in front of a cheering crowd gathered in the Plaza de Mayo in the autumn drizzle of May 25, 1810, one of the celebration days of today's Argentina. Henceforward, loyalty to the imprisoned Ferdinand was forgotten, and the Plata region was the one colony that was never again to revert to Spanish rule after 1810.

The wars in southern South America now divided into three phases. Colonials there had reason to fear invasion from Brazil. The Portuguese royal family had escaped from Napoleon to come to Rio, and had brought with them the wife of the prince regent, the Spanish princess Carlota Joaquina, Ferdinand's sister and the only member of the royal family not in the clutches of Napoleon. As the Spanish heir she was trying to carve out a kingdom on the Plata and might be able to back her claim with Brazilian troops. To the northwest, Spanish royalist troops were entrenched in Lima and threatened the pampas from the Bolivian Andes. Thirdly, and in all directions, the jealous and ambitious port of Buenos Aires tried to bring all other Spanish colonies on the various Plata tributaries, the old viceroyalty of the Plata, under the direct control of that city. Actually more troops and funds were expended in this effort than in any fighting against Spain and Brazil.

While thus involved in a three-pronged fight, the people of Buenos Aires proceeded to conduct a quarrelsome government similar to Colombia's *Patria Boba*. Mariano Moreno, enthusiastic newspaper editor and admirer of the United States, held out for the formation of a republic. His bitter disputes with conservative leaders who favored inviting a European prince to serve as constitutional monarch in a "Kingdom of the Plata" disrupted efforts at real government. Moreno's enemies were pleased when he died en route on a mission for help from England and was buried at sea. "It took all that water to put out so much fire," they said. His death brought no peace to Buenos Aires and one government followed another in confusion, while men and resources were drained off to fight elsewhere.

General of these armies fighting the other colonies was Manuel Belgrano. From 1811 to 1813 he was busy in the foothills leading to Bolivia. He subjugated a separatist movement in Córdoba and fought on up into the *altiplano* as far as Lake Titicaca. After meeting varying fortune, he was turned back out of Upper Peru by the firmly entrenched Spanish loyalists. Then they followed his ragged troops on down into the pampas where the Spaniards were stopped and pushed back. After 1815 the royalists were stopped from invading modern Argentina by a gaucho guerrilla band under a local chieftain named Martín Güemes, who fought them for two years in the foothills and so scorched the earth there as to keep them out of the fertile lowlands throughout the rest of the independence period.

Belgrano had meantime turned the attention of Buenos Aires and its armies to Paraguay in 1811. Creole sentiment there was as strongly separatist as that of the port, but the Paraguayans, always considering themselves superior to the pampa colonists, were determined not to be dominated by either port or mother country. Paraguayan troops defeated Belgrano when he invaded their river territory; then the Paraguayans combined under a fantastic lawyer, Dr. José Gaspar Rodríguez de Francia, to set up their own junta and make their own declaration of independence on October 12, 1813. "These are the arguments which I bring against the supremacy of Fernando Séptimo," Dr. Francia said as he laid two loaded pistols on the table at a junta meeting. No one brought loaded pistols to bear against his own supremacy, and he became the dictator of Paraguay till his death in 1840, keeping it an isolated hermit kingdom, and calling himself *El Supremo*, the Supreme One.

More complicated were the events on the eastern shore of the Uruguay River, along the Eastern Strip, the *Banda Oriental*, that was to become the modern nation of Uruguay. A four-sided struggle took place there till 1821. Belgrano and his troops from the port again entered the picture. Opposed to him were three factions. The first was a loyalist force under Elío firmly entrenched in Montevideo. Brazilian troops, invited to relieve Spanish troops besieged in Montevideo by patriotic forces, made up the second faction and later laid claim to the Eastern Strip. Finally, as a third force, there was a band of ardent gauchos from the interior under a romantic leader named José Gervasio Artigas, who wanted a Uruguayan autonomy apart from both Spain and Buenos Aires. Spain withdrew by 1814; quarrels at home brought disgrace to Belgrano; but Artigas and his ragged army of gauchos and their families continued a guerrilla campaign until only a few fighting men were left alive. Then Artigas escaped to live out a lonely exile in Paraguay. Meanwhile, the Brazilians again occupied the area in 1816 and formally annexed the *Banda Oriental* in 1821. The gauchos and the Montevideans alike were to wait for independence until another series of three-way fights in 1825.

Some semblance of unity on the Plata without Bolivia, Paraguay, and Uruguay had been achieved by the Buenos Aires government. The Plata cities of Córdoba, Tucumán, Mendoza, and Santa Fé had little choice save to join with Buenos Aires in the face of the constant threat of Spanish invasion from Upper Peru. Buenos Aires conceded to the idea of a loose federation without agreeing on a constitutional principle. Thus a congress met at the city of Tucumán to decide on a government for the entire pampas region. They failed to agree on a constitution, but independence for the whole area was actually declared here for the first time on July 9, 1816, and the United Provinces of South America was proclaimed. This was a union in name only, however. Each province maintained an army, as much to keep down Buenos Aires as to ward off a re-invasion by Spain. A state of anarchy persisted, and the quarrel between Buenos Aires and the hinterland colored Argentine affairs for many decades.

Now the real hero of South America enters the story, José de San Martín. He was born an Argentine creole in 1778, but had gone to Spain as a very young cadet and had served faithfully as an officer in the wars against Napoleon. In 1812 he returned to his native land, determined to work for freedom there. Though only thirty-four years old, he could claim twenty-two years of military experience in the Spanish army. As a member of the Lautaro Lodge of the Masons in Buenos Aires, he came to the attention of the junta by offering to help train patriot soldiers in the methods he had learned in Spain. By 1814 he was commander in chief in charge of patriot troops fighting in the foothills north of Tucumán.

Suddenly San Martín resigned this post on the excuse of ill health and asked to be made military governor of the community of Cuyo province on the edge of the Andes across from Chile. All this was part of his long-range plan, which eventually freed South America from Spanish troops. San Martín knew that as long as any part of South America was in royalist hands, independence was in jeopardy. He had decided that Lima, the Spanish stronghold, could not be approached through well-fortified Upper Peru. With Mendoza as a base, "to cross into Chile with a small well-disciplined army is my course, there can be no other." Combined forces from the pampas and Chile could then go on to Peru.

At Mendoza he set about steering that course. All western Argentina helped him, the men training in the army, making special shoes for mules and horses to cross the mountains, casting cannon and shot, while women spun and wove cold-weather uniforms and prepared compact rations for the army which was to cross over the Andes at over 12,000 feet. Down in Buenos Aires Supreme Director Juan Martín de Pueyrredón, from 1816 to 1819 head of government and San Martín's personal friend, knew his plans and sent him sporadic help of men and money, as well as endless unnecessary instructions. But the citizens of Mendoza bore the bulk of the costs.

What had taken place in Chile meanwhile? Throughout the summer of 1810 Chilean creoles had agitated against the Spanish authorities and finally threw them out in a mass meeting on September 18, 1810, today Chile's principal national holiday. In the junta and the congress which proceeded to meet, two parties developed, the radicals led by the young Bernardo O'Higgins, natural son of a former Irish-born viceroy, and the landed aristocrats, led by the Carrera family. While the two factions bickered, Spanish forces from Lima met the "army" of creoles led by O'Higgins at Rancagua in October of 1814 and put them completely to rout. The junta's rule was ended; leaders of both factions escaped to Mendoza, where San Martín listened to each side and conferred his trust on O'Higgins' party.

Now with reinforcements from O'Higgins, San Martín had 2,500 foot soldiers and 700 mounted men ready for the mountain passes. The artillery pieces went by a special pack train which carried a cable bridge, anchors, and grapnels to get the cannon over narrow bridges and rough precipices. Nearly half the 2,000 mules and horses were lost en route, but the men got through; within three weeks they were in the fertile valley of Chile. Here a decisive victory was won against the Spanish soldiers at Chacabuco on February 12, 1817. The troops entered Santiago the next day, where a *cabildo abierto* soon declared O'Higgins "Supreme Dictator." One more battle, on the plains of Maipú a year later, April 5, 1818, had to be fought to make Chile forever free of Spanish royalists. Chilean independence was declared February 12, 1818; then Bernardo O'Higgins joined with San Martín in making plans to get their joint armies up to Lima.

the conquest of Peru, last Spanish stronghold

A sea-borne attack was the only solution, but how was it possible without ships? After Chacabuco and again after Maipú, San Martín had returned across the Andes and the pampas to Buenos Aires for help and money. An agent sent to the United States was able to procure two vessels with Buenos Aires money and dispatch them around the Horn to Valparaiso, but this was the last help San Martín was to get from his native land. The current dictator blamed him for wasting lives and funds in Chile, and "recalled" the Argentine army. San Martín resigned his Buenos Aires commission and he and his soldiers henceforth were in the employ of Chile.

That nation meanwhile had joined with English commercial interests and purchased a frigate, renamed the *Lautaro*. This and the American ships, together with two captured Spanish frigates, made the "Chilean Navy," the first in Latin America. To turn the navy into an "invasion fleet" O'Higgins hired a brilliant English naval officer in bad repute at home, Thomas Lord Cochrane. Cochrane captured more Spanish ships on forays up the coast, converted several fishing boats, and had a total of twenty-four ships and 1,600 sailors by August 1820. The soldiers totaled 4,430, 1,805 of them Chileans, 2,313 of San Martín's original men from Mendoza, and 332 soldiers of fortune—Irishmen, Englishmen, and Americans. With San Martín in command this motley fleet, carrying additional supplies to outfit the 15,000 volunteers he hoped to organize among the patriots of Peru, set sail from Valparaiso. Through widespread propaganda San Martín wanted to stir the Peruvians to win their own independence.

In Peru there were Spanish armies totaling over 16,000 men. A weak little independence movement led by poets and college professors had come to nothing, for Lima was full of Spanish aristocrats, and the Spanish viceroy during the Napoleonic period had been a strong and aggressive man. An uprising in Cuzco in 1814—a replica of the former Tupac Amaru revolution—had been suppressed. Creole leaders had been executed while the revolt was young. Thus there had been no independent government in Peru, no junta supposedly acting for Ferdinand during his imprisonment, though there was increasing unrest.

San Martín and Cochrane came at an opportune moment. Many Indians joined their armies; towns along the southern Peruvian coast welcomed them. A new viceroy sent from Spain was willing to dicker rather than fight. San Martín suggested a deal by which independence would be declared and then a young prince of the royal Spanish house would become the constitutional monarch of South America, such a scheme having probably been part of San Martín's philosophy from the first. The viceroy stalled the proceedings, evidently hoping for reinforcements from Spain. They never came, because of that revolt of the soldiers in Cádiz.

San Martín was not willing to be lulled by a truce as Bolívar had been. He came up the coast, landed south of Lima, won many converts without much fighting, and scared the most conservative loyalist families into fleeing to the interior. Now Lima rushed to invite San Martín in. The wild demonstration that met him there on July 12, 1821, touched the heart of even this very austere and selfless man. He told the Peruvians simply that "all I wish is that this country should be managed by itself alone." When a suitable government had been established by the Peruvians, "I shall consider that I have done enough, and leave them." He participated in a Peruvian declaration of independence on July 28, 1821, and then, as Protector of Peru, proceeded to worry over driving the strong Spanish forces out of the Andes valleys. He had quarreled with Lord Cochrane, who took many of the sailors and went back to Chile. The royalists in the interior mountains were gaining strength. There was criticism of San Martín in Lima. San Martín knew he would need help from other patriot forces in order to liberate Peru.

Meanwhile, a rival "Liberator" had appeared to the north. Bolívar's forces had conquered Ecuador, and that northern leader was now dancing and dining in Guayaquil, and glancing southward toward the last Spanish royalist stronghold. Most historians think that Bolívar was very jealous of San Martín; in his writing he claimed to be afraid of San Martín's plans for an over-all constitutional monarchy. San Martín himself knew the two should cooperate and get this Spanish business finished; he announced early in 1822 that he would sail up to Guayaquil to work out some plan with Bolívar. Quite a correspondence between the two resulted, all very flowery and mutually congratulatory. Then San Martín arrived in Guayaquil, on July 25, and was welcomed to "Colombian soil" by Bolívar.

There followed two days of meetings between the two at a house near the waterfront in Guayaquil, now marked as a shrine of South American history. No one else was present; no minutes were kept. Did they discuss a joint command? a plan of campaign? a future government for all South America? Did Bolívar refuse to join his forces for the victory unless he had supreme command and San Martín was completely out of the picture? At any rate, it was one of the most dramatic meetings in history and it resulted in one of the most unselfish acts. Next day, July 27, San Martín took ship and returned to Lima. From there he wrote Bolívar that the loyalists in the mountain strongholds outnumbered him two to one, but that some immediate action should be taken and he would be willing to resign his command to Bolívar and return to Chile if the northern forces would come to Peru. A Peruvian congress met in September 1822, to take over the government of Lima. In an eloquent speech before it, San Martín resigned to return home as a civilian leaving all behind him. In both Chile and Buenos Aires he found himself unpopular as an ill-advised waster of public funds. Already in ill health, he went quietly to live in Paris on a small pension he received, ironically enough, from a former companion-in-arms in the fight for Spain against Napoleon. Only after his death in 1850 did this self-effacing hero receive honor from the South American nations as a patriot and liberator.

After waiting for an "urgent" invitation from Peru which did not come immediately, Bolívar sailed to Callao in September 1823, and was given supreme command of the weakening Peruvian situation. Again Sucre, the able lieutenant, planned the campaign. With 6,000 Venezuelans and Colombians who had come to Peru with Bolívar, combined with 4,000 Argentines and Chileans, he prepared to meet the Spanish host of 16,000. In a dramatic charge on August 6, 1824, on the Plains of Junín, Bolívar's own horsemen, without firing a shot and fighting only with swords and lances like medieval knights, routed the cream of the Spanish cavalry and drove them back to Cuzco. Mestizos and Indians deserted from the Spanish forces, soon leaving less than 10,000 royal troops, of which only 500 were regulars from Spain.

With Bolívar busy organizing the government and attending social functions in Lima, Sucre took the initiative after Junín and brought his whole army to a well-chosen narrow valley at Ayacucho. Here on December 9, 1824, after a single morning's battle, the entire Spanish army together with the viceroy himself surrendered to the patriots. This battle is considered the final victory in the wars for independence.

Only Upper Peru, the towns of Chuquisaca, Potosí, and La Paz, remained unorganized. They had tried for liberty and independence three times in the period from 1808 to 1822, but had never succeeded. In the spring of 1825 both Bolívar and Sucre, with peace established everywhere, came to La Paz to create a separate nation. Independence was declared in La Paz on August 6, 1825. The citizens, not Bolívar himself, named the state Bolivia, but Bolívar had practically a free hand in writing its constitution throughout 1826. He created a strong executive presidency, elected for life, and left Sucre to fill the post. But the young Sucre did not get along with the high-altitude dwellers of La Paz, and after a short, stormy regime he resigned to go back to Quito. The city of Chuquisaca was renamed Sucre in his honor, so that his name as well as Bolívar's is preserved on the map. Bolívar himself went back to Gran Colombia in 1826 to report to the congress that the Spaniards were gone from South America forever. Once peace was established, Bolívar found no place for himself. Gran Colombia was to disintegrate within a very few years into the states of Venezuela, Colombia, and Ecuador, while Bolívar died of tuberculosis, alone and in poverty. But at least South America was freed from Europe.

*the independence movement
in Spanish North America*

In Mexico, royalist control was stronger throughout the independence area than in South America and it held separatistic revolutions in check more successfully, so that when independence did come for Mexico it came as a conservative compromise in the form of a short-lived empire. However, the movement there contained two civil wars—peninsular versus creole and white versus Indian—to a larger extent than in South America. The first revolution, under Hidalgo, was more of a social and racial revolt and was led by lower clergymen in the name of religion and the lower classes; the creoles opposed and crushed it, only to complete the work of independence themselves after the liberal revolution in Spain in 1820 rather than join in with that constitutional movement.

The news of Napoleon's invasion of Spain caused confusion in Mexico and became an excuse for each faction to claim the right to take over the government. The creole-dominated *ayuntamiento* rejected Napoleon, declared for a junta in the name of Ferdinand, and wanted popular sovereignty and equality with the people and provinces of Spain. The *gachupín*-dominated *audiencia* also rejected Napoleon, declared for a junta in the name of the king, and refused to accept any idea of popular sovereignty and equality with Spain. The viceroy José de Iturrigaray, an ambitious and opportunistic creature of Godoy, thought that he could not lose in such a situation, that if he worked with Napoleon, he might even become king of Mexico. He was flattered by the creoles and fell into their trap—thinking himself safe when on their side.

When the creoles threatened to act first, the *audiencia* staged a coup d'état led by Gabriel Yermo. The viceroy was deposed, a puppet placed in his office, and a new viceroy awaited from Spain. Outwitted and outplayed by the *gachupines*, the creoles organized "literary" and secret societies and went underground. In August 1810, Francisco Xavier Venegas, the viceroy, arrived from Spain, and quiet reigned in the capital.

Not so in the northern cities. In Querétaro a secret group was led by Miguel de Hidalgo y Costilla, a gentle old creole parish priest of the nearby village of Dolores. An intellectual of "enlightened" ideas, he had often clashed with his superiors over improvements for his Indian charges. He and other conspirators in Querétaro, discouraged at the acceptance of the new Spanish viceroy by Mexico City liberals, decided to declare Mexico independent at a large regional fair set for December 1810. Unfortunately, the plot leaked out and a young captain named Ignacio Allende, a fellow conspirator, dashed through the night of September 15 out to the village of Dolores to warn Hidalgo of his threatened arrest.

Awakened at midnight, Hidalgo tolled his church bells, and before the startled Indian parishioners who assembled he proclaimed: "Long live Ferdinand VII! Long live religion and death to bad government!" With these words, Hidalgo meant to start a rebellion in which his ultimate goal was independence. This was the famous *Grito de Dolores*, or Shout, enacted by a leading official in towns of Mexico at midnight on every September 15, to this day. After that first *Grito*, Hidalgo, his parishioners, Allende, and the troops under his command set out with the banner of the Virgin of Guadalupe to capture the city of Guanajuato. This was a social revolution in the name of religion, backed by the lower classes, led by a priest, and opposed by the Church and both the *gachupines* and creoles as well.

Hidalgo's army amassed before Guanajuato within the week numbered a rabble of 50,000 Indians and mestizo peons, unarmed save for farm tools, and expecting Hidalgo to lead them to a better economic life. When the undisciplined army took the city they looted the homes of the aristocracy and killed many creole families.

As they advanced on other cities, as far as within sight of the capital, Hidalgo and Allende quarreled over disciplining the "army" and over planning military strategy. In Guadalajara by November, Hidalgo tried to form a government, set up a printing press, and formulate a policy. Though he was hoping for actual independence from Spain, he wanted to free the peons, procure lands for Indians, abolish Indian tribute, and give legal encouragement to native crafts and industries. The old priest had no time to work out this program peacefully—Indians were not to receive such recognition until another century had passed. On January 17, 1811, near Guadalajara, his forces met a complete defeat at the hands of trained regulars, when their munitions wagon exploded and set fire to the dry grass all around them. Both Allende and Hidalgo were captured as they fled northward. As a priest, Hidalgo went through a "defrocking" ceremony; then he and Allende were executed like common criminals.

The revolution did not die with them. Another parish priest, José María Morelos, had been sent by Hidalgo with a patrol of twenty-five men to plan some way to capture the port of Acapulco. There he had escaped the slaughter of the revolutionary leaders, and with 9,000 volunteers formed a guerrilla army in the hills of southwestern Mexico. A much better military planner and organizer than Hidalgo, Morelos continually harried the Spaniards and then slipped through their noose. While Napoleon fought in Spain, Morelos was able to hold a great part of southern Mexico. He had time, which Hidalgo never had, to form a government, to declare independence on November 6, 1813, at the town of Chilpancingo on the Acapulco road, and to frame a constitution at the village of Apatzingán in October, 1814, which set up a republic and abolished slavery and social and racial distinctions.

After 1814 more soldiers came from Spain to fight Morelos. On one occasion he was defeated while encamped on a rocky height by a young creole officer in the royalist army named Agustín de Iturbide, who scaled the rocks and surprised the patriots. Who was to foresee that when independence came six years later, it was to be Iturbide, turncoat that he was, who would get the credit? Defeat followed defeat for Morelos. Determined to maintain the legal basis of the revolution, he sacrificed himself to save the congress. When his whole government was surrounded, he sent the best of his army to conduct the congressional delegates to safety, while he allowed himself to be captured in a delaying action.

Morelos in his turn was defrocked and executed on December 22, 1815, still thinking that his congress was saved and that his government would live. But the congress disbanded and many patriots were captured. Although the royalists held Mexico firmly until the Revolution of 1820 in Spain, a mulatto named Vicente Guerrero held a group of guerrillas together in the hilly country south of Acapulco—today called the State of Guerrero; and a mestizo leader, Félix Fernández, who renamed himself Guadalupe Victoria in honor of Hidalgo's revolution, lived for many years as a starving hermit, surviving to become the first president of the Mexican Republic.

To the conservative in Mexico City, members of the *audiencia,* landed aristocrats, and upper clergymen, the constitutionalism of the 1820 revolt in Spain, with its radicalism, anticlericalism, and ideas of popular sovereignty, was more dangerous than an independent Mexico. Thus we have the anomaly of independence being achieved by the very men who fought Hidalgo and Morelos. They looked for a military leader to help them achieve such "conservative" independence, and found him in the self-seeking creole officer Agustín de Iturbide, who for some time had been in disgrace for grafting off the silver trains from northern Mexico which his troops had been sent to guard. He ingratiated himself with the right people through Church connections and soon found himself in command of the Spanish imperial forces, supposedly the tool of the new conspiracy.

As a first step he got in touch with the one remaining guerrilla leader of the former revolution, the leader Guerrero. With him he formulated the "Plan of Iguala." Mexican history for the next century was to be dominated by plans and proclamations of axioms or principles by the leaders of a rebellion, hatched in and named after some obscure village, and backed by an armed force. This first Plan was to set up an independent monarchy in Mexico, to offer the throne to Ferdinand himself if he would like to come to the New World, or to any young prince he might suggest. A congress was to meet and a constitution to be written making "Three Guarantees"—independence, equality of all races, and the established position and privileges of the Catholic Church.

This Plan, backed by the Army of the Three Guarantees commanded by Iturbide, quickly won victories, both military and political. The viceroy resigned and went to Spain; a new viceroy, Juan O'Donojú, sent by the constitutionalists in power at home, bowed to Iturbide's forces and signed a treaty with the Mexicans at Córdoba on August 24, 1821. This treaty incorporated all the ideas of the Plan of Iguala, except the insistence on a Spanish prince. By now the wily Iturbide was suggesting that if no European prince could be had, then a Mexican congress could appoint one of its own choosing. He dominated the interim junta and paraded his soldiers down the main avenues of Mexico City, while the Treaty of Córdoba was being rejected by the Spanish government. Soon Iturbide and congress quarreled over making the constitution. Some loyal soldiers in the army staged a planned barracks coup d'état and cheered for Emperor Agustín Iturbide the First. A purchased "rump" congress rubber-stamped this home-town choice, and Emperor Agustín I was crowned in Mexico City's cathedral, July 25, 1822.

While Iturbide set up an elaborate court with pomp exceeding that of any viceroy, leaders on all sides grew scornful of him. Guadalupe Victoria, now out of hiding, and the old Indian Guerrero were disillusioned; the creoles had no more power than before, the lower classes were living as poorly. When congress opposed Iturbide's expenditures, he dissolved it, jailing many of its members.

A young creole officer named Antonio López de Santa Anna, who was to dominate Mexican politics for three decades, took advantage of the disaffection to join with Guerrero and Victoria in a new Plan, this one formed at Casa Mata. This Plan accomplished the abdication and exile of the now unpopular Iturbide before his empire had lasted a year. In the fall of 1823 a new congress assembled, a new constitution providing for a federal republic was written, and Guadalupe Victoria became president. Nevertheless, there was to be no peace, for the army was controlled by the ambitious Santa Anna. Mexico was an independent republic, yes, but the old colonial creole class still ruled.

Iturbide's "revolt" against Spain was being closely watched in Central America. There had been short-lived juntas in 1810 in several of the Central American cities. Disaffection continued through the period of wars elsewhere; Panama held a *cabildo abierto* and joined Gran Colombia in 1821. When a *cabildo abierto* in Guatemala City declared independence on September 15, 1821, apparently forecasting a Central American republic, Iturbide sent an armed force to bring that area also under his power. The leaders in Guatemala voted in favor of Iturbide's empire. Before this union could be organized, however, his empire fell, and a congress called in Guatemala in July of 1823 voted to create the republic of the United Provinces of Central America. This federated republic, with its capital at Guatemala City, ruled the areas of Nicaragua, Costa Rica, El Salvador, Honduras, and Guatemala until it broke up into separate republics in 1839. Chiapas, a northernmost province ruled from Guatemala, stayed with the 1824 Republic of Mexico, and remains a state of Mexico to this day.

Santo Domingo, ruled from Haiti since 1795, had become restive under French Negro rule and expelled those invaders in 1814. In 1821 a revolt proclaimed independence for the Spanish-speaking part of the island and voted to join Gran Colombia; but Boyer came in, conquered it, and joined it to Haiti. It was twenty-two years later, in 1844, that Santo Domingo became a republic, an independence scarcely challenged by the homeland. In fact, nothing remained of the Spanish empire in the New World after 1825 save the islands of Cuba and Puerto Rico, which lived under the European yoke until the Spanish–American War of 1898.

Note: Readings for this chapter are given at the end of Chapter 17.

chapter 17

THE END OF AN ERA;
THE BEGINNING
OF A NEW ONE

problems of the green young nations

The new republics, the "Green Young Nations," sixteen of them by 1830, faced a tremendous job of rebuilding. Vast areas were devastated during the long period of fighting; the cattle industry was ruined where marauding soldiers slaughtered the herds for food; mining was set back by the loss of laborers and damage to installations; plantations lay wasted when freed slaves wandered away or had been drafted into armies and when *gachupín* owners of property went back to Spain. The wars broke up families, drove people from place to place, siphoned off young leaders, disrupted city life, drove away the trained bureaucrats from public work, left taxes uncollected and government obligations unpaid. Even church organization broke down because most bishops and archbishops had been loyal to Spain and anti-clerical feelings grew to become a factor in subsequent politics.

The wars for independence had been essentially political movements. The removal of the mother country left a vacuum which the new republics were hard-pressed to fill. They had to set up governments that had a legal basis and that the people accepted. They had to secure recognition in the eyes of the world as legal political entities. The fine words that had been written and spoken by heroic leaders on how these governments should be run came up against hard realities even while the wars were being fought.

Differences rose between classes and among regions. Constitutions were framed but the idealistic documents were completely ignored. Conservatives and liberals were quick to line up against each other—though political parties in the modern sense did not develop during the war. Finances were chaotic, and the lack of trained administrators increased the chaos. Where fighting had gone on, the military leader had become the government leader, and when peace came, he often remained as dictator. One problem was solved early, and that was the securing of recognition by other nations of the world, for without this recognition, weak and unformed nations labor under severe political and economic handicaps.

the foreign relations of the newly independent countries

The Spanish colonies proclaimed their own independence but needed recognition of that fact from Spain. European powers had sympathized with Spain and would not recognize the new nations if the mother country did not. As late as 1827, the Spanish foreign minister proclaimed Ferdinand's "unalterable resolution never to abandon his rights" and his refusal of all offers of mediation contemplating an acknowledgement of the independence of the new states. It was nearly ten years later that a liberal-minded *Cortes* under a new young queen, Isabella II, was able to reconsider the question and to send a favorable bill to the Queen, who, in December 1836, proclaimed the independence of Mexico. This was tardily followed by recognition of the other republics all of which came at a time when most of the revolutionary leaders were dead and the countries had been living without Spanish direction for fifteen years and more.

And what about the United States, whose own revolution had inspired the Latin American independence movement? A young nation herself, she could only express sympathy, watch the struggle, fight her own War of 1812 against the English, and declare her neutrality. When Ferdinand returned to the Spanish throne in 1814, the United States needed his friendship in order to settle the western boundary of the Louisiana Purchase and to acquire Florida. So she raised the revolting colonies to the status of belligerency, tightened neutrality laws, and sent commissioners to gather information.

The motives of the American government were mixed, confused by the conflict between its ideological sympathies and commercial interests, and between its fear of Europe and hopes of neutrality. Individual Americans sympathetic to the revolution, had gone adventuring with Miranda, served under Bolívar and Lord Cochrane, filibustered on Mexico's borders and privateered in the Caribbean. The revolution had sympathizers like Joel Poinsett, a wealthy South Carolinian who had been an American agent in Buenos Aires and Chile from 1810 to 1814, and who was destined to be the first American minister to independent Mexico. In Congress Henry Clay led the agitation for recognition of the states to the south; while Secretary of State John Quincy Adams opposed any official step that might anger Spain.

He wanted to wait until the United States could be absolutely sure the Latin American states could exist permanently and maintain law and order within their boundaries. A commission sent by Adams to check on conditions in Latin America disagreed on the desirability of recognition.

But by 1820, the Spanish American revolts promised success and Florida was safely purchased. Strict neutrality seemed no longer necessary. And Latin America was clamoring for recognition. San Martín was in Lima in 1821 and Iturbide had won independence for Mexico. Monroe urged recognition. In June 1822, the President formally received Manuel Torres, a *chargé d'affaires* from Colombia, and then, in rapid succession, other states were recognized.[1] Commercial and friendship treaties were signed.

To the "Green Young Nations," British recognition was more important than that of the weak new country to the north. British mercantile interests were eager for Latin American trade, but Spain was England's ally in the Peninsular War. She did not want to antagonize the Spaniards by recognizing the colonies. When Ferdinand was restored to the throne, he began to enforce trade regulations against English ships. Yet imperial England was in no position openly to condone interference in anyone's colonial empire. She played the double game of maintaining friendly relations with Spain and yet carrying on illegal commerce with Spanish America and permitting individual Englishmen privately to participate in the wars. English bankers openly made loans to the patriot governments.

When revolution came to Spain in 1820, the Quadruple Alliance attempted to put down the revolts with French troops and Austrian money. Britain withdrew from the Alliance at the Congress of Verona because she feared the powers in the Alliance would attempt to extend their interference to the Spanish colonies in the New World. She took note of Bolívar's successes, and of America's recognition of South America. British commercial interests were bringing increasing pressure toward English acceptance of the new states. So when the agents and commissions sent out by Parliament to investigate the situation reported back favorably, Britain took the logical step of recognizing most of the new nations and signing treaties with them by 1826.

France was under the domination of Metternich's system until the Revolution of 1830 which put Louis Philippe on the throne. Recognition of the Latin American republics followed, beginning with a treaty with Venezuela in 1832. Papal recognition began with Colombia in August 1835.

The Monroe Doctrine was a by-product of the Quadruple Alliance attempt to put down revolts against Spanish legal government. It was important not so much for what it did at the time as for what it was later to become. Actually it was simply a statement which President Monroe included in his message to Congress on December 2, 1823, to the effect that the United States would not tolerate the intrusion of an Old World political system in the Western hemisphere. When the French and Austrians had first

---

[1] The United States recognized Columbia and Mexico in 1822, Buenos Aires and Chile in 1823, Central America and Brazil in 1824, Peru in 1825.

threatened intervention, the British foreign minister, George Canning, suggested that the United States and Britain should issue a joint declaration. But John Quincy Adams, then Secretary of State in the United States, was jealous of American prestige and wanted to "go it alone," knowing quite well that the policy would still receive the protection of the British navy. So he influenced the President to state in his message that the United States would regard any attempt to extend the political systems of the European powers to any portion of this hemisphere as "dangerous to our peace and safety." Balancing this, it was the policy of the United States not to interfere in the internal concerns of European powers. The New World was no longer considered open to further colonization by any Europeean power. The United States would brook no interference with the new governments that had established their independence. Monroe's statement was also directed toward the Russians in the North Pacific area.

Metternich called the doctrine "indecent." England welcomed it with mixed feelings for she was tacitly included in the policy even though it was unilaterally issued. In the new Latin American states, where it was noted at all, it was received with pleasure. Santander, who was in charge of Colombia during Bolívar's absence in Peru, called it a "policy consolatory to human nature." But Lucas Alamán, a leading political philosopher in Mexico, was alarmed by the statement, seeing it as a "possible threat of North American imperialism." Actually, its major importance was the fact that it allowed Latin America to work out its own destiny. Up to this time, it had been a frontier of Europe; now it was part of the independent American continent, free to organize itself without the danger of intervention.

As early as 1814, Bolívar had conceived the idea of calling a Pan American Congress, one that might make the Isthmus of Panama the eventual site of a world capital. Just before the battle of Ayacucho, he invited the new states to send delegates to Panama, in the hope that "treaties of mutual cooperation" would be made there and a Pan American federation established. But of all the nations invited, only Mexico, the new Central American Federation, Colombia, and Peru sent delegates. He himself did not get to the meeting for he was still in Lima. Brazil, Chile, and Bolivia accepted the invitation but their delegates never arrived. Two representatives were appointed by the United States, but one died en route and the other arrived too late. The British and Dutch sent observers. The plan for a confederation suggested by the Peruvians was opposed by the Colombians. A proposal to submit boundary disputes to arbitration was accepted by the delegates but was ratified only by Columbia. The tragic outcome of this failure was a century of bloody wars over boundaries. Thus Bolívar's dream of a Pan American Federation came to naught.

philosophical ideas of the leaders

Bolívar found time in the midst of constant activity to plan a government for all South America. Eloquent in speech and writing, he set down his political program in memorials, letters, and *pronunciamientos*. Analyzing the reasons for the failure of his first republic, he said of the Venezuela government in a Memorial to the Citizens of New Granada in December 1812 that "We had philosophers for governors, philanthropy for legislation, dialectics for tactics, and sophists for soldiers." He foresaw the difficulties democracy would have in a land in which the people who had known only the colonial rule of Spain were incapable of a prudent and orderly exercise of the right of suffrage. His clear concept of the future of the Spanish American countries, depicted in his letter from Jamaica where Bolívar was in exile in 1815 was an unusually accurate prediction of the political confusion to come.

In a speech at the Congress of Angostura in 1819 Bolívar stated that "social perfection and perfect systems of government are noble ideals but legislators deal with men, not angels." Therefore the new states should have a strong executive, senators that served for life, and closely safeguarded voting restricted to the well-prepared. The Congress followed his advice and provided for a limited suffrage, a strong executive, and a lifetime term for senators. When in 1826 he was challenged to defend his plan for a strong presidency for Bolivia that was actually a monarchy in disguise, he said that "Spanish America contained neither great wealth nor powerful ecclesiastics nor an ambitious clergy nor great nobles. Without these to support them tyrants could not be permanent. . . ." He was certain there need be no fear of monarchs being established in America. It is true, as it happened, that in only one instance, that of the López family in Paraguay, was an attempt made to pass power over to sons, and that instance brought tragic results to the nation, but it is also true that some of the powerful dictator chieftains, the *caudillos* of Latin America's 19th century, were as powerful as kings.

Bolívar feared both the establishment of one big state and the breaking up of Latin America into many small states. If a single monarchical state would be established, "the clumsy colossus would die of convulsion." What he favored was one republic for northern South America, his idealistic scheme for Gran Colombia—and perhaps an equally large unit for the south, each a big, strong republic based on "the sovereignty of the people, the division of power, civil liberty, prohibition of slavery, the abolition of monarchy and of privileges." He was opposed to federalism because it provided too weak an executive.

The ignorance of the citizens, the inexperience of the people in government and the dissolution of Gran Colombia brought Bolívar bitterness before his death. "Those who have worked for the cause of Latin American freedom have ploughed the sea!" he wrote despairingly in 1829. "We have tried all systems; nothing has proved effective. Mexico has fallen; Guatemala is destroyed; there are new revolutions in Chile. In Buenos Aires they have killed the president. Bolivia had three presidents in two days, and two of them have been murdered." He saw Latin America as "a chaos of passions, difficulties, and disorders." In the newly freed nations he found "neither faith nor truth, whether it be among men or among nations. Treaties are mere scraps of paper, constitutions are books, elections are battles, freedom is anarchy." Anarchy had driven him out of leadership in his own Caracas, and then had deposed him as president at Bogotá after

Gran Colombia fell to pieces. He was saved from assassination when he was warned in time by a faithful mistress, Manuela Sáenz, to jump out of a window and hide under a bridge. A victim of tuberculosis, contracted during his campaigns in Ecuador, Bolívar caught cold while en route to Cartagena in 1830 to help stop a rebellion. Attended by a French doctor a few days before his death, he asked what had brought the doctor to the New World and was told it was the wish to find liberty—which he had found. "You have been more fortunate than I, doctor," said Bolívar, "for so far I have not."

San Martín, being more conservative from the start, was not so completely disillusioned. He had felt from the beginning that "a federated republic" could not be established. Although the war in Peru was to him "a war of new and liberal principles against prejudice, bigotry, and tyranny," he seems always to have preferred a constitutional monarchy with an imported European prince as the best way to end civil strife. Elected executives could not run republics successfully because public opinion was too new a mechanism for effective use. He felt that backward and sparsely inhabited Argentina, or the United Provinces of the Plata, could not survive in competition with the Brazilian monarchy next door. San Martín, not interested in permanent leadership, retired from Peru and, when he found himself unwelcome in Chile and his native Argentina, went to live a quiet life in exile in Paris. His death in 1850 went unnoticed in Buenos Aires. Its centenary in 1950 was celebrated there for an entire summer.

Other leaders met death without gratitude from the countries they had helped found. Miranda, who had not been concerned with democratic procedures beyond the establishment of independence and who pictured his ideal countries as monarchies, died miserably chained in a dark Spanish prison. Mariano Moreno, the fiery writer for independence and republicanism in Buenos Aires, had died at sea en route to England. O'Higgins died after being exiled from his beloved Chile by the new state's ambitious politicians. Sucre, elected to the lifelong presidency of Bolivia under the Liberator's model constitution, found, as he wrote to Bolívar, "anarchy, confusion, and ingratitude" surrounding him, and when in disillusionment he retired to Quito, his Bolivian enemies sought him out and assassinated him. Nariño, who had languished like Miranda for years in a Spanish prison for circulating the French Declaration of the Rights of Man, and who had escaped to fight in Colombia and to serve there as vice-president, was accused by enemies of having misappropriated funds and died penniless, leaving as he said, "to my children my memory and to my country my ashes." Iturbide was captured and shot when he dared to return secretly from exile in 1824. Artigas died alone in Paraguay with only an old Negro servant at his bedside. Vicente Guerrero, mulatto follower of Morelos in Mexico, served one term as president and then was executed by his successor. In fact, of all the heroic leaders, only the tough *llanero* Páez managed to die of old age in his eighties, but he died in exile in the United States.

Those who wanted complete idealistic democracy, those who had helped write the many flowery constitutions full of liberal guarantees, those who planned for constitutional monarchies or impractical republics, those who dreamed of great federations, and those who had fought city against city,—all these fighters and philosophers could say with Bolívar, "We who have worked for the cause of Latin American freedom have ploughed the sea."

the fine political philosophies in the hard light of reality

By 1826 the entire Western Hemisphere, except Canada and the Caribbean colonial possessions, was independent. The new nations owed their independence to European rivalries and foreign aid, and also to certain uniquely New World factors.

When they attempted to form governments, they all ran into some of the same problems. One was whether to adopt "centralism" or "federalism" as the pattern set up by the new constitutions,—whether to allow each province a governor, a legislature, and a maximum of self-rule or to provide for a strong central government in a single national capital. It would have seemed natural for the four viceroyalties of Mexico, Peru, the Plata, and New Granada to form four large new nations with the seats of *audiencias* serving as state or provincial capitals. But the viceroyalties immediately began to fall apart. Chile, formerly ruled from Lima but naturally separated from royalist Peru by a long desert, was one of the first sections to proclaim a republic. Upper Peru, which had been part of the Plata viceroyalty stayed loyal to Spain until after Ayacucho, and then became the new republic of Bolivia. Uruguay and Paraguay were lost to the United Provinces of the Plata before they could be federated at the 1816 Congress of Tucumán, and even the regions which remained loosely joined to Buenos Aires resented its domination and engaged in constant strife with the port.

The viceroyalty of New Spain under Iturbide seemed destined to remain intact from Texas to Costa Rica, but the Central American provinces soon left the "empire" to form their own federation, only to split before 1840 into five quarrelsome little states. Mexico itself, after ousting Iturbide and setting up a republic in 1824, proceeded to establish a federation modeled almost exactly on that of the United States to the north. The Caribbean islands, which had been ruled from Mexico City by the viceroy of New Spain, each followed a different pattern of history and never joined in any great federation. In spite of civil war and dissension, the 19 artificially created little states managed to survive, but geographic differences, bad roads, and difficult terrain, as well as lack of homogeneity in social and racial groups, worked against the unification of the newly independent states.

Bolívar had meant to include in the confederation of Gran Colombia the whole area of Bogotá, Venezuela, the Popayán region, the Quito and Guayaquil regions, Cartagena, and Panama. At the time he resigned as president of this unwieldy union, Páez had already made himself dictator of an independent Venezuela, and a general named Juan José Flores had united Guayaquil with Quito in an armed revolt against Bogotá. Even Cartagena planned to form a separate republic. Each faction accused the other of violating Bolívar's 1821 Cúcuta federal constitution, yet each group left to form its own independent republic. In Brazil, too, each region felt itself a separate entity, but monarchy held 19th century Brazil together. In spite of the high hopes for unity and express wishes of most of the leaders of the revolution, Latin America formed itself by 1830 into 16 nations and the empire of Brazil, all except the latter republics, at least in form.

Constitution-making has been a favorite literary pastime of Latin America's heroes, and the constitutions put into effect in the 1820s were elaborate and well-meaning. They provided for executives who were elected or at least non-hereditary, for legislatures elected by at least partial manhood suffrage, and for a system of judicial tribunals. They contained Bills of Rights and guarantees of personal freedom. These constitutions were provided for people who had no traditions of constitutional government and no loyalty to the idea of a nation. The rights were "guaranteed" by army leaders and strong men who had no expectation of putting them into actual practice or men who could call constitutional conventions of their followers if the letter of the law did not suit them and have new constitutions written that were more to their liking. Generally the people were loyal not to a nation but to a leader or a small region. Theory and practice in government were to be in perpetual conflict throughout the 19th century.

Various impractical concepts were embodied in the constitutions and Bills of Rights. A society stratified into such distinct social classes could not immediately accept high-sounding pronouncements on the equality of man. A region unused to popular voting could not peacefully hold elections and expect the losers, if well armed, to accept defeat cheerfully. A people accustomed to a state-supported Church that proclaimed all dissenters heretics could not understand references to freedom of religion and separation of Church and state. Acceptance of these ideas came to Latin America slowly with industrialization and increased contact with the outside world.

Some peaceable division into two main political parties is a necessary adjunct of a democratic state. Two such parties did rise in most Latin American states, one often calling itself the Liberals and the other the Conservatives. In most countries the people devoted to constitutionalism were the Liberals, and included townspeople, intelligentsia, people who were interested in trade and commerce, ambitious for education, suspicious of a dominating, tax-supported Church, and often active members of Masonic lodges. Opposed to them was the aristocracy, the old landlord class that needed no foreign commerce, that wanted the slow life of colonial times unchanged, and that wanted eldest sons to inherit the land and younger sons to become leaders in the conservative, established Church or privileged officers in a conservative army. These Conservatives, in Argentina for example, were more apt to be federalists rather than centralists or *unitarios* because they could continue to dominate the provincial cities and agricultural regions while the capital became more sophisticated and industrialized under centralist Liberals.

The two parties might call themselves *Blancos* and *Colorados* as they did in Uruguay, or *Pelucones* and *Pípiolos* as in Chile, but their fundamental beliefs remained parallel throughout Latin America. Socially and culturally Liberals were interested in reason, science, and the new philosophies of change, while Conservatives wanted to preserve the *status quo* and the old classical culture, the old colonial regime. The two groups quarreled over the secularization of education, the separation of Church and state, the extension of suffrage, the break-up of the large estates, and the superiority of civilian over military government. These disputes still go on today in some of these nations. But even the Liberals could not envisage universal suffrage and completely fair and open elections. Both groups therefore in every country rallied around individual heroes, and personal rule whether by benevolent patriarch or malevolent tyrant became the 19th century pattern in Latin America.

The Spanish colonial heritage made this pattern inevitable. Individualism was exaggerated in its sharply separated caste system. People habituated to what the Latins call *personalismo* or loyalty to a leader, combined with loyalty to a small region, people who had no experience in government except for the limited activity of *cabildo* and revolutionary *junta,* could not be expected to break away from personalism and localism in one generation.

Fifteen years of warfare had destroyed whatever government had existed, and had shackled militarism on the people. The victorious generals who had taken over administration during the fighting refused to accept the obscurity of private life once the regions returned to civilian stability. The soldiers themselves, accustomed to plunder and adventure, were unwilling to return to shop and field. And the common people, finding chaos around them instead of the Utopia idealists had promised them, could find nothing more attractive than the brilliant uniforms of the generals. It was far more dramatic to gain control by sabre and musket than by congresses and constitutional decrees. Military leaders pitted one class against the other, and used coercion to achieve stability and change in lands 95 percent illiterate. The change from royal institutions to formal democracy, even in theory, was too abrupt.

Already by the time of the victory of Ayacucho, *caudillismo* or military dictatorship had begun to develop. The illiterate masses saw little difference between the revolutionary liberators and the later *caudillos*. Each gained, or lost, his power on personal grounds. *Caudillismo* was to last well into the beginning of the 20th century, a product of Latin America's peculiar social and political conditions.

economic and social conditions
at the time of independence

What had the revolution accomplished, then, for the common people if it brought them neither unity nor democracy, not even orderly government? Of what use were all the declarations of independence and "Plans" and impassioned speeches and editorials, all the long marches, the guerrilla fighting, the firing squads, the secret meetings, and all the loss of life and devastation and heartache through fifteen years of war?

For members of the creole class it was a victory, for now all offices were open to them and the new republics were organized and run by them. For the small middle class of merchants and mineowners, freedom had been achieved from the restrictions of colonial Spain—even though long decades of reconstruction lay ahead. For the town-dwelling *mestizo*, some improvement resulted from the fact that he moved up to a position second from the top, where the creole had been before, but materially he gained little.

But the Indian, inert and apathetic, illiterate and still tied to the land of aristocratic creoles, was no better off under the republic than he had been under Spain. Race, the more white blood the better, remained the basis of class stratification. Debt slavery and peonage on the *hacienda* replaced the *encomienda* and the *mita* of the Spanish colonial day, and the Indian seldom sensed the difference. Much as the fighters for independence had sentimentalized about "noble Indians" and glorified Lautaro, Cuauhtémoc, or Atahualpa, when they became their own masters, they gave no thought at all to the masses of Indians about them.

Negroes were probably better off because for most of them the revolutions brought legal freedom. In 1821, Bolívar's Congress of Cúcuta had declared that henceforth the sons of slaves would be born free. A worldwide antislavery movement emerged in the next two decades, headed by the Englishman, William Wilberforce, and the constitutional statements about freedom for slaves were actually enforced.

The position of the Catholic Church was both strengthened and weakened. Free now from the *real patronato,* it could look directly to the Vatican, which soon made concordats or formal treaties with the new governments. Control by the Inquisition was over, as was the missionary urge from Spain which had meant heavy expense on the frontier. The Church needed no support from a mother country for it kept most of its New World lands until the 20th century. On the other hand, the hierarchy was disorganized for a time because so many key leaders had returned to Spain, and the prevailing social change permitted the rank and file of parishioners to become more susceptible to new ideas.

Establishment of a stable government is a first requisite for economic and social progress, and stable government was to be decades away. Each nation had economic chaos on its hands as well as political upheaval. Plantations were not producing, mines had been flooded and abandoned, roads had been neglected, harbor facilities had fallen into decay. The new industrialism which was bringing changes rapidly to the United States was unknown to Latin America at this time. Its new governments, lacking a tax basis, were burdened with bankrupt economies. Little improvement in living conditions was possible.

Landowners, however, freed now from royal taxation and dominating the government, were able to build a new prosperity for themselves and maintain their old colonial caste. Merchants found profit in free trade outside the Spanish empire. Foreign merchants began to filter into the new nations, bringing with them foreign capital. England became the creditor of the new republics, making loans and investing private capital in mines and industries before the middle of the century to a total of over $100,000,000. Foreign money kept the middle class alive and helped it to thrive until it became dominant in the 20th century.

A fresh cultural wind was blowing soon in urban centers. Bolívar found Bogotá flourishing when he returned from the wars. Rossini's new music was played, harpsichord concerts were held, elegant fashions were worn by the new élite. They were interested in universities, libraries, collections of natural history specimens, botanical gardens. Their most popular learned figure was Dr. Félix de Restrepo, a pupil of Mutis, a native of Antioquia, who taught mathematics, geography, and astronomy rather than the old-fashioned classics and lectured in Spanish rather than Latin.

Students and intellectuals read literature that Latin America had not known before. Bogotá had both a regular newspaper and a literary journal. Mexico City's two political factions, Centralists and Federalists, each had a periodical publication. Caracas, Guayaquil, Santiago, Angostura, Arequipa, Cuzco, and Panama, where there were none before, now had printing presses from which flowed pamphlets, literary journals, and poetry, carrying the new doctrines of "freedom" to all literates. This was part of a new nationalistic culture.

In this writing rather than in any social and economic change, is found the revolutionary spirit of the time—stirring hymns for the new nations which called the Spaniards "insolent despots" and "bloody tigers," poetry which described the glories of the battles and the New World's natural and geographic wonders. The writers of the 1820s and '30s were not outstanding literary lights but their works are revered today as symbols of the newly acquired freedom.

The two best-known writers were José María Heredia, a poet, and Andrés Bello, a writer who helped develop a new South American literature. Heredia, born in Cuba but sentenced as a revolutionary student to perpetual exile, wrote about the beauties of nature and Indian traditions while teaching in New York or wandering in parts of Latin America. Bello, a Venezuelan-born Spaniard, friend of von Humboldt, spent ten years in England on missions for Bolívar. In Santiago during the last years of his life he founded the University of Chile and published the most widely accepted grammar of the Spanish language. Less famous writers were legion. Every issue of the contemporary literary journals was filled with poems glorifying the independence battles and local heroes.

The most famous poem was the "Ode to Junín" written by José Joaquín Olmedo, native of Guayaquil, friend of Bolívar, representative of Guayaquil at the first Spanish *Cortes* in 1810, and first vice-president of Ecuador after independence. The long and heroic poem on the battle just before Ayacucho is learned by heart today by school children throughout Latin America. Honored during his life, which he lived out naturally into old age, Olmedo bridged the end of the old era and the beginning of the new.

READINGS: INDEPENDENCE PERIOD

Alexis, S., *Black Liberator: The Life of Toussaint Louverture* (1949).

Anderson, R. C., *Diary and Journal, 1814–1826* (1964).

Angell, M., *Simón Bolívar* (1930).

Arnade, C. W., *Emergence of the Republic of Bolivia* (1957).

Beals, C., *Eagles of the Andes* (1963).

Belaúnde, V. A., *Bolívar and the Political Thought of Spanish American Revolution* (1938).

Bemis, S. F., *John Quincy Adams and Foundation of American Foreign Policy* (1949).

————, *Latin American Policy of the United States: An Historical Interpretation* (1943).

Benson, N. L., *Mexico and the Spanish Cortes, 1810–1822* (1966).

Bernstein, H., *Origins of Inter-American Interest, 1700–1812* (1945).

Biggs, J., *The History of Don Francisco de Miranda's Attempt to Effect a Revolution in South America* (1808).

Blossom, T., *Nariño Hero of Colombian Independence* (1967).

Brackenridge, H. M., *Voyage to South America Performed by Order of the American Government* (reprint 1971).

Brooks, P. C., *Diplomacy and the Borderlands: The Adams-Onís Treaty of 1819* (1939).

Bushnell, D., *The Santander Regime in Columbia* (1957).

————, ed., *The Liberator, Simón Bolívar: Man and Image* (1970).

Caruso, J. A., *The Liberators of Mexico* (1954).

Chandler, C. L., *Inter-American Acquaintances* (2nd ed., 1917).

Chapman, C. E., *Republican Hispanic America* (1937).

Clissold, S., *Bernardo O'Higgins and the Independence of Chile* (1968).

Coester, A., *Literary History of Spanish America* (rev. ed., 1928).

Cole, H., *Henry Christophe: King of Haiti* (1967).

Collier, S., *Ideas and Politics of Chilean Independence, 1808–1833* (1967).

Costa Peers de Nieuburg, E., *English Invasion of the River Plate* (1937).

Craine, E. R., *United States and the Independence of Buenos Aires* (1961).

Davis, H. P., *Black Democracy: The Story of Haiti* (rev. ed., 1936).

Davis, T. B., *Carlos de Alvear* (1955).

Dawson, T., *South American Republics* (2 vols., 1903–1904).

Englekirk, J. E., et al., *Outline History of Spanish American Literature* (3rd ed., 1965).

Fisher, L. E., *Background of the Revolution for Mexican Independence* (1934).

————, *Champion of Reform—Manuel Abad y Queipo* (1955).

Fitzgerald, G. E., *The Political Thought of Bolívar: Selected Writings* (1971).

Galdames, L., *History of Chile*, trans. I. J. Cox (1941).

García Calderón, F., *Latin America: Its Rise and Progress* (1913).

Graham, G. S., and R. A. Humphreys, ed., *The Navy and South America, 1807–1823* (1962).

Graham, H., *Independence in Latin America* (1971).

Graham, M. D., *Journal of a Residence in Chile, during the Year 1822 and a Voyage from Chile to Brazil in 1823* (repr. 1969).

Grahame, R. B. C., *José Antonio Páez* (1929).

Griffin, C. C., *The United States and the Disruption of the Spanish Empire, 1810–1822* (1937).

Guzmán, G., *Camilo Torres*, trans. J. D. Ring (1969).

Haigh, R. M., *Martín Güemes: Tyrant or Tool* (1968).

Hall, B., *Extracts from a Journal* (2 vols., 1824; repr. 3 vols., 1969).

Hamill, H. M., Jr., *The Hidalgo Revolution: Prelude of Mexican Independence* (1965).

Hasbrouck, A., *Foreign Legionaries in the Liberation of Spanish South America* (1928).

Henao, M. M., and G. Arrubla, *History of Colombia*, trans. J. F. Rippy (1938).

Henríquez Ureña, P., *Literary Currents in Hispanic America* (1945).

Humphreys, R. A., ed., *British Consular Reports on Trade and Politics of Latin America* (1940).

————, *The "Detached Recollections" of General D. F. O'Leary* (1970).

————, *Evolution of Modern Latin America* (1947).

————, "The Historiography of the Spanish American Revolutions," *Hispanic American Historical Review*, XXXVI (1956), 81–93.

————, *Liberation in South America, 1806–1827: Career of James Paroissien* (1952).

————, *Tradition and Revolt in Latin America* (1969).

————, and J. Lynch, *Origins of the Latin American Revolutions, 1808–1826* (1965).

Jane, G., *Liberty and Despotism in Spanish America* (1929).

Johnson, J. J., *Simón Bolívar and Spanish American Independence 1783–1830* (1968).

Kaufmann, W. W., *British Policy and the Independence of Latin America, 1804–1828* (1951).

Keen, B., *David Curtis DeForest and the Revolution of Buenos Aires* (1947).

Kinsbruner, J., *Bernardo O'Higgins* (1968).

Koebel, W. H., *British Exploits in South America* (1917).

Lecuna, V., and H. A. Bierck, eds., *Selected Writings of Bolívar* (2 vols., 1952).

Levene, R., *History of Argentina*, trans. W. S. Robertson (1937).

Leyburn, J. G., *The Haitian People* (1941).

Lerman, M., *Hidalgo: Mexican Revolutionary* (1970).

Lloyd, C., *Lord Cochrane* (1947).

Lockey, J. B., *Pan Americanism: Its Beginnings* (1920).

Lovett, G. H., *Napoleon and the Birth of Modern Spain* (2 vols., 1966).

Lynch, J., *Spanish Colonial Administration, 1782–1810* (1958).

Madariaga, S. de, *Bolívar* (1952).

Manning, W. R., *Diplomatic Correspondence of the United States Concerning the Independence of the Latin American Nations* (3 vols., 1925).

Martineau, H., *A History of the Thirty-Years Peace, 1816–1846* (4 vols., 1877–1878).

Masur, G., *Simón Bolívar* (1948).

McAlister, L. N., *The "Fuero Militar" in New Spain, 1764–1800* (1957).

McNerney, R. F., trans. and ed., *Bolívar and the War of Independence* (abrdg. trans. of O'Leary Narracion) (1969).

Mecham, J. L., *Church and State in Latin America* (rev. ed., 1966).

————, "The Papacy and Spanish American Independence," *Hispanic American Historical Review*, IX, 154–75.

Mehegan, J. J., *O'Higgins of Chile* (1913).

Metford, J. C. F., *San Martín, the Liberator* (1950).

Miranda, F. de, *New Democracy in America* (1960).

Mitre, B., *Emancipation of South America*, trans. W. Pilling (1893).

Morris, R. B., *The Emerging Nations and the American Revolution* (1970).

Moses, B., *Intellectual Background of the Revolution in South America* (1926).

————, *South America on the Eve of Emancipation* (1908).

————, *Spain's Declining Power in South America* (1919).

Munro, D. G., *Five Republics of Central America* (1918).

Nicholson, I., *The Liberators—A Study of Independence Movements in Spanish America* (1969).

Noll, A. H., and A. P. MacMahon, *Life and Times of Miguel Hidalgo y Costilla* (1910).

Parkes, H. B., *History of Mexico* (2nd ed., 1950).

Parton, D. M., *Diplomatic Career of Joel Roberts Poinsett* (1934).

Paxson, F. L., *Independence of the South American Republics* (1903).

Peers de Nieuwburg, E. A. J. C., *English Invasion of the River Plate* (1937).

Perkins, D., *The Monroe Doctrine, 1823–1826* (1933).

Peterson, H. F., *Argentina and the United States, 1810–1960* (1964).

Prago, A., *The Revolution in Spanish America* (1970).

Pike, F. B., ed., *Latin American History* (1969).

Priestley, H. I., *Mexican Nation* (1923).

Rappaport, A., *The Monroe Doctrine* (1964).

Reports on the Present State of United Provinces of South America—drawn up by Messers Rodney and Graham (repr. 1969).

Rippy, J. F., *Joel R. Poinsett, Versatile American* (1935).

————, *Rivalry of the United States and Great Britain over Latin America, 1800–1830* (1929).

Robertson, W. S., *France and Latin American Independence* (1939).

————, *Hispanic American Relations with the United States* (1923).

————, *Iturbide of Mexico* (1952).

————, *Life of Miranda* (2 vols., 1929).

————, *Rise of the Spanish American Republics* (1918).

Rojas, R., *San Martin: Knight of the Andes*, trans. H. Brickell (1945).

Rydjord, J., *Foreign Interests in the Independence of New Spain* (1935).

Savelle, M., *The Origins of American Diplomacy. The International History of Anglo-America 1492–1763* (1967).

Schoellkoph, A., *Don José de San Martín* (1924).

Shafer, R. J., *Economic Societies in the Spanish World, 1763–1821* (1957).

Shepherd, W. R., *Hispanic Nations of the New World* (1920).

Sheridan, P. J., *Francisco de Miranda, Forerunner of Spanish American Independence* (1960).

Sherwell, G. A., *Antonio José de Sucre* (1926).

Simpson, L. B., *Many Mexicos* (3rd ed., 1950).

Spell, J. M., *Rousseau in the Spanish World Before 1833* (1938).

Sprague, W. F., *Vicente Guerrero, Mexican Liberator* (1939).

Stevenson, W. B., *On the Disturbances in South America* (1830).

Street, J., *Artigas and the Emancipation of Uruguay* (1959).

Tatum, E. H., *The United States and Europe, 1815–1823: A Study in Background of the Monroe Doctrine* (1936).

Temperley, H. V., *The Foreign Policy of Canning, 1822–1827* (1925).

Thorning, J. F., *Miranda: World Citizen* (1958).

Timmons, W. N., *Morelos of Mexico: Priest, Soldier, Statesman* (1963).

Trend, J. B., *Bolívar and the Independence of Spanish America* (1948).

Turnbull, A. D., and N. R. Van der Veer, *Cochrane the Unconquerable* (1929).

Warren, H. G., *The Sword was their Passport* (1943).

Waxman, P., *The Black Napoleon: The Story of Toussaint L'Ouverture* (1931).

Webster, C. K., *Britain and the Independence of Latin America, 1812–1830* (2 vols., 1938).

————, *Foreign Policy of Castlereagh, 1815–1822* (2nd ed., 1924).

Whitaker, A. P., *The United States and the Independence of Latin America, 1800–1830* (1941).

————, *Western Hemisphere: Its Rise and Decline* (1954).

Wilgus, A. C., ed., *Colonial Hispanic America* (1936).

————, *South American Dictators* (1937).

Wise, G. S., *Caudillo: Portrait of Antonio Guzmán Blanco* (1951).

Worcester, D. E., *Sea Power and Chilean Independence* (1962).

*four important
Latin American
nations since
independence*

PART IV

Out of the chaos of the 1820's the new Latin American nations struggled for identity, their ports desolate, transportation primitive, Indian masses poor and neglected. The capitals made a show of high society, centering around this or that successful general. Such generals became *caudillos*, literally "Men on Horseback." They remained in power until they died, often by assassination, or were defeated in an armed uprising by another military leader, who in turn made himself dictator. Thus the nineteenth century witnessed the era of *caudillismo* throughout the newly created independent Spanish American republics. The followers of any dictator were personally loyal to him, and seldom to any ideal or political party. Persons were more valued than programs. Groups struggled for the spoils of power, and "revolution" followed "revolution," each one a change of leader only. Socially, the "old regime" lived on. Rival cities struggled for control of a new nation, and provincial areas fought for control against a centralized capital.

However, by the middle of the century, the civilizing effects of economic betterment, the influence on the old oligarchies of a newer business class, led to peace and union in the interests of economic prosperity. Immigrants from Europe increased the numbers of a skilled laboring class. European capital reopened mines and built railroads. Thus the end of the nineteenth century saw the decline of the *caudillo* leadership in the modernizing nations. This is especially true of the three most important Spanish-speaking nations, Mexico, Argentina and Chile. Brazil's story in the 19th century is quite different since its independence came without bloodshed, through a young prince of the royal family of Portugal. Not until 1889 did a military coup oust the emperor and set up a Republic. The new Republic, however, suffered some of the troubles of its sister Spanish American Republics in the 1890's, and the early twentieth century.

By the 1970's, the capital of these four nations boomed with new buildings, high-rise apartments of aluminum, chrome, and glass. Each capital has made some attempt at model housing for factory workers, though miserable shanty slums house the stream of in-migrants from the poverty-stricken countryside. Leaders in the city are from the new middle class, bankers and factory owners, replacing the landlords of rural estates who held the wealth and power in the 19th century. The white collar workers and the industrial laborers who worked for these leaders have also become a force in politics. Only in Mexico was social change accomplished after a long civil war, 1910 to 1920.

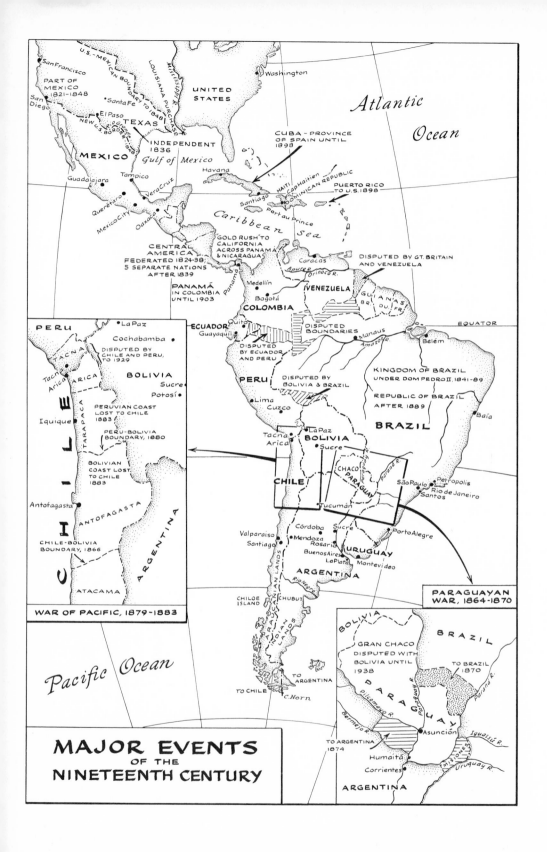

MAJOR EVENTS OF THE **NINETEENTH CENTURY**

Atlantic Ocean

Pacific Ocean

San Francisco

PART OF MEXICO 1821-1848

San Diego

El Paso

NEW U.S. BORDER 1848

TEXAS

MEXICO

Guadalajara

Querétaro

Mexico City

Oaxaca

Santa Fe

U.S.-MEXICAN BOUNDARY TO 1848

LOUISIANA PURCHASE

MISSISSIPPI R.

UNITED STATES

Washington

Gulf of Mexico

Tampico

VeraCruz

INDEPENDENT 1836

Havana

CUBA—PROVINCE OF SPAIN UNTIL 1898

Santiago

HAITI

Cap Haitien

Port au Prince

DOMINICAN REPUBLIC

PUERTO RICO TO U.S. 1898

Caribbean Sea

CENTRAL AMERICA FEDERATED 1824-38; 5 SEPARATE NATIONS AFTER 1839

GOLD RUSH TO CALIFORNIA ACROSS PANAMA & NICARAGUA

PANAMÁ IN COLOMBIA UNTIL 1903

Medellín

Bogotá

COLOMBIA

ECUADOR

Quito

Guayaquil

DISPUTED BY ECUADOR AND PERU

VENEZUELA

Caracas

Apure R.

Orinoco R.

DISPUTED BY GT. BRITAIN AND VENEZUELA

GUIANAS BR. DU. FR.

EQUATOR

DISPUTED BOUNDARIES

Manaus

Amazon R.

Belém

KINGDOM OF BRAZIL UNDER DOM PEDRO II 1841-89

REPUBLIC OF BRAZIL AFTER 1889

Baía

PERU

Lima

Cuzco

DISPUTED BY BOLIVIA & BRAZIL

BRAZIL

Tacna

Arica

La Paz

BOLIVIA

Sucre

CHACO

PARAGUAY

São Paulo

Petropolis

Rio de Janeiro

Santos

CHILE

Tucumán

Paraná R.

Porto Alegre

Valparaiso

Santiago

Córdoba

Mendoza

Rosario

Sucre

URUGUAY

Buenos Aires

La Plata

Montevideo

ARGENTINA

Rio Negro

PATAGONIAN INDIANS LANDS

CHILOE ISLAND

CHUBUT

TO ARGENTINA

TO CHILE

C. Horn

WAR OF PACIFIC, 1879-1883

PERU

La Paz

Cochabamba

DISPUTED BY CHILE AND PERU, TO 1929

TACNA

Tacna

Arica

ARICA

BOLIVIA

Sucre

Potosí

Iquique

TARAPACA

PERUVIAN COAST LOST TO CHILE 1883

PERU-BOLIVIA BOUNDARY, 1880

BOLIVIAN COAST LOST TO CHILE 1883

Antofagasta

ANTOFAGASTA

CHILE-BOLIVIA BOUNDARY, 1866

ATACAMA

C H I L E

ARGENTINA

PARAGUAYAN WAR, 1864-1870

BOLIVIA

BRAZIL

GRAN CHACO DISPUTED WITH BOLIVIA UNTIL 1938

PARAGUAY

TO BRAZIL 1870

Pilcomayo R.

Bermejo R.

Paraguay R.

Paraná R.

TO ARGENTINA 1874

Asunción

Iguassú R.

Humaitá

Corrientes

MISIONES

Uruguay R.

ARGENTINA

In recent years even dictators have had to win the approval of the masses. The old politico-religious controversies have been replaced by socio-economic issues. The "state" is not merely a system for keeping power in the hands of a landed oligarchy or a military clique; it is a new "vital state" which builds housing projects, owns and operates railroads, oil wells, refineries, and electric power projects. Such a state has a "development" division for controlling agriculture and industry, sets up Five-Year Plans, runs Tennessee Valley-type area projects, and works through state-controlled labor unions. The army has been increasingly professionalized and agriculture more diversified. These projects are so tremendous that the big Latin American nations today, though they enjoy more world prestige than ever before, are more concerned with internal problems than with the international situation.

Indeed nationalism—the drive for economic and political independence—is a major objective. Internal problems are by no means fully solved: laborers are often restless; farm workers want immediate land reform. The now "urbanized" families in big city apartments have lost some of the traditional Latin American "family feeling," while their members have turned away from Church-dominated activities toward movies, television, and commercialized sports. Public education, with its goal of reaching every family, and government assumption of charity and welfare work, have also limited the Church's force in the twentieth century. Thus, as we study the large nations—Mexico, Argentina, Brazil, and Chile, and their dynamic cities—we will find ourselves talking about social legislation, rising living standards, education programs, or middle-class growth, rather than about gaucho *caudillos*, barracks revolutions, and struggles of Church versus state. Industrialization and urbanization are the keynotes as, in the second century of their life, these nations seek to catch up with leading nations in the world.

chapter 18

THE POLITICAL HISTORY OF MEXICO AS A NATION

The life of one Mexican Indian typifies the whole struggle upward of the Mexican nation. Benito Juárez was born in 1806 in a poor village of the non-Spanish-speaking Zapotec Indians in the Sierra of Ixtlan—which is still five mule-pack days from the city of Oaxaca. Orphaned at three, an old uncle took him in. He slept on the dirt floor of the uncle's adobe shack, and earned a handful of tortillas for a day's sheep herding. Of the Spanish language, of the arts of reading and writing, of the mysteries of Oaxaca City, he heard vaguely from muleteers passing through the Sierra. But when a sheep was stolen and he was held accountable, he ran away and walked all the long distance to see Oaxaca City for himself. He was then twelve years old.

A kind family, well-to-do, of Italian origin and so without the prejudice of the Spaniard against the Indian, took him in as a servant boy. A priest, a close intimate of the family, adopted him and sent him to school. He grew up to take a degree in law and to marry the daughter of the family where once he was cook's assistant. A brilliant young lawyer, he served in the Oaxaca legislature and in time became governor of the state. He was hailed for his integrity, held to be the highest known at that time in Latin American politics. In the 1860's he saved Mexico from disastrous foreign invasion. A short, dark Indian, reserved and taciturn, he is revered as an "Abraham Lincoln" by most Mexicans today, for he held his nation together through a bitter civil war as well as a foreign invasion.

launching the new republic

While Juárez was growing up, Mexico went through a chaotic period. At the outset of independence, the bulk of its population was illiterate, for the Indians and mestizos had never been given an opportunity to learn to read and write. Peonage continued to exist, and did so well into the 20th century. In spite of the plethora of "rights-of-man" *pronunciamientos*, a wide gulf remained between the aristocrats and the masses. In such an atmosphere *caudillismo* thrived. Down to 1910, Mexico's history may be told through the lives of three famous leaders—a creole *opéra-bouffe* figure named Santa Anna, the unsmiling Indian lawyer Juárez, and a benevolent, paternalistic tyrant of mestizo blood named Porfirio Díaz. In and around the story of these three, other figures rose and fell in brief presidential terms, only two of whom completed their term of office.

The story began, as told above, with Agustín de Iturbide, who, after fighting on the Spanish side, placed himself at the head of the independence movement in 1821, presided over the separation from Spain, and set himself up in 1822 as Emperor Agustín I. Later that year Antonio López de Santa Anna, commander of Veracruz and former soldier in the Spanish service in Mexico, in conjunction with the old liberal revolutionists, started a revolution for a republic which forced the already unpopular Iturbide to abdicate. The latter was given a pension on condition that he would go into exile and never again return to Mexico, but when he violated the agreement a year later, he promptly was shot.

Now for the first time the liberal republicans had a chance to govern. Santa Anna stood back to let Vicente Guerrero, Guadalupe Victoria, and the intellectual creoles set up the constitution of 1824, modeled after that of the United States. But the United States had separate states to unite, whereas Mexico was a single unit which had always been ruled by one viceroy. The constitution-makers arbitrarily created 19 separate states, designing a federation which would prove to be very difficult to govern. What dedicated liberals wanted was a decentralized, Jeffersonian-type republic. Anti-Church and anti-army, they believed local self-government could be successful. Opposing them were the Centralists who had behind them the money of the Vera Cruz merchants and the silver mines of the North as well as the prestige of the Church party. They wanted the élite of Mexico City, whose spokesman was the brilliant lawyer and man of letters, Lucas Alamán, to run the nation. Santa Anna sided with them.

The liberal Federalists' opportunity lasted from 1824 to 1828, with Guadalupe Victoria, surviving leader of the days of Morelos, as president. They had four years of peace but had to contend with problems of finances, foreign recognition, and lack of an adequate civil service. Another problem rose from disputes between two branches of Free Masons, both very active in the new government—the Scottish Rite Masons of the Centralists who were backed by the British minister and the York Rite Masons supported by the American minister, Joel Poinsett.

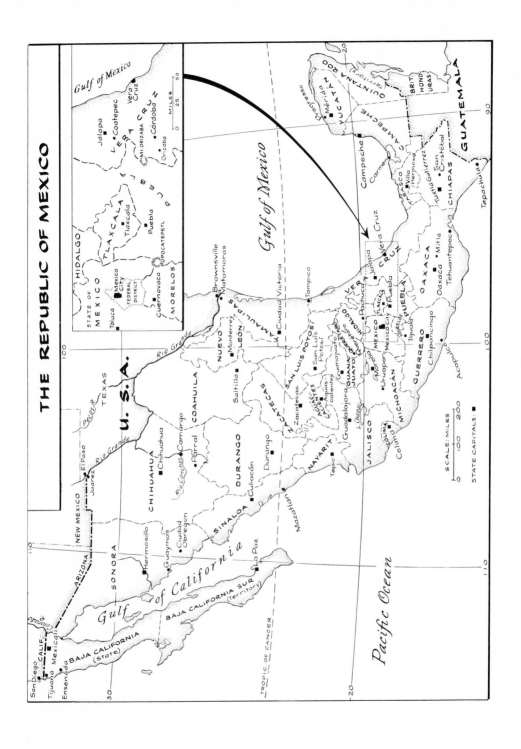

THE REPUBLIC OF MEXICO

Guadalupe Victoria was the only president for decades to come who lasted a straight, legal, four-year term. In the election of 1828, the Centralist and Scottish Rite candidate won, but the Federalists protested the election. With the backing of Santa Anna and his Vera Cruz garrison, they put Vicente Guerrero, that other survivor of the days of Morelos, into the presidency. A chaotic four years followed. Guerrero was overthrown, tried for treason, and executed. The vice-president who succeeded him was ousted by Santa Anna, who for the time being was a Federalist. In 1833, under a new "plan," Santa Anna got himself elected.

But Santa Anna temporarily retired to his lush plantation at Manga de Clavo in the hills above Jalapa. Then he allowed the Federalist vice-president to govern for him and face the unpopular issues. There was no money in the treasury and the two parties were hopelessly split. Valentín Gómez Farías, an intelligent liberal leader, tried to institute basic reforms and run the government efficiently, but was unable to do so because of the forcible opposition of the church groups and the creole aristocracy—just as Santa Anna knew they would, for, despite independence, the colonial regime of the creole had lived on. When cholera broke out in 1834, Santa Anna came out of retirement to quell the riots its spread had caused in Mexico City. Gómez Farías, who had been blamed even for the cholera, quietly went into exile in New Orleans, and Santa Anna now proclaimed himself a Centralist and set up a new constitution. Mexico was to be dominated by Santa Anna until 1855, while the nation fought a powerful neighbor and lost half its territory.

the age of Santa Anna and the American war

Santa Anna was hardly a man of heroic stature. At eighteen, he was a lieutenant in the crack Spanish regiment of Vera Cruz, with little sympathy for Hidalgo. In 1821, he was sent with troops to fight against Iturbide in his move for independence and clashed with the rebels at 4:00 A.M. on March 29th. At 2:00 P.M. the same day he joined the rebels and before midnight they made him a colonel. Santa Anna was always quick to change his plans or even the nation's plans if such change seemed to his advantage. When Iturbide failed to promote him a year later, he was one of the first to proclaim for a "Republic." He admitted afterwards that he scarcely knew the meaning of the word.

His military exploits in the next two decades were almost comic. He followed his troops in the war against Texas, taking with him an elaborate retinue, including a carriage full of fighting cocks. Later in Mexico he took part in skirmishes against French troops who were trying to take the Vera Cruz customs house in payment of debts, and lost his leg. He had the dismembered limb buried with pomp and a funeral discourse said over it; afterwards he always used his wooden leg to arouse sympathy and publicize his patriotism. (Years later, angry crowds dug up the bones and dragged them through the streets.) He ruled as virtual dictator under this Constitution of 1836, the so-called Seven Laws with its *Poder Conservador,* and his later one of 1843, the *Bases Orgánicas Políticas,* sometimes called "constitutional despotism."

In December 1844 Santa Anna's personal enemies and earnest patriots of all factions drove him to exile in Cuba and returned to the federalist principles of the Constitution of 1824. But the war with the United States, which so many feared, now came upon them and, for lack of a better general, Santa Anna was brought back into the limelight.

A major cause of the "War with the United States" lay in the frontier region of Texas. More sparsely populated than either New Mexico or California at the time of Mexican independence, Texas had settlements only at San Antonio, La Bahía, El Paso del Norte, and a few mission stations among the Tejas Indians. American cotton growers were tempted by the well-watered lands around San Antonio. Moses Austin and his son, Stephen, had planned to found colonies of Catholic Americans in Texas before Mexico's independence. Stephen carried out the plan by getting the consent of the new Mexican government in 1821. Three hundred families of non-slave-holding Catholic Americans were to get 177 acres apiece for farming. Men of the families were to be "of good character" and were to become Mexican citizens. Austin's colonists were welcome because they would be a buffer, it was thought, against both Indian and Yankee to the north. But in actuality, they only encouraged more Yankees to come—slave-holding Protestants determined to stay American citizens. With no strong Mexican army in Texas to stop them, at least 12,000 Americans had entered by 1827.

Naturally Mexicans interpreted this migration and the attitude of the colonists who came after Austin as acts of aggression, and took steps to correct the situation. Laws were passed to prevent further immigration; Texas was no longer considered a separate governmental unit, but was combined with the state of Coahuila, making a majority of the citizens in the state thus created Mexican and forcing Texas to deal with government officials at Saltillo, hundreds of miles away. The original American settlers, who felt they had come in good faith with the promise of autonomy under a Federalist regime, joined with the many newly arrived squatters, the bad element of border "roughnecks," and the determined slave importers, who proceeded to violate the laws recently passed in Mexico City to emancipate the slaves.

The results of this Texas trouble are well known to most Americans. The Texans declared their independence, formed a provisional government, created a Texan army, and asked aid from the United States. A group of Texans was besieged in the Alamo Mission station at San Antonio and killed to the last man; the Mexican army under Santa Anna was defeated by the Texans in 1836 on the San Jacinto River. The Texans captured Santa Anna and most of his army and forced the opportunistic general, as a price for his liberty, to recognize their new nation with the Rio Grande as boundary. They then set up the "Lone Star" Republic and waited nine years for the United States to annex the territory as a part of the union. Mexico repudiated Santa Anna and announced that Texas was still a state of Mexico and annexation by the United States would be a cause of war. Mexican leaders even attempted to get the aid and friendship of European nations. Activities of American warships on the California coast made the Mexicans fearful for the safety of their entire frontier. The United States also felt she had grievances. There were large unsatisfied claims of many American citizens for forced loans and loss of life and property in the disorders of the continuous revolutions of the Santa Anna period. However, from the Mexican point of view, the war that followed was due to direct aggression. An official book of "Lessons in Mexican History," written for use in Mexican primary schools, says of the cause of the war in the United States: "That country wanted to enlarge its territory at all costs, and chose as the only method to do this the most unjust one, that of conquest."

When the United States Congress voted to annex Texas, the Mexican minister asked for his passport and went home. A bitter boundary dispute had arisen over the exact Texas line. General Zachary Taylor had troops on the Nueces River; when he advanced to the Rio Grande and crossed into the disputed territory along the border, war started. Taylor's troops won an easy battle at Matamoros, then were almost stopped by the patriots at Monterrey. Santa Anna was returned from exile on an American warship and was passed through the American lines so he could offer the Mexican president a negotiated peace. Finding himself in popular favor, he announced that he would shed his last drop of blood for the mother country; he made no attempt at negotiations, but led a poorly armed and underfed group of Indian conscripts northward. These troops fought to a stalemate at Buena Vista, but Santa Anna himself got away in a carriage and came back to Mexico City and again proclaimed himself a hero.

Meanwhile Americans had invaded elsewhere. Troops under Stephen Watts Kearny and John C. Frémont and sailors under John D. Sloat and Robert F. Stockton took New Mexico and California. Other American forces under Winfield Scott had landed at Vera Cruz and climbed up to the plateau, fighting their way through the hill towns. In Mexico City there was no strong leadership, no unified government. The American troops stormed Chapultepec Castle, then a military training barracks. The boy cadets who were left to defend it have become Mexico's real heroes of the "War with the United States." Nine of them, averaging about fifteen years of age, jumped over the precipice at the foot of the castle rather than be captured. They are called the *Niños Héroes*, the heroic children, and there is a great monument to them in Mexico City, while many towns have named streets for them.

After the fall of Chapultepec, American soldiers occupied Mexico City, while their generals made peace. By the Treaty of Guadalupe Hidalgo of February 2, 1848, Mexico lost all her frontier region, and not only all claim to Texas, but California, Arizona, and New Mexico as well. However, payment of $15,000,000 was made by the United States into the impoverished Mexican treasury, and all claims that American citizens had against Mexico were settled by the northern republic.

Santa Anna, in disgrace over his defeat, was exiled to Colombia. The war had left Mexico exhausted; the government had been annihilated; economic conditions were chaotic. Any semblance of national unity had been destroyed. A liberal party of antiprivilege and anticlericalism began to grow, led by the writer Dr. José María Luís Mora. The conservative ruling class, still rallying around that other political writer, Lucas Alamán, actually asked Santa Anna back as "dictator." He was recalled in lieu of anyone else who could hold the difficult presidency for more than a few weeks at a time. This time Santa Anna called himself "His Most Serene Highness" and ruled with an elaborate court and a complete disregard of finances. He had to sell the area called the Gadsden Purchase to the United States for $10,000,000 in order to get funds. He soon squandered this money and in 1855 the liberals threw him out for good in a revolution under the Plan of Ayutla. In 1872, forgotten and poverty-stricken, he returned from nearly two decades of exile, and four years later died unnoticed in Mexico City. The first act of Mexico's tragic nineteenth-century drama was over as its "hero" went off into the wings.

the era of Benito Juárez

The years following the fall of Santa Anna gave rise to a period of social revolution known as the Era of Reform. The old Indian Juan Álvarez, illiterate *caudillo* of the state of Guerrero who had served under Morelos, was put into the presidency by a group of creole intellectuals. His cabinet included two anticlerical leaders, Miguel Lerdo de Tejada and Benito Juárez. Each of these reformers gave his name to a law: the *Ley Lerdo,* which broke up the large agricultural estates of the Church and offered them for sale in smaller tracts, and the *Ley Juárez,* which abolished the special courts and privileges of churchmen and military officers. Both of these laws were departures from the established mores of the creole aristocrats who had continued to rule Mexican affairs in colonial fashion. The resultant rift between political factions led to the resignation of Álvarez and the transfer of power to the vice-president, Ignacio Comonfort. Meanwhile a constitutional convention had been meeting throughout this stormy year of 1856, and it eventually produced the famous Constitution of 1857, a basis for much of the legal procedure in Mexico today. The principles of the *Ley Lerdo* and the *Ley Juárez* were included in this idealistic document, which became the "banner of liberalism" and the target of conservatives.

Who were liberals and who conservatives at the midpoint of nineteenth-century Mexico? The conservatives were the creole landed aristocracy, changed only from colonial times by the removal of the *gachupines,* or Spanish-born. By 1850 the sons and grandsons of these landlords had become spoiled playboys living in Mexico City or Paris, while overseers despoiled the Indian peons. Added to this class were the privileged and entrenched clergy, still in most cases the second and third sons of the wealthy families. Clerical and military leaders were never brought before the common civil courts but were tried in separate courts, where they were not exposed to stringent punishment. Throughout the next half-century these groups joined every military leader who would preserve for them their vast landed estates, their special position in society, and their *fueros,* or privileges in the eyes of the law.

Opposed to them were many creole intellectuals who had been educated in the philosophies of Rousseau and the political idealism of Jefferson. The Indian leader Benito Juárez joined them in the hopes of a greater equality of races and classes. Since the Church encouraged the aristocracy and was the stronghold of wealth, the liberals considered the land-rich Church their real enemy. The *Ley Lerdo,* designed to break up the estates of the Church and offer them for sale to private owners, meant to end the economic position of the Church. Unfortunately it was so worded as to allow also the private sale of communally owned Indian lands which speculators proceeded to grab cheaply. Church lands, too, fell into the hands of already-rich buyers who could afford them, and the law failed in its attempt to create a class of small farmers. Then came the law to abolish the legal privileges of Church leaders, advanced by Benito Juárez who as Chief Justice of the Supreme Court was now, under the new constitution, next in line for the presidency.

After his prominence in Oaxaca, Juárez had spent a period of exile, at Santa Anna's request, working as a cigar maker in New Orleans, and then rose to national prominence as Chief Justice. In 1857 Ignacio Comonfort, who had attempted an about-face, had been forced to resign and an armed conservative force backing the opportunist General Félix Zuloaga took over Mexico City. The liberals withdrew to Querétaro and proclaimed the Chief Justice president in accordance with the new constitution. Mexico now had two presidents, and plunged into the three years of civil war called the War of Reform. The conservatives had the money and the trained army officers on their side; the liberals were merely bands of guerrillas. Juárez was forced to escape with his cabinet to the Pacific coast, to take ship there to Panama, and to cross the Isthmus and eventually reach Vera Cruz. There he was able to entrench himself, to proclaim it the real Mexico under the true constitution of 1857, and to control the proceeds of the customs house in order to carry on the war. He also decreed more anticlerical reforms, proclaiming the complete separation of Church and state, religious tolerance, the legality of divorce, the secularization of marriage and burial and the end of high clerical fees for them, as well as the establishment of public schools as opposed to Church schools.

Meanwhile in the other regions of Mexico liberals fought bitterly against conservatives, both sides containing many opportunists, both sides committing massacres, destroying opposing villages, and robbing churches. The conservatives lost the final battle in 1860, and the side of anticlerical revolution won the day with Juárez. The losers had made it a holy war, for "*religión y fueros,*" and its bitterness left a deep mark on a devout nation.

The war over, tired Mexico settled down to enjoy an era of reform, with Juárez elected president in 1861 in his own right. But Mexico was prostrate; the treasury was empty; the monthly deficit of the government ran to 400,000 pesos. His nation was heavily in debt to European governments and European banking houses, and many European citizens had claims against Mexico for losses during the War of Reform. It was impossible to pay even the interest on these debts after the war; Juárez could only declare a moratorium for two years. Spain and England were righteously indignant, and willing to join in an effort to collect the debts from the customs at Vera Cruz. But France had other plans. A series of bonds floated by a French-Swiss banker named Jecker made up a large part of the Mexican debt. France was at that time ruled by the ambitious Napoleon III, anxious to win popularity at home by a spectacular foreign policy. He acquired the Jecker bond claims and through them saw a chance to make a puppet state out of Mexico.

The tripartite endeavor to hold the Vera Cruz customs house as a way to collect debts ended in Juárez' promise to pay and the withdrawal of England and Spain. But France remained and sent 6,000 troops inland to intervene in Juárez' government. The French were driven back at the gates of Puebla on May 5, 1862, by the ill-armed but fiercely patriotic Mexicans. One of the young officers defending Puebla that day was named Porfirio Díaz. So complete was the French rout that May 5, *El Cinco de Mayo,* has become one of the most important Mexican national holidays, though this victory only brought a larger-scale French intervention.

Exiles from Mexico and adherents of the Church and the conservative party had sold Napoleon and his devout wife on the alleged popularity a strongly Catholic European monarch would have in Mexico, the need for such stability to "save the persecuted Church," and the chance to build up a strong monarchy to check the expanding United States. The French emperor offered the throne to a young Austrian archduke, Maximilian of Hapsburg, and his wife Carlotta. They were to come to Mexico as monarchs of an independent empire, to be backed by French troops. They were led to believe that all classes of society would welcome them, that a plebiscite in favor of such an empire had been held, and that Juárez and his government comprised a small, unpopular faction.

Maximilian and Carlotta—young, eager, ambitious—were doubtless sincere; they were certainly much more liberal-minded than their Mexican backers, and were anxious to do something to ease the peonage of the Indians, to reform Church procedure, to make themselves popular with all levels of Mexican life. But they had been raised in the hothouse of European royal palaces; they were "benevolent" in the tradition of Divine Right Kings; they were in absolute ignorance of Mexican ways of life and thought of the new Mexican liberalism growing out of the War of Reform. Polite society in Mexico City received them in style. They created a "court," an elaborate and expensive one; they remodeled Chapultepec Palace as an ornate royal dwelling; they affected ways of Mexican dress and Mexican food. Without children of their own, they adopted the young grandson of Agustín de Iturbide as heir to this "phantom crown."

Meanwhile Juárez, recognized by the United States but harried by the French soldiers, retreated northward until the president himself was living in El Paso del Norte, which is now called Cuidad Juárez, barely inside the territory of Mexico. Down in Mexico the whole project was costing more French lives and money than Napoleon III had anticipated. Maximilian could not balance his budget. He made no debt payments; he trained no army of loyal Mexicans to replace the French soldiers; what popular enthusiasm he had aroused soon waned. And, once the American Civil War was over, Secretary of State Seward wrote notes to Napoleon III about this violation of the Monroe Doctrine. Soon all French troops were withdrawn from Mexico.

Maximilian grew desperate. Informed in October 1865 that Juárez had crossed into El Paso on the American side, he declared all followers of Juárez outlaws, to be shot as rebels. Many of them were executed when captured by Maximilian's small conservative army. Such action turned the scale. Mexican sympathies were now with Juárez. Carlotta sailed to France to urge Napoleon not to abandon them. When, after frantic appeals to the papacy, she realized the hopelessness of their position, she lost her mind, and lived sixty years in a European castle incurably insane, never realizing that Maximilian had reached an equally tragic end. For he had decided to lead his small remaining forces himself, met the Mexican nationalist army at Querétaro, was captured with two of his Mexican generals, condemned to death by a quickly organized Republican "court," and shot on June 19, 1867. The three years of his "empire," though well known in world history, comprised a mere incident in the struggle of Mexico toward liberal constitutional government. But the intervention had created a new consciousness of "Mexicanism." The land-owning Church leaders were discredited by their aid to the foreigners. Juárez, himself a deeply religious Catholic, had won his fight against the Church in politics and in economic power, though the national economy was again prostrate.

In July of 1867 Juárez came back into the city without fanfare, dressed in a black business suit, sitting in a small middle-class carriage, which can still be seen in the museum at Chapultepec among the splendid furnishings brought by Carlotta. Though his term under the Constitution of 1857 had expired, he was elected again in 1868, and tried for four years to carry out his aims: balanced budget, free education, encouragement to manufacturing, democratic elections, and tolerance to all faiths. In 1872 he ran for re-election; his victory was tarnished by an unsuccessful military revolt in favor of the younger Porfirio Díaz; death by heart attack took him suddenly soon after the election, his work unfinished.

the age of "Díaz-potism"

Now Porfirio Díaz came to the center of the stage, carrying with him the banner of reform at first, becoming conservative as he entrenched himself in power. This central figure in the third act of Mexico's tragedy had come from somewhat the same background as Juárez. His widowed mother, an innkeeper of Indian blood in Oaxaca City, had labored hard to keep up a hostelry which muleteers would frequent when they came in from the Sierra. She was able to send Porfirio to the small public school of Oaxaca in the 1830s; he went on to attend the college which Juárez had attended, and even to take classes in law taught by the latter when he was director of the law school and governor of Oaxaca. But Juárez was a man of civilian legality; Porfirio Díaz, though on the Juárez side against Santa Anna in the War of Reform and in the Maximilian episode, came to prominence as a military leader. From the underprivileged class as a boy, he became an *hacendado* between military uprisings, making enormous profits on sugar plantations. Though he came to power because of his righteous promises for democratic popular government, he did all but kill it in Mexico.

When Juárez' well-meaning successor tried to succeed himself after a four-year term, Díaz "pronounced" against "re-election" as the greatest sin in Mexican politics. With a private army behind him, he proclaimed another Plan (of Tuxtepec) and made himself provisional president in November 1876. He also arranged his "constitutional election" shortly thereafter. At the end of his four-year term he gracefully kept his promise of no re-election and had his friend, Manuel González, serve in his stead from 1880 to 1884. But Díaz' appointees remained in all important positions, and when they went out for corruption on a large scale, the legal president took the blame for the scandal, just as Díaz had planned he should. Thus Díaz was easily elected again on a "reform" ticket in 1884. He remained president through constant "re-elections" until 1911.

This was the Age of Porfirio Díaz. After years of disorder and civil war Mexico enjoyed a long period of comparative stability under the strong rule of one man, who was nearly always "unanimously" re-elected. In the half century before him, Mexico had lived under two emperors, thirty-six presidents, nine "provisional presidents," twelve "regents," and five "supreme councilors." Now Díaz was the government; there existed only rubber-stamp congresses and courts and his personally appointed state governors to approve his every action.

Yet for years Díaz kept many kinds of people loyal to him. He won the conservative landlords by hushing all talk of dividing estates, for of course he was a large estate-owner himself. The clerical creoles were pleased with him, for though he made much of honoring the Constitution of 1857, he tacitly consented to do nothing to change the position of the Church—a policy in which he was abetted by his very devout young second wife, on whom the clerical class had a strong influence. Díaz held the ambitious intellectual creoles by giving them honorary positions in the government. The educated mestizos were the civil servants in his widespread bureaucracy; with him they lived, and without him they starved. Only the Indians gained nothing, but slid ever farther down the social and economic scale. Rival generals had been given offices in the Díaz troops, the *Federales,* or in his mounted police squads, the *Rurales.* On all those who dared voice political protest, Díaz' army used the *Ley de Fuga,* the law of flight. The political discontents were taken prisoner on one pretext or another, and then "killed while attempting to escape." *Pan ó palo,* bread or the club, was his watchword; and those who wisely decided to accept "bread" in the form of jobs or concessions fared well.

However, Díaz himself had a clear conscience; he was personally honest and he considered himself Mexico's greatest benefactor. Under the *Ley Lerdo,* which had subdivided Indian villages and estates owned by Church groups, foreign investors came into Mexico with millions to spend in acquiring oil lands and cattle-grazing grounds, in developing mines and building railroads. The millions they made from these investments seeped rapidly out of Mexico, for Díaz was a good friend to all foreign companies. They were allowed to exploit Mexican laborers as they pleased, take over unsurveyed Indian lands in open "steals," and pay little or no taxes as they siphoned all the profits to their shareholders in the United States, England, or Germany. Díaz was called "the father of the foreigners and the stepfather of the Mexicans." No one can deny the great material prosperity of the country; the mileage of railroads was expanding every year, the port of Vera Cruz bustled with activity such as it had never seen in the heyday of the Spanish Empire. Textile factories hummed in Mexico City and Guadalajara. Mines were in full production; mine smelters worked silver with new methods at San Luis Potosí and Zacatecas; henequen plantations in Yucatan made twine for all the world; and the famous Blue Hole in the Tampico oil fields produced more oil than any single strike of oil in history up to 1910. Mexico City was served by trolley lines, lit with gas lights, connected by Pullman line via two routes to the United States. And all this in a country that had known no industrialization whatsoever before Díaz' second term in 1880.

But it was all at the expense of the lowest classes of society. The Indians remained tied to the land by imaginary debts kept on the overseers' books from one generation to another, and thus they were never able to leave. In Yucatan the henequen plantations were worked by the grueling labor of the Maya Indians, who were practically enslaved. When they began to die off, the proud, independent-spirited Yaquis of Sonora were rounded up by the *Rurales* and sent to plantation "prisons" in Yucatán. The peons received such low wages they could not buy shoes and so were ostracized in the towns; barefoot people could not walk the main streets nor sit in the public plazas, according to laws passed to "raise the standards of decency." Through it all rode the mounted police, the famous *Rurales* in their silver-decorated sombreros and their grey uniforms with red ties—splendid on their fine horses, busy "putting down banditry and giving confidence to travelers." They made Mexico "one of the safest countries in the world for all except Mexicans."

Equally famous was another group of Díaz' friends, the *Científicos,* educated creole intellectuals, lawyers, and economists, who influenced him in his old age. Led by the financial genius José Ives Limantour, who balanced the budget and stabilized the Mexican peso in world commerce, these scientifically minded politicians agreed that if the native Mexicans could not run the country efficiently and use the nation's natural resources, the foreign companies were the logical ones to do so. These young creoles honestly believed that dictatorship was the only possible government for their country and they did their utmost to modernize it. They themselves became a new class of rich men in the early 1900s, while Díaz and most of the members of his senate and cabinet were growing old and fossilized. In many ways the rule of 1910 was a type of colonialism with Díaz as the doddering but all powerful viceroy, but without the checks of the laws of the Indies and the royal inspectors. In spite of the great material progress and a thin veneer of sophisticated city culture, the "Peace of Don Porfirio" was a calamity for Mexico. He headed an irresponsible autocracy, a neocolonialism under the dictatorship of the creoles.

In 1910, when Díaz celebrated the centenary of the Hidalgo revolt with the largest street fiesta ever held in Mexico City, and carloads of champagne, the nation hailed him as the *Tata*, a kind grandfather. But the growing undercurrent of dissatisfaction was to bring ten years of violent civil war in the new twentieth-century Mexico. The curtain goes down on Don Porfirio, ending the last act of the nineteenth-century drama.

ten years of revolution—with a capital "R,"
1910–1920

The "Revolution," spelled with a capital "R," which came to Mexico a century after Hidalgo's revolt against Spain, began as a struggle against Porfirio Díaz and all he stood for, and evolved into an era of social change which is still in progress. Francisco Madero's attempt at housecleaning after the fall of Díaz sparked the revolution. but years of counterrevolution and chaos followed his regime until a period of stabilization under the dictatorship of generals from the northern state of Sonora evolved into a clear-cut revolution.

Out of the ten years during which men of various degrees of idealism struggled for mastery came a remarkable new constitution, a new national feeling, and a new prestige for those of Indian blood. Those who adhered to the new constitution became a powerful, all-controlling party which little by little brought about the things for which the revolutionists had yearned. The Mexican Revolution assumed importance throughout Latin America as the first major effort to uproot the system of great estates and peonage, to curb foreign control over natural resources, and to raise the living standards of ths masses.

In 1908, Francisco I. Madero, the younger son of a very rich landowning family, a five-foot-tall idealist with little knowledge of economics or of the weaknesses of human nature, had written a book called *The Presidential Succession in 1910*, which was immediately a sell-out. A second edition of the book urged Don Porfirio to hold an election for a vice-president who would then take over the old man's duties. Shortly before it was published, Don Porfirio stated in an interview with an American reporter named James

Creelman that Mexico was ready for democracy, that an opposition party would be welcome and that the election of 1910 would be open and free. Don Porfirio was surprised when he learned that the Mexican public was reading the American article and taking his word as truth. His opponents now rallied behind Madero and urged him forward as a candidate in a campaign for "effective suffrage and no re-election."

The Democratic Party was openly organized in January 1909 and Madero was nominated. Don Porfirio reverted to his old tactics when he saw that the opposition party was being taken seriously and threw Madero in prison. Then he held his largest fiesta, the centennial celebration of September 16, 1810. The celebration over, Madero was allowed to escape to San Antonio, Texas; Díaz then held the "election" and proclaimed himself winner of the presidency for another term.

In protest, the exiled Madero issued the Plan of San Luis Potosí on October 5, 1910, declaring the election fraudulent, asking for new elections, calling Mexicans to arms against the dictator. He had little hope for an armed insurrection but the people of the state of Chihuahua rose up and took the city of Ciudad Juárez in the name of Madero on May 10, 1911. Limantour, Díaz' efficient financial adviser, recognized the growing revolt and realized Díaz' cause was lost. He persuaded the old man to resign. Tortured by an infected wisdom tooth, nagged by his imperious young wife, the aged Don Porfirio was put safely on a boat for Paris, where he lived on his foreign investments in peace and plenty until 1915.

Madero came into Mexico City as a hero on June 7, 1911, and won the subsequent elections without challenge. But his supporters soon fell out among themselves, each group thinking it alone was destined to regenerate Mexico. His Plan of San Luis Potosí contained little actual planning, no recognition of the peasants' land hunger nor of the middle class opposition to the power of foreign capital. He did not realize he had stirred the masses to new hope against the creole landowners and the *científicos*. "Effective suffrage" was but a dream in a largely illiterate nation and the "no re-election" provision simply made it impossible for Madero to insure his own power.

Handicapped by his small stature and squeaky voice, lacking civil service experience as well as common sense, moved by a mystic belief in spirits and destiny, Madero found the situation hard to control. His rich relatives—especially his brother Gustavo who had millions invested in mines—became so powerful that he began to look like just another aristocrat. When he tried to call a congress, he found that his Democratic Party did not even have a titular majority. For the proponents of direct action, he was too mild and polite. For the land-hungry peasants his devotion to mere election reform seemed traitorous, and less than a month after his inauguration, the peasants under an Indian leader named Emiliano Zapata revolted in Morelos. They would fight, they declared in the Plan of Ayala, for redistribution of the landed estates. Their slogan was *Tierra y Libertad*, Land and Liberty. Cried their ballad singers:

But no land was being given; "And if now Madero fail us,
We'll fight on," declared Zapata, "we the people of Morelos,
We, the suffering campesinos, who have lived till now in squalor,"
And he thereupon proclaimed revolt, the Plan of Villa Ayala.[1]

On the right, the conservative army and the forces of "Díazpotism" also made trouble. A drunken ex-Porfirian army officer named Victoriano Huerta, who had been sent to put down an anti-Madero revolt in Chihuahua, later defected when he had an army behind him, and joined the anti-Madero forces in Mexico City. And Don Porfirio's nephew, Félix Díaz, backed by the Church, pronounced himself master of Vera Cruz. Unwilling to punish such rebels by death, the trusting Madero allowed all segments of the opposition to rally against him.

Into this confusion was injected the reactionary meddling of the American ambassador, Henry Lane Wilson, a Taft appointee still in office when Woodrow Wilson was elected president. Henry Lane Wilson represented the colony of rich American businessmen in Mexico City who considered Madero an insane radical endangering the status quo which favored American capital. When Huerta's army began to bombard the forces of Félix Díaz in Mexico City, the ambassador, on February 16, 1913, invited both leaders to the American embassy and urged them to make peace and join in demanding Madero's resignation. While this Pact of the Embassy was being discussed, the Huerta faction was capturing Madero's wealthy brother Gustavo and torturing him to death.

Street fighting was deliberately promoted by the two factions opposing Madero during the Tragic Ten Days of February 9th to 18th. Madero felt himself helpless and his cause lost. Thus Francisco Madero and his vice-president resigned. They were taken into "protective custody" by Victoriano Huerta, and, during the night of February 22, 1913, were "shot while attempting to escape." Ambassador Wilson was recalled by the State Department for supporting the men who murdered the president. The conscienceless Huerta declared himself the provisional president of Mexico. The *Porfiristas* were again in control; the army supported the perpetually intoxicated dictator while terrorism ran rampant, and the treasury was rifled.

Woodrow Wilson refused to recognize this government and attempted to influence Mexico toward a liberal constitution. He was willing to intervene and sell arms to Huerta's opponents, a group of anti-*Porfiristas* in the north rallying to the standard of Venustiano Carranza and calling themselves "Constitutionalists." But this gave Huerta occasion to claim he was the victim of American aggression and to gain support for his unpoular rule.

An unfortunate and confusing incident took place at Tampico in April 1914 which seemed to prove the claim. American sailors landing in the

[1] Gruening, *Mexico and Its Heritage*, p. 648.

town for supplies were taken temporarily into custody. Although they were released "with regrets," their commanding officer asked for an apology in the form of a 21-gun salute. Huerta refused, and thus became the champion of Mexican honor and sovereignty against the foreign aggressor. He was unable to get arms to fight his northern enemies from the United States, so he dealt with German agents, at a time when world opinion was anti-German. The American government, offended by the refusal to salute in apology and bent on preventing delivery of weapons from a German vessel, unwisely shelled and occupied Vera Cruz harbor. Lives were lost on both sides in the street fighting which ensued. The incident further popularized Huerta and his "anti-American" regime. Wilson was able to prove he was not practicing "Dollar Diplomacy" only when he agreed to accept the mediation of Argentina, Brazil, and Chile. But his insistence that "Huerta, the Murderer" must go continued. The victories the "Constitutionalists" in the north were winning with smuggled arms led to the forced resignation of Huerta on July 14, 1914.

chaos which led to a constitution

Victoriano Huerta's troops had met defeat at Zacatecas and other towns in the northern mining region at the hands of the *Constitucionalistas* led by Pancho Villa and Álvaro Obregón. Singing marching songs about the beautiful Valentina or the sweet Adelita, or about *La Cucaracha,* the soldiers fought together until they had defeated Huerta. Then they quarreled among themselves and fought in a three-way civil war until, in 1917, as one sad song said, "only three cornfields" were left.

Venustiano Carranza, the leader under whom the present remarkable constitution of Mexico was drafted, was a dignified old man with a white goatee who had been civilian governor of Coahuila under Díaz and had been responsible for bringing that state into the Madero fold. His state had refused to recognize Huerta, and in 1913 he had combined with the revolutionists in Chihuahua under the slogan, "Return to the Constitution of 1857." He began calling himself First Chief of the Constitutionalist Army.

Álvaro Obregón, boss of the state of Sonora, brought that region and its Yaquis into the Constitutionalist camp. He had been a mechanic in the Americanized north and had prospered enough to become a small landowner. Intelligent, practical, concerned for the common people and the rising class of industrial workers, a personable leader of men, he stood sincerely for Madero's principles and was capable of making long-range plans to assure their success. He understood the economic problems of the Revolution, and he was willing to bide his time and cooperate with Carranza.

Not so the notorious bandit Doroteo Arango, the Robin Hood of the North, who called himself Pancho Villa, and was the leader of the forces from Chihuahua and Durango. Chief of a band of outlaws and cattle thieves, he had brought his personal army of 40,000 ex-cowboys into the

Constitutionalist camp. He, like Carranza, was ambitious for the presidency, and the two were potential enemies. His presence in the Constitutionalist camp brought further American intervention when he became personally angry at the United States because of the favoritism it was showing to Carranza and, crossing the border, he "shot up" the town of Columbus, New Mexico. In retaliation, United States cavalry forces under Pershing chased him through the sagebrush of northern Mexico in an open violation of Mexican sovereignty. Villa kept up his private war with Carranza until the latter was legally ensconced as president, when he retired to a large-scale ranch and some small-scale banditry until, in 1923, he was murdered in a private quarrel. The cause of the Revolution gained little from him but Mexican and American writers in the mid-1960s began to give more credit than was warranted to this picturesque Robin Hood as an inspirational revolutionary force.

The leader of the rural masses in the south, Emiliano Zapata, had no personal ambition whatever. An illiterate tenant farmer of Indian blood, his ghost is said to ride still on his swift white horse through the hills of Morelos and Guerrero, restless, according to legend, until every peon owns his plot of land. His ideals were formulated by the intellectual Antonio Díaz Soto y Gama, who sought the division of the great estates into small holdings, the return of the Indian lands robbed by Díaz to the villages, and the creation of *ejidos* or community-held lands for landless Indian villages. The peasants of southern Mexico followed Zapata in the belief that the equal distribution of land was the solution to all problems. They were willing to fight on Carranza's side if the Constitutionalists were the most likely to guarantee such distribution. Zapata's forces burned haciendas, killed landlords, and proceeded to farm the land themselves. They fought their way to Mexico City by the winter of 1914 and spring of 1915, where they found the army of Villa coming down from the north. The two "outlaw" leaders met and posed amicably for pictures while Zapata's Indians begged for food and Villa's cowboys roamed the city streets engaging in drunken rapine.

Meanwhile the opportunist Carranza, after a futile bid for compromise with the more "respectable" Constitutionalists, decided to set himself up as a Revolutionary "savior" to outdo the "outlaws." He issued a series of proclamations in 1915 promising that under his leadership, Indian lands would be restored, foreign capital ousted, workers' conditions improved, free public education made compulsory, and Church influence removed from politics. Joined now by many liberal leaders, his combined forces under Obregón ousted Villa from the capital, who thereupon returned to cattle rustling and harassing the United States.

Zapata was defeated by another Carranza general, the brutal Pablo Gonzalez, and driven back to his own mountains. There his forces continued to fight for land distribution until in 1919 Gonzalez' agents had him assassinated.

By March of 1915, Carranza was provisional president in Mexico City. Popular now for his liberal promises, he gained further favor by quarreling with the United States over damages done to Americans during the three-way fighting in Mexico City and other towns and over Pershing's "invasion" of Mexican soil in pursuit of Villa. Attacking Wilson—who found the whole situation an embarrassment during his reelection campaign—as the imperialist leader of the Colossus of the North, Carranza gained friends at home from all sides. During World War I he remained anti-United States although technically neutral.

After years of internecine fighting, Mexico was in a terrible plight with its paper money worthless, land untilled, and guerrilla bands roaming the provinces. Carranza had meant, once in power, to forget his proclamations on agrarian and industrial reforms. But the intellectuals in his camp applied pressure until he called a constitutional convention at Querétaro, a convention which was to produce the ultra-modern Constitution of 1917, a document far ahead of its time. Labor leaders, land reformers, opponents of foreign capital, and supporters of public education came to Querétaro and put their stamp on the new document.

As one could expect from a modern Latin American nation, the 1917 Constitution included such measures as a federal government that preserved the states but gave strong powers to the central executive, a president elected for a four-year term but ineligible for re-election, a representative assembly and a senate. But Articles 3, 27, 33, 123, and 130 were new departures in constitutions, bringing in anticlerical, antiforeign, and socialistic ideas. Articles 3 and 130 were a declaration of independence from the clergy. They aimed to drive the Church out of politics and to confine its program to religion, by limiting priest activities, re-emphasizing marriage as a civil contract, removing schools from church control, and making public elementary education compulsory.

Article 14 guaranteed the right of private property, but Article 27 made the nation the legal owner of all oil and minerals under the soil. "Subsoil rights" could never be granted to private parties, only leased. Community Indian lands, *ejidos,* were always to belong to the villages. Under this provision, later presidents, even at the risk of American intervention, confiscated the holdings of foreign petroleum companies, broke up foreign-owned cattle ranches, divided hundreds of large estates among Indian villagers, and gradually worked toward the ideals of Zapata. Article 33 gave the president power to deport foreigners at his discretion and to forbid foreigners from meddling in politics.

Article 123 was intended to be the Magna Carta of Mexican labor, a rising class that grew up during the Revolution. Labor's friends wrote right into the constitution the eight-hour day, the minimum wage, the abolition of child labor, the end of peonage, the obligation of employers and landowners to provide adequate schools and decent housing, industrial accident and unemployment compensation, and the recognition of union organizations and the rights of collective bargaining. No other country in the world in 1917 had such provisions written into its constitution. But they were a statement of aspirations rather than of facts. Articles 27 and 123 were promises to the landless poor and underpaid city laborers, designed to bring all the peasants and workers of the country into the Revolutionary camp.

The history of Mexico for the next four decades was centered on the struggle to put this new constitution into effect. It was a struggle against the same old enemies that reformers in Mexico had faced since the time of Iturbide. Improvement was painfully slow and achievement at times imperceptible, but this 20th century reform was to be genuine.

Carranza accepted the reforming articles, but during the three years of "peace" after his inauguration as legal president in March 1917, no progress was made. The faithless old man broke his promises to the peasants by giving out only a tiny percentage of the free land hoped for by the Zapatistas. He reneged on his promises to labor by breaking a strike called by the labor leader Luis Morones. Morones himself escaped arrest and went to Saltillo, where he formed a new federation of labor in 1918, the *Confederación Regional Obrera Mexicana,* which was to be known for a decade as the powerful CROM. Its leaders, the *Grupo Acción,* entered politics for the purpose of defeating Carranza and installing Obregón in office.

By the provisions of his own constitution, Carranza was unable to run for re-election, so he attempted to stay in power through a puppet. But disappointed intellectuals joined with the *Grupo Acción* to raise an "Army of Sonora" to oust the Carranza regime. It was hardly necessary for this Army to fight any battles, so disgusted were all elements with the waste, corruption, and bad faith under Carranza. When Obregón marched into Mexico City in May 1920, Carranza attempted to escape with five million pesos from the treasury, but he was murdered while he slept in a mountain hideout.

Under the leadership of Obregón, Mexico found real peace by November 1920. It was more nearly united than at any previous time in its history. The first phase of the Revolution had ended.

the northern dynasty

Whoever was to bring stability to Mexico in 1920 must rehabilitate the country, refill an empty treasury, reconstruct agriculture and industry, work out relations with the Church, establish an educational system, set up some more workable political machinery and secure for Mexico a respected position abroad and sovereignty at home. At the same time the promises of the Revolution must be fulfilled and the hopes of the idealists realized. A large order! Because it was undertaken with some success for 14 years by men who came from Sonora, this period is called the time of the Northern Oligarchy. Northern Mexico with its lesser population and great distance from the center of control and conservatism in the south was always a land of Revolution and liberalism.

Álvaro Obregón, the Sonora leader, was elected under the Constitution of 1917 and inaugurated in November 1920. Something of a dramatic hero because he had lost an arm fighting Villa, the popular, plump, and peaceful Obregón knew that true democracy was still impossible; he hoped only to be a practical and able dictator. He was one of the few Revolutionary leaders in Mexico who understood Mexico and its problems. Never an ardent believer in "land for the Indians," he soothed the *Zapatistas* by allowing free villages to apply to an Agrarian Commission for land. However, since this was to be done on the Indians' initiative, and little favorable publicity was given the program, the requests were very modest; less than 3,000,000 acres were distributed. He depended from the first on the labor movement, and backed Luis Morones, making him a labor czar. The CROM, Morones' labor federation, handled all labor disputes and permitted no rival unions to rise. The union treasury, and Morones himself, waxed rich and wasteful, but labor achieved a slowly rising standard of living. The President appointed an eminent educational philosopher, José Vasconcelos, Minister of Education. A thousand elementary schools were built in the four years of Obregón's administration, 1920–1924. The problems of land reform and Church-state relationships were left to be solved in the next decade. Obregón prepared the ground by consolidating his power over the army, the agrarians, and the workers, setting the course the Revolution was to take for the next fourteen years.

Recognition by the United States was an important factor in the achievement of stability for the Mexican government. But the United States disapproved of Obregón on all the traditional old issues—the unpaid debts, the defaulted bonds, the injured American citizens. Besides there was the anxiety of American companies who had half a billion dollars invested in oil wells and mines, most of it in lands granted by Díaz, and who faced confiscation if Article 27 were enforced. They were also worried about the laws for labor in Article 123 which would cause them to lose their margin of profit if enforced since they would have to pay American wages to Mexican oil workers. When Obregón's agents asked Secretary of State Charles Evans Hughes for recognition, Hughes sought assurance that the 1917 law would not be retroactive but was willing to accept a "verbal agreement" to this effect. Finally, on August 30, 1923, the United States recognized Obregón.

The "stabilization of the Revolution" advanced in the next presidential election. Obregón had appointed another Sonoran, Plutarco Elías Calles, as his Secretary of *Gobernación* or Internal Affairs, a position which for three decades was to be a stepping stone to the presidency. It was the understanding of members of the Northern Oligarchy that Calles would succeed Obregón. An election was held, Calles was duly elected, and on December 1, 1924, Obregón turned over the office to his successor.

Calles was ardently interested in public education and opposed to the Church as a power in politics. He was an able administrator and perfected the Obregón system. Radical at first. he became much more conservative when he grew wealthy and was entrenched in power. But by 1925, a variety of reformist programs had gotten under way, made possible by the new stability achieved under Obregón and Calles. As will be explained in the next chapter, these included such measures as compulsory rural education, land reform, campaigns of sanitation and hygiene, cooperative rural banks, and road construction.

The Catholic hierarchy, opposing the Madero revolution, had refused to recognize the Constitution of 1917, had tried to organize Catholic unions in opposition to Morones, had kept the now illegal parochial schools open and had urged the people to boycott the new public elementary schools. In 1926 the well-entrenched Calles struck back by enforcing the anti-clerical provisions of the Constitution. In protest, the priests left the churches, refusing to hold services and withholding the sacraments. The three-year strike on the part of the clergy (discussed as a social problem in the next chapter) had serious political consequences. Deeply religious people organized rebel bands which they called *Cristeros*—proudly adopting the government's epithet for themselves—and these bands became rallying points for all of Calles' enemies. The *Cristeros* burned schools, stoned teachers, blew up trains, and in retaliation, Calles' armies committed parallel atrocities.

This polarization brought tragic results after the election of 1928. It had been evident for some time that Obregón and Calles intended to rotate the presidency between them. Calles had the constitution amended to set up a six-year presidency but allowing intermittent terms. Eliminating possible opposition candidates Obregón, as the only candidate, won the "election," and the continuation of the Northern Dynasty seemed assured, for Obregón was widely trusted and respected as a democratic leader. But at a political luncheon after the election, a fanatic Catholic youth, pretending to draw a sketch of the President, drew a gun from his sketch materials and assassinated him. This left Calles alone in control.

Calles was able to remain in control as *Jefe Máximo* by organizing a well-knit political party, the *Partido Nacional Revolucionario*. "When Calles spoke," it was said, "no dog barked." From his home in Cuernavaca, Calles dictated while three different "stooges" of various shades of liberalism served until 1934 in Mexico City as presidents. But the Revolution could not be completely betrayed, and the old slogans of *Tierra y Libertad*, of "land, education, free elections, no re-election" were declaimed more loudly than ever before. The Church, actually broken in political power, made peace with the Calles régime in 1932. When the time for the 1934 election came around, it was expected that another Calles stooge would be elected by the well-oiled machinery of the PNR. In order to pacify the left wing of his party, Calles chose his liberal cabinet minister, Lázaro Cárdenas. In the minds of the ruling group, the "Revolution" was at an end.

the Cárdenas regime

Cárdenas, if Calles had but known it, was to mean a change in the party policy and an end to the Northern Dynasty and the Calles dictatorship. Calles should not have been surprised at the impatience being shown at his "new-rich" complacency and at the urgency for change in the tenor of the nation. The Great Depression had brought new forces into play and reformers were calling for a Mexican "New Deal." Calles himself at the convention of the National Revolutionary Party in May, 1933, had talked about a "Six Year Plan" to develop the country industrially, improve and enforce the labor laws, build new highways and ports, accelerate the land division program, and to spend 20 percent of the federal budget on new schools. All this, he and Cárdenas promised, would be done by 1940. Pressure was upon him from agrarian leaders and from a new far-left labor organizer named Lombardo Toledano, whose movement had discredited the now rich and fat Morones and his CROM. Calles had to discuss popular programs to show he was still with the people.

Lázaro Cárdenas, the "puppet" chosen to keep up the talk about the Plan, had already improved conditions in exactly the manner outlined by the Plan in his own state of Michoacán when he was governor. Born May 21, 1895, one of eight children in a poor family of Indian blood, he had gone off to join the army of Zapata at the age of eighteen. Here he drank deep of the real Revolutionary spirit, and he never forgot his determination to carry out the hopes for land and schools. Serving afterward under Villa and Carranza, he rose to the rank of general by the age of twenty-five. Honest, able, and good at political strategy, Cárdenas carried on enough anticlerical activity as governor of Michoacán to bring him to Calles' attention; he became party leader of the PNR and then secretary of *Gobernación,* the post which always seemed to lead to the presidency. He had enemies within the party and among the conservatives—they said he "smelled of *petate,*" the Indian's straw-mat bed—but in Mexican politics by 1934 that was as valuable a piece of propaganda as for an American candidate a century ago to have been "born in a log cabin." Cárdenas' adoption of the Six Year Plan described in Calles' speech signified the most advanced and active stage of the Revolution.

Cárdenas was completely devoted to the common people; he took his campaign to the grass-roots, traveling on foot and burro-back to listen to the complaints of the peons. He was the first president to visit the rural areas. Inaugurated in December 1934, Cárdenas was the first president since Díaz who did not come from the north, the first to be elected peacefully for a regular six-year term, the first not to have his election challenged by an armed rebellion, the first to serve out his six years and retire into a secondary position when the six-year term ended.

He was still faced with all Mexico's old problems, however. As to his attitude toward them, this story was currently told to show that he meant to be president of all the people of Mexico.

> One morning while the President was transacting business in the capital, his secretary laid a list of urgent matters and a telegram before him. Here is the list and the comment Cárdenas wrote nonchalantly on each item.
> Bank reserves dangerously low—tell the Treasurer.
> Agricultural production falling—tell the Minister of Agriculture.
> Railroads bankrupt—tell the Minister of Communications.
> Serious message from Washington—tell the Minister of Foreign Affairs.
> Then he opened the telegram—"My corn is dried up, my burro died,

my sow was stolen, my baby is sick. Signed, Juan Pablo, village of Huitzipituzco."

"Order the presidential train at once," said Cárdenas, "I am leaving for Huitzipituzco."[2]

This concern for the peon's problems had not been a part of Calles' plan. Cárdenas purposely made a breach with the *Callistas* and the whole corrupt set of military leaders and men of wealth who had allowed the Revolution to die. He closed up their sources of graft and corruption and backed an anti-Calles labor group in a series of strikes. By June of 1935 labor was united behind Cárdenas; Congress had split into a pro-Cárdenas and a pro-Calles faction within the party; and Cárdenas had ousted Calles' friends from his cabinet. Cárdenas also made friends with leading churchmen in a move toward greater tolerance, so that now Church, labor, peasantry, and politicans were on his side. Calles was soon isolated and exiled to the United States. Then Cárdenas had only to deal with a local *caudillo* in San Luis Potosí, whose revolt was put down by arms—the last private-army rebellion in Mexican politics.

To develop mass support and forestall the threat of conservative reaction, Cárdenas proceeded to reorganize the one strong party, changing its name to *Partido de la Revolución Mexicana*, the PRM. Its basis was made functional and regional; it was to be primarily a workers' and peasants' party. Cárdenas armed the peasants, won over the rank and file of the army, and organized labor. The day of labor czar Morones was gone, and he followed Calles into exile. The new labor leader, Lombardo Toledano, was a very controversial figure, perhaps a Communist, and certainly a troublemaker afterward among labor groups throughout the Western Hemisphere. But at this time Toledano was a friend of Cárdenas and was willing to organize all Mexican labor behind the Cárdenas movement. His powerful union, the *Confederación de Trabajadores Mexicanos*, or CTM, demanded that the Six Year Plan be put into effect. It was to remain a strong influence in the politics of the 1930s and 1940s.

Cárdenas' measures to help the peasantry (more adequately described in the next chapter) mark a turning point in the social and economic progress of the Mexican people. However, it was politically important that 47 million acres of land were distributed among nearly a million peasants in more than 12,000 villages. Often with the land came a new piped water supply and a new rural school. Cárdenas himself was often present at the ceremonies of distribution. He strongly supported the program of *ejidos* or communal village holdings, and organized cooperative *ejidal* banks, crop and machinery loans, and irrigation projects.

Education had prospered under Calles; Cárdenas was to take Mexican rural schools so far toward modernization as to make them an example for the world. The school program became famous for its integration

---

[2] Anita Brenner, *The Wind That Swept Mexico* (New York: Harper & Row, Publishers, 1943), p. 85. The anecdote as told here is paraphrased and shortened.

of the Indian in the national life of Mexico. When the Church continued to fight Cárdenas' school policy, he relaxed the enforcement of the anticlerical laws. On the economic front, the world was recovering from the depression, and the standard of living began to improve in Mexico under Cárdenas' New Deal measures. Prices rose, but consumption rose with them, as state revenues increased and a flood of tourists began to pour money into Mexico. Meanwhile Cárdenas decreased foreign capital through expropriation of agricultural lands and other holdings, reducing United States investments by one-third. Mexico was strong enough and prosperous enough to challenge the power of foreign capital, the largest remaining problem Cárdenas had inherited from the Revolution.

In November 1936, Cárdenas signed a forceful expropriation law which allowed him to take over any property "held and monopolized to the exclusive advantage of a few persons" if it was justifiable "for public and social welfare." At first used to take over land for agricultural projects, the law was applied by Cárdenas to industries which refused to conform to the labor laws of Article 123. Since railroads and oil were key factors in Mexico's economy, he wanted the government to control both. In June 1937 he nationalized all railroads with over 700 miles of track and gave them to the railway workers' cooperative. Mining and oil companies had to watch their step in dealing with labor; if their workers complained of constitutional violation, it might be a cause for confiscation. The large American and English oil-drilling companies had been quarreling with the government and the workers for twenty years. In 1937, faced with a sharp rise in the cost of living, a new petroleum workers' union, affiliated with the strong CTM federation, demanded higher wages and better working conditions and even a share of the management in the Mexican oil fields. The government ordered the dispute settled by the Industrial Arbitration Board set up under the Constitution of 1917. The Board examined the financial record of the companies and ordered the pay raise, giving the companies six months to comply. The companies refused and appealed the case to the Supreme Court, which turned them down.

When no settlement of the strike was reached at the end of the six months, Cárdenas simply "nationalized" the oil fields on March 18, 1938, a day still celebrated in Mexico. It was the beginning of Mexico's economic independence. Backed by popular enthusiasm, Cárdenas turned the oil fields over to an Administration for National Petroleum and created the Pemex agency, which still produces and sells all petroleum products in Mexico. The rising generation of trained Mexican technicians learned to handle the drilling and refining, and the World War II demand for petroleum products made nationalization an economic success.

Though there was some agitation in the United States for American intervention, it was now the heyday of the Good Neighbor Policy. The days of Henry Lane Wilson were gone forever. Franklin Roosevelt insisted that the oil companies arbitrate their dispute with Mexico on the understanding that the Mexican government would pay a "fair price" for the expropriated properties. The English company El Águila was also forced to arbitrate. The negotiation meetings continued for several years until finally, during the administration of Ávila Camacho, Cárdenas' successor, a settlement was reached under which the Mexican government paid about $24,000,000 for the petroleum land being worked by Pemex. This amount was paid in full by the end of another decade. Thus Cárdenas emerged victorious in the most aggressive "foreign affair" ever launched by Mexico.

As the world divided between pro-Fascists and anti-Fascists, Cárdenas sided with the Spanish Republicans against Franco. Forced to sell oil to the Nazis as his only possible customer, he broke with them when they paid him only in barter, and when England severed relations over the affair. When World War II began, he threw his support to the Allies.

At home Cárdenas became a legendary hero of Zapata-status to the Indians, and a leader of successful labor groups. Ready to retire in 1940, he allowed the more conservative elements of the PRM to choose the next president. He had never pleased the rising new industrialists, a growing class of small businessmen who hoped for a lull in the Revolutionary program. Party action, with Cárdenas' blessing, settled on Manuel Ávila Camacho, a colorless army general and devout Catholic who, true to pattern, had been in Cárdenas' cabinet. Conservatives of many types—a strange mixture of Morones' old labor leaders, fanatical Catholics, and big business-men—opposed this choice. Added to them were the neo-Fascist organizations of young terrorists financed by Italian and German Fascist agents and called variously Gold Shirts and *Sinarquistas,* that were making a strong appeal to young urbanites in 1939 and 1940. Together these groups formed a new party and backed a millionaire general named Juan Andreu Almazán, who had been a Huerta supporter during the Revolution. Sure of the power of the PRM as a smooth-running political machine, Cárdenas allowed the Almazán party to run a free campaign of criticism and held an open election. In spite of some fraudulent voting and a little violence here and there, it could truthfully be said that Ávila Camacho won the election. Almazán went into retirement, for his Fascist friends were soon in disrepute as Mexico joined the United States in the war effort. Thus Cárdenas ended his remarkable six-year term in which he had rescued Mexico from the *caudillismo* of Calles and had served his nation as a constructive builder and a leader of great popularity.

presidencies and politics since 1940

By the end of Cárdenas' regime the term Revolution had come to mean the party. The first of the purely party presidents was the honest, dogged conciliator, Manuel Ávila Camacho. The new President meant to consolidate Mexico's gains. His motto was moderation. Mexico settled down to an internal peace it had never known before while Mexican national resources were channeled into the United Nations' effort against the Nazis. Ávila Camacho ousted Lombardo Toledano from power and permitted Calles, in late years an antilabor man, to come back from exile. However, wartime wages kept the growing urban labor class happy and social security benefits and other labor measures became law under Camacho, while war expansion nurtured a new young capitalism at home. A new class of farmers came into being, small private owners of land wealthy enough to clear untilled land and work it by machinery. A campaign to teach adult illiterates, the "each one teach one" program, was launched by the Secretary of Education, Jaime Torres Bodet. Ávila Camacho took the army out of politics and made it professional and efficient. A Mexican air force was trained under American tutelage. The Pan American highway was extended with American cooperation during the war; Mexican laborers, the *braceros,* came by the thousands to help the United States harvest its wartime crops. Lázaro Cárdenas came out of retirement to lead Mexico's war effort after the declaration of war against the Axis on May 30, 1942. Differences with the United States were settled, trade treaties signed, and lend-lease granted to Mexico. Under a mutual defense agreement, strategic materials poured into the United States' war effort. *Sinarquismo* and other Latin American Fascist groups were crushed by the president. Ávila Camacho is remembered today as the president who enhanced Mexico's international prestige and industrial growth during World War II.

Camacho's *Secretario de Gobernación* was Miguel Alemán, an able former governor of Vera Cruz and a modern-minded planner interested in expanding industry. Camacho's nominee for the presidency when his term ended in 1946 was Alemán. The national party was now strongly institutionalized. Military influences had been removed. The party bases had become agrarian, labor, and popular. This new party met in January 1946 to change its name to *Partido Revolucionario Institucional,* the PRI, and to form a Plan Alemán for increased agricultural production and industrialization. The Plan Alemán denounced foreign ideologies and declared that its followers would "make Mexican institutions work better." Ezekiel Padilla opposed the candidacy of Alemán and the election was held on July 7, 1946. That election was probably quite fair for the announced returns gave Alemán only 77 percent throughout the nation and only 52 percent in sophisticated Mexico City. When Alemán succeeded to the presidency, the election law itself was improved, with women being granted full rights of voting and the populated northern part of Lower California coming in as a state. No longer was the PRI an exclusive lodge of Revolutionary generals; it had become by mid-century a middle-of-the-road combination of labor, agrarians, and the new middle class; the Revolutionary generation was dying out.

Miguel Alemán was a young civilian, a member of a new generation which had not taken part in the 1910–1920 Revolution. He launched a well-integrated program to make industrialization the heart of Mexican economy under government direction. His presidency was a period of grandiose public works—irrigation projects, highways, enormous new public buildings like the National University, river control, valley-wide programs for hydroelectric projects in Michoacán and Vera Cruz states. Thousands of acres of previously uncultivated land were added to Mexico's skimpy arable regions; factories run by electricity sprang up in Monterrey, Mexico City, Guadalajara; trucks displaced mule-train transportation everywhere on the new roads of Mexico. Much of this development was accomplished with loans from the United States; much of the money was dribbled away in waste; many of Alemán's friends and, it is said, Alemán himself became a great deal richer than before. The PRI continued strong enough to win elections without resort to fraud or force.

In 1952, party leaders chose the winning candidate, the austere, 61-year-old accountant Adolfo Ruíz Cortines. Ruíz Cortines had the support of laborers, peasants, and the growing middle class. At the time of his peaceful election in 1952, Mexico was industrially a hundred years ahead of its position in 1932. Cárdenas had distributed the land, Ávila Camacho had brought economic peace, Alemán had hastened industrialization; and if Alemán took many *mordidas* or bribe bites out of the new wealth, Ruíz Cortines was a man pledged to an administration that would end graft and corruption in the government. "There is nothing wrong with Mexico," he said, "which honesty, diligence, and intelligent use of available resources will not cure." He pledged to reduce the cost of livng and modernize agriculture to increase the food supply. When in 1953 and 1954 the industrial boom began slowing down, inflation had set in, and Mexico faced a recession, Cortines devalued the peso in a swift move and the whole nation tightened its belt. Gold reserves picked up by 1956, foreign capital made new investments, and prosperity was on the increase. Cortines attacked the major problems of Mexico with firmness and intelligence. These were the fundamental problems of balancing food production and agriculture with industrialization, and of providing prosperity for the rapidly growing population.

On November 4, 1957, the PRI with Ruíz Cortines' blessing nominated for the 1958 presidential elections the popular Secretary of Labor, Adolfo López Mateos. López Mateos, 47 years of age and a moderate leftist, was the choice of ex-president Cárdenas, still a powerful elder statesman with millions of labor and farm supporters. López Mateos had worked as a teacher to pay for his law degree. As Labor Minister he had handled 13,382 labor disputes, of which only thirteen developed into strikes. He was considered a "square shooter" by both labor and management. In December 1958 he was inaugurated for six years of "smooth bossing of the current combination of state and private enterprise." He said at the time of his inauguration: "Mexico must create national wealth from capital, outside capital if necessary, to make jobs for an additional one million Mexicans a year. The human factors involved, that is, whether the worker gets enough to eat and whether his malaria is cured, are the responsibilities of modern capitalism."

The young and vigorous president moved ahead in fields that had recently been neglected. He vastly increased land distribution, though he realized that *ejido* cultivation of marginal lands was uneconomical. An agriculture depending on individual ten to twenty acre holdings, as envisioned by Zapata, could never feed an industrialized urban Mexico. He encouraged the clearing of virgin lands by machinery and the development of large-scale planting by corporations in which the government had a financial share. For city workers, he set up a plan for compulsory profit-sharing schemes in industry and pushed public housing in Mexico City—attempting to outstrip the growth of shanty-towns around new factory districts. To help industry, he enforced the "Mexicanization" program under which a majority of the stock of companies doing business in Mexico must be held by Mexican nationals. All businesses in Mexico were subject to a fairly collected income tax, and an increasing portion of the budget thus balanced was spent on education. Among the accomplishments for which López Mateos will be remembered is the provision of three school books apiece for every rural school in Mexico.

In foreign affairs, he maintained independence without isolation. Mexico was the only country which recognized Fidel Castro's Cuba, yet Mexico became no open refuge for Latin American Communists. Mexico refused to back the Organization of American States in the military action of 1965 in Santo Domingo, yet cooperated completely in every other Pan American activity. "Mexico," said López Mateos, "insists on national sovereignty, non-intervention in internal affairs of other states, and juridical equality of states." Though disagreeing with the United States on Cuba and Santo Domingo, López Mateos' own relations with the United States were exceedingly friendly. An old dispute about the land inside the city of El Paso along the bed of the Rio Grande, an area called Chamizal, was settled by an agreement with President Kennedy that gave Cuidad Juárez, Mexico, the disputed city blocks. Another dispute was settled when President Johnson signed a treaty guaranteeing the desalinization of irrigation water from the Colorado River that reached the eastern side of Baja California. Both nations agreed in December 1964 to end the *bracero* program as no longer necessary for the economy of either side.

In the traditional pattern, the PRI party chose López Mateos' Secretary of *Gobernación* as his successor. In a fair election, with opposition candidates openly campaigning, Gustavo Díaz Ordaz was elected in July 1964 for the six-year term. The son of a postal worker in Puebla, Díaz Ordaz, a middle-class lawyer more conservative than López Mateos, inherited a prosperous and united nation facing no major problems. Mexico's 69th president since 1824, he meant to "put economic growth over doctrinaire politics," to increase the net gross national product, and to exceed the very large population increase annually. "Work and Concord" was his motto. He meant to be remembered as a fair and just president of a prosperous nation, but world-wide student unrest hit Mexico in July 25, 1968.

When riot police in Mexico City put down fighting between college preparatory and vocational or polytechnic high schools, demonstrations against the brutality of the police were staged in which students from the National Polytechnic Institute and the University of Mexico joined forces in protest. Some 150,000 students went on strike. Federal troops were used to disband them. The "United Front" of the students made a series of demands, including the release of all political prisoners and the repeal of the law allowing government arrest of dissidents. President Díaz Ordaz appointed his Minister of Interior, Luis Echevarría to handle the strike. Tension mounted as disorders continued with violence on both sides. On October 2nd, a mass meeting of thousands of people, many of them adults, was held in the downtown Plaza of the Three Cultures. Soldiers and police fired into the crowd. The official count was 50 dead but poet-writer Octavio Paz claims 350 were killed. Hundreds were arrested. All this took place just before Mexico City was to serve as host for the Olympics. Student leaders agreed to call off the strike and the Olympics were held without incident. Schools throughout the nation were closed for the academic year, and, to allay middle-class opposition, some political prisoners were freed.

To the surprise of dissidents, the PRI nominated Echevarría for the presidency in 1970. A weekly newspaper supporting the one opposition candidate, González Morfín of the rightist National Action Party, lost its allotted supply of newsprint paper after it carried a story about the responsibility of Echevarría in the deaths of students in 1968. But Echevarría carried out a vigorous campaign, visiting all state capitals and many remote corners of the country, flooding the country with millions of posters and securing extensive newspaper coverage. He reportedly won more than 80 percent of the votes, a vote which included that of young people aged 18 to 20 who were voting for the first time in Mexico. Also elected in November of 1970 were 178 PRI members of the House of Representatives and 60 PRI members of the Senate, while 20 seats in the Lower Chamber were given to the PAN party and two opposition splinter parties.

In May, 1971, student groups rioted again, demanding release of all political prisoners still held since the riots of 1968. When tough city hoodlums attacked the students and killed 13, the police made no attempt to interfere. Echevarría was said to be "stunned," but was backed by a group of senior army officers and the peace was kept. But the student groups, and many other liberals including the distinguished writers, Octavio Paz and Carlos Fuentes, hoped to start another liberal party, the Movement of Popular Consultation, or MPC. Meanwhile, guerrillas on the ultra-left, as elsewhere in Latin America, harassed the government by robbing banks and kidnapping influential industrial leaders to raise "fight funds." The PRI countered by promising to hold primary elections within the party and reforming petty graft. Growing prosperity was on Echevarría's side in 1972, for economists judged Mexico as "no longer a developing nation." Echevarría said Mexico "must search for ways to strengthen its democratic institutions and to work for the more just distribution of the national wealth." He hoped modernization and increased productivity would correct the imbalance between high costs and low salaries.

Echevarría, an incredibly tireless worker, plunged into the whole of economic and social reforms, re-raising the banner of the revolution and tackling the problems with intelligence. He instituted government programs designed to promote agriculture, and aid the rural poor. He had to stimulate the national economy which had lagged in 1971 and forward the goals of spreading the national patrimony. His problem was to stem the flow of rural population to the already overcrowded urban centers. Thus industrial enterprises became important to his government. He attempted to remove some of the effects of the "mordida," and passed a revamping of the tax structure, especially income tax. Echevarría in 1972 seemed to be turning slightly to the left to counter the slightly rightist administration of his predecessor. Yet his system seems to be steering somewhat of a middle ground to get the support of all with a minimum of opposition.

Did the Mexicans win the Revolution of 1910? Certainly all levels of society gained more from it than they did from the 1810 independence movement. In Latin American history it was especially significant for it came before the Russian Communists could be blamed for every popular rebel movement and it was unquestionably a home-grown product. It was a struggle for land, bread, and justice against a ruling class that was a holdover from the 19th century. The Mexican nation is painfully inching its way toward the satisfaction of these hungers. Through science, industrialization, and technology, it is fast becoming a Westernized, capitalistic society. The revolutionary era, as we shall see, has had a profound effect on the society, the economic life, and the culture of the land south of the Rio Grande.

Note: Readings for this chapter are combined with those on social and economic problems at the end of Chapter 19.

chapter 19

FROM INDIANISM
TO INDUSTRIALIZATION
IN PRESENT-DAY MEXICO

the land and the people who live on it

What was the stage setting in mid-19th century for Mexico's dramatic story? Madame Calderón de la Barca an American woman writing in English of her visit to Mexico in the 1830's had found Vera Cruz "desolate and deserted," with the Spanish trade gone and the yellow fever rife as ever. Then she had journeyed from the port to the plateau in nine days in an eight-horse coach. Once in the capital she found the city delightful. The Alameda was a "fine public park"—as it still is today—and the fashionable ladies, so "gracious and charming," drove around it in their carriages. On the streets she saw the bright dress called the *china poblana*, originally used by girls from Puebla and still worn at fiestas as the national costume of Mexico. During Holy Week there was "so much parading, and religious dancing," such crowding of society carriages and poor mountain Indians and gay *poblana* girls and barefoot soldiers, such elaborate church expense as to upset Madame Calderón de la Barca's concept of a religious Easter.

The Mexico City in which she saw the Easter parade was a city of 150,000 or 200,000 people. It was still in the center of marshland, though the drainage of the city was again being undertaken in 1840 on a small scale. A four-mile-wide Lake Texcoco still existed, and the villages along its edges oppressed all visitors by their shabbiness and squalor. Fruits and vegetables came into the market via the canals, as they had in Montezuma's time. Other traffic was borne into the city "on mules and donkeys, or on the backs of the lower order of inhabitants." Around the square in front of the cathedral, Madame Calderón de la Barca found French tailors and hatters, Spanish wig-makers, German and English shopkeepers—a beginning of the cosmo-politanism that is Mexico City today.

Away from the city, life still revolved around the *hacienda*. The owner was "king amongst his farm servants and Indian workmen." Produc-tion on such an *hacienda* was poor. The *haciendas* were remote from market, transportation was difficult, Indian labor apathetic. Corn and cattle were raised, but the money made was sent to the landlord in the city, or used by a general in his private army for a revolution. The Indians and mestizos lived as they had lived in colonial times untouched by indepen-dence. Madame Calderón de la Barca noted the blanketed Indians of Xochimilco poling their boats among the well-dressed and bejeweled visi-tors on Sundays, selling poppies. "Watching this scene," she wrote, "one might think Mexico a happy and peaceful land; but there is hardly a link between the blankets and the satins, the poppies and the diamonds."

Those who wore the blankets, however, were still nine-tenths of the population in 1850. Away from Mexico City, regional differences among the Indian tribes gave the smaller towns separate color. Madame Calderón de la Barca bought lacquered work in Uruapan from the Tarascans and admired the hand-woven, embroidered blouses and black, pleated skirts, worn in the region for a millennium. If she had visited Oaxaca and Tehuantepec she would have seen more striking costumes and more unchanged ways, pre-served with the native language by half a million Zapotecans. Oaxaca was then a city of about 10,000 people, with a small veneer of the Spanish-speaking ruling class. Puebla, second city of the Republic, had a population of about 60,000 at mid-century.

To the north, Guanajuato, San Luis Potosí, and Zacatecas were still the silver-mining centers they had been in colonial times, though they were being rehabilitated by English capital in the 1840s after years of neglect. Beyond the mining centers and the rich valley of Jalisco around Guadalajara with its 40,000 people lay the country of the cattle ranges, as opposed to *haciendas*. Sonora, Coahuila, Nuevo León still were almost deserts; only a few cattle could be raised. Here, and in the frontier provinces of New Mexico and California which Mexico lost in the 1840s, developed the ranch life of nineteenth-century Mexico, the life of the *rodeo*, the *corral*, the *lasso*, the *vaquero*—the words themselves are a direct heritage from Mexico. In 1845 there were approximately 75,000 Spanish-speaking people in what we call the American Southwest, living an isolated ranch-type life. Following the treaty of Guadalupe Hidalgo these were no longer a part of Latin America.

But in the 20th century, change came to the scene slowly but surely as a result of the accelerative thrust of the Revolution of 1910. The small village of Santa Cruz Etla, located in the hills of Oaxaca in southern Mexico, may be considered as a representative example. Thirty families comprising about 150 people, live along two ridges and in the ravine between. These poor farmers own less than five acres of land apiece, plowing it with oxen to raise barely enough corn and beans to feed the children. For cash to buy city-made articles the young men cut wood in the communally owned forests of the distant *sierra*, burn it into charcoal, and sell it in the kitchens of the distant city. There has never been a resident priest, and a generation ago only one man there could read and write. Then, in 1929, this one literate man procured blueprints from the Mexican federal school authorities and led his fellow townsmen in building a two-room adobe schoolhouse. A year later they hired a young girl from the Oaxaca Normal School as teacher.

One of the present authors has known this village well over the years since the school was started, and has seen the community make other advances with the first literate generation taught in the school.[1] The death rate among children has been lowered by almost 30 per cent because of the new teaching about sanitation and diet and the government anti-malaria and vaccination campaigns. With better seed and iron tools the farmers are growing more corn per acre. In the campaign against illiteracy in the 1940s every adult in the village had the opportunity to learn to read. The community water supply has been improved and deep wells dug for the dry season, while the burro trail to the city has become a road wide enough for heavy trucks.

All is not optimism in Santa Cruz Etla, however, for the depletion of the forest land by centuries of charcoal burners has reduced the wood-cutters' livelihood and eroded away the farmland below. By the 1960s many of the young men of the first literate generation had left the poor land. They went to work on the new highways or on the Oaxaca city waterworks project. Several of them migrated to the far-off Mecca, the national capital, where they found occupation in the new industries, in textile plants and foundries. The oldest son of that first literate man who built the school found work in a tile factory, sent for his younger brothers, and put one of them in business college to learn typing, bookkeeping, and English, while he himself through his labor union and social security was guaranteed more pesos per week than any family had earned per year back in the hills. Several whole families had moved to Mexico City by 1966, although three of them found no place to live save in crowded shanties in Mexico City's new slum fringe. Their children found no school to attend there, while the children back at home were using fine new free textbooks sent to them by López Mateos and Díaz Ordaz.

The story of this village, its improvements at home and the changes coming to the young people, can be repeated in many other regions of Mexico.

Mexico City, center of culture for this progressive nation, increased in population more than ten-fold in the six decades that followed the down-

---

[1] See Helen Miller Bailey, *Santa Cruz of the Etla Hills* (Gainesville, Florida: University of Florida Press, 1958).

fall of Díaz in 1910. In the metropolitan area of the Federal District live over 8 million people, while in all of Mexico, a population of 14 million in 1912 had grown by the early 1970s to more than 48 million. There is more urbanization in Mexico than in any other area of Latin America for it has 52 cities with a population of more than 100,000. Charming, sleepy Guadalajara suddenly became an industrial center of a million and a half people, notable for multistoried buildings and a great complex of textile factories; Monterrey became the Pittsburgh of northern Mexico with 1,200,000 inhabitants; and Puebla, noted for its scores of colonial churches, boasts of enough industry to occupy its population of over 550,000. Whereas in 1910, 77 per cent of the population lived in rural areas, in 1970 less than 50 per cent did so. Yet more than a million rural families still lived at a subsistence level, with an income equivalent of less than 100 dollars in cash a year. Population kept growing in the early 1970's at the rate of 3.4 percent a year.

The problem of illiteracy is yet to be solved; in 1965 Díaz Ordaz reported that 28 per cent of Mexico's people were still unable to read and write. Of the illiterates, more than 500,000, or about 3 per cent, are non-Spanish-speaking Indians, speaking 33 different languages—pre-Columbian tongues never written down. Another 27 per cent of the population are of pure Indian blood although they live in Spanish-speaking communities; 60 per cent are mestizo and 10 per cent white. The Indian people in the remote mountains and the mestizos in the villages like Santa Cruz Etla create a cultural and social problem for modern Mexico. However, in the four decades after the fighting had stopped, the Revolution attempted to solve that problem by means of a new agrarian program.

For an agricultural nation, Mexico's tragedy is lack of fertile land; one-half of the surface is mountainous; of the other half, only 14 per cent has enough natural water for agriculture. Only a little more than half of that is actually sown to crops; the rest lies fallow or is grazed by livestock. The Constitution of 1917 gave the government the right to break up big estates, and by the end of 1926 communal land had been returned to more than 2,000 villages that had lost it under the Díaz regime. It was not until 1932, however, that Mexican courts ruled that the government could give new land to villages that had never owned acreage; finally, the law was also interpreted to allow villagers who lived on estates as feudal peons to receive land, either as private owners or as members of a cooperative or *ejido.*

President Cárdenas increased the pace of *ejido* distribution; he provided financial assistance to these cooperative agricultural projects through the National Bank of *Ejidal* Credit, together with technical assistance in improving the seed stock and handling the newly financed farm machinery. Cárdenas' most ambitious project was at Laguna, in the area of Torreón, an important cotton-growing district. Thirty thousand families were resettled there and were taught the methods involved in a new widescale irrigation project. Similar projects were undertaken in Sinaloa, Morelos, and Sonora. At the end of the Cárdenas regime big owners still held three times as much land as the cooperative villages, although Mexicans revered Cárdenas as the "Father of the *ejido.*"

For twenty years after Cárdenas the land distribution program lagged. Without adequate irrigation the Laguna project could not support the natural increase of population on its cotton lands. There were inadequate methods of financing small farmers outside the *ejido* system. Small family plots of less than ten acres could not produce enough, by hand and oven labor, to send surplus to the growing cities. Then came López Mateos, who gave away more land than any previous president save Cárdenas. Furthermore, his grants were larger, and many of them were on newly irrigated land. The excess population at the Laguna project were given the opportunity to move to tropical lands cleared by bulldozers and drained by new canal systems.

By the 1970's, 50 per cent of all productive land in Mexico had been distributed among more than 2 million peasants. Only one fifth of the nearly 20,000 *ejidos* are operated communally; in the others, each family owns its own land but shares machinery, credit, and marketing facilities with others. Families on lone small farms had such difficulty in surviving that they left the land to swell the shanties of Mexico City. All in all, Mexico by the 1970's had moved away from the communal ownership pattern so ardently desired by the Revolutionaries. The *ejidal* banks survived financially and have expanded their capital. In a single year in the mid-1960s, 133,000 individual *ejido* members received a total of a billion dollars in loans from the bank for seed, machinery, or water conservation projects and had cleared the loans or were making regular payments. More than 500 of these communities are on former large estates expropriated as a unit and now worked cooperatively. Very few enormous estates exist today. A single holding of more than 250 acres is theoretically forbidden by law. In spite of the scarcity of arable land and the continuing increase in population, Mexican farmers today are feeding the city population and little food needs to be imported.

Cooperation with the American government in the use of the Rio Grande water supply is making more land available in the desert north. The great Falcón Dam was finished in 1957, the Amistad Dam on the northern border in 1965. The Lerma Chapala project was built in Jalisco and the Culiacán-Yaqui River project in Sinaloa. In the southern areas of heavy rainfall, the valley regions of Tepalcaltepec and Papaloapán have been developed on the pattern of the Tennessee Valley Authority for long-range flood control, swamp reclamation, transportation improvement, and resettlement of whole villages from dry and eroded areas. Millions of pesos have been spent on reclaiming the Durango "dust bowl" where rainfall was so slight that many families were forced to become migrants. To increase the corn crop for both *ejidos* and small owners a Maize Commission was set up to study why Mexico's corn yield per acre should be only one-sixteenth that of Iowa.

Land newly cleared or newly irrigated often must be fertilized, as must worn-out or eroded land. Artificial fertilizer plants financed by the Mexican-style Reconstruction Finance Corporation, called the *Nacional Financiera*, a typical modern Latin American *Fomento* or government development agency, partially financed by the American Export-Import

Bank. The endemic hoof and mouth disease among cattle was attacked by a joint American-Mexican campaign which sent veterinary scientists throughout the infected areas of Mexico to slaughter the diseased animals and to take other necessary measures.

Modern Mexican leaders, no longer Revolutionary, realize that improved agriculture will not solve the overall problems of a large and rapidly increasing population on poor soil. More research, farmer education, better agricultural methods, more industrialization and mechanization of agriculture, more water on the lands in the north, more flood and erosion control on the lands in the south, all are needed and are being developed more rapidly than in most other parts of the world. Thus the land distribution of Mexico, although it brought free holdings to a great many people who had wanted them, did not increase the food supply commensurate with the higher standard of living desired by an industrialized people. Improved methods of using land and greater industrialization are urgent requirements.

the new industrialization

The tourist driving south in Mexico today along either route of the Pan American Highway through such thriving communities as Monterrey on the east and Hermosillo and Guadalajara on the west would be seeing factories, filling stations, garages, motels, truck assembly plants, housing projects with running water in each unit and schools in the center—all things quite unlike the colonial towns and adobe slums he would have seen three decades previously. Traffic becomes congested and buses and trucks almost push him off the road as he approaches Mexico City, capital of a nation that owns its own oil industry and railroads, that is building up its consumer-goods manufacturing, and that hopes eventually to be self-sufficient in all but the heaviest industry.

The tourist would have been purchasing nothing but government-produced Pemex brand gasoline. The controversy over oil in the 1930's was solved by payments from profits on the government monopoly in the amount of $24 million to eleven American companies whose property had been expropriated and $81 million to British interests. New oil fields and pipelines were developed and by 1950, the Mexican wells had doubled their 1932 production. A new market for Mexican gasoline and fuel oil was found in the local industries and cars and trucks within Mexico itself. Mexico today is using as many barrels of oil at home as it was sending abroad in 1921 when it was the world's second largest oil producer. In 1971, the country was even importing certain grades of crude oil for conversion in Pemex refineries for the use of its factories and motor vehicles. It has the highest developed petrochemical industry in Latin America. Mexican oil is fulfilling the Revolutionary promise of "Mexico for the Mexicans" by helping to make the country self-sufficient.

The hydroelectric projects of the Alemán regime use only a fraction of Mexico's potential yet are providing power for home industries such as the steel foundries in Monterrey and Colima. Mining, once the mainstay of the Mexican economy, is today producing 23 per cent of the total exports of Mexico and employing 2 per cent of the working public. Producing more wealth are the new coke industry, the diesel motor plant in Mexico City, and the plastic and paper factories financed by the *Nacional Financiera.*

For its development program, Mexico needs more technical skills and more capital. Technical education, however, is becoming more easily available. Young Mexicans receive training at Mexico City's Polytechnic Institute, or study on scholarships at United States technical schools, or receive in-service training in both Mexican and American-owned factories. Engineering has become an honored profession in which people of all classes find opportunities. Capital needed for the ambitious new programs was lacking locally but large, long-term loans have been secured from foreign agencies such as the Export-Import Bank and the International Bank for Reconstruction and Development which have largely been used for the public works of the government. Water and sewage systems for the growing new cities alone needed $10 million of new capital every year.

Capital was needed for the country's railroads when privately owned lines were expropriated by the government and their owners paid in full, and when the government-built lines of the Díaz regime were expanded. One of the Cabinet members is a Secretary of Communications and Public Works, one of whose jobs it is to run the railways as a paying proposition. A $15 million loan from the United States Export-Import Bank went into improved track and new rolling stock. The *Nacional Financiera* built new lines to open Yucatán in the south and Lower California in the north to direct contact with the mainland. Three paved highways run down from the United States border to Mexico City, and the central route continues on to the Guatemalan border to meet Guatemala's section of the Pan American Highway. A new transcontinental road and railroad have been built across northern Mexico. Local road improvement has sought to bring every village closer to a market center. Even Santa Cruz Etla can be reached by truck.

Nacional Financiera is actually a corporation in which the government owns a majority of the stock. Joining with other government agencies, it has arranged a series of "six-year plans" following the pattern laid down by Calles. These plans for industrialization are dominated by the New Group, the modern-thinking new businessmen growing out of the northern oligarchy. Under them foreign capital as well as local businessmen have prospered. The New Group made foreign companies welcome in the 1950s; the restrictions put upon their profits and their labor relations are not nearly so strongly enforced as the Constitution of 1917 implied they would. Most new capital has gone into smaller ventures, into assembly plants, into manufacturing with Mexican materials and Mexican skilled workers, rather than into the extractive industries of a bygone age. The need for expanded credit goes on; in the early 1970s Mexico needed another billion for roads and new trucking, six billion for irrigation, additional billions for public sanitation and education projects.

Article 123 of the 1917 Constitution and subsequent legislation provided for the high standards Mexican labor expected—the eight-hour day, equal pay for men and women, natives and foreigners, no child labor, no peonage, safe and sanitary working conditions, accident and sickness benefits, old age pensions, adequate housing and schooling, the right to organize and to strike, severance pay as a guarantee against unfair layoffs. These were far-fetched utopian visions in 1917. But under their impetus, Luis Morones founded the CROM, a trade union like the AFL which later gave way to Lombardo Toledano and his more industrialized CTM. Lombardo Toledano soon became a famous left-wing "labor rouser" throughout Latin America and brought down the suspicion of Communist domination on his labor organization in Mexico. When Ávila Camacho became president, he ousted him from the CTM, bringing that labor group into the National Revolutionary Party and the government into greater control of the labor movement.

Government-sponsored unions claim upward of 2 million members in the rapidly industrializing new Mexico. The larger industrial firms had long remained hostile and foreign capital hesitated to invest in labor-dominated industries, afraid of Morones' type of labor racketeer and Lombardo Toledano's type of ultra left-wing radicalism. However, by 1945 the Mexican National Manufacturers' Association joined with the CTM to back the National Revolutionary Party and to further labor-management plans for Mexican economic development. Mexican labor no longer battles for the nationalization of industry under the "People's Revolution" but concentrates on asking for fair treatment and higher wages.

The first law to carry out the Social Security provisions of 1917 was not passed until 1939; no actual inclusive coverage was provided until 1943. Today there is a Mexican Social Security Institute, with a headquarters building covering two blocks in modern Mexico City. More than a million persons are being benefited by the medical, old age, and unemployment insurance programs. Year by year hospital and clinical services are being established in all urban centers. Before this government-controlled health program was put into effect, there was no medical service available for the families of workers in Mexico; now the law provides free medical treatment and medicine to all workers who contribute a percentage of their wages to the fund. Federally financed low-rent housing projects surround Mexico City and other growing towns. Just to give one example, the *Centro Urbano Presidente Alemán* in Mexico City has room for 6,000 occupants and is a complete city in itself, with recreation facilities, schools, and clinics.

Mexico probably ranks near the top, next to Chile and Argentina, in the living standards of its workers. But the younger sons of the *ejido* members and the small owners, unwilling to share with their older brothers the meager living in the rural homes, come to the city in increasing numbers. Their families continue to surround Mexico City with shanty-town slums where there are inadequate water, sanitation, and schooling. For these immigrants, Mexico's cities must provide 4 million new jobs by 1975, as well as decent housing and good schools for the children.

A problem concerning laborers, peculiar to Mexico, was the situation regarding "wetbacks" and *braceros*. When, during World War II, workers were urgently needed in the United States, 300,000 Mexican contract workers came to the United States under a 1943 treaty as *braceros* and many thousands of other workers crossed the Rio Grande illegally as *wetbacks*. Another 100,000 were admitted by agreement in 1945. The agreements were renewed until as many as 600,000 contract workers had come to the United States, and an equal number probably came as "wetbacks." Arrangements for the legal entry of *braceros* were discontinued in December 1964. By 1970, United States law limited the number of legal Mexican immigrants into this country to 90,000 a year and permitted another 116,000 to come as temporary workers. In the spring of 1971, Mexican authorities estimated that more than a million Mexican nationals were working in the United States and that many of them had their wives and children with them.

Meanwhile, attracted by the magnet of potential work in the United States, a large number of unskilled workers had left their homes in Mexico's city slums or rural areas and had moved north to the Mexican-American border in the hope of getting into the United States. In 1970, an official Mexican Border Industrial Program was organized by which American companies arranged to take the half-finished parts of small manufactured articles across the border, have them assembled by Mexican labor and returned to the United States without the payment of taxes on either side. Nine such companies were established in Tijuana and seven in Juárez, where the minimum wage was a quarter of that paid in San Diego or El Paso. Radios, television sets, and mechanical toys were being turned out in quantity. Tijuana's population grew from 20,000 in 1940 to 366,000 in 1970, and Mexicali, in Baja California, became the sixth largest city in Mexico.

Among assembly plants established in central Mexico is a large factory in Puebla that assembles Volkswagens. A worker in the Volkswagen plant earning the equivalent of $50 in United States dollars in the early 1970s can rent a flat in a new high-rise development, buy a refrigerator and a television set, and make a down-payment on a new Volkswagen. Millions of such workers and their families are creating a market for small cars, motorcycles, and transistor radios. In 1970, 13 per cent of Mexican city dwellers owned a car, 20 per cent a washing machine, and 60 per cent a sewing machine. Mexicans were buying pre-fabricated small houses and even "instant" three-room school houses made in assembly-line factories. Many purchasers of a single truck have gone into business carrying goods over the 40,000 miles of Mexico's paved highways.

In the 1960s and early 1970s, the nation's overall economic growth was better than 7 per cent while her gross national product reached $20 billion. The country has the most diversified economy in Latin America, with cotton providing 20 per cent of her export, coffee 10 per cent, and mineral ores 30 per cent. Steel production has been going up 5 per cent a year while for several years truck manufacture and electric power output have shown an annual 10 per cent increase. Tourism has become a major industry, enhanced by the success of the Olympic games, the development of jet airplane travel, and the building of large hotels for guests. Woolworth, Sears, Chrysler, Ford, and General Motors all have manufacturing and assembly plants as well as large retail outlets in Mexico. The country's diversifying economy should advance the creation of the 5 million jobs it will need by 1980. Yet the life of the landless peasants, drawn to the city in the hope of employment and living in abject poverty in shanty-towns and slums, is as wretched as in any place in the world.

education in Mexico

Mexicans met difficulty during the years of dictatorship and war in throwing off the cultural pattern of Spanish colonialism. Creoles continued to educate their children in the traditional fashion, to send their sons to study in Paris, and to ape in art and literature the customs, manners, and tastes of Europe. Juárez, who had a strong interest in a practical education for the masses of people separate from Church authority, expressed the hopelessness of bringing any change:

> Even though the schools multiplied and be well endowed and teachers well paid, there would always be a scarcity of pupils so long as the cause which prevents the attendance of children persists. That cause is the widespread misery under which our people live. The man who cannot supply his family with food views the schooling of his sons not merely as something remote but actually as an obstacle in his daily struggle for existence since it takes from him his assistants.[2]

This sad commentary summarizes the obstacle that still faces education in Mexico today. Juárez as president did, however, liberalize education at the upper level by broadening the curriculum of Mexico City's few secondary schools. But it was not until after 1920 that Mexico's public schools became an expression of a true non-colonial *Mexican* culture.

The followers of the Revolution of 1910–1920 wanted free public education as a part of their program equal in importance to the free distribution of land. Article 3 of the 1917 Constitution goes beyond any requirement for education in other modern constitutions of the world, providing as it does for education as a government trust, limiting parochial education, and making all plans, programs, and methods of teaching the responsibility of the state. To carry out this heavy responsibility in a land with few teachers and little tradition of state-supported education, Obregón, in 1921, appointed José Vasconcelos, a Revolutionary leader in his student days and by then director of the National University, to be the first Administrator of Federal Education. Under Calles, his pioneer efforts were carried on by Moisés Sáenz, who attempted to carry out the promise to found rural

---

[2] Quoted in Ernest Gruening, *Mexico and Its Heritage* (New York, Appleton-Century-Crofts, Inc., 1928).

schools in all villages. By 1930 there were more than 3,500 new village schools such as the one in Santa Cruz Etla.

These rural schools were the epitome of the Revolutionary doctrine, built by the people themselves and staffed by very young idealists who could hardly be trained fast enough for the demand, and who served as health, cultural, and recreational leaders for the new order. Some of the teachers met with violent opposition; a few were even attacked, in the religious upheaval of the *Cristero* movement. In Cárdenas' time every new *ejido* grant obligated the villagers to build a school; 1,600 new schools went up by his order on large ranches, and additional hundreds were started in factory communities financed by the owners of the industrial development. In the mid-1940s it could be said that in proportion to per capita income, Mexico was spending a larger share for education than the United States.

In the 1970s there were more than 40,000 public elementary schools in Mexico with more than four million students. For each of these schools a teacher had been recruited and trained and was being paid well by Latin American standards, two-thirds from federal and one-third from local funds. Although much credit is due to Cárdenas, actually Ávila Camacho, Alemán, and López Mateos founded more schools than he did; and under later presidents public secondary and technical training showed rapid improvement. Dedicated and sincere men have served in the position of Minister of Education.

Only areas of very sparse population, or Indian-speaking tribal communities in the more remote mountain areas, do not now have public schools; and only one-tenth of Mexican children are now in private or church-supported elementary schools. However, since laws for compulsory attendance are not enforced, no penalties are visited on parents who keep their children out of school; and, since teachers and classrooms are still in short supply as well, 2.5 million children throughout the nation are deprived of elementary education. Most rural and village schools only offer four grades, each grade requiring more factual and advanced material than the corresponding grade in the United States, and ordinarily taking two years to finish. Because a sixth-grade certificate is required for admission to the city secondary school, most rural children have no opportunity for any advanced education.

But formal advanced education has not been the goal for the agricultural population. Simple reading and writing have been augmented with such a wide social program that the elementary rural schools in Mexico have become a model for other parts of Latin America. Scientific agriculture, better care of livestock, improved feeding of infants, control of public health, purification of water supply—these are the things about which simple textbooks have been written and which the teachers have been trained to emphasize. Vasconcelos and Sáenz had to push the normal training-school program rapidly to get teachers prepared for such service; Santa Cruz Etla and thousands of other communities waited from one to three years after their building was finished for a trained teacher. Boys and girls from the villages, especially in areas of Indian culture, have been granted liberal scholarships to encourage them to go to normal schools and return as teachers in their own communities. The rural teachers of Mexico have been a zealous, dedicated group, actual "missionaries" in a non-religious sense.

Their work was from the first augmented by "cultural missions." Since the young teachers sent out to the hill communities in the 1930s were so poorly trained and the communities themselves so unused to schools, groups of trained specialists were sent on circuit to help them. Nurses, gardeners, art-craft workers, recreational leaders, and musicians were formed into units which traveled with mobile libraries and craft rooms from community to community. Successful from the first, cultural missions became a permanent feature of Mexican life, and their example has inspired educators in other parts of Latin America.

To reach the non-Spanish-speaking tribes, the cultural mission program was augmented by bringing promising young Indians into Mexico City for advanced education and training in leadership. The success of these young tribal Indians in the city schools convinced many skeptical Mexicans of the great potential lying dormant in the Indians. But this program failed when the young people so trained did not want to go back and serve the communities they had come from; schools were then founded out in the Indian-speaking regions where teachers were trained on their own home grounds. Today there is a school teaching Spanish in most large Indian-speaking communities. Thus, eventually, all village centers of Indian-speaking groups—the Otomí, the Mixtec, the Zapotecans, the Tarascans, the Huichols, the Chamulas, the Yucateca Maya—will be "Mexicanized" and literate in the Spanish language.

Among the Spanish-speaking people in town and country in the 1930s, 60 per cent did not know how to read and write. In 1944 in a wartime emergency, Ávila Camacho decided to launch a program to teach illiterate adults to read. Doctor Jaime Torres Bodet, afterward chairman of UNESCO and again Secretary of Education for López Mateos in 1959, was appointed to take charge of this program. A primer was prepared to teach adults letter by letter in a very simple way, a primer with which any person who knew how to read and write was able to teach any illiterate person. This "each one teach one" plan was widely publicized throughout Mexico and inspired another "missionary movement" on the part of hundreds of thousands of literate people. Those who could read taught more than a million others to read between 1944 and 1946. Recent presidents have launched a new campaign, using regular trained teachers and granting them extra pay for after-hours work with adults. Today the plan is being copied, through UNESCO by other underdeveloped areas of the world. In 1967, Díaz Ordaz even drafted American companies into the literacy campaign. For example, out of a total of 15,568 "literacy centers" in 19 states, 70 were set up in that year by the Coca Cola Company and its local bottling agencies.

One of the aims of the literacy program has been to give information about malaria, tuberculosis, and venereal disease. To thousands of villages an improved water supply, piped into the village plaza and made free of typhoid contamination, came hand in hand with the new rural school. The Department of Education has cooperated with the Department of Public Health in giving teachers courses in rural medicine. There is a campaign against malaria, a campaign against tuberculosis, a campaign against venereal disease, just as there is a campaign against illiteracy. Other Latin American nations come to Mexico for information about the anti-malaria campaign, and the Pan American Sanitary Bureau has been working closely with it.

Medical students are few in comparison with the number needed, partially because so few students have adequate secondary school training. Even in the city elementary schools, in the six years of free public education offered, 37 per cent of the pupils are in the first grade, 21 per cent in the second grade, and 1 per cent in the sixth grade. Without a sixth-grade certificate secondary education is impossible. Since the demand is still small, the government builds 3,000 elementary schools for every ten secondary institutions of any kind. Though public high schools have been improved, secondary schooling has remained largely a private enterprise, and in the final "live and let live" policy which the government worked out with the Church under Ávila Camacho it has been an accepted fact that more than two-thirds of the secondary education is done by Church authorities. There are also the Latin American-type *colegios* or privately run schools, with varying standards of subject matter and instruction.

This whole secondary school set-up brings only the cream of the brilliant and the sons of the well-to-do into the institutions of higher learning. However, Mexico has become famous in Latin America for her splendid new university buildings. In 1952 the National University of Mexico, eighty-five years older than Harvard, was given a $15 million campus, a beautiful University City in a new suburb some twenty miles outside Mexico City. This plant, with its startling and ultra-modern functional architecture and its Aztec motif, its capacity for 25,000 students, and its library, laboratory, visual education, and sports facilities—certainly one of the finest physical plants for a university in the Western Hemisphere—replaced a great many scattered units throughout Mexico City, which had the medical school here, the law school there, the teacher-training schools elsewhere. The university was filled to capacity in the late 1960s in spite of the lack of secondary school graduates.

There are also an 8 million-peso Polytechnic City which houses a technical school, a National School of Agriculture, a School of Tropical Medicine, a Workers' University, and the University of the Americas, an international institution on the American plan, as well as a smaller university in each state capital. The Monterrey Technical Institute, founded in 1942, is the Cal Tech of Mexico. American students who go to school in Mexico find student life quite different from that in the United States. They miss the sociability of college life in America. Though there are now some full-time faculty salaries for the out-of-town campus, university professors often teach part-time and sometimes have to make their real living by means of their law practices, their government jobs, or their journalistic activities. Therefore, they do not feel themselves a part of campus life. Campus life itself is almost nonexistent; there are few residence groups or undergraduate organizations, and athletics are only now becoming a part of Mexican student life. The courses, however, are very strict and scholarly; advanced degrees which are given are accepted throughout the academic world.

The University of Mexico is coeducational, and many women study for the professions. The position of women in politics, in law, and in medicine has improved enormously since the Revolution. There is also a Women's University, which it is increasingly stylish for women to attend. The members of the Association of University Women are leaders in public affairs in Mexico City. There are also many colleges which are run by the Church. They maintain the high scholastic standards and much of the prestige they had in colonial times, and today they have no opposition from the government. As has been described in the chapter on politics, page 329, the series of student riots in the summer of 1968 brought the death and imprisonment of many students and almost held up the plans for the Olympics. In most of the large centers of Mexico, secondary schools and universities were closed until the fall of 1969. But when the schools were opened again, university life resumed and standards of teaching and scholarship improved consistently.

culture in renascent Mexico

In artistic endeavor, Mexicans of the 19th century fell far behind their Aztec forebears. The beautiful Indian handicrafts sold in Mexican centers today were not considered objects of artistic beauty a hundred years ago. Villagers made them for their own pleasure and use. It was not until the Indian Renaissance of the 1930s that they were considered "art" and received encouragement in their preservation. The Fine Arts Academy in Mexico City lauded by von Humboldt in the late colonial period had fallen into decay. Mexico City did have 700 students of fine arts in the more stable 1870s, but the art taught in the Academy, discussed in cultured circles in the cities, and hung in drawing rooms was a pale provincial reflection of Europe. The only expression of native art was found in folk art, in saloon paintings, in "the people's murals," and in political cartoons.

Today however, Mexico, more than any other Latin American nation, is proud of her Indian blood and Indian tradition. The "Renaissance" of Mexico was initiated by a handicraft exhibition arranged in 1921 by Secretary of Education José Vasconcelos that emphasized the Indian folk art, music, and folklore. He and his associates said they wished to make Mexico the cultural center of the Western Hemisphere as the United States was its industrial center. Their promotion of regional crafts brought a whole new industry to Mexico as tourists eagerly bought the blue blown glass of Guadalajara, the textiles of Oaxaca, the leather craft of Toluca, the silver filigree from Taxco, the lacquer from Michoacán. The work of Aztec, Tarascan, and Zapotecan craftsmen was revived. Also revived was pride in the Indian heritage. Indian symbolism in literature and Indian themes in musical expression became almost a fad in Mexico City. The upsurge in cultural interest brought on by the Revolution made Mexico the one place in the Western Hemisphere in which people were proud of their Indian ancestry.

Indianism was best shown in the art of the 1920s and 30s, the leader of which was Diego Rivera (1885–1957) who became the most famous artist of the Western Hemisphere. At the time when Madero was president, Rivera was a young artist studying with the post-impressionists in Paris; José Clemente Orozco (1883–1949), the second great Mexican artist of his time, was busy painting scenes of the poverty in Mexico City; and David Alfaro Siqueiros (1898–   ), the third Revolutionary art leader, was drawing cartoons to illustrate Revolutionary song sheets. A congress of soldier-artists held to discuss ways of using art in the new Revolutionary program resulted in the sending of Siqueiros and Orozco abroad, where they met Rivera in Paris. In Barcelona they published a "manifesto" proclaiming the Western Hemisphere art of the future to be a true Indian art. Rivera and his young colleagues returned to Mexico after studying alfresco mural painting methods in Italy and joined with Vasconcelos in the new Indian-based movement. A system of teaching drawing in the new public schools with simple elements of design was originated by an art teacher and artist, Adolfo Best-Maugard. A great cultural fair in Chapultepec in 1921 served to popularize the new trends in art, music and folk dancing.

Rivera was soon putting his study of alfresco methods of painting on the new public buildings of the Revolutionary Party. He painted spectacular murals using a palette of ten bright earth colors on wet plaster. The central motif of each was the Indian, portrayed with crude face, large feet and hands, and dark, earth-red skin. The three-story Department of Education building was covered with almost an acre of paintings of Indian groups of all regions. The Cortés Palace in Cuernavaca, used as the state legislature for Morelos, has the artist's concept of the entire history of Mexico painted across the outside wall facing the town.

Orozco,[3] Rivera, and Siqueiros differed sharply in style and approach but all sought to put across a social message. Painting Indians was not enough. They criticized the clergy, made cartoons of public characters, showed Justice as a debauched drunken person, and the Father God surrounded by harpies instead of angels. Polite society in Mexico City was scandalized; conservatives protested the defiling of public buildings, while Rivera took delight in shocking people even more by playing around with the political philosophy of Communism. At the time of his death in December 1957, Rivera and his work were still controversial; his gigantic underwater design for the Mexico City reservoir caused anger and confusion when it was created, and some smug amusement when its colors began to wash away. But Rivera had succeeded in bringing the Indian element into modern art, and recent Mexican artists of a milder school have continued his work of making Mexican art a distinctive New World force. Miguel

[3] See the photograph of the Orozco mural featuring Benito Juárez.

Covarrubias (1904–1959), in illustrating American books, has made readers conscious of Zapotec culture. Sculpture is also using Aztec motifs, and the name of Manuel Centurión is known among world sculptors.

By the 1960s the *Indianismo* which the Revolutionary artists set out to promote had been left behind, and seemed almost a forgotten cause. David Alfaro Siqueiros, long held in jail for his Communist activities, was busy in 1960 and 1965 painting "the largest mural in the world" in a Cuernavaca hotel. Its subject was the "whole history of humanity emerging into the modern world." Rufino Tamayo, Mexico's leading painter in the early 1970s, painted with the flamboyant Mexican colors, but chose themes common to all humanity. He considered El Greco and Picasso his masters rather than Rivera and Orozco. Busily painting into his seventh decade, Rufino Tamayo was considered an artist "of the Americas and of the world," more than was Rivera, the artist of Mexican "Indianismo." Juan O'Gorman, born in 1905 of mixed Mexican and Irish descent, has produced the two most famous recent murals, the mosaic of Mexican history on four sides of the University library and the mural of the Hidalgo revolt which is in the Chapultepec Castle history museum. Today art-conscious Mexico is moving further in the direction of artistic diversity and its art schools are a Mecca for art-minded tourists and students.

Music has always been the great love of Mexico. In the 18th century, native opera troups appeared even in Guadalajara, in the silver-mining towns, and went by ship to Spanish California. Madame Calderón de la Barca went to the Italian opera in Mexico City. She saw pianos in every upper-class house she visited and heard daughters play and listened to singing in family circles. Young men played the guitar, not only for "courting purposes." Tea parties called *tertulias* centered around group singing. Popular songs were printed as *corridos*, running-ballads, and sold as penny sheets. And they were often concerned with subjects such as presidential campaigns, the War against the United States, or Santa Anna's or Maximilian's "empires"—they were, in effect, the forerunners of the many famous ballads of the later Revolutionary period. The popular Mexican folk songs sung today in staged fiestas in California and New Mexico—such as *Cielito Lindo* and *Rancho Grande*—were sung in Mexico in the 1840s and 1850s. Throughout all three acts of the 19th-century drama, the color, the music, the native charm of the people were there on the center of the stage.

In the Revolutionary period, music in Mexico began to follow new patterns. Some of the classical musicians started with the Indian folk tune and created from it a sophisticated modern music form wholly Mexican. The first Revolutionary compositions were the camp songs that are still popular as folk songs. Carlos Chávez (1899–   ) a brilliant composer and the founder of the Mexico City Symphony, brought both Indian and Revolutionary themes into his works, and, as Director of the National Conservatory of Music, has started many young students working in this new direction. The son of a Spanish father and Indian mother, he has conducted in the United States, where much of his music is played, and is considered one of the foremost musicians in Latin American history, second perhaps only to the great Brazilian, Villalobos. As is happening in other fields of art, Mexican music is undergoing diversification, and its styles vary from the academic and the Indian to the ultra-modern.

Few writers of the 1800s are considered worthy of attention today. A feeble new literature appeared in the early days of the Republic which attempted to tell the truly Mexican story. The poems of King Nezahualcoyotl were translated and popularized in the 1830s; and sad epics about "The Vision of Montezuma" and "The Prophecy of Cuauhtémoc" were written by Ignacio Rodríguez Galván (1816–1842)—all this while contemporaneous Indians of Aztec blood were scorned in the streets. Lyric poets were still copying French patterns in the 1860s but a new native beauty in poetic expression began to emerge after the French intervention when the desire was to publish personal feelings rather than to copy things said in Europe. In the 1890s, two poets who were not crushed by the Díaz regime were outstanding—Justo Sierra (1848–1912), son of another poet by that name, and Manuel Gutiérrez Nájera (1859–1895), who wrote lyrical love poetry. And then at the turn of the century came a modernist movement and a magazine devoted to *modernista* poetry paralleling the work of young poets in Central and South America. Except for this late blooming, the culture of 19th-century Mexico generally reflected Díaz' own envy of European society.

Several novels that are popular reading today appeared in the 19th century although no single novel is listed among the great pieces of Spanish literature. These novels tell of romantic love in the midst of the War of Reform or the battle against Maximilian, or of heroes in jail for their political belief or dying in the armies of the Republic. Most of them were written by men who fought in such armies themselves. One of the first unromanticized novels about the Indian love of the land was *La Parcela* (*The Plot of Ground*) written by José López Portillo y Rojas (1850–1923), a work that was a forerunner of the many "land-hungry" novels of the 1920s.

Writers turned naturally to the writing of history at a time when life was as exciting and tragic as it was in Mexico during this period. Vicente Riva Palacio (1832–1896), a commander in the Juárez army, wrote historical novels so accurate they were amost history, writing some of them from a jail cell when the liberals were not "in." He founded a literary magazine and wrote a clever series of biographies of his contemporaries. Francisco Bulnes (1847–1924), a prolific journalist and a political and social leader among the *científicos*, wrote complete, though pro-Díaz, histories of the period during which he lived.

Two political leaders of opposing parties in Santa Anna's time wrote historical materials. José Mariá Luís Mora (1794–1850) defied Iturbide, agitated for the Republic, and fought so well with his pen that he became the cultural leader of the liberals. Lucas Alamán (1792–1853) the conservative political philosopher and exact opposite of Mora, was a meticulous but partisan historian and excellent prose writer. Newspapers, in existence at the time of these writers, were throughout the century never more than political tools for the party in power and negligible as a cultural influence.

A popular Mexican theater was born during the Revolution of 1910, given as tent shows following the armies for the entertainment of the common people. At first called "crude, improvised, and disreputable but alive," this drama has come into its own as a musical theater in Mexico City's downtown area. Musical shows caricaturing political evils are very popular in Mexico, some of them handed down from the Revolution itself. More important today are motion pictures, a big industry in Mexico. Mexican-made movies are shown throughout Latin America, play to packed houses in the Spanish-speaking theaters of the American Southwest, and are regularly shown in the Spanish neighborhoods of New York. Many of their stars are better known in Venezuela or Argentina than American actors. Best known of all has been Mario Moreno, the comic character and pantomimist known as Cantinflas, whose work has been praised in Spain as "the highest form of dramatic art possible" with one character.

Twentieth-century Mexico's deep interest in its Indian culture has been fostered by the office of *Asuntos Indígenas* or things Indian, founded by Cárdenas and the National Institute of Fine Arts established by Alemán. Its objective was to become "guardian and permanent judge of what is purely Mexican throughout the coming generations" and of preserving "that combination of Indian and Spanish which makes Mexican culture today." *Indianismo* and the Revolution have been kept alive in literature. The Revolution, more interested in strong, deep feelings than the light, lyrical ones so popular previously, produced a new type of Revolutionary novel that was concerned with the masses.

One of the new novelists was Gregorio López y Fuentes (1891–1966), who was born of a well-to-do family and worked as a journalist in the days of Obregón, producing a daily column of sketches of common people in the Revolution. A series of these columns about the disorganized adventures of a band of Revolutionary soldiers became his first novel, *Campamento*. His second novel, *Tierra,* actually the life of Zapata, has helped keep the Indian hero a shining figure in the eyes of a non-Revolutionary second generation. In the novel *El Indio,* the main character is the Indian village, a community like Santa Cruz Etla, which is brought from semibarbarism into contact with the world by means of a school, a new road, and a church. To secure material for this famous novel, López y Fuentes served as a rural teacher. His style—presenting an incident here, an incident there—is one of setting atmosphere and mood rather than of intricacies of plot.

Martín Luis Guzmán (1887–   ), a journalist with the forces of Villa and Carranza, wrote of his experiences in *The Eagle and the Serpent* and in *La Sombra del Caudillo* or *Shade of the Chieftain*, books of narrative history that have the dramatic impact of novels. He did much to make Pancho Villa's memory seem heroic with his publication of the memoirs of Villa, and today is considered one of Mexico's most noted historians.

Mariano Azuela (1873–1952), the third of this group of great novelists, was a liberal young doctor who served for several months in 1915 as head of a guerrilla band and had to flee to El Paso, Texas, when Carranza was victorious. There he published in serial form in a Spanish-language paper a novel based on his life as leader of a Revolutionary band. The novel became popular as *Los de Abajo* (*The Underdogs*) after he returned to the practice of medicine in post–Revolutionary Mexico City. A humble Indian from Zacatecas becomes a guerrilla band leader in this most famous of modern Mexican novels, and is followed by his men into the army of Villa, where they fight, kill, love, drink, and sing in a manner completely engrossing to the reader. The novel shows the enthusiastic spirit of the Revolution and at the same time much of its aimlessness and futility. The men, when fighting Carranza, were forced to retreat and, boxed up in a canyon, they were, as "those below," *Los de Abajo,* wiped out by soldiers on the hills above.

Current writers seem less interested in *Indianismo* and the Revolution. Octavio Paz (1914–   ), the leading poet, has said, "We want to be contemporaneous with all mankind." His own poems and essays deal with subjects such as art, mysticism, religion, and psychology. A career diplomat who has lived in Paris, he has been widely translated into other languages and has in turn translated Japanese, Portuguese, and Swedish poets into Spanish. *Américas* magazine judges his influence to have been enormous on young writers in the Western hemisphere. Octavio Paz has written in "Life of the Poet":[4]

> *Words? Yes, made of air*
> *and in the air dissolved.*
> *Let me lose myself among words,*
> *let me become the air on living lips*
> *a breath that goes wandering without barriers,*
> *scent of a moment in the air diffused.*

Poetry is still the literary hobby of many public figures in Mexico. Jaime Torres Bodet, the world-renowned intellectual who headed UNESCO, founded as Secretary of Education the "each one teach one" literacy program, and served as ambassador to France, would like to be remembered for his six novels and his 17 published volumes of poetry. His poetry reflects his concern for mankind. As he writes in "Civilization,"[5]

> *A man dies within me every time a man dies somewhere,*
> *assassinated by the fear and hate of other men.*

Elsewhere Torres Bodet writes of the need for:

> *a truth based on love proclaimed aloud,*
> *time acquired meaning*
> *and neither pain, nor anguish, nor effort*
> *will have been in vain.*

[4] Reprinted from an edition of translations by Muriel Rukeyser, *Selected Poems by Octavio Paz,* Bloomington, Ind., Indiana University Press, 1963, p. 23, by permission of the publisher.

[5] Reprinted from *Américas,* August 1969, pp. 9, 10, by permission of the publisher.

The broader appeal of the new novels is also shown in the works of Juan Rulfo (1918–   ), whose famous novel *Pedro Páramo,* written in 1955 and published in English in 1959, is about peasants in his native Jalisco where he himself was once a homeless orphan. It has a universal appeal to all who have known homelessness or deprivation. A similar psychological approach is found in Carlos Fuentes' (1929–   ) *The Death of Artemio Cruz* (1962) and other recent social novels.

Notable also is the work of literary critic Alfonso Reyes, anthropologist Manuel Gamio, and Director of the Museum of Anthropology Ignacio Bernal. Also notable is Alfonso Caso, the author of 180 works on archeology and social anthropology who retired in 1970 after 21 years as head of the National Indian Institute. Caso has complained that interest in the Indians today is on the decline. He says that modern industrialized Mexico is neglecting the Yaquis, the Zapotecans, the Tarahumares, and the Chamulas, and that the budget to provide improvements, water supply, school and health service to the non-Spanish community is inadequate. "Indianismo" is still, however, part of the dynamic heritage of all Mexicans, interwoven with Mexican public life. Few developments in modern Latin America have been as significant as the educational movements, aesthetic influences, and literary fires of creation that were rekindled out of the Indianist-mestizo world when the violence of the Mexican Revolution of 1910 was over.

READINGS: MEXICO

Adams, R. N., et al., *Social Change in Latin America Today* (1960).

Alba, V., *The Mexicans: Making of a Nation* (1968).

Alexander, R. J., *Organized Labor in Latin America* (1965).

Alisky, M., *State and Local Government in Sonora, Mexico* (1962).

————, *Government of the Mexican State of Nueva Leon* (1971).

Arquin, F., *Diego Rivera: The Shaping of an Artist 1889–1921* (1971).

Ashby, J. C., *Organized Labor and the Mexican Revolution under Lázaro Cárdenas* (1967).

Astiz, C. A., ed., *Latin American International Politics: Ambitions, Capabilities and the National Interest of Mexico, Brazil and Argentina* (1969).

Atkin, R., *Revolution: Mexico 1910–1920* (1970).

Atwater, J. D. and R. Ruiz, *Out From Under: Benito Juáres and Mexico's Struggle for Independence* (1969).

Aubov, R. T., *Nacional Financiera and Mexican Industry* (1966).

Avila, M., *Tradition and Growth: A Study of Four Mexican Villages* (1969).

Azuela, M., *Two Novels of Mexico: The Flies, The Bosses,* trans. L. B. Simpson (1956).

————, *The Underdogs* (various editions).

Bailey, H. M., *Santa Cruz of the Etla Hills* (1958).

Baker, R. D., *Judicial Review in Mexico: A Study of the Amparo Suit* (1971).

Ball, J. M., *Migration and the Rural Municipio in Mexico* (1971).

Banco Nacional de Comercil Exterior (Mexico), *Mexico 1963. Facts, Figures, Trends* (1963).

Barker, E. C., *Life of Stephen F. Austin* (2nd ed., 1949).

———, *Mexico and Texas, 1821–1835* (1928).

Barkin, D., *Regional Economic Development: The River Basin Approach in Mexico* (1970).

Bazant, J., *Alienation of Church Wealth in Mexico Social and Economic Aspects of the Liberal Revolution 1856–1875* (1971).

Beacham, H., *The Architecture of Mexico: Yesterday and Today* (1969).

Beals, C., *Porfirio Díaz, Dictator of Mexico* (1932).

Bell, B., ed., *Indian Mexico: Past and Present* (1965).

Bells, A. H., *Rehearsal for Conflict: The War with Mexico, 1846–1848* (1947).

Benveniste, G., *Bureaucracy and National Planning: A Sociological Case Study in Mexico* (1970).

Bennett, R. L., *The Financial Sector and Economic Development: The Mexican Case* (1965).

Bermudez, A. J., *Mexican Petroleum Industry* (1963).

Bernstein, H., *Modern and Contemporary Latin America* (1952).

Bernstein, M., *Foreign Investments in Latin America* (1966).

Bernstein, M., *Mexican Mining Industry, 1890–1950* (1965).

Bert, V. M., *Central Banking in Mexico: Monetary Policies and Financial Crises, 1864–1940* (1957).

Beteta, R., *Jarano*, trans. J. Upton (1970).

Bett, V. M., *Central Banking in Mexico: Monetary Policies and Financial Crises, 1864–1940* (1957).

Binckley, W. C., *Texas Revolution* (1952).

Blaisdell, L. L., *The Desert Revolution—Baja California, 1911* (1962).

Blasio, J. L., *Maximilian, Emperor of Mexico: Memoirs of His Private Secretary* (1934).

Blumberg, A., *The Diplomacy of the Mexican Empire 1863–1867* (1971).

Booth, G. C., *Mexico's School Made Society* (1941).

Born, E., et al., *The New Architecture of Mexico* (1937).

Braddy, H., *Cock of the Walk: The Pancho Villa Legend* (1955).

———, *Pancho Villa at Columbus* (1965).

———, *Pershing's Mission to Mexico* (1966).

Brand, D., *Mexico: Land of Shadow and Shade* (1965).

Brandenburg, F. R., *The Development of Latin American Private Enterprise* (1964).

———, *Making of Modern Mexico* (1964).

Brenner, A., *Idols Behind Altars* (1929).

———, *The Wind that Swept Mexico: History of the Mexican Revolution, 1910–1942* (1943).

Brothers, D. S., and L. Solís, *Mexican Financial Development* (1966).

Brushwood, J. S., *Mexico and Its Novels* (1966).

———, *The Romantic Novel in Mexico* (1954).

Cadenhead, I. E., *Jesús González Ortega and Mexican National Politics* (1972).

Calderón de la Barca, Mme., *Life in Mexico During a Residence of Two Years in That Country* (many editions).

Callahan, J. M., *American Foreign Policy in Mexican Relations* (1932).

Callahan, J. M., *American Foreign Policy in Mexican Relations* (1932).

Callcott, W. H., *Church and State in Mexico, 1822–1867* (1926).

————, *Liberalism in Mexico, 1857–1929* (1931).

————, *Santa Anna* (1932).

Calvert, P., *The Mexican Revolution 1910–1914: The Diplomacy of Anglo-American Conflict* (1968).

Caponiari, A., ed., *Major Trends in Mexican Philosophy* (1966).

Caruso, J. A., *Liberators of Mexico* (1954).

Castañeda, C. E., ed., *Mexican Side of the Texas Revolution* (1928).

Castañeda, J., *Mexico and the United Nations* (1958).

Charlot, J., *Mexican Art and the Academy of San Carlos, 1785–1915* (1962).

————, *The Mexican Mural Renaissance, 1920–1925* (1963).

Chase, G., *Contemporary Art in Latin America* (1970).

Cheetham, N., *Mexico: A Short History* (1970).

Clark, M. R., *Organized Labor in Mexico* (1934).

Clendenen, C. C., *The United States and Pancho Villa* (1961).

Cline, H. F., *Mexico: Revolution to Evolution, 1940–1960* (1962).

————, *The United States and Mexico* (rev. ed., 1962).

Cockroft, J. D., *Intellectual Precursors of the Mexican Revolution 1900–1913* (1968).

Coe, M. D., *Mexico* (1962).

Cole, W. E., *Steel and Economic Growth in Mexico* (1967).

Corti, E. C., *Maximilian and Charlotte of Mexico*, trans. C. A. Phillips (2 vols., 1928).

Corwin, A. F., *Contemporary Mexican Attitudes Towards Population, Poverty and Public Opinion* (1963).

Cosío Villegas, D., *American Extremes* (1964).

————, *Change in Latin America: The Mexican and Cuban Revolutions* (1961).

————, *United States versus Perfirio Díaz* (1963).

Costeloe, M. P., *Church Wealth in Mexico: A Study of the "Juzgado de Capellanías" in the Archbishopric of Mexico 1800–1856* (1968).

Cotner, T. E., *Military and Political Career of José Joaquín de Herrera, 1792–1834* (1949).

————, and C. E. Castañeda, eds., *Essays in Mexican History* (1958).

Craig, R. B., *The Bracero Program: Interest Groups and Foreign Policy* (1971).

Crawford, W. R., *Century of Latin American Thought* (1961).

————, *A Mexican Ulysses* (Vasconcelos) (1963).

Cronon, E. D., *Josephus Daniels in Mexico* (1960).

Crow, J. A., *Mexico Today* (1957).

Cumberland, C. C., *The Mexican Revolution: Genesis Under Madero* (1952).

————, *The Mexican Revolution: The Constitutionalist Years* (1972).

————, *Mexico: Struggle for Modernity* (1968).

————, ed., *The Meaning of the Mexican Revolution* (1967).

————, *Social and Economic History of Mexico* (1966).

Dabbs, J. A., *The French Army in Mexico, 1861–1867* (1963).

Daniels, J., *Shirt Sleeve Diplomacy* (1947).

Davis, M. L., and C. Pack, *Mexican Jewelry* (1963).

Davis, T. C., et al., *Mexico's Recent Economic Growth* (1967).

Dawson, D., *The Mexican Venture (French Intervention)* (1915).

De la Cueva, M., et al., *Major Trends in Mexican Philosophy*, trans. A. R. Caponieri (1966).

Derossi, F., *The Mexican Entrepreneur* (1971).

Dozier, C. L., *Land Development and Colonization in Latin America. Case Studies of Peru, Bolivia, and Mexico* (1969).

Ducoff, L. J., *Human Resources in Central America, Panama and Mexico, 1950–1980* (1960).

Dulles, J. W. F., *Yesterday in Mexico: A Chronicle of the Revolution, 1919–1936* (1961).

Dunn, F. S., *Diplomatic Protection of Americans in Mexico* (1933).

Dunn, H. H., *Crimson Jester: Zapata of Mexico* (1933).

Ewing, R., ed., *Six Faces of Mexico* (1966).

Fagen, R. R., and L. A. Cornelius, ed., *Political Power in Latin America: Seven Confrontations* (1970).

Feller, A. H., *The Mexican Claims Commission, 1923–1934* (1935).

Fergusson, E., *Mexico Revisited* (1955).

Fernández, J., *A Guide to Mexican Art, from Its Beginnings to the Present* (1970).

————, *Political Administration in Mexico* (1969).

Flandrau, C. M., *Viva Mexico* (1908).

Fox, D. J., and D. J. Robinson, *Cities in a Changing Latin America: Two Studies of Urban Growth in the Development of Mexico and Venezuela* (1969).

Freithaler, W. O., *Mexico's Foreign Trade and Economic Development* (1967).

Gaither, R. B., *Expropriation in Mexico* (1951).

Galarza, E., *Merchants of Labor: The Mexican Bracero Story* (1964).

Garber, P. N., *Gadsden Treaty* (1923).

García Cubas, A., *Republic of Mexico in 1876* (1876).

García Naranjo, N., *Porfirio Díaz* (1930).

Gardiner, C. H., "Survey: Foreign Travellers' Account of Mexico, 1810–1910," *Americas*, III (1952).

Gil, C. C. et al., *Atlas of Mexico* (1970).

Gill, T., *Land Hunger in Mexico* (1951).

Glades, W. P. and C. W. Anderson, *Political Economy of Mexico* (1963).

Glick, E. B., *Straddling the Isthmus of Tehuantepec* (1959).

Gomez, Robledo, A., *Bucareli Agreements and International Law* (1960).

González Casanova, P., *Democracy in Mexico*, trans. D. Selti (1970).

González Peña, C., *History of Mexican Literature*, trans. G. B. Nance and F. J. Dunstan (1943).

Gordon, W. C., *The Expropriation of Foreign Owned Property in Mexico* (1941).

Government of Mexico, *Mexico's Oil* (Documentary compilation—1940).

Great Britain, Board of Trade, Overseas Economic Survey—Mexico (1949).

Green, G., *Another Mexico* (1939).

Gregg, R. D., *Influence of Border Troubles on Relations between the United States and Mexico, 1876–1910* (1917).

Grieb, G., *The United States and Huerta* (1969).

Griffen, W. B., *Cultural Change and Shifting Populations in Central Northern Mexico* (1969).

Gros, B., ed., *National Planning, Power, Purpose, Performance* (1955).

Gruening, E., *Mexico and Its Heritage* (1928).

Guzmán, M. L., *Eagle and the Serpent*, trans. H. de Onís (1936).

————, *Memoirs of Pancho Villa* (1965).

Hackett, C. W., *The Mexican Revolution and the United States, 1910–1926* (1926).

Haddox, J. H., *Vasconcelos of Mexico; Philosopher and Prophet* (1967).

————, *Antonio Case: Philosopher of Mexico* (1971).

Hale, C. A., *Mexican Liberalism in the Age of Mora 1821–1853* (1968).

Haley, P. E., *Revolution and Intervention. The Diplomacy of Taft and Wilson with Mexico 1910–1917* (1970).

Hamill, W. H., *Dictatorship in Latin America* (1965).

Hancock, R. H., *Role of the Bracero in the Economic and Culture Dynamics of Mexico* (1959).

Hanke, L., *Mexico and the Caribbean* (revised, 1966).

Hanna, A. J., and Hanna K. A., *Napoleon III and Mexico: American Triumph over Monarchy* (1971).

Hansen, R. D., *The Politics of Mexican Development* (1971).

————, *Mexican Economic Development: The Roots of Rapid Growth.*

Haslip, S., *The Crown of Mexico, Maximilian and His Empress Carlota* (1971).

Hedrick, B., et al., eds., *The North Mexican Frontier: Readings in Archaeology, Ethohistory, and Ethnography* (1971).

Helm, M., *Man of Fire: J. C. Orozco an Interpretive Memoir* (1953).

Henry, R. S., *The Story of the Mexican War* (1950).

Horowitz, J. L., ed., *Masses in Latin America* (1970).

Houston, J. A., *Latin America in the United Nations* (1956).

Howland, C. P., ed., *Survey of American Foreign Relations* (1931).

Hunley, N., *Dividing the Waters* (1966).

Iduarte, A., *Nino, Child of the Mexican Revolution* (1970).

Inter-American Committee for Agricultural Development, *Information Basic to the Planning of Agricultural Development in Latin America: Mexico* (1964).

International Bank for Reconstruction and Development, *Economic Development of Mexico* (1953).

James, D., *Mexico and Americans* (1963).

Johnson, K. F., *Mexican Democracy: A Critical View* (1971).

Johnson, J. J., *Military and Society in Latin America* (1964).

————, *Political Change in Latin America* (1958).

Johnson, M. C., *Education in Mexico* (1956).

Johnson, R. A., *The Mexican Revolution of Ayutla, 1854–1855* (1939).

Karsen, S., *Jaime Torres Bodet* (1971).

Katz, F., *German-Mexican Relations 1870–1920* (1971).

Kelchner, W. H., *Latin American Relations with the League of Nations* (1930).

Kennedy, P. B., *The Middle Beat: A Correspondent's View of Mexico, Guatemala and El Salvador*, ed. S. R. Ross (1971).

King, T., Mexico; *Industrialization and Trade Policies since 1940* (1970).

Knapp, F. A., *The Life of Sebastián Lerdo de Tejada, 1823–1889* (1951; 1968).

Kneller, D. F., *Education of the Mexican Nation* (1951).

Koslow, L. E., *Mexico in the Organization of American States* (1969).

LaCascia, J. S., *Capital Formation and Economic Development in Mexico* (1969).

Landsberger, H. A., *Latin American Peasant Movements* (1970).

Lansford, W. D., *Pancho Villa* (1965).

Levenstein, H. A., *Labor Organizations in the United States and Mexico: A History of Their Relations* (1971).

Lewis, O., *Children of Sanchez: Autobiography of a Mexican Family* (1961).

————, *Life in a Mexican Village: Tepoztlán Reconsidered* (1951).

————, *Pedro Martínez, A Mexican Peasant and His Family* (1964).

Lieuwen, E., *Mexican Militarism: The Political Rise and Fall of the Revolutionary Army* (1968).

Link, A. S., *Wilson: Confusion and Crises, 1915–1916* (1964).

López Mateos, A., *The Economic Development of Mexico during a Quarter of a Century, 1934–1959* (1959).

López y Fuentes, G., *El Indio* (various editions).

MacCorkle, S. A., *American Policy of Recognition Towards Mexico* (1933).

Machado, M. A., Jr., *Aftosa: A Historical Survey of Foot-and-Mouth Disease and Inter-American Relations* (1969).

Madariaga, S. de., *The Eagle and the Bear* (1962).

Maddox, J. S., *Mexican Land Reform* (American Universities Field Staff—1957).

Maier, J. and R. W. Eatherhead, eds., *Politics of Change in Latin America* (1964).

Maissin, E., *The French in Mexico and Texas, 1838–1839* (1961).

Manning, W. R., *Early Relations between the United States and Mexico* (1916).

Maret, R., *Mexico* (1971).

Martin, P. A., *Latin America and the War* (1925).

Martin, P. F., *Maximilian in Mexico: The Story of the French Intervention* (1914).

Matías, R., *Mexico and the United States* (1898).

May, H. K., and J. A. Fernández Arena, *Impact of Foreign Investments in Mexico* (1972).

Mayer, B., *Mexico As It Was and As It Is* (1944).

McBride, B. M., *Land System of Mexico* (1923).

McGaurum, D. A., *Church Growth in Mexico* (Protestantism) (1963).

McNeeley, J. M., *The Railroads of Mexico: A Study in Nationalization* (1964).

McWhiney, G. and S., eds., *To Mexico with Taylor and Scott 1845–1847* (1969).

Mecham, J. L., *Church and State in Latin America* (rev. ed., 1966).

Mendieta, G. de, *The Ecclesiastical History of Mexico* (1969).

Merrill, J. C., *Gringo: The American as seen by Mexican Journalists* (1963).

Meyer, M. C., *Mexican Rebel: Pascual Drozco and the Mexican Revolution 1910–1915* (1967).

―――――, *Huerta: A Political Portrait* (1972).

Millon, R. P., *Mexican Marxist: Vicenta Lombarde Ioledano* (1966).

―――――, *Zapata: Ideology of a Peasant Revolutionary* (1969).

Moore, W. E., *Industrialization and Labor: Social Aspects of Economic Development*, Chapters 9, 10, and 11 (1951).

Mörner, M., *Race and Class in Latin America* (1970).

Morton, V., *Terán and Texas* (1948).

Morton, W. M., Woman Suffrage in Mexico (1962).

Mosk, S., *Industrial Revolution in Mexico* (1950).

Myers, B. S., *Mexican Painting in Our Time* (1957).

Myers, S. D., ed., *Mexico and the United States* (1938).

National Planning Association, *Sears Roebuck de Mexico* (1953).

Nava, J., *Mexican-Americans Past, Present, and Future* (1969).

Needler, M. C., *Politics and Society in Mexico* (1971).

Nicholson, H., *Dwight Morrow* (1935).

Nicholson I., *The X in Mexico* (1965).

O'Hea, P., *Reminiscences of the Mexican Revolution* (1966).

Orozco, J. C., *José Clemente Orozco: An Autobiography*, trans. R. C. Stephenson (1962).

Padgett, L. V., *The Mexican Political System* (1966).

Pan American Union, *Materiales para el Estudio de la Clase Media en la America Latina* (6 vols., 1950–1951).

Papers on Mexico and Central America (Eighth Conference of Rocky Mountain Council on Latin American Affairs, 1961).

Paredes, A. O. comp. *Folk Tales of Mexico* (1970).

Parkes, H. B., *History of Mexico* (3rd rev. ed., 1960).

Paz, Octavo, *An Anthology of Mexican Poetry* (1960).

―――――, *The Labyrinth of Solitude: Life and Thought in Mexico* (1962).

Peck, J. J., foreword by R. E. Pourade, *The Sign of the Eagle: A View of Mexico, 1830 to 1855* (1970).

Phipps, H., *Some Aspects of the Agrarian Question in Mexico* (1925).

Pike, F. B., *Conflict Between Church and State in Latin America* (1944).

―――――, ed., *Latin American History* (1969).

Pinchon, E., *Zapata the Unconquerable* (1941).

Poinsett, J. R., *Notes on Mexico made in the Autumn of 1822* (repr. 1969).

Poleman, T. T., *The Papaloapan Project: Agricultural Development in the Mexican Tropics* (1964).

Portes Gil, E., *The Conflict between the Civil Power and the Clergy* (1935).

Potash, R. A., "Historiography of Mexico since 1921," *Hispanic American Historical Review*, XL (1960), 383–424.

Powell, J. R., *The Mexican Petroleum Industry, 1938–1950* (1956).

Pozas, J., *The Chamula: An Ethnological Recreation of the Life of a Mexican Indian* (1962).

Price, G. W., *The Origins of the War with Mexico* (1967).

Priestley, H. I., *Mexican Nation* (1923).

Purcell, A., *Frontier Mexico, 1875–1878: Letters of William L. Purcell* (1963).

Quirk, R. E., *Affair of Honor* (1964).

————, *The Mexican Revolution: 1914–1915* (1960).

————, *The Mexican Revolution and the Catholic Church 1910–1929* (1963).

————, *Mexico* (1971).

Ramirez, J. F., *Mexico During the War with the United States,* trans. W. V. Scholes (1950).

Ramos, S., *Profile of Man and Culture in Mexico* (1962).

Read, J. L., *The Mexican Historical Novel, 1826–1910* (1939).

Reed, A., *Orozco* (1956).

Reed, J., *Insurgent Mexico* (rev. ed., 1969).

Reed, N., *The Caste War of Yucatan* (1964).

Relyea, P. S., *Diplomatic Relations between the United States and Mexico under Porfirio Díaz, 1876–1910* (1923).

Retinger, J. H., *Morones of Mexico: A History of the Labour Movement in that Country* (1926).

Reyes, A., *Mexico in a Nutshell* (1964).

Reynolds, C. W., *The Mexican Economy: Twentieth Century Structure and Growth* (1910).

Rice, Sister E. A., *Diplomatic Relations Between the United States and Mexico as Affected by the Struggle for Religious Liberty in Mexico, 1925–1929* (1959).

Rippy, J. F., *United States and Mexico* (rev. ed., 1931).

————, *Joel R. Poinsett, Versatile American* (1935).

Rivera, D., and B. O. Wolf, *Portrait of Mexico* (1937).

Rives, G. L., *United States and Mexico, 1821–1848* (2 vols., 1913).

Robinson, D. J. and D. Fox, *Cities in a Changing Latin America: in Urbanization in Mexico and Venezuela* (1969).

Rodman, S., *Mexican Journal. The Conquerors Conquered* (1958; 1965).

Rodriguez, A., *A History of Mexican Mural Painting* (1969).

Roeder, R., *Juárez and His Mexico* (2 vols., 1947).

Romanell, R., *Making of the Mexican Mind* (1952).

Romero, M., *Geographical and Statistical Notes on Mexico* (1898).

Rosenblum, M., *Heroes of Mexico* (1969).

Ross, J. B., *Economic System of Mexico* (1971).

Ross, S. G. and J. B. Christenson, *Tax Incentives for Industry in Mexico* (1959).

Ross, S. R., *Francisco L. Madero* (1955; 1963).

————, ed., *Is the Mexican Revolution Dead?* (1965).

Ruiz, R. E., *An American in Maximilian's Mexico* (1959).

————, *The Mexican War—Was It Manifest Destiny?* (1963).

————, *Mexico: The Challenge of Poverty and Illiteracy* (1963).

————, ed., *Interpreting Latin American History* (1970).

Rukeyser, M., trans., *Selected Poems of Ortavo Paz* (1963).

Rutherford, J., *Mexican Society During the Revolution: A Literary Approach* (1971).

Sánchez, G. I., *Mexico: A Revolution in Education* (1936).

Sartorios, C., *Mexico about 1850* (1961).

Schmeckebier, L. E., *Modern Mexican Art* (1939).

Schmitt, K. M., *Communism in Mexico* (1965).

Scholes, W. V., *Mexican Politics during the Juárez Regime, 1855–1872* (1957).

Schwartz, K., *A New History of Spanish American Fiction*, 2 vols. (1972).

Scott, R. E., *Mexican Government in Transition* (1959).

Shafer, R. J., *Mexico's Mutual Adjustment Planning* (1966).

Sherman, W. L. and R. E. Greenleaf, *Victoriano Huerta: A Reappraisal* (1960).

Shipway, V. and W., *The Mexican House, Old and New* (1960).

Sierra, J., ed., *Mexico—Its Social Evolution* (2 vols., in 3, 1900–1904).

————, *Political Evolution of the Mexican People*, trans. C. Ramsdell (1970).

Simmons, M. E., *The Mexican Corrido as a Source for Interpretive Study of Modern Mexico, 1870–1950* (1957).

Simpson, E. N., *The Ejido: Mexico's Way Out* (1937).

Simpson, L. B., *Many Mexicos* (3rd ed., 1952).

Singer, M., *Growth Equality and the Mexican Experience* (1969).

Smart, C. A., *Viva Juárez* (1963).

Smith, A. K., *Mexico and the Cuban Revolution: Foreign Policy-Making in Mexico under President Adolfo López Mateos (1958–1964)* (1970).

Smith, J. H., *Annexation of Texas* (1911).

————, *War with Mexico* (2 vols. (1919).

Smith, R. F., *The United States and Revolutionary Nationalism in Mexico 1916–1932* (1972).

Smith, T. L., ed., *Agrarian Reform in Latin America* (1965).

Sprague, W. F., *Vicente Guerrero, Mexican Liberator* (1939).

Spratling, W., *A Small Mexican World*, ed. L. B. Simpson (1964).

Stavanhagen, R., ed., *Agrarian Problems and Peasant Movements in Latin America* (1970).

Stephenson, R. C., ed., *José Clemente Orozco: An Autobiography* (1962).

Sterne, E. G., *Benito Juárez: Builder of a Nation* (1967).

Stevenson, R., *Music in Mexico* (1952).

Steward, J. H., ed., *Contemporary Change in Traditional Societies*, vol. 3: *Mexican and Peruvian Communities* (1967).

Stewart, V., *Forty-five Contemporary Mexican Artists* (1951).

Strassman, M. P., *Technological Change and Economic Development: The Manufacturing Experience* (1968).

Strode, H., *Timeless Mexico* (1944).

Tannenbaum, F., *The Mexican Agrarian Revolution* (1929).

————, *Mexico: The Struggle for Peace and Bread* (1950).

————, *Peace by Revolution* (1933).

Teitelbaum, L. M., *Woodrow Wilson and the Mexican Revolution, 1913–1916* (1967).

Tennery, T. D., *The Mexican War Diary* (1970).

Thompson, W., *Recollections of Mexico* (1846).

Thord-Gray, L., *Gringo Rebels (Mexico, 1913–1914)* (1960).

Timmons, W. H., *Morelos of Mexico* (1970).

Tischendorf, A., *Great Britain and Mexico in the Era of Porfirio Díaz* (1961).

Tomasek, R. D., *Latin American Politics: Studies of Contemporary Scene* (rev. ed., 1970).

Toor, F., *A Treasury of Mexican Folkways* (1947).

Townsend, W. C., *Lázaro Cárdenas: Mexican Democrat* (1952).

Tucker, W. P., *The Mexican Government Today* (1957).

Turlington, E., *Mexico and Her Foreign Creditors* (1930).

Turner, F. C., *Dynamic of Mexican Nationalism* (1965).

Turner, J. K., *Barbarous Mexico* (2nd ed., 1969).

Ugalde, A., *Power and Conflict in a Mexican Community: A Study of Political Integration* (1970).

U.C.L.A., *Nacional Financiera and Mexican Industry: A Study of the Financial Relationship between the Government and Private Sector in Mexico* (1970).

United Nations . . . , *The Population of Central America (Including Mexico), 1950–1980* (1954).

United States, Department of Commerce, Bureau of Foreign Commerce *Investments in Mexico—Conditions and Outlook* (1956).

Urquidi, M., *Mexico's Recent Economic Growth: The Mexican View* (1967).

Venezian, E. L. and W. K. Garble, *The Agricultural Development of Mexico, Its Structure and Growth Since 1950* (1969).

Verissimo, E., *Mexico* (1960).

Vernon, R., *Dilemma of Mexico's Development* (1963).

————, *Public Policy and Private Enterprise in Mexico* (1964).

Ward, H. G., *Mexico in 1827* (2 vols., 1829).

Weyl, N., and S., *The Reconquest of Mexico, the Years of Lázare Cárdenas* (1939).

Whetten, N., *Rural Mexico* (1948).

Whitaker, A. P., ed., *Mexico Today, in Annals of American Academy of Political and Social Sciences*, No. 208 (1940).

Wilgus, A. C., ed., *Caribbean: Mexico Today* (1964).

————, ed., *The Caribbean: at Mid-century* (1951).

Wilkie, J. W., *The Mexican Revolution: Federal Expenditures and Social Change Since 1910* (1970).

———— and A. Michaels, ed., *Revolution in Mexico: Years of Upheaval 1910–1940* (1969).

Wilkie, R., *San Miguel: A Mexican Collective* (1970).

Wionczeh, M. S., *Public Policy and Private Enterprise in Mexico* (1964).

Womack, J., *Zapata and the Mexican Revolution* (1969).

Wood, B., *Making of the Good Neighbor Policy* (1961).

Wright, H. K., *Foreign Enterprise in Mexico* (1971).

Wyllys, R., *French in Sonora* (1932).

Zea, L., *Culture and Man of Our Times* (1959).

————, *The Latin American Mind* (1963).

chapter 20

THE POLITICAL
DEVELOPMENT
OF BRAZIL AS AN
INDEPENDENT NATION

the empire: peaceful break with the homeland

Brazil had many of the grievances against the homeland that were felt in Spanish America, but the Brazilians escaped the bloody revolution and the harrowing travail of rebirth as an independent nation that were experienced in other parts of South America. No strong movement for independence developed in this sprawling colony with its population of 3,617,000 that was less than one-fourth white and about one-half Negro slaves. A few educated intellectuals and literary discussion clubs talked of the Enlightenment and the North American independence movement. The only plot to establish a republic was a small one in Minas Gerais, a mining area in the interior, where Joaquim José de Silva Xavier, known in history as Tiradentes or the "Toothpuller," led an abortive revolt in 1789 and drafted a constitution. But this "precursor" was soon executed. The independence for which he suffered martyrdom was to come gradually, and under the leadership of the royal house of Braganza from Portugal.

Portugal in 1807–1808, found herself, like Spain, facing invasion by Napoleon. But the Portuguese royal family, in a dramatic flight, escaped from Lisbon in time to escape Napoleon's troops. On November 29, 1807, convoyed by British naval vessels, the Queen, the mentally ill María I; the Prince Regent, her middle-aged son John; his wife, his two little sons, and a staff of valets, secretaries, and lesser noblemen amounting to over 10,000 persons sailed out of Lisbon harbor while the cannons of Napoleon's general could be heard in the outskirts of the city. Though library, archives, and furniture were brought along, the packing was incomplete and many of the wardrobe trunks were left on the deck. With only evening dress and a little soap and water, this motley court set sail for Portugal's colony in the New World. After six weeks of rough Atlantic weather, the courtiers hove to off the port of Baía in January 1808. The surprised Brazilians, after the first shock at having royalty in their midst, welcomed them effusively to the New World and lent them all the velvets and lace available in the backward colonial city. Prince John, the regent, an easy-going, plump, intelligent man, had been something of a laughingstock in Portugal. Here he felt warmed and welcomed. His coming, in the long run, was to make a Brazilian war for independence unnecessary.

In borrowed velvets, he went on with his whole entourage toward Rio where word of his coming had preceded him. When he arrived on March 7, 1808, all the best houses in town were turned over to the royal court. The demented Queen mother was ensconced in a Rio convent—where she died eight years later. In those eight years, her son had made Rio de Janeiro the capital of the whole Portuguese empire and the largest city in South America. Brazil was a kingdom, no longer a colony, of equal status with Portugal. On March 20, 1816, after his mother's death, Prince John was crowned in Rio, although Napoleon had already been for many months in exile on St. Helena. Brazilians were heavily taxed to support the Portuguese court, and some of them never got their houses back, to say nothing of their laces and velvets; but the country prospered as it never had as a colony. The harbor was improved and running water was brought into the city. Rio became a center of society; schools, libraries, and printing presses were established, an institute of fine arts was started, botanical gardens were set up, and scholars and scientists were invited to Brazil.

The Portuguese who had come with the king remained the aristocracy and received the favored jobs in government, while they treated the rich Brazilians with arrogance and regarded their own stay in Brazil as a temporary exile. John's wife, Carlota Joaquina, the witchlike woman who was the Spanish King Ferdinand's sister, involved him in difficulties with the Brazilians as well as with the Argentines. In the wars with Buenos Aires which followed, John gained Uruguay, which he called the Cisplatine Province. He had only one Brazilian revolution to quell, a revolt in Pernambuco; the Brazilians soon rallied again in loyalty to King John.

Finally conditions at home in Portugal changed John's successful rule in Brazil. Napoleon's troops had long since evacuated, and there was the postwar depression and unrest in the mother country. The absence of the court and the king contributed to the instability, and Portuguese leaders demanded that John come back to make Lisbon again the capital of the empire and Brazil once more a colony. It was feared that "republicanism" might rear its ugly head in the homeland; revolution had broken out in Portugal, liberals had called a constitutional convention, influenced by the 1820 revolt in Spain, and several Brazilian states had elected delegates to go to it. If the monarchy was to be preserved on both sides of the Atlantic, John must return. Reluctant to do so after his thirteen years of contentment in Rio, nonetheless, for patriotic and dynastic reasons, he left for home on April 26, 1821, taking with him his hag of a wife and 3,000 Portuguese courtiers. John's eldest son, Prince Pedro, was left in Brazil as regent.

Both John and his son knew that the spirit of independence was making gains in the neighboring Spanish colonies; they could foresee an ultimate break between Brazil and Portugal. Two years later, Dom Pedro was to write to his father in Portugal: "I still remember and shall always keep in mind, what Your Majesty told me in the ship's cabin two days before sailing—Pedro, if Brazil must break away, I would rather see you, of whose respect I am certain, take it, than some unknown adventurer!"

Events had moved rapidly in those two years. True to the liberal attitude he meant to maintain, John VI on his return to Lisbon had met with a congress or *côrtes* in Portugal. Soon he quarreled with its members about the status of Brazil. The *côrtes* members wanted Brazil subservient to Lisbon. They abolished the institutions set up by John in Brazil, renewed the Portuguese monopoly on commerce with the "colony." They ordered Pedro, known to be poorly trained for the European throne, to be brought to Portugal to finish his education. When these orders were known in Brazil, Pedro was flooded with requests to remain in Rio.

Pedro himself was torn between allegiance to his family and allegiance to his followers in Brazil. The "Patriarch of Brazilian Independence," José Bonifâcio de Andrada e Silva, an intellectual scientist who had been educated at Coimbra in Portugal, was the strongest influence on Pedro. He believed that a constitutional monarchy under the young monarch separate from Portugal was the best solution of all Brazil's difficulties. On January 9, 1822, Pedro disobeyed the order to go to Lisbon, and sent a reply to his many petitioners—"*Fico!*"—I will remain.

Now Pedro was in the difficult position of defying the homeland. The Portuguese garrison in Rio had tried to force Pedro and his family on board a ship bound for Lisbon, but a local militia was raised which got control, first of the hills and then of the city, and forced the Portuguese garrison itself, not Prince Pedro, to go home. Meanwhile Pedro appointed a new cabinet in which his mentor José Bonifâcio was prime minister, hoping to unify the varying factions in all the provinces. During the spring he made a tour of Minas Gerais and received enthusiastic support there. In May he took the title of "Perpetual Defender of Brazil"; in June he issued a call for an assembly to draft a constitution. Then he went for a horseback tour of another of his provinces—São Paulo.

Here on September 7, 1822, as his horseback party was halted on the little stream of Ypiranga near São Paulo, couriers caught up with him to bring him a message from Portugal abolishing his new cabinet and ordering the prosecution of its members. It had been forwarded from Rio with a note from his intelligent and popular young wife: "The apple is ripe; harvest it now or it will rot." He knew what "harvest" meant. Standing up in the saddle, he unsheathed his sword. "Comrades," he yelled in the famous *Grito de Ypiranga*, "the Portuguese *côrtes* wishes to reduce Brazil to slavery; we must forthwith declare her independence. Independence or death! We are separated from Portugal!"

On his return to Rio he was proclaimed "Constitutional Emperor of Brazil," and soon after crowned as Pedro I on December 1, 1822. Thus revolution had come from the top without violence and with little real support or knowledge on the part of the masses. Political and social reforms were no part of it. In striking contrast to Spanish America, Brazil had won its independent position without a battle; Portugal was in no position to make war on her giant colony. Besides, Pedro soon acquired an experienced naval commander, the ubiquitous Lord Cochrane, and had enough men in his army to continue the fight in the three-cornered wars in Uruguay. England recognized the new state—a good place to promote British trade— and the mother country had no choice but to yield to pressure of her long-time British allies and confer recognition also. This was done in 1825; United States recognition had already come the year before. The wars for independence in Spanish America had lasted fifteen years; Brazilian independence was accomplished in little more than fifteen months.

The new emperor had promised to call an assembly, and elections were held for it immediately. Church dignitaries, plantation owners, and mining prospectors met in Rio, May 3, 1823, an incongruous array symbolic of the assorted groups which were to run Brazil. They discussed humanitarian ideas, and disagreed with the obstinate and strong-minded young ruler. José Bonifâcio and his two brothers resigned from the government in July of 1823, and founded an anti-Pedro newspaper. By November, Pedro had exiled the Andrada brothers, dissolved the assembly, and appointed a new Council of State to draft his own Constitution.

This document, promulgated in 1824 and remaining in effect till 1891, provided for a constitutional monarchy and a legislature of two houses. The members of the lower house, the Chamber of Deputies, were elected for a four-year term, but its laws were subject to approval by the Emperor. The Senators, members of the upper house, were chosen by the Emperor for life from lists submitted to him. The Constitution also provided for a Council of State, or Cabinet, whose members were also chosen by the Emperor to serve for life, or at the Emperor's discretion. These powers for the monarch, called inclusively the "moderative power," brought the ruler into many subsequent conflicts with the Chamber of Deputies. The Emperor also appointed governors for the provinces into which the nation was divided, while the elective assemblies of these provinces had only consultative powers. Although the Constitution guaranteed freedom of press and religion, it declared Catholicism the religion of the state, and the person of the Emperor sacred. It did provide that the ruler could not meddle in Portuguese affairs.

Immediately the popularity of the young monarch began to decline. He did not call the legislature which his constitution had provided until

1826, and when it met he quarreled with it and governed without regard for a parliamentary majority. On his southern frontier, he lost the Cisplatine Province of Uruguay after a three-year war; in the north, Pernambuco revolted again and formed a Federal Republic of the Equator with three other northern states, which took six months and Lord Cochrane's fleet to put down. Within another two years there were riots against him in Baía and demands for his abdication in Minas Gerais, for he was turning more and more toward his old Portuguese friends, and was shocking Rio society propriety as well.

His personal life brought him as many critics as did his arbitrary government. He had been only twenty-three years old in 1822, handsome and warm-hearted, with little formal education. As the problems of government became too heavy for him he picked up many "undesirable" friends on the outer rims of society, and caused his pleasant and popular wife, the Austrian Princess Leopoldina, a mortal sickness by openly establishing a São Paulo girl in Rio as his mistress. Even though he married a Bavarian princess when his empress died, and forsook his mistress for the new bride, he had lost what little remaining loyalty the people had for him.

Meanwhile, his father had died in Lisbon, and the Portuguese throne was once more empty. Though Pedro had arranged that his oldest child, his seven-year-old daughter Maria da Gloria, be crowned Queen of Portugal, he feared the plans of his own younger brother and his scheming Spanish-born old mother back in Portugal. By 1830 he was so concerned in Portugal's affairs as to create the "Portuguese Question" in Brazil. His critics accused him of being unconstitutional and anti-Brazilian. There were street brawls in Rio, defection in the army, and indiscipline in general. Return to Portugal seemed the Emperor's only way out, in spite of the progress toward individual liberty and constitutional government made under him.

On April 7, 1831, Pedro wrote out his abdication in favor of his second child, a five-year-old son. José Bonifâcio had been allowed back from exile in 1828; now Pedro, once his enemy, named him tutor for the little prince. Then Pedro sailed back to Lisbon, his birthplace, to live the remaining three and a half years of his stormy life fighting for his daughter's right to the Portuguese throne. The little son, guided by José Bonifâcio, was to rule as a constitutional monarch, Dom Pedro II, a true native-born Brazilian without any "Portuguese Question" in his life.

There followed a period known as the regency, a time of stress for Brazil through the 1830s. The abdication did not solve Brazil's problems, and they could not be solved by a five-year-old boy. There were revolts up and down the coast for the next ten years. In Rio a board of three regents ruled in the child's name for three years, 1831–1834, with the child's former tutor, José Bonifâcio de Andrada, on the board, aided by the able Minister of Justice, Father Diogo Antonio Feijó. This governing group was backed by the moderates and by the liberal friends of Pedro I. But disorder in the provinces and lawlessness in the city continued. In 1834 congress amended the constitution to give the provinces more authority, and abolished the triple regency. Father Feijó then became the sole regent. After two years of strong government in the name of the young monarch, Father Feijó was replaced by the conservative Pedro Araujo Lima. The regency period taught the Brazilians that a strongly centralized power was essential to maintain order and preserve the union. During this period political parties began to form, and the leaders received training in parliamentary government. Tired of a conservative regency, a group of liberals formed a coalition in July 1840 to declare Prince Pedro king in fact as well as name. The constitution had required that he be eighteen years old, and he was only fifteen, but the General Assembly overrode this unconstitutionality. The prince declared himself "willing to rule," and on July 11, 1841, he was crowned Emperor Pedro II.

Pedro II, a remarkable benevolent despot

The boy prince—his father and his pretty new stepmother gone forever to Portugal—had been reared scientifically by tutors. His mother Leopoldina had had scholarly interests unusual for her time. By the age of six, the boy was already a "rare and unusual child," who could read and write Portuguese and English and was taking lessons in French. This precocious interest in languages persisted into old age; at sixty he was eagerly learning to speak ancient Hebrew. The cultural history of Brazil from 1840 to the 1880s is bound up with this remarkable emperor. He was to rule with a firm hand, but in a soft velvet glove. The "Age of Pedro II" was Brazil's Golden Age.

Ruler in his own right at fifteen, he was married at eighteen to a plain-faced Italian princess, three years his senior, who bore him four children, two sons and two daughters. Both sons died in early childhood; his oldest daughter, Isabella, became his heir and was strictly trained in the responsibilities of the throne. The royal family remained happy in its domesticity, democratic in manner and dress, and never kept elaborate court. The emperor was interested in education, read widely in educational philosophy, and visited schools on trips to America and Europe. He was the best-educated person in Brazil in his lifetime. He also accomplished so much in the way of international improvements, unification, and foreign relations as to compare favorably with any enlightened European ruler of the last two centuries. A dignified, reserved, handsome man six feet four inches tall, he was described, even in his old age, as a "library on top a locomotive."

His first task as emperor was to wipe out the heritage of civil war left over from the regency, the so-called Ragamuffins' (Farrapos) War which had been raging in Rio Grande do Sul for years, and revolts in other regions as well. One by one his armies controlled these separatist movements. By 1848 all such splinter rebellions were permanently settled. This had meant the development of a centralist government in which the emperor and his advisors chose the provincial governors. Pedro II used his personal power wisely; he had maintained his father's constitution of 1824, in which the cabinet was responsible to the ruler not the legislature, but he believed in the British cabinet system, and aimed to choose most of his

ministers from the majority party in the Chamber. The Chamber of Deputies was elected indirectly by manhood suffrage, limited by property and
literacy restrictions on voting. Pedro himself chose the members of the
Senate, but showed care and rare impartiality in his choice. Although the
indirect election system kept the power in the hands of the land-owning and
slave-holding class, while the masses of free laborers and slaves had no
voice in the government, the political stability and the long years of progress
and economic development improved conditions gradually for all classes.
Two parties existed side by side—conservatives who believed in keeping the
power in the central government and controlling the provinces from Rio and
in high suffrage qualifications, and liberals who stood for subordination of
executive to legislative powers, autonomy in the provinces, and progressive
social and economic measures with a broader suffrage basis. In the latter
part of the reign, by 1871, a Republican Party emerged, but the first thirty-
five years of Pedro II's rule were without serious party strife.

In foreign affairs, the pacifistic-minded emperor had few war
troubles on his hands, once all his provinces were brought into satisfied
union with the center. Since revolutions were constantly occurring in the
eight Spanish American countries bordering on Brazil, there were bound to
be repercussions. Pedro II intervened in such revolts only twice, however.
He sent troops to aid in the overthrow of the Argentine dictator Rosas, and
he was one of the allies in the war against the dictator Francisco Solano
López of Paraguay in the 1860s. Brazil won this five-year war and gained
thousands of square miles on the Paraguay border. But the Brazilians
suffered 50,000 casualties and spent $300,000,000; Pedro himself was never
so popular in military circles again. Brazil learned from this war to settle
difficulties by arbitration while concentrating on internal improvement.

In Pedro's dealings with the United States, he was a highly honored
figure and visitor of state, though his slave-minded subjects sympathized
with the South in America's Civil War and invited Confederate leaders to
migrate to Brazil after 1865. He traveled in France as a scientist and a poet
and spent some days with Victor Hugo. He was welcomed on several occasions in Portugal where the son of his sister, Maria da Gloria, was ruler.
Tolerant and open-minded abroad, he also believed in real religious tolerance at home. His government aimed to help all religions and encourage
European immigration by maintaining ministers of any sect to which groups
of new immigrants might belong. Though he was a practicing Catholic
himself, Church authorities began to rise against him near the end of his
reign because of his leadership in the Masonic lodge in Rio which was
regarded as anticlerical by the leading bishops, and because of his belief in
separation of Church and state.

the slavery issue and the downfall of Pedro II

Of the nearly ten million people in Brazil a century ago, only 400,000
belonged to the landowning, slave-owning class, and only 142,000 of these
qualified as voters. A third of the people were slaves. Some worked on the

docks at Rio and Baía, many were house servants in the cities, and some acted as burden bearers on the city streets and country roads. The great majority of them were slaves on plantations growing sugar or coffee. Life there in 1850 was very much as that described for 1650. The Negroes in Brazil—the Bantus, the Sudanese, the Minas, the Angolas, the Guinea natives, all with their varying degrees of agricultural and handicraft skills from African villages and their native folk ways—had largely been mixed into a homogeneous group.

On the plantations and in the homes, slaves were not often mistreated and manumission was common. Since there was no color prejudice, freed slaves could go to the cities and enter business, so that their descendants often became men of importance. There was a growing abolition movement; clubs were organized, propaganda printed, and a political issue was being created. By law, in 1850, Brazil had abolished the slave trade.

By the 1870s abolition had become a subject for speeches, essays, poems, and politics. A young idealist named Antônio de Castro Alves (1847–1871), called the Harriet Beecher Stowe of Brazil, "wept with shame" that Brazil still carried on the buying and selling of slaves. His poem *The Slave Ship* describes conditions under which slaves were shipped clandestinely from Africa. To conciliate the abolitionists Viscount Rio Branco, the conservative prime minister, drafted a law called "Freedom of the Unborn Child," or the Rio Branco Law of 1871. Every child born to a slave mother henceforth was to be free. Rio Branco planned to have all slaves over sixty-five liberated as the next step, though the rural aristocracy, a powerful vested interest and largely in the conservative party, was naturally opposed to all liberation.

Dom Pedro had a long-term solution for Brazil's work-force problem. He had freed the slaves on the royal plantation; he forbade any of the modernizing public work to be built with slave labor. On his visits to the United States he had seen the labor problem being solved by hundreds of thousands of European immigrants. Already Dom Pedro had had the Petropolis railway built by German immigrants, and had settled them in villages afterward, while he supported their Lutheran minister. So successful was this venture that Dom Pedro brought more Germans to work his plantation with modern German farming methods. In 1840 there were 15,000 European immigrant colonists in Brazil; between 1874 and 1888, 600,000 had come in. Especially after 1870, Italians by the thousands had settled in São Paulo state alone, under a sharecropping system which was to make possible São Paulo's coffee industry.

With an increasing substitute source of labor, the opposition to slavery increased, and the abolition movement grew more powerful than that in the United States, inspired by the poems of Castro Alves. The William Lloyd Garrison of Brazil was Joaquim Nabuco, scion of an aristocratic family of Pernambuco and a young protégé of the emperor. Elected to the Chamber of Deputies in 1878, he devoted his impassioned speeches to the cause of immediate abolition, reading Castro Alves' poems aloud, and arousing sympathies with stories of cruelty under the slave system. Defeated in the Chamber, he founded an Anti-slavery Society, with branches all over the country, wrote a powerful book, *O Abolicionismo,* in 1883, and was soon re-elected. Dom Pedro himself paid Nabuco's expenses on an extensive speaking trip for the cause of abolition throughout the empire. The propaganda bore fruit, for two states passed local abolition laws, the law freeing slaves over sixty-five was approved, and when younger slaves deserted by the thousands, the army refused to catch them.

It was Joaquim Nabuco's movement, strangely enough, that helped bring about Dom Pedro's fall from power. Physically, the Emperor's gigantic frame was beginning to give out. Forced by diabetes to withdraw from his active life, Dom Pedro went to Europe in 1887 for treatment, leaving his middle-aged daughter Isabella to act as regent. Never as popular as her father, Isabella was married to the very unpopular Frenchman, Count d'Eu. She was sincere and impulsive, however, and intensely pro-abolitionist. On May 13, 1888, she signed the law which the Chamber and then the Senate had passed freeing the slaves in one stroke with no compensation to owners. In 1870 there had been 1,700,000 slaves in Brazil, but the law of 1888 freed the 750,000 who still remained slaves after eighteen years of gradual emancipation. Dom Pedro, very ill in Italy, immediately rallied when told of the emancipation act and sent cables; "My blessings and congratulations, to everybody, what a nation! What a people!" He was soon well enough to come home, and received a warmer welcome than usual.

But Pedro II did not realize the undercurrent of feeling against the monarchy in general—the strength of the republican movement, the impatience at some of Dom Pedro's high-handed ways. Many liberals had intended to bide with Dom Pedro until his death, and then establish a republic rather than accept Isabella. Now, with her impulsive act freeing the slaves, she had lost the support of the conservatives as well. The most reactionary slave-owners and landlords were willing to work with the most ardent young republicans. Army leaders joined the strange alliance. The young lieutenants had been indoctrinated in the war college by a remarkable mathematics teacher, Colonel Benjamin Constant, a fanatical republican. There was also a clique in the army in sympathy with the disgruntled plantation owners, led by General Deodoro da Fonseca. Many other politicians thought that a republic controlled by the army would be preferable to Isabella.

Other changing conditions were working against the monarchy. An electoral reform law, widely heralded in 1881, had set up direct elections for deputies, but had limited the vote to the well-to-do, and kept the same class of society in power. A conservative prime minister had used the law to restrict the budding Liberal Party, so the emperor had lost much liberal-minded support. He had never had the support of the new industrialist class. At the other extreme the clergy, fearing Pedro's Free-Masonry, opposed the separation of Church and state. When the press supported the Republican party factions on the one hand and the slave-owning nobility on the other, it needed only the defection in the army under Deodoro da Fonseca to bring about the end of the empire.

Hatching an intrigue very similar to the "palace revolutions" so common in Spanish America in the 1800s, Fonseca was able to take control of the city. The revolutionary clique asked for Pedro's resignation and got the confused old gentleman on shipboard and off to Europe with his family before he could actually realize what had happened, or before the rest of the country knew the empire was dead. Many people who witnessed the "revolt" thought it was merely another parade. The Republic of Brazil was proclaimed under army auspices on November 15, 1889. Dom Pedro himself was brokenhearted; he died in Europe two years later without any chance to see a vindication of his reign, though it was two generations before Brazil was so well governed again. Thirty years later his remains were brought back to Rio on a battleship and buried in state.

Brazil today appreciates Dom Pedro. He had been the cohesive force that held the nation together. His liberal constitutional monarchy had given Brazil experience in parliamentary government at the same time that Spanish America was going through the chaotic period of *caudillismo*. His ability, patriotism, and rugged honesty had meant a half-century of almost continual peace and material prosperity, a high place in international affairs, and an advance in culture and education.

The old emperor, the remarkable Pedro II, had been forced to abdicate in the autumn of 1889. The empire was overthrown without a struggle and practically without bloodshed. The new government was engineered by the army leaders, the former slave owners, and the liberal-minded Republicans. In the new Republic of Brazil the European immigration and the coffee and rubber booms which were started under Pedro II continued and, although the government was often chaotic, the modernization of Brazil went ahead apace. In fact, the Republic was a reflection of the shift in economic weight from the sugar of the north to the coffee of the south with its need for free immigrant laborers. The republican *coup d'état* was followed by fifteen months of confusing provisional rule and then by a period of military-dominated governments. The military was supported by an oligarchy of the wealthy landowners. The sincere and likeable Deodoro da Fonseca, general and former loyal friend of Pedro II, found himself in charge of the new republic on November 16, 1889. His first decree was to create the United States of Brazil, a federal republic. Then he set up a commission of five to prepare a draft for a constitutional convention, secured recognition of his regime by foreign powers, and kept peace under martial law until the constitution was written fourteen months later.

The new constitution, modeled somewhat after the imperial constitution of 1824 and somewhat after the federal plan of the United States, was adopted in 1891. It provided for the twenty states that had existed under the empire, with Rio de Janeiro in a federal district, and a new federal district mapped out on the Goiás plateau. The constitution granted central powers to the federal government, including rights to intervene in the states. The states had many self-governing rights, however, but these rights have often been violated by powerful presidents. Election of the president and the federal congress was to be by a direct majority of all males who could read and write, perhaps ten per cent of the population at the time. The Senate was to represent the states; the Chamber of Deputies was to be chosen on a basis of population; Church and state were to be separated and all religions tolerated.

The fine constitution did not bring stability to the new republic. Deodoro himself—for modern Brazilians call their politicians by their first names—was elected first president with General Floriano Peixoto, a cold, efficient military man, as vice-president. Within six months of the election Floriano's army officers were quarreling with the new civilian congress and with Deodoro himself. When the President acted arbitrarily and sent congress home, revolts in favor of the congressmen broke out in the provinces. Deodoro himself sadly resigned, blaming "the ingratitude of those for whom I sacrificed myself," and turned the government over to Floriano, giving way to a military dictatorship less than two years after the Republicans had so hopefully taken over the country. This was a testing time for the survival of the new republic, while military *caudilhismo* over-weighed civilian control at the same time that finances were in a state of chaos.

As might be expected, there was soon widespread revolt against the cold Floriano because of his praetorian regime, his intervention in the states, and the bad state of his finances. This time the fight turned into another navy-versus-army siege. The gauchos of Rio Grande do Sul, some still loyal to Pedro II, were on the side of the dissatisfied and neglected navy; Rio city was on the side of the army and the president. The navy and merchant fleet revolted on September 3, 1893, and attempted to close Rio harbor and keep supplies out of the city; foreign warships came to the city's aid, and it was the sailors, not the city dwellers, who almost starved without supplies. The fleet finally escaped south to join the Rio Grande do Sul ranchers and to fight there in a last effort to restore the monarchy in June 1894. Defeated by soldiers from São Paulo, the rebels escaped into Uruguay; the republic was destined to survive under civilian rule.

The whole affair had consolidated the majority of Brazilians behind the President. He was allowed to serve out his term in peace, and give way in 1894 via a peaceful election to a distinguished civilian lawyer from São Paulo, Dr. Prudente José de Moraes Barros. But the treasury was empty, and the army officers, though successful against the monarchist navy, were jealous of the new civilian leaders and determined to embarrass them if possible by accusing them of monarchist sympathies. They found an excuse for such accusation in Brazil's outer fringes to the north.

The *sertão*, that region of the northeast in Ceará, in behind Baía and Pernambuco, had gone through drought after drought. Among the poor farmers of the region a mentally unbalanced religious fanatic named An-tônio Maciel, called Antônio the Counselor, began to preach against all organized authority. He wandered from town to town urging "sinners" to join him and his throng of ragged believers. Expelled from the settled coastal area, he took his followers, now numbering in the thousands, to the far western edge of the state of Baía where he set up a religious state which he named Canudos. Thousands of huts were built; the frenzied population did just enough farming to feed themselves, and they augmented their colony by means of forays along the coast for food, livestock, and new converts. Their destructive raids produced just the scandal the military leaders had been looking for. They persuaded the people in Rio that Canudos was a dangerous antirepublican movement. Division after division of federal troops were sent over the foot trails of the dry *sertão* to "conquer" Canudos, but the city-bred soldiers died from lack of water or were picked off by guerrillas. Finally artillery was hauled in by oxen, siege laid to the straw and adobe town, and the religious leader killed in the siege. Canudos had held out more than a year until nearly every defender had died. When the handful of survivors surrendered, starved and pitiful, the Rio military leaders looked absurd. How could these ragged back-countrymen have been a menace to the republican government, a secret conspiracy to restore the monarchy? Today the incident is looked upon as an heroic event in Brazilian history; Antônio the Counselor is a sort of poor man's hero. The only good that came out of the episode is Euclides da Cunha's greatest of Brazilian regional studies, *Os Sertões*, translated into English under the title *Rebellion in the Backlands*. From the point of view of economic history, Canudos belongs to a long series of events leading to the opening of the interior. The incident, together with the dastardly attempt on the life of the president in 1897, brought to a close an era marred by the twin evils of factionalism and militarism.

an era of peace and development

The year 1898 ushered in a dozen years of reconstruction and progress, the longest period of comparative peace and undisturbed material prosperity since the abdication of Dom Pedro. "King Coffee" was bringing wealth and political power to planters in São Paulo. Mining and industrialization made Minas Gerais almost equally powerful. As a result of this balanced equation, Brazilian politics under the republic began to revolve on the axis of "São Paulo versus Minas Gerais." Between 1898 and 1914 the peculiarities of national politics faded away before the economic and social changes to be discussed in the next chapter.

Factionalism and militarism as the controlling influences in Brazilian politics had lost ground. The next three presidential terms were devoted to peacetime developments. The first of these presidents was Manóel Ferraz de Campos Salles of São Paulo, under whose administration (1898–1902) finance-minded leaders negotiated loans in Europe to fund the national debt caused by the revolts and the debacle at Canudos. The national credit was stabilized through an increased tariff and economies in government spending. In 1902 Francisco de Paula Rodrígues Alves, a capable, well-equipped civilian *paulista,* was elected to the presidency in an uneventful contest. Energetic and scientific-minded, he has been called Brazil's most able civilian leader; he is famous for beautifying Rio, developing natural resources, building railroads. It was in his regime that the world renowned scientist

Dr. Oswaldo Cruz was given full government support to rid Rio of the yellow fever, as described in the next chapter. In 1906 a *mineiro*, Affonso Augusto Moreira Penna, continued both the civilian rule and great material progress.

Baron Rio Branco, son of the author of the antislavery law, was appointed as minister of foreign affairs by Rodrígues Alves in 1902 and served under four administrations until his death in 1912. With increased Brazilian prestige and strengthened continental solidarity as his objectives, Rio Branco became one of the best-known Brazilians abroad and made Brazil a leader in peace movements at the Hague and at Pan American meetings. The third Pan American conference was held in Rio in 1906 and the American Secretary of State attended personally. The foreign service was reorganized and strengthened, and in 1905 Brazil obtained the first cardinalate in South America. Twenty-nine different arbitration treaties were negotiated during Rio Branco's years of service. In some of these treaties he acted as arbitrator; in others he represented Brazil or negotiated settlements of boundaries long disputed with her neighbors—the border with Argentina's Misiones territory and the boundaries with Holland, England, and France in the Guianas. Bolivia, fronting on the southwest in a little-known region of wild rubber trees, claimed a section of the Amazon drainage basin called Acre and revolts occurred there; Rio Branco negotiated the Treaty of Petropolis in 1903 which gave this area to Brazil. Rio Branco guaranteed to build Bolivia a railroad from her border around a falls and out to a navigable Amazon tributary, the Madeira, a route at long last made available by highway construction in 1967.

factionalism through World War I

The presidency continued to be shuttled back and forth between *paulistas* and *mineiros*. Regional loyalties dominated Brazilian politics rather than political parties as such; and each outgoing president had been able to pick his successor. In 1910 two groups each held nominating conventions, unprecedented in Brazilian history. Actually they were still regional groups and their party strife ushered in another era of *caudilhismo* versus republicanism which lasted more than two decades. One of these 1910 parties dominated by a local *caudilho* from the cowboy country of Rio Grande do Sul named Pinheiro Machado, chose Hermes da Fonseca, a military leader who bore the magic name of his revered uncle and first president. Minas Gerais and Baía boycotted this convention and called another one, nominating the publicist Ruy Barbosa, who had written much of the 1891 constitution. After a spirited campaign and 74 days of vote-checking by congress, Hermes da Fonseca was declared elected despite angry protests of fraudulent balloting. Hermes served out his term to 1914. He was a decided retrogression from the caliber of presidents Brazil had had since 1898 and brought corruption, inflation, and military control to the country.

World War I, which came just as Hermes' presidency ended, had greater repercussions for Brazil than for any other Latin American nation. Brazil was the only country actually to participate in the war—which coincided with the presidency of Wenceslau Braz, a *mineiro*, a great improvement over Hermes. Because of restrictions on international trade in the first two years of the war, Brazil almost suffered economic disaster, but after 1917, the Allies purchased more food and raw material and her situation improved. She severed relations with Germany in April 1917, shortly after the United States entered the war, and in October made an actual declaration of war. Some aviators and some medical units were sent to the European front, and the Brazilian navy was active in patrolling the South Atlantic, but, more important, increasing amounts of foodstuffs flowed into Allied storehouses. Politically the President took steps under martial law to control the large sections of German population, but, as it turned out, the Germans remained more loyal to Brazil than had been expected. In general, World War I served as a unifying force in the regional-minded Brazilian nation; it forced Brazil to diversify agriculture and start some local manufacturing. Most important was the fact that it brought her into world affairs; in fact, since the United States did not join the League of Nations, Brazil came to be the leading American nation in League affairs.

The whole era of 1918 to 1930 was to be one of politico-military intrigue and revolutionary ferment, furthered by the post-war slack and continued regional conflict. The election campaign of 1922 was marked by fraudulence and armed revolt, sparked by the determination of São Paulo to resume control of the central government but meeting the opposition of rancher leaders of Rio Grande, mine workers of Minas, and army officers resisting civilian control of the military. When a *mineiro* won the election, and the price of coffee sank, São Paulo resorted to an open revolt, a costly affair put down in 1924 with federal troops. As the economic slump worsened and unemployment in the cities rose, for the first time the inarticulate workers and immigrant agricultural tenants found a spokesman, the frankly left-wing, Moscow-oriented Luiz Carlos Prestes, an insurrectionary who was exiled to Argentina but who reappeared in Brazilian affairs to harrass the government for decades.

In 1926, a *paulista* won the election, a rich coffee planter with the "coffee first" philosophy named Washington Luiz. But the new President could do nothing to stop the downhill slide of coffee as the whole world plunged into the depression of the 1930's. A nation with a landowning system that was feudal, labor that was destitute and illiterate, commerce and finance that was dependent on an outside world rapidly going to pieces, financially could do little to stem the tide of disaffection, and the republic was ripe for the only successful revolution in its history.

the era of Vargas

From 1889 to 1930 the Republic of Brazil had gone through an era of military dictatorship, an era of prosperity under civilian presidents coming alternately from São Paulo and Minas Gerais, and an era of economic depression. Political parties as such hardly existed, in spite of occasional nominating conventions. Each state had its own political machine, run by rubber kings or coffee planters or rich mine owners or sugar barons or cattle ranchers as the case might be, but always a small, closed oligarchy. The people themselves had little part in any of them. In the fifteen weaker and smaller states there was little interest in the federal government. In the five big states, few participated in the elections, either for federal or for local officials. Regional rivalries dominated politics in the capital; the governors of each state were *caudilhos* at home and strong powers in Rio when the president came from their region.

Washington Luiz, leaving office in 1930, had the chance, as was the custom for outgoing presidents, to "suggest" his successor, provided he, a *paulista*, chose a *mineiro*. His mistake was that he chose instead the governor of São Paulo, Júlio Prestes. This action threw the politicians of Minas Gerais into the camp of the ambitious leaders in Rio Grande do Sul who had been hoping for a chance at the presidency. Liberals and even radicals of Luiz Carlos Prestes' "cells" joined the Rio Grande group to oppose Washington Luiz' pro-planter regime; army men also threw their weight toward Rio Grande in opposition to Washington Luiz' policy of ignoring the army in politics. All these factions formed a new liberal alliance, which proclaimed a reform program. The alliance sounded two mottoes: "no choice of a president by his successor" and "attention to other crops and to industry equal to that given coffee." Its members wanted protection of industry, compulsory and secret voting, and public education for the children of laborers. The man on whom all concentrated to defeat the *paulista* was Getúlio Vargas, a lawyer and a cattle rancher from the pampas of South Brazil. When the election returns showed a majority for the *paulistas*, the self-confident Júlio Prestes took a tour of the United States as president-elect, while economic disorder continued at home, coffee prices fell to the bottom, further foreign loans were refused, and many planters were ruined. The succession of *paulista* presidents was blamed. The election of 1930 brought the social and political discontent into full force.

Some Northern leaders, the Rio Grande group led by Oswaldo Aranha, and many *mineiros* entered into a plot to put Vargas into power. Vargas, completely in control, began a triumphant march north; and cities along the way welcomed him as "conquering hero and liberator." In Rio a handful of generals brought the army to his side. Only outgoing president Washington Luiz opposed the "revolution" and he was held in prison until his legal term of office ended, a month later; then he was exiled to Europe. On November 3, 1930, Vargas entered Rio as the provisional president.

The year 1930 marked a turning in Brazilian history as dramatic as the change from empire to republic had been. Politically, a powerful trend toward centralism and executive domination replaced the easy-going federalism of the old Republic. Economically, the drive for diversified agriculture and industrialization almost swept coffee from its lofty perch; mining and manufacturing made gains. Socially, the neglected laboring classes were to find in Vargas a champion whose coming had been long delayed.

This champion was Getúlio Vargas, born in 1883 on a large cattle ranch on the Rio Grande do Sul frontier where he worked with the gauchos on his father's estates. As a boy "he grew up with a lasso in his hands and a horse between his knees." After a turn in the army, he took a law course and then founded a newspaper in Porto Alegre. He got in state politics and served in the legislature but, having maintained his army officer's status, he rose to the rank of lieutenant colonel through participation in the recurring revolts in volatile Rio Grande. A small unassuming man of friendly word and ready smile, his rise was meteoric; he was federal minister of finance, then governor of Rio Grande do Sul state. In 1930, as the "poor man's president," he lived simply as a devoted family man and worked sixteen hours a day at the presidency. Interested in American business methods, he was friendly to the United States in spite of some flirtation with the Axis. Shrewd and clever as a politician, he played state against state and group against group, and held no grudges. Unassuming, tolerant, and modest, he was untouched by scandal during the fifteen years of his first "reign."

From 1930 to 1934, he was called "interim or provisional president" and was given dictatorial powers. He managed to keep political control and survived from one four-year period to the next. Though his rule was completely autocratic, he sought to broaden the economic and political base of Brazil and inaugurated a sort of New Deal that helped agriculture by limiting sugar and coffee and encouraging diversified crops like grain, citrus fruits, and silk; that tried to bring crop improvement into the drought-ridden northeast; and that aided manufacturers by setting up an international protective tariff while at the same time encouraging commerce by abolishing interstate tariffs and state export taxes. He instituted exchange controls and supported laborers with minimum wage and child welfare laws. All civil rights, however, were suspended. When friends of Julio Prestes, the legally elected president, staged an armed revolt in São Paulo as a last stand for states rights and the old aristocracy, the three-months-long struggle was crushed by hard-fighting federals.

Vargas called a constitutional convention in May 1933, under pressure from the revolt. Most of its members were elected by secret ballot cast by all literate men and women, while a small portion were delegates chosen by labor, trade, and professional organizations. The constitution it produced in 1934 was the first Brazilian constitution since 1891. With the aim of solving the depression, it gave the president and the central government wide economic powers, and the legislature specific representation from industries and professions. The federal government was to own subsoil resources, to regulate and control the mines, to form national corporations in various industries, and to own banks and insurance companies. Various social measures were incorporated into the constitution. The president was to be elected by direct secret ballot, to serve for four years, and not be eligible for immediate re-election. Dom Getúlio was legally elected to the presidency under the authority of the constitution and inaugurated for his first actual "term" on July 20, 1934. This began his period of constitutional government.

The country began slowly to recover from the depression under the increased national intervention and control over industry that was initiated. Preoccupied with the activities this involved, Dom Getúlio allowed the growth of radicalism and fascism to become pressing problems. Luiz Carlos Prestes, the Communist leader, staged a revolt which Vargas crushed in 1935. The far right gave him the most trouble for Hitler had come to power in Germany and Mussolini worked on the loyalties of the thousands of Italians in Brazil. A noisy "Young Fascist" group called the Green Shirts or *Integralistas* entered politics. Vargas, feeling himself destined to stay in power, used the dangers of uprisings on both left and right as his excuse and staged a *coup d'état* against his own Constitution. Thus he again made himself dictator, on November 10, 1937. Desirous of remaining "constitutional," he presented the new Constitution of 1937 which set up "the corporate state of Brazil," the *Estado Novo*, supported by the army. Under it Vargas could rule by decree through a National Economic Council. What he was establishing was a dictator-controlled, planned economy, or economic nationalism, its executive centralization aiming at an integrated society under a personalized control.

Vargas promised to subject this constitution to approval by national plebiscite. While he delayed, the green-shirted *Integralistas*, still unjailed, tried an assassination plot which Getúlio personally foiled. A group of these German-financed young men attempted in May 1938 to take Brazil's White House, the Guanabara Palace. Getúlio and his daughter fired shots into the intruders from behind the curtains of the reception room. The incident brought German influence in Brazilian politics to an abrupt end, and endeared "their Getúlio" to the masses more than ever. So he never put the *Estado Novo* to a plebiscite but maintained his "amiable despotism" and called his rule a "disciplined democracy." "Don't speak; Getúlio will do it for you; don't think—the DIP [the propaganda bureau] will do it for you."

The Brazilian people paid a price for dictatorship but they did gain in economic progress and a higher living standard. A National Economic Council, a Five Year Plan of 1940, and a central education ministry all helped Vargas improve as well as control his country. The decade of the 1930's saw the number of children in secondary school increase from 60,000 to 300,000, the number of elementary school buildings double, road mileage increase 100 percent, airports multiply tenfold. It saw the Volta Redonda plan for steel production, the São Francisco Valley Authority (described in the next chapter), the search for petroleum, drought control in Ceará, the system of coffee quotas, all of them originally Vargas' ideas, worked out by his able henchmen. Labor had him to thank for an eight-hour day and minimum wage, poor farmers for the opening up of the frontier to free settlement, poor city dwellers for new housing projects and workers' restaurants serving inexpensive food in balanced rations. In effect the whole program of the *Estado Novo* was a gigantic public welfare plan imposed from the top. Vargas' regime brought greater national unity to Brazil. Brazilians who had been accustomed to say first, "I am a *paulista*," "I am a *mineiro*," "I am a baíano," all learned to say on first thought, "I am a Brazilian."

Meanwhile the German element in Brazil, and, later, the large Italian population as well, were being wooed by the powerful Nazi propaganda machine. In 1934, Vargas had undertaken barter trade agreements with the Germans to help ease the depression, but when he realized how the trade agreements were being broken by the Naxis, he asked the German ambassador to leave. In 1937–1938, two years before Europe went to war, he outlawed the German language press and clubs, proclaimed Portuguese the only language to be taught in Brazilian elementary schools, and, to bolster the economy, made a reciprocal trade treaty with the United States. The easy-going and racially tolerant Brazilians were offended by Hitler's increasing racial discrimination, and they turned more and more toward the United States.

On December 7, 1941, Pearl Harbor was attacked by the Axis; on December 8th, Brazil declared "continental solidarity"; on the 9th, she froze Axis funds; on the 13th, she suspended pro-Axis newspapers. January 1942 brought Brazilian leadership in the Rio conference to defend the Western Hemisphere, and by August 22nd Brazil was openly at war. Brazil's aid to the Allied cause was of enormous importance at this time for the route to Africa from the bulge of Brazil at Natal was the one free step to North Africa and Mediterranean Europe. The United States Fourth Fleet was based at Recife. Brazilian aviators and naval men were trained for the defense of the Hemisphere by American officers. The Brazilian navy helped patrol the South Atlantic and in convoy duty. In 1944, a Brazilian infantry force fought under Mark Clark in Italy, the only Latin American land force to fight abroad in World War II. Moreover raw materials—rubber, mica, beryllium, quartz, iron ore, copra, vegetable oils, and foodstuffs—poured from Brazil into the Allied coffers.

With Brazil so active in World War II and in the United Nations affairs which followed, the Brazilian Secretary of Foreign Affairs also became a world figure. This was Oswaldo Aranha, that old friend of Getúlio's from Rio Grande, a statesman and thinker far ahead of his fellow gaucho. He had studied in Paris as a youth and fought with Vargas in the endless rebellions of Rio Grande. He had come to Rio with Vargas. As ambassador to the United States, he had been called "the most popular Latin American ambassador who was ever in Washington" and "the essential link between Brazil and North America." After the war he became a leader in the United Nations Security Council.

In February, 1945, the world was surprised to learn that "Getúlio," the permanent president, was retiring to his ranch in Rio Grande and that Eurico Gaspar Dutra was to become president of Brazil. Dutra, Minister of War under Vargas, a quiet army man born in Cuibá in Mato Grosso, had worked behind the scenes to hold the army together in support of Vargas. When the war was almost won, Vargas responded to army pressure and general criticism of his dictatorial methods and announced his retirement before the end of the year. Dutra won the elections and was inaugurated January 31, 1946, the first inauguration of a popularly elected president since 1926. Vargas, returning to his home in Rio Grande, successfully ran for the Senate.

the post-World-War-II period

The quiet, colorless Dutra took over peacefully and promised to sweep away the fascist overtones of Vargas' regime, to restore the rights of states, and to call a new Constitutional Convention and cooperate with the United States. The new Constitution, written in 1946, was essentially conservative. It provided for a five-year presidency with never a second term, made the legislature a real law-making body, reasserted the local direct election of state governors (who had all been appointed by Vargas in recent years) and granted individual rights and guarantees. It also assured the continuation of Vargas' social and economic reforms. Dutra made few other changes. Economic nationalism and promotion of industrialization continued during his term. and business leaders became powerful in the government. Nationally controlled TVA-type development plans were begun, and railroads and highways built, though the lower classes felt increasing hard times under inflation.

In 1950, at the close of Dutra's term, two candidates emerged, an army man and a lawyer from Minas Gerais, with little to distinguish them. Suddenly the new Labor Party presented "Our Getúlio" as its candidate, supposedly an unwilling candidate responding to an irresistible popular demand. He spoke to crowds and made sweeping promises to better economic conditions. With no national issues to the fore, the most colorful personality won, and Vargas was brought back to the presidency in the elections of October 1950—his first actual election by a free democratic choice in open competition.

In governing this second session, Vargas was forced to use a more conciliatory spirit since the new Labor Party did not win the required backing in congress. His own education, welfare, and health programs had so improved Brazil that political democracy was the next logical step. But Vargas was not his old innovative self—he was older and in ill health. He did not choose able men, and graft and corruption surrounded him. Brazil itself had changed in outlook and was politically and economically more nationalistic than it was in Vargas' earlier years.

The Army acquiesced in Vargas' election but later opposed him in his new reforms and his concessions to labor. The plans Vargas had for further industrialization and development of natural resources required money and technical training which Brazil in its deteriorating financial condition could not provide. Vargas and his vice-president, João Café Filho, an editor from northern Brazil—whom Vargas had been forced to accept as his running mate in a "deal" he had made with the governor of São Paulo— were faced with a challenge to stop Brazil's serious inflation and to check the leniency of Brazilians toward Communist infiltration.

Vargas was unable to stop the inflation. Two years after he had promised to reduce food prices, living costs had gone up another 30 percent. Some 250,000 factory workers in São Paulo staged hunger strikes. Vargas' economists pegged coffee at a price that almost drove it off the American market, and a $2 million deficit resulted in overseas trade. In the spring of 1954 army and conservative leaders were asking Vargas to resign. Deputies in congress joined the military men. People in the streets carried "Down with Vargas" signs. Vargas seemed to be scorning his opponents, but then on the last Tuesday in August 1954, more than a year before his five-year term was to expire, he called his cabinet into meeting shortly after midnight and the next morning he wrote out his resignation. And then he shot himself. He left a note saying, "To the wrath of my enemies I leave the legacy of my death. I take the sorrow of not having been able to do for the humble all that I desired." The masses of Rio mourned "Our Getúlio" in a sorrowful public funeral.

Dom Getúlio's dramatic death at the age of 71 did not do anything to check inflation or solve Brazil's other fundamental problems, domestic and international. João Café Filho unwillingly and unhappily took over the government of a restless nation. Knowing that the constitution forbade him to succeed himself, he set about restoring order. The honesty exemplified in Café Filho's own simple personal life contrasted with the corrupt last days of the Vargas regime. The congressional elections returned a right-of-center majority to Congress. The price of coffee in the United States went down and Brazilian trade picked up. But for the very urgent problem of inflation, he could find no solution.

In the 1955 presidential elections, a strong and active Social Democratic Party entered a three-candidate race and nominated the governor of Minas Gerais, a popular personality of Slavic immigrant ancestry named Juscelino Kubitschek, with controversial João Goulart as the vice-presidential candidate. Kubitschek launched the biggest presidential campaign in Brazilian history, using the slogan, "Power, Transportation, and Food." He made 1,215 different speeches. In a fair but close election, held under tense conditions in which 10,000,000 Brazilians voted, the Social Democrats were elected by a 36 percent plurality.

The personable and "Americanized" Kubitschek represented a new class of society in the presidency. A poor boy from Diamantina on the frontier, who had worked as a telegraph operator to put himself through medical school, he was a Vargas man through his years as mayor of Belo Horizonte, delegate to the Chamber of Deputies, and successful governor of the rapidly industrializing state of Minas Gerais. In his campaign, he promised to "advance Brazil fifty years in a five-year term," which could be carried out with a combination of his middle-class and labor supporters and with the development of Brazil's great potentialities by larger foreign capital investment and government loans.

Kubitschek started his term in control of the political situation though he was pressed on one side by the army and on the other by the restless labor unions led by his vice-president João Goulart. As part of his five-year plan, he sought to improve the "poorhouse northeast" and the Brazilian interior. His pet project was the building of a new capital in a federal district in the uncleared bush on the Goiás Plateau, a model city to be called Brasilia. He pushed the project in spite of the heavy financial outlay it would involve during stringent times. He wanted to complete building his city in three years and agreed to remain neutral in the 1960 campaign if the capital was officially moved to Brasilia by the date he set. On April 21, 1960, he opened Congress in the new capital building in Brasilia, surrounded by plowed ground and uncleared brush. Many departments of government, including the diplomatic corps, stayed in Rio.

Kubitschek assumed leadership on the Hemisphere scene when he suggested "Operation Pan Americana," a joint development with United States funds that would counteract the anti-Americanism evident when Vice-President Nixon visited South America in 1958. His plan resulted in the program that later was called the Alliance for Progress.

But he could do nothing about Brazil's chronic inflation and deficit spending which threatened the country with bankruptcy, especially as raw materials and coffee entered a period of falling prices. He apologized in his fourth State-of-the-Union message for his inability to check inflation which had caused a 100 per cent rise in the cost of living during his presidency. Industrialization and foreign investment were slowing down because of the lack of sound base for agriculture and the shortage of skilled laborers. Kubitschek, nevertheless, remained personally popular. In January, 1961, he gave way legally to the newly elected Jânio Quadros who was inaugurated at Brasilia with great ceremony.

Quadros' election symbol was "a new broom," which was to sweep Brazil clean of corruption. Brilliant but temperamental, a self-made man accustomed to hard work and complete honesty on the job himself, he demanded these same attitudes in those who worked under him. He hoped to reorganize Brazil's lax civil service, cure inflation by price and wage controls, and stop the endless printing of paper money with which Kubitschek had tried to control the economy. But João Goulart, Kubitschek's left-leaning labor minister had, by the chance of Brazil's presidential election system, become Quadros' vice-president. He had no intention of helping solve inflation by an austerity program and went off on "economic and cultural missions" first to Moscow and then to Peking.

Quadros struggled against odds to solve the rising discontent. When Quadros ordered the printing of unbacked paper money stopped (43 billion *cruzeiros* had been printed under Kubitschek), a wave of strikes broke out in the industrial centers where living costs were far outrunning wages. In the northeast where drought had hit five years in succession, actual starvation existed. Peasant leagues were being organized by Francisco Julião, a "voice of the people," who urged the farm tenants to take farmland by force from the landlords. The influence of Cuba's Fidel Castro was strong among the landless peasants and the drought refugees who poured into the city slums where jobs were scarce and living expensive.

Quadros as President struggled with this economic chaos for seven months. Then suddenly, on August 25, 1961, he resigned and took a freight boat to England. Some Brazilians thought he had become mentally unstable; others said he hoped by this dramatic move to force the public to accept his belt-tightening reforms and "woo" him back. Vice-president Goulart quickly returned from the Far East to take over the government. The majority in Congress feared his leftist influence and officers in the powerful armed forces refused to accept him as president. A compromise was reached in September by which Goulart was to serve more or less like a "limited monarch" under the British cabinet system—a Council of ministers composed of members of Congress was established. Its chairman was to act as a prime minister.

For the next two years neither Goulart nor Congress accomplished anything. They were bogged down in a "parliamentary quagmire" and no laws were passed. The value of the Brazilian *cruzeiro*, formerly worth twenty to the dollar, fell to 1,100 and then, by the spring of 1964, to 1,500 to the dollar. Goulart did nothing to check the urban strikes and the rural revolt. When some enlisted men in the navy mutinied and staged a sit-down strike and their officers had them jailed, Goulart freed them and ordered them restored to regular status. By this move, he lost what little support he had had in the military.

With business, Congress, and local leadership uniting against him, Goulart was overthrown in March 1964 in a bloodless "coup" backed by army units in Rio, São Paulo, and Paraná. Goulart fled to his ranch in Rio Grande do Sul where he had acquired vast holdings during the 31 months of his presidency, perhaps with public money. His brother-in-law Leon Brizzoli, governor of Rio Grande do Sul, had angered Americans by confiscating the American Telephone Company there. Now both branches of the family fled to Uruguay, taking fortunes with them, and leaving their leftist supporters embarrassed and disillusioned.

Congress was persuaded by the military officers to choose Army Chief of Staff General Humberto Castelo Branco as interim president to serve out the presidential term until 1966. Castelo Branco had been in charge of Brazilian forces in Italy during the war, but he was comparatively unknown to civilians. An *Ato Institucional* or Act of Institution, proclaimsd by the military forces that were backing him stated in April 1964, "Revolution is a profound constitutional power." It was the first of such military decrees that were to supersede whatever constituton was in force.

Evidently Castelo Branco did not intend to create a military dictatorship. He pushed a land reform bill through the landlord-controlled Senate which authorized the distribution of land to needy tenants on a long-term credit basis, payment being permitted in bonds for the land expropriated. But Communist sympathizers Julião and Luiz Carlos Prestes were deprived of their rights to vote and participate in politics. So were 400 other politicians, including former leaders such as Kubitschek who were accused of having profited personally from public office. In two years time, Castelo Branco pushed so many worthy pieces of legislation through Congress that many Brazilians praised him for having brought about a "real revolution." And he probably did avert a more violent one from the "left." But local political leaders were not under the control of his government—now firmly based in the new Brasilia—and in October, 1965, his supporters lost governorships and congressional seats in the elections of ten of Brazil's 22 states. Castelo Branco responded by issuing a second *Ato Institucional* or executive decree which disbanded all parties that had not elected at least twelve state legislators in at least seven states. There had been 14 political parties in Brazil in 1964. As a consequence of this Act, only two groups were left legally active, Castelo Branco's own party and a synthetic "loyal opposition."

Under this new political set-up, Castelo Branco "decreed" an election for September 3, 1966, to choose governors in the remaining 12 states. Governors of his own party won with little opposition. Next he "decreed" a Congressional vote on October 3, 1966, to choose a new President. The hand-picked candidate, another tough old soldier, Artur da Costa e Silva, was easily the winner. Next he decreed a new congressional election in which his friends and approved "opponents" were neatly re-elected. Finally he turned Congress into a constituent assembly, sent it a new Constitution, and on January 22, 1967, had it accepted.

The new constitution, together with the very strict control of the press exercised by the President, concentrated power in the executive. The President, who was to be chosen every four years by Congress, maintained the power to initiate all legislation concerning public finance and national security, and to suspend civil rights for individuals. Castelo Branco had himself used his powers to issue a new unit of money and to curb inflation by stabilizing it at 2.20 to the dollar. And he had expropriated unused land from large estates and encouraged a "homestead" type of colonization. When Costa e Silva was peacefully inaugurated on March 15, 1967, Brazilians hoped the precedent established would work for internal peace and improved economic conditions. Castelo Branco himself was killed in a plane crash a few months after the inauguration.

Costa e Silva engaged in two years of hard-driving activity with military backing. He suspended all civil liberties guaranteed in the Castelo Branco Constitution of 1967. He adopted a three year planned growth in basic industries and highways. Then in August 1969 he suffered a cerebral hemorrhage. Even before his illness the military had been completely in the ascendancy. And the response of the liberals, the students, and even the Catholic clergy was boycotts, street riots, kidnapping of diplomats, and terrorism.

When it became evident by October, 1969, that Costa e Silva would not recover, three powerful generals took over the government. They chose General Garrastazú Médici to act as president, to serve until 1974. A special Congress approved his election and declared a new Constitution giving the executive greatly enlarged powers. The rubber-stamp Congress was reduced in size and its members denied immunity from arrest. In mid-1972 hundreds of political prisoners were in jail, including many priests, nuns, and students, and there were dark reports of torture being used in prison.

Garrastasú Médici, after consolidating his power, has stimulated more rapid economic growth in Brazil. His attempt to build popular support has been through programs of "national and social integration." He is much concerned with the national development of his country, and he has paid attention and allotted moneys on educational programs, especially designed to eliminate illiteracy among adults, extending primary and secondary education, and instruction in science. However Brazil under military rule may have subordinated social reform to the more immediate task of economic development. Médici sees Brazil as underpopulated and under-developed and to meet the challenge of the twentieth century has pointedly worked to overcome such obstacles, so that Brazil can take its place in the community of world powers by the end of the century.

By 1972, price increases had been reduced to an inflation rate of less than 20 per cent, although the average Brazilian's standard of living was not greatly improved and the majority of the people continued to live in squalor and despair. Eight years after the army-controlled revolution of 1964, life in rural areas remained at a low level. The military leaders were still dedicated to the principle of private enterprise capitalism, and were confident that prosperity would "drip down from the top" on to the workers. But the Garrastazú Médici regime was making some progress towards equalization of education and passed a 5 billion dollar budget in 1972 to enforce com-pulsory elementary schooling and make secondary education more available to the masses. Brazilians could only hope that Garrastazú Médici was sincere in his promise of elections in 1974. Brazil, with its vast untapped natural resources, awaits only a non-violent transition to constitutional government and increasing capabilities in science and technology to enter upon a new age of unparalleled promise.

Note: Readings for this chapter are given at the end of Chapter 21.

chapter 21

BRAZILIAN
ECONOMIC
AND SOCIAL
DEVELOPMENT

economic, cultural, and social growth
in the days of Dom Pedro

In 1820 Rio de Janeiro stretched a half mile along its bay and had 100,000 people. In 1853 it extended three miles and boasted 350,000 people, though a traveler called it "an unsanitary and bad copy of Lisbon." The same traveler returned in 1869 to see the bay shore settlement "a circuit of many miles," and a home for 600,000 people. It was still a city of narrow streets, pink, blue, and yellow tile houses, and singing street merchants. Well-to-do ladies traveled through the streets in sedan chairs carried by liveried slaves. A traveler considered the Brazilian ladies "too fat and overdressed" and always several years behind the Paris fashions—a cruel remark that can no longer be made of the ladies of São Paulo and Rio. Most of the women stayed at home as they had done in colonial times, were married very young, gave birth to twelve or fifteen children, and were "withered or corpulent at twenty-five."

The home was the center of life; family birthdays and saints' days were celebrated with enthusiasm. Married sons brought their brides home, and several families, all related, lived under the same roof. During Carnival everyone was in the streets, however, for the Rio Carnival was as hilarious then as now. Easter itself was more boisterous than in Spanish America,

SOUTH AMERICA'S
THREE MAJOR POWERS
ARGENTINA, BRAZIL, CHILE

with rocket explosions all day on "Halleluja Saturday," indicating the same love of fun and celebration that persists in Brazil today.

In spite of the hilarity, Rio, like other cities in the tropics before the discovery of the causes of disease, was an unhealthy place in which to live. Dom Pedro called medical conferences as early as 1846 to discuss the high rate of infant mortality. One traveler was informed by a sugar grower near Rio that "not half the Negroes born in this estate live to be ten years old." Swamps behind the city of Rio remained undrained and mosquitoes filled the air, although an elaborate aqueduct project was constructed to bring pure water into the central Carioca Fountain—that fountain from which modern "Cariocas" take their nickname as residents of Rio. Pedro II built a summer resort at Petropolis, in the hills where mosquitoes did not come, to get his family away from the epidemics of yellow fever that so often hit the city.

The sick in the city were cared for by orders of nuns or by "brother-hoods" of laymen similar to the *hermandades* of Spanish America. Because of the charities of such brotherhoods, begging was not very necessary for the poor of Rio, and after 1855 was only done by "licensed" beggars whose claims the authorities had investigated. As to danger in the streets, a Protestant missionary reported in 1855, "I have found few cities more orderly than Rio de Janeiro; and the police are so generally on the alert, that in comparison with New York and Philadelphia, burglaries rarely occur. I felt greater personal security at a late hour of the night in Rio than I would in New York."

In the provinces there was little of the city life of Rio. Baía impressed travelers in 1855 with its commercial houses on the upper level, "edifices which would adorn the business portions of London, Paris, or New York." But the lower town as "old and wretched" even then, crowded with peddlers, "and at times as filthy as the streets of New York." Baía lived on sugar, and sugar was still considered Brazil's staple crop in the 1870s. The Imperial Agriculture Institute of Rio cultivated twenty-one varieties of sugar cane on Dom Pedro's model plantation, distributed large numbers of new experimental plants, and was constantly recommending new methods.

We are so accustomed to thinking of Brazil as the coffee country that we forget that coffee was never planted in Brazil until 1727, and then only when a few plants were smuggled out of French Guiana. Rio de Janeiro's plantation owners planted it as a crop toward the end of the colonial period, and between 1800 and 1860 increased its production a hundredfold. São Paulo, frontier town, home of the historic *bandeirantes,* slumbered in the 1860s with 25,000 inhabitants. It stood fourteenth among cities in a nation not given to cities. In 1872 coffee began to be planted in this cool upland state, tended by immigrant laborers from Europe and not by slaves.

Rio Grande do Sul was England's chief source of hides, dried beef, and tallow before the development of freezing facilities in Argentina. It was a country of independent spirit that threatened to join Uruguay, and later Paraguay. Descriptions of life there among the hard-riding *vaqueros* sound like stories from Argentina more than from tropical Brazil, for the area is geographically an extension of the pampas. Dom Pedro had an interest in the cattle country from boyhood, and he encouraged European immigration there, exhorting the farmers to take up small personal holdings and produce dairy cattle, sheep, hogs, corn, and flax.

The story of the Amazon area in Dom Pedro's time is the story of a "boom" leading to a "bust." Explorers in the 1700s had seen the Indians carrying rubber bags, had learned the Indian process of making latex, and sent out rubber to be used in galoshes, pencil erasers, and raincoats. In 1844, Goodyear, in the United States, patented vulcanized rubber and the balls of latex, smoked from the sap of the Hevea tree, found a world market. In 1840, 400 tons were shipped out of Belém; in 1860, 3,000 tons. Around Belém, an old colonial city in the sugar business, all cultivation of sugar, corn, or mandioca stopped. The rubber trees grew wild upriver; the Indians knew how to find and tap them, and were soon enslaved by rubber merchants. In the 1860s the Amazon was opened to steam travel and in 1867 to world commerce; by 1870, a fleet of English steamers took the rubber directly to Europe. Manáus began to grow as the center 1,000 miles upriver, when Dom Pedro's last years saw a new market for pneumatic rubber tires.

Transportation between the regions of Brazil, still Brazil's great economic problem today, was far more difficult a century ago. Dom Pedro, king at five, had yet seen no other city except Rio when he was twenty-five. From Rio to Baía, one went by sailing vessel; to Minas Gerais or São Paulo by horseback. No wonder Pedro welcomed the ideas of an engineer named Mauá who in 1854 built ten miles of railroad from Rio toward the new resort of Petropolis.

Baron Mauá, who had been a poor orphan boy apprenticed to a British grocer, was responsible for most of Brazil's economic development. He had quickly learned British accounting methods and larger British companies employed him, sent him to England on business, and encouraged him to build Brazil's first foundry in 1854. He was instrumental in sending a line of steamers to Europe and he brought gas lights to Rio. Through him industrialization and banking increased, and immigration began to come to Brazil. Post roads and railroads inland from Rio were built with government money by immigrant labor, not by slaves, a reform idea of Dom Pedro's; he felt that no such public improvements should bear the stigma of having been built with slave labor. With British capital, other short railways were constructed in Dom Pedro's time, from São Paulo to Santos, from Rio to Minas Gerais. By the end of the empire there were 6,000 miles of railroad and about 12,000 miles of telegraph line in Brazil—though in the late 1950s there was still no continuous north-south railway to connect Rio to Baía or Pernambuco. Dom Pedro, the paternalistic ruler, meanwhile created every new thing he could for Brazil—a scientific agricultural committee to fight famine in the dry region of Ceará, a regular line of coastal steamers, a smallpox vaccine institute, a silkworm-rearing establishment, and a cable connection to the Transatlantic cable. All this new industrialization and scientific interest had great significance for Brazil. Foreign commerce, immigration, and business capital were creating a new generation on a new basis of wealth in the 1880s.

Dom Pedro and his father had both been concerned with schools for their people. Under the constitution every village or town was to have a public school, although the passing of laws does not automatically build schools. The central government did not control or pay for elementary schools in the provinces; the capital merely passed laws, hoping that schools would be set up by localities. Only schools in Rio were supported by the imperial government, and in that city in 1844 there was one primary school for every 900 children, schools attended perhaps by thirty or forty students. Education remained the prerogative of the gentleman; only sons of the aristocracy went beyond primary school.

Dom Pedro did all a man could do, single-handed, to alleviate this situation. He was a true schoolteacher at heart. At the age of twelve he had been made a "Protector of the Colégio Dom Pedro," a public secondary school for boys, and he maintained a lifelong interest in it, supporting many needy boys who came to his attention and paying their way through college after they finished high school. He established teacher-training schools at imperial expense, and he tried to standardize examinations for teachers. Through his unfailing efforts in behalf of elementary and secondary schools, education in Brazil was ahead of that in most Spanish-speaking countries, though illiteracy still stood at 90 per cent of the population at the end of his reign. As for higher education, in the last years of the empire Brazil had two faculties of medicine, two academies of law, a school of nurses, a school of fine arts, a music conservatory, and an observatory. In the secondary schools, new egalitarian philosophies were openly taught, and the new generation which learned them was ready to abolish slavery and favor political and educational reform.

In spite of the fact that the great mass of Brazilians were illiterate, a native Brazilian literature was developing. Several novels on native themes were popular during Pedro II's reign. One of the first South American "best sellers" was called *The Little Brunette*, written by Joaquim Manoel de Macedo (1820–1882). The story would seem very sentimental to us today, but most older Brazilians now alive read it and wept over it in their youth. A rock in Rio Bay, which has become famous as a lovers' suicide leap, is named after the heroine. The romantic life of the Indians came into fiction in the books of José de Alencar (1829–1877). The hero of his *O Guarany* is a noble Indian who risks his life to save the daughter of a plantation owner from death in a flood. So famous is this Indian character that South America's best-known opera was written around his story by the Brazilian composer Carlos Gomez for a debut in Milan in 1870. Alencar's masterpiece, *Iracema*, was published eight years afterwards. Later novelists wrote about life more realistically. Joaquim Maria Machado de Assis (1839–1908), a poor mulatto boy who became a literary genius, wrote short stories and novels about human troubles. He lived into the twentieth century, but his best writing was done in Pedro II's time. He has been called the "Brazilian

Somerset Maugham." His *Don Casmurro* has been proclaimed the best Brazilian novel, and his *Jacob and Esau* has been translated into English and became a best-seller in America.

Dom Pedro's own personal interests encouraged scientific writing. When his mother, the Empress Leopoldina, came as a bride, she brought a European botanist with her who had started a compendium of Brazilian flora. It eventually filled forty volumes and identified and described 20,000 species of Brazilian plants; many native scientists worked on it, for it took forty-six years to complete. The American naturalist, Louis Agassiz, came to Brazil to confer on it as the guest of Dom Pedro, and gave a scientific lecture in Rio, an event of the social season. On August 18, 1838, a "committee of twenty-seven illustrious Brazilians" had met to organize the Brazilian Historical and Geographical Institute. Dom Pedro turned a room of the palace over to the society and was one of its most serious members, serving as chairman at 506 of its meetings. Today, this society is the most active of its kind in South America, rivaled in the Western Hemisphere only by the National Geographic Society of the United States. There were many other scientific and literary societies. The interest in botany, geology, and zoology led to the development of a National Museum.

Opera houses were built in Rio and São Paulo, but only foreign compositions were played. In 1839 in a village in the state of São Paulo, Antônio de Carlos Gomes (1839–1896) a "natural" musician, was born. Apprenticed early to a tailor, he studied by himself, but attracted a wealthy *paulista* who financed him at the conservatory branch of the Rio Fine Arts Academy, where Dom Pedro II heard his work and sent him to Italy to study. His native Brazilian *arias* were difficult for Italian orchestras to perform; they could not get the jungle effects with regular instruments. But it was he who set Alencar's romantic story, *O Guarany*, to opera music; it was performed at La Scala in Milan in 1870, a great musical triumph for a Brazilian. More than fifty other operas were composed by Brazilians in mid-century, many of them with native Brazilian themes. The imported European culture provided the "tone," however, when music and drama were performed at the ten theaters and opera houses of Rio.

All this culture and society were described daily in the *Jornal do Comércio*, Rio's largest newspaper. It had been founded in 1821, and was printing 15,000 six-page copies every morning by the 1870s. The year 1876 saw the beginning of "a very cheap daily paper," the *Gazeta de Notícias* which had the large staff of twelve reporters to get out its morning edition. There were then several other journals in Rio, and many more in Baía and Pernambuco.

the twentieth-century coffee industry in São Paulo

São Paulo, which could hardly be listed as a town of culture in the time of Dom Pedro, is the fastest growing city in the world in the 1970s. But the little town of 30,000 on the "frontier" had already begun, when Pedro II fell from power, to look forward to a great future in coffee. To replace the recently freed slaves in the newly created republic came hard-working peasants from northern Italy along with immigrants from Portugal, Switzerland, and Germany. On arrival they were given a small plot of land that usually had been planted with a thousand coffee trees, to be cared for on a sharecropping basis. For the immigrants, this development was an improvement on the peasant status and depleted land they had known in Europe. For São Paulo it was the beginning of a boom. In 1890, not 100,000 people lived in the whole province; by 1970, over 10,000,000 people, more than half of them of Italian descent, lived in São Paulo state and 4,790,000 in the city. Brazil's day as a "sugar" country was over; coffee was king and São Paulo was his throne. One of the most important government agencies in Brazil in the past twenty years has been the Coffee Institute which supervises the industry, sets prices, arranges quotas, and promotes research.

In June and July, whole families of sharecroppers down to the six-year olds, joined by hundreds of seasonal workers, are busy on the red-soiled rolling hills of São Paulo picking the bright red coffee berries. Other workers pour the berries out on the central drying grounds and rake them endlessly in the sun. The dried hull is floated off on the plantation's cleaning plant and the small brown beans graded. Then commission merchants come to take the sacks of graded beans to Santos; the adults turn their attention to the care of the orchard for next year's picking; the children go back to the *fazenda* school and the migrants go back to the city. In such a work cycle, nearly one-third of the world's coffee supply is grown in a single region of 100,000 square miles. Brazil grows 58 per cent of the world's coffee, São Paulo state almost half of Brazil's export crop, Paraná another 25 per cent and Minas Gerais still another 20 per cent. Of all this coffee, the United States takes 58 per cent.

São Paulo has often overproduced coffee; beginning in 1906 the Brazilian government made its first attempt to keep prices up. All prices soared again during World War I, but the 1920s saw one desperate price drop after another. By 1929, the bumper crop was of no value in world markets. Attempts to destroy the crop by burning it in kerosene-soaked piles, or dumping it out at sea caused only extra expense. Growers and pickers were living on government bounty to produce a crop just to be destroyed, and even in spite of this control—"valorization" as it was called—prices continued to drop. A series of conferences in the late 1930s between Brazil and other coffee-producing nations set up a quota system, under which Brazil was to sell about 65 per cent of the world's supply, and all countries would cooperate to keep the price up. World War II and the postwar inflation kept the price up anyway, and the early 1950s brought boom years to São Paulo. Then the world price went too high, and the United States began to cut its consumption. Today many *fazendeiros* have diversified their crops; they are producing materials for São Paulo's own factories and food for São Paulo's own people and hope to survive any future slump in world coffee prices.

São Paulo city, prospering first from the coffee boom and the immigrant tide, is growing even more rapidly in the era of the new diversification. Not only does the coffee production center there, but the city is responsible for over one-half of the industrial production of Brazil. The city government has constructed viaducts, freeways, and tunnels to handle the traffic. Electric power was produced cheaply by damming up two rivers on the plateau and creating artificial lakes thirty miles long. Factories of all types are being built in São Paulo because of the cheap power, the skilled labor, the supply of prosperous consumers. To house its business offices, the city boasted 1400 "skyscrapers" in 1967. Members of the lower middle class can own their own homes, for new subdivisions are constantly offering houses in the suburbs which can be purchased on the installment plan. There are also many smaller boom towns throughout the region, with new ones springing up every year.

Most of the state's products are shipped through the harbor of Santos, the leading coffee port of the world. In 1920 it had 50,000 inhabitants; today it has 300,000. Trucks and railway cars bring São Paulo's coffee to Santos at the rate of a million bags a month. Santos itself, warmer than São Paulo because it is at sea level, also ships 12,000,000 stems of bananas a year. To São Paulo city dwellers Santos is as important today as a beach resort as it is as a port.

other economic regions

A thousand miles to the north of bustling São Paulo lies another great economic region which rose to a boom on a single crop—the Amazon River Valley with its rubber. The turn of the century saw rubber used for tires on the new horseless carriages, as well as in the waterproofing of cloth. To get the raw material Brazilian middlemen kept Indian rubber collectors in debt slavery, sending them out in the forest to tap the wild rubber trees. Manáus was the center of this boom, a jungle town a thousand miles up the Amazon. Money flowed freely; huge mansions and even an elaborate opera house were erected, streets were paved, extensive docks built—all on the one product, rubber. The peak year was 1912; almost as much rubber was exported that year as coffee.

But the bubble burst. British botanists who had smuggled out rubber-tree seeds in violation of Pedro II's monopoly had started plantations in Malaya, where a steady supply of patient hand labor waited to care for the trees. Plantation rubber of uniform quality stole the Brazilian market; the Manáus boom ended in 1915 and with it the livelihood of many hundreds of Brazilian Indians and half-breeds from the coast who had settled the little river towns along the Amazon.

In the 1930s the American industrialist Henry Ford hoped to revive the Amazon rubber industry, thus making the Western Hemisphere independent of Malayan rubber. Ford developed experimental plantations in the Amazon basin at Belterra and on the Tapajós and planted more than two million trees of carefully grafted, disease-free stock. Much was expected of this venture when World War II cut off the supply of Far Eastern plantation rubber, but the war ended before Ford had begun to clear any profit.

When Malayan rubber again entered world markets in 1946, Ford turned over his experimental plantations to the Brazilian government, which has continued the project of improving the native rubber stock through the work of the Agronomical Institute of Northern Brazil. The botanists in charge hope that the Amazon Valley, which is 40 per cent of the land of Brazil, will break the tyranny of a single-crop system, and are experimenting with rice planting and jute for burlap sacking, as well as with Ford's rubber stock, working out plans for drainage and flood control. To grow rice and jute in commercial quantities Brazil needs machinery and workers, which the Amazon does not yet have.

Meanwhile, World War II's rubber boom put Manáus back on the map. Goodyear and Firestone established branch factories in Rio and São Paulo using Amazon rubber. The end of the war did not bring a collapse, because the rising standard of living in Brazil's cities and the "boom" in São Paulo brought more automobiles for Brazilians. Today Manáus is a cosmopolitan little city of 180,000 people. Through it and its Atlantic port of Belém, with its 400,000 people, stream thousands of tons of other Amazon products—maghogany, carnauba, wax, rotenone roots for insecticides, Brazil nuts, babassu oil, and coconuts. Timber and other forest products, mostly from the Amazon, are the fourth most important export of Brazil.

In the northeast of Brazil, Baía, and Pernambuco, sugar had been king until the slaves were freed just before the establishment of the republic. Already in 1889 more coffee and more rubber were produced than sugar; by 1936 sugar comprised only 2 per cent of the total export. But all sugar consumed in Brazil is grown there, so that Baía and other sugarcane regions produce 25,000,000 sacks a year. Pernambuco no longer needs to live by sugar mills alone. The area grows quantities of cotton, and its capital, Recife, now a city of almost 2 million, is a cotton textile-mill center.

Baía is today a port for shipping cacao, the chocolate-producing bean. Brazil is one of the world's chief exporters, sending 200,000,000 pounds of cacao beans to the United States a year. The crop is sold in world markets through a cooperative called the Cacao Institute of Baía. The trees, which produce cacao beans in large pods hanging from the limbs and trunk, can be grown either in plantation formation or in anyone's back yard; both small and large landowners therefore can belong to the Baía cooperative. Baía is also the center of Brazil's tobacco and cigarette trade. Still a proud city, Baía has about 950,000 people and is much more than a museum piece for it is the center of the musical culture contributed to Brazil by people of African blood.

A special problem exists farther north, in the interior of the bulge, the *sertão*. Here the land is unusable because of recurrent drought. In 1956 Kubitschek established the Northeastern Social and Economic Development Agency, the SUDENE. Its program for irrigating unused acreage, producing electric power from irrigation dams, and dividing unused land into small holdings to be paid for on long-term credit continued into the 1970s under other Presidents, with financial help from the United States under the Alliance for Progress. This is the overcrowded, poverty-stricken area where the pro-Communist organizer Julião gained so many recruits in 1962 and 1963 that it was feared Fidel Castro's influence would make Brazil's northeast another Cuba. Castelo Branco hoped to satisfy Julião's followers through the activities of SUDENE while he had their leader put in jail. In the 1970's, the optimism of 1960 in this region was changed to pessimism when a great drought hit a million Brazilians in the nearly rainless year of 1970. Of what use were the new irrigation canals when there was no water to run in them, or the improved fertilizer and good seed when the land was blowing away? The SUDENE was forced to report in June 1970 that one million people were starving, that the made-work road-building projects were providing food for 200,000 men but not for their large families of children. Other road-building jobs were available in the region west of Brasilia but the men of the Northeast were too weakened by hunger to get to this area.

In great contrast to the despairing Northeast, however, is the prosperous state of Rio Grande do Sul far to the south. This area has 14 million head of cattle. Brahma stock has been used to breed hybrids, and the resultant fine hides, unscarred by ticks, make Brazil the second largest source of hides in the world. The meat is of a fine quality for freezing and refrigeration. Brazil's meat capital is Porto Alegre, which means "Happy Harbor." Located 700 miles south of Rio, it has 800,000 inhabitants who live more in the manner of Argentines than Brazilians.

Together the four "c's"—cacao, cotton, cattle, and coffee—make Brazil a great agricultural nation. One outcome of the coffee-caused depression has been tremendous diversification in agriculture. Cotton is the second largest export—Brazil is the fifth largest cotton producer in the world. It also raises most of its own food—all its beans, manioc, and maize; three-fourths of its wheat requirement is produced in the states south of São Paulo. Brazil has great potentialities as a world food basket in the 21st century, for even today less than 5 per cent of its area is cultivated.

Despite all this agricultural development, the mass of Brazil's population still live within 100 miles of the coast. Under Vargas, the government made an organized attempt to settle the interior. Exploring parties composed of botanists, agriculturists, doctors, and engineers surveyed routes into the Mato Grosso and western Goiás, the two great undeveloped regions whose rivers feed both the Plata and the Amazon. Goiâna, the new capital of Goiás, was founded in 1942, and along with other nearby towns is booming. Anapolis, a "hamlet" when Brasilia was first planned, is now an important trading center of sixty thousand. Cattle thrive in this area. It is favorable to the growth of corn, cane, and cotton. What Iowa, Missouri, and Texas were to North America in the first half of the 19th century, Goiás and Mato Grosso are to South America in the second half of the 20th.

urbanization, mining, and industry

In the spring of 1956, one adobe hut stood on the 4,000-foot plateau of Goiás in the vast area called the Federal District of Brazil. This was to be the home of Brazil's new federal capital under the Constitution of 1946. The capital that President Kubitschek promised to build in three years' time was to help create a strong national feeling among the many jealous regions of Brazil. Kubitschek announced an international competition among architects and city planners for the design of a new city in the wilderness. The design of the Rio de Janeiro architect, Lucio Costa, who won the prize, called for an arrangement of streets and buildings that resembled an airplane. It was to be encircled by a winding lake 25 miles long and to contain sufficient modern housing units for a capital city of 300,000.

Kubitschek hired Oscar Niemeyer, a Brazilian of Swiss ancestry and a former student of Costa's who had helped design the United Nations building in New York, to work out a scale model of the government buildings planned for the Brasilia area. He enthusiastically approved the model Niemeyer worked out in his Rio studio. Niemeyer and his family moved to a shanty in the trackless federal district, moving by truck from the nearest hamlet 80 miles away, following the bulldozers that were building a road. Then came the concrete mixers to pour the buildings into forms as planned —two tall shafts of green glass for the Senate and House office buildings, an upturned saucer for the meetings of the Senate, an overturned saucer for the meetings of the House, a glass-enclosed block for the President's house, and rows and rows of model apartments for government workers, each with its school and playgrounds. On April 1, 1960, the anniversary of the death of Tiradentes, the early martyr for Brazilian independence, the Brazilian congress met in the new buildings. Kubitschek was already living in the President's mansion.

Kubitschek by 1970 had been dishonored by the military dictators, but 500,000 people were living in Brasilia, making it Brazil's tenth largest city. Diplomats from all over the world had set up embassies in the new city. But Brasilia, like many other fabulous modernized cities in Latin America, had troubles behind its glass and aluminum facade, especially when refugees from the drought-stricken northeast came to the city and found neither work nor housing. They built shanties for themselves along dirt trails in the uncleared brush outside the city limits, slums which held more people than the fancy housing projects downtown. There was no running water in these slums, nor electricity. There were no schools. Even in the beautiful center of Brasilia, buildings went unfinished and the liberal-minded university was closed by the military government.

The 21st century should see the vast Amazon area opened up by various road-building projects. The road between Brasilia and Belém at the mouth of the Amazon 800 miles away had been completed. Another 500 miles of new highway indirectly reaches Recife on the Atlantic. A new Trans-Amazon Highway, paralleling the Amazon and reaching the Peruvian border was inaugurated in September 1970 and is expected to be finished by 1975. It is to open up an area of 3 million square miles.

Another new highway was planned to link the capital of Mato Grosso to Santarém, 600 miles up the Amazon. The government was clearing

Above, *market salesmen in Kano, Nigeria, West Africa.* (*Photo by Helen Miller Bailey.*)

Below, *descendants of slaves, who form the bulk of the population in the Caribbean Islands today.* (*Photo by Helen Miller Bailey.*)

The palace built by Diego Columbus in Santo Domingo as repaired by the present Dominican government and furnished with authentic articles, including a portrait of Don Diego and his famous father. (Photo courtesy of Américas Magazine.)

The Spanish colonial aqueduct brought water into the mining town of Querétaro, Mexico. (Photo by Helen Miller Bailey.)

A trade fair and festival in Chichicastenango, Guatemala. (Photo by Helen Miller Bailey.)

Pack trains in a muleteer's inn in the mountains above Toluca, Mexico. Thus was carried most of the freight of the Spanish colonies. (Photo by Helen Miller Bailey.)

Young teacher-training students in an historical pageant in Oaxaca, Mexico, carry in their faces the evidence of the three classes of colonial times. The tall girl is of pure Spanish blood, the girl to her left is mestizo, *and the girl with the flowers is pure Indian, of the Zapotecan tribe, as are most of the girls in the background. (Photo by Helen Miller Bailey.)*

Guatemalan Indians combining ancient Mayan rites with Christian worship in the Church of Santo Tomás, Chichicastenango. (Photo by Helen Miller Bailey.)

Façade of San Francisco Acatepec Church, Puebla, Mexico, showing ornate Spanish tile used in decoration. (Photo by Helen Miller Bailey.)

Folk dancers of Mexico still wear the ranchero costumes similar to those worn in Spanish colonial times. (*Photo courtesy of the Los Angeles County Board of Supervisors.*)

Fortifications of Cartagena, built as a protection against the English, still stand high above the city. (*Photo by Helen Miller Bailey.*)

Independence Monument to Haitian Heroes, near Cap Haitien. Toussaint stands first among the figures with Dessalines and Christophe behind him. Soldiers and flag bearers are on each side. The figures are of life-size bronze on a natural hillside. (Photo by Helen Miller Bailey.)

Jean Jacques Dessalines, first ruler of an independent nation in Latin America, who declared Haiti free of France, January 1, 1804. (Photo courtesy of the Pan American Union.)

Francois ("Papa Doc") Duvalier, strong-man of recent Haitian politics, who "left" the presidency on his death to his nineteen-year-old son. (Photo by Wide World Photos.)

Portrait of Simón Bolívar in the Pan American Union Building. (Photo courtesy of the Pan American Union.)

The port of Guayaquil, where Bolívar met San Martín. (Photo courtesy of the Pan American Union.)

Monument in Caracas to the leaders of the revolution under Bolívar. (Photo by Helen Miller Bailey.)

Meeting room of Bolívar's first Pan American Congress, maintained as an historic site in Panama City. (Photo courtesy of El Halcon-Panama.)

Father Miguel Hidalgo, who gave the first cry, the grito, for Mexican independence. (Photo courtesy of the Pan American Union.)

Mural of Benito Juarez and the Constitution of 1857, painted by the modern Mexican artist Orozco for the Mexican National Museum of History. (Photo courtesy of the Pan American Union.)

The old Cabildo, meeting place of the governing council of the Provinces of the Plata, stands as a monument in downtown Buenos Aires. (Photo by Helen Miller Bailey.)

Pedro II in 1887. (Photo courtesy of the Pan American Union.)

Stern-wheel steamer on the Magdalena, first introduced in 1852. (Photo by Helen Miller Bailey.)

José Gervasio Artigas, gaucho *founder of Uruguay, in whose name the* Thirty-Three Immortals *fought Brazil for the* Banda Oriental. (*Photo courtesy of the Pan American Union.*)

Dr. Carlos Finlay, the Cuban who discovered the cause of yellow fever. (Photo courtesy of the Pan American Union.)

At the top of his huge mountain citadel, Haitian Emperor Henri Christophe placed one cannon for each of the 365 days of the year, unwilling to believe that Napoleon would never invade the New World. (Photo by Helen Miller Bailey.)

Guerilla bands led by Emiliano Zapata fought for the Revolution of 1910 to 1920 for "Tierra y Libertad!" (Photo courtesy of United Press International.)

Álvaro Obregón, leader of the Men of Sonora, who brought internal peace to Mexico by 1920. (Photo courtesy of the Pan American Union.)

President López Mateos of Mexico greeting President Johnson of the United States in Los Angeles in 1964. Señora López Mateos, Mrs. Johnson, Secretary of State Rusk and his wife, and Senator Kuchel of California join the applause. (Photo courtesy of the Los Angeles County Board of Supervisors.)

Mosaic decoration on the main library of the new University of Mexico. (Photo courtesy of the Pan American Union.)

Diego Rivera, creative and controversial Mexican mural painter. (Photo courtesy of the Pan American Union.)

Carlos Chavez, Mexican composer, preparing for recording native-theme music. (Photo courtesy of Américas Magazine.)

São Paulo from the air seems a forest of skyscrapers. (Photo by Helen Miller Bailey.)

Getúlio Vargas, World War II dictator of Brazil. (Photo courtesy of the Pan American Union.)

The Congress buildings at Brasilia, designed by Oscar Niemeyer. (Photo by Helen Miller Bailey.)

Belém, half-way up the Amazon, has its shanty-town slums as houseboats out in the river. (Photo by Helen Miller Bailey.)

Provisional President Castelo Branco greeting American Fulbright Summer Seminar Teachers in Brasilia in 1964. Dr. Eloisa Barbosa Fuiza, University of Ceará, stands at far right as interpreter. (Photo by Helen Miller Bailey.)

Gilberto Freyre, the famous Brazilian sociologist, on the porch of his home in Recife. (Photo by Helen Miller Bailey.)

Heitor Villa-Lobos, Brazilian composer, the Western Hemisphere's most famous musical leader. (Photo courtesy of the Pan American Union.)

Plaza del Congresso and the Capitol building, Buenos Aires. (Photo courtesy of Braniff Airways.)

Hipólito Irigoyen. Photograph sent to the Pan American Union on his inauguration as president of Argentina, October 1916. (Photo courtesy of the Pan American Union.)

Chilean poetess Gabiela Mistral, reading poetry at the Pan American Union, at the time of her Nobel Prize award, 1946. (Photo courtesy of the Pan American Union.)

Salvadore Allende, controversial Marxist president of Chile in the early 1970s. (Photo by Wide World Photos.)

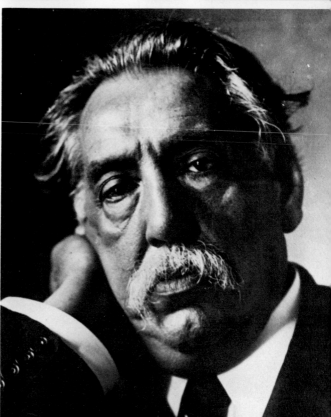

Dr. José Batlle y Ordóñez, "Grand Old Man" of Uruguayan politics to 1929. (Photo courtesy of the Pan American Union.)

Above, *Valparaiso harbor, still a busy port even though the Panama Canal stole half of its business.* (Photo by Helen Miller Bailey.)

Below, *Gatún Locks on the Caribbean side of the Panama Canal.* (Photo courtesy of the Panama Canal Company.)

Above, *extension agent from the Altiplano Experiment Station, Bolivia, encouraging Indian farmers to plant lettuce and other green vegetable crops.* (*Photo courtesy of the International Cooperation Administration.*)

Below, *playground at a public housing project, Bogotá, Colombia.* (*Photo courtesy of the Pan American Union.*)

Fidel Castro, who led the anti-Batista revolution in Cuba in 1958. He was beginning to "mellow" in the early 1970s. (Photo by Wide World Photos.)

The Centrales, or sugar refineries, were taken over by Cuba's Castro. (Photo by Helen Miller Bailey.)

Conga drum team in the Havana Carnival. (Photo courtesy of Pan American Airways.)

Cuban modernist painter Wilfredo Lam. In his veins flows the blood of four races, Spanish, Negro, Caribbean Indian, and Chinese. (Photo courtesy of the Pan American Union.)

*Specialized educational opportunities offered to young Latin Americans
through international or United States agencies: agricultural experiment station growing bell peppers in Haiti, fine arts classes in the Dominican Republic, and radio technology class using U.S. equipment in Asuncion,
Paraguay. (Photo courtesy of the International Cooperation Administration
and Américas Magazine.)*

affair as in Peru or Colombia. One religious holiday, the Carnival or last days before Lent, as celebrated in Rio, has become famous all over the world. The songs from Rio's Carnival become hit tunes for the year. During the four days of the celebration the streets are a mass of happy, friendly people. Costumed *Cariocas* dance in and out of strange houses and shoot each other with squirt guns full of perfume. No one does any work; the entire population is in the streets. The whole festival is less "organized" than any Mardi Gras in New Orleans, and has little of the "promotion" and advertising of Pasadena's Tournament of Roses.

Although the working people enjoy Carnival, their daily life in the cities is on a very low standard. The white-collar workers have a hard time making ends meet, as a pair of shoes costs a clerk's weekly salary, and bookkeepers or teachers make far less proportionately than they would make in the United States. The day laborers and factory workers find it very expensive even to buy shoes. The hills of Rio are covered on one side with fancy hotels or luxuriant tropical vegetation; on the other side, the shanties of the poor fill the entire hillsides with *favelas*. There are 232 separate *favela* communities totaling more than a million inhabitants on the hills of Rio, each with its own governing council. The councils cannot provide schools or running water or electricity, and cannot control the criminal element, but they do try to keep up the stone steps and the "goat trails" that connect the hillsides with the city streets. Even in progressive, bustling São Paulo there are back streets of tenements where workers live on less than a dollar a day.

The Brazilian government has not let these conditions go unheeded. Dom Getúlio, for all his political motives, had set the pattern of working-man's security as a part of government obligation. Article 157 of the post-Vargas Constitution of 1946 lists seventeen "rules for workingmen which legislation shall observe," including plans for profit-sharing, paid vacations, and maternity benefits, as well as rights of collective bargaining and industrial accident compensation. Any visitor to Brazil can see these laws for workers unenforced in many ways. Nevertheless they are there in the supreme law of the land, a goal for Brazil to work towards, that of improving human resources as she develops natural resources.

Rural life in Brazil varies with the area. Sharecroppers on the coffee *fazendas* are controlled by the *fazendeiro*, living in "company" houses and buying at "company" stores, while the migrant workers who help with the coffee picking wander back to the city slums when the harvest is over. Polish villagers in the interior of Paraná or Santa Catarina live in neat wooden houses, carry on diversified farming, and travel by bus four or five days on dirt roads to reach a city. Towns on the São Francisco or the Amazon are built of wood and thatch, with perhaps one main front street on the river lined with neat houses of brightly painted plaster or colorful mosaic tile. Here live the store owner, the teacher in the government-supported elementary school, the members of the government council. The towns support themselves on "thatch and patch" agriculture or on the river traffic, live on beans, rice, and mandioca flour, and pay little attention to color lines between their "upper-class" citizens in the painted houses and the rubber gatherers or cattle herders in the forests.

Such towns have one great problem in common with the cities: the poor health of their people. Statistics collected in 1947 proved that the birth and death rates were both high, that the life expectancy of the Brazilians in general was so short that almost half of the population was under fifteen, and that people were not surviving into middle age. One-third of the rural population was afflicted with malaria and one-fifth with hookworm; tuberculosis and syphilis claimed a very high rate in the urban population, while dysentery was endemic in both city and country. Fewer than 10 per cent of the houses had running water or sanitary facilities; 75 per cent of the houses were not connected to a sewer system. Forty per cent of all nurses and doctors in the nation lived in Rio and São Paulo, so the countryside and the smaller towns went without.

Into this depressing picture came the *Servício Especial de Saude Pública*, an outgrowth of World War II and American interest in making friends in Latin America. Through the Nelson Rockefeller Committee, North American public health specialists came to Brazil as part of a joint two-nation project. They worked out a plan for rural health and sanitation, financed at first by the United States, but paid entirely by Brazil for the last two decades. After experiments with water-filtering systems, nursing programs, mass inoculations, and many small clinics in an area of Minas Gerais, the program was started in the Amazon Basin. Here thirty health centers were set up, seventeen launches fitted out as "healthmobiles" to serve the river towns, and a fifty-bed hospital built at Santarém, a town halfway up the river to Manáus. Girls with elementary school diplomas were trained as visiting nurses and midwives. Engineers from the *Servício* organized improved water supply systems for many towns. Educational campaigns have encouraged more balanced diets. Young doctors from several different regions of Brazil come to the United States for a year's study at Johns Hopkins or other centers for the study of tropical diseases. Endemic diseases are being diminished as a result in incidence and intensity. The *Servício*, cooperating with the Ministry of Health, has also made a great stride forward in the treatment of lepers.

The Oswaldo Cruz Institute has made other spectacular contributions to public health. It is because of the existence of this Institute that Rio de Janeiro is today so free from mosquitoes and there is no yellow fever or malaria in the city. In the early 1900s yellow fever killed tens of thousands in Brazil's cities every year. Then in 1903 a young Brazilian doctor, Oswaldo Cruz, was appointed to head a Brazilian Bacteriological Institute, in charge of a public health program pledged to wipe out yellow fever in Rio in three years. Dr. Cruz carried on a drastic campaign to make the death of every mosquito the goal for Rio dwellers. By 1913 his health program had stopped malaria and yellow fever in the capital and had concentrated on establishing a pure water supply, thus cutting down typhoid. As an organizer and leader, Oswaldo Cruz trained younger men to work after him, and set up research laboratories. Today Rio's health problem is one of malnutrition and organic disease. The three killers—malaria, yellow fever, and typhoid—are gone from Rio, it is to be hoped, forever.

education and culture in Brazil

Unfortunately, Brazil's interest in education has not been as great as her interest in public health. As soon as the republic was established a Ministry of Education was created and Benjamin Constant, that idealistic mathematics professor, was given the job. Interested in higher learning, he developed the technical college course in Rio but neglected primary schools. The Constitution of 1891, the republic's first, put the responsibility of primary education on the shoulders of the new state governments, where it was largely neglected. Finally in 1930 Vargas' new Ministry of Health and Education reorganized the system and campaigned for compulsory primary schools in all regions. At that time more than half the children of elementary age were not in school. President Vargas took education under the wing of the federal government and made education free and obligatory. Today there is a school building of sorts in every Brazilian village large enough to be called a town. But in 1970 there were still four million children in rural areas who had no school to attend, and the nation remained more than 50 per cent illiterate. In Rio, that fine modern city of the *Cariocas*, 14 per cent were unable to read and write.

Brazil is as understaffed for teacher personnel as she was for nurses and doctors. The public health program bogs down when the people at whom it aims its clever pamphlets on disease and sanitation cannot read them. The Constitution of 1946 provided that 10 per cent of federal and 20 per cent of state tax revenues were to be spent on education. However, the Brazilian government is spending only 9 per cent of its budget on education, and this included both local and national budgets. But the new middle class, growing so rapidly in the cities, is now demanding better elementary schools for its children, and high school education as well. Today the Ministry of Education and Culture is tackling the problem. Its national Institute for the Study of Education is doing research on elementary methods and maintaining a central office to help localities. Though the curriculum is "federal," the teacher-training institutes are state-maintained and are neither uniform nor free.

The secondary education situation is still completely inadequate for a practical, industrialized modern nation. The senior high school, the *Colégio* or *Preparatório*, offers only academic courses preparing directly for college. A bare minimum of such schools is provided by the government, and most secondary schools are private ventures, making profit on tuition. Naturally, secondary education becomes a luxury for the children of the upper classes only. To have a secondary school diploma brings more prestige today in Brazil than a bachelor's degree in America. A new interest in trade schools has developed a second type of senior high school. In 1937 there were only 30,000 students in commercial, "business-college type" high schools, trade-technical schools, or vocational schools of any kind, in all of Brazil. Today there are over 700,000. Both São Paulo and Minas Gerais now have agricultural secondary schools offering courses in tractor repair, soil conservation, care of dairy herds, and control of plant diseases.

University education, of the traditional academic type, is of a high standard in Brazil. So respected is an advanced degree that the title of "doctor" has become traditional to use in addressing any well-educated person in the cities. In 1930 the Schools of Medicine and of Law and the Polytechnic School were legally united to form the University of Rio de Janeiro. To this group were added the Schools of Mines, of Dentistry, and of Fine Arts, and the Institute of Music. This whole combined institution is now called the University of Brazil and offers degrees in such "untraditional" fields for a Latin American university as engineering, veterinary medicine, architecture, metallurgy, and political science. State Universities are being modeled after this national pattern; that at São Paulo with its new School of Agriculture is considered one of the best universities in all South America. By 1970 the entire nation could boast forty-two separate institutions of higher learning, including the new glass and chrome University of Brasilia. Students in Rio were so angry at the miniscule amount of the national budget spent on college education as opposed to the expenses of the seldom-used armed forces, that they rioted for a week against the military government in the spring of 1968.

All university students and most secondary school graduates are required to have a reading knowledge of English. Young teachers of English by the dozens have come to the University of Michigan to study "language lab" methods of teaching English as a foreign language and have returned with model "language labs," records, and tape recorders to bring spoken English into Brazilian college and high school classrooms. Many students speak French also. Student life as a whole is much more like European university life than like North American.

The Brazilian college system has produced some eminent scientists. In the fields of geology, soil erosion studies, hydrographic surveys, and other modern applications of soil sciences, the faculty of the School of Mines of Ouro Preto in Minas Gerais has been outstanding. Dr. Emil A. Goeldi has worked in the field of Brazilian zoology; the museum of Amazonian wild life in Belém is named for him. A new interest in the science of sociology is developing. Arthur Ramos produced a great work on the Negro in Brazil; Gilberto Freyre is the leader of the sociological writers and his works on Brazil's social problems have been translated into English, as have also those of Hermane Tavares de Sa and of the Brazilian cultural historian Fernando de Azevedo. The science of aviation has a famous Brazilian on its roll of honor, Alberto Santos-Dumont, who, Brazilians claim, antedated the Wright brothers in the first flight.

For applying the scientific work of its researchers, Brazil deserves special mention among Latin American countries. Mosquito-borne diseases have been controlled; serums have been developed to cure poisonous snake bites. Serums which are produced in the famous snake farm of the Butantan

Institute of São Paulo are sent out all over South America. Contributions have been made to sea navigation and radiology. The Biological Institute of São Paulo has pioneered in the control of plant diseases, and employs eighty-eight scientists and 200 laboratory technicians to care for its experimental gardens, while the Brazilian National Observatory makes astronomical observations for the whole Southern Hemisphere.

It is as fashionable to write for publication in Brazil as it is in Spanish America, and the twentieth century is producing new authors with a new spirit, many of whose works are now being translated into English and receiving worldwide attention. Perhaps the modern concern of Brazilian writers with social problems was forecast by the famous book, *Rebellion in the Backlands*, or, as it was called in the original Portuguese, *Os Sertões*, the name given the drought-stricken region behind Baía and Fortaleza. The revolt against republican authority led by the religious fanatic Antônio the Counsellor had occurred here in 1896 and 1897, and the author, Euclides da Cunha (1866–1909), was a civil engineer with officer's training working on a public project when a São Paulo newspaper sent him to accompany the federal troops and write up the story of the rebellion. In 1907 he made public his detailed and analytical story of the campaign. Brazilian writers formerly interested only in classical themes were influenced to write of the regions of Brazil by this new "classic." A thrilling story, *Os Sertões* reads like a novel, but a novel filled with sociological implications and revealing the psychology of the rural poor.

Other authors followed his lead and began to write about Brazilian themes. Graça Aranha (1868–1931), the "apostle of Brazilian modernism," wrote a novel in the 1920s about Brazil's new "melting pot" for European races, a book called *Canaan*. In São Paulo in 1922 some young intellectuals put on a Modern Art Week, at which, after viewing exhibits, the participants sat around discussing the new freedom in European literature after World War I and deciding that Brazil should also enjoy a new freedom in literature. In the 1950s writers who participated in that famous "week" in São Paulo were still writing. Erico Veríssimo (1905–   ), whose books are translated into English, wrote a novel, *Crossroads,* bringing his home town Porto Alegre into world literature for the first time. His *Of Time and the Wind* began an epic of a south Brazilian family, of which a recent volume is called *The Archipelago* in popular English translation. Veríssimo became the "dean" of Brazilian novelists, has spoken and taught in the United States, and has served as a cultural coordinator for the Pan-American Union.

Regional interest, sociological themes, and modernist style have brought other writers to the fore, particularly Jorge Amada (1912–   ), José Lins do Rego (1901–1957), Graciliano Ramos (1892–1953), and a woman writer Raquel da Queiroz (1910–   ). Most of them are novelists of the Northeast. Popular as the new Brazilian novel is, the vicissitudes of the publishing business make it very difficult to make a living at writing, so Brazil's best writers augment their incomes by translating modern North American novels. In Hemingway and Faulkner modern Brazilian writers find their models—in frank, earthy descriptions of life as it is when people are poor. A book written in the 1960s with this theme by a São Paulo woman, Carolina Maria de Jesus, was a stark description of her own life in the shanty-town *favelas* which, translated into English as *Child of the Dark,* has become a "must" for students of sociology. Another powerful description of shanty-town life was written by Josué de Castro (born 1908), whose novel under the English title of *Men and Crabs* attracted considerable attention in the United States in 1971. It is the story of the author's own childhood on the marshlands of the city of Recife where the poor lived in shanties that stood on stilts above the marshes of the harbor and where he scrounged for food by catching crabs in the mud below.

Poetry also has made an impressive showing, marking the coming of age of literary Brazil. The modern trend was begun with João de Cruz e Sousa (1862–1898) a Negro, son of slaves, whose *Last Sonnets* were published in 1905. Writing indignantly about the wrongs done his race, he initiated a nationalistic and modernistic pattern that has been followed by the young poets of the São Paulo Art Week movement.

At an "Art Biennial in São Paulo," a continuation in the 1960's of the cultural week movement, nations throughout the world have been represented by "non-objective" art entries. In a recent contest, São Paulo was the scene of a battle between the French and Italian schools of modern artists at which the Brazilian judges gave the prize to a young Italian who "pressed heavy doses of paint on rough burlap." Poets attending São Paulo's "week" sell a little magazine called *Street Singers' Guitar* that is full of "the best current poetry for the masses, written with a social purpose." Poets in Belo Horizonte have their own modern poetry movement called *Tendency* that prints the poetry of "the stream of Belo's younger poets." Even the famed sociologist Gilberto Freyre has printed a book of modern verse called *Poetry Perhaps.* Highly admired is Carlos Drummond de Andrade, a Ministry of Education archivist, who writes philosophical verse; he protests modern technological development "for fear personalities will be lost in the great blob," and affirms the enjoyment of life in the present for "time is my master, time *now,* life *now!*"

Apart from the "life now" abstractionists in art, Brazil's best known modern artist is Candido Portinari (1903–1962), a world-renowned muralist. Commissioned to paint a series of murals for government buildings representing "the spirit of Brazil," he drew a long frieze of muscular, sweating coffee plantation workers, to the horror of those who had commissioned him. Portinari himself was born to humble Italian immigrants on a coffee plantation. He worked his way through the Academy of Fine Arts, something unusual in Brazil, and today noted buildings in which his work is found include the Library of Congress in Washington, D.C. In architecture, Rio de Janeiro is a modernist's delight even more than Brasilia as it contains some of the most futuristic buildings in the world. The Swiss architect Le Corbusier influenced the young Brazilians Lúcio Costa and Oscar Niemeyer. They created what amounts to a school of modern tropical architecture by applying the theories of Frank Lloyd Wright to fit into the hills and bays of Rio de Janeiro.

Brazil has a host of distinguished musicians of high talent and originality who have made a valuable contribution to Western Hemisphere music. Outstanding was Heitor Villa-Lobos (1894–1960), another strong advocate of the use of the common people of all racial strains as an inspiration to cultural creation. One of the best-known of recent composers, he used native Indian and Negro folk music as his inspiration. He wrote over 1,500 compositions from simple piano solos to symphonies and operas. Among his followers is Camargo Guarnieri (1907–   ) who has conducted, as has Villa-Lobos, as a guest artist in the United States and whose *Eighth Symphony* has established him as a foremost composer of symphonic music.

The folk music of Brazil with its slave and Carnival themes and the Carnival dance steps of Rio and Baía have become popular in modern America. Considering the Brazilians' fondness for poetry, pageantry, music, and the dance, it is no wonder that there is a very active theater in Brazil, interested in folk plays and native music. In the Ministry of Education and Culture there is a National Theater Service whose director is himself a playwright who has established a National School of the Theater as a part of the University. Brazil is also producing art films. A film on life in Rio won an award at the 1963 Cannes film festival.

Brazilians are music- and rhythm-conscious. It is the musical program that finds favor with Brazilian listeners rather than the variety show or political broadcast. Brazil today has more than 300 radio stations and several television networks. Published regularly are 490 magazines and 252 newspapers.

Also notable is the fact that Brazil is known throughout the world for the fame of its soccer team. Perhaps the most widely-known Brazilian in South America in 1971 was a 29-year-old champion soccer player known internationally as Pelé, born with the name Arantez Do Nasciniente. A gigantic black man, he has made Brazil a three-time winner of the international soccer cup. When he returned to Brazil after bringing victory in July, 1970, for the Brazilian team in the final play-off for the World Cup in Mexico City, President Garrastazú Médici declared a two-day holiday and entertained him in the International Palace in Brasilia. Thus it seems that championship soccer along with radio and newspapers bring the various elements of Brazilian life together more effectually than does the politics described in the previous chapter.

READINGS: BRAZIL

Adams, R. N., et al., *Social Change in Latin America Today* (1960).

Agassiz, L. A., *Journey to Brazil* (1868; 1969).

Alden, D., ed., *Colonial Roots of Modern Brazil* (1972).

Alexander, R. J., *Communism in Latin America* (1957).

————, *Labor Relations in Argentina, Brazil and Chile* (1962).

Armitage, J., *History of Brazil, 1808 to 1831* (2 vols., 1835–1836).

Arraes, M., *Brazil: The People and the Power* (1971).

Astiz, C. A., ed., *Latin American International Politics: Ambitions, Capabilities and the National Interest of Mexico, Brazil and Argentina* (1969).

Avila, F. B., de, *Economic Aspects of Immigration: The Brazilian Immigration Problem* (1954).

Azevedo, F. de, *Brazilian Culture: An Introduction to the Study of Culture in Brazil*, trans. W. R. Crawford (1950).

Baer, W., *Industrialization and Economic Development in Brazil* (1965).

————, *Development of Brazilian Steel Industry* (1969).

Baklanoff, E. M., ed., *New Perspectives of Brazil* (1966).

————, ed., *The Shaping of Modern Brazil* (1969).

Bandeira, M., *Brief History of Brazilian Literature* (1958).

Bardi, P. M., *New Brazilian Art* (1970).

Bauer, W., *Development of the Brazilian Steel Industry* (1970).

Bello, J. M., *History of Modern Brazil, 1899–1964* (1965).

Bergsman, S., *Brazil: Industrialization and Trade Policies* (1970).

Berlinck, M. T., *Structure of the Brazilian Family in the City of São Paulo* (1969).

Bernstein, H., *Modern and Contemporary Latin America* (1952).

Bethell, L., *The Abolition of the Brazilian Slave Trade* (1970).

Bettancourt Machado, J., *Machado of Brazil* (1962).

Bourne, R., *Political Leaders in Latin America* (1970).

Box, P. H., *Origins of the Paraguayan War* (2 vols., 1929).

Brazil Election Fact Book (1965).

Brazil, Ministry of Foreign Relations, *Brazil: 1960* (n.d.).

Brown, R., *Land and People of Brazil* (1960).

Burns, E. B., *Documentary History of Brazil* (1965).

————, *History of Brazil* (1970).

————, *Nationalism in Brazil: A Historical Survey* (1968).

————, ed., *Perspectives of Brazilian History* (1967).

————, *The Unwritten Alliance: Rio Branco and Brazil-American Relations* (1960).

Burton, Sir R. F., *Explorations of the Highlands of Brazil* (2 vols., 1869, repr. 1969).

Calmon, P., with C. de Medeiros, *History of Brazil* (1939).

Calogeras, P., *History of Brazil*, trans. P. M. Martin (1939).

Camacho, J. A., *Brazil: An Interim Assessment* (1954).

Carr, R., ed., *Latin-American Affairs. St. Anthony's Papers No. 22* (1970).

Cava, P. della, *Miracle at Joaseiro* (1970).

Chase, C., *Contemporary Art in Latin America* (1970).

Clements, M. M., *Mechanization of Agriculture in Brazil* (1970).

Conrad, R., *The Destruction of Brazilian Slavery, 1850–1888* (1972).

Cooke, M. L., *Brazil on the March* (1944).

Correa de Costa, J. C., *Every Inch a King* (1950).

Costedo, L., *Baroque Prevalence in Brazilian Art* (1964).

Coutinho, A., *An Introduction to Literature of Brazil*, trans. G. Rubassa (1969).

Cruz Costa, J., *History of Ideas in Brazil* (1964).

Cunha, E. da, *Rebellion in the Backlands*, trans. S. Putnam (1944).

Cunha, L. de A., *Art in Latin America Today: Brazil* (1960).

Da Dubnic, V. R., *Political Trends in Brazil* (1963).

Danbaugh, L. M., *Coffee Frontier in Brazil* (1959).

Dean, W., *The Industrialization of São Paulo 1880–1945* (1969).

de Azevedo, T., *Social Change in Brazil* (1963).

De Castro, J., *Death in the Northeast* (1967).

De Kadt, E., *Catholic Radicals in Brazil* (1970).

————, *The Catholic Church and Social Reform in Brazil* (1970).

Denis, P., *Brazil* (1911).

Dos Pasos, J., *Brazil on the Move* (1963).

Driver, D. M., *The Indian in Brazilian Literature* (1942).

Dulles, J., *Vargas of Brazil: A Political Biography* (1966).

————, *Unrest in Brazil: Political-Military Crises 1955–1964* (1970).

Duncan, J. S., *Public and Private Operation of Railways in Brazil* (1932).

Ellis, H., *The Economy of Brazil* (1969).

Ellison, F. P., *Brazil's New Novel* (1954).

Emerson, P. K., ed., *Studies in Politics in Developing Nations* (1968).

Fagan, R. R., and L. A. Cornelius, eds., *Political Power in Latin America: Seven Confrontations* (1970).

Faust, A. F., *Brazil: Education in an Expanding Economy* (1959).

Fernandes, F., *Negro in Brazilian Society* (1970).

Form, W. H., and A. A. Blum, eds., *Industrial Relations and Social Change in Latin America* (1965).

Frank, L. G., *Capitalism and Development in Latin America: Historical Studies of Chile and Brazil* (1967).

Free, L. A., *Some International Implications of the Political Psychology of Brazilians* (1961).

Freyre, G., *Brazil, An Interpretation* (1965).

————, *Mansions and the Shanties: The Making of Modern Brazil* (1963).

————, *The Masters and the Slaves*, trans. S. Putnam (2nd ed., 1956).

————, *New World in the Tropics* (1959).

————, *Order and Progress. Brazil from Monarchy to Republic* (1970).

Fru, L., *Some International Implications of the Political Psychology of the Brazilians* (1961).

Furtado, C., *Development and Underdevelopment* (1964).

————, *Diagnosis of the Brazilian Crisis* (1965).

————, *Economic Growth of Brazil: A Survey from Colonial to Modern Times* (1963; 1971).

Gauld, C. A., *The Last Titan: Percival Farquhar, Entrepreneur in Latin America* (1964).

Geiger, T., *General Electric Company in Brazil* (1961).

Goldberg, I., *Brazilian Literature* (1922).

Goodwin, P. L., *Brazil Builds: Architecture New and Old, 1652–1942* (1943).

Gordon, L., and E. Grommers, *United States Manufacturing Investment in Brazil: The Impact of Brazilian Government Politics, 1946–1960* (1962).

Graham, L. S., *Civil Service Reform in Brazil* (1968).

Graham, R., *Britain and the Onset of Modernization of Brazil 1850–1914* (1968).

————, *A Century of Brazilian History Since 1865* (1969).

Hahner, J. E., *Civilian-Military Relations in Brazil 1889–1898* (1969).

Hamblock, E., *His Majesty the President* (1935).

Harding, B., *Amazon Throne: The Story of the Braganzas of Brazil* (1941).

———, *Southern Empire: Brazil* (1948).

Haring, C. H., *The Empire of Brazil* (1958).

Harris, M., *Town and Country in Brazil* (1956).

Havighurst, R. J., and J. R. Moreira, *Society and Education in Brazil* (1965).

———, and A. J. Gouvela, *Brazilian Secondary Education and Socio-economic Development* (1969).

Herring, H., *Good Neighbors* (1941).

Hill, L. F., ed., *Brazil* (1947).

———, *Diplomatic Relations Between the United States and Brazil* (1932).

Hirschman, A. C., *Journeys Towards Progress* (1963).

Horowitz, I. L., ed., *Masses in Latin America* (1970).

Horowitz, J., *Revolution in Brazil: Politics and Society in a Developing Nation* (1964).

Houston, J. A., *Latin America in the United Nations* (1956).

Hughlett, L. J., ed., *Industrialization of Latin America* (1946).

Humphreys, R. A., and J. Lynch, *Origins of the Latin American Revolution 1808–1826* (1965).

Hunnicutt, B. M., *Brazil, World Frontier* (1949).

Hunter, J. M., *Economic Aspects of Higher Education in Brazil* (1971).

Hutchinson, H. W., *Village and Plantation Life in Northeast Brazil* (1957).

Ianni, O., *Crisis in Brazil* (1970).

Irwin, R. D., *Industrialization and Economic Development in Brazil* (1965).

James, H. G., *Brazil after a Century of Independence* (1925).

———, *The Constitutional System of Brazil* (1923).

James, P. E., *Brazil* (1946).

Jobim, José, *Brazil in the Making* (1943).

Johnson, A. W., *Sharecroppers of the Sertão* (1970).

Johnson, J. J., *Military and Society in Latin America* (1964).

———, *Political Change in Latin America* (1958).

Joint Brazil–United States Economic Devolopment Commission, *Brazil Technical Studies* (1945).

———, *Development of Brazil* (1958).

Kadt, E. de, *Catholic Radicals in Brazil* (1970).

Keeble, T. W., *Commercial Relations between British Overseas Territories and South America* (1970).

Keith, H. H., and S. F. Edwards, eds., *Conflict and Continuity in Brazilian Society* (1969).

Kelchner, W. H., *Latin American Relations with the League of Nations* (1930).

Kelsey, V., *Seven Keys to Brazil* (1943).

Kuznets, S., W. E. Moore, and J. J. Spengler, eds., *Economic Growth: Brazil, India, Japan* (1955).

Landsberger, H. A., *Latin American Peasant Movements* (1970).

Le Corbusier (pseud. of Jeanneret-Cris, C. E.), *Creation Is a Patient Search: A Self Portrait* (1960).

Leff, N. H., *Economic Policy Making and Development in Brazil 1947–1964* (1969).

Levine, R. M., *Brazil: Field Guide in the Social Sciences* (1966).

————, *The Vargas Regime: The Critical Years 1934–1938* (1970).

Lieuwen, E., *Arms and Politics in Latin America* (rev. ed., 1961).

————, *Generals vs. Presidents* (1964).

Livermore, H. V., ed., *Portugal and Brazil—An Introduction* (1953).

Love, J. F., *Rio Grande do Sul and Brazilian Regionalism 1882–1930* (1970).

Lowenstein, K., *Brazil under Vargas* (1942).

Ludwig, A. R., and H. W. Taylor, *Brazil's New Agrarian Reform* (1969).

Luper, A. T., *The Music of Brazil* (1943).

Macedo Soares, J. C. de, *Brazil and the League of Nations* (1928).

Maier, J., and R. W. Weatherhead, ed., *Politics of Change in Latin America* (1964).

Manchester, A. K., *British Preeminence in Brazil: Its Rise and Decline* (1933).

Marchant, A., *Viscount Mauá and the Empire of Brazil* (1965).

Marighela, C., *For the Liberation of Brazil* (1971. Writings of Opponents of the Regime).

Mariz, V., *Heitor Villa-Lobos Brazilian Composer* (1963).

Martin, P. A., *Latin America and the War* (1925).

Martins, W., *The Modernist Idea: A Critical Survey of Brazilian Writing in the Twentieth Century* (1970).

Maurette, F., *Some Social Aspects of Present and Future Economic Development in Brazil* (1937).

McNeill, M. R., *Guidelines to Problems in Education in Brazil: A Review and Selected Bibliography* (1970).

Mecham, J. L., *Church and State in Latin America* (rev. ed., 1966).

Melo, Father A., *The Coming Revolution in Brazil*, trans. R. Menzel (1970).

Mindlen, N. E., *Modern Architecture in Brazil* (1956).

Momsen, P., *Brazil: A Giant Stirs* (1968).

Mörner, M., *Race and Class in Latin America* (1970).

Morse, R. M., *From Community to Metropolis: A Biography of São Paulo* (1958).

Mosher, A. T., *Case Study of Agriculture Program of AGAR in Brazil* (1955).

Nabuco, C., *Life of Joaquim Nabuco*, trans. R. Hilton et al. (1951).

Nash, R., *Conquest of Brazil* (1927).

Nist, J., *Modern Brazilian Poetry: An Anthology* (1962).

Normano, J. F., *Brazil: A Study of Economic Types* (1933).

Oliveira Lima, M. de, *The Evolution of Brazil* (1914).

Phelps, D. M., *Rubber Development in Latin America* (1957).

Pierson, D., *Negroes in Brazil* (1942).

Pike, F. B., *Latin American History* (1969).

Poppino, R., *Brazil: Land and People* (1968).

Putnam, S., *Marvelous Journey: Four Centuries of Brazilian Literature* (1948).

Randall, L., *A Comparative Economic History of Latin America: Argentina, Brazil, Mexico, Peru, 1500–1914* (1972).

Ramos, A., *The Negro in Brazil* (1939).

Rippy, M., ed., *Cultural Change in Brazil* (1970).

Robock, S. H., *Brazil's Developing Northeast: A Study of Regional Planning and Foreign Aid* (1963).

Rodrigues, J. H., *Brazil and Africa* (1965).

————, *The Brazilians: Their Character and Aspirations* (1967).

Roett, R., *Brazil in the Sixties* (1971).

————, *The Politics of Foreign Aid in the Brazilian Northeast* (1971).

Rosenbaum, H. J., and W. G. Tyler, eds., *Contemporary Brazil: Issues in Economic and Political Development* (1972).

Sa, H. T., de, *The Brazilians: People of Tomorrow* (1947).

Salzano, F. M., *Problems in Human Biology: A Study of Brazilian Population* (1970).

Sanceau, E., *The Perfect Prince: A Biography of Dom João II* (1959).

Saunders, J., ed., *Modern Brazil: New Patterns and Development* (1971).

Sayers, R. S., *The Negro in Brazilian Literature* (1956).

————, ed., *Portugal and Brazil in Transition* (1968).

Schmitter, P. C., *Interest Conflict and Political Change in Brazil* (1971).

Schneider, R. M., *The Political System of Brazil: Emergence of a "Modernizing" Authoritarian Regime 1964–1970* (1971).

Schuh, G. E., *The Agricultural Development of Brazil* (1970).

Schurz, W. L., *Brazil, The Infinite Country* (1961).

Silva, C. M., *Public Functionaries and Brazilian Constitution* (1954).

Simmons, C. W., *Marshal Deodora and the Fall of Dom Pedro Second* (1966).

Simonsen, R. C., *Brazil's Industrial Revolution* (1939).

Skidmore, T., *Brazil Since 1930* (1966).

————, *Politics in Brazil 1930–1964: An Experiment in Democracy* (1967).

Slesser, M., *Brazil: Land Without Limit* (1969).

Smith, T. L., *Agrarian Reform in Latin America* (1965).

————, *Brazil: People and Institutions* (4th ed., 1972).

————, and A. Marchant, *Brazil: Portrait of Half a Continent* (1951).

Spiegel, H. W., *The Brazilian Economy: Chronic Inflation and Sporadic Industrialization* (1949).

Stein, S. J., *Brazilian Cotton Manufacture* (1957).

————, *Vassouras: A Brazilian Coffee Country 1850–1900* (1957).

Stepan, A., *The Military in Politics—Changing Patterns in Brazil* (1971).

Tavares de Sá, H., *The Brazilians, People of Tomorrow* (1947).

Tenenbaum, L., *Tiradentes* (1965).

Thornton, M. C., *The Church and Freemasonry in Brazil 1872–1875* (1948).

Tomasek, R. D., *Latin American Politics—Studies of the Contemporary Scene* (rev. ed., 1970).

Torres-Rioseco, A., *Epic of Latin American Literature* (rev. ed., 1946).

Turner, C. W., *Ruy Barbosa: Brazilian Crusader for the Essential Freedoms* (1945).

United Nations, Department of Economic and Social Affairs, *Economic Development of Brazil* (1956).

United Nations, Economic Commission for Latin America, *Economic Development of Brazil* (1956).

————, *Recent Developments and Trends in the Brazilian Economy* (1951).

United States, Department of Defense, Army Department, *U.S. Army Handbook for Brazil* (1964).

United States, Department of Labor, Bureau of Labor Statistics, *Labor in Brazil* (1962).

Veríssimo, E., *Brazilian Literature: An Outline* (1945).

Wagley, C., *Amazon Town: A Study of Man in the Tropics* (1964).

————, *Brazil, Crisis and Change* (1964).

————, *An Introduction to Brazil* (1963, rev. ed., 1970).

————, ed., *Race and Class in Rural Brazil* (2nd ed., 1963).

————, *Social Science Research in Latin America* (1964).

Webb, M., *Brazil* (1966).

Wiarda, H. J., *Brazilian Catholic Labor Movement* (1970).

Wilgus, A. C., ed., *Argentina, Brazil, and Chile Since Independence* (1935).

Willems, E., *Followers of the New Faith: Culture Change and the Rise of Protestantism in Brazil and Chile* (1971).

William, J. R., Manaus, Amazonas—*A Focal Point For Development in Amazonia* (1971).

Williams, M. W., *Dom Pedro the Magnanimous* (1937).

Wirth, J. D., *The Politics of Brazilian Development 1930–1954* (1970).

Wythe, G., et al., *Brazil: An Expanding Economy* (1949).

Young, J. M., *Brazil: Government and Politics* (1966).

————, *The Brazilian Revolution of 1930 and the Aftermath* (1967).

Zweig, S., *Brazil, Land of the Future* (1941).

chapter 22

ARGENTINA
AND ITS POLITICAL
DEVELOPMENT

the new creole state in the Plata provinces

"God and nature conspired to make the Argentines into a great Latin American nation," say today's citizens of that leading Southern Hemisphere republic, but they followed a tortuous path to achieve that eminence. Endowed with great economic resources on the land surface, but none below, they had been treated as stepchildren by the metal-hungry Spaniards. Since the wide pampas contained only isolated nuclei of creole and *mestizo* cities and they had strongly individualistic and localistic feelings—Córdoba, Santa Fé, Rosario, Mendoza, far across the plains from Buenos Aires and up into the foothills—little feeling of nationalism developed. Not only did Argentina have the usual troubles of the newly independent nations—the inadequately trained leaders, the militaristic *caudillos,* the lack of financial basis—but there ensued the most dramatic struggle between city and country, centralists and federalists, taking place in any New World nation. In the attempts to work out the relationship between Buenos Aires and the provinces almost every theory of government, every type of state and constitution was tried.

After Buenos Aires ousted the viceroy and set up an independent junta on May 25, 1810, Spanish rule was never re-established. For the next six years, however, confusion in the government of the city and quarrels with the pampas provinces postponed any declaration of independence. While Manuel Belgrano, as the junta's military commander in chief, spent the resources and men of the port fighting the interior provinces and trying to force them into union with Buenos Aires, at home the junta changed its personnel and shifted its policy repeatedly between conservatives and liberals.

The conservatives consisted of the rich landowners—whose descendants were to be known as the "oligarchs" of Argentine history—combined with the wealthy merchants of Buenos Aires and the clergy. They wanted the old regime continued if a break must be made with Spain. But the conservatives of Buenos Aires and the interior could not join forces because those in Buenos Aires wanted to dominate the entire area and control all revenues, to which the rich landowners of the provinces would not agree. But in order to frustrate the liberal reformers, the conservatives gave an impetus to federalism and also permitted the growth of *caudillos* in the interior. The liberals hoped to create a prosperous, solvent republic able to coin its own money and pay its bills through efficient customs collection, and also to abolish tithes and ecclesiastic *fueros* and to establish religious tolerance, public schools, and freedom of the press. The contending forces in the period between the establishment of the 1810 junta and the declaration of independence in 1816 created shifts in which the government of the port changed twelve times.

Various towns finally consented to a meeting and in March, 1816, representatives from Buenos Aires, Córdoba, Mendoza, Salta, Rosario and Tucumán met at the nothern town of Tucumán. The conference split on the issue that was to tear Argentine politics apart for generations, whether to have a strong central government centering on the port which the *Unitarios* from Buenos Aires wanted or to have each region autonomous, the demand of the Federalists of the interior. After weeks of deliberation and contention, independence for the Argentine region was proclaimed. Conferees quarreled over suggestions for a limited monarchy and for postponing all plans for a definite form of government, but the Congress did announce that the country should be ruled from Buenos Aires by a "Supreme Director" and it appointed Juan Martín de Pueyrredón to that position.

Pueyrredón served as director for a harassed three years but moved toward centralized authority too fast to please the interior *caudillos*. He resigned, and anarchy reigned in the port city. The year 1820 is called "The Terrible Year Twenty" in Argentine history because of its many uprisings and changes in government. Chieftains in the interior remained practically independent—one of them an Indian chieftain in the province of Corrientes and another a cowboy politician in Santa Fé (who used the head of a donkey as his military headgear). The government in Buenos Aires exhausted its energies fighting such gaucho chieftains.

Finally out of this confusion emerged a wise leader with a strong hand. Bernardino Rivadavia, who had spent some years in England, served as Minister of Foreign Affairs from 1821 to 1824 and as President in 1826–

1827. He favored a democratic government and separation of Church and state. During his administration, the Argentine National University was founded, public schools were opened, primogeniture abolished, and the regions of the pampas were brought into a more friendly federation. As elements of Argentina's potential greatness, he envisioned immigration, foreign capital, and public education. He improved the harbor, introduced sheep-raising into remote Patagonia, and built a national library.

However, his well-meant plan to distribute public lands to farmers through long-term leases, a program called emphyteusis, was later to produce land scandals and create a stronger, more wealthy oligarchy and *latifundia*. By 1827, over 6,500,000 acres had been granted to or rented by only 112 individuals or companies, of whom ten received more than 130,000 acres each. This lavish distribution of land to the wealthy few continued after Rivadavia. Meanwhile, war with Brazil over Uruguay brought Rivadavia disgrace and exile in 1827, and he was followed in 1829—after a period of great anarchy—by Argentina's strongest and most colorful dictator, Manuel Rosas. The Argentine people had come, by the end of the chaotic 1820's, to regard the personal rule of a military chief an acceptable and proper form of government.

the era of a gaucho dictator

The years from 1816 to 1830 had been years of *caudillismo* rampant; but they were also years of growth. The isolated provinces had developed a feeling of nationality they had not had at the time of the Congress of Tucumán in spite of all the power of the local *caudillos*. Some legislation to encourage immigration had been passed and the population of the Plata area had grown from 508,000 in 1818 to 630,000 in 1826. Foreign trade, possible through the port since 1810, had increased by leaps and bounds as hides, tallow, and grain were shipped to Europe. Two incompatible types of society continued to exist side by side—one the urbanized town-dwellers, steadily increasing in number, and the other the cattle rancher aristocrats whose animals ran free on the wide pampas. Working for the ranchers on the unfenced prairie lands were the gauchos, who provided the color and the legends of the middle half of the 19th century.

In the 1830's, the dictator Manuel Rosas was the gaucho's hero. Rosas as a boy had run away from his father's ranch and his mother's discipline and had become a famous "bronco-buster." Not satisfied with the aimless gaucho life, he had become a handler of meats and hides. Backed by his private gaucho force, he served for three years as governor of Buenos Aires province. When Indians threatened settlements to the south, he set out to quell them and left his wife to keep political contact for him in Buenos Aires. Three years later, he was ruling the whole nation.

President Rivadavia had been forced to resign in 1827 because of public dissatisfaction over the outcome of the war in Uruguay. When civil war developed in the Plata provinces, with the *Unitarios* in the capital opposing Federalists from the interior, the Federalists were led by General Rosas. He was elected President but retained his governorship of Buenos Aires province. By 1835 he was, in actuality, dictator of the country.

Rosas first consolidated his power. While he talked "Federalism" and persecuted the city politicians, the *Unitarios*, he slyly built up control in every interior province. He "eliminated" the lesser chieftains, and though *caudillos* remained in Santa Fé, Tucumán, Mendoza, and Entre Ríos, Rosas allied himself with them and controlled them. Inadvertently the country was being unified around Buenos Aires while the sincere patriots who had been working for that end were being tortured in jail or exiled to Montevideo or Chile. Rosas required everything about him—his saddle blankets, the waist-coats of his diplomats, the baggy pants of his gaucho soldiers—to be rosy red. The red sash worn across the vest of a gentleman's evening clothes bore the printed words, "Federalism or death! Death to the filthy, loathsome, savage *Unitarios*." Blue, the color of the "underground" *Unitarios*, was worn in public on pain of death or imprisonment by Rosas' private "aggregate of cutthroats" called the *mazorca*. It has been estimated that during Rosas' power, 3,765 people were garrotted, 1,393 shot, 722 assassinated, 14,920 killed in battle, and 1,660 forced into exile.

Argentina accepted 17 long years of Rosas with little outright objection. Revolts broke out against him but he managed to maintain some degree of internal peace. Meanwhile he negotiated a treaty with England which abolished the slave trade, organized a provincial bank which forced the collection of sufficient taxes to support the federal government, and controlled the Church by forcing out any Church leaders who opposed him and compelling the priests to extol him from the pulpit. Pictures of the dictator and his influential wife Encarnación were carried in religious parades side by side with holy images.

Unsympathetic even with elementary education, Rosas regulated the courses taught at the University and withdrew financial support when he thought professors were too impractical in their teaching or in the slightest degree unfriendly to him. Literary and liberal-minded Argentines lived out his years of rule in exile in Uruguay or Chile. Any newspaper or book printed in Buenos Aires had to be directly approved by Rosas himself. The estate owners, the *estancieros*, supported him for he continued the land policy that allowed them to acquire even larger holdings. Though all his oppression did nothing to promote the country culturally or economically, Rosas did hold Argentina together, by brute force, and saved the Plata area from being cut up by the gaucho *caudillos*—a sort of "negative nation building."

Eventually Rosas wore out his hold on the people by an inept foreign policy. In 1843 he launched a war of intervention in the chaotic affairs of Uruguay which lasted nine years. He became involved with both France and England who were backing Uruguayan politicians in a long siege of Montevideo. Because of his activity across the Plata, the estuary was closed to upriver trade. The interior turned against him because of the continued trade monopoly of Buenos Aires and the blockades caused by his wars. Joining to oust him were the dictator of independent Paraguay, the *caudillo* of the river province of Corrientes, and his former friend, Justo José Urquiza, the wealthiest landowner in Entre Ríos.

On May 25, 1851, Urquiza, with the backing of Brazil, "pronounced" against Rosas, and on May 29th, Brazil made a formal alliance with Urquiza. On February 3, 1852, Urquiza, with soldiers from Entre Ríos and Corrientes, joined by the Brazilian army, was able to defeat Rosas at the battle of Monte Caseros. And with Rosas gone into exile to England, the oligarchy consolidated its power under the Constitution of 1853.

Argentina under the Constitution of 1853 to 1900

Justo José Urquiza, *caudillo* of Entre Ríos province, was not openly for strong central power, but he did promise to organize the nation under a constitutional government and to bring greater economic prosperity by opening the Plata river system to the trade of the world. However, both the city and province of Buenos Aires, comprising the most powerful part of Argentina, were fearful of Urquiza's provincial backing. They resented his triumphal entry into the city at the head of his troops three months previously and rejected the Agreement of San Nicolás he had negotiated with thirteen provinces to renew the federation.

Urquiza then laid siege to Buenos Aires, but the river boats he hoped to use in the blockade went over to the port faction. Urquiza himself barely escaped in a neutral vessel. For the time being, he abandoned hopes of ruling Buenos Aires and withdrew to his estates in Entre Ríos and set up headquarters for his new government in Paraná. His Congress proceeded to meet and call a constitutional convention to plan a stable federated government while Buenos Aires province went ahead and made its own centralized Constitution as if it were an independent nation.

The Argentine Constitution of 1853 drafted at Santa Fé was ratified by 13 of the interior states and was to last with few changes until the Perón era in 1949. Under it the central authorities were to have power to maintain order and national unity without destroying provincial autonomy. Because it was considered a "federalist" plan, it was unacceptable to Buenos Aires. Urquiza, as constitutional president of the Confederation, had to maintain an uneasy truce with the port city while he ruled from far upriver. Well-educated, courteous in diplomacy, a great hand with ladies, temperate in eating and drinking, and withal an efficient administrator and true patriot, Urquiza was a break with Argentina's past and its rough gaucho *caudillos*. He took pains to encourage education and immigration; and he initiated steamboat service upriver to Rosario.

But peace with Buenos Aires was impossible. All products of the interior had to go out through the port. Urquiza made treaties with England, France, and the United States providing for free commerce up the inland rivers, but they availed him nothing, for customs were still collected at the port where ocean-going vessels had to halt. Urquiza retaliated by charging duty on Buenos Aires goods sold inland. In 1859, war finally broke out between the forces of Urquiza and Buenos Aires. Defeat forced Buenos Aires into the Confederation. The government remained at Paraná under Urquiza's control. But the rich port taxes, the best income of the nation, remained in Buenos Aires control. Neither faction was happy.

When delegates from Buenos Aires came to the Congress at Paraná a year later, they were refused recognition because they had not been elected under the true federal Constitution. Insulted, they returned home and their leader, General Bartolomé Mitre, prepared again for war. This time, Mitre won for Buenos Aires at the Battle of Pavón, September 1861. He was declared national as well as provincial leader. Thus the idea of a Federation with the capital at Buenos Aires finally won out in 1861. General Mitre, a symbol of the port or *porteño* spirit, began a constitutional term as president in 1862. For the first time the newly coined term Argentine Nation was used as opposed to Provinces of the Plata, or Republic of the Plata— *argentum* was the Latin word for silver as *plata* was the Spanish.

Bartolomé Mitre, a *Unitario*, is one of the first really modern sons of Argentina. A literary liberal exiled by Rosas, he was a statesman, military general, historian, essayist, and journalist, founder of the great newspaper, *La Nación*, which was to become a force for social betterment in later years. As a writer, Mitre produced a history of independence, biographies of San Martín and Belgrano, a study of ancient Indian dramas, and a translation of the Roman writer Horace. To promote prosperity, Mitre continued railroad building, already begun on a small scale under Urquiza; and he invited British capital, opened public elementary schools, and encouraged the growth of the university. The Constitution of 1853 was now actually in force, with Buenos Aires city still the capital of both the province of Buenos Aires and of the nation.

Unfortunately, after three years of constructive work, he was forced to waste thousands of lives and millions of dollars on the tragic Paraguayan War of the 1860's, a grandiose effort which ended in the devastation of Paraguay. Toward the close of the war, Mitre himself headed the Argentine army which invaded Paraguay. The election of 1868 was held during the war and Mitre refused to run again. He returned victorious, with much of southern Paraguay added to Argentina by treaty, and retired to civilian life and the editing of his newspaper. In the end he was to become one of Argentina's distinguished elder statesmen, intervening in politics many times before his death in 1906.

One of the most progressive literary men South America had produced won the election of 1868. Domingo Faustino Sarmiento first rose to fame as a writer who criticized the gaucho mentality and urged a more sophisticated outlook. He had been a poor boy from the interior whose ambitious mother had, through tireless work with the loom, supported the family and put him through school. He was teaching in a small rural school at the age of fifteen, and was, even then, a *Unitario*. He barely escaped imprisonment by Rosas' local *caudillo*, Facundo Quiroga; he crossed the Andes to become a rural teacher in Chile. Ten years later he was writing for a Chilean paper, and by 1845, owing to his articles on education and to his intellectual contest with the learned Andrés Bello, he became the director of the new Chilean normal school. Chile sent him abroad to study schools; he observed Horace Mann's educational methods, received honorary degrees from American universities, wrote a biography of Lincoln, whom he had met personally, and founded a two-language review called *Both Americas.*

Welcomed to Buenos Aires after Rosas' fall, Sarmiento became a successful newspaper writer and political leader in his native land. He was to serve as director of schools, governor of San Juan, and Minister to the United States. His rise to the presidency was a new departure for Argentina since he was neither a local *caudillo* nor a successful general nor a rich cattleman, just a poor schoolteacher. As president and leader of the *Unitario* party and as a passionate believer in democratic institutions, he came to be regarded as the "Father of Education" for he insisted that "to govern is to educate" and that "an ignorant people will always elect a Rosas." His term of office was a period of great social and political evolution in Argentina. Today a portrait of Sarmiento can be found in almost every schoolroom in Argentina.

Sarmiento doubled the number of European immigrants who came in to farm the pampas. He began modernization of the port and built a sanitary water supply for the city. To enhance new trends in shipping beef for meat, he planned an even more extensive system of railroads. He imported American teachers to conduct his teacher-training institutions, English technicians to build railroads, and German and Swiss colonists to build up the cooler provinces in the unsettled south. Perhaps he tried to hurry his native land too much, for the old *caudillos* rose against him and he had two armed revolts to deal with, twice in the province of Entre Ríos.

In the election of 1874, Sarmiento backed his Minister of Education, the Córdoban Nicolás Avellaneda—who won the election and succeeded in establishing and consolidating order under a very progressive regime. Sarmiento continued in the government as a senator and as Minister of the Interior. When, under a series of weaker presidents in the 1880's, he saw his hopes for democratic elections fading away, he left politics and devoted his time to literature. He left 52 volumes of published works at the time of his death in 1888. The administration of Mitre had moulded the nation; that of Sarmiento continued Mitre's work. By 1880, Argentine society had been transformed by education, immigration, railroads, and foreign capital.

During all this period Argentine expansion to the south had been hindered by Indian tribes on the southern pampas. In 1878–1879, General Julio Roca, a sort of Argentine Custer, led an army of gauchos—actually the last militia in Argentine history that was costumed in gaucho fashion—in a war of extermination against the savages. Just as in the United States, the Sioux, the Comanche, the Apache, and the Pawnee were driven out of the fertile lands of the Mississippi Valley onto reservations in the semi-desert, so the pampas hunters were driven into bleak Patagonia or were transported into work colonies in semi-tropical Santa Fé and Entre Ríos. The land was opened to colonization, but it was ruthlessly squandered in scandalous speculation. The gauchos themselves, in drifting back from this last Indian war, were giving up the old "hell-for-leather" existence and becoming settled tenant farmers or hired cowhands.

The successful Indian campaigns made Julio Roca the presidential candidate of the Federalist and interior party in 1880 on the old issue of the port versus the pampas. Year after year the problem of a permanent capital for the nation had been fought over in the elections. When Roca won the election because of the backing of the interior provinces, the *Unitarios* challenged the election with arms and another civil war resulted. With Roca's victory in the war, a compromise was worked out which holds to this day. A new town, La Plata, was created to serve as capital of Buenos Aires province, a province which since has had little more influence in national affairs than any other large province. Buenos Aires city, with its great port, was separated from the province, as the constitution writers had suggested way back in 1853, and made into a federal district which included only the city and its suburbs.

All political troubles in Argentina were not solved by this formula, however. Both port and pampas were controlled by the oligarchs, the established old families of rich cattlemen. Provincial governors controlled the legislatures at home and their delegations to the national congress at Buenos Aires. They were in turn controlled by the great landed families. Whoever was president had to work through this "machine" to get his policies approved and enforced. Voting was restricted to a few, and there was no secret ballot. Reformers were powerless against the oligarchical families, who falsified the election returns and monopolized political appointments.

After General Roca's oligarchy-serving term expired in 1886, there followed a period of graft in government under his corrupt brother-in-law, Miguel Juárez Celman. Business struggled with inflation as the rapidly modernizing country tried to readjust itself to the change from an economy of wide-open prairies. The world-wide financial panic of 1891 bore quickly on Argentina with its dependence on British financial houses. Liberal-minded citizens, calling themselves the *Unión Cívica,* had organized a nationwide revolt against the oligarchs. When a middle-of-the-road compromise candidate, Luis Sáenz Peña, was elected to the presidency in 1892 as a way to settle both revolt and scandal, the *Unión Cívica* split in two. Its more liberal faction, the *Unión Cívica Radical,*—destined to be the famed Radical Party of the 20th century—plotted to overthrow the compromise. In 1898, during a war scare with Chile, the privileged few were able to put into office old General Roca, still the tool of the oligarchs. Their heyday was passing, however, for the Radicals were to come to power after one decade had passed in the new century. Roca's second term, 1898 to 1904, was an effective oligarchic dictatorship, necessitating frequent interventions in the provinces. But commerce increased and the port was improved.

The boundary disputes which troubled the 1890's strengthened the principle of arbitration. Argentina and Brazil both claimed part of the province of Misiones west of the Uruguay River. This dispute was settled when arbitration by President Cleveland awarded the area to Brazil. Not so simple was the dispute with Chile over the boundary line in Tierra del Fuego and in the Andes passes. The question was whether the Andes line should be the watershed or the line of the highest peaks—for in the Andes the two are not the same. War threatened at the turn of the century but again the dispute was arbitrated. The United States minister decided the northern end of the line and King Edward VII of England established the southern end. In honor of this peaceful settlement, the statue of Christ of the Andes was erected on the highest peak of the boundary, a symbol of peace between Argentina and her neighbors.

Argentine politics at the turn of the century

In the latter half of the 19th century an economic revolution had begun to transform the pampas. Industrialization and urbanization were to be the keynotes of the coming 20th century. The European immigrants who had already displaced the gaucho made Argentina in 1900 seem more like the United States of the same period than like any other part of Spanish-speaking South America. A cowboy tradition was passing. A prairie was being fenced in. Scattered nomadic Indians had been sent to remote reservations. Farmlands were offered to immigrants and a European immigrant population was pouring in. Swiftly-expanding railways were crossing the nation. A temperate prairie climate produced wheat and beef by new scientific agriculture. All these things make the story of the changing Argentina. By 1900 the pampas had been transformed by a new all-white population raising cereals and wheat to meet increasing European demands. Is that the story of some tango-dancing, gaucho-singing Latin nation, or is it a repetition in the Southern Hemisphere of the Yankee's own story?

These trends had been apparent when the twentieth century opened, as the beef industry, and with it the nation, rushed toward modernization. Argentina by 1900 had become one of the world's greatest suppliers of food. An economic revolution had come first to the pastoral industries, and then to the agricultural, brought about by better methods of breeding, planning, and shipping, and accompanied by the increase of foreign capital and the wave of immigration. But with the subsequent industrialization and urbanization had come a growing disparity between the wealthy few and the needy masses. The tide of European immigration had brought about a change in the racial composition of the population and had built up a large minority which had no effective defense of its interests through labor unions or political parties until the twentieth century. Immigration had given a great stimulus to the development of both a proletariat and a middle class, but the middle class of itself was not stable enough to form a political party which could put up a united front of opposition. Thus the oligarchy of landowners along with an element of "new-rich" commercial leaders continued to rule as the twentieth century opened. But the forces of economic and population change were gathering to produce a new political power and to give Argentina the best political party system in Latin America at the time.

Already in 1895 a census showed that one-half of the population could read and write, that railway lines, mostly financed in England, had doubled in mileage, and that foreign immigrants, many of them trained in commerce and mechanical trades, were ploughing up and fencing the open pampas as tenants, or were building a new commercial class in the cities. Though many of the provinces were backward frontier areas which felt the pinch of rural poverty, Buenos Aires was a city of wealth—wealth which was no longer concentrated in the hands of the estate owners but was being amassed by the sons of the commercially-minded immigrants. Along with the immigrant factory workers and stevedores, these new-rich leaders were soon to press for a voice in the government. The *Unión Cívica* had already formed during the revolts of the 1890's to challenge the entrenched political party of the large estate owners, the "oligarchs."

The election of 1904 was a protest vote against the oligarch's power, a protest which was spread over five weak candidates, and which allowed Manuel Quintana, the official oligarch candidate, to win the plurality. Opposing this choice was a new left-wing group called the Radicals which had split off from the moderately anti-oligarch *Unión Cívica Nacional* in the election of 1891. Its leader was Hipólito Irigoyen, who held the Radicals in a tightly knit opposition group that protested by the indirect method of "abstaining" from holding government jobs and from voting in elections.

In 1905, to challenge the minority president, Irigoyen dropped his undercover leadership of the quiescent Radicals and groomed himself as champion of the new laboring class of factory, dock, and railway workers. The generation that had ruled the stormy Argentina of the last two decades was passing. The congressional elections of 1906 brought a well-organized group of Irigoyen's followers and a few Socialists into the legislative body, where they carried on a struggle for the passage of laws forbidding factory work on Sunday, limiting the work hours for women and children, and creating a labor office.

Against the growing influence of the Radicals, oligarchs cooperated with the new commercial class to win the presidency in 1910 with a compromise candidate, Roque Sáenz Peña. It was an era of social pressures on politics, and Sáenz Peña was ready to do more than merely "compromise."

the era of Irigoyen and his Radical Party

Irigoyen's party was not "radical" by today's English connotation of the word; he said little about land division and economic rights for labor, and asked only for political rights—universal suffrage and fair elections. Immigrant farmers, small tradespeople, and factory workers joined his party and achieved some representation in the Congress. The general level of political education was rising. The newspaper, *La Prensa*, though usually representing the landed aristocrats, and *La Nación*, representing the middle class, agitated for actual constitutional two-party government, fair elections, and free trade. Trade unionists were interested in social reform. The University of Buenos Aires had become the defender of academic freedom and secular liberty and a center of research and inquiry. All these forces rallied behind Irigoyen and helped him form a political machine, the powerful and growing Radical Party.

Roque Sáenz Peña, with experience as Minister of Foreign Affairs and as an ambassador in Europe, knew that the forces of democracy must be heeded and that a wider suffrage would encourage more immigrants to become naturalized citizens. He believed that reforms should come from the top. In 1912, through his personal insistence, the famous Roque Sáenz Peña Law was passed which required that every man at the age of eighteen enroll his name for military service and register as a voter. Ballots were to be secret and only people who had actually registered were to vote. Both ideas were theretofore unknown in Argentina. Voting was made compulsory, with a fine of twenty pesos for failure to vote. A little enrollment book was given each voter containing identification, record of military service, and space for recording attendance at the polls for every election. The oligarchy yielded grudgingly to the Radicals on this law.

The Sáenz Peña Law was the magic "open-sesame" for Irigoyen's party. The first elections under the law, the congressional elections of April, 1912, saw the Radicals turn out to vote in large numbers. They won many seats in the Chamber of Deputies, and soon also had three important provincial governorships, while the Socialists won a majority in the municipal government of Buenos Aires.

Argentina seemed headed for true democracy. It was by then the richest country in Latin America, with a population of 8,000,000 and a capital city of 1,500,000 serving as one of the great argricultural shipping ports of the world. Social legislation was expanded. Employers were now responsible for accidents in industry; a national commission had been set up to provide cheap housing for industrial workers; laborers' wages could not be attached by creditors. World War I, which temporarily dislocated the Argentine economy by 1916, created boom demands for pampas meat and wheat.

The election of 1916, its votes counted with "scrupulous impartiality," brought Hipólito Irigoyen to the presidency with a large popular vote, ushering in a period of Radical rule to last until 1930. He was one of the most unusual characters in Argentine history, a colorless, shabby-looking hulk of a man who was called *El Peludo*, the mole, and his followers the *Peludistas*. Neither an inspiring orator nor a flamboyant writer, with no private fortune to spend and no family loyal to him in his lonesome life, he seems the antithesis of Latin American demagogic leaders. Born in 1853, the son of an illiterate Basque stable boy and a well-educated Buenos Aires woman, Hipólito devoted himself to the struggle against the oligarchy; he was in and out of various jobs but always active in the new *Unión Cívica Radical* party. His own words were always deeply philosophical, and his followers, who seldom understood him, considered him a saint. He exerted a mystical leadership, plotting endless intrigues against the oligarchy, now in the provinces and now in the city.

At first in 1916 he had declined the nomination made by the lesser leaders of his own party insisting that what he wanted was victory for his ideals of equality and justice. The exuberant Radicals, meeting in an openly recognized political convention, persisted. They said that if Irigoyen would not accept the nomination, the loosely joined party would disband. To the convention's emissaries, he finally said in the quiet of his study, "Do with me what you will." Then he went out into the country, refusing to campaign or to open his mail. Even at the inauguration he would not make a speech and tried to slip away from the hysterically joyful crowd.

Irigoyen was right, however, in saying he would not be a good administrator. Congress, which still contained a large minority of oligarchs, failed to respond to him. The Radical party consisted of a heterogeneous middle-class core, but with many diverse elements. Irigoyen's program of "honesty and equality" was so abstract as to accomplish little that was concrete. The new laboring class in Buenos Aires city profited from his philosophy for he persuaded Congress to recognize the right of labor to form unions. He also improved public health and brought running water and sewers to all large towns. In crises he ran the nation as he ran the party, as a dictator without trust in subordinates. He intervened in the provinces, and the press was critical.

During the war he had been faced with an unexpected foreign problem because he insisted on strict neutrality. There were many Germans in Argentina, but sympathy in the nation was almost wholly with the Allies, who were buying Argentina's food products. German submarine warfare hit Argentina hard; it became very difficult for neutral food-laden ships to trade with England. In the fall of 1917 when two Argentine vessels were sunk, it was discovered that the German ambassador in Buenos Aires had acted as informer for his government as to the whereabouts of the ships. He had advised his government to either permit Argentine ships to get through or sink them without a trace, and had characterized the Argentine president as "a notorious ass." Irigoyen, determined to remain neutral, simply asked the ambassador to leave and accepted an apology from Germany, without severing diplomatic relations, declaring war, or taking any direct part in aiding the Allies. This strict neutrality was bitterly opposed by a pro-Allied Congress which passed nearly unanimous resolutions to sever relations with Germany. Meanwhile, food prices became inflated because of the overseas wartime demand; there were hardships and food riots at home, which diminished still further the popularity of Irigoyen.

The Radical party, with all its segments, was still strong enough for Irigoyen to handpick his successor, for the Constitution of 1853 had provided that no president could succeed himself until after a six-year interval. Thus in 1922 Marcelo T. Alvear, a Radical party leader, became president. A more practical man than Irigoyen, he faced a difficult administration because of the postwar depression and the collapse of Argentine beef markets abroad. Alvear proved to be no puppet of Irigoyen. He broke away to form a new anti-personalist faction of the Radical party. Under him inheritance taxes and taxes for schools were enacted, and rapid advances in labor rights were gained. He also became involved in a long dispute with the papacy because he interfered with Church appointments. Relations with the papacy were severed for two years, until a solution was reached in 1926 under which Catholicism was recognized as the "official" religion, the president was to have no power to make Church appointments, and all other faiths were to be freely tolerated.

Alvear had some difficulties with the United States, which had just passed the high Fordney McCumber Tariff Act, tending to close the markets of America to Argentine meat and wheat. There was also bad feeling caused by the exclusion of Argentine beef from the United States market because of the supposed taint of hoof and mouth disease. At the Pan American conference at Havana in 1928 Argentine delegates protested American unwillingness to consider tariff reform, though to no avail until much later.

At the end of Alvear's middle-of-the-road term in 1928, Irigoyen suddenly decided to run again. Now he was seventy-six years old, a senile hermit, though still popular in memory. The combined conservative factions could not prevent his election. His second term was a tragedy for the old man, a farce for Argentina. Under his leadership, the costs of living and unemployment both rose. He was easily controlled by a corrupt staff who charged visitors a high price for appointments with him. After two years of budget deficits, corruption in government, unsolved labor disputes, and loss of prestige abroad, the restless workers and critical middle classes were willing to follow a military clique led by the oligarch general José Uriburu, which threw the ineffectual Irigoyen out in a "spontaneous" revolution in 1930. The plot, which was hatched by the army, was assisted by rioting university students. Irigoyen died friendless and alone on July 3, 1933. Now the party remembered him—in death he was the symbol of democracy, although in life he had been the despised old "mole." Thousands jammed the street before the cheap little flat where he had died; people stood bareheaded for hours with tears running down their faces.

In the two years of Irigoyen's second administration, he and his henchmen had quarrelled with Congress, interfered in the provinces far beyond the power of the president, and had split the Radical party. Even so the military revolt was a shock to Argentines, who had considered their country too mature for barracks revolutions. Constitutional government, which had been making strides since 1900, came to a halt in Argentina with the revolution of September 6, 1930.

Argentina through world-wide depression and war

The *coup d'état* of 1930 was made by an army junta which took over the entire government, removed every Radical from office, postponed elections month after month, and threatened repeal of the Roque Sáenz Peña fair-election law. This was the first violent overthrow of government under the Constitution of 1853, and it succeeded only because of the world economic situation and the desperate position of Argentine agriculture with the loss of foreign markets. With the failure of the Radicals, the country had no place to turn save to the Conservatives. Head of the junta was General José Uriburu, member of an old landlord family.

The army controlled the government; the city of Buenos Aires lived as if in a state of siege, with Congress dissolved and the municipal government not functioning. Uriburu intervened in the local governments of twelve of the provinces, called off or postponed elections, and kept all opposition leaders in prison. The nation accepted all this because Irigoyen's last term had been so chaotic. The Conservatives accepted martial law because they hoped to return to power in spite of the country's Radical majority.

Eventually civilian opposition and division in the army forced Uriburu's hand and a rigged election was held in November, 1931, after thirteen months of promises. Augustín P. Justo, a retired general and former Radical party member and Minister, leading a supposedly new coalition of old oligarch landowners, city industrialists and anti-Irigoyen Radicals, was elected to serve until 1938. Justo broke with Uriburu in 1932 but the idea of military dictatorship remained under the surface. He showed some awareness of social responsibilities when he passed income and inheritance tax laws and allowed formation of more powerful unions. Under Justo the Conservatives ended laissez-faire and introduced a controlled economy. Guided by an able Finance Minister, Frederico Pineda, exchange controls, protective tariffs, bilateral agreements and other measures brought Argentina out of the depression. But the prosperity benefited only the oligarchy, through the cattle industry and foreign trade. The middle and lower classes were worse off. The Conservatives were determined that Argentina should never return to Radical rule. Justo himself dissolved Congress during his last two years, because of threatened Radical control.

Even elections held in the 1930's brought in presidents who were tinged with European fascism. From 1934 to 1937, German Nazis came in large numbers into Argentina as "immigrants." They learned Spanish and married Argentinians. In 1939 Hitler could claim 1,300,000 German "nationals" in Argentina although the census showed only 43,625 newcomers who had been born in Germany. But Buenos Aires had 131 Nazi organizations and 203 German-language schools. Meanwhile Franco had won the Spanish Civil War and had a *falange* in Argentina. The Fascists spread their influence among army officers and young Conservative nationalists. A commission to identify and list such anti-Argentine agencies was appointed but not put into effect. One of the best known of Argentine diplomats, Carlos Saavedra Lamas, worked to achieve the "solidarity of the American states under Argentine guidance." At home and abroad, Argentina was building up a strongly militaristic nationalism.

The left-wing Radicals, after the death of Irigoyen, had no leader; and democratic politics in Argentina had by 1937 reached a new "low." Congress passed only three laws that year, one to authorize expenditures and the other two to permit the president to take vacations. Not even a budget was passed. The Radicals had won control of Congress in 1936 and in the election of 1938 were strong enough to force a coalition compromise, a

Liberal president and a Conservative vice-president. Many voters boycotted the polls and preferred to pay a fine rather than vote. Many employers and big ranchers collected their employees' voting booklets and on election day had them counted in a lump. Naturally the coalition was elected.

Roberto M. Ortiz, who had been in Alvear's cabinet, was chosen as the liberal "front man" to lull the masses into acceptance of the continued dictatorship. But Ortiz was staunchly opposed to the Nazis and Fascists, and was sympathetic to the Allies although he maintained neutrality. He interfered in several "rigged" elections in the provinces, and he insisted on fair elections for Congress in 1940. Anti-Nazi coalition groups made plans for socio-economic reforms, which, ironically enough, were to become the basis of Perón's promises six years later. Their candidates won control of the lower house although the Senate remained in conservative control. Ortiz himself, a diabetic, lost his eyesight and the conservative vice-president, Ramón Castillo, favorite of army and landlords, had to act for the blind president. When Ortiz died in 1942, the brief interlude for democracy was over as Castillo took full control.

Castillo's sympathies had been pro-Axis, and now the repercussions of World War II were strongly felt in Argentina. Castillo made a feint for American aid to secure lend-lease military equipment in exchange for strategic tungsten. Then he used the equipment to enforce a strong military dictatorship. Castillo rigidly censored the press in favor of the Nazis, prohibiting pro-Allied meetings and openly encouraging pro-Axis propaganda. The Conservatives, who had lost much of their prewar trade in agricultural products with the British, were lulled into thinking that Hitler would win, and that Argentina's future lay in commercial relations with a victorious Germany. Popular sentiment was still strongly pro-Allied, however—especially since Germany continued to sink Argentine ships and to use the German consulates in Argentina as bases for propaganda aimed at all Latin America. At home Castillo, backed by police force, represented the Conservatives. His government was one of fraud and repression while the cost of living went on up. When Castillo attempted to impose his hand-picked successor, a group of army generals quietly engineered a revolution and drove him from office.

June, 1943, saw a "permanent" president, the even more pro-Axis General Pedro Ramírez, representing the victorious army faction. He dissolved all political parties, outlawed the Confederation of Labor, recessed Congress, and cancelled elections, while he ruled ruthlessly by decree and with the backing of the Catholic Church. Military interventors were sent into all fourteen provinces to assume control from the elected governors, and even the mayors of large cities were replaced by army officers. Nazi propaganda continued to pour out of Argentina, especially in the newspaper *El Pampero*. When enthusiasm for the Allied cause broke into demonstrations in the street, the pro-Axis government of generals and admirals quickly clamped down, padlocked the democratic newspapers, set student rioters and striking meat-packers to jail, and continued its pro-Axis rule by decree.

But the next decade was to be an age of "colonels," not of generals.

The army group which had ousted Castillo in 1943 realized that the monopoly of power in the hands of the landowning oligarchs was out of date. The *estancieros* could not satisfy the needs of a modern state. The "middle-class" military leaders made plans for a more popular backing among the lower classes, while they remained strongly pro-Axis in foreign affairs. Closest to the soldiers and strongest in policy-making among the military were a group of colonels, led by Colonel Juan Domingo Perón, then serving as Under-Secretary of War. Month by month President-General Ramírez became the tool of the colonels. When Ramírez attempted an "about face," hoping that by severing relations with the Axis he would save himself and would receive help from the United States, he was forced to resign in February 1944 and turned over his colonel-controlled seat to former Minister of War Edelmiro Farrell, puppet of the colonels' clique.

England and the United States ignored the government of Farrell and Perón; America called home her ambassador, and shipments of gold to Argentine banks were cancelled. The colonels still did not respond to Allied pressure and in February of 1945 sent no delegate to the inter-American conference at Chapultepec Castle in Mexico City. There the other Western Hemisphere nations resolved that any country that did not join the war against Germany could not join the United Nations to be formed the next month at the Charter Meeting in San Francisco. Only then did the Argentine government conform and declare war on Germany and Japan, March 27, 1945, when American and Russian soldiers were well inside the borders of Germany and marching on Berlin. Then Argentina was admitted to the good graces of the inter-American group and soon became a respected member of the United Nations.

Argentina's troubles with the United States about Nazi activity were not over, however. Ambassador Spruille Braden openly opposed Perón in Buenos Aires, while the United States State Department prepared a "Blue Book" showing in detail how Buenos Aires had been the headquarters of Nazi activity. Braden was recalled and his criticism only served to make Perón more popular at home. It was April 1946 before the United States welcomed Argentina into postwar friendship, accepting Argentine pledges to clean up Axis influences. By this time the Axis issue was dead, and Perón had won the February 1946 elections.

a decade of Perón in the saddle

At home Perón called himself neither pro-Allied nor pro-Nazi, but pro-Argentine. Argentina was by now enjoying unprecedented prosperity, selling her foodstuffs to the victors. She claimed to be "the one spot in the Western World unbothered by the war." There was a building boom going on in Buenos Aires; well-dressed shoppers went in and out of the smart shops on Calle Florida where displays were rich and plentiful. Meat prices were high abroad; other South American nations, cut off from Europe, were buying the new industrial products of Buenos Aires' factories. Workers in the port and out on the pampas were better paid than ever before. All Argentina was willing to back any general, or even any colonel, who preserved this prosperity.

And Juan Domingo Perón was more than a mere colonel. At first not a "headliner" in the military government, he soon got himself promoted from Under-Secretary of War to Minister of War, Labor, and Welfare, and finally in 1944 under Farrell he called himself Vice-President. By then he had begun a policy of social and economic revolution. Three thousand of his opponents were in prison camps, and he was in control of the labor unions. As Labor Minister he had created a civilian army of backers, the new basis of power the "colonels' clique" had planned.

Born October 8, 1895, Perón was one of many bright young lieutenants graduated from the Argentine military academy at eighteen; he was famous as a skier, boxing champion, swordsman, and crack pistol shot. In 1930 he was teaching at the academy; in 1936 he was military attaché to the embassy in Chile; in 1939 he was sent on a special mission to Italy where he learned to admire and copy Mussolini's methods. Early in the colonels' regime he settled a widespread meat-packers' strike by a quick personal tour of the factories and workers' quarters, where he made friends with the labor leaders by treating them as honored equals and greeting them with the warm Latin embrace. Stubborn labor leaders found themselves in exile in Tierra del Fuego; "cooperative" labor leaders helped the Minister of War and Labor to found puppet unions. A widower, charming in manner, tall and prepossessing, Perón was full of vitality at fifty in the spring of 1945.

In October 1945 army leaders decided Perón was too powerful and had him imprisoned on a pretext. A parade of union members, led by his current girl friend, a radio actress named Eva Duarte, protested his arrest. In a few days Perón was out of prison; the day of his return was a labor holiday for the next decade. Within the week he and Eva were married. By October 17 he was the complete dictator of Argentina. In 1946 he was the candidate for the presidency of both army and labor. The big landowners, the oligarchs, opposed him because of his promises to the poor that he would break up the large estates, but they had no candidate of their own.

Perón's greatest power lay in the working masses in the large cities. For a half century each Argentine city worker's dream was to have a job or social position calling for the wearing of a white shirt, a *camisa*. We would call it "the urge to be in the white-collar class," to be among the *camisados*, the wearers of starched shirts. Perón told his followers among the laborers to scorn all this; they were the "unshirted ones," the *descamisados*, the men in work clothes, the real future of Argentina. It was not necessary to rig the election of February 1946. Perón was the friend of the masses, the champion of social justice, the enemy of the "imperialistic Yankees." The Church, the army, and the pro-Axis foreign groups were all on his side. Everyone voted in the secret ballot booths, each on his own registration enrollment book, perhaps for the first time. Impartial observers considered 1946 the fairest election in Argentina since 1916. Perón was not afraid to announce openly his 56 per cent of the vote. The Congress was composed of 90 per cent of his followers, the Radical opposition was weakened, governors of his own choosing were in the provincial capitals, and his own personal enemies were in exile in Montevideo or in work camps in Tierra del Fuego. Perón thus moved into six dramatic years of power.

The drama was enhanced by the beautiful Eva Duarte, now the First Lady. It was unprecedented for an Argentine president to marry an actress of unknown origin. But Eva Duarte was an illegitimately born adventuress playing for high stakes; blonde, intelligent, and charming, she did not fear social ostracism by the wives of the oligarchs. Her appeal to the women of the *descamisados* brought her husband more popular support than any social "freeze-out" would have taken away. As shrewd as Perón, she defied tradition still further by entering politics as the Minister of Social Welfare and was only stopped by the army when the *descamisados* wanted to nominate her for vice-president. The money voted her department by Congress was put in the Eva Perón Foundation. With it and millions from private "contributions," she founded orphanages, homes for working girls, and cheap chain groceries where food was supposedly sold at cost. "I never keep books," she said, "I just work from the heart." She became Secretary of Labor also, managing labor unions, calling strikes on and off at will when they seemed good publicity for Perón. She controlled the radio, the theater, and the newspapers in Argentina. "Eva is the soul of the workers! Perón is the father of the people!" announced the posters, while Eva proclaimed the emancipation of Argentine women and organized a *Peronista* Women's Party. Theatrical as the régime seemed, its base was its popularity among the working class, a new thing in Argentine politics. *Peronismo* was actually a political party opposed equally by the conservative old oligarchs and the remnant of Irigoyen's Radicals.

In 1947 a Bill of Rights for Workers was passed by Perón's Congress, later to be incorporated in his new constitution of 1949. Perón's *descamisados* got vacations with pay at new beach resorts for workers, higher wages, sickness benefits, tenure on the job, and bonuses at Christmas —at a time when the free unions under their own leaders had gained little or nothing for their members in the forty years since Roque Sáenz Peña. Rights of Labor, yes—but not the right to strike. In all this love song there was an undercurrent of tension and bitterness.

Still labor leaders did not openly oppose Perón and the Argentine workers in general waxed fat. The old Radical party still existed, with a token number of seats in Congress, but it was the only "opposition" permitted. New parties could not organize; any existing party could be dissolved for "endangering the social peace." Perón meanwhile consolidated his own power by purging the Supreme Court and the university faculties, controlling elementary education, and organizing his own personal political party, the *Partido Peronista*. He was bent on preserving his totalitarian power and stopping all possible incipient revolt. For this purpose he proclaimed a law of *desacato* (don't be "disrespectful" or you will be arrested); he maintained a large police force against mob action, and kept tight control over the army.

The boldest opposition came from the eighty-year-old newspaper *La Prensa*. The rich and powerful *La Prensa* had always criticized what it pleased in every administration, meanwhile achieving world fame for its excellent coverage, and local prosperity for its circulation and fat advertising. It continued to criticize what it didn't like about the Peróns, though the government cut its newsprint paper supply.

Finally in 1951 the newspaper was accused of being "foreign-bossed" because it carried dispatches from the United Press. *La Prensa's* owner, Gainza Paz, escaped to Uruguay and the new editions began to sing Perón's praises as the circulation dropped.

Perón's economic policy was to convert Argentina into a powerful and self-sufficient modern state. He wanted to break the *estanciero* class and its hold on the food export trade, and to end Argentine dependence on foreign markets. He proposed to make Argentina the industrial giant of South America, economically independent, and launched a Five Year Plan to achieve that end, an elaborate blueprint for industrial progresss filling 128 pages. The agricultural crops of the Argentine pampas were to be bought from the producers at a fixed price by the government, then sold abroad at gouging prices in a starved world market. Money thus made was to pay for the grandiose industrialization schemes.

By 1949 the schemes had begun to bog down. The world market for Argentine food fell off as Marshall Plan funds made war-torn Europe more nearly self-supporting. International prices for beef dropped, while the purchases of heavy machinery abroad for the new industry overbalanced the sale of the food exports. Meanwhile large and small farmers alike began to complain of the differential between Perón's price to them and Perón's price abroad. Rural workers left the farms and came to the cities for the high wages being paid factory workers. Perón had to reverse himself and turn his attention to agriculture. Argentina lacked the coal and iron necessary for industrialization; what Perón needed to import first were not expensive oil drills and dynamos and Bessemer converters but "90,000 tractors, 20,000 combined harvesters, and 100,000 gang plows."

Perón's new industry was to be financed with Argentine, not foreign, capital. For a century English capital had controlled Argentina's banks, meat-packing plants, railways, and small manufacturers. Perón's rise was contemporary with the worldwide decline of English capital. The English railway companies sold to Perón outright, as they were not realizing 1½ per cent on their billion-dollar investment. For little more than half this investment Perón received thousands of miles of track, a great deal of it obsolete, much outworn equipment, and responsibility for 150,000 employees. For months Perón's railway cost him $300,000 a day and the public was bitterly disappointed at the result of this much-touted venture into national ownership.

So Perón's six-year term went by. During that period he had carried his revolution into every branch of national life. He had expanded manufacturing, set prices, brought many social gains to labor, controlled the press, cut down the power of the oligarchy, and tried to eliminate foreign financial influence. Now he determined to entrench himself in power. According to the constitution in force since the fall of Rosas in 1853, no president could succeed himself. Copying Mexico's Porfirio Díaz, Perón called a constitutional convention in 1949, which meekly amended the law of presidential succession. The new "Perónized" constitution allowed indefinite re-election of the president by popular vote including woman suffrage, abolished the electoral college, expanded the economic power of the government, and set forth Perón's social program. Now Perón could run again in 1951. However, a plan to have Eva elected vice-president met with chilly opposition from Perón's own army officers, traditional in their views when it came to the position of Argentine women in society. Eva's name was withdrawn under pressure, at the same time that she became suddenly critically ill. When her illness was diagnosed as incurable cancer, the presidential campaign turned into a sad and muted affair. The Radical party was given little opportunity to present the issues to the people, for Perón owned the press and radio and could send his police to harry opposition meetings. It was unnecessary for the army to supervise the election; it was easily rigged and as easily won by Perón. The surprising fact was that despite all this, the Radicals won a third of the votes cast.

For this second six-year administration—unprecedented since the days of Rosas, to whom many of Perón's enemies compared him—there was an equally unprecedented austere inauguration. Eva was ill unto death; Argentine economy was equally weak. An ambitious second Five Year Plan got off to a bad start. Beginning in February 1952 there were "meatless days" weekly in every restaurant, this in a land where the poorest families were accustomed to juicy steaks. Owing partly to Perón's overemphasis on city workers and manufacturing, partly to unwillingness of farmers to plant crops or sell young steers in the face of Perón's low fixed prices, partly to a two-year drought, the meatless days were a shock to well-fed Argentinians. Throughout 1952 and 1953 this austerity continued.

In 1952 Argentina's living costs were skyrocketing, her peso was devaluated, her foreign trade balance was unfavorable. In the midst of this economic dilemma, Eva died, July 26, 1952. Multitudes of *descamisados* mourned hysterically at her funeral; all streets, towns, plazas, and school rooms named for President Mitre, long since forgotten, were declared by Congress to be renamed for Eva Perón. Her body was to be embalmed and laid to rest in an open glass shrine.

Throughout the decade Perón had considered Argentina a world power, the future leader of the Western Hemisphere. He had spent money lavishly to help his friends get elected in Ecuador, Chile, and Bolivia. Presentations in Argentine movies, radio programs, books and papers actually made Argentina seem a world force to be reckoned with. Perón renewed the Argentine claim to the Falkland Islands, long held by Britain, and "incorporated" them into the Argentine nation, and he published maps which showed a slice of Antarctica as Argentine territory.

In his second administration, Perón's chief problem was how to shift emphasis from "social justice" to "sound business." He was forced to reverse some of his policies. To prove he could rule without Eva, he ousted her favorites in the government and labor organizations. His policy after November 1952 when productivity lagged and economic difficulties increased was to "get along with the oligarchs, go back to the beef industry and to agriculture as the basis of national wealth." Plans for Eva's glass burial place were quietly changed and names of places called after President Mitre were quietly *not* changed. Let Argentina forget Eva and the new industrialization while workers from the congested city were urged to return to the land to increase agricultural production. Perón played off one faction against another, *descamisados* and industrialists against landowning oligarchs and army officers, shopkeepers and employers against workers. But in spite of his cleverness and shrewdness, he saw his schemes had to fail and his devoted minions in the army and the unions beginning to doubt him.

In 1954 in the mistaken hope of stirring up liberalistic loyalties, Perón quarreled with the Catholic Church, which had taken advantage of labor discontent and formed a Catholic labor party. Accusing the priests of meddling in politics, he imprisoned them, closed Catholic papers, prohibited religious processions, raided university students' clubs, and dismissed religious teachers. When he legalized divorce and prostitution and legitimatized illegitimate children, the Church leaders cried, "It is Christ or Perón!" This opposition which the Church organized was the first anti-Perón movement able to survive and grow.

Military officers joined underground liberals in September 1955 to throw Perón out of the *Casa Rosada*, or "Pink House," as the Executive mansion is called. The mobs that broke into Perón's several private houses found evidences of enormous hidden wealth and luxurious living. It became evident that Perón had been a large-scale grafter. Argentina was left with over $1,200,000,000 of debt, and an internal debt of 70 billion pesos. He was fortunate to escape upriver to Paraguay en route to Spain. Yet inadvertently he had wrought an irrevocable social revolution in Argentina with the shift in political power away from the oligarchs.

the new direction of Argentine politics

The inheritors of Perón's wrecked economy were to be plagued for a generation or more by dismaying problems he had left. For the *Peronismo* could not be denied. Argentines had been caught up in the revolution of rising expectations. They had passed out of the underdeveloped stage of economic development and now in an intermediate stage hoped to skip quickly to the stage of industrialization without paying for the Perón interlude. A palace coup in November 1955 installed a little-known infantry officer named Pedro Eugenio Aramburu and hoped its "caretaker's" government could keep itself in power until elections could be held and could avoid provoking violent revolution among the many dissident Argentine factions. It faced the task of "de-Peronization" or cleaning out ten years of favoritism and corruption. It also had to stabilize the economy in a country in which the cost of living index went up 34 per cent in 1956. Aramburu did succeed in controlling inflation to some extent by keeping wages frozen but this increased his unpopularity among the working class. Periodically outbreaks against the government had to be put down by force.

Aramburu acted with political sagacity when he called a constituent assembly in August 1957 which met at Santa Fé and set up a plan for electing a president, a congress, and all provincial governors. A split developed among the active anti-*Peronistas*, members of the old Radical party—the more conservative Radicals following former presidential candidate Ricardo Balbín and the more liberal "Intransigent Radicals" following Arturo Frondizi. The coolly intellectual Frondizi, one of 14 children of an Italian immigrant, a leftist in his law-school days, was willing to work with foreign capital. To industrial leaders he promised high tariffs, to the Church removing "free divorce" from the Radical platform, to the socialists of his youth the nationalization of electric power and telephone companies. In foreign affairs he promised to line Argentina up with the West.

One promise he made backfired, his offer of amnesty to imprisoned *Peronistas*. Frondizi won easily when Perón from exile ordered his million and a half followers to vote for Frondizi, but when *Peronistas* held an enthusiastic street celebration at the Frondizi inauguration, Frondizi broke it up with tear gas. Because he had "a deep personal belief that no one should be persecuted for his political ideas," he did put through the promised general amnesty bill. Then when Perón backers, still in control of labor because of the large measure of autonomy permitted unions, attempted to paralyze the nation with a strike, Frondizi ended six months of pussyfooting with the *Peronistas* and broke it up with armed force.

Frondizi kept down administrative spending, cut wages to bring down inflated prices, and curbed the military in its expectation of favors. He imported foreign capital to prospect for further petroleum deposits, hoping to end the $300 million yearly import of gasoline and oil, thus making a frontal assault on the economic nationalism rooted in the country for a generation. The International Monetary Fund made a $329 million loan to Argentina, the largest to any single Latin American nation up to that time. In 1960 he joined the newly-formed Latin American Trade Association, the common market plan.

But many Argentines were violently opposed to Frondizi's austerity regime and he faced crisis after crisis—32 threats against his presidency and his life. In the 1960 congressional election, *Peronistas* cast more protest blank ballots than the Frondizi party received votes, and then as a result of a reform which Frondizi put through in the election law, 26 different parties were brought into the Congress in the congressional elections of March 1962, including a large block of Perón backers. In panic the army declared the election invalid. A group of officers arrested Frondizi and held him under house arrest for 14 months. Once more democracy had failed in Argentina and the army was in control of the capital.

In elections arranged by the army for July 1963, 24 different parties put up candidates for Congress and seven persons were nominated for president. Coalitions with minor parties gave Dr. Arturo Illia, of the more conservative wing of the old Radical party, a majority in Congress over both the Frondizi and Perón factions.

When Dr. Illia, a physician from Córdoba, came to the presidency in 1963, Argentines were so relieved to have a "stable, mature moderate" in the presidency that the Stock Exchange posted its biggest trading day in history the day the election was proclaimed. But his popularity was short-lived. His philosophy was to "sit quietly back and let the land of beef and wheat run itself." He did cancel the contracts for petroleum prospecting granted to foreign companies by Frondizi, and Argentina began importing oil at high prices again. He had some success in satisfying *Peronista* workers with higher pay and more jobs, an attempt to get them out of politics. They were a working class party without a leader The labor leaders made no great outcry when Illia refused Perón, who had come to visit in nearby Rio, a visa to enter Argentina. When his pretty young third wife came to Buenos Aires to lead the *Peronistas* in 1965, she drew very small crowds. But the working-class voters had gained political power under Perón greater than that of any other Latin American labor group save that in Mexico. In the 1965 congressional election, the Labor party won 35 per cent of the total vote, signaling the one great and lasting achievement of Perón in Argentina, that of bettering the lot of the workers.

The next five years, from 1966 on, were marred by three military coups. The first military government lasted from June, 1966, to May, 1969, and the second from May, 1969, to March, 1971. The third was trying desperately to keep the government and economy going until the promised elections in 1973. Each change was backed by the army, though at the top there was disagreement among generals. Dr. Illia, when his presidency had brought the country to a stalemate in 1966, was replaced by his army commander-in-chief Juan Carlos Onganía, a "strong man" who was simply declared Argentina's 31st president by the army. He proceeded to clamp down on all vestiges of democratic government, forbidding labor unions to strike and setting rigid price and wage controls in an effort to channel food stuffs into the export trade. Then in 1969, the shooting of a student rioter by a policeman triggered a wave to university protests across the nation. The students were soon joined by workers and even some shopkeepers. The *Peronistas*, still well-organized, kidnapped former president and anti-Perón strongman Aramburu, seeking vengeance, supposedly, for the 27 *Peronistas* executed by Aramburu 14 years previously. It was assumed that he had been murdered when his watch and keys were found in a rented bank vault, and the army generals, blaming Onganía for encouraging the *Peronistas,* forced him to resign in June 1970. Army general Alejandro Lanusse headed a three-man-military junta that had taken over when Onganía was dismissed and had chosen Roberto Marcelo Levingston as president, an obscure general then serving in Washington on the Inter-American Defense Board. President Levingston quarreled with Commander-in-Chief Lanusse, tried to dismiss him, and found himself dismissed, with Lanusse becoming the eighth president of Argentina since Perón was ousted in 1955. Lanusse, once considered a liberal, had been leader in two of the five coups in the 16-year period that followed Perón. Before that, he had been jailed for four years because of participation in an anti-Perón revolt.

For nearly a decade the cost of living had been increasing at more than 30 per cent a year, rising to 60 per cent inflation in 1966. Onganía had resorted to measures like "belt-tightening," and President Levingston in his turn lowered the value of the peso and planned to ration beef to make more of it available for export and bring in foreign exchange. The Argentines launched a black market which defeated this program and the economy continued to decline into 1972, with a 60% decrease in manufacturing between January, 1970, and January, 1972.

In dealing with labor, the military presidents met little success. Onganía had hoped to use the CGT, the General Council of Workers, as a pro-government tool, and when he failed, he cracked down on irregularities in labor's activities, cancelled the legal status of the railway workers' union, and in October, 1968, provoked a general strike. President Levingston had to contend with three nation-wide strikes. In the field of civil rights, Onganía declared a 4-year moratorium on political activity. He had acted to take over the universities, launched a campaign for Catholic morality among the students, and provoked student demonstrations against social injustice which many Catholic priests joined. Levingston, a less rigid person, acted to make long-range plans for elections and hoped the nation might "drift" under military control into political reform. Lanusse promised the restoration of "constitutional normality" and annulled laws prohibiting political activities. Political groups began to reform immediately, and a nationalist coalition proclaimed a platform that emphasized gradual socialization of the economy. By 1972, forty per cent of the nation's economic activity, apart from agriculture, was in the hands of state enterprises. Evidently Lanusse hoped to bring together the diverse political factions of the country behind a plan to hold free elections in 1973. He called his attempts at liberal politics and nationalized economics "The Great National Accord."

The labor camp is greatly divided in its devotion to Juan Domingo Perón. Lanusse, who had been imprisoned by Perón for four years in the 1950's, was willing to allow the *Peronistas* to support their own candidates for the 1973 elections in the hopes that the old dictator had lost his appeal. But Argentines were surprised when the 77-year-old Perón landed by plane from his European exile on November 18, 1972, to a tense but subdued welcome, hoping to field his own candidates.

Thus Argentina found itself in the third quarter of the 20th century far from solving its historical problems. Nominally it was still under the rule of military men, though they might be "softening." Its working people were unable to forget the bonuses and favors that had been promised them by Perón, but unable to gather round a new hero. And the rich landlords still owned the fertile hinterland and showed no signs of accepting any land reform, in spite of the nationalization of industries in Buenos Aires. But a majority of the Argentines, like the cattle grazing on their rich pampas, remained for the most part plump and happy.

Note: Readings for this chapter are given at the end of Chapter 23.

THE LIFE
OF THE ARGENTINES
AS THEY CHANGED
FROM GAUCHOS TO
MODERN SOPHISTICATES

the gaucho in ninteenth-century Argentine life

Temperate in climate, European blooded, agriculturally rich Argentina! How similar it seems at first glance to the United States! How different it is in many respects from the colorful, tropical Latin America of mid-hemisphere! With its pure-blooded cattle on parade at the stock shows, its thousands of square miles of wheat acreage, its meat-packing plants and frozen-beef industry—balanced by its sophisticated modern metropolis and its chic little stenographers strolling past the smart fashion shops at their noon hour, its highly unionized stevedores working the busy port and living in model housing, the preponderance of European immigrant stock with little trace of the Indian—all these things make Argentina and its capital seem a mixture of Chicago, Kansas, and New York. Where today is the gaucho with his guitar? Where are the tango dancers with their Latin rhythms? Nowadays the gaucho with his guitar is merely a symbol of Argentina in its early days of independence. He is seldom found outside the night clubs and occasional shows on Buenos Aires television.

In the first half of the 19th century, the gauchos were the lowest class in society, the raw materials for the *caudillos'* armies. By the second half of the century, as the cities and the pampas both filled with immigrant peoples from Europe, their life had become legendary like that of the cowboy in America. The gaucho was the national hero, the central figure in drama, poetry, dance, and novel, a mixture of Buffalo Bill, Daniel Boone, and Robin Hood. As was sung by Martín Fierro, the most famous of the gauchos:

> *A son am I of the rolling plain,*
> *A gaucho born and bred;*
> *For me the whole great world is small,*
>
> *Believe me, my heart can hold it all,*
> *The snake strikes not at my passing foot,*
> *The sun burns not my head.*[1]

To most Argentines, Martín seems a real person although actually he is a fictitious character created in a long, rollicking poem by José Hernández (1834–1886), an Argentine born on a cattle ranch near Buenos Aires in the 1840's. He lived to edit a Buenos Aires newspaper and to serve in the Argentine legislature, but during his own lifetime he was always identified with Martín Fierro himself.

The unlettered gauchos came to know the whole of Martín's rhymed story from their own singers, the *payadores,* who sang songs about the gauchos and their adventures on the pampas that were "brown with the grazing herds." All the gaucho needed beside his rope and saddle was "the plain below and sky above, a horse, and a thatch and a bit of love." As Hernández ended the story, Martín became an outlaw and went south to live with the Indians. But the gauchos were not content to have Martín go off like that and Hernández had to bring him back years later, in 1879, in *The Return of Martín Fierro,* a complete new edition of verses on the wandering minstrel's adventures.

Santos Vega was another guitar-playing cowboy who may perhaps have actually existed. Hilario Ascasubi (1807–1875) had written down a series of poetic adventures of cowboys supposedly told him by this singer. Every *pulpería* or country saloon had its guitar ready for the wandering *payador.* If two *payadores* showed up, a singing contest ensued, each singer extemporizing; and if a dispute developed as to who was best, it could become a free-for-all fight. Sometimes the *payadores* joined small companies of traveling players and sang their verses while the stories of gaucho deeds were acted out. From this a native theater, the *dramas criollos,* grew up, a theater that traveled by wagon from town to town giving these famous "horse operas." In some of them were characters of the Jesse James type whose escapes from the law made them frontier heroes. At the turn of the century, the gaucho plays moved into the cities where they were given more formal staging and complicated plots. They set the style for gaucho stories and became the literature of a nation. Dance forms and art also centered around this theme in the entire Plata region.

---

[1] From Walter Owen translation, José Hernández, *The Gaucho Martín Fierro* (Farrar and Rinehart, 1936), p. 4.

The gauchos influenced not only literature, music, and art but also politics and the economy. They supported Rosas, fought the wars in Uruguay, kept the Indians away from the cities. They cared for the cattle which provided the food, and dried the hides to make up the chief export. Their homes were rude—a bed made of hides and a few steer skulls for stools were the only furniture. But the gaucho seldom sat anywhere save astride a horse, and horses were so numerous that any traveler could rope one for his use and not be considered a horse thief. The women, once they were won by the *payadores* songs, were kept busy shearing the sheep, milking cows, weaving coarse cloth, planting Indian corn in small patches, and rearing the children. But this was a life that ended by the 1880s with the fencing of the great estates, the coming of that same barbed wire that changed America's own West, and the introduction of placid, pedigreed cattle fattened in stalls on corn and alfalfa.

*Argentine life as it moved
from the pampas to the cities*

Inadvertently the gaucho was working to bring prosperity via the beef business to the cities that he scorned. Trade statistics for the 1850s indicate a yearly increase of 50,000 in the exportation of hides out of Buenos Aires. Sarmiento in 1845 wrote that Buenos Aires was destined some day to become "the most gigantic city of the two Americas" because she was "the mistress of navigation of a hundred rivers . . . the outlet of thirteen provinces." At that time the city had a population of 100,000, but by 1890 it was a luxurious city of 668,000 with parks and boulevards already "illumined by electricity." Well-to-do families who had grown rich on the pampas were building marble villas in the new suburbs, but the city poor, descendants of gauchos and European immigrants who did the work of docks and packing houses, lived in crowded tenements and one-room shanties.

Sarmiento was distressed in the 1850's because the grazing provinces had so few urban centers. In the province of Córdoba, he noted, "of 160,000 souls scarcely 20,000 dwell in its only city." Rosario had started a regular stagecoach service by 1860 and a boat service on the Paraná to attract trade from Asunción. But few of the sophistications Sarmiento admired found their way into the back country. And when, on the one hand, the wagon-freight charges were added to the price the inland farmers paid for city-made goods, and, on the other hand, they received 30 per cent less profit on their hides, tallow, and horsehair than farmers near Buenos Aires, it was no wonder the inland provinces hated the political power of the port.

But education and culture expanded as both port and inland towns began to grow. In 1850, Argentina had 205 public schools, with 12,000 pupils and 241 teachers, while 35 years later it had 1,900 schools, with 4,080 teachers and 164,600 students. Illiteracy in 1868 was 78.8 per cent; in 1893, it was only 54.4 per cent. The leading Argentine university was still the old colonial one of Córdoba, but the University of Buenos Aires was soon to rival it. In 1870, Sarmiento traveled from one to the other by a newly opened railroad to dedicate an astronomical observatory he had presented to Córdoba. By 1890, Buenos Aires had 15 modern theaters and concert halls in which European and local troupes presented the most sophisticated of current plays and the most classical of operas—something which a generation earlier would have delighted the progressive soul of Sarmiento.

It is Domingo Faustino Sarmiento (1811–1888) who ranks as the best prose writer of the period. Most of his fame rests on his *The Life of Juan Facundo Quiroga,* published in 1834, which is a biographical study of a corrupt gaucho politician in whose province Sarmiento was born. Subtitled *Civilization and Barbarism,* the book contains much of Sarmiento's progressive philosophy, his criticism of the backward though colorful gaucho era, and his forecast of future greatness for Buenos Aires.

Esteban Echevarría (1805–1851) introduced romanticism in Argentina in his *La Cautiva*—although his unfinished novel, *The Slaughterhouse,* is considered his masterpiece. José Mármol (1817–1871) wrote a romantic novel, *Amalia,* in which the heroine was too sweet and the villain too black, but it courageously described conditions in Buenos Aires under Rosas and earned for him the title of "Rosas' Poetic Hangman" because it served the cause of the opposition party. Juan Bautista Alberdi (1810–1884), one of South America's most profound political thinkers, is remembered as the philosopher behind the Constitution of 1853.

And there was always poetry about politics and against dictators, written surreptitiously and circulated in the "underground." But as conditions became more stable, the urge to write such poetry seemed to diminish. Poets in the latter half of the 1800s copied European writing fashions without infusing into their work any of the "breath of the New World." A notable exception is Luis L. Domínguez (1819–1898) whose poem, *El Ombú,* is written in praise of the one tree that grows natively on the pampas, a poem today loved and memorized by schoolchildren.

> *Every territory on earth has a conspicuous feature:*
> *Brazil, its glowing sun, Peru, its mines of silver,*
> *Montevideo, its hill.*
> *Buenos Aires—my beautiful country*
> *Has its magnificent pampas,*
> *The pampas have the ombú.*

> *. . . There are no leafy groves there,*
> *But sometimes there appears on the top of a little hill,*
> *Which rises so that it can be dimly seen,*
> *The ombú, solemn, lonely, of elegant, graceful growth,*
> *Which rises to the clouds like a light house of the sea.*[2]

[2] Translated by Alice Stone Blackwell, in *Some Spanish American Poets* (New York: Appleton-Century, 1929), pp. 338–39. Reprinted by permission of the University of Pennsylvania Press, copyright owners.

The cities were growing into the pampas and other trees were planted which dwarfed the native *ombú*. Railroads were being built and blooded cattle were being introduced and refrigerated ships were being developed to preserve and ship the tender steaks to the world market. This is the true "revolution" of Argentina, the change in agriculture and shipping that took place by 1900.

wheat and meat: the bases for Argentina's prosperity

In 1872 a system of artificial refrigeration had been invented; in 1882 a meat-freezing plant was built in Buenos Aires; by 1900 these freezing plants were slaughtering more animals than the old salt-meat and hide works had handled. Salting plants had needed thick-hided cattle whose stringy flesh salted easily and whose hide was the greatest value. Freezing plants wanted high-grade meat, tender and fat. A new type of steer was already being raised on the pampas to meet this need, steers bred from Hereford and Angus stock brought in from England. In the same decade wire fencing came to herd in the purebreds. Alfalfa was planted to feed them; the open range was reduced to farming land. Not gaucho riders but tenant farmers were needed, tenants who would settle down to raise corn and alfalfa for the fat cattle and wheat for the new flour mills of Buenos Aires. To handle the trade in meat and wheat, Buenos Aires built new docks in 1889 and dredged the channel of the Plata to meet them. From the port 6,000 miles of railroad stretched across the pampas by 1890, calling for a capital investment of $53,000,000, much of it British capital, much of it contracted under the guidance of an American engineer named William Wheelright. The towns of the hinterland were now connected with the port and the long wagon hauls ended.

Who were the people doing all this new work, ploughing land, building railroads, planting alfalfa, freezing beef carcasses? Leaders like Alberdi, Sarmiento, and Mitre knew that thrifty, hard-working farmers and artisans must come to these sparsely settled temperate lands of South American from temperate Europe. In 1876 a law was passed in the Argentine congress providing for "the organizing of immigrants, payment of their passage, and substantial aid after their arrival." There was never free homestead land on the pampas as there was in North America—the great estate owners wanted docile tenant workers, not freeholding neighbors—but for many south Europeans, Italians especially, a Catholic land, without a hard winter, offered more inducement than did the Dakotas or Nebraska. Many Italians came as harvest hands when the wheat lands opened up; they were called *golondrinas*, swallows who went home when summer was over. But two or three harvest seasons decided them: they would stay in the new country and farm the pampas lands as tenants, land so much more fertile than their hilly tenant farms in Italy. More than a million Europeans came to Argentina to settle between 1857 and 1898. In Buenos Aires in 1890, as in

New York or Boston, 25 per cent of the people were foreign-born. Foreigners far outnumbered Argentines in commerce and industry, and contributed to the stable new middle class.

The economic revolution that transformed the pampas took place in the latter half of the 19th century. The influx of European immigrants made Argentina seem more like the United States by 1900 than like any other part of Spanish-speaking South America. A cowboy tradition was passing. A prairie was being fenced in. Scattered nomadic Indians had been herded into remote reservations. Farmland was offered to the immigrants. Swiftly expanding railways were crossing the nation. New scientific methods were producing wheat and beef on the prairie. All in all it seemed like a repetition in the Southern Hemisphere of the Yankees' own story.

The transformation continued until in the last half of the 20th century, the pampas were producing 300 pounds of beef a year per capita, in contrast to 145 pounds per capita in the rich United States. Argentina has 30 head of cattle per person compared with 5 head in the United States. Some 75 per cent of the beef eaten in England over the last three decades has come from Argentina. Meat in cheaper cuts is sent to France and Germany, in Kosher form to Israel, and in cans of corned beef even to beef-rich United States.

Beef raising transformed the pampas into a society of tenant farmers and large estates, with a social hierarchy of beef-raisers, a cultural tradition of stock shows and cattle judging, and a cultural heritage of gaucho song and story. The 1900's saw the revolution on the pampas completed—the fenced-in pastures, the growing of alfalfa for a year-round food supply to keep the beef fat, the coming of windmills and watering troughs so that the pampered cattle need never wander far for water. The scientific breeding of beef cattle, and the importation of Shorthorns, Durhams, Herefords, and Aberdeen Angus from England, was carried on by a closed corporation of the oligarchs, the Rural Society. To compete in the grand championship shows so popular by 1900, the estate-owner's entries had to have pure blood lines and pedigrees registered in the records of the Rural Society. Winning animals in the yearly livestock shows brought 50,000 to 150,000 pesos apiece at exciting public auctions attended by the highest society. In five decades, the weight of individual animals increased 50 per cent. Improved land use permitted 4,000 head to be pastured on ten square miles where 1,000 had been pastured in 1900. One third of the cattle are in the rich province of Buenos Aires where the weather is so mild that the cattle can live outdoors all year round, making the building of frostproof barns unncessary.

To the north, in the provinces of Misiones, Corrientes, and Entre Ríos, *criollo* cattle, the stock descended from cows brought by the Spaniards, are raised for local consumption. In these regions, the hoof and mouth disease is endemic in a mild form. In 1924 this disease in a highly contagious form broke out in the United States' beef-producing regions, and the frantic American cattle-owners persuaded Congress to clap a quarantine on all raw beef imports from mildly infected Argentina. The quarantine has persisted because of American beef-producers' fear of competition of cheaply-raised Argentine imports, and has produced more hard feeling against the United States in Argentina than any of the so-called acts of "imperialism."

Argentines consume more fresh milk, butter, and cheese than all the rest of Latin America, for there are many dairy farms close to the port city. Well-kept truck gardens produce fresh fruits and vegetables for the Buenos Aires markets. Argentina leads the United States in corn export—even though its aborigines never did learn to plant the corn of the Maya and Aztecs. It exports more wool and frozen mutton than any country except Australia and New Zealand. This was made possible after 1902 when a territorial dispute over Patagonia with Chile was settled and Basque and Scottish shepherds came to wind-swept territories of Patagonia and Chubut to care for thousands of head of the best wool-producing breeding stock. In wheat export, Argentina is second only to Canada. A powerful "oligarchy" of wheat ranchers in the district around Rosario produce the wheat by means of the labor of tenant farmers. Rosario has docks on the Paraná accessible to steamers of 10,000 tons and is one of the world's chief wheat-shipping ports. In the wheat and corn belts, rice and barley are grown, as well as flax for linseed oil. Of the linseed oil used in the world's paint industry, 80 per cent comes from Argentina.

North and West of the Plata area sugar and cotton thrive; the Tucumán region produces sugar for the urban population, while the Argentine Chaco is now producing enough cotton to feed Buenos Aires' new textile mills and to export considerable quantities to English mills as well. Here in the north are vast national forests where hardwoods and *quebracho* for tanning are produced under state control. Mendoza located in the Andean piedmont is the center of the "Garden of the Andes," raising grapes, making wine, and producing fruits.

In the southern Andes and the northern semi-tropics there are still forests, which comprise 32 per cent of Argentina's over-all acreage. Another 14 per cent consists of unproductive regions of the Chaco or the middle Andes. Ten per cent of Argentina is in planted crops in corn and wheat and other foods; while the remaining 41 per cent of Argentina's land is the great pasture of the pampas.

Argentina's hopes for industrial importance

Argentina lacks fuel and iron, yet its industrialization has progressed steadily since its first few factories in the 1890's, until today industry employs more people than does agriculture. The major industry is the preparation of meat. Buenos Aires meat-packing plants are as large as any in Chicago; in fact, to the grief of many nationalistic Argentines, the three largest are owned by the same firms as those in Chicago—Armour, Wilson, and Swift. The fourth largest is an English company, Anglo-Argentine, and the single large plant that is Argentine-owned ranks only fifth. Since the meat must be prepared for shipment overseas, the most modern techniques must be used in these giant *frigoríficos,* as the refrigerated packing plants are called. The whole beef-packing industry changed after World War II from emphasis on chilled beef to "deep-freeze" beef and it is no longer necessary to have the carcasses on board the British refrigerated boats within a few days after they have been slaughtered.

Foreign investments have helped build Argentine industry, which now has 500 plants producing agricultural machinery, plows, harvesters, tractors, windmills, and even silos. The railroads and docks were built largely by English capital, but were sold at a loss to Perón and are running now rather inefficiently under government ownership. The investment of the Chicago meat-packers is worth $50 million; other manufacturing plants absorbed a hundred million; and assembly lines for automobiles and farm machinery have accounted for another hundred million. So prosperous *porteños,* tired of using American products from Fords to vacuum cleaners, enthusiastically accepted Perón's Five Year Plan to industrialize Argentina and make the nation self-sufficient in both heavy industry and consumer goods.

Within the decade of the 1960's, Argentina did fulfill the quotas of the Plan in some fields. Textile manufacturing was up 300 per cent over 1940. The manufacture of leather, ceramics, chemicals, medicine, cement, furniture, paper, tires, rubber goods, and processed and packaged foods increased rapidly. A great deal of American capital was "squeezed out" by Perón-aided local industries and by the "tussle over red tape" that the government created for foreign capital, as well as by his demand that profits made in Argentina be kept in pesos and ploughed back into Argentine development. Perón's successors found it necessary to reverse his "anti-American capital" policy and began to woo United States investors.

Plans recently made to deconcentrate the new industry depend on the development of hydroelectric power, the projects for which must be developed in the Andes 600 miles away. Hard coal is not mined in Argentina. The nationally-owned oil wells in the Chaco could not produce one-fourth of Argentina's yearly needs, and geologists searched for oil in Patagonia. Because of the nation's desperate need for oil, President Frondizi made contracts with ten American and British companies in 1958 to continue the search for oil. Within five years under these contracts, and with the development of existing wells and setting up of refineries, Argentina was producing enough oil for local use and saving the burden of spending $300 million a year on imported oil. But the unpopularity of this grant to foreigners helped to lead to Frondizi's downfall. His successor, Dr. Illia, cancelled these contracts and turned the producing wells and refineries over to a group of inexperienced civil servants. Their failure to find great resources, plus financial obligations, made it necessary, within a few years, for Onganía to bring back foreign oil companies to Argentina.

Argentina cannot get along without foreign trade, no matter how successful she is at developing home-consumption industries. Her trade, long centering on England, has shifted since 1939 to the United States—

which is the source of most of Argentina's imports and ranks second in consuming Argentine goods. Much of this trade is now carried in Argentine-owned ships.

the open pampas of the gaucho now filled in

The world-famous, Nicaragua-born poet, Rubén Darío, who had made Argentina his "second motherland," wrote in honor of the 1910 centenary of Argentina's independence a "Hymn to Argentina" in which he exclaimed:

> *Welcome all nations to the new promised land!*
> *Here is the region of El Dorado,*
> *Here is the terrestrial paradise.*
> *Here the longed-for good fortune,*
> *Here the golden fleece.*[3]

He appealed to dissatisfied Italians, Jews, Spaniards, Swiss, Germans, to "all the disinherited of the earth," to come to the "Plata's shores," this "mystic Eden" that promised everyone a full life. How like it is to the appeal in America's Statue of Liberty! Argentina too abounded in stories of immigrants who came in penniless and made millions. There were, of course, a hundred thousand untold stories of not-so-successful tenant farmers on the pampas and struggling factory workers in the city.

Perhaps a million Italian and Spanish farm workers came as *golondrinas* or swallows for three months of harvest labor in the corn and wheat fields during the season of Europe's own winter and returned home in the cheap steerage. But there were millions who stayed to fill in the pampas and build the new barbed wire fences and plant the alfalfa now so necessary for the pedigreed steers. The immigrants also changed Buenos Aires into a fast-growing, industrialized metropolis, stimulating both the middle class and the proletariat to make Argentina the commercial leader of the Southern Hemisphere, and to add greatly to the social and cultural diversity of the nation.

Every 20 years, the population doubled. Some 65 per cent were descendants of Europeans and 30 per cent were European-born. In the 1920's, immigration boomed when postwar conditions in Italy made life particularly difficult. Nearly two million Italians chose to stay in Argentina, as well as nearly a million Spaniards and hundreds of thousands of Swiss, Austrians, and Russians, almost all of them farm and city laborers. Thousands of English businessmen and engineers live in Buenos Aires; German technicians have come in great numbers; Scotch, Welsh, and Basque sheep farmers have found success in Patagonia. Argentines of Italian blood constitute 40 per cent of the nation's population, but they are an Argentinized type, product of the Argentine melting pot. Immigrants are still coming in,

---

[3] Isaac Goldberg, *Studies in Spanish American Literature*, New York, Brentano's, 1920, p. 177.

encouraged again by Argentine government agents in Europe. In the early 1970's, Argentina was about 90 per cent white, 8 per cent mestizo, and one to two per cent Indian. In 1970, the total population exceeded 24 million. Of the 8 million Argentines gainfully employed in 1966, 21 per cent worked in agriculture, 36 per cent in industry, 20 per cent in transportation, and 22 per cent in permanent service.

Though all the governments since Roque Sáenz Peña had talked about free lands for colonizers, and about cheap small holdings on the pampas, those immigrants who came to find such lands were almost always disappointed. The land was already owned, in the large holdings of the cattle barons who saw no advantage in selling off small acreage. Railroads, built by British capital to serve the large ranchers, did not need to bring in small freeholders to settle new lands as did the railroad builders of the United States. Italian immigrants, used to tenancy at home, were satisfied with the larger tenant farms, the better crops, the greater freedom of movement, and the unlimited meat rations they found on the pampas.

The great estate owners heard few complaints against their system. For them the new refrigeration, the better transportation, the improved stock, and the cheap labor had turned the wild pampas of 1850 into one of the world's richest gardens, and they themselves had become one of the world's most prosperous classes. "As rich as an Argentine" became a by-word on the French Riviera, where many Argentine estate-owning families had villas—families who also maintained houses in Buenos Aires, and who visited the palatial mansions on their pampas lands once a year. The hundred wealthiest families owned more than ten million acres among them; 272 individuals and corporations owned one-sixth of Buenos Aires province, 2,000 owned about one-fifth of the total area of Argentina. Many of these *propiedades* or holdings are still held today by family "corporations," interlocked complexities of inheriting sons and cousins, many of whom never see the land. Recent governments have done almost nothing about land distribution.

In the center of such an estate, or *estancia*, is a palatial mansion house, surrounded by thousands of trees artificially planted on the treeless pampas two or three generations before, and now further surrounded by swimming pools, tennis courts, and polo fields. Here an expert overseer maintains a staff of servants in preparedness for the rare occasions when the owners visit, and supervises the villages of the tenants who care for the hundreds of thousands of head of beef and dairy cattle and sheep, and perhaps a thousand race horses and polo ponies on the stud-farm.

In this feudal organization, the day laborers received in the 1960s the equivalent of about $40 a month in cash—a ranch hand's wage three generations ago in the American West. Planted crops are cared for by tenants or sharecroppers, who use the owners' machinery, receive meat rations, garden plots, small adobe dwellings, free horses, and elementary education for their children from the owners—a life better than that of most European peasants or that of peon farmers in several other parts of Latin America. Such alfalfa land was often broken in from native grass pasture by hiring tenants to plow and plant wheat for four or five seasons. Then alfalfa, which has to be replanted only once in six or seven years, would replace the wheat, and day laborers the tenants. These tenants, now footloose, might move on into the corn belt to farm 150 acres for another owner. Always living in adobe houses, usually comfortless and dirt-floored, never feeling any pride in or love for the land, the tenant feels little need to improve his community, no civil interest in schools or good roads. His women are tied to drudgery in the fields beside him; his children seldom rise above his station. Unless he is content to live little better than did Martín Fierro in the days of the gaucho riders on the open pampas, the tenant has no "out" save to migrate to the city as an industrial laborer. Tenant migration has caused a farm labor shortage and forced recent governments to urge city workers back to the country. But some agricultural workers have achieved success in the city and have joined the middle class. This class of shopkeepers, small owners, clerks, and professional people is rapidly growing in post-Perón Argentina and is estimated to include about 45 per cent of Argentines today. At the top, the rich landowners, their estates still undivided though their political power is largely ended, remain Argentina's aristocracy.

urban living conditions

Of more than 23,000,000 Argentines, over 9,000,000 live in the modern Buenos Aires metropolitan area, making it the largest Latin city in the world. Six million live in the "rural areas" and another 6,000,000 in towns of 10,000 or more away from the Plata mouth. Thus even the provinces of Argentina are more urbanized than most other Latin American countries, though none of the other cities is more than 15 per cent as large as Buenos Aires. Córdoba, seat of Spanish colonial culture before Buenos Aires was born, center of the cloistered university life, and now heavily industrialized with 846,000 inhabitants, still feels itself superior to the "port." Even the language sounds different in the two cities. The nineteenth century rivalry between port and provinces continues to exist, though in milder form.

The families who own the largest estates have set the style in Buenos Aires for fifty years—200 families which have intermarried to a confusing degree, families of old creole stock with a sprinkling of Italian or English names. Devoutly Catholic, yet cosmopolitan in their interest in things European and in their knowledge of French language and literature, they have held to social castes and have controlled politics and politicians, save only Irigoyen and Perón. They maintain exclusive clubs, set fashions, and promote horse racing and particularly polo, a rich man's game even in Argentina, that land of wiry horses. A "new-rich" class has come into being with the recent industrial development. Its members do not play polo with the oligarchs, but support the many soccer teams which play in international competition with the soccer-minded Brazilians and Uruguayans. They maintain swank apartments in town, villas on the local beaches near Mar del

Plata, and buy the automobiles now finished in the Argentine assembly plants from American-made parts.

The white-collar workers of Buenos Aires seldom own cars; they are the commuter class, living in the suburbs and riding daily in and out of the city on the crowded, government-run buses and the new subway trains, now propelled by Japanese-made electric engines. This class of society was caught between the aristocrats and the Perón-pampered *descamisados*. It is traditional that a white-collar worker be a *camisado*, that he wear a white shirt and a neat black business suit to his poorly paid job, even though he takes off coat and shirt for a white smock as soon as he gets to work, for he can afford but one suit every two years. Though he can pay for two trips a day back and forth in order to have his three-hour lunch at home, though he can afford American movies, good books, a radio, or even a television, he still lives in substandard housing; the high city rent is his biggest problem. Perón added to this class by creating a very large number of positions for new bureaucrats, and thus tied to himself many of the white-collar workers. To cut down this heavy expense of civic workers has been one of the problems of the post-Perón presidents. The cost of living and inflation continued to spiral in the late 1960's in spite of attempts to freeze rents and prices, and the peso continued to fall in value.

In La Boca, slum section of Buenos Aires, there used to live as crowded and underprivileged a mass of stevedores and factory workers as in any city in the Western Hemisphere. In the 1950s these workers, numbered among the *descamisados*, were the political tools by which Perón's government remained in power, and hence they were privileged above other Latin American workers. Higher-paid than any other workers in South America, save those in Venezuelan oil fields, these workers took vacations at the seashore at Mar del Plata for the first time. They also began paying for social security, for pensions, health and accident benefits—not receiving as much as Perón had promised, but more than they would have dreamed of a decade before.

Buenos Aires, in 1880 a big provincial town, sprawling, unsanitary, and unattractive, is today one of the ten largest cities of the world—the Paris of the Southern Hemisphere. One Argentine in every four lives there. The city, in which the culture is still Spanish and Catholic to the core, has not kept pace with the population growth, the drift of rural workers to the cities, and the influx of postwar immigrants. There are dwelling units enough to provide one for every four people; large families are no longer the general rule, and young married couples are less prone to live with the old folks. But city planners have been trying for three decades to bring the city up to date. Today the creation of parks and the widening of streets, begun in the 1880s by far-sighted municipal authorities, has continued, making Buenos Aires in this respect a rival of Washington, D.C.

The outskirts are changing too. Thirteen new industrial areas, each centered around one or more new factories, sprang up in the 1950s. Such decentralization goes a long way toward solving the problems of this fast-growing city; workers housed in adequate dwellings near their own factories can go home for their long lunch and yet pay rents within their means. But there are slums in Buenos Aires as in all big Latin American cities. La Boca district itself has been replaced by model housing, but new in-migrants to the cities settled in new shanty towns now called *villas miserías*.

Beyond the busy city, across the park of the Plaza Colón, lies the port, through which flows 80 per cent of all the trade of Argentina. The days of landing in the mud flats in high-wheeled oxcarts seem a millennium ago, not a mere century, at this most modern of harbors, with its electrical equipment and installations worth more than $100,000,000. Ships of all nations and of all sizes come into Buenos Aires; Argentina's own merchant fleet now serves all South America. Railroads and highways from the entire pampas, from Mendoza, from the Bolivian border and from Asunción, Paraguay, route the freight into Buenos Aires port.

This busy and glittering cosmopolitan city has its ordinary share of social problems. For generations social work was done by the ladies of the aristocratic class, or their employees, through charity organizations with Church backing. And then, when Eva Perón was not accepted by the ladies of the aristocracy, she founded her own charity organization backed so lavishly by public money. Today modern procedures have brought other more efficient innovatons—care of the aged through union benefits or employees' pensions, treatment of child delinquents in juvenile courts and "cottage-village" institutions. Pitiful beggars, abject poverty, child criminals are not seen on the streets of Buenos Aires. A National Director of Public Health presides over advanced methods in epidemic control, water and milk inspection, and maternal and child health programs, so that life in the *villas miserías* is better than life in the *favelas* of Rio de Janeiro.

Women themselves have changed. In 1947 women were granted the right to vote as a symbol of the new era. Daughters of the oligarchs go to the theater with their fiancés unaccompanied by family chaperones. Daughters of the new rich go to the university and become lawyers and doctors and social workers. Daughters of white-collar and *descamisado* workers learn to be stenographers; they walk through the city streets unmolested and uncriticized in their new freedom. Divorce is still unacceptable in a deeply Catholic country, but marriages themselves are happier, no longer made entirely by parents for family convenience. The Church itself, never ostentatious in Buenos Aires, where Carnival and Holy Week parades of the Seville type are seldom seen, has always been a behind-the-scenes force in society. However, it has not had the control over education customary in other Latin American countries; Argentina has been a public-school nation since the days of Sarmiento.

Argentine cultural life

Buenos Aires considers itself a highly cultured city, a center of university life, of museums, of symphony orchestras. Its culture is reminiscent of Europe, not of the New World. Argentines, chic, sophisticated, have their eyes on whatever is the cultural trend in Paris, not on the culture patterns of the "crass barbarians" of North America. They consider themselves a "white race" and their cartoonists tend to lampoon the darker-skinned nations of Latin America. Many Argentines feel themselves superior to Brazilians and Mexicans and Paraguayans, and this superiority is often taught from the primary grades up. A visitor in Argentina would certainly find no *Indianismo* of the kind he would find in Mexico.

Greater interest seems to be shown in well-performed classical-style European music by the wealthy classes in Argentina than by those in the United States. The reversal of summer and winter makes it possible for the finest soloists, opera troupes and orchestras to appear in Buenos Aires for a brilliant musical season after they are through with their European bookings. Many European artists prefer an appearance in Buenos Aires, perhaps with stops in Montevideo and Rio de Janeiro, to a schedule in the United States. The Argentines regard their great Colón Theater as "the most important opera house in the Western Hemisphere."

Copying new music trends in Paris, a modernist group formed a *Grupo Renovación* in 1929 to create new classical-style and "absolute" music. This musical revolution was led by two brothers, José María and Juan José Castro. Juan José Castro (1895–   ), the conductor of the Buenos Aires Philharmonic Orchestra and a guest conductor in the United States, composed every type of music save opera and launched many young modernists by playing their works. His brother, José María Castro (1892–   ), a cellist, was the leader of a chamber music society in the 1940's and 1950's and composer of works for the cello. Juan Carlos Paz, an early co-founder of the *Grupo Renovación*, developed an interest in ultra-modern music. The students of these three innovators progressed from classical European music styles and ultra-nationalist themes to newer and more experimental styles, and today musicians like Mario Davidovsky, Armando Krieger, and Antonio Tauriello are turning Buenos Aires into "the most important center of musical creativity in Latin America."

Best known in this group as a world figure is Alberto Ginastera whose first compositions were nationalistic pieces called *The High Plains* and *The Estancia,* but who more recently has composed pieces entitled simply *Second Quartet for Strings* and *Concerto for Piano,* described as written with "dodecaphonic hues and universalist trappings" to mark a milestone in New World composition." Writing with a grant from the city of Buenos Aires, he produced in 1964 an opera called *Don Rodrigo* which was the first operatic work out of Latin America to receive worldwide attention since *O Guaraní.* It concerned the last Visigoth king of Spain whose reign was ended by the Arab invasion. But the musical score, calling for many new types of instruments, including pealing bells strung throughout the theater and operated electronically, set a new pattern for opera music. The success of *Don Rodrigo* was followed by *Bomarzo* and led to the commissioning of *Beatrix Cenci* for the inauguration of the Kennedy Center in Washington in 1971. Ginastera, as head of the Latin American Institute for Advanced Musical Studies in the early 1970's, trained in composition twelve "music fellows" a year from other Latin American countries, whose music is printed in Buenos Aires, for no other Latin American capital has adequate music publishing houses.

Argentine composers of the serious "new" movement are well-known in Europe, and Spain's greatest modern composer, Manuel de Falla, spent many years in Buenos Aires where some of his best works were first played. The love of music in daily life was enhanced in Argentina by the Italians. American jazz dance music came to the country via Paris and has monopolized the time of many little café orchestras. But to find the real gaucho music, the songs of the *payadores,* the visitor has to search out places catering to tourists. The tango, the best known of the country's dance forms, has been replaced in local popularity by two-steps and even "rock and roll."

To promote nationalistic music, Perón ordered every radio musical program to play at least one piece by an Argentine composer, and he decreed that each legitimate theater company present two native Argentine plays for every foreign play given. Aramburu removed such controls, and today the Argentine theater is flourishing. Both the theater and the very prosperous movie industry do a great deal with gaucho themes from Argentina's history.

The Walt Disney of Argentina is Molina Campos who kept alive the nostalgia for the pampas life into mid-century by his humorous drawings of gauchos and horses. They helped him to become financially the most successful artist in Buenos Aires. Bernalde de Quirós is known as a formal painter of the old-time gaucho in his baggy trousers, with the white lace *chiripás* and the bright red poncho of the Rosas period. From the point of view of world renown, Argentina's best artist has been Benito Quinquela Martín, a foundling himself who grew up to be a coal heaver, who has immortalized the life of the poor stevedores of the La Boca slums. Self-taught in art as well as in letters, Quinquela Martín painted his own people and brought prosperity to himself and to his street in La Boca where today in a free art school children of the stevedores who show talent are trained in a waterfront studio founded by Quinquela Martín.

Twenty newspapers are published daily in Buenos Aires, counting the two giants already mentioned, *La Prensa* and *La Nación. La Prensa,* founded in 1869 by José Carlos Paz and remaining in the hands of his family, was financially successful, pro-democratic and pro-United States. It resembled the *London Times* in its neat appearance and the *New York Times* in its prestige and coverage. Then Eva Perón forced it to close. After the fall of Perón it was returned to Gainza Paz, current member of the founding family, and resumed publication in 1956. *La Nación* the rival newspaper, was founded by Bartolomé Mitre the year after he retired from the presidency, and was curtailed but not closed out by the Perón policy. In variety and number of magazines for sale, Buenos Aires newsstands seem to compare favorably with those in the United States, displaying literary reviews, women's magazines, professional magazines, trade journals, and learned reviews especially in the field of history.

In the production of books, Buenos Aires is now, according to the president of the Argentine Publishers' Association, "the leading publishing center of books in Spanish." Of all the nations in the world, only the United States published more books in the last decade. Most Argentine books come out in paperback editions, but these same little volumes can be seen in bookstores from Chile to Southern California and Texas, so Argentina is one country of Latin America where a writer of books can support himself by writing and does not need to hold a teaching or clerical job on the side. Argentine films, like those of modern Mexico, are also distributed throughout the Hemisphere.

The steady reduction of the percentage of illiteracy reflects the expanding culture of the Argentine masses. Public education is free and compulsory for children from six to fourteen years of age. Sarmiento's methods of free public elementary education make Argentina's school system one of the best in Latin America. Entrance into most trades requires a certificate of sixth grade course completion. Secondary education is entirely college preparatory or technical in the English and French pattern.

The universities of Argentina are a far cry from the small classical university at Córdoba a century ago. The six universities are all nationally owned, the largest at Buenos Aires, the second at La Plata, and the smaller institutions in the provinces of Tucumán and Cuyo, and at Santa Fé and Córdoba. The student body is as interested in politics as is the average American student body. Although traditionally Argentine students have had a large part in campus policy-making, all self-government in the universities was stopped by Onganía after street fights between police and students and faculty groups.

The six universities have 36 different campuses, for each subject-matter division is still in a separate building, across town, perhaps, from other "faculties." Professors are usually part-time lecturers who may be practicing lawyers or doctors or even members of Congress. Argentina's intellectual elite is heard in non-academic as well as academic circles at home and abroad. Second generation Argentines from many backgrounds are found in its ranks—for example, the Italian José Ingenieros, sociologist; the German Alejandro Korn, philosopher; and the French *literateur*-historian Paul Groussac.

Argentine literature, many critics feel, leads the Spanish-speaking world. Just as Martín Fierro, the gaucho, stood out as a literary figure in the 19th century, so does another gaucho in the 20th century, Don Segundo Sombra, hero of a novel by that name by Ricardo Güiraldes (1866–1927). The author lived among gauchos as a youth; his father was an *estancia* owner. The central character of this famous 1929 novel was a footloose singer and horse-breaker, prototype of all gauchos; and the narrator of the story was a young boy who worships him, a sort of Argentine Huckleberry Finn. The two of them wander on the pampas, breaking horses for hire, working cattle on long drives, and all the while Don Segundo solioquizes about life and draws upon his store of the folklore developed in the days of the unsettled pampas. In the end the boy comes into an inheritance and leaves to learn city ways. In a way he symbolizes modern Argentina, nostalgia for the past, dramatizing the adventure on the open road, loving its free life, yet in maturity turning away from that life. Realistic and down-to-earth, the book is an Argentine rather than a European product.

The gaucho theme, so dominant in literature and drama in 1900, is still in evidence today. The best remembered drama of the first decade of the 20th century is a stage success by playwright Florencio Sanchez (1875–1910) entitled *My Kid* which told the story of a struggle between a gaucho father and a city-educated son. In the 1920's, boisterous gaucho novels were popular. There was nothing nostalgic in the rough, tough life of the gaucho and back country people portrayed in the novels of Benito Lynch (1885–1951), but they were being read while their author's classes in literature were being censored at the University of La Plata by Perón's agents. The Zane Grey of Argentina was an ultra-conservative political leader, Gustavo Martínez Zuviría, born in 1883, whose pen name was Hugo Wast, and who produced fiction about horses, cowhands, cattle farms and frontier life that has more literary merit and actual realism than their American counterparts. His books, such as the *House of the Ravens*, *Black Valley*, and *Stone Desert*, read in translation, give the North American reader the "feel" of Argentine back-country life.

Today it is realistic novels dealing with social problems that predominate. Manuel Gálvez, for one, born in 1882, was listed as the outstanding Western Hemisphere candidate for the Nobel Prize in literature on two different occasions. His novels have dealt with subjects such as rural teachers, the influence of the Church on university education, and the life of prostitutes in Buenos Aires. Many other writers might be mentioned. In the mid-1950's Latin American critics rated Eduardo Mallea (1903–   ), the author of psychological novels with a pessimistic tone, as Argentina's "best."

Recently a Buenos Aires newspaper took a poll on reading tastes in the city and found that poetry occupied the lowest place on the list; and it concluded that there were more writers than readers of poetry. It seemed almost incredible in a country in which since the 16th century statesmen, journalists, teachers, and priests liked to write verses. But in Argentina, as in France and Spain, there arose a school of young writers who wrote poetry for poetry's sake. They were influenced by the great Nicaraguan poet Rubén Darío—who was himself practically an Argentine after the turn of the century. Calling themselves the *Ultra-istas*, they pursued the "Absolute" in poetry. Listed as Argentina's finest poet was Darío's close friend, Leopoldo Lugones (1874–1938), an avowed socialist and ardent nationalist, active in the fields of education and international intellectual cooperation. His poems in English translation lose their music and novelty of form and seem very abstract to the American student.

Argentina's greatest living novelist and poet in the early 1970's was Jorge Luis Borges who, born in 1899, was in the early 1970's old, blind, and melancholy. As a young man he had taken over the leadership of the *Ultra-istas* on the death of Rubén Darío, but in 1971 he was writing nostalgic short stories about life on the pampas. A book of his stories, published in

English under the title, *The Aleph and Other Stories,* links the Greece of the wandering Homer to the Argentina of the wandering gaucho. Returning in imagination to the shepherd life of the ancient Greeks, he identifies in spirit with Homer, also old and isolated by blindness. In the spring of 1971, in São Paulo, Brazil, he was awarded the first Inter-American literature prize of $25,000 in recognition of his genius.

READINGS: ARGENTINA

Adams, R. N., ed., *Social Change in Latin America Today* (1960).

Alexander, R. J., *Communism in Latin America* (1957).

————, *An Introduction to Argentina* (1969).

————, *Labor Relations in Argentina, Brazil, and Chile* (1962).

————, *Perón Era* (1952).

Amadeo, S. P., *Argentine Constitutional Law* (1943).

Arciniegas, G., ed., *The Green Continent,* trans. H. de Onís, (1944).

Astiz, C. A., ed., *Latin American International Politics: Ambitions, Capabilities, and the National Interest of Mexico, Brazil and Argentina* (1968).

Baily, S. L., *Labor, Nationalism and Politics in Argentina* (1967).

Bank of London and South America, *The Prebisch Plan* (1955).

Barager, J. R., et al., *Why Perón Came to Power* (1968).

————, *Perón and the Argentine Democratic Parties, 1943–1946* (1972).

Bernstein, H., *Modern and Contemporary Latin America* (1952).

Blanksten, G. I., *Perón's Argentina* (1953).

Box, P. H., *Origins of the Paraguayan War* (2 vols., 1929).

Bourne, R., *Political Leaders in Latin America* (1970).

Braden, S., *Diplomats and Demagogues: The Memoirs of Spruille Braden* (1971).

Bruce, J., *Those Perplexing Argentines* (1954).

Bunkley, A. W., *Life of Sarmiento* (1952).

————, ed., *A Sarmiento Anthology* (1948).

Burgin, M., *Economic Aspects of Argentina Federalism, 1820–1852* (1946).

Cady, J. F., *Foreign Intervention in the Rio de La Plata, 1838–1850* (1929).

Campbell, A. B., *The Battle of the River Plate* (1940).

Carr, R., ed., *Latin American Affairs. St. Anthony's Papers No. 22* (1970).

Chase, G., *Contemporary Art in Latin America* (1970).

Cochrane, T. C., and R. E. Reina, *Entrepreneurship in Argentine Culture* (1962).

Coester, A., *Literary History of Spanish America* (rev. ed., 1928).

Conil Paz, A. A. and G. E. Fenrar, trans. J. J. Kennedy, *Argentina's Foreign Policy: 1930–1962* (1966).

Corbett, C. D., *The Latin American Military as a Socio-Political Force: Case Studies of Bolivia and Argentina* (1972).

Correas, E., *Sarmiento and the United States* (1961).

Cowles, F., *Bloody Precedent* (1952).

Crawford, W. R., *A Century of Latin American Thought* (1944).

Criscenti, J. T., *Argentine Constitutional History, 1810–1852* (1961).

Darwin, C., *Charles Darwin's Diary of the Voyage of the H.M.S. "Beagle,"* ed. N. Barlow (1933).

Davis, T. B., *Carlos de Alvear, Man of Revolution* (1955).

Denis, P., *The Argentine Republic* (1922).

Díaz Alejandro, C. F., *Essays in the Economic History of the Argentine Republic* (1970).

————, *Exchange-Rate Devaluation in a Semi-Industrialized Country— Experience of Argentina, 1955–1961* (1965).

Eidt, R. C., *Pioneer Settlement in Northeast Argentina* (1971).

Englekirk, J. E., et al., *Outline History of Spanish American Literature* (3rd ed., 1965).

Fagen, R. R. and L. A. Cornelius, eds., *Political Power in Latin America: Seven Confrontations* (1970).

Fernández, J. A., *The Political Elite in Argentina* (1970).

Ferns, H. S., *Argentina* (1969).

————, *Britain and Argentina in the Nineteenth Century* (1960).

Ferrer, A., trans. M. M. Urquidi, *Argentine Economy* (1967).

Fienup, D. F., et al., *The Agricultural Development of Argentina* (1969).

Fillol, T. P., *Social Factors in Economic Development: The Argentine Case* (1961).

Fitts, D., ed., *Anthology of Contemporary Latin American Poetry* (1942).

Flores, M., *The Woman and the Whip* (1952).

Ford, A. G., *The Gold Standard, 1880–1914: Britain and Argentina* (1962).

Foster, W. D. and R. F., *Research Guide in Argentine Literature* (1970).

Gibson, H., *History and Present State of the Sheep-Breeding Industry in the Argentine Republic* (1893).

Goldwert, M., *Democracy, Militarism and Nationalism in Argentina, 1933– 1966* (1972).

Gordon, W. G., *The Economy of Latin America* (1950).

————, *Political Economy of Latin America* (1965).

Greenup, R. and I., *Revolution before Breakfast: Argentina, 1941–1946* (1947).

Haigh, R. M., *Martin Güemes: Tyrant or Tool* (1968).

Haigh, S., *Sketches of Buenos Ayres, Chile and Peru* (1831).

Hamill, H. M., Jr., *Dictatorship in Latin America* (1965).

Hanson, S. G., *Argentine Meat and the British Market* (1938).

Haring, C. H., *Argentina and the United States* (1941).

————, *South American Progress* (1934).

Head, F. B., *Journey Across the Pampas and among the Andes* (repr. ed., G. H. Gardiner) (1967).

Henríquez Ureña, P., *Literary Currents of Latin America* (1945).

Hernández, José, *The Gaucho Martín Fierro*, trans. Walter Owen (1936), another ed. trans. by C. E. Ward (1968).

Herring, H., *Good Neighbors* (1941).

Horowitz, I. L., *Masses in Latin America* (1970).

Houston, J. A., *Latin America in the United Nations* (1956).

Hudson, W. H., *Far Away and Long Ago* (1918).

————, *Green Mansions* (1943).

————, *Tales of the Pampas* (1939).

Humphreys, R. A., *Evolution of Modern Latin America* (1947).

Imaz, J. L. de, *Los Que Mandan*, trans. C. A. Astiz (1970).

Ireland, G., *Boundaries, Possessions and Conflicts in South America* (1938).

Jefferson, M., *Peopling the Argentine Pampas* (1926).

Jeffrey, W. H., *Mitre and Argentina* (1952).

————, *Mitre and Urquiza: A Chapter in the Unification of Argentina* (1952).

Johnson, H. K., et al., *Argentina's Mosaic of Discord 1966–1969* (1969).

Johnson, J. J., *Military and Society in Latin America* (1954).

————, *Political Change in Latin America* (1958).

Jones, T. B., *South America Rediscovered* (1949).

Joseph, R., *Argentine Diary* (1944).

Joslin, D., *A Century of Banking in Latin America: Bank of London and South America Limited, 1862–1962* (1962).

Kelchner, W. H., *Latin American Relations with the League of Nations* (1926).

Kennedy, J. J., *Catholicism, Nationalism and Democracy in Argentina* (1958).

Kirkpatrick, F. A., *History of the Argentine Republic* (1931).

Kirkpatrick, J., *Leader and Vanguard in Mass Society: A Study of Perónist Argentina* (1971).

King, J. A., *Twenty-four Years in the Argentine Republic* (reprint 1971).

Kroeber, C. L., *Growth of Shipping Industry in the Rio de La Plata, 1794–1850* (1957).

Levene, R., *History of Argentina*, trans. W. S. Robertson (1937).

Lichtblau, M. L., *Argentine Novel in the Nineteenth Century* (1959).

Lieuwen, E., *Arms and Politics in Latin America* (rev. ed., 1961).

————, *Generals vs. Presidents: Neomilitarism in Latin America* (1964).

Lipp, S., *Three Argentine Frontiers* (1969).

Luper, A. T., *Music of Argentina* (1942).

Macdonald, A. F., *Government of the Argentine Republic* (2nd ed., 1954).

Main, M. F., *Woman with the Whip: Eva Perón* (1952).

Martin, P. A., *Latin America and the War* (1925).

McGann, T. F., *Argentina: The Divided Land* (1965).

————, *Argentina, United States and the Inter-American System, 1880–1914* (1958).

Mecham, J. L., *Church and State in Latin America* (rev. ed., 1966).

————, *Survey of United States–Latin American Relations* (1965).

————, *The United States and Inter-America Security* (1961).

Nichols, M., *The Gaucho* (1942).

————, *Sarmiento* (1940).

North, J., *Civil-Military Relations in Argentina, Chile and Peru* (1966).

Owen, F., *Perón: His Rise and Fall* (1957).

Paito, J. A., *Argentina, 1930–1960* (1961).

Paz, A., and G. Ferrari, *Argentine Foreign Policy, 1930–1962*, trans. Kennedy (1966).

Peffer, E. L., *Foot and Mouth Disease in United States Policy* (1962).

Pendle, G., *Argentina* (3rd ed., 1963).

Perón, E., *My Mission in Life* (1953).

————, *Writings of Eva Perón* (1955).

Perón, J. D., *Theory and Complete Doctrine of General Perón* (1946).

————, *Voice of Perón* (1950).

Peters, H. E., *The Foreign Debt of the Argentine Republic* (1934).

Peterson, H. F., *Argentina and the United States, 1810–1960* (1964).

Phelps, D. M., *Migration of Industry to South America* (1936).

Phelps, V. E., *International Economic Position of Argentina* (1938).

Pike, F. B., ed., *Latin American History* (1969).

Potash, R. A., *The Army and Politics in Argentina, 1928–1945* (1969).

Rennie, Y. E., *Argentine Republic* (1945).

Richardson, R. L., *Florencio Sanchez and the Argentine Theatre* (1933).

Rippy, J. F., *Latin America and the Industrial Age* (1944).

Robertson, J. P., *Letters on South America: Comprising Travels on the Banks of the Parana and Rio de La Plata* (1843; repr. 1971).

Romero, J. L., *History of Argentine Political Thought* (1963).

Ronning, C. N., *Law and Politics in Inter-America Security* (1963).

Rowe, L. S., *Federal System of the Argentine Republic* (1921).

Sarmiento, D. F., *Facundo,* trans. Mrs. Horace Mann (1st publication, 1845); (many editions).

————, *Travels in the United States,* trans. M. A. Rockland (1970).

Schutter, C. H., *The Development of Education in Argentina, Chile and Uruguay* (1943).

Scobie, J. R., *Argentina: A City and a Nation* (1964).

————, *Revolution on the Pampas: A Social History of Argentine Wheat, 1860–1910* (1965).

————, *The Struggle for Nationhood: Argentina, 1852–1962* (1964).

Shea, D. R., *The Calvo Clause* (1955).

Silbert, K. H., *The Conflict Society: Reaction and Revolution in Latin America* (1961).

Smith, O. E., *Yankee Diplomacy: United States Intervention in Argentina* (1953).

Smith, P. H., *Politics and Beef in Argentina: Patterns of Conflict and Change* (1969).

Snow, P. J., *Argentine Political Parties and the 1966 Revolution* (1968).

————, *Argentine Radicalism* (1965).

Solberg, C., *Immigration and Nationalism: Argentina and Chile 1890–1914* (1969).

Taylor, C. C., *Rural Life in Argentina* (1948).

Tinker, E. L., *The Horsemen of the Americas* (1953).

————, *Life and Literature of the Pampas* (1961).

Tomasek, R. D., ed., *Latin American Politics, Studies of the Contemporary Scene* (rev. ed., 1970).

Torres Rieseco, A., *Epic of Latin American Literature* (rev. ed., 1946).

Turner, T. A., *Argentina and Argentinians: Notes and Impressions of a Five Year Sojourn in the Argentine Republic, 1885–1890* (1892).

Waldo, F., ed., *Tales from the Argentines,* trans. A. Brenner (1950).

Waltar, P. J. *Student Politics in Argentina* (1968).

Wedell, A. W., *Introduction to Argentine* (1939).

Weil, F., *Argentina Riddle* (1944).

Whitaker, A. P., *Argentina* (1964).

————, *Argentina Upheaval* (1956).

————, *Nationalism in Latin America* (1962).

————, *United States and Argentina* (1954).

White, J. W., *Argentina, the Life Story of a Nation* (1942).

Wilgus, A. C., ed., *Argentina, Brazil, and Chile Since Independence* (1935).

————, *South American Dictators* (1937).

Williams, J. H., *Argentine International Trade Under Inconvertible Paper Money, 1880–1900* (1920).

Wythe, G., *Industry in Latin America* (2nd ed., 1949).

chapter 24

CHILEAN PROGRESS AS A EUROPEANIZED NATION

"Something like a synthesis of the planet is fulfilled in the geography of Chile," wrote Gabriela Mistral, famous Chilean poetess and Nobel Prize winner for literature. "It starts in the desert, which is like beginnning with sterility that loves no man. It is humanized in the valleys. It creates a home for living beings in the ample fertile agricultural zone, it takes on a grandiose sylvan beauty at the end of the continent as if to finish with dignity, and finally crumbles, offering half life, half death, in the sea."[1] It is this range of geography which created Chile's modern political and economic life. The sterile desert has produced nitrates and copper which in turn have created a politically conscious mining proletariat and an investment of foreign capital; the "ample fertile valley" provides the setting for Latin America's standard struggle between landowners and peasants; the "sylvan beauty at the end of the continent" has been a new frontier for European colonization and the attendant problems. The combinations and interplay of these three social and economic groupings have given Chile a progressive, indeed a radical, outlook, a modern spirit, an urge forward, confined as she is by her geography, by the coast and narrow valleys and steep escarpment.

[1] Gabriela Mistral, "My Country," *United Nations World* (May, 1950), p. 51.

the new nation in the making

As in most other parts of Spanish America, the revolution that won independence was a creole revolution. The creoles supplanted the *chapetones* but retained their characteristics throughout the 19th century. At the close of the colonial period, Chile had about half a million inhabitants, among them perhaps 100,000 usually hostile Araucanian Indians. At the top was the oligarchy of conservative creole landowners who made Chile almost a feudal society. Nearly everyone else was dependent upon them, in a life that was based chiefly on agriculture with the central valley dominant. Santiago, the capital, had about 30,000 people, and no other city of over 5,000 existed. Industrious Basques and northern Spaniards began to immigrate in large numbers before 1830, rising to be shopkeepers and merchants. Though more liberal-minded than the rural landlords, they did not like anarchy, and they joined with the conservatives to keep the peace with a strong, stable government. Thus the white creole landowners and the merchants worked hand in hand, and there was less city-versus-country difficulty in Chile than elsewhere.

The stability did not come with independence, however. Chile, too, had its years of chaos and *caudillismo,* though they were over by 1831. Torn between the two conflicting influences of successful revolt in Buenos Aires and the ultra-royalist feelings of Lima, the isolated frontier province of Chile had had its creole rebels and its royalist factions in the period from 1810 to 1814. In 1818, a year after San Martín won the battle of Chacabuco, Chilean independence was proclaimed. Now Bernardo O'Higgins, who fought for San Martín, was the accepted provisional ruler of Chile, while Chilean troops and ships went north to fight in Peru.

In the emergency O'Higgins called himself Supreme Dictator and ruled with a cabinet or "advisory senate" of five members, which he himself appointed from the various regions of Chile. He continued this rule even after a "constitution" was written in 1822, for that document extended his personal dictatorship for another ten years. O'Higgins forbade cockfighting, gambling, religious processions, and games of dice. Determined to break the power of the old Spanish aristocrats, who had never accepted him as the legal son of Ambrosio O'Higgins, he launched a campaign against the inheritance of land by primogeniture, the unbroken holding of the vast estates of Chile by the eldest son of the eldest son, and abolished titles of nobility. Sternly enforcing safety of travel on Chile's roads, he created a strong centralized police force, which further antagonized the old aristocracy. With very progressive ideas for education, newspapers, schools, and the construction of a drainage canal outside of flood-threatened Santiago, O'Higgins still planned to achieve these things by personal power alone.

Soldiers in the army had not been paid for months. Their leader, Ramón Freire, led a revolt against O'Higgins when the news of his plan for a ten-year extension of power reached them. The aristocratic landowners joined the disgruntled soldiers, set up a new *junta,* and forced O'Higgins to resign rather than face a civil war. He went into permanent exile in Peru, where he was given an estate as a reward for his part in defeating the Spanish loyalists. Thus the father of independent Chile joined the other great leaders of South American independence, to die in exile, unappreciated by his own countrymen.

The seven years after the fall of O'Higgins are usually looked upon as Chile's age of *caudillismo,* the briefest such experience in any of the Spanish American countries. The "stormy petrel" of the period was the military leader, Ramón Freire, whose soldiers had won the revolt against O'Higgins. He served as chief executive, Supreme Dictator, from 1823 to 1826, and ruled as high-handedly as O'Higgins before him. Successful as a general, Freire captured Chiloé Island, the last stronghold of the Spaniards on the Chilean coast. But he did not solve the financial and political difficulties of the country and was forced to resign in 1827. From 1827 to 1829 there were five revolutions and two more attempts at constitution-making; by 1830 the country was in a state of social and economic as well as political chaos. Finally, at the battle of Lircay, April 17, 1830, a conservative faction under Joaquín Prieto won the country and the presidency. The attempt to impose democracy on Chile had failed, and the period of political experimentation was at an end. Henceforth the executive represented the aristocracy; his government was an oligarchy. But within this ruling class his subjects had equality before the law, taxes were collected and the budget balanced, and the country continued to progress. Thus Chile gained government stability earlier than any other Spanish American country and was the first to be placed firmly upon the road to economic and intellectual progress.

decades of progress in mid-century

Now began a period of the "ten-year presidents," each serving two five-year terms under a constitution of 1833, a practical document which was to last longer than almost any other Latin American constitution. These presidents were not *caudillos* like the military dictators elsewhere, but were conservative statesmen representing the landowning aristocracy and the growing commercial and mine-owning class, the high clergy and the military. They often consciously adopted progressive ideas in promoting industrialization, and they preserved order. The party these leaders represented was called in Chilean history the "bigwigs," the *pelucones,* while their organized opponents, the intellectual liberals, city newspapermen, school leaders, and advocates of religious tolerance, were called the "beardless young ones," the *pipiolos.* As the century advanced, *pelucones* became more modernized in their attitudes, while *pipiolos* became less aggressive, and were to give way eventually to workmen's leaders among the miners and factory laborers.

The actual leader of the generation of the 1830s in Chile was not the President Joaquín Prieto, who had won the civil war of 1830, but his

Minister, jointly of Interior, Foreign Relations, War, and Navy, the businessman Diego Portales. Portales has been called the Alexander Hamilton of Chilean history, for he brought honesty into government, stabilized Chilean finance, protected national industries and agriculture by tariffs, and welcomed English merchants who made Chile into a popular investment area for other Englishmen. His was a regime of authority and force; he gagged the extreme opposition and exiled its leaders, and then with "firmness and tact" he kept the milder *pipiolos* and *pelucones* all in line. A codification of Chilean law was completed in 1855 by the great South American scholar Andrés Bello who spent thirty-six years in Chile and helped found Chile's National University. Valparaiso was improved as a harbor, for Portales meant to make it the chief port of South America's west coast.

When he became involved in a tariff war with Peru over the duties charged by Chile on Peruvian sugar, and by Lima on Chilean wheat, Portales sent ships into open warfare in 1836 against the dictator of Peru. Chilean merchants feared the combination of Peru and Bolivia which dictators of both nations were planning, and were anxious that the Bolivian dictator Santa Cruz should not extend his power into Lima as a rival to Chile's prospering trade. Though *pipiolos* at home opposed the war, Portales and Prieto won it in a series of successful sea battles in the next three years. It was a costly war for the Chileans, however, as they not only lost men and supplies, but Portales as well; he was shot by some Chilean troops who were revolting against the president. Prieto staged a great public funeral for Portales, and in the wave of popular sentiment managed to stay in power himself, successfully ending the war after the decisive victory at Yungay, January 28, 1839. Chile's reputation abroad as a well-organized fighting nation was established by this victory.

The decade of the 1840s was dominated by Manuel Bulnes, a hero of the war, under whom Portales' conservative-progressive ideas were continued. The American engineer William Wheelwright, who built English railways across the Argentine pampas, helped to plan such a railroad in Bulnes' administration, as well as to promote steam navigation on the coast of Chile by means of coal mined in Chile itself. As president, Bulnes extended Chile to the Straits of Magellan. The period of the 1840s was one of progress in all lines. Agriculture developed through the introduction of machinery and the formation of a National Society for Agriculture.

At the same time as railroads and steamboats arrived on the scene, a religious controversy developed in this progressive new nation. The financiers and industrialists were Englishmen; Englishmen were Protestants and wanted to hold open Protestant service and be buried in their own Protestant graveyards. *Pelucones*, deeply fanatic in matters of the Church as were conservatives all over Latin America, opposed these "heretics"; and the Church-state issue in Chile became involved in the dispute over the hillside used as a cemetery for Englishmen in Santiago. This holy ground for Protestants was not actually declared legal until 1875. But the decades from 1840 to 1870 saw disputes settled amicably over the establishment of civil marriage, the abolition of compulsory tithes for Church support, and the end of *fueros* for Church officials. The Church remained rich and powerful in its ownership of vast agricultural lands, but had to remove its influence from education when the Chilean school system was reformed along North American lines.

During the 1850s Manuel Montt, supported by a revolt of active young liberals, served as president, staying in power for a decade of continued progress of the Portales pattern. Montt was a poor boy who had been educated on a scholarship; one of his chief interests was education. Thirty years after O'Higgins' first attempt, Montt was able to abolish primogeniture as a first step in dividing the great estates, though by so doing he won the hatred of the oligarchy. His era was a time of economic progress, for Chile was suddenly on a main world trade route. Gold had been discovered in California and the ports of Chile were on the direct sea lane around the Horn to the gold fields. A railroad across Panama soon ended the thriving trade with the California coast, but Chile remained on the world map and English vessels continued to call in great numbers for nitrate of soda. Immigrants came in to work on Wheelwright's Santiago-to-Valparaiso railway and Germans settled in the cool regions below the Bío Bío which seemed so like northern Europe. Political agitation against Montt's high-handed methods was so strong by the end of his "decade," however, that after a revolt in 1859, the administration named José Joaquín Pérez as a "coalition" and compromise candidate. By this time the forces of liberalism were growing more insistent on reform and a new aristocracy of wealth in mining and urban pursuits was developing which aligned itself on the side of the liberals against the landed aristocracy.

Pérez proceeded to rule during a new "era of good feeling" in which the only outbreaks were the seemingly endless troubles among the Araucanian Indians, who remained almost as unpacified as in the days of Lautaro. Pérez himself was the "last of the decenniates," the ten-year presidents. His inauguration began a more liberal period within the oligarchical type of government. In his time political parties became well-organized groups, built around philosophies of conservatism and liberalism in the modern sense rather than around the personalism of individual leaders. The issue of religious freedom dominated the later years of Pérez' regime. In 1871 the constitution was amended to permit complete freedom of private religious worship. At the same time, the presidential term was limited to one five-year period.

The almost equal balance between conservative and liberal factions gradually brought about other liberalizing measures. The ecclesiastical courts were restricted, the non-Catholic cemeteries legalized, though Church and state were not yet separated. Other liberalizing measures—removal of municipal government from presidential control and increases in the power of the legislature—brought greater democracy to bear against the strong executive.

In the 1870s Chile's presidents became involved in a full-scale war with Peru and Bolivia, the War of the Pacific. Apart from the war interest, political life in this period centered on the struggle between the president and congress for the ascendancy. The increased clamor for complete universal suffrage was carried on by miners and city workers. This clamor won recognition for a growing proletarian class who hoped for actual representation in the legislature, decades before their counterparts in other parts of South America were politically conscious. Under Federico Errázuriz (1871–1876) the long and hotly disputed policy of widening the powers of the state over Church was pushed forward. During a serious depression he gave way to Anibal Pinto (1876–1881), and Pinto in turn, during the War of the Pacific, to Domingo Santa María (1881–1886), under whom the War was ended and the anticlerical program reached its climax. By 1891, the end of the war era, the party of congressional control, as opposed to the supporters of a strong presidency, had won the government—but that is part of the story of the War of the Pacific.

wars in Chile, foreign and domestic

Of all the Spanish American nations, only the two west coast nations, Peru and Chile, ever went to war with Spain again after independence. Spain had never recognized Peru, and in the 1860s a serious controversy arose between Peru and its former mother country. Peru refused to pay the reparations demanded by the Spaniards and the latter declared war. Chile, sympathizing for once with the usually scorned neighbor, agitated against Spanish demands, and there was a demonstration in the streets of Santiago which threatened the person of the Spanish minister. A Spanish naval commander, just driven out of Callao harbor by the Peruvians, demanded an apology and a salute from Chile. Chile refused to be so "insulted." Forgetting bitter internal politics, all Chile joined in a "defensive and offensive" alliance with Peru, Bolivia, and Ecuador, declaring war September 24, 1865. Though the Chilean navy had only one usable war vessel, Chile stole the Spanish flagship and fought the Spanish navy to a draw, only to have Spain bombard Valparaiso to the tune of $10,000,000 damage. England forced Spain to pay for damages done the British-owned docks at Valparaiso and the affair ended in a moral victory for Chile. But Chileans had learned the necessity of building a powerful navy if they were to be a power on the west coast.

Many more Chileans died in the ceaseless war against the Araucanian Indians in the south throughout the second half of the century than died in the "war with Spain." A native rebellion of 1859, led by powerful *caciques* among these "Apaches of South America," produced two years of guerrilla fighting. When peace was restored, the government set the policy of permanently occupying the Indian country through the erection of forts and the building of towns. European settlers founded communities further and further inside the Araucanian frontier. But the Araucanians were not subdued; they rose up again in the Pérez administration, led by a fanatical French trader who called himself King Orelie Antoine I. In his name, revolt flamed along the frontier until the border guards brought him in as a captive; the courts declared him insane and expelled him from the country. A "treaty" between the Araucanians and the Chilean government in 1883 recognized the tribal government and traditions and held the Indian lands in reservation. Later the Araucanians were given representation in the Chilean congress, but their lands slowly "melted away" and became small patches, crisscrossed by railroad and telegraph lines and separated by the new towns of the European settlers.

The northern border along the nitrate deserts brought aggressive warfare on the part of the Chileans against their erstwhile allies in the naval war with Spain. The exact frontier line between the coastal lands of Chile and Bolivia had never been decided. When nitrates from that desert region came into demand in world trade, an agreement on the 24th parallel was reached, with a share of all proceeds from mines between the 23rd and 25th parallels to be divided between both countries. Chile had the engineers, the capital—borrowed from British firms—and the workers; they went in and made the desert profitable. When Bolivia protested, Chile gave up her claims above the 24th parallel, while Bolivia promised not to add any new taxes on the Chilean firms already there. In 1878 a Bolivian *caudillo* taxed a Chilean company in violation of the treaty and the war was on.

The course of the ensuing War of the Pacific, from 1879 to 1883, is more a part of the story of Bolivia and of Peru than of Chile, since it was fought almost entirely in their area, and influenced their history. Chile was a much more modernized nation with better-trained and better-equipped forces, and she soon had the mastery on land and sea. Chilean troops captured Arica early in 1880; the Chilean fleet blockaded the Peruvian coast and carried out destructive naval raids on Peruvian coastal towns. Chile was so determined on a complete victory that she refused terms set up by an American board of mediators and continued the war in 1881. In January of that year Lima itself was captured and sacked by the victorious Chilean army. Two more years of naval blockade and occupation ensued before the Peruvian government would admit defeat. The peace was finally signed at Ancón on October 20, 1883. Tarapacá was ceded to Chile; Tacna and Arica were to be controlled by Chile for ten years, until a plebiscite would decide which country should have ultimate sovereignty. Such a plebiscite was not held, and Chile continued in possession of the nitrate workings. A separate truce signed with Bolivia in 1884, made into a formal treaty in 1904, gave Chile the Bolivian seacoast on the Pacific and cut Bolivia off from a port entirely, except for the rights of access by railroad. This railway right and the Tacna-Arica question remained open sores in Latin American diplomacy for almost half a century.

Chile emerged from the War of the Pacific one of the richest and most powerful of the South American republics, prosperous from her conquests and exploitation of mineral resources of the north as well as from new markets for her agricultural products to the south. But the *inquilinos*, as the tenant farmers were called, and the *rotos* or proletarian workers, who continued to eke out only a bare subsistence, had achieved no recognition, and the country was not yet a modern democracy. Bribery, fraud, and strong-armed methods were used by the presidents, especially Santa María, to maintain control of congress. However, an alliance of liberal factions brought José Manuel Balmaceda, an able diplomat and cabinet member, to the presidency in 1886.

Balmaceda started a five-year term as president with every chance of success. The nitrate income was assured, new public works were begun, a sanitation and pure drinking-water campaign started. Who would have thought the fine beginning would end in tragedy? But public improvements cost money; the country was in debt because of the War of the Pacific; congress opposed the president's policy. Thus, in order to put his democratic measures into effect, Balmaceda the reformer, on behalf of the inert masses, became an unconstitutional dictator. Over a budget dispute in 1891 the conservative majority of congress revolted and was joined by the navy. The army rallied to Balmaceda's side; fierce fighting resulted, the most serious civil war in Chilean history. The navy captured first the nitrate coast and revenues and then Valparaiso. Balmaceda was defeated and took refuge in the Argentine legation. There he ended the bitter struggle by committing suicide, September 19, 1891, one day after the termination of his legal term of office. He is remembered as the man who struck the first blow in behalf of the masses against the oligarchy in preparation for a social revolution which was to come to fruition after 1920.

One last "foreign fracas" of the nineteenth century took place as a result of the civil war. During the fighting a ship named the *Itata,* carrying arms for the congress party, was seized by the United States Navy, an act considered unneutral by the Chileans. Shortly afterward the American warship *Baltimore* was in Valparaiso, and the anti-American Chileans became involved in a brawl with the "liberty-happy" sailors. When two sailors were killed, America forced Chile to pay an indemnity and to apologize, an act which hurt the ambitious Chileans and augured no goodwill for the United States.

Jorge Montt, leader of the successful conservative forces in the Civil War of 1891, was chosen president in that year and instituted a new era of pseudo-parliamentary government which lasted until 1920. Domestic peace had come to Chile by the election of 1896; economy budgets had cleaned up the deficits the civil war produced; freer elections were the order of the day. Federico Errázuriz, son of a former president, the winner of the fair and hotly contested 1896 election, was declared president by a margin of two votes in congress, and this close a tie brought no armed revolt on the part of the losers. Chile faced the 1900s with a stable equilibrium betweeen congress and president which was to last till 1920.

proletarians and aristocrats in Chilean politics to 1930

The workers confined in the desert and in the valley were not able to move forward and express themselves as a political force until the era of World War I. At Balmaceda's death in 1891, the party of the Chilean Congress had won the "revolution," and for many years no strong president monopolized the scene. This period of parliamentary government was unstable, however. The multiplication of political parties made congressional responsibility impossible. Conservative landowners, heirs to the *pelucones,* held a large block of parliament seats. The old liberals, the *pipiolos,* progressive-minded industrial leaders, with their interest in railways, mines, and urbanization, had become more conservative, and were willing to continue blocs in the Chilean parliament to make a "right-wing liberal plus left-wing conservative combination." This party grouping kept the presidency in the background, and served to prevent the working people from participation in the government for 25 years; electoral fights were simply fights between wealthy aristocrats. Politics, it seems, was an aristocratic sport—controlled through bribery and fraud.

The landholding and merchant-class oligarchs had kept the peace well in the nineteenth century through the complete submission of the lower classes. But like many other dominant social groups, the Chilean oligarchs had lingered on beyond their time. By the early 1900s their rule was inadequate; they had become hopelessly inefficient and corrupt. The broad education program, made compulsory in 1913, had led to a gradual awakening of the masses. Foreign immigration and the colonization of south-central Chile had created a small class of independent farmers. Now the million or more city dwellers were willing to unite with them and with the downtrodden peasants and miners against the inefficient and corrupt oligarchy. The friction of the 20th century was caused chiefly by the exploitation of the *inquilino,* the peasant on the land, and by the abuses heaped on the industrial laborers.

The nitrate industry, unique in Latin America, had produced an alert, organized laboring class. Santiago and Valparaiso, temperate-climate cities, were filled with *rotos,* laborers poor in earthly goods but conscious of their voting power. These workers were not afraid, in the democratic climate of Chile, to call a general strike when the worldwide panic of 1907 brought depression in the nitrate region. City workers combined with small property owners in a new and truly liberal Democratic Party. Miners formed a Socialist Labor Party. By the election of 1915, the bloc formed by these two parties was strong enough to challenge the conservative coalition in a bitterly fought election won by Juan Luis Sanfuentes, in which the social plight of the people was an issue. In spite of violations of her neutrality, Chile remained neutral during World War I while both sides sought her rich nitrates. When the conservatives again won the presidency, only the prosperity brought by the War and the opening of the Panama Canal kept the new parties from revolt. The conservatives were frightened into passing South America's early social legislation—workmen's pensions, accident compensation, and railroad workers' retirement laws—in the period from 1916 to 1919. These were the first gains made by Chile's now class-conscious workers, but they had no voice and no leader. When peace in Europe brought a nitrate slump, the desert provinces themselves brought forth a leader of the people in the person of the senator from Tarapacá, Arturo Alessandri.

Alessandri, a tall man with "an enormous leonine head sunk deep in hulking shoulders"—the Lion of Tarapacá—was to dominate politics in Chile for two decades, one of South America's "great men" of recent times. Elected with a majority of one electoral vote by a combination of all liberal parties in 1920, he was the first president of the people and was committed to labor and middle-class demands for social and economic reforms. Alessandri had already had experience in "cleaning-up" local politics in the nitrate provinces, and in working with immigrant laborers—his own father had come from Italy to work in the mines. He pledged to separate Church and state (a task not yet accomplished by 1920 even in progressive Chile), to lay income taxes on the rich, to control the nitrate industry through a government bureau, to increase the welfare benefits for labor, to expand public education, and even to allow women to vote.

In order to do all these things Alessandri needed strong executive power, so he forced the passage of a new constitution. The old Diego Portales constitution, in effect since 1833, had given the real power to the president and to the upper house controlled by the landowning senators. When Alessandri was blocked by Congress and forced to use arbitrary methods, his supporting coalition fell apart. All these political difficulties were increased by the great economic depression which hit Chile and brought unemployment, unrest, and lowering of government revenues. Forced out temporarily by a military *junta* which opposed him, threatened by the loss of the labor groups to more radical Marxian leaders, he spent some months in exile in Italy. Then he was invited back by a younger military group and finally effected his constitutional changes in 1925. This new document, approved by a plebiscite, gave a more powerful president, directly elected, a six-year term. It advanced the chamber of deputies above the senate in importance, and it created provincial assemblies with more autonomy, thereby giving Chile its first semblance of states in a federal system. In religious matters the new constitution completely separated Church and state and made a strong statement guaranteeing the freedom of all religions. Labor's right to social improvements was recognized and the government assumed protection of trade unions. This constitution ended the rule of the oligarchs and prepared the way for further development of democratic institutions. Alessandri saw the constitution ratified, called new elections under its provisions, initiated some banking and budget reform measures, and was then forced to resign again by the powerful groups opposing him. He turned his power over to a colorless new president and went back to Italy.

One of the younger army officers who had invited Alessandri to return the first time had been a typical *caudillo* type, a twentieth-century "man on horseback" named Carlos Ibáñez del Campo. An admirer of Mussolini's new Italian government, Ibáñez promised all things to all men— stability to the conservatives, social security to the *rotos*. Ibáñez served as Minister of War for two years under the new constitution, was appointed vice-president, and then took over the presidency himself while the leading liberals went into exile. A 1927 election confirmed Ibáñez, for many Chileans were alarmed at the threat of class warfare and were willing to support a military government. The now powerful army pushed through modernization budgets and encouraged industrialization so that armament materials could be locally made. When the nitrate market continued to slump as synthetic substitutes were developed in Europe, Ibáñez borrowed abroad to keep his army well supplied and to keep his supporters among the laborers quiet by giving them jobs on foreign-financed public works. To maintain employment in the mines he formed a government-controlled nitrate corporation, the *Compañía de Salitre de Chile,* or cosach, Chile's first experiment in government ownership. Ibáñez passed some advanced labor laws, started a modest agrarian reform, extended education, and ended the long Tacna-Arica dispute. Repressive dictator though he was from 1925 to 1931, Ibáñez was efficient and might have been successful, had it not been for the world-wide depression, which hit hard at a one-export country like nitrate-producing Chile. His popularity collapsed when prosperity ended.

When opposition to Ibáñez increased among all factions, he tightened his military control until students, professors, workers, and sailors joined in a bloody riot and threw him out in July 1931. There followed eighteen months of utter political chaos. Within that period nine different governments rose and fell, some of them conservative conspiracies, some military *coups,* and one a socialist government which lasted 100 days. The liberals were split in every way; there were two general strikes and a fleet mutiny. But eventually the armed forces demanded that efficient, legal government be restored. Political parties regrouped in the midst of the depression, and by popular demand held a constitutional election in October 1932.

politics through depression and war to the present

In the election of 1932 Alessandri staged a comeback, pledging constitutional rule, law, order, stability, and a semisocialistic program. Alessandri was overwhelmingly elected from a field of five candidates, and his second presidency lasted the full legal six years. He himself had become more conservative. That he was less the workingman's friend than during the 1920s, and more the supporter of the nitrate companies, can be explained by his attempt to stabilize the nitrate industry. With decreasing demand for the product abroad, prices had to be kept up by the government. The cosach of Ibáñez' time had become the tool of the big nitrate companies who owned half the stock of the government company. Alessandri abolished it and returned ownership to private hands, setting up instead a government marketing and price-setting agency. Each company had its quota of the shrinking world market; soon no one was satisfied and wages went down while food prices went up. Alessandri, busy trying to preserve economic stability, sponsored no further social legislation. In 1936 he actually used the army to stop a serious railway strike. He and his Finance Minister, Gustavo Ross, pulled Chile through the serious depression of the 1930s in spite of high living costs and unemployment. His second term was an era of industrial improvement, though he undertook no social reform and never tackled the land distribution problem.

So the masses turned to a new leader, Pedro Aguirre Cerda, a man sincerely concerned with land reform, public health, education, and the unemployment caused by the nitrate slump. He had been one of eleven children of a poor farmer, had gone to school with the *rotos,* had earned a law degree and become Minister of Education, building up an investment in vineyards on the side. Thus the landowners did not hate him, while the intellectuals were his best friends. "If I had the power, I would strew Chile with schools as a farmer sows wheat on rich land," he said.

Aguirre Cerda, elected in a very close vote by a coalition of parties in October 1938, called his government a Popular Front, a term being used for the multiparty anti-Nazi governments in Europe at the time. This popular front called for *"pan, techo y abrigo"* (bread, clothes, and shelter) for every Chilean; it was a coalition of the Radicals with labor and the left, with leadership in the hands of the middle class and business elements of the Radical Party. By 1941 Aguirre Cerda's government was a Radical Party government. But because Aguirre Cerda compromised with Communist labor leaders on the one hand, and served as president of the Wine Growers' Association on the other, he pleased no one. Caught in the middle, he attempted to devote himself to public health and child welfare. Meanwhile the German immigrants in southern Chile were forming a very strong pro-Nazi party as the world entered World War II. Ignoring the world situation, Aguirre Cerda planned to expand the Chilean social program. When a disastrous earthquake killed more than 20,000 people, Aguirre Cerda's welfare funds were so depleted that he formed a Development Corporation, the *Corporación de Fomento,* or CORFO, for long-range industrialization and for WPA-type employment to improve the balance of trade and increase effective production. Too strong for the conservatives, too pro-Chilean for the Nazis, too weak for the labor leaders, the CORFO only brought dissatisfaction. Bewildered and disappointed, Aguirre Cerda died in November 1941, having served only half his term.

Both Alessandri and Ibáñez, as well as a Nazi leader, all hoped for election to succeed Aguirre Cerda. Juan Antonio Ríos, wealthy friend and follower of Aguirre Cerda and leader of the right wing of the Radical Party, took advantage of the confusion and won the election, while much of the Western Hemisphere was plunged into war following Pearl Harbor. Ríos kept a precarious balance between the loud Nazi minority and the strongly pro-American majority. This majority popular opinion was able to force a break in diplomatic relations with the Axis powers in January 1943; by such a break, though an act short of actual belligerency, Chile became eligible for the same type of United States financial aid which American wartime policy was extending to direct Allies in the Hemisphere. Meanwhile the Allies were also making heavy purchases of nitrates and copper. On February 12, 1945, just before the Hemisphere Meeting at Chapultepec, President Ríos declared war against Germany and Japan and signed the United Nations declaration, though the Chilean Congress did not approve his action until April 12, only a month before the United Nations met to frame the charter at San Francisco. However, the German element in Chile, so much more New-World-minded, never constituted the threat to the Allies which the smaller Nazi group did in Argentina. At home Ríos conducted an intelligent, businessman's administration, and encouraged industrialization.

When Ríos died in June of 1946, another leader from the nitrate regions, Gabriel González Videla, leader of the Radicals, won the bitterly fought special election. A friend of the United States who was widely acclaimed as a charming and popular figure when he visited President Truman in the White House, González Videla was a well-known Western Hemisphere figure in 1948. With a flashing smile, and a chic wife who was one of Santiago's leading social workers, González Videla was an informal president. He was available to all citizens, danced at rural fiestas, and was willing to "wait in line at the movies." Called by his own admirers a "clever tightrope walker" in his treatment of postwar Fascists, Communist sympathizers among the dissatisfied labor leaders, and estate owners afraid of land reform, González Videla served out his six-year term. But he could not control postwar inflation and lost his labor support when the cost of bread went up 30 per cent. With the help of industrialization programs financed by the successful CORFO, González Videla had achieved comparative prosperity by 1949. The *fundo* system with its feudal *inquilino* peasants continued to exist side by side with a democratic government and a strong city labor movement. In 1950 González Videla's Chile was praised for "remaining the bright spot for parliamentary republicanism and democracy in Latin America." John Gunther, American news writer, said of Chile's progress, "She will never have a tyrant like Ibáñez again."

What a surprise, then, when Ibáñez was returned to office in the fair and peaceful elections to choose González Videla's successor in September 1952. His campaigning, perhaps financed by Argentina's Perón who had been a close friend of Ibáñez in the 1940s, came at a time when "strong men on horseback" were winning elections elsewhere in Latin America. Ibáñez, who had created the Agrarian-Labor Party in 1949, courted every kind of dissident group, made appeals to workers in an inflation-wracked Chile in which the cost of living had increased 900 per cent since his first term, and promised strong orderly government to the Conservatives. Elected when the weak, traditional parties were rejected by the voters, Ibáñez could not make himself absolute dictator of democratic-minded Chile, for he was faced with a hostile congress. As a man in his mid-seventies he tried to grapple with the continuing economic ills of a country which produces one item for export, which has an outmoded landholding system, but an alert electorate. When the voters began to suspect that he was working closely with Perón, his government nearly fell. Ibáñez had to keep his promises of making administration more efficient, developing industries, promoting electrification and land reclamation schemes, and building roads. The cost of living was still high and labor was restive while Ibáñez changed his cabinet eighteen times in five years. The American firm of Klein and Saks made economic recommendations to fight the chronic upward cycle of inflation. Ibáñez attempted to halt inflation by austerity, economies, and controls, and turned the tide until mid-1957. Then his attempts were thwarted by one of the worst droughts in the history of Chile's central valley, floods in the north, and at the same time a 40 per cent drop in the price of copper on the world market. Ibáñez' programs of land reclamation, irrigation, electrification, and new small industries, as well as his balanced budget and his efficient tax system did not quite overbalance these catastrophes. Politics upset Ibáñez' sincere efforts and in 1957 the Radical Party and rightist groups, which were anti-Ibáñez, gained control of Congress. A fair and open election was held on September 15, 1958, at which, according to constitution and tradition, the people were to choose a president by plurality vote whom the Congress would then approve. There were five candidates, including the supposedly popular socialist, Salvador Allende.

Both Ibáñez and the radical Allende lost the election to a moderate right-winger with a magic name, Jorge Alessandri, the austere but enlightened son of Arturo Alessandri, the old Lion of Tarapacá. Jorge was a manufacturer who controlled Chile's papermaking business, and had been a conservative senator in the 1950s. He attempted to "govern above party," and disciplined private-business monopolies as well as wasteful public utilities to control inflation and keep the cost of living down. But it was not that easy in the early 1960s. The economy was still dependent on exports of nitrates and copper, and there was heavy unemployment in both those industries. The unproductive feudal agricultural system was a century out of date. The peasants left the land to find work in the crowded cities where there was no work. The value of the Chilean peso had fallen so low as to call for a new currency called the *escudo*. The Communist party, legally recognized in politically tolerant Chile, had a wide appeal. It claimed more than 100,000 members by 1960, and the socialist leader Salvador Allende curried their support, as the severe earthquakes of the early 1960s and the long drought of the late 1960's added to the misery of the urban and rural poor.

Jorge Alessandri passed Chile's first agrarian reform law in November 1962, but the law applied only to land which was not currently being worked. This reform law only helped farm families with some capital to invest in developing unused marginal lands. It helped very few *inquilinos* gain possession of their own land. An income tax to pay for new urban housing units on a government-supported building plan called CORVI brought Jorge Alessandri little popularity or support. In his last address to Congress at the end of his term in May 1964 he claimed that industrial production had increased by 33 per cent in the six years of his administration, but did not add that the cost of living had increased 190 per cent in the same period.

So the election of 1964 brought out two candidates urging greater social progress, both of them to the left of Jorge Alessandri. Salvador Allende led a large group of leftists called *Frente de Acción Popular,* or FRAP, asking for complete nationalization of the copper and nitrate industries. His opponent Eduardo Frei, born in Santiago of Swiss parents in 1911, had been a university professor. His devout Catholic faith called for social and economic reform through Christian leadership. He organized a Christian Democratic Party similar to Catholic Action parties in Europe, the first such liberal religious party in the Americas. He planned to achieve his reforms by acting as a strong executive through a congress controlled by Christian Democrats. He hoped to create a "mixed society in Chile of private, public, and cooperative ownership."

In the historic Chilean election of September 4, 1964, women voted for the first time in Chile, and they voted two to one for Frei. He received a majority of 400,000 votes in a very fair election. But votes for Frei were not merely anti-communist. They were votes against the landed oligarchy and the foreign control of business as well, "anti-communism with constructive alternatives." Frei's slogan was "Revolution in Liberty."

Frei's alternatives were to buy up large shares in the nitrate and copper companies for the Chilean government. Let these companies be privately managed but let the government sit on the board of directors. Let locally-owned smaller industries have some government management and invite in new foreign capital as well. Let the money earned by the government in these new "participation" endeavors be used to buy up more and fertile lands from the oligarchy with small down payments and settle a million *inquilinos* on the land. Let 100,000 urban housing units, not a mere 20,000, be built. In the congressional election of March 1965, Frei's party won the majority in the Chamber of Deputies.

Frei's biggest obstacle came from his failure to win control of the senate. His enthusiastic majority in the house passed his bill to buy into the copper industries, and the American and British companies, vastly preferring such a plan to nationalization, set up committees to work with government agents. New jobs were created by the thousands. Finally the oligarch-controlled senate passed his plan to purchase copper shares, although they had stalled on other reforms. Meanwhile he personally went on "good-will" trade missions, was welcomed in Italy, France, England, and West Germany, and came home with promises of several big investments in electric power production and in diversified industries. "The world has faith in our country," Frei reported when he returned to Chile in August 1965. He was also receiving full support from Alliance for Progress financing in the spring of 1966. Some of the funds thus loaned were to build up agricultural industries so that Chile would no longer have to import $140,000,000 worth of food yearly. A report to American financing firms in October 1965 said that President Frei was "maintaining democracy while promoting cooperatives" in "Savings and Loan" housing, small businesses, and new farm processing plants.

As a substitute for communism in solving some of Latin America's ills, Frei's Christian Democratic Party was being watched with interest throughout Latin America as the 1970s approached. In foreign affairs Chile opposed the United States in Santo Domingo, renewed relations with Russia, and allowed the Communist Party legal status at home. Frei himself hoped to become a leader in economic integration in the Western Hemisphere.

Frei's six-year record was excellent despite the fact that the earthquakes of 1965 and droughts of 1968 to 1970 came during his term. He had bought for the government a 51 per cent share in three large American-owned copper companies, and had expropriated 1,224 private estates and had the land distributed to 30,000 families. Some 260,000 housing units had been built, and 600,000 more children were in school than had been in 1960. Families from the *callampas*, the slums of cardboard and packing-case shacks, had been moved into the new housing units near the new schools. A redistribution of some of the nation's wealth had taken place. In 1965, 25 per cent of the wealth had been owned by 5 per cent of the population, but by 1970, this 25 per cent of the wealth was owned by 10 per cent of the people, while the lowest 25 per cent of the population owned twice as much as previously. This progress, unfortunately, was not fast enough to eliminate the *callampas*. As fast as people moved out, families from the drought-affected areas moved in. As Chile approached the presidential election of November 1970, inflation was cut by 10 per cent. Nevertheless, prices continued to rise.

Frei's party, the Christian Democrats, had to select another candidate since Frei was not allowed to succeed himself. They chose a man to the left of Frei but unacceptable to the leftists because of his personality. So in spite of the popularity of Frei's program, his party ended by gaining only 28 per cent of the vote. The rightists still backed former president Jorge Alessandri, then 74, to many Chileans a "father figure," who won 35 per cent of the vote. To everyone's surprise, Salvador Allende, the perennial Socialist Party candidate, the "runner-up" against Frei in 1964, was the winner with 36 per cent of the vote. He won not with the small Socialist Party vote but with a coalition of leftists called the Popular Unity Coalition which included 45,000 dedicated and well-organized Communists.

In December 1970, Congress, with 112 members of the various left-of-center parties and 88 members of the Allessandri party, met to declare Allende president. About 14,000 wealthy Chileans, horrified that a Communist had won the plurality in the popular election, withdrew their funds from the banks and left the country. The rest of the nation seemed jubilant, thinking all problems would be solved in the next few months.

Allende, who had been a student activist at the university from which he was graduated with a medical degree, only practiced medicine for two years. Then he helped organize the Chilean Socialist party and was elected to Congress at the age of 29. When later he served as Aguirre Cerda's Minister of Public Health, he developed a strong interest in the administrative aspect of health problems. Someone said he had the "folksy air" of a country doctor. Although he was a friend and admirer of Fidel Castro, he said Castro had put on "a sugar-and-rum revolution," but the Chilean revolution would have the taste of "meat pies and red wine." He promised that the revolution would be "shockless." He requested that all religious groups in Chile be represented at the religious services held in honor of his inauguration, and the archbishop of Santiago consented to an ecumenical service. Even the United States diplomats did not seem to be too alarmed at the emergence of a new "Communist base" in South America run by the first Marxist president ever elected by a free vote.

Allende agreed to respect political and civil liberties and to guarantee the existence of political parties and freedom of the press and of education. Unions were to be free from state control and the armed forces free from political interference. But he was firm in his determination to nationalize the economy. He said nationalization would extend to copper, extractive minerals, the financial system including insurance, strategic monopolies, and industries vital to the nation such as electricity and gas, transport, and communication. He promised that the state would "control and restrict foreign capital" and that in rural areas all estates over a fixed acreage would be expropriated, to be replaced by cooperatives. Peasant representatives would replace large landowners on state committees.

He announced plans for a new constitution that would provide for a single-chamber legislature and a whole series of departmental and local assemblies for which elections would be regularly held. The literacy requirements for voting still in force in 1970 would be abolished and universal suffrage would be in effect. A "massive drive" would be made in the educational sphere and a large-scale construction of low-cost dwellings would be started with mortgage payments pegged at 10 per cent of the family income. In foreign affairs, he meant to maintain friendly relations with the United States but to reject all foreign economic aid that carried political strings. He planned to recognize all Communist-dominated nations and to work for a more "representative" inter-American institution than the Organization of American States. He moved to establish diplomatic relations with Peking and to re-establish them with Havana.

On some points he had moved rapidly by the end of his first six months in office. He fully nationalized the mines, which had been 51 per cent government-owned under Frei, and seized full control of the *El Teniente* Copper Mine, an American investment in the largest copper mine in the world. By June 1970, two of Chile's largest textile plants and half the nation's banking were government-owned. He was having enough powdered milk distributed to give every child a quart of milk a day, and 500,000 pairs of shoes were given to rural school children. The "people's courts" he had promised were not started for fear they might turn into "kangaroo courts" against counter-revolution. His price control program seemed to be effective, cutting back inflationary rises by another 20 per cent.

His most serious problems were in the area of land distribution. When illegal seizures of land were made by the landless, he had to send policemen to guard the lands of the well-to-do peasants against invasion by squatters on more than 5,000 small farms and 750,000 planted acres. But through "legal expropriations," his committees were engaged in giving away another 800,000 acres. Mapuche and Araucanian Indians, who had long been promised good farm lands, had moved meanwhile by force into good lands of small farmers near their reservations. Agriculture Minister Jacques Chonchol, himself of Indian descent, worked out plans to move the Indians into completely new, uncleared lands and provide them with good farm houses, but the Indians refused to move. Daniel Colompil, the first Mapuche Indian Affairs director in Chilean history, pointed out that the Mapuche had "bad roads, no schools, nothing, and 60 per cent of our children die before the age of one." Still they would not leave the farms near their reservation, but would insist on "This land or death!"

Squatters on non-government land were not only a rural problem for Allende. Following a street riot in January 1971, rioters "permanently" occupied some 4,250 privately-owned city apartments. Allende had to warn that penalties for property seizures would be established and enforced.

Thus leftist were dissatisfied with Allende's slow pace and rightists were angered by the swiftness of his actions. In the United States it was reported that Chile's Marxist president was beginning to "sound and act like a man who is fighting for his political life," for his congressional support had weakened and the "Independent Radical Party" had withdrawn from the coalition. It was difficult to maintain the coalition of the remaining five parties. Though Allende had promised to hold hearings on the amounts owed the large copper companies after nationalization, his judges ended up by assessing the companies for excessive profits made from 1955 to 1970. He further confiscated holdings of the International Telephone and Telegraph Company after that company's agents were accused of spending large sums in Chile to prevent his election. To urge the Chilean masses to work harder to help his "Revolution" succeed, he invited Fidel Castro to visit Chile in the fall of 1971 and make speeches urging the people to "contain their impatience and restrain their demands."

Allende has accomplished much in the face of opposition, but it is questionable whether he can up his pace because some irreversible changes have taken place in Chilean politics and society and in economy. Economically he may have acted too rapidly, for the reserves in gold have practically vanished. In addition to an extremely high foreign indebtedness, production and trade have fallen severely and food must be imported and paid for. Like his predecessor, Allende has been hampered by Congressional opposition. It may be that a true assessment of Allende's progress and program cannot be made until after Congressional elections scheduled for March, 1973. What can be said is that the economical problems are critical, but Allende has demonstrated that he is a shrewd politician.

the variegated economy in the regions

Nowhere in the world was there such a nitrate deposit as in the west coast regions of Tarapacá, Antofagasta, and Atacama. Chile had fought and won the War of the Pacific, acquiring the richest of the nitrate beds from Bolivia and Peru. Chilean and foreign investors began to develop refineries there, which brought a surge of labor into the region, both Chilean and immigrant. Heavy investment eventually caused overspeculation and it seemed in 1914 that the industry and its golden stream of revenue might collapse. The world needed fertilizer, but not at the high prices Chile was charging. World War I brought a boom demand for nitrates as explosives; the same war almost ended the Chilean nitrate business when German chemists, isolated from the Chilean product by England's blockade, developed methods of fixing nitrogen from the air. By 1926, 80 per cent of the world's nitrates were made by synthetic plants in Europe and the United States. Chile's exports were cut to 10 per cent of the 1914 total. Many nitrate-producing centers became ghost towns; the ragged workers flooded the ranks of the unemployed in the cities.

Meanwhile the Guggenheim Company of America, knowing that cotton in the United States South would grow better in Chilean nitrate than in synthetic fertilizers, invested millions in new plants near Antofagasta. There followed various government attempts to equalize the profits from big and little companies, maintain employment and social improvements for the workers, and keep both Chilean and foreign capital happy. In 1965 the quantity of nitrate exports, in spite of efficient new methods, the discovery of new beds, and a fertilizer market in such rapidly developing regions as Israel, was only slightly higher than the amounts exported in 1900.

The easily decomposed masses of nitrate ore lie just below the surface, and can be "mined by steam shovel." In a wetter climate the nitrates would have drained into the ocean ages ago; only the rainless climate of the Atacama coast saved the ores for Chile. Enormous steam shovels have replaced the *roto* workers and their oxcarts of thirty years ago. With ten such shovels in operation at the great Guggenheim workings called the *María Elena*, an acre of ground is cleared of ore in a week, a square mile in ten years. Though the nitrate deposits will thus last indefinitely, 15,000 tons are hauled to the cleaning plant daily from these ten shovels. The ore needs only to be pulverized and washed in a stream of hot water. The nitrates and the valuable by-product iodine are dissolved, and the waste materials are spewed out in endless piles over the empty desert. The nitrate solution is then cooled to form crystals for shipment.

In between the shovels and piles of waste lies the company town of María Elena, where the workers live in houses much better than those of the peasants on Central Valley estates. They send their children to modern schools and attend workers' clubs and recreation centers. They also attend union meetings, for the nitrate workers are articulate and highly organized, and have therefore been an extremely left-wing force in Chilean politics. Before Allende's nationalization program, the workers were completely dependent on the company for life. Settlements in this uninhabitable area require water to be piped from the snow in the Andes hundreds of miles away, food and even green potted plants to be shipped in, and fuel oil for the refinery water heaters to be brought down from Peru. In order to prevent overproduction, the government has had to concentrate its control on María Elena and another equally large plant called the *Pedro de Valdivia* and enforce a quota system.

Chile ranks next to the United States in world copper production. In 1950 copper export brought in 70 per cent of the foreign exchange and paid a very large share of the nation's taxes. The fall in the price of copper hurt Chile badly. In the copper as in the nitrate business, foreign capital has dominated, and the Chuquicamata, the world's largest copper mine, in the mountains not a hundred miles above María Elena, has been owned by America's Anaconda Company. Living conditions for copper miners have been inferior to those for the nitrate workers because their unions were not active until the 1960's. In the 1950's workers were receiving a pittance in comparison to the wages paid copper miners in Montana or Arizona, and foreign companies were at loggerheads with the Chilean government over demands for insurance for indemnities, expensive safety precautions, and government royalties. The monopoly of the copper industry in the hands of American companies led to animosity against the Yankees. The program of President Frei for partial government ownership of the Anaconda and Kennicott Companies went peacefully into effect in the spring of 1967 with the Chilean government purchase of 51 per cent of the stock with long-term bonds. The program was destined to change at the hands of Allende in the 1970's.

Tungsten is produced in Chile, and the iron ore deposits at El Toro feed the new steel mills at Huachipato. Coal from Lota in the south near Concepción is not mined for export but only for local fuel and power. Oil will rapidly replace coal in the Chilean economy if the new wells being developed in the Straits of Magellan area come into heavy production. The output of hydroelectric power has been doubled with government encouragement since World War II. Streams from the Andes entering the agricultural valleys have a tremendous potential for power development and bring greater promise of industrialization than do coal and petroleum.

In 1939, the Chilean Development Corporation or CORFO was founded to raise the standard of living, stabilize employment, and allay social unrest by making loans to private business. CORFO's steel plant, financed partly by a loan from the Export-Import Bank of the United States, is now large enough to provide steel for Bolivia and Ecuador as well as Chile. Its cotton and woolen mills, fruit canneries, and cement plants make home-consumption industries an important element in the economy of Valparaiso, Santiago, and Concepcíon. Electric power has been a main feature of its program, and factories powered by electricity provide employment for the *rotos* displaced by machine methods introduced into the nitrate and copper regions in the north. CORFO has served to coordinate industry with agriculture, mining, and fishing, to improve the balance of trade and thus to make Chile less dependent on mineral exports.

It is the political power of the worker that prompts the government effort to raise the standard of living. The first Chilean strikes took place in the 1880's. By 1916 miners' and nitrate workers' unions secured the passage of laws making employers liable for accidents on the job and providing for one free day in seven. By 1946, the Chilean Workers' Federation (CTCH) had over a quarter of a million members. Because of the better education and increased industrialization of Alessandri's time, Chile's labor accomplished more and accomplished it earlier than did unions in other parts of Latin America. Also helpful were the unusual working conditions in the ore-extracting industries where workers had to be cajoled into going to the northern desert and pampered into staying. The situation was quite different from that of humble peasants tied to the land.

Legal recognition was provided the unions by Alessandri's labor code and a large measure of social security was achieved in the following decade. Under the Preventive Medicine Law, 80 per cent of Chile's population gets some form of medical insurance. In every occupation, workers' *cajas,* meaning cash boxes, are organized into which payments are made by the worker, the employer, and the government. The money thus raised provides not only pensions and unemployment benefits but also sets up cooperative shops, maintains a rotating loan fund, and provides facilities for buying homes.

For the city workers, the health programs have brought such benefits as lowering the infant mortality rate, cutting tuberculosis deaths, and, since 1920, raising life expectancy for workers and miners from 31 years at birth to 44, an increase of thirteen years in four decades. But two people out of every 25 in Chile still have tuberculosis, a rate augmented by malnutrition in rural areas. A problem which factory workers in Santiago and nitrate workers in María Elena faced in the early 1970's was the same one faced by their counterparts in the United States, which rises from the fact that although salaries had doubled in the previous decade, the cost of food, clothes, rent, and transportation had trebled.

Unfortunately Chilean social advances have not reached the agricultural countryside. Back in the mid-19th century, Chile's land tenure system seemed to be even more "oligarchical" than the system of the great *estancias* on the pampas to the east. The *fundo* owners, like the *hacendados* of Mexico, were the ruling class. Their sons studied law in Santiago and became the leading politicians among the *pelucones.* The tenant farmers, the *inquilinos,* worked for the landlords in payment for the small plots of ground they were allowed to cultivate for themselves. In the 1970's, the *inquilino* still works the landlord's *fundo* or estate, and the *huaso* or Chilean gaucho herds the rancher's cattle. They use the same primitive methods, eat the same diet, wear the same style *poncho,* and probably live in the self-same houses as did their ancestors in the 1830's.

The poverty of the Chilean *inquilinos* is an affront to the democratic faith of the Chileans. There has never been a "land" revolution in Chile. Half of Chile's population lives on the land but that land has been held in big estates. In the Central Valley, less than 400 families have held more than half the cultivated land, and some single estates have exceeded 250,000 acres. The conservatives in politics who from 1891 to 1920 controlled the senate and through it the government constitute this closed class of estate owners. A little more modernized than Argentina's oligarchs, they recently began offering some estates for sale in small holdings while they invested family fortunes in new industries. Also, under a homestead law, lands on the southern frontier and in sub-marginal, hard-to-irrigate areas have been offered as homesteads, but the large holdings and the attendant inefficient methods and depressed state of the peasantry are still Chile's major agrarian problems.

The agriculturally rich Central Valley can support wheat, orchards, vineyards, and pasture because the gradual western slope down from the Andes facilitates irrigation from the surging rivers of melted mountain snow. Three-fifths of Chile's lands are in wheat, which can be grown in the area south of the 35th parallel without irrigation. Chile has always been a wheat-bread-eating rather than a corn-tortilla-eating country. Small farmers thresh the wheat on the threshing floors with oxen; the largest *fundos* use American combine harvesters. But fundo *agriculture* generally is still run by oxen. Reapers and tractors were not introduced until the 1940's. A plan for aiding small farms with machinery proposed by President Ríos was increasing agricultural production by 1945. Chile's Central Valley produced fruits—citrus and deciduous, including apples, peaches, and pears—which make the Valley a rival of California's central valley. Wines from Chile compete with those from Mendoza on the tables of Lima or Rio. On the irrigated pastures graze cattle as fat as those of Argentina's pampas. In the cool south sheep raising by Scots and Basques has become a very specialized industry.

The *fundo* house, less palatial than that on the Argentine *estancia*, is usually a one-story Spanish-style building around a series of patios, behind which are acres of family orchards, gardens, and vineyards along with granaries, wineries, workshops, implement sheds, and stock corrals. Beyond lies the village of the tenants, the *inquilinos*, and the day laborers, who comprise 40 per cent of the Chilean population and who remain the submerged class as urban Chile moves rapidly ahead. Most of Chile's social legislation does not apply to *inquilinos* and they continue to work the master's land for the equivalent of 50 cents a day. Rural schools, supplied by the landlords, are inadequate compared with those provided at nitrate plants. The Communists have found the *inquilinos* willing listeners to their talk of radical unions for agricultural laborers. To counteract their activity, the land-owners accepted a bill which would permit formation of unions of all field workers who could read and write, but with 90 per cent illiteracy among adult *inquilinos*, effective organization may have to wait a generation. Some enlightened *fundo* owners have forestalled unrest by creating workers' cooperatives, clinics, loan agencies, and adult classes in their own villages. When European immigrants came in large numbers, they went to the southern frontier or became miners in the rapidly developing nitrate workings of the north, or they stayed in the cities where there was a new aristocracy of commerce and mining. Thus the cities grew and advanced while the *fundos* remained unchanged.

The difficulties of transportation across the Andes and the desert have delayed industrialization in Chile as much as has its feudalism. Chile has an internal spinal column of longitudinal rails and five railway lines linking her to her neighbors. Railroads now are government owned. She has an all-weather section of the Pan American Highway that runs to La Paz, Bolivia. The greatest difficulty is the long haul along the length of Chile, the

2,000 miles from Puerto Montt on the far south to Pisagua on the Peruvian border, for much of the domestic commerce goes this long way by steamer. The government owns a fleet of cargo and passenger vessels, and coastal trade is confined by law to Chilean vessels.

Chile's "western frontier" has been the country south of the Bío Bío River, Valdivia's own last line of settlement. Beyond Concepción was the forest, the beautiful lake region of today's new tourist interest, and the Araucanian Indian reservations. President Ibáñez opened much southern land for small-farm settlement in 1928, a region in which more than two-thirds of the people were of German ancestry, having been attracted to the region for five decades by its fir trees and cold winters. It was among these people, increasing by 6,000 new German migrants a year in the 1920's, that pro-Nazi parties harassed President Ríos during World War II—although the hard-working immigrants for the most part remained loyal to Chile. Near the straits of Magellan lies Punta Arenas, Chile's and the world's southernmost city, which supports itself by shipping out the wool grown in the region.

Araucanian Indians, about 170,000 of them, still largely occupy the territory between 40° and 50° south latitude. Descendants of the brave bands of Lautaro, they have themselves never been conquered by force of arms. To Chileans, Lautaro is a great national hero but his descendants are simply poor Indians on marginal lands. Many Araucanians are fiercely anxious to preserve the independence guaranteed them by "treaty" with the Santiago government in 1883, but their large communal land holdings are melting away, some of it granted in small shares to individual tribal members who want them, but some unfortunately has been given out as homesteads to non-Indian Chilean citizens. Araucanian handicrafts and strikingly designed wool textiles are sold to tourists as typical of "native" Chile but the Indians themselves, although they comprise 4 per cent of the population, are scarcely a factor in Chilean life.

Chilean culture: a European and Yankee mixture

Today Santiago is as sophisticated as Buenos Aires, in a more beautiful setting. In 1890, the city with its suburbs had 250,000 inhabitants, among whom a middle class was rapidly developing. British merchants, accepted in Santiago society, encouraged beautification of the city. Santiago had a School of Architecture as early as 1850, and a little later a School of Fine Arts and a National Conservatory of Music. The University of Chile had been founded in 1843, with Andrés Bello as its first rector. The Argentine statesman Sarmiento, exiled in Chile by Rosas, had started a teacher-training school and set a pattern for elementary education. By 1890 there were many provincial and city high schools, both public and private. One child in four went to school, an average better than in most European countries at the time. Lawyers, doctors, dentists, engineers, and pharmacists were being trained. Chile had libraries and museums, and cultural societies of literary-minded people who gave public lectures and conducted scholarly contests. In 1860 Chile had two daily newspapers; in 1890, it had seven in Santiago alone and twenty more throughout the country.

Today Santiago is the fourth largest city in South America with a population of three million. One third of Chile's 10 million population and 60 per cent of its industrial workers live in the Santiago metropolitan area. Its big, new civic center is "the finest group of public buildings in Latin America," according to one city planning authority, "in that it achieved dignity without monumentality." Its famous parks and gardens include the beautiful Santa Lucía Hill, once the despised Protestant cemetery. Thousands of cooperative workers' apartments have been built by the *cajas*, the workers' social security agencies, and the old unsanitary slums with a family to each room have been torn down. The city contains some 54 per cent of Chile's new manufacturing industry and its continuing industrialization tempts the *inquilinos* in from the farms to taste the higher standard of living in the city, so Santiago, like other Latin American capitals, has newcomers crowding into "mushroom" towns or *callampas*.

Valparaiso has had a greater struggle in becoming a large, modern city in spite of its position of importance as the main harbor and commercial center on South America's west coast. An earthquake which hit the port in 1906 was one of Latin America's major disasters, causing greater loss of life than that of San Francisco a few months earlier. Like San Francisco, the city rose again in greater beauty and prosperity than before, and today has a population of over 300,000. Viña del Mar, the famous beach resort, is only fifteen minutes' drive from the city.

The most severe South American earthquake in modern times, which killed 5,000 people, hit the beautiful valleys of southern Chile in 1960. This loss of life was almost repeated by another series of earthquakes in April 1965, with damages totalling $300 million. Homes and schools destroyed in 1960 had not yet been repaired when the quake struck in 1965, and Frei's government had to call for worldwide aid for the people stricken in the cold south Chilean winter.

Normally the mountains and lakes of the southern national parks make Chile a world-famous summer vacation and winter ski area. In the cities, moving picture houses show American, Argentine, and Mexican films, and the theater presents *zarzuelas* or short musical comedies and traditional drama that is second to none in Latin America. Chile boasts an excellent dramatic school and a large playwriters' group theater, encouraged by annual prizes given by the government for the best new plays. In local village fiestas, the *inquilinos* dance the *cueca*, the pigeon-strutting courtship dance of the 17th century and stage yearly rodeos in a popular "wild west" manner.

Although Chile is much better off in public schooling than other Latin American countries, of every 100 youngsters entering elementary schools, only 30 reach the sixth grade and only five complete high school. Only two would enter college. Secondary schools follow the classical European pattern and for the most part offer only college preparatory work.

Some practical progress is being made and schools for nurses and social workers have been created as well as vocational and technical high schools. Young men in Chile are eager to take mechanical and engineering courses practical for progress in Chile's new industry. A group of socially conscious city women in Santiago has started the Institute for Rural Education which sends out literature and materials to the poorest *inquilino* schools.

University life is active in Chile, among whose large universities are included the National University of Chile with over 6,000 students, the Catholic University, the University of Concepción, and the Santa María Technical University of Valparaiso. University development was enhanced by Frei's 1966 law which promised free education for every Chilean child through the university level. Chilean university students turned away from the Communist movement to support President Frei but joined Allende to welcome Fidel Castro as a visitor in the spring of 1972. Instead of taking summer vacations, they have gone out by the thousands as a "domestic peace corps" to build 5,000 rural classrooms and teach 150,000 people to read.

In rural areas, reported a former member of Frei's cabinet, 90 per cent of the population lack potable water and sanitary facilities. Population increased 3.7 per cent every year but only one child in three receives medical attention the first year of his life. Over 30 per cent of the population, he said, still lived in unhealthy and inhuman conditions.

But about 89 per cent of the Chilean people can read and are sophisticated enough to read newspapers. Santiago's daily *El Mercurio* ranks among the best in the Western Hemisphere. The five other papers in Santiago have varying and uncensored political opinions; and local papers in the provinces carry influence because of the great distance from the capital. Papers in the United States often quote the weekly magazine *Ercilla* and the clever *Topaze* which satirizes politics.

Señora González Videla, a social worker, led the successful campaign which earned Chilean women the right to vote in presidential elections. Chile has women doctors, newspaper writers, and political organizers. A woman is the director of the National School of Social Work; a woman doctor has been in charge of public health work in Santiago; a woman lawyer has served as Chief of the United National Division on the Status of Women. Chile sent a woman as minister to the Netherlands in 1946, the world's fifth country to appoint a woman diplomat.

A Chilean woman, Gabriela Mistral (1889–1957), one of the modern world's best-known poets, served as cultural attaché in the Chilean embassies in Paris and Rome and on committees for the League of Nations, was guest advisor in Mexico's rural education program in 1922 and exchange professor at Vassar College and Columbia University in New York, and continued in her old age visits to other Latin American countries as a consultant on education. Born Lucila Godoy, she spent a girlhood of privation and struggle for education, and as a young adult wrote verse under the pen name of Gabriela, which signifies "angelic annunciation," and of Mistral, the name for the warm wind of Provence. Chilean school children know hundreds of her poems, which are about nature and children and death, and about her hopes for humanity and her ideal of service. In 1945 she received the Nobel prize for literature.

Chile has produced many writers well-known at home. Chilean literature was emancipated from 18th-century form at the time when the young Argentinian Sarmiento engaged the sage Chilean Andrés Bello in a lively controversy about classicism and newer ideas. Sarmiento won by converting José Victorino Lastarria (1817–1888), who became the guide of the new generation of writers.

The second half of the 19th century saw the rise of a truly Chilean national literature. The most famous writer of the period was Alberto Blest Gana (1830–1920), whose stories of Chilean life are so realistic that he is called the Balzac of South America. There is an element of universality in his novel *Martín Rivas,* written in 1862, about a middle-class young man who is trying to "crash" aristocratic Santiago society that strikes a chord in readers everywhere even though the characters move about in a Latin atmosphere of aristocrats' parties, church ceremonies, and popular fiestas.

Chilean poetry was strongly influenced by Rubén Darío when he lived in Chile in the 1890's and by the ever popular Alberto Blest Gana who was still writing satires on Chilean life when in his eighties. In 1915, the poet Pedro Prado (1886–1952), heir to these great writers, founded a noted literary and artistic circle called *Los Diez* or "The Ten." He was the writer of symbolic novels but is also known for a long poem he wrote about the resurrection of Lazarus that is regarded as one of "the finest poems in Spanish of the modernist era."

The third of the best-known contemporary poets in Chile goes by the name of Pablo Neruda. Born Neftalí Reyes in 1904, a leader of Chile's Communist party, a politician who was active in Congress against González Videla in 1949, he is the author of poems written in an ultra-modern mood. Regardless of his politics, he won Chile's national prize for literature in 1945, and in 1971 the Nobel Prize in Literature. His poems may be abstract or obscure, but he has many imitators throughout Latin America.

The Chilean novel has been a notable contribution to recent Spanish literature. Typical is *El Roto,* written in 1920 by Joaquín Edwards Bello (1887–1968) which is a powerful description of the life of the city worker in Santiago's slums. Indicative of the socially conscious attitude of Chile's readers is the fact that this novel, along with *Esmeraldo's Cradle* by the same author, has been so popular. The best-known short stories are by Manuel Rojas (1896–   ). He writes about migratory field hands and railroad workers, writing from experience, for he worked as a youth on the Trans-Andean Railway. His journalistic writings have served to make him manager of the University of Chile Press. His *Lanchas en la Bahía,* written in 1932, stamp him as a worthy novelist as well.

Chile produced a group of historians worthy of that title in competition with any European; particularly, in the 19th century, Benjamín Vicuña Mackenna (1831–1886), revolutionist, journalist, politician, and diplomat, who authored and edited nearly 100 volumes, who, along with Miguel Luis

Amunátegui (1828–1888) and Diego Barros Arana (1830–1907), formed a trio of outstanding historians. Then in the next generation came José Toribio Medina (1852–1930), whose name is well-known to any serious student of Latin American history. He wrote, compiled, and edited more than 200 volumes of historical material. All these books were printed by Chile's own booming publishing business which produces thousands of inexpensive, paperbound books, including translations of modern American writing.

The University of Chile has its own Faculty of *Bellas Artes* which together with the National Conservatory of Music and the National Academy of Fine Arts fosters a new Chilean art and music. Chile's best-known composer, the dean of the *Bellas Artes* faculty, Domingo Santa Cruz Wilson (born in 1899), won the prize offered in 1941 for music written in honor of the 400th anniversary of the founding of Santiago. The work was a symphony in three parts based on praise of the "mighty mountain stream Maipó, the giant mountain Aconcagua, the beautiful lakes of the South." Another composer is the "original and colorful" Carlos Isamitt (born in 1885) who uses Chilean folklore with Araucanian themes to create his ballets and symphonies. He was also a painter and recorded Araucanian faces as well as songs. Juan Orrego Salas, who studied in New York on a Rockefeller grant, found subjects for ballets, cantatas, and piano compositions in the United States, and was welcomed home with his works as the finest of Chile's young composers. The world-renowned ballerina Margot Fonteyn danced in Santiago in 1960 and a new interest in native Chilean ballet developed as a consequence. The ballet *Candelaria*, composed by Carlos Riesco and produced by the Chilean dancer Octavio Cintolesi, was based on folklore from northern Chile and brought about an "integration of the arts in an authentic national ballet idiom."

Chile has had an active school of sculpture for more than a century. One of the best modern sculptors was the great-granddaughter of Andrés Bello, Rebecca Matte de Iñíquez, who died in 1929. To encourage painting, the Faculty of *Bellas Artes* gives prizes for painting; and the Chilean Congress itself votes 100,000 pesos as the yearly budget for art premiums. Chile's greatest contemporary painter is Robert Matta Echaurrén (born in 1912), an artist of international reputation. Chile's geography has given a special quality to Chilean art as well as to its music, literature, and politics. Her prize-winners have most often been landscape artists who painted the color of Chile, the light in her valleys and the perpetual snow on her mountain summits.

READINGS: CHILE

Agor, W. H., *Latin American Legislatures: Their Role and Influence* (1971).

————, *Chilean Senate: Internal Distribution of Influence* (1971).

Aguilar, L. E., ed., *Marxism in Latin America* (1968).

Alexander, R. J., *Communism in Latin America* (1957).

————, *Labor Relations in Argentina, Brazil and Chile* (1962).

Bernstein, H., *Modern and Contemporary Latin America* (1952).

Bonilla, F. and M. Glazer, *Student Politics in Chile* (1970).

Bourne, R., *Political Leaders in Latin America* (1970).

Bowen, J. P., *The Land and People of Chile* (1966).

Bowers, C. G., *Chile Through Embassy Windows, 1939–1953* (1958).

Bowman, T., *Desert Trails of Atacama* (1924).

Burnett, B. G., *Political Groups in Chile: The Dialogue between Order and Change* (1971).

Burr, R. N., *By Reason or Force: Chile and the Balance of Power in South America, 1830–1905* (1965).

———, *Stillborn Panama Congress: Power Politics and Chilean-Colombian Relations during the War of the Pacific* (1962).

Butland, G., *Chile* (3rd ed., 1956).

———, *Human Geography of Southern Chile* (1953).

Campbell, M. V., *Development of the National Theatre in Chile to 1842* (1953).

Carr, R., ed., *Latin American Affairs, St. Anthony's Papers No. 22* (1970).

Chisholm, A. S. M., *Independence of Chile* (1911).

Cleaves, P. S., *Development Processes In Chilean Local Government* (1969).

Clissold, E., *Chilean Scrapbook* (1952).

Coester, A., *Literary History of Spanish America* (rev. ed., 1946).

Cohen, A., *Economic Changes in Chile, 1929–1950* (1960).

Collier, S., *Ideas and Politics of Chilean Independence 1808–1833* (1967).

Crosson, P. R., *Agricultural Development and Productivity: Lessons from the Chilean Experience* (1970).

Davis, W. C., *Last Conquistadores: The Spanish Intervention in Peru and Chile, 1863–1866* (1950).

Dawson, T. C., *South American Republics* (2 vols., 1903–1904).

Debray, R., *The Chilean Revolution Conversations with Allende* (1971).

Dennis, W. J., *Tacna and Arica* (1931).

Edwards, A., *The Dawn* (1931).

———, *My Native Land* (1928).

Edwards, T. L., *Economic Development and Reform in Chile: Progress under Frei, 1964–1970* (1972).

Elliott, G. F. S., *Chile, Its History and Development* (1927).

Ellsworth, P., *Chile, An Economy in Transition* (1945).

Emmerson, D. K., ed., *Studies in Politics in Developing Nations* (1968).

Englekirk, J. E., et al., *Outline History of Spanish American Literature* (3rd ed., 1965).

Evans, H. C., *Chile and Its Relations with the United States* (1927).

Fagen, R. R. and L. A. Cornellus, ed., *Political Power in Latin America: Seven Confrontations* (1970).

Feinberg, R. E., *The Triumph of Allende: Chile's Legal Revolution* (1972).

Fergusson, E., *Chile* (1943).

Fetter, F. W., *Monetary Inflation in Chile* (1951).

Finer, H., *The Chilean Development Corporation* (1947).

Frank, L. G., *Capitalism and Development in Latin America: Historical Studies of Chile and Brazil* (1967).

Galdames, L., *History of Chile,* trans. L. J. Cox (1941).

Gil, F. G., *Genesis and Modernization of Political Parties in Chile* (1962).

————, *The Political System of Chile* (1966).

————, and C. J. Parrish, *The Chilean Presidential Election of September 4, 1964* (1965).

Gross, L., *The Last, Best Hope: Eduardo Prei and Christian Democracy* (1967).

Halperin, E., *Nationalism and Communism in Chile* (1964).

Hancock, A. U., *History of Chile* (1893).

Hanson, E. P., *Chile, Land of Progress* (1941).

Haring, C. H., *South American Progress* (1934).

Herrick, B. H., *Urban Migration and Economic Development in Chile* (1966).

Herring, H., *Good Neighbors* (1941).

Hirschman, A. O., *Journeys Towards Progress* (1963).

————, *Latin American Issues, Essays and Comments* (1961).

Horowitz, I. L., *Masses in Latin America* (1970).

Houston, J. A., *Latin America and the United Nations* (1956).

Hughlett, L. S., *Industrialization of Latin America* (1946).

Hurtado, T. T., Carlos, *Population Concentration and Economic Development: The Chilean Case* (1966).

International Bank for Reconstruction and Development, *Agricultural Economy of Chile* (1952).

Jefferson, M., *Recent Colonization in Chile* (1921).

Johnson, J. J., *Pioneer Telegraphy in Chile, 1852–1876* (1948).

————, *Political Change in Latin America* (1958).

Kaempfer Villagrán, G., *Bloody Episodes of the Worker's Struggle in Chile, 1850–1925* (1962).

Kaufman, R. R., *The Chilean Political Right and Agrarian Reform* (1967).

Kelchner, W. H., *Latin America and the League of Nations* (1926).

Landsberger, H., *Latin American Peasant Movements* (1970).

Lindsell, H., *Chilean-American Controversy of 1891–1892* (1943).

Mamalakis, M., and C. W. Reynolds, *Essays on the Chilean Economy* (1965).

Markham, C. R., *War Between Peru and Chile, 1879–1882* (1883).

Martin, P. A., *Latin America and the War* (1925).

May, C. P., *Chile: Progress on Trial* (1968).

McBride, G. M., *Chile, Land and Society* (1936).

Mecham, J. L., *Church and State in Latin America* (rev. ed., 1966).

————, *Survey of United States–Latin American Relations* (1965).

Merrill, R. N., *Evaluation of Chile's Housing Program* (1962).

Miers, J., *Travels in Chile and La Plata* (1846, repr. 1970).

Millington, H., *American Diplomacy and the War of the Pacific* (1948).

Mistral, G., *Selected Poems,* trans. L. Hughes (1957).

Moors, J. V., *Elites, Intellectuals and Conservatives. A Study of Industrial Relations System in Chile* (1966).

Moreno, F. J., *Legitimacy and Stability in Latin America: A Case Study of Chilean Political Culture* (1970).

Myhr, R. O., *Chile's Path to Socialism: Observations on Allende's First Year* (1972).

NACLA Staff, *New Chile* (1972).

North, J., *Civil-Military Relations in Argentina, Chile and Peru* (1966).

Nunn, F. M., *Chilean Politics 1920–1931: The Honorable Mission of the Armed Forces* (1970).

Pan American Union, *Gabriela Mistral, 1882–1957* (1958).

Pendle, G., *The Land and People of Chile* (1960).

Petras, J., *Chilean Christian Democracy: Politics and Social Forces in Chilean Development* (1970).

Pike, F. B., *Chile and the United States, 1880–1962* (1963).

Poblete Troncoso, M., and B. G. Burnett, *Rise of the Latin American Labor Movement* (1960).

Roberts, S. A., *José Toribio Medina, His Life and Works* (1941).

Schutter, C. H., *The Development of Education in Argentina, Chile and Uruguay* (1943).

Shaw, P. V., *The Early Constitutions of Chile, 1810–1833* (1931).

Sherman, W. R., *Diplomatic and Commercial Relations of the United States and Chile, 1820–1914* (1926).

Silvert, K. H., *Chile: Yesterday and Today* (1965).

————, *The Conflict Society: Reaction and Revolution in Latin America* (1961).

Slater, W., *The Heroic Image in Chile: Arturo Prat, Secular Saint* (1972).

Smole, W. J., *Owner-Cultivatorship in Middle Chile* (1963).

Solberg, C., *Immigration and Nationalism: Argentina and Chile 1890–1914* (1970).

Stavenhagen, R., ed., *Agrarian Problems and Peasant Movements in Latin America* (1970).

Stevenson, J. R., *The Chilean Popular Front* (1942).

Strawbridge, G., *Ibañez and Alessandri: The Authoritarian Right and Democratic Left in Twentieth Century Chile* (1971).

Subercaseaux, B., *Chile: A Geographic Extravaganza* (1943).

Subercaseaux, G., *Monetary and Banking Policy of Chile* (1922).

Swift, J., *Agrarian Reform in Chile: An Economic Study* (1971).

Thiesenhusen, W. C., *Chile's Experiments in Agrarian Reform* (1966).

Tomasek, R. D., ed., *Latin American Politics: Studies of the Contemporary Science* (rev. ed., 1970).

Torres Rioseco, A., *Epic of Latin American Literature* (rev. ed., 1946).

Weaver, E. S., *Regional Patterns of Economic Change in Chile* (1968).

Wilgus, A. C., ed., *Argentina, Brazil, and Chile Since Independence* (1935).

————, *South American Dictators* (1937).

Wollman, N., *The Water Resources of Chile* (1968).

Wolpin, M. D., *The Impact of Cuban Politics on Chile* (1972).

Zañartu, M. and J. J. Kennedy, eds., *The Overall Development of Chile* (1969).

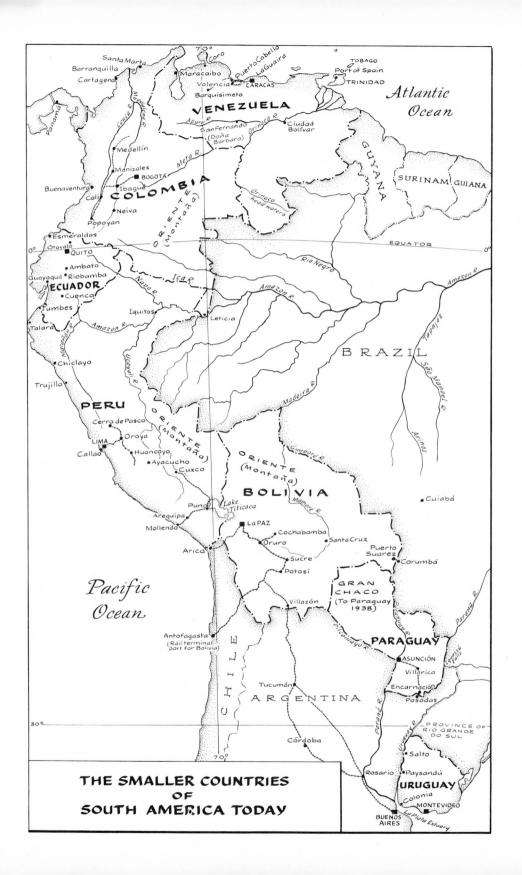

THE SMALLER COUNTRIES
OF
SOUTH AMERICA TODAY

sixteen small nations of Latin America, each in search of identity

three Immortals; former guerrilla leader Rivera, as inspector general of the new army, did not accept the leadership of governor Lavalleja. As head of the army, Rivera, who was to dominate politics through thirty-four years of feuding, got himself elected first president under the Constitution of 1830—a centralistic constitution, incidentally, which was in force to 1919, in spite of the chaos of the country. Gaucho, patriot, and warrior, three times president, Rivera founded the *colorado* party, a name applied to the more liberal-minded city dwellers who followed him. Through this party he left the impression of his personality on nineteenth-century Uruguay. Since his strength lay in riverbank and coastal centers, regions associated with the trade and commerce of La Plata, he feared Argentine domination, and therefore was more pro-Brazilian in outlook. He tried to govern a country in which Brazilian coins were the only ones in circulation, actual slavery was still the order of the day, owernship of ranches in the backlands was in constant dispute, and the Charrúa Indians roamed at will, pillaging the frontier. Furthermore, the country had no financial credit whatsoever.

In 1835 Rivera peacefully gave way to his successor, Manuel Oribe, and retired as head of the army, only to lead another revolt when his financial accounts were questioned. For seven years a feud continued between Rivera's *colorados*, with Brazilian troops on their side, and the party called the *blancos*, organized among the back-country landowners by Lavalleja's supporters with help from the Argentine dictator Rosas. This conservative Blanco party of the landowning aristocracy looked to Argentina as a counterweight against the possibility of Brazilian domination. The long fight in the backlands came to the doors of Montevideo in 1843. Thus began the so-called Great War—the conservative rural *blancos* and Argentina's Rosas on one side, the *colorados*, the Montevideans, and the Brazilians on the other, while Montevideo withstood a nine-year siege.

Strange to say, it was not the city-dwellers who suffered. Supplied by the French and British navies, which were blockading Rosas' Argentina, they ate well, went to the theater, and maintained their normal life. It was the backlands, the estates and villages of the Blancos, which were to feel the pinch, cut off as they were from imported supplies and city trade. Bandits from both sides and from the allied countries stole the cattle and horses; gauchos left the plains and went into the armies. No schools and no roads were built. The war itself wavered first to one side, then to the other. Rivera was first exiled, and then was in and out of the besieged Montevideo through the next four years as he broke his exile, and was finally released legally when the siege was lifted. The Great War was over and the Argentine dictator Rosas was defeated at home in Buenos Aires in 1852.

Before a stable government could be established in Uruguay, however, Rivera and Lavalleja had died, both of them, strangely enough, from natural causes or sheer exhaustion. The peace made with Brazil gave that aggressive nation a large section of the northern frontier. The *colorado* government which opposed it fell from power and a *blanco* government, with 4,000 Brazilian soldiers behind it, tried to rule the country. Peace finally came when the Brazilians withdrew and left the *blancos*, the country ranchowners, to rule the city for a stormy decade. The leader of the suppressed *colorados,* Venancio Flores, was able to work up a revolt from exile. He gained support from both Brazil and Argentina, both of which countries feared that the increasing chances for stability under the *blancos* would end their hopes for territory. By 1863, when Flores reinvaded his homeland, there was an ambitious dictator in neighboring Paraguay, Francisco Solano López, who hoped to add Uruguay to his "empire" by aiding the now friendless Blancos against these new enemies. By such intervention Paraguay became involved in the Great Paraguayan War which lasted from 1864 to 1870. The war was fought outside of Uruguay, and is a story in itself. Uruguay was simply the pawn over which that war was started, but when the war ended Argentine-Brazilian intervention in Uruguay ended also.

Flores, whose plan to take over the presidency from the *blancos* had brought Paraguayan intervention in the first place, served as president and actual dictator in Montevideo while the war raged. His power was brought to an end by assassination in February 1868. He is usually considered the last of the gaucho *caudillos.* Later presidents were professional soldiers who brought gradual peace and a softening of the *colorado-blanco* bitterness.

Tranquility did not come for another decade, however. *Blanco* fought Colorado for two more years after the Paraguayan War was over in 1870, until Argentina arranged a negotiated peace. This strange agreement gave the Blancos $500,000 and the police control of four interior provinces, but left the capital and the presidency in the hands of the Colorados; the device of bribery was a less costly solution for party rivalry than was civil war. The Blanco landlords seemed satisfied with control of their backlands, and this "deal" set a pattern for later agreements.

For 30 more years, however, Blancos and Colorados quarreled over the presidency. One military president, Colonel Lorenzo Latorre, resigned in disgust in 1880, saying, "Uruguay is ungovernable."

But economic and social advance brought increasing maturity to the politics of Uruguay. The population increased from 70,000 to 900,000 in eighty years. British who had come to intervene stayed to go into business. Italians, Germans, and Spaniards came to farm the pampas or to settle in Montevideo, uninformed and unconcerned about traditional party feuds. They and their descendants created a middle class of lawyers, doctors, and merchants. A railway line was begun in 1867; the first meat-packing plant was built by a German firm in 1861. Gauchos could find jobs in such plants or in the well-run ranches which supplied them; they did not have to look to a private armed band for employment. Landowners and merchants, in their turn, became more interested in developing their properties than in the wars of Blancos and Colorados. The bitterness between those parties, though it did not die out, became less acrimonious in the third and fourth generation away from the Thirty-three Immortals, and aroused no interest among the newly arrived immigrants to whom the rich land looked so good.

One of the fathers of progressive modern Uruguay was José Pedro Varela, a youth who lived only 34 years, but who in his short life had known

Sarmiento and Horace Mann. He organized the "Friends of Popular Education" in the 1870s and got the dictator, Colonel Latorre, to create the position of "Inspector of Primary Education and Instruction" for him to fill. His new ideas on free, compulsory education, liberalized curriculum, and improved teaching methods grew more popular after his death.

Montevideo, growing in sophistication in spite of endless civil wars and long siege, was not without culture. There had been a national university there since 1849; the National Library dates from 1816. The Ateneo, which dates from 1880, gives recitals, conferences, and lectures open to the public. The new peace between political parties brought out a flowering of intellectual accomplishment among the bright young men of Montevideo who could turn their attention away from the Colorados and Blancos and toward arts, letters and sciences.

Uruguayan politics in the twentieth century

Bright young Montevideo writers had one political leader to thank for most of the stability and freedom under which they wrote. A great Uruguayan statesman, José Batlle y Ordóñez, often referred to as the "Founder of Modern Uruguay," was responsible for much of the "revolutionary" legislation from 1903 to 1920. Born in 1856 during the years of active Blanco-Colorado fighting, he had been sent by his well-to-do Colorado family abroad to study in a different environment; when he was not yet thirty he had founded the great modern newspaper *El Día* which brought a new kind of liberalism to the Colorado party. After service in Congress, this newspaper editor was elected to the presidency in 1903. He was immediately faced with a Blanco uprising which had to be quelled with military force, but Batlle was soon bringing the Blancos into the government. At the end of his term one of his associates, Claudio Williman, was elected president in a fair election, while Batlle went abroad to represent Uruguay at international conferences at The Hague, and to study the government of Switzerland. He was elected president again on his return in 1911.

A great lion of a man with an enormous head and a shock of unruly hair, Batlle had a forceful personality. As a member of Congress after his second presidency, as editor of *El Día*, as a leader of the National Council of Administration after 1920, Batlle continued to stamp his personality and his progressive ideas on the wax of Uruguay until his death in 1929. In his lifetime Uruguay emerged as a nation socially ahead of any other small Latin country.

Batlle, true friend of democracy, believed the basic problems of Uruguay had stemmed from dictatorship and instability. "Reform" to him meant three things: (1) improving politics by compulsory suffrage, mass public education, and wide representation of all parties and classes; (2) controlling the national economy by state operation of banks, public utilities, and some industries; and (3) raising the standard of living by all types of social security and labor legislation. He saw his first principle bring about free elections during his own lifetime; on the second and third he fought a bitter fight with gradual success, aided by popular opinion and by his ability to influence the policies of his successors in the office of presidency. Batlle was contemporaneous with Scandinavian leaders in urging government competition with private industry, with Theodore Roosevelt in breaking the power of monopolistic companies, with the more progressive state governments in the United States of Wilson's time in setting minimum wages and establishing the rights of unions to strike.

All was not smooth sailing for the Utopia. Uruguay remained neutral in the World War I conflict then raging, but the little nation had to fix prices and control exports in order to avoid inflation in the upset of world trade. In 1917 an Uruguayan ship was torpedoed by the Germans and Uruguay severed relations with the Central Powers, though there was no actual declaration of war. Trade with the Allies kept Uruguay prosperous.

In the tide of peace and prosperity, Batlle had suggested a plural executive, a cabinet government by committee rather than by a powerful president. Much of Batlle's program was incorporated in a new constitution which went into effect in 1919, the first since 1830. The president was to be directly elected, but his powers were cut to those of a mere chairman, sharing executive power with an elected nine-member Council of Administration, serving six years on a staggered plan. The minority party was always to have a third of the members, elected by a system of proportional representation. The new constitution called for compulsory voting, separated Church and state, provided for government participation in industry, and included much labor legislation.

The president had responsibility for foreign affairs. The first to hold office under the new plan, Baltasar Brum, a former Minister of Foreign Affairs during World War I and a close associate of Batlle, brought Uruguay to world attention. He is famous in Latin America for having issued in 1920 his Brum Doctrine, proposing that the Monroe Doctrine be made a multilateral pact of all the Americas in keeping out aggression, and not a mere policy of the United States. He also made Uruguay an active member of the League of Nations. Agreeing with Batlle that the president should not be a power in domestic affairs, he and his successors after him up to 1931 all turned more power over to the Council.

Prosperity ended for the world in 1929, and for Uruguay as well. Depending on world markets for meat, hides, and wool, Uruguay's Administrative Council found it difficult to control the unemployment of the depression years. Gabriel Terra, a lukewarm Batlle man serving as president, quelled disturbances with repression. When he was opposed by the National Council and by Congress, he dissolved both institutions and made himself dictator. Opposition newspapers were closed, opponents arrested. Terra was forced to call a new constitutional convention in 1934; the resulting plan of government returned to a strong presidential government and abolished the Administrative Council. Though the conservative property-owning class had more influence with the Terra regime than in the previous two decades, Terra did not abandon the social and economic reforms of his predecessors. His political policy was more repressive, yet minority rights were still protected. One-half of the new senate and one-third of the cabinet posts were to be filled by the president's opponents. To prevent the two traditional parties from splitting up into several "fragment parties," the law provided that each party could run as many candidates as it pleased, but that "all ballots cast for any of a party's candidates are credited to the one who received the largest number of votes." Thus the most popular candidate within the most popular party won. Terra stepped down from the presidency in 1938; his successors, beginning with his brother-in-law Alfredo Baldomir, returned to the Batlle tradition.

World War II involved Uruguay in an unexpected way. The Declaration of Panama had declared the waters of the Western Hemisphere "out of bounds" for the belligerents, and Uruguay had joined in it. Uruguay then acted belligerently herself when British cruisers drove the German pocket battleship *Graf Spee* into refuge in Montevideo harbor. When the great ship overstayed her limit in neutral waters, she was scuttled, perhaps by the captain, in Montevideo Bay, and her crew interned; Uruguay answered international protests by announcing that her action was in accordance with the Declaration of Panama. Uruguay was then one of the first Latin American nations to sever relations with the Axis powers after Pearl Harbor, conceding the use of bases to the United States and securing military equipment through lend-lease, as opposed to the pro-Nazi attitude of "big neighbor" Argentina. In February 1945, in time to qualify for membership in the United Nations, Uruguay declared war on the Axis.

Luis Herrera, the aging Blanco leader, was an old political warhorse, pro-Nazi and proclerical in opinion though an intellectual historian on the side. He ran for the presidency in 1942, and again in 1946, but a series of political "coups," minor constitutional changes, and Colorado winnings kept him from office. In 1946 Herrera won a plurality of votes as a person but was forced to concede to the Colorado candidate with a lesser total vote because the combined Colorado party vote was greater—the law being that "the highest candidate in the highest party wins." Of the three Colorado candidates in 1946, one was Batlle's own son, editor of the family paper *El Día*, and another was Batlle's favorite nephew and heir-apparent in politics, Luis Batlle Berres. Though Tomás Berreta, the third candidate, won the plurality, Batlle Berres became vice-president, and succeeded to the presidency on the death of the aged Berreta.

Again in 1950 the law of "the highest candidate in the highest party" defeated Herrera and elected Andrés Martínez Trueba. The new president bent all his efforts to restore the Batlle type of government which was contained in a new constitution ratified by a plebiscite in 1951. Under it there was again a nine-member federal executive council, but this time with no president at all. Instead the council ruled Uruguay as the federal council of seven rules Switzerland, the chairmanship rotating among the members by the year. There was also a cabinet, which depended on the majority within the assembly and rose or fell with that majority according to the English system. The council was put into operation with Trueba as its first chairman.

That literary-minded old warhorse Herrera got a seat on the executive council at last in 1952 and again in 1954, but his chance to serve as chairman, and thus as national president, was blocked by the political make-up of the body. Luis Batlle Berres, José Batlle's nephew, and Cesar Batlle Pacheco, José Batlle's son, both served on the council and became bitter rivals within the Colorado party. When acting as the chairman in 1956, the nephew Luis came to visit in the United States; he was described as a "mild, chubby, rather sad-eyed little man," famous for his constant support of a losing soccer team and for his concern with child welfare projects.

However, the inflation and the competition in world markets that all one-crop Latin American nations faced sent up prices of manufactured articles in Montevideo and brought down the real value of fixed pensions. Uruguay, the most welfare-minded economy in Latin America, had difficulties. There were strikes and unemployment; the wool market dropped; nationalized industries were being mismanaged. In the elections of December 1958 a new rural leader, Benito Nardone, a folksy radio star who had taken to the country precincts to arouse political support of Herrera's long-losing Blanco Nationals, was able to win a majority vote for the Blancos on the nine-man council, a break for the Blancos after ninety-three years of Colorado control. Blanco Herrera, by then eighty-five, was leader-emeritus of an aging faction of the old Blancos which bickered with Nardone's more modern-minded Blanco friends. The Batlle cousins continued to split the Colorado or urban party. In the 1962 elections Blancos won the National Council, but the Colorados held the Congress.

The Colorados had not realized that their cozy little welfare state was good for city workers only, and that the countryside, source of the nation's wealth, was a century behind. Not only did farm workers receive few social benefits, but the rich farm land itself was being used to only one-third of its possible capacity. In the ten years from 1956 to 1966, Uruguay's share in the world meat market had fallen from 9 per cent to 7 per cent, in wool from 16 per cent to 10 per cent. Without the foreign exchange brought into Montevideo by meat and wool exports, the city itself was declining. A government facing bankruptcy could not afford the generous pensions at fifty-five and the high unemployment insurance and yearly wage increases the city workers wanted. Pension payments fell three years in arrears by 1965, and the value of the peso had plunged. Meat prices were so much higher across the border in Brazil that farmers drove their cattle into Rio Grande do Sul and let the Montevideo *frigoríficos* work on half time. To people in the city, unpaid and out of work, Cuban *Fidelismo* began to look good. Anti–United States feeling mounted and crowds heckled official American visitors. President Nardone had to beef up an army of 10,000—the first efficient military force in Uruguay in the twentieth century—to deal with rioters. A thousand army men ran the electric and telephone services when the electric workers' union went on strike, and thus proved that most of the 12,000 striking workers in the government-run industry were "featherbedding."

In the midst of this economic chaos, both Batlle Berres and Benito

Nardone died in 1964. In March of 1965 Washington Beltrán, fifty-one-year-old editor of the Batlle newspaper *El Día,* became president of the council. By this time the council seemed no more than a third house of the legislature. Beltrán hoped to strengthen the executive power. In August 1965 he sent a commission to the United States for advice and financial help. A plan was made to refund $500 million of Uruguay's national debt in Washington, in return for austerity at home. This meant cuts in wages and pensions, so 500,000 members of the National Confederation of workers went out on strike. In the midst of strikes and inflation, the Council asked for a vote to return to a single executive. On November 27, 1966, by a large majority, the voters voted for a new constitution providing for a single strong president for a five year term, and elected retired Air Force General Oscar D. Gestido. He took office on March 1, 1967. Just before the election, the Blancos still in power had granted 90 percent salary increases to civil service employees, of which there were 250,000 or a third of the working people of the nation. Hence when Gestido took office he had to default, and fired one third of these government employees. When the remaining civil servants went on strike he took action under an emergency law of August, 1967. He froze wages, jailed many of the strikers, and broke the strike with army men. Declaring a limited state of siege to enforce his measures, he devalued the *peso* one hundred per cent in one day.

But Gestido soon died of a heart attack, and was replaced by Jorge Pacheco Areco, the vice President. He was a relatively unknown editor who lacked Gestido's reputation and personal popularity. Forced to continue Gestido's repressive measures to keep peace in the city, Pacheco joined with some of the more conservative Blancos to keep Uruguayan democracy "afloat" until the general elections of 1972. Batlle's system of two-party democracy under a mild socialist economy was certainly being challenged.

Much of the trouble was the failure of the economy in the early 1970s. The generous pension system created a heavy financial strain on the state; one person drew a government pension for every two and a half persons who were employed. Inflation had pushed the cost of living up 182 per cent in 1967 and 1968. The market for sheep's wool, which was facing worldwide decline in demand due to the popularity of synthetic wool-like fabrics, was now being monopolized by improved fleece from New Zealand and Australia. A foot-and-mouth disease epidemic had cut down the beef exports. There was increasing graft and corruption among the government employees and much tax evasion and profiteering among the population. Many old-line Communists were strongly intrenched in the labor movement and Montevideo served as a nerve center for Communist bloc activity in South America.

In addition to these troubles, Montevideo citizens faced a wave of terror created by 500 or so young activists who called themselves the Tupamaros, a word derived from Tupac Amarú, the last of the Incas. With seemingly no constructive long-range plans, but only the immediate goal of overthrowing the Pacheco government, they robbed banks and casinos, sabotaged or destroyed radio stations and bombed restaurants and recreation spots in an attempt to stop the tourist traffic. Then in July of 1970, they achieved wide publicity throughout the world by kidnapping foreign envoys and important Uruguayan government officials. One of their captives, an American advisor in city police methods, was murdered. In January 1971 they captured the British ambassador, and held the Brazilian ambassador until he was ransomed by his own wife for $250,000. Later in the year more than a hundred of the terrorists broke out of jail. A more military minded man, Juan María Bordaberry, succeeded to the presidency early in 1972, and was granted unlimited powers by the Congress to make "internal war" on the Tupamaros. On April 14, 1972 the terrorists launched a new wave of violence leaving 12 people dead. Uruguay's long struggle for true democracy was not to win out in the early 1970s.

Uruguay as an economic and cultural unit

Uruguay's economy, more so than that of Argentina, is dependent on the two economic tyrants, wool and meat. Helpless when world prices in these commodities fluctuate, Uruguay has attempted to overcome the handicap of the one-crop economy by social and economic experimentation through government ownership in industry. The state owns the Bank of the Republic, the Mortgage Bank, and the State Insurance Bank, which has a monopoly on all forms of insurance—life, fire, marine, and accident. The State Electricity Board controls all light, power, and phones; a government corporation runs the harbor and manages all fuel and alcohol, and even all cement in this treeless country where building is seldom done with wood. A government-run *frigorífico* processes a quarter of the nation's meat for export. Radio stations, beach hotels, ballet troupes are government business. A fishing fleet and a fish cannery, a truck and bus line, a taxicab concession, all are owned by the state. Uruguay points with pride to the fact that little foreign capital has been necessary in her development. Although the number of government employees is top-heavy, the program has achieved a good deal of success, perhaps because the country is so small. Only one city is involved, and it would have been difficult to build up any large private capital in a country without coal or iron. Uruguay weathered the depression, the effects of World War II, and the postwar boom, but her welfare state has been expensive, and she faced actual bankruptcy due to inflation in the 1970s.

Meanwhile the people have happily supported themselves aided by many types of social security from the government. Batlle's personal enemies had bitterly opposed his 1911 plans for social legislation. "Why should we," they wrote in their own paper, "an underpopulated country hardly known abroad, continually astonish the world with the radicalism of our laws?" "You have not seen anything yet," the editor of *El Día* snapped back, "We may be a poor and obscure little republic, but we can have forward-looking little laws." These words became so famous they were used in pushing legislation for two generations. Maximum work hours, minimum wages, unemployment and accident insurance, and workmen's compensation were the order of the day. The year 1916 saw an old-age pension law. The Spanish word most often used for "retired" in Montevideo is *jubilado,* and older workers have happily looked forward to *jubilación* for more than a generation. A modern "Children's Code" is concerned with all children, legitimate and illegitimate, from conception through high school.

When the term "city" is used, only Montevideo is meant. With its wide boulevards and fine beaches and its more than million and a half people, it dominates the little country just as Providence dominates Rhode Island. Paysandú, second urban center, has less than 100,000 people collected around plants for canning corned beef and for processing leather. Steamers go up the Uruguay River to the farming center at Salto where orange and tangerine groves cover thousands of acres and honey is produced in quantity for export. Railroads and modern highways radiate from Montevideo and into Paraguay, Argentina, and southern Brazil. The Pan American Highway connects towns from Montevideo all the way to São Paulo.

Between the Uruguay River on the west and Montevideo on the east lie the rolling grasslands, home of the old Blanco aristocrats. Still wealthy today, these estate owners live much more simply than do the Argentine *estancieros* or the Chilean *fundo* owners. There is little need of farm buildings around the rambling estate houses, for in the mild climate on the edge of the subtropics cattle live outside the year round, and feed never has to be stored. Due to the use of so much land for grazing, there has been little opportunity for small freeholding farmers, and the government has to subsidize a wheat-planting program in order to get enough flour for Montevideo's bakers without importing it. High wages in the city and machine methods on the estates have driven the agricultural workers off the land; most of the social legislation refers to city laborers. One of Uruguay's greatest economic needs today is the counterbalancing of excessive urbanization by mechanized, improved agriculture. Meanwhile the population has continued to grow as European immigration flows into this already predominantly white country, which by 1970 had a population of 2,886,000.

Across the rolling Uruguayan pampas, there are very few small village units around a rural school and church as there are in Mexico or Brazil. The Basque shepherds and their staff of riders contact other communities only at lambing or shearing time. Although mutton and wool from the Merino, Lincoln, and Romney strains of purebreds brought in from Europe are of a high grade, Uruguayan beef is considered inferior on the world markets because of the absence of special care and feeding methods on the open ranges. Uruguayan economists are concerned that Argentine beef and Australian wool bring higher prices than Uruguayan, and wonder whether some of the advanced social thinking spent on improving conditions for city workers should not have been applied also to improving the care and diet of the livestock and thus bringing in more money from world markets.

Since, in spite of the limited economy, Uruguayan life is easy and pleasant, it is not surprising that Uruguayan writers are among the best in

Latin America. Uruguayans had been writing poetry since the time of the Thirty-three Immortals, and gold medals had been awarded for nationalistic and romantic poetry as early as the 1850s. By 1865 *La Revista Literaria* was being published in Montevideo; many of its successful poetry contributors were revolutionists and soldiers as well as writers, but they wrote of romance rather than realism. A famous epic poem of Indian life, called *Tabaré*, was published by Juan Zorilla de San Martín (1855–1931) in 1888, and is considered a masterpiece of Uruguayan literature. Other "masterpieces" dealt with the life of the colonial aristocracy—for example, the versified novel called *Celiar*, written by Alejandro Magariños Cervantes (1825–1893). Today Magariños' best-known book is his novel of gaucho life, *Caramarú*.

The 1890s saw Uruguay produce a novelist worthy of international attention, Eduardo Acevedo Díaz (1851–1924), whose trilogy of novels about the Uruguayan ranchers and their part in the many wars between factions are full of descriptions of landscapes and manners as well as understanding of the bitterness of the strife. *Estancia* owners, beautiful relatives from the city, gauchos, Charrúa Indians, and Brazilian soldiers take part in the interwoven plots of the three novels, but it is the character and the vivid description of them that are important in the literary history of South America.

The essayist José Enrique Rodó (1872–1917) has been called the "greatest modernist prose writer," second only to Rubén Darío as a Latin American literary light. He died in 1917, but not before he had written a thin little book called *Ariel*. The refined and cultured spirit of the aristocratic Latin American—not of the gaucho or the Indian—is the true Ariel of Shakespeare's play, *The Tempest*, while North American materialism, which Rodó considered an evil menace, is the crude gorilla-like Caliban, villain of the play. Thus Latin Americans should be proud of their own culture; there should be a "spiritual unity" among the Spanish-speaking people of the New World; they are the true Americans. Since Rodó was editor of a literary review widely read in all Spanish-speaking countries, his influence in arousing intellectuals against the United States is felt to this day.

Another Uruguayan "greatest in Spanish America" in the twentieth century was the short story writer Horacio Quiroga (1878–1937), who knew the jungle country of the Argentine province of Misiones and spent several years in the Chaco. His jungle stories made the outdoors a popular subject for story material. The backlands world of the gaucho was still the central theme of several well-known Uruguayan works at mid-twentieth century. As in all Latin American countries, Uruguayan poets are as numerous as journalists or politicians—young "ultraists" who write obscurely and live the Bohemian life, such as Julio Herrera y Reissig (1875–1910), and more serious public figures who write poetry as an avocation, among whom are several women. Uruguayans are active in literary criticism and have some well-known literary periodicals. Markets for books being small, the authors must finance their writings, but the Ministry of Public Instruction offers prizes and purchases a number of copies.

Opera and drama are so good in Montevideo that the discriminating Argentines cross the long ferry route to see the state-sponsored Uruguayan shows. All Montevideo theater activity comes under a government agency called SODRE, the initials for Official Service of Radio and Culture Diffusion. SODRE takes summer stock into the backlands, operates schools of opera and ballet, manages the symphony, and conducts art competitions and art classes. "High-quality, low-priced entertainment and artistic training" is SODRE's motto. One of South America's greatest artists was the Uruguayan painter Pedro Fegari (1861–1938). The more recent Uruguayan painter, Joaquin Torres García (1874–1949) went to Spain as an art student and worked with the Spanish abstractionists Miró and Picasso. He returned to Montevideo to introduce Picasso's style to South America. Called the "Latin American artist who did most for universal painting," he founded a studio and gallery in Montevideo which bears his name and from which current Uruguayan artists send traveling exhibitions to New York.

Uruguay is a literate nation, a nation of newspaper readers. Education is the highest single item on the national budget, since Uruguay feels no need for armament spending. Actual compulsory attendance is enforced, not merely written into beautiful law as in other small Latin American lands. All Uruguayan schools are tuition-free, including the university, and there are thousands of high school graduates who continue on to college. Uruguayan college life seems very much like that of the United States, with an intense interest in school sports. The Uruguayans in general are very sports-minded, and they follow international soccer with the zest common to baseball fans in the United States.

Paraguay: isolated under its first dictators

Paraguay, inland country to the northwest of Uruguay with a name so similar, had started out more auspiciously than its coastal sister. Its history had been fascinating, though of third-rate importance. Isolated in the heart of the continent, almost completely an Indian country, with Asunción the oldest Spanish city in the Plate area and the center of the greatest Jesuit successes, the whole nation had no access to the sea except through Argentina. Saved by a powerful, unchallenged dictator from the usual costly civil war after independence, and building up an isolated but self-sufficient agricultural economy, this inland nation of Guaraní-speaking mestizo peoples had every chance for peace. Paraguay remained a one-party state under three dictators, the second succeeding the first at his death from old age, the third chosen by his father the second, as his rightful heir. But with the succession of this "crown prince" in the 1860s Paraguay's peace ended, and the little nation was plunged into a war against three other nations which practically annihilated the Paraguayan people.

Independence had come to Paraguay as a by-product of the movement centered at Buenos Aires. General Belgrano had tried to force Paraguay under the sway of the junta of Buenos Aires of 1810. Dr. José Gaspar Rodríguez Francia, who led the Paraguayans, was able to rid his country of both Spanish and Argentine interference. An assembly called in Paraguay made him "first consul" and finally perpetual dictator, which he remained for twenty-nine years, longer than anyone else in South American history. Dr. Francia declared complete independence in 1813, refused to participate in the Congress of Tucumán in 1816, and kept his country in splendid isolation until his death in 1840.

Dr. Francia was an educated man, one of the few in Asunción, with a degree from the University of Córdoba. As dictator he ruled without congress, ministers, or tribunals, although he refused any salary, made no attempt to enrich himself, and hired watchers to keep a close tab on the national treasury. His foreign policy was one of complete isolation; no visitors came in save for two or three scientists who were under constant surveillance during their brief botanical forays. No Paraguayans went out. Traffic downriver was all but closed.

A lean, haughty man, misanthropic but devoted to peace and prosperity in Paraguay, Dr. Francia does not follow the pattern of cowboy or soldier *caudillos*. His people called him *El Supremo*, and took off their hats when he passed; for this his law required that every Paraguayan wear a hat to take off, even though he might wear little else. Death, torture, and exile came swiftly to anyone who opposed Dr. Francia. As he isolated Paraguay from the rest of the world, so he isolated himself from humanity, living alone with four servants. He even set spies to spy on his spies.

Dr. Francia made long-range plans for his backward state; he avoided the holocaust of civil war experienced by most other new Latin American nations and he forced economic self-sufficiency. When Argentina charged a heavy duty on river traffic, Dr. Francia quit foreign trade and insisted that the Paraguayans raise their own corn and cane, cotton and tobacco, *yerba mate* and beef, rather than depend on Argentine crops for food. Only munitions to fortify the frontiers and arm the secret police came from abroad; the people did without everything else. Livestock increased; local trade between villages was encouraged by fairs. Money was unnecessary when every trade was made by barter. Jesuit missionaries would have seen little difference in the way of life in Paraguay from 1640 to 1840. The only outside enemy that Dr. Francia had to fight was a great army of locusts; he drafted all males from fourteen to sixty to replant the half-grown harvest the locusts had destroyed. Legend has it that thus Dr. Francia learned that two crops of wheat and corn would grow in a year in this semitropical land, and ordered that such be planted henceforth.

The Asunción of Dr. Francia's last years had only 20,000 people, but it was Paraguay's only city. There were very few two-story houses, and "sand still substituted for pavement," according to one of the few visiting scientists. "Ravines continued their errant ways, and served as efficient sewers in wet weather" and the "shops were miserable stores like those of the countryside in Argentina."

The Paraguayan natives did not let such criticism bother them. More generous and happy natured than the trade-minded Montevideans, Paraguayans went barefoot, but wore the embroidered white drawers of the

Argentine gauchos below their baggy pants and tied them with scarlet sashes. Though the majority of these Paraguayans were of mestizo stock, all spoke the Guaraní language, which had been written down by the Jesuit missionaries. When some Paraguayans were taught to read and write under Francia, it was Guaraní they learned first before Spanish, for Dr. Francia was very much pro-Guaraní. A few well-to-do families in Asunción aped the styles of Buenos Aires—their meagre contact with the outside world, two weeks travel downriver. In such a nation no literature developed. Church authority was limited strictly by the anticlerical *El Supremo*, but no other social force arose to take its place.

At the age of seventy-four *El Supremo* rode in his formal carriage past his reverential subjects for the last time. On September 20, 1840, he was dead, though the people could not believe he would ever die. He left no heir and no tradition of electing one. Francia's secretary Patiño, after hiding the news of *El Supremo's* death as long as he could, called a junta to govern, with himself as secretary. The junta threw the secretary into jail, where he committed suicide. After six months of government by a confused junta, a congress was called in March 1841 which proceeded to set up the same type of "consul" government Dr. Francia had started in 1811. Chief consul was Carlos Antonio López, who served in that capacity three years. In 1844 he called a congress to adopt a constitution making himself president for ten years; this "election" process was repeated ten years later and signified "approval" of his rule until his death in 1862.

There could not be two *Supremos*, so Carlos López was called *Excelentísimo*. López was a huge, corpulent, pear-shaped man, mild mannered and "respectable looking"; his regime was one of stability equal to that of Dr. Francia and of much greater modernization and material prosperity. He reorganized the judicial system, collected taxes on a fair basis, brought in the first newspaper, abolished slavery, and tried to encourage primary education. Sixteen young Paraguayans were sent at his own expense to study in Europe. A railroad fifty-five miles long was built from Asunción toward the Uruguayan border, bridges were built across the Paraná, and ferry service was established between towns.

Carlos López meant to establish a place in foreign affairs for Paraguay, a reversal of Francia's policy. He arranged for his country's recognition by Argentina for the first time, but he was not as successful in other forays into foreign relations as he had hoped. Paraguay's boundaries with Argentina and Brazil remained unsettled, a problem his son was to use as a reason for war. He quarreled with the United States over an American steamship company formed to commence regular steamship traffic and whose first cargo was wrecked on the Brazilian coast. England also had an altercation with López and forced the release of a captured British subject by blockading a Paraguayan ship which was in Buenos Aires harbor. France was also angered by López when promises to French settlers induced to settle the frontier were not kept. All these clashes hurt Paraguay's prestige abroad at a time when the nation was definitely hoping for importance and position. At least Carlos López did not involve the nation in any foreign debt; he had developed the country's resources, opened it to foreign commerce, and left to his son and successor an economically prosperous land.

the Paraguayan War of Francisco Solano López

Carlos López' most serious mistake was in the choice of his son as successor. Francisco Solano López was a boy of fourteen when his father came to power, untrained, ignorant, and barefooted. Soon he was given a commission in the army, assigned special tutors, and taught to speak French and to ape the manners of the small colony of diplomats in Asunción. Long before he was thirty he was the commander in chief of the armed forces and built a large military machine in order to play politics against his strong neighbors, Brazil and Argentina. Francisco, the "crown prince" who by now imagined himself the "Napoleon of the New World," went to Paris to buy ships and arms for a River Plate empire and to make an impression on Parisian society. Already bored with his half-Guaraní girl of Asunción, he acquired a mistress in Paris, a footloose Irish girl named Elisa Lynch. She shared his plans for a South American Napoleonic empire and returned with him to lead Asunción society. Carlos López persuaded his subservient congress a month before his death to proclaim Francisco his legal successor. When the *Excelentísimo* died, Paraguay's slow and peaceful life came to an abrupt end, for Francisco, his mistress, and his army immediately took control of the government. On October 16, 1862, he was declared Supreme Chief and General of the Armies.

Francisco Solano followed his father's internal policies and actually made some improvements in communications and transportation. He established the first telegraphic line in South America and dreamed of making Asunción a great city so that his paramour would not feel so downcast at having left Paris. But his foreign policy was so ambitious as to be disastrous. To push it, he built up in two years the largest, best-trained army that South America had ever seen.

Meanwhile Argentina and Brazil skirmished over the *blancos* and the *colorados* in Uruguay. When Brazil supported the *colorados* in Uruguay, López supported the *blancos*—sufficient excuse for war. In November 1864 López seized a Brazilian steamer which had heretofore been allowed peaceful transit up the Paraguay River as the only route by which Brazilians could reach their undeveloped province of Mato Grosso. Then he sent an army into the Brazilian area. In order to attack the Brazilian troops in Uruguay as soon as war was openly declared the next month, Francisco López invaded the Argentine province of Corrientes. Though Argentina and Brazil had been traditional enemies in the long disputes in Uruguay, they now united against Francisco López; he was not to have the pleasure of fighting them one at a time. Indeed, his side lost out in Uruguay, and that small nation then joined the Triple Alliance fighting against Paraguay.

Historians are prone to put all the blame for the ensuing war on López, but this is a misinterpretation of fact. The war had its origins in

Brazilian encroachments upon Paraguayan territory, in Brazilian and Argentine meddling in Uruguay, and in Paraguayan desires to play a decisive role in the politics of the Plata area. It is true, however, that Francisco López precipitated the war, and upon him rests the responsibility of the tragic results for Paraguay. The costly and bloody war lasted nearly six years.

The Paraguayans fought with fanatical bravery throughout, though the odds against them were overwhelming. Once López' troops had lost the offensive, the combined enemy troops fought right up the Paraguay River toward the heart of the nation. Brazil sent her naval squadron up the river to win Brazil's only naval engagement among the water hyacinths. Pedro II's son-in-law, the Comte d'Eu, fought in this useless war, as did the great Argentine statesman Bartolomé Mitre, wasting his ability and Argentina's resources when he was the elected president. Paraguayans swam out into the river to attack Brazilian ships, or stole along in canoes camouflaged with the water hyacinths. Three thousand Paraguayans held muddy trenches along the river against 15,000 invaders, and, with but a handful of soldiers, maintained a fort at Humaitá on the Paraguay River for months against the allied fleet. Six thousand howling Guaraní attacked 40,000 allied soldiers in a narrow pass and were almost entirely wiped out. No individual Paraguayan would admit defeat. Francisco López had taught each of his Guaraní soldiers to consider himself worth six of the enemy. But they were doomed to defeat because of the lack of adequate leadership, the inferiority of numbers and resources, and the extreme isolation of Paraguay.

After four years, every male in Paraguay from eleven to sixty was at the front on the river approaches above Corrientes; women and children worked without wages behind the lines. Elisa Lynch is said to have led a women's battalion into the last days of fighting. Francisco López himself escaped with 2,000 survivors when the enemy occupied Asunción. In the wilderness 150 miles north of the city the allies tracked him and cut him down, leaving his body to rot in the sun, where Elisa found it and covered it with dirt dug with her own bare hands.

The conquering allies set up a provisional government, then signed a peace treaty with this new government in June of 1870, a treaty which exacted a heavy indemnity. The prostrate Paraguay was unable to make any such payments, so the allies kept occupation troops in Paraguay for six more years. Argentina and Brazil each wanted territory from Paraguay; she was forced to grant 55,000 square miles of land northeast of the Paraguay River to Brazil and all claim to Misiones and the region beyond the Pilcomayo to Argentina. Some of this territory has not yet been surveyed. The border disputes concerning frontiers set by the treaty dragged on. Eventually Argentina's dispute was settled by the arbitration of President Hayes of the United States in November of 1878, who gave the disputed Pilcomayo Chaco lands to Paraguay.

When the allies withdrew they left chaos in the government of the devastated country. After the Paraguayan War, when other nations were settling into stability, the era of palace revolutions, changing *caudillos*, and upset constitutions had only begun in Paraguay. Twenty-two   presidents were to serve Paraguay in the forty-two years between 1870 and 1912, a year in which some stability began. It would be pointless to list the names of the individuals involved in these uncertain administrations and of the rebellions that overturned them. The Constitution of 1870 had intended to establish a centralized government. The *colorado* party, which was founded under the aegis of General Bernardino Caballero in 1874, remained in power until 1904, when the Liberal Party, founded in 1887, came to power in one of the more "popular" revolts. There was no real party government, however, and gunplay, not ballots, changed the administration. Not until 1912 was a president elected who filled out a full four-year term in office.

Socially, the Paraguayan War, the War of Francisco Solano López, was even more of a disaster. It is estimated that there were 525,000 people in Paraguay when Francisco López came to power. In 1871 the victorious allies counted 221,079, of whom 106,254 were women, 86,079 children and 28,746 adult men. Such a shortage of men led to promiscuity, to large numbers of illegitimate children, and to a race of lazy males in a land where the women did all the work. Also, the land which the women now had to farm was devastated, the orange orchards were neglected, the horses and cattle dead. Schools were closed and newspapers unprinted for a generation. There were no writers, for people had forgotten how to read.

Paraguay: a twentieth-century victim of its nineteenth-century troubles

Paraguay is an isolated country with no access to the world save through other nations' territory. Naturally this landlocked nation of a million and a half Indians and mestizos is predominantly rural. The average Paraguayan lives amongst the bounty of his own little farm, goes to the sagging colonial church in the middle of his town's weedy little plaza, and does not worry about politics. He is likely to own his little farm of about ten acres, planted in corn, mandioca, beans, and garden vegetables. Perhaps five or six acres will be planted in cotton, the one crop that ever gets to a city market. His family may own a run-down cow or two, some donkeys, pigs, and chickens. His women sit at home or in the village market place making the famous *ñandutí* lace or some other local handicraft specialty. His hut is made of bamboo poles and adobe, with little furniture inside, and kitchen utensils all outside. The family sits outside also to drink *yerba maté*, the Paraguayan tea, from the *bombilla*, or tube stuck in a gourd, and to eat the *puchero* or stew made from boiled beef, vegetables, and mandioca root.

Several years ago the Rockefeller Foundation made a health survey in a district of such family farms. More than 30 per cent of the people had malaria; bad water brought frequent typhoid epidemics; lack of mineral content in the water produced a high incidence of goiter. There was one case of leprosy for every 500 people, seventeen cases of tuberculosis for every thousand. The Rockefeller Foundation workers were looking particularly for hookworm, and they found more than 80 per cent of the rural population infected in the area studied. Illiteracy also ran 80 per cent.

Naturally, there are Paraguayans for whom life is neither so unhealthy nor so simple. Reporting 411,500 people in 1968, one-sixth of all Paraguayans, Asunción was more in touch with the world than ever before in the mid-1960s. Airplanes now come in and out every day; steamers dock twice a week, at the end of the three-day trip up the Paraguay from Buenos Aires. The train across eastern Paraguay runs the 230 miles to Encarnación on the Alto Paraná, and on across the Argentine province of Misones to connect with Montevideo and Buenos Aires once a week. A modern paved highway has been built 475 miles across the Chaco to the Bolivian border. Asunción itself has electricity and a modern water and sewer system, financed with an American loan. Along one bank of the river is a fine residential district; banks and government buildings seem imported from a good-sized North American city, but ladies who want to shop in big department stores must go downriver to Buenos Aires. Although hovels along the waterfront are mere country-type straw huts, and 60 percent of the city dwellers are illiterate, the city has enough soccer fans to support a league of fifteen different teams, and to back a national team which is skillful enough to compete with the invincible Uruguayans. Villa Rica, a good-sized town, lives off sawmills and sugar refineries; Concepción with 34,000 inhabitants has meat-packing plants and a tannery. Encarnación on the Alto Paraná facing Argentina at the end of the railway is considered a port, but it seems no more than a country village without an actual main street save the railway tracks, although it has a population of 35,000.

North and west of Asunción are wild lands of the Chaco, a region where "there is not even a tree without thorns." On the far side of the Chaco are the foothills of the Andes, but the rivers which rise there are lost in lagoons and marshes during the flood season, February to April, while the marshes turn into hard-packed dry beds during the rest of the year. In spite of the new highway, only a vast development program with millions in modern capital to spend could preserve the water through the dry season for livestock and humans. Oil is hoped for in the Chaco. Many of the Indians of the Chaco are primitive migrants, who move from water hole to water hole as the dry season advances. Temperatures vary from almost freezing in the fierce winds of July and August to around 115° in December, the highest temperatures recorded in South America. Such conditions dominate three-fifths of Paraguay's actual area.

There has been some settlement in the Chaco, especially a group of 1,700 Mennonites from Canada, whose cooperative agricultural colonies prospered after bitter years of drought. Sixteen hundred more Mennonites came to the colony in 1929 from Soviet Russia, and another 2,300 from displaced persons' camps in 1949. The success of this latter group led the International Refugee Organization to send a large number of Ukrainians to the area north of Asunción on the edge of the Chaco; individual European settlers, artisans, and independent farmers have not come to any part of Paraguay in any great numbers. The rush of Italians, Basques, Germans, and Swiss to southern South America stopped far downriver on the pampas. On the Paraguayan continuation of the pampas, the Gran Chaco, the only successful inhabitants are the Indians most of whom have seen no white men, wear no clothes, paint their bodies with geometric designs, and hunt game with bow and arrow. President Stroessner was hoping in the early 1970s to build up the equally undeveloped northeast on the Brazilian border, where he opened a $30 million hydroelectric project.

The Chaco produces some tanning extract from the hard wood called *quebracho,* which is logged by private concerns—the principal one Argentinean—having their own railways and logging camps. From the more wooded area of Paraguay, timber for beams, girders, and railroad ties is shipped downstream to treeless Argentina to make up the major export. The wild forests of Paraguay also produce the *yerba maté,* the Paraguayan tea so popular in Argentina, but plantation-type development within Argentina itself has stolen most of the market from the wild leaf. Cotton farming in the populated southern area of Paraguay has to fight locusts and a special tropical "pink boll worm" and can hardly compete with Argentina and United States cotton. Paraguay's tough, lean, tick-bitten cattle are descended from the cattle brought upriver by Irala, with little admixture of improved breeds. Only meat concentrates and canned beef are exported since neither flesh nor hides are of a quality fit for world trade. Oranges brought to the Guaraní missions by the Jesuit fathers have flourished almost in a wild state; during the 1920s and 1930s boatloads of them, gathered piecemeal from each tiny ranch, went downriver to Buenos Aires. Then Argentina began to refuse the scrubby little seedlings as inferior to her own navel oranges. Paraguay grows enough food to feed herself and, in addition to those products already mentioned, exports tobacco and petit-grain oil. Thus it can be seen that Paraguay depends upon agriculture, livestock, and forest products.

Small wonder that during World War II when Paraguay was given a chance by the United States Coordinator of Inter-American Affairs to choose some type of technical aid, she chose scientific agricultural advice. By 1950 a fourfold program had jointly been worked out to be partially financed by the Paraguayans: kill orange blights and improve tree stock by grafting, augment cattle diet by grain feeding, raise milk production, and preserve stored crops from rats and weevils by means of underground silos. Botanists, plant pathologists, dairy and livestock experts started the pilot project. Farmers in villages reached by truck roads were brought to the model farms in groups by bus. More than 11,000 farmers also received loans from the *Servicio Técnico Inter-americano de Cooperación Agrícola,* or STICA, as the joint agency was called. At the time, the plan was considered a pattern for other Point Four projects, but it would take another generation of interested farmers before these methods influenced Paraguay greatly.

It is not surprising that a nation which for so many years devoted its energies to war should still be backward in education. Though the law says primary education is free and compulsory, elementary schools are inadequate and the law is not enforced. In Asunción and the larger towns the "educated classes" are increasing, however; the university has 2,000 students and there is now an agricultural school as well as the medical and law schools. The Guaraní language, a source of much national pride, is actually a cultural drawback. Though there is some fine literature in Guaraní, it has no circulation outside Paraguay. Spanish itself is twisted by the Paraguayans, and many suffixes and prefixes of Guaraní origin make new words in the Spanish of even Asunción's elite.

Transportation remains the great hindrance. In spite of the dawning air age the rivers are still the main through freight routes. Vessels of seven-foot draft, most of them belonging to an Argentine company, come up to Asunción; vessels of five-foot draft go on up to Corumbá in Brazil's Mato Grosso, 1,800 miles from the Atlantic, and maintain a service from Corumbá to Asunción and thence to Buenos Aires every three weeks. All Paraguay reaches the outside world only through Argentina or the new roads which join those in the interiors of Bolivia and Brazil.

An isolated nation, a poor economy, a crippling war in the 1860s, military occupation for nearly a decade, a decimated population, thirty years of changing presidencies—what hopes were there for Paraguay in the early 1900s? A popular revolution in 1904 threw out the long-entrenched Colorado rule and ushered in Liberal party rule. But the change did not produce stability, and Paraguay continued to be ruled by a rapid turnover of *caudillos.* From 1870 to 1932 there were twenty-nine different presidents. The *cuartelazos,* or barracks-room revolutions, continued. Often they boiled out of the *cuarteles,* the soldiers' quarters, into the streets. A major and ten companions captured the artillery barracks to make one such revolution, "mounted guns at street corners to command approaches to public buildings, and waited till sunrise to start the shooting," according to Paraguayan history. Another change in government was brought by a politician who imported 200 farmers from a town forty-five miles away, farmers who knew nothing about the government in the city, but fought hard for the fun of it. An outgoing president quelled a revolution against his successor by mounting a naval piece on a railway car. His opponents won by "seizing a locomotive, packing it with high explosives, and sending it careening madly down the rails." This particular little by-play took place in 1911. The year 1912 saw a peacefully elected German-Paraguayan, Eduardo Schaerer, come to the presidency, bringing a short respite of peace, prosperity, and progress to Paraguay, and actually serving out his full term, the first president since the López family to do so.

It is strange that the presidents of this early part of the new century were intellectuals; they are called the "Generation of 1900," and their era, the "Golden Age of Paraguayan Culture." Dr. Cecilio Báez (1862–1919), leader of the liberals who ushered in Liberal party rule, was a college teacher who occupied the highest posts in state and University, a leader in the fight for religious tolerance, and a prolific writer in both French and Spanish on Paraguayan history and diplomacy. His contemporary, Manuel Domínguez (1867–1935), served as vice-president and foreign minister, while he also spent his spare time writing lyrical poems and patriotic essays on Paraguay's past. A third outstanding figure of the literary-political "Generation of 1900" was Manuel Gondra (1871–1927), expert on the problems of the Chaco, and twice president, who was also an historian of note and a literary critic.

Although the "Generation of 1900" established a bank, chartered the steamship company from Buenos Aires, and built the railway to Encarnación, their Golden Age cannot in any way be compared to the era of Sarmiento in Argentina or of Batlle in Uruguay. Their literary works were only read by each other; their music was performed in the parlors of the tiny group of elite; their art gallery, founded in 1910, was visited by their own wives and children and a few diplomats. All these gentlemen presidents were intellectuals in the sense of nineteenth-century liberal principles; they discussed philosophies the world had gone on to prove in practice a century earlier elsewhere. One of the last "literary presidents" was Eligio Ayala (1879–1930), whose term from 1924 to 1928 was another period of progress. As a group, these presidents never engaged in any drastic economic and social reforms; they had no interest in the masses and thus the masses had no interest in them or in the government in Asunción, for it concerned the mass of the people not at all. With such a limited economy and with such small-scale *cuartelazo* revolutions, Paraguay remained uninfluenced by the troubles of other nations—no involvement in any foreign war, no banking crises, labor troubles, unemployment, or revolts for land subdivision. When the world depression cut off Paraguay's foreign markets after 1930, there was some city unemployment and political agitation among intellectuals for reform, but Paraguay's attention was soon directed elsewhere.

For 1932 brought Paraguay a second devastating foreign war, this one over the uninhabited Chaco Boreal. Bolivia, another poor country with backward Indian peoples ruled by dictators, had claimed the Chaco since 1810, saying that it had been a part of the jurisdiction of the *audiencia* of Charcas and, as such, Bolivian property since independence. After Bolivia lost her seacoast in the War of the Pacific in 1883, she strove to get a footing on the Paraguay River and a trade route out by that river to the Atlantic. By 1927 there were border clashes in the Chaco. Then, when the Tacna-Arica dispute was settled in 1929 and hopes of reclaiming the Bolivian seacoast were dead forever, Bolivia began to press Paraguay through diplomatic channels. There was a series of conferences in Buenos Aires to adjudicate the claims; neither side would give an inch. An "incident" at a frontier fort occurred in 1928, a half-hour's fight in which five Bolivians were killed, and soon national popular indignation was whipped up in both countries. Argentina and Brazil joined with a commission of inquiry of the Pan American Union to try and stop impending disaster, but they only postponed it for four years.

In 1932 two thousand Bolivian troops were in the Chaco in January when all was an immense swamp. They were still there six months later when the earth lay baked and cracked. Paraguay had one division to every six from Bolivia, one general to every five Bolivian, sixteen cannons to Bolivia's more than a hundred, 12,000 rifles to Bolivia's boasted 100,000. Paraguay's soldiers went barefoot because no shoes were ever issued to them to wear in the coarse grass or across the thorny brush or the rough ground. But her soldiers fought upriver from home. The Bolivian commander in chief was a Nazi-trained German imported for the job; he had ideas of a blitzkrieg to be fought with modern war machines, but he had to bring machines and men down from the Andes by narrow mountain trails. His privates were Aymará and Quechua Indians, used to life at 12,000 feet altitude. All Bolivian tactics came to naught when the Indians died like flies in the low, oppressive, hot Chaco. The Western Hemisphere sat back horrified at the grueling conditions of this fighting, in which Indian fought Indian in "that Hell of green and gray." Says an historian of Paraguay, "Then let their masters gather around and draw lines on maps, on maps that will never show where brown men died for nothing!"

A truce attempt was made in 1933, and the League of Nations set up a Chaco Commission, but neither side accepted its decision. By September 1934 Paraguay had captured 22,000 square miles of the territory beyond Bolivia's line of forts, and the German commander of Bolivia's forces resigned. Both countries agreed to the request of the Argentine foreign minister to talk peace terms in Buenos Aires in June 1935, while a tense truce hung over the Chaco. The final boundary was set in July 1938, ten years after the first border incident. Paraguay received the territory she had fought for; Bolivia was given the right to come down to the Paraguay River by a railroad, which was not yet built twenty years later. Paraguayan progress had again been retarded by a senseless war.

Any political leader who agreed to the privileges granted Bolivia in the settlement could not be popular in postwar Paraguay. A new revolutionary movement, not a mere *cuartelazo*, called itself the New Paraguay, and in 1936 gained control of the presidency for its leader Rafael Franco, thus bringing to an end the Liberal party government. Franco attempted to institute some social and economic reforms, and announced a fine modernizing program from which all his successors have drawn ideas. But he failed to fulfill his promises and fell from power. After three years of more *confusionismo*, the social reform was taken up again by General José Félix Estigarribia, hero of the long campaign of attrition in the Chaco. Estigarribia came to the presidency in 1939 hoping to procure loans from the United States to build up the country, expand university education, and improve marginal lands. He helped frame the new constitution of 1940, which provided for a strong president elected for five years. Estigarribia set to work eagerly under this document, but unfortunately for Paraguay, who needed his vitality so badly, this handsome, progressive president was killed in an airplane accident after one year in office.

The hero of the Chaco was followed in the presidency by Higínio Morínigo. He was not of a pattern of the intellects of the Golden Age; his Indian mother is reported to have said that if she had known her son was to become president, she would at least have sent him to school. His only advantage was the boom trade of World War II, in which he played Argentina against the Allies for financial favors. While he joined the United States in a declaration of war and thus made Paraguay a member of the United Nations, he extracted every possible economic advantage out of friendship with the United States and Brazil, at the same time staying on the best of terms with pro-Nazi Argentina. At home the press was taken over by him, and his jails and concentration camps were full of his enemies. He did develop Paraguay economically, stimulating food production, aiding agriculture and some industry. But laborers, students, journalists, and intellectuals who opposed him and dared to strike in 1948 were ruthlessly repressed. When *cuartelazo* after *cuartelazo* tried to overthrow him, he placed the city under five months' siege. This sort of thing went on till 1947. In February of 1948 with Asunción tired of such civil war, Morínigo, after eight years of tyranny, allowed his Finance Minister, Natalicio González, to be elected. With Morínigo's retirement *confusionismo* returned to Paraguay, which had five presidents in the next seventeen months. Then the army placed the aged Frederico Chávez in the presidency with the backing of Perón in Argentina. Chávez was the equal of Morínigo as a dictator and held the Colorado Party under his heel until overthrown by the head of the army, General Alfredo Stroessner. Stroessner, who came in via *cuartelazo* in 1954, was also a Perón man, and helped the strong man in Buenos Aires to "escape" upriver to "visit" him, on his way to exile.

In November 1957 Stroessner was nominated by the party for another five-year term, beginning with the "election" held in February 1958. Paraguayan labor remained the poorest paid in Latin America, but when its leader dared to call the first strike in twelve years in September 1958, Stroessner had his army quickly stop it.

In 1963 Stroessner called an "election" in which an opposition candidate ran, but Stroessner was neatly elected for another six years. In 1969 heavy-handed Stroessner had stayed in power longer than any other Latin American ruler then living, and was elected again for the early 1970s with a majority in both houses. He remains as one of the few real caudillos left in South America. Meanwhile, his poverty-stricken Paraguayans still suffered—not only from the same malnutrition and lack of schooling, but now also from a new inflation. There has been some economic progress with the improvements in scientific agriculture, health, and education; exchange has been made free and money stabilized. There are new rail links to Brazil and new oil pipelines from Bolivia, as well as two new hydroelectric projects, but the masses feel such improvements little as yet. Stroessner's country is still 90 per cent illiterate, though he has provided jobs on the new roads and electric projects, and was hoping to welcome foreign investments and new industries. To build up a good image abroad, he denounced "Cuban Communism," sent soldiers to join American marines in Santo Domingo in 1965, and backed United States policies in the Western Hemisphere. To continue legally in office Stroessner called a convention to modernize the Constitution which met in March, 1967.

In 1971, Stroessner began his sixteenth year as president-dictator. It has been estimated that 800,000 Paraguayans have fled to neighboring Brazil and Argentina since Stroessner took office, leaving the population in 1970 at just less than 2,500,000. Although Stroessner claimed to be softening his dictatorship in the early 1970s, there was little evidence of improvement.

Thus in the last quarter of the twentieth century Paraguay seemed destined to be what it had always been—a poverty-stricken, backward, isolated, dictator-controlled country. It has the potential of becoming the paradise of Guaraní legend, but the tragedy of this natural Arcadia is that it can neither live in idyllic solitude in the twentieth century nor compete with the nations that surround it.

READINGS

Aguirre, A., ed., *Uruguay and the United Nations* (1958).

Alisky, M., *Uruguay: A Contemporary Survey* (1969).

Arnold, A. F., *Foundations of an Agricultural Policy in Paraguay* (1971).

Barrett, W. E., *The Woman on Horseback* (1938).

Bourne, R., *Political Leaders in Latin America* (1970).

Box, P. H., *Origins of the Paraguayan War* (2 vols., 1929).

Brannon, R. H., *Agricultural Development in Uruguay* (1968).

Browning, W. E., *The River Plate Republics* (1928).

Cady, J. F., *Foreign Intervention in the Río de la Plata, 1838–1850* (1929).

Canon, M. M., *Social and Labor Problems of Peru and Uruguay: A Study in Contrasts* (1945).

Chase, G., *Contemporary Art in Latin America* (1970).

Coester, A., *Literary History of Latin America* (rev. ed., 1928).

Craig, C. W. T., *Paraguayan Interlude* (1935).

Crawford, R. W., *Century of Latin American Thought* (1961).

Davis, H. E., *Social Science Trends in Latin America* (1950).

Decoud, J. S., *History of Paraguay* (2nd ed., 1902).

Dombrawski, K. von, *Land of Women* (1935).

Elliot, A. E., *Paraguay: Its Cultural Heritage, Social Conditions and Educational Problems* (1931).

Fenwich, C. G., *Inter-American Regional System* (1949).

Fernández, Artucio H., *Nazi Underground in South America* (1942).

Finot, E., *Chaco War and the United States* (1934).

Fisher, F. R., *et. al.*, *Investments in Paraguay* (1955).

Fitzgibbon, R. H., *Uruguay: Portrait of a Democracy* (1954).

Fretz, J. W., *Pilgrims in Paraguay* (1953).

Gordon, R., *Argentina and Uruguay* (1916).

Gordon, W. C., *Economy of Latin America* (1950).

————, *Political Economy of Latin America* (1965).

Graham, R. B. C., *Portrait of a Dictator, Francisco Solano López* (1937).

Hanson, S. G., *Economic Development of Latin America* (1951).

————, *Utopia in Uruguay: Chapters in the Economic History of Uruguay* (1938).

Harris, C. G., *Uruguay: Economic and Commercial Conditions in Uruguay* (1950).

Harris, S., *Economic Problems of Latin America* (1944).

Henderson, I. L., *Paraguay: Economic and Commercial Conditions* (1952).

Henríquez Ureña P., *Literary Currents in Hispanic America* (1945).

Hopkins, E. A., *et. al., Paraguay 1852 and 1968* (1970).

Hudson, W. H., *The Purple Land* (1885).

International Bank for Reconstruction and Development, *Uruguay* (1951).

Ireland, G., *Boundaries, Possessions and Conflicts in South America* (1938).

James, P., *Latin America* (rev. ed., 1950).

Johnson, J. J., *Political Change in Latin America* (1958).

Josephs, R., *Latin America: Continent in Crisis* (1948).

Klein, M. A., *A Forest Survey of Paraguay* (1946).

Koebel, W. H., *Paraguay* (1917).

———, *Uruguay* (1911).

Kolinski, C. J., *Independence or Death: Story of the Paraguayan War* (1965).

Krause, A. E., *Mennonite Settlement in the Paraguayan Chaco* (1952).

La Foy, M., *The Chaco Dispute and the League of Nations* (1946).

Lewis, P. H., *Politics of Exile: Paraguay's Febrerista Party* (1968).

Lindahl, G., *Uruguay's New Path: A Study of Politics During the First Colegiado, 1919–1933* (1964).

Macdonald, A. F., *Latin American Politics and Government* (2nd ed., 1954).

Martin, P. A., *Latin America and the War* (1925).

Mecham, J. L., *Church and State in Latin America* (rev. ed., 1966).

Murray, J. H., *Travels in Uruguay* (1871).

Pendle, G., *Paraguay: A Riverside Nation* (3rd ed., 1963).

———, *Uruguay: South America's First Welfare State* (3rd ed., 1963).

Peterson, S. E., *Forest Products of Paraguay* (1945).

Pincus, J., *The Economy of Paraguay* (1968).

Raine, P., *Paraguay* (1956).

Reh, E., *Paraguayan Rural Life: Survey of Food Problems, 1943–1945* (1946).

Rengger, J. R., and M. Longchamps, *The Reign of Doctor Joseph Gaspard Roderick de Francia in Paraguay* (1827).

Robertson, J. P. and W. P., *Francia's Reign of Terror* (1839).

———, *Letters on Paraguay* (2 vols., 1838).

Rodó, J. E., *Ariel,* trans. F. J. Stimson, (1922).

Ronde, P. de, *Paraguay: A Gallant Little Nation* (1935).

Rout, L. B., *Politics of the Chaco Peace Conference, 1935–1939* (1970).

Schutter, C. H., *The Development of Education in Argentina, Chile, and Uruguay* (1943).

Service, E. R., and H. S., *Tobatí: Paraguayan Town* (1954).

Smith, H. L., and H. Littell, *Education in Latin America* (1934).

Taylor, P. B., *The Executive Power in Uruguay* (1951).

———, *Government and Politics of Uruguay* (1962).

Thompson, R. W., *Germans and Japs in South America* (1942).

———, *Land of Tomorrow: A Story of South America* (1937).

Tomasek, R. A., ed., *Latin American Politics: Studies of the Contemporary Scene* (rev. ed., 1970).

Torres Rioseco A., *Epic of Latin American Literature* (rev. ed., 1946).

United Nations, Department of Economic Affairs, *Economic Survey of Latin America, 1948,* and for later years; for example, 1955, 1956, 1957.

United Nations, Economic Commission for Latin America, *Economic and Legal Status of Foreign Investments in Selected Countries: Paraguay* (1951).

United Nations, Food and Agriculture Organization, *Agricultural Development of Uruguay* (1951).

University of Texas, Institute of Latin American Studies, *Political, Economic and Social Problems of the Latin American Nations of Southern South America* (1949).

Uruguay Institute of International Law, *Uruguay and the United Nations* (1958).

Vanger, M. J., *José Batlle y Ordoñez: Creator of His Times* (1963).

Warren, H. G., *Paraguay: An Informal History* (1949).

Washburn, C. A., *History of Paraguay* (2 vols., 1871).

White, E. L., *El Supreme* (1916).

Wilgus, A. C., ed., *South American Dictators* (1937).

Willis, J. L., *Historical Dictionary of Uruguay* (1970).

Wood, B., *The United States and Latin American Wars, 1932–1942* (1966).

Wythe, G., *Industry in Latin America* (2nd ed., 1949).

Ynsfran, P. M., ed., *Epic of the Chaco: Marshal Estigarribia's Memoir of the Chaco War, 1932–1935* (1950).

Ysita, E., *National Economy of Uruguay, 1941–1946* (1948).

Zook, P. H., *Conduct of the Chaco War* (1960).

chapter 26

THREE STRUGGLING REPUBLICS OF THE HIGHER CENTRAL ANDES

*the common heritage of "caudillismo" and
the limitations of geography*

When in the 1860's, the American minister to Ecuador, Frederick Has-saurek, traveled by mule train from Guayaquil to Quito, he could find no food for sale along the road. When he stopped to buy eggs or other provisions, the people told him, "We have nothing to sell, sir; the soldiers were here and took all we had." Andean revolutions, to be successful, had to originate with or be supported by the soldiers. And the troops, whether loyal to the outgoing dictator or his outlawed opposition, were poorly paid and ill-clad, and supported themselves usually by requisitioning supplies from the villagers. Revolutionary leaders, the minister reported, resorted to the "customary mode of Spanish American warfare . . . featuring forcible impressments, forced loans and contributions; in addition they seize all the horses, mules, cattle, provisions, Indians, and other property they can lay their hands on." The government party, he added, acted the same way. The ordinary commerce of the Andean republics was "periodically paralyzed by such troubles." Recruiting officers carried away farm laborers and beasts of burden. And "the middle class always become poorer, the poor remain poor, and the number of wealthy families is diminished."[1] It was in this kind of atmosphere that Bolívar's dream of confederation evaporated. He was forsaken by the nations he had founded. And the subsequent history of the three Central Andean countries is well summarized by the comments of the American visitor.

A Peruvian poet, José Chocano (1875–1934), wrote in the early 20th century:

> *Over the whole continent, the Andes run,*
> *Braiding their mighty knots in the shining air,*
> *Lifting a shield of granite in the sun,*
> *And crowned with silver helmet gleaming fair.*[2]

A lover of natural beauty, he was not concerned with the problems that these "mighty knots" of the Andes brought to the nations resting upon them. The three nations of Ecuador, Peru, and Bolivia, which formerly made up the Inca empire, each have a central core of Andes ridges towering over none-too-fertile valleys or plateaus, ridges that separate them from vast undeveloped areas to the east. Because of their difficult geography, and because they have Indian masses still living in crannies in the "shield of granite in the sun," they have much in common in their histories and their many unsolved problems.

The history of Ecuador is a "Tale of Two Cities." Over one-third of her people live on the verdant stretch of coastal plains which supports the port of Guayaquil, the country's largest city, and its over 600,000 people, by producing bananas and cacao for export. Three-fifths of her people live in the *sierra* and its highland valleys where lie the nation's capital, Quito, with its almost 600,000 people, the white and mestizo towns of Ambato, Riobamba, and Cuenca, and the scores of little villages of changeless Andean Indians. Five per cent of Ecuadorians live in the Amazonian *oriente*, many of them uncivilized savages.

Peru is also three separate worlds. Most of its coast is parched desert but it contains a few irrigated valleys, and, near the port of Talara, some oil fields. Some 5,000,000 Peruvians or about 35 per cent of the population live in these coastal areas. In the Andes *sierra* live 6,500,000 Peruvians or about 55 per cent of the population, most of them Indians who take no part in Peru's modern "money economy." In the Amazon area, the *montaña*, which constitutes 60 per cent of Peru's land area, live only 13 per cent of Peruvians, centering on the large river port of Iquitos which ships rubber and mahogany out down the Amazon. Iquitos serves a region bigger than Texas. Few people from Lima ever managed to get to Iquitos, which has been accessible only by plane or by truck-road and river-launch trips that took two weeks' travel time.

---

[1] F. Hassaurek, *Four Years Among the Spanish Americans* (New York: Hurd and Houghton, 1868).

[2] From Isaac Goldberg, *Studies in Spanish American Literature* (New York, Brentano's, 1920), p. 283.

Bolivia also has its three regions. The *altiplano* or high plateau, the home of the Aymará Indians, contains the capital cities and silver-mining centers. The *yungas* or the area of deep narrow valleys centering on Cochabamba are the garden and granary of Bolivia. The third region is the *selvas* or tropical plains of the Department of Santa Cruz which thin out in the southeast into the Paraguayan Chaco.

Division into such distinct natural regions has caused difficulties in transportation and communication that have retarded national integration. In each of the three Andean countries, this division is an important key to understanding the divisiveness within each nation and the conflicts that developed with neighboring nations.

Ecuador, an ultra-religious state in the nineteenth century

In area, Ecuador is one of the smallest of today's South American nations; and it is nearly the smallest in population and in her amount of foreign trade. She has not always been so small. Half of her original territory was lost as the result of boundary disputes. Much of the lost land was in the *oriente,* that jungle-covered area of the eastern slope of the Andes where the sources of the Amazon rise. Quito, her capital, and most of her larger towns are located in the central Andean valley. Her port city Guayaquil and the area that is the source of her exports of bananas and cacao is in the tropical coast which constitutes one-fourth of her territory.

Guayaquil, the progressive port, had always been at odds with Quito, the conservative and very religious mountain capital. The two cities had been kept united in one nation through the influence of Bolívar and Sucre. After they left the country, the nation was kept united by a very young lieutenant from Venezuela, Juan José Flores. This uneducated but charming 26-year-old led Ecuadorians in 1829 to victory over the Peruvians who had tried to annex Quito. He called a *cabildo abierto* which on May 13, 1830, declared Ecuador an independent state, competely separate from any control by Bogotá. That day was "the last day of despotism and the first day of the same thing," for Flores was to be Ecuador's first *caudillo*. He had won the loyalty of the Ecuadorians. Eventually he was to lose to Colombia the towns of Popayán and Pasto but he did gain in the boundary settlement for Ecuador the Galápagos Islands far out to sea. He did not succeed in his efforts to define the boundary with Peru.

Flores had fought 23 battles for Bolívar and knew how to handle men. For fifteen years he dominated the nation through a political alliance with the conservatives of Church and army and the wealthy class of the Quito area. Liberal leaders at Guayaquil were opposed to Flores as a Venezuelan and to his regime, which they thought arbitrary. They organized a series of revolts led by Vicente Rocafuerte, who represented those Latin American liberal intellectuals who were opposed to the political power of the Church. They succeeded by 1845 in exiling Flores to Spain and in writing a new constitution. *Florianismo* was ended, but not in Flores' mind. He persuaded the Spanish queen to let him have ships with which to retake the west coast colonies and re-establish monarchy in the Andean region. British intervention ended this disgraceful attempt of a vengeful ex-*caudillo* to bring back Spanish power. In the 1860's, the forgiving Ecuadorians, who had loved Flores as a young lieutenant with Bolívar, allowed him to return as a subaltern government official.

Rocafuerte quarreled with Colombia over the Popayán boundary almost to the point of war. He accomplished no lasting liberal reforms and retired by the request of the conservatives in 1849. The remaining years down to 1860 were tumultuous ones, with many short-lived *caudillos* rising and falling, some exiling the Jesuits and some bringing them back. The last of the eleven different *caudillos* who were in and out of office was the liberal Guillermo Franco, who set up his capital in Guayaquil. He was driven out by a conservative army under Gabriel García Moreno, assisted by the returned Flores. This broke the power of the liberals for a long time to come. A convention called in September 1860 named García Moreno president, which introduced García Moreno's "Golden Age."

The first statesman Ecuador produced, García Moreno, is still hailed by conservative Catholic South Americans as the champion of their religion. A stern and occasionally cruel officer in Bolívar's campaigns, later a newspaper editor and lawyer in Guayaquil, he had traveled to Europe during its 1848 revolutions and had become imbued with the idea of progress. But to him the requisite for progress was civil peace, the requisite for peace was national unity, to national unity, religion. "Liberty and equality" to him were synonymous with anarchy and therefore evil. He was so deeply devout as to believe he had divine guidance in everything he did for Ecuador.

For his nation he organized the finances, broke up the army, founded an auditing system for government expenses that he himself supervised, and waged war on smuggling and speculation and upon corruption within the government itself. He was responsible for two constitutions. The one in 1861 set up a strong executive and the later one in 1869 made the nation's ties to the Church so strong his enemies called it "the Charter of Slavery to the Vatican." But he did strengthen civil law, making it superior to the military. He brought some modernization and material progress and increased trade to other countries. The mule trail between Quito and Guayaquil was widened enough for carriages and oxcarts and made passable the year round. The Church-managed schools were increased threefold. As strict with priests as with civil servants, he did not hesitate to make changes in Church leadership. Wealthy in his own right, he turned his salary as president over to Church charities. He introduced the Australian eucalyptus tree to the barren slopes of the Andes, where they grow today in profusion. He modernized the Ecuadorian school of medicine and founded an astronomical observatory.

Congress had approved his constitution which gave him a six-year term and allowed re-election, and voted overwhelmingly in 1873 to consecrate the nation to the "Sacred Heart of Jesus." But his re-election to a third term, to start in 1875, caused a revolt among his enemies. On August 6 of that year, as he came out of the cathedral onto the main Quito plaza, he was stabbed to death. The nation was right to mourn him deeply for he was an unselfish leader of devoted purpose.

García Moreno was, however, an opponent of free suffrage, religious tolerance, and public education. His domineering and impetuous character provoked opposition and his intolerant religious despotism clashed with the slowly growing liberalism of the country. He left no heirs among his advisers, no one trained to carry on. For 20 years, Ecuador floundered through civil war, economic depression, and organized brigandage. It wrote two more constitutions, bringing to eleven the total number for the little nation in the years between 1830 and 1895.

some progress for Ecuador in the twentieth century

Progress was made in the port city of Guayaquil—this in spite of recurrent yellow fever epidemics that made it one of the world's most feared pestholes. Gradually a Liberal party grew up to dominate local politics in the city. The port people, the *costeños*, were opposed to the feudalistic, religious, mountain-girt capital and its *Quiteños*. In the 19th century, they had no leader and could not win over the government. But halfway through the 1890's, a new leader emerged and a period of liberalism began. Eloy Alfaro, a mestizo born in a coastal village, came to the presidency in 1895 and brought about a revolution in government and a relaxation of religious conservatism. Until 1916, he and his bitter rival within the party, Leonidas Plaza Gutiérrez, rotated the presidency. Though dictators, they created a civilian, secular government and separated Church from state. They completed the Quito-Guayaquil railroad, stabilized the tax system, and endeavored to establish sanitary systems and a system of public secular education.

Succeeding presidents stayed in power with the support of a combination of the Quito landed aristocracy and the growing class of financiers and shippers in Guayaquil dependent on the cacao trade. World War I and the depression following it brought hardships in this one-crop country to workers at the port and to landless peasants, and they formed a left-wing party which actually held the presidency a few months in 1926. But military *juntas*, often backed by Quito bankers, seized power and ruled the country in the stormy thirties. Since 1925, Ecuador has had 35 different presidents.

But during this period changes were taking place in political consciousness with the appearance of a laboring class and the growth of a small but gradually increasing middle class. New issues were considered important and new political alignments were being made. Political instability increased because of hardships caused by the depression and by loss of territory but some action was taken to solve economic problems. Some social labor legislation was enacted, the production of food was increased, trade was expanded, and women were granted the suffrage.

In 1940, an alliance of liberals made possible a "legal" election which one Ecuadorian historian calls only "normally fraudulent." The man elected president was Carlos Arroyo del Río, a wealthy corporation lawyer. Dissatisfaction rose during his term because a boundary dispute with Peru led to war and a loss of territory. Moreover, though Arroyo del Río declared war on the Axis during World War II and granted bases to the United States, the inflation brought on by the boom in balsa, cacao, and rubber from the *oriente* caused worker unrest. Hoping to assure his reelection in 1944, the president in retaliation against workers' groups gagged the press and exiled the opposition leaders. But the opposition combined behind Velasco Ibarra, one of the exiles. When the president refused to allow his opponent to return from Colombia to campaign, in August 1944, he suddenly found himself in exile and his opponent in the presidency.

But the new president was an opportunist who, once in office, deserted the liberals. He had promised during his campaign "peace, work, and freedom," but now he threw the Arroyo del Río men in jail, cancelled local elections, and announced a switch to the right. This created an explosive situation which brought on the typical *cuartelazo* revolt so common in Ecuador. In 1947 Velasco Ibarra took flight, and the country had four different presidents in quick succession.

The next president showed that Ecuador could be governed freely and democratically through constitutional institutions. A coalition of labor, intellectuals, and liberal businessmen, called the National Civic Democratic Movement, found a leader in Galo Plaza Lasso, a six-foot son of a former president who had put himself through the university in the United States by working in a factory when his land-rich father disapproved of his modern ideas. Imbued with scientific American farming methods, he returned to Quito to make his ancestral acres the finest modern farm in Ecuador. In 1948, after narrowly defeating the Conservative candidate, he went to work with a coalition of liberals behind him, to make all Ecuador a "modern farm." He encouraged foreign capital, founded development associations for the tropical areas, opened highways, and started self-supporting Indian handicraft industries. His enemies were free to print what they pleased and to organize as they wished. Production for export doubled and the standard of living began to rise.

In the 1952 election, Galo Plaza refused to back any candidate as his successor and the smooth turncoat, Velasco Ibarra, became president of Ecuador for the third time. He controlled the powerful Guayaquil newspapers and was supported by Galo Plaza's personal enemy, the mayor of Guayaquil. He won about 42 per cent of the 351,000 votes cast in a three-cornered election. Galo Plaza went back to his farm, and later served as a UN inspector in the Near East, while many of his "development schemes" were neglected in Ecuador; but he had, nevertheless, started his little country in the direction of stability.

Velasco Ibarra managed to complete his legal term. The Conservative party candidate, Camilo Ponce Enriques, who won the 1957 election made some improvements in agriculture, mining, small industries, and highways, backed by loans from the United States. In the 1960 election Galo Plaza ran against Velasco Ibarra, but Velasco was the more spellbinding orator. Tension was caused by his narrow margin of victory. The rightists feared his friendliness toward Castro's Cuba and the landlord class refused to pay the taxes he had laid on the wealthy. And when Velasco Ibarra had his vice-president, Carlos Arosemeña, thrown in jail for opposing him, the air force and navy interfered. They threw Velasco out of the presidency and put Arosemeña in. But Arosemeña was a playboy who soon embarrassed his backers by being drunk at official receptions, so on July 11, 1963, the combined armed forces replaced Arosemeña with a military junta headed by Admiral Ramon Jijón.

The admiral remained in power until 1966. His government pushed the reform schemes of Galo Plaza, and actually collected a graduated income tax, using the funds to pay professionally trained government workers hired by Ecuador's first civil service and to bring some degree of work limits and elementary schooling to highland Indians. Ecuador seemed to be achieving some modernization and it was hoped it would return to democratically elected government in the latter part of 1966, but in March, student riots against government intrusion in the university resulted in the resignation of the junta. Appointees of the junta during the next two years planned a series of agrarian and resettlement projects. Then, in the presidential election held in 1968, the old veteran *político* and silver-tongued charmer, José Velasco Ibarra, was legally elected for the fifth time.

Three of Velasco Ibarra's four previous presidencies had ended by "barracks revolts" against him. He promised this time to collect taxes from the rich landowners, but the conservative Supreme Court declared his new law unconstitutional. Then violent student revolts broke out that lasted seven days, subdued only by a three-hour battle won by tanks and tear gas. Velasco declared Ecuador "ungovernable," knowing the military would persuade him to stay on, and three days after the students were subdued, in June 1970, he assumed dictatorial power. Erratic yet magnetic, Velasco had a personal popularity that blinded people to his faults, and the armed forces supported him as "no worse than any other visible alternative." But a visible alternative appeared February 16, 1972, in the person of Brigadier General Guillermo Rodríguez Lara, army commander-in-chief, who led a bloodless take-over of the presidency and sent Velasco Ibarra off quietly on a plane into exile. It was in the middle of pre-Lenten Carnival, and few Ecuadorians took any notice.

Velasco had challenged the United States in 1970 by insisting that Ecuador's coastal jurisdiction reached 200 miles out to sea. The Ecuadorian navy, which incidentally, was provided by United States military aid, seized 17 California-based fishing boats in one month alone, January 1971, and held them for $500,000 fine, later paid by Washington. But United States economic AID and the provision of $28,000,000 military hardware were canceled. In February 1971, Velasco complained to the Council of Ministers of the Organization of American States, but all the Council could do was to urge both parties to "settle their differences by negotiations." In the meantime, Velasco had made a contract with Gulf-Texaco to open new oil fields east of the Andes and to build a pipeline to bring the oil out to Esmeraldas on the Pacific, the first major oil development in Ecuador. This development would surely continue under any change of presidents. It was opened in 1972 and is a great boon to Ecuador's economy.

Peru: deterioration from the days of the viceroyalty

Peru was once the flower of the colonial regime but its transition from colonialism to independent nationhood was long and tortuous. Life in its cities, in Lima, Arequipa, and Cuzco, was less comfortable and more insecure and dangerous for all classes of society in the 19th century than it had been in the 18th or even the 17th century. It became a domain of petty *caudillos* who, after Ayacucho, staged 40 revolts in less than 50 years. Increasing its internal chaos were wars with Bolivia, Spain, and Chile, wars in which Peru suffered territorially as well as socially and politically.

Although Peru was fourth in size among Latin American republics and had a wealth of natural resources, climate and geography made progress difficult. There is little rain in the arid coastal plain, transportation is difficult in the *sierra*, where the Indian population has changed little since Inca times, and good agricultural land is lacking in its vast Amazonian *montaña*. Its resources brought trouble instead of progress, for the guano and nitrate deposits caused war with Chile, silver declined when the Spaniards departed, and copper and oil had to wait until the 20th century for development.

Actually, Peruvians had not wanted independence as desperately as other South Americans. Freedom was imposed by outsiders. The aristocrats and Indians joined to support the last of the Spanish soldiers before Ayacucho. To many Peruvians Bolívar was not a Liberator but a meddling northerner. In fact sporadic warfare broke out between Colombian and Peruvian forces for three years, and Peru's chief problem of the 1820's was to get rid of foreigners. But Peruvians could not agree among themselves after the foreigners were gone and a series of "small-time" tyrants took over, most of them veterans of the campaigns against Spain, the so-called Marshals of Ayacucho. The first contest was between Andrés Santa Cruz, an aristocratic mestizo who hoped for a federation of Peru with Bolivia, and General Agustín Gamarra, who was opposed to the idea. Their forces struggled in the high Andes plateaus; Santa Cruz ousted Sucre's government in Bolivia, forced Gamarra out, and remained as dictator himself. Gamarra went back to Lima, where he was elected Peruvian president in 1829. His four-year term became chaotic, not only due to intrigues in Lima but due also to the agitation of Santa Cruz in Bolivia for a port on the Peruvian coast.

When a three-way struggle rose in Lima and its interior Andean valleys in the mid-1830's for control of Peru, one of the three leaders who had no legal army of his own asked help of the well-entrenched Bolivian dictator Santa Cruz. Santa Cruz had been waiting for a chance to gain control of Peru and his forces soon defeated the two other opponents in the struggle. He was able to found the Peru-Bolivia federation he wanted, made up of Bolivia, North Peru and South Peru, with its capital at La Paz. Unpopular with many Peruvians, the federation was viewed with alarm by Portales of Chile and Rosas in Argentina. Chile won its side of the ensuing small war but lost its leader in subsequent strife at home. The Bolivians drove Rosas back to Tucumán but Santa Cruz himself was defeated elsewhere in the Andes and driven out of Peruvian politics for good. Peru was splintered into sections.

At the time of Santa Cruz' defeat in 1838, eight different presidents claimed power in various regions of Peru. The old warhorse Gamarra held power briefly while he made a new war on Bolivia. In its one battle he was killed—the one military dictator in the age of *caudillos* to have had "the saving grace to die on the battlefield." In the battle, 3,000 of the 5,000 soldiers with him were killed or captured. The one surviving Peruvian officer was Chief of Staff Ramón Castilla.

Castilla seized power in 1844 but Peru was a shambles. The Indians were still the half-starved peons and burden-bearers, and blacks were still bought and sold as slaves. Lima was a dirty, backward, decaying city. Castilla was a military man with little education but he was able to push Peru along the path toward stability. He was probably Peru's ablest 19th-century ruler. He planned railroads and telegraph communications, consolidated finances, and develped the guano fertilizer industry on the offshore islands as a national monopoly. He had been elected for a six-year term, but at the end, gave way to a puppet in 1851 who spoiled his record with graft in the guano business. Castilla returned for a second term that lasted until 1862, during which the slaves were emancipated and the Indian villages freed of the tribute collected since early colonial times. Castilla's constitution was to remain in force for 59 years. Unfortunately Castilla's gains were erased by a war with Spain, by bankruptcy over the fertilizer business, and by a long, tragic "War of the Pacific" with Chile over nitrate beds.

In the revolution that followed the war with Spain, which preoccupied Peru until 1867, Castilla was killed in the fighting. The governments coming after him exploited the guano business wastefully and went deeply into debt to English and French bankers. Extravagance and financial mismanagement bred revolt. One hopeful development was the election in 1872 of the first civilian president of Peru, Manuel Pardo, who was backed by a *civilista* party. Pardo reorganized the government, gave offices to lawyers and businessmen, established schools, and reduced the army. But the civilian leaders faced bankruptcy because the guano deposits were becoming exhausted; and when the government tried to nationalize the deposits of nitrates, from which artificial fertilizers were being developed by Chilean and English companies, Chile went to war. Chilean troops entered Lima in 1881. Peru had no government able to oppose them. When peace was signed with Chile, generals once again fought over the presidency.

One of the surviving generals, Andrés Cáceres, was legally elected president in 1886 but he could accomplish little in a country demoralized by war, burdened with foreign debt, and bankrupted by the loss of its only revenue-producing section, the nitrate provinces. English bondholders organized an advisory corporation of economic experts who took ever the management of the remaining guano deposits, the railroad, and the port and worked out plans for the payment of the debt. Peru started on the road to economic recovery and social advance. She suffered a setback in the election of 1890 when the military and *civilista* again came to blows and the military party won. But in 1895, Nicolás Piérola was elected president to serve until 1903. Piérola had organized a Democratic party and rallied the democratic forces against the military. An improved economy had brought more political freedom, and the granting of full suffrage had forced the administration to make concessions to the civilian party. Piérola established a new monetary system, permitted civil marriage, and reformed the army. Peru enjoyed peace for the thirteen years from 1895 to 1908. At the dawn of the new century, the people of Lima were doubtless living a better life than they had in 1830. But for the descendants of the Incas, who comprised 80 per cent of the population in the Andes, the century had brought no changes whatsoever.

Peruvian politics in the twentieth century

The most outstanding personality in the early 20th century in Peru was a successful Lima businessman and smart financier named Augusto B. Leguía who served two terms as president with an eight-year period in between. He was elected in an open election in 1919, and then maintained an army-and-conservative-backed dictatorship until 1930. On paper he appeared to be an enlightened and progressive ruler, but "his practices belied his protestations."

During the interim between his terms, Peru passed through the crisis of World War I by severing relations with Germany after the United States entered the war—and the trade brought by the war helped create a prosperous new merchant class. In the postwar period of the 1920's, Leguía borrowed nearly a hundred million dollars from English and American banking houses, some of it to be used on internal improvements such as highways, irrigation projects, and railroads but some to be used for himself and his friends—and all of it to be defaulted on during the depression. He did lay the foundation for the modernization of Peru but only the settlement of the long-festering Tacna-Arica dispute seemed a permanent gain during this period. For the Indians and city workers, Leguía did nothing.

To protest Leguía's undemocratic methods, a student strike took place at the University of San Marcos, led by a young "hothead" named Víctor Raúl Haya de la Torre. Martial law was clamped down on Lima for three days. Haya de la Torre was exiled, but he had managed to come to public attention. For more than 25 years, he was to be a world figure in the fight for political and social equality against dictatorship.

Haya de la Torre had been influenced while in the university by socialistic writers such as José Mariátegui, who later turned to Communism.

Haya in exile moderated his own views after travel in Russia disillusioned him. But a year in Mexico fired him with enthusiasm for the "Indianism" revolution. He made converts among young liberals in Argentina and Chile and called his movement the *Alianza Popular Revolucionaria Americana,* or APRA. *Aprismo* advocated land reform for the Indians and social legislation for city workers. It planned public improvements in irrigation, electrification, and transportation that would actually serve the people, industrialization as a prerequisite to improved living standards, and national socialized development of natural resources rather than development through foreign capital. In spite of difficulties, APRA was to serve as the vehicle for the spread of democratic ideas within Peru's feudal structure.

In 1931, the army overthrew Leguía and placed Colonel Luis M. Sánchez Cerro into power. Opposition to Leguía in Peru had already brought Haya de la Torre back from exile in 1930 as head of an accepted APRA party. He was the most popular presidential candidate in 1931 and probably won the election, but the vote was counted by the government and the *caudillo* Sánchez Cerro was declared president. To deflect domestic unrest, Sánchez Cerro seized Leticia on the Amazon and got into trouble with Colombia. Then in April 1933 the president was assassinated, and the blame was placed on APRA. Haya de la Torre and 27 of his party members in congress were forced into exile and the party was outlawed.

Congress chose Marshall Oscar Benavides as president. He attempted to allay public unrest by actually putting some of APRA's reforms into effect—workers' housing and clinics, mild social security plans on the Chilean pattern—and settled the Leticia question. He ruled as a dictator, however, and no *Aprista* could run for office.

He permitted a one-sided election in 1939 in which Manuel Prado Ugarteche, a moderately liberal man of wealth, came into power. The new president severed relations with the Axis in 1942 and a wartime boom encouraged Peru's industrialization. Most worldwide liberal movements in World War II were pro-American and anti-Nazi, and APRA reversed its anti-Yankee-capitalism stand. The mild President Prado permitted Haya de la Torre to return from exile and APRA pressed for immediate domestic reforms—the secret ballot, universal suffrage, control of absentee-landlordism, separation of Church and state, and education for the Indians. Haya de la Torre championed the Allied cause.

A coalition of factions brought a liberal, Dr. José Luis Bustamente y Rivero, into the presidency in a regularly held election in 1945. Three cabinet posts were given to APRA men. The Democratic Front coalition had gained control of congress. Cleavages soon appeared, for when the reforms began—rural schools, housing projects, surveys for new government-financed irrigation and power projects—to many they were too slow. Bustamente said a "short, careful step" was best.

The entire reform program came to discredit because one man's blood was shed. In January 1947, a powerful conservative newspaper editor was murdered. Other newspapers blamed an APRA man. The coalition cabinet fell and Conservatives in congress blocked the government. Bustamente tried to join with the military and the old established oligarchy. He stalled when one of the new cabinet members, a fanatical rightist named General Odría, insisted that APRA be outlawed again, but he slowed down on APRA's programs. APRA was not only slowed down but knocked out entirely when a naval revolt at Callao in 1948 was also blamed on Haya's followers. An army revolt at Arequipa a few weeks later resulted in the fall of Bustamente.

In the ensuing upset, General Odría became president and soon established himself as an oppressive dictator. Haya de la Torre escaped arrest by taking refuge in the Colombian embassy, where he stayed as a "house guest" for four years while international lawyers debated the legality of such a "right of asylum." In 1954, he was allowed to take a plane to Panama and he spent the next three years in Europe teaching and writing. Odría, who served from 1948 to 1956, was intent on exterminating all APRA organizations but he did not dare abolish the APRA-inspired new schools and public clinics, and the social security plans of the Bustamente coalition. When Haya was allowed to return to Peru in 1957 under a later liberal regime, much of his program had already slowly gained acceptance and his role seemed merely that of "leader emeritus."

During Odría's administration, the nation's economy was bolstered by the demand for copper, cotton, and oil during the Korean War. The government put no restrictions on the new foreign companies and they took out profits at will without paying any royalties. But the American Export-Import Bank helped finance new copper mines and smelting works, and exports doubled in cotton and wool. The government's income tripled, and some of the new income was spent on schools, hospitals, and roads in the interior and on expansion of social security.

Odría allowed the open election of his successor in June 1956; the moderate former president, Manuel Prado, won in a close but fair enough election in which women voted for the first time. President Prado served out his six-year term to 1962. He legalized the APRA party and included many APRA-supported measures in the mild reforms he accomplished with the cooperation of APRA men elected to congress.

The 1962 campaign was a close three-way election in which the tired old leftist leader Haya de la Torre finally won a plurality. But to the Peruvian army it was unthinkable that Haya should be president of Peru, and the generals sent tanks "crashing through the gates of the presidential palace" and nullified the election. Ruling with a four-man junta, they called another presidential election.

This time the election was won by Fernando Belaúnde Terry, a reformer more active than Haya, a Lima architect who had become interested in the city's growing shanty slums through his work on public housing designs. In the 1960's, Lima had one of the worst shanty towns in Latin America as its rainless climate made life possible in hovels roofed with matting. Some 400,000 of Lima's population of 2,400,000 people lived this way. Belaúnde Terry had concentrated on forming a new "Self-Help" political party, called *Acción Popular*, which would work to start a re-development program among Lima slum dwellers and the Andean Indians for which the government would provide the technical assistance and the tools. He had toured every province in Peru by car, truck, mule or launch and campaigned for reconquest of the difficult geography of Peru by the Peruvians themselves. A coalition, in which a new Christian Democratic Party joined, got Belaúnde Terry elected by a narrow vote. He forged ahead with his program and by 1966 was accomplishing more than most leaders in other larger Latin American countries.

President Belaúnde Terry started projects in Lima for streets, sewers, and running water. He pushed a projected network of roads up over the Andes to meet a common trunk road to parallel the Amazon through Brazil and out to the Atlantic. He sought to secure land by paying large owners for inefficiently farmed lands with a small down payment and a 20-year bond program. When this released comparatively little land for resettlement, he planned to open new lands in the cultivable surface of the 62 per cent of Peru's land in the eastern *montaña* and to settle sharecroppers in the area. Students and army officers were sent out on "work years" to teach in Indian schools and to show villagers how to construct their own roads. Navy gunboats were fitted out with crews of doctors, nurses, and technicians and sent around through the canal to ply the Peruvian sections of the upper Amazon and construct clinics and schools.

But a radical change had taken place in army leadership. In October, 1968, Belaúnde Terry was negotiating with the International Petroleum Company, a subsidiary of Standard Oil of New Jersey operating in northern Peru and was threatening nationalization of some of their holdings at Talara if the company did not pay higher taxes. Then suddenly in the dawn of October 3d, an impatient group of younger army officers who wanted Standard Oil completely out of Peru brought 30 tanks up to the presidential palace, and pulled Belaúnde Terry out of bed in his night clothes and whisked him off by plane to exile in Buenos Aires. Then a junta, led by General Juan Velasco Alvarado, took over the government.

Within days General Velasco had appropriated all the Standard Oil holdings in Peru. He assessed the value of wells and refineries at $200 million but insisted that the oil company owed the Peruvian government $609 million for oil taken illegally. The oil itself, said Velasco, belonged to the Peruvian people under Spanish colonial sub-soil grants and could never have been granted legally to the International Petroleum Comany. Borrowing technical experts from Pemex in Mexico, the military *junta* continued to operate the wells and refineries.

Juan Velasco was from the *cholo* or dominantly Indian worker class and grew up in a one-room house with a dirt floor. He had enlisted in the army and had risen up from the ranks to become an officer. In the early 1960's he had been concerned with the road building, land clearance, and rural teaching program of the socially-conscious units within the army. The other members of the junta also came from the lower and middle classes rather than the oligarchic élite. They planned a 20-year program that would extend to 1988, and expropriated foreign holdings in oil and copper, giving their management over to profit-sharing committees from among the workers. They took over the rich coastal sugar plantations and converted them into cooperatives. Also they closed down two opposition newspapers in Lima. Since a great deal of American investment had been confiscated, Peruvian-American relations cooled to the freezing point.

But when Peru was struck by the worst earthquake it had suffered in modern times, relations thawed swiftly when American relief was forthcoming. The earthquake struck northwestern Peru on May 31, 1970, and covered several large towns with mud slides that left 50,000 dead and caused losses up to $300 million. When General Velasco appealed to the American ambassador for help, helicopters and planes loaded with food and other necessities were flown in immediately. Mrs. Richard Nixon, unwelcome in the Andes in 1958, was received enthusiastically when she flew in with one of the relief planes. Forty other nations came to the aid of Peru over the next month.

The junta promised no specific date for elections, but was conciliatory with business interests in an effort to keep the economy stable and rebuild the earthquake damage. Velasco and his generals are trying to bring Peru's 13,500,000 people into the 20th century. Some observers have wondered if the new liberal-minded type of military officers could not accomplish more toward the development of nations such as those in the Andes than could "civilian democracy" dominated by the old oligarchic few. The current rulers say that neither capitalism nor communism has the solutions to Peru's myriad social and economic problems.

In May, 1972, Velasco and his backers had not yet paid a penny for the confiscations of foreign company holdings. They were pushing ahead on the highways into the interior, joining with Ecuador in enforcing the rights of their own fishermen to maintain a monopoly on the deep-sea fishing 200 miles off their coasts, taking a leadership position among South America's "Third World" under-developed nations. Thus, this "modernized" military clique had gone far beyond the hopes of APRA in bringing social improvement to Peru.

Bolivia: the child of Simón Bolívar

Bolivia was to have the saddest history of the age of *caudillismo* for she had to struggle under a succession of ignorant, hard-drinking tyrants, seven of whom met death by assassination. The issues that concerned other Latin American nations—those of centralism and federalism, Church and state, liberalism and conservatism—did concern Bolivia but were a relatively small part of the story. Her history in the 19th century is almost exclusively a tale of dictatorial domination.

Upper Peru, with its cities of La Paz and Chuquisaca (later to be called Sucre) and its unexhausted silver mines of Potosí, was a Spanish colony until after Ayacucho. It had 900,000 square miles at that time, twice as much territory as it has now. It lost half of its area and all of its seacoast to its neighbors—the nitrate provinces and the Pacific to Chile, large regions to Argentina and Paraguay, and some 190,000 square miles of jungle verging on the Amazon Basin to Brazil. With its remaining 424,163 square miles, it still ranks fifth in size in South America. But it is landlocked in the heart of the continent. Its Andean plateau and mining areas are separated from the Pacific coast by a high western *cordillera*. And its three regions are violently divergent, the high plateau or *altiplano* with its cities and mines, its deep narrow agricultural valleys or *yungas* to the east, and the jungles or *selvas* that cover the eastern slopes down into the Amazon drainage basin. Spain had used all this area only as a source of silver. The Aymará Indians there either worked in the silver mines or lived in the bleak farming villages that never seemed to change. The whites who remained there were hangers-on from colonial days who were to mislead the unlettered masses in no less than sixty civil wars in 73 years.

José Antonio de Sucre was Bolivia's first president and one of its few well-meaning ones. He had entered La Paz in February 1825 at the request of Bolívar, a month after the victory at Ayacucho. Chile and Argentina both hoped to obtain a slice of the silver-producing colony, but Bolívar pulled a clever coup when he arrived there himself and declared the area an independent state, separate completely even from his Grand Confederation. An assembly called in August named the whole area of Upper Peru *La República de Bolívar* in honor of its father and protector of the people. Bolívar was given supreme executive power as "Protector and President."

The Liberator wrote his famous *Constitución Vitalicia* which incorporated his ideas for a strong central government and a lifelong president. This proved to be of little concern to Bolivians who changed their constitution many times in the next century. Sucre stayed in La Paz and was elected first constitutional president in December, 1826.

But Bolivia became involved immediately in the Peruvian war to drive Bolívar's Colombians out of the central Andes areas. It was after a mutiny among Sucre's Colombian troops that the Marshalls of Ayacucho, Santa Cruz and Gamarra came up into the *altiplano* and forced Sucre out of office and back to Ecuador. In the ensuing struggle between Peru and Bolivia, it will be remembered, Gamarra became president of Peru and Santa Cruz came to dominate Bolivia, taking office as president on May 4, 1829, the first of a long line of dictatorial *caudillos*.

Andrés Santa Cruz, born near La Paz in 1792 soon after the revolt of Tupac Amarú, was the son of a Spanish colonial official and a wealthy Indian woman of Tupac Amarú's family who claimed to be an Inca princess. Santa Cruz took the legends of his mother's people very seriously, and developed grandiose plans for re-establishing the Inca empire and for humbling Chile, that aggressively modernizing neighbor. Nevertheless he showed tremendous respect for law and order, arranged a codification of law for both Peru and Bolivia, commenced public works, and established seven institutions of higher learning in La Paz, including schools of medicine and fine arts. He proudly proclaimed Bolivia the "only country in America without a foreign debt."

All this was to be wasted, however, for Santa Cruz, like his Inca forebears, believed in paternalistic government and valued efficiency more than democracy. In 1836, his well-trained army took over Peru, and Santa Cruz was legally elected president of Peru as well as Bolivia. This aroused the apprehensions of Rosas in Argentina and Portales in Chile, and led to war. In this war of the 1830s, Santa Cruz quickly defeated Rosas but took defeat after defeat from the Chileans until he finally fell from power in 1839 and was forced into exile by both Peruvians and Bolivians. He spent many years in Europe before his death, it is sad to note, trying to interest Spain and France in a reconquest of South America.

A long period of anarchy and civil war along with a succession of brutal despots followed the fall of Santa Cruz. The Peruvian Gamarra had tried to conquer Bolivia but was defeated in a single battle in 1841. The hero of the battle, General José Ballivián, ruled under a new constitution until 1847. He was doing too good a job, emancipating the slaves and trying to develop the country's resources, for he infuriated the oligarchy and was forced to resign. Within a year after his downfall, the demagogue Manuel Isidoro Belzú came to power with a regime so corrupt that a new word, *belcismo,* came to stand for selfish dictatorship and venal opportunism. During his presidency, "rapine, robbery, and riot" were the normal state of affairs in the land. After eight years, he was ousted.

The reform attempts and civil wars that followed culminated in 1864 in a military overthrow that brought in a regime so debased that it did more damage to the country than fifty years of progress could rectify. Mariano Melgarejo, an illegitimate mestizo who had been an army packboy at nine, became the president of Bolivia as a result of a barracks revolt in which he seized the palace, slew the president, and turned the palace over to his soldiers to loot. During the six years of his rule, he suppressed municipal councils, sent home the Bolivian senate, made rules concerning the duties of bishops and priests, and executed his enemies as traitors. To gain personal funds, which he senselessly squandered on mistresses and high living, he made private deals with Chilean nitrate companies to work the beds on the coast. These deals led directly to the War of the Pacific in which Bolivia lost her nitrate coast. In January, 1871, eight years before the war began, he was defeated and driven out, and shortly thereafter assassinated in a personal quarrel with the brother of one of his mistresses.

The war with Chile was started by a second "hero" of Bolivia, Hilarión Daza, who was meant by nature to be a thug but became president in 1876. An ignorant and drunken reprobate, he seized lands and raised the taxes on the Chilean companies granted concessions by Melgarejo and thus precipitated the War of the Pacific. When Chile waged war for the companies, Daza performed so poorly as a general that Bolivia lost the nitrate area entirely. He was ousted when the war was hardly begun but his successor was defeated so overwhelmingly, he was not even asked to the peace negotiations.

Bolivia's defeat had a chastening effect on the country. A new constitution was promulgated in 1880. Conservative party presidents ran a centralized government, encouraged the revitalization of the old silver-mining industry, and, just before 1900, opened up tin mining which was to bring Bolivia some material progress and importance in the world wars of the 20th century.

Bolivian politics and tin nationalization

In 1899, Bolivia's only internal conflict was the dispute between La Paz and Sucre as to which city should be the nation's capital. A half century later the country was torn over the issues of nationalizing its rich mineral resources and the part the awakened Indian miners should play in the government.

The capital dispute was settled by deciding to hold the supreme court in Sucre and keeping congress in the more accessible La Paz. The middle class business group in La Paz which won the dispute held the presidency afterwards until 1920. They avoided bloody revolts by rotating the administration among the conservative business and tin company "liberals"—chief among whom were José Manuel Pando, Ismael Montes, and Eliodoro Villazón. They instituted middle-class economic reforms, halted by World War I. During this period three giant tin companies developed so much power that they came to dominate the Bolivian government.

The Liberals were overthrown in 1920 by the so-called "Republicans," who ruled for more than a decade. Republican presidents Bautista Saavedra and Hernando Siles floated $60,000,000 worth of loans from private American investors and spent it on personal graft and enormous military expenditures. Bolivia was hit hard by the world depression after World War I. The tin bonanza slackened off and trade decreased, and the ensuing tension caused coalition governments to rise and fall. The country's expensive army was then almost annihilated in the senseless War of the Gran Chaco against Paraguay.

When the protracted peace negotiations to settle the Chaco War were concluded in 1937, Bolivia had acquired only a strip along the Upper Paraguay River which was to be of little worth to her as a shipping point for years to come. Uprisings at home caused by the disruption of the economy during this unpopular war resulted in new alignments of students, discontented veterans of the war, and a new confederation of laborers. When a leader did emerge with a statesman-like program, he found himself unable to enforce any part of it. Germán Busch, a liberal, half Indian, half German, hero of the Chaco War, inherited a defeated country with an empty treasury. Intending to improve conditions for the miners, he was forced to stop strikes by military action when they got out of hand. Meaning to take over the Big Three tin mines, he found he could only weakly try to limit their power and profit. Measures that had been incorporated in his Constitution of 1938 for improved education, rights of labor, rural cooperatives, and national ownership of minerals were side-tracked. In August, 1939, he died by gunshot, probably a suicide.

His death brought no peace. Campaigns against the tin companies were well under way, one by a radical party called the PIR or Leftist

Revolutionaries, which wished to confiscate all tin interests for the workers, and another, an ardently nationalist and socialist Movement of National Revolution or MNR, led by Gualberto Villarroel and Víctor Paz Estenssoro, which wanted all foreigners thrown out of the industry. But in the 1940 election, the conservative *cholo*, Enrique Peñaranda, was elected president with the army probably counting the ballots. His administration was pro-American and brought Bolivia and its tin into World War II on the Allied side. Peñaranda settled a long-standing dispute with the Standard Oil Company of New Jersey which had been forced out of explorations for oil in the Chaco by an anti-foreign regime under David Toro at the time of the Chaco War. He did nothing, however, to alleviate the wretched condition of the tin miners and broke strikes with a heavy hand. One such action, the infamous "Catavi Massacre" in 1942, produced a number of deaths. The reaction to the massacre made it possible for the exiled nationalist MNR leaders, to come home in December 1943 and overthrow the Peñaranda administration to make Villarroel president.

The dictatorial new president was powerless to stop street riots when the price of tin fell in the post-war slump. University students, workers, and businessmen violently revolted against hard times, and in July, 1946, Villarroel himself was ambushed in the government buildings, dragged out into the street, and hanged to a lamppost. The other MNR leaders went into exile again. They changed from their pro-Perón, pro-Nazi emphasis, grouped around the more democratic leader Paz Estenssoro, and concentrated their antipathy on the tin interests. The more radical PIR meanwhile had for the first time founded articulate unions among the miners under Juan Lechín, an ex-soccer player of Syrian ancestry, whose sympathies were on the Communistic side. In the contest between business and tin interests on the one hand and the exiled MNR and the vociferous PIR on the other, compromise presidents kept Lechín in jail and ineffectively tried to handle the many riots and strikes. They held the balance of power until 1951 while the Korean War caused the price of tin to fluctuate and bring inflation in food prices.

In May 1951 a legal election was held. All literate males could vote—which meant that the possible number of voters was limited to 200,000. The MNR was allowed to campaign openly. Paz Estenssoro, for six years an exile in Argentina, undoubtly received a large share of the votes, but he was not proclaimed president. On April 9, 1952, students, liberal intellectuals, and labor leaders combined in a well-organized but bloody revolt and put him into the presidency. This was not the usual *cuartelazo* or barracks and palace revolution but a mass protest against dictatorship and for an elected candidate.

Víctor Paz Estenssoro was a quiet, intelligent economics professor who felt that there was little chance at reform until the tin mines were owned by the government. But he wanted financial support from the United States and recognition from Washington. This latter he gained on the promise that he would refuse to take orders from Moscow. He invited Juan Lechín, now released from jail, into his cabinet as Minister of Mines and went ahead with his long-range plans for national improvement. The essentials of his program included land reform, economic independence, nationalization of the tin industry, social improvements through education, enlarged suffrage, and increased social security benefits.

His land reform program was watched with interest by all of South America, for 70 per cent of the arable land had been owned by the great landed proprietors, half of them absentee landowners. Enough land was expropriated to create more than two million new small landholders. The land was paid for in national bonds, while the new owners were given 25 years to pay off the debt. Each plot of land, its size depending on the use to which it would be put, the water available, and the crop grown, was judged to be sufficient to support a family. Land was also offered to cooperatives, and attempts were made to colonize Indians in the hot lowlands. Every effort was made to fill the chief need, which was to increase the food supply.

Latin America also watched to see what Paz Estenssoro would do about the nationalization of tin. What he did was to assess the mines at a figure smaller than the back income taxes the companies owed the government. Then, in October 1952, he passed a decree of nationalization with great ceremony. The United States continued to send Point Four help for other public improvements and to encourage private American capital in various minor industries, for it was more concerned with the supply of tin than the fortunes of the large international companies. Paz Estenssoro pegged the price of tin at what seemed to him, an economist, to be the most feasible figure and carried out for the miners as many reforms as he could speedily manage. And in 1956 he let a peaceful election replace him with another reform president, Hernán Siles Zuazo. The latter, young and popular, was inaugurated August 5, 1956.

To achieve economic self-sufficiency, recent governments have sought to develop other products besides tin. They have built up the Cochabamba valleys and the eastward transportation facilities via the Amazon and the Paraguay and the Plata. They have explored for oil and developed known reserves. The suffrage has been enlarged to include every adult, no matter what the sex or state of literacy. More than half of the budget for routine government expenses above the cost of tin and land programs went for new primary schools and campaigns against illiteracy. The United States has tried to aid Bolivia to control inflation, keep tin moving, and still diversify the economy. It has granted aid to the extent of one-third of Bolivia's annual budget, and has given technical cooperation for health, education, agriculture, and road building.

The popular Siles Zuazo, in his effort to bring Bolivia out of economic freedom, has visited remote villages, gone down into mines, and has even undertaken a hunger strike to win his points. When world tin prices were depressed due to the dumping of Soviet tin, and unemployment hit the inefficiently run mines, Siles Zuazo resettled thousands of miners on the new agricultural lands or sent them as *braceros* to work in Argentina. Although

United States aid had provided almost as much money in recent years as had the tin mines, half the Bolivians did not seem to know it. Leftist riots against United States journalists in 1959 almost lost Siles Zuazo his North American support.

A coalition to run the country and the MNR or National Revolutionary Party was formed when Juan Lechín, the radical leader of the miners' union, past president Paz Estenssoro, and president Siles Zuazo joined forces. The tin industry was organized as a government corporation called COMIBOL, which in 1959 froze any increase in wages and additional employment in an effort to promote scientific management, and to satisfy American economic advisers. But the miners who remained expected full employment, high wages, and short hours, and could not understand the necessity of introducing new machinery and efficient methods into the tin industry.

Siles Zuazo under the constitution could not succeed himself, but the coalition stayed together and Paz Estenssoro came back to the presidency legally in 1960. For two years Bolivia seemed to be making progress and the tin mines began to show a small profit. The miners, however, became restive when they saw machinery introduced to replace men on the job; and their unions, becoming private armies, used dynamite to destroy mine tunnels and held police and the regular army at bay. They captured newspaper men and detectives as hostages. Farmers sent to farm the new lands in Cochabamba destroyed the tractors clearing the land, deserted the new towns, and walked back by the thousands to the highlands.

Unwilling to give up control in the midst of this crisis, Paz Estenssoro sought to have congress amend the constitution to allow him to run for a consecutive term. The coalition behind him broke up violently at this announcement. Juan Lechín regrouped the PIR party and ran for the presidency himself; and he urged the miners to more violence. A conservative army party nominated a young general, René Barrientos Ortuño. Each party printed ballots of a different color so illiterate voters could make their choice. Paz Estenssoro won a plurality by agreeing to take Barrientos as his vice-president. Disillusioned and ill, Lechín went into exile in Paraguay.

The miners did not submit to defeat without protest. Violence increased as Cuba-trained Communists infiltrated into union leadership. Paz Estenssoro, supposedly the working man's friend, declared martial law. And then, in November 1964, vice-president General Barrientos used the army to overthrow Paz Estenssoro and to take over the government himself. General Barrientos' "siege" against the miners and martial law over the whole country continued until 1966, with violence continuing at the mines and in the city streets. Martial law of course did not solve Bolivia's problems, but the revolutionary junta remained in control for 20 months, with the very able General Alfredo Ovando Candia serving as president during the last few months of the provisional regime. Then in the next presidential election, General Barrientos was legally elected and on August 6, 1967, was inaugurated as Bolivia's 47th president to serve for a four-year term.

Bolivia's "Revolution of the 1960's" was a left-of-the-center movement. It had been trying since 1955 to bring the Bolivian Indian in the mines and on the land into full citizenship in the government; to operate the tin mines effectively as a national resource, with help from foreign investors such as the Alliance for Progress; to diversify the country's economy by developing the eastern interior; and to break up the power of the old élite. And the totalitarian rule of Barrientos seemed a backward step.

In 1969, Barrientos was killed in a helicopter crash. He was succeeded immediately by the vice-president, but the real power reverted to the army leader, Alfredo Ovando Candia, who took the power over himself in September, 1969. But student riots and terrorist activities harassed Ovando, and an army junta overthrew him with a three-day "revolving presidency" from October 5 to 7, 1970. Out of this melée, Juan José Torres emerged as president.

Torres, of part Indian descent, was a 49-year old leftist who promised a "Popular Nationalist Government." He proposed an ambitious "Twenty-Year Plan" of development in industry and agriculture to free the nation from dependence on mining, for which he had the backing of peasants, city workers, miners, students, and the armed forces. Certain elements of the armed forces, however, staged a revolt in January, 1971, against Torres, but he crushed it and consolidated his power. He announced a new constitution that was to be based on "the socio-economic reality of Bolivia" which he promised to submit for a referendum vote before 1973. Meanwhile he doubled the wages for the miners in the COMIBOL, the nationally owned tin mining corporation, although the increase put the corporation in financial difficulties. He also opened the first tin refinery in Bolivia, built by a West German firm.

But the armed forces group, crushed in January, 1971, rose again under a conservative military leader, Colonel Hugo Banzer, and took over the lowland provinces. His men had arms and an efficient organization, said to be financed by an American oil interest whose holdings in Santa Cruz province had been confiscated. In August, 1971, after a day of fighting in which 200 bystanders were killed, the Torres government went into exile. Torres himself had not been a strong leader of the leftist miners and students, and had no personal appeal to the moderates. So no large group supported him and what followers he had were unarmed. On the other hand, Colonel Banzer had no broad following among any large segment of the people, and as of the spring of 1972, had to depend on a coalition of all factions in his cabinet. His three predecessors had each served twelve months or less. There seemed no solution in the early 1970's to Bolivia's internal conflict.

All Latin America has been watching the Bolivia "revolution" with special interest, especially since the fiery Communist Ché Guevara was killed there in 1967. Whether it can achieve political stability, economic progress, and social justice and avoid following the example of Castro's Cuba may prove to be a matter of considerable importance for the future.

wars and international disputes that retarded
the Andes nations

The fact that the boundaries of certain unsurveyed lands had never been settled in colonial times made the three high Andean nations natural enemies in spite of their common bakground. Disputes over boundaries in the *oriente,* the area of the Amazon headwaters and tributaries, created "incidents" between Colombia and Peru, between Peru and Ecuador, and between Bolivia and Brazil that caused strife to drag on well into the 20th century. Unsurveyed acreage in the waterless deserts on the Pacific side of the Andes where valuable nitrates were discovered in the 1840's—that were worked inside Peruvian and Bolivian boundaries by Chilean companies— caused shooting wars to break out.

Their common heritage did bring the three uneasy neighbors into an alliance in the 1860's for a brief "war" against the mother country. The Spanish Crown had never recognized Peru, its most loyal vice-royalty, as an independent nation. Spanish intrigue, urged on by such exiled Latin American plotters as Flores of Ecuador and Santa Cruz of Bolivia, had centered on recapturing these west-coast countries. When some Basques, Spanish citizens, were murdered while at work on a hacienda at Talambo, the agent of Spain demanded compensation under instructions from Spain that implied Peru was still a colony. The current Peruvian dictator, Juan Antonio Pezet, refused to deal with him. A Spanish fleet seized the guano-bearing Chincha Islands off the coast of Peru. When Pezet gave in to the Spaniards, he was ousted by Mariano Ignacio Prado, who declared war on Spain.

When Spain blockaded the coast and bombarded Callao, Chile, always less meek than Peru, leaped to her neighbor's defense. In January, 1866, the "American Union" of Chile, Peru, Bolivia, and Ecuador declared war on Spain. The city of Valparaiso suffered heavy casualties in the naval war and bombardment. Spain's position, however, was untenable due to the distance from Spain and the long coastline to be attacked. She withdrew, and in 1871, the belligerents signed a truce at Washington, D.C. During the subsequent peace, Peru was recognized as a nation, the Chincha Islands were recognized as Peruvian soil, and Chilean merchants at Valparaiso were paid damages for the destruction caused by the bombardment.

But the allies on the west coast soon fell apart. Chile, which had already in the 1830's won a small-scale war against the joint nation of Bolivia and Peru, was now a self-confident, military nation. Her gunboats had done most of the fighting against Spain. Peru, fearing Chilean poaching in the nitrate industry, proclaimed that the nitrates of Arica and Tarapacá, her southernmost provinces where the Chilean companies had been most successful, were to be a Peruvian government monopoly. Bolivia at the same time broke the agreement made by Melgarejo, increased her taxes on the Anglo-Chilean companies, and cancelled some of the concessions. When the powerful Antofagasta Company refused to pay the tax, Bolivian dictator Daza ordered the company sold for taxes. And on February 14, 1879, the day the tax sale was to be held, Chilean armed forces seized the Bolivian port of Antofagasta. Peru, allied to Bolivia, intervened, and Chile declared war on both nations. Thus began the notorious War of the Pacific which was to have many repercussions for South America.

Historians are inclined to blame the aggressive Chile, whose industry and efficiency were far ahead of her more backward enemies. It was a war of contrasts, with the slingshots of the Incas used side by side with the most up-to-date Krupp-made field artillery. But Chile controlled the routes around Cape Horn, and the northern allies had to buy supplies in the United States and smuggle them across Panama, a province of the rigidly neutral Colombia. In the frenzied desert fighting, both sides simply knifed the wounded in the field because water was scarce. Only the Bolivian Indians could fight long without water but they were fighting with Stone Age equipment. Bolivia lost Antofagasta and the whole nitrate coast.

Peru, a weak ally, did not have a navy equal to Chile's. She could not hold Tarapacá and Arica, her provinces north of the 21° line. The Chilean troops proceeded to invade Lima; and American observers were horrified at the "shameful treatment" of the Peruvian capital by the conquering Chilean troops. They looted libraries, universities, private homes, and even the menagerie. Peru's condition was so chaotic as a result that several factions could claim to be its government. Chile recognized one of them and forced the difficult peace of the Treaty of Ancón on October 20, 1883, by which she acquired Tarapacá and a 10-year occupation of Tacna-Arica, the coast provinces up to the 19° line. At the end of that period, an international commission was to hold a plebiscite. Chile moved into the profit-producing provinces. Attempts to hold the plebiscite failed and the dispute lasted into the 1920's as the explosive "Tacna-Arica Problem."

Bolivia was thrown out of the fighting early in the war after Daza's government fell and in 1889 she signed a truce with Chile. By the provisions of the treaty, ratified in 1904, she lost her entire seacoast. Save for the right to ship goods to the ports of Arica and Antofagasta, Bolivia remained a landlocked country. Unfortunately Bolivia had also lost almost as much territory by the treaty of 1867 with Brazil which the ignorant Melgarejo had ceded in the hope of gaining advantages in commerce. Nearly 200,000 square miles on the right bank of the Paraguay and the Marmoré had been handed over to Brazil's Emperor Pedro II. This area almost led to bloodshed in 1903 when the Treaty of Petropolis gave this still disputed rubber-bearing area to Brazil in return for a railroad to be built out to a navigable Amazon tributary to serve Bolivian commerce. Between 1903 and 1909, Bolivia lost not only these areas to Brazil but also areas on the upper Paraguay to Argentina and on her northern border to Peru. As late as the mid 1960's, Bolivia had border difficulties which led to a rupture of diplomatic relations with Chile. The War of the Gran Chaco of 1932–1937, described in the chapter on modern Paraguay, also left deep scars on Bolivia.

The first serious attempt to settle the Tacna-Arica problem left by the War of the Pacific of the 1880s was made in 1898 when diplomats of both sides agreed to let the Queen of Spain organize the plebiscite, but the Chilean congress defeated this plan. Settlement was delayed for a decade until finally, in 1910, Peru broke off diplomatic relations with Chile. In 1922 an agreement was reached between Peru and Chile in Washington, D.C. to accept North American mediation. By this time the provinces were inhabited by a majority of Chileans, so the North American commissioners decided that only those born in Tacna or Arica could register for voting. But only the Chileans registered, for the Peruvian sympathizers boycotted the whole attempt at arranging for a plebiscite and charged Chile with intimidation. Therefore no election was held. Finally in 1929 the two nations negotiated directly and accepted President Hoover's plan to divide the area almost equally, giving Tacna to Peru and Arica to Chile. Since it was Arica that had the port and railway developments, Chile paid Peru $6 million and opened the port to Peruvian commerce. Thus the "Question of the Pacific" was decided 46 years after the close of the war that had raised it.

Peru quarreled with other neighbors over boundaries. In 1932, as told in the chapter on Colombia, Peruvian soldiers from Iquitos attacked the Colombian settlement of Leticia on a branch of the Amazon. This dispute was settled in 1934 by the League of Nations with the return of Leticia to Colombian sovereignty. In the 1940's, Peru was at variance with Ecuador, again over undeveloped areas in *oriente*. Ecuador had been forced in 1904 to cede territory to Brazil, and the same year started a long conflict with Peru over the remaining country to the east of Quito where Ecuador claimed a triangle between the Marañon and the Napo. Franklin D. Roosevelt was attempting mediation in 1942 when actual warfare broke out, the war that brought the downfall of President Arroyo del Rio. The following year the two nations were urged by Argentina, Brazil, Chile, and the United States to agree to a settlement by neutral boundary commissioners in a meeting at Rio. The line that was accepted cut Ecuador's *montaña* back to the Andes foothills, but gave her free access to river navigation eastward. The boundary is still not quite settled, however, owing to differing interpretations of certain articles in the Rio protocol and border warfare has flared up several times.

economic backwardness in the Andes

While dictator followed dictator, the descendants of the Incas spun and wove the same patterns of textiles as had their ancestors. The Ambatans and Otovalans of Ecuador, the Quechuas of Peru, the Aymarás of Bolivia lived in their ancestral villages in the mountains under the same type of local *cacique* and scarcely realized the government had changed. If they were free from the *mita* and other oppressions of the Spanish viceroys, they were raided and impressed into the armies by the dictators. The poor of the cities and the farm workers on the large estates were mestizos, usually called *cholos* in the Andean countries. In Peru and Bolivia Indians worked the silver mines, and by mid-century, they had been drafted into the guano and nitrate industries. In none of these countries were the Indians given any education or voting rights even though they comprised more than three-fourths of the population.

One circumstance that inhibited progress was the lack of transportation. President García Moreno had dreamed of a Quito-Guayaquil railroad for Ecuador but it wasn't until 1896 that an American company received a concession to carry out this difficult project. Although only 290 miles long, it was not completed until 1908. Quito lived through the 19th century as it had in 1800, on agriculture and Indian hand labor. Guayaquil was the center of a province, as one visitor noted, that abounded "in timber for ship and house building and an exuberant growth of fruit, especially cacao and plantains," but cacao and bananas had little value in the 19th century and had to wait for the Panama Canal to shorten the port's routes to world markets. At the time the Canal was begun, the port city of Ecuador had only 40,000 inhabitants.

In 1868, an engineer named Henry Meiggs began a railway from the coast at Mollendo up to Arequipa, Peru's second largest town, and continued the line in the 1870's on the difficult run to Puno on Lake Titicaca, and thence to Cuzco. He also built a line from Lima to the silver country of Huancayo, later to become one of the copper centers of the world. Meiggs was a "promoter" in California's gold rush days who was involved in a political scandal but he was acceptable in South America as a nephew of the William Wheelwright who put rails across the Andes to connect Chile and Argentina. Meiggs optimistically predicted that his Lima line would cross on over and meet the navigable Amazon, but this was a feat no west coast railroad had accomplished by the mid-20th century. A highway-building project to connect Lima with Iquitos on the Amazon was started by President Belaúnde Terry and continued by his successors.

Bolivia's capital city of La Paz had no rail connection to the sea until after 1900. Transportation from one to another of Bolivia's geographic regions has only recently been improved. In 1955, a railroad was opened to Brazil's Corumbá on the Paraguay River from which rail connections reach São Paulo. A rail and highway route east via the Madeira River and the Amazon, which was provided for by treaty with Brazil in 1903, was finally opened after great difficulties in 1925. In the 1950's a macademized road around Lake Titicaca finally connected Bolivia and Peru as part of the Pan American Highway system.

Transportation problems still face Ecuador and Peru. The railways built in the last century by Henry Meiggs and Archie Harmon are the rail lines in use today. To reach Cuzco from Peru's port of Callao, one takes a ship south to Mollendo and then takes Meiggs' rail line to Arequipa and Cuzco. A long-delayed line from Quito to the port of Esmeraldas was not completed until 1957. The Simón Bolívar Highway comes into Ecuador from Colombia but only in the last few years has it been possible to drive from Guayaquil on into Peru.

Climate and geography have thus continued to work against these two countries. One scourge has been eliminated—the insect-borne diseases of yellow fever and the plague which gave the port of Guayaquil a reputation as a pest-hole quarantined to American sailors. It was ended when an international commission cleaned up the city's sanitation system in the 1930's. Earthquake destruction has been continuing, as in the Ecuadorian town of Ambato in 1949, in Cuzco in 1950, and again in northwestern Peru in 1970.

The silver mines had supported Peru and Bolivia since colonial days. Then in the 1840's, the digging of guano was started by private companies off the Chincha Islands, where the rainless rocks had been bird-breeding grounds for untold millennia. The dung, which lay 60 to 100 feet deep, had to be shoveled off, loaded into ships, and sent around the Horn to Europe for the manure-starved fields of England and Germany. When Indians from the highlands died at the job, the new guano bonanza millionaires. imported more than 80,000 Chinese coolies to work off their passage in practical slavery in the guano beds. Other islands and coastal areas proved to be just as rich, and Peru's dictators lived well by simply laying monopolistic high taxes on the guano industry.

For the country, the guano boom was disastrous. After 20 years of digging, the original beds were practically exhausted; the seabirds were scared away; and bankruptcy faced both the newly rich promoters and the spendthrift government. At $80 a ton, the manure boom had brought more value than all the gold collected by Pizarro, but as far as the development of Peru was concerned, both were wasted. In the "nitrate era," Peru's and Bolivia's nitrate business fell into the hands of Chile. Unable or unwilling during the guano boom to raise her own food, the city of Lima had begun to import her cereals, fruits, and vegetables from Ecuador and her meat from Chile. This practice was continuing as late as 1910.

Peru and Bolivia both depended largely on the extractive industries for export trade. In 1895 a first shipment of Bolivian tin was sent out on a new railroad to Chile's Antofagasta into a world suddenly interested in preserving food in tin cans. Today Bolivia produces 30 per cent of the world's tin. The old silver mines are worked for tin. The Glory Hole of Potosí has 642 tunnels for tin extraction. In 1952, the Bolivian government nationalized the three big companies, Patiño, Hochschild, and Aramayo, which exploit tin mining centers.

Simón Patiño, founder of Bolivia's tin economy, was a poor Indian from a remote village working as a clerk in a company store at the Oruro silver mine when he grubstaked a prospector from store funds. He lost his job and was left with nothing but the seemingly worthless claim of the prospector. With his Indian wife, he went out to work the claim alone—and it became the most fabulous of the tin mines. By 1930, Patiño owned 70 per cent of Bolivia's mines, controlled a world tin cartel, and enjoyed a personal income greater than that of the Bolivian government. Never socially accepted by the creole aristocracy of La Paz, he took his fortune abroad and "crashed" society on the French Riviera, while exploiting his fellow Indians in the mines at home. On his death, his playboy sons took no greater interest in Bolivia than he had.

Transportation costs from the mountains to Europe's smelters kept the world price of Bolivian tin high. To refine tin in the Western Hemisphere, the United States during World War II built smelters in Baltimore and Texas. American need for tin kept the country concerned about the continued production of the mineral and forced the United States to cooperate with Bolivian political leaders when they nationalized tin in the 1950's. When inefficient management brought severe losses upon nationalization, American economic missions helped to work out plans to keep the mines operating, to build smelters in Bolivia itself, and to improve means of shipment. It was the Indian tin miners, who had been mercilessly exploited by all three companies and who eventually organized a radical union movement, who pushed through the nationalization of the industry.

Peru has the fabulous copper mine of Cerro de Pasco, which, before the recent confiscations had been owned by an American copper company whose investment in it amounted to $30 million. The Indian miners at Cerro de Pasco have been treated better than Bolivian miners; they have schools and sanitary housing provided at first by the American company; but they get wages that are pitifully low compared to those paid copper miners in Montana or Arizona. Peru also produces oil, and is the fourth largest producer in South America. New centers of population have developed around the oil port of Talara. The foreign-owned oil fields which were shipping out 12 million barrels annually, operated under the strict control of the Belaúnde Terry government, but were confiscated by his military successors. Fearful that the Talara fields might soon become exhausted, Peru, in the early 1970's, was exploring for oil in the *montaña* and was developing iron mines and other mineral resources. Both Peru and Bolivia still produce silver. Bolivia has been producing oil in her nationalized properties beyond her own consumption needs and is now shipping out many thousands of barrels daily. Ecuador has recently found some oil in the Santa Elena Peninsula, but it has no mineral exports.

Agriculture in all three nations is little different from what it was in colonial times except for the irrigation projects in northern Peru, which produce cotton and sugar for export by machine methods, and for the new projects which clear land for settlement in Peru's *montaña*. Ecuador has cacao groves on its warm coastal plain which produce abundantly with little cultivation. The cacao pods grow on the trunks and large limbs of trees like cantalopes sprouting from a giant vine stalk, and during the shipping season the side streets of Guayaquil are spread with the drying pods while town traffic is routed through other thoroughfares. Ecuador's economy has risen and fallen with world chocolate prices, and with the control of leaf disease on the plantations. Ecuador also exports bananas from Guayaquil; balsa wood, of use in airplane parts, and *cinchona* bark, the basis of quinine, come into world markets largely from Ecuador.

With so many resources in common and so many problems regional in nature, the three Andean nations have been making plans to form an Andean Common Market. At first calling themselves the Andean Group and inviting Chile, Colombia, and Venezuela to join, they have sought to present a united front in negotiations with foreign investors and to establish by 1980 a common external traiff. In a meeting in Lima in the fall of 1969, the foreign ministers of the Andes Group signed a declaration which proclaimed that in economic matters, preference would be given to native capital and businesses. In April of 1970, Colombia, Chile, and Peru began their 10-year program of gradual tariff reduction by importing free of duty and restrictions some 85 products of the Andean bloc nations.

society and culture in today's "Inca empire"

All three of these nations have large Indian populations with high infant mortality and illiteracy rates and very low per capita income. The "masses" of these nations include a million Aymará and a million and a half Quechuas in Bolivia, nearly four million Quechuas in Peru, and a half million "cousins" of the Quechuas in Ecuador. Direct descendants of the Incas, they still speak the ancient tongues, cling to the mountain farms, work in the mines, and let the stream of modernism flow around them. With their short, broad physique, their great endurance at high altitudes, their stoic attitude toward misfortune and exploitation, they seem impervious to the effects of hunger and cold and historical change.

They maintain the ancient methods of farming, owning, on the average, two acres of land, and ploughing, if not fortunate enough to own oxen, with the hand-operated digging stick of the Incas. They may graze sheep on the bleak hills for wool and meat, and use burros as beasts of burden, but save for the wheat, the sheep, and the donkeys, agricultural life has changed not at all. Houses remain typically Inca—stone or adobe walls, tile roofs, crudely fashioned stools and benches, with nothing to provide warmth against the winds of the Andes. The headmen of the village learn only enough Spanish to deal with tax collectors and other government officials from Lima or La Paz. Most villages have no resident priest, and the rituals of the Catholic faith are performed in bare stone churches with little depth of understanding. In their own groups, Indians have a very high sense of morals, becoming degraded only when their tribal customs are broken down in contact with whites.

For centuries, the Indians' apathy to reform or self-help has been enhanced by the continuous chewing of coca leaves, the raw material from which the drug cocaine is made. This practice is considered by some sociologists a source of degradation and by others a necessary protection for the Indian against the rigors of his life. Coca, originally a wild Andean plant, is today grown from seed in the *yungas* area of Bolivia and has become one of the most profitable crops of the Andes. Great quantities undoubtedly are smuggled out of Bolivia and Peru through Argentina and Chile into the illegal cocaine markets of the world.

Indians who labor in the mines have need of "tranquilizers" for although the mines are at an elevation of 12,000 feet, they are near the equator and the heat in the interior is terrific. Few Indians stay at the mines throughout the entire year but go and come with the agricultural seasons. They are better fed and housed at the mines than in the villages, but at the mines their tribal patterns are broken and nothing takes their place. In Bolivia in recent years the seemingly slow and stolid Indians have been organized into powerful unions, and many *cholos* who speak Spanish maintain Indian costumes and customs in cities and mines.

Indians in Ecuador fare better than in Peru or Bolivia for they live in a pleasant climate on more fertile, better-watered land. Near Ambato and Otovalo, Indian village groups own thousands of rich acres in communal holdings and bring in their produce to those two colorful market towns for the weekly fairs. Farm workers in the central highlands and on the cacao plantations of the coast are more apt to be mestizos working for cash wages rather than Indians tied to the land.

An aesthetic and literary interest in the Andes Indians has been created by the new interest in Inca archeology. Dr. Julio Tello, himself of Indian blood, created a department of archeology in the Peruvian government and founded the Inca and Pre-Inca museum in Lima. Writers such as Jorge Pando Gutiérrez and Franz Tamayo have popularized sociological writings about the living archeology of Indian villages today. United Nations pilot projects have taught the Ecuadorian Indians of Otovalo to use their native looms for the commercial weaving of tweeds, a project which has brought cash money and a higher standard of living into the Ecuadorian valleys. Various cooperative groups in Peru have revived the old handicrafts of silver work and variegated pattern-weaving for the tourist trade.

However, the problem of bringing the Indians, the masses of the poor in the Andes nations, into the full stream of the political and economic life of these nations remains unsolved. Peru's "reform party," APRA, became interested in Indian education, and in 1947, experimental schools were founded among the Quechuas on the plan of the Mexican rural schools to teach children first the Spanish language and then reading, writing, sanitation, and improved agriculture. Peru and Bolivia have improved their elementary school systems, built secondary schools on the American plan for city children, and revised the curriculum in their old classical universities. But it is the very rare and unusual Indian who finds his way into these secondary schools.

All three of these Andean countries lack a middle class, save perhaps Peru, and are controlled by small white elements, European and Spanish. Although all have organized labor confederations, and small industries of textiles and food processing, they all need more diversification of their national economics to strengthen and stabilize worker organizations and to raise standards of living. All have extremely wide gaps between the "white" city and the "Indian country," but urbanization is increasing, especially in Peru, as even mountain Indians seek to escape the hardships of the *latifundia* and the poverty of overpopulated rural villages and to take up the life of urban workers.

In the stormy 19th century, dwellers in Lima, La Paz, or Quito had little interest in literature. Manuel González Prada (1878–1918), a political and social philosopher, was Peru's best-known author in the 1890's. He courageously wrote essay after essay of bitter satire against the power of Lima's old aristocracy, corruption in government, and the oppression of the Indians, and in favor of land reforms, improvement of labor, and more representative government. Reform movements that came later in Peru owe much to him. A woman writer, Clorinda Matto de Turner (1858–1909) had the vision to think of the Indians in terms of contemporary social problems instead of early Spanish legends, writing in her novel *Birds Without Nests* compassionately about the injustices done the mountain Indians by her own generation of whites. Ricardo Palma (1833–1919) is considered Peru's most famous 19th century poet. He wrote ten volumes of *Peruvian Traditions* in which is preserved much of colonial Lima's social history. He is remembered with gratitude for his work in restoring the national library after the vandalism of the Chilean invaders in the War of the Pacific by recovering treasures scattered by the soldiers.

In Ecuador, Juan Leon Mera (1832–1894) wrote a novel of Indian life, *Cumandá, a Drama Among Savages,* which treated the Amazonian Indians of *oriente* as lofty, idealized figures of the James Fenimore Cooper style. The author was interested in Indian folklore and natural science and his passages describing the *oriente* and the daily rituals of its inhabitants are authentic. Ecuador's most famous writer was philosopher and uncompromising liberal Juan Montalvo (1832–1889) who wrote caustic articles on García Moreno and his Church policy from exile in Panama. When he heard news of the dictator's assassination, he is said to have cried, "My pen has killed him."

University life in Quito, and even in Guayaquil, was limited to Church schools that were run as they had been in colonial times. Chuquisaca, renamed Sucre, which was a cultural center before Córdoba, to which young residents of the pampas went to school in the 18th century, had ceased to have any intellectual activity. Melgarejo and Daza had stifled what Santa Cruz had hoped to encourage there. The University of San Marcos in Lima, once the academic center for South America, had been sacked and looted in the civil and foreign wars and could no longer compete for prestige with newer schools in Chile and Argentina. When many of the rulers could scarcely read or write, what hope was there for education and culture?

"Indian" consciousness has not permeated the social and cultural life of the Andes nations as much as has the pride in Aztec tradition in Mexico. In the last three decades, however, it has contributed something new and vital to the cultural development in this area. The best known novelists from each country are those who have analyzed the problems of the Indian masses.

The leading contemporary novelist of Peru, Ciro Alegría (born in 1909), wrote a prize-winning novel, *The Serpent of Gold,* in 1935 which describes the life of Indian people in the Peruvian Amazon and their exploitation by lumber and rubber companies. Better known is his 1941 prize-winning novel, *Broad and Alien Is the World,* which is the crowning work of the modern *novela indiana.* Ecuador's Jorge Icaza (born in 1906) has received national prizes for novels about the problems of Indians and *cholos,* especially for his *Huasipungo,* published in 1934. Alcides Argüedas (1879–1946) of Bolivia wrote a semi-fictional account of Indian problems in *The Race of Bronze,* published in 1919. Besides the sociological studies of Gutiérrez and Tamayo, previously mentioned, few works of Bolivian writers are known outside La Paz and Sucre. Manuscripts of Bolivian literary works are now published at home instead of being sent to Europe or Buenos Aires as was done previously.

In the 1940's, a Society of Amateur Artists was formed in Peru which produced little-theater plays, wrote radio dramas, and printed poetry on the Peruvian Indian situation. It also held exhibitions of native crafts and promoted an interest in the paintings of Indians. In Ecuador, a young mestizo of Quito, Oswaldo Guayasamín (born in 1918), has exhibited over a hundred paintings on Indian themes and grievances. Similarly Bolivia's Antonio Sotomayor (born in 1904), who has studied in the United States and Europe, has made Bolivian Indian life the subject for sympathetic and popular canvases. Peruvian singer Yma Sumac made the United States conscious of Inca themes, but at home the three Andean countries have followed the same old European classical forms in music that they did in the 19th century.

In Peru, where the interest in Indians has been part of a general reform movement, political writings, essays, histories, and editorials have been most successful in producing "Indianism." Essayist Manuel Gonzalez Prada, the fiery 19th-century reformer, previously mentioned, who became milder in middle age, was most influential on younger writers. If there was any intellectual ferment in the 1930's and 1940's, it was due in great part to his continued criticism of the thin veneer of culture in upper-class Lima and its effete concern with empty poetry and beautiful style in writing. José Carlos Mariátigui (1891–1930) picked up the torch from Prada and carried it beyond liberalism into radical Marxism. He was a young mestizo from the Lima slums who went to work at twelve, by chance in a printing shop, where he handled manuscripts of liberal writers in Prada's group. At sixteen, he began to write himself and came to the attention of a newspaper which sent him abroad as a young correspondent to visit post-World War I Europe. His first book, *The Contemporary Scene,* published in 1925, bitterly criticized American imperialism in Latin America. The editorials he wrote in *Amanta,* a radical journal he was editing, were published in 1928 under the title *Seven Essays Interpreting the Realities of Peruvian Life,* and called for a world-wide workers' state which would include South American Indians. Luis Alberto Sánchez (born in 1900) is a literary historian and leftist politician whose writings bridge the gap between literature and current history. Peru's political reformer Haya de la Torre, founder of the reform party, APRA, which so stirred Peruvian politics, was in his youth a close friend of Mariátegui but broke with him on the issue of Communism as a cure-all. The writings of Haya, who was a prolific author, and Mariátegui's *Seven Essays* were very widely read throughout South America and Mexico.

Andean poets did not write about Indians for they saw little that was poetic about such limited lives. Best known was a Peruvian, José Santos Chocano (1875–1934), whose verse is found in the introduction of this chapter. He was a contemporary and rival of the great Rubén Darío, but he lived twenty years longer and published many more works. He writes about the beauties of Latin America and expresses idealistic hopes for the future of Latin American people, including the Indians. Peru's world-renowned poet and artist José María Egurén (1882–1942) contributed to musical, lyrical verse rather than "Indianism."

All three nations have suffered from poor budget management and from domination by a few extractive industries, with the result that they have had little money to spend on schools. The University of San Andrés in La Paz has a fine 14-story building but few full-time paid professors. San Marcos University in Lima, oldest in South America, has students who often take part in radical demonstrations but provides a limited classical education to a chosen few. Ecuador, which has elementary and secondary schools that are still dominated by the Church, has four classical-type universities. Ecuador has had a campaign against illiteracy under UNESCO guidance and an "each one teach one" program on the Mexican pattern. Progress has been made but it is slow. In Guayaquil, always more cosmopolitan than Quito, a group of young intellectuals formed a so-called "School of Guayaquil" which promotes a native literature and encourages the publication of books within Ecuador itself.

READINGS

Ache, J. V., *Art in Latin America: Peru* (1961).

Adams, A. A., *The Plateau People of South America* (1915).

Adams, R. N., et al., *Social Change in Latin America Today* (1960).

Agle, W. C., *Eastern Peru and Bolivia* (1901).

Alexander, R. J., *The Bolivian National Revolution* (1959).

————, *Organized Labor in Latin America* (1955).

Alisky, M., *Peruvian Political Perspectives* (1972).

Archaud, C., and F. Herbert Stevens, *The Andes: Roof of America*, trans. E. E. Smith (1956).

Arnade, C. W., *Emergence of the Republic of Bolivia* (1957).

Anstee, M. J., *Bolivia: Gate of the Sun* (1970).

Astiz, C., *Pressure Groups and Power Elites in Peruvian Politics* (1969).

Baines, J. M., *Revolution in Peru: Mariátegui and the Myth* (1972).

Barten, R., *A Short History of the Republic of Bolivia* (1968).

Beals, C., *Fire on the Andes* (1934).

Béjar, H., *Peru 1965: Notes on a Guerrilla Experience* (1970).

Belaúnde Terry, E., *Peru's Own Conquest* (1965).

Bernstein, H., *Modern and Contemporary Latin America* (1952).

Blanco, H., trans. by N. Allen, *Land or Death, The Peasant Struggle in Peru* (1972).

Blanksten, G. I., *Ecuador, Constitutions and Caudillos* (1951).

Bonachea, R. E., and N. P. Valdés, *Che: Selected Works of Ernesto Guevara* (1970).

Bourne, R., *Political Leaders in Latin America* (1970).

Bourricaud, F., *Power and Society in Contemporary Peru* (1970).

Bowen, J. D., *Land and People of Peru* (1963).

Bowman, I., *The Andes of Southern Peru* (1916).

Browning, W. C., *The Republic of Ecuador* (1920).

Buechler, H. C., and J. M., *The Bolivian Aymará* (1971).

Bulnes, G., *Chile and Peru, Causes of the War of 1879* (1920).

Bushnell, G. H. S., *Peru* (1964).

Cárdenas, M., and G. C. Cutler, *Chicha, A Native South American Beer* (1941).

Carey, J. C., *Peru and the United States, 1900–1962* (1964).

Carter, W. E., *Aymará Communities and the Bolivian Agrarian Reform* (1965).

Chapman, C. E., "Melgarejo of Bolivia," *Pacific Historical Review*, VIII, 37–45.

Chase, G., *Contemporary Art in Latin America* (1970).

Cleven, N. A. N., *Political Organization of Bolivia* (1940).

Coester, A., *Literary History of Spanish America* (rev. ed., 1928).

Corbett, C. D., *The Latin American Military as a Socio-Political Force: Case Studies of Bolivia and Argentina* (1972).

Coutu, A. J. and R. A. King, *Agricultural Development in Peru* (1969).

Crawford, R. W., *Century of Latin American Thought,* (rev. ed., 1961).

Davis, W. C., *The Last Conquistadores* (1950).

Dawson, T. C., *South American Republics* (2 vols., 1903–1904).

Debray, R., *Revolution in the Revolution?* (1968).

Dennis, W. J., *Tacna and Arica* (1931).

Dew, B., *Politics in the Altiplano: The Dynamics of Change in Rural Peru* (1969).

Dion, H. C., *Agriculture in the Altiplano of Bolivia* (1950).

Dozier, C. L., *Land Development and Colonization in Latin America. Case Studies of Peru and Bolivia* (1969).

Duffield, A. J., *Peru in the Guano Age* (1877).

Duguid, J., *Green Hell* (1931).

E. C. L. A., *Economic Development of Bolivia* (1958).

Enoch, C. R., *Ecuador* (1914).

————, *Peru* (1908).

Ferguson, J. H., *The Revolutions of Latin America* (1963).

Fifer, J. V., *Bolivia: Land, Location and, Politics Since 1825* (1971).

Ford, T. R., *Man and Land in Peru* (1955).

Form, W. H., and A. A. Blum, eds., *Industrial Relations and Social Change in Latin America* (1965).

Fox, D. J., *Tin in the Bolivian Economy* (1970).

Franklin, A. B., *Ecuador: Portrait of a People* (1943).

Gibson, C. R., *Foreign Trade in the Economic Development of Small Nations: The Case of Ecuador* (1971).

Gomez, R., *The Peruvian Administrative System* (1969).

González, L. J. and G. A. Sánchez Salazar, *The Great Rebel: Che Guevara in Bolivia* (1969).

Goodrich, C., *Economic Transformation of Bolivia* (1955).

Gordon, W. C., *Economy of Latin America* (1950).

————, *Political Economy of Latin America* (1965).

Guevara, E. ("Che"), *Reminiscences of the Cuban Revolutionary War*, trans. V. Ortiz (1969).

————, *The Complete Bolivian Diaries of Che Guevara*, ed. D. James, (1968).

————, *Venceremos: The Speeches and Writings of Ernesto Ché Guevara*, ed. by D. James, W. J. Gerassi (1968).

Guise, A. V. L., *Six Years in Bolivia* (1922).

Hammel, E. A., *Wealth, Authority and Prestige in the Inca Valley, Peru* (1962).

Hanson, S. G., ed., *Economic Development of Latin America* (1951).

Hassaurek, F., *Four Years Among Spanish Americans* (1868).

Heath, D. B., C. J. Erasmus, and H. C. Buechler, *Land Reform and Social Revolution in Bolivia* (1969).

Heath, D. B., and R. N. Adams, *Contemporary Cultures and Societies in Latin America* (1965).

Henth, D. B., *Historical Dictionary of Bolivia* (1971).

Henríquez Ureña, P., *Literary Currents in Hispanic America* (1945).

Hilliker, G. G., *Politics of Reform in Peru: The Aprista and Other Mass Parties of Latin America* (1970).

Horowitz, I. L., *Masses in Latin America* (1970).

Hudson, M. O., *The Verdict of the League: Colombia and Peru at Leticia* (1933).

Hughlett, L. J., *Industrialization of Latin America* (1946).

Ireland, G., *Boundaries, Possessions and Conflicts in South America* (1938).

James, P., *Latin America* (rev. ed., 1950).

Kandell, T. L., ed., *Education in the Latin American Countries* (1942).

Kantor, H., *Ideology and Program of the Peruvian Apristla Movement* (1953).

Kirchoff, H., *Bolivia: Its People and Scenery* (2nd ed., 1944).

Klein, H. S., *Parties and Political Change in Bolivia, 1880–1952* (1969).

Kubler, G., *The Indian Caste of Peru, 1795–1940* (1952).

La Barre, W., *The Aymará Indians of the Lake Titicaca Plateau, Bolivia* (1948).

La Foy, M., *Chaco Dispute and the League of Nations* (1946).

Landsberger, H., *Latin American Peasant Movements* (1970).

Lawson, M. S., and A. Eisen Bergman, *Social Stratification in Peru* (1969).

Leavitt, S. E., *Tentative Bibliography of Bolivian Literature* (1933).

————, *Tentative Bibliography of Peruvian Literature* (1937).

Legg, H. J., *Bolivia: Economic and Commercial Conditions in Bolivia* (1952).

Leonard, O. E., *Bolivia: Land, People and Institutions* (1952).

————, *Canton Chullpas: A Socio-Economic Study of an Area in Bolivia* (1948).

————, *Pichilingue: A Study of Rural Life in Coastal Ecuador* (1947).

————, *Santa Cruz: A Socio-Economic Study of an Area in Bolivia* (1948).

Lieuwen, E., *Generals vs. Presidents* (1964).

Linke, L., *Andean Adventure: A Social and Political Study of Colombia, Ecuador and Bolivia* (1945).

————, *Ecuador: Country of Contrasts* (3rd ed., 1966).

Lockwood, A. N., *Indians of the Andes* (1956).

Lynch, J. V., and P. J. Ferell, *Agricultural Economy of Bolivia* (1961).

Macdonald, A. F., *Latin American Politics and Governments* (2nd ed., 1954).

Mader, C., *The Ecuadorian Presidential Election of June 2, 1968, An Analysis* (1969).

Malloy, J. M., *Bolivia: The Uncompleted Revolution* (1971).

Malloy, J. M. and R. S. Thorn, eds., *Beyond the Revolution. Bolivia Since 1952* (1971).

Mariátegui, J. C. (trans M. Urquial), *Seven Interpretive Essays on Peruvian Reality* (1971).

Merrett, R., *Peru* (1969).

Markham, C. R., *History of Peru* (1892).

————, *War Between Peru and Chile, 1879–1882* (1883).

Marsh, M. A., *Bankers of Bolivia* (1928).

Martin, P. F., *Peru in the Twentieth Century* (1911).

Maúrtua, V. M., *The Question of the Pacific* (1921).

Mautner, H. E., *Doctor in Bolivia* (1960).

McEwen, W. J., ed., *Changing Rural Bolivia* (1969).

Mecham, J. L., *Church and State in Latin America* (rev. ed., 1966).

Meggers, B. J., *Ecuador* (1966).

Michaux, H., *Ecuador: A Travel Journal* (1970).

Miller, R. R., *For Science and National Glory: The Spanish Scientific Expedition to America, 1862–1866* (1969).

Millington, H., *American Diplomacy During the War of the Pacific* (1948).

Monge, C., *Acclimatization in the Andes*, trans. D. F. Brown, (1948).

Mörner, M., *Race and Class in Latin America* (1970).

National Planning Association, *Casa Grace in Peru* (1954).

Needler, M., *Anatomy of a Coup d'état: Ecuador, 1963* (1964).

Nelson, R. H., *Education in Bolivia* (1949).

Niles, B., *Peruvian Pageant* (1937).

North, J., *Civil-Military Relations in Argentina, Chile and Peru* (1966).

Ogilvie, A. G., *Geography of the Central Andes* (1922).

Osborne, H., *Bolivia: A Land Divided* (3rd ed., 1966).

————, *Indians of the Andes: Aymarás and Quechuas* (1952).

Ostria Gutiérrez, A., *A People Crucified: The Tragedy of Bolivia* (1958).

Owen, R. J., *Peru* (1966).

Palma, R., *The Knights of the Cape*, trans. H. de Onís (1945).

Palmer, T. W., *Search for a Latin American Policy* (1957).

Pan American Union, *Peruvian Economy* (1950).

————, *A Statement of the Laws of Bolivia in Matters Affecting Business* (3rd ed., 1962).

Patch, R. W., *Peru's New President and Agrarian Reform and Other Studies* in American Universities Field Staff Reports Service (1964).

Paulston, R. G., *Society, Schools and Progress in Peru* (1971).

Payne, J. L., *Labor and Politics in Peru* (1965).

Petras, J. P., and R. Baporte, Jr., *Cultivating Revolution: The United States and Agrarian Reform in Latin America* (1971).

Pike, F. B., ed., *Conflict between Church and State in Latin America* (1964).

————, *History of Republican Peru* (1966).

————, *Latin American History* (1969).

Platt, R. R., *Ecuador* (2nd ed., 1962).

Plaza, G., *Problems of Democracy in Latin America* (1955).

Poppino, R., *Communism in Latin America* (1964).

Quijano, A., *Nationalism and Capitalism in Peru: A Study in Neo-Imperialism* (1971).

Randall, L., *A Comparative Economic History of Latin America: Argentina, Brazil, Mexico, Peru, 1500–1914* (1972).

Reid, W. A., *Bolivia, the Heart of the Continent* (1919).

Rippy, J. F., *Latin America and the Industrial Age* (1944).

Robinson, D. A., *Peru in Four Dimensions* (1964).

Rosmer, M., *Fishing for Growth: Export-led Development in Peru 1950–1967* (1970).

Russe, J., *Bolivia 1970. Essays on the Most Important Events in Bolivia during 1970* (1971).

Saunders, J. V. D., *The People of Ecuador* (1961).

Schwartz, R. N., *Peru: A Country in Search of a Nation* (1970).

Smith, T. L., *Agrarian Reform in Latin America* (1965).

Stavenhagen, R., ed., *Agrarian Problems and Peasant Movements in Latin America* (1970).

Stephens, R. H., *Wealth and Power in Peru* (1971).

Steward, J. H., ed., *Contemporary Change in Traditional Societies*, vol. 3: *Mexican and Peruvian Communities* (1967).

Stewart, W., *Chinese Bondage in Peru* (1951).

————, Henry Meiggs–Yankee Pizarro (1946).

Stuart, G. H., *The Governmental System of Peru* (1925).

Temple, E., *Travels in Various Parts of Peru, Including a Year's Residence in Potosí* (1833; reprint 1971).

Tomasek, R. D., *Latin American Politics: Studies of the Contemporary Scene* (rev. ed., 1970).

Torres Rioseco, A., *Epic of Latin American Literature* (rev. ed., 1946).

Tudela, F., *The Controversy between Peru and Ecuador* (1941).

Tullis, P. L., *Lord and Peasant in Peru: A Paradigm of Political and Social Change* (1970).

United Nations, *Economic Development of Bolivia* (1957).

————, *Economic Survey of Latin America* (1957).

United States Army, *Handbook of Bolivia* (1963).

United States, Department of Commerce, Office of International Trade, *Investments in Peru* (1957).

Urquidi, C., ed., *A Statement of the Laws of Bolivia* (3rd ed., 1962).

Violich, F., *Cities of Latin America* (1944).

Von Hagen, V. W., *Ecuador and the Galápagos Islands* (1949).

_____, *Ecuador the Unknown* (1940).

Waite, P., *Bolivia* (1914).

Welden, P. D., *Social Change in a Peruvian Highland Province* (1968).

Whitaker, A. P., *United States and South America: The Northern Republics* (1948).

Whitten, N. E., Jr., *Class, Kinship and Power in an Ecuadorean Town: The Negroes of San Lorenzo* (1965).

Wilgus, A. C., ed., *South American Dictators* (1937).

Wilkie, J. W., *The Bolivian Revolution and United States Aid Since 1952* (1970).

_____, *Bolivian Foreign Trade: Historical Problems and MNR Revolutionary Policy* (1971).

Wilson, J. M. P., *Development of Education in Ecuador* (1970).

Wood, B., *The United States and Latin American Wars, 1932–1942* (1966).

Ybarra, Y. T., *Lands of the Andes, Peru and Bolivia* (1947).

Zondag, C. H., *The Bolivian Economy, 1952–1965: The Revolution and Its Aftermath* (1966).

Zook, D. H., *Conduct of the Chaco War* (1960).

_____, *Zaramulla-Maranón: The Ecuador-Peru Dispute* (1965).

chapter 27

COLOMBIA AND VENEZUELA, THE "SPANISH MAIN" COUNTRIES

Gran Colombia: a disappointment to Bolívar

Simón Bolívar, who dreamed of a great federation of northern South America, knew the terrain of the Spanish Main, the modern states of Colombia and Venezuela, better than perhaps any man has since, for he had personally traveled over so much of it on foot, on horseback, in river boat and canoe. He knew every hill between Caracas and La Guaira or Valencia or Coro; he had fought over the rough country from Coro to Cúcuta. Landing at Cartagena he had been up and down the Magdalena on the way to Bogotá, and doubtless he had also been many times in the lower Cauca Valley. Then he came into the Orinoco Valley from Jamaica and led his forces up the Apure and over the high Andes to Bogotá, a trip made only by explorers for geographic societies to this day. In fighting for the freedom of Ecuador he had gone through the mountain passes south of Cali on the upper Cauca and had won Popayán and Pasto from the royalists. But as he lay dying he felt that he had "ploughed the sea"; he knew that this region he loved would never hold together, that it was already torn by local civil wars fought by ambitious leaders. He had predicted that if the regions became separate stable states, Colombia would be "the university," the intellectual center, Venezuela would be the "barracks," the land dominated by the military, while Ecuador would be the "convent," the religion-dominated state.

585

Bolívar used the alliterative Spanish terms *"cuartel, colegio, y convento."* These prognostications came true in the course of the nineteenth century, while transportation remained just as difficult as in Bolívar's lifetime, and regionalism just as strong.

stormy Colombian politics to 1903

Throughout the history of Colombia her political life has been handicapped by the inaccessibility of the inland plateaus which stand at the head of those river valleys into which the country is split by the three ranges of the Andes. Caribbean ports have been connected to the capital by highway only within the last decade, and two-thirds of the country remains practically empty—the Caribbean lowlands, the vast area south of the Andes in the Amazon Basin, and the cold high mountain tops. Of the more than 21,350,000 modern Colombians, 90 per cent live on one-third of the land. Though there is no racial and little class rivalry, the separateness of the regions prolonged provincial rivalry, and the lack of outside contacts kept the issue of Church versus state alive long after it had been settled elsewhere.

Bogotaños considered themselves literary lights, and their city the "Athens of South America." It is true that in their approach to the ensuing bloody civil wars between conservatives and liberals they were more "intellectual" than were other South Americans, and their quarrels were more idealistic and less bound up with personal loyalties to leaders. In her first century of existence Colombia, or New Granada as she was called until 1850, witnessed ten civil wars that were national in scope, and lived under eight constitutions. "Yet no national president has been assassinated," an eminent historian reminds us, and "only two legitimate governments were overthrown by revolution in the entire hundred years." The Colombians were opposed to military dictators; they were concerned about the relation of the Church to politics, the secular control of education, the power of the provincial capitals as opposed to Bogotá. And they were concerned enough to fight each other to the death on the two major issues of Centralism versus Federalism and Church power versus freedom of religion. Nearly 100 insurrections and civil wars resulted from the efforts to settle these two questions, which very soon became interrelated.

The first republic in Bogotá had been so "philosophical" and impractical as to be called *La Patria Boba*. It was easily destroyed by the returning Spanish forces in 1815, and the country had to wait for Bolívar to come to Boyacá over the Andes from the Orinoco to be freed in 1819, after which the New Granadan leader, Francisco de Paula Santander, was given the civil administration of the provinces of New Granada—comprising only one province in the Gran Colombian federation according to Bolívar—while Bolívar went off to fight elsewhere. Santander was a very serious, legalistic person, who was called "The Man of Laws." He was thin, straitlaced, and unsmiling, the opposite of Bolívar and never his personal friend. He believed in enforcing the constitution to the letter. Although a democratic Federalist, he was realist enough to make Bogotá, and not the provincial capitals, the center of all financial and cultural matters. Partially owing to Santander's quarrels with the Venezuelan cowboy leader Páez, Venezuela was the first nation to leave the federation, and the triumphal return of Bolívar himself after Ayacucho did nothing to bring the regions together. The quarrel between Federalism and Centralism waxed stronger; at the Convention of Ocaña in 1827 the Federalists were ousted and Bolívar became a dictator. His opponents even plotted to assassinate him, and as a result of this plot, among other things, Santander was exiled. When Bolívar gave up and went downriver to his death in Santa Marta, his scheme of Gran Colombia was dead also.

In 1832 Santander was called back from exile, given a great ovation, and elected president. Now he could make plans for his government of laws and lay the foundations for the subsequent development of liberalism in New Granada. The tradition left by Bolívar made all government seem personal, however, and all financial and administrative troubles in the chaotic new republic were blamed personally on Santander. In retaliation for this criticism Santander stifled all opposition, insisting that the opposition was delaying the progress his Liberal followers hoped for. The Church and its lay supporters in congress, who represented the Conservative provinces of Popayán and Pasto, opposed his plans for secular education and development of the economy. Santander was faint and ill; he gave his last speech before congress in defense of his forward-looking policies, withdrew, and died shortly afterward, in May 1840, the last Colombian survivor of Bolívar's co-workers in the Gran Colombian dream. After his death, opposition by the Church and army led to civil war and the accession as president of Pedro Alcántara Herrán. Herrán and his successor brought the Conservative party to power under the new constitution of 1843.

The Conservative party, now identified with the Centralists and the Church leaders, produced a dictator-president by 1845. This was Tomás Cipriano de Mosquera—author, scientist, soldier, and statesman of remarkable versatility, whose term of office was a period of enlightened progress. Although a Conservative born in Popayán, he secretly had many liberal ideas. He introduced steam navigation on the Magdalena, approved a liberal education program in the university, encouraged foreign trade, and signed a treaty allowing United States interests to build the railroad across the Isthmus of Panama. His outstanding cabinet member, Mariano Ospina, a native of Medellín, helped build that city and its province of Antioquia into a rich coffee-producing area. Disputes with the strong and well-educated Liberals over religious issues caused a split in his party and put these Conservative leaders out by 1849. This change produced a very liberal anticlerical federalistic constitution in 1853. But the separation of Church and state provided by the new document could not come peaceably in this tense nation of clashing idealisms, and the resulting civil strife brought an army dictatorship to Colombia in 1854.

When the Liberals split, with their right wing combining with the Conservatives against army dictatorship, four former presidents converged on Bogotá with their "personal" armies to oust the "national army" from political power. Though Colombian Liberals were industry-minded and thus were Centralists, and the Conservatives represented the far-flung provinces and were Federalists, the progressive developer of Medellín, Mariano Ospina, became the Conservative president from 1857 to 1860. Deeply devout as well as interested in commerce, Ospina drafted a new constitution—the Granadine Confederation—providing for alliance between Church and state again. This extremely federalistic instrument gave opportunity for local *caudillos* to become strong again, and in 1863 the confederation was overthrown by the private army of the former dictator Mosquera. His administration was signalized by a vicious attack on the Church. His constitution of 1863, using the name United States of Colombia, was one of extreme states' rights and anticlericalism, and lasted until 1886. Guerrilla warfare continued, valley against valley, province against capital. While busy fighting on the Ecuadorean border in an attempt to recreate Gran Colombia, Mosquera was unseated in the capital by a barracks revolution and sent into exile in 1867. Although he had started his career as a patriotic Conservative, he is remembered for the autocracy of his old age. During the next thirteen years the Liberals held power but with many revolts and civil wars.

It is strange that during all this chaos Colombia made more progress toward economic modernism than did the other Andean Republics. A group of young politicians who believed in complete freedom of worship, free education, and limitations on any strong executive created a new party, the Radicals. They found supporters among the small shopkeepers and working people in the cities, and among the professional classes, but their mild "radicalism" so aroused Church leaders, who actually felt that the faith was dying, that Colombia was racked by one of her worst armed uprisings in 1876. The old Liberal party was hopelessly split between radicals and moderates. Making friends on both sides—the more conservative shopkeepers and the more liberal landowners and Church leaders—the moderates won the day, formed a coalition, and ruled the country for a decade and a half of comparative peace and considerable material progress. Part of the debt from the civil war was paid with the sum of $10,000,000 received from the French concern, led by Ferdinand de Lesseps, which had contracted to build the Panama Canal.

Rafael Núñez, a poet and a scholar in his own right, a social philosopher, a keen intellectual, and one of South America's great nineteenth-century figures, was leader of the reorganized party, now called the Nationalists. Very much inclined toward radicalism as a young man, he had become more conservative as he grew older. In his most famous poem, *What Do I Know?*, he worries about the difference between good and bad. "They are so inextricably mingled that a poet cannot separate them." Perhaps this poem explains his willingness to lead the Liberals while he carried on the Conservative party's program. After years of experience in congress and in the foreign service, Núñez had been elected to the presidency in 1880 with much Conservative and Church backing. Civil war was still imminent; his strong-arm methods of stopping it made him the darling of the Conservatives, and he is called the "Regenerator." He brought about order and stability, and then went on to abolish the constitution and break the autonomous power of the provinces, while providing nationwide tax support for the Church. He muzzled the press, restricted suffrage, and exiled Liberal leaders, while he remained personally popular with a host of Liberal and even Radical friends. His pro-Church, strongly centralistic constitution of 1886 lasted until 1936; he himself served as president until his death in 1894. So powerful was his influence that he ruled, not from Bogotá, but from his own plantation outside Cartagena far away on the coast. He remains a literary name in Colombia for his writings on philosophy and political science. His influence was felt in recent times in Colombia where the issues of Church and state in education, and of the free practice of missionaries of other than the Catholic faith have been very controversial questions.

At his death, the long repressed left-wing Liberals and Radicals broke out again in open warfare. There was no peace, only truces from month to month, and finally, in 1899 to 1902, the famous "Thousand Days of Civil War." So chaotic was the entire country by that time, so powerful the provinces against the capital, that the remote little state of Panama was actually ruled by the port of Cartagena rather than by the inland capital of Bogotá. This situation made it easy for the United States to encourage a revolt in Panama during the Canal crisis of 1903; the shock of this loss led to a more stable Colombian government by 1904.

Colombian politics in the twentieth century

Colombia's first misfortune in the twentieth century was the loss of Panama. Under Rafael Núñez, regionalism had developed in that isolated province before 1900. When the United States was anxious to negotiate for the Panama area in 1901 to 1902, Colombia was torn by the War of the Thousand Days, and was lacking any strong leadership. The United States, which had pledged with England in the Clayton-Bulwer Treaty of 1850 that no nation would maintain exclusive control over any canal to be built, had looked askance at Colombia's concession to de Lesseps' French firm in 1878. Forced by the tropical conditions to abandon the site, the French firm arranged to sell its rights to the United States. Then the American government made a treaty with Colombia's foreign minister Herrán, arranging for the use of a six-mile-wide zone for a cash payment and an annual fee. Regional elements in the disorganized Colombia senate blocked the passage of the treaty. Meanwhile, in 1901 the Clayton-Bulwer Treaty was abrogated and Theodore Roosevelt tacitly encouraged the incipient revolt in Panama. On November 2, 1903, the province of Panama became an independent nation. Its loss was a shock to Colombia and became a cause of dissent and disunity. Finally, in 1922, American oil companies anxious to begin drilling in Colombia brought pressure to bear on Harding to improve relations. The United States paid Colombia $25 million for her loss and the matter was closed.

Rafael Reyes, the president active in the attempt to secure redress for loss of Panama, had emerged as strong man from the civil strife of 1903, and held the presidency from 1904 to 1909. Famous for explorations on foot over hundreds of miles in the Colombian Amazon, Reyes later made a career in the army, then won the presidency as leader of the Conservatives. Reyes was actually an unconstitutional dictator, but he rehabilitated Colombia economically, supported by a landowners' and army officers' bloc. He improved communications by building railroads from the highland cities to Buenaventura on the Pacific, and by dredging the Magdalena River route. He stabilized the currency and restored Colombia's foreign credit. In 1909 his handpicked National Assembly extended his term in office, at the same time that he arranged a first, unpopular settlement with the United States over Panama. These two steps produced so much popular resentment that Reyes was forced to resign and to go into exile.

The disappearance of Reyes opened the way for the Conservatives to bring in a more traditional regime, through which that party ruled Colombia till 1930. Under a constitutional provision for minority representation, the Liberal party opposition enjoyed full democratic rights and was invited into coalition cabinets. Meanwhile Colombia prospered from the opening of the Panama Canal, as both her coasts could be visited by ships from either ocean. World War I brought increased trade to neutral Colombia. Once the Panama controversy was settled and American oil prospectors came to Colombia after 1922, the new oil boom commenced which today brings millions in revenue to Colombia. Under Pedro Nel Ospina (1922–1926) and his successor Miguel Abadía Méndez (1926–1930), Colombia's small industries were expanded, her whole economy improved, and coffee production encouraged. The Cauca Valley, with its industrial center of Medellín, became a leader in the nation, and contributed statesmen to the Conservative party. Cali, former stronghold of clerical conservatism, became a center of liberalism.

Worldwide depression, the rise of an articulate laboring class, the fall in the price of coffee, and a strike of the banana workers against the United Fruit Company plantations on the coast all combined to change parties by 1930 and bring the Liberal leaders into power. Enrique Olaya Herrera, former minister to the United States, was elected by a large majority, after a vigorous campaign against a split Conservative party replete with promises of social reform and betterment of living conditions. In 1934 a completely Liberal administration succeeded him under Alfonso López. Thus the Liberals ushered in the period 1930–1946, and gave Colombia a new deal. They guided the nation through economic recovery, reorganization of national education, war with Peru, settlement of the Church question, and the constitution of 1936. The period encompassed an era of increased economic nationalism, industralization, cooperation with the United States, and a swing back to conservatism. The Liberals weathered World War II even though Colombia had been a target for Nazi business operations and home of one of the major German-owned airlines in South America, the SCADTA. The line was nationalized as a threat to the

Panama Canal as soon as Colombia broke relations with Germany after Pearl Harbor. Colombian newspapers and public opinion were all pro-American, and actual war was declared in November 1943. The war period even saw a feeble revival of the old idea of Gran Colombia, when Ecuador and Venezuela conferred with Colombia on several common problems in 1942 and 1943. It was a time also of expanded Colombian agriculture and industry, increased education, and advanced labor laws.

During the 1930s and the 1940s visitors praised "cultured, progressive Colombia, the true democracy." The Liberal presidents of the 1930s, Olaya Herrera and Dr. López, were newspaper editors and writers in the field of history and economics. However, Dr. López had instituted a new constitution in 1936 which, together with various pieces of legislation, stirred up old religious resentments by placing government inspectors over Church schools and making charities government-regulated. The constitution, setting up a unitary government, also provided for social security, income and real estate taxes, and some government control over business. It did much for labor and education. After a term under another Liberal newspaperman, Eduardo Santos, from 1938 to 1942, Dr. Alfonso López was elected a second time. But in ultra-devout Colombia the anticlerical president could not hold his cabinet together in his second term. López was forced to resign in 1945, and his term was completed by the moderate Alberto Lleras Camargo, who was later to serve as a leader in the Organization of American States. By this time the Liberals had split widely into two factions, thereby enabling the Conservatives to gain control in the 1946 election, as many Liberals abstained from voting in protest at the growing Conservative power and at their own party dissension. By plurality vote in a three-cornered election the Conservative and devout Mariano Ospina Pérez was easily elected to serve to 1950.

All this time Liberals and Conservatives alike had appealed only to a relatively small educated minority. Long before 1946 among the left-wing Liberals there had arisen a champion of the people, of the city workers and the landless peasants of Colombia—Jorge Eliécer Gaitán, Minister of Education. As a self-made young lawyer, he had represented a group of banana workers on strike. In spite of the restrictions of the Conservative president, Gaitán became a popular orator, in Conservative opinion a rabble-rouser. His own position became so dangerous that he asked for—and failed to receive—personal police protection. Then, when dignitaries of all Latin American states were meeting in Bogotá on April 9, 1948, to hear General George Marshall, American Secretary of State, the meeting was suddenly interrupted. Gaitán had just been assassinated on a Bogotá street! The screaming pro-Gaitán crowd lynched the assassin, while the embarrassed government moved the foreign delegates to the suburbs. The matter did not end there, however; mobs burned anti-Gaitán newspaper offices, and ran riot for several days, while government leaders put the blame on the very small Colombian Communist Party. Thus began the *violencia*, the banditry which, until the 1960s, was not politically motivated.

Fear of civil war and internal danger shocked the parties into cooperation, and the Conservatives and Liberals combined to support a coalition government, but only for a very short time. By autumn armed clashes in the provinces had grown into a guerrilla campaign which lasted for years. Gaitán was more powerful in death than in life. The underfed masses, to whom no one had appealed so strongly before, could not forget him, while the archconservatives feared further disorder. President Ospina Pérez turned reactionary, and the year 1949 was one of disorder and tension. As police control tightened, Liberals again boycotted the polls, and Laureano Gómez, an archconservative, pro-Spanish, and Catholic newspaper editor whose press had been burned by the rioting mobs of April 1948, was elected almost "unanimously" for the term beginning in August 1950. There followed three years of terror. Protestant groups, tolerated by the Liberals and hated by Conservatives, were attacked; a Perón-type army was built up by Laureano Gómez. The Conservatives themselves rioted in September 1953 when religious fanatics and youths from the "best Bogotá families" destroyed a Liberal newspaper plant and even burned the home of the revered past president, Dr. Alfonso López. Laureano Gómez declared a nationwide "state of siege"; armed bands on both sides took to the hills. Each side called the other Communists or Fascists. In the single year of 1952 the guerrilla fighting caused 12,000 deaths. A new constitution gave Laureano Gómez "supreme power in military emergencies." The dominant Conservative party split, and despite widespread opposition, the country turned to the army for relief from atrocities and a rapidly spreading civil war.

In June of 1953 a coalition was formed between the right-wing Liberals and the more progressive Conservatives to try to bring some sort of peace into chaotic Colombian affairs. General Gustavo Rojas Pinilla, endorsed by the Church and leading a moderate element within the army, made a truce with the guerrillas in the provinces, lifted the press censorship, and became head of a provisional government on June 13, 1953. Within two years Rojas Pinilla became a more oppressive military dictator than Laureano Gómez had been, while the rural areas maintained their guerrilla warfare and attacks on Protestant missionaries continued. Whereas before 1950 Rojas Pinilla had lived in a modest rented house, by 1957 he was a multimillionaire and Colombia's number one cattleman and had exported millions for his own future use (which were to be needed in May 1957, when he was exiled). His iron rule was shot through with graft, while Colombia faced a huge debt and a fall in the value of the peso.

Colombia's traditional faith in democracy and opposition to military rule finally turned against Rojas Pinilla when he made a barefaced attempt to perpetuate himself in power in the spring of 1957. A banking and commercial strike forced even the army to oppose him. University students rioted against his "re-election by his handpicked assembly." On May 10, 1957, Rojas Pinilla was forced to resign. A military junta appointed by Rojas Pinilla chose as provisional president Gabriel Paris, who later added a civilian advisory committee to the military junta. The Liberal Dr. Alberto Lleras Camargo, active in foreign affairs and first Latin American Secretary General of the Organization of American States, who had remained the real leader of the Liberals, was called in for consultation. Meeting with the Conservative leaders in August of 1957, Lleras Camargo drew up a formula for alternating national and local offices between Conservatives and Liberals for the next four four-year presidential terms. The first such term was to begin under an openly elected president in August 1958. The plan was accepted by the weary Colombians with "cautious optimism" in an 18-to-1 vote in December 1957. Each party agreed to make its own choices in a sort of "party primary" for the 50 per cent of national, provincial and local offices it was allowed. With the evenly divided congress chosen, Lleras Camargo was elected president in May 1958. In August the junta peacefully resigned; Lleras Camargo was inaugurated August 18, 1958, in the midst of nation-wide celebration. Lleras Camargo's policy called for a severe monetary and stabilization program, a higher standard of living in the rural areas, the development of raw materials and local manufacturing—all under an austerity program to check inflation. Lleras Camargo worked hard to bring some semblance of order to the country.

The coalition plan called the *Frente* held together through Lleras Camargo's legal term and brought the fair election of a mild Conservative in 1962. The most pressing problem, the violence in the backlands, became less political and more a matter of local banditry and crime. Well-trained Colombian army men were sent into remote villages to teach school, organize local self-help groups, and alleviate the fear of bandit gangs. This program was continued by the Conservative president from 1962 to 1966, León Valencia, the son of a well-known poet. He continued the well-organized campaign against rural terror, cutting the number of deaths by two-thirds. He did have to face falling coffee prices, urban unemployment, and a 45 per cent increase in the cost of living. In the 1966 elections, there were splits in both parties which threatened the system of alternating the presidency for 1966–1970 which had been worked out so well by Lleras Camargo. But a distant cousin of his, Carlos Lleras Restrepo, peacefully gained the presidency and was inaugurated for a four-year term on August 7, 1966. Lleras was not exactly popular, but he was an efficient and dedicated reformer. His administration placed heavy emphasis on technocracy. During his four-year term economic conditions in Colombia were good, the price of coffee was stable, and employment was high. Lleras' *Frente* group controlled not only Bogotá, but the twenty-four other cities of more than 100,000 people in this rapidly urbanizing nation.

But there were divisions in the *Frente's* leadership, and the Liberals and Conservatives both put up a candidate in the election of 1970. Thus the last four-year term under the *Frente* plan was upset by the appearance of a third candidate, Rojas Pinilla, the previous dictator, whose political rights had been restored in 1968. He entered the election arena and tried to win the voters by radio appeals and street meetings which were led by his daughter, a popular senator. The masses had forgotten his vicious rule and remembered only his appeal to the "little people of Colombia." They surged to the polls in support of him. It was the Conservative's turn for the presidency and they had nominated a young diplomat named Misael Pastrana Borero. Pastrana received 40 per cent of the vote and Rojas Pinilla 38 per cent.

When the official count of the ballots declared Pastrana elected, the city poor cried "fraud" and took to the streets again. Lleras Restrepo declared the city of Bogotá in a state of siege, and restored order after two days of rioting. The Archbishop of Bogotá was appointed head of a committee to recount the ballots and declared Pastrana the winner by 60,000 votes. Pastrana, a little known young man, chose a young cabinet. He hoped to appeal to the youth of the nation, who had come to maturity since the end of the *violencia*, in a country where two-thirds of the population are under twenty-one. He faced the same type of social unrest, strikes among workers and "Revolution of Rising Expectations" happening all over Latin America in the early 1970s. Observers hoped that the end of Pastrana's term in 1974 would see the peaceful end of the sixteen-year *Frente*'s agreement and the achievement of its objectives. A long step in that direction seems to have been indicated in the local elections held in Colombia on April 16, 1972, when friends of Pinilla were soundly defeated, the liberal majority won in most regions, demonstrating popular support for Pastrana. It proved above all that violence was not wanted in Colombia.

A good part of the Colombian tension had been due to religious difficulty, which, in Colombia of the 1950s as in Mexico of the 1920s, has to be discussed as a political rather than as a social issue. Colombians are deeply and sincerely Catholic with an almost medieval fervor. Under the early Liberals, Protestant missions were established among the rural mountaineers, where the Catholic Church had had no social program. Several Protestant sects gained converts in the cities, and a YMCA was founded in Bogotá. But in such a strongly Catholic country, Protestantism still seemed as antisocial as heresy had been in medieval times; Protestant mission schools which used "foreign money" to "win away" children already baptised Catholic, by means of attractive picture books and recreation programs, were actually considered wicked. After 1948, mob outbreaks against such Protestant establishments increased; there were more incidents of violence against Protestants in the early 1950s in Colombia than in the rest of Latin America in a whole century.

The Protestants themselves showed poor judgment, carrying on street services in front of Catholic churches on Sunday morning, loudly attacking Catholic dogma and institutions, and disagreeing among their various sects. Priests led children in stoning Protestant meetings; the lives of native Colombian converts were not safe. Modern-minded Catholic leaders, distressed at the situation and the bad publicity it brought to Colombia, proposed compromise plans of limiting Protestant missionaries to a quota and in turn guaranteeing police protection of those already there, while other forward-looking Catholic laymen advocated Catholic social action and welfare programs as a countermeasure to the spread of Protestantism. In the increasing industrialization of Colombia and in the rise in the standard of living taking place throughout this stormy period lay the hopes for more tolerant attitudes. The coalition government of 1958 ended the persecution of Protestants in Colombia and again granted visas to Protestant missionaries.

In 1968, Pope Paul VI, in the first papal visit to Latin America in history, attended the International Eucharistic Congress in Bogotá. His words there were conciliatory to all divisions of Christian belief, and came as a surprise to the older, more dogmatic members of the Colombian hierarchy.

Losing Panama at the beginning of the century and frightening Pan American delegates with street riots at the mid-point, Colombia had a minor international fracas in between. The "Leticia Affair" in the 1930s was a small-scale war with Peru over a remote jungle outpost on the Amazon for a group of galvanized iron warehouses and thatched huts at the tip of the wedge-shape territory which Colombia owns. In 1932, when a Peruvian dictator sent soldiers to try to expel the Colombian inhabitants, war between Colombia and Peru resulted; in the eyes of the world this was a senseless war, for both nations had defaulted on foreign-held bonds in the depression and yet spent millions of dollars in fighting. Finally the League of Nations arbitrated the dispute and gave the river town back to Colombia. In the late 1960s the Colombian government was building roads toward the Amazon and developing the Leticia area.

Other Colombian foreign relations have been very successful. Colombians had been active in the League of Nations—a Colombian had served as president of the League Assembly—and Colombia was one of the first nations to support the United Nations. A token force of Colombian troops fought in Korea; Colombian troops served with Scandinavians in a UN police patrol in the Suez dispute of 1956. Foreign investors have had no unhappy time in Colombia. American oil interests built one of the world's famous pipelines, the Barca; the United Fruit Company developed large holdings in the Santa Marta area, and, when the company had labor troubles, the Conservative government backed the American company.

Venezuela launched as a nation

Venezuela, seventh in area in Latin America, supports more than ten million people. The *llanos* in the Orinoco Basin which figured so dramatically in Bolívar's campaigns are still sparsely settled and underdeveloped. The plains on the coast around Maracaibo are often stricken by drought; the foothills of the eastern Andes facing the Orinoco are covered with humid jungle. South and east of the Orinoco, in the Guiana Highlands, lies a jungle area still not explored. The grazing lands of the *llanos* are too dry in the dry season for the stock, too flooded in the wet. Only in the cooler valleys near the coast where lie Caracas and other modern towns is life really pleasant. Geography, which treated Venezuela so badly, still left billions of dollars worth of oil beneath her hills and tidelands. The people who live in this

"poor-rich" country are 60 per cent illiterate. The *Caraqueños,* those fortu-
nates who live in Caracas, inhabit ultra-modern apartment houses and ride
on freeways paid for by the oil royalties in a country with the highest per
capita income of Latin America, but the mountain Indians and the Orinoco
llaneros live just as they did in Bolívar's time. The age of *caudillos,* up to the
1950s, went right on in the spectacular new buildings of the capital.

Venezuela in the nineteenth century was even more turbulent than
Colombia, and its turbulence lasted longer. Civilian executives, who made
so many contributions to Colombian life, made no such gains for Venezuela.
Soldiers of Indian blood controlled the Andes and the *llanos,* with one
spectacular city-dweller from Caracas varying the pattern in the 1870s. An
ignorant populace in an area devastated by the War for Independence had
no experience in good government. Seldom were the geographic regions of
the country unified; the very difficulty of transportation bred military control. As Bolívar had said, Venezuela was to be "the barracks."

There were perhaps half a million inhabitants in Venezuela at the
end of the devastating wars for independence. Of these perhaps a quarter
were whites, and a hundred thousand were pure-blooded Indians—either
the peon farmers of the Andes or the uncivilized tribal groups beyond the
Orinoco. Along the coast were almost as many Negroes, the heritage from
the slavery of colonial days. Many of them were still held in bondage until
freed by the tardy government in 1830, though the first constitution had
abolished the slave trade. The remaining inhabitants were mixtures of
white, Indian, and Negro, divided by class line drawn according to wealth
and land ownership. By the time of independence Venezuela was a land of
poverty, ignorance, and illiteracy, sparsely settled with few large towns. The
landowning creole class had been largely wiped out in Bolívar's War to the
Death; only in the cities did any number of wealthy conservatives remain,
and the recently freed masses opposed their control. From 1810 to 1888
there were forty-two important revolutions, a figure which does not include
riots or minor coups. Seven dictators and eleven constitutions governed
Venezuela during the nineteenth century. Venezuelans could say, "A constitution is just a yellow-backed booklet to be found in the archives."

In the light of such general disorganization and lack of unity, it is
not strange that Venezuela was the first state to break away from Bolívar's
Gran Colombia confederation. In doing so, the Venezuelans were following
a *llanero,* their cowboy hero of independence, José Antonio Páez. Born in
1790 and involved in a murder at seventeen, this illiterate youth ran away to
the Apure, where he worked as a wandering cattle herder and horse breaker
till he joined Bolívar's army. While Bolívar was busy in Bogotá, Quito,
Guayaquil, and Lima, Páez had acted as the actual dictator of the Venezuelan area in Bolívar's name. Members of the congress in Bogotá accused
him of high-handed methods in violation of the new Gran Colombia
constitution and asked him to resign his leadership in Caracas. When his
actions were approved by a convention of his henchmen, he declared
Venezuela a "sovereign state" and himself responsible only to Bolívar. Soon
Bolívar faced troubles of his own in Bogotá, while a citizens' assembly in

Caracas called for a constitutional convention to draft a government for Venezuela alone. This congress met in April 1830 at Valencia, and as a consequence of its actions Páez became Venezuela's first president. His new constitution "freed" the slaves and guaranteed "civil rights" and free public education, but it restricted citizenship and suffrage. In all his years as dictator Páez found little time to really carry out these noble commitments.

Thus began the Age of Páez, which lasted with occasional interruption until 1863. The Indians and mestizos from the *llanos* were devoted to their cowboy leader and called him "The Lion of the Apure"; his rough sense of humor and his skill at horsemanship delighted his illiterate followers. He realized that he knew little about government, and was anxious to take suggestions; the only trouble was that he could not distinguish good suggestions from bad. Opposed at first by the white aristocracy, he was able to make friends with the Caracas leaders after he became personally very wealthy from confiscated cattle. The records indicated that his regime was honest as compared with those of other *caudillos* in South America. He handled the "Church Question" without antagonizing the clerical leaders, although he abolished tithes and special privileges for the clergy. This cowboy of the open ranges, turned cattle rustler, turned general, made a "none-too-bad" president.

Páez' first term was over in 1835, and he retired gracefully in favor of his elected successor, but he was back in the presidency by 1838, as the constitution had forbidden only direct succession of a president by himself, but had made no mention of a return to power after an interim presidency. The next four years were the period of Páez' greatest success. Páez felt that he personally was so popular that he did not have to maintain a large army, so he used tax money to build more roads and to improve the economy of Venezuela. When his term expired again he continued in the background; by now he was the strong friend of the dominating creole aristocracy of landowners, and the humble *llaneros* were neglected and forgotten.

But a liberal group was in the making. An opposition newspaper had been founded in 1840, edited by Antonio Leocadio Guzmán, who appealed to the masses, demanding universal suffrage and improved conditions for the freed slaves. During a suit for libel Leocadio Guzmán defended himself eloquently, became a popular hero, and joined a plot to overthrow the Páez regime in the elections of 1846. After this first organized movement against Páez had failed and its leader Guzmán was thrown in prison, the old dictator retired to his ranch. He was sure that the conservatives were strongly enough entrenched in the congress and allowed the party of two brothers, José Tadeo and José Gregorio Monagas, a coalition group, to dominate the presidency. The Monagas family ("liberal-oligarchy") soon split with Páez (ultra-conservative) and stayed in control for more than a decade. The liberal Leocadio Guzmán Blanco formed a liberal-federalist coalition against the centralist conservative army. Thus started the Federalist War, which went on for several years up and down the western Andes and across the *llanos*. It brought to a head thirty years of unrest and discord and gave rise to new class conflicts. It ended only when Páez, who had been taken from his ranch by the army faction and sent into exile, returned to make himself dictator again in 1861.

The Lion of the Apure returned, an old man, to a Venezuela torn by years of civil war. The two years during which he remained in Venezuela on his return from exile were years of constant guerrilla fighting. He eventually made an agreement in 1863 which allowed a regime under Juan Cristomo Falcón to come to power, and which provided for Páez' own permanent retirement. As a cattle buyer for an American company the old dictator journeyed to Buenos Aires, where he was lionized as the last surviving lieutenant of Bolívar—in fact, the only one who had the opportunity to survive into old age. After a triumphal tour of other South American countries he died in exile in New York at eighty-three, his fortune intact, after having authored his autobiography. Under Falcón and the federalists the name "United States of Venezuela" was adopted, but this regime was not peaceful and the country was torn by revolution.

Venezuela: the age of Guzmán Blanco

With Páez out of the way, two new political groupings were formed. These were called, for a change, the *Azules*, the Blues, and the *Amarillos*, the Yellows. The leaders were the same enemies as before: the army for the Blues, Antonio Guzmán Blanco for the Yellows. As was to be expected, civil war raged for two years, and Blues and Yellows alternated in the shaky government. But Antonio Guzmán Blanco was destined to come out on top. On April 27, 1870, he entered Caracas at the head of an army, took the oath as president on July 20, made himself dictator, and spent the next two years putting the armed bands of Blues to rout. Either he or one of his henchmen served as "president" from then until 1888. This era of peace and, by Venezuelan standards, of culture and prosperity is known as the Age of Guzmán Blanco. Its colorful and refined dictator does not follow the pattern of the rough soldiers, cowboys, or Andean peasants who have ruled Venezuela for the greater part of her history. Caracas-born and trained, he at least had the best education that city could offer, and he followed in the footsteps of his father, that able journalist and lawyer among the more liberal creoles.

Guzmán Blanco has been described by any number of varying adjectives: intellectual, ingenious, virile, pompous, ridiculous, extravagant, poetic, artistic, versatile, and vainglorious. He was lavish in bestowing honors on soldiers, scholars, and public-spirited citizens. (These honors were always medals with his own profile and name on them.) Anxious for scholastic recognition beyond his own education in law, he sought every possible degree that any learned man anywhere could earn or receive as an honor, and eventually he was awarded every one save that of Doctor of Divinity. Each literary and learned society in Venezuela—and he sponsored and encouraged all existing ones and founded new ones—made him an honorary member, and he made scholarly addresses to each. Every book published during his administration—and he prided himself on the literary output of his state-financed scholars and writers—bore his name on the flyleaf: "Published in the administration of Antonio Guzmán Blanco." Time after time the congress declared him president, then chose a puppet when his term expired, then ousted the puppet and returned Guzmán Blanco. During the reigns of the more docile puppets he traveled abroad with his family and became a well-known literary light and patron of the arts in the best circles in Paris. His beloved daughter married a well-born Frenchman, and Guzmán Blanco, that man of the world, considered her home on the Champs Elysées his secondary headquarters. While he commuted between Paris and Caracas, his rubber-stamp congress voted him "Illustrious American, Regenerator, and Pacificator."

Venezuela itself, its *llanos,* its rugged Andes, and its unexplored jungles, did not fare too badly under this "cultured" Pacificator, so seemingly foreign to its own spirit in every respect. He increased the taxes, collected them fairly enough, and reduced the debt. With the revenues he built roads into the Andes, and even a railroad from La Guaira to Caracas. As Grand Master of the Masonic Lodge of Venezuela he opposed the economic and political powers of the Church, secularized education, proclaimed civil marriage, and invited foreign Protestant missionaries into Venezuela. Primary education was made free and public and, in the written law at least, compulsory. Secondary schools and technical institutes were established in the leading towns. He encouraged industry and codified laws, and he gave Venezuela a period of peace and order. All this constructive work was done by "decree legislation," however; when Guzmán Blanco was in Paris, he regularly sent home "laws" to be enacted by the interim puppets for the "good of the people." Through it all, he maintained himself and his friends in the utmost luxury. With his intensely personal and arbitrary government he was as much a *caudillo* as was any other South American tyrant, albeit a benevolent and refined one.

Venezuelan literary historians point with pride to the writings published in Venezuela in this Age of Guzmán Blanco, but none of the many writers whose works were published with Guzmán Blanco's administration credited on the flyleaf is considered important enough to be listed in the standard Spanish American anthologies. In fact, Venezuela produced no great literary figure after Andrés Bello until the turn of the twentieth century. The writers of the time, 1870–1890, were so anxious to please the dictator in his love for all things French, that they were almost academic in aping the romantic style of Victor Hugo. When Zola became more popular in Paris, young Venezuelans became less romantic and more realistic. In any style they won fame if Guzmán Blanco liked them. The most widely read novel of the period necessarily appeared after Guzmán Blanco's prizes were no longer offered. It was *Peonía,* written in 1890 by Manuel Romero García (1865–1917). Its plot centers on a dictatorial father whose sons and daughters cannot rebel against him because of Venezuela's unjust laws; it treats of the social conditions in Venezuela. *Peonía* is considered the first of the nationalistic or creole novels of Venezuela. Under the artificiality of Guzmán Blanco, in spite of his sponsorship of liberalistic courses in the university and his organization of the Academy of Social Sciences and Fine Arts, frank, critical, or naturalistic literature had no chance.

Artificial or not, literary efforts and cultural societies went into a decline with Guzmán Blanco's own decline of power. When he went for another "vacation in Paris" in 1887, his current puppet was faced with an uncontrollable uprising. The dictator was too old, he was absent too much, his old generals were dead. This time Guzmán Blanco sensed the turn of events and remained in Paris, where in 1899 he died at seventy, peacefully in bed amidst luxurious surroundings. Strife in Venezuela between his possible successors lasted from 1887 to 1892. On October 6 of that year, Joaquín Crespo, former puppet president (1880–1881), came into Caracas at the head of a victorious army championing *"legalismo,"* as had Guzmán Blanco before him. Crespo was called "The Hero of Duty" and had a large popular following. His national assembly drew up another constitution under which Crespo held power as an able and efficient dictator, though without Guzmán Blanco's dramatic flair and without continuing his encouragement of the arts.

Crespo's administration, peaceful at home, was involved in the first serious external problem ever faced by Venezuela. Great Britain claimed that the western boundary of British Guiana extended into Venezuelan territory—an old boundary dispute going back to 1844 when English prospectors had crossed the vague line in search of gold. During his presidency Crespo requested that the dispute be submitted to arbitration and appealed to Grover Cleveland, the American President. Under the Monroe Doctrine— in fact in one of its early applications in South America—the United States threatened war on England if she did not submit to arbitration. American Secretary of State Richard Olney declared that "the United States is practically sovereign on this continent and its fiat is law upon the subjects to which it confines its interposition." England tacitly agreed by accepting arbitration. The rulings of the boundary commission meant a defeat for Venezuela, however, since a lion's share of the territory in dispute went to British Guiana. Much of this area, as well as the entire third of the Venezuelan nation that lies south and east of the Orinoco, remained completely unexplored into the twentieth century.

The turn of the century saw the end of Crespo, last of Guzmán Blanco's lieutenants, who was killed in a battle over his successor. This opened the way for a new dictator, General Cipriano Castro, neither a *llanero* like Páez nor a cultured *Caraqueño* like Guzmán Blanco, but a hard-riding cowboy from the western mountains. As the "Lion of the Andes" he rode into power in October 1899, became provisional president until July 1902, and "full constitutional president" until 1909. His ruthless regime began a thirty-year period of rule by Andean soldiers and peasants which characterizes the first quarter of the twentieth century. That century, though still marked by military dictatorship, was to bring a new gushing prosperity, the "Age of Petroleum," an era of its own.

dictatorship pattern broken in oil-rich Venezuela

The twentieth century had dawned in Venezuela with a cruel, vindictive, and irresponsible military *caudillo,* Cipriano Castro, in power—power he held for nine years, during which he bankrupted Venezuela and built up a tremendous personal fortune outside his native land. When finally exhausted from debauchery, he went to visit a kidney specialist in Germany, leaving a trusted henchman, Juan Vicente Gómez, in control. Castro never got back into Venezuela, for Gómez took over and kept him an exile.

Thus commenced the "Age of Gómez," a time of tyranny and cruelty, although not without some material progress. It lasted twenty-seven years. Illegitimate son of a poor mountain Indian woman, himself a peasant who never learned to read and write, Gómez had risen to prominence as one of Castro's army of cattlemen and by 1900 was a wealthy rancher. By 1910 all Venezuela was his ranch. He never married, but fathered scores of illegitimate children who lived around him on fat government jobs. His personal holdings were fabulous; he was said at his death to be worth $30 million, but none of his good fortune ever trickled down to the Indian masses. He maintained order by force and cruelty; common people called him *El Brujo*, the sorcerer, and could not believe he would ever die. When his death in bed from old age was announced in December 1935, the city of Caracas literally went on a drunken spree of celebration.

But Gómez' rule, like that of Porfirio Díaz in Mexico, was not all bad. As a benevolent despot he was interested in promoting public works and sanitation, although he frowned on mass education. He employed smart, scientifically trained young men to do the actual work of government. His foreign relations were harmonious and he preserved a prosperous neutrality during World War I. Most important for the future, oil was discovered in Lake Maracaibo during his rule, and Gómez was smart enough to turn it to his own profit. Foreign capital was allowed to develop the petroleum, but an eighth-part of all oil produced had to be turned over as taxes to his government. Maracaibo turned out to be a fabulously rich field; Gómez' government paid off the national debt, reduced domestic taxes to a minimum, and lived fat off the oil revenues. He gave some material prosperity to Venezuela in agriculture, stock raising, and industry, although they were monopolies. In sharp contrast to the rest of Latin America, Venezuela was hurt very little by the depression, and the prosperity of the government from the oil taxes has persisted to the present day.

Into the orgy of celebration at the dictator's death came Gómez' Minister of War, General Eleazar López Contreras, to bring peace and order; the congress declared him president for the next five years. López Contreras served his country well; a new constitution was made providing for a national labor office and some social insurance. Under it López Contreras broadened the franchise slightly and formed a new liberal government, but in reality he was a continuation of the rule of Venezuela's masters of great estates and businessmen. He organized a Three Year Plan to use the fat revenues for the improvement of transportation, water works, and schools. Though World War II cut into the flow of oil revenues, he maintained Venezuela's prosperity and peacefully designated his successor, General Isaías Medina, in a rigged election in 1941.

Isaías Medina continued Contreras' policy, cooperated with the Allies in World War II, and declared war in February 1945. He completed Contreras' Three Year Plan and adopted a Four Year Plan of public works and agricultural production; he improved harbors and developed low-cost housing. Meanwhile a liberal faction called *Acción Democrática* was growing into a political party of middle-class professionals and businessmen, with some labor support. Convinced that Isaías Medina was planning to dictate the next election, the liberals joined with a group of dissatisfied young army men. Consolidating behind Rómulo Betancourt, who became provisional president, a military junta overthrew Isaías Medina in October 1945. As provisional president from October of 1945 to February of 1946, Betancourt established democratic government under a new constitution. He also attempted social legislation, expanded education, started land reform, and tried to lower the cost of living. Rómulo Gallegos, beloved leader of *Acción Democrática* and a famous novelist, was elected president in February 1946, in the first honest election in Venezuela.

A Caracas school teacher under whom many of the young men in his government had studied history, Rómulo Gallegos was recognized as one of the great writers in the Spanish language. Now at sixty-five, he tried his hand at the presidency under a new constitution with great plans for improving the country. In July 1948 he came to the United States to dedicate a statue of Bolívar, calm in the belief that the Age of *Caudillos* was over in Venezuela. But a group of corrupt older army officers, stopped in their customary graft during Gallegos' administration, were not content to let it be, and precipitated a coup d'état on November 23, 1948. This palace revolution, about which the populace first heard over the radio that morning, set up a three-man junta which soon sent the idealistic Rómulo Gallegos to exile in Cuba.

The three-man junta called their revolt "a democratic necessity in the face of Communist influence." Then they put 4,000 opponents in jail, outlawed the *Acción Democrática*, and disbanded congress. Newspapers were censored; the university was closed. One member of the triumvirate was assassinated in November 1950, the second retired from active administration, and the third, Marcos Pérez Jiménez, was proclaimed provisional president and then actual president by 1953.

Pérez Jiménez was a dictator in the old *caudillo* tradition. Son of a small coffee planter, he had been educated in the War College in Lima and had taught at Venezuela's military academy. His urge to oust the democratic Rómulo Gallegos government stemmed from his dissatisfaction with a major's rank. As president he was a model family man, staging parties and pageants for the public, and shunning the fancier society of oil-rich Caracas. Slated to finish his "legal term" in 1958, he had his congress "declare for a plebiscite to be held on December 15, on his continuing in office for another term to begin in April 1958." Because of his advantageous "deals" with the oil companies, the middle- and upper-class people of Caracas lived well indeed, attended school in streamlined glass buildings, inhabited model apartment houses which excelled those of Rio, and enjoyed a prosperity unparalleled elsewhere in Latin America. The slums of Caracas, the *llanos,* and the Andes remained much the same as in Bolívar's time, however, as far as the masses of the inhabitants were concerned. The Pérez Jiménez government ran an "orderly" administration and pointed with pride to many improvements in Caracas. But its opposition was in exile and it showed no respect for human dignity. Thus it rated as one of the worst dictatorships in South America as of January 1958.

Early that month a group of air force officers rose in revolt against Pérez Jiménez, and when other branches of the military failed to join them, thousands of air force personnel were crowded into jail. By January 10, Pérez Jiménez had jailed a group of liberal priests also, and thus came into sharp conflict with the Church. Now the army generals lost their timidity and forced the dictator to name a new chief of police to replace his hated "stooge" Hector Estrada. Estrada fled precipitately to join Perón with Trujillo in Santo Domingo, but the crowd in the streets had now lost its timidity also. Church leaders rang the church bells continuously on February 1; students left classes to swarm in the streets; the "underground" against Pérez Jiménez came out above ground. At 2:00 A.M. February 2, 1958, the dictator and an eleven-car caravan of friends drove to the airport and to refuge on a "visitor's visa" at Miami. Venezuelans rioted twenty-four more hours, then settled down to rule by a five-man junta—four civilians and only one military officer. Head of this group was a rear-admiral, Wolfgang Larrazábal, who governed throughout the summer of 1958 and supervised a legal election on December 7, 1958. Larrazábal, himself a candidate, had the support of the left-wing, anti-United States faction and of the vociferous though small Communist party.

It was the *Acción Democrática* of Rómulo Gallegos' day, out from hiding since the exile of Pérez Jiménez, which won the election. Its candidate was one of its founders, Rómulo Betancourt, provisional president in 1945 and 1946, who had been spending years of exile observing democracy at work in Costa Rica and Puerto Rico. Imprisoned with ball and chain in his student days by Juan Vicente Gómez, Betancourt had worked for democracy in Venezuela through thirty years of adulthood, twenty-one of them spent abroad. Now he was president after a fair election, and was inaugurated February 14, 1959. Pérez Jiménez had left the country with nothing but disorder. Now Betancourt—honest, hard working, socially conscious, but economy-minded—brought some stability to his nation.

One of his first problems was to work out a new arrangement with the oil companies, whereby a fairer share of their profits came directly to the Venezuelan people, but in which the oil companies themselves had a chance to negotiate. His opponent Larrazábal did not allow him this chance, but led the retiring junta, in the last days before Betancourt's inauguration, to "slap" a 67 per cent tax on oil profits, without any negotiations. Accused already of "too much friendliness to United States oil," Betancourt could not reverse the junta's decision, though he hoped to encourage foreign investment. He needed additional funds to attack unemployment, build schools for the 600,000 Venezuelan children crowded out, and fulfill the promise of better living held tantalizingly before the people by the grandiose freeways, housing projects, and half completed hospitals which Pérez Jiménez and Larrazábal's junta had built with the 50-50 oil royalties.

Four years later Betancourt, though harassed throughout his term by the strongest *Fidelista* Communist party outside Cuba, by "cloak and dagger" spies and secret arms caches from nearby Havana, was able peacefully to turn over his office to Raúl Leoni in February 1963. This was the first time in 152 years that one legally elected president served out his entire term of office and turned over his job to a legally elected successor.

The military had not intervened in politics from 1958 to 1966. This period under Betancourt and Leoni was one of the principal challenges to totalitarianism in Latin America. The new president had been a revolutionary against Gómez in his youth, had been imprisoned, tortured, and exiled, but in the presidency he seemed a placid, plodding man, bald and portly at fifty-eight. However, he formed coalitions between the *Acción Democrática* and three other moderate parties, and thus pushed a reform program faster than had Betancourt. Under a Four-Year Plan he inaugurated irrigation projects in the dry land south of Maracaibo, and distributed farm land in other areas of Venezuela to more than 60,000 families, including settlers in 700 new cooperative villages. Although there were 350,000 families still waiting for lands promised them under Betancourt's 1960 Agrarian Law, this progress seems rapid in a nation in which two per cent of the population had always owned 70 per cent of the farm land. The Four-Year Plan also included the building of 380,000 new housing units and the diversification of industry in one-product, oil-rich Venezuela.

The *Acción Democratica* leadership split into factions in 1968. In a very close election, the Christian Socialist Party, headed by Rafael Caldera and containing many idealistic young Catholic reformers, won the presidency in 1968 by a very small plurality. Caldera, a sincere 54-year-old lawyer, was inaugurated in March of 1969 without incident. He was the first opposition leader to win the presidential office through democratic processes in Venezuela's independent history. But Caldera still had to combat congress, controlled by the more moderate parties. His promises to "Venezuelanize" the oil industry "as opportunities present themselves" were still awaiting such "opportunities" in the early 1970s. Venezuela was rapidly becoming a modern, self-sufficient nation in agriculture, less dependent on foreign oil revenues and pushing toward very rapid urbanization.

Venezuela had begun the century with the fear of foreign invasion. Cipriano Castro, the Lion of the Andes, who became dictator in 1899, soon earned himself the name "International Bad Boy" because he made no payments on debts contracted by his predecessors. In 1902 British, German, and

Italian warships set up a blockade along the Venezuelan coast to force payment on these debts, an incident known as the Second Venezuelan Crisis. Again the United States exercised the Monroe Doctrine. Theodore Roosevelt persuaded England and Italy to settle the matter by arbitration, and threatened the Germans with armed force. The subsequent arbitration awarded a compromise amount to the three powers. Actually, Castro never paid it, and Venezuela remained in bad repute until the matter was settled by Gómez, who, though more crude at home than Castro, was more suave abroad.

In World War I Gómez pursued a policy of neutrality, selling oil rights to whoever could come and pay for them. As the world's needs for oil increased after 1920, he granted leases to Dutch, American, and British companies. American companies, in an oil-conscious world, deliberately made friends in Venezuela by their fine housing projects for workers in the oil fields, and their policy of hiring as many Venezuelan citizens as possible.

By World War II this happy economic friendship between the United States and Venezuela was bearing fruit. Reciprocal trade agreements had been signed in November 1939. When the Nazis took Holland the next year and threatened the Dutch Caribbean islands so near Maracaibo, the two nations were jointly responsible for their defense. The United States granted Venezuela lend-lease funds to train her army and replace her tankers sunk by German submarines. A German-owned railway in Venezuela was expropriated by the government. Thus Venezuela played her full part in inter-American defense, broke with the Axis, declared war, and joined the United Nations. Her relationships with the powers whose companies own the oil concessions have remained friendly and cooperative under every presidency since.

However, resentment flared against the United States because she had "maintained such comfortable relations with the dictator" and had welcomed him in exile. In the recession of 1957 and 1958, oil imports to the United States were cut, and with them much of Venezuela's tax money. When Vice President Nixon arrived on a visit to Caracas in May of 1958, this resentment boiled over and he was spit upon and stoned in the street. Communists and rightists combined in using the latent anti-United States feeling as a whip against Rómulo Betancourt's government. Leoni continued Betancourt's foreign policy of support for self-determination and political democracy. In the 1960s Venezuela's most serious foreign problem was to stop infiltration of Communist terrorists and their armaments from *Fidelista* Cuba. However, she was able to get the Organization of American States to condemn such arms shipments.

Observers could report in 1971 that the ten-year Castro-Communist guerrilla campaign in Venezuela, Fidel's largest foreign effort, had ended when money from Cuba no longer reached the, by then, isolated rural bands. The urban terrorists in Caracas had been crushed by Venezuelan police in 1967. President Rafael Caldera in 1970 put out a general amnesty for the terrorists and 80 of them who came in were pardoned.

economic development along the Spanish Main

Economically this whole area still held to the colonial patterns until after 1850. There was livestock raising, subsistence agriculture, some wheat production in the savanna of Bogotá, some tobacco culture, and some coffee planting on the coast near Santa Marta. Medellín and Cali in the Cauca Valley became boom towns of the coffee business at the same time that São Paulo began to emerge as a coffee center in Brazil. European immigrants came into the Cauca province of Antioquia ready to work as sharecroppers in the coffee lands or as small shopkeepers or artisans in the new towns. The workers in the small industries became an articulate class in the struggle between the right and left wings of the Liberal party just before the days of Núñez. It was one thing to make good cigars or produce finer-flavored coffee beans than São Paulo; it was another thing to get them out to the world. In Colombia the problem was river transportation. In the days of Rafael Núñez the dictator preferred to stay at Cartagena, rather than take the long stern-wheeler trip to Bogotá. From Bogotá the forty miles across the savanna to towns on the other side of the valley were not traversed by a carriage road until after 1850.

In Bolívar's last days the upriver trip on the Magdalena was made in canoes. Two steamers of the Mississippi River type were making the trip in the rainy season by 1852. As late as 1875 there was no accommodation for women; the paying gentlemen brought their own hammocks to sling on the deck; the sailors tied up every night and fished for their dinner. At the overnight stops they got off and cut wood for fuel. At the end of the boat trip the travelers had to buy their own mules for the trip to Bogotá. In 1887 a railroad was begun to Girardot, the head of navigation on the Magdalena. There had been a railway across the Isthmus of Panama, the remote Colombian province, since the California gold rush, but it was of no value to Colombia's domestic development. President Núñez had dreams of connecting Bogotá by rail to the port of Buenaventura on the Pacific; he dredged parts of the Cauca and made it navigable into Antioquia province. By mid-nineteenth century, however, little improvement in the ground transportation to Bogotá had been made; it was still impossible for travelers from the capital to reach the Caribbean by road or rail. Throughout the 19th century Venezuela remained a minor cattle raising area, its agriculture centered around Caracas and the Orinoco *llanos* used only for pasture.

That the standards of living rose in the twentieth century in both Colombia and Venezuela is due partially to the petroleum industry. In 1907 a concession to exploit petroleum deposits in Lake Maracaibo was granted by the Venezuelan dictator Castro to an American company. By 1917 the company at Maracaibo exported 60,000 barrels; in 1965 the production of Venezuela ran to nearly three-and-a-half million barrels a day. About two-thirds of Venezuelan oil comes from the Maracaibo, and one-third from the Orinoco region. Standard Oil has considered the Venezuela holdings a very valuable property, contributing two-thirds of Standard's production outside the United States.

Refined at first in the Dutch West Indies, Curaçao, and Aruba, just off the Maracaibo coast, a large part of the oil is now refined in three coastal refineries, bringing employment and profit to Venezuelans, and more good will to the companies. In the last decade the American companies made a two-billion-dollar profit, of which they re-invested more than a billion right back into Venezuela; the Venezuelan government received more than two billion itself from all these operations.

Perhaps learning a lesson from Cárdenas' anti-oil company action in Mexico, the American management in Venezuela's fields determined to promote good relations. "The oil in Venezuela belongs to Venezuela," says a public relations announcement of an American company. "By means of an arrangement that is mutually profitable to Venezuela and ourselves, we are converting the country's greatest natural resource into the country's greatest source of income." To carry out these fine words, the company not only paid the high royalty, but employed 94 per cent native personnel, even in skilled technical positions, for which they trained young Venezuelans on scholarships. Oil camp communities provided better housing and better schools, hospitals, and recreational facilities than were available to most other Venezuelan working people.

On the other hand, the oil workers' high wages and the government's high profits produced inflation in a nation otherwise economically poor. Since the country did not produce sufficient foodstuffs, and very little consumer goods, prices on such things skyrocketed with the higher wages and more sophisticated demands. Living costs for the workers and the city white-collar classes almost wiped out the advantages of high wages. Presidents through the 1930s and 1940s adopted a policy of "sow the petroleum profits back into the nation." A *Corporación de Fomento,* or Development Corporation, was set up to use the money in public works, housing projects, hydroelectric plants, and agricultural training and soil and livestock improvement for the *llanos* and the mountain farms. Whole blocks of model tenements were built in Caracas, hospitals erected, compulsory health programs started, and better highways into the backlands built.

Colombia, the second largest petroleum producer in South America, also shares in the oil bonanza, with her deposits lying in the same geologic formation as those of the Maracaibo Basin. The fields which have been developed at the bend of the Magdalena nearest the Venezuela line are producing 5 per cent of Colombia's exports. Most of this oil is carried to the coast at Cartagena by means of the Barca pipeline, a spectacular project through the jungle, eight inches in diameter and 335 miles long. Agricultural exports, bananas and coffee, loom larger in the Colombian economic pictures than do such products in Venezuela.

Iron ore reserves in Venezuela are placed at one billion tons, usable for the outside world because they are accessible to year-round navigation on the Orinoco. In 1940 Bethlehem Steel staked out a concession to open up this area, using open-pit mining with electric shovels and thirty-ton diesel trucks in the jungle wilderness. United States Steel has also gone into the region above Ciudad Bolívar. This new iron and steel development was a boon to the Leoni administration in its attempt to diversify the economy. If, as some petroleum authorities prophesy, Venezuelan oil reserves are exhausted by 1980, the slack will be taken up by this boom on the Orinoco. By 1965 a pre-planned town on the Orinoco, Santo Thomé, had 70,000 inhabitants; the Guayana Development Corporation on the Orinoco had built a hydroelectric project on the Caroni River, an Orinoco tributary, to provide power to process the ore. In its first year the steel complex, the "Ruhr of Venezuela," produced 70,000 tons, in its second year, 1964, 300,000 tons. Nickel deposits are also being worked in the area. Colombia has built its own steel refinery at Paz del Río, 280 miles northeast of Bogotá, second in production only to Brazil's Volta Redonda steel plant throughout all South America, and capable of satisfying Colombia's own increasing manufacturing needs.

True to the *Conquistadores'* dreams, gold, diamonds, and emeralds are still being mined along the Spanish Main. Diamond mining in the Venezuelan highlands southeast of the Orinoco is on the increase. Colombia is producing fifteen million dollars' worth of gold from the central *cordillera* annually, and is today the world's chief source of emeralds.

In local manufacturing—textiles, cement, printing, food industries, chemicals, building materials, soap, aluminum products, refined sugar—the two countries are not self-sufficient, although Colombia may be so in another decade. More than 50,000 such establishments are listed, but few of them employ large numbers of people. Foreign trade—in oil, ores, coffee, and bananas—has trebled for the whole region in the last three decades, helping the countries cushion themselves against worldwide fluctuations. Each nation has since established a Department of *Fomento* or Development, which has loaned money to local consumer-goods industries.

Industrialization of agricultural countries produces a new class of industrial laborers, and with them social and political tensions. Though oil workers fared well in Venezuela, the whole policy of the military government was very repressive against trade unions there. Identifying labor unions with the outlawed *Acción Democrática*, the Pérez Jiménez junta dissolved the unions. While still active in the 1940s, labor had been able to write into law the eight-hour day and the forty-eight-hour week. However, these measures have not been enforced outside the oil industry. Dr. Alfonso López, as liberal president of Colombia before 1946, was very pro-labor; his congress passed a basic wage-hour-vacation law in February 1945. During his day the Colombian Federation of Labor held the balance of power in elections. Strongly behind Gaitán, labor went into an eclipse politically under the governments which followed his death.

The typical Colombian laborer is not a city dweller, but rather is a coffee plantation worker living in the Cauca Valley near Medellín or Cali under much the same conditions as his counterpart in São Paulo, though more often eventually owning his own small acreage and becoming a freeholder, not a laborer. Two-thirds of the working population of Colombia are in agricultural, pastoral, and forestry pursuits. Coffee, specially labeled for flavor as "Colombian Coffee" in the world's markets, comprises over 70 per cent of the nation's exports by value. Tuning in on the quota system for world coffee production devised under Brazilian leadership in 1940, Colombia kept up her trade during World War II and did not suffer from Brazilian competition. The sloping highlands in which Colombian coffee is grown do not lend themselves to large plantation methods; some producers must get their product down to the river freighters by muleback as they did thirty years ago. The coffee planters, long an entrenched aristocracy in the Cauca Valley, remain the backbone of the Conservative party, and do not take to new methods, although Medellín, capital of the Cauca state of Antioquia, is a center for urban Liberal ideas.

A special case study of the economy of Colombian coffee was made by the Alliance for Progress in the late 1960s. Coffee exports comprised two-thirds of Colombia's exports in 1960, and the world coffee quota agreements of 1962 obligated the Colombian government to cut that by half. A ten-year investment plan to be financed by the World Bank was to increase cotton production, oil seeds, bananas, and livestock. Seventeen per cent of the increase was to be in new manufactured products. Of the billions of investment promised by international financing, about 400 million was spent. The end of *La Violencia* was bringing peace to the countryside in the 1970s and some of the plans for new crops and improved livestock could be introduced. Colombian development in the decade of the 1960s had been one of the minor victories of the Alliance for Progress in its attempt to change one-crop economies. Bananas, developed by the American United Fruit Company on the Caribbean around Santa Marta, account for 10 per cent of Colombia's foreign trade.

Agriculture in Venezuela employs about half of the population. Long neglected and backward, it has profited from the "sow the petroleum revenues back into the soil" policy. This operates through trained agronomists and veterinarians who are part of an "extension service" to improve methods of planting and breeding among Venezuela's depressed farmers and cattlemen. Schools of practical agriculture were opened, with active clubs organized for farm youth on the 4-H pattern. Both Colombia and Venezuela need to put more land under cultivation; in Colombia in the last two decades the population has increased twice as fast as the amount of new land planted. There is need for more diversified farming, for taking land out of grazing and putting it into crops, for mechanization and technological development of agriculture to feed the growing cities. To help in such improved agriculture, Colombia has an Institute of Colonization and Immigration to colonize government-held lands cooperatively. Venezuela has also brought in a number of immigrants, both for agriculture and as artisans, under the National Agrarian Institute Colonization Program.

Much potentially usable acreage is accessible via the Orinoco, which could be a lifeline for a new Venezuela, reaching the vast undeveloped grassland region. Though long navigated by boats from Trinidad to Ciudad Bolívar, the Orinoco is only now open to scheduled transportation farther inland. Colombia's rivers are more useful to her, as the valleys of the Magdalena and the Cauca and the plateau of Bogotá comprise the principal settled area of the country. A new network of highways connecting the Caribbean with Bogotá, and Bogotá westward to the Cauca Valley and on to the Pacific at Buenaventura was finished in the 1960s. At its mouth the Magdalena is so shallow that only in the last twenty years has it been deepened to make Barranquilla a real ocean port. It is possible to travel by car or bus on the all-weather Simón Bolívar Highway, a section of the Pan American Highway, from Caracas to Bogotá to Popayán to Quito. In 1952 a new superhighway, built with oil revenue, was opened from Caracas to La Guaira, the modernized Caribbean port; other roads into the Venezuelan interior were built in the 1960s. The Orinoco River was spanned by a bridge at Angostura, the longest suspension bridge in Latin America, which opened to traffic in 1970.

Aviation is the answer to northern South America's transportation problems. AVIANCA, the national Colombian aviation company, carries commuters on one-hour trips from Bogotá to Medellín or from Cartagena to Cali. Industrial leaders, politicians, coffee planters, and the growing middle class use planes as North Americans would use interurban trains.

cultural and social patterns
in the Spainsh Main countries

Racially there is more of an admixture of Negro blood in these two countries than in any other South American nation save Brazil. Of the 21 million Colombians, about 20 per cent are pure white, another 2 per cent pure Indian, living as tribal groups in remote areas, perhaps 46 per cent mestizo, and 32 per cent Negro or mulatto, many of them dockworkers in the ports where their slave ancestors were the stevedores of the Spaniards. Venezuela with its ten million inhabitants has much the same pattern, except that there are more primitive Indians in remote sections, descendants of the Caribs. There is so much mixture that there is little racial prejudice, although the large and rapidly growing capital cities are mostly white or mestizo. The population of Caracas, with only 250,000 people three decades ago, now numbers more than 2,500,000 inhabitants in its metropolitan area. About one-half as many people live in all Venezuela as in Colombia, though Vene-zuela's area is one fourth smaller. All administrations in Venezuela have encouraged immigration since World War II; thousands of Italian artisans and farmers came to settle, as did other European groups, including many displaced persons sent by the International Refugee Organization after 1946.

Bogotá, now a city of over two million, high in the mountains, gray and chilly the year round, has had its face lifted in recent years by careful architectural planning under the Swiss designer Le Corbusier. Housing projects and a new government center show a different face to the city than it had before it was looted and burned at the time of the Gaitán murder.

Housing loan cooperatives have been founded, patterned after those of Chile. A modern slum clearance project of 12,000 units was dedicated by John F. Kennedy on his 1962 visit to South America and is named Kennedy City.

The growth of Medellín, the "Manchester of South America," with a population of 1,090,000, has been so phenomenal that, as in São Paulo, all the buildings seem new. "Everyone in Medellín makes good money and lives well," say the Colombians. Manizales, a town just over a century old, already has a population of over 280,000, and thrives on the new highway across the ridges to Buenaventura on the Pacific. Cali, in the upper Cauca, is the third city with 920,000. It seems new and bustling also, as does Barranquilla, with a population of 640,000—an important port since the dredging of the river mouth. Only in Cartagena, sleeping behind its walls built to keep out the buccaneers, does the visitor see much of the old Spanish colonialism of New Granada.

Caracas has a new face too—skyscrapers downtown, lines of apartments with curving balconies of the Rio-Copacabana Beach type, new homes in the suburbs, four-level traffic ways downtown, and a fabulous new university that rivals that of Mexico for its ultra-modern campus. But the shacks on the sides of the surrounding hills, housing the poorest workers, are still as bad a slum as anywhere in South America. Maracaibo, Venezuela's second city, has 433,000 people, with its many oil workers and technicians, its busy port with tankers lined up at the wharf.

Education at the elementary level in both countries is behind that of Chile, Argentina, or Mexico. Alfonso López in his first term in 1934 had tried to modernize Colombia's primary school system and free it from religious domination. A decade later, only one child in two was in any school at all, and of those who finished elementary school, only one in four went to secondary schools, most of which were run by the Church. A school Finance Law of December 1949 required that 30 per cent of the national budget be devoted to primary education, and that local governments provide adequate buildings and hire trained teachers at a standard salary, but because of the continuing guerrilla warfare this has been impossible to enforce in the rural areas. Venezuela has made some valiant efforts recently to increase its schools and to spread elementary and adult education. However, rural schools are practically nonexistent, though Caracas schools have been recently reorganized by an Uruguayan educator imported for the purpose. Illiteracy is unusually high among Venezuela's poor, although Betancourt and Leoni doubled the number of children attending school.

In university education, both capitals have a proud tradition. Their long-established national universities have both moved into "University Cities"—large campuses with fine buildings in the suburbs. The young men of Bogotá are said to go back into the center of the city to do their homework, where they can sit at the sidewalk cafés and discuss politics or recite poetry while they are trying to study. But the "all-one-campus plan" is tending to give faculty and students alike more of a feeling of identification with what North American students would call "real campus life." Venezuela has two other university-level schools; Colombia has fourteen, including the new free University of the Andes founded in 1948. However, none of these college-level schools carries on the training of primary teachers, which is one of the greatest professional needs of both countries. There has always been a high standard of education in Bogotá and Caracas for the sons of the wealthy and professional classes at the top, who are often not interested in training for jobs as technicians, engineers, or commercial leaders. Professional "student" Communists organized riots on both national campuses in late 1966, causing the governments to cut down on university autonomy.

Nineteenth-century Colombia laid the foundations not only for dictators like Mosquera and Núñez, and for interregional strife and religious fanaticism, but also for the respect of culture in all its forms. Isolated as it was, Bogotá was nevertheless an intellectual center. Its dictators wrote history and poetry; its young liberals read John Stuart Mill and admired paintings by the French impressionists. In 1851 only 30,000 people lived in Bogotá; both Cartagena and Popayán were larger. By 1880 Bogotá had doubled in population; 1900 gave her more than 100,000, with "many fine hygienic new houses" and a tramway. The streets were of mud and cobblestone, which the pedestrian long had to share with the mules, as there were no sidewalks till the 1880s.

Bogotaños praised their national library, although it was so small as to boast only one librarian who closed it during his frequent illness. In their much-lauded scientific museum were still the specimens collected by Mutis and von Humboldt, and very little that was new. Notable progress was made in Colombia in the fields of jurisprudence and historical writing, however.

And what did the poets write—anything new at all? Poems of the 1850s dwelt on the scenery of Colombia, the rivers, the mountains, the "strange and varied flora." Several concerning the beautiful Falls of Tequendama near Bogotá were published in the literary journals. In the single year 1854 more poetry and more prose was published than in a decade before or after; one product was a poetic drama in five acts written by Felipe Pérez, telling the story of the explorations of Gonzalo Pizarro. So numerous are the Colombian writers on nationalistic themes—history, scenery, patriotic fervor—that it is impossible to list them. Many, like Rafael Núñez (1825–1894) himself, produced a wide variety of works and were active in public life as well. For example, Manuel María Madiedo (1817–1900) wrote "whole volumes on social science, logic, and law." Editor of a paper, widely versed in European philosophy, acquainted with several languages, Madiedo wrote well-known poems on the "Great River Magdalena, free and strong, beautiful and rebellious," and on "the ocean before the walls of Cartagena," as well as odes to Bolívar, Sucre, and the battle of Ayacucho. At the turn of the century Rafael Pombo (1833–1912), then sixty-seven years old, was Colombia's best-known poet. In his lines *To Bolívar*, Pombo wrote of the shortcomings of his own time as compared to the heroics of the independence era:

Hero, thy last antagonist is Time.
Thy triumph waxes as the years decay.
For even our errors and our meannesses
Make thee stand out still greater every day.[1]

Most famous literary work of this period in all northern South America is Jorge Isaacs' novel *María*. Isaacs (1837–1895) was the son of a Jamaica planter of English-Jewish origin, who married a Colombian girl and came to live on a plantation in the Cauca Valley near Cali. After attending boarding school in Bogotá, Isaacs supported himself by writing, and in 1867, before he was thirty, had produced one of the best-known love stories of the Spanish language. Though its author failed in business and died in poverty, his book is still widely read in Spanish, French, and English. It is almost autobiographical; the heroine María is a cousin of a Jewish plantation-owning family in Jamaica who is adopted by them. When the hero Efraín returns from boarding school he falls in love with his beautiful cousin; their touching love story, opposed on religious grounds, ends in the death of the heroine. But it is the description of Colombian life, the views of the Cauca River, the hero's trip home across country from Bogotá, the warm stories of family life, that make the novel alive. A modern critic has said that the scenes in *María* are "real country-side thinly veiled by words."

In the twentieth century the black-suited, earnest, upper classes of Bogotá still take their culture seriously. In Bogotá, the "Athens of South America," even mechanics enter union-run poetry contests. Classical music is taken equally as seriously. Although Colombia has produced no Heitor Villa-Lobos, Guillermo Uribe-Holquín (born in 1880) has been Colombia's outstanding composer, a violinist and long-time director of the National Conservatory of Music in Bogotá. There are symphony orchestras in Bogotá, in Cali, Medellín, and Barranquilla. Music is important in the social life of Caracas, also; that city's "oil-supported" symphony has almost a hundred members, and has won recognition throughout South America. Caracas is regular host to an all-Western Hemisphere music festival and symphony competition. Most of this musical interest is centered in European-style music, however, and has little of the folk spirit of the music of Brazil, where Negro peoples are also important segments of the population.

Poetry, the cultural interest of all Bogotá citizens, the subject of whole sections of the Sunday newspapers, of hours of special radio programs, of many small magazines, is European-classical in type, with little of the modern spirit or of the native pulse. For all Bogotá's love of poetry, the one well-known poet of these northcoast countries is the Venezuelan, Rufino Blanco Fombona (1874–1944), a writer in many fields—history, essay, literary criticism and, unfortunately for him, political satire. Blanco Fombona, like his friend Rubén Darío, was a citizen of all Latin America. Forced into

---

[1] Translated by Alice Stone Blackwell, in *Some Spanish American Poets* (New York: Appleton-Century, 1929), p. 394. Reprinted by permission of the University of Pennsylvania Press, copyright owners.

exile by Gómez after several periods of imprisonment in Gómez' foul prisons, he supported himself in other Latin American capitals by editing anthologies and writing editorials attacking the United States for its Caribbean intervention program of the early 1900s. Blanco Fombona's novel, *A Man of Gold,* a bitter satire on the politicians of Caracas who had kept him in prison, was widely read outside Gómez' Caracas.

Colombia's most widely read novel of the 1900s gives a true native picture of Colombia's Amazonian backlands called *The Vortex,* a severe criticism of the exploitation of the rubber workers. It was written in 1924 by José Eustacio Rivera (1889–1928), who was a member of a Colombian-Venezuela Boundary Commission in that area, and who himself became lost in the jungle, traveled with river Indians, and almost died of malnutrition.

World-wide attention in 1971 centered on a new novel of rural life in a fictional Colombia town, said to symbolize the story of all South American towns. Written by Gabriel García Márquez, it is called in English translation *One Hundred Years of Solitude.* The town it describes is so isolated that the residents know little about the modern world. But its inhabitants, all inter-related, witness thirty-two political revolutions within the town in one century, as well as endless feuds and violence within families. The long, involved book seems a comic-tragic analysis of the long Colombian *Violencia,* and the excesses of local upheavals in all Spanish South America.

Poets and novelists of Colombia joined in a school of thought called *Los Nuevos,* the New Ones, after World War I, and attempted to modernize Colombian literary expression. Present-day novelists, historians, and literary critics are members of this modernist group. Best known in the United States is Germán Arciniegas (born in 1900), who writes popular biography and fictional history of the romance of colonial Spanish America, and who has brought his own country to the attention of world readers.

Venezuelan literature in the 19th century was dominated by the political leader Guzmán Blanco, and no novel written there is remembered today for its literary merit. In 20th century Venezuela other novelists have been overshadowed by the former president Rómulo Gallegos (born in 1884), whose novel *Doña Bárbara,* remains the greatest novel of the region in the twentieth century, famous for its descriptions of the *llanos,* and ranking with Isaacs' *María* and Güiraldes' *Don Segundo Sombra* among South America's greatest novels. Its symbolic hero returns from his city education to the ranch he inherited, filled with progressive new ideas, and finally succeeds in driving out Doña Bárbara, a wicked woman who had usurped land and demoralized the countryside. Rómulo Gallegos, himself typifying the hero when he served briefly as president of a Venezuela demoralized by the Doña Bárbara-type dictators, spent years in exile while his book was widely read. In 1969, Rómulo Gallegos, returned in honor from exile, died quietly in Caracas at the age of 85. His obituary notice read, "His civilizing purpose flowed with the steady irreversible course of a flooding river."

Philosophers, literary critics, and historians are very popular in both countries. Baldomiro Sanín Cano, born in Colombia in 1861, has been acclaimed as one of Latin America's greatest teachers, literary critics, and philosophers. His Venezuelan contemporary, José Gil Fortoul (1862–1943), has written the best constitutional history of Venezuela. Both countries have been interested in their history and have published much documentation concerning their heroes. Writers in these countries, as in most Latin American countries, cannot live solely by their pens, but must supplement their writing by other occupations.

READINGS: SPANISH MAIN COUNTRIES

Alexander, R. J., *The Communist Party of Venezuela* (1970).

————, *Organized Labor in Latin America* (1965).

————, *Prophets of Revolution* (1962).

————, *Venezuelan Democratic Revolution* (1964).

Allen, H. J., *Venezuela: A Democracy* (1940).

Arcaya, P. M., *The Gómez Regime and Its Background* (1936).

Area Handbook for Venezuela (American University, Washington, D.C. 1971).

Arciniegas, G., *Caribbean: Sea of the New World* (1946).

————, *Green Continent: A Comprehensive View of Latin America by Its Leading Writers,* trans. H. de Onís (1944).

Bernstein, H., *Modern and Contemporary Latin America* (1952).

————, *Venezuela and Colombia* (1964).

Bonilla, F. and J. A. Silva Michelena, eds., *The Politics of Change in Venezuela,* 3 vols. (1967–1970).

Burggraaf, W. J., *The Venezuelan Armed Forces in Politics, 1935–1959* (1972).

Bushnell, D., *The Santandar Regime in Gran Colombia* (1954).

Callcott, W. H., *Caribbean Policy of the United States, 1890–1920* (1942).

Chase, G., *Contemporary Art in Latin America* (1970).

Coester, A., *Literary History of Spanish America* (rev. ed., 1928).

Crist, R. E., *Cauca Valley, Land Tenure and Land Use* (1952).

————, *Venezuela* (1959).

————, *Venezuela: Search for a Middle Ground* (1969).

Davis, H. D., ed., *Economic Development of Venezuela* (1961).

Dawson, T. C., *South American Republics* (2 vols., 1903–1904).

Dennis, A. L. P., *Adventures in American Diplomacy, 1896–1906* (1928).

Dix, R. H., *Columbia: The Political Dimensions of Change* (1970).

Dow, J. K., *Colombia's Foreign Trade and Economic Integration in Latin America* (1971).

Eder, G., et al., *Taxation in Colombia* (1965).

Emerson, D. K., ed., *Studies in Politics in Developing Nations* (1968).

Fagen, R. R. and W. A. Cornelineo, *Political Power in Latin America: Seven Confrontations* (1970).

Fals Borda, B. O., *Peasant Society in the Colombian Andes* (1955).

————, *Subversion and Social Change in Colombia* (1969).

Fergusson, E., *Venezuela* (1939).

Fiscal Survey of Colombia (1965).

Fluharty, V., *Dance of the Millions: Military Rule and Social Revolution in Colombia, 1930–1956* (1957).

Fox, D. J. and D. J. Robinson, *Cities in a Changing Latin America. Two Studies of Urban Growth in the Development of Mexico and Venezuela* (1969).

Friedman, J., *Regional Development Policy: A Case Study of Venezuela* (1966).

————, *Venezuela—From Doctrine to Dialogue* (1965).

Galbraith, W. O., *Colombia: A General Survey* (1953).

Gibson, W. M., *The Constitutions of Colombia* (1948).

Gilmore, R. I., *Caudillismo and Militarism in Venezuela, 1810–1910* (1964).

Gordon, W. C., *Economy of Latin America* (1950).

Graham, R. B. C., *José Antonio Páez* (1929).

Grummond, J. L. de, *Caracas Diary 1835–1854: Journal of John G. A. Williams* (1954).

————, *Envoy to Caracas—The Story of John G. A. Williams, Nineteenth Century Diplomat* (1951).

Guzman, G., *Camilo Tórres* (1969).

Havens, A. E. and W. L. Fernn, eds., *Internal Colonialism and Structural Change in Colombia* (1970).

Heaton, L. E., *Agricultural Development in Venezuela* (1970).

Henao, J. M., and G. Arrubla, *History of Colombia*, trans. J. F. Rippy (1938).

Hirschman, A. O., *Journeys Towards Progress* (1963).

Holt, P. M., *Colombia Today and Tomorrow* (1964).

Horowitz, I. L., *Masses in Latin America* (1970).

Hudson, M. O., *The Verdict of the League: Colombia and Peru at Leticia* (1933).

Hunter, J., *Emerging Colombia* (1962).

Inter-American Development Bank, *Economic Development of Venezuela* (1961).

————, *Fiscal Survey of Colombia* (1965).

International Bank of Reconstruction and Development, *The Basis of a Development Program for Colombia* (Currie Report) (1950).

Jankins, A. P., and N. M. Malloy, *Venezuela, Land of Opportunity* (1936).

Jones, C. L., *Caribbean Since 1900* (1936).

Landsberger, H., *Latin American Peasant Movements* (1970).

Lazardo, R., *Venezuela, Business and Finance* (1957).

Leavitt, S. E., and C. García-Prada, *Tentative Bibliography of Colombian Letters* (1934).

Levy, F. D., Jr., *Economic Planning in Venezuela* (1969).

Lieuwen, E., *Generals Versus Presidents* (1964).

————, *Petroleum in Venezuela: A History* (1954).

————, *Venezuela* (1963).

Lipman, A., *The Colombia Entrepreneur in Bogotá* (1969).

Lombardi, J. V., *Decline and Abolition of Negro Slavery in Venezuela 1820–1854* (1971).

Mack, G., *The Land Divided: A History of the Panama Canal and Other Isthmian Canal Projects* (1944).

Marsland, W. D., and A. L., *Venezuela Through Its History* (1954).

Martz, J. D., *Acción Democrática: Evolution of a Modern Political Party in Venezuela* (1965).

————, *Colombia: A Contemporary Political Survey* (1962).

Masur, G., *Simón Bolívar* (1948).

McGreevey, W. P., *Economic History of Colombia 1845–1939* (1971).

Mecham, J. L., *Church and State in Latin America* (rev. ed., 1966).

Michelene, A. S., *The Illusion of Democracy in Dependent Nations* (1971).

Mikesell, R. F., et al., *Foreign Investments in Petroleum and Mineral Industries* (1970).

Miner, D. C., *The Fight for the Panama Route: History of the Spooner Act and the Hay-Herran Treaty* (1940).

Moron, G., *History of Venezuela* (1964).

Mutschler, D. E., *The Church as a Political Factor in Latin America* (1971).

National Planning Commission, *Creole Petroleum Corporation in Venezuela* (1955).

Niles, B., *Colombia, Land of Miracles* (1924).

OAS/IDB, *Fiscal Survey of Colombia* (1965).

Parks, E. T., *Colombia and the United States, 1765–1934* (1935).

Parsons, J. J., *Antioqueño Colonization in Western Colombia* (1949; 1969).

————, *Antioquia's Corridor to the Sea* (1967).

Payne, J. L., *Patterns of Conflict in Colombia* (1968).

Perkins, D., *History of the Monroe Doctrine* (new ed., 1955).

————, *Monroe Doctrine, 1826–1867* (1933).

————, *Monroe Doctrine, 1867–1907* (1937).

Pike, F. B., ed., *Latin American History* (1969).

Powell, J. D., *Political Mobilization of the Venezuelan Peasant* (1971).

Public International Development Financing in Colombia (1963).

Ratcliff, D. F., *Venezuelan Prose Fiction* (1933).

Ray, T. F., *The Politics of the Barrios of Venezuela* (1969).

Reener, R. R., *Education for a New Colombia* (1971).

Reichel-Dalmatoff, G., *Colombia* (1965).

Rippy, J. P., *The Capitalists and Colombia* (1931).

————, *Latin America and the Industrial Age* (1944).

Roberts, W. A., *Caribbean: Story of Our Sea of Destiny* (1940).

Romoli, K., *Colombia: Gateway to South America* (1941).

Rourke, T., *Gómez: Tyrant of the Andes* (1936).

Rout, L. B., *Which Way Out? An Analysis of the Venezuelan–Guyana Boundary Dispute* (1971).

Royal Institute of International Affairs, *Venezuela: A Brief Political and Economic Survey* (1956).

Rudolph, D. K., and G. A., *Historical Dictionary of Venezuela* (1971).

Scruggs, W. E., *Colombia and Venezuelan Republics* (1905).

Serxner, S. J., *Unión Democrática of Venezuela: Its Origin and Development* (1958).

Silva, Michelena, J. A., *The Illusion of Democracy in Dependent Nations* (Politics of Change in Venezuela), Vol. 3 (1971).

Spence, J. M., *The Land of Bolívar, or War and Peace and Adventure in the Republic of Venezuela* (2 vols., 1878).

Stavenhagen, R., ed., *Agrarian Problems and Peasant Movements in Latin America* (1970).

Taylor, P. B., *Venezuela Golpe de Estado de 1958: The Fall of Marcos Pérez Jiménez* (1968).

Taylor, P. C., *A Case Study of Relationship between Community Development and Agrarian Reform* (1961).

Torres Rioseco, A., *Epic of Latin American Literature* (rev. ed., 1946).

Traba, M., *Art in Latin America Today: Colombia* (1959).

United States, Department of Commerce, Office of International Trade, *Investments in Colombia* (1953).

————, *Investments in Venezuela* (1953).

Urrutia, M., *The Development of the Colombian Labor Movement* (1969).

Watters, M. A., *History of the Church in Venezuela* (1933).

West, R. C., *The Pacific Lowlands of Colombia* (1957).

Whitaker, A. P., *United States and South America: The Northern Republics* (1948).

Whitbeck, R. H., *Economic Geography of South America* (rev. ed., 1940).

Wilgus, A. C., ed., *Caribbean Area* (1934).

————, *Caribbean: Contemporary Colombia* (1962).

————, *Caribbean: Venezuelan Development* (1963).

————, *South American Dictators* (1937).

Wise, S. G., *Caudillo: Portrait of Antonio Guzmán Blanco* (1951).

Wohlrabe, R. A., *Land and People of Venezuela* (1959).

World Bank Country Economic Reports, *Economic Growth of Colombia: Problems and Prospects* (1971).

Wood, B., *The United States and Latin American Wars, 1932–1942* (1966).

Wurfel, S. W., *Foreign Enterprise in Colombia: Law and Policies* (1965).

Wythe, G., *Industry in Latin America* (2nd ed., 1940).

Ybarra, Y. T., *Young Man of Caracas* (1941).

chapter 28

SIX NATIONS
IN CENTRAL AMERICA

common problems of Middle America

Central America consists of six tiny republics, the five which had broken apart from the Central American Federation of a century ago and Panama which became independent of Colombia in 1903. Combined, the six republics cover about 218,000 square miles, less than half the area of Peru. A great part of the entire region is undeveloped mountain or jungle. The total population of the six states in 1970 was estimated at 16,322,441, about two-thirds the population of Argentina. In the export of important raw materials, Central America in no way approaches such countries as Peru or Venezuela. In industrial production it is where Argentina was a century ago. Its largest city, Guatemala City, has an estimated 850,000 people. San Salvador with 340,500 people, and Tegucigalpa in Honduras with 253,000, and San José de Costa Rica with 192,000 are national capitals. Over one-half of the Guatemalans, perhaps 20 per cent of the Hondurans, and at least 10 per cent of the Panamanians are non-Spanish-speaking Indians whose way of life has changed little since 1492.

Why, then, is this area important? Geographically it is the Hemisphere at its narrowest point, close to the United States, located, with Mexico, between the United States and South America. There the United

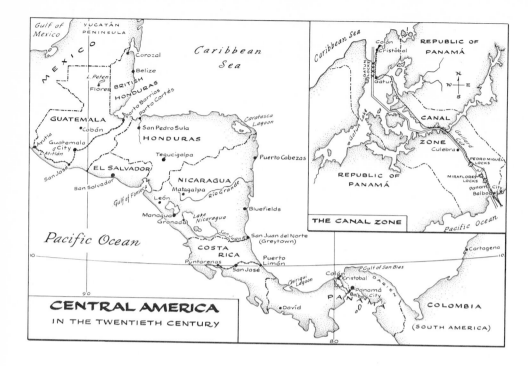

CENTRAL AMERICA
IN THE TWENTIETH CENTURY

States built a canal, negotiated for a unilateral right to build one on another route, and plans to build on still a third route. The United States has intervened in the area to keep other nations from gaining influence. In 1912, Secretary of State Philander Knox said that "our tremendous national interest, created by the Panama Canal," makes the safety, the peace, and the prosperity of Central America and the Caribbean of "paramount interest" to the government of the United States, for which reason the United States must "apply a remedy in these regions where the malady of revolution and financial collapse is most acute."

A united federation, union as a single nation, had for some time seemed the solution for these "acute maladies," but attempts made to form it had failed throughout the 19th and early 20th centuries. One of the most fascinating of 19th century travel stories was written by John L. Stephens of New York who represented President Van Buren on a mission in 1839 to the federation of five states, the United Provinces of Central America, that had been set up after separation from Mexico in 1823. His book entitled *Incidents of Travel in Central America, Chiapas, and Yucatan,* makes vividly apparent the various factors working against federation. In a trip of ten months, Stephens visited all five of the regions that are today's Central American republics, met dictators and generals, watched frontier-type congresses at work, and argued himself out of border difficulties and jail terms owing to constantly changing regulations against strangers.

Stephens ended up enthusiastic about the scenery and the ancient Mayan ruins, mildly tolerant of the backward people, and pessimistic about the unstable government. In fact he wasted considerable time trying to contact federal authorities, to find the government to which he was accredited. Where was the capital of the federation? Was it Guatemala City (which impressed him as a new town for it had been rebuilt after the 1776 earthquake had destroyed the old capital)? No, Guatemala City was in the control of an Indian named Rafael Carrera, a despot supported only by the Guatemalan conservatives and abjured by the other regions. Was it at Quetzaltenango, Guatemala's second city, which had just declared itself a separate province in the federation? No, just before Stephens' arrival a mob of frenzied women had stoned to death the federal vice-president who had come to collect federal taxes. It was not San Salvador, although the federal military commander maintained his headquarters there, for only the people of that city themselves considered it the federal capital. In Nicaragua and Costa Rica Stephens met independent dictators who had left the federation the year before his visit.

In short, he found only confusion in Central America—its towns as far apart as the island capitals in the Caribbean, the mountains and forests between them more difficult to cross than the Caribbean Sea between the islands, and much less frequently traveled. The fine *Provincias Unidas del Centro de América,* founded with such idealism in 1823, suffered from disunity from the first. The smaller capitals resented the power of the federal capital, Guatemala City, and the Guatemala state government could not live happily side by side with the federal government. The typical struggle between centralism and federalism was combined with the standard Latin American struggle between liberalism and conservatism, this in an area where the Indian masses were living as in pre-Colombian times and the Church was unusually powerful.

Manuel José Arce, elected first president of the federation and caught in the crossfire of liberals and conservatives, attempted to please everyone and succeeded in satisfying no one. A church group in El Salvador was disappointed at not having El Salvador created a separate diocese and started a revolt against the federal government, which brought on civil war. A young Honduran creole, Francisco Morazán, won a victory for the combined Honduran and Salvadorean liberals and was elected president of a temporarily pacified federation in 1830.

Morazán, then only thirty years old, is the hero of the Central American federation story. So great was his threat against the conservatives, however, that they went to every length to turn the people against him. They told the ignorant mountain Indians of Guatemala that Morazán and the liberals would upset the true religion. One such Indian, a swineherd of nineteen named Rafael Carrera, who told the Indians he was the Archangel Rafael, roused them against Morazán and marched on Guatemala City with his horde of followers. Morazán came up from El Salvador with liberal troops and drove out Carrera, who melted back with his Indians into the cornfields and mountain tops, only to rise up again with conservative backing to take Guatemala City a year later.

When he visited the city, Stephens was anxious to meet Carrera, whose name had been mentioned in hushed tones by everyone he had met. Carrera was then 23-years old, a small dark Guatemalan Indian like many the tourist today sees trudging to market. He had learned to read and write since coming to power. His cry had been "Long Live Religion and Death to Foreigners!" yet Stephens was the first foreigner he had ever met, and one of the last. He ruled ruthlessly as the tool of conservative forces, backed by a well-paid army and the religious devotion of the Indian masses. But he improved constantly as an administrator and for a quarter century brought peace to Guatemala, albeit it was the peace of death. Although he was often the target of attempted assassinations and twice temporarily exiled, he ruled the separate republic of Guatemala for many years and died of natural causes in 1863.

The federal power that Stephens so diligently searched out in 1839 died in that year. He was present at the last meeting of the federal congress when a small group of hostile delegates, in a dark, gloomy room with no other visitor save himself and two small urchins, argued over the methods of forced collection of church tithes from the Indians, a practice that had been legally abandoned in the first brave days of 1821. Morazán, the federal leader, attempted three years afterward to oust a current Costa Rican dictator but was defeated with his Honduran and Salvadorean army and executed in Costa Rica. The subsequent record of Central America is the story of five different republics. Attempts to reunite Central America after Morazán's downfall were uniformly unsuccessful. Guatemala's great families and the Church preferred their own local government. Costa Rica, even more isolated geographically, had no stomach for civil wars and federation. At various times, however, the other three countries did attempt to achieve federation.

In 1906, El Salvador and Honduras combined to fight Manuel Cabrera, the current dictator of Guatemala, but the United States and Mexico intervened. Fighting stopped, and a conference was held at San José de Costa Rica to formulate treaties which would help avoid such wars in the future. All attended except the Nicaraguan dictator Zelaya, who wanted a federation under his own leadership. In the following year, after two more interventions to preserve the peace, the five Central American nations sent representatives to meet in Washington to plan some way to avoid these little wars. A Central American Court of Justice was established, before which all future border controversies were to be heard. The Court was given a chance, in 1916, to settle controversies concerning the rights of El Salvador and Costa Rica in any future Nicaraguan canal. The Court recognized these two claims, but Nicaragua and the United States paid no attention and denounced the convention which set up the Court. And the Central American Court of Justice never met again. The Washington meeting in 1907 had also set up the Central American International Bureau to deal with common cultural and economic problems. Six conferences were held under its auspices from 1909 to 1914, but its many conventions were never ratified and in 1921 the Bureau ceased to function.

In 1920, on the downfall of dictator Manuel Estrada Cabrera in

Guatemala, four of the Central American states attempted union again. El Salvador, Honduras, and Costa Rica accepted a plan for an executive representing all the states equally, but another revolution in Guatemala brought in a faction that was opposed to it. In 1923 a second conference in Washington resulted in a treaty of peace and eleven conventions on various subjects signed by the five nations, but no mechanism to preserve this peace was set up, and the treaties remained empty locutions. The five nations did, however, work together during World War II, all declaring war against the Axis and all active after 1945 in the United Nations and the Organization of American States. Within the framework of the OAS, five of the Central American states formed a regional "League of Nations" called the ODECA. It did not establish a political union but organized a common Supreme Court in 1962 and it maintains a permanent secretariat. It has held several conferences of foreign ministers and educational ministers, and its economic successes led to the establishment of the Common Market described below.

Economically the nations have lived off coffee, bananas, and "patch and thatch" farm plots. The North American-owned United Fruit Company developed the banana industry for which Middle America is famous. Roots from West African banana stock had been brought to Santo Domingo by a priest in 1516, but the slow-moving sailing ships of the day could not transport such a perishable product to far-away markets. By 1900, refrigerated ships made the popularization of bananas possible. Before long the United Fruit Company was clearing jungle land along the Caribbean coasts of Costa Rica, Honduras, and Guatemala, building ports and wharfs, and operating its own ships.

Botanists experimented with the plants, improved the root stock, and worked out efficient methods of planting. Banana plants produce only one bunch of bananas. Cutters must watch the green fruit for the exact day of cutting since it is never to be cut after ripening. The plant that has produced the one bunch then withers away, and the root stocks must be carefully cultivated so that a second plant will spring up and produce another bunch in eight or nine months. Thousands of square miles of "banana coast" are covered with rows of these self-perpetuating plants on land that two generations ago was jungle.

This was a new industry, and it has not all been simple. The mestizos and highland Indians of the Central American countries were unaccustomed to and uninterested in heavy daily wage work in the tropics, so the Company imported Negro laborers from the West Indies. This brought discrimination in an area where there had been few slaves in colonial days. Negroes, most of them underprivileged and uneducated, became the poor of Puerto Barrios in Guatemala, of Port Limón in Costa Rica, and of Puerto Cortés in Honduras. A blight or disease of the banana plants or a political upheaval between the dominating company and a nationalistic government could mean economic upheaval for the workers. Workers were left destitute when the company abandoned plantations and went on to develop new plantings elsewhere, perhaps near Santa Marta in Colombia or David in Panama.

In later years the reorganized United Fruit Company was to take better care of its employees. It taught them diversified farming, provided primary education, and even founded several fine vocational and experimental agricultural schools. The company worked with the new unions of banana plantation laborers and allowed the governments without interference to set wage and housing standards. In Guatemala, coffee is important as a second crop, and in El Salvador it is the one crop. Grown on small farms, with hand methods, it finds a ready market in America because of its flavor.

Many of Central America's most pressing problems can be traced to its broken terrain which makes transportation and communication difficult. Railroads are not numerous, and generally they run from the capitals to the coast. The capitals of the Central American republics have recently been connected, however, with the completion of the Pan American Highway, built with United States aid.

Foreign capital has also developed the forest extractive industries of hardwood lumbering and chicle gathering. It was mahogany that brought the British to Belize in the first place, and it still provides revenue there and in Guatemala and Honduras. Chicle trees grow wild in the Petén region of Guatemala where they are tapped by native and West Indian workers. Used as a basis for chewing gum, chicle makes up a third of Guatemala's exports. The ever increasing tourist trade also brings a large revenue to Guatemala. Its Maya ruins are accessible by plane, and its highland lakes are breathtakingly beautiful. Each of the mountain Indian villages specializes in a different weave of a brightly colored pattern, valued now by art- and craft-conscious Americans.

Isolation, a yearly income per family of $275, a dependence on coffee and bananas for foreign exchange, and a lack of modern industry and its products—all these things the five nations had in common. To improve the area economically, ODECA held meetings which resulted in the signing of five trade agreements from 1955 to 1962; and in November 1962, the Central American Common Market, an economic union, came into effective being. "Our five nations, averaging two million people each," explained Dr. Pedro Abelardo Delgado, a Guatemalan economist and its first secretary-general, "cannot possibly find the resources to develop their economies if they work separately. So we combine." A common monetary unit, the Central American peso, was set up on a par with the United States dollar, and by 1966 all the paper transactions among the five nations were carried out in this unit, which by 1970 was to be in actual circulation, replacing the colones, córdobas, lampiras, and quetzales of the separate countries. The paper work was handled by the CABEI, the Central American Bank for Economic Integration, which, with United States aid, financed 60 per cent of any approved local industry which would cut the area's dependence on coffee and bananas—such as tire plants in Guatemala, cement in Costa Rica, refrigerated meat in Guatemala, and automobile assembly in Salvador. In the former United Fruit Company town of San Pedro Sula in Honduras, 16 such new factories were in operation by 1966. Inter-Central American trade leaped from $32 million in 1960 to over $130 million in 1970. The growth rate of the gross national product of the region grew from 4.5 per cent a year in 1963 to almost double that figure in 1970, the best growth rate in the Western Hemisphere.

In 1968 the Common Market was still employing only Dr. Delgado and its six secretaries, housed in a six-room house next to a grocery store in Guatemala City, but its activities had spread to other fronts. In 1965, 850,000 Central American school children had received free copies of first and second grade school books printed by the Common Market's educational committee. Ministers of agriculture had met to set minimum prices on corn, rice, and beans from country to country. A thousand miles of village-to-village roads had been started. In June 1969, however, the outbreak of war between Salvador and Honduras, nations standing to benefit most from Common Market exchange of laborers, slowed down these optimistic advances for the 1970's. The war, described below, was fought by a country, Honduras, whose problem was underdeveloped area and a country, Salvador, whose problem was over-population.

Socially this is an area of great contrasts and inequalities. The major part of Central America is mestizo. But there are Negro workers from the West Indies on the Caribbean coast, half-naked primitive Indians in Honduras and Panama, and picturesque and isolated San Blas Indians off the Panamanian coast. Best known of all pure Indian groups in Latin America today to North Americans are the spinners and weavers of Guatemala's hill towns. Tourists have seen the elders of Chichicastenango in hand-embroidered black wool burning pagan incense on the steps of the church of Santo Tomás, or the men of San Martín Chile Verde in red-striped clothing walking the long mountain miles to market in Sololá on Lake Atitlán. Anthropologists study their religious beliefs, sociologists their land ownership systems, artists their textile designs. They still constitute a large majority of Guatemala's total population. Bringing them modern schooling is difficult as their language is Maya-Quiché or Zutuhile or Cakchiquél. Only the men who go to market know any Spanish. There is an increasingly large group of semi-urbanized Spanish-speaking Indians and mestizos in Guatemala, known as *Ladinos*.

El Salvador, Nicaragua, and Honduras are mestizo, while the highland area of Costa Rica away from the coast is almost entirely European white. In the towns the culture patterns seem similar to those of many other parts of Latin America. At the turn of the century, Central America produced one great cultural hero, the Nicaraguan poet, Rubén Darío, who had a profound effect on Latin American literature and whose work is described below on page 633. No figure anywhere near his equal has appeared in the divided little countries in the 20th century. One modern poet, Joaquín Pasos (1905–1947) reflects the Central American environment. The director of Guatemala's National Library, Rafael Arévalo Martínez (born in 1884) has achieved some fame as a novelist, writing on themes connected with nature. Carlos Mérida (born in 1893) and Humberto Garavito have painted the Indian life of Central America and earned some recognition in the United

States. The Costa Rican Joaquín García Monge is the world-famous editor of a literary review, *Repertorio Americano,* published in San José and considered one of the most important cultural periodicals in today's Latin America and a consistent voice for democracy.

Guatemalan politics: communism or caudillismo

In Guatemala in the 19th century political parties were divided on real issues. Lines were sharply drawn between the Conservatives, made up of the clergy, nobility, and many great landowners and merchants, and the Liberals composed of the mestizo and creole professional men and other less privileged groups. It was the Conservatives, led by Rafael Carrera, who overthrew the Central American federation and dominated Guatemala until Carrera's death in 1865. Carrera intervened several times in the neighboring states to knock over Liberal regimes and substitute Conservative ones.

In 1871, however, the Liberals came into power. The Liberal dictator, Justo Rufino Barrios, was an industrious and forward-looking man who during his presidency (1873–1885) destroyed the political influence of the Church and the aristocracy. He developed the production of coffee and bananas, proposed public improvements, including road building and schools, and separated Church and state. The large Guatemalan towns with Spanish-speaking rather than Indian population had primary schools at that time supported by tax funds. As president, Barrios made trips to the United States and Europe and talked of getting factories and railroads into his country and connecting the capital with the Caribbean port which today bears his name.

His ambition was to head a Guatemala-dominated Central American federation, and to that end he announced a decree unilaterally in 1885 that declared the union re-established. This time it was the armies of El Salvador that opposed the federation, and in the ensuing battle between the two countries, Barrios himself was killed and the idea of federation was again deferred.

By this time the Liberal regime was so entrenched that the death of its leader did not upset it. His policies of continued growth of trade and agriculture were continued under two regimes. Then at the close of the century, in 1898, President José María Reyna Barrios, the great leader's nephew, was assassinated, which gave rise to the long-term, notoriously corrupt dictatorship of Manuel Estrada Cabrera.

In Barrios' time, Guatemala City, the capital, had some 5,000 houses and enough sophisticated creoles to provide real political parties and an understanding of the issues between liberals and conservatives. Quetzaltenango, second town of the nation, was still a half-Indian village. In these two "cities" and a few lesser ones lived the 30 per cent of the population who were at all Europeanized. In the villages of the western highlands lived the 70 per cent who were Indians, little changed since Maya times, speaking variations of the Maya dialect, yet subject to the heavy taxes and the forced-labor draft by which Barrios paid for his country's progress.

Today Guatemala, largest of the Central American republics, is one of the prime tourist attractions of the Western Hemisphere, listed in guidebooks as "the most fascinating spot within a night's flight of the United States." But in this ancient land of the Maya, the food on which Communist doctrine thrives is still present—underprivileged masses of people, exploitation by a few foreign companies, class and race discrimination, a peonage system of land tillage, and a high rate of illiteracy. These conditions were starkly present under *caudillismo* throughout the first half of the 20th century.

Manuel Estrada Cabrera had been vice-president when President José María Reyna Barrios was assassinated in 1898. Although a civilian, Cabrera proceeded to set up a military despotism which kept him in power for 22 years. Old age was his only serious enemy; in 1920, his own congress voted him mentally incapacitated to hold office and a revolution threw him out. Guatemala had profited not in the least by his long tenure. Four presidents and eleven years later, he was followed by another dictator.

Jorge Úbico was Guatemala's second *caudillo* of the 20th century. An absolute ruler, he nevertheless improved the lot of the Indians to such an extent that they called him "Tata" or grandfather. He legally ended peonage, enforced better treatment for plantation workers, and in the larger hamlets built some schools for their children. He also balanced the budget and had money left over for schools for the Spanish-speaking children in every large town, and for roads connecting the towns with the capital. Úbico favored Central American cooperation and joined in conferences with his fellow-dictators in neighboring countries. Although there was a German majority in the coffee-rich town of Cobán and the province of Alta Vera Paz, Tata Úbico during World War II maintained strong sympathies with the Allies, declared war against Germany right after Pearl Harbor, and allowed American troops to use Guatemalan bases. Thus wartime prosperity came to Guatemala.

During a world war to end dictatorship, Úbico resorted to repressions of speech and press that caused repercussions among the students and laboring people of his own capital. Although a very small percentage of Guatemalans, this new group put on a general strike in 1944 which paralyzed all business in the modern little city. The strikers got Tata Úbico out of power in July, a year before VE day. An interim triumvirate, a Committee of Liberation, took over the government, held elections in December of 1944, and chose Juan José Arévalo as president for a six-year term. The new group tackled the problems of Guatemala in a new constitution in 1945 which granted unusually broad social reforms. Here began the faint suspicions that the Communist party was becoming a strong influence in Guatemala.

The condition of the Indians had not improved although they were emancipated from ties to the land, for they still did not own the farmland themselves. In the city, the newly politically conscious labor group listened to any radical who inveighed against "Yankee imperialism, colonialism, and monopoly." Many people opposed to North American companies were especially hostile to the United Fruit Company which had exerted so much influence over Úbico. The North American companies offered to make adjustments and to improve labor relations, and called attention to the new housing and hospitals they have provided for plantation workers, but Arévalo, who had been out of touch with things after years of exile in Argentina, answered vaguely with fine phrases about "mystic socialism." This went on for six years of speechmaking and little action while Communist infiltration gained control of the city workers' group.

In the 1951 election, the left-wing groups backed a personal friend of Arévalo, Jacobo Arbenz Guzmán, who had been his Minister of Defense and boss of the Guatemalan army. Although not himself a Communist, Arbenz, a half-Swiss military career man who had risen under Úbico to dominance of the army, was "radical" in his sympathies for Indians and labor. But he was personally ambitious and used such sympathies for his own ends. His wife, who had been educated abroad, was an idealistic Marxist, and one of his closest associates was an avowed Communist named Fortuny who dominated the Labor Party. Arbenz easily won the election and was inaugurated March 15, 1951.

Arbenz had promised "action." Within the next year, his government had nationalized the United States–owned electric company, had expropriated 234,000 acres of the Pacific holdings of the United Fruit Company, and was threatening to take over the 174,000 acres on the Atlantic. Private landowners, large estate owners, who kept land out of cultivation were in danger of having their property taken over by the government. The land was to be redistributed to small owners and to Indian villages. No Communists were actually in the Arbenz cabinet. The party, however, controlled the Guatemalan newspapers and the press published vituperative articles against the United States. By 1953, the party held 46 out of 57 seats in Congress and was in control of the radio and the press. Moscow radio programs were heard loud and clear throughout the country.

The United States faced a dilemma. If it intervened on behalf of the United Fruit Company, it would bring down on its head all the old charges of imperialism which the Good Neighbor Policy had hoped to silence. When Guatemala threatened armed reprisals against neighboring states who were giving refuge to the enemies of Arbenz, the United States hoped that the reaction in these countries would permit using joint public opinion pressure rather than direct intervention. At the OAS meeting in Caracas in the spring of 1954, Secretary of State Dulles pushed through a resolution condemning Communist activity in the Western Hemisphere. In May 1954, Arbenz received a shipload of armaments from Communist Poland, and the dictator of Nicaragua, Somoza, as well as leaders in Costa Rica and Honduras where anti-Arbenz exiles were active, feared the arms would be used in a big Central American melée. But under new mutual assistance agreements the United States could now send arms and planes to these smaller neighbors without fear of too much criticism.

At this tense moment, *caudillismo* came to the fore again. On the Honduras border a former Secretary of War under Úbico, Carlos Castillo Armas, representing the rightist army faction, was collecting arms and training a band of peasants for an invasion. In Guatemala City only a very small minority of factory workers knew what Communism was all about and Arbenz' hold on the populace was weakening. The army was ready to desert Arbenz and join Castillo Armas—who had planes and pilots to fly over and drop leaflets on the capital. While the United Nations and the Organization of American States viewed the situation with alarm, and called for a meeting in July, the ragged rebel army crossed the border into Guatemala.

Subsequent critics of American policy blamed the CIA, our anti-Communist agency, for what happened in Guatemala at this time. Castillo Armas' forces came triumphantly into the city. Arbenz finally found exile abroad and the two leading Communists, José Manuel Fortuny and a writer Carlos Manuel Pellecer, disappeared into Europe behind the iron curtain. In October, Castillo Armas, who had been in military control of the city since summer, was elected by a whopping 99 per cent of the vote and started a term that was supposed to run until 1960.

To settle the confusion in the land relocation program, Castillo Armas allowed small holders who had been given lands to maintain them if they had been planted; and he then announced a long-range, five-year rural improvement program that included regulations for installment buying of small farm plots. Carrying out plans for developing undeveloped lands, and for finishing the Pan American Highway from Mexico to bring more dollar-spending tourists, needed time. But Castillo Armas was a career army man with no administrative experience. To his backers, who had hoped for efficiency and democracy rather than mere military *caudillismo* as an answer to the social problems that had aroused Communist sentiment in the first place, he brought only disappointment. In the meantime, the United Fruit Company agreed to pay taxes on the same plan that Standard Oil Company did in Venezuela and to turn over more unused land for distribution; but the land was in the tropics and not in the highlands where the Indians made their meager living.

Castillo Armas was in power long enough to promulgate a new constitution which was a "model of good intentions." No one was ever to know if he intended to be a constitutional president and hold a legal election at the end of his term, for he was assassinated by a pro-Arbenz army guard in August 1957. A military junta took control until an election could be held in November. The city vote was won by Miguel Ydígoras Fuentes, ambassador to London and delegate on UN committees, a man described as a "crusty old soldier." But, by a fraudulent counting of rural votes, his opponent claimed a victory. Three days of street fighting followed the announcement of Ydígoras' defeat. Then another military *junta* took control, cancelled the election, held an indecisive second election, tossed the choice to congress—which arranged a truce between the two factions. Ydígoras was peacefully inaugurated in March 1958.

In the early 1970s, Guatemala's population neared 5 million, but the Maya-Quichés, the Zutuhiles, the Cakchiqueles, and all the other descendants of the Maya—who are the majority of all Guatemalans—still lived in their thatched villages at the bases of the volcanoes around the shores of azure-blue Lake Atitlán and in the deep *barrancas* and high ridges of Alta Vera Paz and Huehuetenango. The local tribal *alcaldes* are the only government in all such communities that touches the people, most of whom have never heard anything at all about Communism and doubtless do not realize when elections are to be held.

Ydígoras was not to serve out his six-year term. A moderate, he concentrated on activating the new Central American Common Market agreements and hoped to rally support by quarreling with England over Belize. Ardently anti-Communist, he allowed Cuban exiles to train for the Bay of Pigs landings on Guatemalan soil. When the landings failed, Guatemala City student leftists rioted and Ydígoras proclaimed a state of martial law. By 1963, moderates were joining leftists in opposition. Military leaders, under Enrique Peralta Azurdía, in fear of the opposition leader, former president Arévalo, staged a coup and ran the country until the end of 1965.

Finally in February 1966, after three years of military government, Peralta permitted a free and open election. In a three-cornered fight between two colonels and a civilian, the civilian won by a plurality. Julio César Méndez Montenegro, a quiet, moderate dean of the University of Guatemala Law School, did not win an absolute majority and the election was decided in the newly elected congress in May 1966. But by November 1966, rightists in the army and Communist guerrillas in the back country were giving Méndez Montenegro so much trouble that he declared a "state of siege" which lasted into 1967.

But the terror did not end. A wave of kidnapping and killing of American and European diplomats began—two military advisers from the United States were killed in January, 1968, the West German ambassador in April, and the American ambassador in September of the same year. This terrorism forced the election of a strong right-wing candidate in 1970, Colonel Carlos Arana Osoria, on a platform of "law and order." Peacefully inaugurated on July 1, 1970, he proclaimed a month later a five-year plan for agricultural improvement of the whole nation. Apparently Colonel Arana had acquired a social conscience along with his zest for law and order. His plan called for land distribution, resettlement of landless Indian populations, education designed to wean the Indians away from subsistence life on corn and beans to the planting of diversified crops, multiplication of the rural school program, and nationalization of foreign-owned projects. Whichever way he tried to do it, whether by "law and order" or by land reform, the job of maintaining himself in power and suppressing violence was going to be exceedingly difficult. Meanwhile, former president Arévalo, once considered a dangerous leftist, was devoting himself to a UNESCO program to set up television sets in every village which had electric power in order to bring literacy in the Spanish language to Guatemala's Maya-speaking Indians. Another hopeful note was the work of the Institute of Nutrition for Central America and Panama, INCAP, which is fighting malnutrition and its accompanying protein deficiency diseases with the new protein additive Incaparina, something which can be manufactured cheaply in Guatemala City and distributed to the poorest village in the country.

Guatemalan writer Miguel Angel Asturias in 1967 received world recognition when he won the Nobel Prize for Literature. He is the author of social protest novels, one of them a criticism of dictatorship, translated into English as *The President,* and another a study of the Indian peasantry entitled *Men of Corn.*

Nicaragua: canal rights,
intervention, and dictators

Nicaragua, situated where the Isthmus begins to narrow down, is blessed with lakes and river connections which made it a possible route from the Atlantic to the Pacific. This fact warped its history in the 19th century and continued to be a factor in its intra-Hemisphere relations well into the 20th. Because of the possibilities of a canal in the area and the necessity of preventing European nations from building it, the United States was involved there, rightly or wrongly, until the era of Franklin Roosevelt.

Larger than Guatemala, Nicaragua has a third as many people. Only a very small fraction of its population of 1,942,000 are primitive Indians; perhaps ten per cent are blacks on the Caribbean coast; the remainder are mestizos. The economy is based on agriculture, with coffee, cattle, and, a new interest, cotton, predominating. A third of its people live in the three cities (actually only large towns) of Granada, León, and Managua which huddle in mountain valleys along the lake shore just a ridge from the Pacific. On the Atlantic side, Nicaragua is as dense a jungle as is the Petén region of Guatemala. It was a *caudillo*-ruled country in 1900 and still is today.

After Nicaragua withdrew from the Central American union in 1838, it became the scene of bitter internal fighting until the 1850's. Then, because of the discovery of gold in California in 1848, this disorderly little nation suddenly came to world attention while the other middle America nations remained isolated. Gold-seekers from the east coast of the United States could reach San Francisco by taking ship to Greytown on the Caribbean coast, then paddling upriver to Lake Nicaragua, crossing the lake by sail to the cities of central Nicaragua, and finally taking a stage-coach for a 40-mile trip across the range to reach the tiny port on the Pacific where they could wait for a sailing ship to San Francisco. Altogether it was a much shorter journey than crossing the United States in a covered wagon.

The American promoter, Cornelius Vanderbilt, organized a successful company to care for all stages of this trip. He met opposition, not from the Nicaraguans but from the British, who considered the area their own sphere of influence owing to their possession of British Honduras. The Clayton-Bulwer Treaty of 1850 resulted from the ensuing negotiations, by which Britain and the United States agreed that neither nation would obtain or maintain exclusive control over the proposed canal, nor would occupy any part of Central America, nor give any of them exclusive privileges. The crossing was made by Vanderbilt's company until a railroad was built across Panama.

Vanderbilt's success seemed an invitation for other American adventurers to make a strike in Nicaragua. In June 1855, William Walker, most famous of the "land pirates" or filibusters, landed in Nicaragua with 58 followers from the California mining towns. A Tennessean who had already taken a bunch of fellow adventurers on an unsuccessful invasion of Lower California, Walker felt destined to carve a pro-American empire out of the region of Vanderbilt's route. Walker and his followers became Nicaraguan citizens so they could help a revolutionary faction oust the current government. In 1856, he had himself elected president of Nicaragua and drew hundreds of adventurers from the United States to help him "win an empire." Before long he was in control of Vanderbilt's steamers and stage coaches and was dictator of the country. Financed by a group of New Yorkers who were jealous of Vanderbilt, and assisted by Southerners who dreamt of extending the slave states, Walker made an attempt to gain control of all Central America. He was a gentlemanly little man, not at all the pirate type, but he inspired a new fear of federation in all the neighboring republics. Central America rallied to save Nicaragua, and even Great Britain made moves to oppose Walker. Juan Rafael Mora, a far-sighted Costa Rican president, attacked and defeated Walker's troops. When the Walker troops "holed up" in the Nicaraguan city of Granada, an epidemic of cholera laid the American volunteers low. While the allies laid siege to the city, Walker escaped on the lake and then went downriver to an American vessel in the Caribbean.

The result was that Granada lay in smoking ruins, that cholera raged unchecked in many Central American towns, that steamers and stage coaches were damaged, and that American "enterprise" was the object of fear and hatred in Central America for years. Walker persisted in believing in his "destiny," however. Landing in New Orleans as a hero, he soon found new followers and made two subsequent attempts to control Nicaragua and Honduras. He was finally caught by the British navy off the coast of Honduras, turned over to the government at Tegucigalpa, and executed in September, 1860.

Nicaragua was wracked by disputes as to which of its cities should be the capital. León was a city of liberal politics; Granada, rebuilding after the war against Walker, was the stronghold of the Church and the conservatives; and in between them was a sleepy village called Managua—which finally after a generation of disputes became the capital. Nicaragua ended its long era of chronic civil war when in 1863 conservative rule inaugurated a period known as "Thirty Years of Peace," during which some national progress was made. The year 1881 saw a railroad built along the Vanderbilt stage road to connect the lake cities with the Pacific, a route which brought some small business to Nicaragua until the canal was built at Panama, a region then a province of Colombia.

The Central American republics, sleeping between their revolutions, showed in their little undeveloped capitals small interest in things intellectual and would hardly deserve a section on "culture" in so short a study. But León, Nicaragua, home of the strongest liberal party in the region and a center of culture in colonial times, produced Rubén Darío, the "father of modernism" in Latin American literature. Darío was born in a Nicaraguan village in 1867 of mixed Spanish, Indian, and black stock. Educated by an uncle in León, he wrote poems at sixteen which attracted the attention of well-to-do citizens of that town. Before the age of nineteen, he visited the other Central American capitals and had poetry printed in their newspapers, and was writing poems about love in Paris. While writing for a Santiago newspaper, in 1888, his 20th year, he won a poetry contest in literature-conscious Chile. A volume of his *modernista* poems entitled *Azul* appeared in Chile that year, a volume which critics identified as "Art for Art's Sake." Although he lived in Spain, Colombia, Cuba, and his native Nicaragua, Darío's greatest influence was on the literature of Argentina where during a period of 26 years, he wrote for several newspapers. His personal life was wrecked by restlessness, drugs, and alcohol, and he returned to León in 1916 to die after trying unsuccessfully to make a living by lecturing, writing, and serving as consul.

His book *Prosas Profanas*, the collected works published in 1896, has been called the "zenith of the *modernista* movement." His *Songs of Life and Hope* is his greatest collection of poems. Much of his sensuous poetry has been translated into English, for there is color in his verses in any language. The sight of a girl is the sight of orange flowers; a shell found on the shore is a golden message murmuring of azure mines of hidden treasure beneath the sea; sunny pines are "all bathed in charm, in glory, in blue air"; a rock thrown into the sky was "a pebble of pure gold"; and seeing a bird, "its flight on high with ruby streaked the sapphire sky." Today's modern travel books call Central America "the rainbow republics," but Rubén Darío, their famous poet, was the rainbow poet. When many Chileans, Colombians, and Argentines think of Central America at the turn of the century, their thought is not of petty dictators or lost federations or canal plans but of Rubén Darío, poet of all Latin America who was born and who died in Nicaragua.

At the turn of the century, José Santos Zelaya had been dictator for seven years (1893–1909), which ended a lengthy period of Conservative rule. Unusually ruthless and selfish, he had done few things to promote the progress of his country, but had made many personal enemies, especially among rulers of neighboring countries with whom he constantly interfered. In December, 1909, in the face of civil war and international complications, he resigned in favor of a puppet who turned out to be short-lived. When Juan Estrada, the leader of the anti-Zelaya revolt, came to Managua as president in August, 1910, he found the country so disorganized, so deeply in debt to foreign powers, that he asked the United States for aid. Thus began the United States' fiscal, electoral, and military intervention in this Latin America nation.

Marines were to stay in Nicaragua from 1910 to 1934, save for a few months in 1925. Naval vessels were in the harbor, financial advisers in the customs house, guards at the legation. Technical experts supervised elections and drew up long-range plans for improved administration and debt payment. A national guard, the now famous *Guardia Nacional,* was trained by American Marine officers. All this was justified by American presidents and statesmen as necessary on strategic grounds, for it defended the canal route and protected future canal rights. Financially, such American military control prevented European intervention to collect debts and arranged for their ultimate payment. But in the first three decades of the 20th century, this practice brought the United States enmity from the rest of the Hemisphere. Latin American critics scornfully called the program "Dollar Diplomacy" or, more often, *Imperialismo*.

The chronicle of Nicaraguan developments is a confusing one. Estrada's government, coming into power by force when Zelaya left, fought a bloody civil war for two years. When the war was over, the United States supervised the next two elections, 1913, and 1917, and policed the country to ensure peaceful four-year terms for the winners. Since these winning candidates were leaders of the Conservative party, as anti-Zelayists in the first place, the United States got a reputation of automatically backing Conservatives.

The Bryan-Chamorro Treaty ratified in 1916, secured through the Conservatives, gave the United States an option to build a canal along the San Juan River–Lake Nicaragua route in return for an outright grant of $3 million. When the money was used up—much of it paid on foreign debts under American supervision—Wilson's Secretary of State, Robert Lansing, worked out plans for backing private American investment in Nicaragua through American customs control. A High Commission for Nicaraguan Finance, consisting of two Nicaraguans and one American, approved such loans, allocated the Nicaraguan tariff collections, and managed it all so efficiently that the private bankers, both American and European, were satisfied with payments by 1925 and consented to the termination of American controls.

Thus in 1925, everything seemed peaceful and the Marines were withdrawn. A coalition government, consisting of a Conservative president, Carlos Solórzano, and a Liberal vice-president, Juan B. Sacasa, had been elected under the American-supervised election system and had taken office in January. The Marines left in August. In October the recently defeated presidential candidate, Emiliano Chamorro, staged a revolution to return to power. Back came the Marines and the election supervision system. The American-approved Congress chose a compromise candidate while Mexico threw her weight on the side of the former vice-president Sacasa. Finally Sacasa withdrew, and President Coolidge sent the distinguished Henry L. Stimson to work out an adjustment.

The Stimson Plan included Marine supervision of the 1928 elections as soon as both sides laid down their arms. All agreed save one young lieutenant on the Liberal side, César Augusto Sandino, who is still today a hero in the eyes of many Latin Americans who fear United States power. He and his followers took to the hills and jungles and carried on guerrilla raids for five years. Called a bandit in the conservative press of both Nicaragua and the United States, Sandino was considered a symbol of resistance to

"Yankee imperialism" by the Liberals. He had sworn to fight "as long as a Yankee soldier remained." His program of internal reform advocated co-operatives to raise the standard of living, the creation of a class of small landowners through the break-up of foreign-owned estates, and the development of Nicaragua's resources. Meanwhile American Marines tried to be more impartial in supervising elections than they had been previously, and in the elections of 1928 and 1932 Liberal party candidates won.

The same Juan B. Sacasa who was backed by Mexico in 1926 won the election in 1932. His inauguration coincided with that of Franklin Roosevelt. With Roosevelt came the Good Neighbor Policy, the end of armed intervention which had varied from a large force to a legation guard of only a hundred and which had left behind better schools, better roads, improved health, a balanced budget, satisfied creditors but also a resentful populace. When the United States withdrew, military dictatorship and the *Guardia Nacional* took over the government.

The "bandit" Sandino, still at large, claimed a victory because the Americans had gone, and, with Sacasa in Managua as president, came out of the jungles into the city. But the chief of the *Guardia Nacional*, Anastasio Somoza, trained by the United States Marine Corps, was the famous guerrilla's personal enemy. When the rebel arrived for a peace-making dinner with Sacasa's friends, Somoza had Sandino shot. Throughout the next two decades, while Somoza was unquestioned dictator, the friends of Sandino yearly threw red flowers on the airplane runway built over the site of Sandino's assassination, and the departing planes crushed the blood-red blossoms on the asphalt.

With Sandino dead and the American forces gone, the powerful army leader Somoza was able to eliminate all other candidates for the election of 1936. Sacasa resigned when his term was up. Since there was no other candidate, Somoza won the presidency in what he could claim was a completely honest election. Then for twenty years, until he was assassinated in 1956, he was "Nicaragua."

Anastasio Somoza—called "Tacho"—made millions on the side in his own cattle business while controlling the beef sold in his capital. His sons were considered his probable heirs. One headed the *Guardia Nacional;* the other was president of Congress and was made First Delegate in 1955. The pictures of Tacho's favorite daughter Lillian appeared on the twenty-peso bills which were called "Lillians." He owned 117 different business enterprises. He was said to have learned his expansive business methods while working his way through a bookkeeping and advertising course in Philadelphia. Yet many Nicaraguans praised him as a competent ruler, a benevolent despot who modernized agriculture, built roads, schools, and hospitals, and improved living conditions in his country.

Through World War II, Tacho had been a good friend of the United States, as well as through the "cold war" incident in 1954 in Guatemala. He expected the United States to reciprocate. When president, he returned in state to the United States to be entertained as a guest in the

White House. Tacho, who had learned his English as a busboy in Philadelphia, said to a correspondent, "As I told F.D.R., democracy down here is like a baby, and nobody gives a baby everything to eat right away. I'm giving them liberty, but in my own style. If you give a baby a hot tamale, you kill him." Tacho's personal enemies killed him finally in September 1956, and left his sons to quarrel with the Nicaraguan Liberals over control of the little nation.

Congress appointed Luís Somoza Bayle, leader of the Tacho-controlled assembly, to finish out his father's term to May 1957. Naturally Luis Somoza ran for the presidency himself when an election was held and he won, supposedly by an 89 per cent vote, for a six-year term to last until 1963. He had come to realize that the family's feudal control of the country promoted the spread of Cuban-type Communism, and although his younger brother, "Tachito," remained head of the army, he started a literacy campaign, cut individual land holdings (other than those of his own family) to 1,200 acres (500 hectares), and bid for Alliance for Progress loans within the new Central American Common Market framework. His succesor, René Schick Gutiérrez, a personal friend of the family, succeeded him in an actual election in which a "conservative" candidate ran a weak second.

It was no surprise that in 1967, younger brother "Tachito" was "elected" president "overwhelmingly." His five-year term was to end in 1972. The easily changed constitution prohibits re-election. In 1971, an agreement was reached with two major parties that approved the plan for a triumvirate to rule in 1972, redraft a constitution, and declare that the next presidential election was to take place in 1974.

On February 6, 1972, elections were held for Congress which the Liberals won easily. They were given 60 per cent of the Congress seats while the Conservatives were given 40. Congress selected a triumvirate of two Liberals and one Conservative to rule until elections are held under a new constitution, Nicaragua's sixteenth, in September, 1974. On May 1, 1972, the end of his legal term as president, Tachito Somoza resigned. Then he was elected again for four more years under the new constitution. Apparently Nicaragua is still Somozaland.

El Salvador: pocket-handkerchief country in the coffee business

At midpoint in Central America, facing on the Pacific side only, lies the tiny country of El Salvador, no bigger than Maryland. It is the smallest, most industrialized, most progressive of the Central American republics, and also the most densely populated. The capital of El Salvador (which means "the Savior") is San Salvador (which means "Holy Savior") with a population of 340,544. The city, the small towns and open farming country, and the two small ports have enough people, very thickly settled, to make a population of over 3.5 million.

El Salvador has an ideal climate and altitude for coffee growing, and the country would have shown great economic improvement by 1900 if the Salvadoreans had been free of dictators and palace revolutions. Her history has been one of family rule by benign dictators under constitutions that breathed democratic idealism. But it has had rival families, supported by powerful rival armies, which has meant autocratic rule interrupted by revolutions and party strife.

No powerful estate owners and no foreign banana company dominate El Salvador. The farmland is almost perfect for the production of coffee of a certain flavorful type that brings high prices in the United States. Its coffee *fincas* are small, owned by individual native landholders. The country is prosperous when coffee prices are high, but it suffers from the difficulties of other one-crop countries.

It was El Salvador, the center of a strong Church group, which started the disruption of the Central American federation. It came into existence in the first place because of quarrels with Guatemalan dictators inside the federation. Much of Salvadorean history has been concerned with avoiding or overcoming domination by Guatemalan leaders and intervention by other neighbors. The country has followed a policy of non-intervention in her neighbors' business, and of promoting Central American cooperation and federation. Her presidents have maintained large armies, chiefly to keep themselves in power. In the 1950's, President Osorio took the lead in bringing about the Organization of Central American States, the ODECA, which was set up as a regional arrangement under the OAS. El Salvador has also encouraged the free trade Common Market of Central America.

Twenty families in El Salvador have usually rotated the presidency and joined in the typical *cuartelazo* or barracks revolt to throw opponents out of office. The Meléndez family held the reigns from 1913 to 1927, Carlos Meléndez being succeeded by his brother and then his brother-in-law. The Meléndez presidents kept El Salvador neutral during World War I and brought prosperity to the coffee business. Shortly after they fell from power, depression hit the one-crop country, and riots ensued. The army took over the government, and its candidate, Maximiliano Hernández Martinez became dictator with a ruthless control that lasted from 1931 to 1944.

Before World War II was over, Martinez' own people turned against him in a general strike which caused his fall and brought years of political chaos. The liberal-minded commercial class in the capital, combining with the army, finally was able to control the situation and make Oscar Osorio president in 1949. Osorio, copying the successes of larger nations, and acting under a new, liberal constitution which granted women suffrage and offered protection to labor and small farmers, launched a five-year plan and an Institute for Development. This Institute helped him build up diversified agriculture and industry with the assistance of American experts. In September, 1956, his friend José María Lemus peacefully succeeded him and continued to carry out his development plans.

The Cuban Communism issue led to the downfall of Lemus, however, for he openly backed Guatemala's efforts to help train the Cuban exiles for the Bay of Pigs attempt. Leftists assumed this action meant Lemus had no intention of making social reforms at home. Their strikes and riots brought the army into control again through a military junta.

In July 1962, with the backing of the junta, Colonel Alberto Rivera was inaugurated under a new constitution that extended his term to July 1967. A young man from the poorer classes, he permitted a relatively open political system, although he took stern measures to curb vandalism. He continued the Common Market reforms, used the new Central American textbooks to found 926 new reading-teaching centers staffed by literate army men, and revised the tax structure and collected higher income taxes which were invested in new tax-exempt industries. His five years were a time of progress and development; with full employment and scientific diversification of crops, El Salvador's gross national product increased in the 1960's by 8.1 per cent. In a three-cornered presidential race in July, 1967, Rivera's close associate, Fidel Sánchez Hernández was elected president. Sánchez Hernández lacked the popularity of Rivera but he carried on the policies of his predecessor, and economic progress continued for El Salvador. Under the two administrations widespread electrification, public works, and welfare programs have been pushed, with the government devoting large amounts for education. Unfortunately the brief but costly war with Honduras in July, 1969, had a very adverse effect on the Salvadorean economy. In a hotly contested election held in February, 1972, Colonel Arturo Molina, backed by Sánchez Hernández, was the winner, confirmed by Congressional action on February 25. The popular defeated candidate revolted in March, but it was put down, and Arturo Molina was inaugurated on July 1, 1972.

Yet overcrowded El Salvador did not have farms or jobs enough for all its agricultural workers. Under Common Market agreements, many of them could go to work in Honduras, but, according to Honduras, only 1,036 obtained permission to come. And in June, 1969, 300,000 Salvadoreans were living in Honduras, 12 per cent of the total population of that sparsely populated nation. Highly skilled, the Salvadoreans were getting better jobs and better pay than the Hondurans. Hondurans took action. Some 500 Salvadoreans who had obtained farm land in Honduras were forced out by Honduran troops. In both countries, radio broadcasts inflamed the populace. On June 15th, when the Honduran national soccer team came to San Salvador to play the Salvadorean champions, riots broke out. People on both sides were killed.

Within two weeks, more than 15,000 Salvadoreans had been driven out of Honduras. El Salvador sent its small airforce to bomb eight Honduran towns. By July the Council of the Organization of American States was trying to negotiate. An Inter-American Committee organized relief for the Salvadorean refugees, and the Salvadorean army withdrew from 650 miles of territory which it had occupied in Honduras. A demilitarized zone was set up along the border.

The fundamental problem was that El Salvador has 421 persons per square mile and Honduras, right next door has only 59. It is ironic to note that both armies had been armed and trained by the United States. There were more American military advisers in San Salvador than there were pilots in the Salvadorean army. The tragic consequence was that progress towards unified action in Central America had been set back a decade.

Honduras: land of thick forest
and sparse population

Honduras was not faring very well. It had remained underdeveloped because its population, made up largely of Indians and descendants of slaves, lived widely separated in small communities engaged in agriculture in difficult, tiny, infertile valleys. Moreover other governments continually interfered with Honduran political affairs.

After the breakup of the Central American federation, a long, sustained era of civil wars, foreign wars, and neighboring-state intervention ensued—an uninterrupted succession of disorders. Behind most of the changes of the *caudillos* in Honduras was Guatemalan intervention. Brief intervals of stability came during the regime of Marco Aurelio Soto (1876–1883) and of his successor, Luís Bográn, until 1891. In 1894, Nicaragua imposed on Honduras the ardent Liberal Policarpo Bonilla, whose regime lasted until the turn of the century. In 1903, the Conservative faction forced its way into office.

Honduras contained an abundance of mineral wealth, but the mines that had been worked in colonial times were neglected for two generations after independence. Until foreign investment began to develop the gold-washings in the 1880's, the capital was a country village connected with mule trails to the rest of the nation. Today Honduras is the most backward nation of Central America. Its soil is not good for coffee. It has no good port on the Caribbean and only the tiny port of Amapala on the Gulf of Fonseca facing the Pacific. It has the greatest deposits of mineral wealth between Mexico and Colombia, but few good roads to transport the ores if they were mined. Even so, silver and gold make up nearly a fourth of Honduran exports and mahogany and other hardwoods make up another fourth.

Some 46 per cent of the export trade is in bananas. Honduras is the country that usually comes to mind when the term "banana republic" is used. It is the country whose politics have been most closely controlled by the United Fruit Company. Tegucigalpa, the capital and largest city, with 253,283 out of the small total population of just over 2,582,000, is not on the Pan American Highway, nor on any rail line to anywhere. There is now a new paved road which runs from the port of Amapala across the highway and into the capital.

The air age has brought together the isolated little country. A small air company called TACA, organized on a shoestring in the 1920's with American World War veterans as pilots, began to build landing fields in

Honduran towns and it even flew out the gold ore being mined by primitive methods in the hills. This pioneering air venture, later taken over by the Pan American Airways, put Tegucigalpa in touch with the world.

In politics, Honduras has remained in the "age of *caudillos*," a century behind the times. In the whole history of Latin American civilization, a detailed description of its small-town dictators, *cuartelazo* revolutions, and "permanent" presidents is of little importance. In 1923, an ignorant soldier, Tiburcio Carías Andino, became the power behind the throne, making and unmaking presidents. He became president himself in a fraudulent election in 1932 and lasted until old age forced him to resign in 1948. He ruled by force, allowed no free speech, and kept the jails full of his political enemies, but he did develop mining and aviation and maintained a stable government. When he stepped down, he still controlled his personal political party, and he arranged the election of his successor, Juan Manuel Gálvez.

Gálvez during his term, 1948 to 1954, attempted real constitutional government and took the first steps to modernize the nation's economy. He encouraged organized labor and limited the control of foreign companies. He made a new contract with the United Fruit Company, which included payment of 30 per cent of the company's profits in taxes to the government. A serious strike resulted from the fact that the rights given workers were insufficient, which gave rise to a labor party. The labor party has brought new candidates as well as confusion and violence into recent elections. Strikes in the banana plantations, combined with devastating floods and leaf disease, brought about abandonment of the Honduran plantings by the United Fruit Company for new fields elsewhere. In its later years of Honduran activity, the Company did much for its workers in the way of sanitation, housing, and education.

Gálvez, insisting on free elections, held one in 1954, but in the three-cornered electoral campaign no one received a majority of votes. Vice-president Julio Lozano Díaz took advantage of the impasse and assumed executive power. Acting as a dictator, he concentrated on economic and social development. He engineered his election in October, 1956, but the army ousted him in Honduras' 135th revolution. In September, 1957, elections were held for a constituent assembly and in November the constituent assembly elected Liberal party leader Ramón Villeda Morales as president, bringing to an end the regime of the military junta that had been in power since October 1956. The six year term of Villeda Morales approached its end in peace and progress, with the president signing an agrarian land reform bill and attempting to put Alliance for Progress programs into effect. But Honduras' 136th military coup ousted him sixty days before his term was up in October, 1963. He was replaced by Colonel Osvaldo López Arellano who ran a strong dictatorial-type regime, far from progressive, and representing the views of the military and landowners. The reform laws of Villeda Morales remain on the books but have been conveniently forgotten. Although the constitution forbids re-election, López Arellano wanted to continue in power and tried to change the constitution; but the Nationalists had won additional strength in the off year 1968 elections and Arellano was unsuccessful. Elections scheduled for February 14, 1971 were postponed by the president, but took place on March 28. The election issue ranged over Honduras and the Central American Common Market from which Honduras withdrew January 2, 1971. The declared winner in a close and calm election, in which only about half of the voters cast their ballots, was 68-year-old international lawyer and close friend of López Arellano, who had campaigned to continue López Arellano's policies, Ramón Ernesto Cruz. Ironically Cruz had been denied the presidency eight years before, ten days before the election, by the revolution in 1963 led by Arellano. Cruz who took office on June 6 for a six year term makes little difference in the control of Honduras, for López Arellano, upon leaving the presidency, became commander of the armed forces "in the interest of national unity." Honduras which needs most everything, finds that democracy does not come easy.

Costa Rica: the most democratic Central American state

Costa Rica, with Panama at the southern end of Middle America, has bragged that it has more school teachers than soldiers. An organized army is forbidden by its constitution—it has only a small police force. Its 1,800,000 inhabitants own more than 100,000 farms. The people living on its high central plateau and around and in its two small cities of San José and Cartago, are almost all of pure European stock, descendants of farmers who came from Spain in colonial times. Throughout the nation there is 88 per cent literacy.

At the time of John L. Stephens' visit, Costa Rica was inhabited by some 600,000 hard-working, prosperous farmers. It had been the first region to make a complete break with the idea of federation. Stephens had enjoyed his visit there. He felt that San José was "the only city that has grown up or improved since the independence of Central America." He was impressed with the well-cultivated coffee acreage, held in small ownership, the "progressive women of the country," and with the current dictator who was a simple businessman, "short, stout and plain, not a general," who lived in the same small house in which "his wife had a little store," and in which he had "three clerks writing for him" caring for government business. This simple prosperity lasted through various congress-chosen liberal and conservative "dictators" until the 20th century.

The foundations of Costa Rican stability were laid down under Braulio Carillo when land was parceled out in small units of ownership. José M. Castro was Costa Rica's first really constitutional president. Under Juan Rafael Mora at mid-century, the country had a decade of order and economic advance, followed by a decade of dictators dominated by the conservatives. In 1870, Tomás Guardia rose to power, power that was chiefly military, but even such dictatorship brought peace and economic improvement to the country. Railroads were built and the banana industry developed. This new crop, in addition to coffee, promoted Costa Rica's foreign trade and prosperity. Freer elections and a greater voice on the part of the people in government affairs became the vogue as the 20th century began.

As in the time of Stephens' visit a century ago, the president still lives in a bungalow on a small salary. Rail lines connect its port on the Pacific with its port on the Atlantic only 300 miles away, with over a 4,000-foot plateau in between. In Puerto Limón on the Caribbean live Negro banana workers and stevedores, descendants of West Indians brought in to build the port, against whom there is such discrimination that they are not welcomed in the central plateau.

But in San José, the more than 192,000 inhabitants live as well as do citizens of Montevideo. Cacao, bananas, and coffee bring in foreign exchange and with it prosperity. No foodstuffs need be imported for this is no one-crop economy. Progressive governments have developed hydroelectric power in abundance. Roads east to west are paved highways. Recently even the dairy industry has been encouraged, a thing little known in Latin America save in the larger modernized areas. Better breeding sires have been imported, and butter and dry milk are manufactured—this in Central America where most children have never tasted butter. Pasteurized milk is now sold everywhere in the highland towns. Secondary schools are the accepted standard for all communities, the schools offering vocational training as well as the orthodox classical education.

From 1885 to 1944, with a few flurries occasionally, easily settled to the general satisfaction, there was a new president for every term and no violence in any election. Costa Rica earned the respect of the world for orderly government and democratic elections. Thus it was a shock to the Costa Ricans to have a real civil war, international intervention, and bitter fighting take place in the late 1940's and early 1950's. Rafael Angel Calderón García, the retiring president in 1944, picked Teodoro Picado as his successor with the long-range plan of securing the presidency for himself again in 1948, a scheme contrary to Costa Rican tradition. The election of 1948, though marred by some bloodshed, was fairly won by Otilio Ulate, a liberal newspaper publisher, but the congress, controlled by Picado, declared Calderón García elected anyway. Ulate was arrested.

A new figure now emerged in this atypical Costa Rican situation, the civilian José "Pepe" Figueres, a follower of Ulate, who raised a volunteer army (the country has no standing army) and attempted to put the legally elected Ulate in by force. This would have attracted little attention if it had not been for the armed intervention of Nicaragua's Somoza. After a good deal of skirmishing, a *junta* chose Pepe Figueres himself to act as provisional president. A new constitution provided for woman suffrage and set up unusual protections against abuses of authority. Banks were nationalized, Communists outlawed, small business aided, and the army disbanded. In November, 1948, Ulate returned to the presidency to fill out his legal term. Then Somoza's troops again entered Costa Rica. This time, Figueres and Ulate appealed for help from the OAS. Under prodding from the OAS, a treaty of peace was signed by both countries in February, 1949, and the invading troops were withdrawn and the home army disbanded.

After four years of progress under Ulate, Pepe Figueres, a graduate of Massachusetts Institute of Technology and a local small farmer on the side, became president, in July 1953, in a legal election in which 92 per cent of the registered voters cast their ballots. He arranged that the United Fruit Company, formerly so very powerful at Puerto Limón, would pay 50 per cent of its profits to his government. He was also able to break the Company's monopoly on the cacao, hemp, and palm oil industries and to force it out of the electricity and railroad businesses in Costa Rica. Thus he regained for the government an economic control of the country without ruining the banana business.

He was not yet through with the unfriendly Nicaraguan dictator, Tacho Somoza. In 1955 Tacho bought 25 "mustang" planes, which gave him the largest air force in Central America. That spring, border skirmishes for eleven days drew blood, until the OAS again intervened. In September, 1956, just as a five-man peace commission was ending a long investigation and treaties were being drawn, Tacho was shot down by a gunman; and Pepe Figueres had the time to restore Costa Rica to its former Shangri-La status. As he ended his term in 1958, he was busy improving vocational and technical schools, promoting electric power projects, and trying to control inflation.

The inflation provoked a quarrel among Don Pepe's heirs in the 1958 election and a conservative lawyer, Mario Echandí, won over Don Pepe's choice by 6,000 votes. However, it was a fair election, refereed by UN observers at the request of Don Pepe, the first national leader in the world to thus invite in an international election supervisory team. Echandí ran the country with its smooth civil service already functioning and gave way in 1963 to a member of Figueres' party, who could not succeed himself until eight years had passed, Francisco Orlich. Figueres busied himself as a conciliator in Latin America, serving on OAS teams in Santo Domingo and elsewhere.

Costa Rica, a bright spot in Latin America, had an unsuspected enemy in nature. In August, 1962, the inactive volcano Irazú, near the capital city, began a continuous eruption which rained ashes on the city and the finest Central Valley farmland for two years. Livestock died, vegetation was ruined, and city life was almost impossible. The rain of ashes continued until 1965 and threatened the social fabric of the little nation, although its economy was bolstered by the Common Market.

In the early 1970's, Costa Rica was recuperating from catastrophe, with economic standards well above the Latin American norms. In 1966, José Joaquín Trejos, a mathematics professor almost untried in politics, won a hard-fought election. In 1970, the popular Pepe Figueres, one of the most consistent liberals in Western Hemisphere politics, was elected again for another legal four-year term.

the Panama Canal and the nation around it

> Hail, prodigy of human effort!—
> Hail to you, Inter-Oceanic Canal,—
> Magnificent reality!
> My country bears in her breast
> The deep wound that opened this artery of the dark sea.
> It rends her entrails; and, with emotion,
> She offers herself nobly to the sacrifice
> To exclaim: "For the good of the world!"[1]

So wrote Benigno Palma (1882–1930?), Panamanian poet when the Canal opened in 1915 to world trade. Spanish explorers and kings had dreamed of a ship passage through Panama. Henry Clay, as American Secretary of State, had asked for a report in 1825 on its possibilities. In 1850, England and the United States had stalled each other's ambitions by the Clayton-Bulwer Treaty in which they agreed that neither nation would build a canal to the exclusion of the other. The need for a canal was re-emphasized after the United States' conquest of California and the gold-rush crossings of the 1850s. The fact that such a project was possible seemed to have been proved in the 1870s by the construction of a canal through Suez. In 1879, Ferdinand de Lesseps, builder of the Suez Canal, had received a charter from Colombia, of which Panama was then a province, had financed a stock company, and had begun digging. Here, however, he did not have the flat, sandy isthmus he had at Suez, but an area of mountains, swamps, and yellow fever. In the eight years de Lesseps' Company worked at the diggings, 40,000 laborers and engineers died of the fever and the company went bankrupt before two-fifths of the work was done.

When the forceful Theodore Roosevelt became President of the United States, he determined to promote the completion of the canal. First a new treaty was made with England, the Hay-Pauncefote Treaty, which gave the United States the right to build a canal by itself. Then the agent of the defunct French Company, Philippe Buneau-Varilla, agreed to sell all the French rights as well as the abandoned machinery to the United States for only $40 million. Secretary of State Hay next arranged with the Colombian foreign minister Herrán to lease a zone across the isthmus for the American project. The Colombian senate, torn by factionalism, turned this treaty down in the hope of getting a higher price.

The impatient Roosevelt, the anxious Buneau-Varilla, and a small group of independence-minded Panamanians were in no mood for further treaties. Then a series of events took place which affronted Latin Americans called "the rape of Panama." When the Colombian government sent 500 soldiers to Panama's Caribbean port to quell any possible revolt, the Ameri-

---

[1] Alice Stone Blackwell, *Some Spanish American Poets* (New York: Appleton-Century, 1929), p. 526. Reprinted by permission of the University of Pennsylvania Press, copyright owners.

can-owned Panama Railway refused to transport the "army" across the Isthmus to Panama City, the center of the "revolt." On November 3, 1903, the American gunboat *U.S.S. Nashville* was conveniently in the harbor when the republic of Panama was proclaimed after a street fight in Panama City in which one life was lost. Theodore Roosevelt immediately recognized the new nation, and made plans for a canal treaty with the young republic. Helpless Colombia was outraged but Roosevelt's act was acclaimed in the United States.

But "the dirt began to fly," as Roosevelt himself said. Disclaiming any protectorate over Panama, the United States leased a zone ten miles wide for 99 years. A corps of engineers arranged for the drawing of plans, the hiring of laborers, the maintenance of spur railways, and the allocation of supplies and machinery, all on a scale unprecedented in any human undertaking up to that time. Yellow fever had just been conquered, after the Spanish American War, by the Cuban Carlos Finlay and American doctors in Havana. United States Army Surgeon William Crawford Gorgas wiped the mosquitoes out of Panama so vigorously that the last yellow fever case reported on the canal workings was in 1906.

Colonel George W. Goethals of the United States Army Engineers was in charge of building the canal. When finished it was 45 feet deep, ran through 35 miles of locks, upland lakes, and newly created highland ditch, had 15 miles of approaches dredged out at sea level, to make a total of 50 miles of ship passage. Three locks were built to raise ships a total of 85 feet from the Atlantic, three more to lower them to the Pacific on the other side. The ditch between the locks was blasted out of the mountains. The Chagres River was controlled and its water made available for the locks and the new cut.

For this work, thousands of unskilled workers from the black population of the West Indies were brought in. This created a social problem of discrimination and segregation which the Panamanian Republic was later to inherit. On August 15, 1914, a warship used in the construction made the first transit. Regular freight and passenger traffic was begun the following spring. Ships from all over the world paid toll equally at $1 per ton, averaging $4,500 per ship, and saving 8,000 miles over the "round-the-horn" route.

A ship coming in from the Pacific enters Panama Bay along six miles of dredged channel and proceeds through Balboa Basin to the Miraflores Locks. Here, by means of two stair-step locks the vessel is lifted fifty-five feet to the level of Miraflores Lake, eight miles from the Pacific. The artificially created Miraflores Lake, two miles across, ends at the Pedro Miguel Lock, where the vessel is again raised thirty feet. Now the ship is in the true canal, the Gaillard Cut, a quiet channel cutting through the hills of the Isthmus. It opens out into the old course of the Chagres River, where the waters were dammed up to create the twenty-three-mile long Gatún Lake. After crossing the lake, the ship reaches the Atlantic port of Colón and is lowered through three Gatún locks the eighty-five feet to the level of the Atlantic. The whole journey takes about eight hours, and increasing world trade calls for a clearance of this bottleneck by a second canal.

In the ten-mile leased strip called the Zone, the town of Balboa grew up on the Pacific end, Cristobal on the Atlantic. In these towns the American colony kept itself isolated, shopping at government commissaries and discriminating against colored employees. Panama City, with a population of more than 350,000, is contiguous to Balboa on the Pacific side; its *mestizo* and Negro population has had good reason to resent the exclusive American colony. Most of the remainder of the Panamanians live at the Atlantic port, Colón, with about 60,000 people, connected to Panama City by highway and rail, or in the coconut and banana plantations around David, a town of 15,000 to the north on the Pacific plain. The great part of the interior has not been developed. Though the Pan American Highway has been pushed in the north to the Costa Rican border, the Darien region southeast of the Canal was as impenetrable in the early 1970s as in Balboa's day. Panamanians exist on interoceanic transportation, and on the export of small amounts of cacao, coffee, rubber, sugar, bananas, and mahogany.

When the canal was being built, the United States had agreed to pay Panama $10 million in payment for the lease, and $250,000 annual rental for use of the watercourse. Although greatly benefited by American sanitary control and yellow fever eradication, and by the enormous business boom the canal brought, many groups in Panama have been resentful of the United States. The United States, under a treaty arrangement like the Platt Amendment in Cuba, kept control of Panamanian foreign affairs.

The domestic history of Panama follows closely the pattern of other Caribbean nations. It includes fraud and violence in elections and revolutions stopped by United States intervention. A spirit of nationalism and anti-Americanism developed during the depression, and at the same time politics waxed hot as rival families tried to hold the presidency. In 1932, Harmodio Arias was elected on a platform of changing the treaty binding Panama to the United States. In 1939, several years after Arias fell from power, a new treaty was ratified in which the United States gave up the right to intervene in Panamanian affairs and raised the yearly rent payments for the Canal Zone to $430,000 in return for the right to build strategic air bases near the Canal. This arrangement was disrupted in 1940 when Harmodio Arias's brother, Arnulfo Arias, an ardent pro-Nazi, was elected. He had little long-term influence, however, for he tried to increase his power by changing the constitution, which brought his downfall.

Pearl Harbor brought Panama back to the side of the United States, with Ricardo Adolfo de la Guardia inaugurated as a pro-American president. Throughout the war, good working relations were reached between the United States and Panama over air bases and canal defense. But in Panamanian politics, the "American Question" remained a big issue. The election in 1952 of the very popular pro-American president, José Remón, promised a future of cooperation with the United States and economic and social improvement of Panama. But this rare stability was rudely smashed when Remón was assassinated in January 1955, and his immediate successor was held for trial for the murder.

Panamanian politics promised to follow the turbulent pattern that in

————, *Costa Rica and the Civilization of the Caribbean* (1935).

————, *Guatemala, Past and Present* (1940).

Kamman, W., *A Search for Stability: United States Diplomacy Towards Nicaragua 1925–1933* (1968).

Kantor, H., *Costa Rican Election of 1953: A Case Study* (1958).

Karnes, T., *Failure of Union: Central America, 1824–1960* (1961).

Kelsey, V., and L. de J. Osborne, *Four Keys to Guatemala* (2nd ed., 1961).

Kemble, J. H., *Panama Route, 1848–1869* (1943).

Kennedy, P. P., *The Middle Beat: A Correspondent's View of Mexico, Guatemala and El Salvador*, ed. S. R. Ross (1971).

Kepner, C. D., *Social Aspects of the Banana Industry* (1936).

————, and J. H. Southill, *The Banana Empire* (1935).

Kilijarni, T. V., *Central America: Lords and Lizards* (1962).

La Barge, R. A., *Impact of United Fruit Company on the Economic Development of Guatemala, 1946–1954* (1960).

Landsberger, H., *Latin American Peasant Movements* (1970).

Liss, S. R., *The Canal: Aspects of U.S.-Panamanian Relations, 1903–1966* (1967).

Lloyd, J., *Guatemala, Land of the Maya* (1963).

Lookley, L. C., *Guide to Market Data in Central America* (1964).

Macaulay, N., *The Sandino Affair* (1966).

Mack, G., *Land Divided: History of the Panama Canal and Other Isthmian Projects* (1944).

Martin, P. F., *El Salvador in the Twentieth Century* (1911).

Martz, J. D., *Central America: The Crisis and the Challenge* (1959).

————, *Justo Rufino Barrios and Central American Union* (1963).

May, S., et al., *Costa Rica: A Study in Economic Development* (1952).

————, and Galo Plazo, *The United Fruit Company in Latin America* (1958).

McCain, W. D., *United States and the Republic of Panama* (1937).

McClelland, D. H., *The Central American Common Market* (1972).

Mecham, J. L., *Church and State in Latin America* (rev. ed., 1966).

Mellander, G. A., *The United States in Panamanian Politics* (1971).

————, *Handbook on Cuba* (1962).

————, *Handbook on Panama* (1964).

Miller, H. G., *The Isthmian Highway* (1929).

Milliken, G. A., *United States in Panamanian Politics: The Intriguing Formative Years, 1903–1908* (1970).

Moore, R. E., *Historical Dictionary of Guatemala* (1967).

Munro, D. G., *The Five Republics of Central America* (1918).

————, *Intervention and Dollar Diplomacy in the Caribbean, 1900–1921* (1964).

————, *United States and the Caribbean* (1934).

Niemeier, J. G., *The Panama Story* (1968).

Nunley, R. E., *The Distribution of Population in Costa Rica* (1963).

Nye, J. S., *Central American Regional Integration* (1967).

Olin, M. D., *The Negro in Costa Rica* (1970).

Osborne, L. de J., *Four Keys to El Salvador* (1965).

————, *Indian Crafts of Guatemala and El Salvador* (1965).

Padelford, N. J., "Cooperation in the Central American Region: The Organization of Central American States," *International Organization,* XI (1957).

Palmer, T. W., *Search for a Latin American Policy* (1957).

Pan American Union, *Foreign Trade of Nicaragua, 1945–1955* (1955).

Parker, F. D., *Central American Republics* (1964).

————, *History and Historians of Central America to 1850* (1951).

————, *José Cecilio del Valle and the Establishment of Central American Confederation* (1954).

————, *Travels in Central America 1821–1840* (1970).

Perkins, D., *United States and the Caribbean* (1947).

Pincus, J., *The Central American Common Market* (1962).

Pippin, L. L., *The Remón Era: An Analysis of Events in Panama, 1947–1957* (1964).

Ramsett, D. E., *Regional Industrial Development in Central America* (1969).

Reina, R. E., *Chinautla: A Guatemalan Indian Community* (1960).

Rippy, J. F., *Caribbean Danger Zone* (1940).

Rodríguez, M., *Central America* (1965).

————, *A Palmerstonian Diplomat in Central America: Frederick Chatfield* (1964).

Rosenthal, M., *Guatemala, the Story of an Emergent Latin American Democracy* (1962).

Schneider, R. M., *Communism in Guatemala, 1944–1954* (1958).

Scherzer, C., *Travels—Central America* (2 vols., 1857; 1970).

Scroggs, W. O., *Filibusters and Finances: The Story of William Walker* (1916).

Shepherd, R., and R. M. Kinne, *Central American Common Market: Opportunities Plus* (1964).

Silvert, K. H., *A Study in Government: Guatemala* (1954).

Slade, W. F., *Federation of Central America* (1917).

Solnick, B. B., ed., *The West Indies and Central America to 1898* (1970).

Squier, E. G., *Nicaragua* (2 vols., 1852).

————, *Notes on Central America* (1855; 1970).

————, *Travels in Central America* (2 vols., 1853).

Stephens, J. L., *Incidents of Travel in Central America, Chiapas and Yucatan* (new edition; 2 vols., 1949).

Stewart, W., *Keith and Costa Rica* (1964).

Stokes, W. S., *Honduras: An Area Study in Government* (1950).

Stuart, G. H., *United States in Latin America* (5th ed., 1955).

Suslow, L. H., *Aspect of Social Reforms in Guatemala, 1944–1949* (1949).

Tax, S., *Penny Capitalism: A Guatemalan Indian Economy* (1953).

Tomasek, R. D., *Latin American Politics. Studies of the Contemporary Scene* (rev. ed., 1970).

Torres Rioseco, A., *Epic of Latin American Literature* (1959).

Tower, F. J., *Basic Data on Economy of Honduras* (1961).

Tuman, M. M., *Caste in a Peasant Society* (1952).

Turner, G. P., *An Analysis of the Economy of El Salvador* (1961).

United Nations, Bureau of Social Affairs, *Population of Central America Including Mexico, 1950–1980* (1954).

United States Bureau of Labor Statistics, *Labor Law and Practices in Costa Rica* (1962).

————, *Labor Law and Practices in Guatemala* (1962).

————, *Labor Law and Practices in Honduras* (1961).

Von Hagen, V. W., *Maya Explorer: John Lloyd Stephens and the Lost Cities of Central America and Yucatan* (1947).

Waggoner, G. R. and B. A., *Education in Central America* (1971).

Wallach, H. C., and J. H. Adler, *Public Finance in a Developing Country: El Salvador, A Case Study* (1951).

West, R. E. and J. P. Angelli, *Middle America* (1966).

Whetten, N. L., *Guatemala, Land and the People* (1961).

Wilgus, A. C., ed., *Caribbean Area* (1934).

————, *Caribbean at Mid-Century* (1951).

————, *Caribbean: Central America Area* (1961).

————, *Caribbean: Its Hemispheric Role* (1968).

Williams, M. W., *Anglo-American Isthmian Diplomacy, 1815–1915* (1915).

Wilson, C. M., *Challenge and Opportunity: Central America* (1941).

————, *Empire in Green and Gold: Story of American Banana Trade* (1947).

————, *Middle America* (1944).

Woodward, R. L., *Social Revolution in Guatemala: The Carrera Revolt* (1971).

Ydígoras Fuentes, M., *My War with Communism as told by Mario Rosenthal* (1963).

chapter 29

CARIBBEAN
ISLAND NATIONS

two islands, three separate nations

The French-speaking Republic of Haiti, the Spanish-speaking Dominican Republic, and the sugar-producing Republic of Cuba comprise a total of 74,000 square miles and contain nearly 17 million people. They are strategically important because they command the approaches to the Panama Canal and other possible canal routes. By their proximity to each other and their many common historical experiences, they should have been friends but they have not been, for one reason because their rulers have had a tendency to meddle in the politics of the others. They are dependent on outsiders, and they nurture resentment, with good reason, toward these outsiders. Their favorite target is the United States, which has done them immense good at times and immense harm at others. Their histories are colorful and violent, both similar and dissimilar, as a separate treatment of each nation will show.

Cuba, a colony and a republic

Cuba had lain dormant during the continental wars of independence, and when the wars were over, only Cuba and Puerto Rico remained as Spanish colonies in the New World. In Cuba, government jobs were held by Spanish-born officials, and Havana life was dominated by Spanish society. Spanish

654

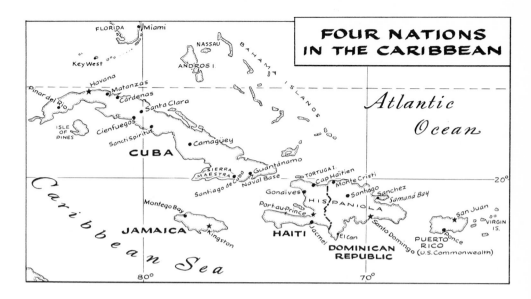

FOUR NATIONS IN THE CARIBBEAN

and white creole families owned the vast sugar plantations, which were worked by slave labor. The governor's post was refilled every few years as soon as the Spanish incumbent had made his fortune in the position. Taxes were heavy on all necessities and many commodities were government monopolies. In 1840, Havana was a neglected, decaying city with thousands of footloose vagabonds and with homeless, starving dogs roaming the city streets.

Cuban patriots today remember the poetry of a poor, self-taught mulatto, Gabriel de la Concepción Valdés (1809–1844) who wrote under the pen name of Plácido. Brought up in an orphanage, a carver of tortoise-shells by trade, he identified himself in his verses as "the tyrant's restless foe" and affirmed that he could with clear conscience "face the rifles, freed from bondage." In 1844, he did face the rifles for he was arrested on a charge of conspiring to free his fellow blacks. His death helped fan the smoldering embers of revolt.

Cuba did not get independence in Plácido's lifetime but the plots and conspiracies against Spain show how great was the dissatisfaction with Spanish colonial policies. Spain was well aware of the danger of losing her last remaining possessions. For various reasons, France, England, Mexico, and Colombia were showing an interest in freeing Cuba. The pro-slavery South in the United States was anxious to annex the slave-holding island. Individual Southerners backed filibustering expeditions to Cuba. A Venezuelan, Narciso López, became an adopted Cuban after fighting both with the patriots and the royalists in his own country and Spain. When a rebellion he planned in Cuba failed in 1848, he escaped to the United States and organized three unsuccessful filibustering expeditions, aided by the pro-slavery men of the American South. On his fourth expedition with "an army of soldiers of fortune," he was captured when no Cubans rallied to him, and was executed.

On October 10, 1868, a group of Cubans, relying on no adventurers from the outside, declared Cuban independence on the plantation of La Damajagua in the so-called *Grito de Yara,* which launched a decade of guerrilla war known as the Ten Years' War. Its civilian leader was Carlos Manuel de Céspedes, later chosen president, and its leading strategist was General Máximo Gómez, a gloomy old *mestizo* who had had experience fighting with the Spanish army in Santo Domingo. Under him the soldiers, ill-armed and barefooted, fought and freed the eastern half of the island. Second in command and most famous was Antonio Maceo, an enormous mulatto who rode a horse like a centaur, sustained many serious wounds, and fought so well he even won respect from his enemies. Maceo and his men slashed through jungles, burned storehouses, and harried the Spanish out of the countryside in the eastern provinces. The Spanish forces, including some youths from Havana society, met fire with fire until open hostilities were ended in 1878 with the Peace of Zanjón, a "no-victors" peace. Freedom for the slaves was won, and luke-warm promises were made by Spain regarding amnesty for the rebels and reforms in the administration. The rebel leaders did not trust these promises, and so they remained in hiding. Maceo and Gómez went into exile. Tomás Estrada Palma, who had succeeded Céspedes as patriot president, went to teach Spanish in a private school in New York. None of the leaders thought the war had ended or considered the peace anything but a truce.

Back in 1854, when the expansionist spirit known as Manifest Destiny prevailed in the United States, her ministers in several European capitals issued a statement, known as the Ostend Manifesto, to the effect that the United States should buy Cuba, paying as much as $120 million, and should threaten Spain with war if she were to refuse. When this statement was ridiculed by the European powers, it was declared "unofficial" by the United States government. With the end of the Civil War in the United States, Southerners ceased trying to annex Cuba, but Cuban agitation for freedom continued in headquarters in New York and Florida. During the Ten Years' War, money was raised to help the rebels and supplies were sent on a Cuban ship that was flying the American flag. When the ship was captured in 1873 and the Americans as well as the Cubans on board were shot, American public opinion was aroused, an interest that was to continue until 1898.

In Cuba the Spanish governor maintained the same dictatorial powers of life and death over people he had had before the Ten Years' War. Graft and oppression were widespread; taxes were siphoned off to Spain; many trade restrictions remained. Moreover, American capital was invested in Cuba and American machinery had saved the sugar-cane industry in its competition with beet sugar. Higher sugar prices brought prosperity to Cuba, but they were counterbalanced by the necessity of paying wages to the newly freed slaves and by the high United States tariffs until the 1890s. Even conservative merchants and planters began to hope for a free Cuba which would have access to world markets. By 1895, the cry of *Cuba Libre!* was on the lips of the majority of Cubans.

The war that freed Cuba was for three years (1895–1898) a struggle of Cubans against Spaniards, and then for 100 days a series of land and naval engagements between Spain and the United States. On February 24, 1895, the revolutionaries staged a series of uprisings in Baire and other eastern towns, and on July 15, the revolutionists in exile had adopted a declaration of independence; Estrada Palma headed a junta in New York which was raising funds; Maceo, who had been in Jamaica since the Ten Years' War, soon joined him; and with them was José Martí, a young poet who organized the revolution and who remains the national hero of Cuba.

Martí, born in Havana in 1853, was involved in early youth in sporadic protests against the government and was sent to prison at hard labor at seventeen. The fetters he wore formed scars which he carried to his death. Released and exiled, he became a typical Caribbean cultural figure, wandering in Central America and Mexico and supporting himself by writing. Ringing words that he wrote for freedom are known to Cuban schoolchildren. Comforting the losers of the Ten Years' War he wrote, "To many generations of slaves must succeed one generation of martyrs." He asserted that war for freedom was inevitable, and founded clubs among Cuban cigar workers in Florida, raising arms for his *Partido Revolucionario Cubano.*

Early in April 1895, Martí and Máximo Gómez landed in the eastern province of Cuba. A month later, they met Maceo. On May 19, in the course of a minor skirmish, Martí, the inspirational leader, who had not followed Gómez' advice to stay out of the foray, was killed. In spite of this loss, the revolt gained momentum, and by the end of 1896, the rebels had succeeded in spreading the war to the western end of the island. Thousands of troops crossed two island-wide fortified lines that had been built by the Spanish to keep the rebels in the east. They cleverly eluded the pursuit of heavy Spanish columns under General Arsenio Martinez Campos. In a skirmish south of Havana while returning from the western region, Maceo also was killed.

Spain was prompted by the large-scale burning of plantations and sugar mills and by a desire to avoid the long guerrilla warfare of the previous insurrection to increase the number of soldiers in Cuba and to replace Martínez Campos, the victor of 1878, with a more energetic commander. She sent up to 200,000 soldiers to Cuba to stop the 25,000 patriots who had joined Gómez. At their head was now General Valeriano Weyler who launched a scorched-earth policy to beat the patriots at their own game. He held the key cities, herded the country people into great fenced areas called *campos de concentración (reconcentrados)* where they could not farm and where thousands of them starved or died of disease. The cities were caught with no food, as General Calixto García held the eastern end of the island and kept food from reaching the capital. Some 52,000 died in Havana alone. The desolation caused repercussions even in Spain, and General Weyler was recalled. Madrid promised greater measures of self-government.

The patriots had written a second declaration of independence and again chose Tomás Estrada Palma as their provisional president. In the

United States, newspapers vied with each other in printing stories about the Cubans fenced and starving in their concentration camps. American investments in sugar plantations were being destroyed and trade was cut off. Then the battleship *Maine*, sent to protect Americans in Havana, mysteriously exploded in February 1898, and 266 men were killed. American public opinion blamed the Spaniards. The Spanish minister in Washington wrote a letter criticizing President McKinley, which was discovered and printed in a New York paper. Calmer leaders in both Spain and the United States tried to avoid hostilities, but public clamor aroused Congress to declare war in April 1898.

Most Americans know the stories of Theodore Roosevelt's Rough Riders on San Juan Hill, the message carried by an American foot soldier to the guerrillas under García, the defeat of the Spanish fleet under Cervera, and the battle of Manila Bay. Fewer Americans realized how unprepared the United States was for the war, or had heard about the brave fighting of Gómez' troops also at Santiago, or of the long Cuban campaigns which made the quick American victory possible. It was the fighting of their own patriots over a thirty-year period that, in the minds of Cubans themselves, won them their independence.

Under the peace treaty, Cuba was recognized as independent by both Spain and the United States. Puerto Rico, Guam, and the Philippines became United States possessions, and America was launched as a world power and influenced Latin American affairs in the 20th century. Cuban foreign affairs, however, were to be hampered by America's Platt Amendment, which allowed American intervention in Cuban affairs, and by the treaty which gave the United States military bases on Cuban soil. Also provided was tariff-free trade for Cuban sugar shipped into the United States, a provision acceptable to both American and Spanish planters who hoped to build up their plantations in Cuba after years of devastation.

The American military government under General Leonard Wood from 1899 to 1902 restored order and granted financial aid. Food was distributed to the people who had been *reconcentrados;* cattle, seed, and cane stock were sent in, and General Wood's interim government rebuilt towns and villages, installed water and sewage systems, set up hospitals, cleaned streets, and rebuilt roads. Elections were held and Cuba drafted a constitution.

An American doctor with Wood, Walter Reed, took the initiative to free Cuba from yellow fever. He consulted a Cuban scientist named Carlos Finlay who had studied its causes and had published way back in 1881 his theory that mosquitoes carried the disease. Dr. Reed's assistants tried to produce yellow fever by all known types of contacts but only the patients bitten by mosquitoes who had fed off yellow fever cases contracted the disease. Armed with this proof, the American army began killing mosquito larvae by draining swamps and pouring oil on breeding places. Cuban-American cooperation thus made possible large-scale, disease-free work in many parts of the tropics, including the Panama Canal Zone.

To aid Cuba on her path toward democracy, more than 3,000

schools were founded under the American military regime where formerly there had been only a few inadequate private schools. In the summer of 1900, more than a thousand young Cubans went to the United States to attend a special session at Harvard and train for teaching in the new schools. With all this aid, Tomás Estrada Palma started his term as president of the Cuban Republic on May 20, 1902. But the new island republic was ill prepared for life in the dawn of the 20th century, due to years of war, of colonial misrule, of racial inequality, of extremes of wealth and poverty, and a total lack of experience in government. Cuba, the island of America's military occupation at the turn of the century, was to be in the 1960's the center of her concern about Western Hemisphere Communism.

Cuba in the twentieth century

The presidency of Estrada Palma started with great hopes for the future promised by the democratic constitution, but when his people were granted local self-government, they did not know how to use it. Soon various areas of the country had become festering sores of revolution against the central power, each one promoted by greedy generals. Estrada Palma tried to get himself re-elected in 1906 but was unable to control the situation. Accordingly he asked William Howard Taft, then the United States Secretary of War, for aid. Taft sent Charles E. Magoon, a Nebraska lawyer, to restore civil government. Magoon supervised the election of José Miguel Gómez, candidate of a so-called Liberal party, and in 1909 withdrew the American occupation forces.

With Gómez began a series of presidents who entered their office poor but retired as millionaries. Tomás Estrada Palma was forced to retire to a little ranch and end his days in poverty. Gómez retired at the end of his term in 1913 with his new private fortune, and Mario García Menocal was elected, to serve two terms, until 1921. His presidency included the period of World War I (in which Cuba joined), a period which brought a boom in prices, the expansion of great estates, and a fantastic speculation in Cuban sugar. His regime is referred to as "the dance of the millions"; a great part of these millions the president and his family and friends acquired personally. Although his regime was unpopular with the "outs," American troops prevented any revolutions against it, preserving it through a second term by backing Menocal against a liberal revolt in the fraudulent 1917 elections. Under the Wilson Corollary to the Monroe Doctrine which the president had propounded to "protect American lives and property," an existing regime, no matter how corrupt, was maintained so long as peace and prosperity were preserved. No governments brought in by revolution would be recognized.

An American commission, headed by General Enoch Crowder, supervised the 1921 election in which Menocal's own candidate, Alfredo Zayas, known as "the peseta stealer," was chosen. But the World War I sugar prosperity collapsed just at this time and General Crowder remained in Cuba to advise Zayas. The United States would lend the now-bankrupt Cubans $50 million, provided Zayas would carry out 15 specific reforms—such as control of graft, economy in the budget, reform of national lotteries, auditing of national bank businesses, and appointment of an "honest cabinet." By 1923, Cuba had recovered in the sugar market and Crowder had become ambassador, so Zayas was able to fire his "honest cabinet" and return to the normal "siege" on the national treasury. President Harding's government refused to interfere for there had been charges of "imperialism" against the United States from other Latin American nations. Zayas' government became a record-breaker for corruption, protection of organized vice, connections with American prohibition-era gangsters, and viciousness in the president's own personal relationships, but the United States continued to support him under the "no successful revolutions" corollary.

Zayas was powerful enough to back his own candidate, General Gerardo Machado, for the next electon and to have him peacefully inaugurated in 1925. The General was to be the archetype of Caribbean dictators through the 1920's. He borrowed heavily from American banks to assure American protection and interest in his behalf. He amended the constitution in the hope of staying in office for life. He imprisoned intellectuals and liberal-minded university students in foul dungeons in the hope of quieting opposition forever.

In 1933, a popular mass uprising brought this barbarous rule to an end with an attack on the presidential palace. Franklin D. Roosevelt, the "Good Neighbor," sent the tactful Sumner Welles to spirit Machado out by plane and help set up a provisional government. But within three weeks came another street riot and Welles had to ask Washington for more protection. Cuban resentment ran high when several naval vessels appeared in response to this request. The provisional government fell and a new force came to power, a combination of a college professor, Ramón Grau San Martín, and a sergeant, Fulgencio Batista. Anti-American demonstrations died down and peace reigned—but only as long as the sergeant, Batista, the real power, wanted it so. Grau, who had been denied recognition by Washington, resigned in 1934 when he disagreed with Batista.

During the next seven years, seven presidents came and went while the little sergeant wielded his puppets and the United States made no protest. This pudgy noncommissioned officer, who made himself a colonel in 1933 and was still dictator in 1958, was a barefoot boy from the canebrakes, of a family so poor his elder brother died of tuberculosis and malnutrition. He had joined the army as an illiterate private at seventeen. There he was issued shoes and taught himself to read and write. Eventually he learned how to take stenographic dictation and to make himself useful as a secretary to officers, and also how to organize a powerful political machine among the other "noncoms." It was the "noncoms" who got the support of the enlisted men, seized the barracks at the time of Machado's fall, and put Batista in power.

For a while Batista was content to be king-maker rather than king. During the period in which he functioned through his presidents, the Platt

Amendment was cancelled as part of the Good Neighbor Policy, and with it United States' legal rights in Cuba. Depression conditions were alleviated by loans from the American Export-Import Bank and by continued preferential treatment for Cuban sugar in the depressed United States market. To keep peace at home, Batista built up the strongest, best-paid, best-fed army of privates Cuba had ever known. Then, to keep them busy, he built primary schools throughout the island and sent the now literate soldiers to teach in them. Cane workers were a little better paid, rural roads were improved, and employers were forced to improve working conditions.

In 1940, just as the great demand for sugar in World War II was to bring a prosperity that Cuba had never known before, the little sergeant decided to run for president himself. He allowed the weak opposition party to campaign, counted the ballots fairly enough, and declared himself by far the most popular candidate. Batista joined the Allies, sold Cuba's sugar and minerals to them, and granted military bases to the United States.

In 1944, Fulgencio Batista, again allowing a fair election, saw his own candidate defeated and the college professor Grau San Martín elected; and he went peaceably to live the life of a millionaire in Daytona, Florida. But Grau, who was supported by a coalition of anti-Batista men that included both conservative and non-Communist labor, had an uneasy hold on politics. A poor administrator, he seemed helpless in the vacuum left by Batista and in the end-of-the-war price boom. His friends and supporters waxed rich at the public trough. He attempted some reforms, tried to promote industrialization and diversified agriculture and attacked the problems of health and illiteracy, but failed because Congress did not cooperate with him.

In 1948, Grau's own candidate, Carlos Prío Socarrás, a strong anti-Communist, was elected. But Prío Socarrás, formerly a friend of Grau, found many evidences of misappropriation of funds in his predecessor's records and as a result an ex-president was tried for graft in office, something unprecedented for Cuba. Grau was cleared, although the funds remained unaccounted for, but now it was clearly on record that it was a public offense for a president to make a fortune while in office. This, however, did not keep Prío Socarrás from retiring in 1952 with a larger fortune that he had had in 1948.

By 1952, the political situation was so confused that Fulgencio Batista seized upon the opportunity to ease himself back into the saddle. In March, 1952, he announced he was taking action to prevent a bloody revolution between opposing factions; and he carefully posted his old friends, the noncommissioned officers, in strategic places in Havana and then came riding into the city, putting over a full-fledged *coup d'état*. Two hours and 16 minutes later, a complete dictatorship was imposed. The United States recognized the Batista regime, and continued its technical and military aid. In 1954, in an actual election, Batista, the only candidate, won a legal four-year term.

The Batista government not only maintained friendly relations with the United States but also kept the peace and raised the standard of living.

Under a Social and Economic Development Plan, inaugurated in 1954, private capital had been invested in new industries, electric power had been doubled, and a housing program pushed. Millions of American dollars had been invested in plantations and refineries, and tourists swarmed through Havana, visiting night clubs and gambling on cockfights and the lottery. Paved highways ran the 750 mile length of the island to connect Havana, a city of over a million and a half people at one end, with Santiago, with nearly 250,000 at the other.

Cuba thus was a country in which the price of sugar was high, wages and working conditions were improving, and children were in school. The elementary schools were even reaching children in rural areas. Health standards were high for a country in the tropics. A mixture of races were living side by side with no evidence of discrimination—Batista himself had a Chinese grandfather and other forebears who were mixed Spanish, Indian, and Afro-Cuban. It could be asked whether the dictatorship of the little sergeant was not an improvement on many eras of dictatorship by generals.

But the sophisticated Cuba of the 1950's came to a crashing end with Fidel Castro in the 1960's. The degrees of wealth and poverty in Cuba were as marked as in any area of the Hemisphere. The rural population had been living in poverty while politicans lived handsomely as they accumulated fortunes to take with them at retirement. So an increasingly well-educated and enlightened populace could not remain satisfied with Batista's "benevolent despotism." Opposition parties through the later 1950's increased their underground activities and university students staged bloody riots. And those who were anxious for political freedom found a champion in the rebel Fidel Castro Ruiz.

Fidel Castro, a visionary idealist from a well-to-do Santiago family, had tried to take Batista's barracks in Santiago with a handful of friends on July 26, 1953, as a protest against Batista's return to power. He and his brother Raúl had been captured in this fiasco and given long prison terms. In 1955, during a general political amnesty declared by Batista, they were freed and allowed to go into exile in Mexico. In Mexico they rallied other Cuban exiles into a closely knit group and took lessons in guerrilla fighting from a Spanish Civil War veteran. They supported their cause, now called the "26th of July Movement," on funds donated by former president Prío Socarrás and many other contributors.

In November, 1956, the Castro brothers and 81 other youthful enthusiasts landed on the shores of eastern Cuba from a 62-foot boat. Escaping from Batista's troops, they found their way into the inaccessible Sierra Maestra hills where they set up rebel headquarters. For two years they harassed Batista's soldiers, arousing worldwide sympathy and attracting recruits and secret support from the villages and towns.

In the face of growing opposition, Batista had announced an election for June 1, 1958 in which a puppet candidate "defeated" the opposition and was expected to be inaugurated on May 20, 1959. But by December 1958, the rebels began to advance with a great popular following. Normal life on the island stopped. Batista declared a "state of emergency." What really caused an emergency was the fact that his own soldiers were deserting by the thousands to the rebels. By New Year's Day, 1959, Batista was in flight to the Dominican Republic. Eight days later, the Castro brothers were in Havana while the crowds were hysterical with enthusiasm.

The rebel soldiers had allowed their hair and beards to grow long in the mountains and the long black beard had become a symbol of the "People's Revolution." This People's Revolution, however, did not result immediately in an election. A little-known Judge Manuel Urrutia, an exiled and energetic fund-raiser for the rebel cause, was declared provisional president. Fidel himself was called "premier"—a title seldom used in Latin America. Brother Raúl was commander-in-chief of the army, and a fiery young Argentine Communist, Ernesto "Ché" Guevara, was economic adviser. When Urrutia grumbled about Communist infiltration, a "puppet" named Osvaldo Dorticós Torrado was declared "legal" president. Public opinion in the United States and other democratic Western nations was turned against the bearded "26th of July" leaders when their followers insisted on vengeance against Batista henchmen and held hurried "kangaroo court" type trials which ordered executions of more than 500 Batista army officers, policemen, and secret service men in the first three months of 1959.

Internationally, the name "Fidel Castro" came to symbolize a new type of Western Hemisphere Communism. It was to mean arming guerrillas among the poorest rural workers and landless peasants in various nations in order to hasten the "socialist revolution." Such armed bands were found in the Dominican Republic, Venezuela, Peru's *montaña*, and Brazil's depressed northeast. Street rioters in Panama yelled "Fidel! Fidel!" when protesting United States' policy in the Canal Zone. The liberal President Betancourt of Venezuela almost fell from power due to the activities of secret "Fidelistas."

The United States had recognized Fidel's government as soon as Batista had fled and had tried to promote the same financial aid it had extended to Batista—but Fidel made it clear that he resented such aid. Eventually, in January, 1961, the United States withdrew recognition, as did all the Latin American states save Mexico. Cuba was not welcomed at later meetings of the Organization of American States, did not join in the Latin American common market or the Alliance for Progress, and it denounced the United States at the United Nations rather than protesting through the regional Organization of American States.

At home, Fidel formally announced that Cuba was a "socialist state" and that he himself would always be a "Marxist-Leninist." He had kept his Communist sympathy quiet in the Sierra Maestra for fear his guerrilla army would lose supporters. Fidel and "Ché" Guevara made visits to Moscow where they received the red-carpet treatment. By the summer of 1960, Fidel had contracted to sell all of Cuba's sugar output to Russia, and the Cuban government had confiscated most of the American sugar properties, investments that totaled $850 million. The United States in turn cancelled the country's contracts to purchase Cuban sugar and gave the Cuban preferential quota to other sugar-producing areas.

Khrushchev, the Russian leader, said in the United Nations in July,

1960, that Russia would defend Cuba if that island was invaded by the United States. This was regarded as an open threat to the Monroe Doctrine. Fidel Castro castigated the United States for its "years of economic aggression" against Cuba in radio and television speeches that went on for hours, night after night. A meeting of the Organization of American States in Costa Rica condemned the intervention of "outside powers," without mentioning Russia, in any Western Hemisphere state.

Cuban exiles, in the United States by this time in large numbers, attempted to organize a Cuban army-in-exile, and their leaders received encouragement, equipment, money, and training from the United States Central Intelligence Agency under President Eisenhower. The army, some 1,500 strong, was secretly trained on Guatemalan soil. When Kennedy became president, he agreed to the plans this army had made for the invasion of Cuba so long as no Americans were directly involved. It was assumed that once the invaders had a foothold on the island hundreds of thousands of Cubans would join the anti-Castro forces. But Castro was warned by his intelligence officers of the plan and thousands of possible supporters of the exiles were jailed and the planned landing place was alerted. As a result, on April 19, 1961, 300 of the exiles' army were killed in the Bay of Pigs and 1,200 were taken prisoners, prisoners who were later ransomed by private individuals in the United States for $53 million worth of drugs and infant foods. The incident strengthened Fidel's hold on his own people and on the imagination of underprivileged people throughout Latin America.

The Bay of Pigs fiasco emboldened the Russians to use Cuba as a base for missiles pointed directly at the United States 90 miles away. In October, 1962, President Kennedy announced that photo-reconnaissance planes had identified an elaborate system of nuclear-missile launching-sites on Cuba. There followed a tense week of formal exchanges between Russia and the United States, after which Russia backed down and removed the missiles. To Fidel's friends in Latin America this confrontation seemed to show American strength and to reveal Fidel's weakness as a tool of the Russians. Castro's attempt to shut off the water from the American naval base at Guantánamo hardly caused a tremor. The United States imposed a quarantine of Cuba which was reported to have lowered the Cuban standard of living by 15 per cent. Yet 748 merchant vessels called at Cuban ports in a three-year period, in spite of the quarantine.

Fidel Castro was willing to allow dissatisfied Cubans to leave Cuba, save only those eligible for military service or skilled in technical trades. The United States undertook to airlift 2,000 persons a month to Miami, with Castro's full consent. Since December, 1965, some 250,000 Cubans were flown from Havana to Miami before Cuba ended the flights in August, 1971. Some half million Cubans have left the country since the Castro take-over, most of them coming to the United States. By 1971, Miami was 25 per cent Cuban.

It was mainly the middle class that left. The lot of the sugar workers at the bottom had always been as wretched as that of any poor laborers in the Americas. Cuba was a one-crop land, in which, in the pre-Castro era, one-third of the six million Cubans lived by cultivating and refining sugar cane. The *guajiros* or peasants lived in huts on the plantations amidst the cane, and were employed only three months out of the year. To solve some of Cuba's most pressing social evils reforms such as guaranteed year-round wages, compulsory subsistence garden plots for families, and adequate schooling for children were needed. If Batista, the rich Cuban plantation owners, and the American sugar refining interests had taken such steps, the eruption of Cuban Communism might have been forestalled.

Cuba's sugar industry was a factory business. The great refineries, called *centrales,* were complexes in the center of the plantations, where oil-heated evaporators and centrifugal separators turned out the white crystals, and assembly lines weighed and bagged them. This outlay of machinery called for heavy investment, and some 70 per cent of the Cuban sugar industry was owned by United States capital. This meant that North American industry often called the tune in Cuban affairs. Cuban sugar, which competed with Louisiana cane and Western beet sugar, was given preferential treatment in the United States, a practice accepted since the "liberation" of Cuba from Spain. Yet it was sugar production that could be held responsible for the poverty of the mass of Cubans. It prevented small ownership, concentrated land in large holdings under absentee owners either in Havana or in New York, kept land out of diversified cultivation, and cut down the production of food crops that might have made Cuba self-sufficient. Although beef and tobacco were grown for export, they constituted only 10 per cent of the country's foreign trade.

Fidel Castro launched his drastic land reform program in the summer of 1959. All large holdings, including those of American sugar companies, were expropriated in return for long-term bonds, on which no payments have yet been made. They were to be redistributed to small holders in 67-acre plots, although by 1965, many of them were recombined into large state farms. Castro's Agrarian Reform Institute also confiscated the grazing lands of the rich cattlemen and made grandiose plans to improve cattle and plant seed strains that would help small farmers toward economic independence.

Between 1960 and 1963, however, Castro and "Ché" Guevara hoped to make Cuba an industrialized nation, and they turned away from this agricultural development. Russian planners had come to Cuba to work out a four-year development program. But already by 1963, the plan had failed, and Fidel returned from a second trip to Moscow in 1963 with new plans to put Cuba back into a sugar-and-cattle producing economy. The new planners pushed for 90 per cent state control of a single vast sugar "factory-in-the-fields," and even small, privately owned farms were expropriated for this purpose. City workers, soldiers, and students were sent out into the fields to harvest the cane. But although the 1964 crop was as large as that produced before 1959, world prices went down, and Russia paid only the equivalent of those lower prices, with the result that the Cuban economy suffered chaos. The refineries began to break down for lack of parts. Russian specialists could not repair them, and they reportedly went home in disgust saying Marxist-Leninist principles were not meant to work with these people in this particular climate.

Abroad, *Fidelismo* suffered a set-back. "Ché" Guevara mysteriously disappeared in the summer of 1965, and in late 1967, his corpse was found among Bolivian Indians, riddled with Bolivian army bullets. Evidently he had planned to start an all-South American revolution through a peasant uprising in the geographic center of the continent, but had failed. Latin American guerrilla groups seemed to have lost steam, and *Fidelismo* turned inwards to make a success within Cuba itself.

Observers assessing Fidel's ten years of "Revolution" in the early 1970's came up with many positive judgments. Children throughout the island were well-cared for by any standard—well-fed, clothed, and "intensely and expensively educated." The number of schools had increased 500 per cent and the number of teachers by 300 per cent. Where there had been 63,000 students in secondary schools in 1958, there were 172,000 in 1971. Every child from every area and level with potential was "sought out" and sent free of expense to high school (often to boarding school) and then on to vocational training, teacher training, technical agriculture school or academic work in preparation for government administration. The program for "up-grading" the population doubled in cost and effort every two years, and in the process wiped out rural illiteracy. An unprecedented public health program had been put into effect which included mass immunization, free clinics in all areas, and the service of hundreds of visiting nurses.

Other advances included improvement of housing for adult rural workers, and the removal of the color bar which was still subtly a problem since slavery had been abolished less than a century earlier. As a result of government action, Fidel could rightly call Cuba a "genuine interracial society." Agricultural specialists were introducing new crops in an effort to get away from the "sugar only" economy and were planting 90 million coffee plants in a "green belt" across the island and 60,000 young citrus trees in an experimental program on the Isle of Pines. Moreover, Fidel had been able to secure the enthusiastic participation of young people in his Youth Militia and "cane-cutter brigades" and in the new jobs he provided for them. They revered him as the "Maximum Leader."

A major failure was the attempt to encourage manufacturing with Russian equipment and technicians. The cane cutting machines invented by Ukrainian specialists were unusable in the tropical heat. Gasoline had to be rationed, and diesel oil was used only for steam plants to produce electric power, available only a few hours a day. Not only did "industrialization" break down but a bumper sugar crop brought disappointment. A great push in 1970 for a 10 million ton sugar crop, more than Cuba had ever previously produced, brought 8,500,000 tons, the greatest crop in Cuban history but short of Castro's goal. Everyone in the nation, including Fidel himself, and even 1,300 young people from the United States, went to cut the cane during the Christmas holiday season. But the bumper crop was secured at the expense of desirable agricultural diversification and of industrial production. Also it failed to gain foreign exchange for Castro since seven million tons had to go to Russia to pay debts that even included the cost of the unusable cane-cutting machines. Fidel was increasingly unhappy about his total dependence on the Russians. They had refused to finance any further his guerrilla groups in South America and held him financially responsible for many useless "aid" programs. "They give us nothing for nothing and then act as if showering us with gold." There seemed to be a tacit agreement between Premier Kosygin of Russia (who wanted increased trade) and President Nixon that the United States would not intervene in Cuba and Russia would not use the island for military bases, an agreement that did not enhance Fidel's regard for the United States. When Latin American diplomats were questioned in 1971 about inviting Cuba to return to the Organization of American States, Fidel castigated that body as a tool of the *Yanquis* and said it would be "a profane indecency" for Cuba to think of rejoining. Currently Russian predominance in the management of the Cuban economy seems to be persisting. Yet Cuba is drawing closer to the Latin American community and seems willing to take a more flexible line toward the United. States. And if the United States persists in its policy of isolating Cuba, some experts warn, it may succeed only in isolating itself.

City life in Havana has been deteriorating, for the urban middle classes have largely left the country and Cuban emphasis recently has been on the rural improvements of the *Campesino* Revolution. Although rents have been low and prices cheap, there is little to buy and people have to queue up for food. Seasonally they are dispatched to the countryside, undernourished as they are, to cut cane in the sun. With jobs scarce in the city and a puritanical prohibition of liquor and tobacco, city dwellers can only conclude that this was "not a revolution for city folks."

Fidel Castro has brought about a real social and economic revolution in Cuba. The ruling landowner class was dispossessed and the landless, jobless peasants have been given great psychological importance. But political life in the democratic sense is dead; there is a complete dictatorship. The press and radio are Fidel's mouthpieces, education has been made the instrument of *Fidelismo,* with resentment against the United States one of the principal keynotes. The economy has been totally changed. Castro's glaring failures and political penetration abroad has reduced his stature throughout the hemisphere.

Thus far the Cuban Revolution has been the most determined effort made to transform the social structure of a Latin American country. Whether Fidel's *Campesino* Revolution will prove to be an inspiring example to other depressed classes in Latin America, and how great its ultimate success will be within Cuba itself, is something the rest of the century will reveal.

Cubans had been making a unique contribution during the first half of this century to Western Hemisphere culture in a modernist movement in poetry, in prose, in music, and in art, that is called "Afro-Cubanism." Typical is the work of a mulatto poet named Nicholas Guillén (born in 1903) whose poems combine the sophistication of Europe with the music and rhythm of the black. Guillén wrote his poems on Negro life and on his own personal sorrows, which he called *sones,* with the syncopated rhythm of the African dance. Cuban rhumba music has four straight beats and a half beat, probably based on the old march of chained slaves, with four steps ahead and one side-ways to throw the chain out of the way. So Guillén's poetry has four and one half beats. One of his famous *sones* was even named "Four Anguishes and One Hope."

Other poets, not all Negro, wrote of the lives of the cane cutters and the city poor on Havana streets. The white Emilio Ballagas (1908–1954) wrote from an intimate knowledge of Negro folklore and psychology. Novelists in the 1930's to 1950's dealt with the problems of the poor field worker, as did Carlos Enríquez (born in 1901) in *Tilín García,* or with the hardships suffered by their ancestors in the slave trade, as did Carlos Montenegro (born in 1900) in *Men Without Women.* Sociologist Dr. Fernando Ortiz produced studies of African lore and its persistence in Cuba that are widely read by anthropologists today. Historians such as Carlos Manuel Trelles y Govín and authorities in international law such as Antonio Sánchez Bustamente y Soria made contributions to scholarship. But literary contributions of this kind no longer reached the Western world after the Cuban revolution in 1959, and for the outside world the journals and five daily papers of Havana no longer existed.

The Cuban music best known abroad is of the rhumba type reflected in much of Ernesto Lecuona's music (born in 1896), as in *"Danza Lucurni."* The famous ballet "La Revambaramba" written by Amadeo Roldán (1900–1939) is heavily influenced by Afro-Cuban themes. Alejandro García Caturla (1906–1940) produced orchestra music, often played in New York, which is, particularly in *Berceuse Campesina,* a "combination of African rhythm and cane cutters' melody." Both Roldán and Caturla have set Guillén's Afro-Cuban poems to music. Cuban painter Wilfredo Lam (born in 1902), half Chinese, half-Negro, was a leader in the Afro-Cuban art movement in Havana.

Haiti's first century as the French-speaking black republic

Unlike its sister republics, Haiti is a French-speaking all-black republic. It is one of the two small unstable republics on the island of Hispaniola, the island which was the first land to be cultivated by Europeans in the New World and the first Latin American country to win independence. The reader will remember the revolt of Toussaint L'Ouverture and his fellow slaves against the French owners of Haiti. The story of Haiti is different from that of the other Western Hemisphere nations from the beginning.

The first independent ruler of this devastated land was the illiterate and embittered Jean Jacques Dessalines, who declared the independence of Haiti on January 1, 1804. This declaration included only the western part of the island, which had few whites left, and had few educated ex-slaves who could help organize a government. The eastern portion remained under French and later Spanish forces.

In an elaborate coronation, Dessalines crowned himself Jacques I, Emperor of Haiti, and held formal court. But the ground lay uncultivated, ex-slaves went to the hills to live in primitive villages, and commerce remained at a standstill. The emperor let Henri Christophe, Toussaint's other ex-slave lieutenant, rule for him in the north of the island. Alexandre Pétion, an educated, liberal-minded mulatto, governed in the south at Aux Cayes. Occasionally Dessalines rode to one camp or the other with his bodyguard to issue proclamations and maintain stern army discipline. On one such occasion, his own dissatisfied troops ambushed and killed him.

It was Henri Christophe's turn to govern. He was perhaps twenty years younger than Toussaint, tall, straight-featured, coal black, and very proud. Nothing is known of his ancestry save that he was born a slave in the British West Indies, was taught the stonemason's trade at eight, ran away to be a cabin boy at twelve, and was sold by the ship captain in the harbor of Cap Haitien to a French naval officer going to fight for North Amrican freedom. Sold again later in Haiti to a free mulatto hotel keeper to serve as waiter and stable boy, he saw the mulatto Ogé, harbinger of Haitian freedom, tortured to death. When Toussaint's army came into the city, he joined as a sergeant.

At the death of Dessalines, Christophe called an election for an assembly that would write a constitution and choose a president. The northern provinces around Cap Haitien, known as the "State of Haiti," picked Christophe. The south, dominated by the mulatto freedmen, made a separate "Republic of Haiti" under Alexandre Pétion. For a decade there were skirmishes between the two areas. Henri Christophe at first called himself chief governor. At the end of a four-year term, he had himself made president for life. And on June 2, 1811, he was crowned Henri I.

Administratively, Christophe tried to follow Toussaint's example rather than Dessalines'. When he came to power, there had been no cultivation of the fields since the time before Napoleon's troops had come. Ex-slaves on the sugar plantations were living in straw huts built inside the roofless ruins of old mansions. All trade was by barter for there was no money in circulation. The West Indian jungle was moving in on the towns.

Using military force, Christophe established order and put the field hands back to work. Coffee was picked on the abandoned plantations and sold to England for cash to start a treasury. A small merchant marine was built in the docks of Cap Haitien to trade with other islands. English artisans were imported to start a weaving mill. In 1812 and 1813, reported the sea captains who handled his trade, 10 million pounds of sugar and equal quantities of coffee, cacao, and cotton were exported.

Christophe prospered personally. He lived in splendor and hired English physicians to care for him and English secretaries to handle his correspondence for he never learned to read and write well enough to do this for himself. He built not only a fancy personal palace, Sans Souci, but also a great citadel on a hilltop, Laferrière, the strongest single fortification in the New World and still a curiosity to tourists. He created an elaborate nobility with dukes, duchesses, and counts. Using his childhood stone-mason's training, he worked tirelessly on the construction projects himself. School buildings were begun in the town of Cap Haitien and teachers from France and the United States were invited to teach there. "While I live, I shall try to build the pride we need," said Christophe. "No one is indolent and dirty, for indolence and filth are forbidden by the emperor!"

But Haitians chafed under his rule. They felt that they had not fought the French only to become the slaves of Christophe. In Pétion's southern republic, villagers sat lazily in the sun and grass grew in the markets of Port-au-Prince; but the subjects of Christophe envied the life there. In 1820 Christophe had a paralytic stroke. His army deserted to Pétion and his people came to Sans Souci to kill him. "We dreamt so much, Toussaint, the Tiger and I, and we have done so little," he said, and blew his brains out with a special silver bullet he had cast just for that purpose.

Alexandre Pétion, born free to a mulatto woman, educated in France at the expense of his white father, had long dreamed of an ideal republic. He was twice elected president, and in 1816 he wrote a constitution which lasted until 1867, providing for a lifelong presidency and forbidding foreign ownership of property in Haiti. He had distributed the lands near Aux Cayes in small plots, leaving it up to the new owners whether they cultivated the plots or not. He was harassed by Christophe's northern soldiers and by internal dissension and civil war. Of all these hard-fighting Haitian leaders, he was the only one to die a natural death in the midst of his indolent people.

During his last illness, in 1819, he designated another free-born mulatto, Jean Pierre Boyer, to succeed him. Boyer's men took over Christophe's army and united Haiti again into one state. They inherited the empty treasury and uncultivated fields of the south, the growing caste system between the educated mulattoes and the black sons of slaves which had developed under Pétion, the anger against the government which had developed in the north under Christophe, and the lawless bandits and primitive villages of the interior.

Boyer ruled Haiti from 1819 to 1843. Not contented with his own disorganized area, he moved into the vacuum left by the removal of Spanish troops from Santo Domingo, the Spanish-speaking eastern half of the island, and ruled that part also. He won final recognition from France at the expense of an enormous indemnity payment and thus was saddled with a French debt that was never paid off. He distributed more land in small plots but his people quit growing the things for export that they had produced under forced labor in Christophe's time. A few educated mulattoes of Boyer's own class became a new aristocracy but there was no progress among the ex-slaves at the bottom.

As time went on, Boyer became more arbitrary. Finally he was overthrown in 1843 and sent into exile. Four years of confusion and barracks revolts followed, during which Haiti lost Santo Domingo, which broke away in 1844. Four different leaders, all Negroes, attempted to maintain the helm by military force until an illiterate ex-slave named Faustín Soulouque crowned himself Emperor Faustín I in 1847. He broke with the mulatto aristocracy and governed through a black army for 12 years.

Soulouque fell in 1859. For the next half century, Haiti averaged one new dictator every two-and-a-half years. Efforts were made to establish a sound currency, improve agriculture, start elementary schools, and to retake Santo Domingo—all to no avail. Some 90 per cent of the people remained illiterate. Black presidents, often illiterate, were backed by the army in throwing out mulatto presidents who often had been educated in Paris but who were concerned only with their own upper-class friends. A compromise ruler between the two racial groups, a dark mulatto named Nicolas Geffrard, held office from 1859 to 1867. He saved funds for elementary schools by cutting the army in half, aided agriculture, won recognition from the United States, and made a Concordat with the Vatican that established an organized French priesthood on the island for the first time since independence. But in 1867, he too was forced to flee and give way to chaos.

The period from 1879 to 1888 was a time of real progress under the administration of Paris-educated president Lysius Salomon. He created a national bank and stabilized the currency, encouraged import trade, opened some schools in country villages, and brought teachers of Parisian French from France to improve the almost unintelligible Haitian *patois* speech. Haiti gained some stature as a nation and became a member of the International Postal Union. But Salomon was ruthless to his opposition, and was followed by chaos. Of his successors, only two served more than a year in office, Florvil Hyppolite (1889–1896), a tyrant who brought some order in finances, and Tiresias Augustin Simon Sam (1896–1902), under whom some railroads were introduced and commerce increased with German investments. In the case of both men, fear of foreign complications sent them into exile. The first threat came in the 1890s when German warships appeared in the harbor threatening to collect by force some of Haiti's confusing debts.

In all these years, nothing effective was done to relieve the poverty, malnutrition, and ignorance of the masses. Public funds were spent on the ruling class, not on public works. Inflation of paper money, unpaid foreign debts, and chaotic government led directly to United States intervention in the 20th century. The only roads were mule trails unrepaired since Christophe's time. The only real workers were the farm women, who brought produce into town on their heads, then sat and sold it in the markets as their forebears had done in the villages of West Africa. Coffee was the only cash crop, but both coffee and sugar lands were left in a "wild state."

"At least two-thirds of the population," said a visitor, "do not speak any language recognized by the civilized world." Yet some excellent verse had been produced in the Haitian *patois*, called "creole," the most noteworthy of which was the work of Oswald Durand (1840–1896) whose love poem *Choucone* is well remembered today. The French bishop who came after the signing of the Concordat found little pure practice of Christianity

in the "cities" of Port-au-Prince and Cap Haitien, for the entire rural populace practiced the superstitious rituals of voodoo. Cut off from the rest of
the French-speaking world, out of tune with the Spanish culture of Latin
America, failing to develop a new middle class as descendants of an enslaved people, Haiti, for all the brave dreams of Toussaint, remained the
most backward Caribbean country until the twentieth century.

Haiti in the twentieth century

Much of Haiti's trouble today stems from the social structure of its population. An all-Negro republic, it nevertheless has a rigid class division. Of the
4,867,000 French and "creole"-speaking people in the country today, some
340,000 live in Port-au-Prince, and the rest in the much smaller centers of
Cap Haitien and Aux Cayes on the two opposite sides of the island or in the
rural area. A deep rift remains between the educated mulattoes, who live
chiefly in the cities, speak like Parisians and comprise perhaps three per cent
of the people, and the rural Negroes, 90 per cent of them illiterate, who
speak their special *patois* and live like West African villagers. In most years
since independence, the Negroes have controlled the army and through it
the presidency. The mulattoes have controlled the congress, the courts, and
the civil service. Turmoil has resulted, and progress has been impeded.

After several decades of more or less stable government, complete
political and financial bankruptcy came to Haiti in 1908. Eight different
presidents held office from 1908 to 1915, each backed by a private army of
cacos, the illiterate mountain farmers. Where did the money come from to
support these private armies? Some of it was left from loans made by
French, English, American, and German bankers who had supported one
president or another—loans that were never repaid. Since 1910, American
banking interests had tried to solidify Haitian finances. They began to fear
European intervention and the loss of their investments in 1915, when a new
leader, Guillaume Vilbrun Sam, was throwing the incumbent, Davilman
Théodore out of the presidential palace. They appealed to the American
government for aid, but the Europeans were fighting World War I and the
United States could not afford to see European forces clashing over Haiti.

The United States, even after tensions lessened, wanted guarantees
against future interference. President Sam tried to throw out the American
banking group, jailed his opponents, and had 167 of his political enemies
assassinated. When news of this became known, a mob attacked the palace,
Sam took refuge in the French embassy, and the mob broke into the building, pulled the president out from under a bed and tore him to pieces. The
next day, July 28, 1915, the United States Navy landed American marines to
protect the legation and took over many of the public services, including the
only source of revenue, the customs house.

The United States arranged a treaty by which the Haitians agreed
to American intervention for ten years. American specialists were to supervise finances, arrange payments to creditors, and control elections—an

arrangement that made Haiti an actual protectorate of the United States. No Haitian territory was to be ceded to any other nation. Americans were to organize the police, and to improve education, health, sanitation, and trade. The Haitian senate, having no choice in the matter, approved the treaty, and in 1917, it was extended to 20 years' duration. In 1918 it was amended to include American approval of legislation and a veto power by the American financial adviser on all expenditures. Then United States experts drafted a constitution for Haiti. It allowed foreigners to own land and encouraged the use of foreign capital.

This American "protection" was not popular. The city's mulatto civil service workers did not like to work under American army bosses. Some were irked over the loss of supervisory jobs and the graft that went with them. In the rural areas, American soldiers set up schools, drained swamps, and built the first real roads in the country; but they did this with the *corvée,* or forced black labor, working the Negro farmers without pay, under American officers, many of them Southerners who treated the Haitians with contempt as inferiors. But sewage systems and pure water supplies were built for Port-au-Prince and Cap Haitien; electricity was brought into these towns for the first time, and telephones were set up in public offices. The financial system was stabilized, efficiency increased, and peace and order reigned—but all revenues went to retire foreign loans. Little was done to alleviate the condition of the people.

Haitians had great pride in their country, the New World's only Negro republic, left unmolested by the white man for more than a century. They did not want to be "improved." They now had no say in their own government but were treated like children. Resentment became rebellion among the country people on the road gangs, and a guerrilla war flared in the backlands for two years. A United States Senate investigation in 1922 ended the worst abuses, and a new High Commissioner, General John H. Russell, was sent from the United States. Louis Borno, an intelligent and well-educated mulatto, was elected president and served two terms, from 1922 to 1930, a period of some achievement and progress. But when Borno's second term came to an end, the anti-American agitation erupted again. Political demonstrations, general strikes, and mob violence endangered American forces. A civilian commission under W. Cameron Forbes which President Hoover sent to investigate the situation formed a plan for withdrawal by 1936 and for sending civilians in place of army officials to direct Haitian affairs. Free, fair, and honest elections were held under Marine supervision according to this plan and in 1930, Sténio Vincent, a leader in the opposition to American occupation was elected president.

Washington by 1934 was developing the Good Neighbor Policy, and Franklin Roosevelt sent a United States Minister to Haiti as to any independent foreign state. Government controls such as police, finances, customs collection, and the school program were all turned over to President Vincent. By 1935, Haiti's finance was considered sound, even in the midst of world depression. In 1941, the American fiscal commission was withdrawn, and Haitian interests owned the national bank which had been American-run since 1910. Vincent changed the American-model constitution to provide for direct election of the president and to allow for his own re-election. He proved a more capable administrator than any of his predecessors. He met the depression by public works projects, and in general improved domestic conditions and Haiti's world position. However, he gave the people little power in the government, believing them not ready for democracy. He controlled affairs through the Haitian Guard and showed no respect for the civil rights of his enemies.

His major enemy was all Haiti's enemy, the Dominican dictator Trujillo next door. Seasonal laborers from Haiti often joined work crews to go across the mountains to help with the sugar-cane harvest in the Dominican Republic. In 1937, more than 60,000 Haitians were working there as migrants, and, because of hard times at home, many were planning to stay. Trujillo, who did not want any more "black blood" in his personal domain, sent his troops and aroused his people to stage a "pogrom," in which more than 15,000 migrants were slaughtered and their bodies thrown to the sharks. The United States government protested. Trujillo ended by paying damages to the Haitian government in the amount of $550,000. It was a tacit admission of responsibility for the death of 15,000 people, each Haitian being worth $37. Because President Vincent let Trujillo off so lightly, he lost popularity, and in 1941 he withdrew from the presidency.

He named as his successor Élie Lescot, a sophisticated Haitian who had been in Washington as the Haitian minister. His administration lasted five years, until 1946, the period of World War II. Right after Pearl Harbor, Lescot declared war on Japan and Germany, and he turned the nation's ports over for use of the Allies. Haitian workers found demand for their labor in producing new crops, and Haiti was kept from excess inflation and trade dislocation. But the end of the war brought a slump in Haiti's importance, and the workers had to go back to their little plots of land. Public dissatisfaction forced Lescot out of the presidency at the end of one term and put in a Negro from the rural area, Dumarsais Estimé, the first Negro after 30 years of rule by the mulatto élite.

He had been raised on a mountain farm, had worked as a rural school teacher and acquired a legal education, and had served as Lescot's Minister of Education. An idealist, interested in compulsory rural education and improved agriculture, he proved an able administrator. To finance public works, he levied an income tax, the first in Haitian history. He paid off the last of the old pre-1922 foreign debts. He was even able to live in peace with strong man Trujillo next door.

In spite of his success, the army which had brought him to power threw him out at the end of his legal term, and turned the presidency over to a military junta headed by General Paul Eugène Magloire. Overriding a measure against military presidents, Magloire was elected in 1951 in a nationwide popular election. A very dark Negro, son of a mountain peasant, Magloire had served in the capital as aide-de-camp to President Sténio Vincent and had been chosen chief of police. He had made and unmade presidents who had preceded him. A black who had served his political apprenticeship under mulattoes, Magloire was determined to end the long rift between blacks and mulattoes in Haitian politics. He meant to concentrate on long-range technological advances which would help both city and country. The country's currency was sound, it was unburdened by heavy debt, the people were small landowners, there were no large plantations and foreign absentee owners. The problem of the Haitians was one of ignorance in the best use of the land.

The black "patch and thatch" farmer of Haiti owns his own land but resents outside teaching. He has no contact with the outside world. His language has no written literature and is scarcely understandable to a Frenchman or a Port-au-Prince intellectual. The poor and illiterate hill and village people had kept their native religion, African animism, and combined it with a thin veneer of Catholicism. This "fetishistic" religion, called voodoo, is of great interest to anthropologists.

For these people, President Magloire in 1951 announced a five-year plan for agricultural improvement. United Nations experts and technicians from the United States helped to develop the badly eroded Artibonite Valley on a TVA-like plan. Some 80,000 acres were to be reclaimed for use over a nine-year period, to produce diversified crops under small farm ownership. Included in the plans were more agricultural schools, the purchase and use of tractors by village cooperatives, cooperative banks for small-farm credit, and a system of county farm agents. Also planned for the late 1950's were better breeding of cattle, better rural elementary education, better health campaigns against the prevalent yaws and malaria—this with the help of the United Nations health agency. To impress his people, Magloire maintained through all this planning and improvement a formal "court" with emphasis on balls and fancy uniforms.

He failed to impress all of them enough. When it became evident that he intended to prolong his legal term, he was forced out of office in December 1956 by a general strike. In the next year, strife-torn Haiti had seven different governments. In September 1957, after eight months of anarchy, junta rule, and near-bankruptcy, Haiti elected François Duvalier president. Ironically, the president, a doctor who had worked in the campaign to eliminate yaws, made his first major speech on the 151st anniversary of the assassination of Jean Jacques Dessalines, the founder of the republic. Feeling himself threatened in mid-1959 by the opposition he himself had exiled and by Fidel Castro's Cubans, he clamped down on the country with strong-arm dictatorial methods. In 1961, he declared himself re-elected for a six-year term, and in 1964, he proclaimed himself president for life.

The uneducated country people loved him and called him "Papa Doc." The educated city people he controlled with his ferocious personal army of terrorists called the *tonton macoute*. He asked the Haitians to vote on the country's 20th constitution, which named him permanent president and gave him sweeping powers, but the ballot used for the vote was simply a piece of paper containing the one word "oui," yes. Duvalier himself said, "I am an exceptional man, the kind the country could produce once every half-century. I am the personification of the Haitian people, and only God can take my power from me."

On April 21, 1971, the 63-year-old dictator died. Before he died he had several times asked his people to vote his only son as his successor. This was the 19-year-old, 200-pound athlete, Jean Claude, an inexperienced young playboy. There were no "no" votes. Jean Claude took over the administration, and said, "My mission is to improve health and education, to abolish hunger, and build a new Haiti that is generous and progressive." He opened Haiti to the return of its citizens from exile.

A year later, Haiti seemed to face a brighter future. No more than one in ten can read and write or has a job, but the fear that pervaded the country has vanished. Exiles have come drifting back. Jean Claude shares authority with his mother and three cabinet members who have established a climate of stability and confidence that has brought financial aid trickling back in, not only from the United States but from various international financial and development agencies. The future is still uncertain but now there is hope.

Modern artistic endeavor in Haiti has received recognition abroad and has, like the Cuban, been built around the African slave theme. In Port-au-Prince, the *Centre d'Art Moderne* provides art instruction and has a gallery for exhibiting the work of Haitians who show an interest in developing native themes. Prizes in Pan American novel contests have been won by two brothers named Philippe and Pierre Marcelin (born in 1904 and 1908 respectively) whose works *Canapé-Vert* and *The Beast of the Haitian Hills* deal with Haitian peasant life. In the 1950s, Haitian art which portrays native farm and market life in a brilliant primitive style became very popular in the United States and Paris. An exotic native-type music with many African characteristics has been developed by several Haitian composers, the most original of whom was Justin Elie (1883–1931) who found inspiration in voodoo chants. Most gifted in recent times is Alain Chérie.

The French-speaking mulattoes have sought to orient themselves toward Parisian culture and have not interested themselves in this renaissance of peasant art and culture. They read their well-edited daily newspapers and French-language reviews, but their writings have not been taken seriously in France and are not known to the rest of the New World. They are cut off by their language from the mainstream of Latin American affairs; and the dictatorship of Duvalier, which silenced many of their publications and drove many of them into exile, forced an even deeper rift between the Negro masses and the mulatto élite.

Santo Domingo: a Spanish-speaking appendage of Haiti

In 1820, the eastern end of Hispaniola, Spain's first colony in the New World, had been the loyal province of Santo Domingo. It was twice as big as Haiti to the west but had less than half as many people in the middle of the century, and its history has been clouded by the shadow of its more spectacular neighbor. Toussaint had held Santo Domingo temporarily in 1801, but the French-speaking Haitians had been ousted by the Spaniards; then in 1821, after a weak republic had been set up, Haitian forces under Pierre Boyer had re-conquered it.

The Dominican people, only 20 per cent black, had no pride in Negro blood and resented Haitian dominance. Their young men were forced into the Haitian army, their university was closed, their church officials were shut off from access to papal authority. What little there had been of culture and religion and of trade and city life in the decadent Spanish colony deteriorated further under the rule of the Haitians. A youth society, the *Trinitaria*, dedicated to "God, Fatherland, and Liberty" planned rebellion. When Boyer was exiled by the Haitians in 1843, they declared their independence in 1844. They were strong enough in the 1850's to expel Faustín Soulouque when he attempted a reconquest. The struggling little republic continued to suffer from Haitian raids and had little success in self-government at home.

For the three decades after Faustín's defeat, Dominicans were dominated alternately by the pro-American Buenaventura Báez, who would have liked to have the country annexed to the United States (and even dickered with President Grant over the possibility), and the pro-Spanish Pedro Santana, who actually brought the independent Santo Domingo back under Spanish control. While the United States was preoccupied with her Civil War, Queen Isabella II, the weak Spanish queen, was proclaimed guardian of Santo Domingo, and her "governor," Santana, ruled in her name with an iron hand. The Dominicans who hated reduction to colonial status went underground, and in the end controlling them proved too costly to Spain. After the "War of Restoration," Spain withdrew, and the pro-American Báez was in control again. But he was to be out of power five times before 1878.

The 1880's brought another absolutist Christophe-type dictator to power in Santo Domingo, Ulises Heureaux, the illegitimate son of former slaves from Haiti and the Virgin Islands. Well-educated, shrewd, he was "an Apollo in physical build, courageous and of extraordinary stamina." In 1882 he began a 17-year dictatorship in which he cowed all opposition by bribery, bullying, and murder. He was an able adminstrator, and during his administration both agriculture and commerce prospered as American capital ventured into sugar. But he turned finances over to the "Santo Domingo Improvement Company" which helped itself and Heureaux personally but sank Santo Domingo further into debt. Shortly after the end of his rule the government owed various foreign countries over $30 million, a debt which brought foreign intervention in the early 20th century. Heureaux did not live to reap the whirlwind his poor finance had sown for he was assassinated in 1899 by a political enemy.

Santo Domingo, nevertheless, maintained a higher standard of culture than its near neighbor, for educated plantation owners and city creoles had not been driven out or killed as had the French whites next door. Its creole families produced some writers who came to be known to all Latin America. Señora Salomé Ureña de Henríquez (1850–1897), who had founded a high school for girls, encouraged teacher-training, and promoted public elementary education, had also found time to write sad poetry on Dominican history which was widely read in other Spanish-speaking countries. Her husband, a noted physician, and president of Santo Domingo in the early 1900's, and both her sons, Max and Pedro, achieved literary fame as great as her own. Santo Domingo also claims one of the advanced political and social philosophers of the 1890's, Eugenio María de Hostos (1839–1903), a Puerto Rican who came to Santo Domingo as an exile in the 1880's and, while teaching, found time to write prolifically in the cause of Cuban and Puerto Rican independence.

the Dominican Republic in the twentieth century

Dominicans consider themselves cultured in the Spanish tradition. They belong to poetry clubs and literary societies, read the best novels of Spanish America, and write novels in the same style. They pride themselves on being descendants of the earliest Spanish colonists. Less than 20 per cent of the total population of 4,325,000 live in the one large metropolitan area of Santo Domingo, but they are in general much more attuned to modern life than the Haitians. Their wealthiest people enter into international society as sophisticated Latins. Yet their country, like Haiti and Nicaragua, was occupied by United States military forces during the first third of the 20th century, and has been dominated by one of the most ruthless of modern dictators during the great part of the second third.

The assassination of the picturesque black dictator, Ulises Heureaux, resulted in five years of revolution and anarchy. If yearly payments had been made on the money that had been borrowed from European firms, they would have consumed all but $100,000 of the national income. In 1903 and 1904, France and other nations threatened to collect the debt payments by force. By arrangement with the almost defunct government, Theodore Roosevelt in October 1904 took over one of the customs houses and acted as receiver for the bankrupt nation, first pledging that the United States would recognize the territorial integrity of the republic. The United States would administer the finances, pay 55 per cent of the customs revenue on the debts, and give 45 per cent to the Dominican government. A later treaty, in 1907, provided that customs receivership should continue as long as bonds were outstanding. Many Americans, and Dominicans, opposed such intervention, but it cannot be denied that the Dominican government received much more revenue under this arrangement than it had when the entire customs were in charge of corrupt officials. More money was collected yearly than the creditors demanded, and much of it was available for local public works.

Politically, however, the interference did more harm than good, even though the United States was at first merely in charge of finances, without military occupation. In the chaotic political upheavals of the country, the United States interests seemed always to be on one side or the other. In 1915, after an especially chaotic period of disorder, a distinguished physician, Francisco Enríquez y Carvajal, was chosen interim president. He was to make arrangements with the United States acceptable to both nations and to supervise the next election. But Enríquez' party rejected the treaty suggested by the United States, whereupon American financial agents refused his government any money. After five months of deadlock, in November 1916, Captain Harry S. Knapp of the United States Navy landed in the Dominican Republic and announced its military occupation for repeated violation of the agreement with Theodore Roosevelt. A direct military government was established under the United States Navy Department. But this direct American rule was not carried out through puppet presidents as was done in Haiti, for the proud Dominicans refused to serve as such puppets. The subterfuge was therefore maintained that this was "an independent state under temporary occupation."

This government, with martial law and occupation troops, lasted eight years. In the way of material betterment, much was accomplished, for finances were efficiently administered, the bureaucracy was trimmed to reason and trained in civil service, schools and sanitation were improved, and a civilian police force was organized. Streets were paved and harbor facilities improved. But even those who approved of military action found much reason for shame in the occupation. The United States army withdrew its best officers when the country became involved in World War I and sent inefficient, prejudiced men and raw recruits into the occupation, none of whom tried to learn the Spanish language or understand Latin American customs. The Dominicans remained hostile and uncooperative. Resentment ran alarmingly high when a distinguished young poet, Fabio Fiallo, was jailed for denouncing the United States. Woodrow Wilson, himself sympathetic, suggested withdrawing all American influence save the control of finances, but for the Dominicans it was "all or nothing at all."

The Harding administration in 1922 sent the resourceful Sumner Welles to work out a plan for effective withdrawal. Horacio Vásquez, the candidate Welles favored, was backed by a coalition of parties and was elected in a supervised but fair vote. When he came to Washington, he was treated as an equal and he returned to be inaugurated for a four-year term. American techincal experts were allowed to remain quietly behind the scenes but American troops were all withdrawn by 1924. With revenues thus stabilized, Vásquez continued the public works program as a purely Dominican venture and gained credit in the eyes of his people. At the end of his term, after a period of prosperity and relative political tranquility, he became ill, and went to the United States for treatment, assuming that he would be re-elected. But as soon as his back was turned, a group of generals under Rafael Trujillo attempted to take over the government. Vásquez had assured the United States there would be no more bloody revolutions. Now he adjusted to the situation when he returned from the hospital by resigning, due to "ill health." Backed by the army, Trujillo took over the government, holding an election in May 1930 in which he himself was elected.

Thus, in 1930, began the "Year One" of the Era of Trujillo.

Opportunistic like Somoza, oppressive like Machado, Rafael Leónidas Trujillo Molina (born in 1893) had been a cattle rustler, like Venezuela's Gómez, before he joined the army. Soon he became chief-of-staff and made the constabulary his private army. And in 1930 he became an absolute ruler and remained so until his death in 1961. Santo Domingo, a city once ruled by Columbus, was renamed Trujillo, as were many villages, plazas, and streets. The dictator owned 20 private residences, a majority of all small industries, and one-fifth of all the agricultural land of the republic, for Trujillo was interested in cattle whether "rustled" or legally confiscated. He served four times as president and had puppets in office between his own terms. His brother Hector served as president, and in May 1957 was re-elected for another full term. Lucrative positions in the government were held by his six brothers, all his minor relatives, and his many children, legitimate and otherwise. Over the entrance to hospitals appeared the inscription, "Only Trujillo Cures You." Those whose democratic idealism he did not "cure" were either dead or elsewhere. His opponents in exile formed a powerful "Caribbean Legion" in 1948 but failed to land on Dominican soil. They collected sympathetic exiles from other dictatorships and fought for Costa Rica in a fracas with Nicaragua.

Slated as Trujillo's "heir" after his death was his 28-year old son and favorite, a pampered young playboy of the international "jet set." But in the meantime, the whole "republic" was his well-kept garden. Nearly 70 per cent of Dominicans worked for Trujillo. Even his office-holding relatives worked long, strictly supervised hours at specific responsibilities, and Trujillo himself was indefatigable, having a businessman's knowledge of his entire "estate," both public and private. He and his family busily salted away hundreds of millions in profit in Swiss banks while he maintained lobbyists abroad to build up a favorable image.

He was despised by other Western Hemisphere peoples, but none hated Trujillo as much as the people of Haiti. He had encouraged the prejudice of his people against the darker Haitians, and when his anti-Haitian policy hit the world's headlines during the massacre of Haitian field workers in 1937, he tried to balance this adverse publicity by offering to take in displaced war refugees from Europe. Few ever arrived. He had declared war on the Axis powers right after Pearl Harbor, profited from the wartime trade, and paid his debts. American control of finances was ended by treaty in 1941. He boasted about being completely out of debt to foreign nations but gladly accepted American economic and military aid in the 1950s for the fight against "Communism."

Rural areas were more prosperous than in neighboring Haiti. The farms were more level and fertile, with more water on level land for irrigation. Sugar remained the major crop. The world's largest sugar refinery, the Rio Haina, was in the Dominican Republic. Exports of bananas, coffee, and cacao had increased. Although a million or more Dominicans still lived on their tiny "patch and thatch" farms, the country as a whole was self-sufficient in food. Anyone who did not like the "patrón" system of farming under Trujillo's henchmen had his farm taken over directly by the dictator.

The Dominican Republic was culturally backward but it did produce a few figures in art and literature who became well-known. The two sons of the great nineteenth-century woman writer and educator Doña Salomé Ureña de Henríquez achieved wider fame than did their mother. Pedro Henríquez Ureña (1884–1946) was a distinguished literary critic and anthologist of Latin American literature. In painting, a leading figure was Abelardo Rodríquez Urdaneta, who for 25 years was director of the Dominican Academy of Fine Arts—which was widely advertised by Trujillo's lobbyists as a cultural center. But 56 per cent of the four million Dominicans were illiterate and lived in a culture little better than it had been in the 16th century.

In mid-1959, Trujillo was blaming *Fidelismo* for the rising tide of discontent among Dominicans and turned to the Organization of American States for help against *Fidelista* infiltrators. He himself had been playing host to dictators, Perón, Pérez Jiménez, and Batista, who had been ousted recently from other Latin American countries. In 1960 Venezuela produced evidence that Trujillo's agents had tried to assassinate the country's liberal President Betancourt and appealed to the Organization of American States to censure Trujillo. A motion was made that its members break relations with the Dominican Republic and place an embargo on trade with Trujillo. Trujillo dealt with the problem of Hemisphere opposition by clamping down on what little opposition he had at home.

A plot against him was formed by younger officers in his own private army, led by Colonel Antonio Imbert Barrera, who were angry at long delays in promotion. In May 1961, three of them ambushed and shot the old dictator on a lonely road as he was driving to meet a current girl friend. Gone was the glory of "God and Trujillo," the "Benefactor of the Patria." Six months of tyranny and chaos followed in Dominican politics. The puppet vice-president, Joaquín Balaguer, vied for power with Trujillo's own brothers and the favorite heir, Rafael Trujillo, Jr. American naval vessels stood off shore to protect American citizens. In January 1962, all members of the Trujillo family and close intimates fled the country to live "happily ever afterward" on their Swiss savings.

A Council of Government ran the uneasy country throughout 1962 and called for an election for December 20th, to be supervised by the OAS. Eight political parties had mushroomed in the confusion, but support grouped on the right around a conservative businessmen's party and on the moderate left around the PRD or Popular Revolutionary Democrats who had outlawed Castro-ite Communists from their midst. The PRD won the election with a 62 per cent of the vote. Their candidate was Juan Bosch, son of Catalán and German parents, a novelist and political science teacher, who had been working against Trujillo from exile for nearly two decades. He was a close friend of Betancourt's and of the Costa Rican liberal "Pepe" Figueres.

With a controlling vote in congress, Bosch started to push the inexperienced new "democracy" toward democratic reforms as rapidly as possible. He tried to distribute Trujillo farm lands to the peasants, but met a legal block in court action from the families who had owned the land before it was confiscated by Trujillo. He tried to nationalize all the Trujillo business enterprises but met the opposition of businessmen who hoped to share in profits themselves. Army men feared that Bosch would end the political power of the officers who had staged the assassination of Trujillo. And so, in spite of American backing, Bosch fell from power after only seven months. In September 1963, a military and civilian junta exiled him to Puerto Rico and took over the government. Leading the coup were Colonel Imbert, who had killed Trujillo, and a fanatical anti-Communist of Lebanese descent, General Elías Wessin y Wessin, who believed every act of Bosch was Castro-inspired. The junta was soon dominated by a businessman of Scottish descent, Donald Reid Cabral, who ruled the country with United States recognition and financial aid.

With six of the political parties still active and protesting, Reid Cabral's rule could not be tyrannical. It was only inept and corrupt. It was torn between the rightist military leaders and the active Communists who fed on the disappointment of the masses in the empty promises of the post-Trujillo governments. Reid set the date for elections on September 1, 1965, but the restive factions could not wait. A revolution led by Bosch sympathizers exploded with violence in the streets of Santo Domingo on April 25, 1965, aided by junior officers who passed out arms to the street fighters in the name of the exiled Juan Bosch. The fighters threatened to attack embassies and hotels where there were hundreds of foreigners.

The United States Marines returned to Santo Domingo after an absence of 31 years. President Johnson was anxious to prevent another Castro-type Communist takeover in the Caribbean. On the excuse that American lives were in danger, he quickly sent thousands of American marines and paratroopers to the Republic. American forces soon controlled the central part of the city. Another section of the city was soon in the hands of the army officers under Colonel Imbert and Wessin y Wessin—although the latter was forced under American pressure to resign as too "rightist" a figure. The other third of the city, the slums and the port, was held by an opportunist named Colonel Francisco Camaaño Deno in the name of Juan Bosch. It was feared that this group contained many Castro sympathizers. Arms and ammunition were found somewhere for 15,000 guerrilla street fighters.

Johnson was widely criticized for this quick, large-scale, unilateral action which was in violation of treaties pledging no intervention without joint action. The name "Johnson Doctrine" was given to attempts to stop the spread of Caribbean Communism by United States military action. By a narrow margin, the Organization of American States voted to send in a military force, the first vote of its kind in history. In the following weeks, Brazil sent 1,200 men and a general to command the entire military effort, and token contingents came from a few other Latin American nations.

The combined force, still largely American, was called the OAS Peace Force. Except for sporadic sniping, this force did bring about a stalemate in August 1965. Among the many different missions that tried to work out a democratic solution to the problem and prevent both a Castro-type takeover and further bloodshed were an OAS mission, Figueres and Betancourt as friends of Bosch, a papal nuncio, and McGeorge Bundy as Johnson's personal representative. But no one could ascertain just how serious the actual threat of Communism had been.

Finally, after four months of negotiations and gunfire, both Imbert and Camaaño resigned their "commands." Bosch and Balaguer, Trujillo's vice-president, had each returned to the island as private individuals. A compromise provisional president, Hector García Godoy, took office September 3, 1965, the Republic's 47th president. Backed by the OAS Peace Force, he cleared both parts of the city of armed men and reinstated regular traffic and food sales, and an uneasy peace settled on the oldest city in the Western Hemisphere.

Riots continued in smaller towns well into 1966. American forces were to be withdrawn after elections which were scheduled for June 1, 1966. Both Joaquín Balaguer and Juan Bosch campaigned actively for the presidency but in a peaceable, moderating spirit. Balaguer won by a 140,000 margin out of the 1,270,000 votes cast. He was peacefully inaugurated on July 1, 1966, and in the following month, the last 8,000 OAS troops, 6,300 of them from the United States, were withdrawn. A few United States officers remained as advisers for President Balaguer's national guard. Free from control by the Trujillo family, Balaguer proved a good administrator. Bosch supporters entered his coalition cabinet as he promised to "operate with a scalpel on those old ulcers of Dominican progress, inflation, corruption, political favoritism, and inefficiency." The Castro leftists were so weakened by the spring of 1967 that they failed dismally in an attempt to call a nation-wide anti-Balaguer strike, since more people than usual came to work on the day of the announced protest.

Balaguer, who used a low-key, conciliatory approach, can be credited with curbing inflation, attracting capital, and balancing the budget. He also meant to keep the press and radio free and the people informed. The gross national product improved more than 6 per cent a year between 1966 and 1970. There had been heavy commitments of United States economic aid. In April 1970, Balaguer announced that he would run again for president, as the amended constitution would have allowed; and despite cries of "*continuoismo*" and fear of a "permanent president," Balaguer won the election against four candidates in an open, hotly debated contest. He was inaugurated peacefully for a second four years in August 1970. He will need a great deal of experience and skill to keep the military in check until 1974 and to keep the country stable and inching toward prosperity.

READINGS: THE CARIBBEAN

Aguilar, L. E., ed., *Marxism in Latin America* (1968).
————, *Cuba 1933: Prologue to Revolution* (1972).
Aimes, H. S., *History of Slavery in Cuba 1511–1848* (1929; 1967).

Alexander, R. J., *Communism in Latin America* (1957).

———, *Organized Labor in Latin America* (1965).

Alexis, S., *Black Liberator—Life of Toussaint L'Ouverture* (1949).

Arciniegas, G., *The Caribbean: Sea of the New World*, trans. H. de Onis (1946).

Atkins, G. P. and L. C. Wilson, *The United States and the Trujillo Regime* (1972).

Balch, E. G., et al., *Occupied Haiti* (1927).

Beals, C., *Crime of Cuba* (1934).

Bemis, S. F., *Latin American Policy of the United States* (1943).

Bernardo, R. M., *The Theory of Moral Incentives in Cuba* (1971).

A Bilingual Report on the Dominican Republic Today (1964).

Blackwell, A. S., *Some Spanish American Poets* (1929).

Blanchard, P., *Democracy and Empire in the Caribbean* (1947).

Bonsal, P. W., *Cuba, Castro and the United States* (1971).

Boorstein, E., *Economic Transformation of Cuba* (1968).

Bosch, J., et al., *The Dominican Republic* (1964).

———, *The Unfinished Experiment: Democracy in the Dominican Republic* (1965).

Buell, R. L., ed., *Problems of the New Cuba* (1935).

Burks, D. D., *Cuba under Castro* (1964).

Caldwell, R. G., *The López Expeditions to Cuba, 1848–1851* (1915).

Callcott, W. H., *Caribbean Policy of the United States, 1890–1920* (1942).

Carr, R., ed., *Latin American Affairs, St. Anthony's Papers No. 22* (1970).

Castro, F., *Fidel Castro Speaks*, ed. by M. Kenner (1969).

Castro Hidalgo, Orlando, *Spy for Fidel* (1972).

Center for Strategic Studies, *Dominican Action 1965: Intervention or Cooperation?* (1966).

Chang-Rodríguez, E., ed., *The Lingering Crisis: A Case Study of the Dominican Republic* (1969).

Chapman, C. E., *History of the Cuban Republic* (1927).

Chase, G., *Contemporary Art in Latin America* (1970).

Chester, E. A., *A Sergeant Named Batista* (1954).

Clytus, J., *Black Man in Red Cuba* (1970).

Coester, A., *Literary History of Spanish America* (rev. ed., 1928).

Corbitt, D. C., *A Study of the Chinese in Cuba 1847–1945* (1971).

Corkan, H., *Patterns of International Cooperation in the Caribbean, 1942–1969* (1970).

Corwin, A. F., *Spain and the Abolition of Slavery in Cuba 1817–1886* (1967).

Courlander, H., *The Drum and the Hoe: Life and Lore of the Haitian People* (1960).

Crasmiller, R. D., *Trujillo* (1966).

Dana, R. H., *To Cuba and Back*, ed. C. Gardiner (1965).

Davis, H. P., *Black Democracy—The Story of Haiti* (rev. ed., 1936).

Dewart, L., *Christianity and Revolution: The Lessons of Cuba* (1963).

De Young, M., *Man and Land in the Haitian Economy* (1953).

Diederich, B. and A. L. Burt, *Papa Doc: The Truth About Haiti Today* (1969).

Dierks, J. C., *A Leap to Arms: The Cuban Campaign of 1898* (1970).

Divine, R. A., *The Cuban Missile Crisis* (1968).

Draper, T., *Castroism Theory and Practise* (1965).

———, *Castro's Revolution-Myths and Realities* (1962).

———, *Dominican Revolt: A Case Study in American Policy* (1968).

Dreier, J. C., *The Organization of American States and the Hemisphere Crisis* (1962).

Dubois, J., *Danger over Panama* (1964).

Espaillat, A., *Trujillo: The Last Caesar* (1963).

Fagen, R. R., *Transformation of Political Culture in Cuba* (1969).

———, and L. A. Cornelius, eds., *Political Power in Latin America: Seven Confrontations* (1970).

Fagg, J. E., *Cuba, Haiti, and the Dominican Republic* (1965).

Fergusson, E., *Cuba* (1946).

Fitzgibbon, R. H., *Cuba and the United States, 1900–1935* (1935).

Foner, P. S., *History of Cuba and Its Relations with the United States* (2 vols., 1962–1963).

Foreign Policy Association, *Cuban Crisis: A Documentary Record* (1963).

Fox, A. B., *Freedom and Welfare in the Caribbean* (1949).

Gilly, A., *Inside the Cuban Revolution* (1964).

Goldenberg, B., *The Cuban Revolution and Latin America* (1965).

Goldwert, M., *The Constabulary in the Dominican Republic and Nicaragua —Progeny and Legacy of United States Intervention* (1962).

Gonzalez, E., *Revolutionary Change in Cuba: Polity, Economy, Society* (1971).

Gott, R., *Guerrilla Movements in Latin America* (1971).

Gray, R. B., *José Martí, Cuban Patriot* (1962).

Hall, G. M., *Social Control in Slave Plantation Societies: A Comparison of St. Dominque and Cuba* (1972).

Halperin, E., *Castro and Latin American Communism* (1963).

———, *Castro's Cuba* (1966).

———, *The Ideology of Castroism and Its Impact on the Communist Parties of Latin America* (1963).

Hamill, H. M., Jr., *Dictatorship in Latin America* (1965).

Harris, S. G., ed., *Economic Problems of Latin America* (1965).

Henly, D. F., *The United States in Cuba, 1898–1902* (1963).

Herskovits, M., *Life in a Haitian Village* (1937).

Hicks, A., *Blood in the Streets: Life and Rule of Trujillo* (1946).

Holly, J. T., *Black Separatism and the Caribbean*, ed. H. H. Bell (1970).

Horowitz, I. L., *Cuban Communism* (1970).

Horowitz, M. M., ed., *Peoples and Cultures of the Caribbean* (1971).

Howland, C. P., ed., *Survey of American Foreign Relations* (1929).

Howland, C. P., ed., *American Foreign Relations in the Caribbean* (1929).

Huberman, C. and P. Sweezy, *Socialism in Cuba* (1969).

Humboldt, A. F. von, *Island of Cuba* (1856).

Iglesias, J., *In the Fist of the Revolution: Life in a Cuban Town* (1968).

International Bank of Reconstruction and Development, *Report on Cuba* (1951).

Ireland, G., *Boundaries, Possessions and Conflicts in North America and the Caribbean* (1941).

Jackson and Castro, *Castro, The Kremlin, and Communism in Latin America* (1970).

James, P., *Geography of Latin America* (2nd ed., 1950).

Jenks, L. H., *Our Cuban Colony* (1928).

Johnson, H., *Bay of Pigs: The Leader's Story of Brigade 2506* (1964).

Johnson, S. H., *The Negro in the New World* (1910).

Johnson, W. F., *History of Cuba* (5 vols., 1920).

Jones, C. L., *Caribbean Backgrounds and Prospects* (1931).

————, *Caribbean Since 1900* (1936).

Karol, K. S., *Guerrillas in Power: The Course of the Cuban Revolution* (1970).

Kernan, M. and J. Petras, eds., *Fidel Castro Speaks* (1969).

Knight, F. W., *Slave Society in Cuba during the Nineteenth Century* (1970).

Knight, M. M., *Americans in Santo Domingo* (1928).

Kurzman, D., *Santo Domingo: Revolt of the Damned* (1965).

Lago, C. M., and R. E. Hernández Morales, *Social Security in Cuba* (1964).

Langley, L. D., *The Cuban Policy of the United States: A Brief History* (1968).

Langley, L. D., ed., *United States, Cuba and the Cold War: American Failure or Communist Conspiracy?* (1970).

Latortue, G. R., *Feudal Haiti: Caribbean Crisis* (1966).

Leon, L. A., *Cuba 1933: A Revolutionary Prologue* (1971).

Leyburn, J. G., *Haitian People* (1941).

Lieuwen, E., *Generals versus Presidents* (1964).

Lizaso, F., *Martí, Martyr of Cuban Independence* (1953).

Lockmiller, D. A., *Magoon in Cuba: A History of Second Intervention, 1906–1909* (1938).

Lockwood, L., *Castro's Cuba, Cuba's Fidel* (1967).

Logan, R. W., *Diplomatic Relations of the United States with Haiti, 1776–1891* (1941).

————, *Haiti and the Dominican Republic* (1968).

Lowenthal, A. F., *The Dominican Intervention* (1972).

MacGaffy, W., and C. H. Burnett, *Cuba, Its People, Its Society, Its Culture* (1962).

————, *Twentieth-Century Cuba, the Background of the Castro Revolution* (1965).

Mallin, J., *Caribbean Crisis: Subversion fails in the Dominican Republic* (1965).

Manach, J., *Martí: Apostle of Freedom,* trans. C. Taylor (1950).

Manigat, L. F., *Haiti of the Sixties* (1964).

Martin, J. B., *Overtaken by Events* (1966).

Mathews, H. L., *The Cuban Story* (1961).

————, *Return to Cuba,* 1964. [A Reply to this was published by Association for Reconstruction of Cuban Economy, Miami University, 1964.]

————, *Fidel Castro* (1969).

McCrocklin, J. H., *Garde d'Haiti, 1915–1934* (1956).

Mecham, J. L., *Survey of United States–Latin American Relations* (1965).

Mellender, G. A., *Handbook on Cuba* (1962).

Mesa-Lago, C., ed., *Revolutionary Change in Cuba* (1971).

Meyer, K. E. and T. Sculc, *The Cuban Invasion: The Chronicle of a Disaster* (1962).

Millet, A. R., *The Politics of Intervention: the Military Occupation of Cuba 1906–1909* (1968).

Millis, W., *The Martial Spirit* (1931).

Millspaugh, A. C., *Haiti Under American Control, 1915–1930* (1931).

Mitchell, H., *Contemporary Politics and Economics in the Caribbean* (1968).

Monchon, J., and K. O. Gilmore, *The Great Deception* (1963).

Montague, L. L., *Haiti and the United States 1714–1938* (1940).

Moreno, J. A., *Barrios in Arms, Revolt in Santo Domingo* (1970).

Mörner, M., *Race and Class in Latin America* (1970).

Morray, J. P., *The Second Revolution in Cuba* (1962).

Munro, D. G., *Intervention and Dollar Diplomacy in the Caribbean, 1900–1921* (1964).

————, *United States and the Caribbean* (1934).

Nelson, L., *Rural Cuba* (1950).

Niles, B., *Black Haiti* (1926).

Noyes, R., *Investment in the Caribbean* (1964).

O'Connor, J., *Origins of Socialism in Cuba* (1970).

Ortiz y Fernández, F., *Cuban Counterpoint: Tobacco and Sugar*, trans., H. de Onís (1947).

Osorio Lizarazo, J. A., *Birth and Growth of Anti-Trujillism in America* (1958).

Pachter, H. M., *Collision Course: The Cuban Missile Crisis and Co-existence* (1963).

Perkins, D., *United States and the Caribbean* (1947).

Petras, J. F. and R. Laporte, Jr., *Cultivating Revolution: The United States and Agrarian Reform in Latin America* (1971).

Phillips, R. H., *Cuba: Island of Paradox* (1960).

Pike, F. B., ed., *Latin American History* (1969).

Political, Economic, and Social Thought of Fidel Castro (1959).

Puech-Parham, A. de, *My Odyssey: Experience of a Young Refugee from Two Revolutions by a Creole of Saint Domingue* (1959).

Rauch, B., *American Interest in Cuba, 1848–1855* (1948).

Rippy, J. F., *Caribbean Danger Zone* (1940).

Rivero, N., *Castro's Cuba* (1962).

Roberts, W. A., *Caribbean: Story of Our Sea of Destiny* (1940).

Roberts, W. A., *The Caribbean* (1940).

Rodman, S., *Haiti: The Black Republic* (1954).

————, *Quisqueya: A History of the Dominican Republic* (1962).

Rodríguez, E. C., *The Lingering Crisis: A Case Study of the Dominican Republic* (1969).

Rotberg, R. J., and C. K. Clague, *Haiti: The Politics of Squalor* (1970).

Rubens, H. S., *Liberty-The Story of Cuba* (1932).

Ruiz, R. E., *Cuba: The Making of a Revolution* (1968).

Salky, A., *Havana Journal* (1971).

Seabrook, W., *The Magic Island* (1929).

Schmidt, H., *The United States Occupation of Haiti 1915–1934* (1971).

Seers, D., ed., *Cuba, the Economic and Social Revolution* (1964).

Slater, J., *Interventions and Negotiation; the United States and the Dominican Revolution* (1970).

Smith, R. F., *Background to Revolution: Development of Modern Cuba* (1966).

————, *The United States and Cuba: Business and Diplomacy 1917–1960* (1961).

————, *What Happened in Cuba: A Documentary History* (1963).

Sobel, L. A., *Cuba, United States, and Russia, 1960–1963* (1964).

Solnick, B. B., ed., *The West Indies and Central America to 1898* (1970).

Stavenhagen, R., ed., *Agrarian Problems and Peasant Movements in Latin America* (1970).

Stuart, G. H., *Latin America and the United States* (5th ed., 1955).

Suárez, A., *Cuba: Castroism and Communism, 1959–1966* (1969).

Suchlicki, J., *The Cuban Revolution: A Documentary Guide* (1971).

————, *University Students and Politics in Cuba 1929–1967* (1969).

Sutherland, E., *The Youngest Revolution* (1969).

Szulc, T., *Dominican Diary* (1965).

————, ed., *The United States and the Caribbean* (1971).

Tang, P. S. H. and J. Malmey, *The Chinese Communist Impact on Cuba* (1962).

Tansill, C. C., *United States and Santo Domingo, 1798–1873* (1938).

Thomas, H., *Cuba: The Pursuit of Freedom* (1971).

Tomasek, R. D., *Latin American Politics. Studies of the Contemporary Scene* (rev. ed., 1970).

Tondel, L. M., ed., *Inter-American Security System and the Cuban in Crisis* (1964).

Underwood, E., *The Poets of Haiti, 1782–1934* (1934).

United States Congress, Subcommittee on Inter-American Affairs of the House Committee on Foreign Affairs Hearings (March 14, 1963).

United States, Department of State, *Events in United States–Cuba Relations: A Chronology, 1957–January 1963* (1963).

————, *United States Policy Toward Cuba* (1964).

United States Senate, Committee on Foreign Relations and Committee on Armed Services, 87th Congress, 2nd Session, *Situation in Cuba* (1962).

University of Miami, Cuban Economic Research Project, *Cuba: Agriculture and Planning, 1963–1964* (1965).

Urrutia, M., *Fidel Castro and Company, Inc.* (1964).

Valdes, N. P. and R. E. Bonachea, *Selected Works of Fidel Castro,* 3 vols. 1971–1972).

———— and E. Lieuwen, *The Cuban Revolution 1959–1969. A Research Study-Guide* (1970).

Vandercook, J. W., *Black Majesty* (1928).

Wallich, H. C., *Monetary Problems of an Export Economy: Cuban Experience, 1914–1947* (1950).

Waxman, S. M., *Bibliography of the Belles-Letters of Santo Domingo* (1931).

Welles, S., *Naboth's Vineyard,* 2 vols. (1928).

Wiarda, H. J., *Dictatorship and Development: The Methods of Control in Trujillo's Dominican Republic* (1968).

―――――, *Dominican Republic: Nation in Transition* (1969).

Wilgus, A. C., ed., *Caribbean Area* (1934).

―――――, ed., *The Caribbean at Mid-Century* (1951).

―――――, ed., *Caribbean: Contemporary Education* (1960).

―――――, ed., *The Caribbean: Contemporary International Relations* (1957).

―――――, ed., *The Caribbean: Contemporary Trends* (1953).

―――――, ed., *The Carribbean: Its Culture* (1955).

―――――, ed., *The Caribbean: Its Economy* (1954).

―――――, ed., *The Caribbean: Its Political Problems* (1956).

―――――, ed., *Caribbean: Natural Resources* (1959).

―――――, ed., *The Caribbean: Peoples, Problems, and Prospects* (1952).

―――――, ed., *The Caribbean: Its Hemispheric Role* (1968).

Wilkerson, L., *Fidel Castro's Political Progress from Reformism to "Marxism-Leninism"* (1965).

Williams, E., *Negro in the Caribbean* (1942).

―――――, From *Columbus to Castro: The History of the Caribbean, 1492–1969* (1971).

Williams, J. J., *Voodoos and Obeahs: Phases of West Indian Witchcraft* (1933).

Williams, W. A., *The United States, Cuba, and Castro* (1962).

Wisan, J. E., *The Cuban Crisis as Reflected in the New York Press (1895–1899)* (1934; 1965).

Wolpin, M. D., *Cuban Foreign Policy and Chilean Politics* (1972).

Wood, H. A., *Northern Haiti: Land Use and Settlement* (1964).

Wright, P. G., *Cuban Situation and Our Treaty Relations* (1931).

Zeitlin, M., *Revolutionary Politics and Cuban Working Class* (new ed., 1970).

―――――, and R. Scheer, *Cuba: Tragedy in Our Hemisphere* (1963).

INTER-AMERICAN COOPERATION
IN THE TWENTIETH CENTURY

PAN AMERICAN CONFERENCES

First - 1889 - Washington.
Second - 1901 - Mexico City.
Third - 1906 - Rio de Janeiro.
Fourth - 1910 - Buenos Aires.
Fifth - 1923 - Santiago, Chile.
Sixth - 1928 - Havana.
Seventh - 1933 - Montevideo.
Eighth - 1938 - Lima.
Ninth - 1948 - Bogotá, creation
  of OAS.
Tenth - 1954 (Inter-American
  Conference) - Caracas.

Several special conferences
  since 1960.
First regular session, OAS
  General Assembly, San
  José de Costa Rica, 1971

PAN AMERICAN HIGHWAY

—————— ALL-WEATHER HIGHWAY ——————
- - - - - - FEEDER ROADS - - - - - - - - -
══════ UNFINISHED SECTIONS, 1970 ══════
COURTESY INTERNATIONAL ROAD FEDERATION

FOREIGN MINISTERS' CONFERENCES

Panamá - 1939
Havana - 1940
Rio de Janeiro - 1942
Washington - 1951
Santiago - 1959
San José de Costa Rica - 1960
Punta del Este - 1962
Washington - 1964
Rio de Janeiro - 1965 (Com-
  mittee to reorganize OAS)

ORGANIZATION OF AMERICAN STATES

The International Organization of the 21
American Republics established by Charter
signed at the Ninth International Conference
of American States, Bogotá, Colombia, 1948

FOREIGN MINISTERS' CONFERENCES

1940 - Act of Havana.
1942 - Rio de Janeiro, united action in
  World War II.
1945 - Mexico City, Act of Chapultepec.
1959 - Santiago (Chile), on intervention.

*Latin America
assumes an
important
place in
international
affairs*

PART VI

In October 1970, the Pan-American Health Organization (the inter-governmental health agencies for the Americas) held its eighteenth Pan-American Sanitary Conference in Washington. Top officials and doctors from 20 Latin American republics were there, as well as representatives from four English-speaking Caribbean Islands and from the United States. France, Holland, and Britain also sent delegates to learn about the progress in tropical medicine. A Chilean doctor was reelected to a four-year term as head of the Pan-American Sanitary Program; he is simultaneously the head of the Secretariat of the Health Division of the Organization of American States and of the World Health Organization of the United Nations. These three agencies carry out a single program. The delegates voted to ask the Organization of American States for a 20-per cent increase in the budget for 1971 over 1970. Of this increased budget, twenty-five per cent was to control infectious diseases, still the major killers in Latin America. Latin America was facing an outbreaak of cholera, the seventh epidemic recorded in Latin America since 1817. The delegates were relieved that cholera is now "almost a benign disease if spotted quickly." It can be detected more easily and calls only for the injection of fluids. The delegates were concerned because five areas of tropical America still show the presence of yellow fever virus. But they reported that in 1969, 30 million people in Latin America had been vaccinated against smallpox in eleven countries under a joint agreement to completely wipe out that disease. These specialists were using the freeze-dried vaccine, which can be carried to the most remote areas. The Pan-American Sanitary Bureau, the first active organization of the Pan-American Union, had reported in 1920 that 176 million people in the Western Hemisphere were threatened by malaria. Now less than ten per cent of that number are still threatened. In such health endeavors, the Pan-American international organizations are leading the world.

Such cooperative effort was not always possible among New World nations. For a century after independence, Latin American nations remained isolated from each other and from the United States. When Latin American nations contacted each other it was to quarrel over boundaries, or to go to war against Francisco Solano López in Paraguay, or to fight about nitrates in the War of the Pacific. Relations with England had centered in economic investments and trade, while Latin American relations with other European countries during the nineteenth century had been of little importance.

Meanwhile, The United States threatened the European nations with war under the Monroe Doctrine if they tampered with Latin American independence, and at the same time rattled the saber of Manifest Destiny at nearby Latin neighbors. After 1900, Latin American nations spent 30 years fearing and hating the United States, thinking of the growing power above the Rio Grande as the "Colossus of the North," bent on overcoming them through "Dollar Diplomacy."

Then came the Good Neighbor Policy of the 1930's, which changed this anti-American attitude slightly for the better. It succeeded in guaranteeing a more united front in World War II; nevertheless, the war provoked further ill will toward the United States. The neglect of the Latin American area by the United States after the end of the war further weakened the friendships that had begun to blossom with the Good Neighbor Policy.

In the late 1940s, the United States was granting large sums to Europe through the Marshall Plan. In the 1950s and 1960s the United States further antagonized Latin America by threats to intervene in countries it felt would go Communist, while spending billions of dollars in Southeast Asia. The promising Alliance for Progress for joint hemisphere improvement hardly got off the ground. As the New World faced the 1970s, the tide had not yet turned toward trust, cooperation and optimism in inter-American relations.

Latin American people tend to expect immediate solutions to political problems as well as to economic and social problems, as they pass from dictatorial to democratically elected governments. The world-wide "Revolution of Expectations" has led people to expect too much too quickly, and hence provoked a wave of anti-American nationalism. Indeed, these "expectations" have in many areas given rise to a return of military-run governments where the world had assumed that democracy was running smoothly. All the Americas, both North and South, need to arrive at a mutual acceptance of each other's values.

Most of the individual stories of trade projects, wartime cooperation programs, and diplomatic relations have been told in the foregoing chapters. The remainder of the book aims to summarize activities from the Hemispheric and from the world point of view. Of these two concluding chapters, the first concerns political developments while the second attempts to describe economic advancement in the Hemisphere, social improvement and cultural exchange.

chapter 30

LATIN AMERICAN
RELATIONS WITH
THE UNITED STATES
AND WITH THE WORLD

In March 1961, the United States joined with the Latin American states in proclaiming a revolutionary program called the Alliance for Progress. It was to use twenty billion dollars over a twenty-year period to house and educate all Latin Americans, to improve rural and urban slums, and to provide social justice. All these things were to be done with American technical "Know-how" but without American "bossing." A month later, April 1961, the United States assisted in the Bay of Pigs invasion, seemingly returning to intervention based on its old belief in "manifest destiny" and right to intervene. These two events coming so close together signified the best and the worst in our American policy toward Latin America through the years. We have been inconsistent for more than a century. We considered ourselves ethnically superior and destined to control. We still thought that United States security was the number-one problem of the Hemisphere. Our first duty was to be secure from England, Germany, and Russia. More recently we believed we must keep out Communism, no matter what happened to the rest of the world. We moved in cycles between condescending concern, military intervention, and complete neglect. So it seems logical that Latin Americans should "hate" us. They resent our well-paid businessmen and official staffs and the lives of conspicuous luxury they lead, and they condemn us for our "dollar diplomacy." It is true Latin Americans have failed to train social scientists with a world view; they teach no objective study of the United States in their universities. But two-thirds of the blame for bad feeling arises from the "Colossus" of the North. Although much of the detailed story of American diplomatic dealings with Latin America has been told chapter by chapter as part of national histories, it is of value to repeat it briefly here from the point of view of the overall United States policy.

United States relations with Latin America to 1959

The Monroe Doctrine, which had been promulgated in 1823, was as much a part of the United States' policy of isolationism and avoidance of entangling alliances at it was a reflection of sympathy with Latin America. Monroe's message to Congress declared to the mother countries, Spain and Portugal, that "we should consider any attempt on their part to extend their system to any portion of this hemisphere as dangerous to our peace and safety." It was its own peace and safety in the face of threatened intervention by the Metternich Alliance which concerned the United States. The Doctrine was practically forgotten once the power of that alliance weakened in Europe. The United States allowed England to take the Falkland Islands from Argentina in 1833 and to strengthen her foothold in Belize and the Honduras coast islands. When British encroachments seemed closer to home in Texas and Oregon in 1844, President Polk made the first new interpretation of the neglected doctrine. England should not even try to "advise" the independent people of this continent who "alone have the right to decide their own destiny."

An actual invasion of an American state during an American war occurred nearly two decades later when Napoleon III's armies placed Maximilian on the throne of Mexico. Secretary of State Seward made only a mild protest against Maximilian in the name of the Monroe Doctrine in 1862 and 1863. When the Civil War was over, Seward took a stronger stand. President Johnson's message to Congress in 1865 considered that it would be a "great calamity to the peace of the world should any foreign power challenge the American people . . . to the defense of republicanism against foreign interference." The American threat combined with the losses in Mexico to end Maximilian's career there.

The Monroe Doctrine was next reinterpreted to mean that disputes between an American nation and a foreign power must be settled by arbitration rather than by war. In 1895 President Cleveland used such an interpretation to force England to arbitrate a boundary dispute between British Guiana and Venezuela which had been causing bad feelings between the two nations for a half-century. Latin Americans had no cause to thank Cleveland for this interference. Cleveland's Secretary of State wrote to his ambassador in England, "Today the United States is practically sovereign on this continent [and] there is a doctrine of American public law . . . which entitles and requires the United States to treat as an injury to itself the forcible assumption by an European power of political control over an

American state." Britain's involvement in the Boer War led her to come to terms with the United States on this issue and settle the boundary by arbitration in 1899.

All this amplification of the Monroe Doctrine did not go unchallenged. An Argentine jurist, Carlos Calvo, had wrritten a treatise in 1868 saying that a sovereign nation was "immune from external intervention no matter what the state's degree of political stability or the quality of its courts." This Argentine statement was used in 1902 by Luis Drago, Argentine Minister of Foreign Affairs, in a note to Washington. "Failure of a state to pay its debts does not justify the use of armed force against it," said Drago. Since sovereign nations could brook intervention from no one, not even a sister nation in the same Hemisphere, all the American nations together should act jointly in "prohibiting the armed intervention by any European power in any American state for the collection of a public debt." Drago considered his proposal as his own Corollary of the Monroe Doctrine; but United States policymakers treated Drago coolly, and the Roosevelt Corollary followed two years later. Drago's own government, changing hands, repudiated his doctrine as "in conflict with Argentine foreign policy." Other Latin American nations, pleased to be asked as equals to The Hague Conference in 1907, brought into that body a wording of the Drago Doctrine which had been formulated at the Third Pan American Conference the year before. The South American bloc was able to get a weakened resolution passed at The Hague: "The Signatories agree not to have recourse to armed force for the recovery of contracted debts." To all intents and purposes this Drago Corollary became a part of the body of international law, a protection against aggression from creditor nations.

The assumption of Hemisphere leadership by the United States prepared the way for Theodore Roosevelt's Corollary to the Monroe Doctrine. Participation in Cuban affairs during the Spanish-American War and plans to build an Isthmian Canal made America conscious of the Caribbean. The Venezuelan dictator Cipriano Castro had incurred debts which the German Wilhelm II threatened to collect by force. Owing to the United States' new prestige, Germany warned the State Department in 1901 that such a step might be necessary, and Roosevelt answered via a message to Congress that the United States did "not guarantee any state against punishment if it misconducts itself, provided that punishment does not take the form of acquisition of territory by any non-American power." Castro was quick to ask the United States to arrange arbitration.

The story of American intervention in the political and financial affairs of the Dominican Republic, Haiti, and Nicaragua has been told from the point of view of those frustrated little nations. When the Dominican Republic threatened to default on its debts to European creditors and the national governments of those creditors made vigorous protests, Theodore Roosevelt sent another message to Congress on the Monroe Doctrine in 1904. "Chronic wrong doing may . . . ultimately require intervention by some civilized nation, and in the Western Hemisphere the adherence of the United States to the Monroe Doctrine may force the United States . . . to the exercise of an international police power." North Americans received this Roosevelt Corollary with patriotic enthusiasm; European creditors felt it guaranteed the payment of debts; but Latin Americans saw it as an excuse for American intervention, to them as bad as or worse than European forced debt-collection. Meanwhile Roosevelt insulted his neighbors even more by quoting his "favorite West African" proverb, "Speak softly and carry a big stick, you will go far."

A "Lodge Corollary" was developed in 1912 when Henry Cabot Lodge assumed that Japanese interests, in attempting to buy property in Magdalena Bay in Lower California, were violating the Monroe Doctrine. Lodge considered the Japanese group a "corporation or association which has a relation to another government, not America," which would give "that government practical power of control for national purposes." Thus foreign companies were discourged from colonization schemes.

In time the Monroe Doctrine itself was softened in United States interpretations. Woodrow Wilson in a speech at Mobile in 1913 "scuttled" the Big Stick and Dollar Diplomacy policies. He hoped to use the Doctrine in support of worldwide self-determination of nations, spoke of it in the Fourteen Points as a successful regional agreement, and was instrumental in having mention of it included as "a regional understanding for securing the maintenance of peace" in Article 21 of the League of Nations Covenant. However, sadly enough, it was on the basis of the United States' own right to interpret the Monroe Doctrine unilaterally that Henry Cabot Lodge led the Senate's opposition to the Covenant. That the Doctrine was "distinctively the policy of the United States" and that the United States had the right to its "definition, interpretation, and application" was insisted upon by Charles Evans Hughes at the Fifth Pan American Congress at Santiago in 1923. Naturally such insistence did not ease Latin America's fears. Hughes and his colleagues did their best to assure Latin American critics that the United States only held such rights in the Canal area and the nearby Caribbean Islands. President Hoover, a good friend of Latin America, was opposed to the early twentieth-century interpretations of the Monroe Doctrine. After 1930 references to the Monroe Doctrine did not include the right of intervention.

To keep the peace in Central America, and possibly to avoid foreign armed intervention, the United States from time to time withheld recognition of governments that had come to power by violence. However, since delayed recognition often weakened a government which the United States opposed, it was considered a subtle type of intervention, and as such became an issue between Latin America and the United States. In 1913 the United States government declared that to receive recognition a nation must demonstrate: "The control of the administrative machinery of the state; the general acquiescence of its people; and the ability and willingness of their governments to discharge international and conventional obligations." Wilson called this the doctrine of "constitutional legitimacy," and attempted to use it to discipline the Revolutionaries in Mexico.

The United States withheld recognition from governments in Central America with varying results. From 1907 to 1921 in Honduras, Nicaragua, Costa Rica, and Guatemala in five different cases United States recognition was withheld after a revolution, and in no case did it bring about a clear-cut change toward peace and stability. Since 1930 the United States has assumed that a de facto government was to be recognized. The statement of the Mexican publicist, Genaro Estrada, sometimes known as the Estrada Doctrine, that "any government which is actually in control of the country is to be acknowledged" is gradually becoming accepted Western Hemisphere practice.

One consistent long-time United States policy that influenced relations with Latin America was built around hopes for an Isthmian Canal. As early as 1846 the United States had signed a treaty with Colombia "conveying to the United States the right of or transit across the Isthmus of Panama, upon any modes of communication that now exist, or that may be hereafter constructed." In 1850 the Clayton-Bulwer Treaty established a partnership between England and the United States in case any canal should be built. With the United States' victory in Cuba in 1898, interest in an American-dominated canal grew. Secretary of State Hay arranged the Hay-Pauncefote Treaty of 1900–1901, in which Britain bowed to the growing power of the United States, accepted her promise of neutrality once the canal was built, and withdrew from the joint partnership of interest. A dispute between supporters of a Nicaragua route and backers of the Panama route was settled in the United States Congress. When Colombia refused to ratify the Hay-Herrán Treaty providing for an American canal project, the Panama Revolution resulted. Then by the Hay-Buneau-Varilla Treaty with Panama, and the purchase of the rights of the defunct French company, the United States proceeded to acquire the Canal Zone, and to dig the "Big Ditch." Subsequent dealings with Nicaragua, such as the Bryan-Chamorro Treaty, though part of the "Dollar Diplomacy" policy of dealing with Central America during the Taft era, centered on the option to the Nicaraguan canal route. With this same policy in mind, the United States acquired the Danish West Indies in 1917, continued its protectorate over Cuba under the Platt Amendment, and maintained the Big Stick policy in the Caribbean.

It was time for some United States president or secretary of state to counteract all the strong anti-American currents. A trend in that direction had already started when Herbert Hoover, as President-elect, made a goodwill trip to Latin America in 1928. He suggested a successful formula for settling the Tacna-Arica dispute and announced that "we have no desire for territorial expansion, for economic or other domination of other peoples." Under Hoover the United States withdrew from Haiti; the Marines left Nicaragua for good in the last month of Hoover's term in office, and a policy of recognizing de facto governments has been pursued up to the present. However, this policy of recognition of any established government brought criticism in the 1950s for supporting dictators.

Franklin Roosevelt first made the new attitude of nonintervention a specific policy in his inaugural address two months after the Marines left

Nicaragua. "In the field of world policy," he said, "I would dedicate this nation to the policy of the good neighbor, . . . the neighbor who respects his obligations and respects the sanctity of his agreements in and with a world of neighbors." A month later, April 1933, he used the same words in a speech before the Pan American Union. Cordell Hull as the new Secretary of State went to the Pan American Conference at Montevideo in December of 1933, reiterated the Good Neighbor stand, and supported a pact to outlaw intervention. These brave words were soon followed by deeds. The Platt Amendment to the Cuban Constitution of 1901 was withdrawn. Haiti and Panama received treaties guaranteeing more equal treatment. In 1936 Roosevelt himself went to a special conference at Buenos Aires. There, as a "traveling salesman for peace," Roosevelt called for united Hemisphere action in the face of any outside aggression, having in mind the Nazi infiltration which was apparent by then. At this meeting no new multilateral Monroe Doctrine was drawn up, but peace machinery between the various American republics was to be strengthened, and the principle of nonintervention was reaffirmed. When Mexico expropriated foreign-owned oil fields two years later, the Roosevelt government ignored the pressure to intervene by armed force, and eventually a satisfactory settlement was reached. Meanwhile, war clouds gathered in Europe, and the next inter-American meetings were concerned with mutual defense against dangerous outsiders.

As World War II changed the position of England and Germany in the world, so it brought further changes in the relationships between the United States and Latin America. By the time the Eighth Pan American Conference was held at Lima in 1938, Hitler had marched on Austria and was threatening Czechoslovakia. The Declaration of Lima, which bolstered the United States' neutrality stand, reaffirmed continental solidarity, and promised collaboration in the face of any forced intervention, showed a new respect for the American position. By September 1939 the foreign ministers of the Latin American nations were ready to come to Panama and declare with the United States that there was to be no hostile act committed by any non-American power in any Western Hemisphere territorial water. The actual steps in the achievement of this continental solidarity will be taken up shortly. The importance here of all these joint statements leading up to World War II is that they show the Latin American nations, with the exception of Argentina and Chile, willing to align themselves with the United States against an enemy who looked more like a colossus than did the power north of the Rio Grande. All the Western Hemisphere felt fear for the Caribbean possessions of Holland and France when Western Europe fell to the Nazis in the spring of 1940. A conference was called in Havana in July, 1940. The Monroe Doctrine ceased to be a one-nation policy, for the Act of Havana proclaimed that "any European possession apt to change sovereignty" should be placed under provisional control by a joint committee, representing all the American states. These committees were to act if Hitler's actions directly threatened any place in the Caribbean. It was also agreed that "any attempt against the inviolability of territory of any American state shall be considered as an act of aggression against the states which sign this declaration."

With the Act of Havana, the ideas of Calvo and Drago and their hopes for multilateral action under the Monroe Doctrine came to fruition. The United States further demonstrated good will by cooperating with the Inter American Financial and Economic Advisory Committee to try to absorb and allocate the surpluses of Latin American products stranded by the blockade of Europe. United States finance helped in defense and security during World War II, building large sections of the Pan American Highway as a hemispheric defense, and sending specialists to train armies to the south in case the Germans or the Japanese should invade the New World. When war was declared on the Axis powers by the United States in December, 1941, all the Latin American nations except Chile and Argentina quickly severed relations and declared war also. The United States was allowed to set up bases at Recife, Natal and Bélem in Brazil, to ship supplies across the Atlantic to West Africa. Meanwhile the office of Coordinator of Inter-American Affairs, known as the Nelson Rockefeller Committee, was set up in the United States State Department as a means to "win friends and influence people." Finally came a meeting held at Chapultepec Castle in February, 1945, six weeks before the United Nations was organized at San Francisco. Here the Monroe Doctrine was expanded to make all the American republics its "co-guardians" even against an American aggressor. Even Argentina was pressured to declare war on Germany, seven weeks before the war ended, so that she could join the United Nations.

The United States suddenly found itself a major world power with heavy responsibilities. Its interest, attention and economic aid had to be spread thinly around the globe. It had Marshall Plan funds to spend freely in Europe but in so doing it did not fulfill Latin American expectations for the large-scale financial assistance tacitly promised during the war.

By 1947, the newly aroused, nationalistic Latin American states wanted "a greater share of the world's good things *now!*" They wanted United States' assistance in improving health, providing practical education, and bringing material progress. They felt that the United States was so concerned with world Communism that it had forgotten them, and contrasted the attentions showered on them during World War II with the neglect of the postwar decade. Although the United States had promised a more generous loan policy in a conference at Petropolis in 1954 and at a meeting of the Finance Ministers at Buenos Aires in 1957, the United States went into an economic recession at home. The raw materials it bought in Latin America declined in price during the same period.

At the same time that this economic pinch began to produce new bitterness, Pérez Jiménez, the hated dictator of Venezuela who had been receiving loans from the United States and royalties from American oil companies, fled for his life from infuriated mobs in Caracas, but found haven in Miami. Somoza, long-time dictator of Nicaragua, was shot by an assassin and the United States rushed him by army plane to an American hospital in the Panama Canal Zone. The playboy son of Trujillo, the autocratic dictator of the Dominican Republic, was acting like an "honored guest" at an officers' school in the United States. In critical Latin American eyes, the United States was causing a slowdown in economic progress in

Latin America while it deliberately hurt the cause of democracy by support-ing the most undemocratic dictators. Then in 1958, Vice-President Nixon toured Latin America as part of a trip to attend the inauguration of Presi-dent Frondizi of Argentina. He was heckled by students in Uruguay, stoned at the University of San Marcos in Lima, and barely escaped an angry crowd in Caracas, where mob action had run Pérez Jiménez out of the country only a few weeks before. During the same year President Eisen-hower sent his distinguished brother, Doctor Milton Eisenhower, president of Johns Hopkins University on a second fact-finding mission to Latin America. Dr. Eisenhower urged an improvement in United States–Latin America relations by working entirely through the Organization of American States and economic plans for "a large program to meet a large problem."

The American people were shocked, but reacted with a searching survey of the United States' postwar Latin American policy. Juscelino Kubitchek, president of Brazil, took advantage of the United States' new attitude to suggest a stronger plan for economic assistance, a new Inter-American bank, and a series of more meaningful conferences. These ideas were to grow into the cooperative plan called the Alliance for Progress. President Eisenhower himself was well received on a goodwill tour to southern South America in 1960.

Part of our neglect of Latin America in the 1950s was due to our concern with the "Cold War" against Russia. At every inter-American meet-ing the United States had hoped for forthright sentiments against Commu-nist infiltration in the Hemisphere, while the Latins minimized this danger. John Foster Dulles, at the Organization of American States meeting in Caracas in 1954, asked for a strong resolution expressing "solidarity against intervention by international Communism." The resolution received a nar-row margin of approval from states who hoped for economic assistance. The Latin American states actually did not intend to approve of *any* interven-tion—including intervention by the United States. Later in the same year an inter-Latin American investigating committee acted slowly to condemn Communist sympathizer Arbenz as president of Guatemala. Meanwhile the United States Central Intelligence Agency gave secret, unilateral help to Arbenz' Guatemalan enemies, and his regime fell. Although the resolution passed at Dulles' insistence was never invoked, the United States was criti-cized by the Organization of American States members for the action against Arbenz.

The year 1959 forced a turning point for the United States. Increas-ingly, the American president had to work through the Organization of American States. Fidel Castro got control of Cuba and the United States attempted to help his enemies in the Bay of Pigs in 1961 without consulting other Western Hemisphere nations. When Russia threatened the United States by using Cuba as a missile base in 1962, President Kennedy conferred immediately with the Council of the Organization of American States. In 1965, public opinion forced President Johnson to consult with the Organiza-tion of American States within two days after sending marines into the Dominican Republic. To understand the influence of the Organization of

American States on Latin American and United States policy, it is necessary to trace the history of Latin American cooperation from the time of Simón Bolívar.

inter-American development from
the Pan American Union to
the Organization of American States

For a century after independence there was no regional cooperation within Latin America. Attempts at Central American union had failed; the Gran Colombian Confederation had broken up soon after independence. Argentina, Brazil, and Chile, calling themselves the ABC Powers, proposed to act as a board of arbitration in regional disputes around 1915, but did not develop a regional union.

There were some few wars between Latin American nations, such as those against the dictator López of Paraguay, the War of the Pacific over Tacna-Arica, and the War of the Gran Chaco. There have been years of friction over unsettled boundaries, disputes over navigation of international rivers, military operations of political refugees across international frontiers, and "incidents" caused by ambitious leaders who coveted the territories and natural resources of their neighbors. But more impressive is the record of pacific settlement of disputes, often with the arbitration of one of the great powers.

That there should be need for arbitration over boundaries is not surprising. By the Doctrine of *Uti Possidetis* of 1810 the new nations were to establish their frontiers on the lines between various Spanish colonial administrative units at the time the independence movements began. The indefiniteness of these lines, some of them not even yet surveyed through jungles and over mountain ranges, produced many "incidents." Some of the possible pairs of nations with common frontiers have made arbitration treaties to settle border disputes; others have refused arbitration on such matters "affecting vital national interests." Through a century and a quarter of such disputes, European kings, American presidents, and international courts of justice have served as boards of arbitration. By the Gondra Treaty of 1923, an outcome of the Fifth Pan American Conference, a Permanent Diplomatic Commission of Investigaton and Conciliation was set up, and its machinery further augmented by the Inter-American Treaty of Good Offices written at the Buenos Aires conference of 1936. Though some border disputes still simmer, the Pan American Union reports that more than seventy-eight disputes have been settled since independence without resort to violence. No recent Latin American squabble has led to a full-scale war, and chances are small that there will ever be such a struggle between any group of Western Hemisphere nations again. This development is largely due to the rise of the Organization of American States.

A union of the American states was a dream of Bolívar's. In his letter from Jamaica in 1815, at one of his periods of deepest discouragement, the Liberator wrote: "Would to God that some day we may have the good fortune to convene . . . an august assembly of representatives of republics, kingdoms, and empires to deliberate upon the high interests of peace and war. . . . Then will we march majestically toward that great prosperity for which South America is destined. Then will those sciences and arts which . . . have enlightened Europe wing their way to a free Colombia which will cordially bid them welcome." When such a meeting was held at Panama City in 1826, its "Treaty of Perpetual Union, League, and Confederation" was ratified only by Colombia of the four nations which attended. Bolívar died, and his dreams disintegrated. The Spanish American states met in partial agreement three more times before the 1880s: the west coast countries in 1847 to draft "a comprehensive plan for peaceful settlement of inter-American disputes" in the face of danger from Ecuador's dissatisfied General Flores and his backers in Spain; Ecuador, Peru, and Chile in 1856 at Santiago; and the Central and northern South American states the same year at Washington, to make a "Continental Treaty." In 1864 a so-called Congress of Hispanic States met at Lima with eight states present to "devise measures of accomplishing Latin American union." All these efforts failed of ratification. Though other conferences met on cultural and social topics, the dream of an American family of nations was almost lost. By the 1880s, however, Latin America was looking for defensive safeguards, and the United States was looking for expanded trade and new places for investment. In 1882 the American President Chester Arthur and his Secretary of State James G. Blaine proposed a Pan American conference at Washington to discuss ways of settling disputes peacefully and to improve commercial relations, but delayed action on it, partially because of the War of the Pacific. Blaine became Secretary of State again under Benjamin Harrison; this time he pushed the idea of the Pan American meeting.

Representatives of eighteen nations came to Washington at Blaine's invitation in October 1889, spent six weeks touring the United States on a special train—which included Pullman cars with hot and cold running water in the washrooms—and then settled down to meetings lasting until April 19. After deliberating over the project of a customs union, suggesting resolutions on a plan of arbitration and on points of international law against conquest, the conference concluded by setting up a Commercial Bureau of the American Republics. Since the meeting was sponsored by the United States, this Bureau was to have permanent headquarters in Washington and to be "charged with the care of all translations and publications and with all correspondence pertaining to the International Union." It was to publish a "bulletin of useful commercial information." This bureau was established in Washington in November 1890, and Mr. William E. Curtis became its first director. Up to this time, most Latin American leaders considered "Pan Americanism" merely a policy of United States aggrandizement. The Bureau continued under United States auspices, but was not to remain purely a commercial affair.

In the spirit of the peaceful pre-World War I world, the American states met again in Mexico City in the winter of 1901–1902. Here The Hague

Convention of 1889 was signed by the Latin American delegates present, and questions of the collection of debts and the arbitration of disputes were discussed. Four years later in 1906 at Rio de Janeiro a Third International Conference was held to continue discussions of The Hague conferences and to request the second Hague meeting to consider "the question of the compulsory collection of public debts." The meeting at Rio, however, accomplished nothing more concrete than to set up a commission of jurists, who, it was hoped, would codify international law for the Americas, and include in the codification a statement against intervention for the collection of debts.

By 1910 the Pan American Sanitary Bureau of 1902 and the Commercial Bureau of 1890 were given a new name, the Pan American Union. The American philanthropist Andrew Carnegie donated funds for the Pan American Union building in Washington, D.C., which still houses all cultural and welfare activities of the Pan American movement. The year 1910 was also the centennial of the independence movement; as part of the celebration the nations met in the Fourth International Conference of American States in Buenos Aires. Here the entire organization changed its name to Union of American Republics, and adopted four treaties relating to copyrights, trademarks, and the collection of debts. The Bureau in Washington was enlarged and strengthened, and was to concern itself with cultural matters and sanitary improvement, as well as to serve as a commercial clearing house.

A Fifth Conference had been scheduled for 1914, following a four year pattern, but it was postponed because of World War I. When the Fifth Pan American Conference finally met in Santiago in 1923, the Latin American states had emerged from World War I with increased status, and were more accustomed to joint action. The Fifth Conference set up four permanent commissions: on economic relations, on labor, on public health, and on intellectual cooperation. Whereas the United States Secretary of State had heretofore served as ex officio chairman of the Union, now there was to be a governing board with one member from each nation and an elected chairman and vice-chairman. The treaty for the pacific settlement of disputes, the Gondra Treaty, was signed. Here at Santiago, too, was made the first suggestion which led to the Pan American Highway.

The year 1928 saw the Sixth Conference meeting at Havana, for conferences were now to be held every five years. This sixth meeting voted to send special delegates to sit upon the Union's governing board, rather than merely have the current ambassador in Washington act in that capacity. Here at Havana the delegates organized the American Institute for the Protection of Childhood, and created new permanent divisions on agricultural cooperation and labor. This Havana meeting also set up a Special Conference on Conciliation and Arbitration, which met at Washington in December 1929, and wrote several agreements for peaceful settlements of international disputes. By 1931 more than sixty technical and scientific conferences had been held on a wide variety of subjects. At the building in Washington the American Secretary of State continued to act as general chairman, even though now "elected" by the members.

By 1933 America was launched on the Good Neighbor Policy under Franklin Roosevelt, and his Secretary of State Cordell Hull went to Montevideo to the Seventh Conference to tell the other delegates so. From 1933 on, the Pan American movement gained greater prestige in Latin American eyes. The Seventh Conference, therefore, was able to accept unanimously a convention of the "Rights and Duties of States," establishing in treaty form the doctrine that "no state has the right to intervene in the internal or external affairs of another." New provisions for enforcing the compulsory arbitration agreements were passed in an effort to stop the war then raging in the Gran Chaco.

Montevideo showed concrete evidence of the spirit of cooperation. As war clouds gathered in Europe, a special Conference for the Maintenance of Peace was held in Buenos Aires in 1936 which produced an agreement that "a threat to the security of any American nation is a threat to all." The nations present also resolved that they would "consult together" on the procedure to follow when such a threat occurred. In 1938 the nations met at Lima, faced with the possiblity of another world war into which Latin America might be drawn, and resolved on a series of meetings of the Ministers of Foreign Affairs of the twenty-one republics to provide concerted action. Thus, when war in Europe spread to America, and the regular meeting of the Ninth Conference had to be postponed in 1943, the foreign ministers had already held a series of meetings on the problem of maintaining neutrality and providing Hemispheric security.

World War II conferences have just been reviewed from the point of view of United States policy. The first of the foreign ministers' meetings was in 1939 at Panama. Here, by the Declaration of Panama, the delegates drew a line some 300 miles offshore around the American continents, and declared that belligerent ships were not to operate within that zone. They also created the Inter-American Financial and Economic Advisory Committee to solve the problems of trade dislocation brought by the war in Europe. By the time of the Rio de Janeiro meeting of the foreign ministers in January 1942, most nations of the Western Hemisphere were in the war, owing to the bombing of Pearl Harbor. The policy of "an attack on one is an attack on all" had "paid off." Plans were made for mobilization of resources to fight the Nazis, and for control of subversive activity. The activities of the Latin American nations prepared them for a strong voice in the postwar deliberations and in the United Nations. When that time came, the Pan American movement was strong enough to be incorporated into the new Organization of American States.

World War II was practically over in February 1945, when delegates of all belligerent states were called to Chapultepec Castle in Mexico City for the Inter-American Conference on War and Peace. The most important decision made in 1945 at Mexico City, termed the Act of Chapultepec, provided that security within the Western Hemisphere depended on collective action of the American states, and would be solved by common corrective action. Such action was to be regional, in accordance with the special situation of the Western Hemisphere and the strength of the Pan

American movement. However, such collective action was to be considered in harmony with the new United Nations. This Act made it possible for the Pan American Union to be reorganized as the Organization of American States, a "regional organization" within the United Nations, but actually an independent and almost equally strong body.

Soon the Act of Chapultepec was to be carried out in the formation of a strong new regional organization. In 1947 an Inter-American Conference for the Maintenance of Continental Peace and Security met at Rio. The "Rio Pact of 1947" forced its signers to unite against any aggression on a member state from the outside world, or from another American state, and was to be prominent in the 1960s in connection with Communism in the Caribbean.

Then in 1948 the Ninth Conference met in Bogotá, to form the Organization of American States. This was the first regional agreement signed under Article 51 of the United Nations Charter. A definite regional charter, which had never existed for the previous loose Pan American movement, was signed as a treaty. This charter set up six major organs: first, the Inter-American Conference, the supreme body of the new organization, to meet every five years to plan general policy and programs; second, the meetings of foreign ministers, such as that called in the Korean emergency; third, the Specialized Conferences to be called on technical matters of all kinds. The remaining three organs are permanent bodies which work throughout the year. They are, first, the Council of the OAS replacing the old Governing Board of the Pan American Union; second, the Pan American Union, a term now applied to the General Secretariat and the permanent clerical workers of all types, with headquarters in Carnegie's building in Washington; and, finally, the Specialized Organizations which had been set up from time to time by the early conferences, or had come into being to fill specific needs. These covered a myriad of activities in health, agriculture, welfare, and economic betterment.

The opening article of this charter says that the signatory states mean "to achieve an order of peace and justice, to promote their solidarity, to strengthen their collaborations, and to defend their sovereignty, their territorial integrity, and their independence." Thus the OAS was more than a regional pact within the UN; it meant no sacrifice of sovereignty, and would continue to exist no matter what the future held for the world organization. To further carry out these purposes, the delegates at Bogotá signed an American Treaty on Pacific Settlement, which outlawed war in the Western Hemisphere, and bound the American republics to "refrain from the threat or the use of force, or from any other means of coercion for the settlement of their controversies, and to have recourse at all times to pacific procedures." A Treaty on Reciprocal Assistance, signed at Rio de Janeiro the year before, had promised joint action in the event of aggression on any American state. The entire OAS plan was unanimously ratified by 1956.

The OAS under this charter soon became far more newsworthy than the Pan-American Union. It maintained a large staff under its secretariat, concerned with a wide variety of social, economic, and cultural programs, pledged in its 1948 charter to maintain peace and to promote human welfare. The OAS constantly expanded its program, enlarged its staff and its budget, and widened its scope. At a conference in Rio de Janeiro in 1965, plans were made to amend the charter to establish a general assembly. As the governing entity of the OAS, this assembly replaces the Inter-American government officials who were meeting only every five years. Directly under the general assembly are three councils of equal rank: the permanent council which carries on the continuing program; the Inter-American Economic and Social Council which has equal weight with the political and diplomatic committees; and, third, the Inter-American Council for Education, Science, and Culture. All member states are represented on each of these councils, and each state has one vote. The first general assembly met in the old Pan-American Union Building in Washington in June, 1970, and planned budget allocations to four different phases of Inter-American economic and social endeavor. Its first regular session began on April 14, 1971, in San José, Costa Rica and was to be held yearly thereafter as an active working group.

the United States attempt to control communism through the OAS

Unfortunately the United States still expected the Latin American states to join with it in controlling Communism in the New World; we considered the OAS pledged to help us maintain our "security." At a foreign ministers' meeting in Santiago, Chile, in the late summer of 1959, which had been called because Trujillo had objected to Castro's interference in the Dominican Republic, the United States asked the meeting for condemnation of Communist intervention anywhere. A planeload of bearded Cuban soldiers who arrived in Chile during the meeting were treated like any unwelcome visitors without visas. The sentiment of the meeting, however, was not with Trujillo, but opposed to any kind of intervention, against dictators or against Communists. The OAS was definitely not going to intervene in Cuba to discipline Castro for his subversive guerrillas.

In June 1960 the United States made a formal report to the OAS on all Fidel Castro's "excesses" in harassing and confiscating American investments in Cuba throughout 1959 and 1960; but expected no action and meant only to have the problem "on the record." Then Venezuela complained that Dominican dictator Trujillo had sent assassins to attack her liberal President Betancourt. Meeting in August 1960 as an "Organ of Consultation" on this specific problem, the Sixth Meeting of Ministers of Foreign Affairs at San José de Costa Rica applied the 1947 Rio pact against aggression for the first time. Member states were asked to break diplomatic relations with Trujillo, forbid the shipment of arms to him, and refuse to buy Dominican products. The United States agreed and withdrew its ambassador, in the hopes that OAS members would then agree to the same kind of treatment against Communist Cuba. American promises to boycott Dominican sugar only led to embarrassment, for the United States Congress refused to cut down on Trujillo's quota of sugar sold in the United States. This was perhaps due to the activities of Trujillo's lobbies in Washington, perhaps to pressure from American firms with large Dominican sugar investments. At any rate, Latin American observers credited this joint action againt Trujillo for the deterioration of his power in the Dominican Republic and the courage of his assassins the following year.

With United States' unilateral action discredited at the Bay of Pigs, the OAS was willing to take some action against Cuba by January 1962. Finally, another Hemipsheric state, Peru, had complained about subversive activity of Castro-trained guerrillas inside her territory. Peru's complaint had been turned over to one of the agencies set up by the 1954 Caracas conference, the Inter-American Peace Committee. The well-documented report of that committee led to a meeting of Consultation of Ministers of Foreign Affairs in January 1962, the first meeting held at the resort of Punta del Este, Uruguay. Neither the OAS charter nor the 1947 Rio Pact against aggression had clearly set down what could be done in such cases of subversion, but the OAS showed itself flexible enough to devise a method of warning against Castro. Seventeen nations voted that "Cuba has voluntarily placed itself outside that system." A resolution was also passed to "apply limited sanctions of trade" against Cuba—a mere gesture for Cuba was by this time sending all her sugar to the Soviet bloc and needed no imports from the Latin American states. Mexico, Bolivia, Uruguay, and Chile still maintained diplomatic relations with Cuba.

This OAS stand served the United States in good stead when President Kennedy announced that Russia was setting up missile bases in Cuba. The President made this announcement at 7:00 p.m., October 22, 1962. Before mid-afternoon on October 23, the Council of the OAS had "unanimously called for the immediate dismantling and withdrawal of all missiles" and other offensive capabilities. Member countries were to take "all individual and collective measures necessary" to prevent more military supplies from reaching Cuba. Thus the OAS Council unanimously backed President Kennedy on the blockade of Russian shipping to Cuba which led to the removal of Russian arms from the island.

In July 1964 Venezuela complained to the OAS that Fidel Castro was making clandestine arms shipments to Venezuelan insurgents, trying to interfere with the peaceful end of Betancourt's presidency and the inauguration of Leoni. The Ninth Consultative Meeting of the OAS Foreign Ministers of Washington, July 26, 1964, accused Cuba of subversive aggression which, "though not an armed attack," called for "mandatory diplomatic and economic sanctions under the Rio Pact of 1947." As a result of this OAS condemnation, Chile, Uruguay, and Bolivia called their ambassadors home from Havana. Only Mexico maintained an embassy there, but she did this more to tell the world that Mexico was not a puppet of the United States than to show any approval of Fidel Castro.

Though bands of Cuban-trained guerrillas continued to appeal to peasants in various underprivileged areas of Latin America, most Latin

American governments had ceased to fear the influence of Fidel Castro by 1971. Russia itself seemed disillusioned in attempting a foothold in the New World via Cuba. Communism there had not been an immediate panacea for the ills of overpopulation, underindustrialization, and grinding rural poverty —a fact which seemed to be proven by Cuba's agreement with the United States to allow several thousand refugees a month to leave the island.

But the Johnson administration feared Communism in the Caribbean. American and OAS attempts to bring stability to the Dominican Republic after the assassination of Trujillo had come to nothing. The junta under Donald Reid Cabral in control there in the spring of 1965 was pressed on the right by Trujillo's old army officers, in the middle by a group of younger army officers, and on the far left by Communists—both a hard core of the old Russian-financed Communist underground from Trujillo's day and a new group of younger people inspired by Fidel Castro. These elements combined to overthrow Reid Cabral in April 1965, and left a vacuum of power, punctuated by street fighting and terror from both right and left. Claiming that a large number of Americans and other foreigners were in danger, President Johnson sent in a detail of marines on April 28 to guard the embassy, the downtown hotels, and an evacuation beach. When these marines were fired upon by the leftist rebels led by Camaaño Deno, more marines and paratroopers were sent in unilaterally by the United States, till the American troops numbered around 15,000. President Johnson was accused by Latin American observers of promulgating a new American policy, the Johnson Doctrine: "the United States will intervene unilaterally to prevent a Communist coup in any Latin American state without waiting for OAS action."

President Johnson immediately declared that he had no intention of invoking this "doctrine" elsewhere in Latin America. The legal counsel of the State Department published a defense of the United States action, saying, "We landed troops in the Dominican Republic in order to preserve the lives of foreign nationals. . . . We continued our military presence in the Dominican Republic for the additional purpose of preserving the capacity of the OAS to function in the manner intended by the OAS Charter"— that is, to secure a ceasefire, re-establish orderly political processes, and supervise a free election.

To bear out this defense of the United States' unilateral action, President Johnson had called the OAS into action on April 29. On May 6 the OAS resolved "to request governments of member states who are willing and capable of doing so to make contingents of their . . . forces available to the OAS . . . to form an inter-American force . . . with the sole purpose of cooperating in the restoration of normal conditions in the Dominican Republic." This historic resolution created a new body in Hemisphere history, an Inter-American Peace Force. By the middle of May 1965 forces from Brazil, five central American states, and a team of civilian doctors from Panama had arrived in Santo Domingo. A Brazilian general, Hugo Panasco Alvrim, was chosen to command the force. American marines were withdrawn, though regular army troops remained wearing the blue and yellow

mission was declared unwelcome and planned visits there were cancelled. On August 3, 1969, the Rockefeller Commission presented Nixon with a report long enough to fill an entire 50-page issue of the Department of State *Bulletin.* Rockefeller called his report "Quality of Life in the Americas." The last 20 pages of the report consisted of various recommendations, the strongest of which was "to make a clear policy in Latin America and stick to it," which he said necessitated being sure that "Congress understands and is willing to go along." He wanted Nixon to upgrade Latin American affairs in the American governmental organization, even suggesting a cabinet secretary of Western Hemisphere Affairs; and he urged that all economic aid be channeled through this new department. He called for the withdrawal of all restrictions on the allocation of United States aid money, of all demands that Latin American purchases were to be made exclusively in America and shipped in American ships, and that no aid was to be given to nations confiscating property of any American company. He realized that many needs of the developing nations could be purchased more cheaply in Europe or Japan and shipped more cheaply in the vessels of several other nations. He recommended that restrictions requiring countries to be helped to buy their military weapons in the United States be canceled. He wanted decision-making powers concerning the use of Alliance funds taken over by the Inter-American Committee for the Alliance for Progress working directly through the OAS. He said that Latin American problems of poverty, unemployment, and illiteracy would continue to produce violence and disorder, and that the United States, working through the OAS, should give aid to any backward nation whether we approved of its government or not. Nixon, however, did not publish this report for three months, and then delayed commenting on it until the end of October 1970.

Meanwhile, a subdivision of the United Nations called the Special Latin American Coordination Committee was meeting at Viña del Mar in Chile, a meeting that was not attended by representatives of the United States, for we were not represented on this particular United Nations Committee. On June 11, 1969, while Rockefeller was in South America, this committee prepared a 6,000-word criticism of American policies which has been called the Consensus of Viña del Mar. Chilean foreign minister Gabriel Valdez, who framed the criticisms, claimed that aid to Latin America was the one that was most successful in selling American products and bringing profits to American companies. In the year 1968, United States companies in Latin America had made five times as much profit as they had invested there. He said it was a myth that the developing nations were actually being aided by United States funds. They were forced to buy United States goods in large quantities in return for the money with which to buy such goods. The United States Congress would only support programs which aid their own constituencies. Tariff restrictions were very high and products of Latin America could not be sold at a profit inside the United States.

The report that Nixon made in October of 1969 in answer to the Rockefeller Report and the Consensus of Viña del Mar was very general. He said that he "recognized many unfulfilled promises" and called for "action not words." He meant to avoid optimism and talked about "implied partnership in improved trade." There should be "regional economic integration, but each nation must make its own decisions about the place of private investment both domestic and foreign, in its development process." Nixon promised to support regular procedures for advance consultation on all trade matters, to be worked out within the OAS system. He promised to "lead vigorously to reduce tariff barriers." He did not take Rockefeller's advice for a cabinet department and merely raised the rank of Assistant Secretary for Latin American Affairs to that of Under-Secretary of State. His only direct action seemed to be to allow United States loan dollars to be spent inside Latin America, rather than to insist that all loan moneys spent on seed, equipment and supplies to carry out improvement projects be spent on purchases inside the United States.

With these soothing statements about "trade rather than aid" Nixon bought another year's time. Then Secretary of State Rogers went to the first General Assembly of the OAS where he met with other foreign ministers in April, 1971. Rogers attempted to calm the angry voices raised against our neglect of Latin America, saying that President Nixon had told him to initiate consultation with the United States Congress to work out tariff agreements on a wide range of items, including the 500 items asked by Latin American delegates. In dollars and cents the tariff arrangements would cover only a small percentage of the total Latin American exports to the United States, but the Nixon administration hoped that psychologically the Latin Americans would feel that they were being treated as "trade equals." With Nixon making overtures for improved trade with China in the spring of 1972, several Latin American leaders expressed fears that even these small hopes toward better trade relations would come to nothing.

Although the goals of the Alliance for Progress were neither attainable nor realistic, much good can be said of the program. Some economic progress has been achieved, as described in the next chapter. The Latin Americans were made aware of the necessity of helping themselves and pulling themselves up by their own bootstraps.

Latin American relations with Europe and the world

In the 1800's, the newly independent nations either feared intervention from European countries or asked them for help. Today Spain's position in world affairs has become negligible and her interest in Latin America merely cultural. England—in the 1800's the dominant world power and principal investor in Latin American industry and transportation facilities—can today afford to take only a minor interest and has become a lesser force. This is even more true of France. Germany, however—"on the make" from 1900 to 1940—became a serious threat to the Western Hemisphere in the 1930's; and, more recently, Russia has been something of a "menace."

Early in the nineteenth century, ties with the mother country had been abruptly broken. Spain later made some feeble attempts at friendship. After Cuba was lost in 1899, Spanish attention was turned to retaining hold of Spanish America through ties of loyalty alone and concentrated on a program of cultural rapproachement based on a reinforcement of *hispanidad,* or hispanic identity.

French investments in Mexico, and the purchase by a relative of Napoleon III of the Swiss Jecker bonds, gave that monarch an excuse for his famous adventure in Mexico, his sponsoring of the ill-fated Maximilian's campaign against Juárez. This was the last attempt made by the French to expand colonialism in the New World. French culture, nevertheless, has continued to be a dominant force in Latin American life.

The colony-hungry German government made several "passes" at Latin America during these days of phenomenal economic growth. In 1897 two German naval vessels appeared in Haitian waters to demand the freedom of a German national who was being held for assaulting a policeman, and to present an ultimatum to the Haitian government. The United States declined to intervene under the Monroe Doctrine; Haiti accepted the ultimatum, freed the German, and made a formal apology. A year later, when the United States went to war against Spain in Cuba, the German Kaiser was openly sympathetic with Spain, as one monarchy to another. Because of the German threat to send forces to Venezuela to collect the debt incurred to German banks by the dictator Cipriano Castro, Theodore Roosevelt formulated the Roosevelt Corollary. He threatened the action of a United States naval squadron in Venezuelan water to prevent the landing of German troops. The dispute was settled by arbitration in 1904.

These incidents helped to build up fear of German expansionism in Latin America. When, in January 1917, the Zimmerman note—a cable from the German Foreign Secretary instructing the minister in Mexico to offer California, New Mexico, Texas, and Arizona to Mexico in return for an alliance with Germany if the United States should go to war—was intercepted and given publicity in America, these fears seemed realized. During World War I eight Latin American nations declared war; five others had sufficient belligerent status to sit in on the Versailles Peace Conference as contracting parties. Defeat ended German expansionism for the time being, cut her merchant fleet down to nothing, bankrupted her foreign investments, and brought her into the depths of depression ahead of the rest of the world. The Weimar Republic could afford no Latin American policy, save an attempt at mutual trade relations.

The Third Reich under Hitler had a more aggressive policy, with political overtones. Every German trader among the Indian tribes, every German storekeeper on the pampas, as well as German pilots with the airplane companies and German bank clerks in the cities all became potential Nazi agents. If such New World Germans were not ardent Nazis they were replaced by ones who were. Many Argentine radio stations and newspapers were controlled by the Nazis as propaganda tools for the whole New World. The German embassy in Buenos Aires was the center of such espionage. Though there were many more German immigrants living in

Chile, with the city of Valdivia a center of German settlement and language, Chile remained more nearly neutral and less suspect to the democratic nations than did Argentina. After Pearl Harbor, only these two southern South American countries failed to break with the Axis. The hatred of things German did not hold over into the 1960s, however, as West Germany, an economically rather than a politically active new state, proceeded to recapture and multiply the trade which all of Germany had held before the war.

Relations with the other Axis powers during World War II were never as dangerous or as unfriendly. Italy was a Latin country, center of the Catholic faith. Millions of people in Argentina and Brazil were of Italian origin. Italian investment was never large; Mussolini's propaganda agents were not very clever. Italy was out of the war by 1943, and few Latin Americans thought of her as a menace. Japanese relations were resumed after the war, and a thriving Japanese-Brazilian trade picked up where it had stopped in 1941. The Japanese merchant fleet was again visiting South American waters in the 1970s; Japanese colonists were being invited to the rice plantations Brazil was attempting to establish on the Amazon.

In the 1960s Latin America felt her interests were often inimicable to those of Europe. Attempting to launch a Latin American Common Market, the grain and meat producing states feared the rivalry of the European Common Market, while banana, coffee, and sugar producing states feared British Commonwealth trade areas in Africa and Asia.

In the post World War II era, Russian infiltration became a danger. There were active Communist parties in several countries, Perón used Russian funds to propagandize against the United States; Guatemala was controlled in 1954 by a pro-Communist government with Russian money; in April 1964 the Castelo Branco revolution in Brazil ousted the Russian sympathizer Goulart. With the rise of Fidel Castro as the Communist leader in Cuba, Russian policy seemed to turn the training and financing of Western Hemisphere Communist groups over to him, under long-range Moscow direction. Appealing to workers, to peasants, and particularly to university students, Castro-type Communists made "¡Yanquis, No!" a youth cry, as much for national patriotism as for international Communism. By the mid-1960s the old-line Cuban Communist Party, loyal to Russia, was being elbowed out of importance in Cuba. Ché Guevara, a world-oriented Communist revolutionary, disappeared from the Cuban scene, and failed in his attempt to arouse the highland Indians in Bolivia, where he was killed late in 1967. In 1971 there were eleven Russian embassies in Latin America, most of them being used as focal points for advice, propaganda and funds to local revolutionary groups. The staffs of the embassies unofficially engage in activity with native extremist parties and leftist presidential candidates. As described elsewhere, the Russians have a toehold in Cuba, though apparently not yet in Chile. In 1972 fourteen nations had trade agreements with Russia; about one-half of Soviet trade with Latin America (except for Cuba) is with Brazil.

As for England, her participation in Latin American affairs was more economic than political and forms a portion of the next chapter. Occasionally England concerned herself with Latin American diplomatic affairs. In 1833 she seized the Falkland Islands while the Argentine dictator Rosas protested. In the Uruguayan difficulties she sent a fleet to blockade the harbor during the siege of Montevideo; in the Maximilian episode she joined with Spain and Napoleon III in an attempt to collect debts, then withdrew when she became suspicious of French plans. As the self-appointed conscience of the world in the fight against the slave trade, she enforced her blockade of the African coast. England exacted from Brazil a promise to end the slave trade as a price for recognition of Brazil as a nation in 1827. When it was later apparent that Brazilians took this promise none too seriously, English warships infringed on Brazilian sovereignty by entering Brazilian ports to stop the slavers. Only when Brazil made the slave trade illegal in 1850 was this problem finally solved.

Accepting the United States as the dominant power in the Caribbean area after the American Civil War, Britain was mainly concerned that any canal built should be neutral and free. In the Clayton-Bulwer Treaty of 1850 both powers pledged themselves to avoid dominating Central America and to assist in the building of a free canal jointly. With the British already holding a piece of Honduran coast at Belize, Britain challenged this treaty almost as soon as it was made by declaring the Bay Islands a British colony. American protests forced her to withdraw, and to give up the toe-hold on the Mosquito Coast of Nicaragua also. A half-century later the Hay-Pauncefote Treaty guaranteed America's right to build the Panama Canal, as long as it was open equally to ships of all nations. England remains a power in the Caribbean; she has an interest in the new self-governing Commonwealth nations of the British West Indies, including Trinidad, Jamaica, and British Guiana on the mainland, which have become members in the UAS. In the 1960s British policy in Latin America was completely tied in with that of the United States in promoting trade, preventing the spread of Communism, and helping raise the standards of living through the Alliance for Progress.

Latin American states had been gravitating toward membership in some type of world organization even before the Pan American system had any strong influence. All save Costa Rica participated in The Hague meetings in 1907, sending outstanding jurists as delegates and influencing The Hague conferences to incorporate "nonintervention" as part of international law. Latin American delegates voted unanimously for Red Cross rules of humanitarian war and accepted settlement of disputes as "obligatory in principle." Dr. Antonio Sánchez de Bustamente of Cuba became a member of the Permanent Arbitration Tribunal of The Hague, and was active two decades later in the League of Nations.

Ten nations became charter members of the League of Nations, and all the others eventually joined. Part of the enthusiasm Latin America felt for the League of Nations was based on antagonism to the United States in the early 1920s; here was a new world organization, in which the Latin American states were equal to European nations, but from which the United States remained aloof. There was a bureau within the League framework to deal with Latin American affairs. As far as the Latin American disputes of the 1920s were concerned, the Chilean delegates opposed any consideration of the Tacna-Arica affair by the League Assembly. In the early 1930s the League, joined by the ABC powers, had unsuccessfully attempted to arbitrate the war in the Gran Chaco, and had successfully formulated a proposal acceptable to Peru and Colombia in the Leticia dispute. Meanwhile, however, the Pan American system was strengthened by the lessening fear of the United States under the Good Neighbor Policy, while the League itself at Geneva was dying on the vine.

At the meeting called at Chapultepec Castle in February 1945 as World War II came to a close, the Dumbarton Oaks proposals had been accepted by the Inter-American system as a basis for a new world federation. Thus the Latin American states went in a body to the San Francisco charter meeting in April 1945, where they advocated the equality of small and large nations. Latin America has had a strong influence in the subsequent development of the UN. Germán Arciniegas, famous Colombian writer, said in the late 1940s, "Latin America was nothing thirty years ago. Now in the United Nations one third part is Latin America. The United States has one vote. Russia, with all its satellites, has maybe six. Latin America holds the balance of power."

The Charter had provided that of the six nonpermanent members of the Security Council elected every two years, two should always be Latin American nations. Thus leading Latin American statesmen have always served on the Council. Zuleta Angel of Colombia was chairman of the Preparatory Committee for the first Assembly, held in London in 1946. Of the fifteen judges elected by this first Assembly to serve on the International Court of Justice, four were Latin Americans, though the judges were chosen purely on the basis of ability, with no relationship to country represented. One-third of the chairmanships of Assembly committees also went to Latin Americans.

At first the Latin American bloc of twenty nations in a total UN membership of fifty or sixty did "hold the balance of power," and Russia charged that this bloc made up a strong pro–United States vote. But Latin America has voted with the United States on some issues and against her on others. In general, these nations held a caucus on each important question before coming to the UN, just as they decided among themselves which of them were to be elected to the Security Council or other UN bodies.

Even after the membership of the United Nations doubled with the admission of the new Asian and African states, Latin Americans continued to play an important part in the deliberations of the General Assembly, in the Security Council, and in varied activities. Judges from at least four Latin American nations have sat in the International Court of Justice. Inter-American organizations have cooperated with UN specialized organizations, as told in the next chapter. This is especially true in the field of health, where the Pan-American Sanitary Bureau of the OAS has led the World Health Organization in disease-control projects. Oswaldo Aranha of Brazil, Benjamin Cohen of Chile, Ana Figueres, a school teacher from Chile, and

Galo Plaza of Ecuador have served as chairmen of the General Assembly or of special commissions.

Activities in Latin American social and economic improvement projects carried out by the various agencies of the UN, the OAS, and the Alliance for Progress are described in the next chapter, providing an optimistic story for the last section of this book.

Note: Readings for Chapter 30 are combined with those of Chapter 31 and are to be found on page 750.

LATIN AMERICAN
COOPERATION
IN ECONOMIC, SOCIAL,
AND CULTURAL
MATTERS

international economic developments

More important in bringing Latin America together today than conferences and diplomats are the truck and the airplane, for increasing travel and improving transportation are vital in Latin America. Trucks can now reach remote hamlets within each nation, and can travel from nation to nation. International motor transit has been made possible by the Pan American Highway system, on which plans were commenced before 1930. The United States government assumed part of the cost of construction under the Inter-American Highway Act passed by Congress in December 1941. American engineers have assisted in the planning and construction, but each section has been built under the direction of the local government involved, and has not been completed until the local government has hired the workers, pushed the work, and paid its share of the bills. When completed, the system will include nearly 16,000 miles of highway and will have cost half a billion dollars. The northern section, known as the Inter-American Highway, has three branches by which the motorist may enter Mexico and proceed to Mexico City. The paved road continues through Guatemala and El Salvador. An all-weather road runs through Nicaragua into Southern Costa Rica, and the Pan American Highway itself was officially completed to the Panama Canal. The Darién Gap connecting southern Panama with Colombia is set for completion by 1978. The 240 miles to be cleared to finish the Pan-American Highway includes the Atrato Swamp, to be bridged with a long viaduct to connect to the finished road at Río León in Colombia. This is the shortest route surveyed to cross this difficult terrain. At Río León the Atrato cutoff will meet the highway of northern South America called the Simón Bolívar Highway from Caracas, first through Colombia and Quito, on into Peru and Bolivia, connecting with roads coming up from Argentina. In 1972 both the Brazilian and Peruvian Governments were working to build the extension east across the Andes to parallel the Amazon and eventually reach the Atlantic.

The highway is thus doing what railways never did: it is connecting groups of Latin American nations. There is no all–Central American rail line; the railroads pioneered in South America by Wheelwright and Meiggs seldom crossed national boundaries. Probably little further international rail building will take place in Latin America, as the airplane is a better answer to transportation problems.

There were commercial airlines in Latin America by 1920. Pan American Airways, a United States firm which held a virtual monopoly in some areas, has been forced to surrender its monopoly to nationally owned lines. There are today more than 200,000 miles of air routes in Latin America. A series of commercial aviation, airmail, and aerial navigation conferences has been held, the earliest as long ago as 1923. Modern trucking and cargo-carrying airlines have improved inter-Latin American trade.

The nations of Western Europe have made profits from Latin American investments for a century and a half. This is especially true of England. Most of the railroads of the nineteenth century were built by English capital, and England was the first nation to profit from Latin American independence. The value of British trade with Latin America in 1823 was $7.5 million, an increase of $2.5 million over the previous year. Not only traders but investors saw such a rich field for profit that Britain was Latin America's investment banker throughout the nineteenth century. British interests built the railways across the pampas and into the Andes; they started the wool industry in Argentina and Uruguay, improved cattle by importing the best British herd sires. English companies started the tramways in both Buenos Aires and Rio de Janeiro, brought steamers to the Pacific coast, financed the Chilean nitrate industry, developed the silver mines in Mexico, and constructed the first *frigoríficos* in Buenos Aires.

By 1870 British investments totaled £85 million. By 1913, the peak year of British economic activity in Latin America, investment had reached £756 million, then more than $4 billion. Of these funds, 32 per cent was in government bonds, 46 per cent in railway securities and shipping, and eighteen per cent in agriculture and mining. By the beginning of World War I, British companies owned 118 railroads, forty-five port facility companies, 112 public utility companies, and thirty-five nitrate companies, as well as almost all the telephone exchanges, electric power distributors, and water works in Latin America. Since the over-all return was said to be under five per cent, it is true that Latin American countries obtained both their capital and their technical assistance at very cheap prices in their first century of growth. But two world wars in the twentieth century destroyed England's economic leadership, in Latin America as well as in the rest of the world. By the 1950s English capital had been partially replaced by American investment and by new locally owned capital. French investment in Latin America has been very small compared with that of the British. French trade reached a peak of $323 million worth of business in Latin America in 1928, most of it with Argentina and Brazil.

German activity before World War I was largely confined to promoting German commerce, investments, and immigration. German firms had investments worth $2 billion in trade yearly, while 700,000 German settlers in Latin America helped keep German companies prosperous. This economic machinery, revived in the 1930s, was of great use to Hitler, under whom it grew to startling proportions. It went through various vicissitudes during World Wars I and II, as described in the nation-by-nation analysis. Today the West German Republic is again making important investments in Latin America and stimulating trade relations by giving careful attention to the client's specifications, extending adequate credit, and providing practical technical aid.

Since 1900 it has been the United States that has loomed largest in the Latin American trade and investment picture. The monetary relations between Latin America and the United States can be divided into three categories: first, the investments made by private American interests; second, the trade relations, the balance of exports and imports between the two regions; and third, the economic aid and governmental loans made as a part of American foreign policy since the 1940s.

The United States was not an investing nation until the twentieth century, and American firms put little into Latin America before the Spanish-American War. By 1910 the banana companies had begun their plantations in Central America, and the American friends of Porfirio Díaz had started to drill for oil in Mexico. American firms are estimated to have invested perhaps $1.6 billion in Latin America by 1914. True, the Taft era was one of "Dollar Diplomacy," but most historians consider that the interventions in Central America and the Caribbean were as much a part of a new American continental strategy as they were a defense of "Wall Street profits." During World War I, American capital began to surpass European capital in the southern republics. The United States itself was a nation of surplus capital, looking for foreign investments.

In the 1930s 43 per cent of all investment abroad by American nationals was in Latin America. American banks had pressed Mexican loans, Bolivian bonds, or Peruvian municipal flotations on their home-town buyers, often without sufficient investigation, and millions of such bonds had been defaulted during the depression. Latin American dictators had often borrowed from American bankers in bad faith, and the money had been wasted. Though the United States was often blamed for "economic imperialism," it never used force to collect these defaulted debts. The United States State Department said "No economic reprisals." Bondholders' protective committees were private affairs, and the government took no responsibility for helping individual American losers. A total of more than $700 million was thus defaulted during the depression.

Individual American companies had not always fared badly; in fact great fortunes were made—by the United Fruit Company, with its fabulous empire in the Caribbean; by the W. R. Grace company, which had a tight hold on shipping, transportation, and banking on South America's west coast; by the Guggenheims, who developed in Chile the largest supply of high-grade copper in the world. Manufacturing did not enter the picture until the new assembly plants of American factories were set up in the rapidly industrializing countries of Mexico, Chile, Argentina, and Uruguay after World War II.

The major part of the United States investments had encouraged the one-crop cultures of many lesser nations and had become monopolies which brought pressure on the weak governments, thereby promoting much ill-will. United States nationals working abroad as employees of American companies usually lived in exclusive American "colonies," seemingly "superior" to the "inferior" natives. They played golf with each other, their wives made no attempt to mix socially, and few such company representatives bothered to learn Spanish. Paid in United States dollars, such families lived well on "the exchange" and took very little interest in Latin American affairs. That United States companies also raised wages and living standards and improved public health in Latin American communities cannot be denied, though most of them neglected to hire local technicians or encourage the training of such among the native populations, and often paid ridiculously small taxes. All except four Latin American countries have passed laws requiring a minimum percentage of nationals to be employed in any foreign venture; many countries have special tax laws which require foreign companies to receive the same tax treatment as local companies. The United Fruit Company and most American oil companies still in business there give the governments of countries in which they operate more than 66 per cent of their net profits.

In the post–World War II world, Latin America was as anxious to attract industrial capital as to discipline it. The Ninth Pan American Conference at Bogotá in 1948 passed a resolution: "The States shall take no discriminatory action against investments by virtue of which foreign enterprises or capital may be deprived of legally acquired property rights. . . ." Signatories could thus guarantee foreign investors fair treatment. American capital saw a green light by the 1950s. An Inter-American Investment Conference was held in New Orleans in 1955 to study additional means of making money in Latin America through the creation of a private International Finance Corporation, approving the floating $35 million worth of loans in eighteen Latin American countries. Some of this was to be in bankers' loans to local Latin American companies, some to American firms with plants abroad. All this provided encouragement in a field which was prospering already. In the 1960s private United States investments in Latin America totaled more than $9 billion while the yearly figures of exports and imports were approaching $8 billion. The taxes American firms paid in Latin America totaled more than their profits, and the companies themselves provided seven hundred thousand jobs. There was bitterness against such companies, however, for they were largely in mining and petroleum, and the Latin Americans accused them of using up non-renewable resources. In the early 1970s, American copper mines were nationalized in Chile and oil wells and refineries in Peru.

Latin American businessmen fared well in direct trade with the United States. When the United States had passed the Smoot-Hawley Tariff in 1930, Latin American trade had been jolted. But by 1933, faced with worldwide depression, the United States was ready to take Cordell Hull's advice on reciprocity. At the Montevideo Pan American Conference in 1933, Hull advocated a resolution "calling upon the American republics to enter upon a program of reciprocal lowering of high tariffs to moderate levels, upon the principle of the unconditional most-favored nation formula by bilateral and multilateral reciprocity agreements." A law of Congress of June 12, 1934, gave the President of the United States the power to make such trade agreements; Hull set up the necessary machinery, and by 1943 had concluded sixteen such trade agreements with Latin American nations. In general, duties were lowered by almost 30 per cent. Today Latin Americans buy millions of dollars' worth of American-made machinery and consumer goods yearly. Sixty per cent of Latin America's imports come from the United States, and only 21 per cent from Europe. In return the United States is Latin America's biggest market, absorbing 44 per cent of their exports. By 1967 United States and Latin American exports and imports were almost equalling each other at about 40 per cent.

Government-to-government aid became a part of United States World War II policy. From 1941 to 1945 American government money poured into Latin America to build up supplies of strategic materials; 34 per cent of all loans made by the Export-Import Bank went to Latin America. After the war, when the Marshall Plan money was being spent in postwar Europe and the stream of funds to Latin America trickled out, Latin American delegates protested at the 1948 conference at Bogotá. Here Secretary of State Marshall promised them more loans—though not direct grants—to build up transportation and hydroelectric and irrigation projects, as well as loans from the Export-Import Bank in greater amounts and assistance from private firms with government approval.

But a harvest of ill-will collected from the halfhearted way in which these post–World War II promises were kept. United States economic aid was being spread out over world areas seemingly less friendly to the United States. Though private American firms had invested the astronomical sum of $9 billion, these dollars were in profit-making ventures, and only helped develop the economically backward regions as an incidental by-product. Although the Organization of American States and the UN launched scores of development projects in Latin America, as will be seen below, and though a fourth part of their cost was borne by United States public funds or private philanthropies, the actual amount spent by United States sources on such cooperative development programs from 1945 to 1960 was very small compared to that spent on military aid to Greece or Turkey or Nationalist China in any one year in the 1950s. Loans were made to Alemán in Mexico, Paz Estenssoro in Bolivia, and others for specific improvements, but the over-all amounts were small compared to the billions the United States spent elsewhere.

Meanwhile, Communist agents worked on Latin American disappointment with American promises, and Soviet trade with the individual Latin American States, although small, was growing. It was practically negligible before 1950, but in 1955 nineteen Soviet trade deals involving $500 million worth of goods were made. A fourth of this trade was with Argentina, a nation which has subsequently carried on 13 per cent of her trade with Iron Curtain countries. By 1958 Russia was the largest single buyer of Uruguayan wool. Soviet trade commissions were visiting Caribbean and Central American countries; Poland and Czechoslovakia were underselling the West to get contracts from Brazil for shipbuilding and railway rolling-stock manufacture. The drop in copper prices brought on by the 1957 recession in the United States forced Chile to sell 15,000 tons of copper wire to Russia, while Red China was anxious to buy the Chilean nitrate fertilizer which American farmers do not use.

In June 1958 Brazilian President Kubitschek called for joint action to end some of the ill-will and ease the Communist threat by means of a cooperative development. As described in Chapter 30, this plan grew into the Alliance for Progress. As far as trade is concerned, the plan was to include a Latin-American Common Market.

Although not actually a Common Market, a Latin American Free Trade Area (LAFTA) did get started in the decade of the 1960's. At a meeting in Montevideo in 1960, Mexico joined with eight South American countries, in an attempt to cut tariffs and promote trade among themselves. Six years later trade among these nine nations had increased 95 per cent. The participants had listed 2,500 items on which the nine nations would charge no tariff for one another. However, only ten per cent of the overall trade was among themselves, although Mexican trade with South America did increase 100 per cent in the decade of the 1960's. New companies were busy sending cement blocks from Monterey to Montevideo and building ships for freight from Vera Cruz to Porto Alegre. The other eight South American members of LAFTA had not shown this much improvement; their trade with each other increased less than 20 per cent. Ecuador and Paraguay hesitated in joining for fear that what little home industry they had would be swamped by manufactured articles from Argentina and Chile.

The LAFTA had not raised the price of coffee, though at least it remained stable. Chocolate prices and profits declined due to world overproduction and large exports from the African states. The LAFTA zone held 180 million people, enough untapped natural resources and enough potential for a boom in the twenty-first century. "It is certain that without integration there will be no economic development in Latin America," said Felipe Herrera, director of the Inter-American Development Bank.

exchange and assistance to attack
social problems

From the time of the first activities of the old Pan American Sanitary Bureau, agencies in the Western Hemisphere have worked toward raising the standard of living, improving health, and solving social problems in the Latin American areas, combining United Nations programs and OAS programs, to set an example for the world in the 1970s as illustrated by the introduction to this section of the book on page 693. Although it must be admitted that the program in reality has not accomplished as much as its outline on paper might indicate, nevertheless the spirit, the promise, and the organized committee work did exist.

Before World War II the Pan American movement consisted of a heterogeneous complexity of separate agencies, bound together by irregular conferences or by the inefficiently expanded old Commercial Bureau in Washington. Most of these activities were correlated with the OAS as specialized agencies by the 1950s. Their mass of paperwork and committee arrangements were headed by the Secretary-General, elected for a term of ten years. Such leading Latin Americans as the Colombian President Alberto Lleras Camargo, the Chilean former president Carlos Dávila, the Ecuadorian Galo Plaza, and the Uruguayan Dr. José Mora have held this post after World War II. The organization worked on a budget of nearly $6 million of which 66 per cent was provided by the United States as the wealthiest and most populous member, and the remainder prorated among the twenty other states according to their ability to pay. The specialized agencies—those concerned with the protection of childhood, with agricultural sciences, with Indian affairs—together with the Institute of Geography and History and, the oldest of all, the Pan American Sanitary Bureau—were all financed from special funds. So also was the OAS Program of Technical Cooperation, which received $2 million a year from its member nations and spent the greater part of it for agriculture, control of animal diseases, conservation, and rural education. One popular method of organizing technical cooperation under the OAS was through the creation of *Servicios* set up by the host country, which cooperated with the technical experts and joined in the financing. There were forty-seven *Servicio* projects operating in Latin America as the decade of the 1970s began.

A report on the specialized activities of the OAS for a five-year period, filled 200 pages with descriptions of concrete activities. A list of the "Forthcoming Inter-American Conferences" for a single year announced eighty-one projected meetings, to be held in various capitals, tropical institutes, rural education centers, or archeological sites throughout the Hemisphere. Preventive medicine, travel conditions, geodetic surveys, nutrition, population problems, tuberculosis treatment, weather prognostication, child psychology, prenatal care, and juvenile delinquency all served as topics for meetings. If such conferences accomplished nothing more constructive than a meeting of minds among the experts, the Hemisphere made progress. Another technical-cooperation project of the OAS dealt with providing low-cost, hygienic housing in the fast-growing cities. This project, called the Inter-American Housing Research and Training Center, was at Bogotá; it trained some fifty technicians a year in its courses. New housing within the range of young people of lower income groups, city planning, slum clearance, and building for earthquake resistance in the Andean countries all occupied the attention of the trainees at Bogotá.

Delegates to Pan American meetings were concerned with health problems as early as 1902. The revolutionary experiments to prove Carlos Finlay's theories on yellow fever had just been finished, and the possibilities of making life safe and sanitary in the tropics appealed to all. There had been ten further meetings on health and sanitation by 1940. The Pan American Sanitary Bureau could report progress of interest to the whole world. The appallingly large figures on the incidence of malaria, yaws, hookworm, venereal disease, smallpox, and yellow fever, country by country, discouraged poorly developed nations with inadequate budgets for welfare projects. Thus the Pan American Sanitary Bureau's board program of scholarship for doctors and nurses, improvement of hospitals, technical assistance in creating sanitary water supply and sewage systems, and quick service in fighting epidemics and providing relief during disasters such as hurricanes and earthquakes gave the Sanitary Bureau a very good reputation from the first, when other Pan American ideas were merely beautiful words. During World War II the United States undertook to expand this work under the direction of the Pan American Sanitary Bureau, financed by the funds of the Rockefeller Commitee. More than 800 individual projects in public health were completed during the war years. In the 1950s the OAS committee had merely to carry on work so well and widely begun; by that time it had the help of the World Health Organization of the United Nations, whose regional office the Pan American Sanitary Bureau had become.

Cooperation in the field of agriculture brought into being a specific agency of the Inter-American Institute of Agricultural Sciences maintained by the OAS at Turrialba, Costa Rica. Here research work on the growing of tropical products such as coffee, cocao, vegetable fats and oils, and fiber was carried on at a 1,250-acre site donated by the government of Costa Rica. Under the Institute of Agricultural Sciences of the OAS a *fiebre aftosa* (hoof and mouth disease) center was set up in Brazil in 1951 to counteract hoof and mouth disease among livestock. A series of meetings on problems in the banana industry were held throughout 1955. Agricultural training centers were supported by the OAS in Cuba, Peru, and Uruguay, all of which were branches of the training headquarters in Costa Rica.

The agricultural, health, and social reform programs of the Pan American Union and the OAS have served as examples for the activities of the United Nations. Often there was official joint action; the OAS has signed agreements for cooperation with the International Labor Organization, UNESCO, the UN Food and Agricultural Organization, and the WHO, or World Health Organization. In all these fields, the Pan American specialists worked out methods of international action to teach the European specialists who came to work with them, and who in most cases had had no international experience. UN teams were then able to run "pilot projects" in backward areas. An example of such a project was a series of meetings on the improvement of the livestock industry—keeping records of milk production per cow, pasturage treatment, vaccines against cattle diseases, crossbreeding to improve cattle strains—held in Brazil in 1952 and attended by 150 delegates from European as well as Latin American nations. UNICEF has worked with the OAS agricultural institute in Costa Rica, hoping to formulate plans to improve dairying everywhere and thus make milk available to all children. The story of joint agricultural activity could fill many pages with reports on locust control, agricultural teaching, care of farm machinery, improvements in farm management—projects in training at the local level carried on with funds from the UN Technical Assistance Administration. There is a parallel and even more successful story concerning the work done through WHO in malaria control, development of insecticides, and large-scale vaccination programs.

The social and technical agencies are themselves always short of funds. By the early 1970s the United Nations agencies were primarily study groups on overall projects, such as: population control, forestry, communication, urban housing, and increased food production. Latin America was still a guide post to United Nations study in the 1970s, for population was outgrowing the food supply and the United Nations Food and Agriculture Organization reported that the next thirty-five years in Latin America would prove whether the entire world could solve its food problems or not.

That the United States itself, apart from OAS or UN cooperation, had an official policy of promoting improvement in Latin America is plainly evident from the list of agencies in Washington concerned with its neighbors to the south. In the Departments of Agriculture, Commerce, and Labor there are sections on encouraging scholarships for Latin Americans and on exchanging statistical studies. The Office of Education has a Division of Inter-American Educational Relations. Many agencies have assisted in financial matters and the State Department has carried on various types of cooperative effort. An interdepartmental Committee on Cooperation with the American Republics was created in 1938 to coordinate all such activities, and a "master plan" for seventy-four different projects was worked out. All such plans were transferred to the Office of the Coordinator of Inter-American Affairs during World War II, and were placed under the direction of Nelson Rockefeller.

Through the Coordinator of Inter-American Affairs, Latin American nations were offered programs in elementary education, in agricultural improvements, and in public health. Paraguay received a model dairy project with thirty head of Holstein cattle and three dairy experts from the University of Wisconsin, paid for by the State Department, as well as projects in silo building and orange-tree fungus control. With American assistance Brazil founded nurses' training schools in the Amazon and São Francisco Valleys, sent out mobile clinics by launch, built purified water supplies in many Amazon towns. By 1950 the Brazilian government was paying 50 per cent of the expenses of this program. Such technical assistance was costing American taxpayers only $18 million nine years after it was started; by 1955 it was being supported 80 per cent by local funds. In 1947 Congress had combined all these activities under a new Institute of Inter-American Affairs, but failed to vote adequate funds to support its activities to the extent set up in World War II.

American public health efficiency had always been admired by Latin Americans. Wheelwright had brought sanitary waterworks to Chile and Peru; the private Rockefeller Foundation had advertised American sanitation throughout the tropics. Even United Fruit spent $54 million on disease control from 1914 to 1941. The Division of Health and Sanitation of the Office of Coordinator of Inter-American Affairs had undertaken 950 projects in seventeen different countries by the end of World War II: 325 "environmental improvement" projects which cleared malarial swamps and improved water supply and sewage control, 214 health centers and hospitals, 300 preventive services in clinics, and eighty-one doctors' and nurses' training schools. Some of this work was continued under assistance schemes or financed directly by the Export-Import Bank when the wartime funds were withdrawn from the Nelson Rockefeller Committee.

The period from 1941 to 1945 also saw many cooperative efforts to improve agriculture, such as the Paraguayan dairy mentioned above. Export crops such as *abacá, cinchona,* and kapok were experimented with in Honduras. Soil conservation service teams went up and down the Hemisphere; an American-Haitian Agricultural Development Society, with American public funds, undertook a long-term program of developing new crops—rubber, oils, seeds, spices, drug plants, and fibers—in the place of sugar and bananas. A group of sixteen Ph.D.'s working jointly for the Rockefeller Foundation and the Colombian government in 1958 had developed new seed strains on a model Colombian farm to double the per-acre production of wheat and barley. During one postwar year there were 650 technicians from the United States stationed in Latin America and an even larger number of Latin American technicians of various kinds studying in the United States. These technicians were not all doctors or teachers or agriculturists; many of them were engineers in industry, transportation, and hydroelectricity.

Not all the social work was done by government agencies. Most famous of all private agencies in the Latin American field is the Rockefeller Foundation, using the private funds amassed by Nelson Rockefeller's grandfather, which spent millions over the years on the control of hookworm and yellow fever through the tropical regions of the world. Of these vast sums, more than $10 million was spent in the American tropics—Mexico, the Caribbean islands, and Central America—from 1913 to 1940. After World War II, the Rockefeller doctors and clinics continued to cooperate with the programs financed by the OAS and the United Nations.

Into this well-planned set-up of programs of the OAS, UN, United

States Federal Government, and United States private philanthropies came the sudden hopes for large funds from the Alliance for Progress.

The new President Kennedy was optimistic for the Alliance in 1961. "This is not just a doctrine of development, not just a blue print for economic advance," he said in 1962. "Rather it is an expression of the noblest goals for our civilization." Kennedy himself seemed to embody the new American attitude in the eyes of Latin Americans. He was young, Catholic, part of a large loyal family group in the Latin American tradition. On a trip with him to Bogotá to dedicate a slum-clearance housing project as part of the Alliance plan, Mrs. Jacqueline Kennedy spoke to the crowds in flawless Spanish. When this handsome young couple were removed from the presidential scene by the assassination on November 22, 1963, Latin Americans wept openly in the streets. Hundreds of thousands put up wreaths and candles in their homes as the traditional signs of mourning for a member of the immediate family. The Kennedy name still lingered over the Alliance for Progress and perhaps helped it to a few small achievements in the mid 1960s.

But Kennedy's appointee, the Puerto Rican Teodoro Moscoso, resigned in discouragement at the lack of interest, the unimaginative plans for projects and the slowness with which money was forthcoming. President Johnson appointed "a hard liner" on Latin America to head the program. Although four billion dollars were allocated to new schools, new textbooks, new irrigation systems, eight thousand miles of roads, and credit unions to help 200,000 small farmers, critics felt that these projects might have been financed anyway under existing programs and the amount of help was "pitifully slow" when contrasted with the needs of the Latin American people. At the Rio de Janeiro OAS Conference in November, 1965, Secretary of State Dean Rusk promised that the United States would continue to finance the Alliance for Progress for a second decade after 1971, and saw the hope for a total investment of $20 billion by 1981. But any such use of American funds depended on the whim of Congress and changing administrations in the White House. There was also a great deal of confusion about overlapping committees in carrying out the goals of the Alliance for Progress.

Should the funds from the United States public treasury be spent through the regular American AID committees, or through decisions made by the Latin American committees in the OAS? In November, 1961, the OAS established an Economic and Social Council of its own, with a panel of Pan-American experts to review long-term plans for economic development and reform.

Alberto Lleras Camargo, ex-president of Colombia, was requested to join with ex-president Kubitschek of Brazil to review the first year of the Alliance's activities and suggest changes. On their advice, two new committees were formed. One was the Association for the Development of Economic Latin America (ADELA), to encourage business investment in Latin America on the part of private corporations in the United States, Europe and Japan; and the other, the Inter-American Committee for the Alliance for Progress (CIAP) which was to work under OAS supervising every project in which international public funds were to be spent.

By 1966, the CIAP clashed with the United States National Association for International Development personnel (AID). The United States Congress put restrictions on the way American tax money was to be spent. No American aid was to go to countries which confiscated American investments or the property of companies such as oil wells. All purchases of supplies and equipment to carry out the new projects had to be made in the United States and carried to Latin American ports in United States ships. Thus the Alliance was being used to further American business profits. The rate of economic growth per capita, even in many nations, was not reaching the minimum for growth set by the original Alliance plan, because the population of these nations was growing more rapidly than the economic improvement. The United States was so deeply involved in Southeast Asia that it had no public funds to spend on improving Latin America. Official Washington had almost completely lost interest. Each project requested by a Latin American nation had to be declared "bankable," that is, sure to become financially solvent and worth a bank loan. Very few of the applications were considered bankable. And in Latin America, the governing classes were interested only in profit which enhanced their own wealth.

Some specific examples of what the Alliance accomplished show how the money could be spent, given the requirement of local reform on the part of Latin American governments. The Mexican village of San Francisco Tepeyecac, less fortunate in its land and water than the Santa Cruz Etla described on page 359, received a deep well, with a pump and motor and the pipes to provide irrigation water for ninety small farms. Thus able to double the corn yield, farmers were granted credit for seed, fertilizer, and small tractors from a new rural credit union, and technical assistance in how to use them. In a four-year period the crop yield could be multiplied four times and the excess sold for cash to buy a variety of food and clothing; the young people would stay on the farms and not move to Mexico City's urban slums. The improvement of this village, a type long hoped for by Mexico's rural planners, had been impossible under Mexico's own program due to lack of funds and personnel for such marginal land. It served as a pilot project for five Mexican marginal valleys. In these valleys, feeder roads, food storage and processing plants increased the economy of each central market town.

A cheap protein food from corn, cotton-seed meal, yeast, and sorghum, developed by a UN project in Panama, is being produced by the millions of pounds to add to the diet of underprivileged children throughout central and northern South America. Ninety thousand residents of one of the first Alliance projects, the slum-clearance housing development in Bogotá dedicated by President and Mrs. Kennedy, named their houses "Ciudad Kennedy." Other Alliance funds carried on jungle road building and clearing for pasture in the Peruvian, Colombian, and Brazilian upper Amazon areas. Underdeveloped little Honduras received its first hydroelectric plant, as well as long-term credit for local industries. AID, with Alliance funds, granted credit to Federal Savings and Loan Associations to spend 1 per cent of their assets in model housing projects in Latin America; Baía, Brazil, long dependent on sugar, received credit for tapping iron deposits, building a 140,000-ton-capacity steel mill, and a wharf for shipping the ore. Air and water pollution control, mobile-health service in rural and city slums in Peru and Bolivia all received funds, after consideration of the promises for social improvement in the countries involved. The success of these projects gave the planners of the Alliance a little spark of hope in the early 1970s.

inter-American cultural movements

Culturally, the Latin American nations long felt themselves tied to Spain and to France, and have been scornful, throughout most of their history, of the "materialistic culture" of the "Yanquis." This feeling, combined with fear of "Dollar Diplomacy," has naturally crept into Latin American poetry. Some of the best writers of Spanish America wrote bitter denunciations of the "Colossus of the North." Rubén Darío, famous Nicaraguan poet, composed an uncomplimentary *Ode to Roosevelt* in the days of the presidency of Teddy the Rough Rider:

> *You are the United States, you are the future invader*
> *Of that ingenious America of native blood,*
> *That prays to Jesus still and still speaks Spanish. . . .*
> *You hold that life is a fire, and progress an eruption;*
> *That where your guns can reach, there you control the future.*
> *No! . . . Beware! For Spanish America lives!*
> *The Spanish Lion has a thousand cubs.*
> *'Twere needful, Roosevelt, to be, . . .*
> *The terrible rifleman and the hunter strong,*
> *Even to keep us in your iron grasp.*[1]

Rufino Blanco Fombona of Venezuela, an equally famous poet, novelist, editor, essayist, and historian who had visited the United States as a haven of refuge in exile, called the northern country a "giant octopus, extending its sinuous tentacles toward the small republics to the south and strangling them one by one." Two other Latin American writers of almost equal stature have been leaders in the diatribe against the United States. Carlos Pereyra of Mexico wrote a scathing series of history books, most of them published in Madrid from 1915 to 1917, entitled variously *The Constitution of the United States as an Instrument of Plutocratic Domination; Bolívar and Washington as an Impossible Parallel;* and *The Crime of Woodrow Wilson.* Manuel Ugarte, son of a wealthy Argentine *estanciero*, took on a twenty-five-year personal campaign against the United States, at home in Buenos Aires, then in the European press, and finally on the lecture platform through half the Latin American capitals. Such writings and lectures,

---

[1] G. Dundas Graig, ed., *The Modernist Trend in Spanish American Poetry* (Berkeley: University of California Press, 1934), p. 68.

which proved very popular among intellectuals and students, were all influenced by the philosophy of the great Uruguayan writer Rodó, whose work *Ariel*, described in a previous chapter, had so criticized North American materialism. To Rodó, the Spanish American spirit was the true culture, and the North American spirit merely a crude materialism.

This attitude was encouraged by the trend called *hispanidad*, or Pan Hispanism, a spirit of cultural solidarity with Spain. Spain had vainly hoped to maintain cultural ties with her former colonies in the early years of independence. Then the Spaniards began a positive attempt to recapture the imagination and devotion of the Spanish-speaking area overseas in the twenty-year period following the loss of Cuba in 1898, hoping for "a spiritual reconquest by Spain of her former empire." This was to be done by means of congresses, student exchanges, and cultural societies.

The first such congress had already been held in Madrid in 1892, honoring the fourth century of Columbus' discovery. October 12 thereafter became the *Día de la Raza*, or day of the Spanish race, even now a big celebration in Latin America, often called also *La Fiesta de la Hispanidad*. During the next eight years Spanish newspapers were full of affectionate expressions of solidarity with the Hispanic American nations. A commercial and literary congress with Hispanic American delegates in Madrid was very successful in 1900; in 1912 the Spanish-speaking nations jointly celebrated the centenary of the Constitution of 1812. A *Casa de América* was set up at Barcelona, and an Hispanic American Academy at Cadiz.

World War I enhanced the movement. Primo de Rivera, dictator of Spain in the 1920s, called Hispanic American medical and aeronautical conferences. The Crown prince of Spain was sent to Chile to celebrate the four-hundredth anniversary of the voyage of Magellan. All this was reflected in Latin America. Almost every city had a Spanish Club. The anti-American writers who opposed the United States in the Ariel-Caliban discussion joined with this Pan Hispanic movement, though the idea was criticized as artificial and reactionary by other Latin American writers such as Leopoldo Lugones in Argentina.

The Pan Hispanic movement might have remained a purely cultural tie of interest mostly to university professors, if it had not been turned into a new *hispanidad* by the success of General Franco in the Spanish Civil War of 1936–1938. Latin Americans were sharply divided by this war—the liberals placing great hopes on the Loyalists; the conservatives and pro–Axis Argentines, as well as the Sinarquistas in Mexico, aiding Franco. Their loud talk was counteracted by the presence in many Latin American countries, especially Mexico, of numerous refugees from the Franco regime. As the Western Hemisphere was drawn into the war against the Axis, only Argentina listened officially to the siren call of *hispanidad*. By the 1950s the movement was almost dead. Ties with Spain remained, but they were strong in the opposite direction; the best novels, the best movies, the good plays in the Spanish language were produced in the New World, and Spaniards were anxious to read and see them. As for cultural relations with Portugal, Brazil is today the unqualified leader of the Portuguese-speaking world, and has unquestionably replaced Portugal in the letters and science of the twentieth century.

Anti-*Yanqui* sentiment had continued through the period just before World War II. The *Unión Latino-Americana,* founded by José Ingenieros in Buenos Aires, that headquarters of anti-Yankee cultural sentiment, published an influential little review called *Nosotros.* After a visit and some sympathy from José Vasconcelos, the Mexican educator in the new Revolutionary Mexican movement, *Nosotros* branched out into a monthly called *Renovación,* which showed much Mexican influence, contained strong articles against United States' activities in Mexico, and was widely read in Spanish-speaking countries. A student group within Mexico which Vasconcelos founded considered itself international and was called the *Unión Juventud Hispano Americana.* The Ibero-American Student Confederation, with its headquarters at Mexico City, is another such anti-North American organization. In the 1970s many Latin American student groups no longer scorned the "materialistic culture" of the United States, joined student groups sponsored by the Pan American Union, with its Yankee tinge, and hoped for scholarships to come to the United States. But there was still much anti-Yankee sentiment in the late 1960's.

As the 1970s approached, many Latin Americans still felt themselves more cultured than English-speaking people, because of the unifying influence of the Spanish language and the increase of books, newspapers, journals of all kinds, and popular literature in Spanish which were reaching the masses as illiteracy declined. Argentina sends it locally printed books in cheap editions all over Latin America. Motion pictures made in Buenos Aires and Mexico City are shown in Mérida, Yucatan; or Cali, Colombia; or Antofagasta, Chile; or Ambato, Ecuador; or Camagüey, Cuba. Book fairs, international book prizes, and the Montevideo annual international film festival are held separate from the many cultural activities of the Pan American Union with its Washington headquarters. As Montevideo holds its Spanish-language film festival, so Caracas holds international festivals of music at which the best Latin American compositions are played and each nation sends its visiting orchestra conductor. A Chilean singer is enthusiastically acclaimed in Mexico City, a Bolivian artist shows in Buenos Aires, a Guatemalan exhibit of Indian weaving goes to Lima. Latin America is proud of its culture. The long-time cultural attachment of Latin Americans to France had been a pro-Latin unifying tie, and not necessarily an anti-Yankee sentiment. For every South American of any wealth and education, Paris was the Mecca. Sophisticated older people in Buenos Aires and Rio still speak French with ease. Franco-Argentine and Franco-Brazilian Institutes encouraged literary exchange. Bastille Day used to be celebrated with frenzy in Mexico City or Buenos Aires. With the decline of French prestige after World War II and the increasing respect for American technical education, students became as anxious to study in New York or Berkeley as in Paris. France served her turn as the inspiration of things liberal and modern in the eighteenth and nineteenth centuries; with her decline as a world power, her cultural influence is slowly waning in Latin America. She is no longer the "Mother Country" of the poets, philosophers, and literateurs. Today the tables are turned, as Paris sponsors shows of Mexican culture and art. But France still holds a lure for many Latin Americans, and French influence still survives in educational and university circles.

Contrary to current apprehensions in the United States, Latin America has not turned culturally toward Russia. In Latin America, communism never became a movement of the masses. Russian-inspired Communist parties have existed in most Latin America countries for over a half-century, and the only place where they ever came to power by election was in Chile in 1970. Many Latin American countries have outlawed the Communist Party although twelve recognize the Soviet Union. In Latin America Communist supporters have swung elections in vote-trading deals, joined "Popular Fronts," aroused students to riot, and influenced such labor and peasant leaders as Vicente Lombardo Toledano in Mexico and Francisco Julião in Brazil. But the hard-line Leninist-Marxists got old and tired. Fidelista movements inspired from Cuba after 1960 appealed to the young, but their efforts were weakened by clashes between Moscow and Peking. Neither old-line Communists nor Bolivian youth leaders came to help Ché Guevara as he lay dying in a remote Bolivian town. Few Latin American intellectuals were attracted to Fidelismo.

Trade unionism had never been a strong inter-American movement, due to the slow development of industrialization. However, Labor has become increasingly active as a political force in those Latin American countries which are rapidly industrializing. A Pan-American Federation of Labor was organized in 1916, and came to be dominated by Luis Morones and his CROM in Mexico. It took a stand against the treatment of laborers by dictators in Venezuela, Peru, and Cuba, and held several joint meetings with the AFL in the United States. Although it sent delegations to South American countries, it never had any influence there. Its influence died in Mexico and the Caribbean with the removal of Morones from politics and the death of Samuel Gompers in the United States. Labor movements in Argentina and Chile, influenced by international Communism in the 1920s, considered it pro-capitalistic.

More radical labor leaders came to the front with Lombardo Toledano in Mexico, and a new Confederation of Latin American Workers, the CTAL, was founded by him in 1938. When he retired as secretary of the Mexican CTM in 1941, he proceeded to give the CTAL all his time. Meanwhile labor leaders in Argentina representing the Argentine General Confederation of Workers met with Toledano's group in Mexico, and served in Argentina as an ardent anti-Axis element. However, all these labor groups were to some extent anti-American also; they feared the United States was trying to keep Latin America an economically "colonial country," exporting raw products forever, and never allowing it to industrialize in competition with the United States. Labor groups made surveys, held discussion meetings, and compared problems on many social issues—child labor, minimum wages, housing, conditions of women in industry. However, most such surveys and meetings were done under the auspices of larger movements, such as the Pan American Union or the International Labor Organization at Geneva. Perón attempted to create a "Latin American Labor Organization" but was unsuccessful.

Today some Latin American labor groups belong to the International Confederation of Free Trade Unions, a group formed after World War II by unions that withdrew from the Communist-dominated World Federation of Trade Unions. Its Latin American regional organization is known as the *Organización Regional Interamericana de Trabajadores*, or ORIT. Most Latin American unions have no international affiliation. At home, however, they are organizing into political parties where such parties are allowed to oppose the military government and are pushing new labor and social legislation.

Russian influence on culture hardly materialized and French influence declined. What about American influence? For a half-century the Latin Americans had looked to the United States for loans, for advice on health, medicine, and farming, for engineers on roads and in industry. They had never considered their northern neighbor cultured enough to teach them anything about literature, art, music, or higher education. Then during World War II the United States made an all-out effort to limit German influence in Latin America. The Nelson Rockefeller Committee set up Divisions of Communications, of Press, of Motion Pictures, of Radio, of Publications, of Art, of Music, Education, and Travel. An inter-American radio program included a network of 100 stations and produced twenty-seven different programs in Spanish and Portuguese known as the "Brave New World" series. Slick-paper picture magazines, cultural institutes connected with the American embassies all openly wooed Latin American friendship. The more than fifty Cultural Institutes enrolled 75,000 students in free classes in English, the speech of the new technology.

Thus some of the prejudice against Americans was overcome. Exchange professors wrote histories of United States literature in Spanish; students came to study on scholarships in liberal arts colleges as well as in technical institutes. In the late 1960s it was estimated that 60 per cent of the scholarships used in the United States by Latin Americans were in health and engineering, 30 per cent in public administration, child welfare, economics, and agriculture, and a good ten per cent in art, music, and literature —fields in which no student would have considered an American university above a European one a decade before.

Translations of North American books took up half the lists of the new best sellers in South America, and Latin Americans were busy reading Hemingway, Steinbeck, O'Neill, Thomas Wolfe, and Edna Ferber as well as Mark Twain and Emerson. Heitor Villa-Lobos and Carlos Chávez conducted symphonies in the United States; American music critics have gone to South America and published histories of American music in the Spanish and Portuguese languages. Meanwhile GI's went to Mexico City College, to the University of San Marcos in Lima, to the University of Córdoba in Argentina to learn more about Latin America on their GI Bill education benefits. Many South and Central American universities offered summer sessions conducted in English for American teachers. Not only did the Latin Americans come to accept the existence of a North American culture, but North Americans began to have a wholesome respect for Latin American culture.

Back at home, Americans became more interested in studying Spanish than a former generation had been in learning French or German. They learned Spanish to go as Fulbright scholars to South America, to visit Argentine or Chilean homes for college credit under the Experiment in International Living, to work in church-sponsored "community help projects" in mountain villages. A thousand young Americans in the Peace Corps served as teachers, recreation directors, nurses, and even brick makers in Spanish-speaking communities. More than 800 Peace Corps volunteers learned Portuguese and served in Brazil. Universities exchanged programs— Stanford with the new University of the Peruvian Andes at Iquitos, Cornell with Buenos Aires, the University of Kansas with the University of Costa Rica. The Carnegie Foundation established a program to assist such exchanges called the CHEAR, the Council on Higher Education in the American Republics.

With the increase of such exchanges, town to town, school to school, student to student, came a new interest in Latin American literature published in English. A sample recent year brought new English editions of the poems of Jorge Luis Borges, Rubén Darío, and Sor Juana Inés de la Cruz. *Don Segundo Sombra, Doña Bárbara, The Eagle and the Serpent,* and other famous novels found their way into English in most college libraries. Classical works by Spanish explorers came out in paperback. In the early 1970s Carlos Fuentes' philosophic novel, *The Death of Artemio Cruz,* Octavio Paz's analysis of the Mexican Revolution called the *Labyrinth of Solitude,* and Gabriel García Márquez, *One Hundred Years of Solitude* were best sellers from Bogotá to Buenos Aires, and were being widely read among the followers of Spanish novels in translation in the United States. The touching Aztec story of the conquest by the Mexican scholar Miguel León Portilla was being widely used as a supplement to the usual texts on the Conquest. It was called in English *"Broken Spears."* Even the anti-American *Ariel* was available to English readers in the new effort to understand Latin America.

At home in Latin America, national programs for education took 20 per cent of local budgets in the 1960s, according to Dr. José Mora of the OAS. The Alliance for Progress gave a spurt to elementary education in rural and urban slums, and to adult education everywhere. Student movements seem to be almost international. Many Americans were scornful of the summer-long riots in Mexico City just before the Olympics in 1968. Students protested at the imposition of new regulations by the government of General Onganía of Argentina. Such demonstrations were not necessarily copies of the events in Berkeley or at Columbia in New York, but rather a tradition in Latin American universities, where students have often organized to protest since the sixteenth century. A reform movement calling for student participation in the government of the university, known as the

Córdoba Manifesto, was still used as a war cry for university students in Latin America throughout the early 1970s. Youth leaders often end up in jail under military dictators, but their experiences do not seem to discourage the next generation of students.

Art and art exhibits are of more interest in Latin America than in most parts of the United States. Among vast plans for the Mexico City Olympics in 1968 were the summer-long cultural Olympics with their art exhibits, musical events and commemorative books of poetry. The OAS continued to sponsor art exhibits from Washington and Latin American capitals. Julio Barragán received the grand prize for painting in a national exhibit in Buenos Aires for work he had been showing in the Pan-American building in Washington in the spring of 1971. An Inter-American Museum Festival has been scheduled in Washington, every four years starting in 1968. There was worldwide interest in the architecture of Latin America, and shows of South American architectural design are often held in New York. In April, 1964, the first Inter-American poetry contest was held in Mexico City with fifteen representatives, and the event has been repeated in other Latin American cities. The OAS has continued the popular summer afternoon concerts at the Pan-American Union Building featuring Latin American performers and composers, the holding of book fairs, and the awarding of international book prizes.

The Regional Technical Aids Center in Mexico City translated technical materials into Spanish for use in the new vocational training in all parts of Latin America. The OAS and the Alliance continued the programs begun in the 1930s to train rural teachers, and joined with UNESCO in model schools for rural teachers from all over the New World at Pátzcuaro, Mexico, and at Rubio, Venezuela. The "each one teach one" method worked out by Dr. Jaime Torres-Bodet for Mexico has been applied in classes for illiterates everywhere. Geographers, historians, astrophysicists, bibliographers, geologists, journalists, and architects have met more or less regularly from 1920 to the present. The preservation of archives, the standardization of university courses and library filing systems, the publication of lists of fellowships and exchange professorships, the preparation of accurate maps, and the reduction of postal rates on educational materials occupied the time of these busy committees.

As a publishing venture, the Pan American Union has an old history. *The Hand Book of the American Republics,* a commercial guide 300 pages long, came out in 1891. The first *Bulletin of the Pan American Union,* a monograph on coffee production, was printed in 1893. By 1911, a meaty magazine, profusely illustrated and full of social and historical material, was published monthly under the title *Bulletin of the Pan American Union.* Its post–World War II successor *Américas* contains stories, art and music criticism, book reviews, political articles, and much chatter about the comings and goings of personalities in the inter-American world. In addition, the Pan American Union's Department of Cultural Affairs publishes *Panorama,* a quarterly cultural review of inter-American affairs. There is also a regular music bulletin, a quarterly *Annals of the OAS,* a *Dictionary of Latin Ameri-*

can Literature, a *Guide to Public Collections of Art in Latin America,* and a quarterly *Inter-American Bibliographic Review.* The list of other printed materials available through the Pan American Union is itself thirty pages long.

The Alliance for Progress, which languished for lack of funds, had at least set up a new spirit of interest in inter-American culture. Under its auspices several Inter-American Conferences of Cultural Directors were held. The Final Act of the most recent of these conferences took the position that: "The various aspects of cultural expression and cultural activity must be incorporated on both the national and regional levels into the joint efforts of the countries participating." Thus the encouragement of cultural activity became an "official" Hemispheric policy.

Note: Readings for Chapters 30, 31 are on p. 750 at end of "Epilogue."

epilogue

HOPES FOR
LATIN AMERICA IN THE
LAST QUARTER OF THE
TWENTIETH CENTURY

"The duty of a revolutionary is to make a revolution," said Ché Guevara, and he spent all his adult life in rebellion. He wrote a manual for revolutionaries in which he said they were to make headquarters in some remote rural area, gain the loyalty of rural farmers who would shelter and feed them, train an army of volunteers in harassing the countryside, and then sweep on to victory as the entire population joined them against the "Establishment" in the capital.

But Ché failed when he tried to carry out his own rules. After success in Cuba with Fidel Castro, he started his "Great Revolutionary Movement" for all South America by choosing the geographic center of the continent, an area near the border of five countries—Bolivia, Paraguay, Chile, Peru, and Brazil—for his headquarters. Late in 1966, he came to La Paz, Bolivia, disguised as an elderly Uruguayan businessman, and soon disappeared from the city, going to his chosen site in a remote canyon south of the city of Santa Cruz. There he met by previous appointment 16 trained guerrillas from Cuba and about 30 other revolutionaries from other parts of Latin America.

But all of his plans went wrong. Old-line Communists from La Paz came out secretly to confer with him, quarreled violently over his methods and long-range plans, and went back to the city in disgust. Moreover, the

are squatters who arrived during the 1960s and have built shanties out of matting on the hillsides. The people who are living in these crowded slums do not have easily accessible drinking water and often have to buy it from venders who carry it in old gasoline tins on the backs of burros. In this whole population explosion only Colombia, Costa Rica, and Chile had a birth control program available through government clinics in 1971. There is a larger proportion of the population living in cities of 100,000 or more in Latin America than there is in Europe.

Can labor organizations help these people? A strong labor organization depends upon loyal members who pay dues. Without strike funds from dues strikers cannot hold out against employers. The only successful strike in the early 1970s had been among well-organized transport workers in Mexico. Again the problem is that large numbers of people came to the city without industrial experience and with few skills which factories could use.

It is interesting to note that young priests and nuns have accomplished more for the city poor than have liberal leaders. Many young priests have defied their bishops to work in the city slums and to organize social revolutionary movements. On the far left fringe, secret revolutionary groups have kidnapped diplomats and foreign specialists in Brazil, in Guatemala, and in Uruguay, and have held such persons for ransom, seeking either large funds to carry on their revolutionary activities or the release of members of their leftist organizations from prison. Leftist leaders freed by such agreements have gone to Mexico, Cuba, or Algeria and then found their way secretly back to Brazil, Guatemala or Uruguay.

At the bottom of the social strata were still the tribal Indians. There were still 20 million people living outside the Spanish or Portuguese-speaking community in the early 1970s. Many of them are "lost in disease, narcotics and desperation." In some places they are being deliberately annihilated. In Brazil there were 230 tribal groups of Indians in 1900. There were 140 left in 1970. They had been reduced by intentional poisoning, slaughtered by firearms or by bombing with dynamite sticks from private aircrafts, or herded into labor camps. In Tierra del Fuego the Indians are now extinct. At least in Bolivia the Indians were better off in 1970 than they had been in 1960. President Barrientos, before his death, upgraded the Bolivian Indian by abolishing the word "Indian" in all legal procedures and substituting the word "farmer." However, Barrientos himself was an Indian. Belaúnde Terry had many plans to improve Indian villages in Peru, but had not been working with Indian groups as such. Mexican Indians, through rural school programs, are being rapidly brought into the Spanish-speaking orbit.

Looking to the last quarter of the century the social problems in Latin America still seem a long way from solution. The old social problems—the rigid class systems based on large landed estates and the great contrasts between the wealthy and the poor—are still there from the 1870s. These problems are now compounded by the population explosion and the urban slums. A committee on education under the Alliance for Progress reported, "How can archaic education systems be transformed to serve the needs of an economically modernizing society? Political stability and economic growth are necessary to educate the city masses!" That committee and the whole Alliance Program gave up in its effort to improve the schools of Latin America, and as of the early 1970s, there were still no schools or teachers for 52 per cent of Latin American primary school children. In the late 1960s a group of teachers representing the most progressive of the nations, including several teachers from the United States, presented a set of goals for Latin American education at a conference at Santiago, Chile. This committee stated that 18,000 more primary school rooms had to be built in Latin America before the mid-1970s. Teacher training is woefully inadequate throughout the Hemisphere and many primary teachers have not had more than sixth grade education. Even more so, there are not enough trained teachers for secondary schools and very few young men who are trained to teach agriculture and science at the high school level. Few universities offer majors in science, technology, or agriculture.

There is, of course, no shortage of students or children who are anxious to go to school, but children are poorly clothed, underfed, and without shoes even in places where winters are chilly. There is usually no type of scholarship program to assist graduates of elementary school to go to high school. The high schools are only found in very large towns or in the center of the great cities, and graduates of the public elementary schools among the poor seldom even plan to go to secondary school so far from home. The secondary school is to the elementary school in much of Latin America in the 1970s what the high school was to the little red schoolhouse of the United States in the Midwest in the 1870s. In many modernized nations today, books, paper, and pencils are supplied to elementary children but not to secondary school students. More secondary schools need to be opened for vocational training. Some way should be found to make students take pride in going to vocational school to up-grade their hopes for technical jobs. The European pattern of secondary school still popular in Latin America prepares only for university education, university courses which emphasize the humanities, classics, and pure science and thus turn out "cultured" young people unprepared for careers as technicians.

The Mexican country children get a chance to finish the sixth grade and learn something about improvements in agriculture. Schools of this type could be spread throughout Latin America and be made a matter of local village pride. In city slums in Caracas, Lima and Rio de Janeiro there is no level ground on which to build the school, and the children who live on the steep hillsides are not encouraged by their parents or by any social workers or religious officials to come down the steep dirt trails to the schools. How can an intelligent electorate grow up in these city slums in the next generation?

According to UNESCO statistics, in the mid-1960s, of every thousand Latin American children who entered school, 500 did not finish the second grade. Another 366 only finish the sixth grade, which is the year of "elementary completion" in most countries. Only 60 out of the 1,000 enter any type of secondary school and only 30 graduate. Of these thirty, only two went on to a university and one in a thousand ever earned a college diploma. In sixteen of the Latin American countries, the average school attendance for people under fifteen years of age in 1965 was two and a half years of school. It is true that school population is growing rapidly, but not as rapidly as the overall population.

University buildings in Mexico City, in Caracas, in Brasilia, in Panama City are extensive and very advanced in design; tuition at such beautiful schools is free. But not enough young people from the poorest classes have finished the secondary schools to prepare themselves to take advantage of the free university education. Student bodies in the university in the 1970s contain many groups of militants demonstrating specifically against political leaders, or for greater social justice, or against the United States and its military aid programs. But they seldom seem to be demonstrating against the poverty and the poor primary schools in the shanty towns. There has been a 400-year-old tradition of quarrels between students and government agencies in Latin America.

A Brazilian student wrote to the Alliance for Progress Committee, "The Alliance failed because it was an alliance with our governments and not with our peoples. We are tired of being promised development and having our wealth siphoned away. We are tired of hunger and misery." Brazilian health students from São Paulo work with public health officials in the Amazon villages, and young Chilean students spend their summers teaching Araucanian Indians to read and write. Mexican Student Action groups are teaching illiterates in Michoacan state. It could be hoped that in the 1970s idealistic student groups will increasingly take on more projects in their own countries, so that they can "follow their own words with their own personal action."

These idealistic students are coming from the new middle class. They might be rioting in the streets all day protesting their "lack of political freedom." But these same students go home at night to modern city flats with hot and cold running water or to separate houses in the suburbs, and sit down to supper with their businessmen fathers, and their fashionably dressed mothers who had been out shopping, driving around in the family Volkswagen, or even doing social work among the poor themselves all day. The emergence of such a prosperous modernized socially-conscious middle class is happening now in the cities of South America, and in Mexico it has been one of the long-range products of the Mexican Revolution of 1910.

The real-life character, who is called Pedro Martínez in Oscar Lewis' sociological study by that same name, grew up in an inaccessible Indian village, a naked orphan child competing with other barefoot illiterate cousins for scraps of tortillas in his uncle's hut. As a barefoot peon, he had fought with Zapata for *"Tierra y Libertad."* He undertook many small businesses of buying and selling livestock and corn while he taught himself to read and write and served as town councilman and judge in his hometown. His activities for the town took him often on foot or burro-back on the trail to Mexico City where he learned many city ways. In his old age he sits on a bench in the new park in his modernized village complaining that

"Zapata's boys fought for nothing!" But while he talks to the sociologist Oscar Lewis about this "lost cause," he is wearing a dark suit and shoes and socks, one of his daughters has become the teacher in a nearby school, and one of his grandsons is applying for admission to a state college which trains high school teachers. The old man can visit another son who owns a bakery in Mexico City by taking the big bus that goes on the highway a two-hour ride into the city three times a day.

READINGS

Adams, M., ed., *Latin America: Evolution or Explosion?* (1963).

Adams, R. N., and C. C. Cumberland, *The United States University Cooperation in Latin America* (1960).

Adams, V., *Peace Corps in Action* (1964).

Aguilar, A., *Latin America and the Alliance for Progress* (1963).

————, *Pan Americanism from Monroe to the Present: A View from the Other Side* (1970).

Aguilar, L. E., ed., *Marxism in Latin America* (1968).

Aguirre, A., ed., *Uruguay and the United States* (1958).

Alba, V., *Alliance Without Allies: The Mythology of Progress in Latin America* (1965).

————, *History of Latin American Labor* (1966).

————, *The Latin Americans* (1969).

————, *Nationalists Without Nations: The Oligarchy versus the People in Latin America* (1968).

————, *Politics and the Labor Movement in Latin America* (1968).

Alexander, R. J., *Communism in Latin America* (1957).

————, *Labor Relations in Argentina, Brazil and Chile* (1962).

Alisky, M., and L. E. Koslow, *Latin American Government Leaders* (1970).

Allen, R. L., *Soviet Influence in Latin America: Role of Economic Relations* (1959).

Alliance for Progress, Official Documents Emanating from the Special Meeting of the Inter-American Economic and Social Council at the Ministerial Level (OAS official records).

————, Committee of Nine, *Evaluation of the General Economic and Social Development Plan of Colombia* (1962) [other countries since].

Álvarez, A., *The Monroe Doctrine* (1924).

American Universities Field Service Staff Reports—Latin American Reports (various dates).

Anderson, C. W., *Politics and Economic Change in Latin America* (1967).

Andreski, S., *Parasitism and Subversion: The Case of Latin America* (1967).

Arciniegas, G., *The State of Latin America* (1952).

————, *Latin America, A Cultural History* (1967).

Artucio, A. F., *Nazi Underground in South America* (1942).

Astiz, L. A., *Latin America International Politics* (1969).

Baer, W., and Kerstenetzky, ed., *Inflation and Growth in Latin America* (1964).

Baerresen, D., M. Carony, and J. Grunwald, *Latin American Trade Patterns* (1965).

Bailey, N., *Latin America: Politics, Economics and Hemisphere Security* (1966).

Bailey, N. A., *Latin America in World Politics* (1967).

Bailey, S. L., *Nationalism in Latin America* (1971).

Ball, M. M., *The OAS in Transition* (1969).

————, *Problems of Inter-American Organization* (1944).

Balseiro, J. A., *The Americas Look at Each Other*, trans. M. Muñoz Lee (1969).

Barber, W. F., and C. N. Ronning, *Internal Security and Military Power* (1965).

Barclay, G., *Struggle for a Continent: The Diplomatic History of South America, 1917–1945* (1971).

Barnett, R. J., *Intervention and Revolution: United States and the Third World* (1968).

Bauer, W. and I. Kerstenetsky, *Inflation and Growth in Latin America* (1970).

Beale, H. K., *Theodore Roosevelt and Rise of America to World Power* (1956).

Beals, C., *et. al., What the South Americans Think of Us* (1945).

————, *Latin America: World in Revolution* (1971).

Beaulac, W. L., *A Diplomat Looks at Aid to Latin America* (1970).

Beckett, G., *The Reciprocal Trade Agreement Program* (1941).

Beller, J., *Jews in Latin America* (1969).

Bemis, S. F., *John Quincy Adams and Foundation of American Foreign Policy* (1949).

————, *Latin American Policy of the United States* (1943).

Benjamin, H., *Higher Education in the Americas* (1965).

Benton, W., *Voice of Latin America* (1961).

Berle, A. A., Jr., *Latin America: Diplomacy and Reality* (1962).

Bernstein, M., *Foreign Investments in Latin America* (1965).

Beyer, G. H., ed., *Urban Explosion in Latin America* (1967).

Bidwell, P. M., *Economic Defense of Latin America* (1941).

Blakemore, H., *Latin America* (1966).

Blasier, C., ed., *Constructive Change in Latin America* (1968).

Braden, S., *Diplomats and Demagogues: The Memoirs of Spruille Braden* (1971).

Bradford, C. I., and C. Pestieau, *Canada and Latin America: The Potential for Partnership* (1971).

Bradley, A., *Trans-Pacific Relations of Latin America* (1942).

Brown, L. R., *Seeds of Change: The Green Revolution and Development in the 1970s* (1970).

Brown, W. A., and O. Redvers, *American Foreign Assistance* (1953).

Bullrich, F., *New Directions in Latin American Architecture* (1969).

Burnett, B. G., and K. F. Johnson, eds., *Political Forces in Latin America: Dimensions of the Quest for Stability* (1968).

Burns, E. B., *Nationalism in Brazil: A Historical Survey* (1968).

Burr, R. N., *By Reason or Force: Chile and the Balance of Power in South America, 1830–1903* (1965).

————, *Latin America's Nationalistic Revolutions* (1961).

————, *Our Troubled Hemisphere: Perspectives on United States–Latin American Relations* (1967).

————, *Stillborn Panama Congress: Power Politics and Chilean-Colombian Relations During the War of the Pacific* (1962).

————, and R. D. Hussey, *Documents on Inter-American Cooperation* (2 vols., 1955).

Cale, E. G., *Latin America Free Trade Association: Progress, Problems, Prospects* (1969).

Callahan, J. M., *American Foreign Policy in Mexican Relations* (1932).

Callcott, W. H., *Caribbean Policy of the United States, 1890–1920* (1942).

————, *The Western Hemisphere: Its Influence on the United States Politics to the End of World War II* (1968).

Calvert, P. A., *Latin America: Internal Conflict and International Peace* (1969).

Campos, R. de Oliveira, *Reflections on Latin American Development* (1970).

Canyes, M., *Meetings of Consultation: Their Origin, Significance and Role in Inter-American Relations* (rev. ed., 1962).

————, *The Organization of American States and the United Nations* (6th ed., 1963).

Carey, J. C., *Peru and the United States, 1900–1962* (1964).

Carleton, W. G., *The Revolution in American Foreign Policy* (1963).

Carnoy, M., *Industrialization in a Latin American Common Market* (1972).

Carr, R., ed., *Latin American Affairs* (1970).

Castañeda, J., *Mexico and the United Nations* (1958).

Castedo, L., *A History of Latin American Art and Architecture from Pre-Columbian Times to the Present* (1969).

Center for Study of Democratic Institutions, *One Spark from Holocaust: The Crisis in Latin America* (1972).

Changing Latin America: New Interpretations of Its Politics and Society (1971).

Chase, A., *Falange, The Nazi Secret Army in the Americas* (1943).

Chase, G., *Contemporary Art in Latin America: Painting, Graphic Art, Sculpture, Architecture* (1970).

Chew, B., *A Sketch of Politics, Relations and Statistics of the Western World* (1827; repr. 1971).

Chilcote, R. H., *Military Intervention and Developmental Tendencies* (1966).

————, *Revolution and Structural Change in Latin America*, 2 vols., (1968).

Clark, J. R., *Memorandum on the Monroe Doctrine* (1930).

Claude, I. L., Jr., *Organization of American States, the United Nations and the United States* (1964).

Cline, H. F., *United States and Mexico* (1953).

Clissold, S., *Latin America: A Cultural Outline* (1965).

————, *Soviet Relations with Latin America, 1918–1968; A Documentary Survey* (1970).

Cole, J. P., *Latin America: An Economic and Social Geography* (1965).

Colonnese, L. M., ed., *Human Rights and the Liberation of Man in the Americas* (1970).

Connell-Smith, G., *The Inter-American System* (1966).

Craig, G. D. trans. and ed., *The Modernist Trend in Spanish American Poetry: Collection of Representative Poems of the Modernist Movement and the Reaction* (1934; repr. 1971).

Crasweller, R. D., *The Caribbean Community: Changing Societies and United States Policy* (1972).

Daniels, J., *Shirt-sleeve Diplomacy* (1947).

Dávila, C., *We of the Americas* (1949).

Davis, H. E., *Latin American Thought. A Historical Introduction* (1972).

Dean, V. M., *Nature of the Non-Western World* (1958).

Debray, R., and R. Blackburn, *Strategy for Revolution: Essays on Latin America* (1970).

DeConde, A., *Latin American Policy of Herbert Hoover* (1951).

Dell, S., *A Latin American Common Market?* (1966).

Del Rio, A., ed., *Responsible Freedom in the Americas* (1955).

Delwart, L. O., *The Future of Latin American Exports to the United States: 1965 and 1970* (1960).

Department of State, *Peace in the Americas* (1950).

Deutschmann, P. J., *et al.*, *Communication and Social Change in Latin America* (1968).

DeVries, E., and J. Medina Echavarría, *Social Aspects of Economic Development in Latin America* (1963).

Dillon, D., *International Communism and Latin America: Perspectives and Prospects* (1962).

Donovan, J., *Red Machete: Communist Infiltration in the Americas* (1963).

Dorner, P., ed., *Land Reform in Latin America: Issues and Cases* (1971).

Dozer, D. M., *Are We Good Neighbors?* (1959).

———, *Monroe Doctrine* (1965).

Dreier, J. C., *The Alliance for Progress: Problems and Perspectives* (1962).

———, *The Organization of American States and Hemisphere Crisis* (1962).

Dubois, J., *Operation America* (1963).

Duggan, L., *The Americas, the Search for Hemisphere Security* (1949).

Dumont, R., *Lands Alive* (1965).

Duncan, W. R., and J. N. Goodsell, eds., *The Quest for Change in Latin America: Sources for a Twentieth Century Analysis* (1970).

Dyer, J. M., *United States–Latin American Trade and Financial Relations* (1961).

Edel, M., *Food Supply and Inflation in Latin America* (1969).

Eister, A. W., *The United States and the ABC Powers, 1889–1906* (1950).

Ellis, H. S., ed., *Economic Development for Latin America* (1962).

Ellis, L. E., *Frank B. Kellogg and American Foreign Relations, 1925–1929* (1961).

Feder, E., *Rape of the Peasantry: Latin America's Landholding System* (1971).

Fenwick, C. G., *The Inter-American Regional System*, 2nd ed. (1961).

Ferguson, Y., ed., *Contemporary Inter-American Relations: A Reader in Theory and Issues* (1971).

Ferns, H. S., *Britain and Argentina in the Nineteenth Century* (1960).

Field, A. J., ed., *City and Country in the Third World: Issues in the Modernization of Latin America* (1970).

Fiscal Policy for Economic Growth in Latin America (1965).

Fitzgerald, G. E., ed., *The Constitutions of Latin America* (1968).

Fitzgibbon, R. H., *Latin America–A Panorama of Contemporary Politics* (1971).

Flores, E., *Land Reform and the Alliance for Progress* (1963).

Form, W. M., and A. A. Blum, eds., *Industrial Relations and Social Change in Latin America* (1966).

Franco, J., *The Modern Culture of Latin America. Society and the Artist,* rev. ed. (1970).

Frank, A. G., *Capitalism and Underdevelopment in Latin America* (1969).

Fulbright, J. W., *Arrogance of Power* (1966).

Furtado, C., *Economic Development of Latin America* (1970).

————, *Obstacles to Development in Latin America* (1970).

Gale, L., *Education and Development in Latin America* (1969).

Gantenbeim, J. W., ed., *Evolution of Our Latin American Policy: Documentary Record* (1950).

Gerassi, J., *The Great Fear: Reconquest of Latin America by Latin Americans* (1963).

Geyer, G. A., *The New Latins: Fateful Change in South and Central America* (1970).

Gil, F. G., *Latin American–United States Relations* (1971).

Glade, W. P., *Latin American Economies: A Study of Their Institutional Evolution* (1969).

Glauert, E. T., and L. D. Langley, *The United States and Latin America* (1971).

Glick, P. M., *Administration of Technical Assistance: Growth in the Americas* (1957).

Goldhamer, H., *The Foreign Powers in Latin America* (1972).

Goldman, R., ed., *Readings in American Foreign Policy* (1959).

Gordon, L., *A New Deal for Latin America: The Alliance for Progress* (1963).

Gordon, W. C., *Political Economy of Latin America* (1965).

Gott, R., *Guerrilla Movements in Latin America* (1971).

Goure, L. M., L. Harvey, and S. Suchlicki, *Soviet Penetration of Latin America* (1972).

Gray, R. B., ed., *Latin America and the United States: Problems and Prospects for the 1970s* (1971).

Green, D., *The Containment of Latin America* (1970).

Griffin, K., *Underdevelopment in Spanish America: An Interpretation* (1969).

————, ed., *Financing Development in Latin America* (1971).

Gross, F. B., ed., *The United States and the United Nations,* Chap. VII (1964).

Grunwald, J. and P. Musgrove, *Natural Resources in Latin American Economic Development* (1970).

Grunwald, J., et al., *Latin American Economic Integration and U. S. Policy* (1972).

Guerrant, E. O., *Roosevelt's Good Neighbor Policy* (1950).

Guggenheim, H. F., *Latin America Now or Never* (1963).

Hamill, H. M., ed., *Dictatorship in Spanish America* (1965).

Hanson, E. P., ed., *South from the Spanish Main* (1967).

Hanson, S. G., *Economic Development of Latin America* (1951).

————, "The End of the 'Good Neighbor Policy,'" *Inter-American Economic Affairs*, X (1953), 45–96.

————, *Dollar Diplomacy Modern Style: Chapters in the Failure of the Alliance for Progress* (1970).

————, *Five Years of the Alliance for Progress* (1967).

Harbron, *Canada and Organization of American States* (1963).

Haring, C. H., *Argentina and the United States* (1941).

————, *South America Looks at the United States* (1928).

Harris, M., *Patterns of Race in the Americas* (1964).

Harris, W., *The Growth of Latin American Cities* (1971).

Hauch, C. C., *The Current Situation in Latin American Education* (1963).

Hauser, P. M., ed., *Urbanization in Latin America* (1961).

Haverstock, N. A., *The OAS: The Challenge of the Americas* (1966).

Heath, D. B., and R. N. Adams, *Contemporary Cultures and Societies of Latin America* (1965).

Herrera, L. F., *Inter-American Bank* (1962).

Hilton, R., ed., *The Movement Toward Latin American Unity* (1969).

Hirschman, A. D., *A Bias for Hope: Essays on Development in Latin America* (1971).

Horowitz, I. L., ed., *Masses in Latin America* (1970).

————, J. de Castro, and J. Gerassi, eds., *Latin American Radicalism* (1969).

Houston, J. A., *Latin America in the United Nations* (1956).

Houtart, K., and E. Pin, *The Church and the Latin American Revolution* (1965).

Howland, C. P., ed., *Survey of American Foreign Relations 1928–1931* (4 vols., 1928–1931).

Hull, C., *Memoirs of Cordell Hull*, 2 vols. (1948).

Humphrey, J. P., *Inter-American System: A Canadian View* (1942).

Illich, I. D., *Celebration of Awareness: A Call for Institutional Revolution* (1970).

Inman, S. G., *Latin America: Its Place in World Life* (rev. ed., 1942).

————, *Problems in Pan Americanism* (2nd ed., 1925).

Imaz, J. L. de, *Los Que Mandan; Those Who Rule* (1970).

Inter-American Conference, Official Documents.

Inter-American Conferences of Foreign Ministers, Handbooks of Delegates of the United States of America and other materials prepared for each meeting.

Inter-American Development Bank, *Annual Reports* (2nd ed., 1963).

————, *Social Progress Trust Fund, Annual Reports* (2nd 1963; 3rd, 1964).

————, *Ten Years of Work in Latin America* (1970).

International Bank for Reconstruction and Development, *World Bank Activities in Latin America: A Report for the Economic Conference of the OAS at Buenos Aires, 1957* (1957).

International Devolpment Board, *An Economic Program for the Americas* (1954).

Ireland, G., *Boundaries, Possessions and Conflicts in South America* (1938).

————, *Boundaries, Possessions and Conflicts in Central and North America and the Caribbean* (1941).

Jackson, D. B., *Castro, the Kremlin and Communism in Latin America* (1969).

Janowitz, M., *The Military in the Political Development of New Nations* (1964).

Johnsen, J. E., *Canada and the Western Hemisphere* (1944).

————, *Latin American Relations with League of Nations* (1930).

Johnson, C., *Communist China and Latin America 1959–1967* (1970).

Johnson, J. J., *The Military and Society in Latin America* (1964).

————, *Political Change in Latin America* (1958).

————, *Role of Military in Underdeveloped Countries* (1962).

————, ed., *Continuity and Change in Latin America* (1964).

Jorrín, M., and J. D. Martz, *Latin American Political Thought and Ideology* (1970).

Jose, J. R., *An Inter-American Peace Force within the Framework of the Organization of American States; Advantages, Impediments, Implications* (1970).

Josephs, R., *Latin America—Continent in Crisis* (1948).

Kane, W. E., *Civil Strife in Latin America. A Legal History of United States Involvement* (1972).

Kantor, H., *Patterns of Politics and Political Systems in Latin America* (1969).

Karnes, T. L., *Major Issues in the Latin American Policy of the United States: A Documentary Narrative* (1972).

Karst, K. L., *Latin American Legal Institutions: Problems for Comparative Study* (1966).

Keeble, T. W., *Commercial Relations between British Overseas Territories and South America 1806–1914* (1970).

Kelchner, W. H., *Latin American Relations with the League of Nations* (1930).

Kidder, F. E., *Latin America and UNESCO: The First Five Years* (1960).

Krause, W., and F. J. Mathis, *Latin America and Economic Integration: Regional Planning or Development* (1970).

La Belle, T. J., ed., *Education and Development: Latin America and the Caribbean* (1972).

LaPorte, R. and J. F. Petras, *Cultivating Revolution: United States and Agrarian Reform in Latin America* (1971).

Lambert, J., *Latin America Social Structures and Political Institutions* (1967).

Landsberger, H. A., ed., *The Church and Social Change in Latin America* (1970).

Latin America Conference on Church and Society, *Social Justice and Latin Churches* (1969).

Latin America Tomorrow, Annals of the American Academy of Political and Social Sciences—Vol. 360, July, 1965.

Latin American Free Trade Association (LAFTA): see Wionczek and also U.S. Tariff Commission publication No. 60.

Latin American Viewpoints, Annals of the American Academy of Political and Social Sciences (1942).

Lauterpach, A., *Enterprise in Latin America* (1966).

Levinson, J., and J. de Onis, *The Alliance That Lost Its Way* (1970).

Lewis, C., *America's Stake in International Investments* (1938).

Lieuwen, E., *Arms and Politics in Latin America* (rev. ed., 1961).

————, *Generals Versus Presidents* (1964).

————, *United States Policy in Latin America: A Short History* (1965).

————, *The United States and the Challenge to Security in Latin America* (1966).

Lindsell, H., *The Chilean-American Controversy of 1891–1892* (1943).

Lipset, S. M., and A. Solari, eds., *Elites in Latin America* (1967).

Liser, M., *Organization of American States,* 4th ed. (1949).

Liss, S. B. and P., *Man, State, and Society in Latin American History* (1972).

Lockey, J. B., *Essays in Pan Americanism* (1939).

————, *Pan Americanism: Its Beginning* (1920).

Lodge, G. C., *Engines of Change: United States Interests and Revolution in Latin America* (1969).

Lofstrom, W., *Attitudes of an Industrial Pressure Group in Latin America* (1968).

Logan, J. A., Jr., *No Transfer, an American Security Principle* (1961).

MacDonald, N. P., *Hitler over Latin America* (1940).

Madariaga, S. de, *Latin America between the Eagle and the Bear* (1962).

Madden, C. H., and L. Rall, *Latin America: Reform or Revolution* (1962).

Maier, J., and R. W. Weatherhead, eds., *Politics of Change in Latin America* (1964).

Mallin, J., ed., *Terror and Urban Guerrillas: A Study of Tactics and Documents* (1971).

Mander, J., *Static Society: The Paradox of Latin America* (1969).

————, *The Unrevolutionary Society: The Power of Latin American Conservatism in a Changing World* (1971).

Manger, W., ed., *The Alliance for Progress: A Critical Appraisal* (1963).

————, *Pan America in Crisis: The Future of OAS* (1961).

————, *The Two Americas: Dialogue on Progress and Problems* (1965).

————, *The War and the Americas* (1944).

Manning, W. R., ed., *Diplomatic Correspondence of the United States Concerning Latin American Independence,* 3 vols. (1925).

————, *Diplomatic Correspondence of the United States: Inter-America Affairs, 1831–1860,* 12 vols. (1932–1939).

————, *Arbitration Treaties Among the American Nations to 1910* (1924; Supplement to 1929).

Maritano, N., *Alliance for Progress* (1963).

————, *A Latin American Economic Community: History, Policies, and Problems* (1970).

Martin, P. A., *Latin America and the War* (1925).

Martínez Piedra, A., ed., *Socio-Economic Change in Latin America* (1970).

Martz, J. D., ed., *Dynamics of Change in Latin American Politics* (1965).

Masters, R. D., *Handbook of International Organization in the Americas* (1945).

Masur, G., *Nationalism in Latin America* (1966).

Mathews, H. L., ed., *United States and Latin America* 2nd ed. (1963).

Mathis, F. J., *Economic Integration in Latin America, The Progress and Problems of LAFTA* (1970).

May, H. K., *Problems and Prospects of the Alliance for Progress: A Critical Examination* (1968).

――――, *The Effects on United States and Other Foreign Investments in Latin America* (1970).

McAlister, L. N., *et al.*, *The Military in Latin America Socio-Political Evolution: Four Case Studies* (1970).

McClellan, G. S., ed., *United States Policy in Latin America* (1963).

McDonald, R. H., *Party Systems and Elections in Latin America* (1971).

MacEoin, G., *Revolution Next Door. Latin America and the 1970s* (1971).

――――, ed., *Latin America in Search of Liberation* (1970).

McGann, T. F., *Argentina, United States and the Inter-American System, 1880–1914* (1958).

Mecham, J. L., *Survey of United States–Latin American Relations* (1965).

――――, *The United States and Inter-American Security, 1889–1960* (1961).

Miller, J., and R. A., Gakenheimer, *Latin American Urban Policies and the Social Sciences* (1970).

Miller, L. B., *World Order and Social Disorder: The United States and Internal Conflicts* (1967).

Moreno, F., and B. Mitrani, eds., *Conflicts and Violence: Cultural and Psychological Factors in Latin American Politics* (1970).

Mörner, M., ed., *Race and Class in Latin America* (1970).

Morrison, D., *Latin-American Mission: An Adventure in Hemisphere Diplomacy* (1965).

Morse, R. M., ed., *The Urban Development of Latin America 1750–1920* (1971).

Motten, C. J., ed., *Latin America: Development Programming and United States Investments* (1956).

Munro, D. G., *Intervention and Dollar Diplomacy in the Caribbean, 1900–1921* (1964).

――――, *United States and the Carribbean* (1934).

National Planning Association, *Studies in Technical Cooperation in Latin America* (Seven studies to 1957).

――――, *Technical Assistance by Religious Agencies in Latin America* (by J. G. Maddox) (1956).

――――, *Technical Cooperation in Latin American Agriculture* (by A. T. Mosher) (1957).

――――, *The Role of the Universities in Technical Corporations in Latin America* (1955).

Nearing, S., and J. Freeman, *Dollar Diplomacy* (1926).

Needler, M. C., *Political Development in Latin America* (1968).

————, ed., *Obstacles to Change in Latin America* (1965).

————, ed., *Latin America and the Caribbean: A Handbook* (1968).

Vernon, R., ed., *How Latin America Views the U.S. Investor* (1965).

Wagley, C., *Latin American Tradition* (1968).

Wagner, R. H., *United States Policy Towards Latin America* (1970).

Walton, R. J., *United States and Latin America* (1972).

Webster, C. K., *Foreign Policy of Palmerston* (1941).

Welles, S., *Time for Decision* (1944).

Whitaker, A. P., *Argentine Upheaval* (1956).

————, *Development of American Regionalism* (International Conciliatio No. 442).

————, *Inter-American Affairs: An Annual, 1941–1945*, Vols. I–V.

————, *United States and Argentina* (1954).

————, *United States and Independence of Latin America, 1800–1830* (1941).

————, *United States and South America: Northern Republics* (1948).

————, *Western Hemisphere Idea: Its Rise and Decline* (1954).

———— and D. C. Jordan, *Nationalism in Contemporary Latin America* (1967).

Wilbur, W. A., *The Monroe Doctrine* (1965).

Williams, E. J., *Latin American Christian Democratic Parties* (1967).

————, *The Emergence of the Secular Nation-State and Latin American Catholicism* (1971).

Winkler, M., *Investments of United States Capital in Latin America* (1929).

Wionczeh, M. S., *Latin American Free Trade Association* (1965).

————, ed., *Latin American Integration: Experiences and Prospects* (1966).

————, *Economic Cooperation in Latin America, Africa and Asia; a Handbook of Documents* (1970).

Wolf, E. R. and E. C. Hansen, eds., *The Human Condition in Latin America* (1972).

Wollman, N., *Water Resources of Chile* (1968).

Wood, B., *Making of the Good Neighbor Policy* (1961).

————, *The United States and Latin American Wars, 1932–1942* (1966).

Wythe, G., *United States and Inter-American Relations: A Contemporary Appraisal* (1964).

Zea, L., *Latin America and the World* (1969).

GLOSSARY OF
UNFAMILIAR TERMS

This glossary aims only to help the reader understand the Spanish, Portuguese, or Indian words which have become a part of Latin American history. Quite often the definition of the same term changes from country to country. A word in Portuguese seemingly very similar to the Spanish will have a different meaning in Brazil. Words with one connotation in colonial times have come to mean something different in the twentieth century. Recent decades have brought a new type of confusing term, the use of capital letters—initials from the Spanish or Portuguese name of a government agency, political party or program—to form a completely new term, in the same way that the United States has used GOP, HEW, or UNESCO. Not all such terms have been included, only those in which the series of letters has developed into an expression of historic importance.

A

abrazo   an embrace, the customary Latin American greeting of welcome and farewell among close friends and relatives, a greeting of cordiality.

Acción Democrática   a middle-class democratic party in Venezuela since the 1940s.

Acción Popular   President Belaúnde-Terry's political party in Peru in the 1960s.

acuerdo   an agreement or resolution; *real acuerdo*—an agreement made with or by parties representing the Spanish crown in colonial times.

adelantado   a private individual given royal permission to explore territory at his own expense, found a colony there, and govern it for the Spanish king; governor of a frontier district during the colonial regime.

aftosa   Spanish word for hoof-and-mouth disease among cattle.

agave   a kind of cactus, similar to the maguey or century plant.

AID   Agency for International Development, United States economic aid agency.

alcabala   a tax on sales levied within the Spanish colonies.

alcalde   a magistrate of local government in the Spanish colonies, a justice of the peace; mayor, head of a municipal district.

alcalde mayor   a Spanish colonial regional governor in a frontier district; *alcaldía mayor* refers to the Spanish colonial regional government, centering on a frontier municipality and based on a European settlement.

alguacil   a constable.

Alianza Para Progreso   the Alliance for Progress, to promote the development of Latin America in the 1960s.

altiplano   the high plateau country above La Paz, Bolivia.

almojarifazgo   an export and import tax charged against colonial trade by the Spanish government.

anata   first years' salary paid to King for appointment to office; *media anata,* payment of half of first year's salary for appointment to office.

APRA   The *Alianza Popular Revolucionaria Americana,* or reform party in Peru led by Haya de la Torre after 1930. *Aprismo* is the name of the movement which it represented; members were called *Apristas.*

Armada de Barlovento   the windward fleet, the coast guard of the Caribbean.

asesor   an assessor, an adviser.

asiento   a contract granted by the Spanish king to ship owners or foreigners allowing them to import slaves into the colonies. Such an *asiento* was granted to England for importing 4,800 slaves a year into the Caribbean colonies of Spain in 1713.

Asuntos Indígenas   Indian problems, hence a government Department of Indian Affairs in modern Mexico.

Ato Institucional   a constitutional act, amendment, or supplementary act in Brazil, such as occurred in 1834, and the one which gave power to Castello Branco in 1964.

audiencia   a group of judges sent from Spain to colonial administrative centers, who had some executive as well as judicial powers; the highest colonial court in Spanish America; also applies to the territorial division over which the *audiencia* has jurisdiction.

auto da fé   public punishment or execution of heretics condemned by the Inquisition.

ayuntamiento   a local town council, sometimes also applied to the city hall. See also *cabildo.*

B

La Banda Oriental　the eastern strip of the Uruguayan coast across the Plata from Buenos Aires; Urugay.

bandeirantes　groups of men who traveled the interior of Brazil in small, organized "traveling cities." Brazilian frontiersman; Portuguese gold and slave hunters in the interior of Brazil.

barranca　a deep canyon.

barriada　shanty town slum in Peru.

barrio　a district within a city or town.

batata　the New World sweet potato, different from the yam.

belcismo　a word for corrupt and selfish dictatorship, derived from the nineteenth century Bolivian demagogue Belzú.

bolas　a type of lasso made with stones tied at the end of long strips of rawhide, used by gauchos to trip up cattle on the Argentine pampas.

bolero　a country dance from Spain, also a sleeveless jacket worn at such a dance.

boucaniers　French term for men who lived on dried beef or *boucan* in the Caribbean area, thus eventually buccaneers, freebooters, or pirates. *Boucaner* is the French word meaning to smoke meat on a wooden frame.

braceros　literally "those with arms," similar to field "hands," referring to farm workers from Mexico under contract to harvest crops in the United States.

C

caballero　mounted horseman, hence a Spanish knight or gentleman.

caballería　a Spanish land grant, or land measure equal to 33½ acres.

Caballeros-Racionales　secret revolutionary societies in Mexico during the war of independence.

cabildo　a town council, or the building where such council meetings were held. See *ayuntamiento*.

cabildo abierto　an open meeeting of a *cabildo* or municipal council to consider gravely important matters, attended by prominent men of the town. Such meetings were a vital factor leading to the wars for independence.

caboclo　Brazilian Indians or mixtures of white and Indian; in recent times any poor farmer in northern Brazil.

cacique　an Indian tribal chieftain, often maintained as a constable or local authority after the Spanish conquest; in recent times a local "boss" or "ward heeler."

cafuso　in Brazil, a person of mixed Indian and Negro ancestry.

cajas　cash boxes, applied to workers' cooperative credit unions in modern Chile.

callampas　shanty-town slums in Chile in the 1960s.

calpullec　the principal civil officer of the Aztecs.

câmaras   Portuguese town councils in Brazil, similar to Spanish *cabildos*.

camaya   a provincial governor in the Inca empire.

campesinos   peasant farmers in Mexico, sometimes called *peones*.

capitania-donatários   tracts of land granted to large-scale proprietors in sixteenth-century Brazil.

capitão mor   boss of local militia in colonial Brazil.

caracas   hereditary chiefs of vassal governments within the Inca empire.

Carioca   a person who lives in Rio de Janeiro.

Casa de Contratación   the Spanish House of Trade which regulated commerce in the New World.

Casa da India   the Portuguese agency for supervising colonial Brazil.

casa grande   a manor house in Brazil.

Casa Rosada   literally the Pink House, home of presidents of Argentina.

catedrático   a university professor.

Caudillo (*caudilho* in Portuguese)   the Spanish word for chieftain or leader, hence a military leader who had a group of followers loyal to him personally; later a military dictator and political "boss." The noun *caudillismo* (*caudilhismo* in Portuguese) refers to military dictatorship and/or "bossism."

centrales   a term for sugar refineries in Cuba.

chapetones   "tenderfeet," a term applied by the Spanish colonials in South America to Spaniards born in Spain.

charro   a Mexican "dude" horseman in colorful costume.

CHEAR   the Council on Higher Education in the American Republics, financed by the Carnegie Foundation.

china poblana   a native costume trimmed with China silk worn by the girls of colonial Puebla, today the national costume of Mexico.

chiripá   a long fringed shawl, part of the costume worn by the old-style Argentine *gauchos*.

cholos   the Bolivian expression for *mestizos*, persons of mixed Indian and Spanish strain.

chunca   an Inca village which held land in common.

científicos   advisers and political supporters of Porfírio Díaz, dictator in Mexico, who made a fetish of scientific efficiency in government administration.

cimarrón   a person of Negro descent or Negro and Indian blood who ran away from a plantation to "go native" in the interior of Brazil or colonial Spain.

cinchona   the Indian term for the bark of the quinine-producing tree.

Cinco de Mayo   "The Fifth of May," a Mexican national holiday honoring a temporary victory over Napoleon III's troops at Puebla on May 5, 1862.

civilista   an adjective referring to civilian rather than military rule.

colegiado   plural executive or council in Uruguay.

colegio   a Latin American secondary school, usually privately financed.

colonos   immigrants from Europe settled in São Paulo state, Brazil, to care for coffee plants; also Andean highland farmers, enjoying use of land in return for labor.

COMIBOL   the Bolivian government corporation to control the tin industry in the 1960s.

Comité de fundos   union of agricultural workers in Chile.

comuneros   rebellious communities which opposed the colonial Spanish royal authorities.

confusionismo   chaos in government.

conquistadores   the general term used for the early Spanish explorers and conquerors.

constituyentes   a constituent assembly convoked to formulate the constitution and basic laws of the land.

consulado   a merchants' guild or "chamber of commerce" representing Spanish merchants in Spain and in the chief colonial cities.

continuoismo   continuous, one-man government; extension of tenure in office.

cordillera   the Spanish word for backbone, referring to the entire chain of the Andean mountains.

CORFO   the *Corporación de Fomento,* a Chilean economic development agency in the 1940s.

corregidor   a special liaison officer between the Spanish king and Spanish towns; later used in the New World for governor of a frontier area based upon Indian settlement, an area called *corregimiento;* also sometimes a *corregidor* was a royal representative for the Indians.

corrido   during the Mexican Revolution, a street ballad about politics, with real and imaginary characters; a folk song.

cortes   (Portuguese: *côrtes*) a parliament or congress in medieval Spain, also applied to the Spanish "underground" meetings held in Cadiz against Napoleon.

COSACH   the *Companía de Salitre de Chile,* the government-controlled nitrate mining development in Chile.

creoles   (Spanish: *criollos*) a term meaning "born of European descent in the New World," never used in colonial times to indicate racial mixture.

criollismo   "nativism."

Cristeros   an anti-revolutionary, pro-Catholic party in Mexico in the 1920s, carrying on underground terrorism.

CTM   the *Confederación de Trabajadores Mexicanos,* new name for Mexico's strong labor organization after 1936.

cuartelazo   a "bloodless" revolution starting in the barracks or soldiers' "quarters," similar to a *coup d'état.*

Cuba Libre!   "Free Cuba!" the war cry for independence among the Cuban guerrillas in 1895.

cueca   a Chilean folk dance.

D

degradados   outlaws or exiles living in the forests of colonial Brazil; castaways on Brazilian shores in colonial days.

desacato   defiance and disrespect of authority; a law of *desacato* was passed by Perón to allow arrest of his political enemies on the excuse of "disrespect."

descamisados "the shirtless ones," hence the "non-white-collar" workers, the urban proletariat, refers especially to those workers who followed Perón in Argentina.

diezmo the ten per cent of income pledged to the church in Spanish colonial times; a tithe.

donatários proporietors of original land grants in early Brazil who founded colonies at their own expense.

dotación grant of land to an individual in accordance with Mexican agrarian law; literally, an endowment, gift, or dowry.

dramas criollos gaucho folk plays, given by wandering troubadours in the pampas towns of nineteenth-century Argentina.

E

ECLA the United Nations' Economic Commission for Latin America.

ejido a community-owned farm in Mexico, originally Indian village or tribal lands; *ejidatario*—a farm worker on communal land.

El Dorado "the Gilded Man" or gold-dust-covered king, hence a myth about such a person in the Colombian Andes.

El Supremo "The Supreme One," a title referring to Dr. Francia, dictator of Paraguay.

emboaba a Portuguese settler newly come to Brazil; especially a derisive term applied to newcomers in the mining regions in colonial Brazil.

empleomanía "job mania."

encomienda a grant by the Spanish kings to a settler of authority over Indians living in an area who were to work; the encomendero had duties to Christianize, civilize, educate, and protect. The grant was given to an individual in recognition of distinguished service.

engenho a sugar mill in Brazil; sometimes also a plantation including such a mill.

Estado Novo "The New State," a term used by Getulio Vargas in Brazil to describe his government in 1937.

estancia a large agricultural estate in the Argentine area; *estanciero* is the term used for the owner of a large cattle ranch in Argentina, member of Argentina's nineteenth-century ruling oligarchy.

F

falange a unit of the followers of Franco in the Spanish Civil War of 1936.

fandango a formal Spanish group dance.

Farrapos "Ragamuffins," a term applied to rebels in the state of Rio Grande do Sul against the Brazilian emperor in the 1830s and 1840s.

favelas Shanty-town slums in Brazilian cities in the 1960s.

fazenda large plantation or estate in Brazil; *fazendero* is the term applied to the man who owned such a plantation, a member of the Brazilian oligarchy.

Federales national militia kept by Porfírio Díaz to maintain his dictatorship in Mexico.

fico Portuguese verb meaning "I will remain," proclaimed by the Brazilian emperor Pedro I, January 9, 1822, when he disobeyed orders to return to Lisbon.

fidalgo Portuguese word for an aristocrat, similar to a Spanish *hidalgo*.

Fidelismo the Latin American Communist movement of the 1960s, centered in Cuba; *Fidelistas* are the followers of Fidel Castro, Cuban dictator of the 1960s, hence Latin American Communists.

fiesta the celebration of a public or religious holiday.

finca a coffee plantation in Central America.

fiscal government attorney.

flota a fleet of cargo ships sent from Spain to Vera Cruz annually during the colonial regime.

fomento governmental internal development; usually done through a government corporation.

FRAP *Frente de Acción Popular,* a socialist communist "Popular Front" in Chile in the 1960s.

Frente coalition government in Colombia in the 1960s.

frigoríficos meat packing and freezing plants in Buenos Aires and Montevideo.

fuero a privilege to claim exemption from the civil or common law in Mexico.

fundo a rural estate in Chile.

G

gachupín "He who wears spurs"; a person born in Spain, residing in New Spain; the Spanish ruling class hated by the colonials in the independence period.

galeones the fleet of Spanish cargo ships sent to Cartagena and Puerto Bello in colonial times.

gaucho (Portuguese: *gaúcho*) horseman of pampas in Argentina, Uruguay; cowboys of South America in song and story.

guanaco a wild species of llama in the Chile area.

gazeta a newsletter, term applied to the first colonial newspapers.

gente de razón people with "ability to reason" in the colonial period, as opposed to slaves and Indians.

Gobernación cabinet office of internal affairs in several Latin American nations.

Godos a sarcastic term for blond or Gothic Spaniards, hence all newcomers from Spain just before the independence period.

golondrinas the Spanish word for swallows, hence migratory workers from Italy who came to Argentina to do harvest work in the Southern Hemisphere summer.

golpe de estado coup d'état; violent overthrow of a government.

GOU *Groupo Officiales Unidos,* group of united officers in Argentina.

gremio   a craft guild of skilled artisans in colonial times.

Grito de Dolores   the "cry" or "shout" made by Father Miguel Hidalgo at the town of Dolores, September 16, 1810; hence the Mexican movement for independence.

Grito de Ypiranga   the "cry" or "shout" for independence made at the stream of Ypiranga near São Paulo by the Emperor Pedro I, September 7, 1822, to announce Brazilian independence.

guajiros   Cuban sugar plantation workers.

guanaco   a wild species of llama in the Chile area.

guano   the dung of sea birds, collected off the coast of Peru; a valuable fertilizer.

Guaraní   name for Paraguayan and Brazilian Indians, hence also the language spoken by the Guaraní tribes.

guardia nacional   a national guard or police force.

H

hacienda   a large, feudal, agricultural estate in Mexico; **hacendado,** owner of a *hacienda,* a powerful landowner in Mexico.

hamaca   Caribbean Indian word for a hammock.

hermandades   brotherhoods of laymen in Catholic society which undertook municipal jobs such as police patrol.

hidalgo   Spanish term for a nobleman, an *hijo de algo,* or son of "somebody."

Hispanidad   an attempt on the part of modern Spain to promote cultural ties with Latin America.

Hispaniola   the name of the island including Haiti and the Dominican Republic.

hondo   deep ocean areas near the Central American coast.

huaso   a Chilean cowherd or *gaucho.*

huna   an Inca tribal group, or family council.

I

IA-ECOSOC   The Inter-American social and economic council of the OAS.

imperialismo   the Spanish term for United States' "imperialism."

Inconfidência   the revolutionary movement in Brazil in the pre-independence period, of which the principal leader was Tiradentes.

Indianismo   the term applied to the cultural interest in Indian backgrounds in modern Mexico.

inquilino   a peasant or tenant farmer in Chile.

Integralistas   pro-German Fascists in Brazil in World War II; the "greenshirts."

Intendencia   a French political institution introduced into the Spanish colonies by the Bourbons in the eighteenth century.

IPAF   the Inter-American Peace Force in the Dominican Republic in 1965–1966.

J

Jefe Máximo   absolute leader of party government; "Chief Boss," the nickname given to Calles in Mexico in the 1920s.

Jefe Político   governor of a district.

jota   a regional or country dance from Spain.

junta   a provisional committee to take over political authority during a revolutionary period.

justicialismo   a term used by Perón to describe his Argentine regime; literally, a "doctrine of justice."

Juzgado de Indias   port authority which controlled shipping from Cádiz during the colonial regime.

Juzgado de Indios   a special court to hear complaints of Indians, created in 1573 to protect the aborigines in the Spanish empire.

L

labrador   farm worker.

Ladinos   modernized Spanish-speaking people of Indian descent in Guatemala.

LAFTA   Latin American Free Trade Association, a trade-promoting agreement in the 1960s.

latifundio   a large landed estate worked under feudal conditions; hence also *latifundismo,* the system of land tenure.

Lautaro   password, name for secret societies opposed to the Spaniards in 1810, from the name of the Araucanian Indian who killed Valdivia.

Lépero   Vagabond, disorderly element in colonial New Spain.

Ley de fuga   "Law of flight," hence justification of "shot while trying to escape," as used by Porfírio Díaz to justify the killing of political prisoners.

liceo   a secondary school.

limpieza de sangre   no mixture of nonwhite blood.

llanero   a cowboy on the plains of the *llanos* or Orinoco Valley.

llanos   the grasslands of the Orinoco Valley.

Luteranos   "Lutherans," hence all Protestants in Spanish colonial times, including especially British pirates.

M

machismo   from the adjective *macho,* or masculine, virile, hence the popularity of masculinity or virility in politics and society.

malambo   a type of folk dance in the Argentine area.

mamelucos   Portuguese half-breeds, mixed European and Indian blood.

mandioca   a root in tropical America providing a starchy food.

maravedi   a little-used Spanish coin.

Mare Nostrum   Latin for "Our Ocean," used by Spain to mean the Caribbean.

masambo   Brazilian word for creole or person born of European stock in the New World.

mas horca   "more gallows," a term used by the Argentine underground against the dictator Rosas and his special police units called *Mazorca.*

maté   a wild plant originating in Paraguay; a popular tea drink is made from the leaves.

mayor domo   administrator of a landed estate.

mayorazco   the right of primogeniture, or inheritance by the eldest son.

Mazorca   an Argentine term for "corn on the cob"—used by the police of the dictator Rosas to imply the closeness and unity of their organization. Pronounced by his enemies as *mas horca,* or "more gallows."

Mesa da Consciencia é Ordens   a Portuguese church council created in 1532 to regulate officials and handle Indian affairs in Brazil.

mesta   a guild of livestock breeders in medieval Spain and in the New World.

mestizo   a person of mixed Spanish and Indian descent (feminine, *mestiza*); *mestizaje,* the culture and way of life in a *mestizo* society.

milpa   a plot of land in Mexico on which Indians grow corn.

minifundo   parcel of land too small to support a family.

mita   forced labor, periodic conscription of Indian labor in Spanish colonies.

mitamaes   Inca colonists sent to newly conquered territories to consolidate control; the Inca military forces encamped within the empire.

MNR   The Movement of National Revolution in Bolivia, less radical than the PIR.

mocambo   fugitive slave settlement in Brazil.

Modernista   "Ultra-modern," referring to the type of poetry written by Rubén Darío.

montaña   the areas of Ecuador, Peru, and Bolivia lying in the foothills of the Andes east of the divide on the edge of the Amazon Basin.

mordidas   "bites," a slang word for bribes to government officials.

mulato   (feminine, mulata) person of mixed Negro and Caucasian stock (English, mulatto).

municipio   township.

N

Nacional Financiera   A Mexican government financing agency for agricultural and industrial loans.

Noche Triste   "The Sad Night," during which Cortés and his followers escaped from the Aztecs on June 30, 1520.

NOVACAP   The Brazilian project for the new capital at Brasilia in the late 1950s.

O

OAS   Organization of American States.

obraje   a textile factory or work shop in the Spanish colonies employing Indian laborers.

ODECA   the federation of Central American States in the 1950s and '60s.

Oficiales Reales   Royal Officials of the Treasury (tax gatherers).

Oidores   judges in the Spanish colonial courts or members of the *audiencia*.

ombú   a bushy tree growing on the Argentine pampas.

Oriente   the eastern slope of the Andes leading out to the Amazon, sometimes called the *montaña*.

ORIT   Inter-American regional organization of labor, a Latin American branch of a worldwide trade union movement.

Ouro Preto   black gold (Portuguese), hence a dark colored ore of high gold content; hence the name given to the Brazilian town near a rich strike of such ore.

P

padre   Spanish word for father, hence a missionary or parish priest.

palmos   "hands," about eight inches, as used in measuring the height of horses or, in the Spanish empire, the height of slaves.

pampas   the level grasslands of Argentina, inland from Buenos Aires; beef and wheat producing area.

pan ó palo   bread or the club, the guiding principle of Porfírio Díaz' dictatorship.

pan, techo y abrigo   bread, clothes, and shelter, the slogan of the Chilean "Popular Front" in 1938.

pardo   mulatto or Negro.

paseo   a walk or stroll, such as through a park, hence often a street near a park.

patio   a central garden or courtyard in a Spanish-style house; also a method of crushing ore under stones by mule-power.

patois   the dialect of French, with many African words added, which is spoken in rural Haiti, sometimes called *creole*.

Patria Boba   "The Foolish Fatherland," referring to the chaotic government in New Granada from 1810 to 1815.

patria chica   the "small fatherland," attachment to local region.

patrón   boss (of hacienda, estancia).

patronato real   a Spanish pact with the papacy; right of Spanish kings to dispose of all ecclesiastical benefits and make church appointments.

Paulistas   people from São Paulo, hence early explorers of the Brazilian interior.

payadores   wandering folk minstrel singers on the Argentine pampas.

pelota   Spanish game of handball.

pelucones   "big-wigs," hence a Chilean political party of older conservative leaders in the nineteenth century.

Pemex   Mexican nationally-owned petroleum industry; the gasoline it sells.

peninsulares   people born in the Iberian peninsula, i.e. in Spain or Portugal rather than in the colonies.

peón   an agricultural worker tied to the land; an indigent agricultural worker.

peonía   a small land grant made to a Spanish foot soldier.

personalismo   a political policy of loyalty to personal leader, rather than to a political philosophy; *personalista* refers to the follower of a dictator for reasons of personal loyalty.

pieza de Indias   a valuable African slave in the "prime" of life.

pípiolos   "beardless young men," hence a Chilean political party of young progressives in the nineteenth century.

plan   a platform or political program, usually advanced by revolutionary leaders.

Plata   the Spanish word for silver, hence applied to the Argentine region where early explorers thought silver abounded.

poncho   a wool blanket or shawl worn by Chilean cowboys.

porteño   an Argentine who lived in Buenos Aires city, as opposed to people who lived on the pampas.

portolani   a medieval sailing chart.

posada   an inn or hostel.

positivism   doctrine of Auguste Comte.

prensa   literally the "press," hence a famous newspaper in Buesos Aires.

preparatorio   an academic secondary school, either public or private. In Brazil the term is written *preparatário*.

presidencia   a regional government in the more remote Spanish colonies, an *audiencia* which is located at a place not having a viceroy or captain-general; hence president of an *audiencia*.

presidio   a spanish garrison, fort, or soldiers' barracks.

PRI   the *Partido Revolucionario Institucional,* the name for Mexico's major political party after 1946.

pronunciamiento   a "pronouncement," or declaration of policy made by a revolutionary leader.

protomédico   a medical inspector, first sent to the colonies in 1571.

Provincias Internas   Interior Provinces, a term applied in 1776 to the northern frontier in New Spain.

pueblo   the Spanish word for a town, sometimes also used for the people of a town; also refers to a tribe of Indians in New Mexico.

pulpería   an Argentine country saloon.

pulque   a mildly intoxicating beverage made by Mexican Indians from the juice of the *maguey* or century plant; *pulquería,* a place where *pulque* is sold.

puna   bleak, arid Andean tableland.

Q

quetzal   a tropical bird, native to Central America; Aztec word for feathers.

quilombo   a village of runaway slaves in the Brazilian backlands.

quinto   the "royal fifth," tax on precious metals mined in the colonies and paid to the Spanish royal treasury during the colonial regime.

quipu   Inca Indian knotted cord used for keeping accounts; a memory aid used in communications.

R

rancho   a farm or cattle ranch.

rancheros   middle-class ranch owners in northern Mexico, not as powerful as *hacendados*.

real hacienda   royal treasury, exchequer.

real de minas   a Spanish colonial mining community.

reales   small Spanish coins, valued at eight to the Spanish colonial *peso*, or "pieces of eight."

reconcentrados   concentration camps in Cuba in 1898.

Reconquista   the Christian reconquest of lands in Spain held by the Moors.

reducción   settlement of converted Indians by Jesuits in Paraguay.

regidores   elected members of the Spanish colonial town councils or *cabildos*.

repartimiento   a temporary allotment of Indian laborers and land to an individual Spanish settler in the early years of the conquest.

residencia   a judicial review of an official's conduct at the end of his term of office.

rotos   Chilean miners and industrial workers.

rumba   a Cuban dance.

rurales   mounted police squads in Mexico created by Porfírio Díaz to maintain order.

S

sabiá   a tropical bird in Brazil whose song symbolized Brazilian national feelings.

Santa Hermandad   the "royal brotherhood," or centralized police force in fifteenth-century Spain.

sarape   a Mexican Indian hand-woven blanket.

savanna   grassland.

selva   forested area; *selvas* (in Bolivia), the tropical plains spreading northeast toward the Amazon.

Sertão   the drought-stricken lands inland from the coast on the "bulge" of Brazil, behind Fortaleza. *Sertanejo* is an inhabitant of the *Sertão*.

Servicio Especial de Sauda Pública   The Brazilian Public Health Service after 1940.

Servicios   service branches of the Organization of American States to encourage technical cooperation in the 1960s.

sierra   Spanish word for mountain range.

siesta   a midday rest period.

simpático   pleasant, cordial, warm-hearted.

sones   sad poems on Cuban life written by Nicolas Guillén.

"Spanish Main"   The mainland of northern South America—i.e., the coasts of Colombia and Venezuela, as opposed to the Caribbean Islands.

SUDENE   the North Eastern Social and Economic Development agency, a Brazilian government program of the 1960s.

T

"Tacho"   nickname for the Christian name Anastasio, hence applied to Anastasio Somoza, dictator of Nicaraugua in the 1940s–1950s.

Tahuantinsuyo   the Inca system of re-colonizing Quechua-speaking people into conquered territory, hence the whole Inca concept of a unified empire.

tango   Argentine-type ballroom dance.

"Tata"   affectionate word for "grandfather," applied by the conservatives to the Mexican dictator, Porfírio Díaz, and others.

teozintle   a wild grass from Central America similar to cultivated corn or maize.

tequila   a strong distilled liquor made from *pulque* or "cactus-plant beer."

tertulias   afternoon tea parties in Mexican society circles.

tierra   the Spanish word for earth or land; agricultural land belonging to peasants in Mexico.

tierra Caliante   the warm coastal regions of Mexico.

Tierra Firme   the northern Caribbean shore of South America, the "Spanish Mainland."

tierra Fría   the area of Mexico of highest altitude near the snow-covered volcanoes.

tierra Templada   the area of Mexico of temperate climate, the plateaus of central Mexico.

"Tierra y Libertad"   "Land and Liberty," the slogan of Emiliano Zapata and his peasant followers in the Mexican Revolution of 1910.

Tlachantín   the elected commander-in-chief of the Aztec army.

tortilla   a flat corn cake, a staple food in Mexico since Aztec times.

Tonton Macoute   the personal bodyguard of Haitian dictator Duvalier in the 1960s.

tribunal   court of justice, tribunal.

tributa   head tax paid by Indians.

Trigarante   pertaining to the "Three Guarantees" of Iturbide under the Mexican *Plan de Iguala*.

tumulto   a riot.

Tupamaro   guerilla terrorists in Uruguay.

U

Ultra-istas   young Latin American authors of ultra-modern poetry.
Unión Cívica Radical   a moderate reform party in Argentine politics at the turn
of the twentieth century.

V

vecino   citizen; resident.
vecindario   neighborhood.
visita   official inspection.
la violencia   civil war in Colombia.

Y

yanacona   laborer in Bolivia.
yerba maté   Paraguayan tea.

Z

zambo   (*zambaígo*) red-black mixture.

AIDS TO
FURTHER STUDY

bibliographical note

The authors have attempted to give full listings of books in English after each chapter, including specialized studies. Here we have confined ourselves to giving some "bibliographies in general" on a number of topics relating to Latin America, to which we have added a list of periodicals by which the student can keep abreast of developments and events in Latin America. For more complete listings, we refer the student to the "Aids to Further Study" given in the second edition of the text.

general bibliographies

Academic Writer's Guide to Periodicals: Volume I Latin American Studies (1971). (A. S. Birkos and L. A. Tambs, eds.)

Adams, E. B., *A Bio-Bibliography of Franciscan Authors in Colonial Central America* (1953).

Albanel, M. N., *Cuba, Dominican Republic, Haiti and Puerto Rico—Selected Bibliography* (1956).

Alisky, M., *Bibliography on Uruguay* (1969).

————, *Latin American Journalism Bibliography* (1958).

American Geographical Society, *Catalogue of Maps on Hispanic America* (4 vols., 1930–1932).

American Historical Association, *Guide to Historical Literature* (1961).

American Universities Field Staff, *List of Publications, 1961–1962* (1963).

————, *A Select Bibliography, Supplement on Latin America* by T. D. Long (1960).

————, *Bibliography of the Andean Countries* (1958).

Andrews, B. H., *Latin America: A Bibliography of Paperback Books* (1964).

Atkinson, W. C., *British Contributions to Portuguese and Brazilian Studies* (1945).

Bartley, R. H. and S. L. Wagner, *Latin America in Basic Collections: A Working Guide* (Hoover Library Publication 1972).

Bayitch, S. A., *Latin America and the Caribbean: A Bibliographical Guide to Works in English* (1967).

Behrendt, R. F. W., *Modern Latin America in Social Science Literature* (1949).

Bemis, S. F. and G. G. Griffin, *Guide to the Diplomatic History of the United States 1775–1921* (1935).

Bernstein, S. P., *Bibliography on Labor and Social Welfare in Latin America* (1944).

Bibliography on Public Administration in Latin America (1954).

Bibliography of Selected Statistical Sources on the American Nations (1947).

Boggs, R. S., *Bibliography of Latin American Folklore* (1940).

Borchard, E. M., *Guide to the Law and Legal Literature of Argentina, Brazil and Chile* (1917). [Other guides for most of the other countries have been produced under the auspices of the Library of Congress.]

Brown, L. C., *Latin America: A Bibliography* (1962).

Browning, L. E., *A Bibliography of Dissertations in Geography, 1901–1969, American and Canadian Universities* (1970).

Burns, E. B., "A Working Bibliography for the Study of Brazilian History," *Americas*, XII, 54–88.

Carlton, R. G. [ed.], *Latin America in Soviet Writings: A Bibliography* (2 vols., 1966).

Carroll, T. F., *Land Tenure and Land Reform in Latin America: A Selective Annotated Bibliography* (1962).

Chapman, C. E., "List of Books on Caudillos," *Hispanic American Historical Review*, XIII (1933), 143–146.

Chatham, J. R. and E. Ruiz-Fornells, *Dissertations in Hispanic Language and Literature; an Index of Dissertations Completed in the United States and Canada, 1876–1966* (1970).

Charnow, S. M., *Latin American Newspapers in United States Libraries: A Union List* (1969).

Chase, G., *Guide to Music of Latin America* (rev. ed., 1962).

Chilcote, R. H., *The Press in Latin America, Spain and Portugal* (1963).

————, *Revolution and Structural Change in Latin America. A Bibliography on Ideology, Development and the Radical Left 1930–1965* (2 vols., 1971).

————, and J. Edelstein, eds., *Latin America* (1972).

Childs, J. B. (ed. for Library of Congress), *Guide to the Official Publications of the Other American Republics* (19 vols.–Latin American Series, 1945–1949).

————, *The Memorias of the Republics of Central America and Antilles* (1932).

Comitas, L., *Caribbeana 1900–1965: A Topical Bibliography* (1968).

Cox, E. G., *Reference Guide to the Literature of Travel*, Vol. II: *New World* (1938).

Daniels, M., *Sources of Information on Contemporary Caribbean International Problems* in A. C. Wilgus, ed., *Caribbean: Contemporary International Relations* (1957).

Davis, H. E., *Social Science Trends in Latin America* (1950).

del Toro, J., *Bibliography of the Collective Biography of Spanish America* (1938 reprint 1971).

Dibble, E. F. and E. W. Newton, eds., *In Search of Gulf Coast Colonial History* (1970).

————, *Spain and Her Rivals in the Gulf Coast* (1971).

Doors to America [Quarterly list of Books] (since 1954).

Dorn, G. M., comp., *Latin America, Spain and Portugal: An Annotated Bibliography of Paperback Books* (1971).

Easton, D. K., *Sources for the Study of Caribbean Culture* in A. C. Wilgus, ed., *Caribbean: Its Culture* (1955).

ECLA Publications, annex in *Development Problems in Latin America* (1970) pp. 279–303.

Economic Literature of Latin America: A Tentative Bibliography (2 vols., 1936).

Education in Latin America: A Partial Bibliography (1958).

Einaudi, L. and H. Goldhamer, *An Annotated Bibliography of Latin American Military Journals* (1965).

Englekirk, J. E., *An Outline History of Spanish American Literature* (3rd. ed., 1965).

Esquenazi-Mayo, R. and M. C. Meyer, eds., *Latin American Scholarship Since World War II: Trends in History, Political Science, Literature, Geography and Economics* (1971).

Fleener, C. J. and R. L. Seckinger, *Guide to Latin American Paperback Literature* (1966).

Foreign Affairs Research, A Directory of Governmental Resources, 1967, 1969.

Fort, G. V., *The Cuban Rebellion of Fidel Castro Viewed from Abroad: An Annotated Bibliography* (1969).

Foster, D. W. and Vr (comps), *Manual of Hispanic Bibliography* (1970).

————, *Research Guide to Argentine Literature* (1970).

Geisse, G. and J. E. Hardoy, eds., *Latin American Urban Research* (vol. II of F. F. Rabinovitz and F. M. Trueblood, series eds. 3 vols.: vol. I, 1971; vol. II, 1972; vol. III, 1973).

Gibson, C., *The Colonial Period in Latin American History* (1958).

————, *Index to the Hispanic American Historical Review, 1946–1955* (1957).

Goldsmith, P. H., *Brief Bibliography of Books in English on Latin America, in English, Spanish and Portuguese, Relating to the Republics Commonly Called Latin America* (1915).

Griffin, C. C., *Latin America: A Guide to the Historical Literature* (1971).

Griffiths, W. J., "Historiography of Central America since 1830," *Hispanic American Historical Review*, XL (1940), 548–567 [There are many other historiographical articles in that publication, which also has valuable reviews of books and lists of books on Latin America.]

Grismer, R. L., *A Guide to the Literature of Latin America* (1939).

————, *New Bibliography of the Literature of Spain and Spanish America* (7 vols., AA–CEZ, 1941–1946).

————, *Reference Index to Twelve Thousand Spanish American Authors* (1939).

Gropp, A. E., *A Bibliography of Latin American Bibliographies* (updates C. K. Jones' second ed., 1948) 1968; Supplement 1971.

————, *Union List of Latin American Newspapers in Libraries of the United States* (1953).

Grossman, G., *Bibliography on Public Administration in Latin America* (rev. ed., 1954).

Guide to the Official Publications of the Other American Republics (19 vols., 1945–1949).

Handbook of Latin American Studies, No. 1–(annual since 1936).

Hardoy, J. E., *Bibliography on the Evolution of Cities in Latin America* (1962).

Haro, H. P., *Latin American Research in the United States and Canada: A Guide and Directory* (1971).

Harvard Council on Hispano-American Studies, a series of bibliographies relating to the Belles-Lettres of the Latin American countries by various editors (14 vols., 1932–1935) [On Argentina, Bolivia, Brazil, Central America, Chile, Colombia, Cuba, Ecuador, Panama, Paraguay, Peru, Santo Domingo, Uruguay and Venezuela.]

Harvard Guide to American History (1952).

Hasse, A., *Index to United States Documents Relating to Foreign Affairs, 1828–1861* (3 vols., 1914–1921).

Haverstock, N. A. and R. C. Schroeder, *Dateline America* (1971).

Hespelt, *et. al.*, *An Anthology of Spanish American Literature* (1946).

Hill, R. R., *National Archives of Latin America* (1945).

Hilton, R., *Handbook of Hispanic American Source Materials and Research Organizations in the United States* (rev. ed., 1956).

Hulet, C. L., comp., *Latin American Poetry in English Translation. A Bibliography* (1965).

————, *Latin American Prose in English Translation. A Bibliography* (1964).

Humphrey, R. A., "The Historiography of the Spanish American Revolutions," in *Hispanic American Historical Review* XXXI (1956), 81–93.

————, *Latin American History: A Guide to the Literature in English* (1958).

Index for the Published News of the New York Times.

Index to Latin American Periodicals (1961; a quarterly).

Inter-American Bibliographical Review (quarterly since 1951).

Inter-American Development Bank, *Socio-Economic Progress in Latin America*, 1967, 1968, 1969.

Jackson, W. W., *Library Guide for Brazilian Studies* (1964).

Johnson, J. J., *et. al.*, *The Mexican-American: A Selected and Annotated Bibliography* (1969).

Joint Publications Research Service. *See* Index to the Microprint Edition of JPRS Reports.

Jones, C. K., *Bibliography of Latin American Bibliographies* (2nd. ed., 1942). [See Gropp]

Jones, T. B., E. A. Warburton, and A. Kingsley, *Bibliography on South American Economic Affairs: Articles in Nineteenth-Century Periodicals* (1955).

Jones, W. K., *Latin American Writers in Translation; A Tentative Bibliography* (1944).

————, *Spanish American Literature in Translation: A Selection of Poetry, Fiction and Drama Since 1888* (1963).

Kantor, H., *Bibliography of José Figueres* (1972).

————, *Latin American Political Parties: Bibliography* (1968).

Keniston, H., *List of Works for the Study of Hispanic American History* (1920).

Ker, A. M., *Mexican Government Publications 1821–1936* (1940).

King, J. F., "The Negro in Continental Spanish America: A Select Bibliography," in *Hispanic American Historical Review* XXIV (1944) 547–559.

Kuehl, W. F., *Dissertations in History: An Index to Dissertations Completed in History Departments of United States and Canadian Universities 1873–1960* (1965).

"Latin American Fiction in English Translation" in D. Dozer, *Latin America: An Interpretive History* (1962), pp. 580–582. [Many more English translations of Latin American literature have since been published.]

Latin American Research Review (three times a year, since 1965).

Lauerhaus, L., *Communism in Latin America: A Bibliography: The Post War Years 1945–1960* (1963).

Lentnek, B. R., L. Carmin, and T. L. Martinson, *Geographic Research on Latin America: Benchmark, 1970* (1971).

Leavitt, S. E., *Hispano-American Literature in the United States: A Bibliography of Translations and Criticism* (1932).

Library of Congress, Hispanic Foundation, *Bibliographic Series* (since 1942).

————, *Latin American Series* (many guides and bibliographies).

————, Law Library, *Index to Latin American Legislation, 1950–1960* (1961) (2 vols., 1961. First Supplement, 1970 (2 vols.).

Libros en Venta (Publications in Spain and Latin America) (Vol. I 1964; Supplements for 1964, 1965, 1966; 1967 and 1968 [published 1969]; and for 1969 and 1970.)

Liebman, S. B., *A Guide to Jewish References in the Mexican Colonial Era* (1964).

Ludwig, L., *Communism in Latin America, a Bibliography: The Post War Years 1945–1960* (1962).

McAlister, L., "Recent Research and Writing on the Role of the Military in Latin America," *Latin American Research Review* II (1966), 5–37.

Marchant, A., *Boundaries of the Latin American Republics, an Annotated List of Documents, 1493–1943* (1944).

Martins, W., *The Modernist Idea. A Critical Survey of Brazilian Writing in the Twentieth Century* (1971).

Mecham, J. L., "Northern Expansion of New Spain, 1522–1822, A Selected Descriptive List," in *Hispanic American Historical Review,* VII (1927), 233–276.

Metford, S. C., *British Contributions to Spanish and Spanish-American Studies* (1950).

Miller, E. W., *The Negro in America: A Bibliography* (2nd. ed., 1970).

Miscov, S., *An Annotated Bibliography of Paraguay* (1972).

Monteiro, P. V. M., comp., *Catalogue of Latin American Flat Maps 1926–1964* (2 vols., 1967–1969).

Moses, B., *Spanish Colonial Literature in South America* (1922; reprint 1970).

Mughiuddin, M. B. and B. J. L. Clark, *Cuba Since Castro: A Bibliography of Revolutionary Materials* (1963).

National Education Association, *Latin American Backgrounds: A Bibliography* (1941).

Navarro, E. G., *Annotated Bibliography of Materials on the Mexican-American.*

Naylor, B., *Accounts of Nineteenth Century South America: An Annotated Check List of Works by British and United States Observers* (1969).

Nesbit, C. T., *Latin American Economic Development: A Selected Bibliography.*

New York University, School of Law, *Bibliographies on the Law and Uses of International Rivers* (1960).

Nott, K. F., *San Martin—100 Years of Historiography* (1960).

O'Leary, T. J., *Ethnographic Bibliography of South America* (1963).

de Onís, H., ed., *The Golden Land* (2nd. ed., 1961).

Okinshevich, L., *Latin America in Soviet Writings: A Bibliography* (2 vols., 1966).

Organization of American States, General Secretariat, *América en Cifras* (1970).

————, *Guide to Writings on the Alliance for Progress* (compiled by P. Vivó 1970).

————, Pan American Union, *Basic Bibliographies* (6 vols., 1965–1969).

————, *Bibliography of the Liberator, Simón Bolívar* (rev. ed., 1933).

————, *Catalogue of Pan American Union Publications: Inter-American Review of Bibliography.*

————, *Librarians, Editors, Authors* (L.E.A.)

————, *Pan American Bookshelf.*

————, *Select List of Books in English on Latin America* (1929). [The Pan American Union has issued many lists of books and bibliographies].

Pan American Union, *Bibliography of Latin American Culture in English Translation* (1963).

————, *Bibliography on Education and Economic and Social Development* (1962).

————, *Books and Libraries in the Americas, Recommendations of the Inter-American Conferences, 1947–1962* (1963).

————, *Guide to Latin American Scientific and Technical Periodicals: An Annotated List* (1962).

————, *Index to Latin American Periodical Literature 1929–1960* (8 vols., 1962; supplement 1961–1965, 2 vols., 1965).

————, *Latin American Higher Education and Inter-American Cooperation* (1961).

————, *Surveys of Investigations in Progress in the Field of Latin American Studies* (1962).

————, *Theses on Pan American Subjects* (by F. E. Kidder) (1962).

————, Department of Economic Affairs, *International Organizations Active in the Field of Agricultural Development, Agrarian Reform and Rural Life in Latin America* (1964).

Paperbound Books in Print (annual–since 1955).

Paperbound Book Guide for Colleges (annual–since 1957).

Pariseau, E. J., ed. and comp., *Cuban Acquisitions and Bibliography* (1970).

Parker, F. D., *Histories and Historians of Central America to 1850* (1951).

Peraza, S. F., *Revolutionary Cuba: A Bibliographical Guide* (1970).

Phillips, P. L., *List of Books, Magazine Articles and Maps Relating to Latin America* (1902).

Pierson, D., *Survey of Literature on Brazil of Sociological Significance Published up to 1940* (1945).

Pierson, W. W., *Hispanic American History: A Syllabus* (rev. ed., 1926).

Potash, R. A., "Historiography of Mexico since 1821," in *Hispanic American Historical Review* XL (1960), 383–424.

Quintero Mesa, Rose (R. R. Bowker Company), *Latin American Serial Documents* (19 vols.; 5 vols. published during 1971).

Rabinowitz, F. F., F. M. Trueblood, and C. J. Savio, *Latin American Political Systems in an Urban Setting: A Preliminary Bibliography* (1967).

Rand Corporation Publications, *Bibliography on Latin American Publications*.

Reader's Guide to Periodical Literature.

"Recent Articles on Historiography" in L. Hanke, *Readings in Latin American History*, I, 309.

"Research in the Spanish Borderlands," in *Latin American Research Review* VII, No. 2 (1972), 3–94.

Roberts, C. P. and M. Hamour, eds., *Cuba in 1968* (1970. Supplement to Statistical Abstract of Latin America).

Romero, M. and W. Raat, *Bibliography on the Mexican-American* (1969).

Sable, M. H., *Communism in Latin America: An International Bibliography 1900–1945; 1960–1967* (1968. For 1945–1960; see Lauerhaus).

————, *Guide to Latin American Studies* (2 vols., 1967).

————, *Master Directory for Latin America* (1965).

————, *Latin American Agriculture: A Bibliography on Pioneer Settlement, Agricultural History and Economics, Rural Sociology and Population, etc., from the Widener Library* (1970).

————, *Latin American Studies in the Non Western World and Eastern Europe* [Bibliography] (1970).

———, *Latin American Urbanization: A Guide to the Literature, Organizations and Personnel* (1971).

A Select Bibliography: Asia, Africa, Eastern Europe, Latin America—Supplement 1969 (1970).

Select Bibliography of Trade Publications with Special Reference to Caribbean Trade Statistics—Annotated (1954).

Shelby, C., *Latin American Periodicals Currently Received in the Library of Congress and in the Library of the Department of Agriculture* (1945).

Simmons, M. E., *A Bibliography of the Romance and Related Forms in Spanish America* (1963).

Sinclair, J. A., *Protestantism in Latin America: A Bibliographical Guide* (1967).

Smith, R. C. and E. Wilder, *Guide to the Art of Latin America* (1948).

Social History of Colonial Spanish History. Series of articles in *Latin American Research Review* VII, No. 1 (1972).

Spell, J. R., *Contemporary Spanish American Fiction Writers* (1944).

State University of New York at Buffalo, Special Studies.

Steck, F. B., *Tentative Guide to Historical Materials on the Spanish Borderlands* (1943).

Stokes, W. W., *Causes of Inter-American Misunderstandings: A Selected Bibliography* (1957).

Suchlicki, J., ed., *The Cuban Revolution: A Documentary Bibliography 1952–1969* (1971).

Taeuber, I. B., *General Censuses and Vital Statistics in the Americas* (1943).

Thompson, E. T., *The Plantation: A Bibliography* (1957).

Thompson, L. S., *Essays in Hispanic Bibliography* (1970).

Topete, J. M., *A Working Bibliography of Latin American Literature* (1952).

Trask, D. F., M. C. Meyer, and R. R. Trask, eds., *Bibliography of United States–Latin American Relations Since 1810* (1968).

Turner, M. (ed.) (R. R. Bowker Company), *Libros en Venta* (1964. Supplements for years 1964–1966; 1967–1968 [1969]; and 1969–1970 [1971]).

UNESCO, *Directory of Current Latin American Periodicals* (1958).

———, *International Bibliography of Social and Cultural Anthropology, of Economics, of Political Science and of Sociology* (annual–since 1955).

Union List of Latin American Newspapers in Libraries of the United States (1953).

United Nations, F.A.O., monographs and lists published yearly.

United Nations, *Latin America, 1935–1949: A Selected Bibliography* (1952).

United States, Department of Agriculture, *Bibliography of Agriculture* (monthly since 1942).

United States, Department of the Army, *Latin America, Hemisphere Partner; a Bibliographical Survey* (1964).

United States, Department of State, Bureau of Intelligence and Research, *Studies in Progress: American Republics*.

United States, Department of State, Office of External Research, *Research Papers Available* (1970) [Issues External Research List Semiannually since 1952].

United States Military Assistance Institute, Library, *Selected Reading List on Latin America* (2nd. rev. ed., 1963) [Supplements on individual country surveys are regularly issued].

United States National Students Association, *Readings on: Latin American Student Movement and the Rise of the Latin American Left* (1965).

University of California at Los Angeles, Center of Latin American Studies, *Guide to Latin American Studies* (1966).

————, *Latin America in Periodical Literature* (monthly 1962–1963).

————, *Master Directory for Latin America* (1965).

————, *Periodicals for Latin American Economic Development, Trade and Investment: An Annotated Bibliography* (1965).

————, *Statistical Abstract of Latin America* (1970).

University of California (Berkeley), *Spain and Spanish America in the Libraries of the University of California: A Catalogue of Books* (2 vols., 1928–1930).

University of Florida Library, *Caribbean Acquisitions* (annual since 1956).

University of Texas, Department of Sociology, *International Population Census Bibliography: Latin America and the Caribbean* (1965).

————, Institute of Latin American Studies, *Bibliography of Dissertations in Latin American History 1960–1970* (1971).

————, *Seventy-Five Years of Latin American Research at the University of Texas* (1959).

Valdés, N. P. and E. Lieuwen, *Revolutionary Cuba: A Research Guide 1959–1970* (1971).

Vaughan, D. R., *Urbanization in Twentieth Century Latin America: A Working Bibliography* (1969).

Violich, F., *Bibliography on Community Development Applied to Urban Areas in Latin America* (1963).

Vivo, A., *A Guide to Writings on the Alliance for Progress* (1970).

Vivo, P., comp., *Sources of Current Information on Latin America* (1971).

Wagley, C., *Social Science Research in Latin America* (1964).

Wagner, H. R., *The Spanish Southwest, 1542–1794* (2 vols., 1937).

Watson, G. H., *Colombia, Ecuador and Venezuela: An Annotated Guide to Reference Materials in the Humanities and Social Sciences* (1971).

Wauchope, R., *Ten Years of Middle American Archaeology: Annotated Bibliography and News Summary 1948–1957* (1961).

Weaver, J. L., ed., *Latin American Development: A Selected Bibliography* [1950–1969] (1969).

Whitaker, A. P., *Latin America Since 1825* (1958).

Wilgus, A. C., *History and Historians of Hispanic America* (1942).

Wish, J. R., *Economic Development in Latin America: An Annotated Bibliography* (1966).

Work, M. N., *Bibliography of the Negro in Africa and America* (1928; reprint 1965).

Zimmerman, I., *Current National Bibliographies of Latin America* (1971).

————, *A Guide to Current Latin American Periodicals* (1961, 1962).

periodicals to keep the student up to date

Alliance for Progress: A Weekly Report on Activities and Public Opinion (Washington, Pan American Union, No. 1, September 7, 1962–April 29, 1963; continued as *Weekly Newsletter* since May 27, 1963).

American Journal of International Law (quarterly since 1907).

Américas (Quarterly review of inter-American cultural history since 1944).

Américas (monthly of OAS since 1949).

Annals of the Organization of American States (quarterly or semi-annually).

Annual Reports of Carnegie Corporation of New York, Ford Foundation, Rockefeller Foundation, John Carter Brown Library, Creole Petroleum Company, Standard Oil of New Jersey (also periodical), Organization of American States, International Monetary Fund and Inter-American Development Bank; and others.

Review of the Economic Situation in Mexico (monthly, Mexico City 1925–).

Banco Nacional de Comercio Exterior (Mexico) *Comercio Exterior de Mexico* (monthly English edition, Mexico City 1951–).

Bank of London and South America, *Fortnightly Review*.

Brazil Culture.

Brazil Journal.

Brazilian-American Survey.

Brazilian Business.

Brazilian Embassy (Washington, D.C.), *Survey of the Brazilian Commerce* (annual 1965, 1966, 1967, 1968,–).

British Bulletin of Publications on Latin America, the West Indies, Portugal and Spain (London).

Bulletin of Hispanic Studies (quarterly).

Bulletin of the Pan American Union (monthly 1893–1948, superseded by *Américas* and *Annals*).

Business Conditions in Argentina (quarterly since 1918).

Business History Review (Winter 1965 issue devoted to Latin America).

Business International.

Business Week.

Caribbean Studies.

Carnegie Endowment for International Peace, *International Conciliation*.

Center for Intercultural Formation, *Reports: Cultures, the Church, the Americas* (published ten times a year).

Central American Bulletin.

Chase Manhattan Bank of New York, *Latin American Business Highlights*, 1950–1960 continued as *World Business* (bi-monthly).

Colombia Today (monthly since November, 1965).

Comparative Political Studies (quarterly journal vol. I, 1968–).

Current History.

Digest (University of Wisconsin).

Doors to Latin America (quarterly) [Bibliographic].

Economic Bulletin for Latin America (semi-annual—UN).

The Economist.

Embassy of Uruguay News.

Encounter.

Evergreen Review.

Export Trade.

Far Horizons.

First National Bank of Boston, *Situation in Argentina* (Buenos Aires, monthly since 1925).

First National City Bank of New York, *Foreign Information Service Bulletin.*

Foreign Affairs (quarterly).

Foreign Commerce Weekly (U.S. Office of International Trade).

Foreign Policy Bulletin (bi-weekly).

Hanson's Latin American Letter (weekly).

Hemisphere Hotline Report (Virginia Prewett Associates—weekly).

Hispania.

Hispanic American Historical Review (quarterly since 1918, with a hiatus of five years). [Numerous articles and monographs, book reviews, bibliographical notes, and news.]

Hispanic American Report (monthly 1948–1962).

Hispanic Review.

Inter American Development Bank, Annual Reports 1960–.

Inter American Economic Affairs (quarterly since 1947).

Inter American Labor Bulletin (monthly O.R.I.T.).

Inter American Municipal Review (Havana, 1950–).

Inter American Review of Bibliography (quarterly since 1951).

Inter American Statistical Institute Estadística (quarterly bulletin since 1943). [Consumer Price Indexes.]

International Affairs (Royal Institute of International Affairs, 1922–1939; 1944–).

International Commerce.

International Financial Statistics (International Monetary Fund).

International Labor Review (I.L.O., Geneva, 1921–).

International Legal Materials: Current Documents 1962–(Continuation of sections in American Journal of International Law).

International Organization (World Peace Foundation Quarterly since 1947).

Journal of Caribbean History (semi-annual, 1970–).

Journal of Church and State (vol. XII, winter 1970—special issue on Latin America).

Journal of Common Market Studies.

Journal of Developing Areas.

Journal of Inter American Studies (quarterly, since 1959).

Journal of International Affairs.

Journal of Latin American Studies (semi-annual, since 1969; Cambridge, England).

Journal of Mexican-American History (Santa Barbara, 1970–).

Lamp (quarterly journal published by Standard Oil of New Jersey).

Latin America–New Orleans (monthly).

Latin America (weekly newspaper–newsletter, London, 1967–).

Latin American Briefs (weekly newsletter of Pan American Union).

Latin American Business Review (Chase Manhattan Bank of New York, monthly).

Latin American Digest (Arizona State University–five times a year).

Latin American Embassies in Washington issue regular publications, e.g. Brazil, Chile, Colombia, Paraguay, etc.

Latin American Report (International Trade Mart of New Orleans, bi-weekly continued as *Ventures in Latin America*).

Latin American Research Review (three times a year since 1965).

Latin American Urban Research (annual, vol. I, 1970–).

Latin American Urban Policies (Sage Publications, Beverly Hills, California).

Latin America and the Caribbean: Analytical Survey of Literature (1969).

Luso-Brazilian Review (semi-annual since 1963).

Mexican Life.

Mexican-American Review (monthly, Mexico City).

Mexico This Month.

Mid America (quarterly).

Modern Language Notes.

Monthly Review.

News from Chile.

New York Times, *Latin American Economic Review* (semi-annual).

North American Congress on Latin America (NACLA), *NACLA's Latin America and Empire Report* (monthly–formerly *NACLA Newsletter;* began 1967–).

Noticias: A Weekly Digest of Hemisphere Reports (since 1945).

OAS Chronicle (bi-monthly, began August, 1965).

Odyssey Review (quarterly since 1961).

Peruvian Times.

Publications of Modern Language Association.

Report of the California Institute of International Studies (quarterly, 1970–).

Review of the Economic Situation of Mexico (English–Monthly since 1925).

Review of the River Plate (Buenos Aires).

Revista Iberoamericana (Iowa City, semi-annual).

Romantic Review.

Royal Institute of International Relations (London), *International Affairs* (quarterly).

————, *World Today* (monthly).

South American Journal (London).

Studies in Comparative International Development (annually, beginning 1965).

Studies on the Left (quarterly).

Texas Quarterly.

Times of the Americas (weekly).

Times of Brazil.

United Nations, Economic Commission for Latin America, Economic Survey of Latin America (annual).

————, Economic Review of Latin America (semi-annual, 1955–).

————, Monthly Bulletin of Statistics (1947–).

————, Report of Central American Economic Co-operative Committee (1955–1966).

————, Latin American Common Market.

United States Chamber of Commerce in Argentina, Economic Survey (Buenos Aires, 1941–1951; 1956–weekly).

University of California, Institute of International Studies, Politics of Modernization Series. [Also issues reprints of various articles.]

University of Florida, Latin American Monograph Series.

University of Pittsburgh, Center for Latin American Studies, Cuban Studies Newsletter (bi-annual, Vol. I, No. 1, published December, 1970).

University of Texas, Latin American Series.

————, Latin American Reprints.

University of Wisconsin (Madison), Center for Internation Communications Studies, Airmail News from Latin America (bi-weekly, since 1969).

Ventures in Latin America (formerly Latin American Report Newsletter—New Orleans).

Vision (weekly in English, New York, since 1964).

Western Political Quarterly.

World Oil (Houston, Texas).

Yearbook on International Communist Affairs (annual—since 1968; published by Hoover Institute of Stanford University).

[See also D. M. Phelps, "Sources of Current Information on Latin America," in Handbook of Latin American Studies, No. 3.]

For Newspapers: the best available are the *New York Times,* the *Christian Science Monitor* and *Washington Post.* Some of the more standard magazines run Latin American news [sometimes departments] as in *Time, Newsweek,* and *U.S. News and World Report.*

Many official publications are published in English by the various department and Bureaus and Commissions of the governments of the United States and Great Britain, United Nations, OAS, Unesco, Caribbean Commission and others. The student is referred to the second edition of *Latin America: Development of Its Civilization* for a list of these as well as for other bibliographic information.

INDEX

social conditions of, 412–14, 416, 427–29, 476, 736, 740, 748
Rio de Janeiro Pact (1947), 708, 709
Rio Grande, 31, 356, 363
Rio Grande do Sul (state), Brazil, 393, 398, 402, 414–15, 421, 425, 528
Rio Haina sugar refinery, 680
Ríos, Juan Antonio, 497–98, 507, 508
Rivadavia, Bernardino, 441–42
Riva Palacio, Vicente, 375
Rivera (explorer), 256
Rivera, Colonel Alberto, 638
Rivera, Diego, 373, 374
Rivera, Fructuoso, 522, 523
Rivera, José Eustacio, 614
Rivera, Primo de, 735
Robles, Marco, 648
Roca, Julio, 446–47
Rocafuerte, Vicente, 550–51
Rockefeller, Nelson, 714–16, 730, 731
Rockefeller Foundation, 538, 731
Rockefeller Commission, 714–15
Rockefeller Committee, 428, 701, 729, 731, 738
Rodó, José Enrique, 532, 735
Rodrígues Alves, Francisco de Paula, 399–400
Rodríguez, Simón, 293
Rodríguez Cabrillo, Juan, 106–7
Rodríguez Galván, Ignacio, 375
Rodríguez Lara, Guillermo, 554
Rodríguez Urdaneta, Abelardo, 681
Rojas, Manuel, 511
Rojas Pinilla, General Gustavo, 592, 593
Roldán, Amadeo, 668
Roman Catholic Church, see Catholic Church
Roman Empire, 7, 8, 16, 39
Roman Law, 7, 10
Romero García, Manuel, 599
Rondon, General Cândido Mariano, 426
Roosevelt, Franklin D., 571, 660, 673, 699–700, 706
  Nicaragua and, 631, 635, 636
Roosevelt, Theodore, 426, 526, 589, 605
  Dominican Republic and, 678, 679
  Panama Canal and, 644–45
  Spanish–American War and, 658
Roosevelt Corollary to Monroe Doctrine, 697–98, 717
Rosario, Argentina, 440, 441, 466, 470
Rosas, Encarnación, 443
Rosas, Manuel, 394, 442–46, 459, 466–67, 523, 563, 719
Rose of Lima, Saint, 208
Ross, Gustavo, 496–97
Rossini, Gioacchino, 318
Rough Riders, 658, 734
Rousseau, Jean Jacques, 265, 268, 281, 291, 336
Royal African Company, 162, 243
Royal and Pontifical University of Mexico, 224

Royal Guinea Company, 161
Royal Naval Observatory, 85
Rubber industry, 36, 397, 415, 419–20
Rubio, Venezuela, 740
Ruíz Cortines, Adolfo, 355
Rulfo, Juan, 378
Rural Society, 469
Rusk, Dean, 711, 712, 732
Russell, General John H., 673
Russia
  Cuba and, 663–67, 702, 709, 710
  Latin America and, 358, 718, 720, 727, 737, 738
  North American explorations of, 256–58
  U.S. and, 311, 695, 702

Sá, Eustacio de, 139
Sa, Hermane Tavares de, 430
Sá, Mem de, 136, 138, 139
Saavedra, Bautista, 564
Saavedra Lamas, Carlos, 453
Sacasa, Juan B., 634–35
Sáenz, Moisés, 368, 369
Sáenz Peña, Luis, 447
Sáenz Peña, Roque, 449–50, 457, 473
Sáenz Peña Law, 450, 452
Sahagún, Friar Bernardino de, 226
St. Augustine, Florida, 111, 244, 246
Saint Domingue, see Haiti
St. Kitts (island), 242
Salomon, Lysius, 671
Salvador, see El Salvador
Salvatierra, Father, 210
Sam, Guillaume Vilbrun, 672
Sam, Tiresias Augustin Simon, 671
San Blas Indians, 625
San Diego, California, 258
San Diego Bay, 107
San Fernando (King Ferdinand), 9
San Francisco, California, 185, 210, 509, 631
San José, Panama, 641, 642
San José de Costa Rica, 619
San Juan, Puerto Rico, 91, 658
San Juan de Letrán (school), 224
San Luis Potosí, Mexico, 109, 193, 214, 340, 342, 351, 360
San Martín, José de, 299–303, 310, 313, 445, 487
San Martín, Juan Zorilla de, 532
San Pedro Sula, Honduras, 624
San Salvador (island), 80, 160
San Salvador, El Salvador, 619, 621, 636
Sanchez, Florencio, 480
Sánchez, Luis Alberto, 578
Sanchez, Manuela, 313
Sánchez Cerro, Luis M., 558
Sánchez Hernández, Fidel, 638
Sandino, César Augusto, 634–35
Sandoval, Gonzalo de, 99, 102
Sanfuentes, Juan Luis, 494
Sanín Cano, Baldomiro, 614–15